TORT LAW

TORT LAW

Text and Materials

FOURTH EDITION

Mark Lunney

Associate Professor, School of Law, University of New England, Armidale, Australia

and

Ken Oliphant

Director of the Institute for European Tort Law, Austrian Academy of Sciences, Vienna, and Professor of Tort Law, University of Bristol

OXFORD

UNIVERSITY PRESS

OXFORD
UNIVERSITY PRESS

Great Clarendon Street, Oxford OX2 6DP

Oxford University Press is a department of the University of Oxford.
It furthers the University's objective of excellence in research, scholarship,
and education by publishing worldwide in

Oxford New York

Auckland Cape Town Dar es Salaam Hong Kong Karachi
Kuala Lumpur Madrid Melbourne Mexico City Nairobi
New Delhi Shanghai Taipei Toronto

With offices in

Argentina Austria Brazil Chile Czech Republic France Greece
Guatemala Hungary Italy Japan Poland Portugal Singapore
South Korea Switzerland Thailand Turkey Ukraine Vietnam

Oxford is a registered trade mark of Oxford University Press
in the UK and in certain other countries

Published in the United States
by Oxford University Press Inc., New York

First published 2000
Second edition 2003
Third edition 2008
This edition 2010

British Library Cataloguing in Publication Data

Data available

Library of Congress Cataloging in Publication Data

Lunney, Mark.
  Tort law : text and materials / Mark Lunney and Ken Oliphant.—4th ed.
    p. cm.
  ISBN 978–0–19–957180–2 (pbk.)
  1. Torts—England. 2. Torts—Wales. I. Oliphant, Ken. II. Title.
  KD1949.L86 2010
    346.4203—dc22   2010018308

Typeset by Newgen Imaging Systems (P) Ltd, Chennai, India
Printed in Great Britain
on acid-free paper by
Ashford Colour Press Ltd, Gosport, Hampshire

ISBN 978–0–19–957180–2

10 9 8 7 6 5 4 3

PREFACE TO THE FOURTH EDITION

In this new edition, we remain committed to the aims set out in the preface to the first: to produce a stimulating resource for use in the teaching of tort law and a work worthy of scholarly attention. The years since the last edition have seen some significant developments, but no major changes at the level of fundamental principle. We have the impression that English tort law is entering a period of relative stability, in which court decisions and legislative interventions reinforce existing approaches and tendencies rather than breaking new ground.

We have tried to resist the temptation to insert new material purely for novelty's sake. New cases that are extracted for the first time in this edition are: *Ashley v Chief Constable of Sussex* [2008] AC 962 (intentional interference with the person); *Smith v Chief Constable of Sussex Police* [2009] 1 AC 225 (duty of care and negligence liability of the police); *Gray v Thames Trains Ltd* [2009] 1 AC 1339 (illegality); and *Farraj v King's Healthcare NHS Trust* [2009] EWCA Civ 1203 (non-delegable duties). We have also included many other recent cases in our introductions and commentaries, sometimes with short extracts, and there are additional extracts from proposed legislation (the draft Civil Law Reform Bill), official reports and academic writings. On reviewing the structure of the book, we felt that liability for invasion of privacy was not accorded sufficient prominence in previous editions—in which our analysis was appended to the chapter on defamation—and we therefore decided to give it a chapter of its own (see Chapter 14 below). We have also added a new section on evaluation and reform to the chapter on the duty of care owed by public bodies (Chapter 10). As in every edition, our aim has been to produce original analysis that is a contribution to scholarly debate in its own right, as well as being an aid to students.

There are many people to whom we should record our thanks, beginning with our current and former colleagues, and our friends elsewhere in the academic world, who have helped to shape our ideas through their published writings and discussions in public and private forums. Both authors must also record their gratitude to generations of law students—in London, Cardiff, Armidale, Bristol and Vienna—for their valuable feedback on previous editions and for helping us to refine our ideas in the course of seminar and tutorial debate. We are also grateful to OUP's anonymous reviewers and to readers who have emailed with comments and suggestions. At OUP we extend our thanks to Helen Swann, our commissioning editor, and Anya Aghdam, for their invaluable assistance in the production process, and to our copyeditor, Julian Roskams, and proofreader, Caroline Quinnell. As in previous editions, we continue to give special thanks to Karen and Annelise for the sort of support that cannot be summarised in a few short words.

We have endeavoured to state the law as of 1 February 2010 though it has been possible to make reference to selected later developments.

Mark Lunney
Ken Oliphant

FROM THE PREFACE TO THE FIRST EDITION

Our aim in preparing this book has been to produce a stimulating resource for use in the teaching of tort law and a work worthy of scholarly attention. It is more than simply a case-book as traditionally conceived. On the one hand, a high proportion of materials extracted in it are not cases but (for example) the diagnoses and prescriptions of law reformers or the critical analyses of academic commentators. The law of tort has generated a rich secondary literature, and we have endeavoured to provide students with easy access to a selection of the best and most interesting examples of that literature. On the other hand, the extent of our own authorial contribution is very considerable. In addition to the short introductions at the beginning of each new chapter (and many of the sub-sections within each chapter), we have written substantial commentaries following on from each extract (or series of extracts). These are designed to shed light on the significance of the material extracted and to identify further, related issues for consideration. Frequently, we have expressed personal views about the topic under discussion (hoping thereby to provoke debate rather than to foreclose it). On a number of occasions, we have developed what we believe to be original analyses worthy of consideration as contributions to scholarly debate.

Tort law cannot be viewed simply as a self-contained collection of legal rules, and we have sought to explore the law from a variety of perspectives that are external to it (amongst them the comparative, the socio-legal, the theoretical, the feminist, and the economic). We believe that each has something to add to our understanding of the law. But, although ours is a pluralist approach to tort law, we have given pride of place to one perspective on the law in particular—the historical. More than most legal subjects, tort law is shaped (scarred, even) by its history. Legal principles are not everlasting and immutable givens: they are the contingent products of history. To understand the law, and to understand (where necessary) how to change it, we must learn the lessons of its history. Rules which appear arbitrary or anomalous in the modern law become explicable only when considered in terms of the law's doctrinal development. Doctrinal developments, in turn, take on meaning only when viewed as a response to external social pressures, which may be specific to a particular time and place. A contemporary account of tort law must therefore—paradoxically—be in some measure historical.

LIST OF ABBREVIATIONS

ABI	Association of British Insurers
AC	Law Reports: Appeal Cases
Admin LR	Administrative Law Reports
AHA	Area Health Authority
AJDA	Les Actualités Juridique: Droit Administratif
ALJ	Australian Law Journal
ALJR	Australian Law Journal Reports
All ER	All England Reports
ALR	Australian Law Reports
Am JLH	American Journal of Legal History
Am L Rev	American Law Review
Am U LR	American Universities' Law Review
APIL	Association of Personal Injury Lawyers
B & S	Best & Smith Reports
BC	Borough Council
BCCI	Bank of Credit and Commerce International
BGB	Bürgerliches Gesetzbuch (German Civil Code)
BGHZ	Entscheidungen des Bundesgerichtshofes in Zivilsachen
BLR	Building Law Reports
BMLR	Butterworths Medico-Legal Reports
Br Col R	British Columbia Reports (Canada)
BWCC	Butterworth's Workmen's Compensation Cases
C & P	Carrington & Payne
Can Bar Rev	Canadian Bar Review
Car & Kir	Carrington & Kirwan Reports
CC	County Council
CCLT	Canadian Cases on the Law of Torts
Ch D	Chancery Division
CLJ	Cambridge Law Journal
CLP	Current Legal Problems
CLR	Commonwealth Law Reports (Australia)
CMLR	Common Market Law Reports
Col LR	Columbia Law Review
Comm L World Rev	Common Law World Review
Con LR	Construction Law Reports
Consumer L Jnl	Consumer Law Journal
Conv	Conveyancer
CP	Consultation Paper (Lord Chancellor's Division)
CPD	Common Pleas
CPR	Civil Procedure Rules

CPS	Crown Prosecution Service
Cr App R	Criminal Appeal Reports
Cr App R(S)	Criminal Appeal Reports (Sentencing)
Crim LR	Criminal Law Review
CUP	Cambridge University Press
DCA	Department for Constitutional Affairs
DHSS	Department of Health and Social Security
DLR	Dominion Law Reports (Canada)
DR	Decisions and Reports of the European Commission of Human Rights
EC	European Community
ECHR	European Convention on Human Rights and Fundamental Freedoms
ECJ	European Court of Justice
ECR	European Court Reports
ECtHR	European Court of Human Rights
EEC	European Economic Community
EG	Estates Gazette
EGLR	Estates Gazette Law Reports
EHRR	European Human Rights Reports
EMLR	Entertainment and Media Law Reports
ER	English Reports
EU	European Union
EUP	Edinburgh University Press
EWCA Civ	England & Wales Court of Appeal, Civil Division
EWHC	England & Wales High Court
Ex D	Exchequer Division
FCFCA	Full Court of the Federal Court (Australia)
FCR	Family Court Reporter
FL Rev	Federal Law Review
FLR	Family Law Reports
FSR	Fleet Street Reports
GLC	Greater London Council
H & N	Hurlstone & Norman Reports
Harv L Rev	Harvard Law Review
Hawaii L Rev	Hawaii Law Review
HCA	High Court of Australia
HL Cas	House of Lords Cases
HMSO	Her Majesty's Stationery Office
HRA	Human Rights Act 1998
ICLQ	International and Comparative Law Quarterly
ICR	Industrial Cases Reports
ILGS	Index-Linked Government Stock
ILJ	Industrial Law Journal

Imm AR	Immigration Appeal Reports
IRLR	Industrial Relations Law Reports
JEnvL	Journal of Environmental Law
JETL	Journal of European Tort Law
J Leg Ed	Journal of Legal Education
J Leg His	Journal of Legal History
J Leg St	Journal of Legal Studies
J Soc Pol	Journal of Social Policy
JLE	Journal of Law and Economics
JLS	Journal of Legal Studies
JPIL	Journal of Personal Injury Law
JSPTL	Journal of the Society of Public Teachers of Law
KB	King's Bench
KCLJ	King's College Law Journal
KIR	Knight's Industrial Reports
Law Com	Law Commission
LBC	Law Book Company
LCD	Lord Chancellor's Department
LEA	Local Education Authority
LGR	Local Government Reports
Lloyd's Rep Med	Lloyd's Medical Law Reports
LQR	Law Quarterly Review
LS	Legal Studies
LS Gaz	Law Society Gazette
LT	Law Times Reports
M & W	Meeson and Welsby
ME	Myalgic encephalomyclitis
Med L Rev	Medical Law Review
Mcd LR	Medical Law Reports
MIB	Motor Insurers' Bureau
Mich LR	Michegan Law Review
Minn LR	Minnesota Law Review
MLR	Modern Law Review
MOD	Ministry of Defence
NAO	National Audit Office
NHBC	National House Building Council
NHS	National Health Service
NILQ	Northern Ireland Law Quarterly
NJW	Neue Juristische Wochenschrift
NLJ	New Law Journal
NSR	Nova Scotia Reports (Canada)
NSWCA	New South Wales Court of Appeal (Australia)
NSWR	New South Wales Reports (Australia)

NTLR	Northern Territory Law Reports (Australia)
NZLR	New Zealand Law Reports
OJLS	Oxford Journal of Legal Studies
OR	Ontario Reports (Canada)
Osgoode Hall LJ	Osgoode Hall Law Journal
OUP	Oxford University Press
PACE	Police and Criminal Evidence Act 1984
PD	Probate Division *or* Practice Direction
PIQR	Personal Injuries and Quantum Reports
PL	Public Law
PN	Professional Negligence
PTSD	Post Traumatic Stress Disorder
QB	Queen's Bench
RPC	Reports of Patent Cases
RPI	Retail Price Index
RSC	Rules of the Supreme Court
RTR	Road Traffic Reports
SASR	South Australian State Reports
SCR	Supreme Court Reports (Canada)
SI	Statutory Instrument
SLT	Scots Law Times
Sol J	Solicitors' Journal
SR (NSW)	State Reports New South Wales (Australia)
Stan L Rev	Stanford Law Review
Stat Law	Statute Law Review
TEC	Treaty establishing the European Community
TEU	Treaty on European Union
Tex L Rev	Texas Law Review
TFEU	Treaty on the Functioning of the European Union
TLJ	Torts Law Journal
TLR	Times Law Reports
Tort LR	Tort Law Review
U Chi L Rev	University of Chicago Law Review
U of Toronto LJ	University of Toronto Law Journal
UCTA	Unfair Contract Terms Act 1977
UKHL	United Kingdom House of Lords
UN	United Nations
UNELJ	University of New England Law Journal
VAT	Value Added Tax
VR	Victorian Reports (Australia)

WALR   Western Australian Law Reports
WLR   Weekly Law Reports
WWR   Western Weekly Reports (Canada)

Yale LJ   Yale Law Journal
YB   Yearbook

ZEuP   Zeitschrift für Europäisches Privatrecht

LIST OF ABBREVIATIONS OF COMMONLY CITED WORKS

Atiyah	P. Cane, *Atiyah's Accidents, Compensation and the Law*, 7th edn. (Cambridge: CUP, 2006)
Baker	J. Baker, *An Introduction to English Legal History*, 4th edn. (London: Butterworths, 2002)
Barendt	E. Barendt et al., *Libel and the Media: The Chilling Effect* (Oxford: Clarendon Press, 1997)
Beever	A. Beever, *Rediscovering the Law of Negligence* (Oxford: Hart, 2007)
Blackstone	W. Blackstone, *Commentaries on the Laws of England* (originally published 1765–69; facsimile edition by University of Chicago Press, 1979)
Clerk & Lindsell	A. Dugdale and M. Jones (eds), *Clerk & Lindsell on the Law of Torts*, 19th edn. (London: Sweet & Maxwell, 2006)
Conaghan & Mansell	J. Conaghan and W. Mansell, *The Wrongs of Tort*, 2nd edn. (London: Pluto Press, 1999)
Cornish & Clark	W. Cornish and G. Clarke, *Law and Society in England 1750–1950* (London: Sweet & Maxwell, 1989)
European Tort Law	Annual beginning with H. Koziol and B. Steininger (eds), *European Tort Law 2001: Tort and Insurance Law Yearbook* (Vienna: Springer-Verlag, 2002)
Fleming	J. Fleming, *The Law of Torts*, 9th edn. (Sydney: Law Book Co, 1998)
Gatley	*Gatley on Libel and Slander*, 11th edn. by P. Milmo and W. V. H. Rogers (London: Sweet & Maxwell, 2008)
Hepple, Howarth & Matthews	M. Matthews, J. Morgan and C. O'Cinneide, *Tort: Cases and Materials*, 6th edn. (Oxford: Oxford University Press, 2008)
Markesinis & Deakin	S. Deakin, A. Johnston, and B. Markesinis, *Markesinis and Deakin's Tort Law*, 6th edn. (Oxford: Oxford University Press, 2007)
Jackson Report	The Right Honourable Lord Justice Jackson, *Review of Civil Litigation Costs: Final Report* (The Stationery Office, 2010)
Jones	M. Jones, *Textbook on Torts*, 8th edn. (Oxford: Oxford University Press, 2002)
Oliphant	K. Oliphant (ed.), *The Law of Tort*, 2nd edn. (London: Butterworths, 2007)
Pearson Commission	Royal Commission on Civil Liability and Compensation for Personal Injury, Chairman: Lord Pearson, *Report*, Cmnd 7054, 1978

Prosser	*Prosser & Keeton on the Law of Torts*, 5th edn. by W. Keeton et al. (St Paul, Minn.: West Publishing Co, 1984)
Salmond & Heuston	*Salmond & Heuston on the Law of Torts*, 21st edn. by R. Buckley (London: Sweet & Maxwell, 1996)
Stanton	K. Stanton, *The Modern Law of Tort* (London: Sweet & Maxwell, 1994)
Stevens	R. Stevens, *Torts and Rights* (Oxford: OUP, 2007)
Street	*Street on Torts*, 12th edn. by J. Murphy (London: Butterworths, 2007)
van Dam	C. van Dam, *European Tort Law* (Oxford: Oxford University Press, 2007)
van Gerven	W. van Gerven et al., *Cases, Materials and Text on National, Supranational and International Tort Law* (Oxford: Hart Publishing, 2000)
Weir	T. Weir, *A Casebook on Tort*, 10th edn. (London: Sweet & Maxwell, 2004)
Winfield & Jolowicz	*Winfield & Jolowicz on Tort*, 17th edn. by W. V. H. Rogers (London: Sweet & Maxwell, 2006)

ACKNOWLEDGEMENTS

We are grateful to all authors and publishers of copyright material used in this book and in particular to the following for permission to reprint from the sources indicated.

Extracts from Crown copyright material are reproduced under the terms of Licence Number C2006010631 with the permission of the Controller of OPSI and the Queen's Printer for Scotland.

EEC Council Directive 85/374/EEC is reproduced from 210 *OJL* 29 (1985), copyright © European Union, http://eur-lex.europa.eu/

The American Law Institute for extract from *Restatement of the Law, Third, Torts: Liability for Physical and Emotional Harm*, copyright © 2010 by The American Law Institute. All rights reserved.

P S Atiyah for extracts from *Vicarious Liabilities* (Butterworths, 1967).

Cambridge Law Journal and the authors for extracts from R Dias: 'Trouble on Oiled Waters: Problems of the Wagon Mound (no 2)', *Cambridge Law Journal* 62 (1967); Conor Gearty: 'The Place of Private Nuisance in a modern law of Torts', *Cambridge Law Journal* 214 (1989); Anthony J E Jaffey: '*Violenti Non Fit Injuria*', *Cambridge Law Journal* 87 (1985); and Glanville Williams: 'Liability for Independent Contractors', 180 *Cambridge Law Journal* (1956).

Cambridge University Press and the author for extract from P Cane: *Atiyah's Accidents, Compensation and the Law* (7th Ed, Cambridge, 2006).

Canada Law Book, a division of The Cartwright Group (www.canadalawbook.ca) for extract from the *Dominion Law Reports*.

Martha Chamallas with Linda K Kerber for extract from 'Women, Mothers and the Law of Fright: A History', 88 *Michigan Law Review* 814 (1990).

Hart Publishing Ltd for extracts from P S Atiyah: *The Damages Lottery* (Hart, 1997), and from A Beever: *Rediscovering the Law of Negligence* (Hart, 2007).

David Ibbetson for 'The Tort of Negligence in the Common Law in the 19th and 20th Centuries'

first published in the first edition of this book and subsequently in *Negligence: the comparative legal history of the law of torts* edited by E J H Schrage (Ducker & Humblot, Berlin, 2001).

The Incorporated Council of Law Reporting for extracts from *Appeal Court Reports* (AC), *Queen's Bench Reports*, (QB) *King's Bench Reports* (KB), and *Weekly Law Reports* (WLR).

The Journal of Law and Economics, The University of Chicago Law School and the author for extract from R H Coase: 'The Problem of Social Cost', 3 *J Law & Econ* 1 (1960), copyright © 1960 by the University of Chicago. All rights reserved.

LexisNexis Pty Ltd for extract from *Torts Law Journal*: R Lewis, A Morris, K. Oliphant: 'Tort Personal Injury Claims Statistics; Is There a Compensation Culture in the United Kingdom?', 14 TLJ158 (2006).

News International Syndication for extract from the *Times Law Reports*, 27.02.1934, copyright © Times Newspapers Ltd, London, 1934.

Oxford University Press for extracts from J H Baker: *Introduction to English Legal History* (3e, Butterworths, 1990); J Baker & S Milson: 'Rattlesdene v Grunestone' and 'The Farrier's Case' in *Sources of English Legal History: Private Law to 1750* (Butterworths,

1986); E Barendt et al: *Libel and the Media: A Chilling Effect* (OUP, 1997); S D Harris et al: *Compensation and Support for Illness and Injury* (OUP, 1984); R Kostal;: *English Law and Railway Capitalism* (OUP, 1994); M Moran: *Rethinking the Reasonable Person: An Egalitarian Reconstruction of the Objective Standard* (OUP, 2006); A W B Simpson: 'Victorian Judges and the Problem of Social Cost: Tipping v St Helen's Smelting Company (1865)' in *Leading Cases in Common Law* (OUP, 1995); and J Stapleton: 'In Restraint of Tort' in P Birks (ed) *The Frontiers of Liability* Vol. 2 (OUP, 1994).

Reed Elsevier (UK) Ltd trading as LexisNexis for extracts from *All England Law Reports* (All ER).

Sweet & Maxwell Ltd for extracts from W Cornish and G Clarke: *Law and Society in England, 1750–1950* (Sweet & Maxwell, 1989); from *Public Law*: Lady Justice Arden: 'Human Rights and Civil Wings: Tort Law Under the Spotlight', *Public Law* 140 (2010); from *Law Quarterly Review*: W Bishop: 'Negligent Representation through Economist's Eyes', 96 *LQR* 360 (1980); P Cane: 'What a Nuisance!', 113 *LQR* 515 (1997); Holdsworth: 'The Origin of the Rule of Baker v Bolton (1916)', 32 *LQR* 431 (1916); B S Markesinis: 'Negligence, Nuisance and Affirmative Duties of Action', 105 *LQR* 104 (1989); and J Stapleton: 'Duty of Care and Economic Loss: a Wider Agenda', 107 *LQR* 248 (1991); and from *Road Traffic Reports* and *Fleet Street Reports*.

Thomson-Reuters (Professional) Australia Ltd for extracts from the *Commonwealth Law Reports* and from J G Fleming: *The Law of Torts* (9e, 1998); P Handford: *Mullaney and Handford's Tort Liability for Psychiatric Damage* (2e, 2006); and from *Tort Law Review*: E Quill: 'Consumer Protection in respect of defective buildings', 14 *Tort L Rev* 105 (2006).

University of Chicago Law School via Copyright Clearance Center for extract from James A Henderson: 'The New Zealand Accident Compensation Reform', 48 *University of Chicago Law Review* 781 (1981), copyright © 1981 by the University of Chicago Law School.

Wiley-Blackwell Publishers via Copyright Clearance Center for extracts from *Modern Law Review*: R Lewis: 'The Politics and Economics of Tort Law: Judicially Imposed Periodical Payments of Damages', 69 *MLR* 418; and from *Legal Studies*: Richard Kidner: 'Vicarious Liability—for whom should the employer be liable', 15 *LS*, 47 (1995); R Lewis: Insurance and the Tort System', *LS* 85 (2005); and K Williams: 'State of Fear: Britain's "compensation culture" reviewed', 25 *LS* 499 (2005).

R B G Williams for extracts from Glanville Williams: 'Liability for Independent Contractors', 180 *Cambridge Law Journal* (1956), and 'The Aims of the Law of Tort', *Current Legal Problems* 137 (1951).

Every effort has been made to trace and contact copyright holders but this has not been possible in every case. If notified, the publisher will undertake to rectify any errors or omissions at the earliest opportunity.

CONTENTS

11 Special Liability Regimes   545

12 Nuisance and the Rule in *Rylands v Fletcher*   640

TABLE OF CASES

TABLE OF STATUTES

TABLE OF STATUTORY INSTRUMENTS

TABLE OF COURT RULES

TABLE OF INTERNATIONAL TREATIES AND CONVENTIONS

TABLE OF EUROPEAN LEGISLATION

1 GENERAL INTRODUCTION

I. Historical Development of Tort Law

1. Origins of Tort Law

The law of tort—the word derives from the French for 'wrong'—is the law of civil liability for wrongfully-inflicted injury, or at least a very large part of it. (Breach of contract and breach of trust are perhaps the other two most important civil wrongs.) Tort itself is a very old legal concept, older even than the concept of crime. According to Sir Henry Maine, 'the penal law of ancient communities is not the law of crimes; it is the law of wrongs, or, to use the English technical word, of torts' (*Ancient Law* (1861), p. 328). It developed in the days before states were sufficiently organised to have a centralised prosecuting authority; the only alternative was to leave the task of punishing wrongful conduct to private individuals. The existence of such remedies was necessary for the maintenance of public order, for in their absence feuds and acts of unrestrained vengeance would no doubt have been common. Tort was a form of legalised self-help. For the injured party, the incentive was often not only the award of compensation, but also the entitlement to an additional punitive element of damages. Under Roman law's action for theft (*actio furti*), for instance, the plaintiff was entitled to recover at least 'double damages', i.e. twice the worth of the thing stolen. Indeed, where the defendant was caught red-handed (in a case of 'manifest theft') fourfold damages would be awarded. As the temptation to take the law into one's own hands would be at its strongest in such a case, a greater than usual incentive was required to ensure that the matter was resolved by lawful means.

Although the Roman law of tort—or 'delict', as it is more usually called—developed in piecemeal fashion, the civilian jurisdictions which took it as their model sought to systematise the principles of tortious liability, eliminating its anomalies and diminishing its complexity (following the analysis of the great natural lawyers such as Grotius). Their Codes—which mainly date from the Napoleonic era and thereafter—reduce the law of tort to its bare essentials. 'Almost the whole of the French law of delict rests on a mere five articles in the *Code Civile* which have remained in force virtually unchanged for 195 years' (P. Zweigert and H. Kötz, *An Introduction to Comparative Law*, 3rd edn., trans. T. Weir (Oxford: OUP, 1998), p. 615). Unlike the French code, the German *Bürgerliches Gesetzbuch* (BGB) resists the temptation of a general clause imposing liability for all the consequences of one's fault, and deals with tort liability under three 'more limited but still broad' principles. The other civilian jurisdictions in Europe (not including Scotland whose law of delict is almost identical with the English law of tort) take varying positions, some more closely aligned with the French approach, some with the German.

The English law of tort stands in stark contrast. 'The Common Law of Torts started out by having specific types of liability just like Roman law, but, whereas on the Continent legal scholars ironed out the old distinctions between the several delicts to the point where a general principle of delictual liability became not only a possibility but an actuality in most legal systems, Anglo-American lawyers have largely adhered to the separate types of case and separate torts which developed under the writ system' (Zweigert and Kötz, *op. cit.*, p. 605). It is perhaps this lack of principle which led the great American judge and jurist, Oliver Wendell Holmes, to pronounce: 'Torts is not a proper subject for a law book' ((1871) 5 Am L Rev 340). Holmes nevertheless overcame his early prejudice, and wrote—in his masterly analysis *The Common Law* (originally published in 1881)—an account of the law of torts which remains a rewarding and insightful read today.

Holmes set himself the task of discovering 'whether there is any common ground at the bottom of all liability in tort, and if so, what that ground is' (*The Common Law*, p. 77). He considered that this was not an easy task: 'The law did not begin with a theory. It has never worked one out' (*ibid.*). He found that discussions of general principle had been 'darkened' by historical controversies that had no contemporary relevance (*ibid.*, p. 78). Nevertheless, he felt that a full account of the law required a knowledge of its history, asserting at the beginning of his great work that '[i]n order to know what it is, we must know what it has been' (*ibid.*, p. 1). Accordingly it is with the historical development of the English law of torts through the forms of action that we begin.

2. The Forms of Action

For most of its history, English common law developed through the procedural mechanisms used to bring an action before the courts. These were known as the forms of action, the writs that it was necessary to purchase from the Chancery so that an action could be commenced in the royal courts. At the very beginnings of the common law these writs were drawn up on an ad-hoc basis, but this soon became impractical and standard-form writs began to develop. Writs set out in a formulaic style the gist of the plaintiff's complaint and instructed the local sheriff to summon the defendant to answer the allegation. There were different writs for different actions within what later became known as the law of tort. It was during this period that the foundations of modern tort law were set down. Although the forms of action were abolished by the Judicature Acts of 1873 and 1875, an understanding of modern tort law is impossible without an appreciation of the writ system and of the most important forms of action that developed under it. Amongst these, undisputed pride of place goes to the writ of trespass—'that fertile mother of actions', to use Maitland's phrase—from which developed the more flexible writ of trespass on the plaintiff's special case (the action on the case or—more simply—'case').

(a) The Writ of Trespass

The writ of trespass was one of the original royal writs (issued in the Crown's name) and it became relatively common after 1250. Trespass was a writ of wrong rather than a writ of right; it complained of a wrong rather than demanded the reinstatement of a right. The mode of trial was by jury and the remedy was damages. A number of different forms of trespass were recognised. The writ of trespass *quare clausum fregit* corresponds to the modern tort of trespass to land; that of trespass *de bonis asportatis* to the modern trespass to goods. The writs dealing with trespass to the person took various forms, corresponding to the modern torts of assault, battery and false imprisonment. What all of them had in common was a requirement that the defendant had acted *vi et armis* ('with force and arms') and *contra pacem* ('in breach of the [king's] peace'). The writ of trespass *vi et armis* for battery, for example, required the defendant 'to show why with force and arms he made assault on the [plaintiff] at [a particular place] and beat, wounded and ill-treated him so that his life was despaired of, and offered other outrages against him, to the grave damage of the self-same [plaintiff] and against our peace' (see *Baker*, p. 545). These requirements were imposed in order to prevent the King's Courts being overwhelmed with business; cases not involving violence and a threat to public safety were left to be dealt with in the local courts.

F. Maitland, *The Forms of Action at Common Law*
(Cambridge: CUP, 1909)

What was a form of action? Already owing to modern reforms [the Judicature Acts of 1873 and 1875] it is impossible to assume that every law student must have heard or read or discovered for himself an answer to that question, but it is still one which must be answered if he is to have more than a very superficial knowledge of our law as it stands even at the present day. The forms of action we have buried, but they still rule us from their graves. Let us then for a while place ourselves in Blackstone's day, or, for this matters not, some seventy years later in 1830, and let us look for a moment at English civil procedure.

Let it be granted that one man has been wronged by another; the first thing that he or his advisers have to consider is what form of action he shall bring. It is not enough that in some way or another he should compel his adversary to appear in court and should then state in the words that naturally occur to him the facts on which he relies and the remedy to which he thinks himself entitled. No, English law knows a certain number of forms of action, each with its own uncouth name, a writ of right, an assize of novel disseisin or of mort d'ancestor, a writ of entry *sur disseisin* in the *per* and *cui*, a writ of *besaiel*, of *quare impedit*, an action of covenant, debt, detinue, replevin, trespass, assumpsit, ejectment, case. This choice is not merely a choice between a number of queer technical terms, it is a choice between methods of procedure adapted to cases of different kinds.

[Maitland then discusses a number of procedural differences between the different actions.]

These remarks may be enough to show that the differences between the several forms of action have been of very great practical importance—'a form of action' has implied a particular original process, a particular mesne process, a particular final process, a particular mode of pleading, of trial, of judgment. But further to a very considerable degree the substantive law administered in a given form of action has grown up independently of the law administered in other forms. Each procedural pigeon-hole contains its own rules of substantive law, and it is with great caution that we may argue from what is found in one to what will probably be found in another; each has its own precedents. It is quite possible that a litigant will find that his case will fit some two or three of these pigeon-holes. If that be so he will have a choice, which will often be a choice between the old, cumbrous, costly, on the one hand, the modern, rapid, cheap, on the other. Or again he may make a bad choice, fail in his action and take such comfort as he can from the hints of the judges that another form of action might have been more successful. The plaintiff's choice is irrevocable; he must play the rules of the game that he has chosen. Lastly he may find that, plausible as his case may seem, it just will not fit any one of the receptacles provided by the courts and he may take to himself the lesson that where there is no remedy there is no wrong.

[Maitland then proceeds to a chronological survey of the major developments in the history of the forms of action.]

1189–1272

The most important phenomenon is the appearance of Trespass—that fertile mother of actions. Instances of what we can not but call actions of trespass are found even in John's reign, but I think it clear that the writ of trespass did not become a writ of course until very late in Henry III's reign. Now trespass is to start with a semi-criminal action. It has its roots in criminal law, and criminal procedure. The historical importance of trespass is so great that we may step aside to look at the criminal procedure out of which it grew. The old criminal action (yes, action) was the Appeal of Felony (*appellum de felonia*). It was but slowly supplanted by indictment—the procedure of the common accuser set going by Henry II, the appeal on the other hand being an action brought by a person aggrieved by the crime. The appellant had to pronounce certain accusing words. In each case he must say of the appellee '*fecit hoc* (the murder, rape, robbery or mayhem) *nequitur et in felonia, vi et armis et contra pacem Domini Regis*' [he did this—the murder, etc—wickedly and feloniously, with force and arms and contrary to the King's Peace].

He charges him with a wicked deed of violence to be punished by death, or in the twelfth century by mutilation. The procedure is stringent with outlawry in default of appearance. The new phenomenon appears about the year 1250, it is an action which might be called an attenuated appeal based on an act of violence. The defendant is charged with a breach of the king's peace, though with one that does not amount to felony. Remember that throughout the Middle Ages there is no such word as misdemeanour—the crimes that do not amount to felony are trespasses (Latin *transgressiones*). The action of trespass is founded on a breach of the king's peace:—with force and arms the defendant has assaulted and beaten the plaintiff, broken the plaintiff's close, or carried off the plaintiff's goods; he is sued for damages. The plaintiff does not seek violence but compensation, but the unsuccessful plaintiff will also be punished and pretty severely. In other actions the unsuccessful party has to pay an amercement for making an unjust, or resisting a just claim; the defendant found guilty of trespass is fined and imprisoned. What is more, the action for trespass shows its semi-criminal nature in the process that can be used against a defendant who will not appear—if he will not appear, his body can be seized and imprisoned; if he can not be found, he may be outlawed. We thus can see that the action of trespass is one that will become very popular with plaintiffs because of the stringent process against defendants. I very much doubt whether in Henry III's day the action could as yet be used save where there really had been what we might fairly call violence and breach of the peace; but gradually the convenience of this new action showed itself. In order to constitute a case for '*Trespass vi et armis*', it was to the last necessary that there should be some wrongful application of physical force to the [plaintiff's] lands or goods or person—but a wrongful step on his land, a wrongful touch to his person or chattels was held to be force enough and an adequate breach of the king's peace. This action then has the future before it.

COMMENTARY

Each form of action had its own procedure. The dominant role played by the action of trespass depended greatly upon the convenience of its procedure. A defendant who did not appear could be fined or outlawed (an aspect of 'mesne' or middle process—the procedure for bringing a defendant to justice—whereby the defendant forfeited his chattels and was subject to other civil disabilities). The mode of adjudication was trial by jury. This was much preferable to the older modes of trial, such as trial by ordeal (in which the plaintiff was subjected to a physical test, e.g. ducking in water to see if he or she would sink) or trial by battle (in which the parties might have to—literally—'fight it out'). No wonder trespass rapidly proved very popular!

(b) Trespass on the Case

The unsatisfactory nature of the requirement that the defendant should have acted 'with force and arms' (*vi et armis*) soon became apparent. Local courts were generally forbidden to entertain suits for more than 40 shillings without royal sanction, and there would have been a failure of justice if non-violent trespasses involving larger sums were excluded from the King's Courts as well. *Baker* writes (p. 61): 'The pressure for change is first seen in attempts to use *vi et armis* writs fictitiously, smuggling in actions under the pretence of force in the hope that no exception would be taken.' Throughout the first part of the fourteenth century there are examples of actions against blacksmiths for killing horses *vi et armis* and *contra pacem* but it seems more likely these are actions for carelessness in shoeing the horse rather than that they indicate a group of equicidal tradesmen. By the middle of the fourteenth century the Chancery clerks had begun drawing up a new writ of trespass. This writ required the plaintiff to plead his special 'case'. If the defendant's act had not been *vi et armis*, the plaintiff had to explain why it was nonetheless wrongful. The earliest forms of this writ involved situations where the parties were in a pre-existing relationship in the course of which the defendant had 'assumed responsibility' to the plaintiff. If the plaintiff had asked the defendant to shoe his horse or to hold a chattel on the plaintiff's behalf, any contact with the animal or chattel could not be *vi et armis*, but it could be wrongful if the shoeing was done carelessly or the chattel lost. The modern law of contract derives from the action on the case for *assumpsit* ('undertaking' or 'assumption of responsibility'), and today a party who has undertaken to do something under a contract and has done it carelessly may be liable in both contract and tort. Examples of the courts' willingness to stretch the writ of trespass *vi et armis* and then to sanction the later action on the case are extracted below.

Rattlesdene v Grunestone (1317)
J. Baker and S. Milsom, *Sources of English Legal History: Private Law to 1750* (London: Butterworths, 1986), p. 300

Suffolk. Richard de Grunestone and his wife Mary were attached to answer Simon de Rattlesdene on a plea why, whereas the same Simon had lately bought from the aforesaid Richard at Orford a certain tun of wine for 6 marks 6s 8d and had left that tun in the same place until he should require delivery, the aforesaid Richard and Mary with force and arms drew off a great part of the wine from the aforesaid tun, and instead of the wine so drawn off they filled the tun up with salt water so that all the wine became rotten and was altogether destroyed to the grave damage of this Simon and against the [king's] peace.

And as to this the same Simon by his attorney complains that whereas the same Simon had bought from the aforesaid Richard at Orford the aforesaid tun, and had left it in the same place until etc, the aforesaid Richard and Mary on the Thursday in the octave of St John the

Baptist in the ninth year of the present king's reign [1 July 1316] with force and arms, namely with swords and bows and arrows, drew off a great part of the wine from the aforesaid tun and instead of the wine so drawn off they filled the tun with salt water so that all the aforesaid wine was destroyed etc, to the grave damage etc, and against [the king's] peace etc whereby he says that he is the worse off and has suffered damage to the value of £10; and therefore he produces suit etc.

And Richard and Mary come by . . . their attorney and they deny force and wrong [and will deny it] when [and where they should] etc. And well do they deny that on the day and in the year aforesaid they ever drew off the aforesaid wine with force and arms or instead of the wine put in salt water or did him any other wrong as the aforesaid Simon complains. And of this [they] put themselves upon the countryside, and so does Simon. And so the sheriff is told to cause to come [a jury on such a day].

COMMENTARY

So vital was the allegation of *vi et armis* that claims that injury was inflicted 'with force and arms'—and often, for good measure, 'with swords, bows, arrows and clubs' (see Milsom (1958) 74 LQR 195)—were made in the most unlikely circumstances. Can it really have been the case in the above action that the defendants drew off a quantity of wine 'with force and arms, namely with swords and bows and arrows'? More likely, this was an action by a disgruntled purchaser of the wine for loss caused by a shipping accident.

The Farrier's Case (1372)
J. H. Baker & S. F. C. Milsom, *Sources of English Legal History: Private Law to 1750* (London: Butterworths, 1986) p. 341

Trespass was brought against a farrier for injuring a horse with a nail; and the writ said to show why, at a certain place, he drove a nail into the quick of the horse's hoof, whereby the plaintiff lost the profit from his horse for a long time.

Percy [for the defendant]. He has brought a writ of trespass against us, and does not say 'with force and arms'. We pray judgment of the writ.

Fyncheden CJ. He has brought his writ according to his case. (So he thought the writ good.)

Percy. The writ should be 'with force and arms', or should say that he drove the nail maliciously; and since there is neither the one nor the other, we pray judgment . . .

Then the writ was held good. And the defendant took issue that he shod the horse, without this that he injured it with a nail . . . etc.

COMMENTARY

This is an early example of an action on the case. The court holds that it is not necessary to include the allegation, necessary in trespass, that the defendant acted *vi et armis*. Rather than relying upon evasory fiction, the court openly accepts that the action in trespass has been stretched beyond its earlier limits.

3. The Development of Fault-Based Liability

(a) Writs of Trespass and Fault

To a contemporary observer it is inconceivable that the law of tort could exist without the fault-based law of negligence. In historical terms, however, the development of negligence as a separate tort is a relatively recent event. To have talked to a medieval or early modern lawyer about the law of 'negligence' would have resulted in a short and puzzled conversation. This is not because notions of fault were unimportant, but rather that its role was obscured by the writ system that dominated the early common law. The formulaic language used on the writs meant that it was not necessary to plead the state of mind or culpability of the defendant. No doubt, if the allegation was that the defendant 'assaulted the plaintiff with force and arms and beat, wounded and ill-treated him so that his life was despaired of', it could safely be assumed that the harm was inflicted intentionally and that the defendant was culpable. But as the writ of trespass was stretched to include cases of accidental injury—a trend that, as was noted above, led to the development of trespass on the case—the defendant's fault could not be taken for granted. It is difficult today to ascertain precisely what role was played in such cases by the concept of fault, but it seems likely that the taking of all reasonable care to avoid the injury of which the plaintiff complained was regarded as a defence. This does not necessarily appear from the language of the early law reports (called 'Year Books'), however, as the reporters were primarily interested in the form of the writ (and legal challenges to its form) and the pleadings. Even later law reporters, who might note the jury's verdict on the facts, frequently said nothing about the likely reason for the verdict. There was thus no record of the evidence put to the jury by defendants 'pleading the general issue', i.e. entering a plea of Not Guilty, but respected authorities conjecture that the issue of fault was often raised at this stage (*Baker*, p. 405; S. F. C. Milsom, *Historical Foundations of the Common Law*, 2nd edn. (London: Butterworths, 1981), pp. 296–300; cf. *Ibbetson*, p. 59, who argues that questions of fault might be reflected in the jury's deliberation as to whether the defendant *caused* the plaintiff's injury).

(b) Negligence and the Action on the Case

Liability for negligently inflicted injuries was first recognised by stretching the scope of trespass, but it found a more natural home in the action on the case. As noted above, the earliest examples of actions on the case involved parties in a pre-existing relationship with each other, e.g. the relationship between vendor and seller. Most of these cases would today be regarded as falling under the law of contract, not tort. Tort concerns itself primarily with parties who are strangers to one another. Liability here was slower to develop than in the case of pre-existing relationships.

Two of the earliest examples of liability imposed in the absence of a pre-existing relationship were for harm caused by the escape of fire and by dangerous animals (the *scienter* action). The liability was premised on the allegation that it was a custom of the realm that a particular activity should be pursued so as not to cause harm. Customs of this nature were also held to apply to innkeepers and common carriers but never developed much further as 'the common custom of this realm is common law and need not be pleaded' (*Beaulieu v Fingham* (1401), in Baker & Milsom, *op. cit.*, p. 557). Liability under these customs was probably stricter than under the modern conception of negligence, although, as noted above, it is difficult to ascertain whether it was wholly independent of fault.

Actions for pure negligence were rare, but, as *Baker* points out (p. 409), this was probably because the existing law covered most situations. Forcible wrongs could be remedied in trespass, but if the wrong was non-forcible it was probably because there had been careless performance of an undertaking, remediable by *assumpsit* (which laid the foundations for the modern law of contract) or because the harm had been caused indirectly. Indirect harm normally involved the escape of something dangerous, like fire or an animal, which was covered by existing actions in case. There was no perceived need to develop a distinct general liability for negligence and the satisfactory nature of the existing remedies made any such development unlikely.

4. Eighteenth-Century Developments

(a) The Beginnings of Negligence

As with much of the development of the common law, the impetus for change came with the attempt of lawyers to modify legal rules for the benefit of their own clients. From the latter half of the seventeenth century, writs began to appear from which the development of a tort of negligence can be traced. However, a general liability for negligence did not sit easily with the forms of action in which it would need to be pleaded. The beginning of the problem can probably be traced to *Mitchil v Alestree* (1676) 1 Vent 295. The plaintiff had been injured in Little Lincoln's Inn Fields when one of the horses the defendants were trying to break in escaped and kicked her. Prima facie this was a forcible wrong, remediable in trespass *vi et armis*. However, it was a defence to trespass to show that the contact had been against the defendant's will, so that in *Mitchil*, if the jury could be convinced that the contact was the result of the independent action of the horse, it might find for the defendant. This encouraged the plaintiff to plead the action in case, by alleging that the defendant's wrong was to break in the horses 'improvidently, rashly and without due consideration of the unsuitability of the place for the purpose'. She was successful. Another reason why the plaintiff might want to choose case instead of trespass *vi et armis* was the development of vicarious liability. It was during the course of the eighteenth century that case became the appropriate form of action in which to sue an employer 'vicariously', i.e. for a tort committed by his employee. Again, case was the correct action even where the employee's act had been forcible *vis-à-vis* the plaintiff.

(b) The Direct/Indirect Distinction

If the forms of action were to mean anything at all, there needed to be some guidance on the circumstances in which trespass *vi et armis* or case was the appropriate form. It was this need that led to the introduction of the infamous direct/indirect distinction between actions of trespass and case. In *Reynolds v Clarke* (1724) 1 Str 634 at 636, Fortescue J ruled:

> [I]f a man throws a log into the highway, and in that act it hits me; I may maintain trespass, because it is an immediate wrong; but if, as it lies there, I tumble over it, and receive an injury, I must bring an action upon the case; because it is only prejudicial in consequence, for which originally I could have no action at all.

This distinction proved difficult to operate in practice. In the famous case of *Scott v Shepherd* (1773) 2 W Bl 892 the defendant threw a lighted squib (firework) into a crowded market, where it was twice thrown on before striking the plaintiff in the face and exploding. The plaintiff pleaded in trespass *vi et armis* and this was ultimately held to be the correct form.

Although the distinction was problematic throughout the history of the two actions of trespass and case, the increase in the number of running-down cases towards the end of the eighteenth century caused particular difficulties. If the plaintiff was hit by a horse-drawn stagecoach, this was a forcible act and hence trespass was the appropriate form of action. However, if the horses had bolted contrary to the intention of the driver this might be a defence to trespass. But, in case, liability might well be imposed if the allegation was that the defendant had carelessly attempted to control the horses. Further, if the coach had been driven by an employee rather than its owner, case had to be brought as this was the proper form for vicarious liability. None of this mattered much if courts were prepared to turn a blind eye to whether or not an action was in the correct form, but in *Day v Edwards* (1794) 5 TR 648, Lord Kenyon CJ held that, in a running-down case, the plaintiff complained of an immediate act and hence trespass was the required form of action. This was reaffirmed by his successor, Lord Ellenborough CJ (see *Leame v Bray* (1803) 3 East 593), but the practical difficulties with a rigid distinction between trespass and case proved insurmountable.

The solution lay in allowing the plaintiff to 'waive' the trespass and sue instead in case. In *Williams v Holland* (1833) 2 LJCP (NS) 190, the Court of Common Pleas decided that this would be allowed where the plaintiff's injury was occasioned by the 'carelessness and negligence' of the defendant, notwithstanding the act was immediate, so long as it was not a wilful act. It thus became the norm to bring case whether the negligence of the defendant produced immediate or consequential damage. The independent action in negligence was thus well and truly established by the time the last vestiges of the forms of action were abolished by the Judicature Acts 1873–5, and the direct/indirect distinction was effectively jettisoned in favour of a new classification: intention and negligence.

For more detailed discussion on the historical development of the tort of negligence see: Kiralfy, *The Action on the Case* (London: Sweet & Maxwell, 1951); Milsom, 'Not Doing is No Trespass: A View of the Boundaries of Case' [1954] CLJ 105; 'Trespass from Henry III to Edward III' (1958) 74 LQR 195–224, 407–36, 561–90; Baker, 'Introduction' (1977) 94 Selden Society 23 (Spelman's Reports, vol. II), ch. VIII; Prichard, 'Trespass, Case and the Rule in *Williams v Holland*' [1964] CLJ 234 and '*Scott v Shepherd* and the Emergence of the Tort of Negligence', Selden Society Lecture (1976); *Ibbetson*, chs 8 and 9.

5. The Classification of Obligations

The task of classifying the various forms of action under the headings we recognise in the modern law—the law of tort, the law of contract, the law of property, etc.—began in England in the early seventeenth century. In the category of those actions imposing personal obligations, as opposed to recognising rights over property, contract (*assumpsit*) came to be regarded as distinct. (Equity, which imposed obligations on trustees and fiduciaries, was always a separate entity.) This left behind a miscellaneous collection of actions in trespass and case which resisted easy classification. These actions were lumped together in books as 'torts', but little thought was given to how they should be rationalised, or whether the law could be simplified, or whether obligations recognised in the courts of equity should be introduced to the classification. The development of general principles of liability had to wait until the period after the abolition of the forms of action in 1875, and many would argue that the task is yet to be completed. The most important advance was the recognition of a generalised liability for negligently-inflicted injuries; liability for intentional acts has still to be so thoroughly rationalised, largely because of a historical attachment to the old writs of trespass.

J. H. Baker, *Introduction to English Legal History*
4th edn. (London: Butterworths, 2002)

The Concept of Tort

The law of torts, or civil wrongs, is extensive and its boundaries are indistinct. An understanding of the process by which a number of miscellaneous causes of action came to be classified as 'torts' must depend partly on semantics. The nearest medieval equivalent of the modern lawyer's 'tort' was 'trespass', because the old French word *tort* (*injuria in Latin*) had a wider meaning; tort denoted any kind of legal injury. In the preceding chapters we traced the development of trespass in the areas of contract and property law, and noticed that in the early sixteenth century there was nothing incongruous about describing a breach of contract as a tort or trespass. But when the action of *assumpsit* became a truly contractual remedy, based on a promise in return for consideration, breaches of contract came to be seen as legally different in a number of ways from other kinds of trespass...By the middle of the seventeenth century contract and tort were seen as being so different that claims in tort and contract could not be joined in the same action. Thus, when an action was brought in 1665 against the hirer of a horse for misusing the animal and not paying the hire, counsel argued that the joinder of the two causes of action was erroneous because one action sounded in tort and the other in 'breach of promise only'. In another case the same year, counsel treated contract and tort as mutually exclusive: 'tort can never be done where there is a special agreement, unless there be duty by statute or common law incumbent'. This is near the modern understanding of the word...Already by 1663 legal indexes were classifying 'tort' in the modern sense, as a subheading under 'actions on the case'.

As different kinds of trespass action acquired separate characteristics in the sixteenth and seventeenth centuries, further subdivisions of the law of torts were made, subdivisions which survived the abolition of the writ system itself. During the last century or so, however, the law of torts has been undergoing a gradual reclassification as a result of the rapid expansion of the tort of negligence. Liability for negligence alone—that is, without reference to other factors—was rarely imposed before 1700, and even at the beginning of the twentieth century Sir John Salmond was denying the existence of a separate tort of negligence. In the practitioners' book, *Clerk and Lindsell on Torts*, negligence did not reach the status of a separate chapter until 1947. It would be easy to conclude that negligence has a short history; but this would be misleading. The negligence approach of the modern law determines liability by focusing on the quality of the defendant's act rather than on the kind of harm done to the plaintiff. The rearrangement of so much of the modern law of tort around the concept of negligence is partly a result of that shift of focus. But there is nothing modern about the concept of negligence in itself; what has changed is its primacy. Negligence and fault have always been familiar ideas, and for at least four centuries before 1700 they played a role in law and legal terminology; but their role was ancillary rather than primary. Negligence was something which a plaintiff might mention together with other factors in his writ, or which a defendant might raise by way of showing that he was not at fault. It was not even confined to actions in tort, in the modern sense of the term...

G. Williams and B. Hepple, *Foundations of the Law of Tort*
2nd edn. (London: Butterworths, 1984)

Since the Judicature Act [1873] judges have been slowly emancipating themselves from the forms of action; they have begun to think in terms of broad rules of law which are not related to the old categories. An outstanding example is the case of *Wilkinson v Downton* [1897] 2 QB 57, decided by an eminent judge of the Victorian era, Wright J:

> Mr Downton, in jest, told Mrs Wilkinson that her husband had been 'smashed up' in an accident and had both his legs broken. The lady suffered a serious shock entailing weeks of suffering and incapacity. At the risk of seeming to have no sense of humour she sued Downton for damages. Wright J held that the action well lay.

There was no precedent for this decision before the Judicature Act. The plaintiff could not have brought an action for trespass, which lay only for the direct physical infliction of harm (or the threat of it). Here the plaintiff had been physically injured, but only as a result of her mental shock following upon the words spoken. She could not have sued for this mental suffering in deceit, because an action for deceit could be brought only where the defendant had made a fraudulent statement on which the plaintiff was intended to rely, and did rely to his detriment; here the plaintiff was not claiming in respect of damage resulting from any conduct on her part in reliance upon the truth of the statement. The damage resulted merely from her belief in its truth, and from the effect that that belief had upon her mind. Notwithstanding these difficulties, the judge felt able to assert the existence of a principle of law without the attempt to relate his decision to any of the ancient writs, as by saying that the concept of trespass to the person could be extended to a 'psychological assault'. Instead, he assumed the existence of a general principle of law according to which a person who intends without justification to cause fear or anxiety to another, in circumstances where grave effects are likely to follow, is responsible if such effects do follow. The judge's attitude can perhaps be expressed in Horatio's words: 'There needs be no ghost, my lord, come from the grave to tell us this.' The decision is an outstanding example of the greater readiness of the courts at the present day to lay down general principles of liability instead of indulging in mere historical research.

COMMENTARY

As we shall see in Chapter 2, the imposition of liability for an intentional act causing indirect harm was not unknown under the forms of action (see *Bird v Holbrook* (1828) 4 Bing 628) but the rationalisation of the result by way of a wide general principle was predominantly a nineteenth-century development. Even then, the courts stopped short of integrating the old writs of trespass to the person—assault, battery and false imprisonment—within the new scheme, and these remained the primary remedy for injuries resulting directly from an intentional act. Wright J's general principle was effectively side-lined: in the next 100 years, it was applied on only a handful of occasions (see Ch. 2.V, below). Perhaps this was just as well, for there now appears to be considerable doubt whether Wright J ever intended his judgment to form the basis for a broad principle of liability (see Lunney, 'Practical Joking and Its Penalty: *Wilkinson v Downton* in Context' (2002) 10 Tort L Rev 168).

A later and more influential example of the introduction of a broad principle of liability was the opinion of Lord Atkin in *Donoghue v Stevenson* [1932] AC 562, in which his Lordship identified a single principle—the 'neighbour principle'—running through all the instances of liability for negligently inflicted harm. If *Wilkinson v Downton* provides a rule for intentionally inflicted harm, and *Donoghue v Stevenson* a rule for negligently inflicted harm, is the rest of the law of tort necessary at all?

6. The Modern Pre-Eminence of Negligence

Without doubt, the tort that has dominated all others since the early twentieth century is negligence; according to one writer it has attained a 'majestic pre-eminence' (M. Millner, *Negligence in Modern Law* (London: Butterworths, 1967), p. 227). However, as we have seen, negligence as an independent action is a relatively modern phenomenon, and the main period of its growth has been in the last 75 years. Why should negligence, as opposed to other torts, have achieved this position? The extract below suggests some possible reasons.

D. Ibbetson, 'The Tort of Negligence in the Common Law in the Nineteenth and Twentieth Centuries' in E. Schrage (ed.), *Negligence: The Comparative Legal History of the Law of Torts* (Berlin: Duncker & Humblot, 2001)

Transformative Factors in the Twentieth-Century Tort of Negligence

From around the beginning of the twentieth century a number of factors combined to alter the nature and structure of negligence liability.

First of all, there were a number of economic changes which altered the basis on which negligence liability operated. Most obvious of these was the increasing preponderance of corporate defendants. This was, of course, not a new phenomenon, as the frequency of actions against railway companies in the nineteenth century amply demonstrates; but the increasingly corporate nature of industrial enterprise by the early twentieth century meant that actions were ever more commonly brought against companies rather than individuals. This undoubtedly brought about a more plaintiff-centred approach to liability, equivalent to that found in actions by railway passengers after the 1850s. As well as the prejudice against wealthy defendants—the maxim of natural jurisprudence, 'It is no sin to rob an apparently rich man'—large corporate defendants were undoubtedly better able to spread losses across their business and so pass them on to customers or shareholders than were individual capitalists or small partnerships. Moreover, in so far as the nineteenth-century legal thinking was built on a moral principle that individuals should only be liable for their own shortcomings, the justification for this in a world of corporate defendants was rather more difficult to see. Added to this there was the increasing availability of liability insurance. Whereas in the nineteenth century individuals might only insure against their losses, from the late nineteenth century it became possible to insure against legal liability; and well into the twentieth century there were doubts about the legality of insuring against the consequence of one's own wrongdoing. Moreover, as the century progressed it became compulsory to take out such liability insurance in respect of certain activities, such as driving a motor vehicle. The same arguments came into play here as in the case of corporate defendants: as between an injured plaintiff and an anonymous (and wealthy) insurance company it was easy to have sympathy with the plaintiff; and losses could be spread widely and relatively painlessly rather than borne by the individual plaintiff or defendant.

Secondly, there was an intellectual shift. The acute individualism which had characterised Victorian England began to give way to a more communitarian approach: no longer was it obvious that an individual who caused harm to another while pursuing his own economic self-interest should be liable only if it could be shown that he had not taken reasonable care. Alongside this, legal commentators began to stress that negligence liability did not depend on a moral principle but on a social one; it was not based on something internal to the defendant but on a failure to live up to an external standard, and that external standard was something which could be determined by public policy. The American jurist Oliver Wendell Holmes was the principal proponent of this view, and even before 1900 it had become so much part of common learning that it was being misunderstood by examination candidates. As corporate and insured defendants became the norm judges and scholars, especially in America, came to formulate the principles of liability in wholly economic, non-moral terms.

Thirdly, this time affecting more the structure of liability than its incidence, the jury disappeared from the trial of negligence actions. This occurred in three stages. First of all, the County Courts Acts [dating from 1846] provided that trial would be without jury in small cases, and might be without jury in other cases within the jurisdiction of the court (though either party had a right to demand a jury). In practice, jury trials in County Courts were very uncommon in any form of action, including negligence actions; they were abolished in 1934. Secondly, after the Judicature Acts 1873–1875 it was possible for some negligence cases to be assigned to the Chancery Division of the High Court; such cases would be heard without a jury. Thirdly, and most significantly, after a prolonged stutter, the jury was to all intents and purposes made optional after the Judicature Acts of 1873–1875, though in actions sounding in tort the option generally appears to have been exercised; temporary provisions restricting the right to trial by jury to a small number of situations (not including negligence) were in force from 1918 to 1925; new rules of procedure were introduced in 1932; and in 1933 the right to trial by jury in negligence actions was effectively abolished. After this, practically all cases were tried by judge alone. In so far as the classic structure of the tort of negligence had been largely generated by the separation between judge and jury, the reintegration of the trial process brought about a reintegration of the elements of the tort of negligence.

COMMENTARY

Ibbetson provides a useful corrective to those tempted to view tort law's development in purely doctrinal terms, as the progressive rationalisation of disparate pockets of liability driven only by legal logic. While tort law's 'intellectual history' should not be disregarded altogether (see especially G. White, *Tort Law in America: An Intellectual History* (expanded edn., New York: OUP, 2003)), it is important to explicate the link between tort law and the social, economic and political environment in which it operates, and to consider how, over the passage of time, tort has responded to changes in that environment. In fact, the influence of external, societal factors upon the law of tort can be traced back a very long way. The writ of trespass *vi et armis*, it may plausibly be argued, was introduced as a means of maintaining the authority of the sovereign and the security of the realm: the writ enabled the King's courts to deal with outbreaks of violent behaviour which would previously have ended up only in the local courts. But it is with the Industrial Revolution that the influence of extra-legal factors becomes most interesting, above all in the development of a generalised liability for negligence.

Tort Law and the Industrial Revolution

According to the very influential but highly controversial thesis of Morton J. Horwitz (*The Transformation of American Law 1780–1860* (New York: OUP, 1977)), tort law was

transformed in the nineteenth century in order to provide a subsidy to the industrial concerns that had sprung up in the aftermath of the Industrial Revolution. (Horwitz concentrated on America, but believed his thesis equally applicable to England.) Horwitz claimed
that the courts of the time abandoned the erstwhile general principle of strict liability (i.e.
liability without fault), as expressed by the Latin maxim *sic utere tuo ut alienum non laedas*
(use your own only in such a way that you do not harm anyone else's), and adopted instead
the fault-based standard of negligence (p. 99):

> At the beginning of the nineteenth century there was a general private law presumption in favour
> of compensation, expressed by the oft-cited common law maxim *sic utere*. For Blackstone, it was
> clear that even an otherwise lawful use of one's property that caused injury to the land of another
> would establish liability in nuisance, 'for it is incumbent on him to find some other place to do that
> act, where it will be less offensive.' In 1800, therefore, virtually all injuries were still conceived of as
> nuisances, thereby invoking a standard of strict liability which tended to ignore the specific charac-
> ter of the defendant's acts. By the time of the [American] Civil War [1861–65], however, many types
> of injuries had been reclassified under a 'negligence' heading, which had the effect of substantially
> reducing entrepreneurial liability . . . [T]he law of negligence became a leading means by which the
> dynamic and growing forces in American society were able to challenge and eventually overwhelm
> the weak and relatively powerless segments of the American economy. After 1840 the principle
> that one could not be held liable for socially useful activity exercised with due care became a com-
> monplace of American law.

The thesis is not without its difficulties. Horwitz's apparent ascription of conscious agency
to the judiciary fails to deal with the very wide range of different attitudes evident in the
decisions of different judges. It ignores the likely hostility to industrial expansion of those
many judges who were members of the landed gentry. And its depiction of a straightforward change from strict liability to negligence liability fails to fit the facts. As Rabin,
'The Historical Development of the Fault Principle: A Reinterpretation' (1981) 15 Ga L
Rev 925 points out, we should regard 'the view that the industrial era was dominated by
a comprehensive theory of fault liability for unintended harm as largely a myth . . . Along
similar lines . . . [it is] a serious mistake to characterize the pre-industrial era as one of
strict liability' (p. 927). Far from replacing strict liability, 'fault liability emerged out of a
world-view dominated largely by no-liability thinking' (p. 928), as was evident in the continuing denial—until well into the twentieth century—of any general duty to consumers
of products and trespassers, and the limitations upon employers' liability to their employees (see further Ch. 11). For further criticism of the Horwitz thesis in its application to
tort law, see Schwarz, 'Tort Law and Economy in Nineteenth Century America' (1981) 90
Yale LJ 1717.

Yet there is no denying that industrialisation had a significant influence on tort law, both
as a catalyst for expansion and as a cause for circumspection. As regards the former, it
seems clear that '[a]dvances in transportation and industry—mills, dams, carriages,
ships—made injuries involving strangers more common', and as a result forced the courts
to move beyond a conception of negligence liability as peculiar to certain pre-existing relationships and to adopt a generalised theory of liability: 'the modern negligence principle in
tort law seems to have been an intellectual response to the increased number of accidents
involving persons who had no pre-existing relationship with one another' (White, *op. cit.*,
p. 16). However, the seemingly unstoppable development of negligence into a generalised
liability was a cause of alarm to at least some members of the judiciary, who urged caution
and sought ways to limit the new liabilities to which entrepreneurs were exposed. This
'backlash' was most apparent in relation to accidents in the workplace, in which context a

number of very effective defences were developed by the courts so as to safeguard the interests of employers (see further Chs 6 and 11.I). However, industrial concerns were never granted an immunity from suit in negligence, and in some areas negligence liability flourished. Consider especially the large number of actions by passengers against railway companies from the mid-nineteenth century on: 'Mass transportation... [gave] rise to mass litigation' (R. Kostal, *Law and English Railway Capitalism 1825–1875* (Oxford: OUP, 1994) p. 255). This was, says Kostal (p. 290), 'the first wave of personal injury litigation in English legal history'.

From Laissez-Faire Individualism to the Welfare State

By the end of the nineteenth century, the prevailing political mood was beginning to change. There was a recognition both that the courts had too jealously protected employers from negligence actions brought by injured employees and that the tort system as a whole was inadequate to the task of providing compensation for the victims of industrial (and other) accidents. In 1897, a no-fault Workmen's Compensation Scheme was introduced by legislation. It was not just a response to the inadequacies of the law of employer's liability; more significantly, it was the first step on the road towards the welfare state. In the twentieth century, the principal burden of providing compensation for the victims of accident, illness or other misfortune was to fall upon taxpayers, not tortfeasors. And it became trite to observe a shift from the laissez-faire individualism of the nineteenth century to the more community-spirited outlook of the twentieth.

Tort law could not remain immune to the changing mood of the times, and the courts sought to adapt its principles in an effort to broaden the scope of tort compensation. Duties of care were recognised in many new types of case, expanding still further the scope of liability in negligence, a development which culminated in Lord Atkin's enunciation of his 'neighbour principle' in *Donoghue v Stevenson* [1932] AC 562 (see Ch. 3.I.2 below). New limits were placed on the defences available to employers in actions brought against them by their injured employees (see Ch. 11.I.1(b) below). And fault came to be determined by reference to an external or objective standard, the standard of the reasonable person (see Ch. 4.IV, below), thereby divorcing legal notions of fault from the moral notions of the ordinary person. As W. Cornish and G. Clarke, *Law and Society in England 1750–1950* (London: Sweet & Maxwell, 1989), p. 538 point out: 'Liability for personal fault had undoubtedly appealed to the strongly individualistic strain in Victorian moralising; but as a basis for a workable system of accident compensation it had required significant compromise.' Its moral trappings stripped away, tort law came to be seen as no more than a component part of the compensation system: it was 'simply a complex of legal rules, largely devoid of moral content and of penal or deterrent effect, the function of which is to mark off the field of recoverable damage' (M. Millner (*op. cit.*), p. 4). Whether tort law could ever be a satisfactory system of accident compensation remained to be seen.

Tort Law and Insurance

It was only with the underpinning of the insurance system that tort law could even aspire to act as a major source of compensation to the victims of accidents. The development of liability insurance in the late nineteenth century, initially as a mechanism for protecting employers against the risk of lawsuits from employees, came to be seen as a justification for tapping the compensation potential of tort law still further (see White, *op. cit.*, pp. 147–50). By the middle of the twentieth century, tort law's function was identified as the transfer of losses away from the victims of accidents and the distribution or spreading of those losses throughout society by means (especially) of the liability insurance system (see James, 'Accident Liability Reconsidered: The Impact of Liability Insurance' (1948) 57 Yale LJ 549). The buck no longer stopped with the negligent actor, but was passed on to his or her insurer and thereafter spread amongst the class of premium-payers as a whole. So vital was insurance thought to be to the effectiveness of the tort compensation system that legislation was introduced to require the commonest targets of negligence litigation car owners and employers—to take out compulsory insurance against their potential liabilities (see, respectively, the Road Traffic Act 1930 (now Road Traffic Act 1988, s. 143ff) and the Employers' Liability (Compulsory Insurance) Act 1969).

Insurers no doubt play a major role in the operation of tort law; whether insurance considerations have brought about change in the substantive doctrines of tort law is another, more disputed matter. Certainly, the predominant judicial attitude is that the insurance position of the parties should have no influence on the adjudication of individual cases. The issue is considered in more detail below (Ch. 1.III.1).

The Modern Tort Crisis

As the twentieth century progressed, tort law in general—and negligence liability in particular—were stretched further and further (see P. Atiyah, *The Damages Lottery* (Oxford: Hart, 1997), chs 2 and 3). It increasingly came to be seen as falling between two stools. On the one hand, it sought to fulfil compensation objectives for which it was fundamentally ill-suited. Compared with social security, tort law was a very expensive method of providing compensation, and, notwithstanding the breadth of the negligence principle, it compensated a very small proportion of all accident victims, namely those injured by another's fault. At the same time, tort law offended against principles of equality as successful claimants received disproportionately high awards compared with those left to rely upon the social security system. By the 1960s and 70s, the notion that tort law could be justified in terms of accident compensation was thoroughly discredited (see especially the first edition of Patrick Atiyah's *Accidents, Compensation and the Law*, published in 1970). The greater the success of the negligence principle in expanding the reach of tort law, the more its inadequacies were exposed: 'in the very moment of its triumph, the shadow of its decline' was falling upon the tort of negligence (Millner, *op. cit.*, p. 234). Reformers, including Atiyah, sought to pursue compensation objectives by other means, for example by the introduction of universal no-fault compensation paid by the state. The high-water mark of such efforts came in 1974, on the other side of the world, when New Zealand abolished its system of tort compensation for personal injuries and replaced it with a no-fault Accident Compensation Scheme (see Ch. 18.II.2(b) below). However, similar reform proposals in Australia were never implemented, while in the United Kingdom the idea never really got off the ground at all: a Royal Commission on *Civil Liability and Compensation for Personal Injury*, chaired by Lord Pearson, confounded the hopes and expectations of advocates of the no-fault endeavour by refusing even to contemplate universal no-fault compensation (Cmnd 7054, 1978). Such is the rhetorical appeal of the notion of fault-based liability that it now seems highly unlikely that it will be abolished in order to make way for any alternative compensation mechanism (see further Ch. 18.II).

At the same time, tort law came under attack from those who believed it had betrayed its moral purpose of promoting justice between individuals. In their eyes, tort law could only be seen as a part of private law, and it risked incoherence if it sought to pursue 'public' goals, for example, the provision of accident compensation, which were inconsistent with the bipartite nature of legal proceedings (see, e.g., E. Weinrib, *The Idea of Private Law*

(Cambridge, Mass: Harvard University Press, 1995)). In short, tort law was about individual, not social, responsibility. Subscribers to this position believed that tort law had overstretched itself in an effort to be something it could not, and should not, become. In particular, it had extended liability to losses that were better left to lie where they fell (e.g. because they were entrepreneurial risks: see the discussion of pure economic loss in Ch. 8); it had encouraged a 'pass the buck' mentality whereby individuals sought someone else to blame for every misfortune that befell them (often on the basis that someone else, often the state, had a duty to take positive steps for their benefit: see Chs 9 and 10); and it had overburdened business and the insurance industry by 'opening the floodgates' of liability. This last concern was particularly highlighted by various 'crises' afflicting the insurance industry in the late 1980s/early 1990s, exemplified by the near collapse of the Lloyds of London insurance market in 1990. Although it was conceded that a number of other factors played a role in these crises (e.g. general economic conditions and a succession of natural disasters), it was also alleged that tort law had played a contributory role by encouraging the spread of (risky) third-party or liability insurance at the expense of (comparatively safe) first-party or loss insurance: it is much easier to predict the potential losses of a single insured person than it is to predict the potential losses of all those other people—who knows how many there could be?—to whom the insured might be held liable (see generally Priest, 'The Current Insurance Crisis and Modern Tort Law' (1987) 96 Yale LJ 1521). To this day the problem of the increasing cost, and sometimes unavailability, of liability insurance has been a common cry of those who bemoan the 'compensation culture' (see further Ch 1.III.3 below).

At the time of writing these tensions show no signs of resolution. The past 30 years or so have seen, in society as a whole, a return to nineteenth-century values of individual responsibility and self-reliance, and fears that tort law might undermine these by 'going too far' have caused the courts to cut back the scope of liability in negligence in certain notable respects (see Chs 3 and 7–10). But tort law has not shed all traces of the loss distribution ideology which prompted its spectacular growth throughout the greater part of the twentieth century. (Consider, in particular, the doctrine of an employer's vicarious liability for torts committed by his or her employees: Ch. 15.) Undoubtedly, the attempt to reconcile the nineteenth-century requirement of individual fault with the idea of a wider social responsibility for accident victims has led to a lack of coherence in the law of tort in general and negligence in particular (see Hepple, 'Negligence: The Search for Coherence' (1997) CLP 69). Yet tort law continues to muddle on, seeking what can only be an uneasy compromise between notions of loss-distribution on the one hand and individualised justice on the other.

II. Theories of Tort

Having looked at this history, let us now consider current views as to the nature and functions of tortious liability. We shall consider two issues. First, what are the aims of tort law—what purposes might it pursue, how effectively does it pursue them? Secondly, how do the aims of tort law differ from those of other branches of the law, and how in doctrinal terms are torts to be distinguished from, say, crimes, contracts and trusts?

1. The Aims of the Law of Tort

Glanville Williams, 'The Aims of the Law of Tort' [1951] CLP 137

An intelligent approach to the study of law must take account of its purpose, and must be prepared to test the law critically in the light of its purpose. The question that I shall propound is the end or social function or raison d'etre of the law of tort, and particularly of the action in tort for damages.

It is commonly said that the civil action for damages aims at compensation, as opposed to the criminal prosecution which aims at punishment. This, however, does not look below the surface of things. Granted that the immediate object of the tort action is to compensate the plaintiff at the expense of the tortfeasor, why do we wish to do this? Is it to restore the *status quo ante*?—but if so, why do we want to restore the *status quo ante*? And could we not restore this status in some other and better way, for instance by a system of national insurance? Or is it really that we want to deter people from committing torts? Or, again, is it that the payment of compensation is regarded as educational, or as a kind of expiation for a wrong?

... There are four possible bases of the action for damages in tort: appeasement, justice, deterrence and compensation.

Appeasement.—Crime and tort have common historical roots. The object of early law is to prevent the disruption of society by disputes arising from the infliction of injury. Primitive law looks not so much to preventing crime in general as to preventing the continuance of this squabble in particular. The victim's vengeance is bought off by compensation, which gives him satisfaction in two ways: he is comforted to receive the money himself, and he is pleased that the aggressor is discomfited by being made to pay. By this means the victim is induced to 'let off steam' within the law rather than outside it.

In modern times the safety-valve function of the law of tort probably takes a subordinate place. We do not reckon on the recrudescence of family feuds as a serious possibility, or even that of duelling. However, it may be thought that unredressed torts would be regarded as a canker in society, and to that extent the law can still be regarded as having a pacificatory aim...

Justice.—With the growth of moral ideas it came to be thought that the law of tort was the expression of a moral principle. One who by his fault has caused damage to another ought as a matter of justice to make compensation. Two variants of this theory may be perceived: (1) The first places emphasis upon the fact that the payment of compensation is an evil for the offender, and declares that justice requires that he should suffer this evil. This is the principal of ethical retribution, exemplified (in criminal law) by Kant's dictum about the moral necessity of executing even the last murderer. (2) The second variant looks at the same situation from the point of view of the victim; it emphasises the fact that the payment of compensation is a benefit to the victim of the wrong, and declares that justice requires that he should receive this compensation.

It may be thought that these two variants are simply two different ways of stating the same thing, but that is not entirely true. (1) Many people who would not subscribe generally to the principle of ethical retribution would nevertheless assert the principle of ethical compensation. Again, (2) one who asserts the principle of ethical compensation does not necessarily say that the wrongdoer must himself be afflicted. If no one else will pay the compensation, the wrongdoer must; but if someone (such as the State or an insurance company) steps in and pays for him, the requirement of recuperation is satisfied even though there is no ethical retribution against the offender.

Those who adopt the doctrine of ethical retribution do not, and cannot, refer it to any other principle. It is a postulate—an ultimate value-judgment which can only be accepted or rejected...

The case is far different with ethical compensation. This does serve a social purpose, independently of any doctrine of punishment or (for that matter) of deterrence. Imagine a small community of comparatively moral people who hardly need a deterrent legal system but who do occasionally commit acts of negligence or even of unruly temper. Even such a community would find educational value in a rule requiring the making of reparation for harm caused by fault. Whereas people do not voluntarily accept punishment for themselves (except for religious reasons by way of penance), good people do accept for themselves the necessity of paying compensation for harm that they have caused. It is not a question of punishment, but of showing in a practical way one's solicitude and contrition, and of obeying the golden rule that we should do as we would be done by . . .

Deterrence.—Ranged against the theory of tort as part of the moral order are those who believe that it is merely a regime of prevention. The action in tort is a 'judicial parable', designed to control the future conduct of the community in general. In England this view seems to have been first expounded by Bentham. Blackstone had expressed the opinion that civil injuries are 'immaterial to the public', but Bentham thought that such a contrast with criminal law could not be maintained, and that the underlying object of civil and criminal law was the same. Both criminal punishment and tort damages were sanctions and therefore evils: the only difference was in the degree of evil. The purpose of threatening them was to secure obedience to rules . . .

Whatever the imperfections of the moral interpretation of tort, the deterrent theory itself fails to provide a perfect rationale. For one thing, it offends against the principle that deterrent punishment must be kept to the effective minimum. According to utilitarian philosophy, of which the deterrent theory is an application, a punishment must not be greater than is necessary to repress the mischief in question. Damages in tort, however, may be far greater than are needful as a warning . . .

Compensation.—Finally there is the compensatory or reparative theory, according to which one who has caused injury to another must make good the damage whether he was at fault or not. This is the same as the theory of ethical compensation except that it does not require culpability on the part of the defendant. If valid, it justifies strict liability [i.e. liability independent of fault], which the theory of ethical compensation does not. The difficulty is, however, to state it in such a form as to make it acceptable. If it is said that a person who has been damaged by another ought to be compensated, we readily assent, moved as we are by sympathy for the victim's loss. But what has to be shown is not merely that the sufferer ought to be compensated, but that he ought to be compensated by the defendant. In the absence of any moral blame of the defendant, how is this demonstration possible?

It is fashionable to say that the question is simply one of who ought to bear the risk. This, however, is a restatement of the problem rather than a solution to it. A more satisfactory version is that known as the entrepreneur theory or, to speak English, the enterprise theory. This regards liability for torts connected with an enterprise as a normal business expense. Nothing can be undertaken without some risk of damage to others, and if the risk eventuates it must be shouldered by the undertaker in the same way as the cost of his raw materials. That this attitude has come into prominence in the present century, though not unknown in the last, is symptomatic of the general search for security at the cost, if need be, of freedom of enterprise . . .

[Williams proceeds to consider whether the rules of the law of tort are consistent or inconsistent with the principal theories of liability. He concludes:]

Our attempt to find a coherent purpose in the present law of tort cannot be said to have met with striking success . . . Where possible the law seems to like to ride two or three horses at once; but occasionally a situation occurs where one must be selected. The tendency then is to choose the deterrent purpose for the torts of intention, and the compensatory purpose for other torts.

COMMENTARY

Of the four possible functions of tort law canvassed by Williams, we can place on one side appeasement (which 'takes a subordinate place' in the modern law) and compensation (which we have already considered in some detail, and will consider further in Ch. 18). It is necessary, however, to say something more on the topics of deterrence and justice.

Deterrence

Notwithstanding Williams's scepticism as to whether deterrence can be seen as one of the functions of tort law, some very sophisticated attempts have been made, especially by members of the law and economics movement in the United States, to demonstrate just that. It is a basic tenet of the economic analysis of law that the incentive provided by the threat of tort liability by and large promotes economic efficiency, and that it is its function to do so. Economic efficiency entails not as great a reduction in the accident rate as is possible, but only such a reduction as is efficient. In the language of Guido Calabresi, one of the founding fathers of the law and economics movement, the aim is to reduce not the number of accidents, but the costs of accidents, taking into account also the cost of safety measures (see *The Cost of Accidents* (New Haven, Conn.: Yale University Press, 1970)). Perhaps the most influential figure in the movement currently is Judge Richard Posner, who argues that tort law's general reliance upon principles of fault-based liability makes it the best mechanism available for ensuring that all efficient precautions are taken in order to reduce the risk of accidental injury (see especially 'A Theory of Negligence' (1972) 1 J Leg St 29). Posner summarises his approach as follows (p. 33):

> [T]he dominant function of the fault system is to generate rules of liability that if followed will bring about, at least approximately, the efficient—cost-justified—level of accidents and safety. Under this view, damages are assessed against the defendant as a way of measuring the costs of accidents, and the damages so assessed are paid over to the plaintiff (to be divided with his lawyer) as the price of enlisting their participation in the operation of the system. Because we do not like to see resources squandered, a judgment of negligence has inescapable overtones of moral disapproval, for it implies that there was a cheaper alternative to the accident.

In other published writing, Posner has gone beyond the claim made in the extract above, viz. that economic inefficiency attracts moral disapproval, to argue that economic efficiency is the foundation of all moral imperatives and hence the main meaning of 'justice' itself (see *The Economics of Justice* (1981)). This somewhat implausible claim is subjected to convincing criticism by Ronald Dworkin in 'Is Wealth A Value?', ch. 12 of *A Matter of Principle* (London: Duckworth, 1985) and in ch. 8 of *Law's Empire* (London: Fontana, 1986). Dworkin accuses Posner of 'moral monstrousness' in suggesting that wealth is a value of intrinsic, or even instrumental, worth.

Even ignoring such extravagant claims about its normative foundations, the descriptive elements of the economic analysis of tort law have attracted a sceptical response from several quarters. S. Sugarman, *Doing Away with Personal Injury Law* (New York: Quorum, 1989), for instance, argues that tort law's role in reducing levels of excessively dangerous activity has been exaggerated. He points to a number of other behavioural controls apart from the law of tort that might exercise such a deterrent effect '[s]elf-preservation instincts, market forces, personal morality, and governmental regulation (criminal and administrative) combine to control unreasonably dangerous actions independently of tort law' (p. 128). And he claims that, seen in terms of deterrence, tort's record has largely been one of a conspicuous lack of success: 'successful lawsuits represent a catalog of tort failures;

people behaved in unacceptable ways notwithstanding the threat of liability' (p. 130). For further criticism, see Abel, 'Torts' in D. Kairys (ed.), *The Politics of Law*, 3rd edn. (New York: Basic Books, 1998).

Justice

The depiction of tort law as designed to serve instrumental goals, for example the compensation of accident victims or the deterrence of accidents, has been disputed by a number of recent commentators. Their view is that tort law does not look forward to the achievement of instrumental goals of this nature, but backwards to a wrong that needs to be redressed. The central idea in tort law, then, is corrective justice. In Aristotle's classic account, corrective justice is contrasted with distributive justice: the former makes good a wrong without any regard to the needs, character, or worth of the individuals concerned; the latter is concerned only with the distribution of goods throughout society as a whole, having regard to every person's needs and desert (*Nichomachaean Ethics, revised edn.* (London: Penguin Classics, 1976), pp. 176–7, 180). In terms of this scheme, tort law would be a system of corrective justice, social security a system of distributive justice. The idea that the function of tort law is to achieve (corrective) justice is perhaps the longest-standing of all theories of tort—it is considered by Williams, above, under the name of 'ethical compensation'—but it has received a particular stimulus over the past 20 or 30 years, largely by way of a backlash to the vogue enjoyed by the instrumentalist accounts of tort law considered above. In particular, it has gained ground as a result of the increasing perception that tort law is ill-suited as a mechanism for achieving a rational system of compensation for incapacity.

One of the leading modern-day proponents of the corrective justice theory is Ernest J. Weinrib, who, in the following passage, describes the elements of tort law and procedure (and of the doctrine and procedure of private law more generally) that support his analysis (*The Idea of Private Law* (Cambridge, Mass.: Harvard University Press, 1995), p. 1).

The most striking feature about private law is that it directly connects two particular parties through the phenomenon of liability. Both procedure and doctrine express this connection. Procedurally, litigation in private law takes the form of a claim that a particular plaintiff presses against a particular defendant. Doctrinally, requirements such as the causation of harm attest to the dependence of the plaintiff's claim on a wrong suffered at the defendant's hands. In singling out the two parties and bringing them together in this way, private law looks neither to the litigants individually nor to the interests of the community as a whole, but to a bipolar relationship of liability.

Weinrib argues that instrumental accounts of tort law cannot make sense of these features because they look only to a desired outcome across society as a whole. 'Only if the plaintiff and defendant are linked in a single and coherent justificatory structure can one make sense of the practice of transferring resources directly from the defeated defendant to the victorious plaintiff' (p. 2). In his view, tort law can perform a rational function only if it abstains from all attempts to achieve instrumental goals, and tort lawyers should give up evaluating tort law in terms of such external (social rather than legal) goals and seek an 'internal' understanding of the law in the notion of corrective justice.

Weinrib's point about the unsuitability of tort law for the pursuit of instrumental goals is well taken (as least in relation to compensation for incapacity). However, as a blueprint for action his account is flawed. Over time, the tort system has come to play a role in our overall system of compensation for incapacity—largely through the 'stretching' of certain of its key doctrines (notably, the concept of fault). This role may be, by and large, only limited, but in some areas it is very significant, for example, in respect of accidents at work and on the roads. If, as Weinrib suggests, the courts should abandon those doctrines which were the product of the stretching of tort law to make it fulfil compensation goals, and should ignore such instrumental concerns in applying the law, then surely this cannot be done without putting in tort law's place some mechanism for ensuring adequate compensation for those who are to lose out. Weinrib is right to consider tort law from an internal perspective, but wrong to look at it in a vacuum, i.e. in isolation from its social context.

Even if it is conceded that tort law's only concern is corrective justice, the question arises of what sort of wrongs it should attempt to redress, and how it should redress them. Aristotle's account of corrective justice was purely formal. It entailed neither a particular conception of 'wrongful conduct' sufficient to give rise to injustice, nor a particular response by way of remedying that injustice. It may thus be regarded as an empty receptacle into which different conceptions of 'wrong' and 'remedy' can be placed. As Posner has pointed out, the concept of corrective justice is compatible with a number of different conceptions of the wrongful conduct whose outcome is to be corrected (see 'The Concept of Corrective Justice in Recent Theories of Tort Law' (1981) 10 J Leg St 187). Similarly, there is a wide range of different remedies that might appropriately be employed to redress a wrong. Admittedly, it is tempting to think that redress must entail the payment of compensation to restore the victim as nearly as possible to the position he would have been in if the injustice had not occurred; this indeed is the principle of the modern law of tort. But there is no reason for thinking that this is necessarily the just outcome. If a very poor person were to cause some small financial injury to a millionaire, would it really be just to demand that he pay compensation in respect of the full extent of that loss, at the cost of personal financial ruin, or would we think that justice had been secured by a sincere apology? It is no doubt true (as Aristotle held) that the wealth, character and desert of an individual are irrelevant in considering whether an injury inflicted or sustained is wrongful, but it is submitted that these factors may be very pertinent to the question of how in justice the wrong should be put right.

There is nothing then in the notion of corrective justice that requires the remedying of wrongful conduct through the law of tort. Nevertheless, the idea that tort law ought to perform such a function has strong intuitive appeal. Those interested in reading further should consult Fletcher, 'Fairness and Utility in Tort Theory' (1972) 85 Harv L Rev 537, Epstein, 'A Theory of Strict Liability' (1973) 2 J Leg St 151 and D. Owens (ed.), *Philosophical Foundations of Tort Law* (Oxford: Clarendon Press, 1995), *passim*. A recent attempt to analyse the English law of negligence in corrective justice terms may be found in A. Beever, *Rediscovering the Law of Negligence* (Oxford: Hart Publishing, 2007).

Can the existence of compulsory liability insurance regimes in respect of road accidents and accidents at work be reconciled with a corrective justice theory of tort law?

2. Doctrinal Classifications: Tort Law and other Legal Categories

J. Fleming, *The Law of Torts* 9th edn.
(North Ryde, NSW: Law Book Co, 1998), pp. 3–5

Perhaps the most profitable method of delimiting the field of tort liability is to describe it in terms of the policies which have brought it into existence and contrast these with the policies underlying other forms of liability. Broadly speaking, the entire field of liability may be divided according to its purposes into criminal, tortious, contractual and restitutionary. Each of these is distinguishable by the nature of the conduct or its consequences and the purpose for which legal remedies are given.

The law of tort and crime, despite their common origin in revenge and deterrence, long ago parted company and assumed distinctly separate functions. A crime is an offence against the State, as representative of the public, which will vindicate its interests by punishing the offender. A criminal prosecution is not concerned with repairing an injury that may have been done to an individual, but with exacting a penalty in order to protect society as a whole. Tort liability, on the other hand, exists primarily to compensate the victim by compelling the wrong-doer to pay for the damage done. True, some traces of its older link with punishment and crime have survived to the present day, most prominently exemplary damages to punish and deter contumelious and outrageous wrongdoing. Yet the principal concern of the law of torts nowadays is with casualties of accidents, that is, of unintended harm. In this wider field, the law is concerned chiefly with distributing losses which are an inevitable by-product of modern living, and, in allocating the risk, makes less and less allowance to ideas of punishment, admonition and deterrence.

The law of contract exists, at least in its most immediate reach, for the purpose of vindicating a single interest, that of having promises of others performed. This it does either by specifically compelling the promisor to perform or by awarding the promisee damages to put him in as good a position as if the promise had been kept. Thus while contract law as a rule assures the promisee the benefit of the bargain, tort law has the different function of primarily compensating injuries or losses. Moreover, by comparison the interests vindicated by the law of torts are much more numerous. They may be interests in personal security, reputation or dignity, as in actions for assault, personal injuries and defamation. They may be interests in property, as in actions for trespass and conversion; or interests in unimpaired relations with others, as in causing injury or death to relatives. Hence the field covered by the law of torts is much broader, and certainly more diverse, than that of contract.

According to another distinction, tort duties are said to be 'primarily fixed by law', in contrast to contractual obligations which can arise only from voluntary agreement. Certainly, in classical theory, the function of contract is to promote voluntary allocation of risks (typically, but not exclusively, commercial risks) in a self-regulating society, while tort law allocates risks collectively in accordance with community values by the fiat of court or legislature. But this distinction, though still fundamentally sound, has become somewhat blurred as the area of self-regulation by contract is being progressively narrowed by regulatory legislation and judicial policing for fairness inspired by collectivist and egalitarian ideals. Besides, contractual terms (where not expressly spelled out) are 'implied' (imposed) by law and [are] usually identical with tort duties arising from one party's 'undertaking' to act for another, as in the case of professional and other services.

The third field of legal liability calling for demarcation from tort, restitution, serves the idea that justice requires the restitution of unintended benefits so as to prevent unjustified enrichment. Common illustrations are the return of money paid under mistake or the recovery of a bribe or profit (rather than loss) from misappropriation. Unlike the law of contract, it has nothing to do with promises and, unlike tort, with losses.

To summarise, criminal liability is distinguished from tort by the fact its object is to punish, not to compensate; contractual liability by reason of the different interests protected and the fact that risks are allocated primarily voluntarily rather than collectively; and restitution because it is concerned with the restitution of benefits, not compensation for losses.

COMMENTARY

The analysis of tort liability put forward by Fleming is similar to that found in other leading tort text books (*Winfield & Jolowicz*, ch. 1; *Salmond & Heuston*, ch. 2). However, it should be noted that the distinction between tort, on the one hand, and other forms of civil liability, on the other, has been challenged. Attempts have been made to find general principles of liability for the law of obligations, of which the current law of tort, contract, and restitution form part (see, e.g., Patrick Atiyah's attempts to find a common foundation for all types of civil liability in the notion of reliance: P. S. Atiyah, *Promises, Morals, and Law* (Oxford: Clarendon Press, 1981), cf. Hedley (1988) 8 LS 137; McBride (1994) 14 LS 35). This may be going too far, but it is certainly true that recent developments have blurred the distinction between tort and other forms of liability. Damages for loss of an expectation of gain under a contract have been awarded in tort (*White v Jones* [1995] 2 AC 207); it has been affirmed that a defendant may be concurrently liable in contract and tort (*Henderson v Merrett Syndicates* [1995] 2 AC 145; see Stapleton (1997) 113 LQR 257); common law causation concepts associated with the law of tort have been imported into the law of trusts (*Target Holdings v Redferns (a firm)* [1996] AC 421); and causes of action like breach of confidence, historically recognised as equitable, are now re-classified as torts. To some observers, such developments can only be regarded as steps towards a common law of obligations (see further J. Cooke and D. Oughton, *The Common Law of Obligations*, 3rd edn. (London: Butterworths, 2000); A. Tettenborn, *Introduction to the Law of Obligations* (London: Butterworths, 1984)). In so far as the result is the abandonment of old distinctions between different heads of liability based only on historical chance (e.g. the historical distinction between common law and equitable wrongs), then they can only be applauded. But it may confidently be asserted that there will always be a need for the separate exposition of the principles of tortious liability (perhaps including, in time, wrongs whose origins are in equity), if for no other reason than that tort is the general law, while contracts and trusts (for example) are institutional arrangements entered into by consent and the conditions for their formation, dissolution, etc. themselves merit independent analysis (see also *Winfield & Jolowicz*, para. 1–14; *Stanton*, p. 10).

III. Modern Influences on Tort Law

In this final section of our general introduction, we highlight a number of external factors that have had a particular influence on the development of tort law in recent years, and can be expected to shape its future.

1. The Influence of Insurance

R. Lewis, 'Insurance and the Tort System' (2005) 25 LS 85

There is no doubt that insurance profoundly influences the practical operation of the law of tort. Liability is not merely an ancillary device to protect the insured, but is the 'primary medium for the payment of compensation, and tort law [is] a subsidiary part of the process'

(P. Cane, *Atiyah's Accidents, Compensation and the Law*). Although the majority of defendants in tort are individual people, they are almost all insured. In nine out of ten cases the real defendants are insurance companies, with the remainder comprising large self-insured organisations or public bodies. Only rarely are individuals the real defendants. Instead, policyholders cede control over their case to their insurer and thereafter usually play little or no part in the litigation process. Insurers determine how the defence is to be conducted and, for example, commonly make admissions without the consent of the insured, and settle cases in spite of the policyholder's objection.

Insurers pay out 94% of tort compensation. Classic studies reveal that it is their bureaucracy that dictates much litigation procedure, and determines when, and for how much, claims are settled. It is their buildings, rather than courts of law, or even solicitors' offices, that are the important centres of tort practice ... Because insurers dominate the system, it is very difficult to view any tort case in isolation: each and every case is affected, no matter whether determined in court or out of it ... Insurers are the paymasters of the tort system: they process the routine payments and they decide which elements of damage they will accept or contest ... Insurers determine the extent that lawyers become involved in disputes, and the tactics that are used in the proceedings. Increasingly cases are being settled at an early stage, and without resort to the issue of court documents. Insurers decide, in particular, whether a case merits the very exceptional treatment of being taken to a court hearing. In effect, they allow trial judges to determine only 1% of all the claims made. Only a few of these are appealed with the result that the senior judiciary are left to adjudicate upon a small fraction of what are, by then, very untypical cases. Whether an appeal court is to be given an opportunity to examine a point of tort law may depend upon the insurer for, if it serves the insurer's purpose for doubt to remain, the claimant can be paid in full and threatened with a costs award if the action is continued. In this sense tort principles themselves have been shaped by and for insurers ...

The importance of insurers to the tort system is reflected in the fact that the claims which are brought closely match the areas where liability insurance is to be found. Thus road and work accidents predominate partly because those are the two major areas where tort insurance is compulsory. They constitute 86% of all the claims brought for personal injury. They dominate the practice of tort even though they are relatively minor causes of disability and incapacity for work. Those suffering injury in areas not covered by insurance are extremely unlikely to obtain compensation. According to one study [for the *Pearson Commission*, 1978], whereas 1 in 4 road accident victims and 1 in 10 work accident victims gain compensation from tort, only 1 in 67 injured elsewhere do so ...

This influence of insurance upon the general pattern of tort liability is matched by its effect upon the level of compensation awarded. The principles upon which damages are assessed implicitly recognise that it is a company with a deep pocket that will pay and not an individual. Although most awards in tort are for very limited sums—little more than £2,500—there are very few individuals who could afford to pay the amounts required in serious injury cases ... If it were not for insurance there would be little hope of restoring the claimant to the pre-accident position in a serious injury case. It is doubtful whether we would even wish to attempt to place full responsibility for the damage on most defendants. The very nature of the tort system would have to change. Without insurance, it is probable that tort liability itself could not survive ...

Whether the rules of tort themselves have been changed to reflect insurance is more difficult to establish. On the one hand, it is certainly true that the foundations of tort remain largely unchanged. Formally, liability still depends upon proof of fault and, even where rules have been revised more in favour of claimants, it is too easy to suggest that insurance is the cause. On the other hand, some judges have acknowledged that they have concerned themselves with who has the deeper pocket, or who was in the better position to distribute, or absorb, a loss.

It is difficult to conclude that loss distribution arguments have influenced only the facts found and not, to some degree, the rules applied. However, substantial change in tort rules has not occurred. Instead it is the overall involvement of insurers with the system which leads us to conclude that insurance has had a major effect.

COMMENTARY

The type of insurance we are concerned with here is liability (or third-party) insurance, which is to be contrasted with loss (first-party) insurance in which the insured pays to be indemnified in the event of some adverse event (e.g. illness or injury), or for someone else to be indemnified (e.g. on his death), usually whether or not another person is liable for the adversity. Liability insurance is essentially parasitic on the tort system as it is triggered only where there is a liability to pay damages to someone else. Loss insurance is largely independent of the tort system—it is concerned simply with loss, not liability—but a loss insurer may get involved in tort litigation where it has a right ('the right of subrogation') to bring a claim in the insured's name, after paying him under the policy, for an injury for which another person is liable. In fact, a tort claim—recorded under the names of two private individuals— could well be, in reality, between two insurers, the claimant's loss insurer and the defendant's liability insurer. The latter usually has full control over the defence by virtue of an express term of the contract of insurance, and need not seek approval from or even consult the defendant about either litigation strategy or settlement. A telling anecdote is recounted by the late Professor Harry Street, author of a well-regarded text on tort law and (with D. W. Elliott) a pioneering socio-legal study on *Road Accidents* (Penguin Books, 1968). In the latter (pp. 209–10), he tells how he was involved in a road accident for which he was sued. His insurer undertook the defence and the claim failed in the county court. He assumed that was that—until to his total surprise he picked up the newspaper one day and read that the Court of Appeal had just heard the claimant's appeal. He had been entirely unaware that any appeal was in prospect.

The courts too are usually unaware whether either or both the parties before them were insured at the relevant time, so they do not know who is in reality going to pay the damages, or who will actually benefit from them. (In road traffic accident cases, however, it is now possible for the claimant to proceed directly, and by name, against the defendant's liability insurer: European Communities (Rights against Insurers) Regulations 2002, SI 2002/3061.) The traditional judicial view is that the insurance position of the parties should not be disclosed in case it influences the court in deciding questions of liability or damages (see, e.g., *Davie v New Merton Board Mills Ltd* [1959] AC 604 at 626–7, per Viscount Simonds, *Morgans v Launchbury* [1973] AC 127 at 136–7, per Lord Wilberforce, and *Hunt v Severs* [1994] 2 AC 350 at 363, per Lord Bridge). However, in a small but not insignificant set of cases, there has been express discussion of the insurance position. A notable example is provided by Lord Denning who—in a typically candid moment—openly approved of judges demanding a higher standard of care from parties (specifically, drivers of motor vehicles) known to be insured in order to secure compensation for the injured person (*Nettleship v Weston* [1971] 2 QB 691 at 699):

[A] person injured by a motor-car should not be left to bear the loss on his own, but should be compensated out of the insurance fund. The fund is better able to bear it than he can. But the injured person is only able to recover if the driver is liable in law. So the judges see to it that he is liable, unless he can prove care and skill of a high standard.

It must be admitted that such expressions of opinion are very rare, and that many judges would doubtless disapprove of Lord Denning's sentiments, especially as they entail a move away from the purported basis of liability for tortious negligence—i.e. fault—in favour of considerations of loss distribution. There is perhaps greater judicial willingness to admit to the influence of insurance considerations in contexts where 'policy' is a relevant factor, e.g. in determining whether it is fair, just and reasonable to recognise a duty of care. In *Vowles v Evans* [2003] 1 WLR 1607, a case considering the liability of a rugby referee to a player, the Court of Appeal expressly acknowledged (at 1614) that the availability of insurance—to both defendant and claimant—could bear on this crucial question of policy. (See also, in slightly difference contexts, *Smith v Eric S. Bush* [1990] 1 AC 831 at 859, per Lord Griffiths, and *Gwilliam v West Hertfordshire Hospitals NHS Trust* [2003] QB 443, considered at p. 574, below.)

A broader question is whether the development and spread of liability insurance has been instrumental in bringing about major structural changes in tort law doctrine (e.g. extensions in the application of the duty of care concept) in the interests of loss distribution. In a subsequent section of the above article, Lewis identifies two diametrically opposed points of view, both well-represented in the literature: on the one hand, that insurance has been the 'hidden hand' that has pulled legal liability rules along with it (see, in the American context, K. Abraham, *The Liability Century: Insurance and Tort Law from the Progressive Era to 9/11* (Cambridge, Mass: Harvard University Press, 2008); on the other, that the influence of insurance has been overstated and actually rather limited. A leading representative of the latter school of thought is Jane Stapleton, who argues that 'neither actual insurance nor insurability are or should be relevant to the reach and shape of tort liability' ('Tort, Insurance and Ideology' (1995) 58 MLR 820 at p. 820). One important point that she makes is that the courts very rarely point to the *claimant's* ability to protect himself by purchasing first-party (loss) insurance as a reason for absolving the defendant from liability. (For a much-criticised example, see *Lamb v Camden Borough Council* [1981] 1 QB 625 at 637–8, per Lord Denning MR.) And rightly so: the result would be the shifting of accident costs—mediated through the pricing of insurance premiums—from tortfeasors to victims, and the diminution of whatever deterrent effect that tort law possesses.

As Lewis argues, the main impact of insurance on the substantive rules of tort may actually have been on the law of damages—an area mostly ignored by other writers—rather than the principles of liability. In fact, a number of recent reforms relating to the assessment of damages—e.g. the new judicial power to order that damages be paid periodically rather than in the traditional lump sum—could not have been contemplated were it not possible to draw upon the insurance industry's technology and financial resources. (See further Ch. 16.) The impact of insurance on liability rules is much more difficult to establish—at least in the United Kingdom, where tort remains largely fault-based. But the influence is perhaps easier to discern in systems such as the French, which over the course of the twentieth century moved decisively in the direction of strict liability, a development which many French commentators have associated directly with the growth of liability insurance (see, e.g., G. Viney, *Introduction à la responsabilité*, 2nd edn. (Paris: LGDJ, 1995), para. 25, translated in *van Gerven*, pp. 23–4).

Insurers themselves are not always happy with reforms which purport to have an insurance rationale, as they may increase insurers' costs and falsify the assumptions grounding their past and present premium rates. (Other things being equal, however, more liability means more business for liability insurers.) Increasingly, they have sought to influence the tort reform agenda by contributing to public debate and applying pressure in the political sphere. Their role in the current debate about 'compensation culture' is considered below.

For further analysis of tort law's insurance context, see Chapter 18, below. For additional discussion of some of the points addressed above, see Davies, 'The End of the Affair: Duty of Care and Liability Insurance' (1989) 9 LS 67, and Morgan, 'Tort, Insurance and Incoherence' (2004) 67 MLR 384.

2. The Influence of Human Rights

A topic of utmost contemporary importance, and no little controversy, has been the effect upon the law of tort of the incorporation of human rights standards into English law. By the Human Rights Act 1998, the courts have an obligation to act compatibly with many of the rights recognised in the European Convention on Human Rights and Fundamental Freedoms. The question of how exactly this is going to affect principles of tortious liability has aroused very great interest and a good deal of uncertainty remains.

Human Rights Act 1998

1.   THE CONVENTION RIGHTS

(1) In this Act 'the Convention rights' means the rights and fundamental freedoms set out in—

   (a) Articles 2 to 12 and 14 of the Convention;
   (b) Articles 1 to 3 of the First Protocol; and
   (c) Articles 1 and 2 of the Sixth Protocol

as read with Articles 16 to 18 of the Convention . . .

2.   INTERPRETATION OF CONVENTION RIGHTS

(1) A court or tribunal determining a question which has arisen in connection with a Convention right must take into account any—

   (a) judgment, decision, declaration or advisory opinion of the European Court of Human Rights;
   (b) opinion of the Commission given in a report adopted under Article 31 of the Convention;
   (c) decision of the Commission in connection with Article 26 or 27(2) of the Convention; or
   (d) decision of the Committee of Ministers taken under Article 46 of the Convention

whenever made or given, so far as, in the opinion of the court or tribunal, it is relevant to the proceedings in which that question has arisen . . .

3.   INTERPRETATION OF LEGISLATION

(1) So far as it is possible to do so, primary legislation and subordinate legislation must be read and given effect in a way which is compatible with the Convention rights.

(2) This section—

(a) applies to primary legislation and subordinate legislation whenever enacted;

(b) does not affect the validity, continuing operation or enforcement of any incompatible primary legislation; and

(c) does not affect the validity, continuing operation or enforcement of any incompatible subordinate legislation if (disregarding any possibility of revocation) primary legislation prevents removal of the incompatibility . . .

6. ACTS OF PUBLIC AUTHORITIES

(1) It is unlawful for a public authority to act in a way which is incompatible with a Convention right.

(2) Subsection (1) does not apply to an act if—

(a) as the result of one or more provisions of primary legislation, the authority could not have acted differently; or

(b) in the case of one or more provisions of, or made under, primary legislation which cannot be read or given effect in a way which is compatible with the Convention rights, the authority was acting so as to give effect to or enforce those provisions.

(3) In this section 'public authority' includes—

(a) a court or tribunal; and

(b) any person certain of whose functions are functions of a public nature

but does not include either House of Parliament or a person exercising functions in connection with proceedings in Parliament.

(4) In subsection (3) 'Parliament' does not include the House of Lords in its judicial capacity.

(5) In relation to a particular act, a person is not a public authority by virtue only of subsection (3)(b) if the nature of the act is private.

(6) 'An act' includes a failure to act but does not include a failure to—

(a) introduce in, or lay before, Parliament a proposal for legislation; or

(b) make any primary legislation or remedial order.

7. PROCEEDINGS

(1) A person who claims that a public authority has acted (or proposes to act) in a way which is made unlawful by section 6(1) may—

(a) bring proceedings against the authority under this Act in the appropriate court or tribunal; or

(b) rely on the Convention right or rights concerned in any legal proceedings but only if he is (or would be) a victim of the unlawful act . . .

(6) In subsection (1)(b) 'legal proceedings' includes—

(a) proceedings brought by or at the instigation of a public authority; and

(b) an appeal against the decision of a court or tribunal.

8. JUDICIAL REMEDIES

(1) In relation to any act (or proposed act) of a public authority which the court finds is (or would be) unlawful, it may grant such relief or remedy, or make such order, within its powers as it considers just and appropriate.

(2) But damages may be awarded only by a court which has power to award damages, or to order the payment of compensation, in civil proceedings.

(3) No award of damages is to be made unless, taking account of all the circumstances of the case, including—

(a) any other relief or remedy granted, or order made, in relation to the act in question (by that or any other court); and

(b) the consequences of any decision (of that or any other court) in respect of that act the court is satisfied that the award is necessary to afford just satisfaction to the person in whose favour it is made . . .

11. SAFEGUARD FOR EXISTING HUMAN RIGHTS

A person's reliance on a Convention right does not restrict—

(a) any other right or freedom conferred on him by or under any law having effect in any part of the United Kingdom; or

(b) his right to make any claim or bring any proceedings which he could make or bring apart from section 7 to 9.

COMMENTARY

The Human Rights Act 1998 (hereinafter HRA) came into force in October 2000. Not all of the Convention rights are incorporated by the HRA, but some of the most important that are incorporated are Article 2 (right to life), Article 5 (right to liberty and security), Article 6 (right to a fair trial), Article 8 (right to respect for private and family life) and Article 10 (right to freedom of expression).

There are several ways in which the HRA may have an impact upon the law of tort. First, s. 3 of the HRA requires a court or tribunal to interpret legislation, as far as possible, in accordance with the Convention rights. Secondly, s. 6 makes it unlawful for a public authority (as defined) to act in a manner that is incompatible with the Convention rights. As courts are public authorities for the purpose of the HRA, it seems that a court must give a judgment which is compatible with the Convention rights even in an action between two private individuals (see *Douglas v Hello!* [2001] 1 FLR 982, *Venables v News Group Newspapers Ltd* [2001] Fam 430). If a public authority does breach s. 6, the 'victim' may bring proceedings under the Act (s. 7) and, if successful, may be awarded compensation or granted some other remedy at the discretion of the court (s. 8) (although note that s. 9, not extracted above, limits the remedies available where it is alleged that a judicial act is in breach of a Convention right: see further Bamforth [1999] CLJ 159). Also important is s. 2, which requires a court or tribunal, when considering any question which has arisen in connection with a Convention right, to take account of, amongst other things, decisions of the European Commission and Court of Human Rights.

The potential effects of the Act are immense, and it is difficult to predict even after some 10 years' experience of its operation what areas of tort law might be affected. One question which warrants extended consideration is how the new statutory remedy against public authorities will be developed and what effect it will have on the liabilities of public authorities at common law (see Ch. 10). How other common law liabilities will be affected by the HRA is considered at relevant points throughout the book, but some particular issues of interest are identified in outline below.

Trespass to the Person (Assault, Battery and False Imprisonment) and Articles 2 and 5

Trespass to the person protects interests in personal security and freedom: assault and battery protect against unwanted or threatened interferences with the person, whilst false imprisonment protects the liberty interest of the individual. Article 2 (right to life) and Article 5 (right to liberty and security) are concerned with similar subject matter, and the question will arise whether the remedies provided in tort are sufficient to satisfy the obligations thereby imposed upon the state. It is important to note that the obligation imposed may be one of positive action. Thus the state might be liable under the Convention not only for breaching the Convention itself but also for failing to take steps to ensure that a third party did not contravene another's Convention rights. For example, the estate of a person who was stabbed to death by another would have a civil action against the actual perpetrator in battery, but might also be able to sue the state for breach of Article 2 if it failed to take reasonable steps to safeguard the deceased's right to life (cf. *Osman v United Kingdom* [1999] 1 FLR 193, and *Van Colle v Chief Constable of Hertfordshire* [2008] UKHL 50, [2009] 1 AC 225, noted at p. 533f, below). Such obligations might be imposed in respect of other Convention rights (see, e.g., *Z v United Kingdom* [2001] 2 FLR 612: Art. 3), but in the tort context are especially relevant in relation to Articles 2 and 5. It has also been argued that these Articles could be interpreted so as to give rights of actions between private individuals (for discussion, see Bamforth [1999] CLJ 159) but in *Austin v Commissioner of the Police for the Metropolis* [2005] EWHC 480 (QB) Tugendhat J saw 'some difficulty' in achieving an alignment between a tort action in false imprisonment and a claim for a violation of Article 5, and in practice the trend seems to be to plead the causes of action in false imprisonment and under the HRA as alternatives. (For later proceedings in *Austin*, see p. 96 below.)

Negligence and the Right to a Court under Article 6

At one time it seemed that the most significant impact of the Act would be through the incorporation of Article 6 of the Convention (right to a fair trial, entailing in turn the right to a court). It was once assumed that Article 6 goes beyond mere procedural safeguards and guarantees, at least to a point, a form of substantive due process. In *Osman v United Kingdom* [1999] 1 FLR 193, the European Court of Human Rights ruled that the applicants had a right under Article 6 to have their allegations of negligence against the police—whom they alleged ought to have prevented an attack by a third party—heard in a full trial; the right was violated when the English court had struck out the action at a preliminary hearing, on the grounds that public policy in any case precluded the recognition of any duty of care. Detailed consideration of this issue is reserved until later (see p. 151ff, below), but it should be noted now that the decision cast doubt over the compatibility with the Convention of English law's basic approach to the tort of negligence. However, in the subsequent case of *Z v United Kingdom* [2001] 2 FLR 612, the European Court of Human Rights appeared to resile from its earlier decision in *Osman*, though not without creating uncertainties of its own (see further p. 152ff, below).

Defamation, Privacy and Articles 8 and 10

Defamation is a tort that protects one's reputation, usually by an award of damages and, if required, an injunction. Most commonly, defendants in defamation cases are members of the media, sued for a false allegation that lowers the reputation of the claimant in the eyes of the general public. Two Convention rights are clearly relevant in this context. Article 8 guarantees a right to privacy, subject to the derogations set out in Article 8(2).

Such a right is wider than the tort of defamation, which protects only reputation. Traditionally, English law does not recognise a liability for invasion of privacy as such, and that approach has been affirmed by the House of Lords even post-HRA (*Wainwright v Home Office* [2004] 2 AC 406). Nevertheless, under the influence of the Convention right, the courts have manipulated established principles of the equitable law of confidence to a very considerable extent, creating what is effectively a tort applying to the wrongful disclosure of private information (*Campbell v MGN Ltd* [2004] UKHL 22, [2004] 2 AC 457).

The right to privacy has to be balanced against the competing right to freedom of expression in Article 10 of the Convention, which HRA, s. 12 explicitly directs the courts to heed when considering the grant of any relief that might affect its exercise. In other common law jurisdictions, the highest courts have balanced these competing concerns in ways that contrast with the traditional approach of the English law of defamation (see *New York Times v Sullivan* 376 US 254 (1964), *Lange v Australian Broadcasting Corporation* (1997) 189 CLR 520) but there are signs that the English courts may be prepared to modify existing rules to ensure that the principles of defamation law are compatible with the Convention (see especially *Reynolds v Times Newspapers* [2001] 2 AC 127 and *O'Shea v MGN Ltd* [2001] EMLR 40; cf. *Loutchansky v Times Newspapers* [2002] QB 783 and *Jameel v Wall Street Journal (Europe) Sprl* [2006] UKHL 44). See further Chapter 13.

Conclusion

The above is merely a sample of the effects the HRA has had—and may have in future—on the law of tort. Only with the further passage of time will the true significance on the Act become clear. Though it is already clear that the European Convention on Human Rights has played a more significant role in the English law of tort than was the case before the HRA, whether the Act will bring about really substantial changes to fundamental tort law principles remains to be seen.

For further discussion and analysis, see J. Wright, *Tort Law and Human Rights* (Oxford: Hart Publishing, 2001).

3. Concerns about 'Compensation Culture'

Tomlinson v Congleton Borough Council [2004] 1 AC 46

The claimant waded into the defendant council's lake, threw himself forward into a dive, and hit his head on the sandy bottom, suffering serious injuries. The lake was on the site of an old quarry, which the council had transformed into a beauty spot. Various water sports were pursued on the lake, and sand had been deposited around it to create a beach, which was a popular place to picnic and sunbathe. As the result of a risk assessment, the council decided to prohibit swimming as unduly dangerous, for example, because a swimmer might be injured by windsurfers. Because warning signs proved ineffective, the council concluded that the only way of dealing with the problem was to make the water less accessible and less inviting. Shortly before the claimant's accident, it allocated a sum in its budget to a scheme to remove or cover over the beaches and replace them by muddy reed beds. The beach off which the claimant was injured was destroyed a few months after the accident. The claimant sued the council under the law of occupiers' liability (see Ch. 11.II), and the case eventually came before the House of Lords.

Lord Hobhouse

[81] ... [I]t is not, and should never be, the policy of the law to require the protection of the foolhardy or reckless few to deprive, or interfere with, the enjoyment by the remainder of society of the liberties and amenities to which they are rightly entitled. Does the law require that all trees be cut down because some youths may climb them and fall? Does the law require the coastline and other beauty spots to be lined with warning notices? Does the law require that attractive waterside picnic spots be destroyed because of a few foolhardy individuals who choose to ignore warning notices and indulge in activities dangerous only to themselves? The answer to all these questions is, of course, no. But this is the road down which your Lordships, like other courts before, have been invited to travel and which the councils in the present case found so inviting. In truth, the arguments for the claimant have involved an attack upon the liberties of the citizen which should not be countenanced. They attack the liberty of the individual to engage in dangerous, but otherwise harmless, pastimes at his own risk and the liberty of citizens as a whole fully to enjoy the variety and quality of the landscape of this country. The pursuit of an unrestrained culture of blame and compensation has many evil consequences and one is certainly the interference with the liberty of the citizen.

Lord Scott

[94] ... [The claimant] was simply sporting about in the water with his friends, giving free rein to his exuberance. And why not? And why should the council be discouraged by the law of tort from providing facilities for young men and young women to enjoy themselves in this way? Of course there is some risk of accidents arising out of the joie-de-vivre of the young. But that is no reason for imposing a grey and dull safety regime on everyone.

COMMENTARY

This is one of the emblematic decisions of the modern law of tort, and we shall encounter it again (see further extracts at pp. 173 and 579). In the passages extracted, Lord Hobhouse and Lord Scott explicitly addressed concerns that the deterrent effect of potential tort liability might lead to the undesirable withdrawal of services and amenities of value to the community at large, and the imposition of (in Lord Scott's words) 'a grey and dull safety regime on everyone'. No doubt the decision will reduce the anxiety previously experienced by councils and other landowners—indeed potential defendants in general—about their potential liabilities, and make it less likely that they will go to such extreme lengths in the interests of risk reduction. The Law Lords also struck out against the dilution of individual responsibility that can result if tort law is too ready to accord the injury victim a remedy. In an official report shortly afterwards (*Better Routes to Redress*, extracted below), the Better Regulation Task Force stated that the decision was 'an important legal precedent...which should make people understand that they need to be responsible for their own actions and should anticipate risk'.

Though *Tomlinson* addressed concerns of compensation in a particularly direct and explicit fashion, it was far from being the first case to contain expressions of judicial concern about the supposed excesses of the tort system. Lord Templeman anticipated the modern 'compensation culture' debate as early as 1986, deriding the assumption 'that for every mischance in an accident-prone world someone solvent must be liable in damages' (*CBS Songs Ltd v Amstrad Consumer Electronics plc* [1988] AC 1013 at 1059). His words were echoed almost 20 years later by Lord Steyn in *Gorringe v Calderdale Metropolitan Borough Council* [2004] 1 WLR 1057 at [2]: 'the courts must not contribute to the creation of a society bent on litigation, which is premised on the illusion that for every misfortune there is a remedy'. In *Corr v IBC Vehicles Ltd* [2007] QB 46 at [63], Ward LJ said that he would 'prefer to forget' Lord Hobhouse's observation relating to the 'evil consequences' of compensation culture, but could not ignore Lord Steyn's more measured expression of concern. What do you think is the difference, if any, between the remarks of the two Law Lords? Can you explain why Ward LJ objected to one and yet was able to assent to the other?

In *Majrowski v Guy's and St Thomas's NHS Trust* [2007] 1 AC 224 at [69], Baroness Hale attempted to explain why the increased scope for claiming compensation in the modern law had raised concern: 'The fear is that, instead of learning to cope with the inevitable irritations and misfortunes of life, people will look to others to compensate them for all their woes, and those others will then become unduly defensive or protective.' Do you think that such fears *ought* to influence how the courts develop and apply the law? In particular, do they have sufficient evidence on which to determine whether or not the fears have any foundation in fact?

The factual evidence for the existence of a 'compensation culture' is considered in the extracts below.

Better Regulation Task Force, *Better Routes to Redress* (2004)

Almost every day there is a report in the media—newspaper, radio or television, suggesting that the United Kingdom is in the grip of a compensation culture. Headlines shout about people trying to claim what appear to be large sums of money for what are portrayed as dubious reasons. But what is not always reported is the outcome. The reality is often very different. Litigating is not easy. Many claims never reach court. Some will, of course, be settled out-of-court; others disappear because the claim had little chance of succeeding in the first place. For a claimant to succeed they have to be able to prove that first someone else owed them a duty of care and then that the same person was negligent.

The term 'compensation culture' is not used to describe a society where people are able to seek compensation. Rather a 'compensation culture' implies that a decision to seek compensation is wrong. 'Compensation culture' is a pejorative term and suggests that those that seek to 'blame and claim' should be criticised. It suggests greed; rather than people legitimately enforcing their rights. Few would oppose the principle that if people's rights are infringed, appropriate action should be available to the injured party to gain compensation from the guilty party. So why the double standards? . . .

Developments in recent years, principally the introduction of 'no win no fee' arrangements—where the claimant only pays their lawyer's fees in the event of success—and the emergence of claims management companies have increased access to justice. But they have also meant that more people have been encouraged to 'have a go' at claiming redress for a wrong they feel they have suffered.

We live in a much richer, but more risk averse, society than ever before. We are also much better informed about our rights, which means we are more aware when there is a case to answer. However some people may be persuaded, by what they have read in the papers or through the contact they have had with claims management companies, to look for compensation where none is available and therefore decide to 'have a go'. This has had both positive and negative impacts. On the positive side the public sector, such as schools, rather than cancelling trips and activities as the media would have us believe, have become much better at assessing and managing risks. Local authorities have put sophisticated systems in place to manage, for example, repairs to their pathways and highways.

However, on the negative side, the 'have a go' culture that encourages people to pursue misconceived or trivial claims:

- has put a drain on public sector resources;
- may make businesses and other organisations more cautious for fear of litigation;
- contributes to higher insurance premiums; and
- clogs up the system for those with indisputable claims...

However the so-called 'compensation culture' cannot be blamed for all these problems. Some have arisen from poor operational practices by companies...

The compensation culture: it's all in the mind...

Almost everyone we spoke to in the course of this study told us that they did not believe that there is a compensation culture in the UK. They argued that the reality is somewhat different, because the number of accident claims, including personal injury claims, is going down..., and that this proves the absence of a compensation culture in the UK. However, it ignores the fact that...people believe that there is a 'compensation culture' in the UK.

It is this perception, and the impact it is having on the UK as a whole, which needs to be tackled. Quoting statistics will not win the argument whilst the papers run 'compensation culture' stories. There is undoubtedly a perception that the public have a greater tendency now than ever before to seek redress if they suffer an injustice or injury, which they believe was someone else's fault. People look for someone else to blame for their misfortune. Advances in science and technology also mean that links between cause and effect are better understood. In the health arena, for example in areas such as passive smoking or occupational exposure to asbestos, this has led to a large increase in claims...

Don't believe everything you read

Regardless of perception, the truth behind the 'compensation culture' is somewhat different to how it is portrayed by the media and commentators. Many of the stories we read and hear either are simply not true or only have a grain of truth about them. The truth behind the famous, or rather infamous, McDonald's coffee case, which is often held up as a shining example of the 'compensation culture', is different to how it is reported or quoted. Newspapers readily use the incident to highlight the 'compensation culture'.

Litigating is not easy

Litigating, or pursuing a case to court, is only one form of redress. The majority of claims never make it to court. In order to litigate successfully the party who accuses (the claimant) another of acting in a negligent manner has to be able to prove that the other party (the defendant) owed them a duty of care and was negligent. This is the tort of negligence...The shift in recent years has been over what kinds of experiences are now appropriate to try to litigate against. Whole new types of claims that were simply not considered by lawyers 20 or 30 years ago are now being pursued. However, despite what the media would lead us to believe such claims do not always succeed...

Keeping the perception alive: the media

The perception of the 'compensation culture' is largely, though not entirely, perpetuated by the media. Whilst appearing to despise the phenomenon, it fills many column inches in newspapers. The media regularly report claims for apparently exorbitant sums, without later reporting the final outcome, which may have been very different. They also report stories from other parts of the world without pointing out that such cases would be unlikely to succeed here...

Impact of the 'compensation culture' perception

The threat of litigation, or just a complaint or claim, can have some positive effects. We have already mentioned improved risk assessments in the case of schools and maintenance work by local authorities. It can also help to improve the provision of goods and services without the need for Government intervention. Those who complain loudest about the current system need to think about the alternatives. However, there are also negative aspects of the 'have a go' culture. Dealing with complaints and claims costs a great deal of money...Of course, some of the claims each local authority handles will be genuine but a large number will be vexatious or frivolous. Dealing with these puts an enormous drain on local authority resources; resources which come from local residents and businesses and which could be better spent for the benefit of the same residents and businesses. Fear of litigation does change behaviour. Reporting incidents that appear trivial, and may be urban myths, will encourage others to change their behaviour. There are more serious examples of an overly cautious approach being taken. Pharmaceutical companies are more wary about developing new drugs for fear of litigation, and some doctors prefer to carry out a caesarean section to a natural birth because it is perceived as less risky (despite caesarean section not being risk free). Excessive risk aversion is not helpful to the UK's prosperity nor well-being.

K. Williams, 'State of Fear: Britain's "compensation culture" reviewed' (2005) 25 LS 499

Claims that Britain is in the grip of a 'compensation culture' and, consequently, a 'litigation crisis' are asserted with increased frequency. Concerns of this kind can be found in the columns of newspapers, in official reports, political discourse, legislative debate, and judicial decisions...

Is there a problem?

The answer to this question is hotly disputed, depending as it does on what exactly is thought to constitute the 'problem', as well as on who is asked. The growth of a 'compensation culture' implies an increased and unreasonable willingness to seek legal redress when things go wrong, whilst 'litigation crisis' implies that this shift in social attitudes has been translated into undesirable (perhaps unbearable) levels of formal disputing...

It seems there may be a number of different problems. Frequently it appears that there are too many (successful) claims; at other times that compensation payouts are too costly, quite commonly that lawyers' fees are excessive; sometimes a mixture of all of these...[But] the statistical evidence is both incomplete and somewhat equivocal...And, of course, even if we could establish with certainty how many claims there are, that would not tell us how many claims is *too* many. It often seems to be assumed, implicitly at least, that any increase is a cause for concern whilst a fall is to be applauded...

There are two other considerations connected with the numbers issue. First, claimant lawyers often point out with considerable (if self-interested) justification that the great majority of injured persons never resort to the law; that it is precisely the *absence* of a compensation culture that characterises our liability system...A second point is whether legitimate, well-founded claims should be counted as part of the 'problem'. After all, one reason why 'compensation crisis' stories find such ready audiences seems to be related to the ways in which they reflect public anxieties about the decline of social and moral values, such as self-reliance and personal responsibility; anxieties that are represented here by tales of greedy lawyers egging on grasping claimants chasing compensation for trivial harms which in an earlier era would have been stoically shouldered without public complaint. Accordingly, any attempt to test for the existence of a 'crisis' should, arguably, look beyond the absolute numbers of injury claims to whether there has been an increase in those that are substantially without merit or are bought off simply for their nuisance value. Unfortunately, there is no direct or reliable evidence to answer this crucial question either…

The 'real' problem and some of its causes

The idea that defendants are beset by ever-increasing numbers of doubtful claims is not proven. Indeed, the 'problem' we started with seems to have come down to this: that whatever may be the *actual* likelihood of irresponsible litigation, many *believe* themselves to be at heightened risk of being unfairly sued. According to the Task Force, this critical misperception or 'urban myth' induces socially and economically damaging risk-averse behaviour. Reputedly, organisations become less innovative, scarce resources that would be better applied elsewhere are unproductively diverted, unnecessarily costly safety precautions are taken, sometimes beneficial activities are fearfully abandoned altogether…

[T]he Task force…make anxious reference to an expanding liability regime…[They] say that new types of claims 'that were simply not considered by lawyers twenty or thirty years ago are now being pursued'—the implication being that the judiciary must take the blame to the extent that novel claims are admitted. Of course, quite how expansions of tort liability affect (insured) defendants or society more broadly is uncertain and disputed…No doubt the great bulk of claims will continue to be based on conventional legal principles applied to perfectly ordinary road traffic and workplace injury cases. On the other hand, the psychological impact of new, especially uncertain liabilities on defendants (and on their insurers' underwriting and pricing policies) may be marked, even where the development in question initially appears to advantage relatively few claimants. In fact, some recent judicial decisions have the potential to affect large numbers (albeit we can only guess how many) and destabilise some (particularly public sector) budgets.

COMMENTARY

A man driving his new Winnebago motor home set it on cruise control, then went into the back to make himself a cup of coffee; the vehicle left the highway, crashed and overturned—and the man successfully sued the manufacturers for failing to advise him not to leave the driving seat! More evidence of the excesses of our compensation culture? Well, no: just one of the myths, often perpetuated by an uncritical news media, that have grown up about the tort system, and are exposed in the Better Regulation Task Force (BRTF) report. In fact, there is no truth in the story at all: 'Winnebago man' did not exist. But this has not prevented his story being reported as fact in numerous national newspapers (including *The Express*, the *Daily Star*, the *Daily Record*, *The People* and *The Mirror*, plus the London *Evening Standard*).

Not quite belonging in the category of pure myth are 'myth-representations'—stories that have some basis in truth but are told in such a way as to present a wholly misleading picture. The famous 'McDonald's coffee case' is the pre-eminent example. Eighty-one-year-old Stella Liebeck got a cup of coffee from a McDonald's drive-through restaurant and suffered third-degree burns after spilling it on her lap in the front seat of her car. She was awarded $2.9 million in damages by a New Mexico jury. Her case has become perhaps *the* emblem of the excesses of the US tort system, and by implication *our* tort system too, and of modern tort law's alleged subversion of traditional values of individual responsibility. But how accurate has been the case's representation in the media and in public debate?

The truth is that the reporting of the case has been sensationalised, partial, misleading and sometimes inaccurate (see W. Haltom and M. McCann, *Distorting the Law* (Chicago: University of Chicago Press, 2004), ch. 6). The plaintiff has been castigated for trying to profit from a trivial accident that was really her own fault; the tort process has been called into question for ignoring her own responsibility for the accident, and for awarding compensation going far beyond her losses. In fact, the truth is much more complex than such media portrayals, and rather different in key respects. Mrs Liebeck was not driving the car, merely a passenger, and the car was not in fact being driven at all at the material time, but parked up. Her injuries were far from trivial: she sustained third-degree burns, was in hospital for more than a week, suffered partial disability for two years after the accident, and was left with permanent scarring on 16 per cent of her body. The jury found McDonald's at fault because the coffee was not just hot—as, of course, it had to be—but excessively hot (considerably hotter than that produced by (e.g.) a domestic coffee machine). The jury did not ignore Mrs Liebeck's share of responsibility for the accident, but found her guilty of contributory negligence and reduced her damages by 20 per cent. After the reduction, the compensatory component of her award was only $160,000, a significant part of this attributable to her medical fees. The rest was punitive damages, the (very large) figure said to represent two days' profits for McDonald's from sales of coffee. In fact, Mrs Liebeck never received anything like the $2.9 million still quoted in news reports. As very commonly occurs in the United States, the award for punitive damages was subsequently reduced very considerably by the judge—to $480,000. Even the combined sum of $640,000 is unlikely to have been what Mrs Liebeck actually received, because—to forestall an appeal—she then accepted an undisclosed sum in final settlement of her claim.

Mrs Liebeck has been commemorated—fairly or not—by the institution of an annual Stella Award for America's most frivolous or outrageous lawsuits of the year: see www.stellaawards.com. While this may seem just a bit of fun, Haltom and McCann, *op. cit.*, argue that a more serious intent lies behind such interventions: the production of, and saturation of the media with, popular narratives ('pop torts') that advance the cause of tort reform. (See also Lunney, 'Letter from America: Tort Reform Illinois Style' (1998) 8 KCLJ 43.)

However the McDonald's coffee case is interpreted, its lessons are not easily applied to England and Wales. Our tort law is very different from that in the United States: no jury determination of liability or assessment of damages for personal injury; no punitive damages for negligence and no contingency fees to feed the lawyers who drive the process. (Our conditional fees are not the same: the successful lawyer gets an uplift on his usual fee, but not—as in the United States—a percentage of the damages.) In fact, when similar coffee cases were brought against McDonald's on this side of the Atlantic, they failed (see *Bogle v McDonald's Restaurants Ltd* [2002] EWHC 490). Why do you think the media has not given the same prominence to the claims that failed as to Mrs Liebeck's claim in the United States?

For further discussion of the tort system in the United States, highlighting differences with England and Wales, see J. Fleming, *The American Tort Process* (Oxford: OUP, 1988).

The Statistical Evidence

The statistical evidence about claims numbers and compensation costs is considered in Chapter 18. Suffice it for now to note that the period which has seen the greatest concern about compensation culture—since broadly speaking the late 1990s, with the rise of the claims management companies (CMCs) and 'no win no fee' litigation—has in fact coincided with relative stability in the annual number of claims for personal injury (see Morris, 'Spiralling or

Stabilising? The Compensation Culture and Our Propensity to Claim Damages for Personal Injury' (2007) 70 MLR 349 at 357–8). Cost is a more complex issue, but it may be noted that the BRTF itself (p. 15) endorsed an estimate of tort costs in the United Kingdom which represents a surprisingly low percentage of gross domestic product (0.6%), and is significantly lower than the comparable figure for most other developed countries, including France (0.8%), Germany (1.3%), Italy (1.7%) and the United States (1.9%).

Translating Rhetoric into Action

The official response to concerns about compensation culture may be traced back to December 2002, when the Department of Work and Pensions established an official review of employers' liability compulsory insurance after significant rises in premiums had raised concerns that the costs of the system were too high and that employers were finding it difficult to secure affordable cover. The review's recommendations (*Review of Employers' Liability Compulsory Insurance: Second Stage Report*, 2003) included the promotion of 'vocational rehabilitation'—helping those who are ill, injured or have a disability to access, maintain or return to employment or some other useful occupation—but were conspicuously lacking in substance. The review did little to settle public fears and a 'media and political frenzy' developed (Morris (2007) 70 MLR 349 at 350), with contributions from across the political spectrum. The insurance industry itself engaged in substantial lobbying and made frequent interventions in the public debate, seeking (according to Morris, p. 365):

> to create a sense of moral and political panic . . . [and] to undermine the legitimacy of those using the tort system and even the tort system itself . . . Insurers have also used the compensation culture as a smokescreen to hide their own role in the sudden and significant increases in liability insurance premiums.

The latter proposition finds some support in an analysis by the Office of Fair Trading (OFT), which noted 'a tendency (perhaps understandable) on the part of the insurance industry, to exaggerate the effect of some drivers of liability insurance premiums, such as changes in tort law' (*An analysis of current problems in the UK liability insurance market* (2003), para. 10.4). In fact, said the OFT, there was 'a consistent pattern of substantial losses and under-pricing of liability risks over many years' in which a significant explanatory factor was '[t]he failure of the market as a whole to anticipate and accurately quantify the effect of a number of emergent risks, including a variety of gradually developing diseases' (paras 10.11–10.12).

Other groups also sought to influence the political process because of concerns about their potential liabilities and the rising costs of liability insurance, amongst them teachers responsible for the organisation of school trips, and companies and volunteer groups engaged in outdoor pursuits. (On the latter, see in particular J. Fulbrook, *Outdoor Activities, Negligence and the Law* (Aldershot: Ashgate Publishing, 2005).) In September 2004, shortly after the publication of the BRTF's report, a private member's bill sought to address concerns that potential volunteers were being deterred from participating in outdoor activities by the fear of liability (Promotion of Volunteering Bill, House of Commons Bill 18, Session 2003–04) but failed to progress to a vote in the House of Commons.

In May 2005, then Prime Minister Tony Blair announced the Government's intention to legislate to address concerns about compensation culture (www.number10.gov.uk/Page7562). The result, a year later, was the Compensation Act 2006. It is the Act's first two sections that are of most interest to us here. Section 1, extracted at p. 175, below, is evidently an attempt to change public perceptions and reassure volunteer groups by restating the well-established common law rule that the deterrent effect of potential liability should be considered in assessing the level of care that would have been exercised by the reasonable person on the facts. Section 2 also restates existing principle: 'An apology, an offer of treatment or other redress, shall not of itself amount to an admission of negligence or breach of statutory duty.' The Government hopes that the provision will reduce the number of cases in which adversarial disputes prevent the early rehabilitation of the accident victim (Hansard, HC vol. 447 col. 422, 8 June 2006). Part II of the Act establishes a regime for the regulation of claims management companies, who were the subject of considerable criticism in the BRTF report: see further p. 948, below.

The Act has itself been the subject of considerable criticism, with questioning of the necessity to devote valuable legislative time to a simple restatement of existing law, and concern that s. 1 will promote new litigation about the meaning of its constituent terms (see further p. 176, below).

Compensation Culture and Tort Reform in Other Countries

The issue of compensation culture is certainly not unique to the United Kingdom, and several other countries have embarked upon legislative reform with a view to constraining the costs of the tort system.

It is in the United States that tort law has been the focus of the most intent political scrutiny and the subject of the most divisive debate. The titles of two recent books give a strong flavour of the positions taken on either side: C. Bogus, *Why Lawsuits are Good for America* (New York: New York University Press, 2001), and P. Howard, *The Collapse of the Common Good: How America's Lawsuit Culture Undermines our Freedom* (Ballantyne Books, 2002). One of the strongest and most consistent proponents of tort reform was former President George W. Bush, though the majority of specific reforms are constitutionally a matter for the state legislatures, and there is therefore only limited scope for federal intervention. Amongst the reforms that have been adopted in different states are caps on the level of damages for non-pecuniary loss, caps on punitive damages, the introduction of proportionate liability for secondary defendants (in place of joint and several liability in full), restrictions on the scope for class actions, and adoption of the (English) 'loser pays' costs rule. As already noted, it must always be remembered, when considering tort law in the United States, that many of the most problematic and controversial matters—e.g. jury assessment of damages, the availability of punitive damages, class actions—are either not to be found at all in England and Wales or only present in a very watered-down form. For further analysis, see Rabin, 'Some Reflections on the Process of Tort Reform' (1988) 25 San Diego L Rev 13; Galanter, 'Real World Torts: An Antidote to Anecdote' (1996) 55 Md L Rev 1093).

Another country to have embarked upon extensive tort reform is Australia. In 2002, the Federal Government convened an expert panel to review the law of negligence in response to the collapse of a leading liability insurer and general concerns about the cost and availability of public liability insurance (*Review of the Law of Negligence: Final Report*, 2002, www. revofneg.treasury.gov.au/content/Report2/PDF/Law_Neg_Final.pdf ('the Ipp report')). The major part of the review's recommendations related to the restatement of existing principles in statutory form, with a view to correcting alleged misunderstandings of the law, promoting greater clarity and certainty, and giving the courts more guidance as to the application of rules and principles that are open to various interpretations (paras 1.12–1.13). As in the United States, tort reform falls constitutionally within the competence of the states, some of whom considered that the Ipp review had not gone far enough and went considerably further in their own legislation (e.g. by introducing greater protection for certain sorts of defendants including public authorities and providers of recreational services: see Civil Liability Act 2002 (NSW), ss. 5M, 5L, 42, 45). However, the extent to which these reforms were needed, or have themselves been responsible for any reduction in insurance costs, has been questioned (Wright, 'National trends in personal injury litigation: Before and after "Ipp"' (2006) 14 TLJ 233). Indeed, Ipp JA—the Chair of the expert panel mentioned above—has himself questioned the breadth of the reforms and commented: 'It is difficult to accept that public sentiment will allow all these changes to remain long-term features of the law' ('Themes in the Law of Tort' (2007) 81 ALJ 609) For discussion of the reforms, see Keeler, 'Personal responsibility and the reforms recommended by the Ipp Report: "Time future contained in time past"' (2006) 14 TLJ 48, and McDonald, 'The impact of the civil liability legislation on fundamental policies and principles on the common law of negligence' (2006) 14 TLJ 268.

More recently, and closer to home, Ireland presents us with another model for possible reform. Since 2004, a new statutory body, the Personal Injuries Assessment Board (PIAB), has had the task of assessing compensation in most cases of personal injury where liability is not contested. Claimants must submit to the procedure and cannot initiate a claim in court without the PIAB's authorisation. Proceedings are conducted entirely on paper, with no oral hearing. Claimants can get assistance from the PIAB's own telephone advice line, but if they want to be represented by a solicitor they must make arrangements at their own expense; they usually also have to bear a significant part of the cost of any medical report. The PIAB assesses the level of damages for non-pecuniary loss ('pain and suffering') by reference to the World Health Organization's International Classification of Diseases, with guideline figures for particular injuries set out in a Book of Quantum. Damages for loss of earnings, medical expenses, etc. are also recoverable. The parties can choose whether to accept or reject the assessment, but, if both accept, it has the same legal effect as a court judgment. If either party rejects the assessment, the case has to be pursued through the courts. The reform aims to allow the resolution of personal injury claims quickly (an average of nine months, as opposed to three years for personal injury claims in the courts) and without the legal expenses and experts fees associated with traditional tort litigation. Some observers in the United Kingdom, especially in the insurance sector, are beginning to advocate a similar reform on this side of the Irish Sea. But the Irish reforms have been criticised for making claimants bear their own legal and expert witness costs, for allowing defendants to put liability in issue *after* the PIAB's assessment of damages, and so pressure claimants into acceptance, and for failing to meet its own objectives because only about a quarter of personal injury claims result in a PIAB assessment (Flynn, *April PI Focus*, 2006, vol. 16 issue 3(33) and 2007, vol. 17 issue 2(10)). See generally Gilhooly, 'PI Changes in Ireland—Implications for England and Wales' [2006] JPIL 104; Quill, in *European Tort Law 2004*, pp. 363–6.

It can be seen that, in the United States, Australia and Ireland, 'tort reform' inevitably refers to *restrictions* on the scope of liability in tort. That is not (yet) true in the United Kingdom. In fact, many of the most recent tort reforms here have *increased* the cost of compensation, or at least effected a significant transfer of the cost from the public to the private sector (see Lewis, 'The Politics of Tort Reform' (2006) 69 MLR 418). These issues are considered in more detail in Chapters 16 and 18.

2 INTENTIONAL INTERFERENCE WITH THE PERSON

I. Introduction

1. Historical Background

The civil wrongs now classified as intentional interference with the person are amongst the oldest causes of action known to the common law. From the early days of the common law, it was undoubtedly a wrong intentionally to cause someone injury, either by hitting them directly or doing some forcible act which had the immediate consequence of injury to another (e.g. throwing a stone). These wrongs were generally remedied in local courts. But the lawlessness that accompanied the reign of Stephen (1135–54), together with the reforms of the legal system made by Henry II (1154–89), encouraged litigants to bring claims before the central (royal) courts. By 1250 the royal writ of trespass had acquired two formal requirements: that the defendant acted *vi et armis* (with force and arms) and *contra pacem* (against the king's peace). The first requirement is self-explanatory; what was targeted was violent or threatening behaviour. The second was included to prevent the royal courts from being flooded with business; only if the force was such as to breach the king's peace would the royal courts have an interest in the case.

However, as Chapter 1 has made apparent, these allegations were only formal, and it became standard practice for a party who wanted the benefits of trial in the royal courts (in terms of mode of trial and procedure) to insert these allegations as a matter of course. Once the case was before the court, evidence as to what actually happened could be presented to the jury; hence the limitation could be overcome. This ultimately led to the creation of a new form of trespass writ, trespass on the case, which did not require the wrong to be *vi et armis* or *contra pacem*. Unlike trespass *vi et armis*, case was not actionable *per se*, that is, it required proof of damage flowing from the interference with the plaintiff. The development of this action, and its relationship with trespass, was considered in Chapter 1, but it is important to remember that, although there was controversy in the late eighteenth and early nineteenth centuries relating to which form of action should be used for unintentional acts causing direct harm, it was never doubted that the proper form of action for intentional acts causing direct harm was trespass *vi et armis*.

The old form of action for trespass to the person was classified into three separate causes of action—assault, battery, and false imprisonment—all of which survive in the modern law. Apart from these actions, there is also in the modern law a general principle of liability for intentional interference with the person under the rule in *Wilkinson v Downton* [1897] 2 QB 57. That decision recognised a liability for intentional infliction of emotional distress—by its nature an indirect consequence of the defendant's act—which can for that reason be regarded as descended from the action on the case. However, the circumstances in which this tort may apply have been considerably reduced by the decision of the House of Lords in *Wainwright v Home Office* [2004] 2 AC 406 (extracted below, p. 69). This chapter will consider the elements of each of these causes of action.

2. Trespass and Fault

As noted above, the historical requirement for bringing the writ of trespass *vi et armis* was directness. This directness requirement was, in theory, capable of being satisfied by either intentional or unintentional conduct. By the time the forms of action were abolished in the 1870s, however, it was generally accepted that unintentional conduct causing direct harm (in modern parlance, negligence) was actionable in case. Thus the substantive, as opposed to procedural, distinction between trespass and negligence was that trespass required intentional conduct and negligence required unintentional conduct. But what if the plaintiff pleaded neither intention nor negligence but merely directness, for example, 'the defendant shot me'? Such a pleading may have been acceptable for the old writ of trespass *vi et armis*, but after the forms of action had been abolished, did that pleading disclose a substantive cause of action? Whilst the issue had a practical significance (illustrated by the extract below) it also raised important questions about the relationship between trespass and negligence.

(a) General

Fowler v Lanning [1959] 1 QB 426

The facts are stated in the extract.

Diplock J

The writ in this case claims damages for trespass to the person committed by the defendant at Corfe Castle, in the county of Dorset, on 19 November 1957. The statement of claim alleges laconically that at that place and on that date 'the defendant shot the plaintiff,' and that by reason thereof the plaintiff sustained personal injuries and has suffered loss and damage. By his defence the defendant, in addition to traversing the allegations of fact, raises the objection that the statement of claim is bad in law and discloses no cause of action against him on the ground that the plaintiff does not allege that the said shooting was intentional or negligent. An order has been made that this point of law be disposed of before the trial of the issues of fact in the action. That order is binding on me, and, in disposing of it, I can look no further than the pleadings. I must confess that at first glance at the pleadings I felt some anxiety lest I was being invited to decide a point which has long puzzled the professors (see the article by Professors Goodhart and Winfield (1933) 49 LQR 359; *Pollock on Torts* (15th ed), p. 129; *Salmond on Torts* (12th ed), p. 311; *Winfield on Tort* (5th ed), p. 213), only to learn ultimately that, just as in *M'Alister (or Donoghue) v Stevenson* [1932] AC 562, there was in fact no snail in the ginger beer bottle, so in this case there was in fact no pellet in the defendant's gun.

The point of law is not, however, a mere academic one even at the present stage of the action. The alleged injuries were, I am told, sustained at a shooting party; it is not suggested that the shooting was intentional. The practical issue is whether, if the plaintiff was in fact injured by a shot from a gun fired by the defendant, the onus lies on the plaintiff to prove that the defendant was negligent, in which case, under the modern system of pleading, he must so plead and give particulars of negligence (see RSC, Ord 19, r 4) or whether it lies on the defendant to prove that the plaintiff's injuries were not caused by the defendant's negligence, in which case the plaintiff's statement of claim is sufficient and discloses a cause of action (see RSC, Ord 19, r 25). The issue is thus a neat one of onus of proof....

In trespass on the case the onus of proof of the defendant's negligence undoubtedly lay on the plaintiff. Where it lay in trespass is much more difficult to determine....

I think that what appears to have been the practice of the profession during the present century is sound in law. I can summarise the law as I understand it from my examination of the cases as follows:

(1) Trespass to the person does not lie if the injury to the plaintiff, although the direct consequence of the act of the defendant, was caused unintentionally and without negligence on the defendant's part.

(2) Trespass to the person on the highway does not differ in this respect from trespass to the person committed in any other place.

(3) If it were [once] right to say...that negligence is a necessary ingredient of unintentional trespass only where the circumstances are such as to show that the plaintiff had taken on himself the risk of inevitable injury (i.e. injury which is the result of neither intention nor carelessness on the part of the defendant), the plaintiff must today in this crowded world be considered as taking on himself the risk of inevitable injury from any acts of his neighbour which, in the absence of damage to the plaintiff, would not in themselves be unlawful—of which discharging a gun at a shooting party in 1957 or a trained band exercise in 1616 are obvious examples....

(4) The onus of proving negligence, where the trespass is not intentional, lies on the plaintiff, whether the action be framed in trespass or in negligence. This has been unquestioned law in highway cases ever since *Holmes v Mather* (1875) LR 10 Exch 261, and there is no reason in principle, nor any suggestion in the decided authorities, why it should be any different in other cases. It is, indeed, but an illustration of the rule that he who affirms must prove, which lies at the root of our law of evidence....

If, as I have held, the onus of proof of intention or negligence on the part of the defendant lies on the plaintiff, then, under the modern rules of pleading, he must allege either intention on the part of the defendant, or, if he relies on negligence, he must state the facts which he alleges constitute negligence. Without either of such allegations the bald statement that the defendant shot the plaintiff in unspecified circumstances with an unspecified weapon in my view discloses no cause of action.

This is no academic pleading point. It serves to secure justice between the parties. If it is open to the plaintiff—as counsel for the plaintiff must, I think, contend—on the pleadings as they at present stand to prove that the defendant shot him deliberately, failure to allege such intention deprives the defendant of his right to apply to stay the action pending prosecution for the felony (*Smith v Selwyn* [1914] 3 KB 98). I should repeat that there is, of course, in fact no suggestion that the shooting here was intentional, and thus felonious. But if counsel for the plaintiff be right, proof of intention would be open on the pleading in its present form.

Turning next to the alternative of negligent trespass to the person, there is here the bare allegation that on a particular day at a particular place 'the defendant shot the plaintiff'. In what circumstances, indeed with what weapon, from bow and arrow to atomic warhead, is not stated. So bare an allegation is consistent with the defendant's having exercised reasonable care. It may be—I know not—that, had the circumstances been set out with greater particularity, there would have been disclosed facts which themselves shouted negligence, so that the doctrine of *res ipsa loquitur* would have applied. In such a form the statement of claim might have disclosed a cause of action even although the word 'negligence' itself had not been used, and the plaintiff in that event would have been limited to relying for proof of negligence on the facts which he had alleged. But I have today to deal with the pleading as it stands. As it stands, it neither alleges negligence in terms nor alleges facts which, if true, would of themselves constitute negligence; nor, if counsel for the plaintiff is right, would he be bound at any time before the trial to disclose to the defendant what facts he relies on as constituting negligence.

I do not see how the plaintiff will be harmed by alleging now the facts on which he ultimately intends to rely. On the contrary, for him to do so, will serve to secure justice between the parties. It offends the underlying purpose of the modern system of pleading that a plaintiff, by calling his grievance 'trespass to the person' instead of 'negligence', should force a defendant to come to trial blindfold; and I am glad to find nothing in the authorities which compels the court in this case to refrain from stripping the bandage from his eyes.

I hold that the statement of claim in its present form discloses no cause of action.

Judgment for the defendant.

COMMENTARY

The issue at stake in *Fowler v Lanning* was not new. As Diplock J noted in his judgment, many of the authorities which he considered pre-dated the modern system of pleading which made it difficult to assess their appropriateness in the modern system. Perhaps the most difficult is *Weaver v Ward* (1616) Hob 134. The plaintiff's declaration alleged assault and battery against the defendant who, in response, pleaded that both parties were in the militia and that the accident had occurred whilst training. The court held that this plea was not valid, and stated that 'no man shall be excused of a trespass (for this is the nature of an excuse, and not a justification...) except as may be judged utterly without his fault'. This might be read as suggesting, contrary to Diplock J's decision, that matters of excuse (in this case, that the defendant had exercised reasonable care) are normally for the defendant to plead, but the particular pleading used by the defendant makes it difficult to discern the exact nature of the court's judgment (see W. L. Morison and C. Sappideen, *Torts: Commentary and Materials*, 8th edn. (North Ryde, NSW: LBC, 1993) pp. 56–9). Nineteenth-century cases tend to support Diplock J's decision by holding that liability depended on some degree of fault being shown by the plaintiff. In *Holmes v Mather* (1875) LR 10 Ex 261 the Court of Exchequer held that, in running-down cases, liability could only ensue if the impact was the result of intention or negligence on the part of the defendant, and in *Stanley v Powell* [1891] 1 QB 86 Denman J took the same view in respect of a shooting accident, a view which was tacitly supported by the Court of Appeal in *National Coal Board v Evans* [1951] 2 KB 861.

Apart from the question of authority, the decision of Diplock J has much to commend it. It forces the claimant to allege facts which constitute intention or negligence, allowing the defendant to know the exact nature of the claim. The defendant does not have to come to trial blindfold, ready to defend evidence of intention and negligence, whichever is raised. The decision may therefore be thought to promote procedural fairness. It also promotes efficiency, as the purpose of the pleadings is to limit the issues in dispute between the parties.

However, the decision has not won universal support in other jurisdictions. There remains doubt in Australia over whether *Fowler v Lanning* represents the law in that jurisdiction (compare *McHale v Watson* (1964) 111 CLR 384, per Windeyer J; *Venning v Chin* (1974) 10

SASR 299; *Hackshaw v Shaw* (1984) 155 CLR 614 at [5] per Deane J; *Stingel v Clark* (2006) 222 CLR 442 at [47] per Gummow J). In Canada, *Walmsley v Humenick* [1954] 2 DLR 232 took the same line as *Fowler v Lanning*, but later cases have followed an earlier Canadian Supreme Court decision (*Cook v Lewis* [1952] 1 DLR 1) which suggests the onus of disproving intent or negligence lies with the defendant (*Larin v Goshen* (1975) 56 DLR 3d 719, *Bell Canada v Cope (Sarnia) Ltd* (1980) 11 CCLT 170). New Zealand appears to follow *Fowler v Lanning* (*Beals v Hayward* [1960] NZLR 131).

Letang v Cooper [1965] QB 232

The plaintiff was sunbathing in the car park of a hotel when she was run over by the defendant's car. As the time for her to bring an action in negligence had expired, she framed her action in trespass, seeking to benefit from the longer limitation period for this cause of action. She was successful before Elwes J but the Court of Appeal reversed the decision.

Lord Denning MR

The sole question is whether the action is statute barred. The plaintiff admits that the action for negligence is barred after three years, but she claims that the action for trespass to the person is not barred until six years have elapsed. The judge has so held and awarded her £575 damages for trespass to the person.

Under the Limitation Act 1939, the period of limitation was six years in all actions founded 'on tort'; but in 1954 Parliament reduced it to three years in actions for damages for personal injuries, provided that the actions come within these words of s. 2(1) of the Law Reform (Limitation of Actions, etc) Act 1954:

> ... in the case of actions for damages for negligence, nuisance or breach of duty (whether the duty exists by virtue of a contract or of a provision made by or under a statute or independently of any contract or any such provision) where the damages claimed by the plaintiff for the negligence, nuisance or breach of duty consist of or include damages in respect of personal injuries to any person ...

The plaintiff says that these words do not cover an action for trespass to the person, and that, therefore, the time bar is not the new period of three years, but the old period of six years.

The argument, as it was developed before us, became a direct invitation to this court to go back to the old forms of action and to decide this case by reference to them. The statute bars an action on the case, it is said, after three years, whereas trespass to the person is not barred for six years. The argument was supported by reference to text-writers, such as *Salmond on Torts* (13th edn.) p. 790. I must say that if we are, at this distance of time, to revive the distinction between trespass and case, we should get into the most utter confusion. The old common lawyers tied themselves in knots over it, and we should find ourselves doing the same. Let me tell you some of their contortions. Under the old law, whenever one man injured another by the direct and immediate application of force, the plaintiff could sue the defendant in trespass to the person, without alleging negligence (see *Leame v Bray*) whereas if the injury was only consequential, he had to sue in case. You will remember the illustration given by Fortescue J in *Reynolds v Clarke* (1725) 1 Stra 634 at 636:

> If a man throws a log into the highway and in that act it hits me, I may maintain trespass because it is an immediate wrong; but if, as it lies there, I tumble over it and receive an injury, I must bring an action upon the case because it is only prejudicial in consequence.

Nowadays, if a man carelessly throws a piece of wood from a house into a roadway, then whether it hits the plaintiff or he tumbles over it the next moment, the action would not be trespass or case, but simply negligence. Another distinction which the old lawyers drew was this: If the driver of a horse and gig negligently ran down a passer-by, the plaintiff could sue the driver either in trespass or in case (see *Williams v Holland* (1833) 10 Bing 112); but if the driver was a servant, the plaintiff could not sue the master in trespass, but only in case (see *Sharrod v London and North Western Ry Co* (1849) 4 Exch 580). In either case today, the action would not be trespass or case, but only negligence.

If we were to bring back these subtleties into the law of limitation, we should produce the most absurd anomalies; and all the more so when you bear in mind that under the Fatal Accidents Acts the period of limitation is three years from the death. The decision of Elwes J, if correct, would produce these results. It would mean that if a motorist ran down two people, killing one and injuring another, the widow would have to bring her action within three years, but the injured person would have six years. It would mean also that if a lorry driver was in collision at a cross roads with an owner driver, an injured passenger would have to bring his action against the employer of the lorry driver within three years, but he would have six years in which to sue the owner-driver. Not least of all the absurdities is a case like the present. It would mean that the plaintiff could get out of the three-year limitation by suing in trespass instead of in negligence.

I must decline, therefore, to go back to the old forms of action in order to construe this statute...

The truth is that the distinction between trespass and case is obsolete. We have a different sub-division altogether. Instead of dividing actions for personal injuries into trespass (direct damage) or case (consequential damage), we divide the causes of action now according as the defendant did the injury intentionally or unintentionally. If one man intentionally applies force directly to another, the plaintiff has a cause of action in assault and battery, or, if you so please to describe it, in trespass to the person. 'The least touching of another in anger is a battery.' If he does not inflict injury intentionally, but only unintentionally, the plaintiff has no cause of action today in trespass. His only cause of action is in negligence, and then only on proof of want of reasonable care. If the plaintiff cannot prove want of reasonable care, he may have no cause of action at all. Thus, it is not enough nowadays for the plaintiff to plead that 'the defendant shot the plaintiff'. He must also allege that he did it intentionally or negligently. If intentional, it is the tort of assault and battery. If negligent and causing damage, it is the tort of negligence.

The modern law on this subject was well expounded by my brother Diplock I in *Fowler v Lanning* with which I fully agree. But I would go this one step further: when the injury is not inflicted intentionally, but negligently, I would say that the only cause of action is negligence and not trespass. If it were trespass, it would be actionable without proof of damage; and that is not the law today.

[Lord Denning went on to decide that, even if he was wrong in the above, the words 'breach of duty' in the Law Reform (Limitation of Actions, etc) Act 1954, s. 2(1) were wide enough to comprehend the cause of action for trespass to the person as well as negligence, and hence the three-year limitation period in that section applied.]

Diplock LJ

A cause of action is simply a factual situation the existence of which entitles one person to obtain from the court a remedy against another person. Historically the means by which the remedy was obtained varied with the nature of the factual situation and causes of action were divided into categories according to the 'form of action' by which the remedy was obtained in the particular kind of factual situation which constituted the cause of action; but that is legal history, not current law. If A, by failing to exercise reasonable care, inflicts direct personal injury on B those facts constitute a cause of action on the part of B against A for damages in respect of such personal injuries. The remedy for this cause of action could, before 1873, have been obtained by alternative forms of action, namely, originally either trespass vi et armis or trespass on the case, later either trespass to the person or negligence. (See *Bullen & Leake's Precedents of Pleadings*, 3rd ed.) Certain procedural consequences, the importance of which diminished considerably after the Common Law Procedure Act, 1852 flowed from the plaintiff's pleader's choice of the form of action used. The Supreme Court of Judicature Act 1873 abolished forms of action. It did not affect causes of action; so it was convenient for lawyers and legislators to continue to use, to describe the various categories of factual situations which entitled one person to obtain from the court a remedy against another, the names of the various 'forms of action' by which formerly the remedy appropriate to the particular category of factual situation was obtained. But it is essential to realise that when, since 1873, the name of a form of action is used to identify a cause of action, it is used as a convenient and succinct description of a particular category of factual situation which entitles one person to obtain from the court a remedy against another person. To forget this will indeed encourage the old forms of action to rule us from their graves.

If A, by failing to exercise reasonable care, inflicts direct personal injuries on B it is permissible today to describe this factual situation indifferently, either as a cause of action in negligence or as a cause of action in trespass, and the action brought to obtain a remedy for this factual situation as an action for negligence or an action for trespass to the person—though I agree with Lord Denning MR that today 'negligence' is the expression to be preferred. But no procedural consequences flow from the choice of description by the pleader (see *Fowler v Lanning*). They are simply alternative ways of describing the same factual situation....

The factual situation on which the plaintiff's action was founded is set out in the statement of claim. It was that the defendant, by failing to exercise reasonable care (of which failure particulars were given), drove his motor car over the plaintiff's legs and so inflicted on her direct personal injuries in respect of which the plaintiff claimed damages. That factual situation was the plaintiff's cause of action. It was the cause of action 'for' which the plaintiff claimed damages in respect of the personal injuries which she sustained. That cause of action or factual situation falls within the description of the tort of 'negligence' and an action founded on it, that is, brought to obtain the remedy to which the existence of that factual situation entitles the plaintiff, falls within the description of an 'action for negligence'. The description 'negligence' was in fact used by the plaintiff's pleader; but this cannot be decisive, for we are concerned not with the description applied by the pleader to the factual situation and the action founded on it, but with the description applied to it by Parliament in the enactment to be construed. It is true that that factual situation also falls within the description of the tort of 'trespass to the person'. But that, as I have endeavoured to show, does not mean that there are two causes of action. It merely means that there are two apt descriptions of the same cause of action. It does not cease to be the tort of 'negligence', because it can also be called by another name. An action founded on it is nonetheless an 'action for negligence' because it can also be called an 'action for trespass to the person'.

It is not, I think, necessary to consider whether there is today any respect in which a cause of action for unintentional as distinct from intentional 'trespass to the person' is not equally aptly described as a cause of action for 'negligence'. The difference stressed by Elwes J [1964] 1 All ER at p 673 that actual damage caused by failure to exercise reasonable care forms an essential element in the cause of action for 'negligence', but does not in the cause of action in 'trespass to the person', is, I think, more apparent than real when the trespass is unintentional; for, since the duty of care, whether in negligence or in unintentional trespass to the person, is to take reasonable care to avoid causing actual damage to one's neighbour, there is no breach of the duty unless actual damage is caused. Actual damage is thus a necessary ingredient in unintentional as distinct from intentional trespass to the person. . . .

[Diplock LJ proceeded to find that the plaintiff's action was for 'negligence, nuisance, or breach of duty' under Limitation of Actions Act 1954, s. 2(1) and was therefore subject to a three-year limitation period where damages for personal injury were claimed.]

Danckwerts LJ, in a short concurring judgment, agreed with **Lord Denning MR**.

Appeal allowed.

COMMENTARY

There is a marked contrast between the two extracted judgments. Lord Denning MR would abolish the action for 'negligent trespass' because trespass connotes intention. Diplock LJ is more circumspect, holding that the label does not matter as long as the procedural consequences do not vary depending on the label. Thus, whilst it is not clear whether an action remains for negligent trespass (see *Winfield & Jolowicz*, para. 4–31; *Salmond & Heuston*, p. 7) what is clear is that a claimant will obtain no benefit from framing an action in negligent trespass as opposed to negligence. Although in most cases it would not matter how the action was framed, it is possible to envisage situations where different consequences might follow depending on which action was pleaded (see Trindade (1971) 20 ICLQ 706; N, Mullany (ed.), *Torts in the Nineties* (Sydney. LDC, 1997), pp. 252–6). Apart from the limitation point considered in *Letang*, the main scope for an action of negligent trespass lies in the different damage requirements: as damage is not a part of the cause of action in trespass an action may be brought in respect of damage which would not qualify as damage for a negligence action (e.g. emotional distress). The decision of the Court of Appeal appears to eliminate the use of trespass in this way.

According to Lord Denning MR, the modern distinction between the causes of action for trespass and negligence lies in the concept of intention. Intentional acts are remediable in trespass; negligent acts in negligence. A claimant would not be allowed to 'dress up' a negligence claim as an intentional tort and seek a longer limitation period. But would a claimant be given greater latitude when attempting the reverse—bringing an action for intentional acts in negligence for the purpose of obtaining a more favourable limitation period? In *Stubbings v Webb* [1993] AC 498 the House of Lords considered the legislative history of the special limitation period of three years (as opposed to the normal six for tort actions) prescribed for actions in 'negligence, nuisance or breach of duty' where damages are claimed for personal injury, including psychiatric injury. The current law is to be found in the Limitation Act 1980, s. 11. (The extract above, *Letang v Cooper*, considers the corresponding provision in the now-repealed Limitation of Actions Act 1954, s. 2(1).) The House of Lords refused to interpret the words 'negligence, nuisance or breach of duty' as including deliberate sexual or physical abuse which meant that the provisions of the Act allowing for the discretionary extension of the limitation period for personal injury claims (s. 33) did not apply. As a result, the plaintiff's actions were subject to the normal six-year limitation period for actions in tort under s. 2 of the 1980 Act, which commenced from the date of the abuse and, as the abuse had taken place between 16 and 28 years earlier, her actions were statute-barred. The decision attracted few admirers (see McGee (1993) 109 LQR 356; Jones (1994) 110 LQR 31; Lunney

(1993–4) 4 KCLJ 79). As Conaghan, 'Tort Litigation in the Context of Intra-familial Abuse' (1998) 61 MLR 132, 141–2 pointed out:

> The Court of Appeal decision [which had interpreted the phrase more broadly] displays a realism and practicality wholly lacking in that of the House of Lords. By choosing to engage in the narrowest interpretative techniques (particularly in relation to the notion of 'duty' as between family members) and relying on their own limited and highly partial understanding of the experience of sexual abuse, their Lordships were able to avoid any examination of the context within which the claim in *Stubbings* (necessarily) evolved and knowingly denied many sufferers of sexual abuse the possibility of a tortious remedy. . . .
>
>   At no point did the House of Lord [sic] in *Stubbings* undertake the necessary exploration of the public policy reasons behind limitation periods and their applicability to cases of childhood sexual abuse.

Despite recommendations from the Law Commission (*Limitation of Actions*, Law Com. No. 270) that the same limitation regime should govern claims for personal injury whether founded on an intentional tort or negligence (para. 4.33), no legislative change was made. The result was that claimants tried to find ways of pleading actions in negligence in relation to conduct that was in essence deliberate sexual or physical assaults, but the Court of Appeal in *KR v Bryn Alyn Community (Holdings) Ltd* [2003] QB 1441 severely limited this kind of pleading by holding that in most cases they were impermissible attempts to avoid the reasoning in *Stubbings v Webb*. Finally, in January 2008 the House of Lords in *A v Hoare* [2008] 1 AC 844 reconsidered its earlier decision in *Stubbings v Webb* and unanimously declined to follow it (as had the High Court of Australia, by majority, in relation to similarly worded legislation in *Stingel v Clark* (2006) 226 CLR 442), holding that the phrase 'negligence, nuisance or breach of duty' was wide enough to encompass personal injury that resulted from a deliberate assault. Lord Hoffmann noted (at [14]), that a more favourable limitation period had been introduced for personal injuries caused by negligence, in the Limitation Act 1975 (re-enacted in Limitation Act 1980, ss. 11(4)(b), 14) by providing for a later commencement date ('the date of knowledge. . .of the person injured') in cases of latent harm. Once this had been done 'there could be no moral or other ground for denying to a victim of intentional injury the more favourable limitation treatment introduced by the 1975 Act for victims of injuries caused by negligence'. Thus, in Handford's words, '[t]he House of Lords has corrected a long-standing anomaly and considerably eased the burden on sexual abuse victims who wish to obtain justice from the courts' ((2008) 16 Tort L Rev 61, 63; cf. Prime and Scanlan, 'Limitation and Personal Injury in the House of Lords—Problem Solved?' (2008) 29 Stat Law 111, who argue that other aspects of the decision not discussed here continue to pose limitation period problems for victims of sexual and physical abuse).

  Although the practical result of *Stubbings v Webb* has been reversed by the decision in *Hoare*, it is suggested that the refusal to allow claimants to pick and choose between trespass and negligence can be defended, especially as the particular limitation difficulty created by the decision in *Stubbings* has now been overcome. If Lord Denning MR was correct to state the modern demarcation line as intentional/unintentional, the decision in *Stubbings* to maintain that demarcation is understandable. However, there would be little merit in maintaining the line if its sole purpose was to maintain outdated or ill-conceived doctrinal boundaries, as was recognised by Diplock LJ in *Letang*, above. His Lordship's reasoning in that case was premised on the notion that the action in negligence and that in negligent trespass are the same, and that the choice of action should therefore make no difference procedurally. But, as Diplock LJ expressly remarked, this does not apply in the case of intentional trespass. It does matter whether the cause of action is negligence or intentional trespass for, amongst other differences, damage is an essential element in negligence but not in trespass, which is actionable *per se*. According to *Fowler v Lanning*, either intention or negligence must be pleaded, and the plaintiff in *Stubbings* pleaded intentional acts of physical and sexual assault, thereby absolving herself of the need to prove damage that was actionable in negligence, or, if damage was caused, that the damage satisfied the remoteness rule applied in negligence (see Buxton LJ in *Wainwright v Home Office* [2002] 3 WLR 405 at 423). In these circumstances, it is not surprising that their Lordships thought this was an intentional trespass, and while the unfortunate consequences of this ruling in terms of limitation periods have been avoided by holding that intentional trespass to the person falls within the phrase 'negligence, nuisance or breach of duty' in s. 11 of the Limitation Act 1980, the decision not to treat negligence and intentional trespass as interchangeable makes sense in light of the division suggested by Lord Denning in *Letang v Cooper*.

For discussion of the potential role of the intentional torts—now broadened after the decision in *Hoare*—in child sexual and physical abuse cases see Paula Case, *Compensating Child Abuse in England and Wales* (Cambridge: Cambridge University Press, 2007) and Laura Hoyano and Caroline Keenan, *Child Abuse: Law and Policy Across Boundaries* (Oxford: OUP, 2007). Note also that abuse victims may be eligible to claim under the Criminal Injuries Compensation Scheme, a state-run compensation scheme for the victims of 'crimes of violence' although it seems that the victim's consent, even if not effective for the purpose of the criminal law, may be sufficient to prevent a 'crime of violence' taking place (see *R v Criminal Injuries Compensation Appeals Panel, ex p. August; R v Criminal Injuries Compensation Appeals Panel, ex p. Brown* [2001] 2 All ER 874; cf. *R (on the application of E) v Criminal Injuries Compensation Appeals Panel* [2003] EWCA Civ 234). Do you think that a child of 13 could give an effective consent to sexual intercourse to an adult of 21? (See *R (on the application of CD) v Criminal Injuries Compensation Appeals Panel* [2004] EWHC 1674 (Admin).) Are such children likely to be *Gillick* competent? (See p. 85, below.)

(b) The Concept of Intention

The distinction between intentional and negligent acts is fundamental to the law of torts. Two questions arise in this context: what does 'intention' mean, and what must the defendant have intended? The latter question is the easier to answer: as far as the intentional torts against the person are concerned the defendant must intend the acts that constitute the tort. In the case of battery, this means that the unlawful contact must be intended (see *Wilson v Pringle*, below) whilst, for assault, the defendant must intend the acts that, objectively, cause apprehension of an imminent infliction of force. So the mere act of intentionally firing a gun will not amount to a battery if there is no-one in sight, but it will be sufficient if the gun is aimed at another who is consequently hit by a bullet. Similarly, throwing a punch when alone is no assault, but may be so if another is in range of the blow.

The first question—what amounts to intent?—is more difficult to answer with certainty. In many cases intent will be obvious. If I aim a blow at your face and consequently hit you, there is no doubt that the contact was intended. Everyone is deemed to intend the natural and probable result of their actions. However, a more difficult case was considered in *Gibbon v Pepper* (1695) 1 Ld Raym 38:

> [I]f I ride upon a horse, and JS whips the horse, so that he runs away with me and runs over any other person, he who whipped the horse is guilty of the battery, and not me. But if I by spurring

was the cause of such accident, then I am guilty. In the same manner, if A takes the hand of B and with it strikes C, A is the trespasser and not B.

In the first of the two cases considered, it seems that the horseman would be found to lack the necessary intent for the reason that the accident could not be attributed to any voluntary act on his part.

The concept of intention is further analysed in the extract, below, from the American Law Institute's *Restatement of the Law (Third), Torts: Liability for Physical and Emotional Harm (2010)*. The *Restatement* is published by the American Law Institute and is a summary of the law which applies in the majority of the states of the United States. Although the extract sometimes refers to an intention to cause harm, the intentional torts against the person only require an intention to cause the particular consequence that constitutes the tort (e.g. in battery, the unlawful contact). The extract should be read with this point in mind.

American Law Institute, *Restatement Third, Torts: Liability for Physical and Emotional Harm (2010)*

Chapter 1—Intent, Recklessness, and Negligence: Definitions

§ 1 Intent

A person acts with the intent to produce a consequence if:

(a) the person acts with the purpose of producing that consequence; or
(b) the person acts knowing that the consequence is substantially certain to result...

Illustration:

1. In a forest area Ken deliberately pulls the trigger of a rifle. He hopes to hit a wild deer, and he is unaware that any person is in the vicinity. The gun discharges. In fact, Nancy is nearby and is struck by the bullet. Ken has intentionally shot his gun. Yet he has not intentionally caused the harm to Nancy; he did not act with the purpose to produce that harm nor did he know that the harm was substantially certain to occur...
2. Wendy throws a rock at Andrew, someone she dislikes, at a distance of 100 feet, wanting to hit Andrew. Given the distance, it is far from certain Wendy will succeed in this; rather, it is probable that the rock will miss its target. In fact, Wendy's aim is true, and Andrew is struck by the rock. Wendy has purposely, and hence intentionally, caused this harm.
3. The Jones Company runs an aluminum smelter, which emits particulate fluorides as part of the industrial process. Jones knows that these particles, carried by the air, will land on neighboring property, and in doing so will bring about a range of harms. Far from desiring this result, Jones in fact regrets it. Despite its regret, Jones has knowingly, and hence intentionally, caused the resulting harms.
4. When Steve, a police officer, seeks to pull to the side of the road a car that has made an illegal turn, the car speeds away. Steve undertakes a chase, and continues the chase even though the car is making every effort to escape, driving rapidly and somewhat wildly. Steve is well aware there is a significant likelihood that someone will suffer physical harm, either personal injury or at least property damage, in the course of the chase. In fact, the escaping car strikes the car owned by Ruth, which she is driving carefully on the highway. Steve, in initiating and continuing the chase, has not intentionally harmed Ruth or her car. Steve did not harbor a purpose that Ruth (or anyone else) suffer any harm; while Steve knew there was a significant likelihood of such harm, the harm was not substantially certain to occur.

5. Joanne, a physician, provides medication to her patient, Mark. Because Joanne has confused one medication with another, the medication she gives Mark is certain to cause harm to Mark. Such harm ensues. Joanne has not intentionally harmed Mark. While Joanne's conduct was substantially certain to cause him harm, Joanne lacked the knowledge that this would happen.

COMMENTARY

A difficult question arises as to whether recklessness as to consequences can amount to 'intention' for the purpose of the intentional torts. The US *Restatement* suggests it does not, although there have been musings to the contrary with respect to English law (Trindade, 'Intentional Torts: Some Thoughts on Assault and Battery' (1982) 2 OJLS 211). The practical significance of the issue may be diminished because, where a claimant has suffered physical injury, his reckless conduct might be categorised as negligent and thus a remedy provided (cf. *Stubbings v Webb*). Nonetheless, there might be procedural advantages in having reckless conduct categorised as intentional rather than negligent (e.g. in terms of limitation periods), and the issue awaits resolution by the courts.

Another difficulty arises when A, seeking to hit B, actually hits C. In the American case of *Talmage v Smith* (1894) 101 Mich 370, the defendant threw a stick towards a group of boys, and there was evidence it was thrown towards a particular boy whom it missed. It struck the plaintiff, who successfully sued in trespass, the Supreme Court of Michigan saying: 'The right of the plaintiff was made to depend upon the intention on the part of the defendant to hit somebody, and to inflict an unwarranted injury upon some one. Under these circumstances, the fact that the injury resulted to another than was intended does not relieve the defendant from responsibility…' This principle of 'transferred intent' appears to have been applied in *James v Campbell* (1832) 5 C & P 372 where the defendant was held liable for hitting the plaintiff, even though he intended to hit a third person and did not know he had struck the plaintiff, the judge holding that this matter went to damages and not to the commission of the battery (see also *Livingstone v Ministry of Defence* [1984] NI 356; *Bici v Ministry of Defence* [2004] EWHC 786 (QB)). Would these actions be better treated as actions in negligence? See Beever, 'Transferred Malice in Tort Law' (2009) 29 LS 400.

II. Assault

Assault is defined in the following terms by Blackstone, vol. III, 'Of Private Wrongs', ch. 8, I, 2–3:

[A]ssault…is an attempt to offer or beat another, without touching him: as if one lifts up his cane, or his fist, in a threatening manner; or strikes at him, but misses him; this is an assault, *insultus*, which Finch describes to be 'an unlawful setting upon one's person'. This also is an inchoate violence, amounting considerably higher than bare threats; and therefore, though no actual suffering is proved, yet the party injured may have redress by action of trespass *vi et armis*; wherein he shall recover damages as a compensation for the injury.

The claimant must establish that the conduct of the defendant created a reasonable apprehension of an imminent battery. These issues are considered in the extracts below.

Stephens v Myers (1830) 4 C & P 349, 172 ER 735

Assault. The declaration stated that the defendant threatened and attempted to assault the plaintiff. Plea—Not Guilty.

It appeared that the plaintiff was acting as chairman, at a parish meeting, and sat at the head of a table, at which table the defendant also sat, there being about six or seven persons between him and the plaintiff. The defendant having, in the course of some angry discussion, which took place, been very vociferous, and interrupted the proceedings of the meeting, a motion was made, that he should be turned out, which was carried by a very large majority. Upon this, the defendant said, he would rather pull the chairman out of the chair, than be turned out of the room; and immediately advanced with his fist clenched towards the chairman, but was stopt by the churchwarden who sat next but one to the chairman, at a time when he was not near enough for any blow he might have meditated to have reached the chairman; but the witness said, that it seemed to them that he was advancing with an intention to strike the chairman.

    Spankie, Serjt, for the defendant, upon this evidence, contended, that no assault had been committed, as there was no power in the defendant, from the situation of the parties, to execute his threat—there was not a present ability—he had not the means of executing his intention at the time he was stopt.

Tindal CJ, summing up to the jury:

It is not every threat, when there is no actual personal violence that constitutes an assault, there must, in all cases, be the means of carrying the threat into effect. The question I shall leave to you will be, whether the defendant was advancing at the time, in a threatening attitude, to strike the chairman so that his blow would almost immediately have reached the chairman, if he had not been stopt; then, though he was not near enough at the time to have struck him, yet if he was advancing with that intent, I think it amounts to an assault in law. If he was so advancing, that, within a second or two of time, he would have reached the plaintiff, it seems to me it is an assault in law. If you think he was not advancing to strike the plaintiff, then only can you find for the defendant; otherwise you must find it for the plaintiff, and give him such damages, as you think the nature of the case requires.

Verdict for the plaintiff, damages 1 shilling.

COMMENTARY

Would the plaintiff have succeeded if, being a particularly timid soul, he had feared being thrown out of his chair even though the defendant had been threatening him from outside the hall? It seems the jury thought him fairly timorous, for even in the 1840s an award of one shilling as damages was paltry.

R v Ireland; R v Burstow [1998] AC 147

A number of issues were raised in these appeals, one of which was whether the maker of silent telephone calls could be convicted of a criminal offence which required the accused to have committed an assault against the victim.

Lord Steyn

It is to assault in the form of an act causing the victim to fear an immediate application of force to her that I must turn. Counsel argued that as a matter of law an assault can never be committed by words alone and therefore it cannot be committed by silence. The premise depends on the slenderest authority, namely an observation by Holroyd J to a jury that 'no words or singing are equivalent to an assault' (see *Meade's and Belt's Case* (1823) 1 Lew CC 184 at 185, 168 ER 1006). The proposition that a gesture may amount to an assault, but that words can never suffice, is unrealistic and indefensible. A thing said is also a thing done. There is no reason why something said should be incapable of causing an apprehension of immediate personal violence, e.g. a man accosting a woman in a dark alley saying 'come with me or I will stab you'. I would, therefore, reject the proposition that an assault can never be committed by words.

That brings me to the critical question whether a silent caller may be guilty of an assault. The answer to this question seems to me to be 'Yes, depending on the facts'. It involves questions of fact within the province of the jury. After all, there is no reason why a telephone caller who says to a woman in a menacing way 'I will be at your door in a minute or two' may not be guilty of an assault if he causes his victim to apprehend immediate personal violence. Take now the case of the silent caller. He intends by his silence to cause fear and he is so understood. The victim is assailed by uncertainty about his intentions. Fear may dominate her emotions, and it may be the fear that the caller's arrival at her door may be imminent. She may fear the possibility of immediate personal violence. As a matter of law the caller may be guilty of an assault: whether he is or not will depend on the circumstance and in particular on the impact of the caller's potentially menacing call or calls on the victim. Such a prosecution case . . . may be fit to leave to the jury. . . .

Lord Hope of Craighead

[I]t has been recognised for many centuries that putting a person in fear may amount to what in law is an assault. This is reflected in the meaning which is given to the word 'assault' in *Archbold's Criminal Pleading, Evidence and Practice* (1997) p 1594 para 19–66, namely that an assault is any act by which a person intentionally or recklessly causes another to apprehend immediate and unlawful violence. . . .

The question is whether such an act can include the making of a series of silent telephone calls. Counsel for the appellant said that such an act could not amount to an assault under any circumstances, just as words alone could not amount to an assault. He also submitted that, in order for there to be an assault, it had to be proved that what the victim apprehended was immediate and unlawful violence, not just a repetition of the telephone calls. It was not enough to show merely that the victim was inconvenienced or afraid. . . .

There is no clear guidance on this point either in the statute [Offences Against the Person Act 1861] or in the authorities. On the one hand in *Meade's and Belt's Case* (1823) 1 Lew CC 184, 168 ER 1006 Holroyd J said that no words or singing can amount to an assault. On the other hand in *R v Wilson* [1955] 1 WLR 493 at 494 Lord Goddard CJ said that the appellant's words, 'Get out knives' would itself be an assault. . . .

The fact is that the means by which a person of evil disposition may intentionally or recklessly cause another to apprehend immediate and unlawful violence will vary according to the circumstances. Just as it is not true to say that every blow which is struck is an assault—some blows, which would otherwise amount to battery, may be struck by accident or in jest or may otherwise be entirely justified—so also it is not true to say that mere words or gestures can never constitute an assault. It all depends on the circumstances. If the words or gestures are accompanied in their turn by gestures or by words which threaten immediate and unlawful violence, that will be sufficient for an assault. The words or gestures must be seen in their whole context.

In this case the means which the appellant used to communicate with his victims was the telephone. While he remained silent, there can be no doubt that he was intentionally communicating with them as directly as if he was present with them in the same room. But whereas for him merely to remain silent with them in the same room, where they could see him and assess his demeanour, would have been unlikely to give rise to any feelings of apprehension on their part, his silence when using the telephone in calls made to them repeatedly was an act of an entirely different character. He was using his silence as a means of conveying a message to his victims. This was that he knew who and where they were, and that his purpose in making contact with them was as malicious as it was deliberate. In my opinion silent telephone calls of this nature are just as capable as words or gestures, said or made in the presence of the victim, of causing an apprehension of immediate and unlawful violence.

Whether this requirement, and in particular that of immediacy, is in fact satisfied will depend on the circumstances. This will need in each case, if it is disputed, to be explored in evidence.

COMMENTARY

The latter of the two extracts is from a criminal case, and it should be noted that assault (as well as battery and false imprisonment) is a crime as well as a tort. The elements of the crime of assault are similar, if not identical, to the tort of assault (although the subjective mental element of *mens rea* is not required in a civil claim) so that criminal assault cases can generally be used as authority for civil cases, although the different context of the decisions should be recognised.

Any successful action for assault requires the claimant to apprehend the direct and immediate application of force to his or her person. As the extracts from *Ireland* show, the question of immediacy is one of fact for the judge or jury. In *Mbasogo v Logo Ltd* [2007] QB 846, the claimant, the head of state of Equitorial Guinea, alleged assault against a group of mercenaries. The mercenaries were an advance party of a larger group whose aim was to overthrow the government but the plot was foiled. It was held by the Court of Appeal that the claim was rightly struck out; it was not clear that the advance group was even armed, still less that it had the capacity to carry out an immediate attack (see also *Thomas v NUM* [1986] Ch 20).

The House of Lords decision in *Ireland* ended any doubt over whether mere words could amount to an assault. It has long been the law that words accompanied by actions could amount to an assault. This could be so even if the words amounted to a conditional threat which exposed the claimant to no immediate danger. In *Read v Coker* (1853) 13 CB 850, 138 ER 1437, the plaintiff was told to leave premises where he conducted his business. He refused, whereupon the defendant collected together some of his workmen, who stood near the claimant with their sleeves and aprons tucked up, and told the claimant they would break his neck if he did not leave. He did leave, but later brought a successful action for assault. In the course of proceedings brought by the defendant for a mistrial Jervis CJ stated: 'If anything short of actual striking will in law constitute an assault, the facts here clearly showed that the defendant was guilty of an assault. There was a threat of violence exhibiting an intention to assault, and a present ability to carry the threat into execution.' (See also *Police v Greaves* [1964] NZLR 295.)

However, not every conditional assault will be actionable. In *Tubervell v Savage* (1669) 1 Mod 3, 86 ER 684, the defendant put his hand on his sword and said to the plaintiff: 'If it were not assize time I would not take such language from you.' The court held that this amounted to a declaration that the plaintiff would not be assaulted; hence there was no action. Whilst the principle is sound, it should be remembered that the main question is whether the conduct creates an apprehension of immediate force. One wonders whether the plaintiff, confronted by a man obviously angry and drawing a sword, would really be calmed by the addition of the words spoken by the defendant. Would it have made a difference if the plaintiff had not known it was assize time? What if he simply did not believe the words spoken? If a person holding a gun says, 'If it wasn't for your ugly face I'd fill you with lead', is this an assault?

A further question that arises is whether the defendant must intend that the claimant apprehends an imminent application of force. It has been suggested that this is so (*Bici v Ministry of Defence* [2004] EWHC 786 (QB)). However, it may be doubted whether the defendant can defeat a claim for assault by arguing that his subjective intention was not to cause the claimant any apprehension if, viewing his conduct objectively, this is exactly what it did. Thus it has been held in a line of earlier cases that pointing an unloaded gun at another may amount to an assault as long as the claimant does not know the gun is unloaded (see *R v St George* (1840) 9 C & P 483; *Logdon v DPP* [1976] Crim LR 121; *contra*, *Blake v Barnard* (1840) 9 C & P 626). The best explanation of these cases is that the defendant must be taken to have intended the natural and probable consequences of his act and the natural and probable consequence of pointing a gun at someone is to create an apprehension of an imminent application of force (unless it is known the gun is unloaded). A related question is whether the apprehension of the claimant is reasonable. There is no assault if there is no means to put the threat into effect but whether this is so should not be governed solely by hindsight. In *Stephens v Myers*, it turned out that the defendant was stopped before he was in a position to hit the plaintiff, but the latter, watching nervously from his seat, was in no position to know this. This is supported by the decision in *Ireland*, which clearly focuses attention on the position of the claimant rather than the intention of the defendant. The victims did not know whether the silent callers were close enough to apply immediate force, but the possibility that they might be was sufficient. Similarly, in another criminal case, *Smith v Chief Superintendent, Woking Police Station* (1983) 76 Cr App R 234, an intruder who looked through the victim's closed window was found guilty of an assault, because it was perfectly reasonable that the elderly victim may have feared the application of immediate force to her. But to be reasonable the apprehension must be related to an overt act of the defendant; in *Mbasogo*, above, it was held that neither the landing of the advance force of mercenaries nor the activities of the main group of mercenaries in another country constituted an overt act giving rise to an apprehension of an imminent application of force.

III. Battery

Battery requires the unlawful touching of another. Blackstone, vol. III, 'Of Private Wrongs', ch. 8, I, 2–3 describes a battery as follows:

> Battery is the unlawful beating of another. The least touching of another's person wilfully, or in anger, is a battery; for the law cannot draw the line between different degrees of violence, and therefore totally prohibits the first and lowest stage of it: every man's person being sacred, and no other having a right to meddle with it, in any the slightest manner.... But battery is, in some

cases, justifiable or lawful. . . . On account of these causes of justification, battery is defined to be the unlawful beating of another. . . .

The defences to a prima facie battery will be considered later in the chapter. The following extract considers what touchings might be considered unlawful.

Wilson v Pringle [1987] QB 237

The plaintiff and the defendant, both schoolboys, were involved in an incident in a school corridor as the result of which the plaintiff fell and suffered injuries. The plaintiff claimed damages, alleging a battery. The defendant admitted that he had indulged in horseplay with the plaintiff but claimed that this was insufficient, as the ingredients of trespass to the person were a deliberate touching, hostility and an intention to inflict injury, and therefore horseplay in which there was no intention to inflict injury could not amount to a trespass to the person. The plaintiff contended that there merely had to be an intentional application of force, such as horseplay involved, regardless of whether it was intended to cause injury.

Croom-Johnson LJ, having considered certain previous decisions on battery, asked the question:

[W]hat does entitle an injured plaintiff to sue for the tort of trespass to the person? Reference must be made to one further case: *Williams v Humphrey* (12 February 1975, unreported), decided by Talbot J. There the defendant, a boy just under 16, pushed the plaintiff into a swimming pool and caused him physical injury. The judge found the defendant acted negligently and awarded damages. But there was another claim in trespass. Talbot J rejected the submission that the action would not lie unless there was an intent to injure. He held that it was sufficient, if the act was intentional, that there was no justification for it. . . .

   The reasoning in *Williams v Humphrey* is all right as far as it goes, but it does not go far enough. It did not give effect to the reasoning of the older authorities . . . that for there to be either an assault or a battery there must be something in the nature of hostility. It may be evinced by anger, by words or gesture. Sometimes the very act of battery will speak for itself, as where somebody uses a weapon on another. What, then, turns a friendly touching (which is not actionable) into an unfriendly one (which is)? . . .

[His Lordship considered *R v Sutton* [1977] 1 WLR 1086 and continued:]

A more recent authority is *Collins v Wilcock* [1984] 1 WLR 1172. . . . The facts were that a woman police officer, suspecting that a woman was soliciting contrary to the Street Offences Act 1959, tried to question her. The woman walked away, and was followed by the police officer. The officer took hold of her arm in order to restrain her. The woman scratched the officer's arm. She was arrested, charged with assaulting a police officer in the execution of her duty, and convicted. On appeal by case stated, the appeal was allowed, on the ground that the officer had gone beyond the scope of her duty in detaining the woman in circumstances short of arresting her. The officer had accordingly committed a battery.

   The judgment of the Divisional Court was given by Robert Goff LJ. It is necessary to give a long quotation to do full justice to it. He said (at 1177–1178):

   . . . The fundamental principle, plain and incontestable, is that every person's body is inviolate . . . The effect is that everybody is protected not only against physical injury but against any form of physical molestation. But so widely drawn a principle must inevitably be subject to exceptions. For example, children may be subjected to reasonable punishment; people may be subjected to the lawful exercise of the power of arrest; and reasonable force may be used in self-defence or for the prevention of crime. But, apart from these special instances where the control or constraint is lawful, a broader exception has been created to allow for the exigencies of everyday life. Generally speaking, consent is a defence to battery; and most of the physical contacts of ordinary life are not actionable because they are impliedly consented to by all who move in society and so expose themselves to the risk of bodily contact. So nobody can complain of the jostling which is inevitable from his presence in, for example, a supermarket, an underground station or a busy street; nor can a person who attends a party complain if his hand is seized in friendship, or even if his back is (within reason) slapped (see *Tuberville v Savage* (1669) 1 Mod Rep 3, 86 ER 684). Although such cases are regarded as examples of implied consent, it is more common nowadays to treat them as falling within a general exception embracing all physical contact which is generally acceptable in the ordinary conduct of daily life.... Among such forms of conduct, long held to be acceptable, is touching a person for the purpose of engaging his attention, though of course using no greater degree of physical contact than is reasonably necessary in the circumstances for that purpose....

This rationalisation by Robert Goff LJ draws the so-called 'defences' to an action for trespass to the person (of which consent, self-defence, ejecting a trespasser, exercising parental authority, and statutory authority are some examples) under one umbrella of 'a general exception embracing all physical contact which is generally acceptable in the ordinary conduct of daily life'. It provides a solution to the old problem of what legal rule allows a casualty surgeon to perform an urgent operation on an unconscious patient who is brought into hospital. The patient cannot consent, and there may be no next of kin available to do it for him. Hitherto it has been customary to say in such cases that consent is to be implied for what would otherwise be a battery on the unconscious body. It is better simply to say that the surgeon's action is acceptable in the ordinary conduct of everyday life, and not a battery. It will doubtless be convenient to continue to tie the labels of the 'defences' to the facts of any case where they are appropriate. But the rationalisation explains and utilises the expressions of judicial opinion which appear in the authorities....

Nevertheless, it still remains to indicate what is to be proved by a plaintiff who brings an action for battery. Robert Goff LJ's judgment is illustrative of the considerations which underlie such an action, but it is not practicable to define a battery as 'physical contact which is not generally acceptable in the ordinary conduct of daily life'.

In our view, the authorities lead one to the conclusion that in a battery there must be an intentional touching or contact in one form or another of the plaintiff by the defendant. That touching must be proved to be a hostile touching. That still leaves unanswered the question, when is a touching to be called hostile? Hostility cannot be equated with ill-will or malevolence. It cannot be governed by the obvious intention shown in acts like punching, stabbing or shooting. It cannot be solely governed by an expressed intention, although that may be strong evidence. But the element of hostility, in the sense in which it is now to be considered, must be a question of fact for the tribunal of fact. It may be imported from the circumstances. Take the example of the police officer in *Collins v Wilcock*. She touched the woman deliberately, but without an intention to do more than restrain her temporarily. Nevertheless, she was acting unlawfully and in that way was acting with hostility. She was acting contrary to the woman's legal right not to be physically restrained. We see no more difficulty in establishing what she intended by means of question and answer, or by inference from the surrounding circumstances, than there is in establishing whether an apparently playful blow was struck in anger. The rules of law governing the legality of arrest may require strict application to the facts of appropriate cases, but in the ordinary give and take of everyday life the tribunal of fact should find no difficulty in answering the question, 'was this, or was it not, a battery?' Where the immediate act of touching does not itself demonstrate hostility, the plaintiff should plead the facts which are said to do so.

Although we are all entitled to protection from physical molestation, we live in a crowded world in which people must be considered as taking on themselves some risk of injury (where it occurs) from the acts of others which are not in themselves unlawful. If negligence cannot be proved, it may be that an injured plaintiff who is also unable to prove a battery, will be without redress....

COMMENTARY

Battery is the unlawful application of force to another, but what constitutes unlawfulness for this purpose? Holt CJ in *Cole v Turner* (1704) 90 ER 958 thought the least touching of another 'in anger' constituted a battery, but this is clearly too narrow. Battery is concerned with the protection of physical integrity, and the intention of the defendant cannot be the sole determinant in whether this integrity has been breached. Hence giving someone an unwanted kiss, or touching a sleeping person, may be a battery despite the absence of animus from the touching.

Nonetheless, it is clear that some forms of touching do not constitute a battery (e.g. a congratulatory pat on the back, forcing past another to exit a crowded bus or train, or tapping another to gain their attention). The rationalisation for this non-actionability is more difficult. One possible rationale, considered in *Wilson*, is that there is implied consent to such touchings. However, in the earlier case of *Collins v Wilcock* [1984] 1 WLR 1172, Goff LJ preferred a general exception embracing all physical contact which is generally acceptable in the ordinary conduct of daily life. This was rejected in *Wilson* as 'not practical'. Instead, the contact needed to be 'hostile' before becoming actionable. However, Lord Goff (as he had by then become) reiterated his earlier views in *Re F; F v West Berkshire Health Authority* [1990] 2 AC 1, where he also disapproved of the 'hostility' requirement as being 'difficult to reconcile with the principle that any touching of another's body is, in the absence of lawful excuse, capable of amounting to a battery and trespass'. Implied consent was also dismissed; it could not apply where a person was not capable of giving consent (e.g. in the case of a child or a mentally disabled person) but it could not be right that every touching of such a person amounted to a battery. It is submitted that, in principle, Lord Goff's view is to be preferred. Hostility is very vague; the only example of a hostile touching given in *Wilson* was the case of *Collins v Wilcock*, where it was suggested that because the contact made by the police constable was 'unlawful' it was hostile. This example is unhelpful, as, by definition, any unlawful touching will amount to a battery and will therefore be hostile. It thus adds nothing to the requirement of unlawfulness. The weight of authority also supports Lord Goff's view (see *T v T* [1988] Fam 52; *R v Brown* [1994] 1 AC 212; *R v Broadmoor Special Hospital Authority, The Times*, 5 November 1997). However, it must be recognised that the boundary of the exception is not always easy to draw. In *McMillan v Crown Prosecution Service* [2008] EWHC 1457 (Admin) the intoxicated appellant had been engaged in anti-social behaviour in a garden outside the entrance to a house. A police constable, who had warned the appellant about her behaviour earlier in the evening, took hold of her arm, without her consent, for the purpose of helping her down the stairs to speak to her in the street. Once in the street her disorderly conduct continued and she was then arrested. There was no suggestion that the police constable intervened to protect the appellant from harm; rather, the constable was attempting a 'negotiated solution' to the problem of removing her from the garden. It was held that the conduct of the police constable fell within the exception. Where there is no consent, nor any lawful arrest, do you think forcibly leading a person from one place to another goes beyond contact that is acceptable in daily life?

Innes v Wylie (1844) 1 Car & Kir 257; 174 ER 800

The plaintiff was a member of a society which attempted to expel him. Under orders from the defendant, a policeman stopped the plaintiff entering the room in which the society was dining. The question of assault was dealt with in the summing up to the jury.

Lord Denman CJ

You will say, whether, on the evidence, you think that the policeman committed an assault on the plaintiff, or was merely passive. If the policeman was entirely passive like a door or a wall put to prevent the plaintiff from entering the room, and simply obstructing the entrance of the plaintiff, no assault has been committed on the plaintiff, and your verdict will be for the defendant. The question is, did the policeman take any active measures to prevent the plaintiff from entering the room, or did he stand in the door-way passive, and not move at all. . . .

Verdict for the plaintiff, damages 40 shillings.

COMMENTARY

As is evidenced by the above, a positive act on the part of the defendant is required before civil liability in trespass can attach: 'not doing is no trespass' (Milsom [1954] CLJ 105). As in other areas of the law, the distinction between misfeasance and nonfeasance is not an easy one. In *Fagan v Metropolitan Police Commissioner* [1969] 1 QB 439, a criminal case. Fagan was parking his car under instruction from a constable. Unbeknownst to him, the car came to rest on the constable's foot, at which point he was asked to move the car. He responded with verbal abuse, and he turned off the car's engine before complying with the constable's request. The majority of the Court of Appeal Criminal Division held that Fagan was guilty of a criminal assault (which for this purpose included a battery) as his act was a continuing one. Accordingly, the offence was complete once he had knowledge of his car's position because at that point he was still acting (i.e. there was a continuing positive act). Bridge J dissented, holding that 'the car rested on the foot by its own weight and remained stationary by its own inertia. The appellant's fault was that he omitted to manipulate the controls to set it in motion again.' This was simply a failure to act, not sufficient to constitute the offence. See also Milsom, 'Not Doing is No Trespass: A View of the Boundaries of Case' [1954] CLJ 105.

Not only must the defendant act positively, the contact or apprehension of contact must be the direct result of the act. This is a hangover from the old forms of action where trespass *vi et armis* could only be brought for direct interferences. Contact may still be direct even if achieved through the use of an intervening object; hence hitting or touching another with a stick will be sufficient. In the criminal law this has been extended so that a person may be guilty of battery if he strikes another with the result that a third person suffers a forcible blow. In *Haystead v Chief Constable of Derbyshire* [2000] 3 All ER 890, the accused struck a woman holding a 12-month-old child with the result that she dropped the child onto the floor. It was held that he was correctly convicted of a criminal assault, as the movement by which the woman had lost hold of the child was entirely and immediately the result of the accused's action in punching her.

Could intentionally taking a flashlight photograph amount to a battery (see *Kaye v Robertson* [1991] FSR 62)?

Direct does not here mean instantaneous; a person who fires a bullet at another is liable in battery even though there is a gap between the act and the contact. The question is one of degree, but it has been held that spitting (*R v Cotesworth* (1704) 3 Mod 172, 87 ER 928), throwing water (*Hopper v Reeve* (1817) 7 Taunt 698, 129 ER 278), or throwing a chair so as to make contact with another person all amount to batteries. In *DPP v K* [1990] 1 WLR 1067, a criminal case, a 15-year-old boy placed sulphuric acid in a hand dryer, which caused injury to another pupil when he later used the dryer. It was held that the perpetrator could be guilty of an assault occasioning actual bodily harm contrary to s. 47 of the Offences against the Person Act 1861. It is submitted that (at least as a matter of civil law) liability in such a case should depend on the length of time between the act and the contact, assuming the requisite intention (*vis-à-vis* the contact) could be shown. A short time between the act and the contact might be sufficiently direct to satisfy the requirement of battery (NB: *DPP v K* has been held to be wrongly decided as a matter of criminal law, but not on this point: see *R v Spratt* [1990] 1 WLR 1073).

IV. False Imprisonment

1. Elements of the Tort

Blackstone, vol. III, 'Of Private Wrongs', ch. 8, II

We are next to consider the violation of the right of personal liberty. This is effected by the injury of false imprisonment, for which the law has not only decreed a punishment, as a heinous public crime, but has also given a private reparation to the party; as well by removing the actual confinement for the present, as, after it is over, by subjecting the wrongdoer to a civil action, on account of the damage sustained by the loss of time and liberty.

   To constitute the injury of false imprisonment there are two points requisite: 1. The detention of the person; and, 2. The unlawfulness of such detention. Every confinement of the person is an imprisonment, whether it be in a common prison, or in a private house, or in the stocks, or even by forcibly detaining one in the public streets. Unlawful, or false, imprisonment consists in such confinement or detention without sufficient authority....

Bird v Jones (1845) 7 QB 742, 115 ER 668

The defendant's employer had appropriated part of Hammersmith Bridge for seating to view a rowing regatta on the river. The plaintiff attempted to pass through the appropriated part of the bridge and managed to enter the enclosure, whereupon the defendant stationed two policemen to block his path and prevent him from entering further into the enclosure. He was told he could freely go back the way he came, but after waiting for over half an hour the plaintiff attempted to push past the policemen, whereupon he committed an assault upon the defendant and was arrested. The plaintiff's case was for wrongful arrest upon a breach of peace. Because of the way the case had been pleaded by the parties, one question the court had to consider was whether the plaintiff had been falsely imprisoned during the period he was obstructed by the policemen.

Patteson J

I have no doubt that, in general, if one man compels another to stay in any given place against his will, he imprisons that other just as much as if he locked him in a room: and I agree that it is not necessary, in order to constitute an imprisonment, that a man's person should be touched. I agree, also, that the compelling a man to go in a given direction against his will may amount to imprisonment. But I cannot bring my mind to the conclusion that, if one man merely obstructs the passage of another in a particular direction, whether by threat of personal violence or otherwise, leaving him at liberty to stay where he is or to go in any other direction if he pleases, he can be said thereby to imprison him. He does him wrong, undoubtedly, if there was a right to pass in that direction, and would be liable to an action on the case for obstructing the passage or of assault, if, on the party persisting in going in that direction, he touched his person, or so threatened him as to amount to an assault. But imprisonment is, as I apprehend, a total restraint of the liberty of the person, for however short a time, and not a partial obstruction of his will, whatever inconvenience it may bring on him....

Coleridge J

And I am of opinion that there was no imprisonment. To call it so appears to me to confound partial obstruction and disturbance with total obstruction and detention. A prison may have its boundaries large or narrow, visible and tangible, or, though real, still in the conception only; it may itself be moveable or fixed but a boundary it must have; and that boundary the party imprisoned must be prevented from passing; he must be prevented from leaving that place within the ambit of which the party imprisoning him would confine him, except by prison-breach. Some confusion seems to me to arise from confounding imprisonment of the body with mere loss of freedom: it is one part of the definition of freedom to be able to go whithersoever one pleases: but imprisonment is something more than the mere loss of this power; it includes the notion of restraint within some limits defined by a will or power exterior to our own....

Denman CJ (dissenting)

I had no idea that any person in these times supposed any particular boundary to be necessary to constitute imprisonment, or that the restraint of a man's person from doing what he desires ceases to be an imprisonment because he may find some means of escape....

As long as I am prevented from doing what I have a right to do, of what consequence is it that I am permitted to do something else? How does the imposition of an unlawful condition show that I am not restrained? If I am locked in a room am I not imprisoned because I might effect my escape through a window, or because I might find an exit dangerous or inconvenient to myself, as by wading through water or by taking a route so circuitous that my necessary affairs would suffer by the delay?

It appears to me that this is a total deprivation of liberty with reference to the purpose for which he lawfully wished to employ his liberty; and, being effected by force, it is not the mere obstruction of a way, but a restraint of the person....

COMMENTARY

Weir (p. 339) points out that, if the plaintiff had been allowed to succeed, it would have subverted the requirement that a claimant needs to show special damage in an action for public nuisance, as false imprisonment is actionable without any damage. It is also one of the four remaining civil causes of action where the claimant is prima facie entitled to trial by jury (the others being fraud, malicious prosecution and defamation). As Weir notes, the plaintiff's advisers in *Griffiths v Williams* (*The Times*, 24 November 1995) must have convinced the trial judge that her allegation of rape also amounted to false imprisonment; the Court of Appeal upheld the jury's award of £50,000. Rape is not a civil cause of action. If a rape victim wants to bring a civil action it must fall within a recognised cause of action, e.g. assault, battery and false imprisonment. Of these, only false imprisonment carries with it a prima facie right to a jury trial.

Would being forced to wait 20 minutes on a wharf for a ferry amount to false imprisonment (assuming there was no other exit from the wharf)? (See *Robertson* (incorrectly called *Robinson* in the Privy Council decision) *v Balmain New Ferry Company* (1906) 4 CLR 379, [1910] AC 295, discussed below at p. 86.)

Because liberty ranks high in the hierarchy of protected interests, any unlawful and intentional interference with that interest, even for a short period, is sufficient to amount to false imprisonment. Some early authorities suggested that knowledge of the imprisonment was necessary to bring an action (*Herring v Boyle* (1834) 1 Cr M R 377, 149 ER 1126) but this was disapproved by Atkin LJ in *Meering v Grahame-White Aviation* (1919) 122 LT 44 (obiter), and in *Murray v Ministry of Defence* [1988] 1 WLR 692 the House of Lords confirmed that knowledge of the imprisonment was not an element of the cause of action, although it would be relevant to the question of damages. However, these cases must now be read in light of the decision of the House of Lords in *R v Bournewood Mental Health Trust (Ex p. L)* [1999] 1 AC 458 where a majority held that a mentally-ill patient who was held in an unlocked ward and did not leave it, but who would have been detained if he had, was not imprisoned. This appears similar to the facts of *Meering* (above): the plaintiff in that case was told to wait in a room, and, unbeknownst to him, two officers were stationed outside the room to prevent him from leaving. Although he did not try to leave the room whilst the officers were outside, it was held he was imprisoned during that period. Lord Goff in the *Bournewood* case clearly thought the situations were distinguishable, but it is not easy to see how. Furthermore, if there must be *actual* restraint before an action can be brought, it seems that there must also be knowledge of the imprisonment, for it is difficult to see how the claimant could be imprisoned in the *Bournewood* sense without knowing about it. This appears to be inconsistent with *Murray v Ministry of Defence* (although it should be noted that the decision in *Murray* on this point was obiter), and it may be that in future the minority speeches of Lords Steyn and Nolan on this point will be preferred. In this regard, note that when the applicant took his case to the ECtHR, the court agreed with Lord Steyn's assessment of the argument that he was free to leave as a 'fairy tale', albeit in the context of Article 5, ECHR (right to liberty and security): *HL v United Kingdom* (2004) 40 EHRR 761 at [91]. In response to the adverse findings of the ECtHR, the UK government amended the Mental Capacity Act 2005 to regulate deprivations of liberty for mentally ill patients in the *Bournewood* situation (see ss. 4, 4A and Sch. A1) thus removing uncertainty over when such patients may be detained. Given the statutory regime now in place, there is little to recommend the majority reasoning in *Bournewood* which was motivated in part by the desire to find that the treatment of patients in Bournewood's situation was lawful.

The question of intention also raises some difficulties in this tort. Must the defendant merely intend the act that amounts to the imprisonment, or is it also required that the imprisonment be intended? In *Prison Officers Association v Iqbal* [2009] EWCA Civ 1312, Smith LJ held that it is the imprisonment that must be intended. Moreover, her Ladyship thought that recklessness as to whether conduct would result in imprisonment would suffice to satisfy the intention requirement. Hence, locking the door of a room thinking it is empty, when there is no reason to think anyone is inside, will not suffice even if someone is actually inside. The victim of negligent imprisonment, although probably without a remedy in false imprisonment, may well be able to sue in negligence instead. It has been held that loss of liberty, even in the absence of any physical injury, constitutes damage sufficient for liability in the tort of negligence: see *W v Home Office* [1997] Imm AR 302, noted (1998) 61 MLR 573, and Nolan, 'New Forms of Damage in Negligence' (2007) 70 MLR 59, 62–70.

2. False Imprisonment and Malicious Prosecution

False imprisonment requires the curtailment of the claimant's liberty to be direct. Where the defendant's own act is responsible for the imprisonment (e.g. where it is he who locks a door), the requisite directness is easily satisfied. But what if the defendant acts through an intermediary? If A tells B to arrest C and B does so, can A be held to have imprisoned C? The following extract considers this issue.

Davidson v Chief Constable of North Wales [1994] 2 All ER 597

The plaintiff's friend, H, purchased a cassette from a store and then joined the plaintiff who was waiting by the cassette counter; they talked for a while before leaving. A store detective watched them and gained the impression that the cassette had been stolen and called the police. When they arrived the store detective told them that H and the plaintiff had stolen the cassette and pointed them out, whereupon the constables arrested them on suspicion of shoplifting. The accusation was denied, but neither H nor the plaintiff could produce the receipt and they were taken to the police station. They were released after two hours when a shop assistant affirmed the cassette had been paid for. At the trial of the plaintiff's action for false imprisonment against the police and the store detective, the police constables gave evidence that they had exercised their own judgment in arresting the plaintiff based on the information given by the store detective. The judge withdrew the case against both defendants from the jury on the grounds that: (1) the police officers had acted lawfully because they had had reasonable grounds to make the arrest; and (2) as the officers had acted independently of the store detective there was no case to answer against the store. The plaintiff appealed.

Sir Thomas Bingham MR

It is plain on the facts that Mrs Yates [the store detective] herself did not arrest, imprison, detain or restrain the plaintiff's liberty directly in any way herself [*sic*]. She gave information to the police constables and according to their evidence they acted on it. If she is liable, therefore, it can only be through the police constables either as her agents or, as Mr Clover who appears for the appellants would prefer to put it, as persons whom she procured to act as they did. It is however plain, as I have indicated, that the police constables acted under s 24(6) of the Police and Criminal Evidence Act 1984. It was accepted that they had reasonable suspicion and acted in pursuance of that section and it is accepted that their action was proper. It, therefore, is correct, as the learned judge observed, that a somewhat anomalous situation arises if the appellant's case is correct, since the defendant would be liable for an act of persons who were not themselves liable in respect of what they had done.

The high watermark of the appellant's case derives from answers which Mrs Yates gave when she was cross-examined by counsel for the plaintiff. In the course of a series of answers she said that she expected information given by a store detective such as herself to carry weight with police officers. She intended and expected the police officers to act upon it. They had always done so in the past. She had never known of any occasion when they had failed to do so and accordingly she regarded the arrest as made on her behalf or for her. . . .

[His Lordship considered the authorities and continued:]

Accordingly, as it would seem to me, the question which arose for the decision of the learned judge in this case was whether there was information properly to be considered by the jury as to whether what Mrs Yates did went beyond laying information before police officers for them to take such action as they thought fit and amounted to some direction, or procuring, or direct request, or direct encouragement that they should act by way of arresting these defendants. He decided that there was no evidence which went beyond the giving of information. Certainly there was no express request. Certainly there was no encouragement. Certainly there was no discussion of any kind as to what action the police officers should take.

The crux of Mr Clover's submission is that this case is different from the case in which an ordinary member of the public gives information to a police officer because this is a store detective, somebody better informed than an ordinary member of the public as to what was likely to happen upon making a complaint, and somebody with a very clear intention and expectation as to what would happen. No doubt the store detective did have an intention and expectation as to what would happen. The fact remains that the learned judge to my mind quite correctly held that what Mrs Yates did and said in no way went beyond the mere giving of information, leaving it to the officers to exercise a discretion which on their unchallenged evidence they did as to whether they should take any action or not.

In those circumstances the learned judge was, as I think, entirely correct to withdraw the matter from the jury since it seems to me inevitable that had he left it to the jury, and had the jury found for the plaintiff, that verdict would have been open to challenge in this court which would have led to its being overruled. I, therefore, dismiss this appeal.

Staughton LJ

Whether a request by itself is sufficient to make a person liable does not arise in this case. What is clear in the passage I have read is that merely giving information is not enough. That does not give rise to false imprisonment. Mrs Yates did no more than that. However much one may look at evidence and analyse what possible consequences might or would arise from the information which she gave, the fact is that all she did was give the information.

I too would dismiss this appeal.

Waite LJ agreed with Bingham MR and Staughton LJ.

Appeal dismissed.

COMMENTARY

As in all torts based on the writ of trespass *vi et armis*, the defendant's act must directly cause the consequences which amount to the tort. Thus in false imprisonment, the imprisonment must result directly from the defendant's act. In *Davidson*, the problem for the plaintiff was the interposition of third parties, the police officers, between the defendant's act and the plaintiff's arrest. One can be liable in false imprisonment even if the arrest has been carried out by a third party, but only in circumstances where the arresting party has acted as an agent or without exercising independent discretion (*Flewster v Role* (1808) 1 Camp 187; *Harnett v Bond* [1925] AC 669). In *Davidson*, the intervening act was by the police, who have statutory authority to arrest in such circumstances, subject to reasonable suspicion of certain matters (Police and Criminal Evidence Act 1984 (PACE) s. 24). If an arrest was made solely on the advice of another it could be argued the officers did not actually act on the basis of their reasonable suspicions. It is therefore likely that, when questioned, a police officer would say that an independent discretion was exercised before deciding to arrest. However, as *Davidson* shows, a person who gives the information on which that discretion is exercised cannot be liable in false imprisonment because the arrest has not been caused 'directly' by that person. The result is that, in many cases (but not all: see *Ahmed v Shafique* [2009] EWHC 618 (QB)), success against one will lead to success against both (because if the constables are not entitled to the defence under PACE they are liable, and if they have not exercised any discretion of their own the store detective is liable as they have merely acted as her agents). Conversely, failure against one will often be fatal to both claims (as in *Davidson*). See also Spencer [1994] CLJ 433.

The decision in *Davidson* should be seen in the light of a number of related torts that require proof of malice if they are to be actionable. The most important of these is malicious prosecution, which was, historically, an action on the case requiring for that reason no element of directness. Even though no liability would arise in false imprisonment if the arrest was made by a party exercising discretion, an action might lie in malicious prosecution if a prosecution was later carried on by the person procuring the arrest. In this action the claimant must establish four elements, three of which are that the defendant acted with malice, that the claimant was 'prosecuted' by the defendant, and that the prosecution was without reasonable and probable cause. The 'prosecution' requirement (that the defendant set the law in motion against the claimant on a criminal charge) has been difficult to prove in modern times where the charge sheet or other originating document is usually signed by the police. An exception is *Martin v Watson* [1996] 1 AC 74. The plaintiff was arrested and charged with exposing his person with intent to insult after the defendant had complained to the police. The charge sheet was signed by a police officer, not the defendant. At the hearing of the charge the prosecution offered no evidence and the magistrates dismissed the charge. Subsequently, the plaintiff brought a successful action against the defendant for malicious prosecution. The Court of Appeal allowed an appeal on the ground that a person who made an allegation to the police, knowing that it was untrue and with the intention that the police should act against the person accused, did not thereby 'set the law in motion' and was not the prosecutor for the purposes of the tort of malicious prosecution. But the House of Lords held that this requirement could be satisfied even though the defendant had not taken any formal steps to charge the plaintiff but had merely provided false or malicious information on which the charge was based, as in those circumstances no real discretion could be exercised by the prosecutor. This would not have helped the plaintiff in *Davidson* because no charge was ever made (nor was there any evidence that the information given by the store detective was deliberately false), but Trindade, 'The Modern Tort of False Imprisonment' (above), has suggested that:

The courts may therefore conclude in the future that a deprivation of liberty brought about by a police officer acting on the basis of deliberately false information supplied by the defendant is a deprivation brought about directly by the defendant for which an action in false imprisonment would lie against the defendant who supplied the wrong information.

If this view was accepted, and a police officer acted on the deliberately wrongful advice of the defendant to arrest the claimant, should the claimant's remedy lie in an action for the tort of maliciously procuring an arrest (a tort related to malicious prosecution where both malice and lack of reasonable and probable cause for procuring the arrest would have to be established by the claimant) or for false imprisonment (established, according to *Davidson*, on showing that the defendant had directed, requested or directly encouraging the officer to arrest the claimant)? Which would be easier to establish for the claimant? Should the law allow only one cause of action in these circumstances? (See *Ahmed v Shafique* [2009] EWHC 618 (QB)).

v. Intentional Infliction of Physical or Emotional Harm

Trespass to the person requires the intentional interference with the claimant to be direct. Is any remedy provided in respect of intentional conduct that causes indirect harm to the claimant? Under the old forms of action, indirect harm was remedied by bringing trespass on the case, in which proof of damage was necessary. Accordingly, where the harm was indirect, actions for both intentional and unintentional interference were brought under the same form of action. However, in *Williams v Holland* it was decided that case could be used for unintentional interference causing direct harm. As a result, unintentional interference (negligence) causing, directly or indirectly, legally-recognised harm was remediable in case. Although the forms of action were abolished in the 1870s, this close association between negligence and case meant that negligence had become the standard cause of action for personal injury except where there was an intentional and direct interference with the claimant (e.g. in cases of assault, battery, false imprisonment). But there might be a reason for seeking a different cause of action, based on intention, if negligence was unavailable and the harm indirect. This was most likely to arise where the injury suffered by the claimant was not recognised as damage for the tort of negligence. In the late nineteenth century negligence did not recognise injury caused by psychiatric means as compensatable. But if the claimant could show that the defendant intended to cause her emotional distress would the courts decide this was sufficient damage to found a cause of action?

In *Wilkinson v Downton* [1897] 2 QB 57 the defendant told the plaintiff, presumably as a practical joke, that her husband had been injured in an accident and that she should go to him immediately. In fact, he was not injured but, unsurprisingly, she did not find it funny and she sued for the adverse health consequences from the shock of believing, at least for a short time, the statement to be true. Wright J stated:

The defendant has, as I assume for the moment, wilfully done an act calculated to cause physical harm to the female plaintiff, i.e., to infringe her right to personal safety, and has thereby in fact caused physical harm to her. That proposition, without more, appears to me to state a good cause of action, there being no justification alleged for the act.

The scope of the so-called *Wilkinson v Downton* tort in modern law was considered by the House of Lords in *Wainwright v Home Office* [2004] 2 AC 406, extracted below.

Wainwright v Home Office [2004] 2 AC 406

The claimants, a mother and son, had been visiting in prison, respectively, their son and brother. Because of concerns over the presence of drugs in the prison, they were required to submit to a strip-search before being allowed to enter. Although the searches were conducted in good faith, the prison officers who carried out the searches failed to comply with the statutory guidelines that imposed strict conditions on the conduct of the searches. The claimants brought an action alleging that the conduct should amount to a tort, whether it be breach of privacy, the liability under *Wilkinson v Downton*, or an extension of trespass to the person, and that the failure to recognise the conduct as tortious would lead to a further breach of the claimant's rights under the ECHR. The claimants succeeded at first instance but, apart from some contact that the Home Office conceded amounted to a battery, failed before the Court of Appeal and before the House of Lords. The extract deals with the *Wilkinson v Downton* issue.

Lord Hoffmann

[36] I turn next to the alternative argument based upon *Wilkinson v Downton* [1897] 2 QB 57. This is a case which has been far more often discussed than applied. Thomas Wilkinson, landlord of the Albion public house in Limehouse, went by train to the races at Harlow, leaving his wife Lavinia behind the bar. Downton was a customer who decided to play what he would no doubt have described as a practical joke on Mrs Wilkinson. He went into the Albion and told her that her husband had decided to return in a horse-drawn vehicle which had been involved in an accident in which he had been seriously injured. The story was completely false and Mr Wilkinson returned safely by train later that evening. But the effect on Mrs Wilkinson was dramatic. Her hair turned white and she became so ill that for some time her life was thought in danger. The jury awarded her £100 for nervous shock and the question for the judge on further consideration was whether she had a cause of action.

[37] The difficulty in the judge's way was the decision of the Privy Council in *Victorian Railways Comrs v Coultas* (1888) 13 App Cas 222, in which it had been said that nervous shock was too remote a consequence of a negligent act (in that case, putting the plaintiff in imminent fear of being run down by a train) to be a recoverable head of damages. Wright J distinguished the case on the ground that Downton was not merely negligent but had intended to cause injury. Quite what the judge meant by this is not altogether clear; Downton obviously did not intend to cause any kind of injury but merely to give Mrs Wilkinson a fright. The judge said, however ([1897] 2 QB 57 at 59), that as what he said could not fail to produce grave effects 'upon any but an exceptionally indifferent person', an intention to cause such effects should be 'imputed' to him.

[38] The outcome of the case was approved and the reasoning commented upon by the Court of Appeal in *Janvier v Sweeney* [1919] 2 KB 316. During the First World War Mlle Janvier lived as a paid companion in a house in Mayfair and corresponded with her German lover who was interned as an enemy alien on the Isle of Man. Sweeney was a private detective who wanted secretly to obtain some of her employer's documents and sent his assistant to induce her to co-operate by pretending to be from Scotland Yard and saying that the authorities wanted her because she was corresponding with a German spy. Mlle Janvier suffered severe nervous shock from which she took a long time to recover. The jury awarded her £250.

[39] By this time, no one was troubled by the *Victorian Railways Comrs* case. In *Dulieu v White & Sons* [1901] 2 KB 669, the Divisional Court had declined to follow it; Phillimore J said ([1901] 2 KB 669 at 683) that in principle 'terror wrongfully induced and inducing physical mischief gives a cause of action'. So on that basis Mlle Janvier was entitled to succeed whether the detectives intended to cause her injury or were merely negligent as to the consequences of their threats. Duke LJ observed ([1919] 2 KB 316 at 326) that the case was stronger than *Wilkinson v Downton* because Downton had intended merely to play a practical joke and not to commit a wrongful act. The detectives, on the other hand, intended to blackmail the plaintiff to attain an unlawful object.

[40] By the time of *Janvier's* case, therefore, the law was able comfortably to accommodate the facts of *Wilkinson v Downton* in the law of nervous shock caused by negligence. It was unnecessary to fashion a tort of intention or to discuss what the requisite intention, actual or imputed, should be. Indeed, the remark of Duke LJ to which I have referred suggests that he did not take seriously the idea that Downton had in any sense intended to cause injury.

[41] Commentators and counsel have nevertheless been unwilling to allow *Wilkinson v Downton* to disappear beneath the surface of the law of negligence. Although, in cases of actual psychiatric injury, there is no point in arguing about whether the injury was in some sense intentional if negligence will do just as well, it has been suggested (as the claimants submit in this case) that damages for distress falling short of psychiatric injury can be recovered if there was an intention to cause it. This submission was squarely put to the Court of Appeal in *Wong v Parkside Health NHS Trust* [2001] EWCA Civ 1721 and rejected. Hale LJ said that before the passing of the Protection from Harassment Act 1997 there was no tort of intentional harassment which gave a remedy for anything less than physical or psychiatric injury. That leaves *Wilkinson v Downton* with no leading role in the modern law.

[42] In *Khorasandjian v Bush* [1993] QB 727 the Court of Appeal, faced with the absence of a tort of causing distress by harassment, tried to press into service the action for private nuisance. In *Hunter v Canary Wharf Ltd, Hunter v London Docklands Development Corp* [1997] AC 655, as I have already mentioned, the House of Lords regarded this as illegitimate and, in view of the passing of the 1997 Act, unnecessary. I did however observe ([1997] AC 655 at 707) that:

> The law of harassment has now been put on a statutory basis... and it is unnecessary to consider how the common law might have developed. But as at present advised, I see no reason why a tort of intention should be subject to the rule which excludes compensation for mere distress, inconvenience or discomfort in actions based on negligence... The policy considerations are quite different.

[43] Mr Wilby said that the Court of Appeal in *Wong's* case should have adopted this remark and awarded Ms Wong damages for distress caused by intentional harassment before the 1997 Act came into force. Likewise, the prison officers in this case did acts calculated to cause distress to the Wainwrights and therefore should be liable on the basis of imputed intention as in *Wilkinson v Downton*.

[44] I do not resile from the proposition that the policy considerations which limit the heads of recoverable damage in negligence do not apply equally to torts of intention. If someone actually intends to cause harm by a wrongful act and does so, there is ordinarily no reason why he should not have to pay compensation. But I think that if you adopt such a principle, you have to be very careful about what you mean by intend. In *Wilkinson v Downton* Wright J wanted to water down the concept of intention as much as possible. He clearly thought, as the Court of Appeal did afterwards in *Janvier's* case, that the plaintiff should succeed whether the conduct of the defendant was intentional or negligent. But the *Victorian Railway Comrs* case prevented him from saying so. So he devised a concept of imputed intention which sailed as close to negligence as he felt he could go.

(4) 'Conduct' includes speech.

(5) References to a person, in the context of the harassment of a person, are references to a person who is an individual.

COMMENTARY

Is there now any scope for the rule in *Wilkinson v Downton* to operate? As far as claims for psychiatric injury are concerned, Lord Hoffmann thought that *Wilkinson* had no role as liability in negligence would provide a satisfactory remedy (cf. the position in Australia (*Nationwide News Pty Ltd v Naidu* [2007] NSWCA 377; *Giller v Procopets* [2008] VSCA 236) and in Canada (Denise Reaume, 'The Role of Intention in the Tort in Wilkinson v Downton' in Jason Neyers, Erika Chamberlain and Stephen Pitel (eds), *Emerging Issues in Tort Law* (Oxford: Hart Publishing, 2007), ch. 21). Some later cases have thought there might still be a role for *Wilkinson* (see *Bici v Ministry of Defence* [2004] EWHC 786 (QB) and *C v D* [2006] EWHC 166 (QB), the latter being a successful post-*Wainwright* claim for psychiatric injury under *Wilkinson).* However, commenting on the latter case, obiter, the Court of Appeal thought it preferable for the law to develop along conventional modern lines rather than through recourse to this obscure tort, whose jurisprudential basis remained unclear (*A v Hoare* [2006] EWCA Civ 395 at [136]; the point was not discussed in the House of Lords). More broadly, Johnston [2004] CLJ 15, 18, commenting on *Wainwright*, notes: 'Lord Hoffmann's analysis on this point may have consigned *Wilkinson v Downton* to the category of historical interest, although the "tort of intention" that he discussed may yet resurface in the future' (see also Lunney, 'Practical Joking and Its Penalty: *Wilkinson v Downton* in Context' (2002) 10 Tort L Rev 168). However, that tort will not encompass claims for mental distress; although Lord Hoffmann did not rule definitively against such a claim, in a passage not extracted, Lord Scott was unequivocally opposed to the idea that the infliction of humiliation and distress by conduct calculated to humiliate and cause distress was, without more, tortious at common law (see also *Mbasogo v Logo Ltd* [2007] QB 846 where a claim for the intentional infliction of mental distress was struck out as unarguable). Whether the intentional infliction of other types of harm might of itself give rise to an action seems to be an unanswered question; Lord Hoffmann hinted (at [44]) that such claims might exist but he had earlier suggested that there would be no such claim for psychiatric injury and no other examples were given.

One reason for the reluctance of both the House of Lords in *Wainwright* and the Court of Appeal in *Mbasogo* (above) to reinvigorate the *Wilkinson v Downton* tort was the existence of the Protection from Harassment Act 1997. It imposes both civil and criminal sanctions in respect of conduct that amounts to harassment. Although no complete definition of 'harassment' is provided, it seems it has two elements: that it is targeted at an individual and that it is calculated to produce the consequences described in s. 7 (s. 7(2) refers to conduct alarming the person or causing the person distress) and is oppressive and unreasonable (see *Thomas v News Group Newspapers* [2002] EMLR 78, [30] per Lord Phillips MR). It is not, however, necessary that conduct cause alarm or distress in fact to amount to harassment; as Baroness Hale pointed out in *Majrowski v Guy's and St Thomas's NHS Trust* [2007] 1 AC 224 at [66], all sorts of conduct may amount to harassment and 'a great deal is left to the wisdom of the courts to draw sensible lines between the ordinary banter and badinage of life and genuinely offensive and unacceptable behaviour'. Although corporations cannot be alarmed or distressed—and hence cannot bring an action under the Act—the employees of a company may bring an action if harassing conduct directed at the company causes them the requisite alarm or distress (*Daiichi UK Ltd v Stop Huntingdon Animal Cruelty* [2005] 1 BCLC 27). Amendments in 2005 extended the Act to cover harassment for the purpose of influencing the conduct of a third person; in these cases at least two persons must be the subject of harassing behaviour. Section 3(1) allows a person who is a victim of harassing behaviour to bring proceedings (usually for an injunction) and s. 3(2) makes it clear that the remedy for harassment is not limited to an injunction but will extend to damages for mental distress and, seemingly, even pure economic loss resulting from the harassment. Breach of an injunction granted under s. 3 may lead to a warrant for arrest and may lead to conviction for a criminal offence (s. 3(3)–(9)) although the civil standard of proof applies to the decision whether to grant the injunction (*Hipgrave v Jones* [2005] 2 FLR 174). It should be noted that harassment falling under s. 1(1A) is treated differently: the only remedy available to the third party whose conduct the harassment is attempting to influence is an injunction.

The scope of conduct potentially affected is very wide, although the incorporation of the European Convention on Human Rights by the Human Rights Act 1998 means that the Act must be interpreted so as to be consistent with the rights to freedom of expression and association contained in the Convention (Articles 10 and 11). In *Thomas v News Group Newspapers* [2002] EMLR 78, it was accepted by the Court of Appeal that, in principle, publication of press articles was capable of amounting to harassment under the Act. However, the newspaper would normally be able to claim that its conduct was reasonable under s. 1(3)(c) unless the alleged harassment was such as to take the publications outside the scope of Article 10(1) (e.g. because they were defamatory, or, as in *Thomas*, incited racial hatred). Commenting on *Thomas*, Finch, 'The Relationship between Freedom of Expression and Harassment' (2002) 66 J Cr Law 134 at 137, argues: 'The reconciliation of the provisions of the Protection from Harassment Act 1997 and the right to freedom of expression, by determining that anything within the protection of the Convention right is reasonable, and cannot, therefore, amount to harassment, is a sensible solution to a potentially tortuous problem.' Even without the influence of the Convention, there had been suggestions that the Act could not be interpreted so as to clamp down on discussion of matters of public interest or upon rights of political protest and public demonstration 'which was so much a part of our democratic tradition' (*Huntingdon Life Sciences v Curtin*, *The Times*, 11 December 1997, QBD, Eady J). See further Mead, 'The Human Rights Act: A Panacea for Peaceful Public Protest?' (1998) 3 *Journal of Civil Liberties* 206.

Liability attaches only to a 'course of conduct', which is defined in s. 7 to mean conduct on at least two occasions or, for harassment falling under s. 1(1A), conduct on at least one occasion in respect of the two persons who must be harassed for the section to apply. Thus the plaintiff in *Wilkinson* could not recover under the Act and would be left to a remedy at common law, a remedy that must be considered precarious given the speeches in *Wainwright*.

Reference should also be made to statutory remedies available in family law for harassing behaviour. The Family Law Act 1996 allows increased scope for the grant of non-molestation orders by the courts by allowing applications not only by a spouse or cohabitee of the respondent but also by any person 'associated' with the respondent (s. 42). This includes any person who lives or has lived in the same household as the respondent 'otherwise than merely by reason of one of them being the other's employee, tenant, lodger or boarder' (s. 62).

VI. Defences

1. Introduction

Four defences—lawful arrest and detention, consent, necessity, and self-defence—will be considered in some detail below. A number of other defences—contributory negligence, *volenti non fit injuria*, and illegality—are considered in Chapter 6, but, as the following extract from *Murphy v Culhane* shows, they might equally arise in an action for intentional interference with the person. Students should also note various other defences of more restricted scope, for example, the exercise of disciplinary powers by parents over children, and prior institution of criminal proceedings against the defendant (see Offences Against the Person Act 1861, ss. 42–45). An issue that has not been unequivocally resolved is whether provocation acts as a general defence in this context in the law of tort (cf. Criminal Justice Act 2003, s. 329 which may allow for provocation to be a defence to a claim for trespass to the person in limited circumstances).

Murphy v Culhane [1977] 1 QB 94

The plaintiff was the widow of a man killed in a criminal affray. She claimed damages under a predecessor of the Fatal Accidents Act 1976. The defendant alleged that the plaintiff's husband and others had come to assault him, and that the death of her husband had occurred as part of a criminal activity originated by him. Judgment was given against the defendant on the basis of the admissions made by him, and he appealed.

Lord Denning MR

Apart altogether from damages, however, I think there may well be a defence on liability. If Murphy was one of a gang which set out to beat up Culhane it may well be that he could not sue for damages if he got more than he bargained for. A man who takes part in a criminal affray may well be said to have been guilty of such a wicked act as to deprive himself of a cause of action or, alternatively, to have taken on himself the risk. I put the case in the course of argument: suppose that a burglar breaks into a house and the householder, finding him there, picks up a gun and shoots him, using more force maybe than is reasonably necessary. The householder may be guilty of manslaughter and liable to be brought before the criminal courts. But I doubt very much whether the burglar's widow could have an action for damages. The householder might well have a defence either on ground of *ex turpi causa non oritur actio* or *volenti non fit injuria*. So in the present case it is open to Mr Culhane to raise both those defences. Such defences would go to the whole claim.

There is another point, too, even if Mrs Murphy were entitled to damages under the Fatal Accidents Acts, they fall to be reduced under the Law Reform (Contributory Negligence) Act 1945 because the death of her husband might be the result partly of his own fault and partly of the default of the defendant: see s. 1(1) and (4) of the 1945 Act. On this point I must explain a sentence in *Gray v Barr* ([1971] 2 QB 554 at 569) where the widow of the dead man was held to be entitled to full compensation without any reduction. Her husband had not been guilty of any 'fault' within s. 4 of the 1945 Act because his conduct had not been such as to make him liable in an action of tort or, alternatively, was not such that he should be regarded as responsible in any degree for the damage. So also in *Lane v Holloway* ([1968] 1 QB 379 at 393), as Winn LJ pointed out. But in the present case the conduct of Mr Murphy may well have been such as to make him liable in tort.

Orr and **Waller LJJ** agreed with Denning MR.

Appeal allowed.

COMMENTARY

In *Barnes v Nayer, The Times*, 19 December 1986, the Court of Appeal affirmed that, in a claim for damages for assault or battery 'if it was possible on the facts properly to say *ex turpi causa* or *volenti non fit injuria*, then probably the two defences described shortly by those Latin tags, could be relied upon'. The court did not, however, agree with other aspects of Lord Denning's judgment (see below). Note also that Lord Denning's comments in relation to a possible reduction of damages under the Law Reform (Contributory Negligence) Act 1945 were doubted by Lord Rodger in *Standard Chartered Bank v Pakistan National Shipping Corporation (No. 2)* [2003] 1 AC 959 at [45]; his Lordship thought they might conflict with the view that contributory negligence was no defence where the defendant intended to harm the claimant.

The traditional view is that, in civil actions, provocation may lead to a reduction in exemplary damages but not in compensatory damages (see *Lane v Holloway* [1968] 1 QB 379). In *Murphy v Culhane*, however, Lord Denning suggested the level of compensatory damages might be reduced where the reaction of the claimant was out of all proportion to the provocation of the defendant. This dictum was subsequently criticised by the Court of Appeal in *Barnes v Nayer* where it was said that the 'better' view was that provocation could only reduce the exemplary (not the compensatory) element of an award of damages. However, a reduction in compensatory damages may be possible if the provocation can be seen as contributory negligence (see *Murphy*; *Malcolm v Walsh*, unreported, CA Civil Division, 13 May 1997), and note Criminal Justice Act 2003, s. 329 (below, pp. 103–4).

2. Lawful Arrest and Detention

Arrest or detention of a person suspected of a criminal offence—but not a civil wrong (see *Sunbolf v Alford*, extracted below)—may be justified by a variety of different powers. These powers are not exclusive to the police, and there are a number of circumstances in which a private individual may make a 'citizen's arrest'. Nevertheless, the powers available to the police are much more extensive than those available to ordinary people. This is not to say that the police have *carte blanche* to use force against, or restrain the movement of, private individuals. The police, like other government agencies, are subject to the 'rule of law', meaning that they must demonstrate clear legal authority to justify interference with the rights of private citizens (see *Entick v Carrington* (1765) 19 State Tr 1029). In the absence of such authority, they may face liabilities for battery, false imprisonment, etc. (see, e.g., *Collins v Wilcock*, above).

Police powers are now extensively catalogued in the Police and Criminal Evidence Act 1984, though other independent powers exist (e.g. the common law power to arrest for breach of the peace). The Act recognises a general power of arrest without warrant for constables

(s. 24) and a more limited power of arrest in respect of indictable offences which may be exercised by private individuals in defined circumstances (s. 24A). Also included in the Act is a power to stop and search a person who is suspected of carrying a stolen or prohibited article in a public place (s. 1; prohibited articles include offensive weapons and housebreaking implements). An officer may use reasonable force in exercising any of the powers recognised in the Act (s. 117). For further details of police powers, see Clayton and Tomlinson, *Civil Actions Against the Police*, 3rd edn. (London: Sweet & Maxwell, 2004).

   In recent times, actions against prison authorities by inmates have become increasingly common. The Prisons Act 1952, s. 12(1), provides that '[a] prisoner, whether sentenced to imprisonment or committed to prison on remand pending trial or otherwise, may be lawfully confined in any prison'. However, efforts have been made to argue that solitary confinement and other restrictions of liberty within the prison for disciplinary reasons may give rise to liability for false imprisonment where there is a breach of the Prison Rules (see further *Hague v Deputy Governor of Parkhurst Prison*, extracted below).

Sunbolf v Alford (1838) 3 M & W 247, 150 ER 1135

The plaintiff and others went to the defendant's inn where they were provided with 'divers quantity of tea and other victuals'. When the defendant asked to be paid for what he had provided the plaintiff refused, whereupon the defendant forcibly took the plaintiff's coat from him as security for the debt. The plaintiff sued in trespass and the defendant pleaded in defence that his action was justified by the non-payment of the debt. The plaintiff issued a special demurrer to that plea, alleging it furnished no legal justification or excuse for the defendant's action.

Lord Abinger CB

Let us look then at the case itself. If an innkeeper has a right to detain the person of his guest for the non-payment of his bill, he has a right to detain him until the bill is paid,—which may be for life; so that the defence supposes, that by the common law, a man who owes a small debt, for which he could not be imprisoned by legal process may yet be detained by an innkeeper for life. The proposition is monstrous....

COMMENTARY

This case should be contrasted with *Robinson v Balmain New Ferry Co*, extracted below, pp. 86–7, and *Herd v Weardale Steel Coke and Coal Co*, discussed in the commentary to *Robinson*.

Hague v Deputy Governor of Parkhurst Prison and Others, Weldon v Home Office [1992] 1 AC 58

In two separate cases the question arose whether a convicted prisoner who had been restrained in a way not permitted by the Prison Rules 1964 while serving his sentence had a cause of action in private law for damages against the prison governor or the Home Office. The causes of action relied upon were breach of statutory duty and false imprisonment. The House of Lords held that no claim for either cause of action was available, but the extract deals only with the false imprisonment issue.

Lord Bridge of Harwich

To ask at the outset whether a convicted prisoner enjoys in law a 'residual liberty', as if the extent of any citizen's right to liberty were a species of right *in rem* or a matter of status, is to ask the wrong question. An action for false imprisonment is an action *in personam*. The tort of false imprisonment has two ingredients: the fact of imprisonment and the absence of lawful authority to justify it. In *Meering v Grahame-White Aviation Co Ltd* (1919) 122 LT 44 at 54 Atkin LJ said that 'any restraint within defined bounds which is a restraint in fact may be an imprisonment.' Thus if A imposes on B a restraint within defined bounds and is sued by B for false imprisonment, the action will succeed or fail according to whether or not A can justify the restraint imposed on B as lawful. A child may be lawfully restrained within defined bounds by his parents or by the schoolmaster to whom the parents have delegated their authority. But if precisely the same restraint is imposed by a stranger without authority, it will be unlawful and will constitute the tort of false imprisonment.

I shall leave aside initially questions arising from the situation where a convicted prisoner serving a sentence is restrained by a member of the prison staff acting in bad faith, by a fellow prisoner or any other third party, or in circumstances where it can be said that the conditions of his detention are intolerable. I shall address first what I believe to be the primary and fundamental issue, viz whether any restraint within defined bounds imposed upon a convicted prisoner whilst serving his sentence by the prison governor or by officers acting with the authority of the prison governor and in good faith, but in circumstances where the particular form of restraint is not sanctioned by the Prison Rules, amounts for that reason to the tort of false imprisonment.

The starting point is s. 12(1) of the Prison Act 1952 which provides:

> A prisoner, whether sentenced to imprisonment or committed to prison on remand pending trial or otherwise, may be lawfully confined in any prison.

This provides lawful authority for the restraint of the prisoner within the defined bounds of the prison by the governor of the prison, who has the legal custody of the prisoner under s. 13, or by any prison officer acting with the governor's authority. Can the prisoner then complain that his legal rights are infringed by a restraint which confines him at any particular time within a particular part of the prison? It seems to me that the reality of prison life demands a negative answer to this question. Certainly in the ordinary closed prison the ordinary prisoner will at any time of day or night be in a particular part of the prison, not because that is where he chooses to be, but because that is where the prison regime requires him to be. He will be in his cell, in the part of the prison where he is required to work, in the exercise yard, eating meals, attending education classes or enjoying whatever recreation is permitted, all in the appointed place and at the appointed time and all in accordance with a more or less rigid regime to which he must conform. Thus the concept of the prisoner's 'residual liberty' as a species of freedom of movement within the prison enjoyed as a legal right which the prison authorities cannot lawfully restrain seems to me quite illusory. The prisoner is at all times lawfully restrained within closely defined bounds and if he is kept in a segregated cell, at a time when, if the rules had not been misapplied, he would be in the company of other prisoners in the workshop, at the dinner table or elsewhere, this is not the deprivation of his liberty of movement, which is the essence of the tort of false imprisonment, it is the substitution of one form of restraint for another.

Mr Harris seeks to surmount these difficulties by submitting that whenever there is a breach of the rules which is sufficiently 'fundamental' this converts an otherwise lawful imprisonment into an unlawful imprisonment. This, as I understand it, is quite a different concept from that of an infringement of residual liberty. The submission is that any breach of the rules which is sufficiently far reaching in its effect on the prisoner, for example the failure to supply him with clothing 'adequate for warmth and health' pursuant to r20(2), undermines the legality of his imprisonment. Logically this would lead to the conclusion that the prisoner who has not been supplied with proper clothing would be entitled to walk out of the prison, but Mr Harris understandably disclaims any such extravagant proposition. It follows that the authority given by s. 12(1) for lawful confinement of the prisoner cannot possibly be read as subject to any implied term with respect to compliance with the Prison Rules and this is fatal to any submission which seeks to make the lawfulness of the imprisonment depend in any sense on such compliance.

In my opinion, to hold a prisoner entitled to damages for false imprisonment on the ground that he has been subject to a restraint upon his movement which was not in accordance with the Prison Rules would be, in effect, to confer on him under a different legal label a cause of action for breach of statutory duty under the rules. Having reached the conclusion that it was not the intention of the rules to confer such a right, I am satisfied that the right cannot properly be asserted in the alternative guise of a claim to damages for false imprisonment. . . .

I turn next to the question posed by the example given in the judgment of Parker LJ in *Weldon's case* [1990] 3 WLR 465 at 480, of a prisoner locked in a shed by fellow prisoners. I think the short answer to this question is given by Taylor LJ who said in *Hague's* case [1990] 3 WLR 1210 at 1267:

> In such a situation an action for false imprisonment would surely lie (for what it was worth), since the fellow prisoners would have no defence under s. 12 of the Prison Act 1952.

The prisoner locked in the shed is certainly restrained within defined bounds and it is *nihil ad rem* that if he were not locked in the shed, he would be locked in his cell or restrained in accordance with the prison regime in some other part of the prison. The restraint in the shed is unlawful because the fellow prisoners acted without the authority of the governor and it is only the governor, who has the legal custody of the prisoner, and persons acting with the authority of the governor who can rely on the provisions of s. 12(1).

This consideration also leads to the conclusion that a prison officer who acts in bad faith by deliberately subjecting a prisoner to a restraint which he knows he has no authority to impose may render himself personally liable to an action for false imprisonment as well as committing the tort of misfeasance in public office. Lacking the authority of the governor, he also lacks the protection of s. 12(1). But if the officer deliberately acts outside the scope of his authority, he cannot render the governor or the Home Office vicariously liable for his tortious conduct. This no doubt explains why Mr Harris did not seek to sustain the decision of the Court of Appeal in his favour on the ground that the plaintiff's pleading should be read as involving an allegation of bad faith.

There remains the question whether an otherwise lawful imprisonment may be rendered unlawful by reason only of the conditions of detention. In *R v Comr of Police of the Metropolis, ex p Nahar, The Times*, 28 May 1983, two applicants for habeas corpus who had been remanded in custody were held pursuant to the provisions of s. 6 of the Imprisonment (Temporary Provisions) Act 1980 in cells below the Camberwell Green Magistrates' Court which were designed only to enable persons to be held in custody for a few hours at a time and which were obviously deficient in many respects for the purpose of accommodating prisoners for longer periods. They sought their release on the ground that the conditions of their detention rendered it unlawful. The applications were rejected, but Stephen Brown J said in the course of his judgment: 'There must be some minimum standard to render detention lawful.' McCullough J said:

> Despite the temporary nature of the detention there contemplated, there must be implied into s. 6 of the 1980 Act some term which relates to the conditions under which a prisoner may lawfully be detained. I say so because it is possible to conceive of hypothetical circumstances in which the conditions of detention were such as would make that detention

unlawful. I do not propose to offer any formulation of that term. Were it broken in any particular case I would reject emphatically the suggestion that the matter would not be one for the exercise of the court's jurisdiction to grant the writ of habeas corpus.

These observations were considered by the Court of Appeal in *Middleweek v Chief Constable of the Merseyside Police*, (1985)[1990] 3 WLR 481. The plaintiff had been awarded damages for false imprisonment by the jury on the basis that his otherwise lawful detention at a police station had been rendered unlawful because it was unreasonable in the circumstances to keep him in a police cell. The defendant successfully appealed, but Ackner LJ, delivering the judgment of the court, said (at 487):

> We agree with the views expressed by the Divisional Court that it must be possible to conceive of hypothetical cases in which the conditions of detention are so intolerable as to render the detention unlawful and thereby provide a remedy to the prisoner in damages for false imprisonment. A person lawfully detained in a prison cell would, in our judgment, cease to be so lawfully detained if the conditions in that cell were such as to be seriously prejudicial to his health if he continued to occupy it, e.g. because it became and remained seriously flooded, or contained a fractured gas pipe allowing gas to escape into the cell. We do not therefore accept as an absolute proposition that, if detention is initially lawful, it can never become unlawful by reason of changes in the conditions of imprisonment.

I sympathise entirely with the view that the person lawfully held in custody who is subjected to intolerable conditions ought not to be left without a remedy against his custodian, but the proposition that the conditions of detention may render the detention itself unlawful raises formidable difficulties. If the proposition be sound, the corollary must be that when the conditions of detention deteriorate to the point of intolerability, the detainee is entitled immediately to go free. It is impossible, I think, to define with any precision what would amount to intolerable conditions for this purpose. McCullough J understandably and perhaps wisely abstained from any attempt at definition in *Ex parte Nahar*. The examples given by Ackner LJ of a flooded or gas-filled cell are so extreme that they do not, with respect, offer much guidance as to where the line should be drawn. The law is certainly left in a very unsatisfactory state if the legality or otherwise of detaining a person who in law is and remains liable to detention depends on such an imprecise criterion and may vary from time to time as the conditions of his detention change.

The logical solution to the problem, I believe, is that if the conditions of an otherwise lawful detention are truly intolerable, the law ought to be capable of providing a remedy directly related to those conditions without characterising the fact of the detention itself as unlawful. I see no real difficulty in saying that the law can provide such a remedy. Whenever one person is lawfully in the custody of another, the custodian owes a duty of care to the detainee. If the custodian negligently allows, or *a fortiori*, if he deliberately causes, the detainee to suffer in any way in his health he will be in breach of that duty. But short of anything that could properly be described as a physical injury or an impairment of health, if a person lawfully detained is kept in conditions which cause him for the time being physical pain or a degree of discomfort which can properly be described as intolerable, I believe that could and should be treated as a breach of the custodian's duty of care for which the law should award damages. For this purpose it is quite unnecessary to attempt any definition of the criterion of intolerability. It would be a question of fact and degree in any case which came before the court to determine whether the conditions to which a detainee had been subjected were such as to warrant an award of damages for the discomfort he had suffered. In principle I believe it is acceptable for the law to provide a remedy on this basis, but that the remedy suggested in the *Nahar* and *Middleweek* cases is not. In practice the problem is perhaps not very likely to arise....

COMMENTARY

It is as well to note that this decision 'does not mean that a prisoner subjected to intolerable hardship is remediless. In appropriate circumstances he may have an action for assault and battery, and, if the conditions of confinement affect his health, he may be able to sue for negligence' (*Street*, p. 249). Moreover, it has recently been held that a prisoner may bring an action in the tort of misfeasance in public office for 'loss of liberty' (*Karagozlu v Metropolitan Police Officer* [2006] EWCA Civ 1691; [2007] 1 WLR 1881), as the commission of the tort necessarily deprives the action from the protection of s. 12 (misfeasance in public office is not considered in this book; for discussion of its elements, see *Winfield & Jolowicz*, paras 7–20–7–23). In *Toumia v Evans (Secretary General of the Prison Officers' Association), The Times*, 1 April 1999, it was held that, following dicta in *Hague*, it was arguable that a prison officer who deliberately locked a prisoner in his cell contrary to the orders of the governor would be liable for the tort of false imprisonment. However, the Court of Appeal's holding that liability in false imprisonment might arise where an officer had failed to release a prisoner (e.g. for exercise or education) from his cell contrary to the orders of the prison governor can no longer stand in light of the recent decision of *Prison Officers Association v Iqbal* [2009] EWCA Civ 1312. The claimant was a prisoner who was kept in his cell throughout the day because of a strike by prison officers. In the normal course of events he would have been allowed out of his cell for several short periods but, as a result of the strike, the prison governor lawfully ordered that all prisoners be kept in their cells throughout the day. Relying on dicta in *Hague* that there may be some residual liberty against persons not acting with the authority of the prison governor, the claimant argued that the failure of the prison officers to open his cell and release him could found a claim for false imprisonment. A majority of the Court of Appeal rejected the claim for two main reasons. First, in the absence of a special duty to act, false imprisonment required a positive act, not a mere omission (see p. 88, below), and the most that could be said against the prison officers was that they had failed to open the cell. Second, the imprisonment had not been caused directly by the action of the prison officers; the immediate cause of the claimant remaining in his cell was the order of the governor and even though it was foreseeable that the governor might make this order as a result of the strike this did not amount to the prison officers procuring the imprisonment (see *Davidson v Chief Constable of North Wales* [1994] 2 All ER 597, discussed above at p. 65). In a powerful dissent, Sullivan LJ rejected the categorisation of the prison officer's conduct as an omission (at 96:

A deliberate refusal to obey a direct order from a prison governor to release a particular prisoner from his cell is not simply an omission, it is fairly described as an act: an act of defiance or disobedience. In practical terms, it is difficult to see why a distinction should be drawn between the liability in tort of prison officer A who deliberately disobeys a governor's instruction and locks a prisoner into a cell having been told not to do so; and prison officer B who deliberately disobeys a governor's instruction and refuses to unlock that prisoner from the cell having been told to do so. Both are fairly described as acting in defiance of, and not with, the authority of the governor.

Moreover, Sullivan LJ did not accept that the actions of the prison officers had not procured the imprisonment; unlike the constables in *Davidson*, the governor was left with 'no practical choice' but to respond as she did. To the extent that the case represented a conflict between the right to strike and the right to liberty, his Lordship thought the latter should prevail. Do you agree?

The question of 'residual liberty' also arose in *R (Munjaz) v Mersey Care NHS Trust* [2006] 2 AC 148 where the question was whether the alleged improper use of 'seclusion' orders under the Mental Health Act 1983 could contribute a breach of Article 5 of the ECHR (right to liberty and security). Only Lord Steyn thought that 'residual liberty' might found such a claim for a patient who was lawfully detained in the institution but alleged the conditions of the detention were unlawful; his Lordship went so far as to say that, in respect of convicted prisoners, *Hague* 'should no longer be treated as authoritative' ([2006] 2 AC 148 at 195).

The defence is one of lawful authority, not reasonable belief that lawful authority existed. Thus a valid order for imprisonment which is subsequently set aside does not give rise to an action for false imprisonment during the period for which it was in force, but a valid order which is misinterpreted may do. This is graphically illustrated by the decision of the House of Lords in *R v Governor of Brockhill Prison, ex p. Evans* [2001] 2 AC 19. In this case a prison governor who incorrectly calculated the release date of a prisoner was held liable in false imprisonment from the date the prisoner should have been released, even though the governor had calculated the date in accordance with pre-existing judicial authority which was only overruled when the prisoner sought judicial review of the governor's decision. Commenting on the Court of Appeal decision (which the House of Lords upheld), Fordham, 'False Imprisonment in Good Faith' (2000) 8 Tort L Rev 53 at 67, argues: 'As long as the officials responsible for detaining a person actually intend to detain him or her, then the fact that they are unaware that the detention was unauthorised is surely irrelevant. The focus of an action for false imprisonment is, after all, primarily on the plaintiff and the wrongful deprivation of his or her liberty.' Do you agree? For comment on the House of Lords' decision, see Cane (2001) 117 LQR 5.

It should be noted that, in cases where the imprisonment is carried out by a 'public authority' under the Human Rights Act 1998, the defence of lawful authority will apply to both a claim for false imprisonment and a claim under s. 7 of the Human Rights Act 1998 for breach of Article 5, ECHR. However, there are significant differences between false imprisonment and a breach of Article 5; imprisonment is a different concept from a deprivation of liberty (see *HL v United Kingdom* [2004] 40 EHRR 761; *R (Gillan and Another) v Commissioner of the Police for the Metropolis* [2006] 2 AC 307) and lawful authority under domestic law does not necessarily satisfy the requirements of Article 5. Discussion of the derogations allowed under Article 5 is beyond the scope of this book, but it is possible that a defence of lawful authority that is recognised in false imprisonment might not be successful in a claim for breach of Article 5, although when the issue has arisen in practice the courts have tended to find that, if the defence succeeds for false imprisonment, it succeeds for any Article 5 claim (see e.g. *Roberts v Secretary of State for the Home Department* [2005] EWCA Civ 1663 at [41]).

3. Consent

(a) General Principles

It has been held that lack of consent is, strictly speaking, an element of the intentional torts, to be pleaded and proved by the claimant (*Freeman v Home Office (No. 2)* [1984] QB 524) but in *Ashley v Chief Constable of Sussex Police* [2007] 1 WLR 398, 410, Clarke MR thought that the correctness of this proposition was open to debate (the point was not considered on appeal by the House of Lords). However, 'as a practical matter... the defendant may need to lead evidence to lay a foundation from which the court will infer consent as a specific issue in his defence to the particulars of claim' (*Winfield & Jolowicz*, para. 25–3). In this weaker sense, therefore, consent may legitimately be treated as a 'defence'. One important issue is when an apparent consent will be vitiated because it was given under duress or without full knowledge of the material facts.

Chatterton v Gerson [1981] QB 432

The plaintiff complained that the defendant surgeon did not advise her as to the possible side effects of the course of treatment he was proposing for her. The plaintiff claimed in both trespass to the person and negligence, but her action was dismissed. The extract relates to the dismissal of the cause of action for trespass.

Bristow J

It is clear law that in any context in which consent of the injured party is a defence to what would otherwise be a crime or a civil wrong, the consent must be real. Where, for example, a woman's consent to sexual intercourse is obtained by fraud, her apparent consent is no defence to a charge of rape. It is not difficult to state the principle or to appreciate its good sense. As so often, the problem lies in its application.

No English authority was cited before me of the application of the principle in the context of consent to the interference with bodily integrity by medical or surgical treatment. In *Reibl v Hughes* (1978) 21 OR (2d) 14, which was an action based on negligence by failure to inform the patient of the risk in surgery involving the carotid artery, the Ontario Court of Appeal said that the trial judge was wrong in injecting the issue, Was it a battery? into the case pleaded and presented in negligence. The majority of the court, having referred to the United States cases on what is there called the 'doctrine of informed consent', decided that the action of 'battery' seemed quite inappropriate to cases in which the doctor has acted in good faith, and in the interests of the patient, but in doing so has been negligent in failing to disclose a risk inherent in the recommended treatment. They reversed the finding of battery. I am told that that decision is now under appeal....

In my judgment what the court has to do in each case is to look at all the circumstances and say, 'Was there a real consent?' I think justice requires that in order to vitiate the reality of consent there must be a greater failure of communication between doctor and patient than that involved in a breach of duty if the claim is based on negligence. When the claim is based on negligence the plaintiff must prove not only the breach of duty to inform but that had the duty not been broken she would not have chosen to have the operation. Where the claim is based on trespass to the person, once it is shown that the consent is unreal, then what the plaintiff would have decided if she had been given the information which would have prevented vitiation of the reality of her consent is irrelevant.

In my judgment once the patient is informed in broad terms of the nature of the procedure which is intended, and gives her consent, that consent is real, and the cause of the action on which to base a claim for failure to go into risks and implications is negligence, not trespass. Of course, if information is withheld in bad faith, the consent will be vitiated by fraud. Of course, if by some accident, as in a case in the 1940s in the Salford Hundred Court, where a boy was admitted to hospital for tonsillectomy and due to administrative error was circumcised instead, trespass would be the appropriate cause of action against the doctor, though he was as much the victim of the error as the boy. But in my judgment it would be very much against the interests of justice if actions which are really based on a failure by the doctor to perform his duty adequately to inform were pleaded in trespass....

Action dismissed.

COMMENTARY

The judgment mentions the decision of the Ontario Court of Appeal in *Reibl v Hughes*. This was confirmed by the Supreme Court of Canada (1981) 114 DLR 3d 1, where it was said that, unless there was fraud or misrepresentation to secure the consent, a failure to advise of risks, however serious, went to negligence and not battery. For a discussion of the issue see Tan, 'Failure of Medical Advice: Trespass or Negligence?' (1987) 7 LS 149, and Maclean, 'The doctrine of informed consent: does it exist and has it crossed the Atlantic?' (2004) 24 LS 386, 398–401.

The Reality of Consent

Consent must be real to be effective, and consent obtained by duress is no defence. Clearly the threat of physical violence will vitiate consent, but the courts have been reluctant to treat less immediate pressures in the same way. The Court of Appeal in *Freeman v Home Office (No. 2)* [1984] QB 524 upheld a prisoner's apparent consent to medical treatment, ruling that the institutional pressures acting upon the prisoner's mind did not affect the genuineness of that consent.

An important question is whether consent can be vitiated by fraud. In criminal law it was long thought that only fraud that went to the essential nature of the contact would vitiate consent. Hence in the criminal law decision of *R v Williams* [1923] 1 KB 340 it was held that there was no consent to sexual intercourse where the accused told the victim he was merely performing an exercise to improve her singing voice. However, changes made by the Sexual Offences Act 2003 (which only applies where there is a sexual assault as defined by the Act) provide that there is no consent if the victim was deliberately deceived by the defendant 'as to the nature and purpose' of the relevant act but it has been held that the statutory wording has not changed the previous law in this respect (*R v B* [2007] 1 WLR 1567; *R v Jheeta* [2007] EWCA Crim 1699). This suggests that fraud as to the 'purpose' of the act remained relevant prior to the Sexual Offences Act 2003 but, if this is so, the decision in *R v Tabassum* [2000] 4 Lloyd's Rep Med 404 remains problematic. In this case, a number of women gave the accused consent to examine their breasts for the purpose of conducting medical research. They gave evidence that the only reason they consented was that they thought he was medically qualified; he was not. The Court of Appeal Criminal Division held that the accused was properly convicted of assault, as the women's consent was to touching for a medical procedure, not for indecent assault. However, there was no evidence that the accused had a sexual motive for his actions; he touched the victims for the purpose for which he told them he would touch them. The gist of their complaint was that he did not possess an attribute—a medical qualification—that they thought he possessed. Such a complaint did not vitiate the patient's consent in *R v Richardson* [1999] QB 444, where a dentist who had been suspended from practice but continued to carry out dental treatment on patients was held not guilty of a criminal assault. This case was distinguished in *Tabassum* on the basis that the sole reason for the decision was that there was no mistake as to the identity of the person performing the dental work, and the question of the nature and quality of the contact was not discussed. However, in *Richardson* Otton LJ stated (at 450): 'In summary, either there is consent to actions on the part of a person in the mistaken belief that he was other than he truly is, in which case it is assault, or, short of this, there is no assault…In essence, the Crown contended that the concept of "identity of the person" should be extended to cover the qualifications or attributes of the dentist on the basis that the patients consented to treatment by a qualified dentist and not a suspended one. We must reject that submission.' Do you think the two cases can be reconciled on the basis suggested in *Tabassum*? For comment on *Tabassum*, see Edwards

(2001) 98 LS Gaz 48 who comments that *Richardson* was distinguished 'on grounds that are hard to identify'.

In an attempt to show up his daughter's boyfriend, a father convinced the boyfriend to commit a sexual act in front of a webcam. The boyfriend thought he was performing for 'Cassie', a 20-year-old woman, but Cassie was the fictitious creation of the father and it was the father at the other end of the computer. In a prosecution against the father for procuring a sexual act, could it be said that the father's fraud went to the 'nature and purpose' of the act performed by the boyfriend? See *R v Devonald* [2008] EWCA Crim 527 and for comment Elvin, 'The Concept of Consent under the Sexual Offences Act 2003' (2008) 72 J Crim L 519.

It may, however, be that in civil law fraud vitiates consent even when it does not go to the essential nature or purpose of the contact. In *Chatterton*, Bristow J suggested that there might be a battery where information about treatment risks was deliberately withheld in bad faith. Support for this proposition comes from the subsequent case of *Appleton v Garrett* (1995) 34 BMLR 23 where the plaintiffs were patients of a dentist who had deliberately and fraudulently performed unnecessary dental work on them. Dyson J held that the defendant's failure to provide any information on whether the treatment was necessary was in bad faith; hence consent was vitiated and trespass to the person established.

This decision seems inconsistent with the position in criminal law, whereby fraud that only goes to the consequences of the contact does not undermine the reality of a person's consent to that contact, whether in bad faith or not. In the controversial case of *R v B* [2006] EWCA Crim 2945, [2007] 1 WLR 1567, the failure of the accused to tell his sexual partner that, to his knowledge, he was HIV-positive can hardly have been in good faith but the Court of Appeal Criminal Division held that this would not be sufficient to vitiate any consent she had given to the act of sexual intercourse (although there might now be an action for in battery for intentionally infecting the victim with an infectious disease: see the American case of *Doe v Johnson* (1993) 817 F Supp 1382, and, for the analogous situation in criminal law, *R v Dica* [2004] EWCA Crim 1103, [2004] QB 1257, noted below). Should a man be guilty of battery any more than rape if he successfully seduces a woman by telling her untruthfully that he is a millionaire? In this context see the discussion in *R v Cuerrier* [1998] 2 SCR 371 in which a majority of the Supreme Court of Canada held that an HIV-positive adult who engages in unprotected consensual sexual activity with another adult, knowing of this condition but without disclosing it to the other party, can be found guilty of sexual assault under the Canadian Criminal Code. (Cf. *R v Dica* [2004] QB 1257 where in similar circumstances to *Cuerrier* the consent to the contact was no defence to a charge of inflicting grievous bodily harm under the Offences Against the Person Act 1861, s. 20, an offence that does not require a battery to be established.) For commentary on this area see generally McEvoy, 'When You have no Right to Remain Silent: Tort Liability for Sexually Transmitted Diseases' (1994) 2 Tort L Rev 175.

Capacity to Consent

In the case of children and those suffering from a mental disability, the question of capacity to consent may arise. The general rule is that the subject of the proposed interference must have the ability to understand what is involved. This was accepted by the House of Lords in *Gillick v Department of Health and Social Security* [1986] AC 112 in considering the capacity of teenage girls to consent to contraceptive treatment. Lord Scarman said that the child's understanding would have to go further than a simple appreciation of the doctor's reasons for touching the child and the purposes behind the touching; the child would have to have an understanding of the wider social and moral implications of the contraceptive treatment.

Where a person lacks the capacity to consent, touching (e.g. in the course of medical treatment) may be justified on the basis of parental consent or the separate defence of medical necessity (see below).

Consents Ineffective for Reasons of Public Policy

In criminal law, '[e]veryone agrees that consent remains a complete defence to a charge of common assault and nearly everyone agrees that the consent of the victim is not a defence to a charge of inflicting really serious personal injury...' (*R v Brown* [1994] 1 AC 212 at 248, per Lord Lowry). However, the limits of consent as a defence in civil law are less clear. Clearly the participants in contact sports or activities consent to the touchings in such pursuits (although intentional acts outside the rules of a sport are no doubt actionable: see the criminal case of *R v Barnes* [2005] 2 All ER 113). However, it has been suggested that injuries inflicted during the course of a mutually agreed fight might be tortious, although damages could not be recovered because the parties were engaged in an illegal activity (*Re F (Mental Patient: Sterilisation)* [1989] 2 WLR 1025 at 1049, per Neill LJ; cf. *Lane v Holloway* [1968] 1 QB 379 at 386, per Lord Denning, who clearly thought consent would operate as a defence provided the injuries were in proportion to the occasion). In *Brown*, above, the House of Lords held by a three to two majority that consent was no defence to consensual acts of sadomasochism amounting to actual bodily harm, but it would be a strange result if a participant in such an activity could sue another in battery because consent was no defence to the civil claim (see *Fleming*, p. 92).

(b) Revocation of Consent

Balmain New Ferry Company v Robertson (1906) 4 CLR 379

The plaintiff entered a wharf to catch a ferry, passing through a turnstile over which was a sign stating that the charge for entry or exit from the wharf was one penny irrespective of whether a ferry had been used. After entering the plaintiff realised he had just missed a ferry, whereupon he sought to leave the wharf. He was restrained by employees of the defendant when he refused to pay the extra penny but finally forced his way out. He brought an action in false imprisonment and was successful at first instance, but the defendant successfully appealed to the High Court of Australia.

Griffith CJ

This agreement involves, in my opinion, an implied promise by the plaintiff that he would not ask for egress by land except on payment of one penny, and, further, a consent on his part that the defendant should be entitled to prevent him from departing in that way until he paid the penny....

O'Connor J

[T]he abridgement of a man's liberty is not under all circumstances actionable. He may enter into a contract which necessarily involves the surrender of a portion of his liberty for a certain period, and if the act complained of is nothing more than a restraint in accordance with that surrender he cannot complain. Nor can he, without the assent of the other party, by electing to put an end to the contract, become entitled at once, unconditionally and irrespective of the other party's rights, to regain his liberty as if he had never surrendered it. A familiar instance of such a contract is that between a passenger and a railway company which undertakes to carry him on a journey. If the passenger suddenly during the journey decided to abandon it and to leave the train at the next station, being one at which the train was not timed to stop, he clearly would not be entitled to have the train stopped at that station. However much he might object, the railway company could lawfully carry him on to the next stopping place of that particular train. In such a case the passenger's liberty would be for a certain period restrained, but the restraint would not be actionable, because it is an implied term of such a contract that the passenger will permit the restraint of liberty so far as may be necessary for the performance by the company of the contract of carriage according to the time of that train. . . .

The first question is, what is the contract to be implied from the plaintiff's payment at and passing through the turnstiles under these circumstances? It is that in consideration of that payment the company undertook to carry him as a passenger to Balmain by any of their ferry boats from that wharf. That is the only contract which could be implied from the circumstances, and the plaintiff was permitted to enter the wharf for the purpose of that contract being performed. It is not denied that the company were ready to perform their part, but the plaintiff, as far as one party can do so, rescinded the contract and determined to go back from the wharf to the street. What then were his rights? They were, in my opinion, no more and no less than they would have been if he had landed from his own boat at the company's wharf. He was on private property. He had not been forced or entrapped there. He had entered it of his own free will and with the knowledge that the only exit on the land side was through the turnstile, operated as a part of the company's system of collecting fares in the manner I have mentioned. If he wished to use the turnstile as a means of exit he could only do so on complying with the usual conditions on which the company opened them. The company were lawfully entitled to impose the condition of a penny payment on all who used the turnstiles, whether they had travelled by the company's steamers or not, and they were under no obligation to make an exception in the plaintiff's favour. The company, therefore, being lawfully entitled to impose that condition, and the plaintiff being free to pass out at any time on complying with it, he had only himself to blame for his detention, and there was no imprisonment of which he could legally complain. . . .

Robinson v Balmain New Ferry Co [1910] AC 295

The plaintiff unsuccessfully appealed to the Privy Council.

Lord Loreburn LC

[I]n the circumstances admitted it is clear to their Lordships that there was no false imprisonment at all. The plaintiff was merely called upon to leave the wharf in the way which he contracted to leave it. There is no law requiring the defendants to make the exit from their premises gratuitous to people who come there upon a definite contract which involves their leaving the wharf by another way; and the defendants were entitled to resist a forcible passage through another turnstile.

The question whether the notice which was affixed to these premises was brought home to the knowledge of the plaintiff is immaterial, because the notice itself is immaterial. When the plaintiff entered the defendants' premises there was nothing agreed as to the terms on which he might go back, because neither party contemplated his going back. When he desired to do so the defendants were entitled to impose a reasonable condition before allowing him to pass through their turnstile from a place to which he had gone of his own free will. The payment of a penny was a quite fair condition, and if he did not choose to comply with it the defendants were not bound to let him through. He could proceed on the journey he had contracted for. . . .

COMMENTARY

In *Herd v Weardale Steel Coke and Coal Co* [1915] AC 67, the plaintiff miner descended into the pit at the beginning of his shift at 9.30 am, and was due to be returned to the surface at 4 pm. On arriving at the bottom of the pit, he refused to do certain work on the ground that it was unsafe, and at 11 am requested to be taken to the surface. The defendant employer ordered that he not be taken up at that time, and it was not until 1.30 pm that he was returned to the surface. There was evidence that the lift was at the bottom of the shaft at 1.10 pm and could conveniently have been used to bring him up. The employer successfully sued the plaintiff for breach of contract, whilst the plaintiff sued in respect of his underground deten-tion, winning at first instance but losing in the Court of Appeal and in the House of Lords. There, Viscount Haldane LC (at 73) said:

My Lords, under these circumstance I find it wholly impossible to come to the conclusion that the principle to which I have alluded, and on which the doctrine of false imprisonment is based, has any application to the case. *Volenti non fit injuria.* The man chose to go to the bottom of the mine under these conditions—conditions which he accepted. He had no right to call upon the employers to make use of special machinery put there at their cost, and involving cost in its working, to bring him to the surface just when he pleased. . . .

Even though the House of Lords' decision is based on the plaintiff's contractual consent to the deprivation of liberty, could the decision be justified on the basis that there was no posi-tive act by the defendant (essential for liability in trespass) but rather an omission to take him to the surface? (It was treated as authority for this proposition in *Prison Officers Association v Iqbal* [2009] EWCA Civ 1312.) The majority of the Court of Appeal thought that if, after the shift had finished, the employer told the employee he would have to wait another hour before being brought to the surface, there would be liability for breach of contract but not false imprisonment (see [1913] 3 KB 771). Would you agree with Vaughan Williams LJ (dis-senting) that the employer did much more than merely fail to provide facilities to bring the plaintiff to the surface but rather that 'it is a legitimate conclusion from the admitted facts that the defendants refused permission to the men to use the lift as penalty or punishment for their refusal to obey the order' (at 784). In the House of Lords Viscount Haldane thought the motive of the defendant irrelevant. Do you agree? (See Glanville Williams, 'Two Cases on False Imprisonment', in Holland and Schwarzenberger (eds), *Law, Justice and Equity (Essays in Tribute to G. W. Keeton)* (London: Pitman, 1967)).

Keng Fen Tan, 'A Misconceived Issue in the Tort of False Imprisonment' (1981) 44 MLR 166

It is . . . clear that at common law a person cannot restrain the liberty of another to enforce a monetary condition as to exit. Such restraint is false imprisonment unless authorised by law. It may be that monetary conditions as to exit, in this context, are never reasonable conditions. It is, however, submitted that even if such conditions do not relate to the collection of debts and even if they are construed as reasonable there may still be liability for false imprisonment. This is so because the reasonableness of the condition as to exit does not determine whether the restraint of liberty used to enforce the condition is or is not false imprisonment. The basis for this proposition is that no person can by imprisonment force another to abide by or conform to any condition, if that other person does not consent to it, unless such compliance is required by law. If compliance is required by contract that other person can choose to abandon the contract and assume liability for the breach. He cannot then be compelled to perform or comply with the contract, unless specific performance is ordered by the court. . . .

[However] in the tort of false imprisonment consent, once given to submission of liberty cannot, in certain situations, be withdrawn for a critical period. These situations arise when a person puts himself voluntarily, for whatever purpose, in a position which necessarily involves a temporary surrender of his liberty and some inconvenience in meeting, for a critical duration, the withdrawal of his consent to submission of liberty. The difficulty in the tort is deciding at what stage and for what duration the consent given to submission of liberty is irrevocable. This must be decided according to the particular circumstance of each case. The decision would involve the balancing and adjustment of two competing claims: the claim to personal liberty and the claim of inconvenience entailed in giving in to such claim. . . .

COMMENTARY

Attempting to reconcile the above authorities is a difficult task, not made any easier by the failure in both *Robinson* and *Herd* to cite *Sunbolf v Alford*. That case, extracted above, is authority for the general rule that one cannot imprison to enforce a civil claim without statutory authority (cf. Police and Criminal Evidence Act 1984, s. 24A which provides private individuals with a limited power of arrest in respect of indictable offences). Arguably, *Robinson* and *Herd* can both be reconciled with that rule—there was no imprisonment in *Robinson* (a point expressly acknowledged by Griffith CJ) and in *Herd* there was no positive act—but it is probably better to regard the cases as being of very limited application or simply as contrary to the general rule. But is the basic principle of *Sunbolf* sound?

4. Necessity

(a) General

F v West Berkshire Health Authority (Mental Health Act Commission intervening) [1990] 2 AC 1

The question for the House of Lords was the lawfulness of conducting a sterilisation operation on a mentally ill 36-year-old female patient ('F'), with the mental capacity of a small child, who had begun a sexual relationship with another patient. Psychiatric evidence suggested a pregnancy would be disastrous and there were doubts whether any other form of contraceptive would be effective, either through non-use or risks to F's health. It was decided that the best course was for her to be sterilised, and her mother, acting as her next friend, sought, as against the health authority, a declaration that the absence of F's consent would not make sterilisation of her an unlawful act. The judge granted the declaration sought and the Court of Appeal and House of Lords affirmed this decision. Their Lordships confirmed the view that the court had no power under its *parens patriae* jurisdiction to make the order, but the extracts are concerned with the common law basis on which the order was made.

Lord Bridge of Harwich

The issues canvassed in argument before your Lordships revealed the paucity of clearly defined principles in the common law which may be applied to determine the lawfulness of medical or surgical treatment given to a patient who for any reason, temporary or permanent, lacks the capacity to give or to communicate consent to that treatment. It seems to me to be axiomatic that treatment which is necessary to preserve the life, health or well-being of the patient may lawfully be given without consent. But, if a rigid criterion of necessity were to be applied to determine what is and what is not lawful in the treatment of the unconscious and the incompetent, many of those unfortunate enough to be deprived of the capacity to make or communicate rational decisions by accident, illness or unsoundness of mind might be deprived of treatment which it would be entirely beneficial for them to receive.

Moreover, it seems to me of first importance that the common law should be readily intelligible to and applicable by all those who undertake the care of persons lacking the capacity to consent to treatment. It would be intolerable for members of the medical, nursing and other professions devoted to the care of the sick that, in caring for those lacking the capacity to consent to treatment, they should be put in the dilemma that, if they administer the treatment which they believe to be in the patient's best interests, acting with due skill and care, they run the risk of being held guilty of trespass to the person, but, if they withhold that treatment, they may be in breach of a duty of care owed to the patient. If those who undertake responsibility for the care of incompetent or unconscious patients administer curative or prophylactic treatment which they believe to be appropriate to the patient's existing condition or disease, injury or bodily malfunction or susceptibility to such a condition in the future, the lawfulness of that treatment should be judged by one standard, not two. It follows that if the professionals in question have acted with due skill and care, judged by the well-known test laid down in *Bolam v Friern Hospital Management Committee* [1957] 1 WLR 582, they should be immune from liability in trespass, just as they are immune from liability in negligence. The special considerations which apply in the case of the sterilisation of a woman who is physically perfectly healthy or of an operation on an organ transplant donor arise only because such treatment cannot be considered either curative or prophylactic....

Lord Brandon of Oakbrook

At common law a doctor cannot lawfully operate on adult patients of sound mind, or give them any other treatment involving the application of physical force however small (which I shall refer to as 'other treatment'), without their consent. If a doctor were to operate on such patients, or give them other treatment, without their consent, he would commit the actionable tort of trespass to the person. There are, however, cases where adult patients cannot give or refuse their consent to an operation or other treatment. One case is where, as a result of an accident or otherwise, an adult patient is unconscious and an operation or other treatment cannot be safely delayed until he or she recovers consciousness. Another case is where a patient, though adult, cannot by reason of mental disability understand the nature or purpose of an operation or other treatment. The common law would be seriously defective if it failed to provide a solution to the problem created by such inability to consent. In my opinion, however, the common law does not fail. In my opinion, the solution to the problem which the common law provides is that a doctor can lawfully operate on, or give other treatment to, adult patients who are incapable, for one reason or another, of consenting to his doing so, provided that the operation or other treatment concerned is in the best interests of such patients. The operation or other treatment will be in their best interests if, but only if, it is carried out in order either to save their lives or to ensure improvement or prevent deterioration in their physical or mental health.

Different views have been put forward with regard to the principle which makes it lawful for a doctor to operate on or give other treatment to adult patients without their consent.... The Court of Appeal in the present case regarded the matter as depending on the public interest. I would not disagree with that as a broad proposition, but I think that it is helpful to consider the principle in accordance with which the public interest leads to this result. In my opinion, the principle is that, when persons lack the capacity, for whatever reason, to take decisions about the performance of operations on them, or the giving of other medical treatment to them, it is necessary that some other person or persons, with the appropriate qualifications, should take such decisions for them. Otherwise they would be deprived of medical care which they need and to which they are entitled....

Lord Griffiths

I agree that those charged with the care of the mentally incompetent are protected from any criminal or tortious action based on lack of consent. Whether one arrives at this conclusion by applying a principle of 'necessity' as do Lord Brandon and Lord Goff or by saying that it is in the public interest as did Neill LJ in the Court of Appeal, appear to me to be inextricably interrelated conceptual justifications for the humane development of the common law. Why is it necessary that the mentally incompetent should be given treatment to which they lack the capacity to consent? The answer must surely be because it is in the public interest that it should be so.

In a civilised society the mentally incompetent must be provided with medical and nursing care and those who look after them must do their best for them. Stated in legal terms the doctor who undertakes responsibility for the treatment of a mental patient who is incapable of giving consent to treatment must give the treatment that he considers to be in the best interests of his patient, and the standard of care required of the doctor will be that laid down in *Bôlam v Friern Hospital Management Committee* [1957] 1 WLR 582....

Lord Goff of Chieveley

[I] turn to consider the question whether, and if so when, medical treatment or care of a mentally disordered person who is, by reason of his incapacity, incapable of giving his consent can be regarded as lawful. As is recognised in Cardozo J's statement of principle, and elsewhere (see e.g. *Sidaway v Bethlem Royal Hospital Governors* [1985] AC 871 at 882, per Lord Scarman), some relaxation of the law is required to accommodate persons of unsound mind. In *Wilson v Pringle* [1987] QB 237 the Court of Appeal considered that treatment or care of such persons may be regarded as lawful, as falling within the exception relating to physical contact which is generally acceptable in the ordinary conduct of everyday life.... I am with respect unable to agree. That exception is concerned with the ordinary events of everyday life, jostling in public places and such like, and affects all persons, whether or not they are capable of giving their consent. Medical treatment, even treatment for minor ailments, does not fall within that category of events. The general rule is that consent is necessary to render such treatment lawful. If such treatment administered without consent is not to be unlawful, it has to be justified on some other principle.

On what principle can medical treatment be justified when given without consent? We are searching for a principle on which, in limited circumstances, recognition may be given to a need, in the interests of the patient, that treatment should be given to him in circumstances where he is (temporarily or permanently) disabled from consenting to it. It is this criterion of a need which points to the principle of necessity as providing justification.

That there exists in the common law a principle of necessity which may justify action which would otherwise be unlawful is not in doubt. But historically the principle has been seen to be restricted to two groups of cases, which have been called cases of public necessity and cases of private necessity. The former occurred when a man interfered with another man's property in the public interest, for example (in the days before we could dial 999 for the fire brigade) the destruction of another man's house to prevent the spread of a catastrophic fire, as indeed occurred in the Great Fire of London in 1666. The latter cases occurred when a man interfered with another's property to save his own person or property from imminent danger, for example when he entered on his neighbour's land without his consent in order to prevent the spread of fire onto his own land.

There is, however, a third group of cases, which is also properly described as founded on the principle of necessity and which is more pertinent to the resolution of the problem in the present case. These cases are concerned with action taken as a matter of necessity to assist another person without his consent. To give a simple example, a man who seizes another and forcibly drags him from the path of an oncoming vehicle, thereby saving him from injury or even death, commits no wrong. But there are many emanations of this principle, to be found scattered through the books. These are concerned not only with the preservation of the life or health of the assisted person, but also with the preservation of his property (sometimes an animal, sometimes an ordinary chattel) and even to certain conduct on his behalf in the administration of his affairs. Where there is a pre-existing relationship between the parties, the intervener is usually said to act as an agent of necessity on behalf of the principal in whose interests he acts, and his action can often, with not too much artificiality, be referred to the pre-existing relationship between them. Whether the intervener may be entitled either to reimbursement or to remuneration raises separate questions which are not relevant to the present case.

We are concerned here with action taken to preserve the life, health or well-being of another who is unable to consent to it. Such action is sometimes said to be justified as arising from an emergency; in Prosser and Keeton, *Torts* (5th ed, 1984) p. 117 the action is said to be privileged by the emergency. Doubtless, in the case of a person of sound mind, there will ordinarily have to be an emergency before such action taken without consent can be lawful; for otherwise there would be an opportunity to communicate with the assisted person and to seek his consent. But this is not always so; and indeed the historical origins of the principle of necessity do not point to emergency as such as providing the criterion of lawful intervention without consent. The old Roman doctrine of *negotiorum gestio* presupposed not so much an emergency as a prolonged absence of the *dominus* from home as justifying intervention by the gestor to administer his affairs. The most ancient group of cases in the common law, concerned with action taken by the master of a ship in distant parts in the interests of the shipowner, likewise found its origin in the difficulty of communication with the owner over a prolonged period of time, a difficulty overcome today by modern means of communication. In those cases, it was said that there had to be an emergency before the master could act as agent of necessity; though the emergency could well be of some duration. But, when a person is rendered incapable of communication either permanently or over a considerable period of time (through illness or accident or mental disorder), it would be an unusual use of language to describe the case as one of 'permanent emergency', if indeed such a state of affairs can properly be said to exist. In truth, the relevance of an emergency is that it may give rise to a necessity to act in the interests of the assisted person without first obtaining his consent. Emergency is however not the criterion or even a prerequisite; it is simply a frequent origin of the necessity which imples intervention. The principle is one of necessity, not of emergency.

We can derive some guidance as to the nature of the principle of necessity from the cases on agency of necessity in mercantile law. When reading those cases, however, we have to bear in mind that it was there considered that (since there was a pre-existing relationship between the parties) there was a duty on the part of the agent to act on his principal's behalf in an emergency. From these cases it appears that the principle of necessity connotes that circumstances have arisen in which there is a necessity for the agent to act on his principal's behalf at a time when it is in practice not possible for him to obtain his principal's instructions so to do. In such cases, it has been said that the agent must act *bona fide* in the interests of his principal (see *Prager v Blatspiel Stamp & Heacock Ltd* [1924] 1 KB 566 at 572, per McCardie J). A broader statement of the principle is to be found in the advice of the Privy Council delivered by Sir Montague Smith in *Australasian Steam Navigation Co v Morse* (1872) LR 4 PC 222 at 230, in which he said:

> when by the force of circumstances a man has the duty cast upon him of taking some action for another, and under that obligation, adopts the course which, to the judgment of a wise and prudent man, is apparently the best for the interest of the persons for whom he acts in a given emergency, it may properly be said of the course so taken, that it was, in a mercantile sense, necessary to take it.

In a sense, these statements overlap. But from them can be derived the basic requirements, applicable in these cases of necessity, that, to fall within the principle, not only (1) must there be a necessity to act when it is not practicable to communicate with the assisted person, but also (2) the action taken must be such as a reasonable person would in all the circumstances take, acting in the best interests of the assisted person.

On this statement of principle, I wish to observe that officious intervention cannot be justified by the principle of necessity. So intervention cannot be justified when another more appropriate person is available and willing to act; nor can it be justified when it is contrary to the known wishes of the assisted person, to the extent that he is capable of rationally forming such a wish. On the second limb of the principle, the introduction of the standard of a reasonable man should not in the present context be regarded as materially different from that of Sir Montague Smith's 'wise and prudent man', because a reasonable man would, in the time available to him, proceed with wisdom and prudence before taking action in relation to another man's person or property without his consent. I shall have more to say on this point later. Subject to that, I hesitate at present to indulge in any greater refinement of the principle, being well aware of many problems which may arise in its application, problems which it is not necessary, for present purposes, to examine. But as a general rule, if the above criteria are fulfilled, interference with the assisted person's person or property (as the case may be) will not be unlawful. Take the example of a railway accident, in which injured passengers are trapped in the wreckage. It is this principle which may render lawful the actions of other citizens, railway staff, passengers or outsiders, who rush to give aid and comfort to the victims: the surgeon who amputates the limb of an unconscious passenger to free him from the wreckage; the ambulance man who conveys him to hospital; the doctors and nurses who treat him and care for him while he is still unconscious. Take the example of an elderly person who suffers a stroke which renders him incapable of speech or movement. It is by virtue of this principle that the doctor who treats him, the nurse who cares for him, even the relative or friend or neighbour who comes in to look after him will commit no wrong when he or she touches his body.

The two examples I have given illustrate, in the one case, an emergency and, in the other, a permanent or semi-permanent state of affairs. Another example of the latter kind is that of a mentally disordered person who is disabled from giving consent. I can see no good reason why the principle of necessity should not be applicable in his case as it is in the case of the victim of a stroke. Furthermore, in the case of a mentally disordered person, as in the case of a stroke victim, the permanent state of affairs calls for a wider range of care than may be requisite in an emergency which arises from accidental injury. When the state of affairs is permanent, or semi-permanent, action properly taken to preserve the life, health or well-being of the assisted person may well transcend such measures as surgical operation or substantial medical treatment and may extend to include such humdrum matters as routine medical or dental treatment, even simple care such as dressing and undressing and putting to bed.

The distinction I have drawn between cases of emergency and cases where the state of affairs is (more or less) permanent is relevant in another respect. We are here concerned with medical treatment, and I limit myself to cases of that kind. Where, for example, a surgeon performs an operation without his consent on a patient temporarily rendered unconscious in an accident, he should do no more than is reasonably required, in the best interests of the patient, before he recovers consciousness. I can see no practical difficulty arising from this requirement, which derives from the fact that the patient is expected before long to regain consciousness and can then be consulted about longer term measures. The point has however arisen in a more acute form where a surgeon, in the course of an operation, discovers some other condition which, in his opinion, requires operative treatment for which he has not received the patient's consent. In what circumstances he should operate forthwith, and in what circumstances he should postpone the further treatment until he has received the patient's consent, is a difficult matter which has troubled the Canadian courts (see *Marshall v Curry* [1933] 3 DLR 260 and *Murray v McMurchy* [1949] 2 DLR 442), but which it is not necessary for your Lordships to consider in the present case.

But where the state of affairs is permanent or semi-permanent, as may be so in the case of a mentally disordered person, there is no point in waiting to obtain the patient's consent. The need to care for him is obvious; and the doctor must then act in the best interests of his patient, just as if he had received his patient's consent so to do. Were this not so, much useful treatment and care could, in theory at least, be denied to the unfortunate. It follows that, on this point, I am unable to accept the view expressed by Neill LJ in the Court of Appeal, that the treatment must be shown to have been necessary. Moreover, in such a case, as my noble and learned friend Lord Brandon has pointed out, a doctor who has assumed responsibility for the care of a patient may not only be treated as having the patient's consent to act, but also be under a duty so to act. I find myself to be respectfully in agreement with Lord Donaldson MR when he said:

> I see nothing incongruous in doctors and others who have a caring responsibility being required, when acting in relation to an adult who is incompetent, to exercise a right of choice in exactly the same way as would the court or reasonable parents in relation to a child, making due allowance, of course, for the fact that the patient is not a child, and I am satisfied that that is what the law does in fact require.

In these circumstances, it is natural to treat the deemed authority and the duty as interrelated. But I feel bound to express my opinion that, in principle, the lawfulness of the doctor's action is, at least in its origin, to be found in the principle of necessity. This can perhaps be seen most clearly in cases where there is no continuing relationship between doctor and patient. The 'doctor in the house' who volunteers to assist a lady in the audience who, overcome by the drama or by the heat in the theatre, has fainted away is impelled to act by no greater duty than that imposed by his own Hippocratic oath. Furthermore, intervention can be justified in the case of a non-professional, as well as a professional, man or woman who has no pre-existing relationship with the assisted person, as in the case of a stranger who rushes to assist an injured man after an accident. In my opinion, it is the necessity itself which provides the justification for the intervention.

I have said that the doctor has to act in the best interests of the assisted person. In the case of routine treatment of mentally disordered persons, there should be little difficulty in applying this principle. In the case of more serious treatment, I recognise that its application may create problems for the medical profession; however, in making decisions about treatment, the doctor must act in accordance with a responsible and competent body of relevant professional opinion, on the principles set down in *Bolam v Friern Hospital Management Committee* [1957]1 WLR 582. No doubt, in practice, a decision may involve others besides the doctor. It must surely be good practice to consult relatives and others who are concerned with the care of the patient.

Sometimes, of course, consultation with a specialist or specialists will be required; and in others, especially where the decision involves more than a purely medical opinion, an interdisciplinary team will in practice participate in the decision. It is very difficult, and would be unwise, for a court to do more than to stress that, for those who are involved in these important and sometimes difficult decisions, the overriding consideration is that they should act in the best interests of the person who suffers from the misfortune of being prevented by incapacity from deciding for himself what should be done to his own body in his own best interests....

COMMENTARY

Commenting on the case, Shaw (1990) 53 MLR 91 writes:

The supposed absence of maternal feelings in mentally handicapped women, their assumed inability to care for any potential offspring and the pain that they might suffer if they were separated from a child are common themes in recent English cases although in the absence of definite criteria for decision making it is hard to tell what weight is placed upon them. Is it acceptable that judges should make public policy choices about the relevance of such factors to the presumed best interests of mentally handicapped people in the closed forum of the courtroom? More, is it appropriate that the basis for such choices, which essentially determine the content of the claim which mentally handicapped people may make upon the resources of society, should be made by reference for the most part only to the clinical judgement of doctors and in isolation from wide questions of resource allocation?

Lord Goff points out that the doctrine does not encompass 'officious intervention', so that the treatment of a non-urgent condition of a temporarily incapacitated patient should await that patient's consent. If the vast majority of the patients would have wished the condition to be treated at the same time as the urgent surgery, does it make any sense to force them into another surgical operation, together with its associated risks, and, in the case of NHS, at the public's expense, rather than treating the problem at once? If the need for surgical treatment exceeds the capacity to provide that treatment (undoubtedly the position in the NHS) can this rule be justified? Conversely, do such utilitarian concerns have any place when considering rights of personal autonomy?

Although the most frequent application of necessity is where the claimant is unable to consent to an activity the aim of which is to benefit the claimant, the defence has a wider application. In the tragic case of *Re A (Conjoined Twins)* [2001] Fam 147, the Court of Appeal held that it would be lawful to operate on conjoined twins for the purpose of saving one of them, even if the result of the operation would the death of the other. The decision of Brooke LJ was partly based on the defence of necessity available to the surgeons who performed the surgery. Although the case dealt with the question of criminal liability, there seems little doubt necessity could also have been invoked as a defence to any claim of battery arising out of the surgery that might have been made by the estate of the dead child. Such a case will, however, be exceptional; the defence will normally not apply if the conduct complained of is not in the best interests of the claimant. Although necessity normally operates as a defence to a potential action for battery, it can also apply to other intentional torts, such as false imprisonment (see *R v Bournewood Community and Mental Health NHS Trust, ex p. L* [1999] 1 AC 458; *Austin v Commissioner of the Police for the Metropolis* [2008] 1 All ER 564 (CA); necessity was not considered on appeal in the House of Lords: [2009] 1 AC 564). Note, however, that the presence of the defence of necessity to a common law claim for false imprisonment may not prevent the same conduct from amounting to a deprivation of liberty contrary to Article 5 ECHR, further illustrating the point, made at p. 82 above, that although there are similarities between false imprisonment and for breach of Article 5, there remain significant differences.

The speech of Lord Goff is careful to reconcile the right of autonomy with intervention based on necessity. To what extent, if any, can necessity be used where a claimant of full capacity refuses to agree to treatment which medical opinion considers to be in his best interests? The following section considers this issue.

(b) Necessity and Personal Autonomy

Early in the twentieth century it was held that prison staff had a 'duty' to prevent a prisoner from conducting a hunger strike where it caused a risk to the prisoner's health (*Leigh v Gladstone* (1909) 26 TLR 139). However, a greater recognition of personal autonomy in modern times has led to a different conclusion. In *Secretary of State for the Home Department v Robb* [1995] Fam 12 a declaration was obtained by prison officials that they might lawfully abstain from providing hydration and nutrition to a prisoner on a hunger strike as long as he retained the capacity to refuse to receive nutrition. Thorpe J accepted that an adult of sound mind had a specific right of self-determination which entitled him to refuse nutrition and hydration. However, the House of Lords has ruled that the police may be liable in negligence for failing to take reasonable steps to prevent a prisoner of sound mind committing suicide (*Reeves v Commissioner of Police for the Metropolis* [2000] 1 AC 380). The result of these cases seems to be that the police have a duty to take steps to prevent the suicide but these steps cannot amount to a battery as this infringes the right of self-determination. Is this a defensible position to take?

Mental Capacity Act 2005

1 THE PRINCIPLES

(1) The following principles apply for the purposes of this Act.

(2) A person must be assumed to have capacity unless it is established that he lacks capacity.

(3) A person is not to be treated as unable to make a decision unless all practicable steps to help him to do so have been taken without success.

(4) A person is not to be treated as unable to make a decision merely because he makes an unwise decision.

(5) An act done, or decision made, under this Act for or on behalf of a person who lacks capacity must be done, or made, in his best interests.

(6) Before the act is done, or the decision is made, regard must be had to whether the purpose for which it is needed can be as effectively achieved in a way that is less restrictive of the person's rights and freedom of action.

2   PEOPLE WHO LACK CAPACITY

(1) For the purposes of this Act, a person lacks capacity in relation to a matter if at the material time he is unable to make a decision for himself in relation to the matter because of an impairment of, or a disturbance in the functioning of, the mind or brain.

(2) It does not matter whether the impairment or disturbance is permanent or temporary.

(3) A lack of capacity cannot be established merely by reference to—

    (a) a person's age or appearance, or

    (b) a condition of his, or an aspect of his behaviour, which might lead others to make unjustified assumptions about his capacity.

(4) In proceedings under this Act or any other enactment, any question whether a person lacks capacity within the meaning of this Act must be decided on the balance of probabilities . . .

3   INABILITY TO MAKE DECISIONS

(1) For the purposes of section 2, a person is unable to make a decision for himself if he is unable—

    (a) to understand the information relevant to the decision,

    (b) to retain that information,

    (c) to use or weigh that information as part of the process of making the decision, or

    (d) to communicate his decision (whether by talking, using sign language or any other means).

(2) A person is not to be regarded as unable to understand the information relevant to a decision if he is able to understand an explanation of it given to him in a way that is appropriate to his circumstances (using simple language, visual aids or any other means).

(3) The fact that a person is able to retain the information relevant to a decision for a short period only does not prevent him from being regarded as able to make the decision.

(4) The information relevant to a decision includes information about the reasonably foreseeable consequences of—

    (a) deciding one way or another, or

    (b) failing to make the decision . . .

5   ACTS IN CONNECTION WITH CARE OR TREATMENT

(1) If a person ("D") does an act in connection with the care or treatment of another person ("P"), the act is one to which this section applies if—

    (a) before doing the act, D takes reasonable steps to establish whether P lacks capacity in relation to the matter in question, and

    (b) when doing the act, D reasonably believes—

        (i) that P lacks capacity in relation to the matter, and

        (ii) that it will be in P's best interests for the act to be done.

(2) D does not incur any liability in relation to the act that he would not have incurred if P—

    (a) had had capacity to consent in relation to the matter, and

    (b) had consented to D's doing the act.

(3) Nothing in this section excludes a person's civil liability for loss or damage, or his criminal liability, resulting from his negligence in doing the act.

(4) Nothing in this section affects the operation of sections 24 to 26 (advance decisions to refuse treatment).

COMMENTARY

The Mental Capacity Act 2005, which came into full effect in October 2007, now determines whether a person has a capacity to consent to medical treatment and, if not, what treatment would be in her best interests (s. 4). However, there has been held to be 'no relevant distinction between the test in s 3(1) of the Act and the pre-existing common law' (*Re MM* (An Adult) [2007] EWHC 2003 (Fam) per Munby J at [74]) with the result that pre-Act cases remain useful guides to determining how s. 3(1) will be applied. In the leading pre-Act case of *Re MB* [1997] 2 FLR 426, the appellant was admitted to one of the respondent's hospitals for a caesarean section, for which she had signed a consent form. However, she would not consent to a venepuncture to provide necessary blood samples. She subsequently refused to consent to the insertion of the veneflon, necessary to anaesthetise the appellant so that the caesarian section could be performed. She did agree to anaesthesia by mask, but, following an explanation to her of the risks attendant upon such a procedure, she withdrew her consent to it and to caesarean section delivery. When she went into labour she agreed to delivery by caesarean section, providing she did not feel the needle involved in the anaesthesia. Later that day, in the operating theatre, she refused to consent to anaesthesia by mask and the surgery was cancelled. The defendant health authority then sought and obtained a declaration that it would be lawful to perform a caesarean section to deliver the foetus. The appellant instructed her lawyers to appeal that decision the same evening. On the following day she agreed to the induction of anaesthesia and she was delivered of a healthy male infant by caesarean section. The Court of Appeal dismissed an appeal against the original declaration. Whilst recognising the right of a competent adult to refuse medical treatment for rational or irrational reasons or for no reason at all, the refusal needed to be made by a person with the mental capacity to make that decision. Applying these principles to the facts of the case, Butler-Sloss LJ held that:

(1) MB consented to a caesarian section; (2) what she refused to accept was not the incision by the surgeon's scalpel but only the prick of the anaesthetist's needle. Capacity is commensurate with the gravity of the decision to be taken. (3) She could not bring herself to undergo the caesarian section she desired because, as the evidence established, 'a fear of needles has got in the way of proceeding with the operation. At the moment of panic her fear dominated all at the actual point she was not capable of making a decision at all at that moment the needle or mask dominated her thinking and made her quite unable to consider anything else'.

Would it make any difference that the failure to undergo the procedure might have endangered the life of the child? After considering case law in the UK and elsewhere, as well as the position under the European Convention on Human Rights, Butler-Sloss LJ thought not, holding that a competent woman who had the capacity to decide may choose not to have medical intervention, even though the consequence may be the death or serious handicap of the child she bears or her own death. As the foetus did not have separate legal personality until it was born alive, it did not have any separate interests (from its mother) capable of being taken into account when a court had to consider an application for a declaration in respect of a caesarean section operation. Whether a pregnant women should be subject to controls for the benefit of her unborn child was a matter for Parliament. This aspect of the decision in *Re MB*, which was obiter, was confirmed in *St George's Healthcare NHS Trust v S* [1999] Fam 26, where the Court of Appeal held that an adult of sound mind had the right to refuse medical treatment even where this would result in the death of the foetus: 'In our judgment while pregnancy increases the personal responsibilities of a woman it does not diminish her entitlement to decide whether or not to undergo medical treatment.' The case also held that the Mental Health Act 1983 could not be used to achieve the detention and subsequent treatment of an individual because her thinking process is 'unusual, even apparently bizarre and irrational, and contrary to the views of the overwhelming majority of the community at large'.

This latter point was taken up Butler-Sloss P in *Re B (Adult: Refusal of Treatment)* [2002] 2 All ER 449. In this case the applicant, a tetraplegic patient, sought a declaration that the failure of hospital staff to turn off the ventilator to which she was attached was unlawful. The consequence of turning off the ventilator was almost certain death. In finding that the applicant had capacity, and granting the declaration, Butler-Sloss P gave the following guidance in respect of a patient's competence to make such a decision:

If there are difficulties in deciding whether the patient has sufficient mental capacity, particularly if the refusal may have grave consequences for the patient, it is most important that those considering the issue should not confuse the question of mental capacity with the nature of the decision made by the patient, however grave the consequences. The view of the patient may reflect a difference in values rather than an absence of competence and the assessment of capacity should be approached with this firmly in mind. The doctors must not allow their emotional reaction to or strong disagreement with the decision of the patient to cloud their judgment in answering the primary question whether the patient has the mental capacity to make the decision.

Butler-Sloss P thought that this case illustrated the serious danger of 'benevolent paternalism which does not embrace recognition of the personal autonomy of the severely disabled patient'. Do you agree?

The purpose of seeking an order in these circumstances is to provide a defence to an action in battery brought by patients who have received medical treatment against their will Where there is capacity to refuse consent, such an order will not be granted (and, as in *Re B*, above, a declaration may be obtained that the treatment was unlawful). This is the converse of the question considered by the House of Lords in *Gillick v West Norfolk Health Authority* [1986] AC 112, namely, the capacity to give (rather than withhold) consent to medical treatment (see above). The two situations are not strictly comparable, however, as the ability of children to refuse consent to treatment is limited. In *Re R* [1992] Fam 11, a 15-year-old girl in local authority care suffered bouts of suicidal and violent behaviour, but during periods of lucidity she refused anti-psychotic drugs. The Court of Appeal ordered, in the exercise of its wardship jurisdiction, that the drugs could nonetheless be administered, Lord Donaldson MR holding that a *Gillick* competent child could give an effective consent to medical treatment, but that, if treatment was refused, consent could be given by anyone exercising parental rights. A similar conclusion was reached in *Re W* [1993] Fam 64, where the appellant had the power to consent to treatment under the Family Law Reform Act 1969. This, however, did not give her a corresponding right to refuse treatment if the court, in the exercise of its inherent jurisdiction, thought the best interests of the child required that the treatment be administered. Do these decisions leave any scope for *Gillick* competent children to refuse treatment if persons exercising parental authority consent on their behalf? (See *Re L (Medical Treatment: Gillick Competency)* [1998] 2 FLR 810.) For further discussion of consent in the context of medical procedures see M. Brazier & E. Cave, *Medicine Patients and the Law*, 4th edn. (London: Penguin, 2007), chs 5–6, and A. Maclean, *Autonomy, Informed Consent and Medical Law* (Cambridge: Cambridge University Press, 2009), pp. 154–6.

Although the Mental Capacity Act 2005 in many ways codifies the common law position, s. 5, which provides a defence to battery (negligence is expressly excluded from the section) in respect of acts done in connection with the care or treatment of an incapacitated person, differs from the common law defence of necessity set out in *Re F*. First, the defence applies if the defendant (1) has taken reasonable steps to ascertain if the person has capacity in relation to the matter in question; (2) reasonably believes that the person does not have capacity; and (3) reasonably believes that it will be in the person's best interests for the act to be done. At common law it was no defence that the defendant reasonably believed that the person lacked capacity if they did not, nor that they believed the acts were in the person's best interest if they were not. Secondly, it is possible that a belief that the act was done in the best interests of the patient may justify the kind of officious intervention that Lord Goff thought was not covered by the defence of necessity at common law, although in determining what is in the person's best interests the defendant must consider, amongst other things, the likelihood that the person may have capacity in the future (s. 4(3)).

For further details on the Act see Bartlett, *Blackstone's Guide to the Mental Capacity Act 2005*, 2nd edn. (Oxford: OUP, 2008).

5. Self-Defence and Related Defences

Ashley v Chief Constable of Sussex Police [2008] 1 AC 962

The deceased was shot and killed by an officer of the defendant when they raided the deceased's flat in the early hours of the morning to execute a warrant to search for drugs. The deceased was naked and unarmed at the time of the shooting but the police officer who shot him alleged the shooting was an act of self-defence. Criminal charges against the officer failed on the ground that there was no evidence to negate the assertion of self-defence, but the personal representatives of the deceased (his father and son) brought actions as dependants, under the Fatal Accidents Act 1976, and for the benefit of the deceased's estate, under section 1(1) of the Law Reform (Miscellaneous Provisions) Act 1934, against the chief constable of the defendant police force for damages for assault and battery, negligence and false imprisonment. One issue for the House of Lords was whether a mistaken but reasonable belief that the officer was under attack could found a defence of self-defence in a civil law action. The other issue (not discussed here) was whether the actions for assault and battery should be allowed to proceed, the defendant having admitted liability in negligence and false imprisonment and agreed to pay all damages flowing from the incident. By a majority, their Lordships agreed that the actions should be allowed to proceed.

Lord Scott of Foscote

Issue 1: the self-defence criteria

16 In para 37 of his judgment Sir Anthony Clarke MR identified three possible approaches to the criteria requisite for a successful plea of self-defence, namely, (1) the necessity to take action in response to an attack, or imminent attack, must be judged on the assumption that the facts were as the defendant honestly believed them to be, whether or not he was mistaken and, if he made a mistake of fact, whether or not it was reasonable for him to have done so (solution 1); (2) the necessity to take action in response to an attack or imminent attack must be judged on the facts as the defendant honestly believed them to be, whether or not he was mistaken, but, if he made a mistake of fact, he can rely on that fact only if the mistake was a

reasonable one for him to have made (solution 2); (3) in order to establish the relevant necessity the defendant must establish that there was in fact an imminent and real risk of attack (solution 3). It was common ground that, in addition, based on whatever belief the defendant is entitled to rely on, the defendant must, in a civil action, satisfy the court that it was reasonable for him to have taken the action he did. Of the three solutions the Court of Appeal held that solution 2 was the correct one. On this appeal the chief constable has contended, as he did below, that solution 1 is the correct one. The claimants have not cross-appealed in order to contend that solution 3 should be preferred.

17 It was held in *R v Williams (Gladstone)* [1987] 3 All ER 411 and is now accepted that, for the purposes of the criminal law, solution 1 is the correct one . . . It is urged upon your Lordships that the criteria for self-defence in civil law should be the same as in criminal law. In my opinion, however, this plea for consistency between the criminal law and the civil law lacks cogency for the ends to be served by the two systems are very different. One of the main functions of the criminal law is to identify, and provide punitive sanctions for, behaviour that is categorised as criminal because it is damaging to the good order of society. It is fundamental to criminal law and procedure that everyone charged with criminal behaviour should be presumed innocent until proven guilty and that, as a general rule, no one should be punished for a crime that he or she did not intend to commit or be punished for the consequences of an honest mistake . . .

18 The function of the civil law of tort is different. Its main function is to identify and protect the rights that every person is entitled to assert against, and require to be respected by, others. The rights of one person, however, often run counter to the rights of others and the civil law, in particular the law of tort, must then strike a balance between the conflicting rights. Thus, for instance, the right of freedom of expression may conflict with the right of others not to be defamed. The rules and principles of the tort of defamation must strike the balance. The right not to be physically harmed by the actions of another may conflict with the rights of other people to engage in activities involving the possibility of accidentally causing harm. The balance between these conflicting rights must be struck by the rules and principles of the tort of negligence. As to assault and battery and self-defence, every person has the right in principle not to be subjected to physical harm by the intentional actions of another person. But every person has the right also to protect himself by using reasonable force to repel an attack or to prevent an imminent attack. The rules and principles defining what does constitute legitimate self-defence must strike the balance between these conflicting rights. The balance struck is serving a quite different purpose from that served by the criminal law when answering the question whether the infliction of physical injury on another in consequence of a mistaken belief by the assailant of a need for self-defence should be categorised as a criminal offence and attract penal sanctions. To hold, in a civil case, that a mistaken and unreasonably held belief by A that he was about to be attacked by B justified a pre-emptive attack in believed self-defence by A on B would, in my opinion, constitute a wholly unacceptable striking of the balance. It is one thing to say that if A's mistaken belief was honestly held he should not be punished by the criminal law. It would be quite another to say that A's unreasonably held mistaken belief would be sufficient to justify the law in setting aside B's right not to be subjected to physical violence by A. I would have no hesitation whatever in holding that for civil law purposes an excuse of self-defence based on non existent facts that are honestly but unreasonably believed to exist must fail. This is the conclusion to which the Court of Appeal came in preferring solution 2 . . .

20 I would, therefore, dismiss the chief constable's appeal against the Court of Appeal's adoption of solution 2. It has not been contended on behalf of the Ashleys that solution 3 might be the correct solution in a civil case but, speaking for myself, I think that that solution would have a good deal to be said for it, as appears to have been the view also of Sir Anthony Clarke MR [2007] 1 WLR 398, paras 63–78. I would start with the principle that every person is prima facie entitled

not to be the object of physical harm intentionally inflicted by another. If consent to the infliction of the injury has not been given and cannot be implied why should it be a defence in a tort claim for the assailant to say that although his belief that his victim had consented was a mistaken one nonetheless it had been a reasonable one for him to make? Why, for civil law purposes, should not a person who proposes to make physical advances of a sexual nature to another be expected first to make sure that the advances will be welcome? Similarly, where there is in fact no risk or imminent danger from which the assailant needs to protect himself, I find it difficult to see on what basis the right of the victim not to be subjected to physical violence can be set at naught on the ground of mistake made by the assailant, whether or not reasonably made...However, and in my view, unfortunately, solution 3 has not been contended for on this appeal, its pros and cons have not been the subject of argument, and your Lordships cannot, therefore, conclude that it is the correct solution. But I would, for my part, regard the point as remaining open.

Lord Neuberger of Abbotsbury

89...Thirdly, there is the argument that the inflictor of an alleged battery has to go further than the Court of Appeal held, and show that he was in fact under imminent threat of attack. The point appears to me to be difficult, and the authorities are not entirely clear on the point: see Sir Anthony Clarke MR's analysis, in paras 63 to 78. Like him, I think that the balance of authority favours the conclusion that a defendant does not have to go that far, although the point is plainly open for reconsideration in your Lordships' House.

90 There are powerful arguments both ways. It is easy to conceive of circumstances where it would be inevitable that either the inflictor or the victim would have a thoroughly understandable sense of great grievance if, as the case may be, there was or was not a valid claim for damages for the infliction of severe violence in circumstances where the inflictor reasonably, but wrongly, believed he was under imminent threat of attack. As the Ashleys have not challenged the Court of Appeal's conclusion on this issue, it appears to me that in this case it should be left open in your Lordships' House.

91 Fourthly, if a reasonable but mistaken belief will do, other questions may need to be considered. One such question is whether, when seeking to justify the reasonableness of his belief, a defendant can rely on factors which were not the claimant's responsibility. There is obviously a strong argument for saying that a defendant can rely on such factors. Otherwise, one would be getting close to holding that the belief must be correct. Further, it could lead to difficulties if one had to decide whether the claimant was responsible for the defendant's belief, especially if only some of the factors which influenced the defendant could be taken into account. However, it can also be said to be unfair on the claimant if matters for which he had no responsibility can serve to justify the reasonableness of the defendant's mistaken belief. The answer may ultimately depend on whether one judges the issue of reasonableness from the claimant's point of view or from that of the defendant...

Lords Rodger, **Bingham** and **Carswell** delivered speeches agreeing with Lord Scott on this point.

COMMENTARY

Although their Lordships were content to rest the defence of self-defence on an honest and reasonable belief in the existence of a threat to the defendant, Lords Scott, Rodger and Neuberger left open the question of whether even a reasonable belief in the existence of the threat should be sufficient to found the defence. Interestingly, Lord Scott considered, at [19], the analogous defence of consent in concluding that a reasonable belief in the existence of a threat was required. However, if the consent analogy had been taken further it would have supported the view that even a reasonable belief would not be sufficient. It is no defence to a claim in battery that the defendant reasonably thought the claimant was consenting unless, perhaps, the claimant induces the defendant to believe that he or she is consenting (see McBride [2008] CLJ 461, 463). Why should a surgeon who mistakenly but reasonably believes she has consent to operate on a patient commit a battery whereas the police officer who deliberately shoots another in the mistaken but reasonable belief he is under attack has a defence? Whilst the different purposes of the law of crime and tort identified by Lord Scott both justify the criminal law standard and explain why it is inappropriate for civil law, there seems no reason for self-defence to stand alone amongst the defences to the intentional torts in allowing a reasonable belief to found the defence.

If a reasonable belief is to be sufficient, what factors can be taken into account in determining reasonableness? In consent the better view is that a reasonable belief in the existence of consent induced by the claimant might prevent the claimant from later claiming there was no consent but Lord Scott at [20] seemed to think this would only go to contributory negligence. Greater difficulties arise where the mistake is induced by the conduct of third parties. If a police briefing was responsible for creating the reasonable belief in an officer that she was under attack, would this suffice to found the defence? Although Lord Neuberger pointed out the problem (at [90]) he provided no solutions, and both Lord Rodger in the House of Lords and Arden LJ in the Court of Appeal expressly left open the question of whether a mistake which was not induced by the person against whom the act of self-defence was committed, but by a third party, would found the defence. (Cf. Lord Scott, who thought it would only go to the question of contribution (see p. 266, below). If it did it would be contrary to the rules that apply to the defence of consent; it is no defence to an action for battery for a surgeon to say he reasonably thought, as a result of a clerical error by hospital staff, that a consent form had been signed if it had not. For further comment on *Ashley*, see Palmer and Steele (2008) 71 MLR 801.)

Apart from the presence of a reasonable belief that the victim was threatening the claimant, the claimant must also show that the response to the threat was proportionate. In *Lane v Holloway* [1968] 1 QB 379, the 64-year-old plaintiff struck the 23-year-old defendant on the shoulder, and the defendant responded by hitting the plaintiff in the eye with such severity that he was in hospital for a month. The Court of Appeal held that the blow was out of all proportion to the original act of the plaintiff so that no defence of consent or self-defence was applicable. The court also held that the provocation of the plaintiff could not be used to reduce compensatory damages (see above).

Analogous principles govern the defence of property and of other persons. In the context of the defence of property, it is generally the case that a warning to leave should be given before any force is applied, but if actual force has already been applied to one's property such a warning may be unnecessary 'for it is but returning violence with violence' (*Green v Goddard* (1702) 2 Salk 641).

Aspects of self-defence and defence of property form part of the statutory defence set out in the Criminal Justice Act 2003, s. 329. The section may provide a defence to an action for trespass to the person where the claimant was convicted of an imprisonable offence on the same occasion as the conduct alleged to amount to trespass to the person. In these circumstances the court must give permission to sue before proceedings can be brought, and permission will not be granted if the defendant did the act because he believed that the claimant was about to commit an offence, was in the course of committing an offence, or had committed an offence immediately beforehand, and that he believed it was necessary to defend himself or another person, protect or recover property, prevent the commission or continuation of an offence, or apprehend, or secure the conviction of, the claimant after he had committed an offence. The defence will not apply where, in all the circumstances, the defendant's act was grossly disproportionate. In many ways the provision merely codifies the common law relating to self-defence and illegality but, as *Winfield & Jolowicz* (para. 4–26) points out, it may provide a defence to an action for false imprisonment where the original arrest of the claimant was unlawful, provided that the claimant was ultimately convicted of an imprisonable offence on the same occasion as the arrest, the defendant had the requisite belief at the time of acting (which is an honest, rather than a reasonable, belief), and that the conduct of the defendant was not grossly disproportionate (although note the wider powers of arrest given to non-constables by s. 24A of the Police and Criminal Evidence Act 1984 (see p. 77 above)). Note that s. 329 applies not only to private individuals but also the police. Should the police be given an immunity (except for grossly disproportionate conduct) from actions in trespass to the person arising from conduct occurring whilst making an arrest merely because the person arrested is ultimately convicted of an imprisonable offence? For criticism of the section as it applies to police, see *Adorian v Metropolitan Police Commissioner* [2009] 1 WLR 1859 per Sedley LJ at [7], and Spencer [2010] CLJ 19.

Note also the power to use reasonable force in the prevention of crime under Criminal Law Act 1967, s. 3.

3 NEGLIGENCE— INTRODUCTION

I. Formulation of a General Duty of Care

1. Historical Introduction

Because of the piecemeal development of civil liability under the forms of action, little thought was given by early common lawyers to the existence of any general principle underlying the various examples of liability. As late as the latter half of the eighteenth century, Blackstone in his *Commentaries on the Laws of England* described trespass on the case as a 'universal remedy given for all personal wrongs and injuries without force' (vol. III, ch. 8, para. 4); he thought in terms only of the form of action, not of the substantive grounds for allowing the action. Similarly, the authors of Digests and Abridgements (early types of practitioner texts) were concerned only to provide examples of factual situations where liability had been held to exist, and to state the correct form of action in which to plead those facts. As *Baker* points out (p. 413), even though *Comyns Digest* (published in 1762) might have had a heading 'Action upon the Case for Negligence', many examples of what would today be considered negligence were included under 'Actions upon the Case for Misfeasance' and no attempt was made to rationalise the specific examples under a general theory of liability. For parties in a pre-existing relationship, liability came to be associated with the assumption of an obligation by promise (*assumpsit*), and this provided the unifying basis for the law of contract. But it was not until a good deal later that the idea of obligation or duty was to play a similar role in the development of a general theory of tortious liability (applicable to parties who had no prior relationship). 'Duty' was first put forward as a unifying concept in the law of tort in Buller's *Nisi Prius* ('An Institute of the Law Relative to Trials at Nisi Prius'), published in 1768, in which it was suggested that:

> Every man ought to take reasonable care that he does not injure his neighbour; therefore, wherever a man receives hurt through the default of another, though the same were not wilful, yet if it be occasioned by negligence or folly the law gives him an action to recover for the injury so sustained. . . . However, it is proper in such cases to prove that the injury was such as would probably follow from the act done.

The notion that liability in negligence was based on the existence of a duty owed by the defendant to the claimant was slow to take hold (see Winfield, 'Duty in Tortious Negligence' (1934) Col LR 41; Prichard, '*Scott v Shepherd* and the Emergence of the Tort of Negligence', Selden Society Lecture, 1976), but by the early part of the nineteenth century it was said that damages could be sought for 'the negligent or wilful conduct of the party sued, in doing or omitting something contrary to the duty which the law casts on him in the particular case' (*Ansell v Waterhouse* (1817) 6 M & S 385). This still left the question when such a duty would be imposed, and the earliest 'discussions' of the tort of negligence usually consisted of nothing more than lists of factual situations where a duty had been held to exist.

Particular problems arose where the defendant acted pursuant to a contractual obligation. By the beginning of the nineteenth century a contracting party might be able to sue the other party to the contract for breach of a tortious duty imposed by law. In addition, it was clear that a stranger to the contract might, in certain circumstances, sue for injury caused by negligent behaviour where the activity was undertaken pursuant to a contract; pedestrians injured by the negligence of a coachman were an obvious example. But the recognition of a duty where the parties were bound by a chain of contracts (e.g. between manufacturer, supplier, and consumer of goods) was a much slower process. The initial tendency was to limit the plaintiff to a claim under his contract, and to rule out any attempt to rely on an obligation arising under a contract to which he was not party. Each of the parties was expected to protect his own interests by securing appropriate warranties in the contracts to which he was party. Many of the early authorities deal with the liability of the manufacturer or supplier of defective goods or equipment, and raised the question: should a plaintiff who was not a party to the initial contract of sale or supply be able to claim the benefit of a warranty given thereunder by the manufacturer or supplier?

Winterbottom v Wright (1842) 10 M & W 109

The plaintiff entered into a contract with the Postmaster General to drive a mail coach. The coach had been supplied by the defendant to the Postmaster General under a contract which provided that during the term of the contract the coach was to be kept in a fit, proper, safe and secure state. The plaintiff alleged that the defendant 'negligently conducted himself, and so utterly disregarded his aforesaid contract and so wholly neglected and failed to perform his duty in this behalf' that the plaintiff was injured when the coach collapsed throwing him from his seat.

Lord Abinger CB

I am clearly of opinion that the defendant is entitled to our judgment....Here the action is brought simply because the defendant was a contractor with a third person; and it is contended that thereupon he became liable to every body who might use the carriage....There is no privity of contract between these parties; and if the plaintiff can sue, every passenger, or even any person passing along the road, who was injured by the upsetting of the coach, may bring a similar action. Unless we confine the operation of such contracts as this to the parties who entered into them, the most absurd and outrageous consequences, to which I can see no limit, would ensue....

There is...a class of cases in which the law permits a contract to be turned into a tort; but unless there has been some public duty undertaken, or a public nuisance committed, they are all cases in which an action might have been maintained on the contract....

Alderson B

If we were to hold that the plaintiff could sue in such a case, there is no point at which such actions would stop. The only safe rule is to confine the right to recover to those who enter into the contract; if we go one step beyond that, there is no reason why we should not go fifty....

Rolfe B

The duty, therefore, is shewn to have arisen solely from the contract; and the fallacy consists in the use of the word 'duty'. If a duty to the Postmaster General be meant, that is true; but if a duty to the plaintiff be intended (and in that sense the word is evidently used), there was none....

COMMENTARY

In *Langridge v Levy* (1837) 2 M & W 519, 150 ER 863, the plaintiff's father bought a gun for his own and his son's use. The defendant falsely told him it was made by a reputable gunmaker; it was not and it later exploded when the plaintiff fired it, causing him injury. The Court of Exchequer allowed the plaintiff's claim because of the fraudulent misrepresentation, but refused to found liability on the basis of a breach of a contractual duty owed to a third party. The plaintiff attempted to use this case as an authority in support of his claim in *Winterbottom v Wright* but, as the court noted, *Langridge* was decided on a narrower ground.

The judges in *Winterbottom v Wright* were clearly influenced by a form of what would today be called the 'floodgates' argument, namely a concern that imposing liability in the instant case would lead to countless more extensions in the scope of the duty. Allied to this was a concern over the proper limits of liability in contractual settings. Once a contractual obligation was held to give rise to a duty in tort which extended beyond the parties to the contract, what other limitation was there? (See Palmer, 'Why Privity Entered Tort—An Historical Re-examination of *Winterbottom v Wright*' (1983) 27 Am JLH 85.)

With hindsight, it seems odd that the common law would allow a claim by the pedestrian injured by the negligent driving of a coachman, but not a claim by the coachman injured by the negligent maintenance of the coach (see Winfield, 'Duty in Tortious Negligence' (1934) Col LR 41). Given this anomaly, it is not surprising that the alignment of tortious product liability with contractual liability was periodically challenged. An exception was developed to the general rule of no liability in tort, resulting in the recognition of a potential liability in respect of articles 'dangerous in themselves' (*Longmeid v Holliday* (1851) 6 Ex 761, 155 ER 752). And a more direct challenge was mounted in the case of *George v Skivington* (1869) LR 5 Ex 1. In that case, the first plaintiff was injured after using hair wash which had been sold to her husband, but for her use, by the defendant. (The husband was the second plaintiff in the action.) There was no fraud; neither did the case fit into the exception to the general rule noted above. Nonetheless, the Court of Exchequer went out of its way to hold that the wife had a good cause of action (see Ibbetson, 'George v Skivington' in C. Mitchell & P. Mitchell (eds), *Landmark Cases in the Law of Tort* (Oxford: Hart, 2010), ch. 3). Kelly CB expressly noted that the action was not upon a contract, and hence no question of warranty arose; rather, an action on the case was brought for 'unskilfulness and negligence in the manufacture of it whereby the person who used it was injured'.

The attempt to clarify the law of liability for defective products brought with it the common law's first attempt at a normative explanation of the duty of care (see extract below).

Heaven v Pender (1883) 11 QBD 503

The plaintiff was painting a ship when one of the ropes holding up the staging on which he was working broke; he fell and was injured. The staging had been erected by the defendant dock owner under contract with the plaintiff's employer. It was found that the rope which snapped was unfit for use at the time it was supplied by the defendant. The plaintiff succeeded in recovering damages in the county court, but the Queen's Bench Division on appeal ordered that judgment be entered for the defendant. The plaintiff appealed to the Court of Appeal.

Brett MR

Actionable negligence consists in the neglect of the use of ordinary care or skill towards a person to whom the defendant owes the duty of observing ordinary care and skill, by which neglect the plaintiff, without contributory negligence on his part, has suffered injury to his person or property. . . .

If a person contracts with another to use ordinary care and skill towards him or his property the obligation need not be considered in the light of a duty; it is an obligation of contract. It is undoubted, however, that there may be the obligation of such a duty from one person to another although there is no contract between them with regard to such duty. . . .

The questions which we have to solve in this case are—what is the proper definition of the relation between two persons other than the relation established by contract, or fraud, which imposes on the one of them a duty towards the other to observe, with regard to the person or property of such other, such ordinary care or skill as may be necessary to prevent injury to his person or property. . . .

The proposition which [the cases] suggest, and which is, therefore, to be deduced from them, is that whenever one person is by circumstances placed in such a position with regard to another that everyone of ordinary sense who did think would at once recognise that if he did not use ordinary care and skill in his own conduct with regard to those circumstances he would cause danger of injury to person or property of the other, a duty arises to use ordinary care and skill to avoid such danger. . . .

Bowen and **Cotton LJJ** delivered separate judgments in favour of allowing the appeal.

Appeal allowed.

COMMENTARY

The attempt of Brett MR to enunciate a general principle defining when a duty of care exists was rejected by the other two judges in the case, who confined their reasoning to the particular facts of the case. And shortly afterwards, the House of Lords affirmed that there was no general principle of liability for negligent misstatements causing monetary loss (*Derry v Peek* (1889) 14 App Cas 337). Brett MR (as Lord Esher) subsequently attempted to resuscitate his general principle by suggesting that it would only arise where there was physical proximity between the parties. In *Le Lievre v Gould* [1893] 1 QB 491, an action by a mortgagee against a surveyor who had prepared certificates for the mortgagor, he stated:

A man is entitled to be as negligent as he pleases towards the whole world if he owes no duty to them. The case of *Heaven v Pender* has no bearing upon the present question. That case established that, under certain circumstances, one man may owe a duty to another, even though there is no contract between them. If one man is near to another, or is near to the property of another, a duty lies upon him not to do that which may cause a personal injury to that other, or may injure his property. For instance, if a man is driving along a road, it is his duty not to do that which may injure another person whom he meets on the road, or to his horse or his carriage. In the same way it is the duty of a man not to do that which will injure the house of another which he is near.... That is the effect of the decision in *Heaven v Pender*, but it has no application to the present case....

Notwithstanding Lord Esher's efforts, the general principle enunciated in *Heaven v Pender* did not result in more extensive liability, as can be seen from Lord Sumner's statement in *Blacker v Lake & Elliot Ltd* (1912) 107 LT 533 at 536 that 'the breach of the defendant's contract with A to use care and skill in and about the manufacture or repair of an article does not of itself give any cause of action to B when he is injured by reason of the article proving to be defective'. The courts continued to think in terms of a general rule of no liability, to which only limited exceptions were made (in respect of articles dangerous in themselves and also, eventually, articles which were not normally dangerous but had become so because of a defect known to the manufacturer). It was not until 1932 that the limited notion of duty explained in *Le Lievre v Gould* was expanded into the notions of closeness, proximity, and neighbourhood—used in a metaphorical rather than literal sense—that define the modern duty of care.

2. *Donoghue v Stevenson*

Lord Atkin of Aberdovey, 'Law as an Educational Subject'
[1932] JSPTL 27

It is quite true that law and morality do not cover identical fields. No doubt morality extends beyond the more limited range in which you can lay down the definite prohibitions of law; but, apart from that, the British law has always necessarily ingrained in it moral teaching in this sense: that it lays down standards of honesty and plain dealing between man and man....

[A man] is not to injure his neighbour by acts of negligence; and that certainly covers a very large field of the law. I doubt whether the whole law of tort could not be comprised in the golden maxim to do unto your neighbour as you would that he should do unto you. It imposes standards ... and and it is of the utmost importance to the community that those standards should be maintained; and it teaches a man to respect his neighbour's right of property and person....

Donoghue v Stevenson [1932] AC 562

The pursuer alleged that she and a friend had entered a café in Paisley, near Glasgow, and her friend had purchased a bottle of ginger beer for her consumption. The dark green colour of the bottle made it impossible to see its contents. The pursuer drank some of the ginger beer, and as she was pouring more into her glass the partly decomposed remains of a snail came out of the bottle. She alleged that she suffered shock and severe gastro-enteritis as a result. The defender argued that the pursuer's claim disclosed no cause of action.

Lord Atkin

My Lords, the sole question for determination in this case is legal: Do the averments made by the pursuer in her pleading, if true, disclose a cause of action? I need not restate the particular facts. The question is whether the manufacturer of an article of drink sold by him to a distributor, in circumstances which prevent the distributor or the ultimate purchaser from discovering by inspection any defect, is under any legal duty to the ultimate purchaser or consumer to take reasonable care that the article is free from defects likely to cause injury to health. I do not think a more important problem has occupied your Lordships in your judicial capacity: important both because of its bearing on public health and because of the practical test which it applies to the system under which it arises. The case has to be determined in accordance with Scots law; but it has been a matter of agreement between the experienced counsel who argued this case, and it appears to be the basis of the judgments of the learned judges of the Court of Session, that for the purposes of determining this problem the laws of Scotland and of England are the same. I speak with little authority on this point, but my own research, such as it is, satisfies me that the principles of the law of Scotland on such a question as the present are identical with those of English law; and I discuss the issue on that footing. The law of both countries appears to be that in order to support an action for negligence the complainant has to show that he has been injured by the breach of a duty owed to him in the circumstances by the defendant to take reasonable care to avoid such injury. In the present case we are not concerned with the breach of the duty; if a duty exists, that would be a question of fact which is sufficiently averred and for present purposes must be assumed. We are solely concerned with the question whether, as a matter of law in the circumstances alleged, the defender owed any duty to the pursuer to take care.

It is remarkable how difficult it is to find in the English authorities statements of general application defining the relations between parties that give rise to the duty. The courts are concerned with the particular relations which come before them in actual litigation, and it is sufficient to say whether the duty exists in those circumstances. The result is that the courts have been engaged upon an elaborate classification of duties as they exist in respect of property, whether real or personal, with further divisions as to ownership, occupation or control, and distinctions based on the particular relations of the one side or the other, whether manufacturer, salesman, landlord, customer, tenant, stranger, and so on. In this way it can be ascertained at any time whether the law recognises a duty, but only where the case can be referred to some particular species which has been determined and classified. And yet the duty which is common to all cases where liability is established must logically be based upon some element common to the cases where it is found to exist. To seek a complete logical definition of the general principle is probably to go beyond the function of the judge, for the more general the definition the more likely it is to omit essentials or to introduce non-essentials. The attempt was made by Brett MR in *Heaven v Pender* (1883) 11 QBD 503, in a definition to which I will later refer. As framed, it was demonstrably too wide, though it appears to me, if properly limited, to be capable of affording a valuable practical guide.

At present I content myself with pointing out that in English law there must be, and is, some general conception of relations giving rise to a duty of care, of which the particular cases found in the books are but rare instances. The liability for negligence, whether you style it such or treat it as in other systems as a species of 'culpa', is no doubt based upon a general public sentiment of moral wrongdoing for which the offender must pay. But acts or omissions which any moral code would censure cannot in a practical world be treated so as to give a right to every person injured by them to demand relief. In this way rules of law arise which limit the range of complainants and the extent of their remedy. The rule that you are to love your neighbour becomes in law, you must not injure your neighbour; and the lawyer's question, Who is my neighbour? receives a restricted reply. You must take reasonable care to avoid acts or omissions which you can reasonably foresee would be likely to injure your neighbour. Who, then, in law is my neighbour? The answer seems to be—persons who are so closely and directly affected by my act that I ought reasonably to have them in contemplation as being so affected when I am directing my mind to the acts or omissions which are called in question. This appears to me to be the doctrine of *Heaven v Pender*, as laid down by Lord Esher (then Brett MR) when it is limited by the notion of proximity introduced by Lord Esher himself and AL Smith LJ in *Le Lievre v Gould*. Lord Esher says: 'That case established that, under certain circumstances, one man may owe a duty to another, even though there is no contract between them. If one man is near to another, or is near to the property of another, a duty lies upon him not to do that which may cause a personal injury to that other, or may injure his property'.... I think that this sufficiently states the truth if proximity be not confined to mere physical proximity but be used, as I think it was intended, to extend to such close and direct relations that the act complained of directly affects a person whom the person alleged to be bound to take care would know would be directly affected by his careless act....

  With this necessary qualification of proximate relationship as explained in *Le Lievre v Gould*, I think the judgment of Lord Esher expresses the law of England; without the qualification I think the majority of the court in *Heaven v Pender* were justified in thinking the principle was expressed in too general terms. There will no doubt arise cases where it will be difficult to determine whether the contemplated relationship is so close that the duty arises. But in the class of case now before the court I cannot conceive any difficulty to arise. A manufacturer puts up an article of food in a container which he knows will be opened by the actual consumer. There can be no inspection by any purchaser and no reasonable preliminary inspection by the consumer. Negligently, in the course of preparation, he allows the content to be mixed with poison. It is said that the law of England and Scotland is that the poisoned consumer has no remedy against the negligent manufacturer. If this were the result of the authorities, I should consider the result a grave defect in the law, and so contrary to principle that I should hesitate long before following any decision to that effect which had not the authority of this House. I would point out that, in the assumed state of the authorities, not only would the consumer have no remedy against the manufacturer, he would have none against any one else, for in the circumstances alleged there would be no evidence of negligence against any one other than the manufacturer; and, except in the case of a consumer who was also a purchaser, no contract and no warranty of fitness, and in the case of a purchase of a specific article under its patent or trade name, which might well be the case in the purchase of some articles of food or drink, no warranty protecting even the purchaser consumer. There are other instances than of articles of food and drink where goods are sold intended to be used immediately by the consumer, such as many forms of goods sold for cleaning purposes where the same liability must exist. The doctrine supported by the decision below would not only deny a remedy to the consumer who was injured by consuming bottled beer or chocolates poisoned by the negligence of the manufacturer, but also to the user of what should be a harmless proprietary medicine, an ointment, a soap, a cleaning fluid or cleaning powder. I confine myself to articles of common household use, where every one, including the manufacturer, knows that the articles will be used by other persons than the actual ultimate purchaser—namely, by members of his family and his servants, and in some cases his guests. I do not think so ill of our jurisprudence as to suppose that its principles are so remote from the ordinary needs of civilised society and the ordinary claims it makes upon its members as to deny a legal remedy where there is so obviously a social wrong.

  It will be found, I think, on examination that there is no case in which the circumstances have been such as I have suggested where the liability has been negatived. There are numerous cases, where the relations were much more remote, where the duty has been held not to exist. There are also dicta in some cases which go further than was necessary for the determination of the particular issues, which have caused the difficulty experienced by the courts below. I venture to say that in the branch of the law which deals with civil wrongs, dependent in England at any rate entirely upon the application by judges of general principles also formulated by judges, it is of particular importance to guard against the danger of stating propositions of law in wider terms than is necessary, lest essential factors be omitted in the wider survey, and the inherent adaptability of English law be unduly restricted. For this reason it is very necessary in considering reported cases in the law of torts that the actual decision alone should carry authority, proper weight, of course, being given to the dicta of the judges. . . .

[His Lordship considered various decided cases, including *Winterbottom v Wright*, and continued:]

I do not find it necessary to discuss at length the cases dealing with duties where the thing is dangerous, or, in the narrower category, belongs to a class of things which are dangerous in themselves. I regard the distinction as an unnatural one so far as it is used to serve as a logical differentiation by which to distinguish the existence or non-existence of a legal right. In this respect I agree with what was said by Scrutton LJ in *Hodge & Sons v Anglo-American Oil Co* (1922) 12 L1 L Rep 183 at 187, a case which was ultimately decided on a question of fact: 'Personally, I do not understand the difference between a thing dangerous in itself, as poison, and a thing not dangerous as a class, but by negligent construction dangerous as a particular thing. The latter, if anything, seems the more dangerous of the two; it is a wolf in sheep's clothing instead of an obvious wolf'. The nature of the thing may very well call for different degrees of care, and the person dealing with it may well contemplate persons as being within the sphere of his duty to take care who would not be sufficiently proximate with less dangerous goods; so that not only the degree of care but the range of persons to whom a duty is owed may be extended. But they all illustrate the general principle. . . .

My Lords, if your Lordships accept the view that this pleading discloses a relevant cause of action you will be affirming the proposition that by Scots and English law alike a manufacturer of products, which he sells in such a form as to show that he intends them to reach the ultimate consumer in the form in which they left him with no reasonable possibility of intermediate examination, and with the knowledge that the absence of reasonable care in the preparation or putting up of the products will result in an injury to the consumer's life or property, owes a duty to the consumer to take that reasonable care.

It is preposition which I venture to say no one in Scotland or England who was not a lawyer would for one moment doubt. It will be an advantage to make it clear that the law in this matter, as in most others, is in accordance with sound common sense. I think that this appeal should be allowed.

Lord Macmillan

On the one hand, there is the well established principle that no one other than a party to a contract can complain of a breach of that contract. On the other hand, there is the equally well established doctrine that negligence apart from contract gives a right of action to the party injured by that negligence—and here I use the term negligence, of course, in its technical legal sense, implying a duty owed and neglected. The fact that there is a contractual relationship between the parties which may give rise to an action for breach of contract, does not exclude the co-existance of a right founded on negligence as between the same parties, independently of the contract, though arising out of the relationship in fact brought about by the contract. Of this the best illustration is the right of the injured railway passenger to sue the railway company either for breach of the contract of safe carriage or for negligence in carrying him. And there is no reason why the same set of facts should not give one person a right of action in contract and another person a right of action in tort. . . .

Where, as in cases like the present, so much depends upon the avenue of approach to the question, it is very easy to take the wrong turning. If you begin with the sale by the manufacturer to the retail dealer, then the consumer who purchases from the retailer is at once seen to be a stranger to the contract between the retailer and the manufacturer and so disentitled to sue upon it. There is no contractual relation between the manufacturer and the consumer; and thus the plaintiff, if he is to succeed, is driven to try to bring himself within one or other of the exceptional cases where the strictness of the rule that none but a party to a contract can found on a breach of that contract has been mitigated in the public interest, as it has been in the case of a person who issues a chattel which is inherently dangerous or which he knows to be in a dangerous condition. If, on the other hand, you disregard the fact that the circumstances of the case at one stage include the existence of a contract of sale between the manufacturer and the retailer and approach the question by asking whether there is evidence of careless-ness on the part of the manufacturer, and whether he owed a duty to be careful in a question with the party who has been injured in consequence of his want of care, the circumstance that the injured party was not a party to an incidental contract of sale becomes irrelevant, and his title to sue the manufacturer is unaffected by that circumstance. The appellant in the present instance asks that her case be approached as a case of delict [i.e. tort], not as a case of breach of contract. She does not require to invoke the exceptional cases in which a person not a party to a contract has been held entitled to complain of some defect in the subject matter of the con-tract which has caused him harm. The exceptional case of things dangerous in themselves, or known to be in a dangerous condition, has been regarded as constituting a peculiar category outside the ordinary law both of contract and of tort. I may observe that it seems to me inac-curate to describe the case of dangerous things as an exception to the principle that no one but a party to a contract can sue on that contract. I rather regard this type of case as a special instance of negligence where the law exacts a degree of diligence so stringent as to amount practically to a guarantee of safety....

The law takes no cognisance of carelessness in the abstract. It concerns itself with careless-ness only where there is a duty to take care and where failure in that duty has caused damage. In such circumstances carelessness assumes the legal quality of negligence and entails the consequences in law of negligence. What, then, are the circumstances which give rise to this duty to take care? In the daily contacts of social and business life human beings are thrown into, or place themselves, in an infinite variety of relations with their fellows; and the law can refer only to the standards of the reasonable man in order to determine whether any particular rela-tion give rise to a duty to take care as between those who stand in that relation to each other. The grounds of action may be as various and manifold as human errancy; and the conception of legal responsibility may develop in adaptation to altering social conditions and standards. The criterion of judgment must adjust and adapt itself to the changing circumstances of life. The categories of negligence are never closed. The cardinal principle of liability is that the party complained of should owe the party complaining a duty to take care, and that the party com-plaining should be able to prove that he has suffered damage in consequence of a breach of that duty. Where there is room for diversity of view, it is in determining what circumstances will establish such a relationship between the parties as to give rise, on the one side, to a duty to take care, and on the other side to a right to have care taken....

Now I have no hesitation in affirming that a person who for gain engages in the business of manufacturing articles of food and drink intended for consumption by members of the public in the form in which he issues them is under a duty to take care in the manufacture of these articles. That duty, in my opinion, he owes to those whom he intends to consume his products. He manufactures his commodities for human consumption; he intends and contemplates that they shall be consumed. By reason of that very fact he places himself in a relationship with all potential consumers of his commodities, and that relationship which he assumes and desires for his own ends imposes upon him a duty to take care to avoid injuring them....

Lord Buckmaster (dissenting)

I do not propose follow the fortunes of *George v Skivington*; few cases can have lived so dangerously and lived so long...So far, therefore, as the case of *George v Skivington* and the dicta in *Heaven v Pender* are concerned, it is in my opinion better that they should be buried so securely that their perturbed spirits shall no longer vex the law....

  The principle contended for must be this: that the manufacturer, or indeed repairer, of any article, apart entirely from contract, owes a duty to any person by whom the article is lawfully used to see that it has been carefully constructed. All rights in contract must be excluded from consideration of this principle; such contractual rights as may exist in successive steps from the original manufacturer down to the ultimate consumer are *ex hypothesi* immaterial. Nor can the doctrine be confined to cases where inspection is difficult or impossible to introduce. This conception is simply to misapply to tort doctrine applicable to sale and purchase....

  The principle of tort lies completely outside the region where such considerations apply, and the duty, if it exists, must extend to every person who, in lawful circumstances, uses the article made. There can be no special duty attaching to the manufacture of food apart from that implied by contract or imposed by statute. If such a duty exists, it seems to me it must cover the construction of every article, and I cannot see any reason why it should not apply to the construction of a house. If one step, why not fifty?...Were such a principle known and recognised, it seems to me impossible, having regard to the numerous cases that must have arisen to persons injured by its disregard, that, with the exception of *George v Skivington*, no case directly involving the principle has ever succeeded in the courts, and, were it well known and accepted, much of the discussion of the earlier cases would have been a waste of time, and the distinction as to articles dangerous in themselves or known to be dangerous would be meaningless....

  I am of opinion that this appeal should be dismissed, and I beg to move your Lordships accordingly.

Lord Thankerton delivered a speech allowing the appeal, whilst **Lord Tomlin** delivered a speech dismissing the appeal.

Appeal allowed.

COMMENTARY

Readers who take for granted the wide scope of the tort of negligence in the modern law may well underestimate the importance of *Donoghue v Stevenson*. Its immediate importance was to impose a duty on manufacturers in respect of the production of certain types of goods, i.e. those which could not be inspected before consumption or use. A similar case had only recently been dismissed in Scotland (*Mullen v AG Barr* [1929] Sess Cas 461—ginger beer bottle containing a mouse) so this action was hardly a foregone conclusion when it reached the House of Lords. That the case ever made it to the Lords was due to the perseverance of the pursuer's lawyers (who had also acted for the pursuers in *Mullen*) who successfully petitioned the House of Lords to allow Mrs Donoghue to proceed as a pauper (the case being before the advent of legal aid). The development of the law of products liability from this beginning will be considered briefly below.

The 'Privity Fallacy'

On a wider doctrinal level, the majority of the House of Lords held that the existence of a contract between the defendant and a third party did not prevent the defendant owing a duty to the plaintiff in tort in relation to the performance of that contract. Hence the 'privity of contract' fallacy was exposed. *Winterbottom v Wright* was distinguished on the ground that the plaintiff in that case had sought to found his claim on the defendant's breach of contract with a third party, not his breach of an independent tortious duty owed directly to the plaintiff ('no duty was alleged other than the duty arising out of the contract': [1932] AC 562 at 589, per Lord Atkin). Whether *Winterbottom* and the cases which followed it could be distinguished so easily is another matter (see Palmer, 'Why Privity Entered Tort—An Historical Re-examination of *Winterbottom v Wright*' (1983) 27 Am JLH 85) but, after *Donoghue*, the existence of a contract between the defendant and a third party has rarely affected the defendant's tort liability to a claimant who suffers personal injury. However, it should be noted that Lord Buckmaster's 'floodgates' concerns, rejected in *Donoghue*, have proved much more persuasive in cases involving pure economic loss.

The 'Neighbour Principle'

Despite the above achievements, the case is probably best known for Lord Atkin's neighbour principle. As can be seen from the majority speeches, it does not form part of the ratio of the case, but the decision has nevertheless been regarded as introducing into the law a general moral principle of 'good neighbourliness'. To answer the question whether A owes B a duty of care necessarily requires a consideration of whether A ought to take care to look after B's interests (see Howarth, 'Negligence after Murphy: Time to Re-Think' [1991] CLJ 58, 68–70). Knowledge of Lord Atkin's personal views helps to explain his conviction that we all have a duty to take care of our 'neighbours'. His biographer has described his Christian faith as a 'strong constant in his life', and a speech he gave to an audience at King's College London in October 1931 (less than two months before *Donoghue v Stevenson* was argued) is replete with references to the relationship between law and morality (see 'Law as an Educational Subject', extracted above); in addition, it is known that Lord Atkin discussed the concept of 'neighbour' with his family and guests over the summer of 1931 (see generally G. Lewis, *Lord Atkin* (London: Butterworths, 1983)).

Lord Atkin's reliance upon a broad moral principle should be contrasted with the more pragmatic approach of Lord Macmillan. Lord Macmillan had originally drafted a speech deciding the case by reference to Scottish law, but it seems likely that Lord Atkin persuaded him (and perhaps also Lord Thankerton) to widen the decision to cover English law as well (see Rodger, 'Lord Macmillan's Speech in *Donoghue v Stevenson*' (1992) 108 LQR 236), a not unreasonable suggestion as the case had been argued on the basis that English and Scottish law were the same. For Lord Macmillan, the 'categories of negligence are never closed' and 'the conception of legal responsibility may develop in adaptation to altering social conditions and standards'. This gives little practical guidance on when a duty of care should be owed and leaves the issue to be decided in each and every specific factual matrix. Although it can hardly be regarded as conducive to certainty in the law, his cautious, case-by-case approach bears very great similarities to that currently favoured by the courts (see especially *Caparo Industries plc v Dickman*, below).

Further historical background on the case can be found in Rodger, 'Mrs Donoghue and Alfenus Varus' (1988) CLP 1; P. Burns (ed.), *Donoghue v Stevenson and the Modern Law of Negligence* (Vancouver: CLE, 1991); McBryde, '*Donoghue v Stevenson*: The Story of the "Snail in the Bottle" Case' in A. Gamble (ed.), *Obligations in Context* (Edinburgh: EUP, 1990). It was never actually determined whether there was a snail in the ginger beer bottle; the defender died before proofs were required and the matter was settled with his estate in December 1934 (see (1955) 71 LQR 472).

3. *Donoghue v Stevenson* in Action—The Development of Liability for Defective Products

Grant v Australian Knitting Mills Ltd [1936] AC 85

The plaintiff bought two pairs of long underwear (known as Long Johns) from a retail shop. The defendants were the manufacturers who had supplied the goods to the retailers and the retailer. After he had worn one of the pairs for a couple of days, the plaintiff's legs began to itch and appeared red. After a week he sent that pair for washing and wore the second pair, and by the time he visited a dermatologist and was advised to dispose of the garments one pair had been washed twice and the other once. Despite this the rash worsened and spread; he was in bed for seventeen weeks and spent a further three months in hospital after a relapse. His dermatologist at one stage feared he might die. He sued the retailers for breach of contract and the manufacturers in negligence. He was successful against both at first instance, but the High Court of Australia overturned the decision on the basis that the goods were not sold in breach of contract and there was no evidence of negligence. The manufacturers provided details of the precautions they took to ensure no chemicals remained in the clothes, and stated that they had received no complaints in respect of 4,737,600 other garments treated in the same manner. The plaintiff successfully appealed to the Privy Council, who held that the Australian High Court could not be satisfied that the inferences drawn by the trial judge as to defectiveness were wrong.

Lord Wright

[W]hen the position of the manufacturers is considered, different questions arise; there is no privity of contract between the appellant and the manufacturers; between them the liability, if any, must be in tort, and the gist of the cause of action is negligence. The facts set out in the foregoing show in their Lordships' judgment negligence in manufacture. According to the evidence, the method of manufacture was correct; the danger of excess sulphites being left was recognised and was guarded against; the process was intended to be foolproof. If excess sulphites were left in the garment, that could only be because someone was at fault. The appellant is not required to lay his finger on the exact person in all the chain who was responsible or to specify what he did wrong. Negligence is found as a matter of inference from the existence of the defects taken in connection with all the known circumstances; even if the manufacturers could by apt evidence have rebutted that inference they have not done so.

On this basis, the damage suffered by the appellant was caused in fact (because the interposition of the retailers may for this purpose in the circumstances of the case be disregarded) by the negligent or improper way in which the manufacturers made the garments. But this mere sequence of cause and effect is not enough in law to constitute a cause of action in negligence, which is a complex concept, involving a duty as between the parties to take care, as well as a breach of that duty and resulting damage. It might be said that here there was no relationship between the parties at all; the manufacturers, it might be said, parted once and for all with the garments when they sold them to the retailers and were, therefore, not concerned with their future history, except in so far as under their contract with the retailers they might come under some liability; at no time, it might be said, had they any knowledge of the existence of the appellant; the only peg on which it might be sought to support a relationship of duty was the fact that the appellant had actually worn the garments but he had done so because he had acquired them by a purchase from the retailers, who were at that time the owners of the goods, by a sale which had vested the property in the retailers. It was said there could be no legal relationship in the matter save those under the two contracts between the respective parties to those contracts, the one between the manufacturers and the retailers and the other between the retailers and the appellant. These contractual relationships (it might be said) covered the whole field and excluded any question of tort liability; there was no duty other than the contractual duties.

This argument was based on the contention that the present case fell outside the decision of the House of Lords in *Donoghue (or McAlister) v Stevenson* [1932] AC 562. Their Lordships, like the judges in the courts in Australia, will follow that decision, and the only question here can be what that authority decides and whether this case comes within its principles. . . .

It is clear that the decision treats negligence, where there is a duty to take care, as a specific tort in itself, and not simply as an element in some more complex relationship or in some specialised breach of duty, and still less as having any dependence on contract. All that is necessary as a step to establish the tort of actionable negligence is to define the precise relationship from which the duty to take care is to be deduced. It is, however, essential in English law that the duty should be established; the mere fact that a man is injured by another's act gives in itself no cause of action; if the act is deliberate, the party injured will have no claim in law even though the injury is intentional, so long as the other party is merely exercising a legal right; if the act involves lack of due care, again no case of actionable negligence will arise unless the duty to be careful exists. In *Donoghue's* case, the duty was deduced simply from the facts relied on, namely, that the injured party was one of a class for whose use, in the contemplation and intention of the makers, the article was issued to the world, and the article was used by that party in the state in which it was prepared and issued without it being changed in any way and without there being any warning of, or means of detecting, the hidden danger; there was, it is true, no personal intercourse between the maker and the user; but though the duty is personal, because it is inter partes, it needs no interchange of words, spoken or written, or signs of offer or assent; it is thus different in character from any contractual relationship; no question of consideration between the parties is relevant; for these reasons the use of the word 'privity' in this connection is apt to mislead because of the suggestion of some overt relationship like that in contract, and the word 'proximity' is open to the same objection; if the term proximity is to be applied at all, it can only be in the sense that the want of care and the injury are in essence directly and intimately connected; though there may be intervening transactions of sale and purchase and intervening handling between these two events, the events are themselves unaffected by what happened between them; proximity can only properly be used to exclude any element of remoteness, or of some interfering complication between the want of care and the injury, and, like 'privity', may mislead by introducing alien ideas. Equally also may the word 'control' embarrass, though it is conveniently used in the opinions in *Donoghue's* case to emphasise the essential factor that the consumer must use the article exactly as it left the maker, that is in all material features, and use it as it was intended to be used. In that sense the maker may be said to control the thing until it is used. But that again is an artificial use, because, in the natural sense of the word, the makers parted with all control when they sold the article and divested themselves of possession and property. An argument used in the present case based on the word 'control' will be noticed later.

It is obvious that the principles thus laid down involve a duty based on the simple facts detailed above, a duty quite unaffected by any contracts dealing with the thing, for instance, of sale by maker to retailer, and again by retailer to consumer or to the consumer's friend. . . .

If the foregoing are the essential features of *Donoghue's* case they are also to be found, in their Lordships' judgment, in the present case. The presence of the deleterious chemical in the pants, due to negligence in manufacture, was a hidden and latent defect, just as much as were the remains of the snail in the opaque bottle: it could not be detected by any examination that could reasonably be made. Nothing happened between the making of the garments and their being worn to change their condition. The garments were made by the manufacturers for the purpose of being worn exactly as they were worn in fact by the appellant; it was not contemplated that they should be first washed. It is immaterial that the appellant has a claim in contract against the retailers; because that is a quite independent cause of action, based on different considerations, even though the damage may be the same. Equally irrelevant is any question of liability between the retailers and the manufacturers on the contract of sale between them. The tort liability is independent of any question of contract . . .

Counsel for the respondents, however, sought to distinguish *Donoghue's* case from the present on the ground that in the former the makers of the ginger beer had retained 'control' over it in the sense that they had placed it in stoppered and sealed bottles, so that it would not be tampered with until it was opened to be drunk, whereas the garments in question were merely put into paper packets, each containing six sets, which in ordinary course would be taken down by the shopkeeper and opened and the contents handled and disposed of separately so that they would be exposed to the air. He contended that, though there was no reason to think that the garments, when sold to the appellant were in any other condition, least of all as regards sulphur contents, than when sold to the retailers by the manufacturers, still the mere possibility and not the fact of their condition having been changed was sufficient to distinguish *Donoghue's* case; there was no 'control' because nothing was done by the manufacturers to exclude the possibility of any tampering while the goods were on their way to the user. Their Lordships do not accept that contention. The decision in *Donoghue's* case did not depend on the bottle being stoppered and sealed; the essential point in this regard was that the article should reach the consumer or user subject to the same defect it had when it left the manufacturer. That this was true of the garment is in their Lordships opinion beyond question. At most there might in other cases be a greater difficulty of proof of the fact.

Counsel further contended on behalf of the manufacturers that, if the decision in *Donoghue's* case were extended even a hair's-breadth, no line could be drawn and a manufacturer's liability would be extended indefinitely. He put as an illustration the case of a foundry which had cast a rudder to be fitted on a liner; he assumed that it was fitted and the steamer sailed the seas for some years; but the rudder had a latent defect due to faulty and negligent casting and one day it broke, with the result that the vessel was wrecked, with great loss of life and damage to property. He argued that, if *Donoghue's* case were extended beyond its precise facts, the maker of the rudder would be held liable for damages of an indefinite amount, after an indefinite time and to claimants indeterminate until the event. But it is clear that such a state of things would involve many considerations far removed from the simple facts of this case. So many contingencies must have intervened between the lack of care on the part of the makers and the casualty that it may be that the law would apply, as it does in proper cases, not always according to strict logic, the rule that cause and effect must not be too remote. In any case the element of directness would obviously be lacking. Lord Atkin deals with that sort of question in *Donoghue's* case at 591 where he refers to *Earl v Lubbock* [1905] 1 KB 253; he quotes the common sense opinion of Mathew LJ: 'It is impossible to accept such a wide proposition, and, indeed, it is difficult to see how, if it were the law, trade could be carried on.'

In their Lordships' opinion it is enough for them to decide this case on its actual facts. No doubt, many difficult problems will arise before the precise limits of the principle are defined: many qualifying conditions and many complications of fact may in the future come before the courts for decision. It is enough to say that their Lordships hold the present case to come within the principle of *Donoghue's* case and they think that the judgment of the Chief Justice was right and should be restored as against both respondents. . . .

Appeal allowed.

COMMENTARY

Unlike *Donoghue v Stevenson*, the above appeal was about the correctness of a judgment on the merits, and not a decision on a preliminary issue of law. Hence the court was required to consider whether all the elements of a cause of action in negligence were complete: there had to be a duty of care, and a breach of that duty which had caused the claimant damage. We shall consider each of the elements in turn in order to provide a general overview of the most important issues that arise in negligence litigation.

Duty

The existence of a duty of care is the primary requirement for a successful claim in negligence. If there is no duty, the failure to take reasonable care cannot give rise to liability. The chief significance of *Donoghue v Stevenson* was in providing a generalised concept of duty which was applicable to a wide range of different situations. Gradually, with the passage of time, the circumstances in which duties of care were recognised moved further and further from the specific factual context of the leading case. And potential limitations on the scope of liability under the principle of *Donoghue v Stevenson* in cases where the plaintiff suffered physical injury were rejected.

The early stages of this process are evident in *Grant*. One question for the Privy Council was whether *Donoghue v Stevenson* applied only to products which the manufacturer supplied in a sealed and opaque container (like the bottle of ginger beer in the earlier case). This was a plausible interpretation of certain passages of their Lordship's speeches in *Donoghue*, but it was rejected by the Privy Council, who ruled that the essential question was whether the product reached the consumer subject to the same defect it had when it left the manufacturer. Another question for the Privy Council was whether the fact that the defect might have been discovered precluded the imposition of a duty of care on the manufacturer, given that Lord Atkin had stated in *Donoghue* that there should be 'no reasonable possibility of intermediate examination'. On the facts, the Privy Council ruled that the presence of the chemicals in the pants could not have been detected by any examination that could reasonably have been made, and so the limitation—which arose only where there was a reasonable possibility of discovering the defect—did not apply. Subsequently, it has been made clear that Lord Atkin's words did not lay down a separate requirement of liability under *Donoghue v Stevenson* and that liability can arise even if a third party did have a reasonable opportunity of inspecting the goods (*Griffiths v Arch Engineering Co Ltd* [1968] 3 All ER 217). It seems therefore that the possibility of intermediate examination goes to the question of causation rather than to the existence of a duty.

Later decisions take the process of 'stretching' the principle still further. It has been recognised, for instance, that a manufacturer owes a duty of care not only to the consumer of the product in question, but to anyone—even a 'by-blow victim'—who is injured by the product (*Stennett v Hancock* [1939] 2 All ER 578). And the range of potential defendants has also been extended, for example, to the repairer of a product who negligently leaves it in a dangerous state (*Haseldine v Daw & Sons Ltd* [1941] 2 KB 343). The result has been, in the last 70 years or so, a rapid expansion in the scope of the tort of negligence as the number of 'duty situations' has multiplied. In so far as physical injury is caused by the positive act of a private individual, it is now safe as a general rule to assume the existence of a duty of care.

Nevertheless, the extension of liability into other types of case has proved problematic—especially where the type of loss that the claimant has suffered is purely economic or psychiatric, or the alleged negligence consists of an omission rather than a positive act, or the defendant is a public body rather than a private individual. In such cases, the courts have limited the circumstances in which a duty of care will arise for a variety of reasons (see Chs 7–10). A major concern has been that the recognition of a duty of care would result in a 'liability in an indeterminate amount for an indeterminate time to an indeterminate class' (*Ultramares Corp v Touche, Niven & Co* (1931) 174 NE 441 at 444, per Cardozo J). This 'floodgates' concern has not, however, been a significant factor restricting liability in simple cases of physical harm caused by another's positive act. Indeed, in *Grant*, counsel for the defendants, paraphrasing Cardozo's famous words, argued with a conspicuous lack of success that the court should not recognise a duty lest it open up a vista of indeterminate liability. The restrictive approach to the recognition of duties in 'problematic' cases should not mask the broad scope of the duty of care applying to 'simple' cases (as defined above). It is quite unthinkable, for instance, that anyone would ever deny the existence of a duty of care in respect of personal injuries caused by accidents in the workplace, collisions on the roads or railways, or dangerously defective products.

Breach

The case also raises the question of breach of duty (i.e. actual carelessness) by the defendant. All the plaintiff could do was point to the existence of the sulphur in the clothing; he could not suggest how or why it was there or who was responsible for it. In response the manufacturer suggested they had received no complaints about the 4,737,600 other garments treated the same way. If these figures are to be believed, the percentage chance that sulphur would remain in a garment was 0.000021. *Weir* (p. 26) suggests that such a low rate of failure should have entitled the manufacturer to a prize rather than a finding of negligence.

If such a high standard of performance can amount to negligence, one might question the extent to which liability is really fault-based. In the United States, the common law liability of the manufacturer to the ultimate consumer developed beyond negligence to strict liability, that is, liability without fault (see Prosser, 'The Fall of the Citadel' (1966) 50 Minn L Rev 791), and a similar regime of strict liability for defective products was introduced in the United Kingdom by the Consumer Protection Act 1987, Part 1 (see Ch. 11.IV). In strict liability the issue is not whether the defendant has exercised reasonable care in manufacturing the product but whether the product in question was defective. Strict liability can be defended on economic grounds: 'The cost of accidents should be "internalised" to the enterprise that is the best cost-avoider; and in so far as that cost is passed on by the producer to the customer, it may not only reflect itself in competitive pricing but the cost will be spread among all consumers of the product' (*Fleming*, p. 551). Seen thus, liability for defective products is simply a cost of business and is dealt with like other costs; the price of a product ought therefore to include an element to reflect the cost of obtaining insurance against that liability. Although strict product liability has been the subject of intense criticism in the United States for some considerable time (see P. Huber, *Liability* (New York: Basic Books, 1990); W. Olson, *The Litigation Explosion* (New York: Truman Tally, 1992)), most of the criticism has been directed at the number of actions and the level of damages rather than at the idea itself. In the United Kingdom, the introduction of strict liability for defective products seems to have excited little opposition. The question whether other strict liabilities should be introduced into English law is considered below, p. 974.

It is worth noting at this point that it was the English common law's preference for a tort—rather than contract—based analysis of the manufacturer's liability that led it to rest that liability on a finding of fault. If the courts had recognised a contractual warranty as to fitness for purpose or quality owed to the ultimate consumer of the product then the resultant liability would have been strict, for the taking of all reasonable care is no defence to an action for breach of warranty. It was perhaps open to the House of Lords in *Donoghue* to set the law along this course by straightforwardly overruling *Winterbottom v Wright*, rather than distinguishing it on the basis that the plaintiff in the earlier action had pleaded his case in contract, not tort. This solution would undoubtedly have required a significant modification of the contractual doctrines of privity and consideration, but it would have accorded consumers the benefits associated with strict liability. Professor Milsom has commented: 'At the time [of *Donoghue*] it seemed a triumph to reach the manufacturer purely on the basis of wrong, and to exclude any trace of contractual analysis. But perhaps it was the contractual position that really needed reconsidering' (*Historical Foundations of the Common Law*, 2nd edn. (London: Butterworths, 1981), p. 400). However, as *Grant* illustrates, the malleability of the fault concept allows tribunals of fact to impose liability even where the manufacturer appears to have done all that could reasonably be expected of it.

Causation

There must be a causal link between the claimant's injury and the defendant's breach of his duty of care. The concept of causation brings together a number of discrete principles, which are well illustrated by the product liability cases. First, it must be established that the defendant's negligent conduct was the factual cause of the claimant's loss, in the sense that the loss would not have occurred but for the negligence. In *Evans v Triplex Safety Glass Co Ltd* [1936] 1 All ER 283, the plaintiffs sued in respect of an allegedly defective windscreen which had broken and showered them with shards of glass. The claim failed because, even assuming negligence on the defendants' part, there was no evidence that this rather than various other possible causes was the actual cause of the windscreen's distintegration: the damage might very well have occurred even if the defendants had taken all reasonable care. (Additionally, the court ruled that the allegation that the defendants had failed to take reasonable care could not be substantiated.) Secondly, there is the requirement of legal causation. Even if the hurdle of but-for or factual causation is overcome, the court may have to consider whether acts or omissions intervening in point of time between the defendant's breach of duty and the claimant's injury 'break the chain of causation' so as to negate the defendant's responsibility for the injury. In *Burrows v March Gas & Coke Co* (1872) LR 7 Ex 96, the defendants supplied the plaintiff with a defective pipe; when a gas-fitter called in to look for the source of an escape of gas searched for it with a lighted candle, he caused an explosion which did damage to the plaintiff. Although the explosion would not have happened but for the defendants' earlier breach of duty, they could not be regarded as a cause of loss which resulted immediately from a third party's reckless conduct. Although the case (which pre-dated *Donoghue v Stevenson*) was in fact decided in contract, there is no doubt that the court would have adopted the same analysis even if it had recognised a tortious duty (albeit that a modern court might well find both parties to be responsible for the accident: see p. 266). Lastly, there is the question of remoteness. A defendant is only responsible for types of loss that are the reasonably foreseeable consequence of his negligence. If the claimant sustains a loss of a different type, that is too remote.

What if the claimant makes use of a product which obviously has a dangerous defect? In such a case it could be said that he was the cause of his own loss, but this will depend on whether he ignored the danger deliberately or inadvertently. In *Grant* Lord Wright stated that 'the man who consumes or uses a thing which he knows to be noxious cannot complain in respect of whatever mischief follows because it follows from his own conscious volition in choosing to incur the risk or certainty of mischance'. The same result is achieved whether the court finds the causal link with the manufacturer's negligence to have been broken or relies instead on the defence that the claimant has voluntarily assumed the risk of harm (*volenti non fit injuria*). If, however, the claimant has not consciously adverted to the danger, it may not be appropriate to allow the manufacturer to escape all liability. This might be a case for the operation of the partial defence of contributory negligence, which provides for a reduction in the damages award in proportion to the claimant's own responsibility for the injury. (Even where the claimant consciously runs the risk of injury, it may be going too far to prevent him from claiming altogether and the court may prefer simply to reduce his damages for contributory negligence.) The interaction of principles of causation with the various defences that can be raised to a negligence action is considered further at pp. 263–8, below.

Damage

Unlike trespass to the person, negligence (descended from the action on the case) is not actionable *per se*: it is necessary to prove that the claimant suffered legally-recognised damage as a result of the defendant's breach of duty. However, not all kinds of damage receive equal treatment from the law of negligence. The law reserves its most general protection for interests in the physical integrity of property and the person. But purely financial interests, for example, are protected only exceptionally. So if a negligently-manufactured product causes physical injury or property damage, there is generally no obstacle to recovery, but if the claim is simply that the product does not work—and so has caused the claimant to incur repair costs or to lose trade or business—this purely economic loss is unlikely to give rise to liability (see Ch. 8). Financial interests are of a lesser order than interests in physical integrity, and the law by and large leaves individuals to make their own (contractual) arrangements for the protection of their financial affairs.

It is crucial to note that English law treats the classification of the claimant's loss as a matter going primarily to the existence of a duty of care. The existence of the duty must be considered separately in respect of each different type of loss suffered by the claimant; a finding that the defendant owed a duty of care in respect of one type of loss does not entail that there is a duty in respect of others. Other legal systems address the nature of the claimant's loss more directly. Under the German civil code, the *Bürgerliches Gesetzbuch* (BGB), for example, the most general principle of liability for negligence, under 823 I BGB, applies only in respect of certain 'protected interests' which, for the most part, are set out in the code itself (see pp. 123–4, below). English law's rather indirect way of attaching significance to the type of loss suffered by the claimant should nevertheless not be allowed to obscure the vital role played by that factor in determining liability in negligence.

II. The Duty of Care in the Modern Law

As we have seen, *Donoghue v Stevenson* established the pre-eminent role of the 'duty of care' concept in the tort of negligence. Fault, causation and damage are all irrelevant if the defendant is under no duty to the claimant, although each of the above may be factors influencing whether a duty will be owed. The Roman lawyer Buckland may have been able to suggest in 1935 that the duty of care was 'an unnecessary fifth wheel on the coach, incapable of sound analysis and possibly productive of injustice' ('The Duty to Take Care' (1935) 51 LQR 637), but the modern law treats the duty concept as an indispensable tool with which to denote when a person should be held responsible for the consequences of his negligence—and when he should be safeguarded against liability in respect of those consequences. In fact, it is helpful to regard the duty concept as primarily concerned with cases of the latter sort: 'duty of care cases are really about giving the defendant an immunity against liability in negligence' (Howarth, 'Negligence after Murphy: Time to Re-Think' [1991] CLJ 58 at 93–4). The reasons why such an immunity should be granted are considered below.

Some modern commentators have argued that there is not a single 'duty of care'; there are numerous 'duties of care' of a relatively high degree of specificity—a duty to do x rather than a general duty to exercise reasonable care in the circumstances (see McBride, 'Duties of Care—Do they Really Exist?' (2004) 24 OJLS 417). One difficulty with this approach is that it tends to conflate the 'duty of care' question with the 'breach of duty' question. As Howarth, 'Many Duties of Care—Or a Duty of Care? Notes from the Underground' (2006) 26 OJLS 449, 466 argues:

> Judges who follow the 'many duties' path tend to use the phrase 'there was no duty' even where the defendant's case is that they acted reasonably, not that there was no legal requirement for them to act reasonably. These judges tend to claim that the question is whether there was a duty to take precisely the precaution the defendant is accused of failing to take. But that view collapses the distinction between the two arguments. Indeed, if such a way of thinking were taken to its logical conclusion, there would never be any separate consideration of breach of duty since the issue would already have been resolved in setting the precise 'duty' involved. The concept of fault would disappear.

In our view, the duty of care is best viewed as a 'control device' for determining when defendants will (or will not) be placed under a generalised duty to exercise reasonable care in respect of their conduct, and held liable in damages for failing to do so, as opposed to giving specific advice to defendants as to how they should have acted in a given situation. The latter determination is made in the breach of duty element of the cause of action in negligence.

1. Introduction: Duty as 'Control Device'

The duty of care's role as a control device can be illuminated by comparing the approach of English law with that of other jurisdictions that do without any concept of 'duty' at all. In France, the *Code civil* imposes a general obligation to pay compensation for losses caused by the fault of another. The control mechanism used to limit liability is the law of causation (*van Dam*, para. 604-3) but this control is exerted in a much less systematic fashion than in English law, and it is apparent that French law has a much more expansive conception of liability for fault than that to be found in the common law. Conversely, the German civil code (BGB) in Article 823 I provides for compensation to be paid where a list of protected interests are infringed intentionally or negligently; these include the life, body, health, freedom, ownership of another (for general analysis, see B. Markesinis and H. Unberath, *The German Law of Torts: A Comparative Treatise*, 4th edn. (Oxford: Hart Publishing, 2002), ch. 2). It is the protected interests (*Rechtsgüter*) that provide the principal limitation on the scope of liability for negligence (and indeed for intentional injury). In English law, that function is performed by the concept of the duty of care, though the set of protected interests is nowhere set out in explicit fashion, while the related question of what constitutes actionable 'damage' has been neglected to a very considerable extent (see further Nolan, 'New Forms of Damage in Negligence' (2007) 70 MLR 59). Additionally, the duty concept's role in delimiting the interests protected in the tort of negligence may be obscured by the sheer variety of factors—including an apparently unlimited set of potentially relevant policy considerations—that affect the decision whether or not a duty of care arises on the facts. To the advantage of the English practice, however, is the possibility of taking account of the protected interests in a more nuanced fashion—allowing for greater or lesser protection according to the perceived importance of the interest infringed in the individual case. A different approach is therefore possible depending on whether the damage takes the form of personal injury, property damage, pure economic loss or some other type of actionable harm.

The *Principles of European Tort Law* (Vienna: Springer, 2005) elaborated by the European Group on Tort Law, an informal study group of tort law experts from different jurisdictions, attempt a synthesis of the best elements of common law and civil law tort traditions. Their 'general conditions of liability', applicable (as in most European systems) to both intentional and negligent conduct, state that '[d]amage requires material or immaterial harm to a legally protected interest' (Article 2:101). The protected interests are then introduced in a fashion which seeks to combine explicit statement (as in the German civil code) with flexibility of treatment (as under the common law).

Principles of European Tort Law, Article. 2:102: Protected Interests

(1) The scope of protection of an interest depends on its nature; the higher its value, the precision of its definition and its obviousness, the more extensive is its protection.

(2) Life, bodily or mental integrity, human dignity and liberty enjoy the most extensive protection.

(3) Extensive protection is granted to property rights, including those in intangible property.

(4) Protection of pure economic interests or contractual relationships may be more limited in scope. In such cases, due regard must be had especially to the proximity between the actor and the endangered person, or to the fact that the actor is aware of the fact that he will cause damage even though his interests are necessarily valued lower than those of the victim.

Some academics go even further than the protected interests approach, arguing that private law duties, including the duty of care, can only be correlative to a right possessed by the claimant. For example, as the claimant has a right to bodily safety, a defendant owes a duty to be careful not to infringe that right (see, e.g. R. Stevens, *Torts and Rights* (Oxford: OUP, 2007)). On this view, the classification of damage is only relevant in so far as it helps to illustrate whether an underlying right of the claimant has been infringed. Part of the attraction for adherents of rights-based approaches to negligence law is the belief that it can generate a law of negligence that is not affected by the policy considerations referred to above (see A. Beever, *Rediscovering the Law of Negligence* (Oxford: Hart, 2007)). The extent to which the law of negligence, or the law of tort more generally, can or should be based on this approach is controversial and it is likely that policy factors will continue to play a role, along with the type of harm suffered by the claimant, in determining the duty of care question.

The function of the duty of care concept in English law, and its role in determining which interests are protected by the English law of negligence, and what counts as actionable damage, were considered by the House of Lords in *D v East Berkshire Community NHS Trust*, below.

D v East Berkshire Community Health NHS Trust [2005] 2 AC 373

The claimants alleged negligence on the part of the defendant's child welfare professionals (doctors and social workers) who had formed the opinion, subsequently shown to be erroneous, that the claimants had been guilty of abuse towards their children. The case is given fuller consideration below (p. 527), where the facts are stated in more detail. For now, it is enough to note that one argument advanced for the claimants was that the duty concept was an inappropriate 'control mechanism' for dealing with the relevant policy considerations, and that the material factors were better taken into account in determining whether or not there had been a breach of duty.

Lord Nicholls

92 A wider approach has also been canvassed. The suggestion has been made that, in effect, the common law should jettison the concept of duty of care as a universal prerequisite to liability in negligence. Instead the standard of care should be 'modulated' to accommodate the complexities arising in fields such as social workers dealing with children at risk of abuse . . . The contours of liability should be traced in other ways.

  93 For some years it has been all too evident that identifying the parameters of an expanding law of negligence is proving difficult, especially in fields involving the discharge of statutory functions by public authorities. So this radical suggestion is not without attraction. This approach would be analogous to that adopted when considering breaches of human rights under the European Convention. Sometimes in human rights cases the identity of the defendant, whether the state in claims under the Convention or a public authority in claims under the Human Rights Act 1998, makes it appropriate for an international or domestic court to look backwards over everything which happened. In deciding whether overall the end result was acceptable the court makes a value judgment based on more flexible notions than the common law standard of reasonableness and does so freed from the legal rigidity of a duty of care.

  94 This approach, as I say, is not without attraction. It is peculiarly appropriate in the field of human rights. But I have reservations about attempts to transplant this approach wholesale into the domestic law of negligence in cases where . . . no claim is made for breach of a Convention right. Apart from anything else, such an attempt would be likely to lead to a lengthy and unnecessary period of uncertainty in an important area of the law. It would lead to uncertainty because there are types of cases where a person's acts or omissions do not render him liable in negligence for another's loss even though this loss may be foreseeable. My noble and learned friend, Lord Rodger of Earlsferry, has given some examples. Abandonment of the concept of a duty of care in English law, unless replaced by a control mechanism which recognises this limitation, is unlikely to clarify the law. That control mechanism has yet to be identified. And introducing this protracted period of uncertainty is unnecessary, because claims may now be brought directly against public authorities in respect of breaches of Convention rights.

Lord Rodger

100 . . . [T]he world is full of harm for which the law furnishes no remedy. For instance, a trader owes no duty of care to avoid injuring his rivals by destroying their long-established businesses. If he does so and, as a result, one of his competitors descends into a clinical depression and his family are reduced to penury, in the eyes of the law they suffer no wrong and the law will provide no redress—because competition is regarded as operating to the overall good of the economy and society. A young man whose fiancée deserts him for his best friend may become clinically depressed as a result, but in the circumstances the fiancée owes him no duty of care to avoid causing this suffering. So he too will have no right to damages for his illness. The same

goes for a middle-aged woman whose husband runs off with a younger woman. Experience suggests that such intimate matters are best left to the individuals themselves. However badly one of them may have treated the other, the law does not get involved in awarding damages.

101 Other relationships are also important. We may have children, parents, grandparents, brothers, sisters, uncles and aunts—not to mention friends, colleagues, employees and employers—who play an essential part in our lives and contribute to our happiness and prosperity. We share in their successes, but are also affected by anything bad which happens to them. So it is—and always has been—readily foreseeable that if a defendant injures or kills someone, his act is likely to affect not only the victim but many others besides. To varying degrees, these others can plausibly claim to have suffered real harm as a result of the defendant's act. For the most part, however, the policy of the law is to concentrate on compensating the victim for the effects of his injuries while doing little or nothing for the others. In technical language, the defendants owe a duty of care to the victim but not to the third parties, who therefore suffer no legal wrong.

COMMENTARY

These extracts highlight a number of important points. First, one of the important functions of the duty of care in English law (but not its only function) is to determine whether or not the claimant has suffered loss that is recognised by law. In fact, we should say 'by the law of negligence' because what constitutes actionable damage may vary from tort to tort. Lord Rodger's examples are of cases where the loss in question may be styled *damnum* but not *injuria*, following a famous distinction made in Roman law: i.e. a loss that the law does not recognise as actionable damage. Secondly, the duty concept allows not just for a distinction between actionable and non-actionable damage, but also for an intermediate category of damage actionable under a limited set of circumstances. The 'ricochet' losses considered by Lord Rodger in [100] provide examples. The relatives of the victim may, in certain limited circumstances, have a claim against the injurer for their own losses that are consequential on the victim's injury, e.g. their mental suffering or their loss of economically valuable services. English law identifies such claims as falling in areas of 'limited duty', and prescribes specific requirements that they must satisfy (e.g. requirements of proximity or voluntary assumption of responsibility) if a duty of care is in fact to be recognised. Thirdly, whether or not a duty of care arises depends not only on the nature of the claimant's loss, but also on a variety of other 'complexities'. Depending on the circumstances of the case, the court may take account of *how* the loss was caused (positive act or omission?), whether it was caused directly by the defendant or through a third party, and whether the claim has a public law dimension because the defendant is a public body, as well as an apparently unlimited set of policy factors relevant to the 'fairness, justice and reasonableness' of imposing a duty of care.

In *D v East Berkshire*, Lord Bingham stated, at [49], that he would regard a shift of emphasis from consideration of duty to consideration of breach as 'welcome', adding that 'the concept of duty has proved itself a somewhat blunt instrument for dividing claims which ought reasonably to lead to recovery from claims which ought not'. Lord Nicholls himself admitted, in the extract above, that the idea was 'not without attraction'. Why then did he (and a majority of the House of Lords) reject the approach?

Nolan (*op. cit.*, p. 125) has argued that it would be conducive to greater clarity in the law if the question of actionable damage were considered separately, and proposes a further distinction between 'never actionable' and 'sometimes actionable' harm:

[I]t seems preferable to deal with the question of whether a given harm is ever actionable under the heading of actionable damage, and to deal with the question of whether a sometimes actionable harm is actionable in this particular case under the separate heading of duty of care, since doing so draws attention to the distinction we have identified, and makes it more likely that the important issues raised by the former question will be addressed openly and comprehensively. Unfortunately, however, there is a tendency to subsume the damage issue into the duty of care question.

It is certainly true that in some cases—identified by Nolan—the damage requirement has received insufficient attention when considered as a duty of care issue. But it should not be thought that this is a general problem; as we discuss in later chapters, there are many situations where the duty of care has been denied or limited because of the particular kind of damage claimed, and the particular difficulties raised by allowing recovery for that kind of damage have been explored as part of the duty analysis. In other words, the same result that Nolan argues for can be achieved through the distinction between 'no duty' and 'limited duty' situations.

In a claim for 'wrongful conception', the parents of a child conceived—against their will—through the defendant's negligence, usually relating to a failed sterilisation operation, seek damages for their losses. What interest do you think that the law is protecting in such cases: the woman's physical integrity, the couple's reproductive autonomy, the family's financial wellbeing, or some other interest? See further p. 135, below.

Logically, the question whether a particular interest is protected is distinct from the question whether it has been damaged on the facts. (Cf. *Principles of European Tort Law*, Article 2:101: 'Damage requires material or immaterial harm to a legally protected interest'.) In practice, 'damage' almost never emerges as a legal issue but only as a matter of proof (i.e. did the claimant in fact suffer the harm). In some very exceptional cases, however, it may be questioned whether what the claimant experienced legally constituted harm at all. One such case was *Rothwell v Chemical & Insulating Co Ltd* [2008] 1 AC 281, a test case in which a number of nominated claimants sued their employers in respect of the appearance of harmless pleural plaques (fibrous tissues on the membrane of the lung) as a consequence of their exposure to asbestos in the workplace. A unanimous House of Lords held that the development of pleural plaques did not constitute personal injury in itself, Lord Hoffmann commenting at [11]:

It was not merely that the plaques caused no immediate symptoms... The important point was that, save in the most exceptional case, the plaques would never cause any symptoms, did not increase the susceptibility of the claimants to other diseases or shorten their expectation of life.

In his Lordship's view, 'damage' was an abstract concept of being worse off, physically or economically. It was not merely a physical change as this might be consistent with an improvement (a successful operation) or with having a neutral effect. Nor could the change be trivial, but exactly how much of a change was necessary before the change amounted to actionable damage was a matter of degree.

Applying analogous reasoning, do you think that property covered in dust by nearby building works is or could be 'damaged'? (See *Hunter v Canary Wharf Ltd* [1996] 1 All ER 482, CA.) What about organic crops in which an unwanted GMO presence is found because of the defendant's GM farming next door? (Cf. *Hoffman v Monsanto Canada Inc* [2005] 7 WWR 665 at [72] (Saskatchewan Court of Queen's Bench), affirmed without reference to this point: 2007 SKCA 47.)

2. The Foreseeable Claimant

An important early step in the process of limiting a wrongdoer's liability for the consequences of his negligence came with the recognition that the 'duty' recognised by the tort of negligence is a relative concept. The duty is owed not to the world at large (as a duty in criminal law would be), but only to an individual within the scope of the risk created, that is, to a foreseeable victim. This idea was explored in the well-known American case of *Palsgraf v Long Island Railroad Co* 59 ALR 1253 (1928) (New York Court of Appeals). The plaintiff was standing on a platform of the defendant's railroad when a train stopped at the station. A man carrying a package tried to get on the train, but appeared to be having difficulties, so a railway guard on the car, who had held the door open, reached forward to help him in, and another guard on the platform pushed him from behind. In doing this, the package was dislodged, and fell on the track. Although there was nothing in its appearance to suggest it, the package contained fireworks which exploded when it fell on the tracks. The shock of the explosion (as the court held) threw down some scales at the other end of the platform some distance away. The scales struck the plaintiff, causing injuries for which she sued. The New York Court of Appeals rejected the plaintiff's claim but on different grounds. Cardozo J held the plaintiff was owed no duty because it was not foreseeable that the allegedly careless acts of the guards could create a risk of harm *to the plaintiff*. The fact that the guards might have owed a duty to others (i.e. those who were foreseeably at risk as a result of the conduct) was irrelevant:

> What the plaintiff must show is 'a wrong' to herself, i.e. a violation of her own right, and not merely a wrong to someone else, nor conduct 'wrongful' because unsocial, but not 'a wrong' to anyone . . . Negligence, like risk, is thus a term of relations. Negligence in the abstract, apart from things related, is surely not a tort, if indeed it is understandable at all. Negligence is not a tort unless it results in the commission of a wrong, and the commission of a wrong imports the violation of a right, in this case, we are told, the right to be protected against interference with one's bodily security. But bodily security is protected, not against all forms of interference or aggression, but only against some.
>
> One who seeks redress at law does not make out a cause of action by showing without more that there has been damage to his person. If the harm was not wilful, he must show that the act as to him had possibilities of danger so many and so apparent as to entitle him to be protected against the doing of it though the harm was unintended. . . . The victim does not sue derivatively, or by right of subrogation, to vindicate an interest invaded in the person of another. Thus to view his cause of action is to ignore the fundamental difference between tort and crime. . . . He sues for breach of a duty owing to himself.

A different approach was taken by Andrews J:

> The proposition is this: Every one owes to the world at large the duty of refraining from those acts that may unreasonably threaten the safety of others. Such an act occurs. Not only is he wronged to whom harm might reasonably be expected to result, but he also who is in fact injured, even if he be outside what would generally be thought the danger zone. There needs be duty due the one complaining, but this is not a duty to a particular individual, because as to him harm might be expected. Harm to someone being the natural result of the act, not only that one alone, but all those in fact injured may complain. . . . Unreasonable risk being taken, its consequences are not confined to those who might probably be hurt. . . .

Andrews J went on to hold that the defendant's negligence was not in fact the 'proximate cause' of the plaintiff's injury. So, despite the fact that he espoused a very different theory of negligence from that of Cardozo J, he reached the same conclusion as to liability on the facts of the case. In his judgment, the concept of 'proximate cause' does the work that the concept of 'duty' does in Cardozo J's. Andrews J's approach has appealed to some English commentators: Buckland (*op. cit.*) writes that the majority view in *Palsgraf* seems 'only to be another way of saying that a man ought not to be responsible for unforeseeable consequences' (at p. 648) and asks what would have happened if the plaintiff had been injured, without the intervention of the scales, by the package violently sliding along the platform: 'As there was no duty to her, it seems she would have had no remedy even in this case, but of course if it had happened it would have been held that she was near enough to have an interest' (*ibid.*). It will be considered further, below, whether the duty concept can usefully perform any function other than that which may already be performed by the concept of causation.

Doubts have been expressed whether the events described in the judgments in the *Palsgraf* decision could have occurred in the fashion envisaged. Although the court accepted that it was the shock of the explosion which threw down the scales, injuring the plaintiff, it has been suggested that the more likely explanation is that the scales were knocked down by people running about in a panic following the explosion (see Prosser, '*Palsgraf* Revisited' (1953) 52 Mich L Rev 1; cf. G. White, *Tort Law in America: An Intellectual History, expanded edn.* (New York: OUP, 2003), pp. 357–8, n. 117). If this version of the facts had been accepted by the New York Court of Appeals, do you think Mrs Palsgraf would have been any more likely to succeed?

It may be noted that Andrews J's approach bears some similarity to that taken under Article 1382 of the French *Code civil*, which does without any concept of 'duty' at all but instead advances a generalised liability for 'fault' (see above).

The requirement that the duty of care can only be owed to a foreseeable plaintiff was explored in England (and Scotland) in the following case.

Hay or Bourhill v Young [1943] AC 92

The pursuer, described in the opinions as a fishwife, was a passenger on a tramway car. After she had alighted at a stop, and as she was lifting her fish-basket from the driver's platform, she heard the sound of a collision between a motor-cycle and a car. The motorcyclist, a certain John Young, had been travelling at excessive speed and had been unable to avoid the car when it had crossed his path in order to make a right hand turn. Young was thrown on the street and sustained injuries from which he died. The accident occurred some 45 or 50 feet away from where the pursuer was standing, but out of her line of sight. After the cyclist's body had been removed, the pursuer approached and saw the blood left on the roadway. She alleged that, as an immediate result of the violent collision and the extreme shock of the occurrence, she wrenched and injured her back and was thrown into a state of terror and sustained a very severe shock to her nervous system. At the time of the incident, she had been about eight months pregnant, and five weeks later she gave birth to a child which was still-born as a result of her injuries. Having failed in her action before the Scottish courts, she appealed to the House of Lords.

Lord Macmillan

The duty to take care is the duty to avoid doing or omitting to do anything the doing or omitting to do which may have as its reasonable and probable consequence injury to others and the duty is owed to those to whom injury may reasonably and probably be anticipated if the duty is not observed.

There is no absolute standard of what is reasonable and probable. It must depend on circumstances and must always be a question of degree. In the present instance the late John Young was clearly negligent in a question with the occupants of the motor car with which his cycle collided. He was driving at an excessive speed in a public thoroughfare and he ought to have foreseen that he might consequently collide with any vehicle which he might meet in his course, for such an occurrence may reasonably and probably be expected to ensue from driving at a high speed in a street. But can it be said that he ought further to have foreseen that his excessive speed, involving the possibility of collision with another vehicle, might cause injury by shock to the pursuer? The pursuer was not within his line of vision, for she was on the other side of a tramway car which was standing between him and her when he passed and it was not until he had proceeded some distance beyond her that he collided with the motor car. The pursuer did not see the accident and she expressly admits that her 'terror did not involve any element of reasonable fear of immediate bodily injury to herself.' She was not so placed that there was any reasonable likelihood of her being affected by the deceased's careless driving.

In these circumstances I am of opinion...that the late John Young was under no duty to the pursuer to foresee that his negligence in driving at an excessive speed and consequently colliding with a motor car might result in injury to the pursuer, for such a result could not reasonably and probably be anticipated. He was, therefore, not guilty of negligence in a question with the pursuer.

Lord Wright quoted Lord Atkin's 'well-known aphorism' in *Donoghue v Stevenson*—'You must take reasonable care to avoid acts or omissions which you can reasonably foresee would be likely to injure your neighbour'—and continued:

This general concept of reasonable foresight as the criterion of negligence or breach of duty (strict or otherwise) may be criticised as too vague; but negligence is a fluid principle, which has to be applied to the most diverse conditions and problems of human life. It is a concrete not an abstract idea.... It is also always relative to the individual affected. This raises a serious additional difficulty in the cases where it has to be determined not merely whether the act itself is negligent against someone but whether it is negligent vis-à-vis the plaintiff. This is a crucial point in cases of nervous shock. Thus in the present case John Young was certainly negligent in an issue between himself and the owner of the car which he ran into, but it is another question whether he was negligent vis-à-vis the appellant.

In such cases terms like 'derivative' and 'original' and 'primary' and 'secondary' have been applied to define and distinguish the type of the negligence. If, however, the appellant has a cause of action, it is because of a wrong to herself. She cannot build on a wrong to someone else. Her interest, which was in her own bodily security, was of a different order from the interest of the owner of the car....

The present case, like many others of this type, may, however, raise the different question whether the appellant's illness was not due to her peculiar susceptibility. She was 8 months gone in pregnancy. Can it be said, apart from everything else, that it was likely that a person of normal nervous strength would have been affected in the circumstances by illness as the appellant was? Does the criterion of reasonable foresight extend beyond people of ordinary health or susceptibility, or does it take into account the peculiar susceptibilities or infirmities of those affected which the defendant neither knew of nor could reasonably be taken to have foreseen? Must the manner of conduct adapt itself to such special individual peculiarities? If extreme cases are taken, the answer appears to be fairly clear, unless, indeed, there is knowledge of the extraordinary risk. One who suffers from the terrible tendency to bleed on slight contact, which is denoted by the term 'a bleeder;' cannot complain if he mixes with the crowd and suffers severely, perhaps fatally, from being merely brushed against. There is no actionable wrong done there. A blind or deaf man who crosses the traffic on a busy street cannot complain if he is run over by a careful driver who does not know of and could not be expected to observe and guard against the man's infirmity. These questions go to 'culpability, not compensation'. . . . No doubt it has long ago been stated and often restated that, if the wrong is established, the wrongdoer must take the victim as he finds him. That, however, is only true . . . on the condition that the wrong has been established or admitted. The question of liability is anterior to the question of the measure of the consequences which go with the liability.

What is now being considered is the question of liability, and this, I think, in a question whether there is a duty owing to members of the public who come within the ambit of the act, must generally depend on a normal standard of susceptibility. This, it may be said, is somewhat vague. That is true; but definition involves limitation, which it is desirable to avoid further than is necessary in a principle of law like negligence, which is widely ranging and is still in the stage of development. It is here, as elsewhere, a question of what the hypothetical reasonable man, viewing the position, I suppose *ex post facto*, would say it was proper to foresee. What danger of particular infirmity that would include must depend on all the circumstances; but generally, I think, a reasonably normal condition, if medical evidence is capable of defining it, would be the standard. The test of the plaintiff's extraordinary susceptibility, if unknown to the defendant, would in effect make the defendant an insurer. The lawyer likes to draw fixed and definite lines and is apt to ask where the thing is to stop. I should reply it should stop where in the particular case the good sense of the jury, or of the judge, decides.

However, when I apply the considerations which I have been discussing to the present appeal, I come to the conclusion that the judgment should be affirmed. The case is peculiar, as indeed, though to a varying extent, all these cases are apt to be. There is no dispute about the facts. Upon these facts, can it be said that a duty is made out, and breach of that duty, so that the damage which is found is recoverable? I think not. The appellant was completely outside the range of the collision. She merely heard a noise, which upset her, without her having any definite idea at all. As she said: 'I just got into a pack of nerves and I did not know whether I was going to get it or not.' She saw nothing of the actual accident, or indeed any marks of blood until later. I cannot accept that John Young could reasonably have foreseen, or, more correctly, the reasonable hypothetical observer could reasonably have foreseen, the likelihood that anyone placed as the appellant was, could be affected in the manner in which she was. In my opinion John Young was guilty of no breach of duty to the appellant and was not in law responsible for the hurt she sustained. I may add that the issue of duty or no duty is indeed a question for the court, but it depends on the view taken of the facts. In the present case both courts below have taken the view that the appellant has, on the facts of the case, no redress and I agree with their view.

Lord Russell of Killowen, Lord Thankerton and **Lord Porter** delivered separate concurring opinions.

Appeal dismissed.

COMMENTARY

The law relating to 'nervous shock' has moved on significantly since this decision, albeit that the reluctance to compensate for harm caused by psychiatric means persists. The matter is considered in full detail in Chapter 7.

In the instant case, Lord Wright submitted that 'the question of liability . . . must generally depend on a normal standard of susceptibility'. He admitted, however, that what the reasonable person would foresee was a matter that was 'somewhat vague' and accepted that some kind of infirmity might be reasonably foreseeable. In *Haley v London Electricity Board* [1965]

AC 778, the House of Lords was faced with a claim by a blind man (the appellant) who, while walking along the pavement, had injured himself when he tripped over a long hammer left on the ground by the respondent company's employee with the object of warning passers-by of a trench which he had been digging at the spot. The appellant was alone but had approached with reasonable care, waving his white stick in front of him to detect objects in his way. It was accepted that the hammer gave adequate warning of the trench for normally-sighted persons, but the appellant alleged that the respondents or their employees should have taken special precautions to guard against the risk that a blind person's stick might miss the hammer. It was put in evidence that about 1 in 500 people were blind; that in Woolwich there were 258 registered blind; that the Post Office took account of the blind in guarding their excavations, using for the purpose a light fence some two feet high; and that more than once the appellant had detected such fences with his stick. The House of Lords held that the duty of care owed by persons excavating a highway was to ensure the reasonable safety of all persons whose use of the highway was reasonably foreseeable, not excluding the blind or infirm.

Are pregnant woman to be encountered less frequently than blind people so that their presence is not reasonably foreseeable? If not, how can these two decisions be reconciled?

If the House of Lords had held that John Young owed a duty of care to Mrs Bourhill, might he also have owed a duty to her child *in ventro*? Consider the following extract.

Congenital Disabilities (Civil Liability) Act 1976

1. CIVIL LIABILITY TO CHILD BORN DISABLED

(1) If a child is born disabled as the result of such an occurrence before its birth as is mentioned in subsection (2) below, and a person (other than the child's own mother) is under this section answerable to the child in respect of the occurrence, the child's disabilities are to be regarded as damage resulting from the wrongful act of that person and actionable accordingly at the suit of the child.

(2) An occurrence to which this section applies is one which—

   (a) affected either parent of the child in his or her ability to have a normal, healthy child; or

   (b) affected the mother during her pregnancy, or affected her or the child in the course of its birth, so that the child is born with disabilities which would not otherwise have been present.

(3) Subject to the following subsections, a person (here referred to as 'the defendant') is answerable to the child if he was liable in tort to the parent or would, if sued in due time, have been so; and it is no answer that there could not have been such liability because the parent suffered no actionable injury, if there was a breach of legal duty which, accompanied by injury, would have given rise to the liability.

(4) In the case of an occurrence preceding the time of conception, the defendant is not answerable to the child if at that time either or both of the parents knew the risk of their child being born disabled (that is to say, the particular risk created by the occurrence); but should it be the child's father who is the defendant, this subsection does not apply if he knew of the risk and the mother did not...

(5) The defendant is not answerable to the child, for anything he did or omitted to do when responsible in a professional capacity for treating or advising the parent, if he took

reasonable care having due regard to then received professional opinion applicable to the particular class of case; but this does not mean that he is answerable only because he departed from received opinion.

(6) Liability to the child under this section may be treated as having been excluded or limited by contract made with the parent affected, to the same extent and subject to the same restrictions as liability in the parent's own case; and a contract term which could have been set up by the defendant in an action by the parent, so as to exclude or limit his liability to him or her, operates in the defendant's favour to the same, but no greater, extent in an action under this section by the child.

(7) If in the child's action under this section it is shown that the parent affected shared the responsibility for the child being born disabled, the damages are to be reduced to such extent as the court thinks just and equitable having regard to the extent of the parent's responsibility.

1A. EXTENSION OF SECTION 1 TO COVER INFERTILITY TREATMENTS

(1) In any case where—
   (a) a child carried by a woman as the result of the placing in her of an embryo or of sperm and eggs or her artificial insemination is born disabled,
   (b) the disability results from an act or omission in the course of the selection, or the keeping or use outside the body, of the embryo carried by her or of the gametes used to bring about the creation of the embryo, and
   (c) a person is under this section answerable to the child in respect of the act or omission, the child's disabilities are to be regarded as damage resulting from the wrongful act of that person and actionable accordingly at the suit of the child.

(2) Subject to subsection (3) below and the applied provisions of section 1 of this Act, a person (here referred to as 'the defendant') is answerable to the child if he was liable in tort to one or both of the parents (here referred to as 'the parent or parents concerned') or would, if sued in due time, have been so; and it is no answer that there could not have been such liability because the parent or parents concerned suffered no actionable injury, if there was a breach of legal duty which, accompanied by injury, would have given rise to the liability.

(3) The defendant is not under this section answerable to the child if at the time the embryo, or the sperm and eggs, are placed in the woman or the time of her insemination (as the case may be) either or both of the parents knew the risk of their child being born disabled (that is to say, the particular risk created by the act or omission).

(4) Subsections (5) to (7) of section 1 of this Act apply for the purposes of this section as they apply for the purposes of that but as if references to the parent or the parent affected were references to the parent or parents concerned.

2. LIABILITY OF WOMAN DRIVING WHEN PREGNANT
A woman driving a motor vehicle when she knows (or ought reasonably to know) herself to be pregnant is to be regarded as being under the same duty to take care for the safety of her unborn child as the law imposes on her with respect to the safety of other people; and if in consequence of her breach of that duty her child is born with disabilities which would not otherwise have been present, those disabilities are to be regarded as damage resulting from her wrongful act and actionable accordingly at the suit of the child . . .

4. INTERPRETATION AND OTHER SUPPLEMENTARY PROVISIONS

(1) References in this Act to a child being born disabled or with disabilities are to its being born with any deformity, disease or abnormality, including predisposition (whether or not susceptible of immediate prognosis) to physical or mental defect in the future.

(2) In this Act—

(a) 'born' means born alive (the moment of a child's birth being when it first has a life separate from its mother), and 'birth' has a corresponding meaning; and

(b) 'motor vehicle' means a mechanically propelled vehicle intended or adapted for use on roads

and references to embryos shall be construed in accordance with section 1 of the Human Fertilisation and Embryology Act 1990 and any regulations made under s. 1(6) of that Act.

(3) Liability to a child under section 1, 1A or 2 of this Act is to be regarded—

(a) as respects all its incidents and any matters arising or to arise out of it; and

(b) subject to any contrary context or intention, for the purpose of construing references in enactments and documents to personal or bodily injuries and cognate matters

as liability for personal injuries sustained by the child immediately after its birth....

(5) This Act applies in respect of births after (but not before) its passing, and in respect of any such birth it replaces any law in force before its passing, whereby a person could be liable to a child in respect of disabilities with which it might be born; but in section 1(3) of this Act the expression 'liable in tort' does not include any reference to liability by virtue of this Act, or to liability by virtue of any such law....

COMMENTARY

The above legislation is an example of Parliament creating by statute a 'foreseeable' claimant. Before the Act was passed there was some doubt whether a child in this position had an action, hence the Law Commission recommended legislation to put the matter beyond doubt and its recommendations formed the basis of the 1976 Act (Law Com. 60, *Injuries to Unborn Children*, 1974). The Court of Appeal subsequently held that a child had a cause of action in respect of pre-natal injuries even at common law (*Burton v Islington Health Authority* [1993] QB 204) but this is of little practical importance as the Act replaces the existing common law in respect of congenital disabilities suffered after its enactment. Even granted that the limitation period does not run against a child until he attains the age of majority, there can be very few common law claims of this sort still pending.

The Act only allows a claim where the child is born alive, so that negligently killing a previously healthy foetus will not attract liability under the Act. Three injury-causing situations are covered by s. 1(2). The first relates to a period prior to conception, and deals with the ability of either parent to produce a healthy child. The second situation deals with conduct that affects the mother during pregnancy and affects her capacity to have a healthy child. The third situation covers negligence relating to the birth of the child. The Human Fertilisation and Embryology Act 1990 extended the Act's coverage to include injury caused by the selection, storage, and use of embryos and gametes during fertility treatment. However, in all these cases, the defendant is liable to the child only if he would have been liable in tort to either parent (or, in the second and third situations, to the mother). The child's claim is therefore derivative to some extent, but, as the defendant's conduct may not cause any damage to the parent, s. 1(3) provides that the actionability of the parent's claim depends upon breach of a legal duty rather than damage (which would be required in an ordinary negligence action). The derivative nature of the claim is further illustrated by s. 1(4), (6) and (7), which ensure that the duty owed to the child is no greater than that owed to the relevant parent. The child must also establish that the negligence caused the injury, which can be extremely difficult in medical negligence cases (see Ch. 5). Given the somewhat convoluted nature of the child's claim, it is not surprising that a leading text has described the Act as 'largely irrelevant' (M. Brazier & E. Cave, *Medicine, Patients and the Law*, 4th edn. (London: Penguin, 2007), p. 292).

Unless the mother's tortious conduct relates to the driving of a motor vehicle (s. 2), the child may bring no claim against its own mother. The Law Commission thought that, on balance, the immunity should not be extended to the father and this is the position under the Act. However, the *Pearson Commission* reached the contrary conclusion (para. 1471) although it recommended that no immunity should apply to either parent where the ante-natal injury arose from any activity for which insurance was compulsory (para. 1472). Which approach do you prefer? Do you think that mother and father should be treated differently? Do you think that the fact of insurance should be treated as relevant to the imposition of liability? (If there are sound policy reasons for granting one or other of the parents an immunity from suit, why should the position be different where the parents are insured against the liability?) For more detailed comment on the Act, see I. Kennedy and A. Grubb, *Medical Law*, 3rd edn. (London: Butterworths, 2000), ch. 12; M. Brazier & E. Cave, *Medicine, Patients and the Law*, 4th edn. (London: Penguin, 2007), ch. 12.

The child may claim in respect of 'disabilities', which are defined so as to cover any deformity, disease, or abnormality with which the child is born. However, what if the child's claim relates, not to any injury it was born with, but to the fact that it was born at all? For example, if a doctor negligently advises that the foetus is healthy when, in fact, it has a serious disease which will render it severely disabled when born, can the child claim damages for the pain and suffering it has suffered by being born alive? Such a claim was rejected by the Court of Appeal at common law on the grounds of public policy: the claim entailed that the child would have been better off not being born at all (*McKay v Essex Area Health Authority* [1982] QB 1166; the position is the same in France and Germany (see *van Dam*, para. 707–2), though only after the legislative reversal of an (in)famous decision to the contrary of the French *Cour de Cassation* (in the *arrêt Perruche*), and the same result was recently reached by the High Court of Australia (*Harriton v Stephens* (2006) 226 CLR 52)). In *McKay*, it was also held, obiter, that such a claim would fail under the 1976 Act because of the wording of s. 1(2)(b). Some jurisdictions still go the other way, however: see, e.g., the Baby Kelly case in the Netherlands (summarised by Faure and Hartlief in *European Tort Law 2005*, pp. 421–2).

Although there are arguments in favour of allowing such an action, the rejection of the claim may not provide much hardship where the parents can bring a 'wrongful conception' or 'wrongful birth' action. Such claims allege that, but for the negligence, the parents would not have conceived the child, or would have had an abortion, with the main head of damages being the cost of bringing up the child. However, in *McFarlane v Tayside Health Authority* [2000] 2 AC 59 the House of Lords held that the cost of raising a healthy but unplanned child was not recoverable in a wrongful birth action. At least this rule, however undesirable it may be thought, was clear, but almost immediately after *McFarlane* was decided the Court of Appeal held that child-rearing costs could be claimed in a case where the child was born with disabilities, though only the *additional* costs associated with the child's disability were recoverable (see *Parkinson v St James and Seacroft University Hospital NHS Trust* [2002] QB 266). Shortly afterwards, the Court of Appeal held that a wrongful birth claim lay for the additional costs of raising a *healthy* child attributable to the disability of its mother but on appeal the claim was rejected by a four to three majority of their Lordships (*Rees v Darlington Area Health Authority* [2004] 1 AC 309). In obiter dicta, three members of the majority cast doubt on the correctness of *Parkinson*, but the final member of the majority appeared to agree with the minority that the additional costs attributable to the child's disability should be recoverable. A different member of the majority thought it arguable that the *Parkinson* claim could be brought where the very purpose of the procedure was to prevent the birth of a disabled child (e.g. some type of screening or testing process to determine whether the child has a disability). Moreover, the majority in *Rees* held that, in any case where negligence resulted in the birth of an unplanned child, an award of £15,000 should be made, seemingly to the parents, to compensate for the loss of autonomy associated with having an unplanned child. Is such an award compensating for a loss to the parents, or for an infringement of their rights? (See Nolan, 'New Forms of Damage in Negligence' (2007) 70 MLR 59.)

Lest it be thought English courts were on their own in struggling with this area, it should be noted that the High Court of Australia split four to three in *Cattanach v Melchior* (2003) 215 CLR 1 in favour of allowing a claim for the rearing costs of a healthy child, only for a number of states legislatively to reverse the result, leaving open the possibility of a *Parkinson*-type claim (see, e.g., *Civil Liability Act 2002* (NSW), s. 71). The position in Canada is uncertain, with some courts awarding, in the case of a healthy child, damages for non-pecuniary loss to both parents to reflect their loss of autonomy (see *Paxton v Ramji* (2008) 92 OR (3d) 401, n 7). In Europe, different jurisdictions take different approaches (see *van Dam*, para. 706–2).

For further discussion of the English cases see Pedain [2004] CLJ 19; Lunney (2004) 1 UNELJ 145; Priaulx, 'Damages for the Unwanted Child: Time for a Rethink' (2005) 73 *Medico-Legal Journal* 152, and more generally N. Priaulx, *The Harm Paradox: Tort Law and the Unwanted Child in an Era of Choice* (Oxford: Routledege-Cavendish, 2007), chs 2, 4 and J. K. Mason, *The Troubled Pregnancy: Legal Wrongs and Rights in Reproduction* (Cambridge: CUP, 2007), chs 3–6.

3. Additional Requirements for the Existence of a Duty

The above extracts illustrate that a duty of care is owed only to those who might foreseeably suffer damage as a result of the defendant's negligence. Foreseeability may be regarded as the factual aspect of the duty of care inquiry. It should be noted, however, that the existence of a duty is not simply a matter of factual investigation into the risks associated with the defendant's conduct (though it has been argued that this may have been what Lord Atkin intended in *Donoghue*: see Heuston, '*Donoghue v Stevenson* in Retrospect' (1957) MLR 1). The better view is that Lord Atkin never thought that his 'neighbour principle' would apply to all types of damage, whether caused by act or omission, no matter how foreseeable (see Smith and Burns, '*Donoghue v Stevenson*—The Not so Golden Anniversary' (1983) 46 MLR 147). In some of the older cases (of which *Bourhill v Young* is an example) a finding that the claimant was unforeseeable masked other policy concerns which militated against imposing a duty of care. Was the decision that Mrs Bourhill was owed no duty of care really attributable to the fact that she was not a reasonably foreseeable victim of John Young's negligent driving? There seems little doubt that the real consideration which motivated the House of Lords was the fact that the damage suffered by the claimant was shock-induced: injury of this type ('nervous shock') has long been thought to raise particular problems and to call for limitations on the circumstances in which a duty is owed (see Ch. 7). However, so long as foreseeability was seen as the touchstone of liability, these policy concerns could be given effect only in covert fashion—by holding that the claimant was unforeseeable. The reasons for this approach are complex, but part of the explanation lies in the reluctance of the courts at that time to acknowledge the influence of policy on judicial decisions.

In more modern times, the courts have shown an increased willingness to bring policy questions into the open, and have recognised that whether a duty of care arises or not is ultimately a matter of policy. Even if a court finds that injury to the claimant was a foreseeable result of the defendant's negligence, it may deny the existence of a duty of care on the basis that underlying policy concerns necessitate a restrictive answer to the question: who at law is the defendant's neighbour? This is what may be termed the legal aspect of the duty of care inquiry. By emphasising that the recognition of a duty is ultimately a legal (not factual) question, the courts have been able to introduce restrictions on the scope of liability in what they consider to be particularly sensitive areas, for example in relation to pure economic loss or psychiatric injury, or to injuries resulting from omissions rather than positive acts.

What is required, in addition to the reasonable foreseeability of injury, in order to give rise to a duty of care has long been a matter of great difficulty. In *Caparo Industries plc v Dickman*, extracted below, Lord Bridge summarised the competing approaches, and laid the foundations for the current approach of the courts.

Caparo Industries plc v Dickman [1990] 2 AC 605

The facts of this case are not relevant for present purposes. They are set out, along with additional extracts, at p. 425, below.

Lord Bridge of Harwich

In determining the existence and scope of the duty of care which one person may owe to another in the infinitely varied circumstances of human relationships there has for long been a tension between two different approaches. Traditionally the law finds the existence of the duty in different specific situations each exhibiting its own particular characteristics. In this way the law has identified a wide variety of duty situations, all falling within the ambit of the tort of negligence, but sufficiently distinct to require separate definition of the essential ingredients by which the existence of the duty is to be recognised. Commenting on the outcome of this traditional approach, Lord Atkin, in his seminal speech in *Donoghue v Stevenson* [1932] AC 562 at 579–580 observed:

> The result is that the Courts have been engaged upon an elaborate classification of duties....In this way it can be ascertained at any time whether the law recognises a duty, but only where the case can be referred to some particular species which has been examined and classified. And yet the duty which is common to all the cases where liability is established must logically be based upon some element common to the cases where it is found to exist.

It is this last sentence which signifies the introduction of the more modern approach of seeking a single general principle which may be applied in all circumstances to determine the existence of a duty of care. Yet Lord Atkin himself sounds the appropriate note of caution by adding:

> To seek a complete logical definition of the general principle is probably to go beyond the function of the judge, for the more general the definition the more likely it is to omit essentials or to introduce non-essentials.

Lord Reid gave a large impetus to the modern approach in *Home Office v Dorset Yacht Co Ltd* [1970] AC 1004 at 1026–1027, where he said:

> In later years there has been a steady trend towards regarding the law of negligence as depending on principle so that, when a new point emerges, one should ask not whether it is covered by authority but whether recognised principles apply to it. *Donoghue v Stevenson* may be regarded as a milestone, and the well-known passage in Lord Atkin's speech should I think be regarded as a statement of principle. It is not to be treated as if it were a statutory definition. It will require qualification in new circumstances. But I think that the time has come when we can and should say that it ought to apply unless there is some justification or valid explanation for its exclusion.

The most comprehensive attempt to articulate a single general principle is reached in the well-known passage from the speech of Lord Wilberforce in *Anns v Merton London Borough* [1978] AC 728 at 751–752:

> Through the trilogy of cases in this House, *Donoghue v Stevenson* [1932] AC 562, *Hedley Byrne & Co Ltd v Heller & Partners Ltd* [1964] AC 465, and *Home Office v Dorset Yacht Co Ltd* [1970] AC 1004, the position has now been reached that in order to establish that a duty of care arises in a particular situation, it is not necessary to bring the facts of that situation within those of previous situations in which a duty of care has been held to exist. Rather the question has to be approached in two stages. First one has to ask whether, as between the alleged wrongdoer and the person who has suffered damage there is a sufficient relationship of proximity or neighbourhood such that, in the reasonable contemplation of the former, carelessness on his part may be likely to cause damage to the latter, in which case a prima facie duty of care arises. Secondly, if the first question is answered affirmatively, it is necessary to consider whether there are any considerations which ought to negative, or to reduce or limit the scope of the duty or the class of person to whom it is owed or the damages to which a breach of it may give rise (see the *Dorset Yacht* case [1970] AC 1004 at 1027, per Lord Reid).

But since *Anns's* case a series of decisions of the Privy Council and of your Lordships' House, notably in judgments and speeches delivered by Lord Keith, have emphasised the inability of any single general principle to provide a practical test which can be applied to every situation to determine whether a duty of care is owed and, if so, what is its scope.... What emerges is that, In addition to the foreseeability of damage, necessary ingredients in any situation giving rise to a duty of care are that there should exist between the party owing the duty and the party to whom it is owed a relationship characterised by the law as one of 'proximity' or 'neighbourhood' and that the situation should be one in which the court considers it fair, just and reasonable that the law should impose a duty of a given scope on the one party for the benefit of the other. But it is implicit in the passages referred to that the concepts of proximity and fairness embodied in these additional ingredients are not susceptible of any such precise definition as would be necessary to give them utility as practical tests, but amount in effect to little more than convenient labels to attach to the features of different specific situations which, on a detailed examination of all the circumstances, the law recognises pragmatically as giving rise to a duty of care of a given scope. Whilst recognising, of course, the importance of the underlying general principles common to the whole field of negligence, I think the law has now moved in the direction of attaching greater significance to the more traditional categorisation of distinct and recognisable situations as guides to the existence, the scope and the limits of the varied duties of care which the law imposes. We must now, I think, recognise the wisdom of the words of Brennan J in the High Court of Australia in *Sutherland Shire Council v Heyman* (1985) 60 ALR 1 at 43–44, where he said:

> It is preferable in my view, that the law should develop novel categories of negligence incrementally and by analogy with established categories, rather than by a massive extension of a prima facie duty of care restrained only by indefinable 'considerations which ought to negative, or to reduce or limit the scope of the duty or the class of person to whom it is owed.

Lord Oliver

I think it has to be recognised that to search for any single formula which will serve as a general test of liability is to pursue a will-o'-the wisp. The fact is that once one discards, as it is now clear that one must, the concept of foreseeability of harm as the single exclusive test, even a prima facie test, of the existence of the duty of care, the attempt to state some general principle which will determine liability in an infinite variety of circumstances serves not to clarify the law but merely to bedevil its development in a way which corresponds with practicality and common sense. . . .

COMMENTARY

Lord Bridge's opinion has come to be regarded as the classic exposition of the modern approach to establishing a duty of care. He denied that any simple formula could offer assistance as a test of liability, but his analysis (contrary to his intentions?) has been understood as laying down a 'three-stage' test for the existence of a duty of care, the ingredients of which are (1) foreseeability, (2) proximity, and (3) the fairness, justice and reasonableness of recognising such a duty.

His approach should be compared with that of Lord Wilberforce in *Anns* (considered by Lord Bridge in the extract above). Lord Wilberforce's approach—taken literally—effectively recognised a presumption of liability in every case where injury to the claimant was reasonably foreseeable, and put on the defendant the onus of identifying reasons of public policy which militated against the imposition of such a duty. Perhaps defendants were not up to this task. Or maybe the courts were just not inclined to listen to them. Whichever was the case, the *Anns* approach was interpreted—for a brief period in the late 1970s and early 1980s—as giving the courts licence to overturn long-established authorities denying the existence of a duty (e.g. in the area of pure economic loss) on the basis that the mere foreseeability of injury gave rise to at least a prima facie duty of care (see especially *Junior Books Co Ltd v Veitchi Co Ltd* [1983] 1 AC 520). Eventually, there arose a concern amongst the members of the higher judiciary that 'a too literal application of the well-known observation of Lord Wilberforce in *Anns* . . . may be productive of a failure to have regard to, and to analyse and weigh, all the relevant considerations in considering whether it is appropriate that a duty of care should be imposed' (*Rowling v Takaro Properties Ltd* [1988] AC 473 at 501 per Lord Keith). The result was the so-called 'retreat from *Anns*' in which the courts reverted to a more cautious and pragmatic approach to the recognition of duties of care and re-established many of the old rules denying the existence of any duty at all in particular circumstances. (Especially notable was *Murphy v Brentwood District Council* [1991] 1 AC 398, which overruled the narrow ratio of *Anns* itself: see further p. 391, below.)

Lord Bridge's three-stage test should not be read simply as a new, improved version of the two-stage test in *Anns*, for Lord Bridge adds the crucial qualification that the law should be developed only incrementally, by analogy with existing duty situations (see especially his reliance upon the passage from the judgment of Brennan J in the High Court of Australia in *Sutherland Shire Council v Heyman* (1985) 60 ALR 1 at 43–4, which he cites in the extract above). Whereas *Anns* invited courts to disregard previously established limits on the number and breadth of duty situations, the *Caparo* approach gives a crucial role to consideration of precisely how far the authorities have already gone. The difference may aptly be characterised as one between an approach that starts from a presumption of duty, and requires the invocation of policy factors if the duty is to be negated, and one that starts from a presumption of no duty, and requires the invocation of policy factors if a new duty is to be established (see *Stovin v Wise* [1996] AC 923 at 949, per Lord Hoffmann).

In fact, having a test for the existence of a duty of care only becomes important in those 'battlegrounds' of the modern law of negligence where the legitimacy of holding a negligent party liable for losses suffered by another is disputed. The major fields of conflict lie in the areas of psychiatric illness, pure economic loss, omissions, acts of third parties, and public bodies. Detailed consideration of these issues can be found in Chapters 7–10. Outside these areas—in the traditional homeland of the tort (which deals with physical harm caused by positive acts)—the existence of a duty will often be indisputable, and the empty recitation of the three stages of Lord Bridge's test would be a waste of time. Already by the time that *Donoghue v Stevenson* imposed a duty of care upon manufacturers of products, it was well established that one road-user owed a duty of care to another (e.g. *Williams v Holland* (1833) 2 LJCP (NS) 190) and that an employer owed a duty of care to his or her employees (*Smith v Baker & Sons* [1891] AC 325). Indeed, in the modern law it is permissible to work on the assumption that, where a private individual commits a positive act of misfeasance which foreseeably causes physical harm to the person or property of the claimant, a duty of care will be owed. This is not because the *Caparo* requirements are of no relevance in such cases—Lord Steyn stated in *Marc Rich and Co AG v Bishop Rock Marine Co Ltd, The Nicholas H* [1996] AC 211 that it was 'settled law that the elements of foreseeability and proximity as well as considerations of fairness, justice and reasonableness are relevant to all cases whatever the nature of the harm sustained by the plaintiff'—but because they are regarded as satisfied in most cases that fit this description. Nevertheless, there are certain exceptional cases—mainly involving property damage rather than physical injury to the person—where the courts have denied the existence of a duty of care even where these types of damage are foreseeable (e.g. where allowing a claim would upset a prior allocation of risks as between parties to a commercial venture: see *Norwich City Council v Harvey* [1989] 1 WLR 828; cf. *British Telecommunications plc v James Thomson & Sons (Engineers) Ltd* [1999] 1 WLR 9, noted by Convery (1999) 62 MLR 766; see also *The Nicholas H*, noted below).

Proximity

According to Weir [1991] CLJ 24 at 25, '[p]roximity is now the key word, though it doesn't open many doors'. Where Lord Wilberforce's two-stage approach had appeared to treat proximity as no more than a synonym for foreseeability (there was a relationship of proximity if harm was foreseeable), the more recent trend is to view this requirement as conceptually distinct (see, e.g., *Peabody Donation Fund v Sir Lindsay Parkinson & Co* [1985] AC 210 at 240–1, per Lord Keith). The effect was to reverse the expansion of duty situations prompted by *Anns* by placing an additional hurdle in the way of a successful claim. Yet the nature of proximity remained elusive. In *Stovin v Wise* [1996] AC 923 at 932, Lord Nicholls explained further:

The Caparo tripartite test elevates proximity to the dignity of a separate heading. This formulation tends to suggest that proximity is a separate ingredient, distinct from fairness and reasonableness, and capable of being identified by some other criteria. This is not so. Proximity is a slippery word. Proximity is not legal shorthand for a concept with its own, objectively identifiable characteristics. Proximity is convenient shorthand for a relationship between two parties which makes it fair and reasonable that one should owe the other a duty of care. This is only another way of saying that when assessing the requirements of fairness and reasonableness regard must be had to the relationship of the parties.

This suggests that considerations of proximity are not in the final analysis clearly distinguishable from those of fairness, justice and reasonableness (i.e. policy), and in many cases the terms are used interchangeably. Yet it may be argued that 'proximity' has acquired a conventional (though not universal) usage as the umbrella term denoting certain particular types of restriction on the scope of the duty of care. Notable amongst these are restrictions upon liability for certain types of loss (e.g. pure economic loss and psychiatric illness) and for nonfeasance (omissions) as opposed to misfeasance (positive acts). Judicial reluctance to recognise a duty of care in these contexts is expressed in legal terms by a finding of no proximity. The absence of proximity is asserted in conclusory fashion and merely indicates that underlying policy concerns warrant a general rule of no liability in the area in question. Conversely, the courts' analysis of the underlying policy considerations may warrant the development of rules which allow proximity (and hence a prima facie duty) to be established in exceptional cases. Such rules are conveniently termed principles of proximity.

Certain commentators have resisted the notion that proximity is just a particular way of looking at considerations of fairness, justice and reasonableness, and have argued that the concept plays an autonomous, and more principled, role in determining the existence of a duty of care. Witting ('The three-stage test abandoned in Australia—or not?' (2002) 118 LQR 214 and 'Duty of Care: An Analytical Approach' (2005) 25 OJLS 33), for example, argues that the function of the test of proximity is to identify those persons most appropriately placed to take care to avoid damage to the claimant, whom he defines as those whose act or omission most closely and directly affected the claimant. According to Witting, this is a question of fact, and the criteria upon which a finding of sufficient proximity are based are 'unequivocal' ((2005) 25 OJLS 33, 40). He does, however, concede that policy plays some role in determining the existence of a duty of care: a finding of proximity is not conclusive as whether or not a duty of care arises is ultimately a normative question (i.e. the third stage of the *Caparo* test—fairness, justice and reasonableness—may operate to deny a duty of care even if there is a relationship of proximity). Witting's argument rests on the notion that a finding of proximity is not a normative question: 'Proximity can be no more than the penultimate question—the "is" upon which an "ought" is based' ((2002) 118 LQR 214, 217). The tendency to define proximity in this way comes from a wider concern to minimise the resort to 'policy' (see below) as a means of determining the duty of care question; if proximity can be seen as a legal *principle* it avoids the value-laden 'legal intuition' that attaches to judicial assessment as to whether a particular policy argument should operate to deny the existence of a duty of care (see Kramer, 'Proximity as principles: directness, community norms and the tort of negligence' (2003) 11 Tort L Rev 70). However, as Cane (2004) 120 LQR 189, 192 points out: '...all rules and principles that state individuals' legal rights and obligations are underpinned by policy arguments because policy arguments are arguments about what individuals' legal rights and obligations ought to be'. Thus, in our view, the finding of a relationship of proximity is—indeed must be—to some extent based on policy factors, and to that extent we would disagree with Witting's analysis. We agree with Hickman [2002] CLJ 13 at 14 that '[t]he requirement of proximity is itself not simply a categorisation of facts from which conclusions about responsibility can straightforwardly be drawn. A finding of proximity is underpinned by policy considerations'. However, as is argued below, we believe that a distinction can be made between the tests of 'proximity' and 'fairness, justice and reasonableness' on the basis of the type of policy considerations that are relevant in determining if the test has been satisfied and the way in which they are invoked.

Fairness, Justice and Reasonableness

Whereas the tendency is to use proximity as the heading for relatively well-settled rules limiting liability for certain types of loss and for nonfeasance, the third stage of the *Caparo* approach can be regarded as the general repository for a miscellaneous set of policy arguments, undefined in nature and unlimited in number, which are invoked haphazardly and in an ad hoc fashion by the courts in determining whether a duty of care should arise. An example which demonstrates the varied nature of the concerns which can be raised is the case of *The Nicholas H* (cited above). The defendants, a shipping classification society, were alleged to have been negligent in certifying a particular ship as seaworthy after it had undergone temporary repairs. Shortly after it left port, the vessel sank, causing the plaintiff's cargo to be lost. Despite the fact that the harm suffered was property damage (for which a duty is normally owed merely upon foresight of damage), a majority of the House of Lords held that no duty arose. The rights and liabilities between shippers and cargo owners were the subject of an international convention ('the Hague Rules'). These limited the ship owner's liability to the cargo owner in respect of the loss of cargo, and Lord Steyn argued that to impose a duty in tort would upset the balance created by these rules. Further, the defendant was an independent and non-profit-making entity, created and operated for the sole purpose of promoting the collective welfare, namely the safety of lives and ships at sea. His Lordship thought that this status might be endangered if a duty was found to exist. Do you find these reasons convincing? Do you think that the House of Lords would have reached the same result if the sinking of the ship had caused the loss of life?

Considerations of fairness, justice, and reasonableness are most commonly invoked where it is thought that the imposition of a duty of care solely on the basis of reasonable foreseeability of damage would be undesirable. Over the course of time, the most important concern has undeniably been the fear of 'opening up the floodgates of liability'. The 'floodgates argument' has no doubt a number of different dimensions (see generally J. Bell, *Policy Arguments in Judicial Decisions* (Oxford: OUP, 1983), ch. 3), but the primary concern underlying its deployment in the modern law is that of overburdening the defendant—not just the defendant in the instant case, but all future defendants in similar cases. This form of the argument has been particularly influential in situations where numerous different claims are likely to arise out of a single incident (consider in particular the treatment of the 'nervous shock' claims arising out of the Hillsborough stadium disaster: see p. 342, below). This is partly a question of fairness: it is thought unreasonable to expose a defendant to liability grossly disproportionate to his fault or to 'liability in an indeterminate amount for an indeterminate time to an indeterminate class' (*Ultramares Corp v Touche, Niven & Co* (1931) 174 NE 441 at 444, per Cardozo J). But it is also, at least in part, an argument that the imposition of large and/or indeterminate liabilities might in certain circumstances have detrimental effects on society as a whole (e.g. because it would result in the curtailment of certain socially-useful activities which come to be seen as carrying a risk of excessive liabilities).

This version of the floodgates argument tends to shade into the argument about 'overkill'. The overkill concern is that the imposition of a duty of care might encourage detrimental practice on the part of potential defendants (see, e.g. *Hill v Chief Constable of West Yorkshire* [1989] AC 53). Although tort liability may have, as one of its purposes, the promotion of due care and attention, it may have the undesired effect of promoting undue care and attention. The (alleged) phenomenon of defensive medicine is perhaps the best example: the argument suggests that medical practitioners might be induced to perform unnecessary tests and undertake unnecessary procedures—adding to the costs of the treatment and perhaps exposing the patient to new or different risks—for the sole purpose of reducing the risk of costly litigation and of consequent increases (in the case of doctors in private practice) in insurance premiums. (Why would the risk of liability if doctors are too defensive not induce them to provide the 'right' treatment?) These arguments have some plausibility, but whether they are borne out by actual practice is a matter of considerable controversy. (On the question of defensive medicine, see M. Brazier & E. Cave, *Medicine, Patients and the Law*, 4th edn. (London: Penguin, 2007), pp. 204–5.) In any case, it may be doubted whether the courts have adequate empirical evidence, or sufficient expertise, to enable them to evaluate these claims with any degree of scientific rigour. Moreover, it is questionable whether the weighing of competing policy interests is something that the courts, as opposed to the legislature, ought to be doing. A leading critic of the current approach to the duty of care question has commented that, if judges insist on making policy choices, 'the legislatures should seize control of the law of negligence, replace the common law with statute, and supplant judges with democratically accountable officials (A. Beever, *Rediscovering the Law of Negligence* (Oxford: Hart, 2007) p. 8). Conversely, attempts by law reform bodies to evaluate the impact of proposed changes to the law have not always been successful. Commenting on the Law Commission's recent consultation paper *Administrative Redress: Public Bodies and the Citizen* (Law Commission Consultation Paper No. 187, 2008), Morgan notes ((2009) 125 LQR 215, 221): 'The Law Commission's evident difficulty in estimating the impact of its proposals for reforming public authority liability throws into doubt any assumption that the legislative process must necessarily be superior.' It seems likely that the debate over the proper role for policy concerns, if any, in the duty of care enquiry will continue for some time.

An area where policy has long played a leading role in the duty of care question is in actions against the police. In the leading case of *Hill v Chief Constable of West Yorkshire* [1989] AC 53, the House of Lords dismissed an action by the parents of the last victim of the 'Yorkshire Ripper', Peter Sutcliffe. The action alleged that there had been negligence in the conduct of the police investigation of earlier murders and that this had resulted in failing to apprehend Sutcliffe at an earlier date which would have prevented her murder. Although their Lordships struck out the claim as disclosing no cause of action partly on the ground that there was no proximity between the parties, a number of policy grounds were also raised that militated against a duty of care being owed. Lord Keith expressed them as follows (at 63):

The general sense of public duty which motivates police forces is unlikely to be appreciably reinforced by the imposition of such liability so far as concerns their function in the investigation and suppression of crime. From time to time they make mistakes in the exercise of that function, but it is not to be doubted that they apply their best endeavours to the performance of it. In some instances the imposition of liability may lead to the exercise of a function being carried on in a detrimentally defensive frame of mind ... Further it would be reasonable to expect that if potential liability were to be imposed it would be not uncommon for actions to be raised against police forces on the ground that they had failed to catch some criminal as soon as they might have done, with the result that he went on to commit further crimes. While some such actions might involve allegations of a simple and straightforward type of failure - for example that a police officer negligently tripped and fell while pursuing a burglar - others would be likely to enter deeply into the general nature of a police investigation, as indeed the present action would seek to do. The manner of conduct of such an investigation must necessarily involve a variety of decisions to be made on matters of policy and discretion, for example as to which particular line of inquiry is most advantageously to be pursued and what is the most advantageous way to deploy the available resources. Many such decisions would not be regarded by the courts as appropriate to be called in question, yet elaborate investigation of the facts might be necessary to ascertain whether or not this was so. A great deal of police time, trouble and expense might be expected to have to be put into the preparation of the defence to the action and the attendance of witnesses at the trial. The result would be a significant diversion of police manpower and attention from their most important function, that of the suppression of crime.

The *Hill* immunity was at its outset applied to a wide variety of circumstances which did not involve challenges to the manner of investigating a crime (see, e.g., *Alexandrou v Oxford* [1993] 4 All ER 328; *Hughes v National Union of Mineworkers* [1991] 4 All ER 278; *Ancell v McDermott* [1993] 4 All ER 355). In *Osman v Ferguson* [1993] 4 All ER 344, the Court of Appeal held that the relevant policy considerations still applied even where the police had received advanced warning that a particular individual posed a danger to the plaintiffs. This decision was later challenged as an infringement of the plaintiff's rights under the ECHR and the result of the subsequent case law on the issue (discussed below in Section III) is that the widest applications of the *Hill* immunity cannot now be supported. However, the House of Lords in *Brooks v Commissioner of the Police for the Metropolis* [2005] 1 WLR 1495 took the opportunity to reaffirm authoritatively the central holding in *Hill's* case, i.e. that the police cannot generally be held liable for careless conduct in investigating crime. The context was a claim by the surviving victim of a notorious racist attack in London, following findings in an official inquiry ('the Stephen Lawrence Inquiry', after the deceased victim) that the police investigation had been marred by a collective failure to treat Brooks with proper concern and respect because of stereotyping based on his skin colour.

The scope of the *Hill* immunity was again before their Lordships in *Smith v Chief Constable of Sussex Police*, extracted below.

Smith v Chief Constable of Sussex Police [2009] 1 AC 225

The claimant was the victim of a violent assault by his former partner and suffered serious physical injuries as a result. Prior to the attack, the claimant had been in contact with the police about a stream of violent, abusive and threatening telephone, text and internet messages, including death threats, that had been sent to him by the ex-partner. Amongst other alleged failings, the relevant police officers did not look at any of these messages and took no steps other than tracing the source of the messages. The claim in negligence was struck out at first instance but the Court of Appeal allowed an appeal. The House of Lords also heard at the same time the appeal in *Van Colle v Hertfordshire Police*, a case based on a breach of Art 2 of the ECHR. The extract deals only with the decision in *Smith*.

Lord Brown

123. Generally speaking, it is accepted that in the discharge of this function the police owe no legal duty of care to individuals affected. Lord Steyn in *Brooks v Commissioner of Police of the Metropolis* [2005] 1 WLR 1495 more than once referred to this as the "core principle in

Hill's case" (*Hill v Chief Constable of West Yorkshire* [1989] AC 53). Can this "core principle", however, accommodate Lord Bingham's "liability principle": the proposition that "if a member of the public (A) furnishes a police officer (B) with apparently credible evidence that a third party whose identity and whereabouts are known presents a specific and imminent threat to his life or physical safety, B owes A a duty to take reasonable steps to assess such threat and, if appropriate, take reasonable steps to prevent it being executed"?

124. For my part I would acknowledge that the facts of the present case are vastly different from those either in *Hill* or in *Brooks* and that it is easier to contemplate civil liability here than in either of those cases. The particular reasons for rejecting the contended for duty of care in each of them were compelling: in *Hill* because it was surely unthinkable that the conduct of the entire Yorkshire Ripper investigation should be subject to minute examination; in *Brooks* because the main complaint was of psychiatric injury caused by the police's cavalier treatment of the claimant when they were first called to Stephen Lawrence's horrific murder, unsure at that stage whether he was a suspect or a witness, and intent above all on finding out who were the killers.

125. I recognise too that the facts of the present case are really very strong—as, indeed, I clearly recall having regarded the facts in *Osman* when originally that case was before the Court of Appeal in 1992: [1993] 4 All ER 344.

126. But all that said, is it really possible to find a satisfactory basis upon which to distinguish this class of case (it would, of course, have to be distinguished on a class basis since, if a duty of care were found to exist, claims a good deal less meritorious than this one would inevitably be brought) from all the many other situations in which the *Hill* principle would clearly apply?

127. Not without hesitation—for Lord Bingham's opinion is undoubtedly persuasive and it is tempting to provide redress in as meritorious a case as this—I conclude not.

128. In the first place, it seems to me difficult to limit "the liability principle" in the way my Lord does. Why, logically, should the principle apply only to threats to "life or physical safety" and not also to property? Paragraphs 54 and 55 of my Lord's opinion, indeed, invite that very question. I do not question for a moment the highly authoritative statements made by the House in *Glasbrook Brothers Ltd v Glamorgan County Council* [1925] AC 270 as to the "absolute and unconditional obligation" on the police to protect property, as well as persons, from criminal injury. But nothing said there suggests that a breach of this obligation would give rise to civil liability for damages and, indeed, the authors of those statements would surely have been astonished by any such suggestion.

129. Secondly . . . who is to judge whether the evidence is both (a) "apparently credible" and also (b) of "a specific and imminent threat"? These, of course, are critical preliminary questions since "the liability principle" would determine whether or not a duty of care arises in the first place.

130. Thirdly, although it is tempting to regard the police's function from which this duty is said to spring as something different from that of "investigating crime" (the function which prompted the *Hill* principle)— as, perhaps, the exercise of a protective function—this really would be a false dichotomy. Not only are the threats themselves criminal offences which, like other reported crimes, fall to be investigated but, as I indicated earlier, the police have to investigate many other risks of physical violence which come to their attention.

131. Fourthly, some at least of the public policy considerations which weighed with the House in *Hill* and *Brooks* to my mind weigh also in the present factual context. I would emphasise two in particular.

132. First, concern that the imposition of the liability principle upon the police would induce in them a detrimentally defensive frame of mind. So far from doubting whether this would in fact be so, it seems to me inevitable. If liability could arise in this context (but not, of course,

with regard to the police's many other tasks in investigating and combating crime) the police would be likely to treat these particular reported threats with especial caution at the expense of the many other threats to life, limb and property of which they come to learn through their own and others' endeavours. They would be likely to devote more time and resources to their investigation and to take more active steps to combat them. They would be likely to arrest and charge more of those reportedly making the threats and would be more likely in these cases to refuse or oppose bail, leaving it to the courts to take the responsibility of deciding whether those accused of making such threats should remain at liberty. The police are inevitably faced in these cases with a conflict of interest between the person threatened and the maker of the threat. If the police would be liable in damages to the former for not taking sufficiently strong action but not to the latter for acting too strongly, the police, subconsciously or not, would be inclined to err on the side of over-reaction. I would regard this precisely as inducing in them a detrimentally defensive frame of mind. Similarly with regard to their likely increased focus on these reported threats at the expense of other police work.

133. The second public policy consideration which I would emphasise in the present context is the desirability of safeguarding the police from legal proceedings which, meritorious or otherwise, would involve them in a great deal of time, trouble and expense more usefully devoted to their principal function of combating crime. This was a point made by Lord Keith in *Hill* and is of a rather different character from that made by Lord Steyn in para 30 of his opinion in *Brooks*—see para 51 of Lord Bingham's opinion. In respectful disagreement with my Lord, I would indeed regard actions pursuant to the liability principle as diverting police resources away from their primary function. Not perhaps in every case but sometimes certainly, the contesting of these actions would require lengthy consideration to be given to the deployment of resources and to the nature and extent of competing tasks and priorities.

134. Just such policy considerations as these (the conflicts of interest involved and the desirability of limiting litigation against those concerned to act in the interests of the wider community) informed the judgments of the House, not only in *Hill* and *Brooks* but also (of the majority) in *D v East Berkshire Community Health NHS Trust* [2005] 2 AC 373 . . . .

Lord Hope, **Lord Phillips** and **Lord Carswell** delivered separate concurring speeches. **Lord Bingham** dissented.

Appeal allowed.

COMMENTARY

The affirmation of a core area where *Hill* applies has not pleased everyone; commenting on the case Burton ((2009) 72 MLR 283, 293) argues, bluntly: 'The denial of a remedy in *Smith* may therefore be seen not just as a failure to provide redress for one victim, but also arguably as a licence for the police to continue to fail victims of crime generally and victims of domestic violence in particular.' It must be remembered, however, that the immunity of the police is not a blanket immunity. The courts have never exhibited the same reluctance to hold the police liable for positive acts of misfeasance, at least where these are the direct cause of a physical injury suffered by the claimant and do not simply provide a third party with the opportunity to injure the claimant (see, e.g., *Marshall v Osmond* [1983] 2 All ER 225: duty owed in high-speed pursuit). Moreover, where it can be held that the police have assumed a responsibility to the claimant, a duty of care might be owed (see *Kirkham v Chief Constable of Manchester* [1990] 2 QB 283, *Reeves v Commissioner of the Police for the*

Metropolis [2000] 1 AC 360, discussed further at p. 265) and in the recent case of *Desmond v Chief Constable of Nottinghamshire Police* [2009] EWHC 2362 (QB) it was assumed that this would also apply to cases that prima facie fell within the *Hill* immunity (see also *Swinney v Chief Constable of Northumbria* [1997] QB 464). In *Smith* Lord Bingham attempted to expand this category of exception by the creation of a new 'liability principle': if a member of the public (A) furnishes a police officer (B) with apparently credible evidence that a third party whose identity and whereabouts are known presents a specific and imminent threat to his life or physical safety, B owes A a duty to take reasonable steps to assess such threat and, if appropriate, take reasonable steps to prevent it being executed (see para. 123 of the extract above). This approach did not find favour amongst the majority; according to Lord Phillips, the duty could be rephrased as 'where the police have reason to believe that an individual is threatened with criminal violence they owe a duty to that person to take such action as is in all the circumstances reasonable to protect that person'. In his Lordships' view, such a duty of care would be in direct conflict with the principle in *Hill*.

In cases where the defendant is a public authority under the HRA (as are the police), it may be possible to circumvent the *Hill* immunity by bringing an action under the HRA for breach of the public authority's s. 6 obligation to act compatibly with the Convention. One aspect of the ECtHR's decision in *Osman v United Kingdom* that has escaped critical reassessment (see Section III, below) is that the police might have a duty to take positive action to protect an individual's right to life (Article 2 ECHR) where they were aware of a 'real and immediate risk'. The nature and extent of that positive obligation lay at the heart of the appeal heard alongside *Smith*, *Van Colle v Chief Constable of Hertfordshire Police*. The claimant's son, who was to be a witness in an upcoming criminal trial, was subjected to threats and intimidation—which were reported to the police and of which they were aware—and then murdered before the trial could take place. A unanimous House of Lords held that the *Osman* test was a stringent one and was not satisfied on the facts of the case. Despite the difficulties of establishing liability under the *Osman* test, the possibility of this claim was one reason their Lordships in *Smith* felt no need to relax the *Hill* immunity. One may wonder how valuable this alternative really is. As Spencer notes: '...if a Human Rights Act claim failed in the *Van Colle* case, such claims are likely to fail in most other cases too' ([2009] CLJ 25, 26). If there is any reform of the common law, however, it is likely to be in the direction of the *Osman* approach as the Law Commission (*Administrative Redress: Public Bodies and the Citizen*, Consultation Paper No. 187, 2008, paras 4.143–4.166) has provisionally recommended a liability regime for public bodies (which would include the police) based on, amongst other things, the presence of serious fault by the defendant. See further Ch. 10 below.

Other Immunities

The number of specific immunities recognised by the courts, at one time or another, has been very significant, although the growing influence of human rights law on the law of tort (Section III, below) has led to many of the old immunities being abolished. One of the most important of the old immunities was that enjoyed by barristers and solicitors in respect of their conduct of litigation, as well as preliminary matters which were intimately connected with the conduct of a case in court (see *Rondel v Worsley* [1969] 1 AC 191; *Saif Ali v Sidney Mitchell & Co* [1980] AC 198). This immunity was abolished by the House of Lords in *Arthur J. S. Hall v Simons* [2002] 1 AC 615, overruling its own previous decisions in *Rondel* and *Saif Ali*. Whilst an immunity continues to be recognised in favour of witnesses giving evidence in, or in anticipation of, legal proceedings (*X v Bedfordshire CC* [1995] 2 AC 633), recent cases have interpreted the scope of the immunity narrowly (*L (A Child) v Reading Borough Council* [2001] 1 WLR 1575, *Darker v Chief Constable of West Midlands Police* [2001] 1 AC 435). However, there remain a number of areas where the public policy reasons for denying a duty of care outweigh other factors so as to provide an effective immunity from suit in negligence. Those acting in a judicial or quasi-judicial capacity, for example, owe no duty to persons foreseeably affected by their conduct (*Yuen Kun Yeu v Attorney General for Hong Kong* [1988] AC 175; cf. *Three Rivers District Council v Bank of England (No. 3)* [2003] 2 AC 1). It has also been held that members of the armed forces involved in a conflict situation owe no duty to take steps to protect their colleagues from the risk of 'friendly fire' (*Mulcahy v Ministry of Defence* [1996] QB 732). The principal concern here is that the threat of liability might take soldiers' minds off the task in hand. Lastly, it may be observed that local authority social services departments have some immunity from suit in responding to actual or suspected child abuse (*X v Bedfordshire CC*, above; see further p. 519, below; cf. *D v East Berkshire Community Health NHS Trust*, p. 527, below).

Immunities from Negligence Liability and a Note on the Striking-Out Procedure

As is illustrated above, the practical effect of denying a duty of care (whether on grounds of proximity or 'fair, just and reasonable') is to provide a complete or partial immunity applying to certain types of defendant or to certain types of activity (or a mixture of both). It is important to recognise that when a court is asked to find that no duty of care is owed between the parties, it is being asked whether it wants the reasonableness of the defendant's conduct to be discussed at all. According to orthodox theory, the decision whether the defendant has acted carelessly (i.e. unreasonably) is logically distinct from the question whether he should be held liable for the consequences of his carelessness. A finding of 'no duty' safeguards the defendant from all claims, no matter how carelessly he has behaved (unless, of course, he has acted deliberately or in bad faith). And whether or not a duty is owed is determined without regard for the defendant's actual degree of fault (if any). Given this background, the law recognised—in the interests of the efficient disposal of actions—that the decision whether the defendant owes the claimant a duty of care may be decided in a preliminary or pre-trial hearing. The issue normally arises when the defendant seeks to strike out the claimant's case as disclosing no cause of action (Civil Procedure Rules, r. 3.4; the procedure applies to all claims, not just those in tort). Striking-out applications are only appropriate for dealing with disputed questions of law (e.g. as to the existence of a duty of care), not disputed questions of fact (e.g. as to the breach of any duty owed) as these latter can only be addressed after a full hearing and the examination and cross-examination of witnesses on both sides. (In fact, under the *Caparo* approach striking out would appear possible only in respect of the legal duty requirements of proximity and fairness (etc.), not the factual requirement of foreseeability.) It follows that, for the purposes of the striking-out application, the court assumes that the facts as pleaded are true, so that (in the case of a properly pleaded negligence action) it will be deemed that the defendant has been careless and that the carelessness has caused the claimant's loss.

The striking-out procedure represents a very significant weapon in the hands of defendants, enabling them to deal quickly and cheaply with ill-founded claims without incurring the expenses associated with full trial. However, the use of the procedure has been thrown into some doubt by developments in the human rights field.

III. Negligence in the Human Rights Era

The implementation of the Human Rights Act 1998 (HRA) has resulted in a number of challenges to the law of negligence. It appears that the Act has both 'vertical' and 'horizontal' effects (i.e. it allows individuals to rely upon specified rights under the European Convention in litigation both against the state and against other private individuals or organisations). Its vertical effect lies in the obligation imposed directly upon public authorities to respect Convention rights (HRA, s. 6). The most notable consequence is the recognition of a positive duty on public authorities (e.g. local councils, government departments, regulators) to safeguard rights to life, physical integrity, private and family life, and personal property (see p. 504, below). The Act's horizontal effect stems from the fact that the courts are 'public authorities' within the meaning of s. 6, and hence (it seems) have a duty to reach decisions compatible with Convention rights even in litigation between private parties. However, as Lord Bingham noted in *Smith* (at [58]), 'the existence of a Convention right cannot call for instant manufacture of a corresponding common law right where none exists'; the horizontal effect of the HRA does not extend that far (see also *Wainwright v Home Office* [2004] 2 AC 406).

How far have the courts been prepared to go in adapting the law of negligence, and the law of tort generally, to the new legal landscape of the HRA? This issue is considered in the extract below.

Lady Justice Arden, 'Human Rights and Civil Wrongs: Tort Law Under the Spotlight' [2010] PL 140

[T]he courts have not extended the law of tort to provide remedies for violations of Convention rights involved in claims for negligence against public authorities but left such claims to be dealt with in proceedings under s. 7 of the HRA...

Conclusions

Early expectations

Before the HRA came into force, there was much debate about the implications of the statutory duty imposed by s.6 on courts not to act incompatibly with Convention rights. Many people expressed the belief that s.6 would lead the courts to develop the law of tort to make it consistent with Convention rights. Our tort law is largely case law, and its development is often policy-driven. Convention jurisprudence reflects the values of the Convention, and thus could provide inspiration for decisions about developing tort law.

Since the commencement of the HRA

The courts have indeed in some cases proceeded to develop the common law by reference to Convention rights. Certainly the law of breach of confidence has been transformed by using Convention rights and values. Undoubtedly, the lack of a remedy at common law for invasions of privacy was widely regarded as a deficiency. In actions for disclosure of information in breach of confidence, English law now "mirrors" the Strasbourg jurisprudence.

But the developments have been subtler than forecast, and it is clear that s. 6 does not have the full effect mooted before the HRA came into force. The law of England and Wales that public bodies should not in general owe a duty of care in the performance of statutory powers has not been qualified so as to provide a remedy where Convention rights have been violated...

Is there a principle?

The position would seem to be that the English courts are not necessarily going to develop the common law in the field of tort by reference to Convention rights and values, but will do so only in specific cases where that is appropriate for domestic law reasons. It will not be appropriate where the Convention goes against the grain of some established principle of domestic law. The disappointed litigant will then be confined to his statutory remedy for violation of Convention rights. At the moment this is in general distinctly less generous than a tort law remedy in English law but if the Strasbourg jurisprudence on damages were to change there might well be a reason to reconsider the position in tort in domestic law rather than persist in the system of parallel remedies.

COMMENTARY

The extract addresses the question of how the implementation of the HRA has impacted upon the duties of care owed by public bodies at common law. Is the existence of a remedy under the HRA a reason for or against the development of a parallel remedy under the general law of negligence? In *D v East Berkshire Community NHS Trust* [2004] QB 558 the Court of Appeal relied upon the passage of the HRA to justify its departure from a previous decision of the House of Lords. The issue was whether social and medical care workers owed a duty of care to children in deciding to separate them from their parents for reasons of suspected child abuse. The House of Lords had previously held that it would not be fair, just and reasonable to recognise a duty of care in such circumstances (*X v Bedfordshire County Council* [1995] 2 AC 633), but the ECtHR subsequently found a violation of the claimants' rights under the Convention (*Z v United Kingdom* [2001] 2 FLR 6). In the *East Berkshire* case, the Court of Appeal ruled that the HRA's creation of a new statutory remedy for the violation of Convention rights had altered the balance of policy considerations as assessed by the House of Lords in the *Bedfordshire* case. Recognising a common law remedy would have no additional chilling effect on the conduct of care professionals. (It may be noted that the statutory remedy was in force at the time of the court's decision, but not at the time of the alleged negligence, so there was no possibility of an action under the HRA itself.) However, the court decided at the same time that no duty of care was owed to the parents of the children, and this was affirmed by the House of Lords in *D v East Berkshire Community NHS Trust* [2005] 2 AC 373. Concern about the chilling effect of the contrary decision was again highlighted. It is striking that these decisions flew in the face of the ECtHR's decision in *TP and KM v United Kingdom*—another claim arising out of the House of Lords' decision in *X v Bedfordshire*—that care professionals may in some circumstances violate the Convention rights of parents whose children have been taken into care. If, as seems to be the case, the parents would now have a claim under the HRA, the question arises why the courts have not recognised here the same decisive change in the balance of policy considerations as they have in relation to the claim by the child.

Whatever willingness, albeit partial, of the Court of Appeal in D to modify the law of negligence should be contrasted with the position taken by a majority of the House of Lords in *Van Colle v Hertfordshire Police; Smith v Chief Constable of Surrey* [2009] 1 AC 225. According to Lord Hope and Lord Brown, there was no need to extend the common law to provide a remedy for breach of a Convention right; the two systems (common law negligence and the statutory cause of action under the HRA) could exist in parallel. For

Lord Hope, the presence of a remedy under the HRA was a ground for *refusing* to extend the common law: 'any perceived shortfall in the way that it [the common law] deals with cases that fall within the threshold for the application of the *Osman* test can now be dealt with in domestic law under the 1998 Act.' Moreover, the case for extending the common law to cover a breach of Article 2 was weakened by the fact that the standard for liability to be imposed on the state under the *Osman* test is more stringent than that imposed in negligence. In other words, imposing liability in negligence might actually *expand* liability for breach of Convention rights beyond that recognised by the ECHR. More fundamentally, Lord Brown argued that actions in tort and under the HRA for breach of Convention rights served different purposes: tort law actions provided compensation for loss whilst claims for breach of Convention rights aimed at upholding minimum human rights standards and providing vindication of those rights. However, as Steele, 'Damages in Tort and under the Human Rights Act: Remedial or Functional Separation?' [2008] CLJ 606, points out, this distinction is too stark as tort law frequently allows awards that can be seen to vindicate rights (for example, in the tort of false imprisonment). She comments (at 609):

As ever, it remains legitimate to ask whether tort's remedies are appropriate and proportionate to the objective sought. As we have seen, the House of Lords seems on occasions to have supplied an answer to this question which is far from the one predicted by commentators: the extension of monetary remedies in tort is an inappropriate and unnecessary protection of Convention rights' given the enactment of the HRA. This sceptical response has not however been reached on the basis of clear analysis of the nature of the tort remedies beyond compensation for material damage, and it is unnecessarily stark.

Ultimately, the question remains, as Lord Bingham asked rhetorically in his dissenting opinion in the *East Berkshire* case (at [50]), whether 'the law of tort...should remain essentially static, making only such changes as are forced upon it, leaving difficult and, in human terms, very important problems to be swept up by the Convention'?

Article 6 and the Duty of Care

A more fundamental challenge to basic doctrines of tort law and procedure came from the view that denying liability in negligence on the basis that no duty of care was owed to the claimant might infringe Article 6, ECHR, which provides:

In the determination of his civil rights and obligations or of any criminal charge against him, everyone is entitled to a fair and public hearing within a reasonable time by an independent and impartial tribunal established by law.

This general right is regarded as giving rise to the more specific 'right to a court'. Applying this to negligence claims, the question arises whether a claimant's right to a court is satisfied where the claim had been struck out at a preliminary hearing on the basis that it was not fair, just and reasonable that a duty of care be recognised. In *Osman v United Kingdom* [1999] 1 FLR 193 the applicants were the unsuccessful plaintiffs in *Osman v Ferguson* [1993] 4 All ER 344, an action against the police, in which they alleged that a careless police investigation had resulted in insufficient steps being taken against a certain individual, PL, to prevent him causing harm to the applicants' family. As a result, PL killed the applicants' husband and father, and injured one of the applicants. Applying *Hill v Chief Constable of West Yorkshire*, above, the applicants' claim in negligence against the police was struck out at a preliminary hearing by the Court of Appeal on the basis that the police owed no duty to the applicants. The applicants took their case to the ECtHR, unsuccessfully alleging breaches of Articles 2 and 8 but successfully arguing a breach of Article 6. The decision on Article 6 is difficult and much of it, in practice if not in theory, has been departed from by later courts, but an important part of the decision was that the Court of Appeal had failed to balance the policy factors against imposing a duty of care (as set out in *Hill*) against the factors in the individual case which would militate in favour of a duty of care, and this resulted in a disproportionate immunity from civil action being granted to the police. According to the ECtHR, the Court of Appeal should have considered other factors such as the degree of negligence, the seriousness of the harm suffered, and the justice of the particular case in deciding whether a duty of care should be owed. The problem with this was that these were not factors which English law, according to orthodox principles, took into account in determining the existence of a duty of care. The English approach was to deal under the heading of duty with considerations (of both proximity and policy) applicable to all cases of the same general description as the case at hand; the question was whether there should be liability if negligence was proved in this type of case, and the facts of the individual case were not relevant.

By contrast, the ECtHR appeared specifically to require domestic courts to assess whether it would be proportionate to apply a general immunity of the type under consideration in view of the particular merits of the individual case. Accordingly, whilst the ECtHR did not expressly state that the striking-out procedure of itself contravened Article 6, the traditional manner in which such striking-out decisions were decided prima facie appeared to contravene Article 6.

The reaction to *Osman* in England varied considerably, although, as Hickman, 'The "Uncertain Shadow": Throwing Light on the Right to a Court under Article 6(1) ECHR' [2004] PL 122, fn 65 points out, 'the few who were favourably disposed to the judgment saw it as curing ills largely unconnected with the right of access to court'. When the issue came again before the ECtHR in *Z v United Kingdom* [2001] 2 FLR 612, arising out of the House of Lords' decision in *X v Bedfordshire*, the ECtHR took a different approach to Article 6 and the duty of care from that which it adopted in *Osman*. The key passages of the Court's judgment follow:

96. Moreover, the Court is not persuaded that the House of Lords' decision that as a matter of law there was no duty of care in the applicants' case may be characterised as either an exclusionary rule or an immunity which deprived them of access to court. As Lord Browne-Wilkinson explained in his leading speech, the House of Lords was concerned with the issue whether a novel category of negligence, that is a category of case in which a duty of care had not previously been held to exist, should be developed by the courts in their law-making role under the common law. ... The House of Lords, after weighing in the balance the competing considerations of public policy, decided not to extend liability in negligence into a new area. In so doing, it circumscribed the range of liability under tort law.

97. That decision did end the case, without the factual matters being determined on the evidence. However, if as a matter of law, there was no basis for the claim, the hearing of evidence would have been an expensive and time-consuming process which would not have provided the applicants with any remedy at its conclusion. There is no reason to consider the striking out procedure which rules on the existence of sustainable causes of action as per se offending the principle of access to court. In such a procedure, the plaintiff is generally able to submit to the court the arguments supporting his or her claims on the law and the court will rule on those issues at the conclusion of an adversarial procedure. ...

98. Nor is the Court persuaded by the suggestion that, irrespective of the position in domestic law, the decision disclosed an immunity in fact or practical effect due to its allegedly sweeping or blanket nature. That decision concerned only one aspect of the exercise of local authorities' powers and duties and cannot be regarded as an arbitrary removal of the courts' jurisdiction to determine a whole range of civil claims (see *Fayed v UK* (1994) 18 EHRR 393 at 429).... [I]t is a principle of Convention case law that art 6 does not in itself guarantee any particular content for civil rights and obligations in national law, although other articles such as those protecting the right to respect for family life (art 8) and the right to property (art 1 of Protocol 1) may do so. It is not enough to bring art 6(1) into play that the non-existence of a cause of action under domestic law may be described as having the same effect as an immunity, in the sense of not enabling the applicant to sue for a given category of harm.

Article 6 and the Duty of Care post-Z

It is clear after *Z* that the striking out of a negligence claim on the basis that it is not fair, just and reasonable to impose a duty of care on the defendant does not necessarily infringe Article 6. The ECtHR recognised that a holding that it is not fair, just and reasonable to impose a duty of care precludes liability from arising in the first place—in the language of the Court it related to the applicable principles governing the substantive right of action in domestic law. It did not operate to give an immunity from a liability which would otherwise have arisen. As the Court noted in para. 98: 'It is not enough to bring Art 6(1) into play that the non-existence of a cause of action of domestic law may be described as having the same effect as an immunity.' Many commentators consequently concluded that Article 6 has no relevance at all to striking-out claims in negligence (see, e.g., Gearty, 'Osman Unravels' (2002) 65 MLR 87).

The case-law since *Z* has generally assumed that Article 6 has little, if any, role to play in negligence cases. In *Matthews v Ministry of Defence* [2003] 1 AC 1163 (a case which did not concern the existence of a duty of care) the House of Lords accepted a distinction, advanced in previous decisions of the ECtHR (see, e.g., *Fayed v United Kingdom* (1994) 18 EHRR 393) between restrictions on the right of access to a court based on substantive law and restrictions of a procedural nature. It was only the latter that attracted Article 6 scrutiny. In these terms the denial of a duty of care on the ground that it was not fair, just and reasonable is substantive, not procedural, and there is no basis for scrutiny under Article 6. In effect, this is to treat Article 6 as wholly non-applicable to matters of substantive law, not merely to assert the substantive law's compliance with Article 6. This seems to be further supported by *Roche v United Kingdom* (2006) 42 EHRR 30, where the ECtHR, in stressing the importance of the substance/procedure divide, stated that Article 6 'can, in principle, have no application to substantive limitations on the right existing under domestic law' (para. 119). An attempt to 'resurrect' *Osman* as a means of challenging the striking-out procedure was comprehensively rejected by the Court of Appeal in *D v East Berkshire Community NHS Trust* [2004] QB 558 (and was not even argued before the House of Lords on appeal: [2005] 2 AC 373), and in the recent case of *Mitchell v Glasgow City Council* [2009] 1 AC 874 Lord Hope was able to assert blandly (at [13]) that there was 'no incompatibility' between the striking out procedure and Article 6.

There is little doubt that the *direct* effect of *Osman* is considerably less than was first thought. However, there is no doubt that the *practical* effect of the decision was greatly to inhibit the use of the strike-out procedure in actions against public authorities—at least for a while. As Gearty (2002) 65 MLR 87 at 94 notes: 'perhaps *Z and others* is too late to save the pre-*Osman* law of negligence? Certainly the liability of public authorities has greatly increased in the period since that now-disgraced decision was handed down, albeit (we are asked to believe) without it having been explicitly or even implicitly "followed" in the traditional English sense'. More recent decisions, however, have shown less reluctance to use the strike-out procedure (see, e.g., *Brooks* and *Smith*, discussed above). It may well be then that, paradoxically, the enduring legacy of *Osman* will lie not in its view of the role of Article 6 in negligence actions, but rather in its reinvigoration of the debate as to the role of the duty of care in the English law of negligence, evidenced both in the submission made to the House of Lords in *D v East Berkshire Community NHS Trust* [2005] 2 AC 373 that the common law should jettison the concept of duty of care as a prerequisite to liability in negligence (see extract at p. 125, above), and, more generally, as to whether the law of negligence should expand to provide a remedy for breach of other Convention rights.

For an analysis resisting the inevitability of the above interpretation, and arguing that there may still be some mileage in the Article 6 reasoning in *Osman*, see Oliphant, 'European Tort Law: A Primer for the Common Lawyer' (2009) 62 CLP 440, 465–6.

4 BREACH OF DUTY

I. Introduction

Liability in the tort of negligence is premised on fault. It must be shown that the defendant was in breach of his duty to take reasonable care of the claimant—assuming such a duty to exist. The inquiry is into the content of the duty of care, as opposed to its existence (the topic of Ch. 3). The classic definition is Alderson B's in *Blyth v Birmingham Waterworks Co* (1856) 11 Ex 781 at 784:

> Negligence is the omission to do something which a reasonable man, guided upon those considerations which ordinarily regulate the conduct of human affairs, would do, or doing something which a prudent and reasonable man would not do.

The test is therefore essentially *practical*, referring to the hypothetical conduct of a reasonable person: what would a reasonable person have done in the circumstances? Nevertheless, a tendency to focus upon the risk run by defendants once led some courts to regard breach of duty as an essentially *statistical* question, referring only to the degree of probability or foreseeability that the risk in question might eventuate. Thus the question was put whether the foreseeability of the claimant's injury was 'reasonable', as if this referred to some absolute standard. In fact, whether or not the defendant's conduct gave rise to a reasonably foreseeable risk of harm is truly relevant only in addressing the question, what would the reasonable person have done in the circumstances?

The relationship between the concept of foreseeability and the 'reasonable person test' is addressed in the following extracts.

Bolton v Stone [1951] AC 850

The plaintiff, Miss Stone, was injured when a cricket ball struck her. The ball, which had been hit by a batsman playing in a cricket match at a local cricket club, travelled approximately 100 yards before it hit her, clearing a fence some 78 yards from the pitch which, at the point where the ball left the ground, was 17 feet high. The evidence suggested that balls had not been hit out of the ground more than six times in thirty years. The plaintiff sued the committee and members of the club, alleging negligence and nuisance in not taking steps to avoid the danger of a ball being hit out of their ground. Oliver J at first instance found for the defendants, but the Court of Appeal reversed his decision, ruling that the defendants were guilty of negligence. On the defendants' appeal to the House of Lords, the only issues in dispute related to the action in negligence.

Lord Oaksey

My Lords, I have come to the conclusion in this difficult case that the decision of Oliver J ought to be restored. Cricket has been played for about ninety years on the ground in question and no ball has been proved to have struck anyone on the highways near the ground until the respondent was struck, nor has there been any complaint to the appellants. In such circumstances was it the duty of the appellants, who are the committee of the club, to take some special precautions other than those they did take to prevent such an accident as happened? The standard of care in the law of negligence is the standard of an ordinarily careful man, but, in my opinion, an ordinarily careful man does not take precautions against every foreseeable risk. He can, of course, foresee the possibility of many risks, but life would be almost impossible if he were to attempt to take precautions against every risk which he can foresee. He takes precautions against risks which are reasonably likely to happen. Many foreseeable risks are extremely unlikely to happen and cannot be guarded against except by almost complete isolation. The ordinarily prudent owner of a dog does not keep his dog always on a lead on a country highway for fear it may cause injury to a passing motor cyclist, nor does the ordinarily prudent pedestrian avoid the use of the highway for fear of skidding motor cars. It may very well be that after this accident the ordinarily prudent committee man of a similar cricket ground would take some further precaution, but that is not to say that he would have taken a similar precaution before the accident...There are many footpaths and highways adjacent to cricket grounds and golf courses on to which cricket and golf balls are occasionally driven, but such risks are habitually treated both by the owners and committees of such cricket and golf courses and by the pedestrians who use the adjacent footpaths and highways as negligible, and it is not, in my opinion, actionable negligence not to take precautions to avoid such risks.

Lord Reid

My Lords, it was readily foreseeable that an accident such as befell the respondent might possibly occur during one of the appellants' cricket matches. Balls had been driven into the public road from time to time, and it was obvious that if a person happened to be where a ball fell that person would receive injuries which might or might not be serious. On the other hand, it was plain that the chance of that happening was small. The exact number of times a ball has been driven into the road is not known, but it is not proved that this has happened more than about six times in about thirty years. If I assume that it has happened on the average once in three seasons I shall be doing no injustice to the respondent's case. Then there has to be considered the chance of a person being hit by a ball falling in the road. The road appears to be an ordinary side road giving access to a number of private houses, and there is no evidence to suggest that the traffic on this road is other than what one might expect on such a road. On the whole of that part of the road where a ball could fall there would often be nobody and seldom any great number of people. It follows that the chance of a person ever being struck even in a long period of years was very small.

This case, therefore, raises sharply the question what is the nature and extent of the duty of a person who promotes on his land operations which may cause damage to persons on an adjoining highway. Is it that he must not carry out or permit an operation which he knows or ought to know clearly can cause such damage, however improbable that result may be, or is it that he is only bound to take into account the possibility of such damage if such damage is a likely or probable consequence of what he does or permits, or if the risk of damage is such that a reasonable man, careful of the safety of his neighbour, would regard that risk as material? I do not know of any case where this question has had to be decided or even where it has been fully discussed. Of course there are many cases in which somewhat similar questions have arisen, but, generally speaking, if injury to another person from the defendants' acts is reasonably foreseeable the chance that injury will result is substantial and it does not matter in which way the duty is stated. In such cases I do not think that much assistance is to be got from analysing the language which a judge has used. More assistance is to be got from cases where judges have clearly chosen their language with care in setting out a principle, but even so, statements of the law must be read in light of the facts of the particular case. Nevertheless, making all allowances for this, I do find at least a tendency to base duty rather on the likelihood of damage to others than on its foreseeability alone.

The definition of negligence which has, perhaps, been most often quoted is that of Alderson B in *Blyth v Birmingham Waterworks Co* (1856) 11 Ex 781 at 784:

> Negligence is the omission to do some thing which a reasonable man, guided upon those considerations which ordinarily regulate the conduct of human affairs, would do, or doing something which a prudent and reasonable man would not do.

I think that reasonable men do, in fact, take into account the degree of risk and do not act on a bare possibility as they would if the risk were more substantial. A more recent attempt to find a basis for a man's legal duty to his neighbour is that of Lord Atkin in *Donoghue v Stevenson*. I need not quote the whole passage: for this purpose the important part is (p. 580):

> You must take reasonable care to avoid acts or omissions which you can reasonably foresee would be likely to injure your neighbour.

Parts of Lord Atkin's statement have been criticised as being too wide, but I am not aware that it has been stated that any part of it is too narrow. Lord Atkin does not say 'Which you can reasonably foresee could injure your neighbour': he introduces the limitation 'would be likely to injure your neighbour' . . .

Counsel for the respondent in the present case had to put his case so high as to say that, at least as soon as one ball had been driven into the road in the ordinary course of a match, the appellants could and should have realised that that might happen again, and that, if it did, someone might be injured, and that that was enough to put on the appellants a duty to take steps to prevent such an occurrence. If the true test is foreseeability alone I think that must be so. Once a ball has been driven on to a road without there being anything extraordinary to account for the fact, there is clearly a risk that another will follow and if it does there is clearly a chance, small though it may be, that somebody may be injured. On the theory that it is foreseeability alone that matters it would be irrelevant to consider how often a ball might be expected to land in the road and it would not matter whether the road was the busiest street or the quietest country lane. The only difference between these cases is in the degree of risk. It would take a good deal to make me believe that the law has departed so far from the standards which guide ordinary careful people in ordinary life. In the crowded conditions of modern life even the most careful person cannot avoid creating some risks and accepting others. What a man must not do, and what I think a careful man tries not to do, is to create a risk which is substantial . . . In my judgment, the test to be applied here is whether the risk of damage to a person on the road was so small that a reasonable man in the position of the appellants, considering the matter from the point of views of safety, would have thought it right to refrain from taking steps to prevent the danger. In considering that matter I think that it would be right to take into account not only how remote is the chance that a person might be struck, but also how serious the consequences are likely to be if a person is struck, but I do not think that it would be right to take into account the difficulty of remedial measures. If cricket cannot be played on a ground without creating a substantial risk, then it should not be played there at all. I think that this is in substance the test which Oliver J applied in this case. He considered whether the appellants' ground was large enough to be safe for all practical purposes and held that it was. This is a question, not of law, but of fact and degree. It is not an easy question, and it is one on which opinions may well differ. I can only say that, having given the whole matter repeated and anxious consideration, I find myself unable to decide this question in favour of the respondent.

I think, however, that this case is not far from the border-line. If this appeal is allowed, that does not, in my judgment, mean that in every case where cricket has been played on a ground for a number of years without accident or complaint those who organise matches there are safe to go on in reliance on past immunity. I would have reached a different conclusion if I had thought that the risk here had been other than extremely small because I do not think that a reasonable man, considering the matter from the point of view of safety, would or should disregard any risk unless it is extremely small . . .

In my judgment, the appeal should be allowed.

Lord Radcliffe

My Lords, I agree that this appeal must be allowed. I agree with regret, because I have much sympathy with the decision that commended itself to the majority of the members of the Court of Appeal. I can see nothing unfair in the appellants being required to compensate the respondent for the serious injury that she has received as a result of the sport that they have organised on their cricket ground at Cheetham Hill, but the law of negligence is concerned less with what is fair than with what is culpable, and I cannot persuade myself that the appellants have been guilty of any culpable act or omission in this case . . .

It seems to me that a reasonable man, taking account of the chances against an accident happening, would not have felt himself called on either to abandon the use of the ground for cricket or to increase the height of his surrounding fences. He would have done what the appellants did. In other words, he would have done nothing. Whether, if the unlikely event of an accident did occur and his play turn to another's hurt, he would have thought it equally proper to offer no more consolation to his victim than the reflection that a social being is not immune from social risks, I do not say, for I do not think that that is a consideration which is relevant to legal liability.

I agree with the others of your Lordships that, if the respondent cannot succeed in negligence, she cannot succeed on any other head of claim.

Lord Porter and **Lord Normand** delivered separate concurring speeches.

Appeal allowed.

COMMENTARY

This is a pivotal case in the modern law of negligence. It broaches a cluster of crucial issues relating to the duty to take reasonable care. Is it a breach of this duty for the defendant to run the risk of *foreseeable* injury to the claimant, however improbable that result might be? Is *a greater probability* of harm required? Or is the magnitude of the risk not the ultimate test of breach of duty?

Their Lordships clearly answered the first question in the negative. It is on the second and third questions that there is room for doubt as to what their Lordships decided.

In places, their Lordships seem to focus upon *the degree of probability* as the crucial factor in determining whether there was negligence. But it would be wrong to look at the probability of harm in isolation: it is only one of the factors which bear upon what is really the crucial question, namely whether the risk was such as would make a reasonable person take precautions to guard against it. This question emphasises not so much the magnitude of the risk but *the practical response* to the risk expected from a reasonable person. As Lord Reid states: 'the test to be applied is whether the risk of damage to a person on the road was so small that a reasonable man in the position of the appellants, considering the matter from the point of view of safety, would have thought it right to refrain from taking steps to prevent the danger.' This analysis is confirmed in the next case extracted below, *The Wagon Mound (No 2)*.

Having dealt with the key point to come out of the decision of the House of Lords, it is worth addressing a number of other issues raised by the case which should be borne in mind throughout the rest of this chapter.

Questions of Fact and Law

Whether or not there is a breach of duty is a question of fact; whether or not the defendant owes the claimant a duty of care is a question of law (at least in so far as the requirements of proximity and fairness, justice and reasonableness are concerned). Nevertheless, the distinction between questions of fact and law still has important practical consequences, for example in relation to appeals and the application of the rules on precedent. Questions of fact were once questions for the jury rather than the judge, but jury trial has been effectively abolished for most tort actions, including actions in negligence (see Senior Courts Act 1981, s. 69; *Ward v James* [1966] 1 QB 273; *H v Ministry of Defence* [1991] 2 QB 103).

Whilst there are of course no limits to an appellate court's power to review disputed questions of law, questions of fact are treated differently. The basic approach of the appellate courts in relation to questions of fact was set out by the House of Lords in *Benmax v Austin Motor Co Ltd* [1955] AC 370, a case on the infringement of letters of patent. Their Lordships drew a distinction between *primary facts* and *inferences* drawn from primary facts. An appellate court should not interfere with a trial judge's finding of primary facts (e.g. as to the sequence of events leading up to an accident) unless it appears perverse or against all the evidence. But inferences from those facts are treated differently. In *Benmax*, Lord Reid stated: 'in cases where the point in dispute is the proper inference to be drawn from proved facts, an appeal court is generally in as good a position to evaluate the evidence as the trial judge, and ought not to shrink from that task, though it ought, of course, to give weight to his opinion' (at 376). In *Qualcast (Wolverhampton) Ltd v Haynes* [1959] AC 743, Lord Denning commented:

Since *Benmax v Austin Motor Co Ltd* [1955] AC 370, the Court of Appeal no longer takes refuge in that most unsatisfactory formula: 'Although we should not have come to the same conclusion ourselves, we do not think we can interfere.' If the Court of Appeal would not have come to the same conclusion themselves, it does what the Court of Appeal ought to do—what it is there for—it overrules the decision. But, short of that, it should accept the conclusions of fact of the tribunal of fact. This means that questions such as whether the injury to the claimant was reasonably foreseeable and whether the defendant took reasonable care in view of the risk of injury are fully open to review by an appellate court.

Precedential Value of Decisions on Breach

As decisions on breach of duty are decisions of fact, and negligence actions almost inevitably have slightly different facts, it follows that the ruling in one case has no precedential value in another case, even if the facts are superficially the same. Hence, *Bolton v Stone* does not decide that cricket clubs can never be held responsible for injuries sustained from a ball hit out of the ground, as Lord Reid indicated in the extract above. The point is illustrated clearly by the contrast between *Bolton v Stone* and the later decision of the Court of Appeal in *Miller v Jackson* [1977] QB 966, in which a majority of the Court of Appeal found a cricket club liable in negligence in circumstances in which balls were hit out of the ground into neighbouring gardens several times each season.

The situation is somewhat different when separate claims arise out of the same basic facts, for example where a number of people are injured by an accident allegedly attributable to the defendant's negligence or by use of an allegedly defective product supplied by the defendant. In such a situation, it is common for one, or a representative sample, of the actions to be brought forward as a 'test case' while the other actions are stayed (i.e. put on hold). Often this results in a 'split trial', with the common issues (e.g. the alleged negligence of the defendant's conduct) ruled upon in an initial hearing and the issues which are peculiar to each individual action (e.g. the quantum of damages) dealt with at a later date if necessary. As English law has not adopted the concept of a class action such as exists in the United States, the decision in the test case is not formally binding upon the other actions in the test case scheme. Nevertheless, the courts have a discretion to strike out any action where it would be an abuse of the process of the court, and they have shown themselves willing to take this course of action where one party seeks to relitigate matters already adjudicated upon in the test case (see *Ashmore v British Coal Corp* [1990] 2 QB 338).

A Note on Terminology—Special and General Duties

Lord Oaksey asked: 'was it the duty of the appellants…to take some special precautions other than those they did take to prevent such an accident as happened?' It is important to distinguish questions of this nature—questions whether there was a duty to take specific precautions—from the question whether the defendant owed the claimant a duty of care. The former goes to *the content* of the duty of care, or—to look at things the other way around—whether there was a *breach of duty*: it is the failure to take the specified precautions which is alleged to be careless. The latter goes to *the existence of a duty*: without a duty of care, the defendant cannot be held legally responsible for the claimant's injury, no matter how carelessly the defendant might have behaved. For criticism of the former use of the term 'duty', which can lead to confusion, see Howarth, 'Negligence after *Murphy*: Time to Re-think' [1991] CLJ 58 at 72–81, and 'Many Duties of Care—Or a Duty of Care? Notes from the Underground' (2006) 26 OJLS 449 at 466.

Compensation and Culpability

As we have seen, Lord Radcliffe thought that there would be nothing unfair in requiring the appellants to compensate the respondent in respect of her injury even though they were not culpable. In effect, this was to advocate strict liability, that is, liability without fault. That was not, however, the law of the land. Nevertheless, it transpires that the cricketing authorities allowed Miss Stone to keep the damages and costs that she had been awarded in the Court of Appeal, and did not seek to recover the costs they incurred in their successful appeal against liability in the House of Lords. Despite this goodwill gesture, it is almost certain that Miss Stone was left out of pocket, as she would have had to bear her own costs in the House of Lords (see Goodhart (1952) 68 LQR 3). For further context, see Lunney, 'Six and Out? *Bolton v Stone* after 50 Years' (2003) 24 J Leg Hist 1.

Whether fault on the part of the defendant is the appropriate criterion for determining whether a claimant should be paid compensation is an issue of general importance that we shall return to later on (see Ch. 18.II).

Overseas Tankship (UK) Ltd v The Miller Steamship Co Pty Ltd, The Wagon Mound (No. 2) [1967] 1 AC 617

The facts are set out in the opinion of the Privy Council, below.

Lord Reid delivered the opinion of the Privy Council

This is an appeal from a judgment of Walsh J, dated 10 October 1963, in the Supreme Court of New South Wales (Commercial Causes) by which he awarded to the respondents sums of £80,000 and £1,000 in respect of damage from fire sustained by their vessels, Corrimal and Audrey D, on 1 November 1951. These vessels were then at Sheerlegs Wharf, Morts Bay, in Sydney Harbour undergoing repairs. The appellant was charterer by demise of a vessel, the Wagon Mound, which in the early hours of 30 October 1951, had been taking in bunkering oil from Caltex Wharf not far from Sheerlegs Wharf. By reason of carelessness of the Wagon Mound engineers a large quantity of this oil overflowed from the Wagon Mound on to the surface of the water. Some hours later much of the oil had drifted to and accumulated round Sheerlegs Wharf and the respondents' vessels. About 2 pm on 1 November this oil was set alight: the fire spread rapidly and caused extensive damage to the wharf and to the respondents' vessels.

An action was raised against the present appellant by the owners of Sheerlegs Wharf on the ground of negligence. On appeal to the Board it was held that the plaintiffs were not entitled to recover on the ground that it was not foreseeable that such oil on the surface of the water could be set alight (*Overseas Tankship (UK) Ltd v Morts Dock and Engineering Co Ltd* [1961] AC 388). Their Lordships will refer to this case as the *Wagon Mound (No 1)* . . .

In the present case the respondents sue alternatively in nuisance and in negligence. Walsh J had found in their favour in nuisance but against them in negligence. Before their Lordships the appellant appeals against his decision on nuisance and the respondents appeal against his decision on negligence. Their Lordships are indebted to that learned judge for the full and careful survey of the evidence which is set out in his judgment (see [1963] 1 Ll Rep 402 at 406–8). Few of his findings of fact have been attacked, and their Lordships do not find it necessary to set out or deal with the evidence at any length; but it is desirable to give some explanation of how the fire started before setting out the learned judge's findings.

In the course of repairing the respondents' vessels the Morts Dock Co, the owners of Sheerlegs Wharf, were carrying out oxy-acetylene welding and cutting. This work was apt to cause pieces or drops of hot metal to fly off and fall in the sea. So when their manager arrived on the morning of 30 October and saw the thick scum of oil round the Wharf, he was apprehensive of fire danger and he stopped the work while he took advice. He consulted the manager of Caltex Wharf and, after some further consultation, he was assured that he was safe to proceed: so he did so, and the repair work was carried on normally until the fire broke out on 1 November. Oil of this character with a flash point of 170 °F is extremely difficult to ignite in the open; but we now know that that is not impossible. There is no certainty about how this oil was set alight, but the most probable explanation, accepted by Walsh J is that there was floating in the oil-covered water some object supporting a piece of inflammable material, and that a hot piece of metal fell on it when it burned for a sufficient time to ignite the surrounding oil.

The findings of the learned trial judge are as follows (see [1963] 1 Ll Rep 402 at 426):

(i) Reasonable people in the position of the officers of the Wagon Mound would regard furnace oil as very difficult to ignite on water.

(ii) Their personal experience would probably have been that this had very rarely happened.

(iii) If they had given attention to the risk of fire from the spillage, they would have regarded it as a possibility, but one which could become an actuality only in very exceptional circumstances.

(iv) They would have considered the chances of the required exceptional circumstances happening whilst the oil remained spread on the harbour waters, as being remote.

(v) I find that the occurrence of damage to [the respondents'] property as a result of the spillage, was not reasonably foreseeable by those for whose acts [the appellant] would be responsible.

(vi) I find that the spillage of oil was brought about by the careless conduct of persons for whose acts [the appellant] would be responsible.

(vii) I find that the spillage of oil was a cause of damage to the property of each of [the respondents].

(viii) Having regard to those findings, and because of finding (v), I hold that the claim of each of [the respondents] framed in negligence fails.

It is now necessary to turn to the respondents' submission that the trial judge was wrong in holding that damage from fire was not reasonably foreseeable. In *Wagon Mound (No 1)* [1961] AC 388 at 413 the finding on which the Board proceeded was that of the trial judge:

[the appellants] did not know and could not reasonably be expected to have known that [the oil] was capable of being set afire when spread on water.

In the present case the evidence led was substantially different from the evidence led in *Wagon Mound (No 1)* and the findings of Walsh J are significantly different. That is not due to there having been any failure by the plaintiffs in *Wagon Mound (No 1)* in preparing and presenting their case. The plaintiffs there were no doubt embarrassed by a difficulty which does not affect the present plaintiffs. The outbreak of the fire was consequent on the act of the manager of the plaintiffs in *Wagon Mound (No 1)* in resuming oxy-acetylene welding and cutting while the wharf was surrounded by this oil. So if the plaintiffs in the former case had set out to prove that it was foreseeable by the engineers of the Wagon Mound that this oil could be set alight, they might have had difficulty in parrying the reply that then this must also have been foreseeable by their manager. Then there would have been contributory negligence and at that time contributory negligence was a complete defence in New South Wales.

The crucial finding of Walsh J in this case is in finding (v): that the damage was 'not reasonably foreseeable by those for whose acts the defendant would be responsible'. That is not a primary finding of fact but an inference from the other findings, and it is clear from the learned judge's judgment that in drawing this inference he was to a large extent influenced by his view of the law. The vital parts of the findings of fact which have already been set out in full are (i) that the officers of the Wagon Mound 'would regard furnace oil as very difficult to ignite on water'—not that they would regard this as impossible: (ii) that their experience would probably have been 'that this had very rarely happened'—not that they would never have heard of a case where it had happened, and (iii) that they would have regarded it as a 'possibility, but one which could become an actuality only in very exceptional circumstances'—not, as in *Wagon Mound (No 1)*, that they could not reasonably be expected to have known that this oil was capable of being set afire when spread on water. The question which must now be determined is whether these differences between the findings in the two cases do or do not lead to different results in law.

In *Wagon Mound (No 1)* the Board were not concerned with degrees of foreseeability because the finding was that the fire was not foreseeable at all. So Viscount Simonds had no cause to amplify the statement that the 'essential factor in determining liability is whether the damage is of such a kind as the reasonable man should have foreseen' (p 426). Here the findings show, however, that some risk of fire would have been present to the mind of a reasonable man in the shoes of the ship's chief engineer. So the first question must be what is the precise meaning to be attached in this context to the words 'foreseeable' and 'reasonably foreseeable'.

Before *Bolton v Stone* the cases had fallen into two classes: (i) those where, before the event, the risk of its happening would have been regarded as unreal either because the event would have been thought to be physically impossible or because the possibility of its happening would have been regarded as so fantastic or far-fetched that no reasonable man would have paid any attention to it—'a mere possibility which would never occur to the mind of a reasonable man' (per Lord Dunedin in *Fardon v Harcourt-Rivington* [1932] All ER Rep 81 at 83)—or (ii) those where there was a real and substantial risk or chance that something like the event which happens might occur and then the reasonable man would have taken the steps necessary to eliminate the risk.

Bolton v Stone posed a new problem. There a member of a visiting team drove a cricket ball out of the ground on to an unfrequented adjacent public road and it struck and severely injured a lady who happened to be standing in the road. That it might happen that a ball would be driven on to this road could not have been said to be a fantastic or far-fetched possibility: according to the evidence it had happened about six times in twenty-eight years. Moreover it could not have been said to be a far-fetched or fantastic possibility that such a ball would strike someone in the road: people did pass along the road from time to time. So it could not have been said that, on any ordinary meaning of the words, the fact that a ball might strike a person in the road was not foreseeable or reasonably foreseeable. It was plainly foreseeable; but the chance of its happening in the foreseeable future was infinitesimal. A mathematician given the data could have worked out that it was only likely to happen once in so many thousand years. The House of Lords held that the risk was so small that in the circumstances a reasonable man would have been justified in disregarding it and taking no steps to eliminate it

It does not follow that, no matter what the circumstances may be, it is justifiable to neglect a risk of such a small magnitude. A reasonable man would only neglect such a risk if he had some valid reason for doing so: e.g., that it would involve considerable expense to eliminate the risk. He would weigh the risk against the difficulty of eliminating it. If the activity which caused the injury to Miss Stone had been an unlawful activity there can be little doubt but that *Bolton v Stone* would have been decided differently. In their Lordships' judgment *Bolton v Stone* did not alter the general principle that a person must be regarded as negligent if he does not take steps to eliminate a risk which he knows or ought to know is a real risk and not a mere possibility which would never influence the mind of a reasonable man. What that decision did was to recognise and give effect to the qualification that it is justifiable not to take steps to eliminate a real risk if it is small and if the circumstances are such that a reasonable man, careful of the safety of his neighbour, would think it right to neglect it.

In the present case there was no justification whatever for discharging the oil into Sydney Harbour. Not only was it an offence to do so, but also it involved considerable loss financially. If the ship's engineer had thought about the matter there could have been no question of balancing the advantages and disadvantages. From every point of view it was both his duty and his interest to stop the discharge immediately.

It follows that in their Lordships' view the only question is whether a reasonable man having the knowledge and experience to be expected of the chief engineer of the Wagon Mound would have known that there was a real risk of the oil on the water catching fire in some way: if it did, serious damage to ships or other property was not only foreseeable but very likely. Their Lordships do not dissent from the view of the trial judge that the possibilities of damage (see [1963] 1 Ll Rep 402 at 411) 'must be significant enough in a practical sense to require a reasonable man to guard against them', but they think that he may have misdirected himself in saying (at 413)

> there does seem to be a real practical difficulty, assuming that some risk of fire damage was foreseeable, but not a high one, in making a factual judgment as to whether this risk was sufficient to attract liability if damage should occur.

In this difficult chapter of the law decisions are not infrequently taken to apply to circumstances far removed from the facts which give rise to them, and it would seem that here too much reliance has been placed on some observations in *Bolton v Stone* and similar observations in other cases.

In their Lordships' view a properly qualified and alert chief engineer would have realised there was a real risk here, and they do not understand Walsh J to deny that; but he appears to have held that, if a real risk can properly be described as remote, it must then be held to be not reasonably foreseeable. That is a possible interpretation of some of the authorities; but this is still an open question and on principle their Lordships cannot accept this view. If a real risk is one which would occur to the mind of a reasonable man in the position of the defendant's servant and which he would not brush aside as far-fetched, and if the criterion is to be what that reasonable man would have done in the circumstances, then surely he would not neglect such a risk if action to eliminate it presented no difficulty, involved no disadvantage and required no expense.

In the present case the evidence shows that the discharge of so much oil on to the water must have taken a considerable time, and a vigilant ship's engineer would have noticed the discharge at an early stage. The findings show that he ought to have known that it is possible to ignite this kind of oil on water, and that the ship's engineer probably ought to have known that this had in fact happened before. The most that can be said to justify inaction is that he would have known that this could only happen in very exceptional circumstances; but that does not mean that a reasonable man would dismiss such risk from his mind and do nothing when it was so easy to prevent it. If it is clear that the reasonable man would have realised or foreseen and prevented the risk, then it must follow that the appellants are liable in damages. The learned judge found this a difficult case: he said that this matter is 'one on which different minds would come to different conclusions' (see [1963] 1 Ll Rep 402 at 424). Taking a rather different view of the law from that of the learned judge, their Lordships must hold that the respondents are entitled to succeed on this issue...

Appeal and cross-appeal allowed.

R. W. M. Dias, 'Trouble on Oiled Waters: Problems of *The Wagon Mound (No. 2)*' [1967] CLJ 62 at 68–70

Conduct is careless if it falls short of the standard of the reasonable man's behaviour in the circumstances; and the pattern of his behaviour is determined with reference to the foreseeable likelihood that some harm may occur. Normally if a reasonable man would have foreseen a harmful result as likely to happen, he would have governed his conduct so as to avoid it. If, however, the chance of the happening was remote, he may well have persisted notwithstanding that chance; in which case the reasonableness of his behaviour rests on a balance between the degree of likelihood that the danger will materialise, the cost and practicability of measures needed to avoid it, the gravity of the consequences and the end to be achieved by the activity, including its importance and social utility. A remote likelihood of harm will in some cases be outweighed by one or other of these considerations. Thus, every time that one drives a car or flies an aeroplane it is foreseeable that there is at least a chance of disaster. But it is not for that reason negligent to drive cars or fly aeroplanes, since the balancing considerations outweigh the risk…

From all this it will be seen that foreseeability of the likelihood that harm may occur is implicit in the determination of carelessness. With regard to foreseeability of the individual actually affected and the kind of occurrence that actually follows, it has been remarked that this relates to actionability rather than to the careless quality of the defendant's conduct. The two do coalesce whenever the only foreseeable result is harm to a particular person and of a particular kind. The conduct is then said to be careless *qua* that person and *qua* that result simply because no other consideration enters in. Breach of duty and remoteness become, as Denning LJ once said, 'different ways of looking at one and the same problem' (see *Roe v Minister of Health* [1954] 2 QB 66 at 85). Nevertheless it is important to keep the two apart, as when conduct sets up a chain reaction. One consequence might be foreseeable as quite likely to occur, another only as a remote possibility, and yet another not at all. Even though the defendant's conduct is careless with reference to the first, a successful action may or may not lie in respect of the other two. To put it in another way, the question of actionability with regard to these two does not affect the careless quality of the conduct that produces them…

COMMENTARY

The Wagon Mound (No. 2) is a very complicated case, not least because of the difference in relation to a crucial matter of fact between it and the earlier case that arose out of the same incident, *The Wagon Mound (No. 1)* [1961] AC 388. In the earlier case, the plaintiffs had conceded that the fire damage for which they sought compensation was not reasonably foreseeable—they had to do so or else they would have been found contributorily negligent (unless perhaps it was reasonable for them to have run the risk, in view of the cost involved in their shutting down their welding operations) and at that time contributory negligence was a *total* defence to liability under New South Wales law.

The real importance of the case lies in its examination of the nature of the requirement of foreseeability in the modern law of negligence and its role in determining whether the defendant was acting in breach of duty. The reasoning of the Privy Council on these crucial issues can be summarised as follows:

(i) in any case where there is more than a far-fetched possibility of injury to the claimant, the defendant's conduct may amount to a breach of duty if he failed to take such precautions to remove or minimise the risk as would have been taken by the reasonable person;

(ii) there is no precise point on the scale of probabilities that has to be attained before a finding of negligence is justified and once the trial judge had held that there was a remote but not far-fetched possibility that the oil might catch fire and damage the plaintiff's vessel, it was not necessary to prove additionally that there was any greater degree of probability that damage might result;

(iii) breach of duty is determined rather by looking at the likelihood of the risk relative to all the other circumstances of the case, including the difficulty of taking precautions to guard against the risk; the real issue is the practical question whether the risk was such as to require the taking of such precautions;

(iv) here, given the ease of preventing the oil-spill and the lack of any public benefit associated with the activity (spilling oil into Sydney Harbour served no useful purpose, unlike (arguably!) the playing of cricket in *Bolton v Stone*), it was negligent not to take steps to prevent the oil from leaking because of the (admittedly slight) risk of fire.

The Privy Council's impeccable analysis demonstrates the triumph of the practical over the statistical approach to breach of duty (as explained on p. 155, above). But, as Dias notes, it does not entail the same approach to questions of foreseeability arising in other contexts, for example in relation to remoteness of damage. On this, see further Ch. 5.III, below.

II. Reasonable Care: Relevant Considerations

In the previous section, we saw that the degree of foreseeability of injury to the claimant does not provide in itself a test of the defendant's negligence. This is to be assessed in the light of a cluster of interlinked considerations, all looked at together. The court must embark upon a practical inquiry into what (if anything) the reasonable person would have done to remove or minimise the risk in question. In the extracts that follow, we see the courts rejecting attempts to limit the range of factors that may impinge upon the inquiry into breach of duty.

One attempt to provide a systematic approach to the factors relevant in assessing the defendant's negligence was provided by the American judge Learned Hand J. In *United States v Carroll Towing Co* (1947) 159 F 2d 169 he held that a decision as to whether particular conduct was negligent required three factors to be considered: the probability that the event would happen ('P'), the gravity of the injury that would be caused if the event occurred ('L'), and the cost of preventing the event ('B'). Thus the 'Learned Hand formula' held that there was a breach where B < PL (where the cost of preventing the injury was less than the cost of the injury discounted by the probability of it happening). This formula has been held up by later scholars as an example of the economic analysis of law, imposing liability only where it would be economically efficient to do so (Posner, 'A Theory of Negligence' (1972) 1 J Leg Stud 29). A difficulty with this approach, however, is that it assumes that 'L' (the injury) can be given an accurate value. As is discussed in Chapter 16, this is not necessarily the case: although the law attributes a value even to personal injuries, this cannot be other than arbitrary. In any event, it may be thought somewhat distasteful to allow the infliction of harm on an individual in the name of economic efficiency (see, e.g., the American case of *Grimshaw v Ford Motors* (1981) 119 Cal App 3d 757, where it was alleged that Ford calculated that it would be less expensive to pay off the victims of accidents caused by a defect in their car, which was liable to burst into flames following a collision, rather than recall the model and repair the defect). Nonetheless, it cannot be denied that some form of balancing of interests must take place in the breach inquiry, and to that end the Learned Hand formula may be viewed as a useful guide, even if the equation cannot be worked out with scientific accuracy.

(For a critical analysis, see Green, 'Negligence = Economic Efficiency: Doubts>' (1997) 75 Tex L Rev 1605; Wright, 'Hand, Posner, and the Myth of the "Hand Formula"' (2003) 4 Theoretical Inquiries in Law 145.)

1. Gravity of the Potential Harm

Paris v Stepney Borough Council [1951] AC 367

The plaintiff was employed as a fitter in a garage owned by the defendant borough council. To the council's knowledge, he had the use of only one eye. While he was using a hammer to remove a bolt on a vehicle, a chip of metal flew off and entered his good eye, so injuring it that he became totally blind. The defendants did not provide him with goggles to wear, and there was evidence that it was not the ordinary practice for employers to supply goggles to men employed in garages on the maintenance and repair of vehicles. The trial judge, Lynskey J, allowed the plaintiff's claim for damages but this decision was reversed in the Court of Appeal for reasons which were clearly stated by Asquith LJ (see [1950] 1 KB 320 at 324):

> The plaintiff's disability could only be relevant to the stringency of the duty owed to him if it increased the risk to which he was exposed. A one-eyed man is no more likely to get a splinter or a chip in his eye than is a two-eyed man. The risk is no greater although the damage may be to a man with only one good eye than to a man with two good eyes. But the quantum of damage is one thing and the scope of duty is another. A greater risk of injury is not the same thing as a risk of greater injury; the first alone is relevant to liability.

The plaintiff appealed to the House of Lords.

Lord Normand

My Lords, this appeal involves a question of general importance affecting the common law duty which an employer owes to his employee. It is this. A workman is suffering, to the employer's knowledge, from a disability which, though it does not increase the risk of an accident's occurring while he is at work, does increase the risk of serious injury if an accident should befall him. Is the special risk of injury a relevant consideration in determining the precautions which the employer should take in fulfilment of the duty of care which he owes to the workman?...

It is not disputed that the respondents' duty of care is a duty owed to their employees as individuals. The respondents contend, however, that, though it is not a duty owed to the employees collectively, they must take account in fulfilling the duty only of any disability that increases the risk of an accident's occurring. For that proposition no authority was cited, and, in my opinion, it is contrary to principle. The test is what precautions would the ordinary, reasonable and prudent man take? The relevant considerations include all those facts which could affect the conduct of a reasonable and prudent man and his decision on the precautions to be taken. Would a reasonable and prudent man be influenced, not only by the greater or less probability of an accident occurring but also by the gravity of the consequences if an accident does occur?...

The court's task of deciding what precautions a reasonable and prudent man would take in the circumstances of a particular case may not be easy. Nevertheless, the judgment of the reasonable and prudent man should be allowed its common every-day scope, and it should not be restrained from considering the foreseeable consequences of an accident and their seriousness for the person to whom the duty of care is owed. Such a restriction, if it might sometimes simplify the task of the judge or jury, would be an undue and artificial simplification of the problem to be solved. If the court were now to take the narrow view proposed by the respondents the cleavage between the legal conception of the precautions which a reasonable and prudent man would take and the precautions which reasonable and prudent men do in fact take would lessen the respect which the administration of justice ought to command . . .

In the present case . . . the balance of the evidence inclines heavily against the appellant on the question of the usual practice of others, but that evidence necessarily dealt with the normal case when the employee suffers from no special disablement. In the nature of things there could scarcely be proof of what was the usual precautions taken by other employers if the workmen had but one good eye. Since Lynskey J did not deal with the evidence on practice and made no finding about the precautions which should be taken in the ordinary case and without reference to individual disability, I think that his judgment is essentially a finding that the supply of goggles was obviously necessary when a one-eyed man was put to the kind of work to which the appellant was put. The facts on which the learned judge founded his conclusion, the known risk of metal flying when this sort of work was being done, the position of the workman with his eyes close to the bolt he was hammering and on the same level with it or below it, and the disastrous consequences if a particle of metal flew into his one good eye, taken in isolation, seem to me to justify his conclusion. Even for a two-eyed man the risk of losing one eye is a very grievous risk, not to speak of the foreseeable possibility that both eyes might be simultaneously destroyed, or that the loss of one eye might have as a sequel the destruction of vision in the other. It may be said that, if it is obvious that goggles should have been supplied to a one-eyed workman, it is scarcely less obvious that they should have been supplied to all the workmen, and, therefore, that the judgment rests on an unreal or insufficient distinction between the gravity of the risk run by a one-eyed man and the gravity of the risk run by a two-eyed man. I recognise that the argument has some force, but I do not assent to it. Blindness is so great a calamity that even the loss of one of two good eyes is not comparable, and the risk of blindness from sparks of metal is greater for a one-eyed man than for a two-eyed man, for it is less likely that both eyes should be damaged than that one eye should, and the loss of one eye is not necessarily or even usually followed by blindness in the other. What precautions were needed to protect two-eyed men, and whether it could properly be held, in the teeth of the evidence of the usual practice, that goggles should have been supplied for them, were not questions which the learned judge had necessarily to decide. Therefore, though there might have been advantages of lucidity and cogency if the precautions needed for the protection of the two-eyed men had first been considered and the increased risk of damage to which the one-eyed man is exposed had been expressly contrasted, I would allow the appeal and restore the judgment of Lynskey J.

Lord Oaksey and **Lord Macdermott** delivered separate concurring opinions. **Lord Simonds** and **Lord Morton of Henryton** dissented.

Appeal allowed.

COMMENTARY

Lord Simonds and Lord Morton of Henryton agreed with the majority that the gravity of the injury was a relevant consideration in assessing whether the defendant had acted with due care, but disagreed with the majority's conclusion that there was a breach of duty on the facts of the case. Their dissent was premised on the propositions that the risk to the plaintiff was not materially greater than that to the other workers engaged on the same task—such an accident would be serious in its consequences to any worker whether one-eyed or two-eyed—and it was a risk which could reasonably be run.

The decision of the House of Lords reflects the broader proposition that the content of the defendant's duty of care must be tailored to the known, or reasonably foreseeable, characteristics of the individual claimant. The issue arises not only where the claimant is at risk of more serious injury than other potential victims of the tort, but also where the risk is more likely to eventuate (a question of the foreseeability or probability of harm). A number of the cases involve the claimant's unusual susceptibility to injury, e.g. an allergy (*Withers v Perry Chain* [1961] 1 WLR 1314) or a vulnerability to stress-related illness (*Hatton v Sutherland* [2002] 2 All ER 1, extracted p. 363, below). For an interesting application of the same principle, see *Haley v London Electricity Board*, p. 131, above.

It is important to note that the principle applied in such cases is *not* the 'thin skull rule' considered at p. 275 below. The content of the defendant's duty of care reflects the claimant's susceptibility to injury only when it is known or reasonably foreseeable. The thin skull rule comes into play afterwards—once it has been established that the defendant was in breach of duty—and provides for the liability to extend to the consequences of the claimant's susceptibility even where it is unknown and not reasonably foreseeable. To make things even more complicated, a special rule applies in psychiatric illness cases involving 'secondary victims' (i.e. those who witness another's death or injury): they must prove that psychiatric illness was, in the circumstances, foreseeable to a person of 'ordinary fortitude' or 'customary phlegm', unless (perhaps) the defendant actually knows that the claimant was a person especially susceptible to suffering psychiatric illness (see p. 350, below). This is best viewed as a policy-motivated restriction on the existence of the duty of care in such cases, and does not affect the general rule that the content of the defendant's duty is tailored to the individual claimant in the sense described above.

In *Paris v Stepney*, the Law Lords accepted that the employer had no duty to provide safety goggles to its mechanics generally, but reasonable expectations of safety change over time and failure to provide safety goggles in the same situation today would almost certainly be negligent. On the 'time dimension' of negligence, see Section III, below.

2. The Cost of Precautions

Latimer v AEC Ltd [1953] AC 643

As the result of an exceptionally heavy rain storm, the defendants' factory was flooded and the water, mixed with an oily liquid ('mystic') which normally collected in channels in the floor, left the floor exceedingly slippery. The defendants spread sawdust on the floor, but there was not enough to cover the floor in its entirety. The plaintiff was injured when he slipped on a portion of the floor which was not covered with sawdust and fell. He sued for damages alleging both a liability under the Factories Act 1937 and negligence at common law. The claim under the Factories Act was rejected but the negligence claim was allowed at first instance. The Court of Appeal upheld the trial judge's decision on breach of statutory duty but allowed the defendant's appeal as regards negligence, holding that a breach of duty had not been established. The House of Lords affirmed the Court of Appeal decision, but the extracts relate only to the negligence action. Their Lordships' consideration of the central question of breach of duty was influenced by the fact that the appellant's allegation that the respondents should have shut down the works did not appear in the initial pleadings and was only advanced at a late stage of the trial, after all the evidence had been introduced.

Lord Porter

[U]ndoubtedly the respondents did their best to get rid of the effects of the flood, employing such of the day workers as could be spared and obtaining volunteers from them for work in the interval between day and night work and from the night shift at a later period, but in the learned judge's opinion it was not possible for them to take any further steps to make the floor less slippery. I understand his view to have been, however, that, inasmuch as the effect of the storm left the gangway in question, and possibly other portions of the works, somewhat slippery and therefore potentially dangerous, they should have shut down the whole works if necessary, or at any rate such portion as was dangerous...

   On the issue of common law negligence...the direction which should be given is not in doubt. It is to determine what action, in the circumstances which have been proved, would a reasonably prudent man have taken. The probability of a workman slipping is one matter which must be borne in mind, but it must be remembered that no one else did so. Nor does the possibility seem to have occurred to anyone at the time. It is true that after the event Mr Milne, one of the respondents' witnesses, expressed the opinion that he would not have gone on to the floor in the condition in which it was and that it would be too dangerous to do so. But this was after the event, and, though he was the respondents' safety engineer and was present until late that night, it seems never to have occurred to him that there was any danger or that any further steps than those actually taken were possible, or required for the safety of the employees. The seriousness of shutting down the works and sending the night shift home and the importance of carrying on the work on which the factory was engaged are all additional elements for consideration, and without adequate information on these matters it is impossible to express any final opinion. Moreover, owing to the course taken at the trial, there is no material for enabling one to judge whether a partial closing of the factory was possible, or the extent to which the cessation of the appellant's activities would have retarded the whole of the work being carried on. In my view, in these circumstances, the appellant has not established that a reasonably careful employer would have shut down the works, or that the respondents ought to have taken the drastic step of closing the factory...

Lord Tucker

[I]t appears to me desirable in these days, when there are in existence so many statutes and statutory regulations imposing absolute obligations on employers, that the courts should be vigilant to see that the common law duty owed by a master to his servants should not be gradually enlarged until it is barely distinguishable from his absolute statutory obligations.

Lord Asquith

At common law the question can only be whether, having regard to the nature and extent of the risk created by the slippery patches on the floor, a reasonably careful employer would have suspended all work in this 15-acre factory and sent the night shift home: or whether, having done all he could (and did) do with the sawdust at his disposal, the 40 production service men in the afternoon, and the 24 volunteers between the end of the day shift and the beginning of the night shift, he would have allowed the work to proceed. The learned trial judge concluded that a reasonable employer would have closed down. I agree with practically everything else he said in a most careful judgment. But, of course, this conclusion was crucial...

What evidence the learned judge had before him suggests to my mind that the degree of risk was too small to justify, let alone require, closing down. The evidence of the plaintiff himself is that 'you always get a certain amount of grease about'... Yet the plaintiff says that except for the accident to himself on this occasion in August, he has never known any accident happen to anyone in the factory through these causes. I cannot resist the conclusion that on this occasion, notwithstanding the extent of the flooding, the risk was inconsiderable, and that the learned judge's conclusion cannot stand. Treated as a finding of fact, it cannot be supported on the evidence, which, as to the onerousness of the suggested of remedial measure, was non-existent. Treated as an inference of fact, it was open to the Court of Appeal and is open to your Lordships' House to draw a different inference, and I would do so.

I agree that the appeal should be dismissed.

Lord Oaksey and **Lord Reid** delivered separate concurring opinions.

Appeal dismissed.

COMMENTARY

Why were the defendant employers not held to be negligent in failing to have sufficient reserves of sawdust to cover the entire area of the floor?

In *Bolton v Stone*, above, at 867, Lord Reid stated that, in determining whether the defendant cricket club had been negligent: 'I do not think that it would be right to take into account the difficulty of remedial measures.' This remark has been seized upon by one well-regarded commentator as evidence that in English law 'the cost of precautions is irrelevant... [T]he consideration that the cost to the defendant of precautions would exceed the ex ante quantification of the plaintiff's injury does not exonerate the defendant from liability. The defendant can therefore be liable even for a cost-justified action' (E. Weinrib, *The Idea of Private Law* (Cambridge, Mass.: Harvard University Press, 1995), p. 149). The present case, not mentioned by Weinrib, makes it clear that his interpretation of the English authorities is quite wrong. But what explanation can be given for Lord Reid's dictum, and his subsequent signing up to the apparently inconsistent decision in *Latimer*? The answer lies in the qualification he gave to the words quoted: 'If cricket cannot be played on a ground without creating a substantial risk, then it should not be played there at all.' It is clear that Lord Reid was saying no more than that, even if it would be impractical for the defendant to pursue his activities in a safer fashion, he can still be found guilty of negligence if the risks associated with those activities were so great as to require him to desist altogether. It must be admitted, however, that cases of this nature will be very rare (though the House of Lords accepted in *Latimer* that there might indeed be cases where a factory would have to be shut down in view of the riskiness of keeping it in operation).

The precautions necessary to protect the claimant may sometimes run counter to the claimant's own wishes. Suppose an employee has an unusual sensitivity to chemicals used in the workplace, and the employer has no alternative work available. Does the latter's duty of care require the employee to be dismissed, or is it enough that the employee is informed of the risks and decides to continue the employment? In *Withers v Perry Chain* [1961] 1 WLR 1314 at 1320, Devlin LJ stated: 'there is no legal duty upon an employer to prevent an adult employee from doing work which he or she is willing to do'. But in *Coxall v Goodyear Great Britain Ltd* [2002] EWCA Civ 1010, [2003] 1 WLR 536 at [29] Simon Brown LJ denied that this was an absolute rule, and found that the case before himself was one of those exceptional cases in which, despite the employee's desire to remain at work, there was a duty to dismiss him for his own good and to protect him from danger. Brooke LJ agreed the employer was liable on the facts, but only for failing to discuss the employee's options with him once his susceptibility was known. Does Simon Brown LJ's approach give effect to what another judge once derided as 'the nursemaid school of negligence' (*Savory v Holland & Hannen & Cubitts (Southern) Ltd* [1964] 1 WLR 1158 at 1166, per Diplock LJ)?

3. Utility of the Defendant's Conduct

Watt v Hertfordshire County Council [1954] 1 WLR 835

A lifting jack in the defendant's fire station was rarely used. It stood on four wheels, two of which were castored, and it weighed between two and three hundredweight. Only one vehicle at the station was specially fitted to carry it. While that vehicle was properly out on other service, the station received an emergency call to an accident in which a woman had been trapped under a heavy vehicle two or three hundred yards away. The sub-officer in charge ordered the jack to be loaded on a lorry, which was the only other vehicle there capable of carrying it and on which there was no means of securing it. Whilst carrying a number of firemen employed by the defendants and the jack to the scene of the accident, the driver of the lorry had to brake suddenly and the jack moved inside the lorry and injured one of the firemen. The trial judge, Barry J, dismissed the fireman's claim against the defendant. The fireman appealed.

Singleton LJ

It is not alleged that there was negligence on the part of any particular individual, nor that the driver was negligent in driving too fast, nor that the sub-officer was negligent in giving the order which he did. The case put forward in this court is that, as the defendants had a jack, it was their duty to have a vehicle fitted in all respects to carry that jack, from which it follows, I suppose, that it is said that there must be a vehicle kept at the station at all times, or that, if there is not one, the lifting jack must not be taken out. Indeed [counsel] claimed that, in the case of a happening such as this, if there was not a vehicle fitted to carry the jack, the sub-officer ought to have telephoned to the fire station at St Albans and arranged that they should attend to the emergency. St Albans is some seven miles away, and it was said an extra ten minutes or so would have elapsed if that had been done. I cannot think that is the right way to approach the matter. There was a real emergency; the woman was under a heavy vehicle; these men in the fire service thought they ought to go promptly and to take a lifting jack, and they did so. Most unfortunately this accident happened...

The employee in this case was a member of the fire service, who always undertake some risk—but, said [counsel for the plaintiff] not this risk...

The purpose to be served in this case was the saving of life. The men were prepared to take that risk. They were not, in my view, called on to take any risk other than that which normally might be encountered in this service. I agree with Barry J that on the whole of the evidence it would not be right to find that the employers were guilty of any failure of the duty which they owed to their workmen. In my opinion, the appeal should be dismissed.

Denning LJ

It is well settled that in measuring due care you must balance the risk against the measures necessary to eliminate the risk. To that proposition there ought to be added this: you must balance the risk against the end to be achieved. If this accident had occurred in a commercial enterprise without any emergency, there could be no doubt that the servant would succeed. But the commercial end to make profit is very different from the human end to save life or limb. The saving of life or limb justifies taking considerable risk, and I am glad to say there have never been wanting in this country men of courage ready to take those risks, notably in the fire service.

In this case the risk involved in sending out the lorry was not so great as to prohibit the attempt to save life. I quite agree that fire engines, ambulances and doctors' cars should not shoot past the traffic lights when they show a red light. That is because the risk is too great to warrant the incurring of the danger. It is always a question of balancing the risk against the end. I agree that this appeal should be dismissed.

Morris LJ delivered a short concurring judgment.

Appeal dismissed.

COMMENTARY

In *Daborn v Bath Tramways Motor Co Ltd & Trevor Smithey* [1946] 2 All ER 333 at 336, Asquith LJ encapsulated the law's approach in such cases in a celebrated dictum:

As has often been pointed out, if all the trains in this country were restricted to a speed of five miles an hour, there would be fewer accidents, but our national life would be intolerably slowed down. The purpose to be served, if sufficiently important, justifies the assumption of abnormal risk.

Does the law's approach unfairly prejudice claimants who are members of the emergency services and daily run substantial risks for the good of society at large? In *King v Sussex Ambulance NHS Trust* [2002] ICR 1413, Buxton LJ expressed some disquiet about the approach taken in *Watt* in the analogous context of injury suffered by an ambulance officer whilst on an urgent call-out. He asked, rhetorically (at [47]):

[W]hy should those who run the risk on behalf of the public, suffer if the risk eventuates? If, as this court held in *Kent v Griffiths* [extracted p. 473, below], the public interest obliges the service to respond to public need, why should it not be equally in the public interest to compensate those who are foreseeably injured in the course of meeting that public need?

In his view, the 'men of courage' that Lord Denning referred to in *Watt* were unduly disadvantaged when compared with workers in the private sector. The latter might very well be able to recover in negligence if exposed to equivalent risks for their employer's commercial benefit rather than the general public good.

Buxton LJ appears to be arguing that compensation should be paid to injured members of the emergency services irrespective of fault. Do you think that the tort system ought to provide compensation in such circumstances, or is this something for which advance provision should be made, if considered desirable, in the service members' contracts of employment?

Tomlinson v Congleton Borough Council [2004] 1 AC 46

As noted above (p. 32), the claimant suffered serious injuries when he waded into a lake at the defendant council's country park, threw himself forward in a dive and hit his head on the sandy bottom. The lake was a popular public amenity, used for various water sports, and the surrounding beach was used for picnicking and sunbathing. The council prohibited swimming as they regarded it as unduly dangerous, for example, because of the risk of collision with wind-surfers. They displayed prominent notices which said: 'Dangerous water: no swimming', distributed warning leaflets, and employed rangers to enforce the no-swimming policy. Despite these efforts, many visitors continued to swim in the lake and the council concluded that the only way of dealing with the problem was to make the water less accessible and less inviting. Shortly before the claimant's accident, the council approved a scheme to cover over the beaches with soil and establish reed beds in their place, but this was not implemented until after the claimant's accident. The claimant brought an action under the Occupiers' Liability Acts 1957 and 1984 (see Ch. 11.II), failing at first instance, but succeeding (by a majority) before the Court of Appeal. The case then went to the House of Lords.

Lord Hoffmann

[46] My Lords...I think that there is an important question of freedom at stake. It is unjust that the harmless recreation of responsible parents and children with buckets and spades on the beaches should be prohibited in order to comply with what is thought to be a legal duty to safeguard irresponsible visitors against dangers which are perfectly obvious...

[47] It is of course understandable that organisations like the Royal Society for the Prevention of Accidents should favour policies which require people to be prevented from taking risks. Their function is to prevent accidents and that is one way of doing so. But they do not have to consider the cost, not only in money but also in deprivation of liberty, which such restrictions entail. The courts will naturally respect the technical expertise of such organisations in drawing attention to what can be done to prevent accidents. But the balance between risk on the one hand and individual autonomy on the other is not a matter of expert opinion. It is a judgment which the courts must make and which in England reflects the individualist values of the common law.

[48] As for the council officers, they were obvious motivated by the view that it was necessary to take defensive measures to prevent the council from being held liable to pay compensation. The borough leisure officer said that he regretted the need to destroy the beaches but saw no alternative if the council was not to be held liable for an accident to a swimmer. So this appeal gives your Lordships the opportunity to say clearly that local authorities and other occupiers of land are ordinarily under no duty to incur such social and financial costs to protect a minority (or even a majority) against obvious dangers.

Lord Browne-Wilkinson, Lord Hutton, Lord Hobhouse and **Lord Scott** gave separate concurring opinions.

Appeal allowed.

COMMENTARY

It is scarcely credible that the claimant should have succeeded before the Court of Appeal with an argument that entailed the effective destruction of a valuable public amenity enjoyed by thousands of visitors each year; as one of the authors has written elsewhere: 'an argument that the exercise of reasonable care requires attractive beaches to be replaced by ballast and muddy reeds justifiably attracts the strong language used by their Lordships in rejecting it' (Lunney (2003) 11 Tort L Rev 140, 145). Lord Hoffmann was absolutely right to emphasise that the costs of 'compensation culture' are not simply pecuniary—here, the cost of the scheme to destroy the beaches was relatively small—but also the general undermining of personal autonomy and the loss of individual liberty. This accorded entirely with the established law on the relevance of social utility to the determination of whether or not the defendant has exercised due care.

The House of Lords' decision came too late to preserve the beach previously enjoyed by the people of Congleton, but seems to have heralded a more restrictive judicial approach to the resolution of similar claims under the Occupiers' Liability Acts (see Ch. 11.II, below). The tone of the extract above seems to suggest that Lord Hoffmann (like Lord Hobhouse and Lord Scott, extracted at p. 32, above) was consciously speaking to a wider audience than just the legal profession, and intended his remarks to be given wider publicity—as indeed they were by the general news media.

The particular significance of the case in this context is its very clear recognition that the social utility of an activity extends to such intangible considerations as its contribution to individual flourishing through the scope it allows for autonomous risk-taking. (See also the further extracts at p. 579, below.) The deprivation of liberty and undermining of personal responsibility that would result from 'a grey and dull safety regime' (as Lord Scott put it, at [94]) must therefore be taken into account in deciding whether the defendant's duty of care required him on the facts to eliminate or reduce the risk in question.

Compensation Act 2006

Section 1: Deterrent Effect of Potential Liability

A court considering a claim in negligence or breach of statutory duty may, in determining whether the defendant should have taken particular steps to meet a standard of care (whether by taking precautions against a risk or otherwise), have regard to whether a requirement to take those steps might—

(a) prevent a desirable activity from being undertaken at all, to a particular extent or in a particular way, or

(b) discourage persons from undertaking functions in connection with a desirable activity.

Explanatory Note

The purpose of this provision is to address what was suggested by the Better Regulation Task Force (BRTF) report of May 2004 (*Better Routes to Redress*) to be a common misperception, that can lead to a disproportionate fear of litigation and consequent risk-averse behaviour... What amounts to reasonable care in any particular case will vary according to the circumstances. In some cases, what would be required to prevent injury of the kind suffered may be such that to demand it of the defendant would be to demand more than is reasonable. This provision is intended to contribute to improving awareness of this aspect of the law; providing reassurance to the people and organisations who are concerned about possible litigation; and to ensuring that normal activities are not prevented because of the fear of litigation and excessively risk-averse behaviour.

COMMENTARY

This provision was a direct response to concerns about 'compensation culture' highlighted in Chapter 1.III.3). The government accepted the diagnosis of the problem advanced by the Better Regulation Task Force in its 2004 report, *Better Routes to Redress* (extracted p. 34, above), namely, that it was the public's *misperception* that a compensation culture existed, rather than the actual number of claims being brought, that had adverse consequences, e.g. the inducing of risk-averse behaviour. Section 1 is designed to ease the fear of potential defendants that the courts are too willing to find negligence where there is any evidence that an accident was preventable. But the deterrent/discouraging effect of requiring a particular precaution in the interests of risk reduction is, in principle, something that should be taken into account at common law. Section 1 restates the current law: it was not intended to change the law, but only to change perceptions.

As we explained in our earlier discussion, the public debate has often been lead astray by the media's uncritical repetition of a number of compensation culture myths, and it is worth highlighting here a particular subset of those myths dealing with risk-averse behaviour induced by liability fears, e.g. the cancellation of events, the withdrawal of public amenities, and the prohibition of traditional activities in public spaces like school playgrounds. Williams, 'Politics, the media and refining the notion of fault: section 1 of the Compensation Act 2006' [2006] JPIL 347 at 349–50 exposes as fiction one story that was reported more than 30 times in almost all the national newspapers and repeated even by the then Prime Minister, Tony Blair: that the Bury St Edmunds council had taken down the hanging baskets in the town centre because of fears that they would be sued if the baskets fell down. In fact, the town's traditional floral installations were displayed as usual that year, and won the annual Best Large Town award in the regional flower show. The only, very slight basis of truth in the story was that some of the older lamp posts in the town centre had been replaced because they were no longer safe to carry the weight of the baskets. Williams comments (at 349): 'False or exaggerated liability stories of this sort are politically significant, and not just infantilising "infotainment", because they help (indeed, sometimes seem designed) to influence legislative and judicial "tort reform" agendas.' However, *Tomlinson v Congleton BC* demonstrates that not all the stories are myths: the council did indeed approve a plan to dig up its attractive beach and replace it with muddy reed beds, and had actually implemented the plan in the period between the claimant's accident and the trial. Whether this action was justified is another matter: in retrospect, it looks like a considerable overreaction.

During the Compensation Bill's progress through Parliament, cl. 1 (as it was then) was criticised in the House of Commons Constitutional Affairs Select Committee's report on the bill, on the basis that it was unnecessary, would lead to 'costly satellite litigation' to determine the meaning of its terms (e.g. 'desirable activity'), and might have unforeseen consequences (e.g. creating an excessive shield against liability). See *Compensation Culture: Third Report of Session 2005–06* (2006), vol. 1, House of Commons (HC) 754-1, §§ 67–8. Notwithstanding the criticism, the government reiterated its support for the clause, and its belief that the reform would perform a valuable role in tackling perceptions that lead to risk-averse behaviour. It dismissed the Committee's fears that the clause would promote costly satellite legislation: the desirability of an activity was already a factor the courts could take into account, and would have no greater, nor any lesser, significance than it had at present. In fact, rather than promoting unnecessary litigation, the clause would help to reduce the number of ill-conceived, speculative and frivolous claims. (See Secretary of State for Constitutional Affairs and Lord Chancellor/Secretary of State for Health, *Government Response to the Constitutional Affairs Select Committee's Reports: Compensation culture and Compensation culture: NHS Redress Bill* (2006), Cm. 6784, §§ 38–49.)

It may, however, be doubted whether the provision will provide the intended comfort for those who perceive themselves to be at risk of liability in tort. If the problem is their misperception of the law, it is not clear how passing more law is going to help. In addition, as Morris points out ('Spiralling or Stabilising? The Compensation Culture and Our Propensity to Claim Damages for Personal Injury' (2007) 70 MLR 349 at pp. 368–9), s. 1 is rather narrowly drafted and certainly does not offer wider reassurance that people will not be liable if they adopt reasonable standards and procedures: 'If the Government genuinely wants to get the wider message across, it seems strange to pick on only one aspect of the breach issue' (*ibid.*, at p. 369). An interesting comparison is provided by the tort reform legislation passed in many Australian jurisdictions, where more specific defences to actions in negligence limit the liability of certain classes of defendant (e.g. those providing recreational services: see, e.g., Civil Liability Act 2002 (NSW), ss. 5L, 5M).

At the time of writing, the only case to have applied Compensation Act 2006, s. 1 was *Hopps v Mott MacDonald Ltd* [2009] EWHC 1881 (QB). A civilian engineer involved in reconstruction work in Iraq following the invasion of 2003 was injured by an explosive device while travelling in a Land Rover under British army protection. Amongst the issues arising was whether his employers should have ensured he was transported in an armoured vehicle. Applying s. 1, Christopher Clarke J stated (para. 93):

It seems to me that in determining whether particular steps (e.g. confinement to the airport until armoured vehicles were available for transport) should have been taken I am entitled to have regard to whether such steps would prevent the desirable activity of reconstruction of a shattered infrastructure after a war in a territory occupied by HM forces, particularly when failure to expedite that work would carry with it risks to the safety of coalition forces and civilian contractors in Iraq as a whole.

After weighing the relevant factors, he concluded that the use of an unarmoured vehicle on the occasion in question was not unreasonable. The relevant events occurred in 2003, but the judge rejected an argument that the application of s. 1 entailed impermissibly giving the statute retrospective effect (para. 92):

Firstly, the section must, as it seems to me, be applicable to this claim since it is a claim which the court is 'considering'. Secondly the purpose of the section is to draw attention to, and to some extent, to expound the principle of the common law expounded by the House of Lords in *Tomlinson v Congleton Borough Council*.

This entirely accords with the view of Field J in *Uren v Corporate Leisure (UK) Ltd* [2010] EWHC 46 (QB), para. 19, that in his opinion s. 1 'adds nothing to the common law'.

III. Negligence Judged from the Defendant's Standpoint

In determining whether there has been a breach of duty, the court must place itself 'in the shoes' of the defendant: would a reasonable person, in the same circumstances as the defendant found himself, have acted as the defendant did? This inquiry has a temporal dimension: what could reasonably have been expected from the defendant ought not be affected by hindsight or by subsequent developments in technological skill or scientific knowledge. Account may however be taken of transient considerations, for example that the defendant had to act in 'the agony of the moment', and in emergencies, fast-moving sports, and other contexts demanding split-second judgements the defendant is not to be judged as if there had been time available for calm reflection.

Roe v Minister of Health [1954] 2 QB 66

The plaintiffs underwent surgical procedures at the first defendant's hospital in 1947. In each case, the plaintiff was administered a spinal anaesthetic consisting of Nupercaine by the second defendant, Dr Graham, a specialist anaesthetist. The Nupercaine was contained in glass ampoules which were, prior to use, immersed in a phenol solution. After the operations the plaintiffs developed spastic paraplegia which resulted in permanent paralysis from the waist downwards. In an action for damages for personal injuries against the first and second defendants, the trial judge found that the injuries to the plaintiffs were caused by the Nupercaine becoming contaminated by the phenol which had percolated into the Nupercaine through molecular flaws or invisible cracks in the ampoules, and that at the date of the operations the risk of percolation through molecular flaws in the glass was not appreciated by competent anaesthetists in general. The trial judge dismissed the plaintiffs claims. They appealed.

Denning LJ

The only question is whether on the facts as now ascertained anyone was negligent. Leading counsel for the plaintiffs said that the staff were negligent . . . in [amongst other things] not colouring the phenol with a deep dye . . . If the anaesthetists had foreseen that the ampoules might get cracked with cracks that could not be detected on inspection they would, no doubt, have dyed the phenol a deep blue; and this would have exposed the contamination. But I do not think their failure to foresee this was negligence. It is so easy to be wise after the event and to condemn as negligence that which was only a misadventure. We ought always to be on our guard against it, especially in cases against hospitals and doctors. Medical science has conferred great benefits on mankind, but these benefits are attended by considerable risks. Every surgical operation is attended by risks. We cannot take the benefits without taking the risks. Every advance in technique is also attended by risks. Doctors, like the rest of us, have to learn by experience; and experience often teaches in a hard way. Something goes wrong and shows up a weakness, and then it is put right. That is just what happened here. Dr Graham sought to escape the danger of infection by disinfecting the ampoule. In escaping that known danger he, unfortunately, ran into another danger. He did not know that there could be undetectable cracks, but it was not negligent for him not to know it at that time. We must not look at the 1947 accident with 1954 spectacles. The judge acquitted Dr Graham of negligence and we should uphold his decision . . .

This has taught the doctors to be on their guard against invisible cracks. Never again, it is to be hoped, will such a thing happen. After this accident a leading text-book, Professor Macintosh on *Lumbar Puncture and Spinal Anaesthesia*, was published in 1951 which contains the significant warning:

> Never place ampoules of local anaesthetic solution in alcohol or spirit. This common practice is probably responsible for some of the cases of permanent paralysis reported after spinal analgesia.

If the hospitals were to continue the practice after this warning, they could not complain if they were found guilty of negligence. But the warning had not been given at the time of this accident. Indeed, it was the extraordinary accident to these two men which first disclosed the danger. Nowadays it would be negligence not to realise the danger, but it was not then.

One final word. These two men have suffered such terrible consequences that there is a natural feeling that they should be compensated. But we should be doing a disservice to the community at large if we were to impose liability on hospitals and doctors for everything that happens to go wrong. Doctors would be led to think more of their own safety than of the good of their patients. Initiative would be stifled and confidence shaken. A proper sense of proportion requires us to have regard to the conditions in which hospitals and doctors have to work. We must insist on due care for the patient at every point, but we must not condemn as negligence that which is only a misadventure... These appeals should be dismissed.

Somerville and **Morris LJJ** delivered concurring judgments.

Appeal dismissed.

COMMENTARY

The 'time dimension' of the inquiry into breach of duty is especially important in actions arising out of the use of dangerous substances whose toxicity is only gradually discovered by medical science. Asbestos is a case in point (see N. Wikeley, *Compensation for Disease* (Aldershot: Dartmouth, 1993)). The risk of various asbestos-related conditions (including the respiratory disease asbestosis, and the invariably fatal cancer mesothelioma) has been known since about 1930, and the Inspector of Factories began warning of the risk to employees handling asbestos in 1945. But the risk to those exposed only occasionally to asbestos only subsequently became apparent. In *Smith v P & O Bulk Shipping Ltd* [1998] 2 Lloyd's Rep 81 the High Court rejected a claim in respect of an employee exposed to asbestos in his workplace environment in the period 1954–71. He did not work directly with asbestos, but would often pass others who were working on it and sometimes came into contact with asbestos dust in the air. The High Court held that a reasonable employer would not have known in 1971 that there was a danger to health to those not working directly with or on asbestos, and hence the failure to take precautions against such exposure was not negligent. It will be apparent that much depends in such cases on the nature of the victim's contact with the asbestos, and there is no single date of imputed knowledge that can be relied upon in all cases of asbestos exposure. Similar issues arise in relation to the provision of personal safety equipment (e.g. ear muffs or goggles) to guard against other hazards of the workplace. See, e.g., the discussion of the date of imputed knowledge in the context of industrial deafness in *Thompson v Smith Shiprepairers* [1984] QB 405.

There can be an interesting interplay in such cases between the breach of duty analysis and principles relating to the existence of a duty of care. A defendant employer, for example, may be in breach of duty to its employees for exposing them to asbestos, but not to residents in the vicinity of its factory who contract an asbestos-related illness because of emissions from the factory (cf. *Margereson v J. W. Roberts Ltd* [1996] PIQR P358, where the plaintiffs succeeded in their action for damages, having been allowed as children to play in loading bays where they were foreseeably at risk from asbestos) or members of an employee's family who contract such illness from asbestos dust on the employee's clothes (*Maguire v Harland and Wolff* [2005] EWCA Civ 1, [2005] PIQR P21), if the risk to such persons was not foreseeable at the relevant time. Such cases are best analysed under the foreseeability stage of the inquiry into the existence of a duty of care, rather than in relation to breach of duty. The employer's negligence was a breach of duty to the foreseeable victims (the employees) but not the unforeseeable victims (the local residents and family members) because the employer owed the latter no duty of care.

A comparison may be drawn between the time dimension in the common law of negligence and the position under the statutory product liability regime introduced by Consumer Protection Act 1987, Part 1. By s. 4(1)(e) of the Act, it is a defence to a claim under the statutory product liability regime that 'the state of scientific and technical knowledge at the [time the product was supplied by the producer] was not such that a producer of products of the same description as the product in question might be expected to have discovered the defect if it had existed in his products while they were under his control'. This so-called 'development risks' defence only applies, however, where the defendant could not possibly have known of the relevant risk, and liability can therefore arise under the statutory scheme in cases where it would not at common law, for example because the defendant could not reasonably have avoided a known risk (Ch. 11.III below; note also the 'time dimension' in the definition of 'defect' in s. 2 of the Act).

Wooldridge v Sumner [1963] 2 QB 43

An experienced horseman, Mr Holladay, competing at the National Horse Show, galloped his horse round a corner of the competition arena. About two feet away from the edge of the arena there was a line of shrubs with a number of benches interspersed between them. Surrounding the arena and behind the shrub and benches was a cinder track. A film cameraman, who had little experience of dealing with horses, was standing about twenty-five yards from the corner by one of the benches, although he had been told by the steward of the course to go outside the competition area while the horses were galloping. The horse went into and behind the line of the shrubs. When the plaintiff saw the horse approaching him, he stepped back or fell into its course and was knocked down and injured. In the cameraman's action against the owner of the horse, the trial judge found that the rider brought the horse into the corner much too fast and that the horse when it crashed into the line of shrubs would have gone out on to the cinder track if its rider had allowed it to do so, where it would not have harmed the plaintiff. He awarded the plaintiff damages for negligence. The defendant appealed.

Diplock LJ

It is a remarkable thing that, in a nation where, during the present century, so many have spent so much of their leisure in watching other people take part in sports and pastimes, there is an almost complete dearth of judicial authority as to the duty of care owed by the actual participants to the spectators...

What is reasonable care in a particular circumstance is a jury question, and where, as in a case like this, there is no direct guidance or hindrance from authority, it may be answered by inquiring whether the ordinary reasonable man would say that, in all the circumstances, the defendant's conduct was blameworthy.

The matter has to be looked at from the point of view of the reasonable spectator as well as the reasonable participant... because what a reasonable spectator would expect a participant to do without regarding it as blameworthy is as relevant to what is reasonable care as what a reasonable participant would think was blameworthy conduct in himself...

A reasonable spectator attending voluntarily to witness any game or competition knows, and presumably desires, that a reasonable participant will concentrate his attention on winning, and if the game or competition is a fast-moving one will have to exercise his judgment and attempt to exert his skill in what, in the analogous context of contributory negligence, is sometimes called 'the agony of the moment'. If the participant does so concentrate his attention and consequently does exercise his judgment and attempt to exert his skill in circumstances of this kind which are inherent in the game or competition in which he is taking part, the question whether any mistake he makes amounts to a breach of duty to take reasonable care must take account of those circumstances.

The law of negligence has always recognised that the standard of care which a reasonable man will exercise depends on the conditions under which the decision to avoid the act or omission relied on as negligence has to be taken. The case of the workman engaged on repetitive work in the noise and bustle of the factory is a familiar example. More apposite for present purposes are the collision cases where a decision has to be made on the spur of the moment...

It cannot be suggested that the participant, at any rate if he has some modicum of skill, is by the mere act of participating in breach of his duty of care to a spectator who is present for the very purpose of watching him do so. If, therefore, in the course of the game or competition at a moment when he really has not time to think, a participant by mistake takes a wrong measure, he is not, in my view, to be held guilty of any negligence.

Furthermore, the duty which he owes is a duty of care, not a duty of skill. Save where a consensual relationship exists between a plaintiff and a defendant by which the defendant impliedly warrants his skill, a man owes no duty to his neighbour to exercise any special skill beyond that which an ordinary reasonable man would acquire before indulging in the activity in which he is engaged at the relevant time. It may well be that a participant in a game or competition would be guilty of negligence to a spectator if he took part in it when he knew or ought to have known that his lack of skill was such that, even if he exerted it to the utmost, he was likely to cause injury to a spectator watching him. No question of this arises in the present case. It was common ground that Mr Holladay was an exceptionally skilful and experienced horseman.

The practical result of this analysis of the application of the common law of negligence to participant and spectator would, I think, be expressed by the common man in some such terms as these: 'A person attending a game or competition takes the risk of any damage caused to him by any act of a participant done in the course of and for the purposes of the game or competition, notwithstanding that such act may involve an error of judgment or a lapse of skill, unless the participant's conduct is such as to evince a reckless disregard of the spectator's safety'. The spectator takes the risk because such an act involves no breach of the duty of care owed by the participant to him...

As regards the speed at which Mr Holladay went round the bandstand end of the arena, I doubt whether his error of judgment would have amounted to negligence, even if one were to ignore completely the fact that his judgment had to be exercised rapidly in the excitement of the contest although not at a moment of intense crisis. For it does not seem to me that any miscalculation of the speed at which [the horse] could take the corner could be reasonably foreseen to be likely to injure any spectator sitting on or standing by the benches twenty to thirty yards from the point at which a horse taking the corner at too great a speed would cross the line demarcated by the shrubs. The likelihood was that, if a horse was forced by its momentum to go beyond that line, it would run out on to the cinder track without coming into contact with any of the shrubs... If it ran out on to the cinder track, there would be no peril to spectators who remained, as reasonably knowledgeable spectators would remain, on the benches in line with the shrubs... In fact... [t]he horse was deflected from its course before it reached the benches, and no spectator would have been injured had not the plaintiff in a moment of panic stepped or stumbled back out of his proper and safe place among the other spectators in the line of benches into the path of the horse. Such panic in the case of a person ignorant of equine behaviour and, as the judge found, paying little or no attention to what was going on, is understandable and excusable, but, in my view, a reasonable competitor would be entitled to assume that spectators actually in the arena would be paying attention to what was happening, would be knowledgeable about horses, and would take such steps for their own safety as any reasonably attentive and knowledgeable spectator might be expected to take. When due allowance is made for the circumstances in which Mr Holladay had in fact to exercise his judgment as to the speed at which to take the corner, his conduct in taking the corner too fast could not in my view amount to negligence.

As regards the second respect in which the learned judge found Mr Holladay to be negligent, namely, in his attempt to bring back the horse into the arena after it had come into contact with the first shrub...here was a classic case where Mr Holladay's decision what to do had to be taken in the 'agony of the moment' when he had no time to think, and if he took the wrong decision that could not in law amount to negligence. The most that can be said against Mr Holladay is that, in the course of, and for the purposes of, the competition he was guilty of an error or errors of judgment or a lapse of skill. That is not enough to constitute a breach of the duty of reasonable care which a participant owes to a spectator. In such circumstances, something in the nature of a reckless disregard of the spectator's safety must be proved, and of this there is no suggestion in the evidence.

Sellers and **Dankwerts LJJ** delivered separate concurring judgments.

Appeal allowed.

COMMENTARY

Their Lordships also found that the plaintiff had failed to prove a causal link between the defendant's negligence (even if that could be established) and the injury he sustained. The accident could just as well have been caused by something the horse saw or thought he saw. Dankwerts LJ (at 59) expressed some regret that the court was 'unable to have the story from the horse's mouth'.

Mr Holladay subsequently won the competition in which he was taking part, causing Sellers LJ to comment: 'there can be no better evidence that Mr Holladay was riding within the rules'. Goodhart, however, in a note in (1962) 78 LQR 490 at 492, advises caution on this point, for the competition judges were assessing the horse, not the rider, and their attention may not have been fixed on the speed at which the corner was rounded.

'A reckless disregard of safety'

According to Diplock LJ, it was necessary to show that the defendant was guilty of something more serious than an error of judgment or a lapse of skill; something in the nature of a reckless disregard of the spectator's safety had to be proved. The correct analysis of this dictum has proved problematic. Does the test of *reckless disregard* displace the ordinary standard of care in relation to contact sports and certain other activities (on the basis that competitors and spectators are deemed to waive the ordinary standard of care)? Or does it merely attempt to paraphrase, in ordinary language, the trite proposition that, in assessing whether the defendant is in breach of the duty of care, some latitude must be allowed where the alleged negligence arises in the context of a fast-moving sporting activity?

The two different approaches were summarised as follows by Sir John Donaldson (as he then was) in *Condon v Basi* [1985] 1 WLR 866 at 868, a successful claim in respect of a leg-breaking tackle in a Sunday-league football match:

One is to take a more generalised duty of care and to modify it on the basis that the participants in the sport or pastime impliedly consent to taking risks which otherwise would be a breach of the duty of care...The other...is saying, in effect, that there is a general standard of care, namely the Lord Atkin approach in *Donoghue v Stevenson* [1932] AC 562 that you are under a duty to take all reasonable care taking account of the circumstances in which you are placed, which, in a game of football, are quite different from those which affect you when you are going for a walk in the countryside.

His Lordship conceded that it generally made no difference which approach was preferred. Nevertheless, it is submitted that there are good reasons for preferring the latter. Displacing the ordinary standard of care raises awkward questions as to which activities are to attract the modified standard, and seems to be an unnecessary complication given that the ordinary standard can quite happily accommodate the sporting cases. (See further Kidner, 'The Variable Standard of Care, Contributory Negligence and *Volenti*' (1991) 11 LS 1.)

On-the-Pitch Incidents

Condon v Basi makes it clear that actions arising out of sporting events may be brought not only by bystanders (as in *Bolton v Stone*) and spectators (as in *Wooldridge*) but also by participants. Such actions have become increasingly common, perhaps because serious injury may deprive those engaged in professional sport of the ever-increasing financial rewards that are on offer. In *Elliott v Saunders*, 10 June 1994, unreported, Chelsea footballer Paul Elliott failed in his action for damages against Dean Saunders arising out of an injury suffered in a two-footed challenge by the then Liverpool striker in a Chelsea–Liverpool Premiership match in 1992; the injury ended his career. Drake J held that Elliott had failed to prove that Saunders had any intent to jump at him rather than the ball or was otherwise guilty of dangerous or reckless play. He accepted Saunders' evidence that he had jumped at the ball with two feet only so as to evade injury from Elliott's challenge (which the referee considered dangerous and had penalised) and that he had attempted to play the ball and not the player. The Judge was fortified in his opinion by the fact that Elliott's team-mate, Vincent (better known as Vinnie) Jones, a well-known 'hard man' of the game, made no immediate protest at the tackle even though he was very close by. (See further Gardiner and Felix, '*Elliott v. Saunders*: Drama in Court' (1994) 2(2) Sport and the Law Journal 1.)

The decision in *Elliott v Saunders* did not, however, signal the end of attempts to use the law of tort to gain compensation for football-field injuries. Later the same year, it was reported that John O'Neill, the Norwich City and Northern Ireland international defender, received £70,000 in an out-of-court settlement in respect of injuries sustained in a tackle with Wimbledon's John Fashanu; there was no admission of liability (*Independent*, 14 October 1994). Subsequently, Brian McCord, a former Stockport County player, succeeded in an action against Swansea City and its captain, John Cornforth, over the tackle that ended his career in 1993 (*McCord v Swansea Football Club*, *The Times*, 11 February 1997). Kennedy J found that the tackle was late and over-the-top (the defendant's foot was about 18 inches off the ground); although the defendant was not 'playing the man' he was guilty of an intentional foul 'which carried a real risk of serious injury'. His Lordship ruled that the tackle was 'inconsistent' with the player's duty of care and that the plaintiff was entitled to damages. This is believed to be the first occasion on which a professional footballer obtained judgment against another player in respect of a dangerous tackle. (But it was not the last: see *Watson v Gray, The Times*, 26 November 1998; *Collett v Smith* [2009] EWCA Civ 583, (2009) 106(26) LSG 18.)

Referees have also been the target of tort claims by injured players, for example, where they fail to follow standard procedures introduced in the interests of player safety. See *Smoldon v Whitworth* [1997] PIQR P133 and *Vowles v Evans* [2003] 1 WLR 1607, both successful actions for damages in respect of injuries suffered in a collapsed rugby scrum, the former when the referee failed to apply the standard phased sequence of engagement, the latter when the referee allowed a substitute to play in the front row even though he lacked the necessary training and experience.

In *Smoldon v Whitworth*, the Court of Appeal specifically rejected the view that 'reckless disregard' had to be proven in order to establish a breach of duty. The court reiterated its position in *Caldwell v Maguire* [2002] PIQR P6, a claim by one professional jockey against two others whose riding, he alleged, had caused him to fall. The court considered that it was not helpful to say anything other than that something more serious than an error of judgment, oversight or lapse of skill was required. On the facts, however, it was 'not possible to characterise momentary carelessness as negligence' (at [28], per Tuckey LJ) and the claim failed. The same approach was subsequently applied in respect of horseplay between teenage boys (*Blake v Galloway* [2004] 1 WLR 2844; see also *Orchard v Lee* [2009] EWCA Civ 295, [2009] PIQR P16).

Compensation and Culpability (Again)

These actions raise again the question of compensation and culpability. Should compensation be restricted to those who are injured by another's fault? One expedient might be for players to be required to have insurance against the risk of catastrophic injury (whether caused by negligence or not), and this was advocated as a possible solution by the Court of Appeal in *Smoldon v Whitworth*. '[T]he trouble there,' according to Drake J in *Elliott v Saunders*, 'is that the insurance company who has to meet the injured party's claim, would be likely to want to sue the player who caused the injury in order to recover the compensation they had paid out, so the dispute would still end up in the law courts.' The judge thought that it would be better to keep the law of personal injuries out of sport altogether, and advocated, in relation to professional football, 'a system of no fault liability in which every injured player would receive full compensation, irrespective of whether the injury was caused by someone's fault, or by pure accident.' As in other spheres where the replacement of tort liability with a no-fault system of compensation has been proposed, this radical suggestion has yet to be acted upon. But the mere fact that it has been made may be seen by some as further evidence of the problematic nature of 'fault' as the basis of a system of compensation for accidental injury.

IV. The Objective Standard of Care

Lack of skill or experience is no defence to an action in negligence, as is affirmed by the Latin maxim *imperitia non exculpatur*. The law assesses whether there has been a breach of duty by reference to an objective standard of care. For every activity, there is a certain minimum degree of care and skill that a defendant must exercise on pain of being found guilty of negligence. The question posed by the courts is, 'What level of care and skill was required by the activity which the defendant was pursuing?' rather than 'What could this particular defendant have done?' The objective standard 'eliminates the personal equation and is independent of the idiosyncrasies of the particular person whose conduct is in question' (*Glasgow Corporation v Muir* [1943] AC 448 at 457, per Lord Macmillan). As Honoré has noted, the effect of such an approach is the imposition of strict liability, that is liability without (moral) fault, in cases where the defendant is physically or mentally unable to reach the standards of the reasonable person ('Responsibility and Luck' (1988) 104 LQR 530).

A rather uncharitable view of the objectively reasonable person is given by the humorist A. P. Herbert in the fictitious case of *Fardell v Potts* (The Reasonable Man), in *Uncommon Law* (London: Metheun, reprinted 1982):

> He is an ideal, a standard, the embodiment of all those qualities which we demand of the good citizen...This noble creature stands in singular contrast to his kinsman the Economic Man, whose every action is prompted by the single spur of selfish advantage and directed to the single end of monetary gain...All solid virtues are his, save only that peculiar quality by which the affection of other men is won. For it will not be pretended that socially he is much less objectionable than the Economic Man. Though any given example of his behaviour must command our admiration, when taken in the mass his acts create a very different set of impressions...Devoid, in short, of any human weakness, with not a single saving vice, *sans* prejudice, procrastination, ill-nature, avarice and absence of mind, as careful for his own safety as he is for that of others, this excellent but odious creature stands like a monument in our Courts of Justice, vainly appealing to his fellow-citizens to order their lives after his own example.

Tongue in cheek, Herbert has his judge conclude—after a review of the authorities—that 'legally at least there is no reasonable woman' (p. 4). Mayo Moran takes Herbert's 'perceptive mockery' as the starting point of her recent book, *Rethinking the Reasonable Person* (extracted below), and argues that he presaged the later insight of various critical commentators who question the use of an idealised person as a legal standard (p. 1).

M. Moran, *Rethinking the Reasonable Person: An Egalitarian Reconstruction of the Objective Standard* (Oxford: OUP, 2003), pp. 301–2, 195

The reasonable person—an idealized person—is the common law's characteristically ingenious solution to the complex problem of articulating a standard of appropriate attentiveness to others across an almost infinite variety of individuals and situations. The genius of the reasonable person is largely found in the way he seamlessly weaves together the normative components of the standard—attentiveness to others—with biographical or empirical qualities—age, intelligence, level of education, mode of transportation, etc. Thus constructed, the reasonable person has the undoubted virtue of making an otherwise abstract normative standard seem familiar and knowable. But these very virtues are inextricably linked to his most serious vices. In fact, the use of an idealized person often seems a poor way to capture the idea of what attentiveness to others requires, precisely because it makes it so difficult to distinguish between those qualities of the idealized person that matter normatively and those that do not. Beyond this, the personification of a normative ideal may also incline the decision-maker to read ordinariness into the reasonableness component of the standard...

The reasonable person standard purports to derive its objectivity from an appeal to shared rather than individual qualities, and to the extent that it thus relies on customary norms it is essentially a standard of ordinariness. However, if the objective standard draws its notion of what is reasonable in large part from a conception of what is normal or ordinary, then we can expect many problems with these conceptions to 'seep' into determinations under the objective standard. In fact, while in the law of negligence reference to what is customary may seem useful in identifying behaviour long regarded as reasonable, there are also significant dangers here. This is because conceptions of what is normal or ordinary have also exhibited serious and systematic defects: they have consistently located some people beyond the innermost enclave of concern. For many groups including women, those disadvantaged on racial, religious, or ethnic grounds, the poor, and those with mental and physical disabilities, conceptions of what is normal or natural have been and continue to be used to justify discriminatory treatment.

COMMENTARY

Moran's basic argument is that the law's personification of the idea of reasonable care has tended towards a blurring of the distinction between *proper* behaviour and *ordinary* behaviour as the reasonable person is invested with more and more of the defendant's own characteristics and attributes. The only significant check on this process is that the characteristics and attributes must be 'normal', but normality is a slippery and politically-contested notion that, as Moran observes, has often been used to justify discriminatory treatment of historically disadvantaged groups. Because the law has been too preoccupied with ordinariness, she argues, it has paid insufficient attention to the question of which characteristics and attributes are normatively relevant. Elsewhere in her important and challenging book, she substantiates her claims in a detailed analysis of the standard of care demanded of children and the developmentally disabled. She persuasively argues—in the case of the former—that gender stereotypes frequently intrude into the inquiry, with the courts particularly inclined to excuse the 'normal' heedlessness of playing boys ('boys will be boys!': see further Section 3, below). This gendering of an apparently neutral legal standard is particularly evident, she submits, when the standard of care is considered in the mirror-image context of contributory negligence by the claimant. She explains (at pp. 128–9):

[A]ssumptions about what kind of behaviour is natural for girls as opposed to for boys effectively results in different standards for contributory negligence. The normal boy, it seems, seeks risks and is therefore not chastised for so doing; in contrast, the normal girl seeks safety and avoids risks and is held to that standard.

Other feminist legal scholars have argued, more radically, that the very notion of 'reasonableness' inevitably reflects a male perspective—not just because it is usually interpreted by male judges, but because it is itself a construct of patriarchal society—and should be discarded. See, e.g., Martin, 'A Feminist View of the Reasonable Man: An Alternative Approach to Liability in Negligence for Personal Injury' (1994) 23 Anglo-Am L Rev 334. For Moran, by contrast, it is not the 'reason' part of the reasonable person standard that should be abolished, but the 'person'. Instead of personifying the standard of reasonable care, we would do better to inquire directly into the question of whether the conduct in question betrays that culpable indifference to others that is properly called 'negligence'.

1. Lack of Skill and Experience

Nettleship v Weston [1971] 2 QB 691

The defendant asked the plaintiff, a friend, to teach her to drive. He agreed only after ensuring that he was covered under the defendant's comprehensive car insurance policy. During the course of a lesson and when the defendant was driving, she failed to straighten the car after having turned a corner with the result that it mounted the pavement and hit a lamp-post. The plaintiff broke his kneecap as a result of the collision, and sued for negligence. The trial judge dismissed his claim on the basis that the defendant only owed him a duty to do her best, and that she did not fail in that duty.

Lord Denning MR

The Responsibility of the Learner-Driver Towards Persons on or near the Highway

Mrs Weston is clearly liable for the damage to the lamp-post. In the civil law if a driver goes off the road on to the pavement and injures a pedestrian, or damages property, he is prima facie liable. Likewise if he goes on to the wrong side of the road. It is no answer for him to say: 'I was a learner-driver under instruction. I was doing my best and could not help it.' The civil law permits no such excuse. It requires of him the same standard of care as any other driver . . . The learner-driver may be doing his best, but his incompetent best is not good enough. He must drive in as good a manner as a driver of skill, experience and care, who is sound in mind and limb, who makes no errors of judgment, has good eyesight and hearing, and is free from any infirmity . . .

The high standard thus imposed by the judges is, I believe, largely the result of the policy of the Road Traffic Acts. Parliament requires every driver to be insured against third-party risks. The reason is so that a person injured by a motor-car should not be left to bear the loss on his own, but should be compensated out of the insurance fund. The fund is better able to bear it than he can. But the injured person is only able to recover if the driver is liable in law. So the judges see to it that he is liable, unless he can prove care and skill of a high standard . . . Thus we are, in this branch of the law, moving away from the concept: 'No liability without fault'. We are beginning to apply the test: 'On whom should the risk fall?' Morally the learner-driver is not at fault; but legally she is liable to be because she is insured and the risk should fall on her . . .

The Responsibility of the Learner-Driver Towards Passengers in the Car

Mrs Weston took her son with her in the car. We do not know his age. He may have been 21 and have known that his mother was learning to drive. He was not injured. But if he had been injured, would he have had a cause of action? I take it to be clear that, if a driver has a passenger in the car, he owes a duty of care to him. But what is the standard of care required of the driver? Is it a lower standard than he or she owes towards a pedestrian on the pavement? I should have thought not. But, suppose that the driver has never driven a car before, or has taken too much to drink, or has poor eyesight or hearing; and, furthermore, that the passenger *knows* it and yet accepts a lift from him. Does that make any difference? Dixon J thought it did. In *Insurance Comr v Joyce* (1948) 77 CLR 39 at 56, 57 he said:

> If a man accepts a lift from a car-driver whom he *knows* to have lost a limb or an eye or to be deaf, he cannot complain if he does not exhibit the skill and competence of a driver who suffers from no defect . . . If he knowingly accepts the voluntary services of a driver affected by

drink, he cannot complain of improper driving caused by his condition, because it involves no breach of duty.

We have all the greatest respect for Sir Owen Dixon, but for once I cannot agree with him. The driver owes a duty of care to every passenger in the car, just as he does to every pedestrian on the road; and he must attain the same standard of care in respect of each. If the driver were to be excused according to the knowledge of the passenger, it would result in endless confusion and injustice. One of the passengers may know that the learner-driver is a mere novice. Another passenger may believe him to be entirely competent. One of the passengers may believe the driver to have had only two drinks. Another passenger may know that he has had a dozen. Is the one passenger to recover and the other not? Rather than embark on such enquiries, the law holds that the driver must attain the same standard of care for passengers as for pedestrians. The knowledge of the passenger may go to show that he was guilty of contributory negligence in ever accepting the lift—and thus reduce his damages—but it does not take away the duty of care, nor does it diminish the standard of care which the law requires of the driver . . .

The Responsibility of a Learner-Driver Towards His Instructor

The special factor in this case is that Mr Nettleship was not a mere passenger in the car. He was an instructor teaching Mrs Weston to drive. Seeing that the law lays down, for all drivers of motor cars, a standard of care to which all must conform, I think that even a learner-driver, so long as he is the sole driver, must attain the same standard towards all passengers in the car, including an instructor. But the instructor may be debarred from claiming for a reason peculiar to himself. He may be debarred because he has voluntarily agreed to waive any claim for any injury that may befall him. Otherwise he is not debarred. He may, of course, be guilty of contributory negligence and have his damages reduced on that account. He may, for instance, have let the learner take control too soon, he may not have been quick enough to correct his errors, or he may have participated in the negligent act himself: see *Stapley v Gypsum Mines Ltd* [1953] AC 663. But, apart from contributory negligence, he is not excluded unless it be that he had voluntarily agreed to incur the risk.

[His Lordship proceeded to consider, and reject, the defence of *volenti non fit injuria*, and continued:]

Conclusion Thus Far

In all that I have said, I have treated Mrs Weston as the driver who was herself in control of the car. On that footing, she is plainly liable for the damage done to the lamp-post. She is equally liable for the injury done to Mr Nettleship. She owed a duty of care to each. The standard of care is the same in either case. It is measured objectively by the care to be expected of an experienced, skilled and careful driver.

Salmon LJ delivered a separate concurring judgment. **Megaw LJ** dissented on the question of contributory negligence.

Appeal allowed.

COMMENTARY

The Court of Appeal found for the plaintiff but (Megaw LJ dissenting) reduced his damages by 50 per cent for contributory negligence. For analysis of the case in the context of the defence of *volenti non fit injuria*, see p. 287, below.

The Court of Appeal's approach did not commend itself to the Australian High Court (*Cook v Cook* (1986) 162 CLR 376), which held that, although the standard owed would normally be that of the reasonably competent driver, special circumstances might exist which would alter this standard. An example of such circumstances would be where the driver was, to the knowledge of the passenger, a learner; hence 'the standard of care which arises from the relationship of pupil and instructor is that which is reasonably to be expected of an unqualified and inexperienced driver in the circumstances in which the pupil is placed'. The duty owed to other road users remained that of a careful qualified driver. However, in *Imbree v McNeilly* [2008] HCA 40, the High Court changed its mind and overruled *Cook v Cook*, for reasons both principled and practical. At the level of principle, the variable standard of care recognised in *Cook v Cook* was inconsistent with the essential requirement that the standard of care should be objective and impersonal. Further, the *Cook v Cook* approach required the drawing of difficult distinctions, e.g. between a lack of skill due to inexperience and a lack of care, and left undefined the level of competence that was to be assumed in a learner driver (was it to vary depending on how long the learner had been having lessons?). The decision brings Australian common law into line with English law as established by *Nettleship v Weston*.

Inexperience in the Professions

In *Wilsher v Essex Area Health Authority* [1987] QB 730 (reversed on different grounds at [1988] AC 1074), a majority of the Court of Appeal held that the standard of care required of members of a medical unit was that of the ordinary skilled person exercising and professing to have that special skill, and that the standard was to be determined in the context of particular posts in the unit rather than according to the general rank or status of the people filling the posts. The duty had to be tailored to the acts which the doctor had elected to perform rather than to the doctor himself. It followed that inexperience was no defence to an action for medical negligence. However, Glidewell LJ held that an inexperienced doctor who was called on to exercise a specialist skill and made a mistake nevertheless satisfied the necessary standard of care if he had sought the advice and help of his superior when necessary. By contrast, the dissenting member of the court, Sir Nicolas Browne-Wilkinson V-C, expressly rejected the view that there was an objective standard which could be determined irrespective of the experience of the individual doctor and the reason why he was occupying the post in question. In his opinion, the ordinary standard of a skilled doctor did not apply to a houseman (a junior doctor) or to a doctor just beginning to train in a speciality. He explained (at 777):

The houseman has to take up his post in order to gain full professional qualification; anyone who...wishes to obtain specialist skills has to learn those skills by taking a post in a specialist unit. In my judgment, such doctors cannot in fairness be said to be at fault if, at the start of their time, they lack the very skills which they are seeking to acquire...In my judgment, so long as the English law rests liability on personal fault, a doctor who has properly accepted a post in a hospital in order to gain necessary experience should only be held liable for acts or omissions which a careful doctor with his qualifications and experience would not have done or omitted.

If this view were to prevail, should patients be told of the status of the surgeon about to operate on them so they can decide whether to go ahead or wait for a more experienced surgeon?

Alternative Medicine

Is a practitioner of alternative medicine to be assessed by the standards of orthodox medicine? In *Shakoor v Situ* [2001] 1 WLR 410, the defendant was trained in traditional Chinese herbal medicine and practised with the imprimatur of an association promoting medicine of that type, but he was not qualified as a doctor in the United Kingdom. One of his patients died following a course of treatment prescribed by the defendant for the cure of benign skin blemishes, whose only treatment in western medicine was removal by surgery. The agreed expert evidence was that the death was caused by an extremely rare and unpredictable toxic reaction to the herbal treatment. The question was whether the prescription was negligent. The judge ruled that the defendant's conduct ought not to be assessed by the standards of orthodox medicine, because 'the fact that the patient has chosen to reject the orthodox and prefer the alternative practitioner is something important which must be taken into account'. It was immaterial whether the patient's decision was 'enlightened and informed or based on ignorance and superstition' (at 416). But it was not enough to consider only whether the defendant had exercised the degree of skill appropriate to his 'art', for the fact that he was offering an alternative to orthodox medicine had a number of implications (at 417):

First of all, the practitioner has to recognise that he is holding himself out as competent to practise within a system of law and medicine which will review the standard of care he has given to a patient. Secondly, where he prescribes a remedy which is taken by a patient it is not enough to say that the remedy is traditional and believed not to be harmful, he has a duty to ensure that the remedy is not actually or potentially harmful. Thirdly ... [a]n alternative practitioner who prescribes a remedy must take steps to satisfy himself that there has not been any adverse report in [orthodox medical] journals on the remedy which ought to affect the use he makes of it. That is not to say that he must take a range of publications himself. It should be enough if he subscribes to an 'association' which arranges to search the relevant literature and promptly report any material publication to him. The relevant literature will be that which would be taken by an orthodox practitioner practising at the level of speciality at which the alternative practitioner holds himself out.

Applying these principles, the judge found that the defendant was not in breach of his duty of care to the deceased since there was nothing in the orthodox medical journals to indicate that his herbal treatment was too hazardous to prescribe, or should have been prescribed only with a warning of the risk of an adverse reaction.

Of course, it is also possible to sue on the basis that the alternative practitioner failed to exercise the skill and care appropriate to his art. As J. Stone and J. Matthews, *Complementary Medicine and the Law* (Oxford: OUP, 1996) demonstrate, however, establishing what this standard is will not always be a straightforward matter for the court (pp. 167–8):

The closer the therapy to a medicalized model and the more formalized and standardized its techniques, the easier it will be ... to establish a standard of care. In therapies which are more intuitive or esoteric, this may prove to be extremely difficult.

There are conceptual difficulties in applying legal standards of objective reasonableness to holistic practitioners. If the therapy is truly patient-centred it is not objective and it could be argued that the therapy given was the only appropriate treatment for that particular patient at that particular point in time. So individualized can the treatment claim to be that it would be almost impossible for another practitioner who did not observe the patient at that time to say whether he would or would not have treated them in the same way. Individualized treatment may work against a patient, in that almost any treatment could be justified retrospectively by the practitioner. Thus, in practice, it could be very hard for a plaintiff to disprove the practitioner's assertion that what he did was the appropriate thing at that particular time…

The ability to establish a standard of care will depend on the extent to which the therapy has agreed competencies. Once a therapy has established what the basic competencies are, it can then ensure that every practitioner is trained in them. One of the biggest difficulties is that at present, many smaller therapies have not even begun to define what the competencies required of their skill are.

Sporting Skill

In *Condon v Basi* [1985] 1 WLR 866, one of the football cases summarised above, the Court of Appeal rejected what Conor Gearty [1985] CLJ 371 describes as 'Basi's wonderful argument that he was such a bad footballer he owed no duty not to break his opponents' legs with awful tackles'. Nevertheless Sir John Donaldson MR stated (at 868): 'there will of course be a higher degree of care required of a player in a First Division football match than of a player in a local league football match…'. Gearty queries whether this is desirable, suggesting that it effectively gives rise to a 'Cloggers' Charter':

This gives a new dimension to knock-out competition. Imagine Melchester Rovers, the league leaders, away to non-league Thugs United in the third round of the FA Cup. Must Roy continue to play his immaculate game under threat of a personal injuries action whilst all about him the manicured and expensive legs of his team-mates are hacked to the ground by the legitimately incompetent?

Quite apart from our sympathy for Roy of the Rovers, we should note that Sir John Donaldson's comments on this matter were obiter and were subsequently doubted by Drake J in *Elliott v Saunders*, unreported, QBD, 10 June 1994. Subsequently, in *Vowles v Evans* [2003] 1 WLR 1607 at [28], in an analogous context, the Court of Appeal accepted that there was 'scope for argument' whether the degree of skill to be expected of a referee depends on his grade or that of the match he is refereeing, but stated that a volunteer called to stand in from amongst the spectators when the nominated referee failed to show up or was injured 'cannot reasonably be expected to show the skill of one who holds himself out as referee, or perhaps even to be fully conversant with the laws of the game'. Is the quoted proposition consistent with *Nettleship v Weston*?

2. Physical and Mental Disability

Mansfield v Weetabix Ltd [1998] 1 WLR 1263

The plaintiffs were the owners of a shop that was badly damaged when it was hit by a lorry owned by the first defendant and driven by the second defendant, Mr Tarleton. At the time of the accident, and unbeknownst to him, Tarleton was in a hypoglycaemic state whereby his brain was starved of oxygen and unable to function properly. The trial judge found him to have been negligent. Both defendants appealed.

Leggatt LJ

Mr Tarleton had an impaired degree of consciousness because of the malfunction in his brain caused by the deficiency in glucose.

The judge followed *Roberts v Ramsbottom* [1980] 1 WLR 823. In it a motorist was involved in an accident when unknowingly he was suffering from a stroke and was unaware of his unfitness to drive. Neill J considered several criminal cases about automatism before saying, at p. 832:

> I am satisfied that in a civil action a similar approach should be adopted. The driver will be able to escape liability if his actions at the relevant time were wholly beyond his control. The most obvious case is sudden unconsciousness. But if he retained some control, albeit imperfect control, and his driving, judged objectively, was below the required standard, he remains liable.

He gave no reason for being so satisfied. In my judgment, consideration of criminal cases can only introduce confusion. In them the question is whether the defendant was driving. Hence the need, if the defendant is to escape conviction, to show that he was in a state of automatism. In civil cases that is not the test. So Neill J erred when he considered criminal and civil cases indifferently, and assumed that to escape liability in a civil case a defendant must show that he was in a state of automatism . . . Nonetheless, *Robert's* case was, in my judgment, rightly decided on the alternative ground that the defendant 'continued to drive when he was unfit to do so and when he should have been aware of his unfitness:' see pp. 832–833 . . .

The other case upon which Collins J principally relied was *Nettleship v Weston* [1971] 2 QB 691, in which this court held that the duty of care owed by a learner driver to her instructor is to be judged by the same objective standard as that owed to passengers and other road users by qualified drivers. But although this case shows that there should be no relaxation of the standard of care, it does not refer to cases in which a driver is unaware that he is subject to a disability . . .

There is no reason in principle why a driver should not escape liability where the disabling event is not sudden, but gradual, provided that the driver is unaware of it. A person with Mr Tarleton's very rare condition commonly does not appreciate that his ability is impaired, and he was no exception. Although by the time of trial Mr Tarleton was dead, and there was no direct evidence of his actual state of awareness, the judge held that he 'would not have continued to drive if he had appreciated and was conscious that his ability was impaired.' Of course, if he had known that it was, he would have been negligent in continuing to drive despite his knowledge of his disability. So also if he ought to have known that he was subject to a condition that rendered him unfit to drive: *Waugh v James Allan Ltd* [1964] 2 Lloyd's Rep 1 . . .

In my judgment, the standard of care that Mr Tarleton was obliged to show in these circumstances was that which is to be expected of a reasonably competent driver unaware that he is or may be suffering from a condition that impairs his ability to drive. To apply an objective standard in a way that did not take account of Mr Tarleton's condition would be to impose strict liability. But that is not the law. As Lord Wilberforce said in *Snelling v Whitehead, The Times*, 31 July 1975, a transcript of the speeches in which is before the court:

> The case is one which is severely distressing to all who have been concerned with it and one which should attract automatic compensation regardless of any question of fault. But no such system has yet been introduced in this country and the courts, including this House, have no power to depart from the law as it stands. This requires that compensation may only be obtained in an action for damages and further requires, as a condition of the award of damages against the driver, a finding of fault, or negligence, on his part . . . it is . . . not disputed that any degree of fault on the part of the [driver], if established, is sufficient for the plaintiff to recover. On the other hand, if no blame can be imputed to the [driver], the action, based on negligence, must inevitably fail.

In the present case the plaintiffs may well have been insured. Others in their position may be less fortunate. A change in the law is, however, a matter for Parliament. Meanwhile, since in my judgment Mr Tarleton was in no way to blame, he was not negligent. I would therefore allow the appeal.

Aldous LJ

The standard of care that Mr Tarleton was obliged to show was that which is expected of a reasonably competent driver. He did not know and could not reasonably have known of his infirmity which was the cause of the accident. Therefore he was not at fault. His action did not fall below the standard of care required.

Sir Patrick Russell agreed with Leggatt and Aldous LJJ.

Appeal allowed.

COMMENTARY

Is this decision reconcilable with *Nettleship v Weston* (above)? How was the defendant in *Nettleship* any more 'at fault' than the defendant in *Mansfield*?

In *Roberts v Ramsbottom* [1980] 1 WLR 823, Neill J held that the defendant could escape liability only if the incapacity amounted to automatism, as defined in criminal law where the defence requires a *total* loss of consciousness or control over one's actions. This was disapproved in *Mansfield* but the decision was upheld on the alternative ground that the defendant was at fault for continuing to drive whilst aware of the unfitness, as he had been 'feeling queer' and had earlier hit the back of parked van. However, just before the accident in *Mansfield*, the defendant driver had collided with the trailer of a car ahead of him, and, although the defendant was dead by the time of the trial and so could not give evidence, the policeman who attended the accident said he was 'behaving strangely'. Why was the defendant not liable, as in *Roberts*, for continuing to drive in the light of these circumstances?

Should a no-fault compensation scheme be introduced in respect of road traffic accidents, as Lord Wilberforce seems to have been suggesting in the passage quoted from *Snelling v Whitehead*, above? See p. 978, below.

3. Age

Mullin v Richards [1998] 1 WLR 1304

The plaintiff, a 15-year-old schoolgirl named Teresa, was injured whilst playing at school with the first defendant, another girl of the same age. The two girls were fencing with plastic rulers during a class when one of the rulers snapped and a fragment of plastic entered Teresa's right eye, causing her to lose all useful sight in that eye. She brought proceedings for negligence against the other girl and the local education authority. The judge dismissed the claim against the education authority but found that both girls had been guilty of negligence of which Teresa's injury was the foreseeable result. Accordingly, he held that the claim against the other schoolgirl succeeded, subject to a reduction of 50 per cent for contributory negligence. The defendant schoolgirl appealed, contending that the judge had erred when considering foreseeability by omitting to take account of the fact that she was not an adult.

Hutchison LJ

By her notice of appeal, the first defendant contends … [*inter alia*] that the judge erred when considering foreseeability by omitting to take account of the fact that the first defendant was not an adult but a 15-year-old schoolgirl. What he should have done, it is contended, was to consider objectively what a normal and reasonable 15-year-old schoolgirl would have foreseen …

The argument centres on foreseeability. The test of foreseeability is an objective one; but the fact that the first defendant was at the time a 15-year-old schoolgirl is not irrelevant. The question for the judge is not whether the actions of the defendant were such as an ordinarily prudent and reasonable adult in the defendant's situation would have realised gave rise to a risk of injury, it is whether an ordinarily prudent and reasonable 15-year-old schoolgirl in the defendant's situation would have realised as much. In that connection both counsel referred us to, and relied upon, the Australian decision in *McHale v Watson* (1966) 115 CLR 199 esp at 213–214 in the judgment of Kitto J. I cite a portion of the passage I have referred to, all of which was cited to us by Mr Lee on behalf of the appellant, and which Mr Stephens has adopted as epitomising the correct approach:

> The standard of care being objective, it is no answer for him [that is a child], any more than it is for an adult, to say that the harm he caused was due to his being abnormally slow-witted, quick-tempered, absent-minded or inexperienced. But it does not follow that he cannot rely in his defence upon a limitation upon the capacity for foresight or prudence, not as being personal to himself, but as being characteristic of humanity at his stage of development and in that sense normal. By doing so he appeals to a standard of ordinariness, to an objective and not a subjective standard.

Mr Stephens also cited to us a passage in the judgment of Owen J (at 234):

> the standard by which his conduct is to be measured is not that to be expected of a reasonable adult but that reasonably to be expected of a child of the same age, intelligence and experience.

I venture to question the word 'intelligence' in that sentence, but I understand Owen J to be making the same point essentially as was made by Kitto J. It is perhaps also material to have in mind the words of Salmon LJ in *Gough v Thorne* [1966] 1 WLR 1387 at 1391, which is cited also by Mr Stephens, where he said:

> The question as to whether the plaintiff can be said to have been guilty of contributory negligence depends on whether any ordinary child of 13½ can be expected to have done any more than this child did. I say 'any ordinary child'. I do not mean a paragon of prudence; nor do I mean a scatter-brained child; but the ordinary girl of 13½.

I need say no more about that principle as to the way in which age affects the assessment of negligence because counsel are agreed upon it and, despite the fact that we have been told that there has been a good deal of controversy in other jurisdictions and that there is no direct authority in this jurisdiction, the approach in *McHale v Watson* seems to me to have the advantage of obvious, indeed irrefutable, logic …

The judge, it seems to me, found negligence without there being material on which he could properly do so. He seems indeed from the language he used to have regarded it as axiomatic that if there was a fight going on, such as he found there was, a play fight, that imported that injury was reasonably foreseeable and from his finding that the ruler broke that there was necessarily dangerous or excessive violence. For my part, I would say that in the absence of evidence one simply does not know why the ruler broke, whether because it was unusually weak, unlike other rulers; whether because it had been damaged in some way; or whether because rulers of this sort are particularly prone to break; one does not know. What certainly one cannot infer, and the judge was, I consider, not entitled to infer, was that there was here excessive violence or inappropriate violence over and above that which was inherent in the play fencing in which these two girls were indulging. This was in truth nothing more than a schoolgirls' game such as on the evidence was commonplace in this school and there was, I would hold, no justification for attributing to the participants the foresight of any significant risk of the likelihood of injury. They had seen it done elsewhere with some frequency. They had not heard it prohibited or received any warning about it. They had not been told of any injuries occasioned by it. They were not in any sense behaving culpably. So far as foresight goes, had they paused to think they might, I suppose, have said: 'It is conceivable that some unlucky injury might happen', but if asked if there was any likelihood of it or any real possibility of it, they would, I am sure, have said that they did not foresee any such possibility. Taking the view therefore that the learned judge—who, as I have said, readily and almost without question accepted that on his findings of fact there was negligence on the part of both these young ladies—was wrong in his view and there was no evidence on which he could come to it, I would allow the appeal and direct that judgment be entered for the first defendant.

Sir John Vinelott and **Butler-Sloss LJ** delivered short concurring judgments.

Appeal allowed.

COMMENTARY

Butler-Sloss LJ cited with approval (at 1312) certain additional dicta from the judgment of Kitto J in *McHale v Watson*, including the following:

in the absence of relevant statutory provision, children, like everyone else, must accept as they go about in society the risks from which ordinary care on the part of others will not suffice to save them. One such risk is that boys of twelve may behave as boys of twelve . . .

The same applied, she added, to the risk that 'girls of 15 playing together may play as somewhat irresponsible girls of 15'. Whether boys' play is or ought to be distinguished from girls' play may be questioned. Moran (*Rethinking the Reasonable Person*, pp. 80–1) is particularly troubled by the Australian High Court's nostalgic reconstruction of boyhood in *McHale*, and its celebration of boyish imprudence.

[T]he boy appears as a child of nature—specially responsive to the whims and impulses of the natural world. Beyond this implicit assertion of what the state of boyhood is, however, one can discern a deeper commitment, a commitment to a certain understanding of what is both constitutive and most valuable in the state of boyhood. The characteristic freedom of boyhood is, it seems, defined by the absence of any constraints arising out of the interests of others. So one could not impose liability for boyish imprudence without destroying the most fundamental and valuable characteristic of boyhood as well . . . The delightful freedom of boyhood springs, it seems, from the liberty to ignore the interests of others.

In contrast, Moran finds Butler-Sloss LJ's insistence that girls will be girls 'almost revolutionary' (p. 90). But she doubts the desirability of extending the possibilities of irresponsibility to girls, rather than demanding a reasonable standard of attentiveness to others from both girls and boys.

In the extract above, Hutchison LJ seems to question whether it was right to treat the child's intelligence as a relevant factor. In so far as this suggests that the child's *experience* may be taken into account, is this consistent with *Nettleship v Weston*? (Cf. the approach of Kitto J in the passage cited by Hutchison LJ.)

It was agreed that, in assessing breach of duty, the foreseeability of injury should be assessed from the point of view of a reasonable child of the defendant's age. Presumably the defendant's age is also relevant in relation to the other elements of the 'breach equation' (e.g. in inquiring how easy it would be for the defendant to take precautions to guard against the risk of harm).

See further *Orchard v Lee* [2009] EWCA Civ 295, [2009] PIQR P16.

4. Special Skills

Philips v Whiteley (William) Ltd [1938] 1 All ER 566

The plaintiff made an appointment to have her ears pierced at the defendant's jewellery department. Whiteleys employed a Mr Couzens to perform the operation. For this purpose, he used an instrument he brought with him, having disinfected it by placing it in a flame before leaving his shop. Before actually piercing the ears, he rinsed his fingers in a glass of water into which he had poured a quantity of lysol, a disinfectant. Shortly after the ear piercing, the plaintiff developed an abscess in her neck which required surgery to have it opened and drained. The operation was skilfully done, leaving only a very small scar. The plaintiff brought an action against the defendant, alleging that the operation was negligently performed and that the abscess was due to that negligence.

Goddard J

In this case, the first thing that I have to consider is the standard of care demanded from Mr Couzens—or, I should say, from Whiteleys, because Whiteleys were the people who undertook to do this piercing. It is not easy in any case to lay down a particular canon or standard by which the care can be judged, but, while it is admitted here, and admitted on all hands, that Mr Couzens did not use the same precautions of procuring an aseptic condition of his instruments as a doctor or a surgeon would use, I do not think that he could be called upon to use that degree of care. Whiteleys have to see that whoever they employ for the operation uses the standard of care and skill that may be expected from a jeweller, and, of course, if the operation is negligently performed—if, for instance, a wholly unsuitable instrument were used so that the ear was badly torn, or something of that sort happened—undoubtedly they would be liable. So, too, if they did not take that degree of care to see that the instruments were clean which one would expect a person of the training and the standing of a jeweller to use. To say, however, that a jeweller warrants or undertakes that he will use instruments which have the degree of surgical cleanliness that a surgeon brings about when he is going to perform a serious operation, or indeed any operation, is, I think, putting the matter too high. The doctors all seem to agree in this case that, if a lady went to a surgeon for the piercing of her ears, he would render his instruments sterile. After all, however, aseptic surgery is a thing of very modern growth. As anybody who has read the life of Lord Lister or the history of medicine in the last fifty or sixty years knows, it is not so many years ago that the best surgeon in the land knew nothing about even antiseptic surgery. Then antiseptic surgery was introduced, and that was followed by aseptic surgery. I do not think that a jeweller holds himself out as a surgeon or professes that he is going to conduct the operation of piercing a lady's ears by means of aseptic surgery, about which it is not to be supposed that he knows anything.

If a person wants to ensure that the operation of piercing her ears is going to be carried out with that proportion of skill and so forth that a Fellow of the Royal College of Surgeons would use, she must go to a surgeon. If she goes to a jeweller, she must expect that he will carry it out in the way that one would expect a jeweller to carry it out. One would expect that he would wash his instruments. One would expect that he would take some means of disinfecting his instrument, just in the same way as one knows that the ordinary layman, when he is going to use a needle to prick a blister or prick a little gathering on a finger, generally takes the precaution to put the needle in a flame, as I think Mr Couzens did. I accept the evidence of Mr Couzens as to what he says he did on this occasion—how he put his instrument in a flame before he left his shop, and how he washed his hands, and so forth. I think that he did. I see no reason to suppose that he is not telling me the absolute truth when he says what he did, and... for all practical purposes that is enough. That is to say, for the ordinary every-day matters that would be regarded as enough. It is not a degree of surgical cleanliness, which is a very different thing from ordinary cleanliness. It is not the cleanliness which a doctor would insist upon, because, as I say, Mr Couzens is not a doctor. He was known not to be a doctor. One does not go to a jeweller to get one's ears attended to if one requires to have a doctor in attendance to do it. If one wants a doctor in attendance, one goes to his consulting room or one has him come to see one. I do not see any ground here for holding that Mr Couzens was negligent in the way in which he performed this operation. It might be better, and I think that it probably would, if he boiled his instrument beforehand at his place, or if he took a spirit lamp with him and boiled his instrument at the time, but in view of the medical evidence, the evidence of Dr Pritchard, which I accept, I see no ground for holding that Mr Couzens departed from the standard of care which you would expect that a man of his position and his training, being what he held himself out to be, was required to possess. Therefore, the charge of negligence fails.

[His Lordship also found for the defendants on the alternative ground that, even if the charge of negligence was proven, it was much more likely that the abscess from which Mrs Philips suffered was due to the subsequent infection of the puncture rather than a dirty needle.]

Judgment for the defendants.

COMMENTARY

Goddard J opted for the lower of the two standards he had to chose between: the standard of a jeweller, not that of a doctor. How can this be reconciled with *Nettleship v Weston* where the court decided to adopt the standard of a qualified driver, instead of the less demanding standard of the average learner driver for which the defendant had argued? The answer seems to be that, in *Nettleship*, the defendant was trying to *lower* the standard *below* that which normally governs driving on the roads, while, in *Philips*, the plaintiff was trying to *raise* the standard *above* that which the court deemed was appropriate to ear-piercing at the time in question. In each case, the court simply re-asserted the 'normal' standard of care for the activity in question. Of course, where the defendant professes a special skill, then the standard of a person possessed of such skill will be applied (see *Maynard v West Midlands Regional Health Authority* [1984] 1 WLR 634: more is expected of a specialist than of a general practitioner).

An interesting case to consider in this context is *Wells v Cooper* [1958] 2 QB 265. The plaintiff was injured after he slipped and fell when, as he was seeking (with permission) to enter the defendant's house, the door knob he was pulling came away from the door. The door knob had been fixed by the defendant. It was held that the standard expected of him was that of a reasonably competent amateur carpenter, which the court noted was lower than the standard expected of a professional carpenter. The Court of Appeal found that he had not been negligent, noting that the job in question was a 'trivial domestic replacement'; it added that, had the job been something more ambitious, the defendant might have been negligent merely in undertaking the task. What sort of task do you think a competent amateur carpenter would be negligent merely in undertaking?

If a first-aid volunteer attends to an injured person, by what standard should his conduct be judged? Should one distinguish between the standard of care of a first-aider and that of a trained doctor where the aim of first-aid treatment is simply to get the patient into a condition where he can be transported to hospital? (See *Cattley v St John's Ambulance Brigade*, noted by Griffiths (1990) 53 MLR 255, and compare the position of the volunteer stand-in rugby referee considered by the Court of Appeal in *Vowles v Evans*, p. 191, above.)

First-aiders may be expected to have at least some training. But what of the person professing no special training or skill who is obliged to give emergency medical care through force of circumstances? How would you formulate the standard of care to apply in such a case?

v. Common Practice

The decision whether or not the defendant is in breach of duty must be looked at in the light of other normative systems which regulate the activity in question. In the industrial sphere, the court may attach relevance to the existence of a common practice throughout the industry in question of taking, or not taking, a particular precaution against injury. Similarly, in the case of doctors, architects, lawyers and other professionals, it is necessary to take account of the rules and regulations promulgated by the relevant professional body, and to consider the state of expert opinion in the field. On the one hand, this is a matter of fairness to the defendant: is it reasonable to expect the defendant to 'plough a lone furrow' (to borrow a phrase from Mustill J in *Thompson v Smith Shiprepairers* [1984] QB 405 at 416) when others in the same sector of activity abide by lower standards? On the other hand, it reflects a realistic assessment of the courts' limited expertise in relation to certain technical matters, and of their consequent need to defer to the expert.

1. Common Industrial Practice

In *Morton v William Dixon*, 1909 SC 809, Lord Dunedin P set out principles which have been applied on many subsequent occasions:

> Where the negligence of the employer consists of what I may call a fault of omission, I think it is absolutely necessary that the proof of that fault of omission should be one of two kinds, either—to show that the thing which he did not do was a thing which was commonly done by other persons in like circumstances or—to show that it was a thing which was so obviously wanted that it would be folly in anyone to neglect to provide it.

The two propositions Lord Dunedin advances here should be regarded as rules of thumb, not absolutes. First, failure to take a common precaution may indeed be sufficient evidence to warrant a finding of negligence, but it does not necessarily connote negligence. In *Brown v Rolls Royce* [1960] 1 WLR 210, the House of Lords declined to hold the defendant employers liable to a machine-oiler in their factory who had contracted dermatitis. The employee alleged that his condition resulted from contact with oil which would have been avoided had he been supplied with barrier cream. Even though barrier cream was commonly supplied by other employers to men doing work of this kind, there were strong differences of medical opinion about the practice and the defendants had acted throughout with the advice of their medical officer. The House of Lords emphasised that Lord Dunedin's propositions might impose a provisional, evidential burden on the defendants, but they had no compelling legal force (see especially at 215–16, per Lord Denning).

Secondly, the courts will be wary of finding that something which is commonly done by others in like circumstances is negligent unless it amounts to plain folly. In *Stokes v GKN* [1968] 1 WLR 1776 at 1783, Swanwick J stated: 'where there is a recognised and general practice which has been followed for a substantial period in similar circumstances without mishap, [the defendant] is entitled to follow it...'. Even where the practice has not been 'without mishap', it may be reasonable to follow it if the risk is 'an inescapable feature of the industry' (*Thompson v Smith Shiprepairers Ltd* [1984] QB 405 at 415, per Mustill J). But a defendant is not entitled to rely upon common practice where 'in the light of common sense or newer knowledge it is clearly bad' and 'where there is developing knowledge, he must reasonably keep abreast of it and not be slow to apply it' (*Stokes* at 1783, per Swanwick J). In *Thompson*, Mustill J (at 416) reinforced this statement by holding that negligence could consist in 'an absence of initiative in seeking out knowledge of facts which are not in themselves obvious'; he added, however, that, while the employer 'must keep up to date...the court must be slow to blame him for not ploughing a lone furrow'.

2. Professional Standards

Bulam v Friern Hospital Management Committee [1957] 1 WLR 582

McNair J

[W]here you get a situation which involves the use of some special skill or competence, then the test whether there has been negligence or not is not the test of the man on the top of a Clapham omnibus, because he has not got this special skill. The test is the standard of the ordinary skilled man exercising and professing to have that special skill. A man need not possess the highest expert skill at the risk of being found negligent. It is well established law that it is sufficient if he exercises the ordinary skill of an ordinary competent man exercising that particular art... A doctor is not guilty of negligence if he has acted in accordance with a practice accepted as proper by a responsible body of medical men skilled in that particular art.... Putting it the other way round, a doctor is not negligent, if he is acting in accordance with such a practice, merely because there is a body of opinion that takes a contrary view. At the same time, that does not mean that a medical man can obstinately and pig-headedly carry on with some old technique if it has been proved to be contrary to what is really substantially the whole of informed medical opinion. Otherwise you might get men today saying: 'I don't believe in anaesthetics. I don't believe in antiseptics. I am going to continue to do my surgery in the way it was done in the eighteenth century'. That clearly would be wrong.

COMMENTARY

The so-called '*Bolam* test' (on which, see further Montrose, 'Is Negligence an Ethical or a Sociological Concept?' (1958) 21 MLR 259) attracted the attention of the House of Lords in two cases in the 1980s. In *Maynard v West Midlands Regional Health Authority* [1984] 1 WLR 634, the House of Lords held that a doctor's exercise of clinical judgment in a manner thought appropriate by a body of competent medical opinion could not be regarded as negligent simply because the trial judge 'preferred' an alternative body of medical opinion. In *Sidaway v Board of Governors of Bethlem Royal Hospital* [1985] AC 871, their Lordships held that the test applied not only to matters of medical diagnosis and treatment, but also to the question of the amount of information that a medical practitioner must give to a patient as to the risks involved in a proposed course of treatment. Lord Scarman (at 881) summarised the result of the *Bolam* test as follows: 'the law imposes the duty of care; but the standard of care is a matter of medical judgment'. 'What seems to have happened,' according to I. Kennedy and A. Grubb, *Medical Law: Text with Materials*, 2nd edn. (London: Butterworths, 1994), 'is that the House of Lords in *Maynard* and also…in *Sidaway* elevated to the status of an unquestionable proposition of law derived from *Bolam* that professional practice *will not* be reviewed by the courts.' This is particularly disturbing given that in decisions from *Sidaway* onwards 'the courts have used the test to allow doctors to determine other matters beyond their competence, such as the extent of the patient's right to be informed of risks and alternatives; the "best interests" of incompetent patients; and the very value of patients' lives' (Keown, 'Reining in the *Bolam* Test' [1998] CLJ 248 at 249).

However, certain earlier decisions had suggested that the protection given to medical practitioners by the *Bolam* test would not be absolute. In *Hills v Potter* [1984] 1 WLR 641, Hirst J qualified the test by stipulating that the body of medical opinion must be 'both respectable and responsible and experienced in [the] particular field of medicine'. And, in a long-overlooked decision from 1968, the Court of Appeal affirmed that the defendant doctor acted negligently in taking an easily avoidable risk which elementary teaching had instructed him to avoid, notwithstanding that other doctors admitted in court that they would have done the same (*Hucks v Cole* [1993] 4 Med LR 393). The question of the extent of the *Bolam* protection was considered again (albeit indirectly) by the House of Lords in *Bolitho v City and Hackney Health Authority* [1998] AC 232, extracted below.

Bolitho v City and Hackney Health Authority [1998] AC 232

Lord Browne-Wilkinson

[T]he court is not bound to hold that a defendant doctor escapes liability for negligent treatment or diagnosis just because he leads evidence from a number of medical experts who are genuinely of opinion that the defendant's treatment or diagnosis accorded with sound medical practice. In the *Bolam* case itself, McNair J [1957] 1 WLR 583, 587 stated that the defendant had to have acted in accordance with the practice accepted as proper by a '*responsible* body of medical men.' Later, at p. 588, he referred to 'a standard of practice recognised as proper by a competent *reasonable* body of opinion.' Again, in…*Maynard's* case [1984] 1 WLR 634, 639, Lord Scarman refers to a 'respectable' body of professional opinion. The use of these adjectives—responsible, reasonable and respectable—all show that the court has to be satisfied that the exponents of the body of opinion relied upon can demonstrate that such opinion has a logical basis. In particular in cases involving, as they so often do, the weighing of risks against benefits, the judge before accepting a body of opinion as being responsible, reasonable or respectable, will need to be satisfied that, in forming their views, the experts have directed their minds to the question of comparative risks and benefits and have reached a defensible conclusion on the matter.

There are decisions which demonstrate that the judge is entitled to approach expert professional opinion on this basis… [Lord Browne-Wilkinson referred here to *Hucks v Cole* [1993] 4 Med LR 393 amongst other cases.] These decisions demonstrate that in cases of diagnosis and treatment there are cases where, despite a body of professional opinion sanctioning the defendant's conduct, the defendant can properly be held liable for negligence (I am not here considering questions of disclosure of risk). In my judgment that is because, in some cases, it cannot be demonstrated to the judge's satisfaction that the body of opinion relied upon is reasonable or responsible. In the vast majority of cases the fact that distinguished experts in the field are of a particular opinion will demonstrate the reasonableness of that opinion. In particular, where there are questions of assessment of the relative risks and benefits of adopting a particular medical practice, a reasonable view necessarily presupposes that the relative risks and benefits have been weighed by the experts in forming their opinions. But if, in a rare case, it can be demonstrated that the professional opinion is not capable of withstanding logical analysis, the judge is entitled to hold that the body of opinion is not reasonable or responsible.

I emphasise that in my view it will very seldom be right for a judge to reach the conclusion that views genuinely held by a competent medical expert are unreasonable. The assessment of medical risks and benefits is a matter of clinical judgement which a judge would not normally be able to make without expert evidence. As the quotation from Lord Scarman makes clear, it would be wrong to allow such assessment to deteriorate into seeking to persuade the judge to prefer one of two views both of which are capable of being logically supported. It is only where a judge can be satisfied that the body of expert opinion cannot be logically supported at all that such opinion will not provide the benchmark by reference to which the defendant's conduct falls to be assessed.

COMMENTARY

Lord Browne-Wilkinson's apparent modification of the *Bolam* test has been applauded by some (e.g. Scott (1998) 148 NLJ 64) as challenging the autonomy of the medical profession. But Keown [1998] CLJ 248 comments: '*Bolitho* is good as far as it goes, but it does not go as far as it should. For one thing, it is not clear whether medical opinion may be disregarded only if it is illogical. What if the logic is flawless but the premise unsound or unpersuasive?' However, as Teff, 'The Standard of Care in Medical Negligence—Moving on from *Bolam*' (1998) 18 OJLS 473 notes (p. 483), 'the measured approach now endorsed by the House of Lords in *Bolitho* should reduce the risk of legitimating the lowest common denominator of accepted practice'. See further Brazier and Miola, 'Bye-bye *Bolam*: a medical litigation revolution?' (2000) 8 Med L Rev 85.

A particular difficulty lies in the court's ability to judge the merits of a particular course adopted by a medical practitioner. Unless there is an error of a very basic kind (in which case it is highly unlikely to have the support of a responsible body of medical opinion), or a logical inconsistency in the supporting expert evidence (see, e.g., *Penney v East Kent Health Authority* [2000] PNLR 323), the court may not be sufficiently versed in medicine to challenge what was done.

Lord Browne-Wilkinson made clear that he was leaving aside the question of risk disclosure, but in *Pearce v United Bristol Healthcare NHS Trust* [1999] PIQR P53 the Court of

Appeal seems to have used his judgment as a springboard allowing for more stringent judicial review of the failure to advise of treatment risks than was previously apparent. While purporting to follow the House of Lords in *Sidaway*, Lord Woolf MR nevertheless felt emboldened to state the following principle of law (at 59): 'if there is a significant risk which would affect the judgment of a reasonable patient, then in the normal course it is the responsibility of a doctor to inform the patient of that significant risk, if the information is needed so that the patient can determine for him or herself as to what course he or she should adopt'. It is notable that, rather than talk of the conduct of the reasonable doctor, Lord Woolf here focuses on the interests of the reasonable patient. Significantly, when the Australian High Court adopted a similar approach in *Rogers v Whitaker* (1992) 175 CLR 479, it thought it was rejecting *Bolam*. The impact of the Court of Appeal's decision should not, however, be overstated. The court rejected an even more radical approach which would have required the disclosure of risks which would be significant to the actual patient. And notwithstanding the change of judicial tone, the court still found against any duty of disclosure on the facts: a 0.1–0.2 per cent risk of stillbirth was not 'significant'. See further Grubb (1999) 7 Med L Rev 61; Maclean, 'The doctrine of informed consent: does it exist and has it crossed the Atlantic?' (2004) 24 LS 386 at 407–10.

The law of professional negligence

The *Bolam* test has also been used in respect of other professionals. In *Gold v Haringey Health Authority* [1988] QB 481, the Court of Appeal held it applied to any profession or calling which requires special skill, knowledge, or experience. In fact, the test can also be applied to those who are not members of a profession but must nevertheless exercise a special skill (see, e.g., *Adams v Rhymney Valley DC* (2001) 33 HLR 41: selection of window locks by local authority). In these other contexts, professional and non-professional, the court may not feel the same reluctance to declare a widespread practice to be negligent as they do when evaluating the care and skill exercised by medical practitioners. A significant decision in this regard is *Edward Wong Finance Co Ltd v Johnson Stokes & Master (A Firm)* [1984] AC 296, a successful claim against conveyancing solicitors. Lawyers are both more prepared and more competent to judge professional conduct when it involves members of their own profession. (Cf. the views of Lord Hoffmann, 'The reasonableness of lawyers' lapses' (1994) 10 PN 6: 'The underlying truth seems to be that judges regard conveyancing as an activity which should give a result to the client. The solicitor is insured and it seems only fair that the risk of a mistake should be borne by the underwriters rather than the client.')

Determining how the standard of care owed by different professionals should be applied in concrete situations, and what weight should be attached on the facts of the case to guidelines and standards published by the relevant professional body, is a large part of the law of professional negligence, a flourishing area of legal practice. For detailed and authoritative analysis, readers are referred to the leading work: *Jackson and Powell on Professional Liability*, 6th edn. (London: Sweet & Maxwell, 2006).

VI. *Res Ipsa Loquitur*

The maxim *res ipsa loquitur* (meaning 'the thing speaks for itself' or, more loosely, 'the accident tells its own story') allows the claimant to succeed in an action for negligence even where there is no evidence as to what caused the accident and, therefore, whether it was attributable to negligence on the part of the defendant. The leading case is *Scott v London and St Katherine Docks Co* (1865) 3 H & C 596 where the principle was stated as follows (at 601, per Erle CJ):

> There must be reasonable evidence of negligence. But where the thing is shown to be under the management of the defendant or his servants, and the accident is such as in the ordinary course of things does not happen if those who have the management use proper care, it affords reasonable evidence, in the absence of explanation by the defendants, that the accident arose from want of care.

The precise nature of the maxim has been the subject of considerable debate.

1. Purpose and Effect

P. S. Atiyah, 'Res Ipsa Loquitur in England and Australia'
(1972) 35 MLR 337

There are two basic views as to the purpose and effects of the maxim.

1. The first is that the maxim is not a distinct rule of law (or evidence) in its own right and that in all cases of negligence the ultimate or legal burden of proof rests upon the plaintiff. According to this view the maxim is no more than a summary way of describing a situation in which it is permissible to infer from the occurrence of an accident that it was probably caused by the negligence of the defendant. However, on this view, the inference of negligence is merely permissible (not obligatory) and if at the conclusion of the case the tribunal of fact is not satisfied that the accident was more probably than not caused by the negligence of the defendant, the plaintiff must fail.

2. The second view is that the maxim involves more than this and that it does represent a distinct rule of law (or evidence) in its own right. According to this view a *legal* burden of proof may be cast on the defendant in certain circumstances and the maxim therefore represents an exception to the general principle that the *legal* burden of proof always rests on the plaintiff throughout a negligence action. On this view, once the maxim operates, the plaintiff is entitled to a verdict even though, at the conclusion of the evidence, the tribunal of fact remains in doubt whether the accident was more probably than not caused by the negligence of the defendant. A plaintiff could not, of course, be entitled to a verdict in such a situation unless the legal burden of disproving negligence is upon the defendant…

[A] strong case can be made for saying that on policy grounds the second view is preferable and that, so far as English law is concerned, the first view is inconsistent with the actual decision in many recent cases.

The policy grounds for preferring the second view can be simply stated. The normal principle that the legal burden of proof rests on the plaintiff is liable to lead to unjust results in many cases in which the plaintiff does not know but the defendant does know the facts relevant to the issue of negligence or not. In particular, where accidents are caused due to sudden vehicle failure on the roads, or to unexplained disasters (such as explosions) in factories, the plaintiff may be in grave difficulties because he will have no information as to the standards of inspection, maintenance, etc which the defendant has adopted. The defendant may be able to adduce evidence on these matters but the plaintiff will frequently be unable to do so.

COMMENTARY

Atiyah admits that there are some strong judicial expressions of opinion favouring the first of the two views he describes. He cites a dictum of Megaw LJ in *Lloyde v West Midlands Gas Board* [1971] 2 All ER 1240 at 1246 as an example:

I doubt whether it is right to describe *res ipsa loquitur* as a 'doctrine'. I think that it is no more than an exotic, though convenient, phrase to describe what is in essence no more than a common-sense approach, not limited by technical rules, to the assessment of the effect of evidence in certain circumstances. It means that a plaintiff prima facie establishes negligence where: (i) it is not possible for him to prove precisely what was the relevant act or omission which set in train the events leading to the accident; but (ii) on the evidence as it stands at the relevant time it is more likely than not that the effective cause of the accident was *some* act or omission of the defendant or of someone for whom the defendant is responsible, which act or omission constitutes a failure to take proper care for the plaintiff's safety.

His Lordship stated that the maxim was most properly applied to a situation where the defendant, at the close of the plaintiff's case, submits that there is no case to answer and that it is not even necessary to adduce evidence to contradict the plaintiff's allegations.

One of the reasons why Atiyah rejects the Megaw approach and prefers the second of the two views he outlines is that only this second view can satisfactorily describe the result in *Henderson v Henry E. Jenkins & Sons* [1970] AC 282. Mr Henderson was killed after the brakes on the defendant's lorry failed. It was subsequently discovered that the pipe carrying the brake fluid was badly corroded and that the brake failure must have been caused by a large hole in the corroded part of the pipe. The instantaneous development of this hole was very uncommon. In evidence it was shown that neither the vehicle manufacturers nor the Ministry of Transport recommended the removal of the pipe for inspection, although only 60 per cent of it was visible in situ and the remaining 40 per cent (in which part of the pipe the hole had occurred) was particularly prone, by reason of its position, to corrosion. Evidence also established that the degree and speed of corrosion was largely determined by the use to which the vehicle was put (e.g. type of loads carried, places visited, unusual occurrences). The defendant firm produced evidence that the lorry had been inspected in accordance with the manufacturer's instructions; however, the House of Lords held that, in order to prove it had exercised all reasonable care, the firm should have produced evidence that the lorry had not been carrying corrosive loads of any kind. Atiyah, *op. cit.*, cites this case for his proposition that English law is committed to the second of the two views he outlines as to the nature of the doctrine of *res ipsa loquitur*. He reasons:

It is difficult to see how anyone approaching the evidence dispassionately could reasonably take the view that the plaintiff had proved that negligence of the defendants was more probable than not. Even on the view most favourable to the plaintiff it could only be said that it had been proved that probably something unusual had happened to the lorry. There was no evidence *at all* what this 'something unusual' was, whether the defendants knew or ought to have known of it, and what precautions should have been adopted to deal with it. The truth was that the issue of negligence or no-negligence was simply not proved either way; there may or may not have been negligence, and the decision for the plaintiff seems necessarily to involve that the legal burden of disproving negligence was held to be on the defendants.

It is curious, however, that a case which Atiyah relies upon to demonstrate the true nature of the doctrine of *res ipsa loquitur* makes no express mention of the doctrine at all.

During the course of his opinion in *Henderson*, Lord Pearson (at 301) made the following comments on the legal and evidential burdens of proof:

My Lords, in my opinion, the decision in this appeal turns on what is sometimes called 'the evidential burden of proof', which is to be distinguished from the formal (or legal or technical) burden of proof...For the purposes of the present case the distinction can be simply stated in this way. In an action for negligence the plaintiff must allege, and has the burden of proving, that the accident was caused by negligence on the part of the defendants. That is the issue throughout the trial, and in giving judgment at the end of the trial the judge has to decide whether he is satisfied on a balance of probabilities that the accident was caused by negligence on the part of the defendants, and if he is not so satisfied the plaintiff's action fails. The formal burden of proof does not shift. But if in the course of the trial there is proved a set of facts which raises a prima facie inference that the accident was caused by negligence on the part of the defendants, the issue will be decided in the plaintiff's favour unless the defendants by their evidence provide some answer which is adequate to displace the prima facie inference. In this situation there is said to be an evidential burden of proof resting on the defendants. I have some doubts whether it is strictly correct to use the expression 'burden of proof' with this meaning, as there is a risk of it being confused with the formal burden of proof, but it is a familiar and convenient usage...

This passage of Lord Pearson's opinion is praised by A. L. Goodhart—'it would be difficult to find elsewhere a clearer statement of the law on this point' (see (1970) 86 LQR 145)—but Atiyah finds Lord Pearson's denial that the formal burden of proof shifts inconsistent with his later remark that, if the plaintiff raises a prima facie case, 'the issue *will* be decided in the plaintiff's favour unless the defendants by their evidence provide some answer which is adequate to displace the prima facie inference' (Atiyah's emphasis). This remark suggests, Atiyah submits, that Lord Pearson did indeed treat the legal burden of proof as reversed.

See, further, *Ng v Lee* (below).

2. Application of the Maxim

Ng Chun Pui v Lee Chuen Tat [1988] RTR 298

The first defendant was driving a coach owned by the second defendant westwards in the outer lane of a dual carriageway in Hong Kong. Suddenly the coach crossed the central reservation and collided with a public light bus travelling in the inner lane of the eastbound carriageway. One passenger in the bus was killed, and the driver and three other passengers were injured. The plaintiffs (those injured and the personal representatives of the deceased) commenced an action against the defendants claiming damages for negligence. At the trial the plaintiffs did not call oral evidence and relied on the doctrine of *res ipsa loquitur*, contending that the fact of the accident alone was sufficient evidence of negligence by the first defendant. The defendants called evidence which established that an untraced car being driven in the inner lane of the westbound carriageway had cut into the outer lane in front of the coach, and to avoid hitting the car the first defendant had braked and swerved to the right whereupon the coach had skidded across colliding with the bus. The judge gave judgment for the plaintiffs on liability holding that the defendants had failed to discharge the burden of disproving negligence. On appeal the Court of Appeal of Hong Kong reversed that decision and found that the plaintiffs had failed to prove negligence. The plaintiffs appealed to the Judicial Committee of the Privy Council.

Lord Griffiths delivered the opinion of the Judicial Committee

The plaintiffs called no oral evidence and relied upon the fact of the accident as evidence of negligence or, as the judge put it, the doctrine of *res ipsa loquitur*. There can be no doubt that the plaintiffs were justified in taking this course. In ordinary circumstances if a well maintained coach is being properly driven it will not cross the central reservation of a dual carriageway and collide with on-coming traffic in the other carriageway. In the absence of any explanation of the behaviour of the coach the proper inference to draw is that it was not being driven with the standard of care required by the law and that the driver was therefore negligent. If the defendants had called no evidence the plaintiffs would undoubtedly have been entitled to judgment.

The defendants however did call evidence and gave an explanation of the circumstances that caused the first defendant to lose control of the coach. This evidence was given both by the driver of the coach, i.e. the first defendant, and a passenger sitting in the front of the coach. Their evidence corresponded closely with the contemporary accounts that both of them had given to the police. The judge accepted their evidence and made the following findings of fact:

> The evidence led by the defendants shows clearly that the coach was proceeding along a straight stretch of the road possibly a little in excess of the speed limit of 40 miles per hour. But the speed of the coach is not alleged to be one of the elements of negligence and I am not particularly concerned with that. The coach was travelling in the fast or outer lane and in that lane there was other traffic about two coach lengths ahead of it. In the inner lane there was a vehicle about 10 to 20 feet ahead and between that vehicle and the coach there was a blue car travelling a little faster than the coach. Suddenly that blue car, which did not subsequently stop and has not been traced, cut into the fast lane some six to eight feet ahead of the coach. That was clearly a very dangerous manoeuvre and the first defendant reacted to it by braking and swerving a little to his right. The coach then skidded across the central reservation, as I have said, colliding with the public light bus.

The judge however was of the view that, despite those findings of fact, because the plaintiffs had originally relied upon the doctrine of *res ipsa loquitur*, the burden of disproving negligence remained upon the defendants and they had failed to discharge it. In their Lordships' opinion this shows a misunderstanding of the so-called doctrine of *res ipsa loquitur*, which is no more than the use of a Latin maxim to describe a state of the evidence from which it is proper to draw an inference of negligence. Although it has been said in a number of cases, it is misleading to talk of the burden of proof shifting to the defendant in a *res ipsa loquitur* situation. The burden of proving negligence rests throughout the case on the plaintiff. Where the plaintiff has suffered injuries as a result of an accident which ought not to have happened if the defendant had taken due care, it will often be possible for the plaintiff to discharge the burden of proof by inviting the court to draw the inference that on the balance of probabilities the defendant must have failed to exercise due care, even though the plaintiff does not know in what particular respects the failure occurred. One of the earliest examples of the operation of this doctrine is *Scott v London and St Katherine Docks Co* (1865) 3 H & C 596...

So in an appropriate case the plaintiff establishes a prima facie case by relying upon the fact of the accident. If the defendant adduces no evidence there is nothing to rebut the inference of negligence and the plaintiff will have proved his case. But if the defendant does adduce evidence that evidence must be evaluated to see if it still reasonable to draw the inference of negligence from the mere fact of the accident. Loosely speaking this may be referred to as a burden on the defendant to show he was not negligent, but that only means that faced with a prima facie case of negligence the defendant will be found negligent unless he produces evidence that is capable of rebutting the prima facie case. Resort to the burden of proof is a poor way to decide a case; it is the duty of the judge to examine all the evidence at the end of the case and decide whether on the facts he finds to have been proved and on the inferences he is prepared to draw he is satisfied that negligence has been established. In so far as resort is had to the burden of proof the burden remains at the end of the case as it was at the beginning upon the plaintiff to prove that his injury was caused by the negligence of the defendants…

Appeal dismissed.

COMMENTARY

His Lordship adopted the dicta of Lord Pearson in *Henderson v Henry E. Jenkins & Sons* and Megaw LJ in *Lloyde v West Midlands Gas Board* quoted above as 'most clearly expressing the true meaning and effect of the so-called doctrine of *res ipsa loquitur*'. An example of the application of the maxim to a road traffic accident, to the plaintiff's benefit, is *Widdowson v Newgate Meat Corporation* [1998] PIQR P138. The plaintiff, who suffered from a serious mental disorder, was injured when struck by a car driven by one of the defendants whilst walking on the edge of the inside lane of a dual carriageway. The plaintiff was not competent to give evidence, and the driver chose not to, although in an earlier statement to police he could offer no explanation for the accident. There was also no evidence of why the plaintiff was on the road at the time or of where he was going. Nonetheless, the Court of Appeal allowed an appeal against the dismissal of the action, holding that there was no absolute rule against invoking the doctrine in road accident cases. Here, there was evidence that the plaintiff had an awareness of road safety, it was a clear night, and the driver would have had a long clear view of the road in front. This was sufficient to establish a prima facie case and, in the absence of evidence from *either* of the parties involved in the accident, the defendants could not rebut that inference. However, the plaintiff's damages were reduced by 50 per cent for contributory negligence, because he was not wearing brightly coloured clothing nor (so it seems) had he moved onto the grass verge as the car approached. Do you agree that the facts were sufficient for the maxim to apply and raise a prima facie case? And, if it was, how could damages be reduced for contributory negligence? Does this case support Atiyah's view of the role of the maxim?

As *Widdowson* demonstrates, the importance of the maxim to the claimant is that it re-establishes a prima facie case. However, this is so only where the *res* (the happening of the event) is itself evidence of negligence. In *Fryer v Pearson, The Times*, 4 April 2000, noted by Witting (2001) 117 LQR 392, the Court of Appeal doubted whether the presence of a sewing needle in the defendant's carpet was more consistent with fault on the defendant's part than the absence of fault. Where the *res* is more complicated, moreover, it is very unlikely that the maxim will apply as further evidence will be required to ascertain whether the facts are consistent with carelessness or not. Clinical negligence litigation provides a good example. In *Ratcliffe v Plymouth & Torbay Health Authority* [1998] PIQR P170, the Court of Appeal made the point that the maxim may apply in the medical negligence context if the *res* is sufficient to give rise to an inference of negligence which is supported by ordinary human experience and does not require expert evidence (e.g. surgeon cuts off right foot instead of left, swab is left in operation site, or patient wakes up during surgical operation despite general anaesthetic). Such cases will be rare, and more frequently the claimant's case will rely on, or at least be buttressed by, expert evidence adduced on his behalf. Thus, even if the defendant were to call no evidence, the judge would be deciding the case on inferences he was entitled to draw from the *whole* of the evidence (including expert evidence), and not on the application of the maxim in its purest form.

The Future for *Res Ipsa Loquitur*

Because of the uncertainties surrounding its application and effect, there have been calls for the courts to avoid recourse to the maxim (see, e.g., Witting (2001) 117 LQR 392). Such calls have been heeded in Canada (*Fontaine v Loewen Estate* [1998] 1 SCR 424), but, in *Schellenberg v Tunnel Holdings* (2000) 200 CLR 121, the High Court of Australia declined to do away with the doctrine, Gleeson CJ and McHugh J holding that it represented a mode of inferential reasoning, not a rule of law, and viewed in this way was fully consonant with the general body of tort law (at 141). This also appears to be the view taken by the Court of Appeal in *Fryer v Pearson*, although May LJ thought that lawyers should stop using unhelpful Latin phrases to describe straightforward principles of law (at [19]; see also McInnes (2000) 8 Tort L Rev 162 at 164, commenting on *Schellenberg*, who notes that the maxim is 'endowed with the seemingly mystical qualities that frequently attend upon Latin appellations'). No matter how this practice is described, however, it seems clear that the court may still infer negligence from the occurrence of the accident itself. If it does so, it is very probable that the defendant will be found liable unless he produces evidence to rebut the inference raised by the *res*. In such circumstances, the practical difference between a reversal in the legal burden of proof, which Atiyah in 1972 contended was *res ipsa loquitur*'s effect, and a reversal of the evidential burden is more apparent than real.

5 CAUSATION AND REMOTENESS

It is axiomatic that before liability can attach to a defendant a causal link must be established between the negligence and the injury for which the claimant claims compensation. As in other areas of the law, however, deciding whether this requirement of a cause of action has been satisfied may present considerable difficulties. Stapleton, 'Cause in fact and the scope of liability for consequences' (2003) 119 LQR 388 has argued that the 'causation' inquiry consists of two separate strands. The first and most obvious hurdle that must be overcome is to show an historical connection between the defendant's negligence and the injury (factual causation). This is normally decided by the application of the but-for test: but for the defendant's negligence, would the claimant have suffered the injury that he or she did? Difficulties arise when this question cannot be answered because there is insufficient evidence, or where the answer produces a result which seems contrary to common sense. In these cases courts have, on policy grounds, relaxed in the claimant's favour the ordinary rules for determining the existence of an historical connection between the negligence and the damage for which the claimant is claiming. If factual causation is satisfied, the claimant must then show that the defendant should be legally responsible for the damage the claimant has suffered. This question of legal causation (or in Stapleton's words, the question of whether the damage falls within the scope of liability for consequences) may involve consideration of the effect of intervening acts, whether of the claimant or of a third party, occurring between the defendant s negligence and the claimant's injury. It may also entail a decision as to the appropriate limit to place on the defendant's liability as a matter of policy. The damage may have been factually caused by the defendant but it may be decided that the defendant should not have to pay for the full extent of the damage because it is considered too remote. Whilst we retain the traditional terminology of legal causation and remoteness in this chapter, it is important to remember, as Stapleton points out, that this second stage is a normative inquiry, and that drawing the line between recoverable and irrecoverable damage inevitably requires, and reflects, a value judgement as to the proper limits of liability. These issues will be considered in this chapter.

I. Factual Causation

1. The But-For Test

The first test the claimant must overcome in establishing causation is the but-for test. If the claimant's injury would have occurred irrespective of the defendant's negligence, the negligence is not causative of the claimant's loss. However, satisfying the but-for test may of itself be insufficient to establish causation for there may be a number of factual causes (mere 'conditions') satisfying that test. For example, if one negligently throws a lighted match on to a newspaper, there are at least two causes of the resultant fire—the presence of oxygen in the atmosphere and the negligent act of throwing down the match. As a matter of law, however, the oxygen is disregarded as a cause: 'it is part of the normal environment and therefore is disregarded when identifying the cause of some abnormal event' (*Reeves v Commissioner of Police for the Metropolis* [2000] 1 AC 360 at 391, per Lord Hobhouse). As Lord Asquith noted in *Stapley v Gypsum Mines* [1953] AC 663 at 688, a 'broad common-sense view' is taken in deciding whether one of two or more conditions is the 'real' or 'legal' cause.

But-for causation is established on the balance of probabilities: if it is more likely than not that an event was the cause, it is treated as if it were the cause. The application of the balance of probability standard of proof to the but-for test is considered in the extracts below.

Barnett v Chelsea and Kensington Hospital Management Committee [1969] 1 QB 428

The plaintiff was the wife of one of three nightwatchmen who had gone to the defendant's hospital after drinking some tea and becoming ill. The plaintiff's husband looked particularly ill, but the casualty officer, who was also unwell, told them to go home and consult their own doctors. The men went away but several hours later the plaintiff's husband died from what was held to be arsenical poisoning. In an action against the defendant hospital the judge found that there was evidence of negligence, but that this negligence did not cause the injury to the plaintiff's husband.

Neild J

It remains to consider whether it is shown that the deceased's death was caused by this negligence or whether, as the defendants have said, the deceased must have died in any event. In his concluding submission counsel for the plaintiff submitted that Dr Banerjee should have examined the deceased and, had he done so, he would have caused tests to be made which would have indicated the treatment required and that, since the defendants were at fault in these respects, therefore the onus of proof passed to the defendants to show that the appropriate treatment would have failed, and authorities were cited to me. I find myself unable to accept this argument and I am of the view that the onus of proof remains on the plaintiff, and I have in mind (without quoting it) the decision quoted by counsel for the defendants in *Bonnington Castings Ltd v Wardlaw* [1956] AC 613. However, were it otherwise and the onus did pass to the defendants, then I would find that they have discharged it, as I would proceed to show.

There has been put before me a timetable which, I think, is of much importance. The deceased attended at the casualty department at 8.5 or 8.10 am. If Dr Banerjee had got up and dressed and come to see the three men and examined them and decided to admit them, the deceased (and Dr Lockett agreed with this) could not have been in bed in a ward before 11 am. I accept Dr Goulding's evidence that an intravenous drip would not have been set up before 12 noon, and if potassium loss was suspected it could not have been discovered until 12.30. Dr Lockett, dealing with this, said 'If [the deceased] had not been treated until after 12 noon the chances of survival were not good'.

Without going in detail into the considerable volume of technical evidence which has been put before me, it seems to me to be the case that when death results from arsenical posioning it is brought about by two conditions; on the one hand dehydration and on the other disturbance of the enzyme processes. If the principal condition is one of enzyme disturbance—as I am of the view that it was here—then the only method of treatment which is likely to succeed is the use of the specific antidote which is commonly called BAL. Dr Gouding said this in the course of his evidence:

> The only way to deal with this is to use the specific BAL I see no reasonable prospect of the deceased being given BAL before the time at which he died,

and at a later point in his evidence:

> I feel that even if fluid loss had been discovered death would have been caused by the enzyme disturbance. Death might have occurred later.

I regard that evidence as very moderate, and that it might be a true assessment of the situation to say that there was no chance of BAL being administered before the death of the deceased. For these reasons, I find that the plaintiff has failed to establish, on the grounds of probability, that the defendants' negligence caused the death of the deceased.

Judgment for the defendants.

2. Challenges to the Orthodox But-For Approach

(a) Loss of a Chance

Hotson v East Berkshire Area Health Authority [1987] AC 750

The plaintiff, aged 13, injured his hip in a fall from a tree and was taken to a hospital run by the defendant health authority. His injury was not diagnosed, and after suffering severe pain for five days he was taken back to the hospital. His injuries were then recognised and he was given emergency treatment, but his injury later developed into a medical condition (avascular necrosis) which resulted in a deformity to his hip and left him with limited mobility by the time he was 20. In his action against the health authority negligence was admitted but the authority argued that the delay had not affected the plaintiff's ultimate condition. The trial judge found that there was a 25 per cent chance that with proper medical treatment the plaintiff would have avoided avascular necrosis, and awarded him 25 per cent of the damages he would have received if he could have shown the avascular necrosis was caused by the defendant's negligence. The judgment for the plaintiff was upheld by the Court of Appeal, and the defendant appealed to the House of Lords.

Lord Bridge of Harwich

...The plaintiff's claim was for damages for physical injury and consequential loss alleged to have been caused by the authority's breach of their duty of care. In some cases, perhaps particularly medical negligence cases, causation may be so shrouded in mystery that the court can only measure statistical chances. But that was not so here. On the evidence there was a clear conflict as to what had caused the avascular necrosis. The authority's evidence was that the sole cause was the original traumatic injury to the hip. The plaintiff's evidence, at its highest, was that the delay in treatment was a material contributory cause. This was a conflict, like any other about some relevant past event, which the judge could not avoid resolving on a balance of probabilities. Unless the plaintiff proved on a balance of probabilities that the delayed treatment was at least a material contributory cause of the avascular necrosis he failed on the issue of causation and no question of quantification could arise. But the judge's findings of fact . . . are unmistakably to the effect that on a balance of probabilities the injury caused by the plaintiff's fall left insufficient blood vessels intact to keep the epiphysis alive. This amounts to a finding of fact that the fall was the sole cause of the avascular necrosis.

The upshot is that the appeal must be allowed on the narrow ground that the plaintiff failed to establish a cause of action in respect of the avascular necrosis and its consequences. Your Lordships were invited to approach the appeal more broadly and to decide whether, in a claim for damages for personal injury, it can ever be appropriate, where the cause of the injury is unascertainable and all the plaintiff can show is a statistical chance which is less than even that, but for the defendant's breach of duty, he would not have suffered the injury, to award him a proportionate fraction of the full damages appropriate to compensate for the injury as the measure of damages for the lost chance. There is a superficially attractive analogy between the principle applied in such cases as *Chaplin v Hicks* [1911] 2 KB 786 (award of damages for breach of contract assessed by reference to the lost chance of securing valuable employment if the contract had been performed) and *Kitchen v Royal Air Force Association* [1958] 1 WLR 563 (damages for solicitors' negligence assessed by reference to the lost chance of prosecuting a successful civil action) and the principle of awarding damages for the lost chance of avoiding personal injury or, in medical negligence cases, for the lost chance of a better medical result which might have been achieved by prompt diagnosis and correct treatment. I think there are formidable difficulties in the way of accepting the analogy. But I do not see this appeal as a suitable occasion for reaching a settled conclusion as to whether the analogy can ever be applied.

As I have said, there was in this case an inescapable issue of causation first to be resolved. But if the plaintiff had proved on a balance of probabilities that the authority's negligent failure to diagnose and treat his injury promptly had materially contributed to the development of avascular necrosis, I know of no principle of English law which would have entitled the authority to a discount from the full measure of damage to reflect the chance that, even given prompt treatment, avascular necrosis might well still have developed. The decisions of this House in *Bonnington Castings Ltd v Wardlaw* [1956] AC 613 and *McGhee v National Coal Board* [1973] 1 WLR 1 give no support to such a view. . . .

Lord Mackay of Clashfern

[W]hat was the plaintiff's condition on being first presented at the hospital? Did he have intact sufficient blood vessels to keep the affected epiphysis alive? The judge had evidence from the authority's expert which amounted to an assertion that the probability was 100% that the fall had not left intact sufficient vessels to keep the epiphysis alive while he had evidence from Mr Bucknill, for the plaintiff, which although not entirely consistent suggested that the probability was perhaps between 40% and 60%, say 50%, that sufficient vessels were left intact to keep the epiphysis alive. The concluding sentence in the judge's fourth finding of fact makes it plain, in my opinion, that he took the view, weighing that testimony along with all the other matters before him, that it was more probable than not that insufficient vessels had been left intact by the fall to maintain an adequate blood supply to the epiphysis and he expressed this balance by saying that it was 75% to 25%, a result reached perhaps as counsel for the plaintiff suggested by going for a figure midway between the competing estimates given by the parties' experts in evidence. Although various statistics were given in evidence, I do not read any of them as dealing with the particular probability which the judge assessed at 75% to 25%. In the circumstances of this case the probable effect of delay in treatment was determined by the state of facts existing when the plaintiff was first presented to the hospital. It is not, in my opinion, correct to say that on arrival at the hospital he had a 25% chance of recovery. If insufficient blood vessels were left intact by the fall he had no prospect of avoiding complete avascular necrosis whereas if sufficient blood vessels were left intact on the judge's findings no further damage to the blood supply would have resulted if he had been given immediate treatment, and he would not have suffered the avascular necrosis.

As I have said, the fundamental question of fact to be answered in this case related to a point in time before the negligent failure to treat began. It must, therefore, be a matter of past fact. It did not raise any question of what might have been the situation in a hypothetical state of facts. To this problem the words of Lord Diplock in *Mallett v McMonagle* [1970] AC 166 at 176 apply:

> In determining what did happen in the past a court decides on the balance of probabilities. Anything that is more probable than not it treats as certain. . . .

On the other hand, I consider that it would be unwise in the present case to lay it down as a rule that a plaintiff could never succeed by proving loss of a chance in a medical negligence case . . .

Lord Ackner

To my mind, the first issue which the judge had to determine was an issue of causation: did the breach of duty cause the damage alleged? If it did not, as the judge so held, then no question of quantifying damage arises. The debate on the loss of a chance cannot arise where there has been a positive finding that before the duty arose the damage complained of had already been sustained or had become inevitable. . . .

In a sentence, the plaintiff was not entitled to any damages in respect of the deformed hip because the judge had decided that this was not caused by the admitted breach by the authority of their duty of care but was caused by the separation of the left femoral epiphysis when he fell some 12 feet from a rope on which he had been swinging.

On this simple basis I would allow this appeal. I have sought to stress that this case was a relatively simple case concerned with the proof of causation, on which the plaintiff failed, because he was unable to prove, on the balance of probabilities, that his deformed hip was caused by the authority's breach of duty in delaying over a period of five days a proper diagnosis and treatment. Where causation is in issue, the judge decides that issue on the balance of the probabilities. Unless there is some special situation, e.g. joint defendants where the apportionment of liability between them is required, there is no point or purpose in expressing in percentage terms the certainty or near certainty which the plaintiff has achieved in establishing his cause of action.

Once liability is established, on the balance of probabilities, the loss which the plaintiff has sustained is payable in full. It is not discounted by reducing his claim by the extent to which he has failed to prove his case with 100% certainty. The decision by Simon Brown J in the subsequent case of *Bagley v North Herts Health Authority* (1986) 136 NLJ 1014, in which he discounted an award for a stillbirth because there was a 5% risk that the plaintiff would have had a stillborn child even if the hospital had not been negligent, was clearly wrong. In that case, the plaintiff had established on a balance of probabilities, indeed with near certainty, that the hospital's negligence had caused the stillbirth. Causation was thus fully established. Such a finding does not permit any discounting: to do so would be to propound a wholly new doctrine which has no support in principle or authority and would give rise to many complications in the search for mathematical or statistical exactitude.

Of course, where the cause of action has been established, the assessment of that part of the plaintiff's loss where the future is uncertain, involves the evaluation of that uncertainty. In *Bagley*, if the child had, by reason of the hospital's breach of duty, been born with brain injury, which could lead in later life to epilepsy, then it would have been a classic case for the evaluation, *inter alia*, of the chance of epilepsy occurring and discounting, to the extent that the chance of that happening fell below 100%, what would have been the sum of damages appropriate if epilepsy was a certain consequence....

Lord Goff and **Lord Brandon** agreed with Lord Bridge, Lord Mackay and Lord Ackner.

Appeal allowed.

Gregg v Scott [2005] 2 AC 176

The defendant misdiagnosed a lump under the claimant's left arm as harmless; it was in fact cancerous, and the misdiagnosis lead to delay in treatment of nine months, during which time the disease had spread. The claimant sued in respect of his consequent loss of expectation of life. The trial judge ruled that the misdiagnosis was negligent, and went on to consider what would have happened if the claimant had been diagnosed with due care. For present purposes, it is enough to note the judge's finding that the claimant's prospects of recovery (taken to mean disease-free survival for 10 years from the date of the negligence) would have been 45 per cent, i.e. less than even, even if a proper diagnosis had been made, and that the delay had reduced the likelihood of the claimant's survival for that period to 25 per cent as at the date of trial. The claim failed at first instance and, by a majority, before the Court of Appeal. Two arguments were presented to the House of Lords on appeal (as they had been to the Court of Appeal). The first was that, as the delay had caused the tumour to grow, this meant that the claimant had suffered a physical injury, and the lost chance of recovery could therefore be compensated as a loss consequential upon physical injury. The second was that the lost chance of recovery was itself a compensatable head of damage. The first argument appealed only to Lord Hope (see commentary, below) and the extracts deal primarily with the second issue.

Lord Nicholls (dissenting)

[1] This appeal raises a question which has divided courts and commentators throughout the common law world. The division derives essentially from different perceptions of what constitutes injustice in a common form type of medical negligence case. Some believe a remedy is essential and that a principled ground for providing an appropriate remedy can be found. Others are not persuaded. I am in the former camp.

[2] This is the type of case under consideration. A patient is suffering from cancer. His prospects are uncertain. He has a 45% chance of recovery. Unfortunately his doctor negligently misdiagnoses his condition as benign. So the necessary treatment is delayed for months. As a result the patient's prospects of recovery become nil or almost nil. Has the patient a claim for damages against the doctor? No, the House was told. The patient could recover damages if his initial prospects of recovery had been more than 50%. But because they were less than 50% he can recover nothing.

[3] This surely cannot be the state of the law today. It would be irrational and indefensible. The loss of a 45% prospect of recovery is just as much a real loss for a patient as the loss of a 55% prospect of recovery. In both cases the doctor was in breach of his duty to his patient. In both cases the patient was worse off. He lost something of importance and value. But, it is said, in one case the patient has a remedy, in the other he does not.

[4] This would make no sort of sense. It would mean that in the 45% case the doctor's duty would be hollow. The duty would be empty of content. For the reasons which follow I reject this suggested distinction. The common law does not compel courts to proceed in such an unreal fashion. I would hold that a patient has a right to a remedy as much where his prospects

of recovery were less than 50–50 as where they exceeded 50–50. Perforce the reasoning is lengthy, in parts intricate, because this is a difficult area of the law . . .

Medical Negligence

[20] Against this background I turn to the primary question raised by this appeal: how should the loss suffered by a patient in Mr Gregg's position be identified? The Defendant says "loss" is confined to an outcome which is shown, on balance of probability, to be worse than it otherwise would have been. Mr Gregg must prove that, on balance of probability, his medical condition after the negligence was worse than it would have been in the absence of the negligence. Mr Gregg says his "loss" includes proved diminution in the prospects of a favourable outcome. Dr Scott's negligence deprived him of a worthwhile chance that his medical condition would not have deteriorated as it did . . .

[24] Given this uncertainty of outcome, the appropriate characterisation of a patient's loss in this type of case must surely be that it comprises the loss of the chance of a favourable outcome, rather than the loss of the outcome itself. Justice so requires, because this matches medical reality. This recognises what in practice a patient had before the doctor's negligence occurred. It recognises what in practice the patient lost by reason of that negligence. The doctor's negligence diminished the patient's prospects of recovery. And this analysis of a patient's loss accords with the purpose of the legal duty of which the doctor was in breach. In short, the purpose of the duty is to promote the patient's prospects of recovery by exercising due skill and care in diagnosing and treating the patient's condition.

[25] This approach also achieves a basic objective of the law of tort. The common law imposes duties and seeks to provide appropriate remedies in the event of a breach of duty. If negligent diagnosis or treatment diminishes a patient's prospects of recovery, a law which does not recognise this as a wrong calling for redress would be seriously deficient today. In respect of the doctors' breach of duty the law would not have provided an appropriate remedy. Of course, losing a chance of saving a leg is not the same as losing a leg: see Tony Weir, *Tort Law* (2002), p 76. But that is not a reason for declining to value the chance for whose loss the doctor was directly responsible. The law would rightly be open to reproach were it to provide a remedy if what is lost by a professional advisor's negligence is a financial opportunity or chance but refuse a remedy where what is lost by a doctor's negligence is the chance of health or even life itself. Justice requires that in the latter case as much as the former the loss of a chance should constitute actionable damage . . .

Identifying a Lost Chance in Medical Negligence Cases

[34] I come next to a further twist in the story. It concerns an additional complication. It is a difficult part of this appeal. With "loss of chance" cases such as *Chaplin v Hicks* [1911] 2 KB 786, identifying the "chance" the claimant lost is straightforward enough. The position of the claimant in the Chaplin case, had there been no wrong, could not be decided satisfactorily because no one could know what would have been the outcome of the beauty contest if the claimant had appeared at the interview. It was this uncertainty which made it appropriate to treat her loss of a chance as itself actionable damage. Otherwise she would have had no remedy. The chance she lost was the opportunity to attend and be considered at the interview. Thus, in this type of case the claimant's actual position at the time of the negligence, proved on balance of probability if disputed, is not determinative of the crucial hypothetical fact: what would have been the claimant's position in the absence of the wrong?

[35] The position with medical negligence claims is different. The patient's actual condition at the time of the negligence will often be determinative of the answer to the crucially important hypothetical question of what would have been the claimant's position in the absence of the negligence. *Hotson v East Berkshire Heath Authority* [1987] AC 750 is an instance of this.

The relevant factual question concerning Stephen Hotson's condition immediately prior to the negligence was whether his fall from the tree had left sufficient blood vessels intact to keep his left femoral epiphysis alive. The answer to this question of actual fact ipso facto provided the answer to the vital hypothetical question: would avascular necrosis have been avoided if Stephen Hotson's leg had been treated promptly? The answer to the first question necessarily provided the answer to the second question, because the second question is no more than a mirror image of the first. Built into the formulation of the first question was the answer to the second question.

[36] This is not always so. Many cases are not so straightforward. Sometimes it is not possible to frame factual questions about a patient's condition which are (a) susceptible of sure answer and also (b) determinative of the outcome for the patient. As already noted, limitations on scientific and medical knowledge do not always permit this to be done. There are too many uncertainties involved in this field.

[37] The present case is a good example. Identifying the nature and extent of Mr Gregg's cancer at the time of the mistaken diagnosis (the first question), so far as this could be achieved with reasonable certainty, did not provide a simple answer to what would have been the outcome had he been treated promptly (the second question). There were several possible outcomes. Recourse to past experience in other cases, that is statistics, personalised so far as possible, was the best that could be done. These statistics expressed the various possible outcomes in percentage terms of likelihood.

[38] Thus, for present purposes medical negligence cases fall into one or other of two categories depending on whether a patient's condition at the time of the negligence does or does not give rise to significant medical uncertainty on what the outcome would have been in the absence of negligence. The Hotson case was in one category. There was no significant uncertainty about what would have happened to Stephen Hotson's leg if treated promptly, once his condition at the time of the negligence has been determined on the usual probability basis. The present case is in the other category. Identifying Mr Gregg's condition when he first visited Dr Scott did not provide an answer to the crucial question of what would have happened if there had been no negligence. There was considerable medical uncertainty about what the outcome would have been had Mr Gregg received appropriate treatment nine months earlier . . .

[44] The way ahead must surely be to recognise that where a patient is suffering from illness or injury and his prospects of recovery are attended with a significant degree of medical uncertainty, and he suffers a significant diminution of his prospects of recovery by reason of medical negligence whether of diagnosis or treatment, that diminution constitutes actionable damage. This is so whether the patient's prospects immediately before the negligence exceeded or fell short of 50%. "Medical uncertainty" is uncertainty inherent in the patient's condition, uncertainty which medical opinion cannot resolve. This is to be contrasted with uncertainties arising solely from differences of view expressed by witnesses. Evidential uncertainties of this character should be resolved in the usual way . . .

Contrary Arguments

[After considering, and rejecting, arguments based on 'floodgates', uncertainty, additional costs to the National Health Service, the desirability of parliamentary rather than judicial reform, and the risk that medical practitioners would adopt defensive practices, his Lordship continued:]

[57] An alternative submission advanced on behalf of Mr Gregg should be noted briefly. In the present case the trial judge found that, treated promptly, the initial spread of the cancer and the enlargement of the tumour would probably not have occurred. This, it was said, was physical injury established on balance of probability. This constituted actionable damage. The

consequences flowing from this damage should be assessed in terms of diminution of prospects: what were the chances that without this spread of the cancer the subsequent adverse results would not have occurred?

[58] This submission is superficially attractive. It would enable compensation to be awarded in the present case while retaining the need to prove physical damage on the balance of probability. But this solution would not get to the heart of the problem. It does not provide an answer to the fundamental issue raised at the outset of this speech . . .

Lord Hoffmann

Loss of a Chance

[72] The alternative submission was that reduction in the prospect of a favourable outcome ("loss of a chance") should be a recoverable head of damage. There are certainly cases in which it is. *Chaplin v Hicks* [1911] 2 KB 786 is a well known example. The question is whether the principle of that case can apply to a case of clinical negligence such as this.

[73] The answer can be derived from three cases in the House of Lords: *Hotson v East Berkshire Area Health Authority* [1987] AC 750, *Wilsher v Essex Area Health Authority* [1988] AC 1074 and *Fairchild v Glenhaven Funeral Services Ltd* [2003] 1 AC 32 . . .

[79] What these cases show is that, as Helen Reece points out in an illuminating article ("Losses of Chances in the Law" (1996) 59 MLR 188) the law regards the world as in principle bound by laws of causality. Everything has a determinate cause, even if we do not know what it is. The blood-starved hip joint in *Hotson*, the blindness in *Wilsher*, the mesothelioma in *Fairchild*; each had its cause and it was for the plaintiff to prove that it was an act or omission for which the defendant was responsible. The narrow terms of the exception made to this principle in *Fairchild* only serves to emphasise the strength of the rule. The fact that proof is rendered difficult or impossible because no examination was made at the time, as in *Hotson*, or because medical science cannot provide the answer, as in *Wilsher*, makes no difference. There is no inherent uncertainty about what caused something to happen in the past or about whether something which happened in the past will cause something to happen in the future. Everything is determined by causality. What we lack is knowledge and the law deals with lack of knowledge by the concept of the burden of proof.

[80] Similarly in the present case, the progress of Mr Gregg's disease had a determinate cause. It may have been inherent in his genetic make-up at the time when he saw Mr Scott, as Hotson's fate was determined by what happened to his thigh when he fell out of the tree. Or it may, as Mance LJ suggests, have been affected by subsequent events and behaviour for which Dr Scott was not responsible. Medical science does not enable us to say. But the outcome was not random; it was governed by laws of causality and, in the absence of a special rule as in *Fairchild*, inability to establish that delay in diagnosis caused the reduction in expectation in life cannot be remedied by treating the outcome as having been somehow indeterminate . . .

[84] . . . In the present case it is urged that Mr Gregg has suffered a wrong and ought to have a remedy. Living for more than 10 years is something of great value to him and he should be compensated for the possibility that the delay in diagnosis may have reduced his chances of doing so. In effect, the Appellant submits that the exceptional rule in *Fairchild* should be generalised and damages awarded in all cases in which the defendant may have caused an injury and has increased the likelihood of the injury being suffered. In the present case, it is alleged that Dr Scott may have caused a reduction in Mr Gregg's expectation of life and that he increased the likelihood that his life would be shortened by the disease.

[85] It should first be noted that adopting such a rule would involve abandoning a good deal of authority. The rule which the House is asked to adopt is the very rule which it rejected in *Wilsher's* case [1988] AC 1074. Yet *Wilsher's* case was expressly approved by the House in

Fairchild [2003] 1 AC 32. *Hotson* [1987] AC 750 too would have to be overruled. Furthermore, the House would be dismantling all the qualifications and restrictions with which it so recently hedged the *Fairchild* exception. There seem to me to be no new arguments or change of circumstances which could justify such a radical departure from precedent.

Control Mechanisms

[86] The Appellant suggests that the expansion of liability could be held in reasonable bounds by confining it to cases in which the claimant had suffered an injury. In this case, the spread of the cancer before the eventual diagnosis was something which would not have happened if it had been promptly diagnosed and amounted to an injury caused by the Defendant. It is true that this is not the injury for which the Claimant is suing. His claim is for loss of the prospect of survival for more than 10 years. And the judge's finding was that he had not established that the spread of the cancer was causally connected with the reduction in his expectation of life. But the Appellant submits that his injury can be used as what Professor Jane Stapleton called a "hook" on which to hang a claim for damage which it did not actually cause: see (2003) 119 LQR 388, 423.

[87] An artificial limitation of this kind seems to me to be lacking in principle. It resembles the "control mechanisms" which disfigure the law of liability for psychiatric injury. And once one treats an "injury" as a condition for imposing liability for some other kind of damage, one is involved in definitional problems about what counts as an injury. Presumably the internal bleeding suffered by the boy Hotson was an injury which would have qualified him to sue for the loss of a chance of saving his hip joint. What about baby Wilsher? The doctor's negligence resulted in his having excessively oxygenated blood, which is potentially toxic: see [1987] QB 730, 764–766. Was this an injury? The boundaries of the concept would be a fertile source of litigation.

[88] Similar comments may be made about another proposed control mechanism, which is to confine the principle to cases in which inability to prove causation is a result of lack of medical knowledge of the causal mechanism (as in *Wilsher*) rather than lack of knowledge of the facts (as in *Hotson's* case). Again, the distinction is not based upon principle or even expediency. Proof of causation was just as difficult for *Hotson* as it was for *Wilsher*. It could be said that the need to prove causation was more unfair on *Hotson*, since the reason why he could not prove whether he had enough blood vessels after the fall was because the hospital had negligently failed to examine him . . .

[I]n my opinion, the various control mechanisms proposed to confine liability for loss of a chance within artificial limits do not pass this test. But a wholesale adoption of possible rather than probable causation as the criterion of liability would be so radical a change in our law as to amount to a legislative act. It would have enormous consequences for insurance companies and the National Health Service. In company with my noble and learned friends Lord Phillips of Worth Matravers and Baroness Hale of Richmond, I think that any such change should be left to Parliament.

Baroness Hale

The Loss of a Chance Argument

[209] The second, and more radical, way of redefining the Claimant's damage is in terms of the loss of a chance. Put this way, his claim is not for the loss of an outcome, in this case the cure of his disease, which he would have enjoyed but for the negligence. His claim is for the reduced chance of achieving that outcome . . .

[210] In that case [*Hotson*], the claimant had actually suffered the adverse outcome, avascular necrosis. The risk of suffering that outcome as a result of falling from the tree was 75%. The

defendant's negligent failure to detect the injury to his hip took away the remaining 25% chance of avoiding it. Clearly he could not prove that the negligence had caused the outcome. It was more likely than not that it had made no difference. But might he have proved that it was more likely than not that the negligence had reduced his chance of avoiding that outcome?

[211] The House of Lords treated this as a case in which the die was already cast by the time the Claimant got to the hospital (or at least the Claimant could not prove otherwise). The Defendant had not even caused the loss of the chance of saving the situation, because by the time the Claimant got to them there was no chance. The coin had already been tossed, and had come down heads or tails. But there must be many cases in which that is not so. The coin is in the air. The Claimant does have a chance of a favourable outcome which chance is wiped out or significantly reduced by the negligence. The coin is whipped out of the air before it has been able to land.

[212] This is, therefore, a new case, not covered precisely by previous authority. The Appellant himself describes his argument as the "policy approach". He recognises that it is a question of legal policy whether the law should be developed as he argues it should be. The wide version of the argument would allow recovery for any reduction in the chance of a better physical outcome, or any increase in the chance of an adverse physical outcome, even if this cannot be linked to any physiological changes caused by the Defendant. A Defendant who has negligently increased the risk that the Claimant will suffer harm in future (for example from exposure to asbestos or cigarette smoke) would be liable even though no harm had yet been suffered. This would be difficult to reconcile with our once and for all approach to establishing liability and assessing damage. Unless damages were limited to a modest sum for anxiety and distress about the future, sensible quantification would have to "wait and see". The narrower version of the argument would require that there be some physiological change caused by the Defendant's negligence, bringing with it a reduced prospect of a favourable outcome . . .

[223] Until now, the gist of the action for personal injuries has been damage to the person. My negligence probably caused the loss of your leg: I pay you the full value of the loss of the leg (say £ 100,000). My negligence probably did not cause the loss of your leg: I do not pay you anything. Compare the loss of a chance approach: my negligence probably caused a reduction in the chance of your keeping that leg: I pay you the value of the loss of your leg, discounted by the chance that it would have happened anyway. If the chance of saving the leg was very good, say 90%, the claimant still gets only 90% of his damages, say £ 90,000. But if the chance of saving the leg was comparatively poor, say 20%, the claimant still gets £ 20,000. So the claimant ends up with less than full compensation even though his chances of a more favourable outcome were good. And the defendant ends up paying substantial sums even though the outcome is one for which by definition he cannot be shown to be responsible.

[224] Almost any claim for loss of an outcome could be reformulated as a claim for loss of a chance of that outcome. The implications of retaining them both as alternatives would be substantial. That is, the claimant still has the prospect of 100% recovery if he can show that it is more likely than not that the doctor's negligence caused the adverse outcome. But if he cannot show that, he also has the prospect of lesser recovery for loss of a chance. If (for the reasons given earlier) it would in practice always be tempting to conclude that the doctor's negligence had affected his chances to some extent, the claimant would almost always get something. It would be a "heads you lose everything, tails I win something" situation. But why should the Defendant not also be able to redefine the gist of the action if it suits him better?

[225] The Appellant in this case accepts that the proportionate recovery effect must cut both ways. If the claim is characterised as loss of a chance, those with a better than evens chance would still only get a proportion of the full value of their claim. But I do not think that he accepts that the same would apply in cases where the claim is characterised as loss of an outcome. In that case there is no basis for calculating the odds. If the two are alternatives available

in every case, the defendant will almost always be liable for something. He will have lost the benefit of the 50% chance that causation cannot be proved. But if the two approaches cannot sensibly live together, the claimants who currently obtain full recovery on an adverse outcome basis might in future only achieve a proportionate recovery. This would surely be a case of two steps forward, three steps back for the great majority of straightforward personal injury cases. In either event, the expert evidence would have to be far more complex than it is at present. Negotiations and trials would be a great deal more difficult. Recovery would be much less predictable both for claimants and for defendants' liability insurers. There is no reason in principle why the change in approach should be limited to medical negligence. Whether or not the policy choice is between retaining the present definition of personal injury in outcome terms and redefining it in loss of opportunity terms, introducing the latter would cause far more problems in the general run of personal injury claims than the policy benefits are worth.

[226] Much of the discussion in the cases and literature has centred round cases where the adverse outcome has already happened. The patient has lost his leg. Did the doctor's negligence cause him to lose the leg? If not, did it reduce the chances of saving the leg? But in this case the most serious of the adverse outcomes has not yet happened, and (it is to be hoped) may never happen. The approach to causation should be the same for both past and future events. What, if anything, has the doctor's negligence caused in this case? We certainly do not know whether it has caused this outcome, because happily Mr Gregg has survived each of the significant milestones along the way. Can we even say that it reduced the chances of a successful outcome, given that Mr Gregg has turned out to be one of the successful minority at each milestone? This is quite different from the situation in *Hotson*, where the avascular necrosis had already happened . . . Mr Gregg faced a risk of an adverse outcome which happily has not so far materialised, serious though the effects of his illness, treatment and prognosis have been. The complexities of attempting to introduce liability for the loss of a chance of a more favourable outcome in personal injury claims have driven me, not without regret, to conclude that it should not be done . . .

Lord Phillips gave a separate concurring opinion. **Lord Hope** concurred with Lord Nicholls' dissenting opinion, but added further grounds for dissenting from the majority.

Appeal dismissed.

COMMENTARY

The attraction of the but-for test is its simplicity: if the injury would in fact have occurred even without the defendant's negligence that negligence can be ruled out as a factual cause of the injury. However, this assumes that a definitive answer can be given to the question. If the answer comes out as 'we don't know', or 'we don't know for certain', the test can create problems. In deciding whether a past injury was caused by the defendant's negligence, the standard of proof used is the balance of probability. If it is more likely than not that the negligence caused the injury, it is deemed that it did cause the injury. The probability is converted into a certainty. The extracts from *Barnett* and *Hotson* illustrate this proposition, as the plaintiffs failed because they could not show on the balance of probability that the injury for which they were claiming was caused by the defendant's negligence.

One way of avoiding this difficulty is to re-define the damage that the claimant suffers. What if the plaintiff's claim in *Hotson* could be viewed not as for the injury itself (the necrosis) but the loss of the chance of avoiding the injury that was caused by the negligent original diagnosis? The House of Lords in *Hotson* did not view the case in this way, a refusal which avoided their Lordships having to deal with the question. (For criticism of this approach see Stapleton, 'The Gist of Negligence, Part 2: the relationship between "damage" and causation' (1988) 104 LQR 389.) However, in *Gregg v Scott,* the House of Lords had to meet this argument head-on, as the claimant put his claim on the basis (amongst others) that the negligence had caused not the injury itself but the loss of the chance that the injury might have been avoided with careful medical treatment.

In contract law, it is well established that damages may be awarded for the loss of a chance (*Chaplin v Hicks* [1911] 2 KB 786, cited in *Hotson* and *Gregg*). In tort, where the claimant has established that some recognised damage has been caused on the balance of probability, compensation can be awarded for other damage that might accrue in the future by discounting (i.e. reducing) the full amount payable in respect of such an injury by the probability that it will not occur. (For a recent affirmation of this principle, see *Rothwell v Chemical & Insulating Co Ltd* [2008] AC 281.) This is conceived as a matter simply of the quantification of the loss resulting from the breach of contract or tort. Take a car accident victim who suffers a broken leg and is estimated to have a 30 per cent chance of losing the movement in that leg in the future. Part of the award to such a claimant will be calculated by assessing what the claimant would have received if there was no movement in the leg and then discounting it by 70 per cent to reflect the possibility that full movement may be retained. (This however may be an appropriate case for the award of provision damages under the Senior Courts Act 1981, s. 32A: see p. 877, below.) Given this, why is it not possible to view the loss of the chance of avoiding the injury with proper medical treatment as damage independent from the ultimate injury suffered?

Loss of a Chance in *Gregg*

Despite the powerful arguments in favour of the loss of chance approach advanced by Lord Nicholls in his dissenting opinion, a majority of the House of Lords in *Gregg v Scott* rejected the claim for loss of a chance. However, the reasoning of the majority Law Lords differs significantly. For Lord Hoffmann, the material issue in *Gregg* was no different from that in *Hotson*; in both cases the relationship between the negligence of the defendant and the beneficial outcome the claimant hoped to achieve was shrouded in uncertainty, and the law dealt with uncertainty through the burden of proof. Commenting on *Gregg* in the later case of *Barker v Corus*, extracted at p. 237, below, Lord Hoffmann observed [at 38]:

Gregg v Scott [2005] 2 AC 176 was a case of uncertainty about the cause of a known event. Although this point was to some extent obscured by the fact that Mr Gregg was making a claim for loss of expectation of life and was still alive at the time when he brought his action, there was no finding of uncertainty about what the outcome would be. The judge found as a fact that his expectation of life was substantially less than it would have been if he had not contracted cancer. His loss of expectation of life was therefore damage which he was taken to have suffered at the time when he made his claim, exactly as if he had suffered a broken leg...

The uncertainty in the case was over what had been the cause of the reduced expectation of life. Was it the genetics and lifestyle which caused him to contract cancer, or was it the negligent delay in his diagnosis and treatment? The judge found that the delay had increased the chances of a premature death but not enough to enable him to say on a balance of probability that it would not otherwise have happened. The question before the House was whether Mr Gregg could claim that the damage he suffered was the additional chance of a premature death which had been caused by the delay.

According to Lord Hoffmann, it was not permissible to reframe the claim as one for loss of chance and avoid the evidential difficulties. He therefore disagreed with Lord Nicholls, who drew a distinction between the evidential uncertainty in *Hotson* and the scientific uncertainty in *Gregg*. Not everyone thinks that this is a satisfactory way of distinguishing between the cases (see, e.g., Peel (2005) LQR 364 at 367) but Baroness Hale also thought that *Hotson* was a different kind of case, one where their Lordships did not consider the loss of a chance argument because they held there was no chance to lose. The issue was, however, clearly raised in *Gregg*, because the adverse outcome to which the loss of the chance related (i.e. death by cancer) had not occurred at the time of the trial nor by the time of the appeal to the House of Lords. It was a case in which, to expand upon Baroness Hale's useful metaphor, the tossed coin was still in the air, rather than covered on the back of the player's hand. Thus the claim could only be for the loss of chance of avoiding death by cancer, and Baroness Hale declined to accept it as a form of damage for which compensation would be recoverable as it risked transferring the law of negligence from liability for outcomes to liability for chances. The other member of the majority, Lord Phillips, pointed out the difficulties of trying to assess the statistical chances in a case like *Gregg* where the adverse outcome had not yet occurred but, at [190], he expressly reserved his position on the possibility of a claim for loss of chance '[w]here medical treatment has resulted in an adverse outcome and negligence has increased the chance of that outcome'. Lord Phillips seemed to distinguish *Hotson* as a case where the claim was for the adverse outcome rather than for the loss of a chance of avoiding that outcome, but this avoids the key question of *when* the claimant will be allowed to frame the claim as one for loss of chance so as to avoid difficulties in proving causation of the adverse outcome itself. On the facts, Lord Phillips rejected the claim for loss of chance on the basis that the adverse outcome was still prospective, stating (at [190]): 'Awarding damages for the reduction of the prospect of a cure, when the long term result of treatment is still uncertain, is not a satisfactory exercise.' He was particularly influenced by the consideration that a patient's prognosis is liable to vary by the day. In the circumstances of the case before him, the very fact that the claimant had survived until the date of the House of Lords' hearing demonstrated that his chances of surviving cancer-free for 10 years from the date of his initial treatment were significantly higher than the 25 per cent figure settled upon by the trial judge.

The result, then, seems to be as follows. Lord Hoffmann could not distinguish the case from *Hotson* and saw no reason to take a different approach than was taken in that case. Baroness Hale saw the case as distinguishable from *Hotson* but rejected the award of damages for loss of chance in the 'coin in the air' scenario as well. Lord Phillips agreed the case was distinguishable from *Hotson*, interpreted *Hotson* as a claim for the adverse outcome rather than a loss of chance, kept his options open on the award of loss of chance damages in the *Hotson* scenario, but rejected the claim for the very reason that the coin was still in the air. For the minority, Lord Nicholls distinguished *Hotson* and would have allowed recovery where it was scientific uncertainty that created the evidential difficulty for the claimant. Although he agreed with Lord Nicholls, the other member of the minority, Lord Hope, found an alternative ground for the decision: as the negligence was responsible for some physical change—the growth of the tumour—this constituted 'damage' so as to complete the action in negligence, and the lost chance of avoiding the cancer could be claimed as damage consequential upon the physical 'injury' (see Stapleton (2005) 68 MLR 996 at 998). This argument did not appeal to a unanimous House of Lords in *Rothwell v Chemical & Insulating Co Ltd* [2008] AC 281 where their Lordships refused to find that the development of asymptomatic pleural plaques on the lungs, as a result of exposure to asbestos dust, amounted to physical damage so as to ground a claim for consequential stress and anxiety relating to the chance of contracting mesothelioma in the future. The presence of the plaques did not increase the likelihood of the claimants suffering asbestos-related diseases; they were just a marker to indicate the presence of asbestos fibres. As Leczykiewicz (2008) 124 LQR 552 notes, it is hard to see that mere physical change which does not constitute damage can be the hook on which other heads of damage can be claimed. This is especially so where that change does not increase even the statistical risk of an adverse physical outcome from occurring (see Turton (2008) 71 MLR 1009, 1012). Moreover, the presence of some physical injury does not always solve the evidentiary difficulties; as Lord Phillips pointed out, there was no evidence that the enlargement of the tumour in *Gregg* had actually made any difference to the claimant's prospects of long-term survival.

Damages for Loss of a Chance after *Gregg*

So does *Gregg* preclude altogether the award of damages for the loss of a chance of avoiding personal injury? It is certainly not possible to succeed in such a claim where, as in *Gregg*, the *only* claim available is for loss of chance as the adverse outcome has not yet occurred. Where the adverse outcome has occurred, it is suggested that *Gregg* itself does not prevent a claim for the loss of the chance of avoiding that outcome, though we would argue that *Hotson* in fact stands in the way of such a claim and would need to be overruled if damages are to be awarded (see Stapleton (2005) 68 MLR 996 at 1004). However, whether such a claim should be allowed is another matter. Writing extra-judicially, Lord Hoffmann ('Causation' (2005) 121 LQR 592 at 601) has noted the difficulties that would arise if different causation rules were applied depending on the time when the action was brought:

> What would be startling would be to change the principles of liability, so that if Mr Gregg had died just before the trial, his executor would have to prove that the delay had probably hastened his death, while if he was alive but clearly did not have long to live, it would be sufficient to prove that there was a substantial possibility that the delay hastened his death. That makes no sense.

Moreover, it is not only the House of Lords that has been wary of accepting 'loss of chance' as compensatable damage in negligence, at least in relation to the loss of chance of avoiding a physical injury (see *Lawson v Laferriere* [1991] 1 SCR 541 (Canadian Supreme Court), and also the competing views of Gaudron and Callinan JJ of the High Court of Australia in *Naxakis v Western General Hospital* (1999) 197 CLR 269; at time of writing, the issue is again before the Australian High Court: *Tabet v Gett* [2009] HCATrans 303, 304). If 'loss of chance' is to amount to damage in the tort of negligence, some important questions will need to be addressed. First, as *Gregg* indicates, there is no consensus on when a claimant might be said to have lost a chance. Lord Mackay in *Hotson* argued that, when the plaintiff arrived at the hospital, there was no chance to lose, the plaintiff either having sufficient blood cells alive so that with proper medical treatment he would have made a complete recovery, or not. This was a question of past fact to be determined on the balance of probability, although by the date of the trial this was extremely difficult. As Reece has argued ('Losses of chances in the law' (1996) 59 MLR 188 at 196):

> [T]here was a time in the past when the cause of the necrosis could have been determined. If the blood vessels had been examined after the fall, then it would have been humanly possible to decide whether or not the plaintiff would develop necrosis even if he were treated. At the time of trial the cause was uncertain, but the uncertainty was epistemological not objective.

If, however, there was an 'objective' uncertainty, there being no time in the past at which the cause of the necrosis could have been determined (e.g. because the plaintiff's fate was still 'held in the balance'), then this might be regarded as a real 'loss of a chance' case meriting the award of compensation.

Another difficulty in accepting 'loss of a chance' as damage lies in assessing a value to be given to the chance. It is normally suggested that the chance be evaluated by reference to the ultimate injury to which the chance relates, so that the 40 per cent chance of avoiding the loss of a leg would be calculated by discounting by 60 per cent the damages awarded for the loss of a leg. If the chance is so valued, however, is it an attempt to compensate for the underlying injury itself even though balance of probability causation has not been satisfied? As Voyiakis (2009) 72 MLR 909, 917 notes: 'Knowing how much risk I have imposed on you and how much compensation I would have to pay you if I had caused you actual physical harm does not by itself suggest how much I should pay for having exposed your physical health to danger.' Do you think it is realistic to value the chance in a way other than by reference to the injury to which that chance relates?

Whilst courts have generally been reluctant to sanction loss of a chance in personal injury actions, they have been more lenient where the damage to which the chance relates is economic loss. In *Allied Maples v Simmons & Simmons* [1995] 1 WLR 1602 (noted [1996] CLJ 187; (1996–7) 7 KCLJ 101), the plaintiff sued its solicitors for failure to advise with respect to the deletion of a warranty in a sale of business agreement between the plaintiff and a third party which deprived the plaintiff of protection in respect of any contingent liabilities of the third party. The defendant argued that its negligence did not cause the plaintiff's damage because it could not be shown on the balance of probability that the third party would have accepted such a warranty. Stuart-Smith LJ held that, while the plaintiff had to show on the balance of probability it would have relied on the proper advice if given (see *McWilliams v Sir William Arrol* [1962] 1 WLR 295), it was not necessary to show that the third party would, on the balance of probability, have given some protection to the plaintiff against these liabilities. It was enough that a 'substantial' chance was lost, and compensation could be awarded for that chance (see also *Blue Circle Industries plc v Ministry of Defence* [1999] Ch 289, and the decision of the Australian High Court in *Sellars v Adelaide Petroleum NL* (1994) 179 CLR 332 allowing a claim for loss of a commercial opportunity). Although the different treatment has been seen as anomalous (see Stapleton (2003) 119 LQR 388 at 406–11), it has been suggested (see Coote (1988) ALJ 761 at 772) that it is acceptable to allow claims for loss of a chance where the ultimate injury is economic loss and a duty of care is owed in respect of pure economic loss:

[T]he loss of a chance of financial gain goes to establishing the existence of the actionable tort only where the nature of the tort, or, as regards negligence, the category of case is such that economic loss is sufficient for the purpose. Loss of chance complies with the requirement because the chance itself has an economic value. No artificiality is involved. There would be such artificiality though, if the chance of physical injury or the loss of a chance of physical recovery were to be treated by the courts as amounting to a form of injury in itself.

Does this reasoning, adopted by Baroness Hale in *Gregg*, result in greater protection to financial interests than to personal injury, and, if so, is it desirable?

Perhaps the greatest difficulty with accepting loss of chance as actionable damage, identified by Baroness Hale in the extracts from *Gregg*, is its relationship to balance of probability causation. If the evidence suggests that the claimant's chance is 60 per cent, under balance of probability causation the chance would be converted into a certainty and the claimant would recover 100 per cent of the damages. But if loss of a chance amounts to compensatable damage, why should a claimant with a 40 per cent chance recover only 40 per cent of the amount that would be awarded to compensate his injury whilst one with a 60 per cent chance receives 100 per cent of the award? For criticism of awards of damages for loss of chance in French law, see Khoury (2008) 124 LQR 103, 121–130 and for different approaches to this issue, see Stapleton (1988) LQR 389; Hill (1991) 54 MLR 511; Lunney (1995) 15 LS 1; Reece (1996) 59 MLR 188; Stauch (1997) 17 OJLS 205; A. Porat and A. Stein, *Tort Liability under Uncertainty* (Oxford: OUP, 2001), pp. 116–29 and 195–201; and L. Khoury, *Uncertain Causation in Medical Liability* (Oxford: Hart, 2006), pp. 133–5.

The but-for test requires a hypothetical inquiry into what would have happened if the defendant had not been negligent. It has so far been assumed that the defendant's response in this hypothetical situation is easily ascertainable. But what if the defendant alleges that he would have done one thing, while the claimant alleges he ought to have done another? Can the defendant rely upon the fact that, if he had not been guilty of the negligence of which the claimant complained, he would have caused the injury anyway by negligence of another sort? The issue was raised by the House of Lords' decision in *Bolitho v City and Hackney Health Authority* [1998] AC 232. In *Bolitho*, the defendant's negligence consisted in not responding to a pager message until a time after the plaintiff's child had died. To prove causation it was therefore necessary to ask what the defendant would have done if she had responded to the pager. Her evidence was that she would not have intubated (i.e. inserted a tube into the child's larynx). It was subsequently accepted that this was the only medical procedure that would have saved the child. The House of Lords held that this was not the end of the causation inquiry, as it was necessary to ask whether the failure to intubate would have been negligent. If it was, causation would have been proved, not on the basis of what the defendant would have done but on what she should have done. What if the defendant's negligence consisted in failing to call a third party to examine the claimant? If there was evidence that there was a chance the third party might have intubated, would this fall under the rule in the *Allied Maples* case, allowing the award of damages for the chance that the injury might have been avoided? (Cf. *Khalid v Barnet & Chase Farm Hospital NHS Trust* [2007] EWHC (QB) 644.)

(b) Material Contribution to Injury

In *Hotson* and *Gregg* the House of Lords declined to depart from orthodox principles of tort law in response to the difficulty of proving causation in complex medical cases. But their Lordships have shown themselves more willing to innovate in a series of cases involving exposure to toxic substances in the workplace. The first stage was the recognition of a liability for the employer's 'material contribution' to the employee's injury in a situation where part of the toxic exposure causing the injury was 'innocent' and part of it was attributable to the employer's breach of duty (*Bonnington Castings Ltd v Wardlaw*, extracted below). Unlike in *Hotson* or *Gregg*, the question in such a case is not one of 'alternative' causation, in which it is assumed that it is *either* the defendant's negligence *or* some other factor that was *the* cause, but one of 'cumulative' causation, in which both innocent and guilty exposures are taken to have played a part. It is not necessary for the claimant to demonstrate that he would not have suffered the injury 'but for' the employer's breach, though it appears that the breach must at least have made the injury worse than it would otherwise have been.

The second stage was for the House of Lords to apply the 'material contribution' test in cases where the medical evidence could not say whether the claimant's injury was caused by a cumulative process or a discrete one-off exposure for which the defendant may or may not be responsible (*McGhee v National Coal Board*; *Fairchild v Glenhaven Funeral Services Ltd*; and *Barker v Corus UK Ltd*, all extracted below). Here it cannot be said that the employer's breach of duty has materially contributed to the injury, merely that it materially contributed to *the risk* of injury, and the effect is to relax the ordinary rules of causation. The implications of this very radical development, and the circumstances in which the court may apply the test of material contribution to risk, are considered in Section (c) below.

Bonnington Castings Ltd v Wardlaw [1956] AC 613

The pursuer complained that, after working in the defenders' workshop for eight years, he contracted pneumoconiosis as a result of the inhalation of silicone dust. The dust came from two sources. Some of the dust was created by the operation of a pneumatic hammer in the defenders' workshop. As there was no known protection against dust produced in this way, the defenders were not negligent with respect to this source. The rest of the dust was caused by the workings of the defenders' swing grinders, and arose because the ducts of the dust-extraction plant for these grinders had not been properly maintained. The defenders were found to have been negligent and in breach of statutory duty with respect to the dust from this source. The issue for the House of Lords was whether the defenders' negligence and breach of statutory duty caused the pneumoconiosis of the pursuer.

Lord Reid

It would seem obvious in principle that a pursuer or plaintiff must prove not only negligence or breach of duty but also that such fault caused, or materially contributed to, his injury, and there is ample authority for that proposition both in Scotland and in England. I can find neither reason nor authority for the rule being different where there is breach of a statutory duty. The fact that Parliament imposes a duty for the protection of employees has been held to entitle an employee to sue if he is injured as a result of a breach of that duty, but it would be going a great deal further to hold that it can be inferred from the enactment of a duty that Parliament intended that any employee suffering injury can sue his employer merely because there was a breach of duty and it is shown to be possible that his injury may have been caused by it. In my judgment, the employee must, in all cases, prove his case by the ordinary standard of proof in civil actions; he must make it appear at least that, on a balance of probabilities, the breach of duty caused, or materially contributed to, his injury.

The medical evidence was that pneumoconiosis is caused by a gradual accumulation in the lungs of minute particles of silica inhaled over a period of years. That means, I think, that the disease is caused by the whole of the noxious material inhaled and, if that material comes from two sources, it cannot be wholly attributed to material from one source or the other. I am in agreement with much of the Lord President's opinion in this case, but I cannot agree that the question is which was the more probable source of the respondent's disease, the dust from the pneumatic hammers or the dust from the swing grinders. It appears to me that the source of his disease was the dust from both sources, and the real question is whether the dust from the swing grinders materially contributed to the disease. What is a material contribution must be a question of degree. A contribution which comes within the exception *de minimis non curat lex* is not material, but I think that any contribution which does not fall within that exception must be material. I do not see how there can be something too large to come within the *de minimis* principle, but yet too small to be material....

I think that the position can be shortly stated in this way. It may be that, of the noxious dust in the general atmosphere of the shop, more came from the pneumatic hammers than from the swing grinders, but I think it is sufficiently proved that the dust from the grinders made a substantial contribution. The respondent, however, did not only inhale the general atmosphere of the shop; when he was working his hammer, his face was directly over it, and it must often have happened that dust from his hammer substantially increased the concentration of noxious dust in the air which he inhaled. It is, therefore, probable that much the greater proportion of the noxious dust which he inhaled over the whole period came from the hammers. But, on the other hand, some certainly came from the swing grinders, and I cannot avoid the conclusion that the proportion which came from the swing grinders was not negligible. He was inhaling the general atmosphere all the time, and there is no evidence to show that his hammer gave off noxious dust so frequently, or that the concentration of noxious dust above it when it was producing dust was so much greater than the concentration in the general atmosphere, that the special concentration of dust could be said to be substantially the sole cause of his disease. . . .

In my opinion, it is proved not only that the swing grinders may well have contributed, but that they did, in fact, contribute, a quota of silica dust which was not negligible to the respondent's lungs and, therefore, did help to produce the disease. That is sufficient to establish liability against the appellants and I am, therefore, of opinion that this appeal should be dismissed. . . .

Lord Tucker and **Lord Keith of Avonholme** delivered speeches in favour of dismissing the appeal, **Viscount Simonds** agreed with Lord Reid, and **Lord Somervell** simply concurred.

Appeal dismissed.

COMMENTARY

Where the claimant develops a disease as a result of cumulative exposure to a noxious substance, only part of which is attributable to the defendant's breach of duty, it is not necessary to demonstrate that he would not have suffered the disease at all but for the breach. He need only prove that the breach of duty made a 'material contribution', which Lord Reid, in the extract above, defines as a contribution falling outside the *de minimis* range. (For recent confirmation of this analysis, see *Bailey v Ministry of Defence* [2009] 1 WLR 1052.)

In *Wardlaw*, the pursuer recovered full damages, i.e. damages for all the effects of the pneumoconiosis. The Court of Appeal has now ruled, however, that the claimant in such a case is entitled only to proportionate damages reflecting the extent of the defendant's wrongful contribution to the disease. In *Holtby v Brigham & Cowan (Hull) Ltd* [2003] 3 All ER 421, the claimant developed asbestosis as a result of occupational exposure to asbestos dust over a period of several years, during which he had worked for a number of different employers. The Court of Appeal ruled that each employer could only be held liable for a part of the claimant's total disability and, for want of evidence suggesting any fairer basis of appointment, divided responsibility between them on a 'time-exposure' basis. (See also *Allen v British Rail Engineering* [2001] PIQR Q10: vibration white finger.) The court explained the award of full damages in *Wardlaw* on the basis that the question of apportionment had simply not been raised.

It is important to note that proportionate damages may be awarded only where the claimant's injury is 'divisible'. The clearest examples are where there are two wholly different injuries, e.g., where D1 breaks C's arm and D2 breaks his leg. *Holtby* is a significant case because

it awards proportionate damages in a case where cumulative exposure to a harmful substance causes a single condition which gets progressively worse the longer the exposure lasts.
Its practical result is to throw the risk of the bankruptcy or untraceability of individual
defendants onto the claimant, who must now sue, and recover against, all those who contributed to the injury if he is to get compensation for the whole of his loss. Where, as in
Wardlaw's case, an 'innocent' factor has contributed to the injury, it seems to follow that the
claimant's damages cannot exceed that proportion of his loss that is attributable to the guilty
cause.

Gullifer (2001) 117 LQR 403 has questioned whether proportionate damages are to be
awarded if the periods of 'guilty' and 'innocent' exposure are not consecutive (as in *Holtby*)
but concurrent (as in *Wardlaw*), citing the evidential difficulties of assessing the contribution of the defendant's wrongful act in the latter type of case (see also Green (2009) 125
LQR 44) . But the evidential difficulties may be no less in cases of successive exposure, especially where, as in *Holtby*, the disease manifests itself only many years afterwards. In *Holtby*,
Stuart-Smith LJ stated that 'the court only has to do the best it can using its common sense',
adding that this was necessary in order 'to achieve justice, not only to the claimant but the
defendant, and among defendants' (at 429).

In two decisions dealing with psychiatric injury, the Court of Appeal apparently confirmed that proportionate damages are to be awarded even where the causative factors
operate concurrently. In *Rahman v Arearose Ltd* [2001] QB 351, the claimant was beaten
up in his workplace in a violent attack for which his employer was held responsible. He
was taken to hospital where he received negligent treatment, leaving him blind in his right
eye. Subsequently, he developed various psychiatric disorders which his psychiatric report
attributed, in different degrees, to the attack and the loss of his eye. The Court of Appeal
accepted that the effects of the two incidents had 'a synergistic interaction' and apportioned
responsibility for the resultant disorders between the employer and the hospital authority. (It should be noted that, unlike in the other cases considered here, each defendant was
clearly liable for some harm and the question was how far each liability should extend.) This
approach was approved in *Hatton v Sutherland* [2002] ICR 613, where the Court of Appeal
would have applied it in the context of claims for work-related stress had the issue arisen on
the facts. Hale LJ observed: 'Many stress-related illnesses are likely to have a complex aetiology with several different causes. In principle a wrongdoer should pay only for that proportion of the harm suffered for which he by his wrongdoing is responsible' (para. 36).

In *Barker v Corus (UK) Ltd* [2006] 2 AC 572 at [111]–[112], Lord Walker pointed out that
indivisible damage is not always instantly recognisable, and that there are debatable borderline cases. For example, Keeler (2004) 12 TLJ 20 at 28, has argued that the loss in *Wardlaw*
was the pursuer's incapacity to perform his usual work and was hence indivisible. Given
these doubts it may legitimately be asked whether psychiatric illnesses can appropriately be
treated as 'divisible' injuries. Commenting on the *Rahman* decision, Weir [2001] CLJ 237 at
238 argues: 'Here the Court accepted an absurd report confected jointly by the experts for
the three parties, who tentatively divided up the victim's present condition in terms of the
two causes. They should not have been asked to do this, and their answer should have been
ignored, for there is no scientific basis for any such attribution of causality: the claimant is
not half-mad because of what the first defendant did and half-mad because of what the second defendant did, he is as mad as he is because of what both of them did.' Do you agree?

For doubts as to Hale LJ's approach to apportionment in *Hatton*, see the comments of
Lady Justice Smith in *Dickens v O2 Plc* [2008] EWCA Civ 1144 at [46], and note the decision
of the House of Lords in *Simmons v British Steel plc* [2004] SCLR 920, where their Lordships

showed no inclination to carve up the various causes of the pursuer's psychiatric injury and applied the 'material contribution' test of *Bonnington* to hold the defendant 100 per cent responsible for the injury. More recently, the limited scope of proportionate damages awards in a *Bonnington* material contribution case was recognised in *Ellis v Environment Agency* [2008] EWCA Civ 1117 where May LJ (at [39]) thought that, at least in the Court of Appeal, it should be limited to 'industrial disease or injury cases where there has been successive exposure to harm by a number of agencies, where the effect of the harm is divisible, and where it would be unjust for an individual defendant to bear the whole of a loss when in commonsense he was not responsible for all of it.'

Some of the doubts that have arisen over when proportionate damages can be awarded under the *Bonnington* 'material contribution' test are due to a failure to differentiate between an injury which is *divisible*, and an injury which has a *number of causes*. An instructive case to consider in this context is *Bailey v Ministry of Defence* [2009] 1 WLR 1052. In this case the claimant suffered brain damage as a result of her inability to clear vomit from her throat. The Court of Appeal rightly proceeded on the basis that this injury was indivisible; the brain damage could not be divided up and part attributed to any particular cause. It was, however, attributable to two different underlying causes, which together made the claimant too weak to clear the vomit from her throat: the defendant's negligence and a non-tortious illness. Although some have argued that the 'material contribution' test should not be applied to these situations (e.g. Stauch [2009] CLJ 27), it can sensibly be said that the defendant's negligence materially contributed to the injury by contributing to the claimant's weakened state which resulted in her injury (see Green (2009) 125 LQR 44). As in *Bonnington*, the causes operated concurrently and interdependently to produce the injury, and in these circumstances it was enough that the defendant's negligence had materially contributed to the injury by being one of the causes of it. As the *injury* was indivisible, there was no question of the defendant for being liable for only a proportion of that injury.

Where the claimant's injury is indivisible, no deduction is made to reflect the contribution of innocent causes (see, e.g., *Smith v Leech Brain & Co*, discussed below, p. 275) so if *Bonnington* applies the claimant should recover in full. Furthermore, if two or more defendants have made a material contribution to an indivisible injury, their liability is 'joint and several', meaning that the claimant can sue any one of them for the full amount of his loss (though he cannot recover sums in excess of his full loss by then suing the others). The onus is on the defendant whom the claimant chooses to sue to join those responsible for the same damage as co-defendants to the action, or to seek contribution from them in separate proceedings (Civil Liability (Contribution) Act 1978), and he bears the risk that he cannot find them or that they turn out to be bankrupt (see further p. 266, below).

While working for D1, C inhales quantities of asbestos wholly as a result of his employer's negligence. The quantities are not such as to warrant a diagnosis of asbestosis, but they make him more susceptible to asbestosis in the future. In his subsequent employment with D2, C inhales further quantities of asbestos as a result of D2's negligence, and asbestosis is now diagnosed as a result of the accumulation of fibres in C's lungs. If C sues D1, can it be said that D1's negligence caused the asbestosis? If C sues D2 and establishes liability, will he get proportionate damages reflecting D2's contribution to the total exposure? Or is he entitled to full damages on the basis that D2 must take his victim as he finds him (i.e. with some asbestos in his lungs) and it was the additional exposure to asbestos that caused the injury? Are your answers consistent with *Bonnington* and *Holtby*?

For further consideration of these and other divisibility issues, see K. Oliphant (ed.), *Aggregation and Divisibility of Damage* (Vienna: Springer, 2009).

(c) Material Contribution to Risk

McGhee v National Coal Board [1973] 1 WLR 1

The pursuer was sent by the defender, his employer, to clean brick kilns. This meant that he was exposed to abrasive brick dust, although this exposure was not negligent. However, the defender in breach of duty failed to provide adequate washing facilities, with the result that the pursuer was forced to bicycle home before the dust could be removed. After some days the pursuer began to suffer from dermatitis. In the action against the defender, the failure to provide sufficient washing facilities was held to be negligent but the issue was whether the negligence caused the dermatitis. The medical evidence showed (1) the dermatitis had been caused by the working conditions in the brick kilns; and (2) the fact that after work the pursuer had had to exert himself further by bicycling home with brick dust adhering to his skin had added materially to the risk that he might develop the disease. The medical evidence could not say, however, whether the prolonged exposure to the dust had caused the dermatitis.

Lord Reid

It has always been the law that a pursuer succeeds if he can shew that fault of the defender caused or materially contributed to his injury. There may have been two separate causes but it is enough if one of the causes arose from fault of the defender. The pursuer does not have to prove that this cause would of itself have been enough to cause him injury. That is well illustrated by the decision of this House in *Bonnington Castings Ltd v Wardlaw*. There the pursuer's disease was caused by an accumulation of noxious dust in his lungs. The dust which he had inhaled over a period came from two sources. The defenders were not responsible for one source but they could and ought to have prevented the other. The dust from the latter source was not in itself sufficient to cause the disease but the pursuer succeeded because it made a material contribution to his injury. The respondents seek to distinguish *Wardlaw's case* by arguing that then it was proved that every particle of dust inhaled played its part in causing the onset of the disease whereas in this case it is not proved that every minor abrasion played its part.

In the present case the evidence does not shew—perhaps no one knows—just how dermatitis of this type begins. It suggests to me that there are two possible ways. It may be that an accumulation of minor abrasions of the horny layer of skin is a necessary precondition for the onset of the disease. Or it may be that the disease starts at one particular abrasion and then spreads, so that multiplication of abrasions merely increases the number of places where the disease can start and in that way increases the risk of its occurrence.

I am inclined to think that the evidence points to the former view. But in a field where so little appears to be known with certainty I could not say that that is proved. If it were then this case would be indistinguishable from *Wardlaw's case*. But I think that in cases like this we must take a broader view of causation. The medical evidence is to the effect that the effect that the fact that the man had to cycle home caked with grime and sweat added materially to the risk that this disease might develop. It does not and could not explain just why that is so. But experience shews that it is so. Plainly that must be because what happens while the man remains unwashed can have a causative effect, although just how the cause operates is uncertain. I cannot accept the view expressed in the Inner House that once the man left the brick kiln he left behind the causes which made him liable to develop dermatitis. That seems to me quite inconsistent with a proper interpretation of the medical evidence. Nor can I accept the distinction drawn by the Lord Ordinary between materially increasing the risk that the disease will occur and making a material contribution to its occurrence.

There may be some logical ground for such a distinction where our knowledge of all the material factors is complete. But it has often been said that the legal concept of causation is not based on logic or philosophy. It is based on the practical way in which the ordinary man's mind works in the every-day affairs of life. From a broad and practical viewpoint I can see no substantial difference between saying that what the respondents did materially increased the risk of injury to the appellant and saying that what the respondents did made a material contribution to his injury.

Lord Wilberforce

My Lords, I agree with the judge below to the extent that merely to show that a breach of duty increases the risk of harm is not, *in abstracto*, enough to enable the pursuer to succeed. He might, on this basis, still be met by successful defences. Thus, it was open to the respondents, while admitting, or being unable to contest that their failure had increased the risk, to prove, if they could, as they tried to do, that the appellant's dermatitis was 'non-occupational'.

But the question remains whether a pursuer must necessarily fail if, after he has shown a breach of duty, involving an increase of risk of disease, he cannot positively prove that this increase of risk caused or materially contributed to the disease while his employers cannot positively prove the contrary. In this intermediate case there is an appearance of logic in the view that the pursuer, on whom the onus lies, should fail—a logic which dictated the judgments below. The question is whether we should be satisfied in factual situations like the present, with this logical approach. In my opinion, there are further considerations of importance. First, it is a sound principle that where a person has, by breach of duty of care, created a risk, and injury occurs within the area of that risk, the loss should be borne by him unless he shows that it had some other cause. Secondly, from the evidential point of view, one may ask, why should a man who is able to show that his employer should have taken certain precautions, because without them there is a risk, or an added risk, of injury or disease, and who in fact sustains exactly that injury or disease, have to assume the burden of proving more: namely, that it was the addition to the risk, caused by the breach of duty, which caused or materially contributed to the injury? In many cases of which the present is typical, this is impossible to prove, just because honest medical opinion cannot segregate the causes of an illness between compound causes. And if one asks which of the parties, the workman or the employers, should suffer from this inherent evidential difficulty, the answer as a matter of policy or justice should be that it is the creator of the risk who, *ex hypothesi*, must be taken to have foreseen the possibility of damage, who should bear its consequences.

There are analogies in this field of industrial disease. In cases concerned with pneumoconiosis, the courts faced with a similar, although not identical, evidential gap have bridged it by having regard to the risk situation of the pursuer. Pneumoconiosis being a disease brought on by cumulative exposure to dust particles, the courts have held that where the exposure was to a compound aggregate of 'faulty' particles and 'innocent' particles, the workman should recover, so long as the addition of the 'faulty' particles (i.e. those produced by some fault of the employers) was material, which I take to mean substantial, or not negligible (*Bonnington Castings Ltd v Wardlaw; Nicholson v Atlas Steel Foundry & Engineering Co Ltd* [1957] 1 WLR 613). *Wardlaw's case* was decided with full acceptance of the principle that a pursuer must prove not only negligence but also that such fault caused or materially contributed to his injury (at 620, per Lord Reid) and the pursuer succeeded because negligently-produced dust made a material contribution to the total dust which injured him. . . .

The evidential gap which undoubtedly existed there (i.e. the absence of proof that but for the addition of the 'guilty' dust the disease would not have been contracted) is similar to that in the present case and is expressed to be overcome by inference.

The present factual situation has its differences: the default here consisted not in adding a material quantity to the accumulation of injurious particles but by failure to take a step which materially increased the risk that the dust already present would cause injury. And I must say that, at least in the present case, to bridge the evidential gap by inference seems to me something of a fiction, since it was precisely this inference which the medical expert declined to make. But I find in the cases quoted an analogy which suggests the conclusion that, in the absence of proof that the culpable condition had, in the result, no effect, the employers should be liable for an injury, squarely within the risk which they created and that they, not the pursuer, should suffer the consequence of the impossibility, foreseeably inherent in the nature of his injury, of segregating the precise consequence of their default.

I would allow this appeal.

Lord Simon of Glaisdale, Lord Salmon, and **Lord Kilbrandon** delivered speeches in favour of allowing the appeal.

Appeal allowed.

Fairchild v Glenhaven Funeral Services Ltd [2003] 1 AC 32

The three claimants had each worked for several employers for a substantial period during which time they were exposed, through their employers' negligence (and in one case the negligence of the occupier), to asbestos dust. Each suffered mesothelioma, a cancer caused by exposure to asbestos dust. However, the precise manner in which asbestos caused the cancer was unknown to medical science. It was accepted that, the greater the exposure to asbestos, the more likely it was that a mesothelioma would occur, but there was no evidence to indicate whether the trigger was a single asbestos fibre or an accumulation of asbestos fibres. At trial, two of the claimants lost at first instance on the basis that they had not established on the balance of probabilities the precise source of the asbestos causing their disease, whilst the third was successful on the basis that the defendant employer's negligence had materially contributed to the mesothelioma. The Court of Appeal rejected all three claims, holding that mesothelioma was triggered on a single identifiable occasion and that each of the three claimants could not establish on the balance of probabilities which period of exposure had caused the damage. The claimants appealed to the House of Lords.

Lord Bingham of Cornhill

The essential question underlying the appeals may be accurately expressed in this way. If (1) C was employed at different times and for differing periods by both A and B, and (2) A and B were both subject to a duty to take reasonable care or to take all practicable measures to prevent C inhaling asbestos dust because of the known risk that asbestos dust (if inhaled) might cause a mesothelioma, and (3) both A and B were in breach of that duty in relation to C during the periods of C's employment by each of them with the result that during both periods C inhaled excessive quantities of asbestos dust, and (4) C is found to be suffering from a mesothelioma, and (5) any cause of C's mesothelioma other than the inhalation of asbestos dust at work can be effectively discounted, but (6) C cannot (because of the current limits of human science) prove, on the balance of probabilities, that his mesothelioma was the result of his inhaling asbestos dust during his employment by A or during his employment by B or during his employment by A and B taken together, is C entitled to recover damages against either A or B or against both A and B? To this question (not formulated in these terms) the Court of Appeal (Brooke, Latham and Kay LJJ), in a reserved judgment of the court reported at [2002] 1 WLR 1052, gave a negative answer. It did so because, applying the conventional 'but for' test of tortious liability, it could not be held that C had proved against A that his mesothelioma would probably not have occurred but for the breach of duty by A, nor against B that his mesothelioma would probably not have occurred but for the breach of duty by B, nor against A and B that his mesothelioma would probably not have occurred but for the breach of duty by both A and B together. So C failed against both A and B. The crucial issue on appeal is whether, in the special circumstances of such a case, principle, authority or policy requires or justifies a modified approach to proof of causation.

It is common ground that in each of the three cases under appeal conditions numbered (1) to (5) above effectively obtained. . . .

It is not known what level of exposure to asbestos dust and fibre can be tolerated without significant risk of developing a mesothelioma, but it is known that those living in urban environments (although without occupational exposure) inhale large numbers of asbestos fibres without developing a mesothelioma. It is accepted that the risk of developing a mesothelioma increases in proportion to the quantity of asbestos dust and fibres inhaled: the greater the quantity of dust and fibre inhaled, the greater the risk. But the condition may be caused by a single fibre, or a few fibres, or many fibres: medical opinion holds none of these possibilities to be more probable than any other, and the condition once caused is not aggravated by further exposure. So if C is employed successively by A and B and is exposed to asbestos dust and fibres during each employment and develops a mesothelioma, the very strong probability is that this will have been caused by inhalation of asbestos dust containing fibres. But C could have inhaled a single fibre giving rise to his condition during employment by A, in which case his exposure by B will have had no effect on his condition; or he could have inhaled a single fibre giving rise to his condition during his employment by B, in which case his exposure by A will have had no effect on his condition; or he could have inhaled fibres during his employment by A and B which together gave rise to his condition; but medical science cannot support the suggestion that any of these possibilities is to be regarded as more probable than any other. There is no way of identifying, even on a balance of probabilities, the source of the fibre or fibres which initiated the genetic process which culminated in the malignant tumour. It is on this rock of uncertainty, reflecting the point to which medical science has so far advanced, that the three claims were rejected by the Court of Appeal and by two of the three trial judges.

Principle

In a personal injury action based on negligence or breach of statutory duty the claimant seeks to establish a breach by the defendant of a duty owed to the claimant, which has caused him damage. For the purposes of analysis, and for the purpose of pleading, proving and resolving the claim, lawyers find it convenient to break the claim into its constituent elements: the duty, the breach, the damage and the causal connection between the breach and the damage. In the generality of personal injury actions, it is of course true that the claimant is required to discharge the burden of showing that the breach of which he complains caused the damage for which he claims and to do so by showing that but for the breach he would not have suffered the damage.

The issue in these appeals does not concern the general validity and applicability of that requirement, which is not in question, but is whether in special circumstances such as those in these cases there should be any variation or relaxation of it. The overall object of tort law is to define cases in which the law may justly hold one party liable to compensate another. Are these such cases? A and B owed C a duty to protect C against a risk of a particular and very serious kind. They failed to perform that duty. As a result the risk eventuated and C suffered the very harm against which it was the duty of A and B to protect him. Had there been only one tortfeasor, C would have been entitled to recover, but because the duty owed to him was broken by two tortfeasors and not only one, he is held to be entitled to recover against neither, because of his inability to prove what is scientifically unprovable. If the mechanical application of generally accepted rules leads to such a result, there must be room to question the appropriateness of such an approach in such a case....

Policy

The present appeals raise an obvious and inescapable clash of policy considerations. On the one hand are the considerations powerfully put by the Court of Appeal [2002] 1 WLR 1052 at 1080 which considered the claimants' argument to be not only illogical but 'also susceptible of unjust results. It may impose liability for the whole of an insidious disease on an employer with whom the claimant was employed for quite a short time in a long working life, when the claimant is wholly unable to prove on the balance of probabilities that that period of employment had any causative relationship with the inception of the disease. This is far too weighty an edifice to build on the slender foundations of *McGhee v National Coal Board* [1973] 1 WLR 1, and Lord Bridge has told us in *Wilsher v Essex Area Health Authority* [1988] AC 1074 that *McGhee* established no new principle of law at all. If we were to accede to the claimants' arguments, we would be distorting the law to accommodate the exigencies of a very hard case. We would be yielding to a contention that all those who have suffered injury after being exposed to a risk of that injury from which someone else should have protected them should be able to recover compensation even when they are quite unable to prove who was the culprit. In a quite different context Lord Steyn has recently said in *Frost v Chief Constable of Yorkshire Police* [1999] 2 AC 455, 491 that our tort system sometimes results in imperfect justice, but it is the best the common law can do.'

The Court of Appeal had in mind that... [in *Wardlaw* and *McGhee*, and certain other cases] there was only one employer involved. Thus there was a risk that the defendant might be held liable for acts for which he should not be held legally liable but no risk that he would be held liable for damage which (whether legally liable or not) he had not caused. The crux of cases such as the present, if the appellants' argument is upheld, is that an employer may be held liable for damage he has not caused. The risk is the greater where all the employers potentially liable are not before the court. This is so on the facts of each of the three appeals before the House, and is always likely to be so given the long latency of this condition and the likelihood that some employers potentially liable will have gone out of business or disappeared during that period. It can properly be said to be unjust to impose liability on a party who has not been shown, even on a balance of probabilities, to have caused the damage complained of. On the other hand, there is a strong policy argument in favour of compensating those who have suffered grave harm, at the expense of their employers who owed them a duty to protect them against that very harm and failed to do so, when the harm can only have been caused by breach of that duty and when science does not permit the victim accurately to attribute, as between several employers, the precise responsibility for the harm he has suffered. I am of opinion that such injustice as may be involved in imposing liability on a duty-breaking employer in these circumstances is heavily outweighed by the injustice of denying redress to a victim. Were the law otherwise, an employer exposing his employee to asbestos dust could obtain complete immunity against mesothelioma (but not asbestosis) claims by employing only those who had previously been exposed to excessive quantities of asbestos dust. Such a result would reflect no credit on the law. It seems to me, as it did to Lord Wilberforce in *McGhee* [1973] 1 WLR 1 at 7 that:

> the employers should be liable for an injury, squarely within the risk which they created and that they, not the pursuer, should suffer the consequence of the impossibility, foreseeably inherent in the nature of his injury, of segregating the precise consequence of their default.

Conclusion

To the question posed...[previously in] this opinion I would answer that where conditions (1)–(6) are satisfied C is entitled to recover against both A and B. That conclusion is in my opinion consistent with principle, and also with authority (properly understood). Where those conditions are satisfied, it seems to me just and in accordance with common sense to treat the conduct of A and B in exposing C to a risk to which he should not have been exposed as making a material contribution to the contracting by C of a condition against which it was the duty of A and B to protect him. I consider that this conclusion is fortified by the wider jurisprudence reviewed above. Policy considerations weigh in favour of such a conclusion. It is a conclusion which follows even if either A or B is not before the court. It was not suggested in argument that C's entitlement against either A or B should be for any sum less than the full compensation to which C is entitled, although A and B could of course seek contribution against each other or any other employer liable in respect of the same damage in the ordinary way. No argument on apportionment was addressed to the House. I would in conclusion emphasise that my opinion is directed to cases in which each of the conditions specified in (1)–(6)...above is satisfied and to no other case. It would be unrealistic to suppose that the principle here affirmed will not over time be the subject of incremental and analogical development. Cases seeking to develop the principle must be decided when and as they arise. For the present, I think it unwise to decide more than is necessary to resolve these three appeals which, for all the foregoing reasons, I concluded should be allowed....

Lord Hoffmann

What are the significant features of the present case? First, we are dealing with a duty specifically intended to protect employees against being unnecessarily exposed to the risk of (among other things) a particular disease. Secondly, the duty is one intended to create a civil right to compensation for injury relevantly connected with its breach. Thirdly, it is established that the greater the exposure to asbestos, the greater the risk of contracting that disease. Fourthly, except in the case in which there has been only one significant exposure to asbestos, medical science cannot prove whose asbestos is more likely than not to have produced the cell mutation which caused the disease. Fifthly, the employee has contracted the disease against which he should have been protected.

In these circumstances, a rule requiring proof of a link between the defendant's asbestos and the claimant's disease would, with the arbitrary exception of single-employer cases, empty the duty of content. If liability depends upon proof that the conduct of the defendant was a necessary condition of the injury, it cannot effectively exist. It is however open to your Lordships to formulate a different causal requirement in this class of case.

The Court of Appeal was in my opinion wrong to say that in the absence of a proven link between the defendant's asbestos and the disease, there was no 'causative relationship' whatever between the defendant's conduct and the disease. It depends entirely upon the level at which the causal relationship is described. To say, for example, that the cause of Mr Matthews's cancer was his significant exposure to asbestos during two employments over a period of eight years, without being able to identify the day upon which he inhaled the fatal fibre, is a meaningful causal statement. The medical evidence shows that it is the only kind of causal statement about the disease which, in the present state of knowledge, a scientist would regard as possible. There is no a priori reason, no rule of logic, which prevents the law from treating it as sufficient to satisfy the causal requirements of the law of negligence. The question is whether your Lordships think such a rule would be just and reasonable and whether the class of cases to which it applies can be sufficiently clearly defined.

So the question of principle is this: in cases which exhibit the five features I have mentioned, which rule would be more in accordance with justice and the policy of common law and statute to protect employees against the risk of contracting asbestos-related diseases? One which makes an employer in breach of his duty liable for the employee's injury because he created a significant risk to his health, despite the fact that the physical cause of the injury may have been created by someone else? Or a rule which means that unless he was subjected to risk by the breach of duty of a single employer, the employee can never have a remedy? My Lords, as between the employer in breach of duty and the employee who has lost his life in consequence of a period of exposure to risk to which that employer has contributed, I think it would be both inconsistent with the policy of the law imposing the duty and morally wrong for your Lordships to impose causal requirements which exclude liability....

The question is how narrowly the principle developed in *McGhee's case* and applied in this case should be confined. In my opinion, caution is advisable. *Wilsher's case* shows the dangers of over-generalisation...

Lord Rodger of Earlsferry

[His Lordship held that the principle recognised in *McGhee* should be applied on the present facts, and continued:]

First, the principle is designed to resolve the difficulty that arises where it is inherently impossible for the claimant to prove exactly how his injury was caused. It applies, therefore, where the claimant has proved all that he possibly can, but the causal link could only ever be established by scientific investigation and the current state of the relevant science leaves it uncertain exactly how the injury was caused and, so, who caused it. *McGhee* and the present cases are examples. Secondly, part of the underlying rationale of the principle is that the defendant's wrongdoing has materially increased the risk that the claimant will suffer injury. It is therefore essential not just that the defendant's conduct created a material risk of injury to a class of persons but that it actually created a material risk of injury to the claimant himself. Thirdly, it follows that the defendant's conduct must have been capable of causing the claimant's injury. Fourthly, the claimant must prove that his injury was caused by the eventuation of the kind of risk created by the defendant's wrongdoing. In *McGhee*, for instance, the risk created by the defenders' failure was that the pursuer would develop dermatitis due to brick dust on his skin and he proved that he had developed dermatitis due to brick dust on his skin. By contrast, the principle does not apply where the claimant has merely proved that his injury could have been caused by a number of different events, only one of which is the eventuation of the risk created by the defendant's wrongful act or omission. *Wilsher* is an example. Fifthly, this will usually mean that the claimant must prove that his injury was caused, if not by exactly the same agency as was involved in the defendant's wrongdoing, at least by an agency that operated in substantially the same way. A possible example would be where a workman suffered injury from exposure to dusts coming from two sources, the dusts being particles of different substances each of which, however, could have caused his injury in the same way. Without having heard detailed argument on the point, I incline to the view that the principle was properly applied by the Court of Appeal in *Fitzgerald v Lane* [1987] QB 781. Sixthly, the principle applies where the other possible source of the claimant's injury is a similar wrongful act or omission of another person, but it can also apply where, as in *McGhee*, the other possible source of the injury is a similar, but lawful, act or omission of the same defendant. I reserve my opinion as to whether the principle applies where the other possible source of injury is a similar but lawful act or omission of someone else or a natural occurrence....

Lord Hutton delivered a separate opinion, concurring in the outcome but dissenting on the correct interpretation of *McGhee.*

Appeals allowed.

Barker v Corus UK Ltd [2006] 2 AC 572

The appeal considered a number of cases where employees had died from mesothelioma as a result of exposure to asbestos dust in the workplace. In cases where all the exposure resulted from negligent sources, the actions were brought against the remaining solvent defendants, and these defendants had been found jointly and severally liable (i.e. for the full value of each claim) even though there were other parties who also exposed the deceased to asbestos but who could not be sued as they were insolvent. In one case, the disease was contracted from exposure in three distinct periods: first whilst working for a company that was insolvent by the time the action was commenced, the second whilst working for the defendant, and the third whilst self-employed. It was held at first instance and in the Court of Appeal that the defendant was jointly and severally liable but that there should be a 20 per cent deduction for the deceased's contributory negligence while self-employed. The defendants in all the cases appealed against the finding that liability imposed under the *Fairchild* principle was joint and several, arguing that the liability should only be proportionate to the risk that was created by their negligence (in most cases, the proportion of time spent working for the defendant as contrasted with the deceased's total exposure).

Lord Hoffmann

The Limits of *Fairchild v Glenhaven Funeral Services Ltd* [2003] 1 AC 32

5 My Lords, the opinions of all of your Lordships who heard *Fairchild* expressed concern, in varying degrees, that the new exception should not be allowed to swallow up the rule. It is only natural that, the dyke having been breached, the pressure of a sea of claimants should try to enlarge the gap. Indeed, an attempt to extend the principle of liability for increasing the likelihood of an unfavourable outcome to the whole of medical negligence was narrowly rejected in *Gregg v Scott* [2005] 2 AC 176. But each member of the Committee in *Fairchild* stated the limits of what he thought the case was deciding in slightly different terms...

11 The assistance which can be derived from these various formulations is limited. No one expressly adverted to the case in which the claimant was himself responsible for a significant exposure. Lord Bingham's formulation requires that all possible sources of asbestos should have involved breaches of duty to the claimant; Lord Rodger allowed for a non-tortious exposure by a defendant who was also responsible for a tortious exposure but reserved his position on any other non-tortious exposure. The most that can be said of the others is that they did not formulate the issue in terms which excluded the possibility of liability when there had been non-tortious exposures...

17 It should not...matter whether the person who caused the non-tortious exposure happened also to have caused a tortious exposure. The purpose of the *Fairchild* exception is to provide a cause of action against a defendant who has materially increased the risk that the claimant will suffer damage and may have caused that damage, but cannot be proved to have done so because it is impossible to show, on a balance of probability, that some other exposure to the same risk may not have caused it instead. For this purpose, it should be irrelevant whether the other exposure was tortious or non-tortious, by natural causes or human agency or by the claimant himself. These distinctions may be relevant to whether and to whom responsibility can also be attributed, but from the point of view of satisfying the requirement of a sufficient causal link between the defendant's conduct and the claimant's injury, they should not matter. On this point I am therefore in agreement with Moses J and the Court of Appeal.

Creating a Risk as Damage

35 Consistency of approach would suggest that if the basis of liability is the wrongful creation of a risk or chance of causing the disease, the damage which the defendant should be

regarded as having caused is the creation of such a risk or chance. If that is the right way to characterise the damage, then it does not matter that the disease as such would be indivisible damage. Chances are infinitely divisible and different people can be separately responsible to a greater or lesser degree for the chances of an event happening, in the way that a person who buys a whole book of tickets in a raffle has a separate and larger chance of winning the prize than a person who has bought a single ticket.

36 Treating the creation of the risk as the damage caused by the defendant would involve having to quantify the likelihood that the damage (which is known to have materialised) was caused by that particular defendant. It will then be possible to determine the share of the damage which should be attributable to him. The quantification of chances is by no means unusual in the courts. For example, in quantifying the damage caused by an indivisible injury, such as a fractured limb, it may be necessary to quantify the chances of future complications. Sometimes the law treats the loss of a chance of a favourable outcome as compensatable damage in itself. The likelihood that the favourable outcome would have happened must then be quantified: see, for example, *Chaplin v Hicks* [1911] 2 KB 786 and *Kitchen v Royal Air Force Association* [1958] 1 WLR 563.

37 These are of course cases in which there is uncertainty as to what will be, or would have been, the outcome of a known event; for example, the consequences of a fractured ankle, a beauty contest or a lawsuit. The present case involves uncertainty as to the cause of a known outcome, namely, the mesothelioma. But in principle I can see no reason why the courts cannot quantify the chances of X having been the cause of Y just as well as the chance of Y being the outcome of X . . .

Fairness

40 So far I have been concerned to demonstrate that characterising the damage as the risk of contracting mesothelioma would be in accordance with the basis upon which liability is imposed and would not be inconsistent with the concept of damage in the law of torts. In the end, however, the important question is whether such a characterisation would be fair. The *Fairchild* exception was created because the alternative of leaving the claimant with no remedy was thought to be unfair. But does fairness require that he should recover in full from any defendant liable under the exception? . . .

43 In my opinion, the attribution of liability according to the relative degree of contribution to the chance of the disease being contracted would smooth the roughness of the justice which a rule of joint and several liability creates. The defendant was a wrongdoer, it is true, and should not be allowed to escape liability altogether, but he should not be liable for more than the damage which he caused and, since this is a case in which science can deal only in probabilities, the law should accept that position and attribute liability according to probabilities. The justification for the joint and several liability rule is that if you caused harm, there is no reason why your liability should be reduced because someone else also caused the same harm. But when liability is exceptionally imposed because you may have caused harm, the same considerations do not apply and fairness suggests that if more than one person may have been responsible, liability should be divided according to the probability that one or other caused the harm . . .

Quantification

48 Although the *Fairchild* exception treats the risk of contracting mesothelioma as the damage, it applies only when the disease has actually been contracted. Mr Stuart-Smith, who appeared for Corus, was reluctant to characterise the claim as being for causing a risk of the disease because he did not want to suggest that someone could sue for being exposed to a risk which had not materialised. But in cases which fall within the *Fairchild* exception, that possibility is precluded by the terms of the exception. It applies only when the claimant has

contracted the disease against which he should have been protected. And in cases outside the exception, as in *Gregg v Scott* [2005] 2 AC 176, a risk of damage or loss of a chance is not damage upon which an action can be founded. But when the damage is apportioned among the persons responsible for the exposures to asbestos which created the risk, it is known that those exposures were together sufficient to cause the disease. The damages which would have been awarded against a defendant who had actually caused the disease must be apportioned to the defendants according to their contributions to the risk. It may be that the most practical method of apportionment will be according to the time of exposure for which each defendant is responsible, but allowance may have to be made for the intensity of exposure and the type of asbestos. These questions are not before the House and it is to be hoped that the parties, their insurers and advisers will devise practical and economical criteria for dealing with them...

Lord Scott of Foscote

53 It is essential, in my opinion, to an appreciation of the effect of the *Fairchild* decision to keep firmly in mind that liability was not imposed on any of the defendant employers on the ground that the employer's breach of duty had caused the mesothelioma that its former employee had contracted. That causative link had not been proved against any of them. It was imposed because each, by its breach of duty, had materially increased the risk that the employee would contract mesothelioma. That, coupled with the fact that mesothelioma had been contracted and that it was not possible to tell when the fatal inhalation had taken place, justified, in their Lordships' view, the imposition of liability on each employer who had contributed to the risk...

57 My Lords, the importance of *Gregg v Scott* for present purposes is that *Fairchild* was treated as an exception to the normal requirement of a proved causative link between the breach of duty and the damage for which tortious damages are claimed. *Fairchild* is explained as a pragmatic judicial response to what would otherwise have been an unjust and unsatisfactory denial of a remedy to a mesothelioma sufferer whose disease had been caused by one or other of a number of wrongdoers (in the sense of persons shown to have been in breach of duty) each of whose breach of duty may have caused the disease, and could not be shown not to have done so, but could not be shown to have done so. *Fairchild* cannot, therefore, be taken to have established an overarching principle in the law of tort...

Lord Rodger of Earlsferry (dissenting on this point)

85 The new analysis which the House is adopting will tend to maximise the inconsistencies in the law by turning the *Fairchild* exception into an enclave where a number of rules apply which have been rejected for use elsewhere in the law of personal injuries. Inside the enclave victims recover damages for suffering the increased risk of developing mesothelioma (or suffering the loss of a chance of not developing mesothelioma) while, just outside, patients cannot recover damages for suffering the increased risk of an unfavourable outcome to medical treatment (or suffering the loss of a chance of a favourable outcome to medical treatment). On the other hand, if such a claim had been recognised outside the enclave, the patient would have been entitled to recover damages for the increased likelihood that he would suffer a premature death, whereas inside the enclave a victim who suffers an increased risk of developing mesothelioma cannot recover damages unless he actually develops it. Inside the enclave claimants whose husbands die of mesothelioma receive only, say, 60% of their damages if the court considers that there is a 60% chance that the defendant caused the death and no other wrongdoer is solvent or insured. Outside the enclave, claimants whose husbands are killed in an accident for which the only solvent defendant is, say, 5% to blame recover the whole of their damages from that defendant.

86 Why, then, is the House spontaneously embarking upon this adventure of redefining the nature of the damage suffered by the victims? The majority are not just on a mission to tidy up the reasoning in *McGhee* and *Fairchild*. Their aim is to open the way to making each defendant severally liable for a share of the damages, rather than liable in *solidum* for the whole of the damages. This is said to be a preferable, fairer, solution when the defendants are found liable for creating the risk of illness rather than for causing it.

87 Certainly, as a matter of legal logic, it would be open to the House to hold that since on the reasoning in *McGhee* and *Fairchild* the defendants are ultimately held liable for materially contributing to the victims' mesothelioma, they should be held liable in *solidum* like any other concurrent tortfeasors whose separate wrongful acts combine to produce indivisible harm. That was indeed one of the main submissions for the claimants—and I would accept it. Mr Stuart-Smith countered by arguing that, since the *Fairchild* exception involved adjusting the rules on causation, so equally the House should be prepared to adjust the rules on liability and apportion it among the defendants. That would be a powerful argument indeed if there were actually any logical or otherwise compelling connection between the *Fairchild* exception and the introduction of several liability which the defendants seek. In truth, there is not.

88 So long as all the defendants and possible defendants are solvent or insured, the application of liability in *solidum* causes them no problems and makes life simple for the claimant. A defendant or insurer who pays the claimant's damages can recover the appropriate contribution from the other defendants and their insurers under the Civil Liability (Contribution) Act 1978. In asbestosis cases insurers have been operating such a system among themselves for decades, with contributions being based on the claimant or pursuer's periods of work with various employers. And, following the judgment of the House in *Fairchild* which, in the absence of argument, provided for joint and several liability, insurers introduced a somewhat similar scheme for mesothelioma cases in England and Wales in their *Guidelines for Apportioning and Handling Employers' Liability Mesothelioma Claims* (28 October 2003).

89 ... [T]he real reason why the defendants want to get rid of liability in *solidum* is that quite a number of the potential defendants and their insurers in the field of mesothelioma claims are insolvent. So, if held liable in *solidum*, solvent defendants or, more particularly, their insurers will often find that they have to pay the whole of the claimant's damages without in fact being able to obtain a contribution from the other wrongdoers or their insurers, if any. So their only hope of minimising the amount they have to pay out by way of damages is to have liability to the claimant apportioned among the wrongdoers. Therefore they are asking for the introduction of apportionment because of this entirely contingent aspect of the situation regarding mesothelioma claims. If *Fairchild*-exception claims had first arisen in an area where the wrongdoers and their insurers were in good financial heart, matters could have been resolved satisfactorily for all concerned on the basis of liability in *solidum* and the use of the Civil Liability (Contribution) Act 1978.

90 Of course, it may seem hard if a defendant is held liable in *solidum* even though all that can be shown is that he made a material contribution to the risk that the victim would develop mesothelioma. But it is also hard—and settled law—that a defendant is held liable in *solidum* even though all that can be shown is that he made a material, say 5%, contribution to the claimant's indivisible injury. That is a form of rough justice which the law has not hitherto sought to smooth, preferring instead, as a matter of policy, to place the risk of the insolvency of a wrongdoer or his insurer on the other wrongdoers and their insurers. Now the House is deciding that, in this particular enclave of the law, the risk of the insolvency of a wrongdoer or his insurer is to bypass the other wrongdoers and their insurers and to be shouldered entirely by the innocent claimant. As a result, claimants will often end up with only a small proportion of the damages which would normally be payable for their loss. The desirability of the courts, rather than Parliament, throwing this lifeline to wrongdoers and their insurers at the expense of claimants is not obvious to me ...

COMMENTARY

As noted above (p. 226), the House of Lords in this trilogy of cases recognised an exceptional principle of liability for materially contributing to (i.e. increasing) the risk of the claimant suffering injury. But the first case of the trilogy, *McGhee*, was not immediately recognised as making a radical break with the ordinary requirement of proof of a causal connection between the defendant's tortious conduct and the claimant's injury. In fact, its importance was rather downplayed when the Law Lords had the opportunity to consider it in another case of causal indeterminacy, *Wilsher v Essex Area Health Authority* [1988] AC 1074. There the infant plaintiff was born prematurely and suffered from oxygen deficiency. In treating him, the hospital staff negligently inserted a catheter into his vein rather than his artery, causing the administration of excessive amounts of oxygen. The plaintiff was later found to be afflicted by an incurable condition of the retina which resulted in his virtual blindness. The condition could have been caused by the excess oxygen but it could alternatively have been caused by any one of four other, completely different risks to which the plaintiff was also exposed. At the trial of his action, medical evidence was inconclusive as to whether the excess oxygen caused or even materially contributed to the blindness. The action succeeded at first instance and a majority of the Court of Appeal [1987] QB 730, relying on *McGhee*, affirmed the judgment on the basis that the hospital could be taken as having caused the injury notwithstanding that the existence and extent of the contribution made by its breach of duty could not be ascertained. Sir Nicolas Browne-Wilkinson V-C dissented as he considered that '[a] failure to take preventive measures against one out of five possible causes is no evidence as to which of those five caused the injury' (at 779). The House of Lords allowed the health authority's appeal, Lord Bridge (who delivered the only substantial speech) stating that he was unable to find fault with Sir Nicolas Browne-Wilkinson's dissent. His Lordship also held that *McGhee* was authority for no new proposition of law and was the result of a 'robust inference' of causation from the established facts of the case.

In *Fairchild* the House of Lords expressly rejected Lord Bridge's rationalisation of *McGhee* and held that it had indeed recognised a new principle of law (Lord Hutton dissenting on this point), but accepted that *Wilsher* was correctly decided on its facts. There is a risk of confusion here, however, as the *McGhee* principle borrows the terminology of 'material contribution' that had previously been employed in *Wardlaw's case* (a confusion that seems to appear in the recent decision of the Supreme Court of Canada in *Resurfice Corp v Hanke* [2007] SCC 7; see Tse (2008) 16 TLJ 249)). What must be noted is that, in *Wardlaw*, the breach of duty had materially contributed to the pursuer's disease (by making it worse), but in *McGhee* and *Fairchild* all that could be said was that the breach of duty had materially contributed to *the risk* of developing the disease. There was, as Lord Wilberforce put it in *McGhee*, an 'evidential gap' that made it impossible to draw the inference that the breach of duty had caused any harm at all. The decisions in both *Fairchild* and *Barker* confirm *McGhee* as a very radical decision which allows claimants to bridge that evidential gap and recover damages even though they cannot satisfy the orthodox requirements of causation.

Increase in Risk as an Injury

In both *McGhee* and *Fairchild* the claimant was able to use the defendant's responsibility for increasing the risk that the claimant might suffer an injury as sufficient to establish causation for the injury that ultimately resulted. However, what if the claimant can establish that (1) the defendant has increased the risk of the claimant suffering a particular injury; (2) the injury has not yet occurred; and (3) the claimant has incurred costs to determine whether the injury has occurred or to take steps to prevent it from occurring. Should the claimant be able to recover for these costs? In *Rothwell v Chemical & Insulating Co Ltd* [2008] AC 281 (discussed above at p. 222) the House of Lords rejected the notion that risk itself was compensatable but it has recently been suggested that the economic costs associated with exposure to risk, such as medical costs associated with alleviating or monitoring the risks, or the additional insurance costs borne by the claimant as a result of the increased risk of injury, are recoverable, at least if they are significant (Voyiakis (2009) 72 MLR 909). If fear, and even psychiatric harm, attributable to the creation of the risk are not recoverable (as held in *Rothwell*), is there any reason why economic costs associated with the risk should be recoverable? Moreover, if there are uncertainties in the causal link between the risk and the injury resulting from the materialisation of that risk (such as the link between asbestos dust and mesotehelioma), should a claimant be entitled to all the economic costs associated with the risk or a reduced amount to reflect the possibility that the monitoring costs were not attributable to the defendant's conduct? See further Fleming, 'Preventive Damages', in Mullaney (ed), *Torts in the Nineties* (LBC Information Services, 1997).

Proportionate Damages

In *Fairchild*, the House of Lords was not addressed on the question of proportionate damages, but the issue was raised squarely in *Barker*. A majority of their Lordships decided that, as causation was satisfied by the creation of a risk of injury rather than causing the injury itself—a departure from the orthodox rules of causation—it was appropriate that the extent of a defendant's liability should be limited by the extent of that risk. So in a *Fairchild*-type case, a defendant who was responsible for 50 per cent of the asbestos to which the claimant was exposed would only be liable for 50 per cent of the damages the claimant would have received had causation been proved under ordinary rules. Lord Rodger disagreed: to award proportionate damages would, in effect, be allowing recovery for the loss of a chance, something which had been rejected in *Gregg v Scott*. His Lordship argued that allowing proportionate damages in the *Fairchild*-type case would thus make it an 'enclave' in which special rules applied and would lead to cases being decided differently depending on whether they fell within the 'enclave' or not. Lord Rodger was also motivated by the concern that the creation of proportionate liability shifted the risk of some of the defendants being insolvent onto the claimant: if D1 and D2 were each responsible for creating 50 per cent of the risk and D2 was insolvent at the time of the trial, the claimant only recovered 50 per cent of the damages for the injury. Whilst these criticisms have some force, once it is accepted that the defendant is liable for increasing the risk of injury, it seems natural, unless policy otherwise dictates, to limit the damages to the extent of his contribution to the total risk. Indeed this seems the fairest solution, as it should be recalled that the *McGhee* and *Fairchild* decisions already expose the defendant to a potential injustice in order to avoid a greater injustice to the claimant. Having once tipped the scales in the latter's favour, it is surely going too far to do so again. If the House of Lords had not relaxed the rules of causation, the claimant would have recovered nothing at all and can hardly complain that the concession made to him does not go far enough. Furthermore, awarding full damages would be to heap further injustice on those defendants who (though we can never know it) did not contribute at all to the causal processes producing the disease in question.

The Law Lords' approach accords with a trend towards proportionate liability in cases of causal uncertainty in other European jurisdictions (see, e.g., the decision of the Netherlands

High Court noted by M. Faure and T. Hartlief in *European Tort Law 2006* (Netherlands, no. 22ff)), and with the recommendations of the European Group on Tort Law in its *Principles of European Tort Law* (2005):

Art. 3:103. Alternative causes

(1) In case of multiple activities, where each of them alone would have been sufficient to cause the damage, but it remains uncertain which one in fact caused it, each activity is regarded as a cause to the extent corresponding to the likelihood that it may have caused the victim's damage.

(2) If, in case of multiple victims, it remains uncertain whether a particular victim's damage has been caused by an activity, while it is likely that it did not cause the damage of all victims, the activity is regarded as a cause of the damage suffered by all victims in proportion to the likelihood that it may have caused the damage of a particular victim...

Art. 3:106. Uncertain causes within the victim's sphere

The victim has to bear his loss to the extent corresponding to the likelihood that it may have been caused by an activity, occurrence or other circumstance within his own sphere.

This is a proposal for a general, not merely exceptional, liability on a proportional basis in cases in cases of causal uncertainty. What do you think would be the implications for English law if such a liability were introduced there?

Compensation Act 2006, s. 3

Whatever the theoretical merits of imposing only proportionate liability under the *Fairchild* principle for mesothelioma victims, the decision in *Barker* sparked a wave of protest from victims. The result was that the Compensation Bill which was then before Parliament—and had not been concerned directly with the issue—was amended so as to reverse *Barker*'s effect. Section 3 of the Compensation Act 2006 now provides:

(1) This section applies where—
   (a) a person ('the responsible person') has negligently or in breach of statutory duty caused or permitted another person ('the victim') to be exposed to asbestos,
   (b) the victim has contracted mesothelioma as a result of exposure to asbestos,
   (c) because of the nature of mesothelioma and the state of medical science, it is not possible to determine with certainty whether it was the exposure mentioned in paragraph (a) or another exposure which caused the victim to become ill, and
   (d) the responsible person is liable in tort, by virtue of the exposure mentioned in paragraph (a), in connection with damage caused to the victim by the disease (whether by reason of having materially increased a risk or for any other reason).

(2) The responsible person shall be liable—
   (a) in respect of the whole of the damage caused to the victim by the disease (irrespective of whether the victim was also exposed to asbestos—
      (i) other than by the responsible person, whether or not in circumstances in which another person has liability in tort, or
      (ii) by the responsible person in circumstances in which he has no liability in tort), and
   (b) jointly and severally with any other responsible person.

(3) Subsection (2) does not prevent—
   (a) one responsible person from claiming a contribution from another, or
   (b) a finding of contributory negligence.

(4) In determining the extent of contributions of different responsible persons in accordance with subsection (3)(a), a court shall have regard to the relative lengths of the periods of exposure for which each was responsible; but this subsection shall not apply—

  (a) if or to the extent that responsible persons agree to apportion responsibility amongst themselves on some other basis, or

  (b) if or to the extent that the court thinks that another basis for determining contributions is more appropriate in the circumstances of a particular case...

The result, in effect, is that, if the conditions for imposing liability set out in *Fairchild* are met (see s. 3(1)), the 'responsible person' who is found liable for the exposure is liable in respect of the whole of the damage irrespective of the existence of other sources of exposure, whether from other responsible persons, other non-tortious sources, or the claimant's own actions (although a deduction for contributory negligence is possible: s. 3(3)(b)). This is so even if it is in theory possible for the claimant to prove causation on the traditional balance of probability standard; it has been held that s. 3 enshrines in statute the *Fairchild* requirements for all mesothelioma cases falling within its provisions (see *Sienkiewicz v Grief (UK) Ltd* [2009] EWCA Civ 1159). Responsible persons may claim contribution from other responsible persons and, as provided for by s. 3(7) (not extracted), regulations have been passed to allow a responsible person, if it appears other responsible persons are insolvent, to make a claim on the compensation scheme established under the Financial Services and Markets Act 2000 which currently guarantees payments in the event of an insurer's insolvency generally (see Compensation Act 2006 (Contribution for Mesothelioma Claims) Regulations 2006, SI 2006/3259).

As a result of s. 3, the impact of *Barker* is greatly reduced; it will apply only where the *Fairchild* principle takes effect outside the context of asbestos-induced mesothelioma. Can you give examples of cases covered by the *Fairchild* principle *other than* mesothelioma? (See, e.g., *Novartis Grimsby Ltd v Cookson* [2007] EWCA Civ 1261, [72]–[73] per Smith LJ.)

Conditions for Application of the Doctrine

The limits of the *McGhee/Fairchild* doctrine were set out in *Barker*. It is not necessary that each exposure should be tortious (as was assumed in *Fairchild*) nor that the total exposure should be the result of the same party's conduct, even if some of the exposure was non-tortious (as in *McGhee*). As Lord Hoffmann makes clear, the *Fairchild* exception applies irrespective of whether the other exposures (i.e. the exposure other than that resulting from the defendant's negligence) were tortious or non-tortious, by natural causes or human agency or by the claimant himself. Whilst the policy arguments for relaxing the ordinary rules of causation are certainly strong where all sources of exposure are tortious as the claimant may otherwise 'fall between two guilty tortfeasors' (Fleming, 'Probabilistic Causation in Tort Law' (1989) 68 Can Bar Rev 661; see further, p. 247, below), there seems little reason to distinguish cases depending on the source of the other risks to which the claimant was exposed if liability is based on the creation of a risk (but note Lord Rodger's views (at [100]) on where the claimant was exposed due to his own carelessness).

A Single Agent?

In both *McGhee* and *Fairchild*, the agent that caused the disease (brick dust/asbestos dust) was the agent to which the defendant negligently exposed the plaintiff. This was not the case in *Wilsher*, where it was unknown which of five possible agents was the cause of the condition.

Both Lord Rodger in *Fairchild* and Lord Hoffmann in *Barker* treated this as the distinguishing feature of *Wilsher*. Indeed, Lord Hoffmann, who in *Fairchild* doubted whether the 'single agent' theory was a satisfactory ground of distinction, changed his view in *Barker* and admitted that it was hard to see how *Wilsher* did not fall within the *McGhee/Fairchild* principle unless it was because there were a number of causative agents. It appears, however, that the principle can apply even if the agents are not identical but operate in the same or substantially the same way. It is clear that *Wilsher* is not seen as a case involving a 'similar' agency but their Lordships give no further indication of what a 'substantially similar' agency might be. As Miller, 'Causation in personal injury: legal or epidemilogical common sense?' (2006) 26 LS 544 at 563 argues: 'The most obvious form of similarity—similar capacity to bring about a given injury—must be excluded if the *McGhee/Wilsher* distinction is to survive, because that is precisely what obtained in *Wilsher*, one tortious and four non-tortious mechanisms, each by itself capable of causing retrolental fibroplasia'. Neither did their Lordships indicate why the usual rules of causation should be relaxed in 'similar agency' cases and not in others: if policy grounds justify their relaxation in *McGhee/Fairchild*, why not in *Wilsher*? Are sufferers of industrial diseases to be treated better than victims of medical negligence? (For reasons why this might be justifiable, see Stauch [2009] CLJ 27.) In any case, the 'substantially similar' agency test provides no reason for distinguishing *McGhee* from *Hotson*, of which their Lordships in *Fairchild* made scarcely a mention; in *Barker*, Lord Scott held, curiously, that it was a case involving different agents. In *Hotson*, it will be recalled, the cause of the plaintiff's avascular necrosis was a lack of blood to the femoral epiphysis. The plaintiff's fall was responsible for some of the blood deprivation to the epiphysis, but the period of blood deprivation was extended by the defendant's negligent failure to diagnose and treat. So the defendant's negligence increased the plaintiff's exposure to the same risk as had been created by the fall. Compare the facts of *McGhee*, where the original exposure to the brick dust was innocent but extended in point of time by the defendant's breach of duty. Both cases therefore involved a 'single agency'. Perhaps the real reason for excluding *Hotson* from the operation of the *Fairchild/McGhee* principle is the reluctance, evidenced in *Gregg v Scott*, to extend the principle to medical negligence cases, no doubt because of the perceived expansion in liability that such an extension would create (see Spencer [2006] CLJ 282). But is this a satisfactory ground on which to distinguish the cases?

An Evidential Gap?

It is clear than an important factor in both *McGhee* and *Fairchild* was the existence of an 'evidential gap' which prevented the plaintiff from satisfying the orthodox requirements of causation. The key question, of course, is how such a gap is to be distinguished from a mere inability to prove causation, as was apparently the case in *Hotson*, *Wilsher* and *Gregg*.

One possible line of argument, a version of which was expounded by Lord Nicholls in *Gregg v Scott*, is to distinguish between 'general' aetiological uncertainty, where medical science is uncertain of the potential causes of the condition in question, and uncertainty which is personal to the claimant. In *Hotson*, for example, it was known how the avascular necrosis was caused, and the only uncertainty was whether the plaintiff's condition was irreversible at the time when he should have been treated. This was a matter which could be addressed by evidence particular to the plaintiff's own situation, rather than general scientific speculation about the causes of the disease, and it could be resolved by the judge's view of the probabilities in the individual case (for an application of this line of reasoning, see *Hull v Sanderson* [2008] EWCA Civ 1211). The same was true in *Wilsher*: the potential causes of the plaintiff's blindness were known, but it was uncertain which one was operative on the facts. By contrast, in both *McGhee* and *Fairchild* there was uncertainty about the potential causes of the claimants' condition: could the dermatitis/mesothelioma be caused by a single exposure or only by cumulative exposure? If this distinction between 'general' and 'personal' uncertainty should be accepted, it would provide a solution to the problem that the *McGhee/Fairchild* principle might place claimants in a win/win situation whereby they could first try their luck at establishing orthodox causation so as to recover full damages, and then, if unsuccessful, simply reformulate their claim as one for materially increasing the risk of injury. Under our approach, if there is 'general aetiological uncertainty', the court should treat it as impossible to satisfy the orthodox causation requirements, and limit liability to proportionate damages (under *McGhee/Fairchild*) in every case. Conversely, where the uncertainty is 'personal', the *McGhee/Fairchild* doctrine should not apply, there should be no entitlement to proportionate damages, and the claimant should be left to satisfy the 'all-or-nothing' requirements of orthodox causation. In neither situation would the claimant's prospects be win/win.

Whatever the merits of this argument, however, the decision in *Gregg v Scott* seems to preclude its application as a general rule in cases of scientific uncertainty. Lord Nicholls' view was not accepted by the majority, partly on the ground that there was, in principle, no scientific uncertainty (see the speech of Lord Hoffmann, extracted above). The problem was 'personal' uncertainty. But it is also clear, as illustrated by the speeches in *Barker*, that their Lordships see the *McGhee/Fairchild* exception as of very limited application. As Lord Rodger pointed out in *Barker*, this results in differential treatment of claimants and defendants depending on whether the case can be interpreted as one to which the *McGhee/Fairchild* principle applies. The anomaly is greater when it is recognised, as Lord Hoffmann does in his speech in *Barker*, that 'increase in risk' and 'loss of a chance' are different ways of expressing the same idea. Thus, according to Lord Hoffmann, the House of Lords in *Gregg* did not dismiss the claim because the damage was framed as the loss of a chance but because *that* damage was not recoverable on the facts of the case. Lord Hoffmann in *Barker* suggested that this was because to extend the *McGhee/Fairchild* principle to medical negligence would be inconsistent with *Wilsher*, but if the principle is limited to 'single' agents this was clearly an alternative ground on which to distinguish *Wilsher*. Rather, it seems the principal justification for excluding cases of medical negligence is simply pragmatic.

Assuming that the subject matter of the *McGhee/Fairchild* principle is limited, one question that remains is whether the principle applies only to scientific uncertainty or to cases of personal uncertainty as well. If the single fibre theory had been accepted as correct in *Fairchild* and the general aetiology of mesothelioma thus regarded as certain, would the difficulty that the claimant had in proving which of the defendants was responsible for the fibre that caused the mesothelioma have been sufficient to justify a relaxation of the ordinary causation requirement? If the exception only applies to cases of scientific uncertainty, we would argue that there are cases where the need to prevent the claimant falling between two tortfeasors warrants the application of the *McGhee/Fairchild* principle to cases of personal uncertainty (see 'The Problem of the Indeterminate Defendant', below). A distinction may need to be drawn here between cases where all the sources of exposure are tortious and those in which only some are tortious. In the latter—for example, where the claimant's own negligence resulted in some exposure—there is less reason to relieve the claimant of the ordinary evidential burden because the claimant's injury could have resulted from an innocent source. However, where all sources of exposure are tortious, our view is that the claimant should be able to recover proportionate damages against each defendant on the basis that each has materially contributed to the risk of his contracting the disease. Furthermore, there is even a case for allowing the claimant, as an alternative, to establish causation of the injury according to orthodox principles. Where he can prove that one particular defendant was more likely than not the source of the single guilty fibre, it is arguable that he should be entitled to claim from him the full quantum of damages. In practice, this would be the desirable claim if one or more of the other defendants contributing to the risk were untraceable or insolvent. Even if this results in a win/win scenario for the claimant, it may be justified on the basis that we know him to have been tortiously injured, and therefore entitled to full compensation for his injury, and it would be unfair if he lost out on his entitlement because one or more of those who have breached their duty towards him should be untraceable or insolvent. Better to leave the defendant who, on the balance of probabilities, caused the harm to pick up the bill. As the next section discusses, it is in this situation—that of the 'indeterminate defendant'—that courts have been most willing to relax the usual rules of causation in favour of the claimant.

The Problem of the Indeterminate Defendant

In this final section, we consider various approaches taken by the courts, here and in other jurisdictions, in cases which raise what Fleming has called the problem of the 'indeterminate defendant' (*American Tort Process* (Oxford: OUP, 1988), p. 261). This arises where two or more defendants have acted tortiously towards the claimant, who suffers injury as a result but cannot determine whose tort was the cause. By this definition, *Fairchild* is a case of indeterminate defendants but *McGhee* and the case of the periodically self-employed deceased in *Barker* were not.

A much-discussed example is the 'two hunters' scenario which was discussed by several members of the House of Lords in *Fairchild*. In *Summers v Tice* 199 P 2d 1 (1948), the plaintiff was shot by one of two defendants, each of whom had shot negligently in the plaintiff's direction at roughly the same time. Rejecting an argument that neither was liable because the plaintiff could not prove which of them had fired the guilty bullet, the Supreme Court of California upheld his claim on the basis of a theory of 'alternative liability'. Although only one of the defendants had actually caused the plaintiff's injury, they were equally culpable and the impossibility of anyone else determining who fired the fatal shot meant that it should rest with each of the defendants to absolve himself if he could. See also the factually similar *Cook v Lewis* [1951] SCR 830 where the Supreme Court of Canada adopted comparable reasoning. In fact, in *Fairchild*, following a review of decisions in both civil and common law worlds, Lord Bingham concluded (at [32]) that most jurisdictions would afford a remedy to the claimant in equivalent circumstances.

The decision of the Court of Appeal in *Fitzgerald v Lane* [1987] QB 781 may rest on the same underlying considerations, although the factual circumstances were different. There, a pedestrian was hit successively by two cars whilst crossing the road and subsequently suffered tetraplegia. It could not be determined whether this resulted from the first or the second collision. A straightforward application of the but-for test would have left the plaintiff without a remedy, but the Court of Appeal, by a majority, followed *McGhee* and held both drivers liable. As Fleming has noted, '[i]t is arguable that the plaintiff's equities here overwhelmed the defendants', for...both defendants were negligent so that neither could contend that to allow recovery would conceivably give the plaintiff a windfall' ('Probabalistic Causation in Tort Law' (1989) 68 Can Bar Rev 661). If this is correct, would (or should) the result of *Hotson* have been different if the original injury had been caused by his friend carelessly pushing him off the tree rather than his falling off himself, and both the potential defendants were before the court? If the *McGhee/Fairchild* principle only results in an award of proportionate damages, can the imposition of joint and several liability in such cases be justified?

The problem of the indeterminate defendant also arises in more complicated factual situations. In the American case of *Sindell v Abbot Laboratories* 607 P 2d 924 (1980), there were over 200 manufacturers of a drug which was assumed to have caused vaginal cancerous lesions, but because of the long latency period of the cancer it could not be determined which manufacturer had supplied the plaintiff. Any one of the manufacturers could have been responsible (as the defect was in the genetic make-up of the drug). The court held that the five defendants (all the manufacturers) were liable to compensate plaintiffs only in proportion to their respective market shares. For analysis of the *Sindell* reasoning, see R. Goldberg, *Causation and Risk in the Law of Torts* (Oxford: Hart, 1999) ch. 2, especially pp. 60–72, and L. Khoury, *Uncertain Causation in Medical Liability* (Oxford: Hart, 2006), pp. 114–17.

Do you think that the House of Lords' decision in *Fairchild* provides any basis for the introduction of alternative and market-share liability into English law? In his speech in that case, Lord Hoffmann described the *Sindell* solution as 'imaginative' but declined to speculate as to whether it might be adopted in this jurisdiction. He noted, however, that it fell outside the scope of the *McGhee/Fairchild* principle because 'the existence of the additional manufacturers did not materially increase the risk of injury. The risk from consuming a drug bought in one shop is not increased by the fact that it can also be bought in another shop' (at 130). For a general discussion on the use of statistics in these cases, see Miller, 'Causation in personal injury: legal or epidemiological common sense?' (2006) 26 LS 544.

3. Multiple Sufficient Causes

What happens when the claimant is injured by the defendant's negligence, but, before the trial, an unrelated supervening event occurs which would have caused the claimant the same loss for which he is suing the defendant? At first glance this might be thought a matter relating to damages: the defendant has clearly caused the claimant some damage (i.e. from the date of the tort to the date of the supervening event) so the issue is how much the defendant has to pay. However, the issue has often been addressed in terms of causation. If the defendant's negligence can still be seen as a cause despite the supervening event, it might not seem unfair to hold the defendant liable for the initial injury for the period after the supervening event. Yet whether or not the defendant is regarded as a cause of the plaintiff's continuing injuries, even in respect of the period after the supervening event, the question arises whether it is fair to hold him liable for an injury that the claimant would have sustained anyway. These issues are considered in the extracts below.

Baker v Willoughby [1970] AC 467

The plaintiff was injured in a car accident, which resulted in injury to his left leg and stiffness in his right ankle. Before the trial in respect of this accident, the plaintiff was working in a scrap-metal yard when he was shot by two robbers, which resulted in his left leg being amputated. One issue for the House of Lords was whether the defendant responsible for the original car accident was liable for the damage caused by that accident after the date of the second tort (the shooting). The facts are stated more fully in the speech of Lord Reid.

Lord Reid

The second question is more difficult. It relates to the proper measure of damages. The car accident occurred on 12 September 1964. The trial took place on 26 February 1968. But meanwhile, on 29 November 1967, the appellant had sustained a further injury and the question is whether or to what extent the damages which would otherwise have been awarded in respect of the car accident must be reduced by reason of the occurrence of this second injury.

There is no doubt that it is proper to lead evidence at the trial as to any events or developments between the date of the accident and the date of the trial which are relevant for the proper assessment of damages. The plaintiff may have died (*Williamson v John I Thornycroft & Co., Ltd* [1940] 2 KB 658); or the needs of the widow (*Curwen v James* [1963] 1 WLR 748) or of the children (*Mead v Clarke Chapman & Co, Ltd* [1956] 1 WLR 76) may have become less because of her marriage. And it is always proper to take account of developments with regard to the injuries which were caused by the defendant's tort; those developments may show that any assessment of damages that might have been made shortly after the accident can now be seen to be either too small or too large. The question here is how far it is proper to take into account the effects of a second injury which was in no way connected with the first.

As a result of the car accident the appellant sustained fairly severe injury to his left leg and ankle, with the result that his ankle was stiff and his condition might get worse. So he suffered pain, loss of such amenities of life as depend on ability to move freely and a certain loss of earning capacity. The trial judge did not deal with these matters separately. He assessed the whole damage at £1,600 and making allowance for the appellant's contributory negligence awarded £1,200 with minor special damage. After the accident the appellant tried various kinds of work, finding some too heavy by reason of his partial incapacity. In November 1967 he was engaged in sorting scrap metal and while he was alone one day two men came in, demanded money, and, when they did not get it, one of them shot at him. The shot inflicted such serious injuries to his already damaged leg that it had to be amputated. Apparently he made a fairly good recovery but his disability is now rather greater than it would have been if he had not suffered this second injury. He now has an artificial limb whereas he would have had a stiff leg.

The appellant argues that the loss which he suffered from the car accident has not been diminished by his second injury. He still suffers from reduced capacity to earn although these may have been to some extent increased. And he will still suffer these losses for as long as he would have done because it is not said that the second injury curtailed his expectation of life. The respondent on the other hand argues that the second injury removed the very limb from which the earlier disability had stemmed, and that therefore no loss suffered thereafter can be attributed to the respondent's negligence. He says that the second injury submerged or obliterated the effect of the first and that all loss thereafter must be attributed to the second injury. The trial judge rejected this argument which he said was more ingenious than attractive. But it was accepted by the Court of Appeal.

The respondent's argument was succinctly put to your Lordships by his counsel. He could not run before the second injury; he cannot run now. But the cause is now quite different. The former cause was an injured leg but now he has no leg and the former cause can no longer operate. His counsel was inclined to agree that if the first injury had caused some neurosis or other mental disability, that disability might be regarded as still flowing from the first accident; even if it had been increased by the second accident the respondent might still have to pay for that part which he caused. I agree with that and I think that any distinction between a neurosis and a physical injury depends on a wrong view of what is the proper subject for compensation. A man is not compensated for the physical injury; he is compensated for the loss which he suffers as a result of that injury. His loss is not in having a stiff leg; it is in his inability to lead a full life, his inability to enjoy those amenities which depend on freedom of movement and his inability to earn as much as he used to earn or could have earned if there had been no accident. In this case the second injury did not diminish any of these. So why should it be regarded as having obliterated or superseded them?

If it were the case that in the eye of the law an effect could only have one cause then the respondent might be right. It is always necessary to prove that any loss for which damages can be given was caused by the defendant's negligent act. But it is commonplace that the law regards many events as having two causes; that happens whenever there is contributory negligence, for then the law says that the injury was caused both by the negligence of the defendant and by the negligence of the plaintiff. And generally it does not matter which negligence occurred first in point of time. . . .

[There is a] general rule that a wrongdoer must take the plaintiff (or his property) as he finds him; that may be to his advantage or disadvantage. In the present case the robber is not responsible or liable for the damage caused by the respondent; he would only have to pay for additional loss to the appellant by reason of his now having an artificial limb instead of a stiff leg. . . .

If the later injury suffered before the date of the trial either reduces the disabilities from the injury for which the defendant is liable, or shortens the period during which they will be suffered by the plaintiff then the defendant will have to pay less damages. But if the later injuries merely become a concurrent cause of the disabilities caused by the injury inflicted by the defendant, then in my view they cannot diminish the damages. Suppose that the plaintiff has to spend a month in bed before the trial because of some illness unconnected with the original injury, the defendant cannot say that he does not have to pay anything in respect of that month; during that month the original injuries and the new illness are concurrent causes of his inability to work and that does not reduce the damages. . . .

Lord Pearson

There is a plausible argument for the respondent on the following lines. The original accident, for which the respondent is liable, inflicted on the appellant a permanently injured left ankle, which caused pain from time to time, diminished his mobility and so reduced his earning capacity, and was likely to lead to severe arthritis. The proper figure of damages for those consequences of the accident, as assessed by the judge before making his apportionment, was £1,600. That was the proper figure for those consequences if they were likely to endure for a normal period and run a normal course. But the supervening event, when the robbers shot the appellant in his left leg, necessitated an amputation of the left leg above the knee. The consequences of the original accident therefore have ceased. He no longer suffers pain in his left ankle, because there no longer is a left ankle. He will never have the arthritis. There is no longer any loss of mobility through stiffness or weakness of the left ankle, because it is no longer there. The injury to the left ankle, resulting from the original accident, is not still operating as one of two concurrent causes both producing discomfort and disability. It is not operating at all nor causing anything. The present state of disablement, with the stump and the artificial leg on the left side, was caused wholly by the supervening event and not at all by the original accident. Thus the consequences of the original accident have been submerged and obliterated by the greater consequences of the supervening event.

That is the argument, and it is formidable. But it must not be allowed to succeed, because it produces manifest injustice. The supervening event has not made the appellant less lame nor less disabled nor less deprived of amenities. It has not shortened the period over which he will be suffering. It has made him more lame, more disabled, more deprived of amenities. He should not have less damages through being worse off than might have been expected.

The nature of the injustice becomes apparent if the supervening event is treated as a tort (as indeed it was) and if one envisages the appellant suing the robbers who shot him. They would be entitled, as the saying is, to 'take the plaintiff as they find him' (*Performance Cars Ltd v Abraham* [1962] 1 QB 33). They have not injured and disabled a previously fit and able-bodied man. They have only made an already lame and disabled man more lame and more disabled. Take, for example, the reduction of earnings. The original accident reduced his earnings from x per week to y per week, and the supervening event further reduced them from y per week to z per week. If the respondent's argument is correct, there is, as counsel for the appellant has pointed out, a gap. The appellant recovers from the respondent the x – y not for the whole period of the remainder of his working life, but only for the short period up to the date of the supervening event. The robbers are liable only for the y – z from the date of the supervening event onwards. In the Court of Appeal an ingenious attempt was made to fill the gap by holding that the damages recoverable from the later tortfeasors (the robbers) would include a novel head of damage, viz, the diminution of the appellant's damages recoverable from the original tortfeasor (the respondent). I doubt whether that would be an admissible head of damage; it looks too remote. In any case it would not help the appellant, if the later tortfeasors could not be found or were indigent and uninsured. These later tortfeasors cannot have been insured in respect of the robbery which they committed.

I think a solution of the theoretical problem can be found in cases such as this by taking a comprehensive and unitary view of the damage caused by the original accident. Itemisation of the damages by dividing them into heads and sub-heads is often convenient, but is not essential. In the end judgment is given for a single lump sum of damages and not for a total of items set out under heads and sub-heads. The original accident caused what may be called a 'devaluation' of the plaintiff, in the sense that it produced a general reduction of his capacity to do things, to earn money and to enjoy life. For that devaluation the original tortfeasor should be and remains responsible to the full extent, unless before the assessment of the damages something has happened which either diminishes the devaluation (e.g., if there is an unexpected recovery from some of the adverse effects of the accident) or by shortening the expectation of life diminishes the period over which the plaintiff will suffer from the devaluation. If the supervening event is a tort, the second tortfeasor should be responsible for the additional devaluation caused by him. . . .

Viscount Dilhorne, **Lord Guest** and **Lord Donovan** agreed with Lord Reid.

Appeal allowed.

COMMENTARY

The defendant must take his victim as he finds him. While this might entail paying much larger compensation than was foreseeable (see below under 'Remoteness of Damage'), its corollary is that if the defendant injures an impaired claimant, he is only liable to put the claimant back into the position he was in prior to the commission of the tort, that is to restore him to the same impaired state. A good example is *Performance Cars v Abraham* [1962] 1 QB 33. The defendant negligently drove his car so that it collided with the plaintiff's Rolls Royce, causing minor damage. Two weeks previously the Rolls Royce had been in another minor collision which required a wing of the car to be repainted. The plaintiff's claim for this head of damage was rejected by the Court of Appeal, because the defendant damaged an imperfect car (i.e. one needing a paint job). The defendant was only required to put the plaintiff's car back into that imperfect position.

According to this rule, the plaintiff in *Baker v Willoughby* would only have been entitled to recover from the second tortfeasors (assuming they were ever found, and had any assets!)

the extra damage caused by their shooting, for they damaged an already damaged man. But, as Lord Pearson pointed out, if the first defendant was only liable until the date of the second tort, there might be a gap in the damages. The plaintiff would only receive damages for the first injury up to the time of the second tort and, after that, would receive damages for the increased damage caused by the second tort, but would not receive compensation from either tortfeasor for the effects of the first injury after the date of the second tort. To avoid this, the House of Lords held the first defendant's tort continued to cause the first injury even after the date of the second tort, even though this later tort would have been sufficient to have caused the first injury. Is this a satisfactory solution?

Commenting on *Baker*, MacGregor (1970) 33 MLR 378 at 382–3 queried whether the same result would be reached where the supervening cause was non-tortious. This situation is considered in the following extract.

Jobling v Associated Dairies Ltd [1982] AC 794

The plaintiff injured his back as a result of the defendant's breach of statutory duty in 1973, and the injury only allowed him to take on light work. Prior to the trial of this action, however, he suffered a spinal disease (myelopathy) unrelated to the accident which rendered him unfit to work. The question for the House of Lords was whether damages were payable for loss of earnings after the time he suffered from the spinal disease, the Court of Appeal having held they were not.

Lord Wilberforce

In an attempt to solve the present case, and similar cases of successive causes of incapacity according to some legal principle, a number of arguments have been invoked.

1. Causation arguments. The unsatisfactory character of these is demonstrated by the case of *Baker v Willoughby* [1970] AC 467. I think that it can now be seen that Lord Reid's theory of concurrent causes even if workable on the particular facts of *Baker v Willoughby* (where successive injuries were sustained by the same limb) is as a general solution not supported by the authority he invokes (*Harwood v Wyken Colliery Co* [1913] 2 KB 158) or workable in other cases. I shall not enlarge on this point in view of its more than sufficient treatment in other opinions.

2. The 'vicissitudes' argument. This is that since, according to accepted doctrine, allowance, and if necessary some discount, has to be made in assessing loss of future earnings for the normal contingencies of life, amongst which 'illness' is normally enumerated, so, if one of these contingencies becomes actual before the date of trial, this actuality must be taken into account. Reliance is here placed on the apophthegm 'the court should not speculate when it knows'. This argument has a good deal of attraction. But it has its difficulties: it raises at once the question whether a discount is to be made on account of all possible 'vicissitudes' or only on account of 'non-culpable' vicissitudes (i.e. such that if they occur there will be no cause of action against anyone, the theory being that the prospect of being injured by a tort is not a normally foreseeable vicissitude) or only on account of 'culpable' vicissitudes (such as per contra). And if this distinction is to be made how is the court to act when a discounted vicissitude happens before trial? Must it attempt to decide whether there was culpability or not? And how is it to do this if, as is likely, the alleged culprit is not before it?

This actual distinction between 'culpable' and 'non-culpable' events was made, with supporting argument, in the Alberta case of *Penner v Mitchell* [1978] 5 WWR 328. One may add to it the rider that, as pointed out by Dickson J in the Supreme Court of Canada in *Andrews v Grand & Toy Alberta Ltd* (1978) 83 DLR (3d) 452 at 470, there are in modern society many public and private schemes which cushion the individual against adverse circumstances. One then has to ask whether a discount should be made in respect of (a) such cases or (b) cases where there is no such cushion. There is indeed in the 'vicissitude' argument some degree of circularity, since a discount in respect of possible events would only be fair if the actual event, discounted as possible, were to be taken into account when happening. But the whole question is whether it should be. One might just as well argue from what happens in 'actual' cases to what should happen in discountable cases.

In spite of these difficulties, the 'vicissitude' argument is capable in some, perhaps many, cases of providing a workable and reasonably just rule, and I would certainly not discountenance its use, either in the present case or in others.

The fact, however, is that to attempt a solution of these and similar problems, where there are successive causes of incapacity in some degree, on classical lines ('the object of damages for tort is to place the plaintiff in as good a position as if etc'; 'the defendant must compensate for the loss caused by his wrongful act, no more'; 'the defendant must take the plaintiff as he finds him' etc) is, in many cases, no longer possible. We do not live in a world governed by the pure common law and its logical rules. We live in a mixed world where a man is protected against injury and misfortune by a whole web of rules and dispositions, with a number of timid legislative interventions. To attempt to compensate him on the basis of selected rules without regard to the whole must lead either to logical inconsistencies or to over- or under-compensation. As my noble and learned friend Lord Edmund-Davies has pointed out, no account was taken in *Baker v Willoughby* of the very real possibility that the plaintiff might obtain compensation from the Criminal Injuries Compensation Board. If he did in fact obtain this compensation he would, on the ultimate decision, be over-compensated.

In the present case, and in other industrial injury cases, there seems to me no justification for disregarding the fact that the injured man's employer is insured (indeed since 1972 compulsorily insured) against liability to his employees. The state has decided, in other words, on a spreading of risk. There seems to me no more justification for disregarding the fact that the plaintiff (presumably; we have not been told otherwise) is entitled to sickness and invalidity benefit in respect of his myelopathy, the amount of which may depend on his contribution record, which in turn may have been affected by his accident. So we have no means of knowing whether the plaintiff would be over-compensated if he were, in addition, to receive the assessed damages from his employer, or whether he would be under-compensated if left to his benefit. It is not easy to accept a solution by which a partially incapacitated man becomes worse off in terms of damages and benefit through a greater degree of incapacity. Many other ingredients, of weight in either direction, may enter into individual cases. Without any satisfaction I draw from this the conclusion that no general, logical or universally fair rules can be stated which will cover, in a manner consistent with justice, cases of supervening events, whether due to tortious, partially tortious, non-culpable or wholly accidental events. The courts can only deal with each case as best they can in a manner so as to provide just and sufficient but not excessive compensation, taking all factors into account. I think that this is what *Baker v Willoughby* did, and indeed that Lord Pearson reached his decision in this way; the rationalisation of the decision, as to which I at least have doubts, need and should not be applied to other cases. In the present case the Court of Appeal reached the unanswerable conclusion that to apply *Baker v Willoughby* to the facts of the present case would produce an unjust result, and I am willing to accept the corollary that justice, so far as it can be perceived, lies the other way and that the supervening myelopathy should not be disregarded. If rationalisation is needed, I am willing to accept the 'vicissitudes' argument as the best available. I should be more firmly convinced of the merits of the conclusion if the whole pattern of benefits had been considered, in however general a way. The result of the present case may be lacking in precision and rational justification, but so long as we are content to live in a mansion of so many different architectures this is inevitable. . . .

Lord Russell of Killowen

There remains the question of the decision of this House in *Baker v Willoughby*. . . . I am not prepared to state disagreement with the decision. I am prepared to suggest that physical damage due to a subsequent tort is not to be regarded as a relevant vicissitude. Some of the reasons given in that case are susceptible of being taken as pointing in favour of the appellant in the instant appeal, but they do not persuade me that we are led by *Baker v Willoughby* to take a further step by allowing this appeal. . . .

Lord Keith of Kinkel

I am therefore of opinion that the majority in *Baker v Willoughby* were mistaken in approaching the problems common to the case of a supervening tortious act and to that of supervening illness wholly from the point of view of causation. While it is logically correct to say that in both cases the original tort and the supervening event may be concurrent causes of incapacity, that does not necessarily, in my view, provide the correct solution. In the case of supervening illness, it is appropriate to keep in view that this is one of the ordinary vicissitudes of life, and when one is comparing the situation resulting from the accident with the situation, had there been no accident, to recognise that the illness would have overtaken the plaintiff in any event, so that it cannot be disregarded in arriving at proper compensation, and no more than proper compensation.

Additional considerations come into play when dealing with the problems arising where the plaintiff has suffered injuries from two or more successive and independent tortious acts. In that situation it is necessary to secure that the plaintiff is fully compensated for the aggregate effects of all his injuries. As Lord Pearson noted in *Baker v Willoughby* [1970] AC 467 at 495 it would clearly be unjust to reduce the damages awarded for the first tort because of the occurrence of the second tort, damages for which are to be assessed on the basis that the plaintiff is already partially incapacitated. I do not consider it necessary to formulate any precise juristic basis for dealing with this situation differently from the case of supervening illness. It might be said that a supervening tort is not one of the ordinary vicissitudes of life, or that it is too remote a possibility to be taken into account, or that it can properly be disregarded because it carries its own remedy. None of these formulations, however, is entirely satisfactory. The fact remains that the principle of full compensation requires that a just and practical solution should be found. In the event that damages against two successive tortfeasors fall to be assessed at the same time, it would be highly unreasonable if the aggregate of both awards were less than the total loss suffered by the plaintiff. The computation should start from an assessment of that total loss. The award against the second tortfeasor cannot in fairness to him fail to recognise that the plaintiff whom he injured was already to some extent incapacitated. In order that the plaintiff may be fully compensated, it becomes necessary to deduct the award so calculated from the assessment of the plaintiff's total loss and award the balance against the first tortfeasor. If that be a correct approach, it follows that, in proceedings against the first tortfeasor alone, the occurrence of the second tort cannot be successfully relied on by the defendant as reducing the damages which he must pay. That, in substance, was the result of the decision in *Baker v Willoughby*, where the supervening event was a tortious act, and to that extent the decision was, in my view, correct.

Before leaving the case, it is right to face up to the fact that, if a non-tortious supervening event is to have the effect of reducing damages but a subsequent tortious act is not, there may in some cases be difficulty in ascertaining whether the event in question is or is not of a tortious character, particularly in the absence of the alleged tortfeasor. Possible questions of contributory negligence may cause additional complications. Such difficulties are real, but are not sufficient, in my view, to warrant the conclusion that the distinction between tortious and non-tortious supervening events should not be accepted. The court must simply do its best to arrive at a just assessment of damages in a pragmatical way in the light of the whole circumstances of the case. . . .

Lord Bridge of Harwich

[His Lordship considered the decision in *Baker v Willoughby* and continued:]

Notwithstanding the course taken by the argument, in the speech of Lord Reid in this House (with which Lord Guest, Viscount Dilhorne and Lord Donovan agreed) there is no reference at all to the circumstance that the amputation of the plaintiff's leg was the result of a tort as a factor relevant to the decision. On the contrary, the reasoning in the speech applies equally to the effect of a supervening disability arising from illness or non-tortious accident. . . .

Having reached the conclusion that the *ratio decidendi* of *Baker's case* cannot be sustained, it remains to consider whether the case should still be regarded as authority, as a decision on its own facts, for the proposition that, when two successive injuries are both caused tortiously, the supervening disability caused by the second tort should, by way of exception to the general rule arising from the application of the vicissitudes principle, be disregarded when assessing the liability of the first tortfeasor for damages for loss of earnings caused by the first tort. I find it difficult to attribute such authority to the decision, when both the Court of Appeal and this House were expressly invited to adopt that proposition, and both, in different ways, declined the invitation. . . . In the instant appeal counsel for the respondents was content to accept the decision in *Baker's case* as correct on its facts, so your Lordships have not heard argument on the question. In these circumstances, the proper conclusion seems to me to be that the question should remain open for decision on another occasion, if and when it arises.

Lord Edmund-Davies delivered a speech in favour of dismissing the appeal.

Appeal dismissed.

COMMENTARY

What is the status of *Baker v Willoughby* after this decision? Is it authority in (1) situations generally where there are multiple sufficient causes, (2) situations where the second sufficient cause is a tortious act, or (3) no situation at all?

Is the problem raised by *Baker* and *Jobling* one of causation or the assessment of damages? In both cases there was no doubt that the defendant was liable for some damage to the plaintiff; the issue was for how much. In *Baker*, Lord Reid attempted to answer this question by using a theory of concurrent causation: after the plaintiff had been shot there were two concurrent causes responsible for the damage suffered as a result of the original tortfeasor's (the defendant's) tort. The House of Lords in *Jobling* adopted a different approach. It was a well-established principle that the ordinary vicissitudes of life (of which illness was one) were taken into account in assessing damages. When assessing the damages payable in respect of post-trial losses, this is done globally by way of a percentage discount to reflect the fact that in the future it is not known whether or to what extent events unconnected with the tort would have caused the claimant the same loss for which he is claiming. But where such a vicissitude has occurred pre-trial, it is taken into account, for there is then no need to speculate. But if this is correct, how could the decision in *Baker* be justified? Can the distinction be, as Lord Keith suggested, that the vicissitude in *Baker* was tortious or culpable? This clearly did not appeal to Lord Wilberforce, who decried any attempt at a principled solution and left it for the court to do its pragmatic best depending on the facts of the case. In light of these concerns, the authority of *Baker* remains open to doubt (see especially the speech of Lord Bridge). However, in the later case of *Rahman v Arearose Ltd* [2001] 2B 35, Laws LJ saw no inconsistency between the two cases: 'Once it is recognised that the first principle is that every tortfeasor should compensate the injured claimant in respect of that loss and damage for which he should justly be held responsible, the metaphysics of causation can be kept in their proper place...' If pragmatism is the only way to achieve justice in this area, then both *Baker* and *Jobling* were correctly decided on their own facts.

Even adopting pragmatism as principle, there are difficulties in reaching the 'just' result. Lord Wilberforce referred to the fact that the plaintiff in *Baker* might have been able to claim damages from the Criminal Injuries Compensation Board, and hence be over-compensated. This possibly seems unlikely today, as the benefits payable under that scheme are reduced by the amount of any tort damages recovered (para. 48 of the Criminal Injuries Compensation Scheme, promulgated under s. 1 of the Criminal Injuries Compensation Act 1995). Lord Wilberforce's wider point, however, was that it was difficult for a court to assess whether the denial of the plaintiff's tort claim would leave him under-compensated, as that would depend on the other benefits available to the plaintiff from his employer, private insurance, and social security. The deductibility of other benefits of this nature is considered in Chapter 16, but it should be noted that in some situations double recovery is allowed. In other words, the plaintiff may recover tort damages in respect of a loss for which other benefits are being paid. Given that the court may not know the source or extent of these benefits, is it really capable of fulfilling Lord Wilberforce's mandate to provide 'just and sufficient but not excessive' compensation?

Similar results to *Jobling* have been reached in cases where there is an alternative hypothetical cause which would have resulted in the claimant suffering the same injury but for the defendant's negligence. In the famous American case of *Dillon v Twin State Gas* (1932) 163 Atl 111, a child fell from a bridge towards almost certain death on the rocks below, but was in fact electrocuted by some electric wires which had been hung negligently by the defendant. It was accepted that the defendant's negligence was the cause of the death, but the plaintiff's damages were reduced to reflect his short life-expectancy, namely, the period between the time when the plaintiff hit the wires and when he would have hit the rocks (see also *Smith v Cawdle Fen Commissioners* [1938] 4 All ER 64). Although the practical results are similar (the defendant only pays damages for a limited time) the cases are different. In *Jobling* the event which it was argued had supervened the defendant's negligence had actually happened, whilst in *Dillon* it had not. Accordingly, in *Jobling* it did not matter that the supervening event occurred some time after the original negligence; once it did it had to be taken into account at the trial. Conversely, in the case of hypothetical alternative causes, the temporal relationship between the defendant's negligence and the alternative cause must be close before the alternative cause will be taken to have negatived the causal effect of the defendant's negligence, as in *Dillon*. For example, is it really likely that a court would reduce the damages of a claimant injured through a taxi-driver's negligence whilst on his way to the airport even if the evidence was that, if he had been safely delivered to the airport, the claimant would have caught a plane that crashed?

It is submitted that this approach may also explain the result in the difficult cases dealing with the negligent failure of a surgeon to disclose the risks of surgery to the claimant where the risk materialises: as long as the claimant can show that, if he had been properly advised, he would not have had the surgery at that time, it is irrelevant (at least to the question of liability) that he might later have had the surgery and been exposed to the same risk. The House of Lords has recently affirmed this view, albeit by a bare majority (*Chester v Afshar* [2005] 1 AC 134). As Stapleton points out ('Occam's razor reveals an orthodox basis for *Chester v Afshar*' (2006) 122 LQR 426), the real issue in these cases is not one of cause in fact. Assuming that the patient would not have had the surgery if the risks had been disclosed, there is no doubt that the negligent failure to disclose the risk is the factual cause of the injury. Rather, the key question is the normative one of whether the defendant should be held liable even though, if he had acted carefully, the claimant would have been exposed to exactly the same risk by having the same surgery at a later date (although, as the risk was very unlikely, the chances of the risk materialising during the later surgery was low). Although the majority of their Lordships based their decision on the grounds that to reject the claim would be to empty the surgeon's duty of disclosure of any content, it is possible to view the true question as being the extent to which hypothetical supervening events should be taken into account in determining whether the claimant has suffered a loss. As Gummow J argued in the factually-similar Australian case of *Chappel v Hart* (1998) 195 CLR 232 at 262, '[i]t would...be unjust to absolve the medical practitioner from legal responsibility for her injuries by allowing decisive weight to hypothetical and problematic considerations of what could have happened to Mrs Hart [the claimant] at the hands of some other practitioner at some unspecified later date and in conditions of great variability'.

Where the alternative hypothetical cause is the claimant's own pre-existing condition, damages will be awarded on the basis that the defendant's negligence was the cause of the injury but reduced to reflect the likelihood that the injury might have occurred irrespective of the defendant's negligence (see *Cutler v Vauxhall Motors* [1971] 1 QB 418; *Malec v J. C. Hutton* (1990) 169 CLR 638). Is this equivalent to reducing the claimant's damages to reflect the chance that the injury might not have been caused by the defendant, and hence awarding damages for the chance that the defendant's negligence caused the injury? (See Stapleton (2003) 119 LQR 388 at 425, and Peel (2003) 66 MLR 623 at 629.)

For comment on *Jobling*, see Evans (1982) 45 MLR 329 and Hervey (1981) 97 LQR 210 (the latter dealing with the decision of the Court of Appeal, which was affirmed by the House of Lords).

II. Intervening Acts

In certain situations, the most immediate cause of the damage suffered by the claimant is an act which occurs some time after the defendant's negligent conduct. Unlike the cases just considered, the defendant's negligence was not sufficient, on its own, to cause the claimant's damage. Rather, the damage is the result of the defendant's negligence and some other event; the negligence only creates the opportunity for injury to be caused to the claimant. The question for consideration in this section is the circumstances in which such an intervening event will be held to negate the causative effect of the defendant's breach of duty.

Empress Car Co (Abertillery) Ltd v National Rivers Authority [1999] 2 AC 22

In a criminal prosecution, the issue for the House of Lords was whether the respondent had 'caused' polluting matter to enter controlled waters contrary to s. 85(1) Water Resources Act 1991. The House of Lords upheld the lower court's conviction. The result of the case is not important for present purposes, but Lord Hoffmann's comments on causation are of general applicability, even to the law of tort.

Lord Hoffmann

The courts have repeatedly said that the notion of 'causing' is one of common sense. So in *Alphacell Ltd v Woodward* [1972] AC 824 at 847 Lord Salmon said:

> ... what or who has caused a certain event to occur is essentially a practical question of fact which can best be answered by ordinary common sense rather than by abstract metaphysical theory.

I doubt whether the use of abstract metaphysical theory has ever had much serious support and I certainly agree that the notion of causation should not be overcomplicated. Neither, however, should it be oversimplified. In the *Alphacell* case [1972] AC 824 at 834 Lord Wilberforce said in similar vein:

> In my opinion, 'causing' here must be given a common sense meaning and I deprecate the introduction of refinements, such as causa causans, effective cause or novus actus. There may be difficulties where acts of third persons or natural forces are concerned....

The last concession was prudently made, because it is of course the causal significance of acts of third parties (as in this case) or natural forces that gives rise to almost all the problems about the notion of 'causing' and drives judges to take refuge in metaphor or Latin. I therefore propose to concentrate upon the way common sense notions of causation treat the intervention of third parties or natural forces. The principles involved are not complicated or difficult to understand, but they do in my opinion call for some explanation....

The first point to emphasise is that common sense answers to questions of causation will differ according to the purpose for which the question is asked. Questions of causation often arise for the purpose of attributing responsibility to someone, for example, so as to blame him for something which has happened or to make him guilty of an offence or liable in damages. In such cases, the answer will depend upon the rule by which responsibility is being attributed. Take, for example, the case of the man who forgets to take the radio out of his car and during the night someone breaks the quarterlight, enters the car and steals it. What caused the damage? If the thief is on trial, so that the question is whether he is criminally responsible, then obviously the answer is that he caused the damage. It is no answer for him to say that it was caused by the owner carelessly leaving the radio inside. On the other hand, the owner's wife, irritated at the third such occurrence in a year, might well say that it was his fault. In the context of an inquiry into the owner's blameworthiness under a non-legal, common sense duty to take reasonable care of one's own possessions, one would say that his carelessness caused the loss of the radio....

I turn next to the question of third parties and natural forces. In answering questions of causation for the purposes of holding someone responsible, both the law and common sense normally attach great significance to deliberate human acts and extraordinary natural events. A factory owner carelessly leaves a drum containing highly inflammable vapour in a place where it could easily be accidentally ignited. If a workman, thinking it is only an empty drum, throws in a cigarette butt and causes an explosion, one would have no difficulty in saying that the negligence of the owner caused the explosion. On the other hand, if the workman, knowing exactly what the drum contains, lights a match and ignites it, one would have equally little difficulty in saying that he had caused the explosion and that the carelessness of the owner had merely provided him with an occasion for what he did. One would probably say the same if the drum was struck by lightning. In both cases one would say that although the vapour-filled drum was a necessary condition for the explosion to happen, it was not caused by the owner's negligence. One might add by way of further explanation that the presence of an arsonist workman or lightning happening to strike at that time and place was a coincidence.

On the other hand, there are cases in which the duty imposed by the rule is to take precautions to prevent loss being caused by third parties or natural events. One example has already been given; the common sense rule (not legally enforceable, but neglect of which may expose one to blame from one's wife) which requires one to remove the car radio at night. A legal example is the well-known case of *Stansbie v Troman* [1948] 2 KB 48. A decorator working alone in a house went out to buy wallpaper and left the front door unlocked. He was held liable for the loss caused by a thief who entered while he was away. For the purpose of attributing liability to the thief (e.g. in a prosecution for theft) the loss was caused by his deliberate act and no one would have said that it was caused by the door being left open. But for the purpose of attributing liability to the decorator, the loss was caused by his negligence because his duty was to take reasonable care to guard against thieves entering.

These examples show that one cannot give a common sense answer to a question of causation for the purpose of attributing responsibility under some rule without knowing the purpose and scope of the rule. Does the rule impose a duty which requires one to guard against, or makes one responsible for, the deliberate acts of third persons? If so, it will be correct to say, when loss is caused by the act of such a third person, that it was caused by the breach of duty. In *Stansbie v Troman* [1948] 2 KB 48 at 51–52 Tucker LJ referred to a statement of Lord Sumner in *Weld-Blundell v Stephens* [1920] AC 956 at 986, in which he had said:

> In general . . . even though A is in fault, he is not responsible for injury to C which B, a stranger to him, deliberately chooses to do. Though A may have given the occasion for B's mischievous activity, B then becomes a new and independent cause. . . .

Tucker LJ went on to comment:

> I do not think that Lord Sumner would have intended that very general statement to apply to the facts of a case such as the present, where, as the learned judge points out, the act of negligence itself consisted in the failure to take reasonable care to guard against the very thing that in fact happened.

Before answering questions about causation, it is therefore first necessary to identify the scope of the relevant rule. This is not a question of common sense fact; it is a question of law. In *Stansbie v Troman* the law imposed a duty which included having to take precautions against burglars. Therefore breach of that duty caused the loss of the property stolen. In the example of the vapour-filled drum, the duty does not extend to taking precautions against arsonists. In other contexts there might be such a duty (compare *Mediterranean Freight Services Ltd v BP Oil International Ltd, The Fiona* [1994] 2 Lloyd's Rep 506 at 522) but the law of negligence would not impose one . . .

Knightley v Johns [1982] 1 WLR 349

The first defendant was involved in a serious road accident at the end of a one-way tunnel. A Mr Williams, driving behind him, stopped and used an emergency telephone to report the accident to the police, but the message appeared to have been received and passed on in a somewhat confused form. The police officer in charge at the scene forgot to close the entrance to the tunnel, and, in breach of police force standing orders, commanded two officers on motorcycles, one of whom was the plaintiff, to ride down the tunnel, against the traffic, to close it. The officers obeyed, even though this also constituted a breach of standing orders, and near the entrance to the tunnel the plaintiff was hit by an oncoming car, without negligence on the part of the driver. The trial judge held that neither the commanding officer nor the plaintiff had been negligent and that their actions did not break the causal link between the first defendant's negligence and the plaintiff's injuries. The Court of Appeal allowed the appeal by the first defendant, holding that the police officer had been negligent and that this negligence broke the causal link between the first defendant's negligence and the plaintiff's injury.

Stephenson LJ

On a Friday evening in October 1974 at about 8.20 in the twilight PC Knightley rode his motor bicycle the wrong way along a tunnel in Birmingham into collision with Mr Cotton's oncoming motor car. He sued Mr Cotton for negligence in causing him serious injuries. He also sued Police Inspector Sommerville and the Chief Constable of the West Midlands as the inspector's superior officer for the inspector's negligence in instructing or at the least permitting him to ride the wrong way. But the person he alleged to be first and foremost responsible for his accident and injuries was Mr Johns, because it was his negligence in overturning his motor car in the tunnel which was the cause of all the trouble. . . .

[After reaching the conclusion that the acts and omissions of the plaintiff and the inspector were causes of the plaintiff's accident and injuries for which the inspector was in law liable but the plaintiff was not, his Lordship continued:]

Now comes the question the judge decided first: were they causes concurrent with the negligence of Mr Johns or were they new causes which broke the chain of causation? The judge, putting Mr Johns's case, said:

> What is said is that the action of the police was so unforeseeable that it can no longer be said that the negligence of the first defendant [Mr Johns] had any operative effect on subsequent events. After reviewing some of the relevant authorities he came to his conclusion 'that the injury to the plaintiff was the natural and probable result of the original negligence of Mr Johns' and that consequently 'his negligence was an operative cause of the plaintiff's injury'. . . .

[After considering the authorities, including cases involving the intervention of rescuers, his Lordship continued:]

At one end of the scale is wanton interference or disregard for the rescuer's own safety, which will break the chain; at the other, reasonable conduct which, according to what Lord Haldane said in *Canadian Pacific Rly Co v Kelvin Shipping Co Ltd* (1927) 138 LT 369 at 370 (and what Maugham LJ said in *Haynes v Harwood* [1935] 1 KB 146 at 162), will not. But there may be many intervening actions which cannot be characterised as either reasonable reaction or wanton intermeddling and recklessness. In this intermediate category come . . . tortious or criminal acts (wanton enough in one sense), the latter illustrated by the *Dorset Yacht Co* case, the former by such cases of negligent driving into an obstruction negligently left on the highway as *Rouse v Squires* [1973] QB 889 at 898, where Cairns LJ regarded 'those who deliberately and recklessly drive into the obstruction' as disqualified by their own new act from recovering damages from those responsible for the obstruction. Of those who expose themselves to the danger of being injured by the negligence of others, rescuers are of course in a special category. For they will come to the rescue as often by deliberate and courageous choice as by instinctive reaction and they are unlikely to commit any crime or tort in so doing except the tort of failing to take reasonable care, which might be described as recklessness, for the safety of persons likely to be endangered by their actions, including of course themselves.

That brings me to the peculiarity of the present case, or rather to two peculiarities. One is that the action which injured the plaintiff might well have injured others such as Mr Cotton. The other is that between Mr Johns's negligent action and the plaintiff's own injury were interposed not merely his own decision to ride the wrong way along the tunnel hugging the wall of lane 1 when PC Easthope was riding ahead hugging the wall of lane 2 but a number of other acts and omissions for which he was not responsible, namely what was submitted to be 'the series of acts of ineptitude on the part of the police' in the judge's judgment:

> He submits that the first such act of ineptitude was failing to ascertain from Mr Williams precisely where the collision was. The next one was failing to close the tunnel before going into it in accordance with the standing orders. Having failed to close the tunnel he says it was inept to send the police officers back instead of using the telephone or sending them forward to radio for more assistance. There were, he says, clear breaches of the standing orders . . . and he says it is not foreseeable as likely to happen that police officers will ignore all those standing orders and all these things will happen.

The judge dealt with that submission in this way:

> I think that is looking at the matter from rather too narrow a point of view. It was not suggested, of course, that the first defendant was aware of these standing orders or had any idea what was in them. The issue is whether a motorist driving in that tunnel ought to have foreseen as likely to happen that if he was negligent and created an emergency other members of the public, and in particular police officers, would have to take risks either to rescue him or to protect other motorists. . . . [T]he very fact of rescue must in any view involve unexpected things happening. Although I do not say that a motorist driving through a tunnel such as this should reasonably foresee that if he is negligent a police officer may drive the wrong way out of the tunnel, nevertheless in my view the motorist ought to foresee that if he is negligent and creates an emergency other people are likely to be put at risk and other people, particularly police officers, fire officers and ambulance officers, are likely to take deliberate risks, as I say, either to rescue him and his passengers or to protect other members of the public. In my view the action of the police officers was the very sort of action which is governed by that principle. It cannot be said, looked at in those general terms, that it was something so unexpected, so unforeseeable as not to be something likely to flow from the original negligence of Mr Johns. In my view then the injury to the plaintiff was the natural and probable result or a natural and probable result of the original negligence of Mr Johns. It follows that in my view his negligence was an operative cause of the plaintiff's injury.

It is plain from that clear and persuasive expression of the judge's reasoned opinion that he was asking himself the right question and applying the right law. He was, I think, rightly taking the law to be that, in considering the effects of carelessness, as in considering the duty to take care, the test is reasonable foreseeability, which I understand to mean foreseeability of something of the same sort being likely to happen, as against its being a mere possibility which would never occur to the mind of a reasonable man or, if it did, would be neglected as too remote to require precautions or to impose responsibility: cf Lord Dunedin's judgment in *Fardon v Harcourt-Rivington* (1932) 146 LT 391 at 392. The question to be asked is accordingly whether that whole sequence of events is a natural and probable consequence of Mr Johns's negligence and a reasonably foreseeable result of it. In answering the question it is helpful but not decisive to consider which of these events were deliberate choices to do positive acts and which were mere omissions or failures to act; which acts and omissions were innocent mistakes or miscalculations and which were negligent having regard to the pressures and the gravity of the emergency and the need to act quickly. Negligent conduct is more likely to break the chain of causation than conduct which is not; positive acts will more easily constitute new causes than inaction. Mistakes and mischances are to be expected when human beings, however well trained, have to cope with a crisis; what exactly they will do cannot be predicted, but if those which occur are natural the wrongdoer cannot, I think, escape responsibility for them and their consequences simply by calling them improbable or unforeseeable. He must accept the risk of some unexpected mischances: see *Ward v TE Hopkins & Son Ltd* [1959] 1 WLR 966 at 984, per Willmer LJ and *Chadwick's case* [1967] 1 WLR 912 at 921, per Waller J. But what mischances?

The answer to this difficult question must be dictated by common sense rather than logic on the facts and circumstances of each case. In this case it must be answered in the light of the true view to be taken of the events leading up to Inspector Sommerville's acts, or rather his act and omission, and the plaintiff's, and PC Easthope's, acts. I have expressed my view of all these links in the chain leading from Mr Johns's negligence to the plaintiff's collision with Mr Cotton. I have decided, respectfully disagreeing with the judge, that the inspector was negligent in failing to close the tunnel and, respectfully agreeing with the judge, that the plaintiff was not negligent in riding the wrong way after being ordered to do so by the inspector or in deciding on the spur of the moment to ride his motor cycle close to the wall in lane 1.

I am also of the opinion that the inspector's negligence was not a concurrent cause running with Mr Johns's negligence, but a new cause disturbing the sequence of events leading from Mr Johns's overturning of his car to the plaintiff's accident and interrupting the effect of it. This would, I think, have been so had the inspector's negligence stood alone. Coming as it did on top of the muddle and misunderstanding of Mr Williams's telephone call and followed by the inspector's order to remedy his own negligence by a dangerous manoeuvre, it was the real cause of the plaintiff's injury and made that injury too remote from Mr Johns's wrongdoing to be a consequence of it.

In the long run the question is, as Lord Reid said in the *Dorset Yacht Co* case, one of remoteness of damage, to be answered, as has so often been stated, not by the logic of philosophers but by the common sense of plain men. . . . In my judgment, too much happened here, too much went wrong, the chapter of accidents and mistakes was too long and varied, to impose on Mr Johns liability for what happened to the plaintiff in discharging his duty as a police officer, although it would not have happened had not Mr Johns negligently overturned his car. The ordinary course of things took an extraordinary course. The length and the irregularities of the line leading from the first accident to the second have no parallel in the reported rescue cases, in all of which the plaintiff succeeded in establishing the original wrongdoer's liability. It was natural, it was probable, it was foreseeable, it was indeed certain, that the police would come to the overturned car and control the tunnel traffic. It was also natural and probable and foreseeable that some steps would be taken in controlling the traffic and clearing the tunnel and some things be done that might be more courageous than sensible. The reasonable hypothetical observer would anticipate some human errors, some forms of what might be called folly, perhaps even from trained police officers, and some unusual and unexpected accidents in the course of their rescue duties. But would he anticipate such a result as this from so many errors as these, so many departures from the common sense procedure prescribed by the standing orders for just such an emergency as this? I can see that it is a question on which the opinions of plain men and women in the jury box and judges who have now to perform their function may reasonably differ. I can only say that, in my opinion, the judge's decision carries Mr Johns's responsibility too far: in trying to be fair to the inspector the judge was unfair to Mr Johns....

Dunn LJ agreed with Stephenson LJ. **Sir David Cairns** gave a short concurring judgment.

Appeal allowed.

COMMENTARY

As can be seen from the above extract, the answer to the question of when an intervening act will be held to break the chain of causation is said to be a matter of common sense and to depend very greatly on the precise factual context in question, although the guidelines given by Stephenson LJ are useful pointers to what a court might hold. The tendency to express the principles applied in value-neutral terms should be noted—it also characterises the magisterial and very influential treatise by H. Hart and T. Honoré, *Causation in the Law*, 2nd edn. (Oxford: Clarendon Press, 1985)—but, as numerous commentators have observed, underlying such principles are often contentious notions of personal (as opposed to social) responsibility (see, e.g., *Conaghan & Mansell*, pp. 71–2, Stapleton (2006) 122 LQR 426 at 430–6). This point has even received judicial recognition, at least to some extent, e.g. by McHugh J in the Australian case of *March v E. & M. H. Stramare* (1991) 171 CLR 506 at 534: 'In general...the "but for" test should be seen as the test of legal causation. Any other rule limiting responsibility for damage caused by a wrongful act or omission should be recognised as a policy-based rule concerned with remoteness of damage and not causation.' Whether the matter be regarded as one of common sense or of legal policy, it is still possible to offer some general observations as to how the courts approach different types of case.

Intervention by Deliberate Wrongful Act

In *Weld-Blundell v Stephens* [1920] AC 956 at 986, Lord Summer stated: 'In general...even though A is in fault, he is not responsible for injury to C which B, a stranger to him, deliberately chooses to do. Though A may have given the occasion for B's mischievous activity, B then becomes a new and independent cause.' This is reflected in a line of cases denying liability where damage has been caused by deliberate acts of third parties (here conceived broadly to include all cases where they act voluntarily in order to exploit the situation created by the defendant: see Hart and Honoré, *op. cit.*, p. 136). In such cases, no liability can arise unless the defendant is under an exceptional duty to take care to prevent a third party injuring the claimant. *Jones*, p. 232, discussing the case of *Lamb v Camden London Borough Council* [1981] QB 625, where the council was sued by a landowner for damage to her property inflicted by squatters, argues:

The council's negligence created the opportunity for the squatter's damage but it did not cause it, unless it could be said that they were under a duty of care to prevent the squatters' behaviour. If there is such a duty then the defendant cannot complain that the intervention is a novus actus. The third party's act is the occasion of the breach of duty, not a separate cause.

Lamb was an unusual case, in that there was some property damage for which the council was undeniably responsible, so it could be said that the council already owed a duty in respect of property damage. The question for the court was for what property damage should the council be liable? In cases where the only damage is brought about by the deliberate and wrongful act of a third party, such cases will fail or succeed on whether a duty of care is owed, and, because such a duty entails a liability for the acts of third parties, special circumstances are required before it will be imposed: see *Mitchell v Glasgow City Council* [2009] UKHL 11 and more generally Chapter 9.III.

Intervening Act of Claimant

Prior to the Law Reform (Contributory Negligence) Act 1945 (see Ch. 6), if the plaintiff was guilty of contributory negligence this operated as a complete defence to any claim as the plaintiff was regarded as the cause of his own damage (except where the defendant had the 'last opportunity' to prevent the accident, see Ch. 6). Since 1945, the courts have had the ability to apportion damages where they find that the fault of both the defendant and the claimant are causally relevant, and there is no need to decide, in absolute terms, whether the claimant's intervening act or the defendant's negligence was the sole cause of the damage. In *March v E. & M. H. Stramare Pty Ltd* (1991) 65 ALJR 334 at 341, Deane J stated:

> It is true that, in the context of apportionment legislation which gives the latitude necessary to enable the relief to be fairly adjusted to fit the circumstances, the courts will be unlikely to deny causation in any case where the fault of the defendant contributed to an accident. Nonetheless, the question remains to be determined by a value judgment involving ordinary notions of language and common sense.

A rare post-1945 case where the subsequent act of the claimant was held to break the causal chain is *McKew v Holland and Hannen and Cubitts (Scotland) Ltd* [1969] 2 All ER 1621. The pursuer suffered an injury at work which caused a stiffening and weakening of his leg. Shortly afterwards he went to inspect a flat, access to which was provided by a steep staircase with no handrail. As he was about to descend the stairs, his leg gave way, and, to avoid going down head-first, he threw himself and landed on his right leg, breaking the ankle. The House of Lords rejected an argument that the defender should be liable for this damage. Lord Reid held that, although it was quite foreseeable that the pursuer would attempt to do what he did, the attempt to descend the stairs (but not throwing himself once he was falling) was an unreasonable act for which the defender was not responsible. The claimant was more fortunate in the recent case of *Spencer v Wincanton Holdings Ltd* [2009] EWCA Civ 1404. Here, the defendant's negligence resulted in the claimant's leg being amputated. Whilst waiting for a car converted to suit someone with this disability to become available, the claimant tripped whilst filling his existing car with petrol and as a result was confined to a wheelchair. He had had available a prosthesis and walking sticks but did not use them. The Court of Appeal upheld the trial judge's finding that the defendant was responsible for the additional injury caused by the fall subject to a reduction of one third for contributory negligence. Aikens LJ accepted that there was 'inevitably' a degree of tension between *McKew* unreasonableness (which broke the causal connection) and unreasonableness that merely went to contributory negligence. The difficulty, as Sedley LJ noted, is that the term 'unreasonable' covers a range of conduct from irrationality to simple incaution or unwisdom, and it is only where the degree of unreasonable conduct is very high that *McKew* will apply (see *Emeh v Kensington & Chelsea Area Health Authority* [1984] 3 All ER 1044, 1049 per Waller LJ).

If McKew made an unwise decision to descend the stairs, why should the defendant 'takes his victim as he finds him' rule not apply? See *Wieland v Cyril Lord Carpets* [1969] 3 All ER 1006 and Stiggelbout, 'The scope and rationale of the principle that the defendant "takes his victim as he finds him"' (2009) 17 Tort L Rev 140, 142); cf. *Weir* (p. 233).

Even acts which, if viewed in isolation, might be thought unreasonable may not break the causal chain where the defendant's negligence placed the claimant in a position of danger. In *Sayers v Harlow UDC* [1958] 1 WLR 623, the plaintiff was injured when attempting to climb out of a cubicle in a public lavatory in which she had become trapped due to the defendant's negligence. Although her method of escape involved considerable risk, the Court of Appeal held that the chain of causation had not been broken, but reduced her damages by a quarter for contributory negligence. If the unreasonableness of the claimant's act is the determining factor, one might think it certain that the claimant's suicide should satisfy that test and break the causal chain. However, in *Corr v IBC Vehicles Ltd* [2008] AC 884 a unanimous House of Lords held that the suicide of the deceased did not prevent his widow claiming for loss of dependency under the Fatal Accidents Act, primarily because the suicide was a reasonably foreseeable consequence of the defendant's negligence which had caused the deceased to become depressed, though not insane, or (per Lord Scott) because the employer was liable for the deceased's psychiatric harm and the suicide was attributable to that psychiatric harm. The same result has been reached in other cases where the defendant has been responsible for creating the environment in which the deceased's suicidal tendencies developed. In *Kirkham v Chief Constable of Greater Manchester Police* [1990] 2 QB 283, the suicide of a depressed prisoner was held not to constitute a *novus actus*, at least where the police had a duty to prevent the prisoner from committing suicide. The police had failed to pass on to the prison authorities information that the plaintiff was suffering from clinical depression and was suicidal. More recently, in *Reeves v Commissioner of Police for the Metropolis* [2000] 1 AC 360, the House of Lords held that the suicide in police custody of a prisoner, whether of sound mind or not, did not break the causal chain, provided a duty of care was owed by the defendant to take steps to prevent it. In *Reeves* the police knew that the prisoner had suicidal tendencies, and the defendant conceded that in the circumstances of the case the police owed a duty to take reasonable care to prevent him from committing suicide. According to Lord Hoffmann (at 368): 'Once it is admitted that this is the rare case in which such a duty is owed, it seems to me self-contradictory to say that the breach could not have been a cause of the harm because the victim caused it to himself.' Lord Hobhouse dissented, reaching the same conclusion as Lloyd LJ in *Kirkham* that the voluntary, deliberate, and informed act of a person precluded a causative link between the breach of duty and the consequences of that person's action. As explained above, the answer to these cases lies in a duty analysis (see further Ch. 9): if the defendant is under a duty to prevent another person from causing the very harm that he in fact causes, that person's action does not break the chain of causation (although it might give rise to a defence of contributory negligence, as was held to be the case in *Reeves*). The decision in *Reeves* is in line with the obligations of the state under Article 2 of the ECHR: irrespective of the mental state of the claimant, it was held by the European Court of Human Rights in *Keenan v United Kingdom* (2001) 10 BHRC 319, that once the person in custody had been identified as a suicide risk, Article 2 required reasonable steps to be taken to prevent that suicide. (For the similar position of hospitals detaining patients under mental health legislation, see *Savage v South Essex Partnership NHS Foundation Trust* [2008] UKHL 74.) But there is no *general* duty to prevent persons in custody harming themselves: as long as the police have taken steps to assess whether the person was a suicide risk and decided he was not, no further duty was owed to take steps to prevent him harming himself (*Orange v Chief Constable of West Yorkshire Police* [2002] 2B 347), nor do the police owe a duty to take steps to stop persons they are attempting to arrest harming themselves (*Vellino v Chief Constable of Greater Manchester Police* [2002] 1 WLR 218; note, however, the dissent of Sedley LJ). What if the prisoner is a suicide risk, not because he is mentally disturbed, but because he is a political prisoner attempting to gain publicity for a cause (see Lord Hobhouse in *Reeves* at 385)? For a discussion of *Reeves*, see Nolan (2000) 8 Tort L Rev 91.

Should the intervening acts of the claimant break the causal connection between the defendant's negligence and the loss more readily where the loss is purely economic? In *Calvert v William Hill Credit Ltd* [2009] Ch 330, the Court of Appeal declined to find a bookmaker liable to a pathological gambler for the losses caused by failing to stop him gambling even though it had not implemented a self-exclusion agreement from telephone betting that had previously been requested by the claimant. However, the claim failed because the duty assumed by the defendant did not extend to preventing gambling losses entirely (or alternatively, and perhaps more simply, because the trial judge had held that that there was no but-for causation; the claimant would have suffered the same losses even if the defendant was not careless: Morgan [2009] CLJ 268; see also Mitchell (2010) 18 TLJ 1). However, unlike *Corr v IBC* and *Reeves* (above), where the defendants were responsible in part for creating the impairment of the claimant's mental condition, the defendant in this case did not create the pathological gambling condition. Why, then, is the claimant's conduct not seen as the cause of his own loss?

A category of claimants that receives especially favourable treatment from the courts is rescuers. Generally, a rescuer injured whilst attempting to perform a rescue necessitated by the defendant's negligence will have a claim against the originally negligent party. In *Baker v T. E. Hopkins* [1959] 1 WLR 966 the Court of Appeal allowed a Fatal Accidents Act claim in respect of a doctor who died whilst attempting the rescue of two workers who had been trapped in a well as a result of the defendant's negligence. Morris LJ said (at 975–6): 'There is, happily, in all men of good will an urge to save those who are in peril. Those who put men in peril can hardly be heard to say that they never thought that rescue might be attempted, or be heard to say that the rescue attempt was not caused by the creation of the peril.'

Negligent Acts of Third Parties

Like the Law Reform (Contributory Negligence) Act 1945, the introduction of legislation allowing apportionment of damages between tortfeasors (by a process called contribution, now governed by the Civil Liability (Contribution) Act 1978) has affected the courts' decisions on whether an intervening negligent act will break the chain of causation. Where several tortfeasors are in some way responsible for the same damage suffered by the claimant, it is rare for the court to hold that only one of them is the sole legal cause. Although the claimant may sue every party responsible for the damage, the principle of joint and several liability means that each tortfeasor is liable in full to the claimant; hence the claimant need sue only one. If the person sued can find another person whose fault contributed to the claimant's damage, that other may be joined as a party to the claimant's action and becomes a co-defendant. Thus, when the court is called upon to make the final decision, there may be several defendants before the court, and each of the defendants may be ordered to pay a percentage of the claimant's damage depending on the degree of fault and causal connection between the negligence and the claimant's damage. The claimant still receives 100 per cent of the damages (assuming no deduction for contributory negligence), but those damages are paid by several defendants. (Of course, if one of the defendants is insolvent, the share of the others is increased proportionately.)

It is important to note the difference between issues of contribution between defendants and the question of proportionate liability, discussed above at p. 242. In the former, each defendant is jointly and severally liable for all of the claimant's damage, whereas in the latter, the individual defendant's liability to the claimant is not joint and several and is capped according to that defendant's contribution to the injury. The difference is important where one of a number of defendants is bankrupt or insolvent. Such an event has no impact on the claimant where the remainder of the defendants are jointly and severally liable, for the claimant can recover 100 per cent of the damages against *any* of them. The insolvency or bankruptcy is only relevant to the question from which of the other defendants contribution may be claimed. Conversely, in the case of proportionate liability, the bankruptcy or insolvency of one of the defendants held to have contributed to the claimant's damage will limit the ability of the claimant to recover in full for his injury, as the proportion attributable to the now bankrupt or insolvent defendant will be irrecoverable. In this latter case the risk of insolvency falls on the claimant.

A good example of contribution in practice is *Rouse v Squires* [1973] QB 889. A lorry driver, A, negligently drove his lorry so that it jack-knifed and blocked two lanes of a motorway. A car travelling behind collided with the lorry, but its rear lights remained on. The driver of a second lorry, R, parked his vehicle beyond the accident point and returned to the scene to offer assistance. A third lorry driver, F, parked his lorry just short of the accident, left its lights on to provide illumination, and also provided assistance. Finally, S, the driver of the fourth lorry, negligently failed to notice the accident until it was too late, and his lorry skidded into the back of F's vehicle, pushing it forward so that it caused fatal injuries to F. In the action by F's widow, the trial judge held that S was wholly responsible for the accident, but the Court of Appeal allowed an appeal, holding that the responsibility for the accident should be apportioned in the ratio 25/75 between A, the original lorry driver, and S. Although it was accepted that there might be cases where there was sufficient time for an oncoming driver to notice the accident and take evasive action (in which case there would be a break in the necessary causal link) this was not such a case.

The result in *Rouse* should be compared with *Wright v Lodge* [1993] 4 All ER 299 (noted by Jones (1994) 2 Tort L Rev 133). A small car broke down on an unlit part of a dual carriageway, and, whilst the driver was attempting to start it up again, it was hit by a lorry travelling at excessive speed, injuring the plaintiff, a passenger in the car. As a consequence of the collision, the lorry crossed the median strip and collided with other vehicles, killing one driver and injuring another. At the trial of the plaintiffs' actions against the lorry driver (who joined the driver of the car as a co-defendant), the driver of the car was held to have been negligent in not pushing the car to the verge of the road once it had broken down, and the driver was ordered to pay 10 per cent of the passenger's damages. However, the judge held that the reckless driving of the lorry driver was the sole cause of the injuries to the other drivers hit by the lorry. This result was upheld by the Court of Appeal, Parker LJ holding that:

Causation is also different. In the case of Miss Duncan [the passenger] there is an obvious connection between the presence of the Mini and the fact that it was struck from behind. The connection between its presence and the fact that the Scania [the lorry] went out of control and ended on its side in the westbound carriageway is in my view far from obvious. Suppose for example that the Scania, owing to its excessive speed and failure to observe the Mini until a very late stage had, instead of pulling over, proceeded upright across the westbound carriageway, through a brick wall into the driveway of a house and there injured a guest of the owners who was leaving after a dinner party. I would find it very hard to accept that such injuries were caused at all by the presence of the Mini...

In any event approaching the matter as if he were a jury and taking a common sense view, [the judge] was, as we are, clearly entitled to conclude that the presence of the Scania in the westbound carriageway was wholly attributable to Mr Lodge's reckless driving. It was unwarranted and unreasonable. It was the violence of the swerve and braking which sent his lorry out of control. Such violence was due to the reckless manner in which he was driving and it was his reckless speed which resulted in the swerve, loss of control and headlong career onto, and overturn on, the westbound carriageway. It is true that it would not have been there had the Mini not obstructed the nearside lane of the eastbound carriageway but the passages which I have cited show clearly that this is not enough. It does not thereby necessarily become a legally operative cause.

If the original accident was caused in part by the presence of the car on the dual carriageway, why should causation be denied to the injuries arising as a consequence of the collision? (Cf. *Bland v Morris* [2006] EWCA Civ 56, [2006] RTR 31 where the driver who was partly responsible for the original accident was also held to have some responsibility for the subsequent accident even though this involved later negligence by two other parties.)

Because of a tyre blow-out, partly caused by driver negligence, a car is left blocking part of a motorway. Both the driver and passenger move to the safety of the hard shoulder, but then the passenger returns to the car to retrieve some money he has left there. Whilst searching the car, he is hit by another vehicle which is being negligently driven by its driver. Who is responsible for the passenger's injuries? (See *Patel v McLeish & Bhupinder Singh Danjal*, unreported, Court of Appeal, 21 June 1996.)

Rescue attempts in emergency situations created by a defendant's negligence are unlikely to be held to break the causal chain, even if they cause or increase the damage suffered by the claimant. In *The Oropesa* [1943] P 32, the captain of one of two ships badly damaged by a collision, for which both were to blame, ordered most of his crew into a lifeboat, from where they were collected by the other ship. He later ordered the rest of the crew into another lifeboat, but the high seas capsized it and nine people died. The House of Lords held that the captain's decision did not break the chain of causation between the negligence which created the collision and the death because, even though he may have been guilty of an error of judgment, he was in a 'very perilous plight'.

Will the intervention of negligent medical treatment break the causal chain? In the criminal law it does not necessarily do so (*R v Cheshire* [1991] 1 WLR 844) and a similar position applies in the civil law. Certainly later medical negligence does not *always* extinguish the original tortfeasor's liability, and it has been suggested that only where there has been gross negligence in relation to the intervening medical treatment will the causal link be broken (*Webb v Barclays Bank plc* [2001] EWCA Civ 1141). Where both the original and subsequent negligent parties are before the court it may be that apportionment of the damage is the fairest option (see *Prendergast v Sam & Dee Ltd, The Times*, 14 March 1989; cf. *Rahman v Arearose Ltd* [2001] 2B 351, where it was conceded the intervening medical negligence was the sole cause of some of the claimant's injuries). Apportionment accords with the persuasive argument that, as the risk of negligent medical treatment is one which is entailed by the initial injury, such treatment should not break the causal link (see *Mahony v Kruschich (Demolitions) Pty Ltd* (1985) 156 CLR 522).

III. Remoteness

Although any attempt to encapsulate this complicated concept is problematic, remoteness of damage can be said to represent the law's attempt to place limits on liability for damage for which the defendant's negligence has factually been a cause but for which, as a matter of legal policy, no liability should attach. The previous section considered a similar problem and some commentators consider the two issues under the heading of 'Legal Causation' or 'Scope of Liability for Consequences'. Although the cases are not always clear, a useful analytical tool to apply is the 'scope of risk' approach. A defendant's negligence creates certain risks. If the claimant's damage falls within the risk that is created (i.e. if it is of a type that might foreseeably result from the defendant's negligence), it might be seen as appropriate to make the defendant liable for that damage, although, as the above section shows, other factors may militate in favour of non-recovery. Conversely, if the damage suffered bears no relation to the risk created, why should the defendant be liable? Recent years have seen the development of a new concept—the scope of the duty of care—to limit the defendant's liability. The influence of judicial policy in this area is clear for all to see.

1. *Wagon Mound* and the Scope of Risk Approach

Overseas Tankship (UK) Ltd v Morts Dock & Engineering Co Ltd (The Wagon Mound (No. 1)) [1961] AC 388

The facts appear in the extract.

Viscount Simonds (giving the advice of the Privy Council)

The relevant facts can be comparatively shortly stated, inasmuch as not one of the findings of fact in the exhaustive judgment of the learned trial judge has been challenged. The respondents at the relevant time carried on the business of ship-building, ship-repairing and general engineering at Morts Bay, Balmain, in the Port of Sydney. They owned and used for their business the Sheerlegs Wharf, a timber wharf about four hundred feet in length and forty feet wide, where there was a quantity of tools and equipment. In October and November, 1951, a vessel known as the *Corrimal* was moored alongside the wharf and was being refitted by the respondents. Her mast was lying on the wharf and a number of the respondents' employees were working both on it and on the vessel itself, using for this purpose electric and oxy-acetylene welding equipment. At the same time, the appellants were charterers by demise of the SS *Wagon Mound*, an oil-burning vessel which was moored at the Caltex Wharf on the northern shore of the harbour at a distance of about six hundred feet from the Sheerlegs Wharf. She was there from about 9am on 29 October until 11 am on 30 October 1951, for the purpose of discharging gasolene products and taking in bunkering oil. During the early hours of 30 October 1951, a large quantity of bunkering oil was, through the carelessness of the appellants' servants, allowed to spill into the bay, and, by 10.30 on the morning of that day, it had spread over a considerable part of the bay, being thickly concentrated in some places and particularly along the foreshore near the respondents' property. The appellants made no attempt to disperse the oil. The *Wagon Mound* unberthed and set sail very shortly after. When the respondents' works manager became aware of the condition of things in the vicinity of the wharf, he instructed their workmen that no welding or burning was to be carried on until further orders. He inquired of the manager of the Caltex Oil Co, at whose wharf the *Wagon Mound* was then still berthed, whether they could safely continue their operations on the wharf or on the *Corrimal*. The results of this inquiry, coupled with his own belief as to the inflammability of furnace oil in the open, led him to think that the respondents could safely carry on their operations. He gave instructions accordingly, but directed that all safety precautions should be taken to prevent inflammable material falling off the wharf into the oil. For the remainder of 30 October and until about 2 pm on 1 November, work was carried on as usual, the condition and congestion of the oil remaining substantially unaltered. But at about that time the oil under or near the wharf was ignited and a fire, fed initially by the oil, spread rapidly and burned with great intensity. The wharf and the *Corrimal* caught fire and considerable damage was done to the wharf and the equipment on it.

The outbreak of fire was due, as the learned judge found, to the fact that there was floating in the oil underneath the wharf a piece of debris on which lay some smouldering cotton waste or rag which had been set on fire by molten metal falling from the wharf; that the cotton waste or rag burst into flames; that the flames from the cotton waste set the floating oil afire either directly or by first setting fire to a wooden pile coated with oil and that, after the floating oil became ignited, the flames spread rapidly over the surface of the oil and quickly developed into a conflagration which severely damaged the wharf. He also made the all-important finding, which must be set out in his own words:

> The *raison d'être* of furnace oil is, of course, that it shall burn, but I find the [appellants] did not know and could not reasonably be expected to have known that it was capable of being set afire when spread on water.

It is on this footing that their Lordships will consider the question whether the appellants are liable for the fire damage...

It is inevitable that first consideration should be given to *Re Polemis and Furness, Withy & Co Ltd* [1921] 3 KB 560 which will henceforward be referred to as *Polemis*. For it was avowedly in deference to that decision and to decisions of the Court of Appeal that followed it that the full court was constrained to decide the present case in favour of the respondents...

What, then, did *Polemis* decide? Their Lordships do not propose to spend time in examining whether the issue there lay in breach of contract or in tort. That might be relevant for a tribunal for which the decision was a binding authority; for their Lordships it is not. It may, however, be observed that in the proceedings there was some confusion. The case arose out of a charter-party and went to arbitration under a term of it, and the first contention of the charterers was that they were protected from liability by the exception of fire in the charterparty. But it is clear from the pleadings and other documents, copies of which were supplied from the Record Office, that alternative claims for breach of contract and negligence were advanced, and it is clear, too, that, before Sankey J and the Court of Appeal, the case proceeded as one in which, independently of contractual obligations, the claim was for damages for negligence. It was on this footing that the Court of Appeal held that the charterers were responsible for all the consequences of their negligent act, even though those consequences could not reasonably have been anticipated. The negligent act was nothing more than the carelessness of stevedores (for whom the charterers were assumed to be responsible) in allowing a sling or rope by which it was hoisted to come into contact with certain boards, causing one of them to fall into the hold. The falling board hit some substances in the hold and caused a spark; the spark ignited petrol vapour in the hold; there was a rush of flames and the ship was destroyed. The Special Case submitted by the arbitrators found that the causing of the spark could not reasonably have been anticipated from the falling of the board, though some damage to the ship might reasonably have been anticipated. They did not indicate what damage might have been so anticipated.

There can be no doubt that the decision of the Court of Appeal in *Polemis* plainly asserts that, if the defendant is guilty of negligence, he is responsible for all the consequences, whether reasonably foreseeable or not. The generality of the proposition is, perhaps, qualified by the fact that each of the lords justices refers to the outbreak of fire as the direct result of the negligent act. There is thus introduced the conception that the negligent actor is not responsible for consequences which are not 'direct', whatever that may mean. . . .

[After considering relevant authorities both before and after *Polemis*, his Lordship continued:]

Enough has been said to show that the authority of *Polemis* has been severely shaken, though lip-service has from time to time been paid to it. In their Lordships' opinion, it should no longer be regarded as good law. It is not probable that many cases will for that reason have a different result, though it is hoped that the law will be thereby simplified, and that, in some cases at least, palpable injustice will be avoided. For it does not seem consonant with current ideas of justice or morality that, for an act of negligence, however slight or venial, which results in some trivial foreseeable damage, the actor should be liable for all consequences, however unforeseeable and however grave, so long as they can be said to be 'direct'. It is a principle of civil liability, subject only to qualifications which have no present relevance, that a man must be considered to be responsible for the probable consequences of his act. To demand more of him is too harsh a rule, to demand less is to ignore that civilised order requires the observance of a minimum standard of behaviour. This concept, applied to the slowly developing law of negligence, has led to a great variety of expressions which can, as it appears to their Lordships, be harmonised with little difficulty with the single exception of the so-called rule in *Polemis*. For, if it is asked why a man should be responsible for the natural or necessary or probable consequences of his act (or any other similar description of them), the answer is that it is not because they are natural or necessary or probable, but because, since they have this quality, it is judged, by the standard of the reasonable man, that he ought to have foreseen them. Thus it is that, over and over again, it has happened that, in different judgments in the same case and sometimes in a single judgment, liability for a consequence has been imposed on the ground that it was reasonably foreseeable, or alternatively on the ground that it was natural or necessary or probable. The two grounds have been treated as conterminous, and so they largely are. But, where they are not, the question arises to which the wrong answer was given in *Polemis*. For, if some limitation must be imposed on the consequences for which the negligent actor is to be held responsible—and all are agreed that some limitation there must be—why should that test (reasonable foreseeability) be rejected which, since he is judged by what the reasonable man ought to foresee, corresponds with the common conscience of mankind, and a test (the 'direct' consequence) be substituted which leads to nowhere but the never ending and insoluble problems of causation . . .

At an early stage in this judgment, their Lordships intimated that they would deal with the proposition which can best be stated by reference to the well-known dictum of Lord Summer [*Weld-Blundell v Stephens* [1920] AC 956 at p 984]: 'This, however, goes to culpability, not to compensation.' It is with the greatest respect to that very learned judge and to those who have echoed his words that their Lordships find themselves bound to state their view that this proposition is fundamentally false.

It is, no doubt, proper when considering tortious liability for negligence to analyse its elements and to say that the plaintiff must prove a duty owed to him by the defendant, a breach of that duty by the defendant, and consequent damage. But there can be no liability until the damage has been done. It is not the act but the consequences on which tortious liability is founded. Just as (as it has been said) there is no such thing as negligence in the air, so there is no such thing as liability in the air. Suppose an action brought by A for damage caused by the carelessness (a neutral word) of B, for example a fire caused by the careless spillage of oil. It may, of course, become relevant to know what duty B owed to A, but the only liability that is in question is the liability for damage by fire. It is vain to isolate the liability from its context and to say that B is or is not liable, and then to ask for what damage he is liable. For his liability is in respect of that damage and no other. If, as admittedly it is, B's liability (culpability) depends on the reasonable foreseeability of the consequent damage, how is that to be determined except by the foreseeability of the damage which in fact happened—the damage in suit? And, if that damage is unforeseeable so as to displace liability at large, how can the liability be restored so as to make compensation payable? But, it is said, a different position arises if B's careless act has been shown to be negligent and has caused some foreseeable damage to A. Their Lordships have already observed that to hold B liable for consequences, however unforeseeable, of a careless act, if, but only if, he is at the same time liable for some other damage, however trivial, appears to be neither logical nor just. This becomes more clear if it is supposed that similar unforeseeable damage is suffered by A and C, but other foreseeable damage, for which B is liable, by A only. A system of law which would hold B liable to A but not to C for the similar damage suffered by each of them could not easily be defended. Fortunately, the attempt is not necessary. For the same fallacy is at the root of the proposition. It is irrelevant to the question whether B is liable for unforeseeable damage that he is liable for foreseeable damage, as irrelevant as would the fact that he had trespassed on Whiteacre be to the question whether he had trespassed on Blackacre.

Again, suppose a claim by A for damage by fire by the careless act of B. Of what relevance is it to that claim that he has another claim arising out of the same careless act? It would surely not prejudice his claim if that other claim failed; it cannot assist it if it succeeds. Each of them rests on its own bottom and will fail if it can be established that the damage could not reasonably be foreseen. We have come back to the plain common sense stated by Lord Russell of Killowen in *Hay (or Bourhill) v Young* [1943] AC 92. As Denning LJ said in *King v Phillips* ([1953] 1 QB at p 441)' . . . there can be no doubt since *Hay (or Bourhill) v Young* that the test of liability for shock is foreseeability of injury by shock.' Their Lordships substitute the word 'fire' for 'shock' and indorse this statement of the law.

Their Lordships conclude this part of the case with some general observations. They have been concerned primarily to displace the proposition that unforeseeability is irrelevant if damage is 'direct.' In doing so, they have inevitably insisted that the essential factor in determining liability is whether the damage is of such a kind as the reasonable man should have foreseen. This accords with the general view thus stated by Lord Atkin in *M'Alister (or Donoghue) v Stevenson* [1932] AC 562 at 580:

> The liability for negligence, whether you style it such or treat it as in other systems as a species of 'culpa', is no doubt based upon a general public sentiment of moral wrongdoing for which the offender must pay.

It is a departure from this sovereign principle if liability is made to depend solely on the damage being the 'direct' or 'natural' consequence of the precedent act. Who knows or can be assumed to know all the processes of nature? But if it would be wrong that a man should be held liable for damage unpredictable by a reasonable man because it was 'direct' or 'natural', equally it would be wrong that he should escape liability, however 'indirect' the damage, if he foresaw or could reasonably foresee the intervening events which led to its being done; cf *Woods v Duncan* ([1946] AC 401 at 442). Thus foreseeability becomes the effective test. In reasserting this principle, their Lordships conceive that they do not depart from, but follow and develop, the law of negligence as laid down by Alderson B in *Blyth v Birmingham Waterworks Co* (1856) 11 Exch 781 . . .

Appeal allowed.

COMMENTARY

The extract sets out two approaches to remoteness of damages. The first, derived from the Court of Appeal decision in *Re Polemis and Furness, Withy & Co Ltd* [1921] 3 KB 560, is based on directness. The Privy Council in the above case described this as meaning that if the defendant is guilty of negligence, he is responsible for all the consequences, whether reasonably foreseeable or not, as long as they are a 'direct' consequence of the negligence. However, it is probable that this was limited to situations where the plaintiff was foreseeably endangered by the negligence, as was the case in *Polemis*: it was foreseeable that the falling plank would cause some damage to the plaintiff, albeit not fire damage (see Dias [1962] CLJ 178).

Whatever the precise nature of the directness approach, it was disapproved by the Privy Council in the above case in favour of a test based upon reasonable foreseeability of damage. As liability (duty and breach) was based on the foresight of damage, it was only fair that compensation was based on the same principle; hence the rejection of the split between culpability and compensation. If one has a duty to take care only in respect of certain damage, one should be liable to pay compensation only if that damage occurs. Not everyone agrees that this necessarily follows; as *Fleming* argues (p. 238):

> But in truth, the premise does not compel the conclusion. It may be thought politic that the reason for creating liability should also delimit it, but it is just as tenable, and certainly as logical, to insist that there are good reasons within the framework of fault for holding a proven wrongdoer liable for injury he has caused even if it went beyond all ken. 'The judgment lies in the realm of values and what you choose depends upon what you want' (Gregory, 'Proximate Cause in Negligence—A Retreat from Rationalisation' (1938) 6 U Chi L Rev 36 at 47).

Another problem that arises if foreseeability is used as the basis of remoteness of damage is the relationship between foreseeability of damage at the duty of care stage and foreseeability at the remoteness stage. If it has already been decided, as part of the duty of care inquiry, that the defendant could foresee that the claimant was a foreseeable victim of the defendant's negligence and was owed a duty of care in respect of loss of the type that he actually suffered, why is it necessary to ask at the remoteness stage whether loss of that type was reasonably foreseeable? Is foreseeability at the duty stage different from foreseeability at the remoteness stage? A possible approach is provided by the extract below.

D. Harris, I. D. Campbell and R. Halson, *Remedies in Contract and Tort* 2nd edn. (London: Butterworths, 2002) pp. 315–16

> The tests for duty of care and remoteness are not identical: both use the phrase 'reasonable foreseeabilty', but they are applied at different times in the sequence of events, and are therefore based on different sets of data. The purpose of using foreseeability of risk in the duty of care concept is to draw a conclusion as to whether D's action should be tested by the standard of care of the reasonable man. In the light of his foresight of possible risks would the reasonable man in D's position (immediately before he acted) have considered that he should take care to avoid harming someone in C's position? ...
>
> [Generally] it may be said that at the duty of care stage the risk need not be seen in any detail, nor need there be foresight of a particular way in which D might fall below the standard of reasonable care. There might be many ways in which he could be careless, but the duty test

is phrased in general terms: 'If care is not taken by D in the action he is about to undertake, is there a risk of harm to someone in C's position?' The phrase 'if care is not taken' is applied in a general, unspecified way, without knowledge of the actual act or omission by D which will later be labelled as negligent. But the causation and remoteness tests are applied after D has acted: the information given to the reasonable man has then expanded to include knowledge of the particular act or omission found to be negligent. The test of foreseeability is applied to D's specific action: what types of consequence are foreseeable by the reasonable man in D's shoes, given the knowledge that, in the particular circumstances, he has dropped this plank onto the hold of the ship; or has spilled this oil into the harbour at this place; or has dropped this hardboard cover into this cauldron of chemicals, or has given this piece of inaccurate information. The range of foreseeability will vary according to the nature of the negligent action in question: in most situations where D owes C a duty of care, the duty could be broken by many different acts or omissions on the part of D. The range of foreseeable risks will depend on the actual negligence in question. Some negligent acts will create only the risk of damage by physical impact, others the risk of damage by fire or explosion, others the risk that C will himself choose to take some step in reliance on D's statement, and so on. Knowledge of the particular action may widen foresight: if I drop a lighted cigarette, there may be a foreseeable risk of fire; but in other cases it may narrow the range of foresight: dropping this particular lid into this chemical mixture may create no foreseeable risk of a chemical explosion, but only a risk of splashing from the liquid. . . .

COMMENTARY

In a section not extracted, it is also suggests that whether a duty is owed depends not just on foresight of the risk but also on whether precautions would be taken to prevent that risk. It is suggested, however, that this is really a breach issue and should not be considered as part of the duty inquiry.

Foreseeability: Duty and Remoteness

Nonetheless, the main argument presented by the authors is plausible. They argue that, at the duty stage, the court considers matters prospectively and looks at the whole range of risks that the defendant might create if he is negligent in the activity he is about to undertake. The purpose of the inquiry is to decide whether the law should impose an obligation on the defendant to act carefully. If the risks are sufficiently serious, that warrants the imposition of a duty of care. But at the remoteness stage, the court focuses upon what actually occurred (i.e. at the precise way in which the defendant was negligent) and asks whether injury to the claimant was of a type that was a foreseeable consequence of the defendant's (actual) negligence. The inquiry into what damage was foreseeable at the remoteness stage is for a different purpose: it is to determine whether the claimant's injury was within the risk created by the defendant's negligence. In this respect, hindsight inevitably comes into the equation, for one cannot know what risks were created without knowledge of what happened.

The question arises whether this is how the courts view the role of the concept in the two contexts of duty and remoteness. An immediate difficulty in attributing this approach to the courts is the unforeseeable claimant rule (see p. 128, above). The range of risks arising from any given activity is very large indeed, and it is difficult to see how (except in very unusual cases) a claimant could be regarded as outside the zone of risk unless one takes into account details of what actually happened. It is, for instance, difficult to see how this approach allowed the House of Lords to reach the conclusion in *Bourhill v Young* [1943] AC 92 that the pursuer was not a foreseeable victim of the deceased motorcyclist's negligence (see p. 129, above): surely there was a risk that he might actually have run into her, or indeed any number of other road users. It is clear in such cases that it is the type of harm suffered by the claimant that causes the court to rule that there was not sufficient foreseeability of injury. This points to a second difficulty: if the duty of care is imposed relative to harm of a particular type (whether it be personal injury, psychiatric illness, property damage or pure economic loss) what room is there for a 'foreseeable type of harm' rule at the remoteness stage? One possible answer is that the relevant specification of the type of harm may be narrower at the remoteness stage—where an individual determination is made in respect of the actual facts of the case—than it is at the duty stage—where the duty is made relative to losses of different sorts in order to give expression to general considerations of policy applying to all cases (not just the particular case). For instance, in *Wagon Mound* itself, the duty was clearly owed in respect of 'property damage' taken as a general category—no general consideration of public policy precluded the recognition of such a duty in respect of that category of damage—but the court still held that it would go too far on the facts to impose liability not just for damage caused by the oil resulting from fouling but also for damage caused when the oil caught fire. This concern of fairness, arising in respect of the particular facts of the case, was appropriately considered under the head of remoteness.

Application of the *Wagon Mound* Principle

Whatever the truth of the above, it was clear from its inception that the *Wagon Mound* formula would rarely be used to limit liability where physical injury was caused by negligence. The first concession came in *Smith v Leech Brain & Co* [1962] 2 QB 405, where the plaintiff suffered a burn to his lip as a result of the defendant's negligence. Because of a pre-malignant condition, the burn ultimately resulted in the plaintiff contracting cancer, from which he died. The Court of Appeal allowed his widow's action, holding that *Wagon Mound* did not affect the longstanding rule that the defendant takes his victim as he finds him (the thin or 'egg-shell' skull rule). As long as the type of injury which he suffered (the burn) was foreseeable, the fact that this caused the plaintiff greater injuries than might have been foreseeable was irrelevant. Shortly afterwards, the House of Lords had to decide whether a 10-year-old boy should recover in respect of burns suffered in a paraffin fire. In *Hughes v Lord Advocate* [1963] AC 837, the defender's negligence had consisted of failing to secure adequately the entrance to a man-hole. The pursuer and another boy took one of the warning paraffin lamps around the site and went into the man-hole, and after they had come out the pursuer accidentally knocked a lamp into the hole with the consequence that there was a large explosion and fire. The force of the explosion knocked the pursuer back into the hole and he was badly burned. It was argued for the defenders that the damage was too remote; damage by paraffin burn was foreseeable but not by paraffin explosion. This was rejected by the House of Lords, Lord Reid holding that '[t]his accident was caused by a known source of danger, but caused in a way which could not have been foreseen, and in my judgment that affords no defence'. Both cases illustrate the courts adopting a definition of type or kind of damage favourable to the claimant. Once the claimant has suffered a foreseeable type or kind of damage it matters not that the extent of the injury was more extensive than was foreseeable, or that the injury occurred in an unforeseeable way.

Nonetheless, in the first decade after *Wagon Mound* there were a few successful attempts to deny recovery on the ground that the plaintiff's physical injury was too remote. In *Doughty v Turner Manufacturing Co Ltd* [1964] 1 QB 518, an asbestos lid fell into a vat of molten liquid, and shortly thereafter the plaintiff was burnt when some of the molten liquid erupted. The plaintiff's claim failed on the basis that, although burning by splashing was foreseeable from the falling of the lid, in fact the plaintiff's injury was caused because the temperature of the liquid caused a change in the chemical composition of the lid and was therefore too remote. In *Tremain v Pike* [1969] 1 WLR 1556 the plaintiff contracted Weil's disease as a result of exposure to rats' urine. The defendant had negligently allowed his farm to be overrun with rats, but the hapless plaintiff lost because the judge found that, whilst injuries such as rat bites were foreseeable, the rare disease contracted by the plaintiff was not. The inconsistency of the law in this area can be highlighted by two other decisions, *Bradford v Robinson Rentals Ltd* [1967] 1 WLR 337 and *Vacwell Engineering Co Ltd v B. D. H. Chemicals Ltd* [1971] 1 QB 88. In *Bradford* the plaintiff suffered frostbite as a result of his employer's negligence in requiring him to drive a vehicle without a heater in extremely cold weather. To avoid frosting the windscreen he was forced to leave a window open with the result that he contracted frostbite. It was held that this was a type or kind of injury that was foreseeable as a result of the breach. In *Vacwell*, injuries occurred when chemicals supplied in glass ampoules reacted with water in which the ampoules were being washed and caused a large explosion. Because a small explosion had been foreseeable, all the damage that occurred was recoverable even though its extent could not have been anticipated.

The modern trend, illustrated by *Smith v Leech Brain*, is to define type or kind of injury widely, with the result that the extent of the foreseeable type or kind of injury or the method of its occurrence does not affect liability. Lord Nicholls has doubted whether the distinction drawn in *Doughty* (described above) would commend itself to modern courts (*Attorney-General v Hartwell* [2004] 1 WLR 1273 at [29]), and it may even be that for the purposes of remoteness the relevant type or kind of injury can be as wide as simply 'physical injury', a view which gains support from the decision of the House of Lords in *Jolley v Sutton London Borough Council* [2000] 1 WLR 1082. In this case a child of 13 was injured when a derelict boat he and his friend were trying to repair collapsed on him after the jack they had used to prop up the boat gave way. Although the Council conceded the existence of a duty of care and breach of that duty, it argued successfully in the Court of Appeal that the damage was too remote. Physical injury by, say, falling through rotten planks on the boat's deck was foreseeable, but not physical injury caused when a jack collapsed. The House of Lords, however, agreed with the trial judge that the appropriate classification of the risk was that children would 'meddle with the boat at the risk of some physical injury'. When the question is framed is this broad way, an affirmative answer to the duty question necessarily means the damage is not too remote; as was said in *Foster v Maguire* [2001] EWCA Civ 273 at [24], per Sir Anthony Evans, '…no separate question arises under the heads of causation and remoteness. The kind and description of the damage in fact suffered, namely, physical injury, was reasonable foreseeable…'

An even wider classification may be required as a result of the House of Lords' decision in *Page v Smith* [1996] AC 155, which suggests that physical and psychiatric injury are one type or kind of damage—'personal injury'. The scope of *Page v Smith* remains uncertain; although the House of Lords applied the 'one type of damage' approach in *Simmons v British Steel plc* [2004] UKHL 20, [2004] ICR 585 (as did a number of their Lordships in *Corr v IBC Vehicles Ltd* [2008] AC 884; cf. Lords Mance (at [46]) and Neuberger (at [54])), its application was limited in *Rothwell v Chemical & Insulating Co Ltd* [2008] AC 281 where it was held not to

extend to a psychiatric injury suffered as a result of the claimant's fear of contracting a physical injury *in the future* as a result of the defendant's negligence (for contrasting views of the
effect of *Rothwell* on *Page*, see Steele [2008] CLJ 28; Leczykiewicz (2008) 124 LQR 552).
Where *Page v Smith* does apply, it becomes difficult to see any role for foreseeability of damage in remoteness, for if personal injury was foreseeable at the duty stage it must also be so
at the remoteness stage. The abandonment of the 'type of harm' approach in this context is
supported by Lord Hoffmann's speech in *Jolley* (above), where his Lordship argued that, at
least where children were concerned, the defendant should be liable if he was under a duty
to take steps to avoid some risks and it would have cost no more to avoid the risk that actually
materialised. If this was the case the defendant would be liable for 'the materialisation of
even relatively small risks of a different kind' (*Jolley v Sutton London Borough Council* [2000]
1 WLR 1082 at 1093; cf. *Clare v Perry* [2005] EWCA Civ 39). If this is correct, does it make
any sense to deny liability on the ground that, although property damage to a wharf by being
fouled with oil was foreseeable, property damage by fire was not? Is Nolan (1996–7) 7 KCLJ
96 correct to see *Page* as a requiem for the *Wagon Mound* approach? It is submitted, however,
that until the courts depart from *Wagon Mound (No. 1)*, 'property damage' cannot be a type
or kind of damage for the purpose of remoteness, because property damage was foreseeable
in *Wagon Mound* itself, but this was insufficient to satisfy the test. However, the basis on
which a narrower classification should be made is unclear (see Nolan (2001) 9 Tort L Rev 104,
and, for a critical analysis, see *Conaghan and Mansell*, pp. 66–72).

2. Policy-Based Limitations on Liability

Banque Bruxelles Lambert SA v Eagle Star Insurance Co Ltd [1997] AC 191

In three appeals, the House of Lords had to decide the extent of a valuer's liability in respect
of a negligent valuation upon which commercial lenders had relied in making loans. In each
case it was conceded that the valuation had been negligent. As a result of the collapse of the
property market at the end of the 1980s and early 1990s, the plaintiff lenders failed to recoup
the amounts of the loans when the properties on which they were secured were sold, and the
mortgagors either could not be found or were worthless. The Court of Appeal held that, in a
case in which the lenders would not have made the loan if there had been a non-negligent valuation, they were entitled to recover the difference between the sum which they lent, together
with a reasonable rate of interest, and the net sum which they actually recovered. The valuer
was therefore liable for the whole risk of a transaction which, but for his negligence, would not
have happened, and was liable for all the loss attributable to the fall in the market. The defendants appealed.

Lord Hoffmann

My Lords, the three appeals before the House raise a common question of principle. What is the
extent of the liability of a valuer who has provided a lender with a negligent overvaluation of the
property offered as security for the loan? The facts have two common features. The first is that
if the lender had known the true value of the property, he would not have lent. The second is
that a fall in the property market after the date of the valuation greatly increased the loss which
the lender eventually suffered.

The Court of Appeal (*Banque Bruxelles Lambert SA v Eagle Star Insurance Co Ltd and other appeals* [1995] QB 375) decided that in a case in which the lender would not otherwise have lent (which they called a 'no-transaction' case), he is entitled to recover the difference between the sum which he lent, together with a reasonable rate of interest, and the net sum which he actually got back. The valuer bears the whole risk of a transaction which, but for his negligence, would not have happened. He is therefore liable for all the loss attributable to a fall in the market. They distinguished what they called a 'successful transaction' case, in which the evidence shows that if the lender had been correctly advised, he would still have lent a lesser sum on the same security. In such a case, the lender can recover only the difference between what he has actually lost and what he would have lost if he had lent the lesser amount. Since the fall in the property market is a common element in both the actual and the hypothetical calculations, it does not increase the valuer's liability.

The valuers appeal. They say that a valuer provides an estimate of the value of the property at the date of the valuation. He does not undertake the role of a prophet. It is unfair that merely because for one reason or other the lender would not otherwise have lent, the valuer should be saddled with the whole risk of the transaction, including a subsequent fall in the value of the property.

Much of the discussion, both in the judgment of the Court of Appeal and in argument at the Bar, has assumed that the case is about the correct measure of damages for the loss which the lender has suffered. The Court of Appeal (at 401–402) began its judgment with the citation of three well-known cases, *Robinson v Harman* (1848) 1 Exch 850 at 855, *Livingstone v Rawyards Coal Co* (1880) 5 App Cas 25 at 39 and *British Westinghouse Electric and Manufacturing Co Ltd v Underground Electric Rlys Co of London Ltd* [1912] AC 673 at 688–89, stating the principle that where an injury is to be compensated by damages, the damages should be as nearly as possible the sum which would put the plaintiff in the position in which he would have been if he had not been injured. It described this principle as 'the necessary point of departure' (at 403).

I think that this was the wrong place to begin. Before one can consider the principle on which one should calculate the damages to which a plaintiff is entitled as compensation for loss, it is necessary to decide for what kind of loss he is entitled to compensation. A correct description of the loss for which the valuer is liable must precede any consideration of the measure of damages. For this purpose it is better to begin at the beginning and consider the lender's cause of action.

The lender sues on a contract under which the valuer, in return for a fee, undertakes to provide him with certain information. Precisely what information he has to provide depends, of course, upon the terms of the individual contract. There is some dispute on this point in respect of two of the appeals, to which I shall have to return. But there is one common element which everyone accepts. In each case the valuer was required to provide an estimate of the price which the property might reasonably be expected to fetch if sold in the open market at the date of the valuation.

There is again agreement on the purpose for which the information was provided. It was to form part of the material on which the lender was to decide whether, and if so how much, he would lend. The valuation tells the lender how much, at current values, he is likely to recover if he has to resort to his security. This enables him to decide what margin, if any, an advance of a given amount will allow for: a fall in the market; reasonably foreseeable variance from the figure put forward by the valuer (a valuation is an estimate of the most probable figure which the property will fetch, not a prediction that it will fetch precisely that figure); accidental damage to the property and any other of the contingencies which may happen. The valuer will know that if he overestimates the value of the property, the lender's margin for all these purposes will be correspondingly less.

On the other hand, the valuer will not ordinarily be privy to the other considerations which the lender may take into account, such as how much money he has available, how much the borrower needs to borrow, the strength of his covenant, the attraction of the rate of interest, or the other personal or commercial considerations which may induce the lender to lend.

Because the valuer will appreciate that his valuation, though not the only consideration which would influence the lender, is likely to be a very important one, the law implies into the contract a term that the valuer will exercise reasonable care and skill. The relationship between the parties also gives rise to a concurrent duty in tort (see *Henderson v Merrett Syndicates Ltd* [1995] 2 AC 145). But the scope of the duty in tort is the same as in contract.

A duty of care such as the valuer owes does not, however, exist in the abstract. A plaintiff who sues for breach of a duty imposed by the law (whether in contract or tort or under statute) must do more than prove that the defendant has failed to comply. He must show that the duty was owed to him and that it was a duty in respect of the kind of loss which he has suffered. Both of these requirements are illustrated by *Caparo Industries plc v Dickman* [1990] 2 AC 605. The auditors' failure to use reasonable care in auditing the company's statutory accounts was a breach of their duty of care. But they were not liable to an outside take-over bidder because the duty was not owed to him. Nor were they liable to shareholders who had bought more shares in reliance on the accounts because, although they were owed a duty of care, it was in their capacity as members of the company and not in the capacity (which they shared with everyone else) of potential buyers of its shares. Accordingly, the duty which they were owed was not in respect of loss which they might suffer by buying its shares. As Lord Bridge of Harwich said (at 627):

> It is never sufficient to ask simply whether A owes B a duty of care. It is always necessary to determine the scope of the duty by reference to the kind of damage from which A must take care to save B harmless.

In the present case, there is no dispute that the duty was owed to the lenders. The real question in this case is the kind of loss in respect of which the duty was owed.

How is the scope of the duty determined? In the case of a statutory duty, the question is answered by deducing the purpose of the duty from the language and context of the statute (see *Gorris v Scott* (1874) LR 9 Exch 125). In the case of tort, it will similarly depend upon the purpose of the rule imposing the duty. Most of the judgments in *Caparo* are occupied in examining the Companies Act 1985 to ascertain the purpose of the auditor's duty to take care that the statutory accounts comply with the Act. In the case of an implied contractual duty, the nature and extent of the liability is defined by the term which the law implies. As in the case of any implied term, the process is one of construction of the agreement as a whole in its commercial setting. The contractual duty to provide a valuation and the known purpose of that valuation compel the conclusion that the contract includes a duty of care. The scope of the duty, in the sense of the consequences for which the valuer is responsible, is that which the law regards as best giving effect to the express obligations assumed by the valuer: neither cutting them down so that the lender obtains less than he was reasonably entitled to expect, nor extending them so as to impose on the valuer a liability greater than he could reasonably have thought he was undertaking.

What therefore should be the extent of the valuer's liability? The Court of Appeal said that he should be liable for the loss which would not have occurred if he had given the correct advice. The lender having, in reliance on the valuation, embarked upon a transaction which he would not otherwise have undertaken, the valuer should bear all the risks of that transaction, subject only to the limitation that the damage should have been within the reasonable contemplation of the parties.

There is no reason in principle why the law should not penalise wrongful conduct by shifting on to the wrongdoer the whole risk of consequences which would not have happened but for the wrongful act. Hart and Honoré, *Causation in the Law* (2nd edn, 1985) p. 120 say that it would, for example, be perfectly intelligible to have a rule by which an unlicensed driver was responsible for all the consequences of his having driven, even if they were unconnected with his not having a licence. One might adopt such a rule in the interests of deterring unlicensed driving. But that is not the normal rule. One may compare, for example, *Western Steamship Co Ltd v NV Konninklijke Rotterdamsche Lloyd, The Empire Jamaica* [1955] P 259 at 264 per Evershed MR, in which a collision was caused by a 'blunder in seamanship of ... a somewhat serious and startling character' by an uncertificated second mate. Although the owners knew that the mate was not certificated and it was certainly the case that the collision would not have happened if he had not been employed, it was held in limitation proceedings that the damage took place without the employers' 'actual fault or privity' because the mate was in fact experienced and (subject to this one aberration) competent (see [1955] P 259 at 271). The collision was not, therefore, attributable to his not having a certificate. The owners were not treated as responsible for all the consequences of having employed an uncertificated mate, but only for the consequences of his having been uncertificated.

Rules which make the wrongdoer liable for all the consequences of his wrongful conduct are exceptional and need to be justified by some special policy. Normally the law limits liability to those consequences which are attributable to that which made the act wrongful. In the case of liability in negligence for providing inaccurate information, this would mean liability for the consequences of the information being inaccurate.

I can illustrate the difference between the ordinary principle and that adopted by the Court of Appeal by an example. A mountaineer about to undertake a difficult climb is concerned about the fitness of his knee. He goes to a doctor who negligently makes a superficial examination and pronounces the knee fit. The climber goes on the expedition, which he would not have undertaken if the doctor had told him the true state of his knee. He suffers an injury which is an entirely foreseeable consequence of mountaineering, but has nothing to do with his knee.

On the Court of Appeal's principle, the doctor is responsible for the injury suffered by the mountaineer because it is damage which would not have occurred if he had been given correct information about his knee. He would not have gone on the expedition and would have suffered no injury. On what I have suggested is the more usual principle, the doctor is not liable. The injury has not been caused by the doctor's bad advice, because it would have occurred even if the advice had been correct. ...

Your Lordships might, I would suggest, think that there was something wrong with a principle which, in the example which I have given, produced the result that the doctor was liable. What is the reason for this feeling? I think that the Court of Appeal's principle offends common sense because it makes the doctor responsible for consequences which, though in general terms foreseeable, do not appear to have a sufficient causal connection with the subject matter of the duty. The doctor was asked for information on only one of the considerations which might affect the safety of the mountaineer on the expedition. There seems no reason of policy which requires that the negligence of the doctor should require the transfer to him of all the foreseeable risks of the expedition.

I think that one can to some extent generalise the principle upon which this response depends. It is that a person under a duty to take reasonable care to provide information on which someone else will decide upon a course of action is, if negligent, not generally regarded as responsible for all the consequences of that course of action. He is responsible only for the consequences of the information being wrong. A duty of care which imposes upon the informant responsibility for losses which would have occurred even if the information which he gave had been correct is not in my view fair and reasonable as between the parties. It is therefore inappropriate either as an implied term of a contract or as a tortious duty arising from the relationship between them.

The principle thus stated distinguishes between a duty to provide information for the purpose of enabling someone else to decide upon a course of action and a duty to advise someone as to what course of action he should take. If the duty is to advise whether or not a course of action should be taken, the adviser must take reasonable care to consider all the potential consequences of that course of action. If he is negligent, he will therefore be responsible for all the foreseeable loss which is a consequence of that course of action having been taken. If his duty is only to supply information, he must take reasonable care to ensure that the information is correct and if he is negligent, will be responsible for all the foreseeable consequences of the information being wrong.

I think that this principle is implicit in the decision of this House in *Banque Financière de la Cité SA v Westgate Insurance Co Ltd sub nom Banque Keyser Ullmann SA v Skandia (UK) Insurance Co Ltd* [1991] 2 AC 249. Some banks had lent a large sum of money on the security of, first, property which the borrower had represented to be valuable, and, secondly, insurance policies against any shortfall on the realisation of the property. When the borrower turned out to be a swindler and the property worthless, the insurers relied upon a fraud exception in the policies to repudiate liability. The banks discovered that the agent of their broker who had placed the insurance had, by an altogether separate fraud, issued cover notes in respect of non-existent policies for part of the risk. This had come to the knowledge of one of the insurers before a substantial part of the advances had been made. The banks claimed that the insurers were under a duty of good faith to disclose this information and that, if they had done so, the banks would have so distrusted the brokers that they would have made no advance and therefore suffered no loss.

Lord Templeman (with whom all the other members of the House agreed) dealt with the matter in terms of causation. He said that assuming a duty to disclose the information existed, the breach of that duty did not cause the loss. The failure to inform the lenders of the broker's fraud induced them to think that valid policies were in place. But even if this had been true, the loss would still have happened. The insurers would still have been entitled to repudiate the policies under the fraud exception.

Lord Templeman could only have dealt with the case in this way if he thought it went without saying that the insurers' duty to provide information made them liable, not for all loss which would not have been suffered if the information had been given, but only for loss caused by the lender having lent on a false basis, namely, in the belief that insurance policies had been effected. If that had not been the principle which the House was applying, the discussion of whether the non-existence of the policies had caused the loss would have been irrelevant. I respectfully think that the underlying principle was right and that it is decisive of this case. The Court of Appeal distinguished *Banque Financière de la Cité* on the ground that the insurers could not have foreseen the borrower's fraud. No doubt this is true: it shows that the rule that damages are limited to what was within the reasonable contemplation of the parties can sometimes make arguments over the scope of the duty academic. But I do not think it was the way the House actually decided the case. Lord Templeman's speech puts the matter firmly on the ground of causation and the analysis makes sense only on the footing that he was concerned with the consequences to the lenders of having lent without knowing the true facts, rather than with what would have been the consequences of disclosure. . . .

Lords Goff, **Slynn**, **Jauncey** and **Nicholls** agreed with Lord Hoffmann.

COMMENTARY

The analytical tool used to limit liability by Lord Hoffmann is the 'scope' of the duty of care owed by the valuers to the lenders. The valuers provided incorrect information; hence the liability of the valuers should be limited to the consequences of that information being incorrect. This was assessed as the difference between the valuation as given and what a non-negligent valuation would have been at the time. An earlier Court of Appeal decision can be seen to adopt similar reasoning in respect of a claim by a company for trading losses (*Galoo Ltd v Graeme Murray* [1994] 1 WLR 1360). The company argued that if the defendant auditor had provided an accurate valuation of the company it would have ceased trading and hence incurred no further loss, but it was held that the auditor's actions had only provided the opportunity for the loss to occur. For comment on *Galoo* see O'Sullivan [1995] CLJ 25; Lunney (1995–6) 6 KCLJ 99.

A similar 'scope of duty' approach was used by the House of Lords in *Caparo Industries plc v Dickman* [1990] 2 AC 605, where it was held that auditors did not provide audits for the purpose of providing information to shareholders or investors which they could use to make investment decisions; hence they were not liable when such persons relied on the audit to their detriment. The scope of the duty did not extend to those parties. Any duty of care should be limited to the parties for whom the work was undertaken. A more controversial example is *Stone & Rolls Ltd v Moore Stephens* [2009] 1 AC 1370, where a bare majority of their Lordships held that auditors owed no duty to a company to detect the fraud of its managing director where the managing director was the 'directing mind and will' of the company. Although the case was primarily concerned with the question of when the fraud of a person representing the company can be attributed to the company itself (the 'attribution' question), the majority was also concerned that finding a duty to be owed in such circumstances would be contrary to *Caparo*. As the company was insolvent, the only beneficiaries of finding a duty to exist would be its creditors, but the scope of the auditor's duty of care did not extend that far. (Cf. the powerful dissent of Lord Mance at [267]–[270].)

In *Banque Bruxelles*, the valuers clearly owed a duty of care to the plaintiff lenders, and were liable for something, but because they had only been employed to provide information the limit of their responsibility was the inaccuracy of that information. The valuer's liability might also be reduced if the lender had been guilty of contributory negligence by virtue of its own lending practices the effect of which was to increase the lender's loss (*Platform Home Loans Ltd v Oyston Shipways Ltd* [2000] 2 AC 190; on the difficulties of applying the scope of the duty approach in such cases see Howarth (2000) 8 Tort L Rev 85). For comment on *Banque Bruxelles*, see Wightman (1998) 61 MLR 68, and the decision of the High Court of Australia in *Kenny & Good Pty Ltd v MGICA* (1999) 199 CLR 413 where Lord Hoffmann's general approach was rejected, although two members of the court agreed that the valuer's liability should be limited).

Can any of the analytical tools suggested above adequately deal with the problem of limiting the valuer's liability? Stapleton (1997) 113 LQR 1, commenting on the 'scope of duty' approach, argues:

> …a formulaic 'sphere of risk' approach which relies simply on setting the scope of the duty in terms of the consequences which made the act wrongful is open to the same complaint and danger of manipulation; while Lord Hoffmann asserts that what makes the valuation wrongful is that it was inaccurate so that liability is limited to the results of this, someone else might assert that what makes it wrongful is that it was not a careful valuation, and liability should include the consequences of this such as the risk of the advisee locking himself into a transaction from which he cannot escape if the market begins to fall.

In contrast, both the language of remoteness of damage and a non-formulaic approach to duty have the advantage of signalling that there is no mechanical test which can be applied and that the court has to make a judgment about the extent of legal responsibility, a judgment which one hopes will evaluate the often complex concerns which go to produce the boundaries placed on civil obligations....

Lord Hoffmann has subsequently accepted, extra-judicially, that the 'scope of duty' terminology is inappropriate in this context but still insists upon the closeness of the link between the 'nature' of the duty and the extent of liability for breach of that duty ('Causation' (2005) 121 LQR 592 at 596). However, whether the 'nature' of the duty is conceptually any clearer than its 'scope' may be doubted. Stapleton ('Cause in fact and the scope of liability for consequences' (2003) 119 LQR 388) suggests that the question in such cases is about the circumstances in which a foreseeable type and kind of damage is nonetheless irrecoverable. One example is where the consequences sought to be attributed to the defendant are 'coincidences', coincidences being events the occurrence of which is not generally increased by the defendant's negligence. Thus in *Banque Bruxelles*, the risk of a fall in the market was not generally increased by negligent valuations. Hence the loss caused by the fall was a coincidence and only exceptionally does the law attribute responsibility to the defendant for coincidental losses. Of course, describing the loss as coincidental does not relieve the court from asking the normative question of whether coincidental losses should be recovered; as Stapleton had previously argued ((1997) 113 LQR 1 at 7): 'A line must be drawn between types of foreseeable "but for" consequences. Once arrived at, it can be packaged in duty or remoteness terms but the central problem is the line drawing. Typically, there is no consensus where it should be drawn nor even which factors should weigh in its determination, but it must be drawn with explicit evaluation of the factors taken into account.'

A different approach is adopted by Stauch (2001) 64 MLR 191, who argues that remoteness questions are much more a question of principle than their portrayal often suggests. He comments: 'In particular, the concept has been too readily associated with outcome harm [i.e. the harm the claimant actually suffers] that results from negligent conduct. Instead, the question of whether the risk that made the defendant's conduct faulty subsequently materialised requires us to ask not so much "what" that damage was, but "how" it occurred.' In other words, instead of simply looking to the type of harm suffered, one should first ask what were the foreseeable risks associated with the defendant's negligence. As the notion of risk necessarily entails the potential causing of harm, Stauch argues there will be a foreseeable causal chain between the negligent conduct giving rise to the risk(s) and the causing of harm as a result of the risk materialising. Where the harm is caused in accordance with the foreseeable causal chain, such harm is not too remote; conversely, the greater the degree of diversion from the foreseeable causal chain the more likely it is that the harm will be held to be too remote to be recovered. Although Stauch does not claim that all questions of remoteness can be solved in this way, he argues it is more principled than the 'scope of duty' approach. An example of this approach can be seen in *Clare v Perry* [2005] EWCA Civ 39. It was alleged that the defendant was careless by not taking steps to prevent persons from falling off a wall. The claimant was injured when she attempted to climb down the wall. The Court of Appeal rejected the claim; the risk to which the alleged negligence related was of someone accidentally falling off the wall, not deliberately trying to descend it. In Stauch's terms, the risk of injury by deliberately climbing down the wall diverted sufficiently from the foreseeable causal chain (an accidental fall) so as to deny recovery. One difficulty with this approach, however, may be defining the risks that made the defendant's conduct negligent; as Nolan puts it ((2001) 9 Tort L Rev 101 at 104, commenting on *Jolley v Sutton London Borough Council* [2000] 1 WLR 1082): 'And when it comes to identifying the risk or risks that made the defendant's conduct negligent, consensus is often hard to come by.'

Claimant's Impecuniosity

For a long period it was thought that the speech by Lord Wright in *The Edison* [1933] AC 449 excluded recovery where the claimant's damage was the result of the claimant's impecuniosity. Fine distinctions were drawn to avoid applying the rule *(Dodd Properties (Kent) Ltd v Canterbury City Council* [1980] 1 WLR 433; *Alcoa Minerals of Jamaica v Herbert Broderick* [2002] 1 AC 371) and in *Lagden v O'Connor* [2004] 1 AC 1067 the House of Lords expressly disapproved Lord Wright's view. As Lord Hope argued (at [61]):

The wrongdoer must take his victim as he finds him: talem qualem, as Lord Collins said in *Clippens Oil Co Ltd v Edinburgh and District Water Trustees* [1907] AC 291 at 303. This rule applies to the economic state of the victim in the same way as it applies to his physical and mental vulnerability. It requires the wrongdoer to bear the consequences if it was reasonably foreseeable that the injured party would have to borrow money or incur some other kind of expenditure to mitigate his damages.

6 DEFENCES TO NEGLIGENCE

I. Introduction

Even where a claimant satisfies the prima facie elements of a cause of action in negligence, the defendant may be relieved from liability by a number of defences. Whether these defences negate the existence of a duty of care or operate as defences in the true sense—that is, by denying liability even though a cause of action has been established—has not been conclusively decided in every case, but for practical purposes these exculpatory factors are normally considered after the claimant has pleaded and established a cause of action. The scope for defences in a negligence action is now much reduced. At the end of the nineteenth century the 'unholy trinity' of common employment (whereby employees were deemed to accept the risk of their fellow employees' negligence: see p. 549), *volenti non fit injuria* and contributory negligence provided employers with a choice of defences to escape liabilities to their employees. Today, these defences no longer hold the sway they once did: common employment was abolished in 1948, contributory negligence has been only a partial defence since 1945, and the range of negligence actions in which *volenti non fit injuria* can be used has been vastly reduced, both by judicial decision and statute. In addition, the ability of the defendant to exclude liability for negligence by giving notice has also been reduced, although not eliminated, by the Unfair Contract Terms Act 1977. The only defence to a negligence action that has developed, if only spasmodically, in the last 20 years is that of illegality, partly in response to the elimination of the *volenti* defence in the case of motor vehicle accidents.

II. *Volenti Non Fit Injuria*

The defence of *volenti non fit injuria*, sometimes called voluntary assumption of risk, reflects the common sense notion that '[o]ne who has invited or assented to an act being done towards him cannot, when he suffers from it, complain of it as a wrong' (*Smith v Baker* [1891] AC 325 at 360, per Lord Herschell). An assumption of risk may be either express or implied. Express assumption of risk usually takes the form of an agreement, and the extent, if any, to which the risk has been assumed depends upon construction of the agreement. More difficult are cases of implied assumption of risk, particularly when the defendant seeks to use the conduct of the claimant prior to the creation of the risk as evidence that the claimant has consented to a subsequent act of negligence. In either case, however, the claimant must be held to have assumed the risk; mere knowledge of the risk is insufficient. Although the courts once took an expansive view of the scope of the defence, it is now rare for the defence to be successful in a negligence action in the absence of an express prior agreement.

1. Knowledge of the Risk

Woodley v Metropolitan District Railway Co (1877) 2 Ex D 384

The facts appear in the judgment of Cockburn CJ.

Cockburn CJ

The facts of the case were as follows: the plaintiff was a workman in the employ of a contractor engaged by the defendants to execute certain work on a side wall on their line of railway in a dark tunnel. Trains were passing the spot every ten minutes, and the line there being on a curve, the workmen would not be aware of the approach of the train till it was within twenty or thirty yards of them. The space between the rail and the wall, on which the workmen had to stand while at work, was just sufficient to enable them to keep clear of a train when sensible of its approach. The place in question was wholly without light. No one was stationed to give notice of an approaching train. The speed of the trains was not slackened when arriving near where the men were at work, nor was any signal given by sounding the steam whistle. It is unnecessary to say that the service on which the plaintiff was thus employed was one of extreme danger. While he was reaching across the rail to find a tool he had laid down a train came upon him suddenly, and struck and seriously injured him....

   That which would be negligence in a company, with reference to the state of their premises or the manner of conducting their business, so as to give a right to compensation for an injury resulting therefrom to a stranger lawfully resorting to their premises in ignorance of the existence of the danger, will give no such right to one, who being aware of the danger, voluntarily encounters it, and fails to take the necessary care for avoiding it.... He cannot, I think, make the company liable for injury arising from danger to which he voluntarily exposed himself....

Judgment for the defendants.

COMMENTARY

Woodley is an extreme example of the scope of the defence in the middle part of the nineteenth century in relation to negligence actions by employees against their employer. The case effectively equates knowledge of the risk with assent. However, it was one of the last to take such a view. In 1891, the House of Lords in *Smith v Baker* [1891] AC 325 held that the defence did not apply where the defendant's negligence increased the risk to the plaintiff employee even though the employee knew the risk to which he was exposed. Lord Herschell stated:

[W]here...a risk to the employed, which may or may not result in injury, has been created or enhanced by the negligence of the employer, does the mere continuance in service, with knowledge of the risk, preclude the employed, if he suffers from such negligence, from recovering in respect of his employer's breach of duty? I cannot assent to the proposition that the maxim, *'Volenti non fit injuria'* applies to such a case, and that the employer can invoke its aid to protect him from liability for his wrong.

An example of this more restrictive conception of the defence in the employment context is provided by *Bowater v Mayor, Aldermen and Burgesses of the Borough of Rowley Regis* [1944]

KB 476, where Goddard LJ stated: 'For this maxim to apply it must be shown that a servant who is asked or required to use dangerous plant is a volunteer in the fullest sense; that, knowing of the danger, he expressly or impliedly said he would do the job at his own risk, and not that of his master....' As these conditions can rarely be satisfied, the defence nowadays plays little role in actions between employers and employees (but note *Shatwell*, below). See also *Johnstone v Bloomsbury Health Authority* (below) for the possible impact on the defence of the Unfair Contract Terms Act 1977.

For a discussion of *Woodley* in its historical context, see S. Banks, 'Woodley v Metropolitan District Railway Company', in C. Mitchell and P. Mitchell (eds), *Landmark Cases in the Law of Tort* (Oxford: Hart, 2010), ch. 5.

It has been said that, for the defence of *volenti non fit iniuria* to apply, the claimant must have agreed, expressly or impliedly, 'to waive any claim for any injury that may befall him due to the lack of reasonable care by the defendant: or more accurately, due to the failure of the defendant to measure up to the standard of care that the law requires of him' (*Nettleship v Weston* [1971] 2 QB 691 at 701, per Lord Denning MR). However, the notion of an agreement may be artificial if the defence can apply where the parties have not met or cannot do so (see *Winfield & Jolowicz*, para. 25–9; *Titchener v British Railways Board* [1983] 1 WLR 1427) and the defence has been applied where the plaintiff merely acted voluntarily and with full knowledge of the risk and those actions were a cause of the injury (see Jaffey, '*Volenti Non Fit Injuria*' [1985] CLJ 87). What is clear is that knowledge of the risk is insufficient to establish the defence. The circumstances in which acting with knowledge of the risk will be translated into an assumption of the risk are considered below.

2. Implied Agreement to Accept Risk

Morris v Murray [1991] 2 QB 6

The plaintiff had been drinking with the deceased in a number of public houses over several hours. At the end of this period the deceased, who had a pilot's licence, suggested to the plaintiff that he go on a flight with him in his light aircraft. The plaintiff drove the deceased to the airfield, helped to fuel the plane and attempted to help start it. Flying conditions were poor and all regular club flying at the airfield had been cancelled. Further, the deceased took off down wind on an uphill runway that was wet and slippery. The flight was short and chaotic, as a witness account confirmed:

He said in his statement that when he saw the plane his initial reaction was that he was looking at a model plane. He could not initially reconcile the flying attitude of the plane, that is to say its almost vertical climb and its close proximity to the ground, with anything other than a model aircraft. The plane was evidently recovering from a descent which brought it close to the ground. It climbed to about 300 feet, then stalled and dived into the ground.

The deceased was killed and the plaintiff severely injured. The autopsy on the deceased revealed, from the concentration of ethanol in his body and from his blood alcohol content, that he had consumed the equivalent of seventeen whiskies. At the trial of the plaintiff's action against the deceased's estate for negligence, the defences of *volenti* and contributory negligence were raised. The trial judge rejected the defence of volenti and reduced the plaintiff's damages by 20 per cent because of contributory negligence. The estate appealed.

Fox LJ

The reasoning of Asquith J [in *Dann v Hamilton* [1939] 1 KB 509, noted below] was that a person who voluntarily travels as a passenger with a driver who is known to the passenger to have driven negligently in the past cannot properly be regarded as volens to future acts of negligence by the driver. Should it then make any difference that the driver is likely to drive negligently on the material occasion, not because he is shown to have driven negligently in the past, but because he is known by the plaintiff to be under the influence of drink? Asquith J thought not and held that the plaintiff by embarking in the car, or re-entering it with the knowledge that through drink the driver had materially reduced his capacity for driving safely, did not implicitly consent to or absolve the driver from liability from any subsequent negligence on his part whereby she might suffer harm.

Having reached that conclusion, however, Asquith J continued (at 518) as follows:

> There may be cases in which the drunkenness of the driver at the material time is so extreme and so glaring that to accept a lift from him is like engaging in an intrinsically and obviously dangerous occupation, inter-meddling with an unexploded bomb or walking on the edge of an unfenced cliff. It is not necessary to decide whether in such a case the maxim *volenti non fit injuria* would apply, for in the present case I find as a fact that the driver's degree of intoxication fell short of this degree.

The question before us, I think, is whether, as a matter of law, there are such cases as Asquith J refers to and, if so, whether this present case is one of them.

As to the first of these questions there is a fundamental issue whether the volenti doctrine applies to the tort of negligence at all. In *Wooldridge v Sumner* [1963] 2 QB 43 at 69, Diplock LJ said:

> In my view, the maxim, in the absence of express contract, has no application to negligence simpliciter where the duty of care is based solely on proximity or 'neighbourship' in the Atkinian sense (see *Donoghue v Stevenson* [1932] AC 562 at 580, per Lord Atkin). The maxim in English law pre-supposes a tortious act by the defendant. The consent that is relevant is not consent to the risk of injury but consent to the lack of reasonable care that may produce that risk ... and requires on the part of the plaintiff at the time at which he gives his consent full knowledge of the nature and extent of the risk that he ran....

Asquith J himself raised the same question in *Dann v Hamilton* [1939] 1 KB 509 at 516–517. He drew a distinction between two kinds of case. First, where a dangerous physical condition has been brought about by the negligence of the defendant and, after it has arisen, the plaintiff fully appreciating its dangerous character elects to assume the risk. In that sort of case Asquith J regarded the *volenti* maxim as capable of applying. That, however, is not this case....

The second class of case was where the act of the plaintiff relied on as a consent precedes and is claimed to licence in advance a possible subsequent act of negligence. *Dann v Hamilton* itself was an instance of that class in which Asquith J held on the facts the maxim not to be applicable. But as I have indicated he left open the question of extreme cases....

[I]n general, I think that the *volenti* doctrine can apply to the tort of negligence, though it must depend on the extent of the risk, the passenger's knowledge of it and what can be inferred as to his acceptance of it. The passenger cannot be volens (in the absence of some form of express disclaimer) in respect of acts of negligence which he had no reason to anticipate and he must be free from compulsion....

If the plaintiff had himself been sober on the afternoon of the flight it seems to me that, by agreeing to be flown by Mr Murray, he must be taken to have accepted fully the risk of serious injury. The danger was both obvious and great. He could not possibly have supposed that Mr Murray, who had been drinking all the afternoon, was capable of discharging a normal duty of care.

But as he himself had been drinking, can it be assumed that he was capable of appreciating the risks? The matter was not very deeply examined at the trial, but he was certainly not 'blind drunk'. In cross-examination, he agreed with the description 'merry'. He was capable of driving a car from the Blue Boar to the airfield and he did so for the purpose of going on a flight with Mr Murray. He helped to start the aircraft and fuel it. Immediately before take-off he asked Mr Murray whether he should not 'radio in' (a sensible inquiry). None of this suggests that his faculties were so muddled that he was incapable of appreciating obvious risks. Moreover, he gave no specific evidence to the effect 'I was really too drunk to know what I was doing'. Nor did anyone else give such evidence about him....

In my opinion, on the evidence the plaintiff knew that he was going on a flight, he knew that he was going to be piloted by Mr Murray and he knew that Mr Murray had been drinking heavily that afternoon. The plaintiff's actions that afternoon, from leaving the Blue Boar to the take-off, suggest that he was capable of understanding what he was doing. There is no clear evidence to the contrary. I think that he knew what he was doing and was capable of appreciating the risks. I do not overlook that the plaintiff's evidence was that, if he had been sober, he would not have gone on the flight. That is no doubt so but it does not establish that he was in fact incapable of understanding what he was doing that afternoon.

If he was capable of understanding what he was doing, then the fact is that he knowingly and willingly embarked on a flight with a drunken pilot. The flight served no useful purpose at all: there was no need or compulsion to join it. It was just entertainment. The plaintiff co-operated fully in the joint activity and did what he could to assist it. He agreed in evidence that he was anxious to start the engine and to fly. A clearer source of great danger could hardly be imagined. The sort of errors of judgment which an intoxicated pilot may make are likely to have a disastrous result. The high probability was that Mr Murray was simply not fit to fly an aircraft. Nothing that happened on the flight itself suggests otherwise, from the take-off down wind to the violence of the manoeuvres of the plane in flight.

The situation seems to me to come exactly within Asquith J's example of the case where: the drunkenness of the driver at the material time is so extreme and so glaring that to accept a lift from him is like engaging in an intrinsically and obviously dangerous occupation.... I think that in embarking on the flight the plaintiff had implicitly waived his rights in the event of injury consequent on Mr Murray's failure to fly with reasonable care....

Considerations of policy do not lead me to any different conclusion. Volenti as a defence has, perhaps, been in retreat during this century, certainly in relation to master and servant cases. It might be said that the merits could be adequately dealt with by the application of the contributory negligence rules. The judge held that the plaintiff was only 20% to blame (which seems to me to be too low) but if that were increased to 50%, so that the plaintiff's damages were reduced by half, both sides would be substantially penalised for their conduct. It seems to me, however, that the wild irresponsibility of the venture is such that the law should not intervene to award damages and should leave the loss where it falls. Flying is intrinsically dangerous and flying with a drunken pilot is great folly. The situation is very different from what has arisen in motoring cases.

I should mention that the defence of volenti has been abrogated in relation to passengers in motor vehicles covered by comprehensive insurance (see s. 148 of the Road Traffic Act 1972). It is not suggested, however, that there is any similar enactment relating to aircraft and applicable to this case....

Stocker LJ

Where a plaintiff is aware that his driver is to some extent intoxicated his responsibility can be reflected by an apportionment on the basis of contributory negligence. Whether such a course is appropriate or whether the maxim *volenti* applies depends on the facts of each case. In particular it is relevant to consider the degree of intoxication and the nature of the act to be performed by the driver. In motoring cases it may well be that an apportionment on the basis of contributory negligence will usually be the appropriate course but in my view to pilot an aircraft requires a far higher standard of skill and care than driving a motor car and the effect of intoxication becomes all the more important. It seems to me from the authorities cited that this is the approach which the courts ought to apply to this problem: how intoxicated was the driver? How obvious was this to the plaintiff, and the extent of the potential risk to the plaintiff if he voluntarily accepts the offer of carriage?

In the light of these observations I turn next to the crucial issue in this case. Did the plaintiff voluntarily accept the risk of injury, and of the defendant's likely breach of duty in negligence with full knowledge of the facts?

I therefore first consider the position on the basis that the plaintiff himself was sober, or at least not so intoxicated as the result of alcohol as to be incapable of assessing the risk. I would unhesitatingly answer this question 'Yes'. The facts were: (1) the deceased pilot had consumed at least the equivalent of 17 whiskies and when absorption rate is considered over the period of time involved must, in fact, have consumed rather more. (2) The plaintiff was drinking with him over several hours and knew how much the deceased pilot had had to drink. (3) The risk of accident was manifest to any sober person when the activity to be carried out involves flying an aeroplane. The risk is far greater than driving a car in a similar condition of insobriety. The plaintiff had flown with the deceased pilot before; he co-operated and, indeed, encouraged the deceased pilot throughout; he drove the pilot to the airfield and filled the aeroplane with aviation spirit. The purpose of going to the airfield can only have been to fly in the aircraft. That the pilot was in fact incapable of flying the aircraft is demonstrated by a number of factors. Firstly he took off down wind and uphill, a highly dangerous manoeuvre itself, and in fact only just managed to get airborne shortly before the end of the runway. Evidence suggests that the aircraft was out of control virtually at all times thereafter. (4) The plaintiff not only accepted the offer of being taken for a joyride in the aircraft, but actively sought it....

Thus on the basis that the plaintiff himself was capable of appreciating the full nature and extent of the risk and voluntarily accepted it, I would have no doubt whatever that this maxim would have applied to defeat his claim. If this was not a case of *volenti non fit injuria* I find it very difficult to envisage circumstances in which that can ever be the case.

However, the position is that the plaintiff himself must have consumed an amount of drink not dissimilar to that consumed by the deceased pilot and, therefore, the question falls to be considered whether or not his own condition was such as to render him incapable of fully appreciating the nature and extent of the risk and of voluntarily accepting it....

It has been submitted to this court that the proper test of this, that is to say the plaintiff's appreciation of the risk, and his consent to it, is an objective one.... I do not, for my part, go so far as to say that the test is an objective one (though if it is not a paradoxical situation arises that the plaintiff's claim could be defeated by the application of the maxim if he was sober, but he could recover damages if he was drunk), but unless there is specific evidence either from the plaintiff himself or from some other source that the plaintiff was in fact so intoxicated that he was incapable of appreciating the nature and extent of the risk and did not in fact appreciate it, and thus did not consent to it, it seems to me that the court is bound to judge the matter in the light of the evidence which is put before it for consideration. In this case the plaintiff did not say, 'I did not appreciate the risk as I was too drunk.' What he did say was that, looking back on it, he would not have gone on the flight had he not been drunk. This is a wholly different proposition. The evidence seems to me to establish that the plaintiff was not so drunk as to be incapable of appreciating the risk or of knowing the state of intoxication of the deceased pilot. Amongst the factors which tend to this conclusion seem to me to be that he himself drove the car to the aerodrome with no other object than of going on a flight with the deceased pilot. He himself assisted to start the engine by swinging the propeller and filling it with petrol. He queried with the pilot whether he should 'radio in' to control. I do not feel that he could have done these things if he was seriously incapacitated by alcohol or unaware of knowing just what it was he was doing. He must have known a number of facts such as the amount of drink the deceased pilot had taken and the risks in general terms at least of flying in an aircraft. He was not himself so drunk as to be in a state of incomprehension. He himself assented to the proposition that he was 'merry'. In my view, therefore, there was no evidence before the judge, even if the matter had been fully canvassed, which could have justified the proposition that the plaintiff's own condition was such as to render him incapable of appreciating the nature of the risk and its extent or indeed that he did in fact fail to appreciate the nature and extent of such risk.

To accept a flight in an aeroplane piloted by a pilot who has had any significant amount of drink, let alone the amount which manifestly this pilot had had, is to engage in an intrinsically and obviously dangerous occupation. For these reasons, in my judgment, the judge ought to have found that the plaintiff's claim should be rejected on the basis of the application of the maxim *volenti non fit injuria*. . . .

Sir George Waller delivered a short concurring judgment.

Appeal allowed.

COMMENTARY

In *Dann v Hamilton* [1939] 1 KB 509, the plaintiff, a passenger in a car whose driver had consumed some alcohol, was injured in an accident caused by negligent driving. Although she had the opportunity to leave the car when another person left it, she remained, and in response to the exiting passenger's comment that the two remaining passengers had 'more pluck than she had', the plaintiff remarked, regrettably, 'You should be like me. If anything is going to happen it will happen.' It did, but she was still able to recover from the deceased driver's estate. What is the difference between the cases? According to Fox LJ, the plaintiff in *Dann v Hamilton* was engaged in a quite ordinary social outing to London and back, with a driver who was not drunk when the drive started and who was not drunk until quite a late stage in the day, by which time it was not very easy for the plaintiff to extricate herself without giving offence. The whole situation bore little resemblance to the drunken escapade, heavily fraught with danger from the first, on which the plaintiff and deceased embarked in *Morris*. Do you agree? Would not a reduction in damages due to the plaintiff's contributory negligence have been a fairer option in both these cases? Note that contributory negligence, which would also have operated as a complete defence, was not pleaded in *Dann v Hamilton*, as Lord Asquith (as he had by then become) pointed out at a later date (see (1953) 69 LQR 317). Note also that *volenti* is not now available as a defence to a motor vehicle accident: see s. 149 Road Traffic Act 1988, replacing the earlier s. 148(3) Road Traffic Act 1972.

If the plaintiff had been so drunk that he was incapable of appreciating the risk he was running, would the defence apply? One can hardly accept a risk if one is incapable of appreciating it, but the contrary conclusion means, as Stocker LJ points out, that a sober or slightly intoxicated claimant is barred when a blind drunk may recover. Such a result cannot be justified in terms of culpability: the blind drunk is at least as much at fault.

If one drinks too much and as a result suffers an injury, can the blame be laid at the door of the provider of the alcohol, or should a publican be able to plead *volenti* if sued by a customer injured as a consequence of alcohol served to him when it should have been obvious to the publican that he had had one too many? (See *Munro v Porthkerry Park Holiday Estates* (1984) 81 LS Gaz 1368.) Where such actions have been brought, the cases have been decided (usually against the claimant) on the issue of whether the defendant owed a duty to ensure the claimant was not injured whilst drinking (*Barrett v Ministry of Defence* [1995] 1 WLR 1217; *Jebson v Ministry of Defence* [2000] 1 WLR 2055 (the claimant won but was 75 per cent contributorily negligent); *Cole v South Tweed Heads Rugby League Football Club Ltd* (2004) 217 CLR 469; *CAL No 14 Pty Ltd v Motor Accidents Insurance Board* [2009] HCA 47, (2010) 84 ALJR 1; see further Ch. 9) although the precise question of whether *volenti* would be open as a defence in such circumstances has not been decided in England. However, in Canada—where a provider of alcohol can owe a duty of care to an intoxicated patron—*volenti* has not provided a defence, the preferred option being to reduce the damages for contributory negligence. See generally Solomon and Payne, 'Alcohol liability in Canada and Australia: Sell, serve and be sued' (1996) 4 Tort L Rev 189, and Malkin and Voon, 'Social hosts' responsibility for their intoxicated guests: Where courts fear to tread' (2007) 15 TLJ 34 (considering the Supreme Court of Canada's decision in *Childs v Desormeaux* [2006] 1 SCR 643 that a social host owes no duty to her guests with respect to the consumption of alcohol).

In *Kirkham v Chief Constable of Greater Manchester* [1990] 2 QB 283 the deceased committed suicide in police custody, but this did not prevent his wife claiming damages as he was not of sound mind at the time (per Lloyd and Farquharson LJJ). Farquharson LJ also held that the defence of *volenti* would fail where 'the act of the deceased relied on is the very act which the duty cast upon the defendant required him to prevent'. This latter ground was applied by a majority of both the Court of Appeal and House of Lords in *Reeves v Commissioner of Police for the Metropolis* [1999] QB 169, [2000] 1 AC 360 so as to defeat the defence where the prisoner committing suicide was of sound mind. Their Lordships, affirming the correctness of a concession made by counsel for the Commissioner, held that if the suicide did not amount to a *novus actus interveniens* the defence of *volenti* could not succeed, a position that was accepted in non-prisoner cases by the House of Lords in *Corr v IBC Vehicles Ltd* [2008] 1 AC 884 where the deceased's suicide was attributable to the depressive illness he contracted as a result of the defendant employer's negligence. The dissentients in *Reeves* (Morritt LJ in the Court of Appeal, Lord Hobhouse in the House of Lords) accepted Lloyd LJ's view in *Kirkham* that acceptance by a claimant of the consequences of his own intentional act was a stronger reason for excluding liability than acceptance of the risk created by negligence of the defendant. Do you agree?

Imperial Chemical Industries Ltd v Shatwell [1965] AC 656

The facts of this case are stated in the speech of Lord Reid, below.

Lord Reid

My Lords, this case arises out of the accidental explosion of a charge at a quarry belonging to the appellants which caused injuries to the respondent George Shatwell and his brother James, who were both qualified shotfirers. On 8 June 1960, these two men and another shotfirer,

Beswick, had bored and filled fifty shot holes and had inserted electric detonators and connected them up in series. Before firing it was necessary to test the circuit for continuity. This should have been done by connecting long wires so that the men could go to a shelter some eighty yards away and test from there. They had not sufficient wire with them and Beswick went off to get more. The testing ought not to have been done until signals had been given, so that other men could take shelter, and these signals were not due to be given for at least another hour. Soon after Beswick had left George said to his brother 'Must we test them', meaning shall we test them, and James said 'yes'. The testing is done by passing a weak current through the circuit in which a small galvanometer is included and if the needle of the instrument moves when a connexion is made the circuit is in order. So George got a galvanometer and James handed two short wires to him. Then George applied the wires to the galvanometer and the needle did not move. This showed that the circuit was defective so the two men went round inspecting the connections. They saw nothing wrong and George said that that meant there was a dud detonator somewhere, and decided to apply the galvanometer to each individual detonator. James handed two other wires to him and George used them to apply the galvanometer to the first detonator. The result was an explosion which injured both men.

This method had been regularly used without mishap until the previous year. Then some research done by the appellants showed that it might be unsafe and in October 1959, the appellants gave orders that testing must in future be done from a shelter and a lecture was given to all the shotfirers, including the Shatwells, explaining the position. Then in December 1959, new statutory regulations were made (SI 1959 No. 2259) probably because the Ministry had been informed of the results of the appellants' research. These regulations came into operation in February 1960, and the Shatwells were aware of them. But some of the shotfirers appear to have gone on in the old way. An instance of this came to the notice of the management in May 1960, and the management took immediate action and revoked the shotfiring certificate of the disobedient man, and told the other shotfirers about this. George admitted in evidence that he knew all this. He admitted that they would only have had to wait ten minutes until Beswick returned with the long wires. When asked why he did not wait, his only excuse was that he could not be bothered to wait.

George now sues the appellants on the ground that he and his brother were equally to blame for this accident, and that the appellants are vicariously liable for his brother's conduct. He has been awarded £1,500, being half the agreed amount of his loss. There is no question of the appellants having been in breach of the regulation because the duty under the regulation is laid on the shotfirer personally. So counsel for George frankly and rightly admitted that if George had sued James personally instead of suing his employer the issue would have been the same. If this decision is right it means that if two men collaborate in doing what they know is dangerous and is forbidden and as a result both are injured, each has a cause of action against the other.

The appellants have two grounds of defence, first that James's conduct had no causal connexion with the accident the sole cause being George's own fault, and secondly *volenti non fit injuria*....

[His Lordship held that the appellant could not succeed on the first ground, and then considered the early cases on *volenti non fit injuria* in actions between masters and servants, before continuing:]

More recently it appears to have been thought in some quarters that, at least as between master and servant, *volenti non fit injuria* is a dead or dying defence. That, I think, is because in most cases where the defence would now be available it has become usual to base the decision on contributory negligence. Where the plaintiff's own disobedient act is the sole cause of his injury, it does not matter in the result whether one says 100 per cent contributory negligence or *volenti non fit injuria*; but it does matter in a case like the present. If we adopt the inaccurate habit of using the word 'negligence' to denote a deliberate act done with full knowledge of the risk, it is not surprising that we sometimes get into difficulties. I think that most people would say, without stopping to think of the reason, that there is a world of difference between two fellow servants collaborating carelessly, so that the acts of both contribute to cause injury to one of them, and two fellow servants combining to disobey an order deliberately, though they know the risk involved. It seems reasonable that the injured man should recover some compensation in the former case, but not in the latter. If the law treats both as merely cases of negligence, it cannot draw a distinction. In my view the law does and should draw a distinction. In the first case only the partial defence of contributory negligence is available. In the second *volenti non fit injuria* is a complete defence, if the employer is not himself at fault and is only liable vicariously for the acts of the fellow servant. If the plaintiff invited or freely aided and abetted his fellow servant's disobedience, then he was *volens* in the fullest sense. He cannot complain of the resulting injury either against the fellow servant or against the master on the ground of his vicarious responsibility for his fellow servant's conduct. I need not here consider the common case where the servant's disobedience puts the master in breach of a statutory obligation, and it would be wrong to decide in advance whether that would make any differ-ence. There remain two other arguments for the respondent which I must deal with.

It was argued that in this case it has not been shown that George had a full appreciation of the risk. In my view it must be held that he had. He knew that those better qualified than he was took the risk seriously. He knew that his employers had forbidden this practice, and that it had then been prohibited by statutory regulation; and he knew that his employers were taking strong measures to see that the order was obeyed. If he did not choose to believe what he was told, I do not think that he could for that reason say that he did not fully appreciate the risk. He knew that the risk was that a charge would explode during testing, and no shotfirer could be in any doubt about the possible consequences of that....

I can find no reason at all why the fact that these two brothers agreed to commit an offence by contravening a statutory prohibition imposed on them as well as agreeing to defy their employer's orders should affect the application of the principle *volenti non fit injuria* either to an action by one of them against the other or to an action by one against their employer based on his vicarious responsibility for the conduct of the other. I would therefore allow this appeal.

Lord Donovan

The duty to test from shelter is laid on the shotfirers themselves. George himself was well aware of his duty in this respect, and must have known of the reason for the rule, namely, the risk of premature explosion. When he asked James whether they should proceed to test, not-withstanding that they were both in the open, and obtained his agreement to that course, they were voluntarily accepting this known risk with their eyes open. Against this view of the matter it is argued for the respondent that, though he knew of the risk, he knew it also to be a remote one, and never dreamed that it would mature; and that to be affected by the plea of *volenti* he must be aware of the exact extent of the danger. I cannot accept this argument. George did know the extent of the risk, namely, that it was very remote. What he did not know, of course, was whether the risk would mature. But whoever does? The argument really is this: 'I didn't think it would happen to me.' This is not an answer, once the risk is known, and understood, and accepted. Next it is argued that for the defence based on the plea to succeed, it must be shown that there was no kind of pressure on George to accept the risk, but that it was his free and vol-untary act. In the present case that was not so, it is said, because of the pressure represented by the willingness of James to help to carry out the test in the open; but what James did was to accept George's invitation so to test in the open and thereafter to co-operate. I cannot regard this as affecting George's complete freedom of choice in the matter. He remained perfectly free to change his mind....

When George invited James to join him in testing the electrical circuit without taking shelter George knew the risk he was running and accepted it voluntarily. He did not, of course, in express language, waive such rights as he might have against James if the risk matured and he was injured; but in my opinion that must be taken to be the tacit effect of the agreement between the two of them to test the circuit in the open. The situation lacks nothing of the elements necessary to support the plea of *volenti non fit injuria*. Each knew the risk he ran: each accepted it quite voluntarily. . . .

Lord Hodson, **Lord Pearce** and **Viscount Radcliffe** delivered separate speeches in favour of allowing the appeal.

Appeal allowed.

COMMENTARY

The above extract shows that the defence of *volenti* is not dead in the employment context, although the employer was only liable vicariously through the acts of another employee. As *Hepple & Matthews* (p. 455) suggest, the position might have been different if James had been George's superior and had ordered him to do the work. In that situation, whilst there may have been knowledge of the risk, it would be more difficult to imply acceptance of the risk. For a closely analogous situation, see *Radclyffe v Ministry of Defence* [2009] EWCA Civ 635 where the claimant soldier engaged in the dangerous conduct only because of the encouragement of a senior officer.

Should the result be affected by the claimant's belief as to whether the risk will materialise? There have been suggestions in a number of Australian cases that a genuine belief that the risk would not materialise is inconsistent with a finding of *volenti* (*Canterbury Municipal Council v Taylor* [2002] NSWCA 24; *Carey v Lake Macquarie City Council* [2007] NSWCA 4) but it is hard to see why this should follow. It is the risk of injury, not the injury, that must be accepted; no doubt the Shatwells genuinely believed there would be no explosion, but they knew there was a risk and their conduct suggested that the risk was accepted.

In the Scottish case of *Hugh v National Coal Board*, 1972 SC 252, the pursuer, an apprentice electrician employed by the defenders, was injured when his foot slipped under a train used to convey employees from the mine in which he worked to the lift cage. As the train approached the cage, many employees, including the pursuer, jumped off, a practice which was prohibited by both the defender and by statutory regulation. He was injured when, in the rush, several men fell causing him to lose his footing. Lord Keith, applying *Shatwell*, held that the defence of *volenti* barred the pursuer's claim. Do you agree that the two cases are indistinguishable?

3. *Volenti* and Breach of Duty

Wooldridge v Sumner [1963] 2 QB 43

The defendant was the owner of a horse that was a competitor in a horse show. The horse was being ridden by H. Whilst the horse was executing a gallop around the competition arena, the plaintiff, a film cameraman, was injured when he fell under the horse. The plaintiff, who was unfamiliar and inexperienced with horses, had been attempting to get out of the way of the horse when he fell. He had earlier been told by a steward to go outside the arena when the horses were galloping but had remained. In the plaintiff's action against the defendant in negligence (the plaintiff alleging that H was the servant or agent of the defendant), the trial judge found that H had brought the horse into a corner much too fast. The judge also found that the horse, when it crashed into the line of tubs (behind which the plaintiff was standing), would have gone out on to the cinder track behind the tubs if its rider had allowed it to do so, where it would not have harmed the plaintiff, and awarded the plaintiff damages. The defendant appealed.

[Further extracts from this decision may be found at p. 180, above.]

Sellers LJ

In my opinion, a competitor or player cannot, at least, in the normal case of competition or game, rely on the maxim *volenti non fit injuria* in answer to a spectator's claim, for there is no liability unless there is negligence, and the spectator comes to witness skill and with the expectation that it will be exercised. But, provided the competition or game is being performed within the rules and the requirement of the sport and by a person of adequate skill and competence, the spectator does not expect his safety to be regarded by the participant. If the conduct is deliberately intended to injure someone whose presence is known, or is reckless and in disregard of all safety of others so that it is a departure from the standards which might reasonably be expected in anyone pursuing the competition or game, then the performer might well be held liable for any injury his act caused. There would, I think, be a difference, for instance, in assessing blame which is actionable between an injury caused by a tennis ball hit or a racket accidentally thrown in the course of play into the spectators at Wimbledon and a ball hit or a racket thrown into the stands in temper or annoyance when play was not in progress. The relationship of spectator and competitor or player is a special one, as I see it, as the standard of conduct of the participant, as accepted and expected by the spectator, is that which the sport permits or involves. The different relationship involves its own standard of care....

Diplock LJ

The matter has to be looked at from the point of view of the reasonable spectator as well as the reasonable participant; not because of the maxim *volenti non fit injuria*, but because what a reasonable spectator would expect a participant to do without regarding it as blameworthy is as relevant to what is reasonable care as what a reasonable participant would think was blameworthy conduct in himself. The same idea was expressed by Scrutton LJ in *Hall v Brooklands Auto-Racing Club* [1933] 1 KB 205 at 214:

> What is reasonable care would depend on the perils which might be reasonably expected to occur, and the extent to which the ordinary spectator might be expected to appreciate and take the risk of such perils.

A reasonable spectator attending voluntarily to witness any game or competition knows, and presumably desires, that a reasonable participant will concentrate his attention on winning, and if the game or competition is a fast-moving one will have to exercise his judgment and attempt to exert his skill in what, in the analogous context of contributory negligence, is sometimes called 'the agony of the moment'. If the participant does so concentrate his attention and consequently does exercise his judgment and attempt to exert his skill in circumstances of this kind which are inherent in the game or competition in which he is taking part, the question whether any mistake he makes amounts to a breach of duty to take reasonable care must take account of those circumstances....

The practical result of this analysis of the application of the common law of negligence to participant and spectator would, I think, be expressed by the common man in some such terms as these: 'A person attending a game or competition takes the risk of any damage caused to him by any act of a participant done in the course of and for the purposes of the game or competition, notwithstanding that such act may involve an error of judgment or a lapse of skill, unless the participant's conduct is such as to evince a reckless disregard of the spectator's safety'. The spectator takes the risk because such an act involves no breach of the duty of care owed by the participant to him. He does not take the risk by virtue of the doctrine expressed or obscured by the maxim *volenti non fit injuria*. That maxim states a principle of estoppel applicable originally to a Roman citizen who consented to being sold as a slave. Although pleaded and argued below, it was only faintly relied on by counsel for the first defendant in this court. In my view, the maxim, in the absence of express contract, has no application to negligence simpliciter where the duty of care is based solely on proximity or 'neighbourship' in the Atkinian sense....

Since the maxim has, in my view, no application to this or any other case of negligence *simpliciter*, the fact that the plaintiff, owing to his ignorance of horses, did not fully appreciate the nature and extent of the risk he ran did not impose on Mr Holladay any higher duty of care towards him than that which he owed to any ordinary reasonable spectator with such knowledge of horses and vigilance for his own safety as might be reasonably expected to be possessed by a person who chooses to watch a heavyweight hunter class in the actual arena where the class is being judged. He cannot rely on his personal ignorance of the risk any more than the plaintiff in *Murray v Harringay Arena Ltd* [1951] 2 KB 529 could rely on his ignorance of the risk involved in ice-hockey, excusable though such ignorance may have been in a six-year-old child....

Danckwerts LJ delivered a separate concurring judgment.

Appeal allowed.

COMMENTARY

In the context of the intentional torts, consent is a defence to conduct which falls within the ordinary course of the game; thus a claimant cannot complain of a battery when tackled in a rugby game as tackling is a necessary part of the game (see *Blake v Galloway* [2004] 1 WLR 2844). It was not a necessary part of watching a horse show that the plaintiff in the above case should be struck by the horse, but the defendant did not intend to make such contact, so the plaintiff sought to bring an action in negligence. In this context, the Court of Appeal held that the defendant's liability depended upon breach of duty rather than any acceptance of the risk. As Sappideen et al., *Torts: Commentary and Materials*, 10th edn. (Ryde, NSW: Law Book Co, 2009) point out (para. 16.40), 'To say that a person is *volens* to certain sporting injuries, not caused by negligence, is no different from saying that a person using the highways is *volens* to accidents not caused by negligence. In both cases the injured party has undertaken an activity, which, in its own way, is fraught with danger and in which, it is generally known, injury may be caused without negligence on the part of anyone.'

Although *volenti* in this context does not operate as a defence *per se*, what risks have been assumed by the claimant does affect liability, because any injury caused by a risk which forms part of the sport or competition will not constitute a breach of duty by the defendant player or competitor. Unlike *volenti*, which looks to the conduct of the claimant, the question here is what risk the defendant is entitled to treat the claimant as having accepted (see Kitto J in *Rootes v Shelton* (1967) 116 CLR 383). Thus participants in a game of football (*Elliott v Saunders*, unreported, QBD, 10 June 1994 (discussed above, p. 183)), organisers of a motor car race (*Wattleworth v Goodwood Road Racing Co Ltd* [2004] EWHC 140 (QB)) and occupiers of land used for recreational activities generally (*Tomlinson v Congleton Borough Council* [2004] 1 AC 46) can assume that anyone engaged in the activities in question accepts risks inherent in them (e.g. injury caused by a mistimed tackle or a collision with a tyre-wall on a racetrack, or hitting one's head because of a misjudgement as to the depth of water). In other words, the level of risk which attaches to the defendant's conduct before it is considered careless is affected by the level of risk that is accepted as part of the sport by other participants. Much depends, then, on what risks the defendant is entitled to assume the claimant has accepted. Logically, the answer to this question does not depend on what risks the claimant actually knows of or assumes—for that is what is required to prove the *volenti* defence—but on what risks the defendant knows (or ought reasonably to know) that the claimant is aware of and has assumed. This, of course, is usually to be inferred from the patterns of behaviour of ordinary people in the claimant's position. There is evidence, however, that some courts conflate the analytically separate issues when considering the breach of duty question (see Lunney, 'Personal Responsibility and the "New" Volenti' (2005) 13 Tort L Rev 76). Some risks, however, are clearly outside what the defendant believes the claimant has accepted. In *Watson v British Boxing Board*, unreported, 24 September 1999, Ian Kennedy J (affirmed [2001] QB 1134), the claimant, who was injured as a consequence of a blow to his head in a professional boxing contest, successfully sued the governing body of the sport in the United Kingdom. Although the claimant accepted the risk of injury caused as a result of events in the ring, he did not accept, nor could the defendant assume he accepted, any risk which followed from the inadequate and negligent provision made for medical treatment at the ringside, this being the defendant's responsibility.

In *Elliot v Saunders* (above), Drake J also held, following the Canadian decision of *Mattheson v Governors of Dalhusey University and College* (1983) 57 NSR (2nd) 56, that 'a frequent or familiar infraction of the rules of a game can fall within the ordinary risks of the game accepted by all the participants'. Does this apply to spectators as well? In the American case of *Hunt v Thomasville Baseball Co* (1949) 80 Ga App 572 the plaintiff, a spectator sitting in an unfenced part of the grandstand, was hit by a 'wild ball' thrown in the course of the warm-up for a game of baseball. Townsend J held:

An examination of numerous cases concerned with the liability of an owner for injuries received by a spectator at a baseball game seated in the grandstand and injured by foul balls, flying bats and other like missiles leads us to concur with the majority view that one who buys a ticket for the purpose of witnessing a baseball game and who chooses or accepts a seat in a portion of the grandstand which his own observation will readily inform him is unprotected, voluntarily assumes the risks inherent in such a position, since he must be presumed to know that there is a likelihood of wild balls being thrown and landing in the grandstand or other unprotected areas.

If tennis players regularly throw their racquets into the crowd, does this then become one of the ordinary risks assumed by spectators sitting in that area?

4. Evaluation

A. Jaffey, 'Volenti Non Fit Injuria' [1985] CLJ 87

[W]here the plaintiff's relevant conduct occurred before the defendant's negligent act, the possibility of *volens* is confined to cases where (assuming there is no express agreement) there is some consensual relationship or transaction between the parties, which may carry with it an implied agreement under which the plaintiff forgoes any claim he might otherwise have. This is the point of Diplock LJ's well-known statement in *Wooldridge v Sumner*, 'In my view, the maxim, in the absence of express contract, has no application to negligence simpliciter where the duty of care is based solely on proximity or "neighbourship" in the Atkinian sense.' Where the defendant's duty of care stems merely from the fact of foreseeability of injury to the plaintiff, but there is no relationship or transaction between them, there is nothing from which an agreement can be inferred.

Thus the desirable state of the law would be that put forward by Glanville Williams: the defence of consent or *volenti non fit injuria* (in the tort of negligence) requires an agreement—not necessarily a contract—between the parties under which the plaintiff agrees that identified possible future conduct of the defendant shall not be actionable. There should be no defence of voluntary assumption of risk covering cases where there is no such agreement between the parties made before the defendant's act. In other words the phrase 'voluntary assumption of risk' should be confined to cases where there is such an agreement, though it is more likely to be used in relation to an implied rather than an express agreement. Cases of a plaintiff merely freely encountering a risk of which he is aware should be dealt with under contributory negligence or in exceptional cases, under *nova causa interveniens*. Such a state of the law would not seem to be out of reach of the courts. . . .

What are the circumstances in which an agreement will be implied in a less obvious case [sc. than *ICI v Shatwell*]? As we have seen, there must be a transaction or relationship between the parties. Then, if it is to be held that the parties tacitly agreed that if in the course of the transaction or relationship the defendant by his careless or unskilled conduct should injure the plaintiff the latter would forego any action, it is necessary that the plaintiff must have been fully aware, not merely of the possibility of negligence by the defendant (for that is always possible), but of facts making it highly likely that the defendant would commit some specific act of negligence—for instance the plaintiff knew that the defendant was incapable, or scarcely capable, of avoiding that act. Such knowledge on the plaintiff's part must exist, otherwise there would be no reason why he should have adverted to the possibility of liability on the defendant's part, let alone not agreeing to sue. . . . If the relationship or transaction exists, and also the requisite knowledge the question still remains whether the parties impliedly agreed that the defendant's conduct, if it occurred, should not be actionable. In effect the question is whether such a term should be implied in the relationship, and although the relationship itself may not be a contract, or even an agreement in the proper sense, the classic test of the 'officious bystander' will do very well. If the parties were asked what would be the position if the plaintiff were injured as a result of an act done by the defendant which the parties knew he was very likely to do in the course of the transaction or relationship, would they say, 'Of course there will be no liability if that happens' . . .

COMMENTARY

Is this approach consistent with the result in *Dann v Hamilton*? Or *Morris v Murray*?

In *Haynes v Harwood* [1935] 1 KB 146 the defendant's employee negligently left a two-horse van unattended in a crowded street. A passing youth threw a stone at the horses and they bolted. The plaintiff, a police constable, was injured in the course of successfully restraining the horses. One argument for the defendant, rejected by the Court of Appeal, was that the plaintiff consented to the risk of injury by his actions. This is an example of a case in Asquith J's first category in *Dann v Hamilton*, that is a dangerous physical condition brought about by the negligence of the defendant and, after it has arisen, the plaintiff, fully appreciating its dangerous character, elects to assume the risk (although on the facts there was held to be no consent). Jaffey, however, argues that the defence should not apply at all in this kind of case, there being no transaction or relationship between the parties. As Roche LJ put it in *Haynes* (at 166–7): 'He [the plaintiff] knew nothing of what had been done or by whom, and there was no material for choice or consent such as is contemplated and required by the maxim.' Is there ever any material for choice or consent in the absence of a relationship between the parties?

An alternative approach has been suggested by Tan, '*Volenti Non Fit Injuria*: An Alternative Framework' (1995) 3 Tort L Rev 208. She suggests refashioning the defence as an assessment of the plaintiff's conduct. Accordingly, although the traditional elements of knowledge of the risk, agreement, voluntariness and the degree of danger of the defendant's activity would remain relevant, they would not be determinative. Rather, they would be considered along with other factor such as:

(i)   whether the claimant was a rescuer;

(ii)   whether the claimant was committing a crime or trespass;

(iii)   the extent of the claimant's willing participation in the dangerous activity;

(iv)   the claimant's mental capacity;

(v)   whether the claimant was intoxicated;

(vi)   whether the claimant was merely obeying her employer's instructions.

Tan argues that the flexibility inherent in this approach allows the defence to adapt to changes in social policy; for example the increasing recognition of the social evil of drink-driving. Do you agree? Are cases such as *Morris v Murray* better explained by Tan's approach than by attempting to find an implied agreement to accept the risk of injury due to the defendant's negligence?

III. Contributory Negligence

The claimant, without looking to check for traffic, steps out onto the road and is hit by the defendant's car, which is being driven too quickly. Should the defendant be held liable? Not much assistance is gained by looking at the issue solely as one of causation because the injury would not have been caused at all but for both the claimant's and the defendant's negligence. From the early part of the nineteenth century, however, the common law did attempt to solve the problem through the mechanism of causation. If the contributory negligence was the cause of the damage the claimant was barred from recovery, even though the defendant had also been negligent. This all-or-nothing approach—the plaintiff either received 100 per cent of the damages if the contributory negligence was not the cause of the damage or nothing if it was—offended against notions of justice, although the malleability of the causation concept and the benevolence of the juries that heard the cases allowed this unsatisfactory state of affairs to continue for longer than it might otherwise have done. The law was finally reformed in 1945 to allow the claimant's damages to be reduced, but not eliminated, as a result of his contributory negligence. The role of causation in contributory negligence was thus diminished, although not banished. A court can today concentrate on whether the claimant's conduct amounted to contributory negligence and, if it did, what the proper apportionment of damages should be between the negligent claimant and defendant.

1. Historical Background

Butterfield v Forrester (1809) 11 East 60, 103 ER 926

The plaintiff brought an action on the case against the defendant for obstructing a highway by placing a pole across part of a road. The plaintiff was injured when his horse crashed into the pole and he was thrown off. The pole was visible from a distance of about 100 yards and if the plaintiff had been riding normally 'he might have observed and avoided it.' However, the plaintiff, who had just left a public house, was 'riding violently' at the time of the accident. The action failed because of the plaintiff's contributory negligence.

Lord Ellenborough CJ

A party is not to cast himself upon an obstruction which has been made by the fault of another, and avail himself of it, if he do not use common and ordinary caution to be in the right. In cases of persons riding upon what is considered to be the wrong side of the road, that would not authorise another purposefully to ride up against them. One person being in fault will not dispense with another's using ordinary care for himself. Two things must occur to support this action, an obstruction in the road by the fault of the defendant, and no want of ordinary care to avoid it on the part of the plaintiff.

COMMENTARY

This case reflects the traditional dislike of the common law for attributing an injury to more than one legal cause. Either the defendant's negligence or the plaintiff's negligence was the cause. When civil cases were tried by juries this may not have mattered much, because a jury could find for the plaintiff on the basis that it was indeed the defendant's negligence that caused the damage but only award the plaintiff a fraction of the damages claimed in order to reflect the plaintiff's contributory fault. But the abrogation of jury trial from 1854 onward required judges to deal with this issue. This was made no easier by the decision in *Davies v Mann* (1842) 10 M & W 547, 152 ER 588 which was regarded as the leading authority on the so-called 'last clear chance' doctrine: if the defendant had the last opportunity to avoid the damage then it was deemed to have been caused by his neglect, even if the plaintiff had been guilty of some prior contributory negligence. This became even more complicated with the development of a 'constructive last clear chance' doctrine: but for his own negligence, the defendant would have had the opportunity of avoiding the damage (see *British Columbia Electric Railway v Loach* [1916] 1 AC 719). The civil law jurisdiction of admiralty adopted the eminently more sensible practice of apportioning the loss equally where both parties' negligence was to blame for a collision, an approach expanded by the Maritime Conventions Act 1911, which allowed damages to be apportioned in proportion to the degree in which each vessel was in fault. When the House of Lords applied the statute in *Admiralty Commissioners v Volute* [1922] 1 AC 129, their Lordships declined to apply the last opportunity rule, apportioning liability between the two negligent parties. In 1939, the Law Revision Committee, in its Eighth Report (Cmd. 6032), recommended legislative change to apply the admiralty rules to the common law and this was enacted in 1945.

2. The 1945 Act

Law Reform (Contributory Negligence) Act 1945

1. APPORTIONMENT OF LIABILITY IN CASE OF CONTRIBUTORY NEGLIGENCE

(1) Where any person suffers damage as the result partly of his own fault and partly of the fault of any other person or persons, a claim in respect of that damage shall not be defeated by reason of the fault of the person suffering the damage, but the damages recoverable in respect thereof shall be reduced to such extent as the court thinks just and equitable having regard to the claimant's share in the responsibility for the damage:

Provided that—
   (a) this subsection shall not operate to defeat any defence arising under a contract;
   (b) where any contract or enactment providing for the limitation of liability is applicable to the claim, the amount of damages recoverable by the claimant by virtue of this subsection shall not exceed the maximum limit so applicable.

(2) Where damages are recoverable by any person by virtue of the foregoing subsection subject to such reduction as is therein mentioned, the court shall find and record the total damages which would have been recoverable if the claimant had not been at fault.

   . . .

(5) Where, in any case to which subsection (1) of this section applies, one of the persons at fault avoids liability to any other such person or his personal representative by pleading the Limitation Act 1939, or any other enactment limiting the time within which proceedings may be taken, he shall not be entitled to recover any damages . . . from that other person or representative by virtue of the said subsection.

(6) Where any case to which subsection (1) of this section applies is tried with a jury, the jury shall determine the total damages which would have been recoverable if the claimant had not been at fault and the extent to which those damages are to be reduced . . .

4. INTERPRETATION

The following expressions have the meanings hereby respectively assigned to them, that is to say—

   'court' means, in relation to any claim, the court or arbitrator by or before whom the claim falls to be determined;

'damage' includes loss of life and personal injury;

'fault' means negligence, breach of statutory duty or other act or omission which gives rise to a liability in tort or would, apart from this Act, give rise to the defence of contributory negligence.

COMMENTARY

'Fault' of both the claimant and the defendant is required for the Act to apply, but the s. 4 definition appears to suggest that the defendant's fault may consist of conduct that amounted to contributory negligence, and 'since contributory negligence did not at common law pre-suppose a duty of care, the result of this construction is to allow an action for damages for a fault that would not at common law have been a breach of a duty of care' (Glanville Williams, *Joint Torts and Contributory Negligence* (London: Stevens & Sons, 1951), p. 318). Williams' solution was to read s. 4 as having two parts: for the defendant fault is 'negligence, breach of statutory duty or other act or omission which gives rise to a liability in tort', whilst for the claimant fault is 'negligence, breach of statutory duty or other act or omission which ... would, apart from this Act, give rise to, the defence of contributory negligence'. This interpretation has now been accepted as correct (see the decision of the Court of Appeal in *Forsikringsaktieselskapet Vesta v Butcher* [1988] 3 WLR 565, and of the House of Lords in *Standard Chartered Bank v Pakistan National Shipping (Nos 2 & 4)* [2003] 1 AC 959). The 'fault' that may amount to contributory negligence has been construed widely but Lord Denning's view in *Murphy v Culhane* [1977] QB 94 that the defence might apply where the claimant initiated a criminal affray during the course of which he was injured has been doubted; in *Standard Chartered Bank v Pakistan National Shipping (Nos 2 & 4)* [2003] 1 AC 959 Lord Rodger noted that contributory negligence had never been available where the defendant intended to harm the claimant.

However, other intentional acts of the claimant do fall within the Act. In *Corr v IBC Vehicles Pty Ltd* [2008] AC 884, a majority of their Lordships thought that the suicide of the deceased (for which the defendant was held liable) could nonetheless be conduct justifying a reduction of the damages for contributory negligence. Even though the deceased had been suffering from a depressive illness—which was caused by the defendant's negligence and ultimately caused him to commit suicide—he retained some capacity and, in recognition of the value of personal autonomy, some responsibility had to be attributed to the deceased. O'Sullivan ([2008] CLJ 241, 244) comments:

Mr. Corr's suicide was a fatal symptom of a ghastly illness, no more his 'fault' than if he had died of cancer triggered by the accident. To retort that he was not an 'automaton' shows no understanding of the effect of serious depression. The families of victims such as Mr. Corr deserve better.

The majority in *Corr* were influenced by the decision in *Reeves v Commissioner of Police for the Metropolis* [2000] 1 AC 360, where the 'fault' in issue was the intentional and deliberate suicide of the deceased whilst in police custody. Although Lord Hoffmann accepted that it would be a rare case where such an act did not amount to a *novus actus interveniens*, where it did not (as in *Reeves*) the act could nonetheless amount to fault and hence satisfy the requirement of s. 1(1) of the Act. For Lord Hoffmann, however, a negative answer to the question 'did the suicide break the causal link?' did not preclude a different answer to the question 'did the suicide contribute to the deceased's death?'. Can it sensibly be said that the claimant has been guilty of contributory negligence if he commits the very act the defendant was supposed to be preventing? (See the judgment of Buxton LJ in the Court of Appeal in *Reeves* [1999] QB 169 at 181–3.)

In *Barclays Bank v Fairclough Building Ltd* [1995] QB 214 the Court of Appeal held that the Act did not apply to an action for breach of a strict contractual obligation, even if there was a parallel liability in tort, but it might apply if the liability for breach of contract was the same as, and co-extensive with, a liability in tort which was independent of the existence of the contract (see the Court of Appeal decision in *Forsikringsaktieselskapet Vesta v Butcher* [1988] 3 WLR 565; cf. *Astley v Austrust Ltd* (1999) 197 CLR 1, where the High Court of Australia did not follow *Vesta* and held that the South Australian equivalent of the 1945 Act did not apply at all to claims in contract, although the decision has now been reversed by legislation in most states). For a general discussion of these issues see the Law Commission Consultation Paper, *Contributory Negligence as a Defence in Contract*, Law Com. No. 114, 1989 and the Report, *Contributory Negligence as a Defence in Contract*, Law Com. No. 219, 1993.

Jones v Livox Quarries [1952] 2 QB 608

The plaintiff, who worked in a quarry, rode on the back of a tracked vehicle (a 'traxcavator') on his way to the employer's canteen. This action was contrary to the express instructions of the employer. The plaintiff was injured when the back of the traxcavator was hit by another vehicle and the plaintiff was crushed. In the plaintiff's action against the defendant for being vicariously liable for the negligence of the vehicle's driver, it was alleged that the plaintiff had been guilty of contributory negligence in riding on the back of the traxcavator. The trial judge found the defendant negligent but reduced the award by 20 per cent for contributory negligence. However, he also held that the only risk to which the plaintiff exposed himself by his actions was falling off the vehicle. The plaintiff appealed against the reduction of the award for contributory negligence on the basis that that negligence had not caused the injury.

Denning LJ

Although contributory negligence does not depend on a duty of care, it does depend on foreseeability. Just as actionable negligence requires foreseeability of harm to others, so contributory negligence requires the foreseeability of harm to oneself. A person is guilty of contributory negligence if he ought reasonably to have foreseen that, if he did not act as a reasonable, prudent man, he might be hurt himself; and in his reckonings he must take into account the possibility of others being careless.

Once negligence is proved, then no matter whether it is actionable negligence or contributory negligence, the person who is guilty of it must bear his proper share of responsibility for the consequences. The consequences do not depend on foreseeability, but on causation. The question in every case is: What faults were there which caused the damage? Was his fault one of them? The necessity of causation is shown by the word 'result' in s. 1(1) of the Act of 1945, and it was accepted by this court in *Davies v Swan Motor Co (Swansea) Ltd* [1949] 2 KB 326.

There is no clear guidance to be found in the books about causation. All that can be said is that causes are different from the circumstances in which, or on which, they operate. The line between the two depends on the facts of each case. It is a matter of common sense more than anything else. In the present case, as the arguments of Mr Arthian Davies proceeded, it seemed to me that he sought to make foreseeability the decisive test of causation. He relied on the trial judge's statement that a man who rode on the towbar of the traxcavator 'ran the risk of being thrown off and no other risk'. That is, I think, equivalent to saying that such a man could reasonably foresee that he might be thrown off the traxcavator, but not that he might be crushed between it and another vehicle.

In my opinion, however, foreseeability is not the decisive test of causation. It is often a relevant factor, but it is not decisive. Even though the plaintiff did not foresee the possibility of being crushed, nevertheless in the ordinary plain common sense of this business the injury suffered by the plaintiff was due in part to the fact that he chose to ride on the towbar to lunch instead of walking down on his feet. If he had been thrown off in the collision, Mr Arthian Davies admits that his injury would be partly due to his own negligence in riding on the towbar; but he says that, because he was crushed, and not thrown off, his injury is in no way due to it. That is too fine a distinction for me. I cannot believe that that purely fortuitous circumstance can make all the difference to the case. . . .

In order to illustrate this question of causation, I may say that if the plaintiff whilst he was riding on the towbar, had been hit in the eye by a shot from a negligent sportsman, I should have thought that the plaintiff's negligence would in no way be a cause of his injury. It would only be part of the history. But I cannot say that in the present case. The man's negligence here was so much mixed up with his injury that it cannot be dismissed as mere history. His dangerous position on the vehicle was one of the causes of his damage. . . .

It all comes to this: If a man carelessly rides on a vehicle in a dangerous position, and subsequently there is a collision in which his injuries are made worse by reason of his position than they otherwise would have been, then his damage is partly the result of his own fault, and the damages recoverable by him fall to be reduced accordingly

Singleton and **Hodson LJJ** delivered separate concurring judgments.

Appeal and cross-appeal dismissed.

COMMENTARY

Do you agree that the event which occurred was within the 'penumbra of danger' to which the precautions were directed, though of a slightly different kind from those which caused the precaution to be required? (See *Braverus Maritime Inc v Port Kembla Coal Terminal Ltd* [2005] FCAFC 25.) If, as the trial judge held, the only risk created by the plaintiff's contributory negligence was that of being thrown off the vehicle, did it make sense to reduce the plaintiff's damages when what actually occurred was not within that risk? Even if foreseeability may not be sufficient to establish contributory negligence, should it not be a necessary condition? If a defendant is not liable for a type or kind of damage which is unforeseeable, why should a claimant's damages be reduced when the injury results from an unforeseeable risk? Whilst liability is expanded by adopting a broad classification of type or kind of damage at the remoteness stage of the cause of action in negligence, it has the converse effect when the issue is the claimant's contributory negligence, as illustrated by the extracted case.

Can the claimant's lifestyle choices be taken into account in assessing whether there is contributory negligence? If a claimant continues to smoke cigarettes in the knowledge that this is adverse to his health, there is authority that this can trigger the defence (*Badger v Ministry of Defence* [2006] 3 All ER 173). However, in two recent decisions—one involving a pathological gambler and one involving a claimant addicted to drugs and alcohol—the Court of Appeal has held that the lifestyle choices that created these conditions should not be considered as part of the contributory negligence enquiry where the defendant's negligence consisted of failing to treat or to take account of these conditions (*Calvert v William Hill Credit Ltd* [2008] EWCA Civ 1427, [2009] Ch 330; *St George v Home Office* [2008] EWCA Civ 1068, [2009] 1 WLR 1670). As the lifestyle choices were made well before the defendant's negligence, such events were generally 'too remote in time, place and circumstance' from the defendant's negligence and were, applying the words of Lord Denning in *Jones v Livox*, 'no more than part of the history' (*St George v Home Office* [2009] 1 WLR 1670 at [56] per Dyson LJ).

The issue of causation has been considered elsewhere, but it should be remembered that the 1945 Act only changed the consequences of a finding of contributory negligence. Whether there was, in fact, contributory negligence must still be decided. This appears clearly from the decision of the House of Lords in *Stapley v Gypsum Mines Ltd* [1953] AC 663. Here, a miner was injured when the roof of a stope on which he and another miner, Dale, were working, collapsed. The trial judge held that the defendant was vicariously liable for the breach of statutory duty of its employee, Dale, but reduced the damages because of the deceased's contributory negligence. The Court of Appeal allowed an appeal on the basis that the deceased was the sole cause of his injuries, but the House of Lords reversed, Lord Reid holding:

In these circumstances it is necessary to determine what caused the death of Stapley. If it was caused solely by his own fault, then the appellant cannot succeed. But if it was caused partly by his own fault and partly by the fault of Dale, then the appellant can rely on the Law Reform (Contributory Negligence) Act 1945. . . . The question must be determined by applying common sense to the facts of each particular case. One may find that, as a matter of history, several people have been at fault and that if any one of them had acted properly the accident would not have happened, but that does not mean that the accident must be regarded as having been caused by the fault of all of them. One must discriminate between those faults which must be discarded as being too remote and those which must not. Sometimes it is proper to discard all but one and to regard that one as the sole cause, but in other cases it is proper to regard two or more as having jointly caused the accident. . . .

See also the comments of Deane J in *March v E & MH Stramare Pty Ltd* (1991) 65 ALJR 334 at 341.

3. Apportionment

Stapley v Gypsum Mines Ltd [1953] AC 663

The facts are not relevant for the purpose of the extract.

Lord Reid

A court must deal broadly with the problem of apportionment, and, in considering what is just and equitable, must have regard to the blameworthiness of each party, but 'the claimant's share in the responsibility for the damage' cannot, I think, be assessed without considering the relative importance of his acts in causing the damage apart from his blameworthiness. . . .

Froom v Butcher [1976] QB 286

The plaintiff, his wife and his daughter were injured when, without carelessness on his part, the car which he was driving was struck head-on by the defendant's car. Although the collision was the result of careless driving by the defendant, the injury to the plaintiff was exacerbated by the fact he had deliberately chosen not to wear a seat belt. Prior to the Court of Appeal decision there had been a number of first instance decisions reaching conflicting results as to whether failure to wear a seat belt constituted contributory negligence.

Lord Denning MR

Contributory Negligence

Negligence depends on a breach of duty, whereas contributory negligence does not. Negligence is a man's carelessness in breach of duty to others. Contributory negligence is a man's carelessness in looking after his own safety. He is guilty of contributory negligence if he ought reasonably to have foreseen that, if he did not act as a reasonable prudent man, he might be hurt himself: see *Jones v Livox Quarries Ltd* [1952] 2 QB 608. Before 1945 a plaintiff who was guilty of contributory negligence was disentitled from recovering anything if his own negligence was one of the substantial causes of the injury: see *Swadling v Cooper* [1931] AC 1. Since 1945 he is no longer defeated altogether. He gets reduced damages.... Those provisions must be borne in mind as we take our consideration further.

The Cause of the Damage

In these seat belt cases, the injured plaintiff is in no way to blame for the accident itself. Sometimes he is an innocent passenger sitting beside a negligent driver who goes off the road. At other times he is an innocent driver of one car which is run into by the bad driving of another car which pulls out on to its wrong side of the road. It may well be asked: why should the injured plaintiff have his damages reduced? The accident was solely caused by the negligent driving by the defendant. Sometimes outrageously bad driving. It should not lie in his mouth to say: 'You ought to have been wearing a seat belt.' That point of view was strongly expressed in *Smith v Blackburn* [1974] RTR 533 at 536 by O'Connor J. He said:

> The idea that the insurers of a grossly negligent driver should be relieved in any degree from paying what is proper compensation for injuries is an idea that offends ordinary decency. Until I am forced to do so by higher authority, I will not so rule.

I do not think that is the correct approach. The question is not what was the cause of the accident. It is rather what was the cause of the damage. In most accidents on the road the bad driving, which causes the accident, also causes the ensuing damage. But in seat belt cases the cause of the accident is one thing. The cause of the damage is another. The accident is caused by the bad driving. The damage is caused in part by the bad driving of the defendant, and in part by the failure of the plaintiff to wear a seat belt. If the plaintiff was to blame in not wearing a seat belt, the damage is in part the result of his own fault. He must bear some share in the responsibility for the damage and his damages fall to be reduced to such extent as the court thinks just and equitable. In Admiralty the courts used to look to the causes of the damage: see *The Margaret* (1881) 6 PD 76. In a leading case in this court under the 1945 Act, we looked to the cause of the damage: see *Davies v Swan Motor Co* [1949] 2 KB 326. In the crash helmet cases this court also looked at the causes of the damage: see *O'Connell v Jackson* [1972] 1 QB 270. So also we should in seat belt cases....

[His Lordship considered the arguments for and against wearing seat belts, holding that it was a sensible practice for them to be used, and continued:]

The Share of Responsibility

Whenever there is an accident, the negligent driver must bear by far the greater share of responsibility. It was his negligence which caused the accident. It also was a prime cause of the whole of the damage. But insofar as the damage might have been avoided or lessened by wearing a seat belt, the injured person must bear some share. But how much should this be? Is it proper to enquire whether the driver was grossly negligent or only slightly negligent? Or whether the failure to wear a seat belt was entirely inexcusable or almost forgivable? If such an enquiry could easily be undertaken, it might be as well to do it. In *Davies v Swan Motor Co* [1949] 2 KB 326 we said that consideration should be given not only to the causative potency of a particular factor, but also its blameworthiness. But we live in a practical world. In most of these cases the liability of the driver is admitted; the failure to wear a seat belt is admitted; the only question is: what damages should be payable? This question should not be prolonged by an expensive enquiry into the degree of blameworthiness on either side, which would be hotly disputed. Suffice it to assess a share of responsibility which will be just and equitable in the great majority of cases.

Sometimes the evidence will show that the failure made no difference. The damage would have been the same, even if a seat belt had been worn. In such cases the damages should not be reduced at all. At other times the evidence will show that the failure made all the difference. The damage would have been prevented altogether if a seat belt had been worn. In such cases I would suggest that the damages should be reduced by 25 per cent. But often enough the evidence will only show that the failure made a considerable difference. Some injuries to the head, for instance, would have been a good deal less severe if a seat belt had been worn, but there would still have been some injury to the head. In such case I would suggest that the damages attributable to the failure to wear a seat belt should be reduced by 15 per cent.

Conclusion

Everyone knows, or ought to know, that when he goes out in a car he should fasten the seat belt. It is so well known that it goes without saying, not only for the driver, but also the passenger. If either the driver or the passenger fails to wear it and an accident happens—and the injuries would have been prevented or lessened if he had worn it—then his damages should be reduced. Under the Highway Code a driver may have a duty to invite his passenger to fasten his seat belt, but adult passengers possessed of their faculties should not need telling what to do. If such passengers do not fasten their seat belts, their own lack of care for their own safety may be the cause of their injuries. In the present case the injuries to the head and chest would have been prevented by the wearing of a seat belt and the damages on that account might be reduced by 25 per cent. The finger would have been broken anyway and the damages for it not reduced at all. Overall the judge suggested 20 per cent and Mr Froom has made no objection to it. So I would not interfere.

I would allow the appeal and reduce the damages by £100.

Lawton LJ and **Scarman LJ** agreed with Lord Denning.

Appeal allowed.

Candolin v Pohjola Case C–537/03, 30 June 2005 [2005] ECR I–5745

The case arose out of a car accident in Finland; one passenger died and the remainder were seriously injured. Under Finnish law, compensation was denied to two of the passengers because they should have noticed the driver's drunken state. The primary question for the ECJ was whether these provisions were compatible with a number of directives of the EU, issued to harmonise the laws of member states, relating to compulsory third party liability insurance arising out of motor vehicle accidents. The precise wording of the articles considered in the extract below is not material for present purposes.

Judgment

The Questions Referred for a Preliminary Ruling

...24. As regards the refusal or limitation of the right to compensation paid by the compulsory motor vehicle insurance on account of the fact that the passenger who is a victim of an accident contributed to the injury, it is clear from the aim of the first, second and third directives, and from their wording, that they do not seek to harmonise the rules of the Member States governing civil liability and that, as Community law stands at present, the Member States are free to determine the rules of civil liability applicable to road accidents (Case C-348/98 *Mendes Ferreira and Delgado Correia Ferreira* [2000] ECR I-6711, paragraphs 23 and 29).

25. In that regard, Pohjola and the Finnish, German, Austrian and Norwegian Governments claim that Community law does not impose any limits on the appraisal, under national law on civil liability, of the extent to which the passenger contributed to the occurrence of his injuries.

26. Such an argument cannot be accepted.

27. The Member States must exercise their powers in compliance with Community law and, in particular, with Article 3(1) of the First Directive, Article 2(1) of the Second Directive and Article 1 of the Third Directive, whose aim is to ensure that compulsory motor vehicle insurance allows all passengers who are victims of an accident caused by a motor vehicle to be compensated for the injury or loss they have suffered.

28. The national provisions which govern compensation for road accidents cannot, therefore, deprive those provisions of their effectiveness.

29. Such would be the case specifically where, solely on the basis of the passenger's contribution to the occurrence of his injuries, national rules, established on the basis of general and abstract criteria, either denied the passenger the right to be compensated by the compulsory motor vehicle insurance or limited such a right in a disproportionate manner.

30. It is only in exceptional circumstances that the amount of the victim's compensation may be limited on the basis of an assessment of his particular case.

31. In the determination of whether those circumstances exist and whether the limit on the compensation is proportionate, which is a matter for the national court, the fact that the passenger concerned is the owner of the vehicle the driver of which caused the accident is irrelevant.

32. By providing that insurance for civil liability in respect of the use of motor vehicles covers liability for personal injuries to all passengers other than the driver, Article 1 of the Third Directive lays down only one distinction between the driver and the other passengers.

33. Furthermore, the protective aims recalled in paragraphs 18 to 20 of this judgment require that the legal position of the owner of the vehicle, present in the vehicle at the time of the accident as a passenger, be the same as that of any other passenger who is a victim of the accident.

COMMENTARY

Section 1 of the 1945 Act requires a court to apportion damages according to the claimant's share in the responsibility for the damage. Even though the word 'cause' is not used, the above cases illustrate that the apportionment takes place on a causation plus fault basis. The court must evaluate both the relative blameworthiness of each party's conduct and the extent to which that fault caused the damage. That this is the correct approach is made clear by Dias and Markesinis, *Tort Law*, 2nd edn. (Oxford: Clarendon Press, 1989), p. 122: 'For instance, in strict liability a defendant is liable even though he has not been at fault. A plaintiff who has been at fault, however slightly, would recover nothing if fault is the basis, since his is the only fault "responsible" for the damage. This clearly cannot be.'

Froom v Butcher also affirms that the fault and causation inquiries are directed at the damage for which the claimant claims. Mr Froom's fault did not have anything to do with causing the accident in the first place, but it did contribute to the damage he suffered.

In an area of law where the relevant principles were considered relatively settled and uncontroversial, the ECJ's *Candolin* decision constitutes something of a bombshell. In the motor accident context, the victim's compensation is to be limited for reasons particular to him only 'in exceptional circumstances' (para. 30). Compare this with the finding of one well-known empirical study that contributory negligence was taken into account in almost half of all settlements in personal injury cases (Harris et al., *Compensation and Support for Illness and Injury* (Oxford: Clarendon Press, 1984), p. 91). One wonders how the Court—interpreting a provision that, on its face, does nothing more than to require member states 'to ensure that civil liability in respect of the use of vehicles…is covered by insurance' (Article 3(1))—came to rewrite the domestic law of contributory negligence. As one expert has remarked, 'the Court has set another milestone in a series of cases blatantly disregarding the most fundamental principles of the law of delict' (Koch, *European Tort Law 2005*, p. 599).

A related question is whether the guidelines in *Froom v Butcher* are consistent with the ECJ's ruling. Merkin (2005) 17 *Insurance Law Monthly* 12 has argued that they are but much depends on the interpretation of para. 29 of the judgment; if the guidelines are seen as 'national rules based on general and abstract criteria' which limited the rights of recovery in a disproportionate manner, there may be incompatibility. Certainly the guidelines are aimed at preventing an airing of the individual facts of the case—hence might be seen as applying general and abstract criteria—but it may be difficult to construe the maximum deduction of 25 per cent as disproportionate. This may explain why there has thus far been no challenge to the guidelines on the grounds that they are inconsistent with *Candolin*.

Irrespective of the position under EU law, is it consistent with the broad discretion provided by the 1945 Act to set figures for the appropriate reduction? Although there are examples where other factors, together with the failure to wear a seat belt, have resulted in a departure from Lord Denning's guidelines (see e.g. *Owens v Brimmel* [1977] QB 859 (driving with a drunken driver) and *Ashton v Turner* [1981] QB 137 (driving the getaway car for a robbery)), the broad thrust of *Froom* was affirmed, albeit in a slightly different context, in *J (A Child) v Wilkins* [2001] PIQR P12 where the Court of Appeal reiterated the benefit of guidelines in promoting settlement. Moreover, in the recent first instance decisions of *Gawler v Raettig* [2007] EWHC 373 (QB) and *Stanton v Collinson* [2009] EWHC 342 (QB) arguments that public policy required a reassessment (to increase the deduction) of the guidelines because of the increased awareness of the importance of wearing seat belts were rejected. Nor did the Court of Appeal in *Gawler's* case think the question of revisiting the *Froom* guidelines a matter of urgency ([2007] EWCA Civ 1560). It thus seems unlikely that any change to the guidelines is imminent.

The Court of Appeal has accepted that the failure of a motorcyclist to wear a crash helmet amounts to contributory negligence (*O'Connell v Jackson* [1972] 1 QB 270), and that Lord

Denning's guidelines should also apply in these cases (*Capps v Miller* [1989] 1 WLR 839). It has also recently been held that the failure of pedal cyclist to wear a helmet constitutes contributory negligence (*Smith v Finch* [2009] EWHC 53 (QB)) although it was not necessary for the judge to decide whether the *Froom* guidelines would apply as the injury would have occurred regardless of whether a helmet was worn. See further Fulbrook, 'Cycle helmets and contributory negligence' [2004] JPIL 171. In *Capps*, Glidewell and May LJJ thought a 10 per cent reduction appropriate where the helmet was worn but the strap was not done up. It has also been held that the guidelines are appropriate in determining apportionment between defendants under the Civil Liability (Contribution) Act 1978 when a claimant's damage was caused partly through careless driving and partly by her mother's failure to secure adequately her seat belt.

Can a court order a reduction of 100 per cent in respect of the claimant's negligence? The ECJ decision in *Candolin* precludes this for motor vehicle accidents but 100 per cent deductions were in any case doubted generally by the Court of Appeal in *Pitts v Hunt* [1991] 1 QB 24, and this view has been followed by the same court in *Anderson v Newham College of Higher Education* [2003] ICR 212: 'Whether the claim is in negligence or for breach of statutory duty, if the evidence, once it has been appraised as the law requires, shows the entire fault to lie with the claimant there is no liability on the defendant. ... If there is liability, contributory negligence can reduce its monetary quantification, but it cannot legally or logically nullify it.' This is also in line with the view of the Australian High Court that a reduction of the claimant's damages by 100 per cent is not possible as is it not compatible with a finding that the defendant's negligence was a cause of the damage, a prerequisite for apportionment to occur (see *Wynbergen v Hoyts Corporation* (1998) 72 ALJR 65 but note that deductions of 100 per cent for contributory negligence are now allowed by statute in most Australian jurisdictions).

For a general discussion of the principles governing apportionment, see Gravells, 'Three Heads of Contributory Negligence' (1977) 93 LQR 581.

It should be remembered that in many cases where the question of contributory negligence arises, the defendant will be insured against liability. The result of this is that any reduction in damages attributed to the claimant's contributory negligence is very likely to be borne by the claimant personally, whilst the defendant's liability is distributed through the mechanism of liability insurance. Commenting on this, the current editor of *Atiyah's Accidents, Compensation and the Law* remarks (p. 56): 'In practice, negligent people do not pay for the consequences of their negligence; but contributorily negligent people do pay for the consequences of their contributory negligence. It is not too much to say that the only significant group of people who are called upon to pay for the consequences of their negligence are accident victims themselves.' Is this fair?

4. Defendant's Negligence Creating Emergency

Adams v Lancashire and Yorkshire Railway Co (1869) 4 LR CP 739

The plaintiff was a passenger on a train operated by the defendant. Due to the defendant's negligence, the door of the carriage in which the plaintiff was travelling flew open a number of times. The plaintiff had room to sit away from the door, but, in attempting to close the door, fell out of the train and was injured. The train had stopped at three stations since the door had begun opening and would have stopped at another three minutes later. The plaintiff's action against the defendant failed on the ground of the plaintiff's contributory negligence (which was at that time a complete defence).

Montague Smith J

I quite agree that, if the negligence of a railway company puts a passenger in a situation of alternative danger, that is to say, if he will be in danger by remaining still, and in danger if he attempts to escape, then, if he attempts to escape, any injury that he may sustain in so doing is a consequence of the company's negligence; but if he is only suffering some inconvenience, and, to avoid that, he voluntarily runs into danger, and injury ensues, that cannot be said to be the result of the company's negligence. It is hardly necessary to say, that though I use the words 'danger' and 'inconvenience', yet, if the inconvenience is very great and the danger run in avoiding it very slight, it may not be unreasonable to incur that danger. Here, however, I see no proof that the plaintiff was suffering any inconvenience, certainly none comparable to the danger he ran in endeavouring to close the door in the way he did.

I think the rule is well stated and illustrated by Lord Ellenborough in *Jones v Boyce* (1816) 1 Stark 493. Lord Ellenborough says: 'To enable a plaintiff to sustain the action, it is not necessary that he should have been thrown off the coach; it is sufficient if he was placed, by the misconduct of the defendant, in such a situation as obliged him to adopt the alternative of a dangerous leap or to remain at certain peril; if that position was occasioned by the default of the defendant, the action may be supported'; and again, 'if I place a man in a situation that he must adopt a perilous alternative, I am responsible for the consequences.'

In the present case I think there is no evidence that the plaintiff was placed in such a situation, or that he was justified in undertaking the peril he voluntarily undertook...

The plaintiff's action failed.

COMMENTARY

It is unlikely today that the plaintiff's claim would have failed completely, as a finding of contributory negligence would not operate as a complete defence. The defendant had been guilty of some fault, and, as noted earlier (see *March v E. & M. H. Stramare* (1991) 171 CLR 506), a court is unlikely to find that the claimant was solely responsible for his own damage when the defendant is at fault and apportionment is possible.

The rationale behind taking the emergency situation into account is clear: as the defendant placed the claimant in the emergency situation he cannot be heard to complain that the claimant, judged in the cold light of day, acted unreasonably. Should the same rule apply where the defendant's negligence places the claimant in a position where it would be unfair to judge him by the ordinary standard, not because of an emergency but because the defendant's negligence has deprived the claimant of the capacity to act in such a manner? It would certainly seem harsh to judge the conduct of a claimant who was mentally disabled as a result of the defendant's tort without reference to the disability (cf. *Corr v IBC Vehicles Ltd* [2008] AC 884, discussed above at p. 265).

If the defendant's negligence creates an emergency situation, the conduct of a rescuer who responds to the emergency is judged with the emergency in mind. In *Baker v T. E. Hopkins* [1959] 1 WLR 966, the plaintiff's husband died whilst attempting to rescue two men trapped in a well as a result of the defendant's negligence. In response to the defendant's contention that the husband had been guilty of contributory negligence, Willmer LJ said:

The burden of proof with regard to this allegation is on the defendant company, and in order to succeed I think they would have to show that the conduct of Dr Baker was so foolhardy as to amount to a wholly unreasonable disregard for his own safety. Bearing in mind that danger invites rescue, the court should not be astute to accept criticism of the rescuer's conduct from the wrongdoer who created the danger. Moreover, I think it should be remembered that it is fatally easy to be wise after the event. It is not enough that, when all the evidence has been sifted and all the facts ascertained in the calm and deliberate atmosphere of a court of law, the rescuer's conduct can be shown *ex post facto* to have been misguided or foolhardy. He is entitled to be judged in the light of the situation as it appeared to him at the time, i.e., in a context of immediate and pressing emergency...

5. Children

Gough v Thorne [1966] 1 WLR 1387

The plaintiff, a 13½-year-old girl, was waiting with her brothers to cross a busy road in London. A lorry driver stopped alongside them and, with one hand raised to indicate to following traffic to stop, indicated with his other that they should cross. They did so but as the plaintiff went past the edge of the lorry she was struck and injured by a 'bubble car' being driven at excessive speed. The driver of the car failed to notice the lorry driver's outstretched hand and drove between the lorry and the bollards in the middle of the road. In an action by the plaintiff for damages, the trial judge found that the bubble car driver, the defendant, was negligent, but also that the plaintiff was negligent in advancing past the lorry into the open road without pausing to see whether there was any traffic coming from her right; he assessed the degree of her contributory negligence at one-third. The plaintiff appealed against the finding of contributory negligence.

Lord Denning MR

I am afraid that I cannot agree with the judge. A very young child cannot be guilty of contributory negligence. An older child may be, but it depends on the circumstances. A judge should only find a child guilty of contributory negligence if he or she is of such an age as reasonably to be expected to take precautions for his or her own safety: and then he or she is only to be found guilty if blame should be attached to him or her. A child has not the road sense or the experience of his or her elders. He or she is not to be found guilty unless he or she is blameworthy.

In this particular case I have no doubt that there was no blameworthiness to be attributed to the plaintiff at all. Here she was with her elder brother crossing a road. They had been beckoned on by the lorry driver. What more could you expect the child to do than to cross in pursuance of the beckoning? It is said by the judge that she ought to have leant forward and looked to see whether anything was coming. That indeed might be reasonably expected of a grown-up person with a fully developed road sense, but not of a child of 13½...

Salmon LJ

The question as to whether the plaintiff can be said to have been guilty of contributory negligence depends on whether any ordinary child of 13½ could be expected to have done any more than this child did. I say, 'any ordinary child'. I do not mean a paragon of prudence; nor do I mean a scatter-brained child; but the ordinary girl of 13½. I think that any ordinary child of 13½, seeing a lorry stop to let her cross and the lorry driver, a grown-up person in whom she no doubt has some confidence, beckoning her to cross the road would naturally go straight on, no one in my view could blame her for doing so. I agree that if she had been a good deal older and hardened by experience and perhaps consequently with less confidence in adults, she might have said to herself: 'I wonder if that man has given the proper signal to traffic coming up? I wonder if that traffic has heeded it? I wonder if he ought to have beckoned me across when he did and whether he looked behind him before doing so?' She might not have gone past the front of the lorry without verifying for herself that it was safe to do so; but it would be quite wrong to hold that a child of 13 is negligent because she fails to go through those mental processes and relies unquestioningly on the lorry driver's signal. . . .

Danckwerts LJ delivered a short judgment agreeing with Lord Denning MR.

Appeal allowed.

COMMENTARY

The language 'any ordinary child…not…a paragon of prudence [or] a scatter-brained child; but the ordinary girl of 13' is probably derived from the judgment of Kitto J in *McHale v Watson* (1966) 115 CLR 199, a case decided shortly before *Gough* which dealt with the standard of care of a 12-year-old boy. This judgment subsequently received the approval of the Court of Appeal in *Mullin v Richards* [1998] 1 WLR 1304 (extracted above, p. 193); see also *O v L* [2009] EWCA Civ 295.

   Lord Denning suggests that a very young child cannot, as a matter of law, be guilty of contributory negligence, but this probably requires some qualification. No doubt, as a matter of fact, the younger the child the more difficult it will be to show that the child had sufficient understanding to appreciate the risk being run (see, e.g., *Barnes v Flucker*, 1985 SLT 142, where it was conceded by counsel that 5-year-old children were not capable of being contributorily negligent), but each case will depend on its own facts. A good general guide was provided by Lord Nimmo Smith in the Scottish case of *Galbraith's Curator ad Litem v Stewart (No. 2)* 1998 SLT 1305 (Outer House of the Court of Session), where he stated: 'In my opinion no hard and fast rule can be derived from [the] cases, and the question of a child's contributory negligence must depend on the nature of the particular danger and the particular child's capacity to appreciate it.' Note also that, in comparison with other European jurisdictions, English law provides (at least in theory) greater possibilities for children to have their damages reduced for contributory negligence (see *van Dam*, p. 1215 and, for more information, M. Martin Casals (ed.), *Children in Tort Law. Part II: Children as Victims* (Vienna: Springer, 2006)).

IV. Exclusion of Liability

A defendant may seek to exclude all potential liability to another person in advance of exposing himself to the risk of a possible claim. Although this is commonly done in the form of an agreement or contract between the parties—the student of the law of contract will

be aware of the case and statute law on exemption clauses—it may also be done by an appropriately placed notice. This usually occurs where an owner or occupier of land attempts to
exclude liability for the state of the premises or in respect of some activity carried on upon
that land. However, not every notice which attempts to reduce or limit the defendant's liability will be an exclusion of liability notice. If A is about to use a bridge to cross a river and
sees a notice stating: 'Warning. Bridge Dangerous—Use Bridge Further Upstream', this is
not an exclusion clause. Rather, the clause recognises that the owner or occupier responsible
for that bridge does owe some duty to potential users, and the notice is an attempt to satisfy
the duty owed to them (i.e it goes to breach of duty). Similarly, if the notice had read: 'Cross
Bridge at Own Risk' this might be construed as a *volenti* notice, an attempt to place any
responsibility for injury caused as a result of the state of repair of the bridge with the user of
the bridge. But a notice in the form: 'The Owner of the Bridge will not be held responsible for
any loss or damage howsoever caused due to the state of the Bridge' will be regarded as an
attempt to exclude liability. These categories are not mutually exclusive, and it is possible to
construe a clause in a contract or a notice as performing more than one of the above functions. But some attempt at classification is necessary, particularly in view of the restrictions
placed on the defence of exclusion of liability by the Unfair Contract Terms Act 1977.

1. Unfair Contract Terms Act 1977

Unfair Contract Terms Act 1977

1. SCOPE OF PART I

(1) For the purposes of this Part of this Act, 'negligence' means the breach—

    (a) of any obligation, arising from the express or implied terms of a contract, to take
reasonable care to exercise reasonable skill in the performance of the contract;

    (b) of any common law duty to take reasonable care or exercise reasonable skill (but not
any stricter duty);

    (c) of the common duty of care imposed by the Occupiers' Liability Act 1957 or the
Occupiers' Liability Act (Northern Ireland) 1957.

(3) In the case of both contract and tort, sections 2 to 7 apply (except where the contrary is
stated in section 6(4)) only to business liability, that is liability for breach of obligations or
duties arising—

    (a) from things done or to be done by a person in the course of a business (whether his
own business or another's); or

    (b) from the occupation of premises used for business purposes of the occupier; and ref-
erences to liability are to be read accordingly but liability of an occupier of premises
for breach of an obligation or duty towards a person obtaining access to the premises
for recreational or educational purposes, being liability for loss or damage suffered
by reason of the dangerous state of the premises, is not a business liability of the
occupier unless granting that person such access for the purposes concerned falls
within the business purposes of the occupier.

(4) In relation to any breach of duty or obligation, it is immaterial for any purpose of this Part of
this Act whether the breach was inadvertent or intentional, or whether liability for it arises
directly or vicariously.

2. NEGLIGENCE LIABILITY

(1) A person cannot by reference to any contract term or to a notice given to persons generally or to particular persons exclude or restrict his liability for death or personal injury resulting from negligence.

(2) In the case of other loss or damage, a person cannot so exclude or restrict his liability for negligence except in so far as the term or notice satisfies the requirement of reasonableness.

(3) Where a contract term or notice purports to exclude or restrict liability for negligence a person's agreement to or awareness of it is not of itself to be taken as indicating his voluntary acceptance of any risk. . . .

11. THE 'REASONABLENESS' TEST

(1) In relation to a contract term, the requirement of reasonableness for the purposes of this Part of this Act, section 3 of the Misrepresentation Act 1967 and section 3 of the Misrepresentation Act (Northern Ireland) 1967 is that the term shall have been a fair and reasonable one to be included having regard to the circumstances which were, or ought reasonably to have been, known to or in the contemplation of the parties when the contract was made.

(2) In determining for the purposes of section 6 or 7 above whether a contract term satisfies the requirement of reasonableness, regard shall be had in particular to the matters specified in Schedule 2 to this Act; but this subsection does not prevent the court or arbitrator from holding, in accordance with any rule of law, that a term which purports to exclude or restrict any relevant liability is not a term of the contract.

(3) In relation to a notice (not being a notice having contractual effect), the requirement of reasonableness under this Act is that it should be fair and reasonable to allow reliance on it, having regard to all the circumstances obtaining when the liability arose or (but for the notice) would have arisen.

(4) Where by reference to a contract term or notice a person seeks to restrict liability to a specified sum of money, and the question arises (under this or any other Act) whether the term or notice satisfies the requirement of reasonableness, regard shall be had in particular (but without prejudice to subsection (2) above in the case of contract terms) to—
    (a) the resources which he could expect to be available to him for the purpose of meeting the liability should it arise; and
    (b) how far it was open to him to cover himself by insurance.

(5) It is for those claiming that a contract term or notice satisfies the requirement of reasonableness to show that it does. . . .

13. VARIETIES OF EXEMPTION CLAUSE

(1) To the extent that this Part of this Act prevents the exclusion or restriction of any liability it also prevents—
    (a) making the liability or its enforcement subject to restrictive or onerous conditions;
    (b) excluding or restricting any right or remedy in respect of the liability, or subjecting a person to any prejudice in consequence of his pursuing any such right or remedy;
    (c) excluding or restricting rules of evidence or procedure; and (to that extent) sections 2 and 5 to 7 also prevent excluding or restricting liability by reference to terms and notices which exclude or restrict the relevant obligation or duty.

(2) But an agreement in writing to submit present or future differences to arbitration is not to be treated under this Part of this Act as excluding or restricting any liability.

14. INTERPRETATION OF PART I

In this Part of this Act—

'business' includes a profession and the activities of any government department or local or public authority;

'goods' has the same meaning as in [the Sale of Goods Act 1979] . . .

'negligence' has the meaning given by section 1(1);

'notice' includes an announcement, whether or not in writing, and any other communication or pretended communication; and

'personal injury' includes any disease and any impairment of physical or mental condition.

COMMENTARY

Section 2 of the Act prevents the exclusion or restriction of liability, altogether in respect of loss or damage falling within s. 2(1), and subject to a requirement of reasonableness in respect of loss or damage falling within s. 2(2). In *Smith v Eric S. Bush* [1990] 1 AC 831, it was argued that the effect of the defendant's disclaimer of liability was to prevent a duty from ever coming into existence; hence its effect was not to exclude or restrict the duty because there never was one, and it was not therefore subject to the 'reasonableness' requirements set out in s. 11. This was accepted by the Court of Appeal, but, after considering the policy behind the Act (in particular, ss. 11 and 13), the House of Lords rejected the argument. Lord Griffiths commented (at 857): 'The result of taking the notice into account when assessing the existence of a duty of care would result in removing all liability for negligent misstatements from the protection of the Act.'

The Act limits only the exclusion or restriction of 'business liability' as defined in s. 1(3). This extends not only to liabilities incurred in the course of business activities but also to liabilities arising in respect of the occupation of business premises. In considering the liability of a business occupier, it should be noted that excluding liability in respect of persons entering the premises for educational or recreational purposes does not generally amount to an exclusion of a business liability. This amendment to s. 1(3)(b), made by the Occupiers' Liability Act 1984, was designed to ensure that those who allow visitors onto their land to see, for example, ruins of a castle or a historic home, are able to avoid liability for injuries caused by the state of their premises, unless having visitors falls within their business purposes. Would a farmer who allows tourists entry to his land to view a ruined monastery be attempting to exclude a business liability if he also offered them a bed and breakfast service? Non-business occupiers, by contrast, are totally free to exclude possible liabilities to their visitors (see Occupiers Liability Act 1957, s. 2(1), extracted below at p. 559).

2. *Volenti* and Exclusion of Liability

White v Blackmore [1972] 2 QB 651

The deceased was an experienced 'jalopy' racing driver and a member of the Stroud Jalopy Club. He wished to take part in a series of races due to start at 2 pm on a Sunday afternoon. That morning, he took his jalopy to the field where the races were to be held and had his name entered on the list of competitors before returning home. He returned in the afternoon with a group of other people including his wife, the plaintiff, and paid their admission fees; as a competitor, he did not pay for his own admission. At the entrance to the field and around the track were exhibited notices which stated:

> WARNING TO THE PUBLIC. MOTOR RACING IS DANGEROUS. It is a condition of admission, that all persons having any connection with the promotion and/or organisation and/or conduct of the meeting...are absolved from all liabilities arising out of accidents causing damage or personal injury (whether fatal or otherwise) howsoever caused to spectators or ticket-holders.

There was no evidence that the notices had been in position in the morning when the deceased entered for the races. In the afternoon, the deceased was killed when, in between races in which he was competing, a car collided with a safety rope, the consequence of which was that all the stakes were uprooted and the deceased was thrown into the air. He subsequently died from the injuries. At the time of the accident, he had been near the spectators' enclosure but not behind the enclosure ropes, despite warnings that all spectators should retire behind them before the race began.

His wife sued the chairman of the club and the racing organiser for damages in respect of his death. The trial judge held that the defendants were in breach of the common duty of care owed by an occupier of land to visitors under the Occupiers' Liability Act 1957, but that the deceased was one-third to blame for the accident. The judge also found that the deceased had seen the notices exhibited at the entrance to and around the track and appreciated that they contained conditions governing admission to watch the racing; he also found that similar warnings were a common feature of jalopy races with which the deceased was familiar. He therefore dismissed the claim on the ground that the defence of *volenti non fit injuria* applied. The Court of Appeal rejected the *volenti* defence but by a majority held that the defendants had excluded liability by virtue of the notice.

Buckley LJ

In my judgment the case must turn on the effect of the various warnings which the deceased saw or had ample opportunity to see. If these warnings were, or any of them was, sufficient to exclude any duty of care on the part of the organisers of the meeting towards the deceased, the defendants were not guilty of negligence and consequently they do not need the shield of the doctrine of *volenti*. The learned judge in fact based his decision on these warnings.

I need not repeat the history of the relevant events on the day of the accident. Counsel for the plaintiff has submitted that when the deceased signed on in the morning of that day he entered into a contractual arrangement with the organisers that he should be permitted to come on to the field for the purpose of competing in the races, and that that contract could not be affected by any of the subsequent events of the day. That contract, he says, was not subject to any limitation of liability except possibly one to the effect that competitors taking part in races did so at their own risk. Consequently, counsel submits, the organisers' liability to the deceased when he came on to the field in the afternoon was subject to no relevant limitation. In my judgment, the evidence does not support the suggestion that the parties had any intention of entering into contractual relations when the deceased signed on in the morning. He was thereby indicating to the organisers, as the learned judge thought and as I think, that he proposed to take part in the racing in the afternoon as a competitor and no more. Accordingly I do not feel able to accept this submission of counsel for the plaintiff.

When the deceased returned with his family in the afternoon, the notice... [whose terms are set out above] was prominently displayed near the entrance to the ground. The learned judge found as a fact that the deceased saw that notice and appreciated that it was a notice governing the conditions under which people were to be admitted to watch the racing....

In my opinion, when the deceased came on to the field in the afternoon, he did so as a gratuitous licensee. I have already said that, in my view, no contract was made in the morning. The deceased made no payment for entry in the afternoon. Nothing that occurred in the morning could afford consideration for any contract entered into in the afternoon. In my judgment, no contract between the promoters and the deceased was made in the afternoon. The deceased remained willing to take part in the races and the promoters remained willing to allow him to do so. On the evidence, he was not, in my judgment, either bound or entitled contractually to take part in the races. In this state of affairs he was allowed on to the field free of charge....

What then was the effect of the situation which arose when the deceased returned to the field in the afternoon? It is clear that the occupier of land, who permits someone else to enter on that land as his licensee, can by imposing suitable conditions limit his own liability to the licensee in respect of any risks which may arise while the licensee is on the land (*Ashdown v Samuel Williams & Sons Ltd* [1957] 1 QB 409). The Occupiers' Liability Act 1957, which in s. 2(1) refers to an occupier excluding his duty of care to any visitor 'by agreement or otherwise', has not altered the law in this respect. Counsel for the plaintiff concedes that in the present case the notice displayed at the entrance to the ground was sufficient to exclude liability on the part of the organisers of the meeting to all spectators properly so called, but he contends that a distinction is to be drawn between competitors and spectators for this purpose. It is common ground that the deceased was not a ticket-holder within the meaning of the notice, but, in my judgment, he was a spectator. The learned judge so held, and I think that he was right in doing so. The notice was, in my opinion, sufficiently explicit in its application to the deceased. I feel unable to accept the suggestion that the heading 'Warning to the Public' should be read in a restrictive sense excluding competitors. Reading the document as a whole, I think there can be no doubt that it was addressed to all persons answering the descriptions of spectators or ticket-holders. The deceased was not even a member of the Severn Valley Jalopy Club. He was, in my opinion, a member of the public. The organisers are, I think, shown to have taken all reasonable steps to draw the condition contained in the notice to the attention of the deceased. The learned judge found that warnings of this character were a common feature at jalopy races with which the deceased would have been familiar. He also found, as I have already said, that the deceased saw this particular notice and appreciated its character. He also found that the deceased saw a number of other notices in identical terms posted about the field and that he appreciated what these notices were intended to effect. I think that he came on to the field in the afternoon on the terms contained in the notice displayed at the entrance to the ground.

The liability of the organisers of the meeting to visitors attending it for the purpose of taking part in some races and watching others was in my opinion limited in two respects. Such a visitor, in my judgment, as a competitor and when engaged in the role of a competitor, accepted all the risks inherent in the sport of jalopy racing. The organisers owed no duty to him to protect him against those risks. The express warning to the effect that competitors took part in the races at their own risk, which may have been attached to the signing-on sheet, is consequently, in my view, of little importance. As a spectator, such a visitor was, I think, subject to the condition set out in the warning notice. At the time when the accident occurred the deceased was, in my opinion, a spectator. The limitation on the liability of the organisers in these circumstances is to be found in the notice. The condition set out in the notice was that they were to be absolved from all liabilities arising out of accidents causing damage or personal injury howsoever caused. The use of the words 'howsoever caused' makes clear that the absolution was intended to be of a general character. The effect of the condition must, in my judgment, amount to the exclusion of liability for accidents arising from the organisers' own negligence. For these reasons I consider that the learned judge was right in dismissing the action....

Roskill LJ agreed the appeal should be dismissed. **Lord Denning MR** dissented.

Appeal dismissed.

COMMENTARY

The Court of Appeal unanimously rejected the *volenti* defence because the deceased did not have full knowledge of the risk he was running (arising from the faulty layout of the ropes). He had not willingly accepted that risk of injury arising from the defendants' negligence.

Note that this case was decided before UCTA. Would it have made any difference to the result if the Act had been in force?

In cases where exclusion of liability is allowed, two issues normally dominate. First, have appropriate steps been taken to bring the exclusion to the attention of the party who or through whom the claim is being made? Secondly, on a proper construction of the clause or notice, does the party fall within the notice? In the above case, it was clear that the deceased had seen the notice when he returned to the field in the afternoon, but the plaintiff argued that the conditions under which the deceased was competing were fixed by contract when he left his jalopy at the site in the morning, and could not be unilaterally varied by the defendant in the afternoon. This involved an argument over contractual licences to enter land that need not concern us here, but the proposition was rejected by the majority of the Court of Appeal. The question of the scope of the exclusion clause was also raised; as he was not a spectator or ticket holder the clause did not protect the defendant. This was also rejected by the majority, as at the time of accident he was acting as a spectator and was within the class of persons affected by the notice. Hence the notice exhibited at the entrance in the afternoon was effective to exclude liability. Detailed discussion of these issues are normally left for courses in contract law, on which see Treitel, *The Law of Contract*, 12th edn. (London: Sweet & Maxwell, 2007), ch. 7. Note that although exclusions are often contained in a contractual clause, they need not be (as in *White* where the exclusion was contained in a non-contractual notice).

Is UCTA applicable in a case where the defendant relies on a contractual clause to show that the claimant voluntarily accepted the risk in question? In *Johnstone v Bloomsbury Health Authority* [1992] QB 333, an employment case, the Court of Appeal held that it was at least arguable that such a clause might fall foul of s. 2(1) as an effective *volenti* clause will by definition modify or restrict the duty owed to the claimant (see also the speech of Lord Hobhouse in *Reeves v Commissioner of Police for the Metropolis* [2000] 1 AC 360 at 395). However, the position remains unclear; *Johnstone* was settled before a final decision was reached, and the point has not been taken in other employment cases where it could have been raised (e.g. the occupational stress cases discussed in Ch 9).

UCTA is not the only legislation that precludes the exclusion of liability. Reference should also be made, in particular, to Road Traffic Act 1988, s. 149; Consumer Protection Act 1987, s. 7; and, in the context of employers' liability, Law Reform (Personal Injuries) Act 1948, s. 1(3) and Employers' Liability (Defective Equipment) Act 1969, s. 1(2).

v. Illegality (*Ex Turpi Causa Non Oritur Actio*)

The precise basis of the defence of illegality is difficult to discern (see Law Commission, *The Illegality Defence in Tort*, Consultation Paper No. 160 (2001), Part IV, and (id.), *The Illegality Defence: A Consultative Report*, Consultation Paper No. 189 (2009), Parts 2 and 7). At its broadest the defence is grounded in a general policy objection to allowing those engaged in an illegal activity to receive compensation when injured in its course. This policy is often expressed in the Latin maxim *ex turpi causa non oritur actio* (no action can be founded upon a wicked act). A good example is the case of *Ashton v Turner* [1981] QB 137, where the plaintiff was injured whilst a passenger in a 'getaway' car speeding from the scene of a burglary in which he had participated. The claim against the driver of the car failed because, as a matter of public policy, English law refuses to recognise the existence of a duty of care owed by one participant in a crime to another in respect of an act done in furtherance of the common purpose. Nonetheless it is clear that not every illegal act bars the claimant from recovering in negligence: driving with a broken headlight during daylight hours would not prevent the driver recovering damages if injured by another's negligence, even though he might face a criminal liability for breach of road traffic regulations. The difficulty lies in assessing the circumstances in which illegality will bar a claim.

Gray v Thames Trains Limited [2009] 1 AC 1339

The claimant was a victim of the Ladbroke Grove train crash in 1999. He suffered minor physical injuries as a result of the crash but subsequently developed a serious psychiatric condition. In August 2001, whilst driving, he was involved in an altercation with a drunken pedestrian (a Mr. Boultwood). He left the scene, obtained a knife, and returned to find the pedestrian, stabbing him to death when he did. He was later convicted of manslaughter on the grounds of diminished responsibility and was ordered to be detained in hospital. He sued the defendants (whose employee's negligence had caused the crash) for, amongst other things, loss of earnings during the period in which he was and would be detained as a result of the killing, and general damages for his detention, conviction, feelings of guilt and remorse, and damage to reputation, as well as an indemnity against any claims which might be brought by dependants of the dead pedestrian. At first instance, Flaux J rejected these claims as inconsistent with the rule of law preventing a person obtaining compensation for his own criminal act. The Court of Appeal allowed an appeal in part, holding that whilst general damages were not recoverable, the claim for loss of earnings could be accepted. Both sides appealed to the House of Lords.

Lord Hoffmann

27. My Lords, the question in this case is in my opinion whether the intervention of Mr Gray's criminal act in the causal relationship between the defendants' breaches of duty and the damage of which he complains prevents him from recovering that part of his loss caused by the criminal act. The facts of which were clearly established by the evidence and the verdict at the trial. On the one hand, but for the accident and the stress disorder which it caused, Mr Gray would not have killed and would therefore not have suffered the consequences for which he seeks compensation. On the other hand, the killing was a voluntary and deliberate act. The stress disorder diminished Mr Gray's responsibility but did not extinguish it. By reason of his own acknowledged responsibility, Mr Gray committed the serious crime of manslaughter and made himself liable to the sentence of the court. The question is whether these features of the causal relationship between the injury and the damage are such as to prevent Mr Gray from recovering.

28. It is not sufficient to exclude liability that the immediate cause of the damage was the deliberate act of the claimant himself. Although in general a defendant will not be liable for damage of which the immediate cause was the deliberate act of the claimant or a third party, that principle does not ordinarily apply when the claimant or third party's act was itself a consequence of the defendant's breach of duty. So in *Corr v IBC Vehicles Ltd* [2008] 1 AC 884 an employer whose negligence had caused post-traumatic stress disorder to a workman was held

liable to his dependants for his subsequent death by suicide. Although the immediate cause of the workman's death was his own voluntary and deliberate act, the state of mind in which he had taken his own life had been caused by the employer's breach of duty. In such a case the damages may be reduced, as in *Reeves v Commissioner of Police of the Metropolis* [2000] 1 AC 360, but the defendant's liability is not excluded.

29. It must follow from *Corr's* case that the mere fact that the killing was Mr Gray's own voluntary and deliberate act is not in itself a reason for excluding the defendants' liability. Nor do the appellants say that it is. Their principal argument invokes a special rule of public policy. In its wider form, it is that you cannot recover compensation for loss which you have suffered in consequence of your own criminal act. In its narrower and more specific form, it is that you cannot recover for damage which flows from loss of liberty, a fine or other punishment lawfully imposed upon you in consequence of your own unlawful act. In such a case it is the law which, as a matter of penal policy, causes the damage and it would be inconsistent for the law to require you to be compensated for that damage.

30. Is there such a rule? The appellants say that there is, and that it is one aspect of a wider principle that *ex turpi causa non oritur actio,* (or, as Lord Mansfield said in *Holman v Johnson* (1775) 1 Cowp 341, 343, *ex dolo malo non oritur actio.*) This tag has been invoked to deny a remedy in a wide variety of situations and a good deal of time was spent in argument examining diverse cases and discussing whether the conditions under which the courts had held the maxim applicable in some other kind of case were satisfied in this one. For example, in cases about rights of property, it has been said that a claimant will fail on grounds of illegality only if his claim requires him to rely upon or plead an illegal act: *Tinsley v Milligan* [1994] 1 AC 340. So Mr Scrivener QC, who appeared for Mr Gray, said that his client's action was founded upon the defendants' act of negligence and not upon the unlawful killing. That of course is true; if the defendants had not been negligent, or the damage had no connection with the train crash which could be described as causal, the claim would not have got past the starting post. But that is not the point; in this kind of case, the question is whether recovery is excluded because the immediate cause of the damage was the act of manslaughter, which resulted in the sentence of the court. Likewise, there was an examination of the pleadings to discover whether Mr Gray had been obliged to plead his unlawful act, Mr Purchas QC, (who appeared for the appellants), saying that he had and Mr Scrivener saying that he had not. Again, the pleadings seem to me to have nothing to do with whether there is the rule of law for which the appellants contend. As a result, I did not find any of this discussion very helpful. The maxim ex *turpi causa* expresses not so much a principle as a policy. Furthermore, that policy is not based upon a single justification but on a group of reasons, which vary in different situations. For example, as Beldam LJ pointed out in in *Cross v Kirkby* [2000] EWCA Civ 426, at para 74, in cases in which the court is concerned with the application of the maxim to property or contractual rights between two people who were both parties to an unlawful transaction—

> it faces the dilemma that by denying relief on the ground of illegality to one party, it appears to confer an unjustified benefit illegally obtained on the other.

31. In cases of that kind, the courts have evolved varying rules to deal with the dilemma: compare the approach of the House of Lords in *Tinsley v Milligan* [1994] 1 AC 340 with that of the High Court of Australia in *Nelson v Nelson* (1995) 184 CLR 538. But the problem to which Beldam LJ drew attention does not arise in this case. The questions of fairness and policy are different and the content of the rule is different. One cannot simply extrapolate rules applicable to a different kind of situation.

32. The particular rule for which the appellants contend may, as I said, be stated in a wider or a narrow form. The wider and simpler version is that which was applied by Flaux J: you cannot recover for damage which is the consequence of your own criminal act. In its narrower form, it

is that you cannot recover for damage which is the consequence of a sentence imposed upon you for a criminal act. I make this distinction between the wider and narrower version of the rule because there is a particular justification for the narrower rule which does not necessarily apply to the wider version.

33. I shall deal first with the narrower version, which was stated in general terms by Denning J in *Askey v Golden Wine Co Ltd* [1948] 2 All ER 35,

> It is, I think, a principle of our law that the punishment inflicted by a criminal court is per-sonal to the offender, and that the civil courts will not entertain an action by the offender to recover an indemnity against the consequences of that punishment. . . .

[His Lordship considered a number of English and Commonwealth authorities and continued:]

43. The Court of Appeal rightly held that it was bound by the decision in *Clunis v Camden & Islington Health Authority* [1998] QB 978 to apply the rule and reject the claim for damage suf-fered in consequence of the criminal court's sentence of detention. They did so with regret. The Master of the Rolls, giving the judgment of the Court, said (at paragraph 49):

> There seems to us to be something to be said for the view that the traditional harsh view of public policy expressed in, for example, the *Clunis* case [1998] QB 978 and the *Worrall* case [*Worrall v British Railways Board*, unreported, CA Civil Division, 29 April 1999] should be revisited in a case in which the crime relied upon (whether relied upon by the claimant or the tortfeasor) was itself caused by the tort. In times gone by, it would perhaps have been seen as inconceivable that the murder or manslaughter of another could have been caused by a tort. However, the facts and evidence in the *Corr* case [2008] 1 AC 884 and this case, and perhaps a more developed understanding of clinical depression, show that it is no longer inconceivable. It is far from clear to us why the ends of justice are not sufficiently served by the principles of foreseeability, causation and contributory negligence without the need for a further principle of public policy in such a case.

44. This argument treats the whole question as being whether the crime can be said to have been 'caused' by the tort. As I have said, there is no dispute that there was a causal connection between the tort and the killing. The evidence which the judge accepted was but for the tort, Mr Gray would not have killed. But the rule of public policy invoked in this case is not based upon some primitive psychology which deems mental stress to be incapable of having a connection with subsequent criminal acts. As *Hunter Area Health Service v Presland* (2005) 63 NSWLR 22 shows, it may reflect more than one facet of public policy, but it is sufficient in the present case to say that the case against compensating Mr Gray for his loss of liberty is based upon the inconsistency of requiring someone to be compensated for a sentence imposed because of his own personal responsibility for a criminal act. The Court of Appeal said nothing about this aspect of the matter . . .

50. My Lords, that is in my opinion sufficient to dispose of most of the claims which are the subject of this appeal. Mr Gray's claims for loss of earnings after his arrest and for general dam-ages for his detention, conviction and damage to reputation are all claims for damage caused by the lawful sentence imposed upon him for manslaughter and therefore fall within the nar-rower version of the rule which I would invite your Lordships to affirm. But there are some additional claims which may be more difficult to bring within this rule, such as the claim for an indemnity against any claims which might be brought by dependants of the dead pedestrian and the claim for general damages for feelings of guilt and remorse consequent upon the kill-ing. Neither of these was a consequence of the sentence of the criminal court.

51. I must therefore examine a wider version of the rule, which was applied by Flaux J. This has the support of the reasoning of the Court of Appeal in *Clunis's* case [1998] QB 978 as well as

other authorities. It differs from the narrower version in at least two respects: first, it cannot, as it seems to me, be justified on the grounds of inconsistency in the same way as the narrower rule. Instead, the wider rule has to be justified on the ground that it is offensive to public notions of the fair distribution of resources that a claimant should be compensated (usually out of public funds) for the consequences of his own criminal conduct. Secondly, the wider rule may raise problems of causation which cannot arise in connection with the narrower rule. The sentence of the court is plainly a consequence of the criminality for which the claimant was responsible. But other forms of damage may give rise to questions about whether they can properly be said to have been caused by his criminal conduct.

52. The wider principle was applied by the Court of Appeal in *Vellino v Chief Constable of the Greater Manchester Police* [2002] 1 WLR 218. The claimant was injured in consequence of jumping from a second-floor window to escape from the custody of the police. He sued the police for damages, claiming that they had not taken reasonable care to prevent him from escaping. Attempting to escape from lawful custody is a criminal offence. The Court of Appeal (Schiemann LJ and Sir Murray Stuart-Smith; Sedley LJ dissenting) held that, assuming the police to have been negligent, recovery was precluded because the injury was the consequence of the plaintiff's unlawful act.

53. This decision seems to me based upon sound common sense. The question, as suggested in the dissenting judgment of Sedley LJ, is how the case should be distinguished from one in which the injury is a consequence of the plaintiff's unlawful act only in the sense that it would not have happened if he had not been committing an unlawful act. An extreme example would be the car which is damaged while unlawfully parked. Sir Murray Stuart-Smith, at para 70, described the distinction:

> The operation of the principle arises where the claimant's claim is founded upon his own criminal or immoral act. The facts which give rise to the claim must be inextricably linked with the criminal activity. It is not sufficient if the criminal activity merely gives occasion for tortious conduct of the defendant.

54. This distinction, between causing something and merely providing the occasion for someone else to cause something, is one with which we are very familiar in the law of torts. It is the same principle by which the law normally holds that even though damage would not have occurred but for a tortious act, the defendant is not liable if the immediate cause was the deliberate act of another individual. Examples of cases falling on one side of the line or the other are given in the judgment of Judge LJ in *Cross v Kirkby* [2000] EWCA Civ 426. It was Judge LJ, at para 103, who formulated the test of 'inextricably linked' which was afterwards adopted by Sir Murray Stuart-Smith LJ in *Vellino v Chief Constable of the Greater Manchester Police* [2002] 1 WLR 218. Other expressions which he approved, at paras 100 and 104, were 'an integral part or a necessarily direct consequence' of the unlawful act (Rougier J: see *Revill v Newbery* [1996] QB 567, 571) and 'arises directly *ex turpi causa*' (Bingham LJ in *Saunders v Edwards* [1987] 1 WLR 1116, 1134.) It might be better to avoid metaphors like 'inextricably linked' or 'integral part' and to treat the question as simply one of causation. Can one say that, although the damage would not have happened but for the tortious conduct of the defendant, it was caused by the criminal act of the claimant? (*Vellino v Chief Constable of the Greater Manchester Police* [2002] 1 WLR 218). Or is the position that although the damage would not have happened without the criminal act of the claimant, it was caused by the tortious act of the defendant? (*Revill v Newbery* [1996] QB 567).

55. However the test is expressed, the wider rule seems to me to cover the remaining heads of damage in this case. Mr Gray's liability to compensate the dependants of the dead pedestrian was an immediate 'inextricable' consequence of his having intentionally killed him. The

same is true of his feelings of guilt and remorse. I therefore think that Flaux J was right and I would allow the appeal and restore his judgment.

Lord Rodger of Earlsferry

My Lords,

62. Before the House the defendants continued to fight under the banner *ex turpi causa non oritur actio*—or on a particular application of the maxim. Not surprisingly, therefore, the focus of the discussion in the judgments below, and of counsel's submissions to the appellate committee, tended to be on the application of that maxim. But Mr Scrivener QC was surely right to this extent, at least: there was nothing unlawful or even base or immoral about the circumstances giving rise to the claimant's right of action against the defendants. That right arose on 5 October 1999 when, as a result of their admitted negligence, he was injured in the Ladbroke Grove crash. Although Mr Gray waited until August 2005 before starting proceedings, at that date his right of action was precisely the same lawful right of action as had accrued to him when the accident occurred. So the defendants' real objection cannot be to the lawfulness of the action as such. Rather, they object that the particular 'head of claim' for loss of earnings after 19 August 2001 is precluded by the working of the *ex turpi causa* doctrine.

63. This case is therefore completely different from cases, such as *National Coal Board v England* [1954] AC 403 or *Cross v Kirkby* The Times 5 April 2000; [2000] EWCA Civ 426, (much relied on by the Court of Appeal), where the argument is that, at the time when he was injured, the claimant was engaged in an unlawful activity and so the policy of the law should be to refuse him a right of action for any injuries sustained in those circumstances. The maxim *ex turpi causa non oritur actio* is as good a way as any of identifying the policy which the court is asked to apply in those circumstances. And, of course, in such cases questions can arise about the exact scope of the maxim. In the present (very different) case, however, Mr Scrivener appeared to advance Mr Gray's claim on two bases. In my view the maxim is relevant to the first, but may tend to divert attention from the true nature of the alternative version of the claim and of the defendants' response to it.

64. First, the claimant alleges that the defendants' negligence caused him to develop psychological problems, which in turn led to him committing manslaughter, and so being detained in Runwell Hospital under the 1983 Act, and losing earnings as a result. In my view a claim of that kind undoubtedly falls foul of the *ex turpi causa* maxim since the claimant is asking the defendant to compensate him for the consequences of his own deliberate criminal act in killing Mr Boultwood . . .

70. But Mr Scrivener has an alternative version. He submits that, as a result of his injuries in the crash, Mr Gray was losing earnings immediately before 19 August 2001 and, on the balance of probabilities, he would have continued to do so after that date, even if he had not killed Mr Boultwood. He was therefore entitled to damages from the defendants for his loss of earnings after, just as much as before, 19 August. In effect, on this approach that date had little significance for his claim for loss of earnings . . . .

75. The immediately obvious objection to the claimant's formulation of his claim for loss of earnings is that it proceeds by ignoring what actually happened—he killed Mr Boultwood and was detained as a result. Yet it is well established that 'the court should not speculate when it knows'. In other words, the judge should base any award of damages on what has actually happened, rather than on what might have happened, in the period between the tort and the time when the award is to be made. So, even if the court were satisfied that the claimant would have continued to lose earnings after 19 August 2001, due to the PTSD brought on by the accident, it would be highly artificial to ignore the fact that, by committing manslaughter, the claimant had created a new set of circumstances which actually made it impossible for him to work and

to earn after that date. Why should the defendants pay damages on the basis that, but for his PTSD, the claimant would have been able to work after 19 August, when, as the court knows, because of the manslaughter, at all material times after that date he was actually in some form of lawful detention which prevented him from working? . . .

82. In short, the civil court should cleave to the same policy as the criminal court. For that reason, the events which the claimant triggered on 19 August 2001 should not be regarded as irrelevant to the due assessment of the loss of earnings for which the defendants are liable. Rather, the House should uphold the defendants' contention that, as a matter of policy, they should not be held liable for any such loss after 20 August 2001 when the claimant gave himself up to the police. . . .

84. The claimant has a number of other claims for damages, which were not explored in detail at the hearing. In particular, he has what is described as a claim for an "indemnity" against any future liability in damages to Mr Boultwood's dependants—a claim for economic loss. He also has a claim for his feelings of guilt and remorse. As my noble and learned friend, Lord Hoffmann, says, these claims are not a consequence of the sentence of the criminal court and so cannot be disposed of on the ground of inconsistency. Nevertheless, I agree with him that they should be rejected.

85. In *British Columbia v Zastowny* [2008] 1 SCR 27 , 41–42, para 30, quoted at para 68 above, Rothstein J observed that a person is not entitled to be indemnified for the consequences of his criminal acts for which he has been found criminally responsible. He cannot attribute them to others or seek rebate of those consequences. Yet that is precisely what the claimant is trying to do, both in his claim for any sum he is found liable to pay in damages to Mr Boultwood's dependants and in his claim for his feelings of guilt and remorse.

86. In *Meah v McCreamer (No 2)* [1986] 1 All ER 943 Woolf J rejected an attempt to recover the damages which the plaintiff had been found liable to pay to two women whom he had subjected to criminal attacks. His main reason for rejecting the claim was that the damages were too remote. But he would also have rejected it, at pp 950h–951f, on the public policy ground that the plaintiff was not entitled to be indemnified for the damages which he was liable to pay as a result of his criminal attacks. That seems to me to be an appropriate application of the *ex turpi causa* rule.

87. In the same way, in this case the claimant should not be entitled to an indemnity for any damages he had to pay in consequence of his having assaulted and killed Mr Boultwood. The same goes for his claim for feelings of guilt and remorse. Alternatively, the claims can be treated as simply raising issues of causation and disposed of as Lord Hoffmann explains.

Lord Scott agreed with **Lord Hoffmann** and **Lord Rodger**. **Lord Phillips** and **Lord Brown** delivered separate concurring speeches.

Appeal allowed.

COMMENTARY

Lord Hoffmann's speech in *Gray* divides the illegality defence in two: there is a narrow version which applies to situations where the objection is that the claimant is attempting to avoid penalties imposed on him by the criminal law, and a wider version that one cannot recover for the consequences of one's own criminal act. It has been noted that these divisions—which are apparently intended to be comprehensive—do not fit neatly with the previous categories into which illegality cases had been placed (see Goudkamp (2009) 17 TLJ

205) but, in light of the decision's high authority, this section will consider the illegality defence under the two strands identified in *Gray*.

1. Claimants Seeking to Avoid the Consequences of Criminal Sanctions

As highlighted in Lord Rodger's speech (at [63]), the different strands of the defence apply to two different kinds of case. The narrow version of the defence applies to situations where it is alleged that the defendant's negligence was responsible for the claimant committing a subsequent illegal act which resulted in the imposition of a criminal sanction. In these cases, it is not suggested that the cause of action as a whole is tainted by illegality. Hence in *Gray*, there was no doubt that the claimant could recover for any loss of earnings between the date of the tort and the date of the killing; that part of the claim was not connected with the criminal offence. Earlier cases that would now be considered to fall within the narrow version of the defence (and which are discussed in *Gray*) include *Clunis v Camden & Islington Health Authority* [1998] QB 978 and *Worrall v British Railways Board*, unreported, CA Civil Division, 29 April 1999. In *Clunis*, Christopher Clunis stabbed Jonathan Zito to death on the platform of Finsbury Park Underground Station in London. Clunis, who had a long history of mental illness, was convicted of manslaughter on the ground of diminished responsibility. He later sued Camden & Islington Health Authority in negligence, alleging that its failure to care for him properly caused him to commit the murder for which he was charged. One ground on which the Court of Appeal allowed the claim to be struck out was *ex turpi causa*; the court would not to allow itself to be made an instrument to enforce obligations alleged to arise out of the plaintiff's own criminal act.

A similar result was reached in *Worrall v British Railways Board*, unreported, CA Civil Division, 29 April 1999, where the Court of Appeal upheld a defence of illegality in respect of a claim for damages arising out of the plaintiff's imprisonment for a number of sexual assaults. The plaintiff argued that he had only committed the offences because he had suffered a personality change as a result of an accident caused by the defendant's negligence. No doubt the plaintiff's claim was hindered by the fact that his defence at his criminal trial was not any lack of mental capacity, as in *Clunis*, but alibi (i.e. not that he did not know it was wrong, but that he was not there and therefore did not do it at all!) thereby making it difficult to convince the judges in the later civil actions that the real reason for his conduct was the personality change attributable to the defendant's negligence.

The courts have thus generally refused to allow claims in respect of the consequences of criminal conduct, such as fines, imprisonment, or damages payable to the victim. The results of these cases may be explained by what the Law Commission, in its Consultation Paper (No. 160), *The Illegality Defence in Tort* thought was the best policy rationale for the defence of illegality—consistency in the law (para. 4.70):

> The policy of not allowing someone to profit or benefit from their own wrongdoing may also be seen as an example of the wider need for the law to maintain consistency. It can be argued that it would be inconsistent for the law to proscribe certain forms of conduct on the one hand but to allow someone who has committed such wrongdoing to benefit from it. This appears to us to be a parallel case to that of allowing a claimant to recover compensation for the consequences to himself or herself of his or her criminal act. Just as a person is not allowed to claim to recover

the damage arising out of the criminal act that resulted in conviction and sentence, so he or she is not allowed to take any benefit from that wrongdoing. To hold otherwise would mean that in one case the law would be giving with one hand what it takes with another, in the other case it would be allowing crime to pay. Neither would promote 'consistency' in the law.

The widely divergent views received by the Law Commission in response to this consultation paper lead ultimately to a second consultation paper on the application of the illegality defence in contract, trusts and tort actions (Consultation Paper No. 189, *The Illegality Defence: A Consultative Report*). In this later paper, the Commission noted that, whilst there was a 'large degree of agreement that the illegality defence helped to maintain internal consistency in the law, this was not seen to be the overriding rationale' (para. 2.15). Others remained convinced that the consistency rationale is the only one that can support the illegality defence. Goudkamp, 'Can tort law be used to deflect the impact of criminal sanctions? The role of the illegality defence' (2006) 14 TLJ 20 at 42 argues, for example:

> A serious difficulty besetting sanction-shifting actions [attempts to shift the burden of criminal sanctions from the offender to someone else] is that they are seemingly incompatible with the earlier finding that the plaintiff is liable for their conduct under the criminal law. On one hand, sanction-shifting actions make the allegation that the plaintiff's conduct was not the product of a choice which they made, but was caused by the defendant's tort. Yet, on the other hand, the fact that the plaintiff was held criminally liable in respect of their conduct dictates that their conduct was the expression of a choice on their part. Therefore, in short, sanction-shifting actions raise the question as to how it can be said that a person is capable of making choices and is thus responsible for the outcome of their choices in the criminal context but that, in the tort context, they succumbed, inevitably, to the laws of physics that govern a deterministic world.

Gray, *Clunis* and *Worrall* were all cases where the claimant was held at least partly to be criminally responsible for their conduct (this is the effect of a plea of diminished responsibility). If the claimant is not held criminally responsible for their conduct—as is the case in a successful defence of insanity—the arguments for applying the illegality defence are considerably weaker. In *Gray*, Lord Phillips suggested (at [15]) that, where the defendant's offending behaviour played no part in the decision to order him to be detained in hospital (as might be the case for an accused found not guilty on the grounds of insanity), the illegality defence would not apply. The detention would be the consequence of the accused's mental condition rather than of any criminal act. More controversially, Lord Phillips (at [15]) reserved his position (as did Lords Rodger and Brown) about the situation where the need for detention is the result of a criminal act of the accused but, in the view of the sentencing judge, the defendant should not bear significant personal responsibility for the crime. However, Lord Hoffmann doubted whether it was possible to divide up the purposes for which a sentence was passed to decide which was the 'predominate' purpose. His Lordship also drew attention to a controversial Australian decision of the New South Wales Court of Appeal in *Hunter Area Health Service v Presland* (2005) 63 NSWLR 22. Here the defendant negligently discharged the plaintiff from a psychiatric hospital, and the plaintiff subsequently killed another person, was tried for murder, acquitted on the grounds of insanity but ordered to be detained in a secure facility for the mentally-ill. A majority of the court applied the defence to his claim for damages for the detention. Do you agree with this result or is the approach of Lord Phillips to be preferred? Commenting on *Gray* Goudkamp (2009) 17 TLJ 205, 209 notes: 'Purely rehabilitative sentences are, therefore, compensable. This makes sense since awarding damages in respect of such sentences would not hinder attempts to rehabilitate offenders.' Do you agree?

2. Claimants not Recovering for the Consequences of their Own Criminal Acts

In *Gray*, Lord Hoffmann (at [51]) identified the wider strand of the illegality defence as being based 'on the ground that it is offensive to public notions of the fair distribution of resources that a claimant should be compensated (usually out of public funds) for the consequences of his own criminal conduct.' Prior to *Gray*, the cases that would now be categorised as falling under the wider strand fell into two main categories—cases where the claimant was a participant in a joint illegal activity and was injured in the course of that activity by another participant, and cases where the claimant, but not the defendant, was engaged in an illegal activity at the time the tort was committed. Given the broad definition of the circumstances when the wide version of the illegality defence will apply, it is likely that these traditional categories will remain important in deciding whether the illegality defence applies in a particular situation (cf. Goudkamp (2009) 17 TLJ 205, 214, who queries whether the category of joint illegal enterprise remains as it was not referred to in *Gray*).

(a) Joint Illegal Enterprise

The defence of illegality in this category of case has only been successful in defeating tort claims in 'exceedingly rare' cases (*National Coal Board v England* [1954] AC 403 at 428–9, per Lord Asquith). In the case cited, Lord Asquith thought the necessary prerequisite before the defence could apply was that the act complained of was at the very least a step in the execution of a common illegal purpose. He gave the following example:

> If two burglars, A and B, agree to open a safe by means of explosives, and A so negligently handles the explosive charge as to injure B, B might find some difficulty in maintaining an action for negligence against A. But if A and B are proceeding to the premises which they intend burglariously to enter, and before they enter them B picks A's pocket and steals his watch, I cannot prevail on myself to believe that A could not sue in tort.... The theft is totally unconnected with the burglary.

The leading modern case is *Pitts v Hunt* [1991] 1 QB 24. The 18-year-old plaintiff was severely injured when the motorcycle on which he was a pillion passenger collided with another vehicle. The 16-year-old motorcyclist, who was killed in the accident, had earlier been drinking with the plaintiff and the plaintiff knew he was both unlicensed and uninsured. With the plaintiff's encouragement, the deceased drove the motorcycle in a dangerous and reckless manner so as to deliberately frighten members of the public. The plaintiff claimed damages for negligence against the personal representative of the deceased. The trial judge rejected the claim because the accident occurred in the course of a joint illegal enterprise and was thus barred on the grounds of illegality (*ex turpi causa non oritur actio*), and, in the alternative, because the plaintiff was 100 per cent contributorily negligent. (The Road Traffic Act 1972, s. 148(3) prevented the defendant from relying on a defence of *volenti non fit injuria*: see now Road Traffic Act 1988 s. 149.) The plaintiff appealed against the dismissal of his claim against the deceased's estate but the appeal was dismissed (note that the actual decision in *Pitts* must now be read in light of the ECJ's decision in *Candolin* (extracted above, p. 308) which limits the applicability of defences which would deprive a claimant of the benefit of a policy of compulsory motor vehicle liability insurance 'solely on the basis of the passenger's contribution to the occurrence of his injuries' (para. 29)). Two different approaches were recognised for determining the circumstances when illegality may operate as a defence. The majority of the Court of Appeal adopted the 'inability to set a standard of care' approach. What standard of care would a getaway driver owe to a fellow participant in a burglary when escaping from the scene of the crime? Or a burglar to a fellow burglar engaged in a breaking and entering? The majority of the court disclaimed any ability to determine such questions. The alternative approach, which seems to have been adopted by Beldam LJ, was the 'public conscience' test. Would it shock the public conscience if the claimant were allowed to recover? The majority disliked such an approach, but in truth there seems little difference between the two. It is not that the court cannot set a standard of care but that it will not. This is particularly clear on the facts of *Pitts* itself, because the standard of care owed by a car driver is set at that of the reasonable driver, irrespective of the individual idiosyncrasies of the driver (*Nettleship v Weston*). The court could have used this standard to judge the conduct of the driver but it chose not to for (unstated) policy reasons. This, as Murphy J pointed out in *Jackson v Harrison* (1978) 138 CLR 438 at 463, 'is simply an application of judicial policy'. (See further Law Commission Consultation Paper No. 189, para. 7.15.)

Subsequent to *Pitts*, however, the public conscience test was rejected by the House of Lords in *Tinsley v Milligan* [1994] 1 AC 340, a case concerning a resulting trust, in favour of an approach which asks whether the plaintiff had to rely on the illegality to found the claim. *Jones* (p. 539) describes this approach as 'side stepping illegality by the application of technical rules' and in *Gray* Lord Hoffmann (at [30]) made it clear that the 'reliance' approach was unlikely to be helpful in tort cases (see also *Moore Stephens (a firm) and Stone & Rolls Ltd* [2009] 1 AC 1370; Law Commission Consultation Paper No. 189, para. 7.22). However, it is also clear that the 'public conscience' test can no longer be used in tort cases (see *Moore Stephens (a firm) and Stone & Rolls Ltd* [2009] 1 AC 1370, [97] per Lord Scott; Law Commission Consultation Paper No. 189, paras 7.45–751).

The result is that, although the idea of a 'scale' of illegality did not find favour with the Court of Appeal in *Pitts* (nor with Lord Goff in *Tinsley*), the Law Commission has accepted that the seriousness of the claimant's illegality is a factor to be considered (Consultation Paper No. 189, paras 7.34–7.37). As Buckley (1994) 110 LQR 3, 8, commenting on the decision in *Tinsley*, states: 'If absurd results are to be avoided there will therefore always be some cases in this field which, contrary to the view of Lord Goff, the law will be obliged to admit that there are "degrees of iniquity".' The Law Commission, in both its consultation reports has recognised that the seriousness of the claimant's illegality is important in considering the proportionality between the claimant's illegality and the seriousness of the loss the claimant would suffer if the defence was allowed (No 160, paras 6.29, 6.36; No. 189, para 7.38). As Ward LJ noted, with considerable understatement, 'this is not quite the same as judging whether the claimant's wrongdoing is disproportionate to the defendant's wrongdoing' (*Hewison v Meridian Shipping PTE* [2003] ICR 766 at [72]), an enquiry which the Law Commission in its 2009 paper saw as part of the discredited public conscience test.

Apart from the decision as to the seriousness of the illegality, the wider version of the illegality defence identified by Lord Hoffmann in *Gray* also requires that there be a sufficient causal connection between the illegality and the injury for which the claimant is seeking redress. Although his Lordship thought it might be better to avoid answering this question by reference to metaphors (was the claim 'inextricably linked' or an 'integral part' of the illegality), no further guidance was provided. In *Pitts v Hunt* the injury was suffered whilst actually committing the illegality so there was little doubt as to the causal connection, but other cases will not be as clear. Should a participant in an insurance fraud be subject to the defence where, on the way to the scene where the accident is to be staged, he is injured by the careless driving of fellow participant? (See *Italiano v Barbaro* (1993) 40 FCR 303.) Would your answer be different if the participants had been on their way to commit a murder? If so, are we not, inevitably, back to a version of the public conscience test?

A very different approach to joint illegal enterprise cases, and to the illegality defence in tort more generally, was taken by the Supreme Court of Canada in *Hall v Hebert* (1993) 101 DLR 4th 129. The plaintiff and defendant had been drinking and driving the defendant's 'souped-up muscle car' when it stalled. It was decided to roll-start the vehicle with the plaintiff in the driver's seat, but he lost control of the car and it crashed down an incline and he suffered head injuries. The Supreme Court held that the illegality relating to the drink-driving did not bar the claim. The majority decision of McLachlin J held, first, that the denial of liability based on the plaintiff's conduct operated as a defence and not as a negation of the duty of care; and, secondly, that the defence of illegality rested on the need to preserve the integrity of the legal system. Accordingly, a plaintiff should not obtain relief which would enable him to profit from a wrong or evade the criminal consequences of his action. However, compensatory damages arose from the defendant's wrong, not the plaintiff's wrongful conduct, so to allow recovery would not allow a plaintiff to profit from his own turpitude (although some heads of damage might be irrecoverable, e.g. loss of future earnings as a burglar: see *Burns v Edman* [1970] 2 QB 541). This approach has received academic support (Goudkamp (2006) 14 TLJ 20) and, as noted above, was seen by the Law Commission in its 2001 consultation paper as being the best rationale for the defence. However, as noted above, in its 2009 consultation paper, the Law Commission noted that a large majority of consultees to its original paper did not see consistency as the overriding rationale for the defence and its latest recommendations do not comprehensively embrace the Canadian approach.

(b) Illegality by Claimant Alone

Revill v Newbery [1996] QB 567

The facts appear in the extract.

Neill LJ

This is an appeal by Mr William Newbery from the order of Rougier J dated 1 December 1994 whereby the plaintiff, Mr Mark Revill, was awarded the sum of £4,033 for damages for personal injuries. By the same order Mr Newbery was awarded £400 on his counterclaim. Mr Revill was found two-thirds to blame for the injuries which he suffered.

The facts of the case are set out with admirable clarity by the judge whose account I can gratefully adopt:

At about 2 o'clock in the morning of Saturday, 12 March 1988 the plaintiff, then aged 21, accompanied by a man called Grainger, some 14 years older, who between them had already on that night broken into two car showroom Portakabins, set alight to one of them, stolen keys from the other and, by that means, two motor cars, attempted to break into a brick shed belonging to the defendant on his allotment which abutted Greenwood Avenue, Ilkeston. They did so because Grainger, whose father had owned the next allotment, was well aware that the defendant kept a good many items in the shed of considerable attraction to a burglar. The defendant, who at that time was 76, had rigged up sleeping quarters in the shed and had, for several years, been in the habit of sleeping there in order to protect his property from the frequent attentions of vandals and thieves in the area. . . . Besides the various items depicted in the photographs there were also one air rifle together with pellets and a single barrelled 12-bore shotgun with a supply of No 6 shot cartridges. Wakened by the noise of the plaintiff and Grainger trying to break open the shed, the defendant took the shotgun, loaded it, poked the barrel through a small hole in the door, also illustrated in the photographs, and fired. The charge caught the plaintiff at a range of approximately five feet on the right upper arm, passing clean through it, through the armpit and into his chest.

Mr Revill was subsequently prosecuted for the various offences which he had committed that night and pleaded guilty. Mr Newbery also was prosecuted on charges of wounding but he was acquitted.

Mr Revill then brought the present proceedings. The claim was based on (a) assault, that is, trespass to the person; (b) a breach of the duty owed under s. 1 of the Occupiers' Liability Act 1984; and (c) negligence.

To these claims Mr Newbery raised the defences of *ex turpi causa*, accident, self-defence and contributory negligence. In addition Mr Newbery counterclaimed damages for shock and distress.

The judge rejected the defence of *ex turpi causa* . . . Having considered various authorities, he came to the conclusion that the defence could only apply 'if the injury complained of was so closely interwoven in the illegal or criminal act as to be virtually a part of it or if it was a direct uninterrupted consequence of that illegal act'. In rejecting the defence on the facts of this case he said:

> The discharge of a shotgun towards burglars who are not displaying any intention of resorting to violence to the person is, in my judgment, out of all proportion to the threat involved, even making all due allowance for the agony of the moment, and therefore any injury sustained by such discharge cannot be said to be an integral part nor a necessarily direct consequence of the burglary . . .

[I] must consider the relevance of the defence of *ex turpi causa* and also whether Mr Revill's criminal conduct makes it possible for the court to assess the relevant standard of care.

[**Neill LJ** considered the decision of the Court of Appeal in *Pitts v Hunt*, and continued:]

For the purposes of the present judgment I do not find it necessary to consider further the joint criminal enterprise cases or the application of the doctrine of *ex turpi causa* in other areas of the law of tort. It is sufficient for me to confine my attention to the liability of someone in the position of Mr Newbery towards an intruding burglar. It seems to me to be clear that, by enacting s. 1 of the 1984 Act, Parliament has decided that an occupier cannot treat a burglar as an outlaw and has defined the scope of the duty owed to him. As I have already indicated, a person other than an occupier owes a similar duty to an intruder such as Mr Revill. In para. 32 of their 1976 report the Law Commission rejected the suggestion that there should be no duty at all owed to a trespasser who was engaged in a serious criminal enterprise.

I am satisfied that the liability of someone in the position of Mr Newbery is to be determined by applying a test similar to that set out in s. 1(4) of the 1984 Act. There is in my view no room for a two-stage determination whereby the court considers first whether there has been a breach of duty and then considers whether notwithstanding a breach the plaintiff is barred from recovering by reason of the fact that he was engaged in crime. It is to be noted that the defence of *volenti* is dealt with specifically in s. 1(6).

[**Neill LJ** concluded that the defendant had been negligent and upheld the two-thirds reduction for the plaintiff's contributory negligence.]

Evans LJ

The present case can . . . be distinguished from the 'criminal enterprise' type of case exemplified by *Pitts v Hunt* [1991] 1 QB 24. The issue here is whether the plaintiff in a personal injury claim for damages for negligence is debarred from making any recovery where he was a trespasser and engaged in criminal activities when the injury was suffered. Any broad test of causation is satisfied almost by definition in such a case, because he would not have sustained the injury caused by the defendant unless he had been where he was and acting as he was at the relevant time.

These are the factors of fault and responsibility which are taken into account when assessing the issue of contributory negligence pursuant to s. 1 of the Law Reform (Contributory Negligence) Act 1945. So the question whether there is a complete defence will only have practical relevance in relation to that proportion of the liability which as between the plaintiff and the defendant it is adjudged that the defendant should bear.

This does not mean that the rule cannot apply, because the underlying principle is that there is a public interest which requires that the wrongdoer should not benefit from his crime or other offence. But it would mean, if it does apply in circumstances such as these, that the trespasser who was also a criminal was effectively an outlaw, who was debarred by the law from recovering compensation for any injury which he might sustain. This same consideration also prompts the thought that it is one thing to deny to a plaintiff any fruits from his illegal conduct, but different and more far-reaching to deprive him even of compensation for injury which he suffers and which otherwise he is entitled to recover at law.

It is abundantly clear, in my judgment, that the trespasser/criminal is not an outlaw, and it is noteworthy that even the old common law authorities recognised the existence of some duty towards trespassers, even though the duty was limited and strictly defined and was much less onerous than the common law duty of care. I note also that the Law Commission's Report on *Liability for Damage or Injury to Trespassers and Related Questions of Occupiers' Liability*, Law Com No 75, 1976 discussed the extent of the occupier's duty towards trespassers in the context of 'Other possible limitations upon the duty of care' (see paras. 31–35). It is not suggested that no duty of any sort is owed to the trespasser, and it follows that the law recognises that the plaintiff has some rights, however limited, which the law does recognise and protect.

This is sufficient, in my judgment, to answer the defendant's contention that there is a rule or principle of law which relieves him of all liability or which, conversely, deprives the plaintiff of any right to recover damages in the present case. Such a rule would make it unnecessary to consider the precise scope of the defendant's duty towards the plaintiff or to apply the rules of contributory negligence. The claim would fail in any event. That clearly is not the law. . . .

Millett LJ delivered a separate concurring judgment.

Appeal dismissed.

COMMENTARY

Unlike the earlier extracts, this case did not involve a joint illegal enterprise with one participant claiming against another. Here, the defendant did not commit the negligent act in the course of a criminal activity so that there was no difficulty in setting a standard of care. Neither did Evans LJ think the approach in *Tinsley v Milligan* applicable. Rather, the Court of Appeal held what would now be described as the wide version of the defence inapplicable by a form of policy analysis, relying on the provisions of the Occupiers' Liability Act 1984 (which provides that an occupier owes a limited duty to trespassers), although only obliquely so because Neill LJ held it did not actually apply where the complaint related to an activity carried on by the occupier (in this case, shooting) as opposed to the state of the premises. None the less, his Lordship thought that the Act showed Parliament's intent that burglars who were trespassers should be owed some duty and that the defendant had breached that duty. However, the defendant's complaint was not that the plaintiff was a trespasser; it was that he had come to rob his shed, as had happened frequently before. The term 'trespasser' covers a wide variety of persons, including children who stray onto property and adults who mistakenly cross onto another's property. It is possible to be a trespasser without being culpable, and certainly possible to be one without criminal intent. Thus the fact that Parliament sought to give protection to trespassers as a group may not be much indication as to its position on burglars, although it is true the earlier Law Commission Report on which the Act was based did suggest a duty was owed to trespassers engaged in criminal activity.

It may not be good public policy to encourage unreasonable forms of self-help in the protection of property, but is it correct to say the plaintiff would have been an 'outlaw' if the claim had been refused? The defendant was tried and acquitted of a criminal charge in respect of the incident, so clearly the plaintiff retained the protection of the criminal law. Is a burglar entitled to the further protection of an award of damages in a civil action for an injury which was caused, according to Evans LJ, because he was involved in an illegal activity? This causal connection would certainly seem to satisfy the requirements of Lord Hoffmann's wide version of the illegality defence in *Gray*. The public's attitude was clear in any event; they contributed to a collection which paid the defendant's award. Apparently, however, the public's views are of little importance, for Sedley LJ has commented: 'The public conscience, an elusive thing, as often as not turns out to be an echo-chamber inhabited by journalists and public moralists' (*Vellino v Chief Constable of Greater Manchester Police* [2002] 1 WLR 218 at 233). Do you think this a fair description of those who contributed to the fund?

Evans LJ stated: 'it is one thing to deny to a plaintiff any fruits from his illegal conduct, but different and more far-reaching to deprive him even of compensation for injury which he suffers and which otherwise he is entitled to recover at law'. But this consideration did not prevent the plaintiff being denied compensation in *Ashton v Turner* and *Pitts v Hunt*. If the claimant had an accomplice and was injured partly by the negligence of the accomplice and partly by that of the victim the result would seem to be that the claim against the accomplice would be barred but not the claim against the victim, and, under the rules of joint and several liability, the victim would be liable for 100 per cent of the damages. For further comment see Weir [1996] CLJ 182, and note also the report of *Wiles v Phillips*, *The Times*, 9 May 1997, where a farmer was held liable to a thief for unreasonable use of force in apprehending him, although he was acquitted of criminal charges in respect of the incident in 1992. (An appeal was dismissed by the Court of Appeal in June 1998.) See also *Stone & Rolls Ltd v Moore Stephens* [2009] 1 AC 1370 where, in the very different context of corporate fraud, the

House of Lords held by majority that the illegality of the main shareholder and director of a company protected the company's auditor from liability in negligence for failing to detect the fraud.

Whatever the theoretical justifications for the result in *Revill*, later cases have been less reluctant to apply the defence in comparable circumstances, and less convinced by the reasons that prevented the Court of Appeal doing so in *Revill*. In *Cross v Kirkby*, unreported, CA Civil Division, 18 February 2000, the claimant, who had attacked the defendant with a baseball bat and was then injured when the defendant used it to defend himself, failed in his claim partly on the ground of illegality. Beldam LJ thought the defence would apply where the claim arose out of the claimant's conduct (in the sense that it had a causal connection with it), and that this was clearly satisfied, whilst Judge LJ thought the defence applied as the claim was inextricably linked with the illegality. Both of these approaches are broadly consistent with the wide version of illegality defence set out by Lord Hoffmann in *Gray*. In its original consultation paper (No. 160), the Law Commission argued that none of the possible rationales for the defence supported its application where the claimant was suing for personal injury, stating (at para. 4.85): 'We...doubt whether it is "inconsistent" [see p. 327, above] to allow a claim for personal injury caused by the default of the defendant where the claimant was engaging in illegal or criminal activity at the time he or she was injured.' However, consider the following case: Carlos Vellino, a notorious if petty local criminal, lived in a second floor flat, and when the police went to arrest him one evening he broke away from them and jumped out of his bedroom window, causing severe injury. As he had been known to escape in this way previously, it was alleged the police were careless (should they have had officers waiting to catch him?), but it was held by a majority of the Court of Appeal that the claimant's illegal act of escaping from police custody barred the claim, either by preventing any duty of care from arising or by operating as a defence. Sedley LJ dissented, partly on the ground of the Law Commission's views as to the appropriateness of the defence in personal injury cases. However, if Vellino had successfully made his escape but was later apprehended and imprisoned for escaping, or in the course of escaping he had injured a passer-by who later sued him successfully for damages, his claim in respect of the imprisonment, or for the damages paid out to the passer-by, would clearly have been barred by the defence. In terms of the consistency rationale why should the fact that he injured himself make a difference? The Commission's 2009 consultation was much more equivocal about the scope of the defence, no doubt influenced by the fact that a large majority of those who responded to the initial consultation paper thought the defence should be available to deny a claim for personal injury (para. 7.11).

Both of the Law Commission Consultation Papers have provisionally recommended that the defence remain available in the law of tort (cf. Glofcheski (1999) 19 LS 6, who argues that both the joint illegal enterprise cases and situations like *Revill* can be dealt with by other defences, and that illegality has therefore no role to play in the law of tort). However, in its 2001 consultation paper, the Commission suggested (paras 6.6–6.30) that the defence should be put on a statutory footing, so that the court had a 'structured discretion' in applying the defence, taking into account: (1) the seriousness of the illegality; (2) the knowledge and intention of the claimant; (3) whether denying relief would act as deterrent; (4) whether denying relief would further the purpose of the rule which rendered the claimant's conduct illegal; and (5) whether denying relief would be proportionate to the illegality involved. This approach was rejected in the 2009 consultation paper; it was noted that some consultees to the initial consultation paper thought the statutory discretion might not have sufficient flexibility to deal with the very wide circumstances in which the defence might arise and that, given that the discretion was very broad, the law would still remain uncertain (see also the comments of Tuckey LJ in *Hewison v Meridian Shipping PTE* [2003] ICR 766). Instead, the Commission in its 2009 report recommended that the court should consider in each individual case whether the defence could be justified on the basis of the policies underlying the defence; these included: (1) furthering the purpose of the rule which the illegal conduct has infringed; (2) consistency; (3) the claimant should not profit from his or her wrong; (4) deterrence; and (5) maintaining the integrity of the legal system. These are to be balanced in the circumstances of the individual case against the objective of achieving a just result, taking into account the relative merits of the parties and the proportionality of denying the claim. In its final report (Law Com No. 320, *The Illegality Defence*, 2010), the Commission adhered to its earlier recommendations. It thought the decisions of the House of Lords in *Stone & Rolls v Moore Stephens* [2009] 1 AC 1370 and, in particular, *Gray v Thames Trains* [2009] UKHL 33, indicated that the law was developing along the lines of its recommendations in the 2009 consultation paper (see para. 3.38). No legislative reform was therefore required.

Do you think there is any substantive difference between the approach advocated by the Law Commission and the public conscience test? In particular, would it be possible to find the defence applicable where the court thought the claimant's conduct was disproportionately worse than that of the defendant so that applying the defence would maintain the integrity of the legal system (see para 2.27 of the 2009 consultation paper).

7 NEGLIGENCE: DUTY OF CARE— PSYCHIATRIC ILLNESS

I. Introduction

In its Report on *Liability for Psychiatric Illness* (Law Com. 249, 1999), the Law Commission stated: 'The issue of liability for psychiatric illness provokes a range of strongly-held opinions' (para. 1.2). At one end of the spectrum is the view that psychiatric illness should be treated no differently from physical injury to the person, and damages for the former should be no less extensive than the latter. At the other end is a deep scepticism about the reality of the conditions grouped together under the label of 'psychiatric illness', and about the need to provide compensation for them. Here one finds the view that 'liability for psychiatric illness should be abandoned altogether' (*ibid.*). Use of the derogatory (though frequently used) phrase 'nervous shock' to describe the injuries in question may contribute to a tendency to underestimate their gravity.

Despite certain initial doubts as to whether claims for psychiatric illness should be accepted at all, English law has steered a middle course between these two extreme views. An early mood of scepticism was set by the Privy Council in *Victorian Railway Commissioners v Coultas* (1888) 13 App Cas ???, where Sir Richard Couch, delivering the judgment of the Judicial Committee, pointed to the danger of admitting claims of psychiatric illness (at 225–6):

> [I]n every case where an accident caused by negligence had given a person a serious nervous shock, there might be a claim for damages on account of mental injury. The difficulty which now often exists in cases of alleged physical injuries of determining whether they were caused by the negligent act would be greatly increased, and a wide file opened up for imaginary claims.

The Privy Council held that psychiatric illness suffered by a woman when she was nearly hit by a train after being negligently allowed onto a level crossing by the gatekeeper was not a natural and reasonable result of the gatekeeper's negligence and was therefore too remote. This decision was, however, subjected to considerable criticism by contemporary commentators and the English Divisional Court declined to follow it in *Dulieu v White & Sons* [1901] 2 KB 669, like *Coultas* a 'two party' case in which the plaintiff was actually imperilled (or reasonably believed she was imperilled) by the defendant's negligence. The right to recover damages in such circumstances was confirmed by the House of Lords in *Page v Smith*, extracted below (Section III).

To be contrasted with such cases are 'three-party' cases in which the claimant witnesses the injury (or threatened injury) of another person as a result of the defendant's negligence; here, the claimant may be regarded as a 'secondary' or 'ricochet' victim of the defendant's negligence. For fear of an overwhelming number of claims, English law has restricted liability in such cases by imposing a number of 'proximity requirements' which the claimant must satisfy in order to establish a duty of care. As it is in the witness cases that the courts have most directly confronted the problematic nature of psychiatric illness claims, it is with those cases that we begin.

II. Witnesses

In *Dulieu v White*, Kennedy J stated in an obiter dictum that liability for psychiatric illness was limited by a requirement that there 'must be a shock which arises from a reasonable fear of personal injury to oneself' (at 675). If accepted, this would preclude liability to someone who merely witnesses, or reasonably fears, the injury of another person. But Kennedy J's dictum was rejected by the majority of the Court of Appeal in *Hambrook v Stokes Bros* [1925] 1 KB 141. In that case, the defendants were held liable for a fatal nervous shock suffered by a woman who watched as a driverless runaway lorry careered down a hill towards the spot—just out of her view—where she knew her children to be; she was almost immediately informed that a child answering the description of one of hers had been injured. Atkin LJ dismissed the restriction on liability proposed in the earlier case in the following terms (at 157; see also Bankes LJ at 151):

> It would result in a state of the law in which a mother, shocked by fright for herself, would recover, while a mother shocked by her child being killed before her eyes, could not, and in which a mother traversing the highway with a child in her arms could recover if shocked by fright for herself, while if she could be cross-examined into an admission that the fright was really for her child, she could not. In my opinion such distinctions would be discreditable to any system of jurisprudence in which they formed part.

Although the duty to the mere witness was established in that case, the precise circumstances in which it would arise were not fully specified. A number of questions remained unanswered. Would the duty arise when the witness had no relationship with the person injured or in danger? If not, what sort of relationship was required? Did it make any difference if the psychiatric illness arose not from the perception of a traumatic event, but from being told about it later? Initially, these and other questions were subsumed under the all-embracing question of foreseeability. In *Bourhill v Young* (extracted above, p. 129), the House of Lords rejected a claim by a woman who suffered nervous shock (allegedly causing her to miscarry) as a result of an accident in which the defendant motorcyclist was killed. Although she heard the accident occur, and came immediately to the scene, she was not related to the deceased. On those facts, the House of Lords held that it was not reasonably foreseeable that a person of normal fortitude would have suffered nervous shock. One might have expected that, with increasing public knowledge of psychiatric conditions, psychiatric illness would be regarded over time as reasonably foreseeable in a wider and wider range of situations, and the bounds of the liability would be extended accordingly. This did indeed occur—for a time. But more recently, especially over the last 20 years or so, the courts have sought to limit the scope of liability for psychiatric illness by using the concept of foreseeability in an artificially restricted sense and by making the existence of a duty of care depend also upon the satisfaction of various requirements of proximity.

McLoughlin v O'Brian [1983] AC 410

The plaintiff, Mrs McLoughlin, suffered nervous shock after a car crash in which her husband and three of her children were seriously injured; the injuries of one of her children were fatal. Mrs McLoughlin had been at home some two miles away at the time the accident happened, but news of the accident was communicated to her by a friend an hour or so afterwards. She was driven to the hospital and arrived there approximately two hours after the accident. At the hospital she witnessed scenes which the House of Lords accepted were 'distressing in the extreme' (at 417, per Lord Wilberforce): she saw her children cut and bruised, and begrimed with dirt and oil, and she heard their sobs and screams; while she was with them, her son lapsed into unconsciousness. For the purposes of determining the question of legal liability, it was assumed that she had suffered what was described as severe shock, organic depression and a change of personality as a consequence of these experiences. Her claim was rejected at trial and by the Court of Appeal. She appealed to the House of Lords.

Lord Wilberforce stated that the foreseeability of nervous shock was not enough to establish liability and went on to consider the policy arguments against the extension of liability to meet the facts of the present case:

First, it may be said that such extension may lead to a proliferation of claims, and possibly fraudulent claims, to the establishment of an industry of lawyers and psychiatrists who will formulate a claim for nervous shock damages, including what in America is called the customary miscarriage, for all, or many, road accidents and industrial accidents. Second, it may be claimed that an extension of liability would be unfair to defendants, as imposing damages out of proportion to the negligent conduct complained of. In so far as such defendants are insured, a large additional burden will be placed on insurers, and ultimately on the class of persons insured: road users or employers. Third, to extend liability beyond the most direct and plain cases would greatly increase evidentiary difficulties and tend to lengthen litigation. Fourth, it may be said (and the Court of Appeal agreed with this) that an extension of the scope of liability ought only to be made by the legislature, after careful research. . . .

[S]ome of the arguments are susceptible of answer. Fraudulent claims can be contained by the courts, which, also, can cope with evidentiary difficulties. The scarcity of cases which have occurred in the past, and the modest sums recovered, give some indication that fears of a flood of litigation may be exaggerated: experience in other fields suggests that such fears usually are. If some increase does occur, that may only reveal the existence of a genuine social need . . .

But, these discounts accepted, there remains, in my opinion, just because 'shock' in its nature is capable of affecting so wide a range of people, a real need for the law to place some limitation on the extent of admissible claims. It is necessary to consider three elements inherent in any claim: the class of persons whose claims should be recognised; the proximity of such persons to the accident; and the means by which the shock is caused. As regards the class of persons, the possible range is between the closest of family ties, of parent and child, or husband and wife, and the ordinary bystander. Existing law recognises the claims of the first; it denies that of the second, either on the basis that such persons must be assumed to be possessed of fortitude sufficient to enable them to endure the calamities of modern life or that defendants cannot be expected to compensate the world at large. In my opinion, these positions are justifiable, and since the present case falls within the first class it is strictly unnecessary to say more.

I think, however, that it should follow that other cases involving less close relationships must be very carefully scrutinised. I cannot say that they should never be admitted. The closer the tie (not merely in relationship, but in care) the greater the claim for consideration. The claim, in any case, has to be judged in the light of the other factors, such as proximity to the scene in time and place, and the nature of the accident.

As regards proximity to the accident, it is obvious that this must be close in both time and space. It is after all, the fact and consequence of the defendant's negligence that must be proved to have caused the 'nervous shock'. Experience has shown that to insist on direct and immediate sight or hearing would be impractical and unjust and that under what may be called the 'aftermath' doctrine, one who, from close proximity comes very soon on the scene, should not be excluded.... The High Court of Australia's majority decision in *Chester v Waverley Municipal Council* (1939) 62 CLR 1, where a child's body was found floating in a trench after a prolonged search, may perhaps be placed on the other side of a recognisable line (Evatt J in a powerful dissent placed it on the same side)....

Finally, and by way of reinforcement of 'aftermath' cases, I would accept, by analogy with 'rescue' situations, that a person of whom it could be said that one could expect nothing else than that he or she would come immediately to the scene (normally a parent or a spouse) could be regarded as being within the scope of foresight and duty. Where there is not immediate presence, account must be taken of the possibility of alterations in the circumstances, for which the defendant should not be responsible.

Subject only to these qualifications, I think that a strict test of proximity by sight or hearing should be applied by the courts.

Lastly, as regards communication, there is no case in which the law has compensated shock brought about by communication by a third party. In *Hambrook v Stokes Bros* [1925] 1 KB 141, indeed, it was said that liability would not arise in such a case, and this is surely right.... The shock must come through sight or hearing of the event or of its immediate aftermath. Whether some equivalent of sight or hearing, e.g. through simultaneous television, would suffice may have to be considered.

My Lords, I believe that these indications, imperfectly sketched, and certainly to be applied with common sense to individual situations in their entirety, represent either the existing law, or the existing law with only such circumstantial extension as the common law process may legitimately make. They do not introduce a new principle. Nor do I see any reason why the law should retreat behind the lines already drawn. I find on this appeal that the appellant's case falls within the boundaries of the law so drawn. I would allow her appeal.

Lord Bridge

In approaching the question whether the law should, as a matter of policy, define the criterion of liability in negligence for causing psychiatric illness by reference to some test other than that of reasonable foreseeability it is well to remember that we are concerned only with the question of liability of a defendant who is, ex hypothesi, guilty of fault in causing the death, injury or danger which has in turn triggered the psychiatric illness. A policy which is to be relied on to narrow the scope of the negligent tortfeasor's duty must be justified by cogent and readily intelligible considerations, and must be capable of defining the appropriate limits of liability by reference to factors which are not purely arbitrary. A number of policy considerations which have been suggested as satisfying these requirements appear to me, with respect, to be wholly insufficient. I can see no grounds whatever for suggesting that to make the defendant liable for reasonably foreseeable psychiatric illness caused by his negligence would be to impose a crushing burden on him out of proportion to his moral responsibility. However liberally the criterion of reasonable foreseeability is interpreted, both the number of successful claims in this field and the quantum of damages they will attract are likely to be moderate.

I cannot accept as relevant the well-known phenomenon that litigation may delay recovery from a psychiatric illness. If this were a valid policy consideration, it would lead to the conclusion that psychiatric illness should be excluded altogether from the heads of damage which the law will recognise. It cannot justify limiting the cases in which damages will be awarded for psychiatric illness by reference to the circumstances of its causation. To attempt to draw a line at the furthest point which any of the decided cases happen to have reached, and to say that it is for the legislature, not the courts, to extend the limits of liability any further, would be, to my mind, an unwarranted abdication of the court's function of developing and adapting principles of the common law to changing conditions, in a particular corner of the common law which exemplifies, par excellence, the important and indeed necessary part which that function has to play. In the end I believe that the policy question depends on weighing against each other two conflicting considerations. On the one hand, if the criterion of liability is to be reasonable foreseeability simpliciter, this must, precisely because questions of causation in psychiatric medicine give rise to difficulty and uncertainty, introduce an element of uncertainty into the law and open the way to a number of arguable claims which a more precisely fixed criterion of liability would exclude. I accept that the element of uncertainty is an important factor. I believe that the 'floodgates' argument, however, is, as it always has been, greatly exaggerated. On the other hand, it seems to me inescapable that any attempt to define the limit of liability by requiring, in addition to reasonable foreseeability, that the plaintiff claiming damages for psychiatric illness should have witnessed the relevant accident, should have been present at or near the place where it happened, should have come upon its aftermath and thus have had some direct perception of it, as opposed to merely learning of it after the event, should be related in some particular degree to the accident victim—to draw a line by reference to any of these criteria must impose a largely arbitrary limit of liability. . . .

My Lords, I have no doubt that this is an area of the law of negligence where we should resist the temptation to try yet once more to freeze the law in a rigid posture which would deny justice to some who, in the application of the classic principles of negligence derived from *Donoghue v Stevenson* [1932] AC 562, ought to succeed, in the interests of certainty, where the very subject matter is uncertain and continuously developing, or in the interests of saving defendants and their insurers from the burden of having sometimes to resist doubtful claims.

Lord Edmund-Davies, **Lord Russell of Killowen** and **Lord Scarman** delivered separate concurring speeches.

Appeal allowed.

COMMENTARY

This was the first of four decisions in which the House of Lords developed the modern approach to nervous shock claims (see also *Alcock*, *Page* and *White* below). Perhaps inevitably, *McLoughlin* left certain issues unresolved. Amongst these was the absolutely fundamental question of whether the courts should adopt a restrictive or expansive approach to liability for psychiatric illness. Although Lord Wilberforce was very circumspect in setting out the precise criteria that had to be satisfied before a claim would be allowed, other members of the House of Lords (notably Lord Bridge and Lord Scarman) seemed to adopt a broader approach, following Lord Wilberforce's own 'two-stage' test in *Anns*, under which the reasonable foreseeability of psychiatric injury was on its own sufficient to give rise to a prima facie duty of care. (Ironically, this was clearly not Lord Wilberforce's own approach in *McLoughlin*, perhaps indicating that his two-stage test in *Anns* had been misinterpreted by other members of the House: see further p. 139, above.) Whether this was to develop as English law's true approach to the question of liability for psychiatric illness was addressed in the next case extracted below.

The Need for a Recognised Psychiatric Illness

Where a personal injury is sustained by physical means, a claim is possible not only for the loss of amenity resulting from the injury but also for 'pain and suffering' suffered as a consequence. But the position with regard to 'free-standing' mental injuries is different. Notwithstanding the frequent use of the epithet 'nervous shock' in this area, it is necessary for the claimant to establish a recognised psychiatric illness, not merely grief, distress, anxiety or shock in the ordinary sense of that word (see, e.g., *White v Chief Constable of South Yorks Police* [1999] 2 AC 455 at 501, per Lord Hoffmann). Many recent cases have involved a condition known as post-traumatic stress disorder (PTSD), but the courts are prepared to allow claims in respect of any condition that is medically-recognised. In some cases, the distinction between compensatable and non-compensatable conditions seems—at least so far as the (non-medical) lay-person can tell—rather fine, as perhaps is the case with the distinction between pathological grief disorder and 'mere' grief (see *Vernon v Bosley* [1997] 1 All ER 577 at 610, per Thorpe LJ; Hedley, 'Nervous Shock: Wider Still and Wider?' [1997] CLJ 254). But this is a matter that is primarily medical rather than legal, and so does not call for further attention here. Where *physical* harm (e.g. a heart attack or miscarriage) is suffered by psychiatric means, there is of course no need to show a recognised psychiatric illness.

Alcock v Chief Constable of South Yorkshire [1992] 1 AC 310

This was one of the cases that arose out of the Hillsborough football stadium tragedy in which 96 people died and hundreds more were injured. It was a test case brought by friends and relatives of those caught in the crush at the Leppings Lane end of the ground; the case brought together a number of claims identified as representative of the different legal issues raised by the group of claims as a whole. For the purpose of the test case, it was presumed that the plaintiffs had suffered post-traumatic stress disorder as a result of their experiences. Various relationships with those in the Leppings Lane pen were represented, including those between parent and child, brothers and (unofficial) fiancés. The selected plaintiffs were also situated in different locations at the time of the accident (some in the ground itself, some outside, some at home in Liverpool) and the experiences which caused their condition were contrasting (some had witnessed the events unfold from the other side of the stadium, some had seen live or recorded television coverage, some had identified bodies in the make-shift mortuary erected at the ground). The defendants admitted negligence but disputed that they owed a duty of care to the plaintiffs in the test case. After rulings by Hidden J and the Court of Appeal on the class of plaintiffs owed a duty of care, the case reached the House of Lords where the plaintiffs appealed against the Court of Appeal's ruling in favour of the defendants.

Lord Keith

It was argued for the appellants in the present case that reasonable foreseeability of the risk of injury to them in the particular form of psychiatric illness was all that was required to bring home liability to the respondent. In the ordinary case of direct physical injury suffered in an accident at work or elsewhere, reasonable foreseeability of the risk is indeed the only test that need be applied to determine liability. But injury by psychiatric illness is more subtle, as Lord Macmillan observed in *Bourhill v Young* [1943] AC 92 at 103. In the present type of case it is a secondary sort of injury brought about by the infliction of physical injury, or the risk of phys- ical injury, upon another person. That can affect those closely connected with that person in various ways. One way is by subjecting a close relative to the stress and strain of caring for the injured person over a prolonged period, but psychiatric illness due to such stress and strain has not so far been treated as founding a claim in damages. So I am of the opinion that in addition to reasonable foreseeability liability for injury in the particular form of psychiatric illness must depend in addition upon a requisite relationship of proximity between the claimant and the party said to owe the duty. Lord Atkin in *M'Alister (or Donoghue) v Stevenson* [1932] AC 562 at 580, described those to whom a duty of care is owed as being—

> persons who are so closely and directly affected by my act that I ought reasonably to have them in contemplation as being so affected when I am directing my mind to the acts or omissions which are called in question.

The concept of a person being closely and directly affected has been conveniently labelled 'proximity', and this concept has been applied in certain categories of cases, particularly those concerned with pure economic loss, to limit and control the consequences as regards liability which would follow if reasonable foreseeability were the sole criterion.

As regards the class of persons to whom a duty may be owed to take reasonable care to avoid inflicting psychiatric illness through nervous shock sustained by reason of physical injury or peril to another, I think it sufficient that reasonable foreseeability should be the guide. I would not seek to limit the class by reference to particular relationships such as husband and wife or parent and child. The kinds of relationship which may involve close ties of love and affection are numerous, and it is the existence of such ties which leads to mental disturbance when the loved one suffers a catastrophe. They may be present in family relationships or those of close friendship, and may be stronger in the case of engaged couples than in that of persons who have been married to each other for many years. It is common knowledge that such ties exist, and reasonably foreseeable that those bound by them may in certain circumstances be at real risk of psychiatric illness if the loved one is injured or put in peril. The closeness of the tie would, however, require to be proved by a plaintiff, though no doubt being capable of being presumed in appropriate cases. The case of a bystander unconnected with the victims of an accident is difficult. Psychiatric injury to him would not ordinarily, in my view, be within the range of rea- sonable foreseeability, but could not perhaps be entirely excluded from it if the circumstances of a catastrophe occurring very close to him were particularly horrific.

In the case of those within the sphere of reasonable foreseeability the proximity factors mentioned by Lord Wilberforce in *McLoughlin v O'Brian* [1983] 1 AC 410 at 422, must, however, be taken into account in judging whether a duty of care exists. The first of these is proximity of the plaintiff to the accident in time and space. For this purpose the accident is to be taken to include its immediate aftermath, which in *McLoughlin's* case was held to cover the scene at the hospital which was experienced by the plaintiff some two hours after the accident....

As regards the means by which the shock is suffered, Lord Wilberforce said in *McLoughlin's* case [1983] 1 AC 410 at 423 that it must come through sight or hearing of the event or of its immediate aftermath. He also said that it was surely right that the law should not compensate shock brought about by communication by a third party....

Of the present appellants two, Brian Harrison and Robert Alcock, were present at the Hillsborough ground, both of them in the West Stand, from which they witnessed the scenes in pens 3 and 4. Brian Harrison lost two brothers, while Robert Alcock lost a brother-in-law and identified the body at the mortuary at midnight. In neither of these cases was there any evidence of particularly close ties of love or affection with the brothers or brother-in-law. In my opinion the mere fact of the particular relationship was insufficient to place the plaintiff within the class of persons to whom a duty of care could be owed by the defendant as being foreseeably at risk of psychiatric illness by reason of injury or peril to the individuals concerned. The same is true of other plaintiffs who were not present at the ground and who lost brothers, in one case a grandson. I would, however, place in the category of members to which risk of psychiatric illness was reasonably foreseeable Mr and Mrs Copoc, whose son was killed, and Alexandra Penk, who lost her fiancé. In each of these cases the closest ties of love and affection fall to be presumed from the fact of the particular relationship, and there is no suggestion of anything which might tend to rebut that presumption. These three all watched scenes from Hillsborough on television, but none of these depicted suffering of recognisable individuals, such being excluded by the broadcasting code of ethics, a position known to the defendant. In my opinion the viewing of these scenes cannot be equiparated with the viewer being within 'sight or hearing of the event or of its immediate aftermath', to use the words of Lord Wilberforce in *McLoughlin v O'Brian* [1983] 1 AC 410 at 423, nor can the scenes reasonably be regarded as giving rise to shock, in the sense of a sudden assault on the nervous system. They were capable of giving rise to anxiety for the safety of relatives known or believed to be present in the area affected by the crush, and undoubtedly did so, but that is very different from seeing the fate of the relative or his condition shortly after the event. The viewing of the television scenes did not create the necessary degree of proximity.

My Lords, for these reasons I would dismiss each of these appeals.

Lord Ackner

[W]hile it may be very difficult to envisage a case of a stranger, who is not actively and foreseeably involved in a disaster or its aftermath, other than in the role of rescuer, suffering shock-induced psychiatric injury by the mere observation of apprehended or actual injury of a third person in circumstances that could be considered reasonably foreseeable, I see no reason in principle why he should not, if in the circumstances, a reasonably strong-nerved person would have been so shocked. In the course of argument your Lordships were given, by way of an example, that of a petrol tanker careering out of control into a school in session and bursting into flames. I would not be prepared to rule out a potential claim by a passer-by so shocked by the scene as to suffer psychiatric illness. . . .

Although the television pictures certainly gave rise to feelings of the deepest anxiety and distress, in the circumstances of this case the simultaneous television broadcasts of what occurred cannot be equated with the 'sight or hearing of the event or its immediate aftermath'. Accordingly shocks sustained by reason of these broadcasts cannot found a claim. I agree, however, with Nolan LJ [in the Court of Appeal] that simultaneous broadcasts of a disaster cannot in all cases be ruled out as providing the equivalent of the actual sight or hearing of the event or its immediate aftermath. Nolan LJ gave an example of a situation where it was reasonable to anticipate that the television cameras, whilst filming and transmitting pictures of a special event of children travelling in a balloon, in which there was media interest, particularly amongst the parents, showed the balloon suddenly bursting into flames (see [1991] 3 All ER 88 at 122). Many other such situations could be imagined where the impact of the simultaneous television pictures would be as great, if not greater, than the actual sight of the accident. . . .

[His Lordship proceeded to consider the case of Brian Harrison, who witnessed the tragedy, in which his two brothers were killed, from his seat in the West Stand:] The quality of brotherly love is well known to differ widely—from Cain and Abel to David and Jonathan. I assume that Mr Harrison's relationship with his brothers was not an abnormal one. His claim was not presented upon the basis that there was such a close and intimate relationship between them as gave rise to that very special bond of affection which would make his shock-induced psychiatric illness reasonably foreseeable by the chief constable. Accordingly, the learned judge did not carry out the requisite close scrutiny of their relationship. Thus there was no evidence to establish the necessary proximity which would make his claim reasonably foreseeable....

Lord Jauncey

My Lords, what constitutes the immediate aftermath of an accident must necessarily depend upon the surrounding circumstances. To essay any comprehensive definition would be a fruitless exercise. In *McLoughlin v O'Brian* the immediate aftermath extended to a time somewhat over an hour after the accident and to the hospital in which the victims were waiting to be attended to. It appears that they were in very much the same condition as they would have been had the mother found them at the scene of the accident. In these appeals the visits to the mortuary were made no earlier than nine hours after the disaster and were made not for the purpose of rescuing or giving comfort to the victim but purely for the purpose of identification. This seems to me to be a very different situation from that in which a relative goes within a short time after an accident to rescue or comfort a victim. I consider that not only the purpose of the visits to the mortuary but also the times at which they were made take them outside the immediate aftermath of this disaster.

Lord Oliver and **Lord Lowry** concurred.

Appeal dismissed.

COMMENTARY

The House of Lords made it clear that it was following the approach of Lord Wilberforce in *McLoughlin* notwithstanding hints of a broader approach in one or two places in the earlier decision (especially in the speech of Lord Scarman; in *Alcock*, their Lordships did not accept that Lord Bridge had differed from Lord Wilberforce in any material respect—do you agree?). It is evident therefore that psychiatric illness is to be dealt with more restrictively than other forms of personal injury: the House of Lords lays down a number of specific proximity requirements that must be satisfied in cases where psychiatric illness results from the experience of witnessing a traumatic event. These may be termed the requirements of proximity of relationship, proximity in time and space, and proximity of perception (described by some as the requirements of dearness, nearness and hear-ness).

Proximity of Relationship

It is necessary for the claimant to establish 'a close tie of love and affection' with the person injured or endangered. In a number of cases, such a tie can be rebuttably presumed from the nature of their relationship: parent–child relationships, spousal relationships, and relationships between those engaged to be married are all of this character. In other cases, the claimant must rebut the presumption that there is no close tie of love and affection. Weir has written that this requirement 'will be very messy in practice', and risks causing 'perplexity to advisers and embarrassment to litigants' (*Casebook on Tort*, 7th edn. (London: Sweet & Maxwell, 1992), p. vi). Do you agree? (Cf. the approach of the Law Commission, Section IV, below.)

At first instance in *Alcock*, Hidden J had ruled that all relationships within the nuclear family, including sibling relationships, involved close ties of love and affection (see [1992] 1 AC 310 at 337–8). But the approach of the House of Lords was narrower: the quality of sibling relationships was so varied that the presumption was not applicable in such cases. So no duty was owed, for instance, to Brian Harrison, who witnessed the events from inside the stadium itself knowing that his brother had been standing at the Leppings Lane end. It had indeed been open to him to plead that his relationship with his brother went beyond that which is normal between brothers, but before the decision of the House of Lords no-one would have realised that this was a precondition of liability in such a case. It must be said that it seems rather harsh to disallow a claim for not being pleaded in a way that no-one had previously suggested was necessary. In a subsequent action also arising out of the Hillsborough tragedy, when the plaintiff had the benefit of knowing what he had to prove, the court did in fact accept that he had enjoyed a close tie of love and affection with his deceased half-brother (*McCarthy v Chief Constable of South Yorkshire Police*, unreported; noted in *Daily Telegraph*, 12 December 1996); the judge held that they were part of 'a very close-knit' family.

The requirement of proximity of relationship seems to close the door on claims by mere bystanders (i.e. those with no relationship with the person injured or imperilled). In *Alcock*, Lord Ackner and Lord Keith were prepared to accept that there might be liability where the accident witnessed by a bystander was particularly horrific. One wonders why the terrible scenes at the Hillsborough football stadium were not considered horrific enough. In any case, it is not clear how any 'scale of horrors' could be devised, especially given the subject-ive nature of reactions to such events. This practical difficulty, coupled with a fear that the resultant liability would be based effectively on nothing more than reasonable foreseeabil-ity, led the Court of Appeal to reject the idea of liability to mere bystanders in *McFarlane v E. E. Caledonia Ltd* [1994] 1 Lloyd's Rep 16, a case arising out of the Piper Alpha fire tragedy (see further below). For an argument in favour of the extension of liability to such a case, see Oughton and Lowry, 'Liability to Bystanders for Negligently Inflicted Psychiatric Harm' (1995) 46 NILQ 18.

Proximity in Time and Space

It is clear that the claimant need not actually be at the scene of the accident at the time it occurs. This was first accepted in a number of Commonwealth decisions, for example where a mother ran 100 yards from her home to see the unconscious body of her son (*Benson v Lee* [1972] VR 879) and where a man arrived home minutes after a gas explosion had killed his three children (*Fenn v City of Peterborough* (1976) 73 DLR (3d) 177). Subsequently, in *McLoughlin v O'Brian*, extracted above, the House of Lords held that the aftermath of an accident extended not only *temporally* forward from the accident, but also *spatially* away from the accident scene to the hospital to which the victims were taken. This develop-ment was followed by the High Court of Australia in *Jaensch v Coffey* (1984) 155 CLR 549 where Deane J observed that 'the aftermath...extends to the ambulance taking an injured person to hospital for treatment and to the hospital itself during the period of immediate post-accident treatment' (at 608). Query therefore whether Mrs McLoughlin would have recovered if she had arrived at the hospital after her injured husband and children had been cleaned, operated upon, and bandaged. If not, one sees the force of the rhetorical question put by *Jones*, p. 169: 'Should liability for psychiatric harm depend on a race between the claimant and the ambulance?'

In *Galli-Atkinson v Seghal* [2003] EWCA Civ 697, [2003] Lloyd's Rep Med 285, an extempore decision of the Court of Appeal, the claimant's 16-year-old daughter was killed by a car which dangerously mounted the pavement. The claimant went looking for her, came across the police cordon surrounding the accident, and was told her daughter was dead. She then went with her husband to the mortuary and saw the girl's body, which had devastating and disfiguring injuries. The court ruled that this constituted an uninterrupted sequence of events and that the accident's immediate aftermath extended to the moment at which the claimant left the mortuary. How (if at all) can this decision be reconciled with the ruling in *Alcock* that the relatives who travelled to Sheffield to search for their loved ones and subsequently identified their bodies in the temporary mortuary were not entitled to invoke the aftermath doctrine? (Cf. *Walters v North Glamorgan NHS Trust* [2003] PIQR P16, noted p. 363, below.)

Proximity of Perception

The claimant must suffer psychiatric injury as a result of directly hearing or seeing the accident or its immediate aftermath. There can be no liability where he is merely told about the accident by a third party (*Ravenscroft v Rederiaktiebolaget Transatlantic* [1992] 2 All ER 470n). In *Palmer v Tees Health Authority* [2000] PIQR P1, the claimant sought damages for psychiatric conditions occasioned by the abduction and subsequent murder of her 4-year-old daughter by a psychiatric patient whom the defendant health authority had discharged from its care. The child's body was discovered four days after her abduction, during which period the claimant had suffered from visions and nightmares; she did not see the body until some two or three days later. The Court of Appeal struck out her claim, partly on the basis that the claimant—whatever her fears and whatever she had seen in her imagination—had had no sudden appreciation by sight or sound of the horrifying event. It was immaterial that her fears had subsequently been confirmed by events. But the House of Lords in *W v Essex County Council* [2001] 2 AC 592 found that an alternative approach was arguable. One of the claims there was brought by parents whose children had been sexually abused by a foster-child placed with them by the defendant local authority. The House of Lords declined to strike out the claim on the basis that the parents had only been told of the abuse, without actually witnessing it or its immediate aftermath. If a duty is to be recognised on such facts, however, this is best done by reference to the local authority's assumption of responsibility to the claimants in placing the foster-child with them (see p. 369, below), and not by dilution of the general requirement of proximity of perception.

On the facts of *Alcock*, the House of Lords denied that the experience of watching the events even on live television was equivalent to direct perception of those events, although Lord Ackner was prepared to accept that there might be exceptional circumstances in which liability might arise. What might those circumstances be? Do you think it would have made any difference to the result in *Alcock* if one of the plaintiffs, while watching live television coverage of the tragic events, had been able to identify a close relative being crushed against the fencing at the Leppings Lane end, for example, because the relative was wearing very distinctive clothes?

A difficult and unresolved question is *how much* perception of the accident the claimant must have. In *Alcock*, would it have been enough that a man had witnessed only generalised chaos from the far end of the ground, knowing that his children were standing in the Leppings Lane pens but unaware whether they were in fact injured or imperilled? (See

Mullis [1991] All ER Rev 371 at 376.) The Court of Appeal's decision in *Hambrook v Stokes Bros* [1925] 1 KB 141, where the accident occurred out of sight round a corner, suggests that a reasonable fear for the life or safety of a loved one is sufficient in such a case. But even if this reasoning is accepted in principle, it might be very difficult to disentangle the effects of witnessing the shocking scenes from those of the grief and distress consequent upon being told that the children had in fact been injured or killed. The rule here is that the 'shock' need only be a cause, not necessarily the sole cause, of the claimant's psychiatric condition (*Vernon v Bosley* [1997] 1 All ER 577) though in awarding damages the court should endeavour, where possible, to disentangle the effect of the defendant's negligence from that of other extrinsic causes of the claimant's symptoms (*Hatton v Sutherland* [2002] EWCA Civ 76, [2002] 2 All ER 1; see further p. 228, above). An additional question is whether it would make any difference if (unlike *Hambrook*) the children were not actually injured: even if they were left unscathed after a narrow escape, it is possible to imagine that their parents might still have nightmares afterwards. Should they be able to recover damages?

Claims Against the Primary Victim

In *Greatorex v Greatorex* [2000] 1 WLR 1970, the claimant fire-officer was called to the scene of a car accident in which, by pure coincidence, his son had been injured through his own negligence. He sued his son for damages for the post-traumatic stress disorder he consequently sustained (knowing, of course, that any award would be covered by his son's insurance). Adopting a view that had provisionally appealed to Lord Oliver in *Alcock* (at 418), Cazelet J ruled that a defendant who imperilled or injured herself owed no duty to those suffering psychiatric injury as a result. In his view, the policy arguments in favour of a duty of care were outweighed by those that ran against it. He identifies the two main considerations leading him to this conclusion in the following passage (at 1784–6).

[T]he issue which I have to resolve raises, as it seems to me, a question which impinges upon a person's right of self-determination. . . . Both counsel maintain that self-harming, whether by negligence or deliberately, would not be expected to give rise to any criminal liability. . . . There is, of course, a duty not to cause foreseeable physical injury to another in such circumstances, but in my judgment to extend that duty so as to bring within its compass purely psychiatric injury would indeed be to create a significant further limitation upon an individual's freedom of action. That seems to me to be a powerful objection to the imposition of such a duty. . . .

Home life may involve many instances of a family member causing himself injury through his own fault. Should the law allow one family member, B, to sue another family member, A, or his estate in respect of psychiatric illness suffered as a result of B either having been present when the injury was sustained or having come upon A in his injured state? . . . To allow a cause of action in this type of situation is to open up the possibility of a particularly undesirable type of litigation within the family, involving questions of relative fault as between its members. . . . I appreciate, of course, that one member of the family may already sue another family member in respect of physical injury caused by that other, so that in cases of physical injury there is already the potential for personal injury litigation within the family; but the fact that family members have the same right as others to make a claim for physical injury does not necessarily mean that they should have the right to make a claim for a different kind of harm in respect of which, because of the first *Alcock* control mechanism, others have no such right. Further, where a family member suffers psychiatric harm as a result of the self-inflicted injuries of another family member, the psychiatric illness in itself may well have an adverse effect upon family relationships which the law should be astute not to exacerbate by allowing litigation between those family members. In my judgment, to permit a cause of action for purely psychiatric injury in these circumstances would be potentially productive of acute family strife.

Do you find these arguments convincing? (See further Markesinis, 'Foreign Law Inspiring National Law: Lessons from *Greatorex v Greatorex*' [2002] CLJ 386.)

Liability for Communicating Distressing News

Suppose the live television broadcasts coming from the Hillsborough stadium had included—in breach of the broadcasters' code of practice—close-up pictures of individuals caught in the crush and close to death. Could relatives claim that the television company was at fault in showing the pictures and liable for PTSD suffered as a consequence of seeing them? It is far from obvious that the courts would recognise a duty of care in such a case. The public interest in the dissemination of information might well be taken to preclude the imposition of liability on the negligent communicant of distressing news (*aliter*, perhaps, if there was intent to harm the recipient). What appears to have been the first claim of this nature in the English courts was brought in *AB v Tameside & Glossop Health Authority* [1997] 8 Med LR 91, in which a number of patients of the defendant health authority complained of the way they had been informed that a health worker had been found to be HIV-positive and that they had thereby been exposed to a very remote risk of infection; the patients alleged *inter alia* that they should have been informed face-to-face rather than by letter. The case provides no authority on the matter under consideration, however, as the existence of a duty was conceded by the defendants; in any case, the claim failed because the Court of Appeal held that the defendants had not been negligent in deciding to break the news in the way they did. It is nonetheless noteworthy that Brooke LJ intimated that any duty found to exist might not be a generalised feature of the tort of negligence but only a particular incident of the pre-existing relationship between health authority and patient, a view that accords with the judgments of Gummow, Kirby and Callinan JJ of the High Court of Australia in *Tame v New South Wales* (2002) 211 CLR 317 that no general duty of care is owed by a bearer of bad tidings to their recipient.

Reactions to the case and the issues it raises have varied. Mullany, 'Liability for Careless Communication of Traumatic Information' (1998) 114 LQR 380 argues that counsel's concession of a duty of care was sound, emphasising the effect the bad news may have on the health of the patient, but other commentators regard concerns of free speech as more important. Dziobon and Tettenborn, 'When the truth hurts: the incompetent transmission of distressing news' (1997) 13 PN 70, for instance, argue strongly against the imposition of a duty in view of its restricting effect on speech and news reporting. They suggest that, in the context of *AB* itself, '[t]he threat of litigation on the basis that such information, while accurate, was mistimed, infelicitously drafted or even conceivably sent to someone who would suffer more if told than if kept in ignorance, is likely to stem rather than encourage the timely flow of information to which the patient has at least a prima facie right' (p. 71). But would not the health authorities in any case have a duty to inform fully and expeditiously in such circumstances?

Another type of case in which the liability of the communicant of shocking news might be raised is where the communicant passes on *erroneous* information about the fate of a close relative. In Australia, it has been held that the communicant owes a duty of care to the relative and liability was imposed on state authorities who told the plaintiff falsely that her husband had been admitted to an asylum (*Barnes v Commonwealth* (1937) SR (NSW) 511). The issue was raised in *Allin v City & Hackney Health Authority* [1996] 7 Med LR 167 where the plaintiff recovered damages for PTSD suffered as a result of being told after a difficult birth that her baby had died; six hours later, she learned that the baby had in fact survived. As in *AB*, however, the defendants had conceded that they owed a duty of care, so the case cannot be regarded as authority on the duty issue. Noting the contrast with *Ravenscroft*, Jones has argued that the imposition of liability in such circumstances would be 'bizarre': 'which event is worse,' he asks, 'being told (correctly) that someone has negligently killed your child or negligently being told (incorrectly) that your child has died?' ('Negligently inflicted psychiatric harm: is the word mightier than the deed?' (1997) 13 PN 111 at 113.) Mullany again disagrees, arguing that '[i]t would be offensive if liability could lie under *Hedley Byrne* for economic loss caused by a negligent misstatement but not for psychiatric injury caused by the same wrong' ((1998) 114 LQR 380 at 385).

Customary Phlegm

Another requirement—that there be a reasonable foreseeability of psychiatric illness to a person of normal fortitude or 'customary phlegm'—is considered further below, Section III.

III. Participants

In *Alcock*, Lord Oliver distinguished the case of the witness from that where 'the injured plaintiff was involved, either mediately or immediately, as a participant' in the traumatic event (p. 407). He thought that in the latter type of case the duty owed to the plaintiff was often 'self-evident'; there was no need to satisfy the same proximity requirements as were applied in the witness cases. The term 'participant'—or 'primary victim', which is sometimes used in its place—is not entirely clear in its meaning, but it certainly includes a person who is physically imperilled by the defendant's negligence and suffers psychiatric illness as a result. Liability in such circumstances was accepted as early as *Dulieu v White & Sons* [1901] 2 KB 669, and it was confirmed in *Page v Smith*, extracted below, where the House of Lords considered whether liability should be restricted by any of the proximity factors applicable in the witnesses cases.

In *Alcock*, Lord Oliver identified two other types of participant, viz. rescuers and innocent agents of traumatic events (p. 408):

> It is well established that the defendant owes a duty of care not only to those who are directly threatened or injured by his careless acts but also to those who, as a result, are induced to go to their rescue and suffer injury in so doing. The fact that the injury suffered is psychiatric and is caused by the impact on the mind of becoming involved in personal danger or in scenes of horror and destruction makes no difference. 'Danger invites rescue. The cry of distress is the summons to relief ... the act, whether impulsive or deliberate, is the child of the occasion' (see *Wagner v International Rly Co* (1921) 232 NY 176 at 180–181 per Cardozo J) ...

These are all cases where the plaintiff has, to a greater or lesser degree, been person-ally involved in the incident out of which the action arises, either through the direct threat of bodily injury to himself or in coming to the aid of others injured or threatened. Into the same category, I believe, fall those cases such as *Dooley v Cammell Laird & Co Ltd* [1951] 1 Lloyd's Rep 271, *Galt v British Railways Board* (1983) 133 NLJ 870 and *Wigg v British Railways Board* (1986) 136 NLJ 446 where the negligent act of the defendant has put the plaintiff in the position of being, or of thinking that he is about to be or has been, the involuntary cause of another's death or injury and the illness complained of stems from the shock to the plaintiff of the consciousness of this supposed fact. The fact that the defendant's negligent conduct has foreseeably put the plaintiff in the position of being an unwilling participant in the event establishes of itself a sufficiently proximate relationship between them and the principal question is whether, in the circumstances, injury of that type to that plaintiff was or was not reasonably foreseeable.

The position of rescuers was considered in the second case extracted below, *White v Chief Constable of South Yorkshire Police*, along with the question of whether those who, in the course of employment, attend a disaster caused by the negligence of their employer also fall within the special class of participants. The status of involuntary agents of another's death or injury remains to be definitively resolved by the courts.

Page v Smith [1996] 1 AC 155

The case arose out of a car crash of moderate severity. The plaintiff was driving with due care when, suddenly and without warning, the defendant, coming in the opposite direction, turned into his path. The impact caused some physical damage to the cars but none to the occupants. Three hours later, however, the plaintiff felt exhausted and took to his bed. The exhaustion continued and the plaintiff never fully recovered. At the time of the appeal, despite the lapse of almost eight years, the plaintiff had not yet returned to work. The diagnosis was the recru-descence of a condition known most commonly as myalgic encephalomyelitis (ME), from a mild form of which the plaintiff had suffered sporadically in the past; this now became an ill-ness of chronic intensity and permanency. At first instance, he was awarded damages of over £160,000, but the defendant's appeal to the Court of Appeal was allowed, primarily on the basis that it had not been reasonably foreseeable that a person of normal fortitude would have suffered psychiatric injury. The plaintiff appealed to the House of Lords.

Lord Lloyd

This is the fourth occasion on which the House has been called on to consider 'nervous shock'. On the three previous occasions, *Bourhill v Young* [1943] AC 92, *McLoughlin v O'Brian* [1983] 1 AC 410 and *Alcock v Chief Constable of the South Yorkshire Police* [1992] 1 AC 310, the plaintiffs were, in each case, outside the range of foreseeable physical injury....

In all these cases the plaintiff was the secondary victim of the defendant's negligence. He or she was in the position of a spectator or bystander. In the present case, by contrast, the plaintiff was a participant. He was himself directly involved in the accident, and well within the range of foreseeable physical injury. He was the primary victim. This is thus the first occasion on which your Lordships have had to decide whether, in such a case, the foreseeability of phys-ical injury is enough to enable the plaintiff to recover damages for nervous shock.

The factual distinction between primary and secondary victims of an accident is obvious and of long-standing. It was recognised by Lord Russell in *Bourhill v Young*, when he pointed out that Mrs Bourhill was not physically involved in the collision. In *Alcock* [1992] 1 AC 310 at 396 Lord Keith of Kinkel said that in the type of case which was then before the House, injury by psychiatric illness 'is a secondary sort of injury brought about by the infliction of physical injury, or the risk of physical injury, upon another person'. In the same case Lord Oliver of Aylmerton said of cases in which damages are claimed for nervous shock (at 407):

> Broadly they divide into two categories, that is to say those cases in which the injured plain-
> tiff was involved, either mediately or immediately, as a participant, and those in which the
> plaintiff was no more than the passive and unwilling witness of injury caused to others.

Later in the same speech, he referred to those who are involved in an accident as the primary victims, and to those who are not directly involved, but who suffer from what they see or hear, as the secondary victims (see [1992] 1 AC 310 at 410–411). This is, in my opinion, the most con-venient and appropriate terminology.

Though the distinction between primary and secondary victims is a factual one, it has, as will be seen, important legal consequences....

Foreseeability of psychiatric injury remains a crucial ingredient when the plaintiff is the sec-ondary victim, for the very reason that the secondary victim is almost always outside the area of physical impact, and therefore outside the range of foreseeable physical injury. But where the plaintiff is the primary victim of the defendant's negligence, the nervous shock cases, by which I mean the cases following on from *Bourhill v Young*, are not in point. Since the defendant was admittedly under a duty of care not to cause the plaintiff foreseeable physical injury, it was unnecessary to ask whether he was under a separate duty of care not to cause foreseeable psychiatric injury....

It may be said that ... [this approach] would open the door too wide, and encourage bogus claims. As for opening the door, this is a very important consideration in claims by second-ary victims. It is for this reason that the courts have, as a matter of policy, rightly insisted on a number of control mechanisms. Otherwise, a negligent defendant might find himself being made liable to all the world. Thus in the case of secondary victims, foreseeability of injury by shock is not enough. The law also requires a degree of proximity: see *Alcock* [1992] 1 AC 310 at 396 per Lord Keith, and the illuminating judgment of Stuart-Smith LJ in *McFarlane v EE Caledonia Ltd* [1994] 2 All ER 1 at 14. This means not only proximity to the event in time and space, but also proximity of relationship between the primary victim and the secondary victim. A further control mechanism is that the secondary victim will only recover damages for nerv-ous shock if the defendant should have foreseen injury by shock to a person of normal fortitude or 'ordinary phlegm'.

None of these mechanisms are required in the case of a primary victim. Since liability depends on foreseeability of physical injury, there could be no question of the defendant finding himself liable to all the world. Proximity of relationship cannot arise, and proximity in time and space goes without saying.

Nor in the case of a primary victim is it appropriate to ask whether he is a person of 'ordinary phlegm'. In the case of physical injury there is no such requirement. The negligent defendant, or more usually his insurer, takes his victim as he finds him. The same should apply in the case of psychiatric injury. There is no difference in principle ... between an eggshell skull and an egg-shell personality. Since the number of potential claimants is limited by the nature of the case, there is no need to impose any further limit by reference to a person of ordinary phlegm. Nor can I see any justification for doing so.

As for bogus claims, it is sometimes said that if the law were such as I believe it to be, the plaintiff would be able to recover damages for a fright. This is not so. Shock by itself is not the subject of compensation, any more than fear or grief or any other human emotion occasioned by the defendant's negligent conduct. It is only when shock is followed by recognisable psychiatric illness that the defendant may be held liable.

There is another limiting factor. Before a defendant can be held liable for psychiatric injury suffered by a primary victim, he must at least have foreseen the risk of physical injury. So that if . . . the defendant bumped his neighbour's car while parking in the street, in circumstances in which he could not reasonably foresee that the occupant would suffer any physical injury at all, or suffer injury so trivial as not to found an action in tort, there could be no question of his being held liable for the onset of hysteria. Since he could not reasonably foresee any injury, physical or psychiatric, he would owe the plaintiff no duty of care. That example is, however, very far removed from the present.

So I do not foresee any great increase in unmeritorious claims. The court will, as ever, have to be vigilant to discern genuine shock resulting in recognised psychiatric illness. But there is nothing new in that. The floodgates argument has made regular appearances in this field, ever since it first appeared in *Victorian Railways Comrs v Coultas* (1888) 13 App Cas 222. I do not regard it as a serious obstacle here.

My provisional conclusion, therefore, is that . . . [t]he test in every case ought to be whether the defendant can reasonably foresee that his conduct will expose the plaintiff to risk of personal injury. . . .

In the case of a primary victim the question will almost always turn on whether the foreseeable injury is physical. But it is the same test in both cases, with different applications. There is no justification for regarding physical and psychiatric injury as different 'kinds' of injury. Once it is established that the defendant is under a duty of care to avoid causing personal injury to the plaintiff, it matters not whether the injury in fact sustained is physical, psychiatric or both. . . .

Applying that test in the present case, it was enough to ask whether the defendant should have reasonably foreseen that the plaintiff might suffer physical injury as a result of the defendant's negligence, so as to bring him within the range of the defendant's duty of care. It was unnecessary to ask, as a separate question, whether the defendant should reasonably have foreseen injury by shock; and it is irrelevant that the plaintiff did not, in fact, suffer any external physical injury. . . . It is no answer that the plaintiff was predisposed to psychiatric illness. Nor is it relevant that the illness takes a rare form or is of unusual severity. The defendant must take his victim as he finds him.

Lord Ackner and **Lord Browne-Wilkinson** delivered separate speeches concurring with Lord Lloyd. **Lord Keith** and **Lord Jauncey** dissented.

Appeal allowed.

COMMENTARY

The House of Lords remitted the case to the Court of Appeal to determine the question of causation. The Court of Appeal found for the plaintiff on this issue in *Page v Smith (No. 2)* [1996] 3 All ER 272.

Primary and Secondary Victims

The distinction between primary and secondary victims was said by the Law Commission in its report on *Psychiatric Illness* to be 'more of a hindrance than a help' (para. 5.51). It noted that there was 'confusing inconsistency' as to how the line should be drawn (para. 5.45). In *W v Essex County Council* [2001] 2 AC 592 at 601, Lord Slynn commented: 'the categorisation of those claiming to be included as primary or secondary victims is not as I read the cases finally closed. It is a concept still to be developed in different factual situations.' In our view, such statements risk increasing the confusion. Furthermore, if the category of primary victims is enlarged, this may well undermine the proximity requirements currently applied in secondary victim cases. Even if one favours reforming the law on secondary victims, this is not the best way of going about it.

For the sake of clarity, we shall use the term 'primary victim' to denote the person who is physically harmed or imperilled by the defendant's negligence, whilst leaving it open whether other claimants are also to be relieved of the burden of satisfying the proximity requirements applicable to secondary victims.

How Wide is the Zone of Danger?

In *Page v Smith*, Lord Lloyd appeared confident that there was no problem of 'opening the door too wide' in respect of claims by primary victims. But it is possible to imagine incidents in which a very large number of people are traumatised by a fear of physical injury, for example where a disabled aeroplane limps over a city before finally crashing into a block of flats (see Trindade (1996) 112 LQR 22 at 24, and *Winfield & Jolowicz*, para. 5–56). Are all those who think even momentarily that the plane might come down on them to be regarded as primary victims? Unless the zone of danger is defined narrowly in such cases, there would seem to be the risk of a very large number of claims arising out of a single incident. The courts may therefore rely upon their hindsight as to what actually happened, and who was *actually* at risk in the *specific* collision that occurred, in order to limit the class of those who were foreseeably at risk. (See further p. 369f, below.)

Reasonable Fear not Enough

In *McFarlane v E. E. Caledonia* [1994] 1 Lloyd's Rep 16, the Court of Appeal accepted that a plaintiff could recover for nervous shock caused by a reasonable fear of death or physical injury even if not in fact imperilled. According to Stuart-Smith LJ, the class of participant extended beyond the plaintiff who 'is in the actual area of danger created by the event, but escapes physical injury by chance or good fortune' and embraced 'the plaintiff [who] is not actually in danger, but because of the sudden and unexpected nature of the event…reasonably thinks that he is'. But it was still necessary, as in all primary victim cases, to show that the defendant ought reasonably to have foreseen that a person in the position of the plaintiff might be killed or suffer physical injury (or might fear such consequences). Put another way, even if, judged with the benefit of hindsight, the plaintiff's reaction was reasonable, it still had to be shown that the defendant had (actual or imputed) foresight that the plaintiff might be imperilled or reasonably believe that he was.

McFarlane arose out of the Piper Alpha fire disaster. The plaintiff had been employed as a painter on an oil rig in the North Sea owned and operated by the defendants. On the night of 6 July 1988, while the plaintiff was off duty and lying on his bunk on a support vessel some 550 metres away, a series of massive explosions occurred on the rig. Over the next hour and three-quarters the plaintiff witnessed the explosions and consequent destruction of the rig before he was evacuated by helicopter. The explosions and fire on the rig caused the deaths of 164 men. The closest the plaintiff came to the fire was 100 metres when the support vessel moved in towards the rig in an attempt to fight the fire and render assistance. The plaintiff brought an action against the defendants claiming damages for psychiatric illness suffered as a result of the events he had witnessed. On the trial of a preliminary issue whether the defendants owed the plaintiff a duty to exercise reasonable care to avoid causing him psychiatric injury, the judge held *inter alia* that the plaintiff was owed such a duty, on the ground that he was a participant in the event who had been reasonably in fear for his life and safety and that his injury had resulted from the shock caused by his fear. The defendants' appeal was allowed on the basis that, even if the plaintiff had been reasonably albeit mistakenly in fear of his safety, this did not establish that this was something which the defendants ought reasonably to have foreseen. In any case, the court held that it was not established on the facts that the plaintiff had really been in fear for his own safety. (See also *Hegarty v E. E. Caledonia* [1997] 2 Lloyd's Rep 259, where Brooke LJ noted (at 266) that reasonable fear was only 'one part of the test'.)

The inherently vague nature of the concept of foreseeability, coupled with the infinitely varied facts of individual cases, means that it is impossible to make any scientific assessment of the consistency of judicial rulings on foreseeability. But it certainly appears that the courts have varied between generous and restrictive approaches, perhaps reflecting a view taken on the facts of each individual case as to whether imposing liability might lead to a flood of similar claims arising out of the same incident.

Primary Victims: Must the Harm be Caused by Fear?

It is natural to assume that the primary-victim terminology refers to a case where the claimant reasonably fears that he or she is within the area of physical risk and suffers psychiatric illness *as a result of that fear*. On this view, Kennedy J's opinion in *Dulieu v White & Sons* [1901] 2 KB 669 at 675 that there had to be 'a shock which arises from a reasonable fear of personal injury to oneself' would be an accurate statement of the law on primary victims (although it neglects the duty owed to secondary victims). But some cases seem to proceed on the basis that the claimant need only prove he or she was *actually* within the area of physical risk, irrespective of whether the claimant was aware of this at the time or suffered psychiatric illness as a result of that awareness.

Young v Charles Church (1997) 39 BMLR 146 was a case arising out of the fatal electrocution of the plaintiff's workmate with whom he was erecting scaffolding in the course of employment. While the plaintiff's back was turned, the deceased touched an overhead electric cable with a scaffolding pole and was electrocuted, dying instantly. On hearing a loud bang and hissing sound, the plaintiff immediately looked behind and saw that the workmate had been killed and that the surrounding ground had burst into flames. He ran 600 yards to the security office to summon help and returned to the scene of the accident to wait for the arrival of an ambulance. As a result of what he saw and heard he suffered psychiatric injury and claimed damages for nervous shock as a primary victim of the defendants' negligence and breach of statutory duty. The Court of Appeal found the defendant liable for two alternative reasons: (1) the plaintiff was within the area of physical danger and (2) a special duty was owed by virtue of the employment context (on which, see below). As regards the former basis for the decision, it is notable that the plaintiff seems to have been unaware of the physical danger until after the accident had occurred and to have suffered psychiatric injury not as a result of any fear for his physical safety but as a result of witnessing the aftermath of a horrific accident in which his workmate was killed. In our opinion dispensing with any requirement that the psychiatric illness should result from a fear for one's physical safety appears to blur the distinction between primary and secondary victim cases and to open up a loophole for potential claimants to exploit.

Criticism of *Page v Smith*

In *White v Chief Constable of South Yorkshire* [1999] 2 AC 455, 477–80, Lord Goff (dissenting) stated that the decision in *Page v Smith* 'constituted a remarkable departure from . . . generally accepted principles'. In particular, it 'dethroned foreseeability of psychiatric injury from its central position as the unifying feature of this branch of the law' by making a distinction between primary and secondary victims. Only for secondary victims was it still necessary for the claimant to establish the foreseeability of psychiatric injury; the primary victim had only to show the foreseeability of injury, whether physical or psychiatric. Lord Goff noted academic criticism of *Page v Smith* (e.g. by Handford (1996) 4 Tort L Rev 5 and Trindade (1996) 112 LQR 22), and continued:

In summary the basic grounds of criticism appear to be threefold.

(a) There has been no previous support for any such approach, and there is authority in England and Australia to the contrary. In England, see Lord Oliver's opinion in the *Alcock* case [1992] 1 AC 310, 408 where he regarded the principle of foreseeability of psychiatric damage as applicable in cases concerned with participants, as in the case of secondary victims . . .

(b) The approach favoured by Lord Lloyd appears to be inconsistent . . . with . . . *The Wagon Mound No 1* [1961] AC 388 [extracted p. 269, above] . . . There a particular type of damage to property, viz. damage by fire, was differentiated from other types of damage to property for the purpose of deciding whether the defendant could reasonably have foreseen damage of that particular type, so as to render him liable in damages in tort for such damage. That differentiation was made on purely common sense grounds, as a matter of practical justice. On exactly the same grounds, a particular type of personal injury, viz. psychiatric injury, may, for the like purpose, properly be differentiated from other types of personal injury. It appears to be in no way inconsistent with the making of that common sense judgment, as a matter of practical justice, that scientific advances are revealing that psychiatric illnesses may have a physical base, or that psychiatric injury should be regarded as another form of personal injury . . .

(c) The majority in *Page v Smith* [1996] AC 155 may have misunderstood the so-called eggshell skull rule . . . The maxim only applies where liability has been established. The criticism is therefore that Lord Lloyd appears to have taken an exceptional rule relating to compensation and treated it as being of general application, thereby creating a wider principle of liability.

In *Grieves v FT Everard & Sons Ltd sub nom. Rothwell v Chemical & Insulating Co Ltd* [2007] UKHL 39, [2008] 1 AC 281 the House of Lords referred to Lord Goff's criticisms of *Page v Smith*, but declined to rule that it was wrongly decided. Lord Hoffmann (at [32]) stated:

I do not think that it would be right to depart from *Page v Smith*. It does not appear to have caused any practical difficulties and is not, I think, likely to do so if confined to the kind of situation which the majority in that case had in mind. That was a foreseeable event (a collision) which, viewed in prospect, was such as might cause physical injury or psychiatric injury or both. Where such an event has in fact happened and caused psychiatric injury, the House decided that it is unnecessary to ask whether it was foreseeable that what actually happened would have that consequence. Either form of injury is recoverable.

Lord Hope (at [52]) and Lord Mance (at [104]), by contrast, expressly reserved their opinion on the correctness of the decision in *Page v Smith*, the latter seeing some force in the argument that it causes uncertainty, argument and artificiality. On the facts, however, it was not necessarily to rule on the matter because the present case was distinguishable. Mr Grieves suffered clinical depression in consequence of his becoming aware that he was at risk of suffering mesothelioma or some other asbestos-related illness in the future as a result of his negligent exposure to asbestos dust in the workplace in the years 1961–9. In 2000, an X-ray showed that he had developed pleural plaques around his lungs. Pleural plaques do not themselves constitute actionable damage (as the Law Lords ruled in the other cases heard with *Grieves*), nor do they lead to any asbestos-related conditions, but they signal the presence in the lungs of asbestos fibres which may independently cause life-threatening or fatal diseases. It was this knowledge that triggered the claimant's psychiatric illness. His claim against his former employers failed, their Lordships ruled, because (1) even when approached with the benefit of hindsight, the psychiatric illness was not a foreseeable consequence of the defendant's negligence to a person of ordinary fortitude, but reflected the claimant's longstanding anticipatory fears of developing the disease, and (2) though physical harm (asbestos-related disease) was a foreseeable consequence of the negligence, that was not sufficient to establish liability because *Page v Smith* did not apply to a case where a psychiatric illness was triggered by fear of something that might happen in the future rather than as an immediate response to a past event. For comment and analysis, see Jones (2008) 24 PN 13, Leczykiewicz (2008) 124 LQR 548, Steele [2008] CLJ 28 and Turton (2008) 71 MLR 1009.

Cf. the view of Lord Walker in *Corr v IBC* [2008] UKHL 13, [2008] 1 AC 884 at [40] that *Page v Smith* 'provides a much simpler test for judges trying personal injury cases, even if it sometimes results in compensation for damage in the form of psychiatric sequelae which might not, on their own, have been reasonably foreseeable…'. In that case, where the deceased was driven to take his own life by the depressive illness he developed following a horrendous accident at work, Lord Walker at [42] and Lord Scott at [29] applied *Page v Smith* to hold the employer liable to the deceased's widow for the financial consequences of the suicide. In their Lordship's view it did not matter whether psychiatric harm was a foreseeable result of the employer's negligence so long as some kind of personal injury (physical or psychiatric) was reasonably foreseeable. A majority of the House of Lords agreed the claimant was entitled to recover damages for the suicide, but without applying *Page v Smith* which was considered strictly irrelevant as the employer had conceded the deceased's depressive illness was reasonably foreseeable: see Lord Mance at [46], Lord Neuburger at [55], and (implicitly) Lord Bingham at [13]. For other aspects of the decision, see pp. 265, 292 and 303, above.

White v Chief Constable of South Yorkshire [1999] 2 AC 455

A number of police officers sued their employer, the chief constable, in respect of post-traumatic stress disorder suffered in the aftermath of the Hillsborough football stadium disaster. Three of the officers had been on duty at the stadium at the time. One of these had attempted to help free spectators from the pens and two of them had attended a makeshift morgue set up at the ground. Two other officers had been drafted in to help in the aftermath at the ground shortly after the disaster. All five officers had witnessed chaotic and gruesome scenes. The sixth officer had not been on duty at the ground and had acted as liaison officer between the hospital staff and the casualty bureau; she had also dealt with relatives and later went to the temporary morgue at the ground with personal effects. The chief constable admitted that the disaster had been caused by negligence for which he was vicariously responsible and had accepted liability towards other officers more directly concerned in the events of the disaster, but denied that he owed any duty of care to the officers bringing the claim. Having failed at first instance, five of the officers appealed to the Court of Appeal which held that all bar one of them were entitled to succeed either on the basis that they had encountered exceptionally horrific scenes in the course of their employment or that they were rescuers; no duty was owed, however, to the liaison officer who had never actually gone onto the pitch. The court considered that the fact that members of the police might be described as professional rescuers did not make any difference to the adjudication of the appeal. The Chief Constable appealed to the House of Lords.

Lord Hoffmann

[T]he plaintiffs draw two distinctions between their position and that of spectators or bystanders. The first is that they had a relationship analogous to employment with the Chief Constable. Although constitutionally a constable holds an office rather than being employed, there is no dispute that his Chief Constable owes him the same duty of care which he would to an employee. The plaintiffs say that they were therefore owed a special duty which required the Chief Constable and those for whom he was vicariously liable to take reasonable care not to expose them to unnecessary risk of injury, whether physical or psychiatric. Secondly, the plaintiffs (and in this respect there is no difference between the police and many others in the crowd that day) did more than stand by and look. They actively rendered assistance and should be equated to 'rescuers', who, it was said, always qualify as primary victims.

My Lords, I shall consider first the claim to primary status by virtue of the employment relationship. Mr Hytner QC, for the plaintiffs, said that prima facie an employer's duty required him to take reasonable steps to safeguard his employees from unnecessary risk of harm. The word 'unnecessary' must be stressed because obviously a policeman takes the risk of injury which is an unavoidable part of his duty. But there is no reason why he should be exposed to injuries which reasonable care could prevent. Why, in this context, should psychiatric injury be treated differently from physical injury? .... I think, my Lords, that this argument really assumes what it needs to prove. The liability of an employer to his employees for negligence, either direct or vicarious, is not a separate tort with its own rules. It is an aspect of the general law of negligence. The relationship of employer and employee establishes the employee as a person to whom the employer owes a duty of care. But this tells one nothing about the circumstances in which he will be liable for a particular type of injury. For this one must look to the general law concerning the type of injury which has been suffered. It would not be suggested that the employment relationship entitles the employee to recover damages in tort (I put aside contractual liability, which obviously raises different questions) for economic loss which would not ordinarily be recoverable in negligence. The employer is not, for example, under a duty in tort to take reasonable care not to do something which would cause the employee purely financial loss, e.g. by reducing his opportunities to earn bonuses. The same must surely be true of psychiatric injury. There must be a reason why, if the employee would otherwise have been regarded as a secondary victim, the employment relationship should require him to be treated as a primary one....

Should the employment relationship be a reason for allowing an employee to recover damages for psychiatric injury in circumstances in which he would otherwise be a secondary victim and not satisfy the *Alcock* control mechanisms? I think, my Lords, that the question vividly illustrates the dangers inherent in applying the traditional incrementalism of the common law to this part of the law of torts. If one starts from the employer's liability in respect of physical injury, it seems an easy step, even rather forward-looking, to extend liability on the same grounds to psychiatric injury. It makes the law seem more attuned to advanced medical thinking by eliminating (or not introducing) a distinction which rests upon uneasy empirical foundations. It is important, however to have regard, not only to how the proposed extension of liability can be aligned with cases in which liability exists, but also to the situations in which damages are not recoverable. If one then steps back and looks at the rules of liability for psychiatric injury as a whole, in their relationship with each other, the smoothing of the fabric at one point has produced an ugly ruck at another. In their application to other secondary victims, the *Alcock* control mechanisms stand obstinately in the way of rationalisation and the effect is to produce striking anomalies. Why should the policemen, simply by virtue of the employment analogy and irrespective of what they actually did, be treated different from first aid workers or ambulance men?...

In principle, therefore, I do not think it would be fair to give police officers the right to a larger claim merely because the disaster was caused by the negligence of other policemen. In the circumstances in which the injuries were caused, I do not think that this is a relevant distinction and if it were to be given effect, the law would not be treating like cases alike....

The second way in which the plaintiffs put their case is that they were not 'bystanders or spectators' but participants in the sense that they actually did things to help. They submit that there is an analogy between their position and that of a 'rescuer', who, on the basis of the decision of Waller J in *Chadwick v British Railways Board* [1967] 1 WLR 912, is said to be treated as a primary victim, exempt from the control mechanisms...

There is no authority which decides that a rescuer is in any special position in relation to liability for psychiatric injury. And it is no criticism of the excellent judgment of Waller J in *Chadwick v British Railways Board* [1967] 1 WLR 912 to say that such a question obviously never entered his head. Questions of such nicety did not arise until the *Alcock* control mechanisms had been enunciated.

There does not seem to me to be any logical reason why the normal treatment of rescuers on the issues of foreseeability and causation should lead to the conclusion that, for the purpose of liability for psychiatric injury, they should be given special treatment as primary victims when they were not within the range of foreseeable physical injury and their psychiatric injury was caused by witnessing or participating in the aftermath of accidents which caused death or injury to others...

Should then your Lordships take the incremental step of extending liability for psychiatric injury to 'rescuers' (a class which would now require definition) who give assistance at or after some disaster without coming within the range of foreseeable physical injury? It maybe said that this would encourage people to offer assistance. The category of secondary victims would be confined to 'spectators and bystanders' who take no part in dealing with the incident or its aftermath. On the authorities, as it seems to me, your Lordships are free to take such a step.

In my opinion there are two reasons why your Lordships should not do so. The less important reason is the definitional problem to which I have alluded. The concept of a rescuer as someone who puts himself in danger of physical injury is easy to understand. But once this notion is extended to include others who give assistance, the line between them and bystanders becomes difficult to draw with any precision. For example, one of the plaintiffs in *Alcock*, a Mr O'Dell, went to look for his nephew. 'He searched among the bodies...and assisted those who staggered out from the terraces.' (See [1992] 1 AC 310 at 354.) He did not contend that his case was different from those of the other relatives and it was also dismissed. Should he have put himself forward as a rescuer?

But the more important reason for not extending the law is that in my opinion the result would be quite unacceptable. I have used this word on a number of occasions and the time has come to explain what I mean. I do not mean that the burden of claims would be too great for the insurance market or the public funds, the two main sources for the payment of damages in tort. The Law Commission may have had this in mind when they said that removal of all the control mechanism would lead to an 'unacceptable' increase in claims, since they described it as a 'floodgates' argument. These are questions on which it is difficult to offer any concrete evidence and I am simply not in a position to form a view one way or the other. I am therefore willing to accept that, viewed against the total sums paid as damages for personal injury the increase resulting from an extension of liability to helpers would be modest. But I think that such an extension would be unacceptable to the ordinary person because (though he might not put it this way) it would offend against his notions of distributive justice. He would think it unfair between one class of claimants and another, at best not treating like cases alike and at, worst, favouring the less deserving against the more deserving. He would think it wrong that policemen, even as part of a general class of persons who rendered assistance, should have the right to compensation for psychiatric injury out of public funds while the bereaved relatives are sent away with nothing...

It may be said that the common law should not pay attention to these feelings about the relative merits of different classes of claimants. It should stick to principle and not concern itself with distributive justice. An extension of liability to rescuers and helpers would be a modest incremental development in the common law tradition and, as between these plaintiffs and these defendants, produce a just result. My Lords, I disagree. It seems to me that in this area of the law, the search for principle was called off in *Alcock v Chief Constable of South Yorkshire* [1992] 1 AC 310. No one can pretend that the existing law, which your Lordships have to accept, is founded upon principle. I agree with Jane Stapleton's remark (see P. Birks (ed), *The Frontiers of Liability*, OUP, 1994, vol. 2, p. 87) that:

> once the law has taken a wrong turning or otherwise fallen into an unsatisfactory internal state in relation to a particular cause of action, incrementalism cannot provide the answer.

Consequently your Lordships are now engaged, not in the bold development of principle, but in a practical attempt, under adverse conditions, to preserve the general perception of the law as a system of rules which is fair between one citizen and another...

Naturally I feel great sympathy for the plaintiffs, as I do for all those whose lives were blighted by that day at Hillsborough. But I think that fairness demands that your Lordships should reject them....I would therefore allow these appeals and dismiss the actions.

Lord Griffiths (dissenting on the 'rescuer' question)

What rescuer ever thinks of his own safety? It seems to me that it would be a very artifical and unnecessary control, to say a rescuer can only recover if he was in fact in physical danger. A danger to which he probably never gave thought, and which in the event might not cause physical injury....I do not share the view that the public would find it in some way offensive that those who suffered disabling psychiatric illness as a result of their efforts to rescue the victims should receive compensation, but that those who suffered the grief of bereavement should not. Bereavement and grief are a part of the common condition of mankind which we will all endure at some time in our lives. It can be an appalling experience but it is different in kind from psychiatric illness and the law has never recognized it as a head of damage. We are human and we must accept as a part of the price of our humanity the suffering of bereavement for which no sum of money can provide solace or comfort. I think better of my fellow men than to believe that they would, although bereaved, look like dogs in the manger upon those who went to the rescue at Hillsborough.

Lord Browne-Wilkinson and **Lord Steyn** concurred with Lord Hoffmann. **Lord Goff** dissented (on both 'employee' and 'rescuer' questions).

Appeal allowed.

COMMENTARY

The House of Lords denied that any distinctive duty is owed to a person simply by virtue of his employment relationship with the defendant or his status as a rescuer. As the plaintiffs in this case were not 'personally threatened' or in a relationship of love and affection with any of the deceased, it followed that their claims had to fail. Do you think that the decision leaves the law in a satisfactory position?

Rescuers

In *Chadwick v British Transport Commission* [1967] 1 WLR 912, an action was brought by the plaintiff as personal representative of her late husband in respect of injuries she alleged were caused by the Lewisham train disaster in 1957. In bad weather conditions two trains collided as a result of the admitted negligence of the defendants. Ninety people were killed. The accident happened at 6 pm, some 200 yards from the Chadwicks' house. Mr Chadwick immediately ran out of the house to help. Mrs Chadwick did not see him again until 3 am, when he came in, covered with mud, with blood on his hands. He went out again and did not return until 6 am. He would not go to bed and he was upset and shaking. It was alleged that, whereas before the accident he was a cheerful busy man carrying on a window-cleaning business and with many spare-time activities, the shock of his experiences that night made him psychoneurotic, and he no longer took the interest in life which he had taken and was unable to work for a considerable time. He required hospital treatment for approximately six months. Waller J held that the defendants owed the deceased a duty of care as a foreseeable victim of their negligence and awarded damages of £935 3s 6d for lost wages and £600 for misery and discomfort arising from his diminished enjoyment of life and for his periods of treatment in hospital.

How was this case explained by the House of Lords in *White*? What requirements must a rescuer now satisfy in order to bring a claim for nervous shock? Do you agree with Todd, 'Psychiatric injury and rescuers' (1999) 115 LQR 345 at 347 that the approach adopted by the House of Lords is 'quite arbitrary, its sole purpose being to limit the ambit of liability'?

Despite Lord Hoffmann's fear that treating rescuers as a separate category would introduce difficult questions of definition, the Court of Appeal seems to have successfully dealt with these in *McFarlane v E. E. Caledonia*, noted above at p. 354f. The court held that acts of assistance of a peripheral nature (fetching blankets and supporting the walking wounded) were not enough to make the plaintiff a rescuer.

Unwitting Agents of Misfortune

One type of case left unresolved by the House of Lords in *White* is that involving those who inadvertently, and through another's negligence, become the agent of another person's injury or reasonably believe that they are about to do so. The leading authority is *Dooley v Cammell Laird & Co Ltd* [1951] 1 Lloyd's Rep 271. The plaintiff, a crane operator in a dock-yard, suffered an aggravation of his pre-existing neurasthenia when the rope carrying his load suddenly broke as a result of the defendants' negligence and the load fell into the hold of the ship which he was loading. Although he could not see if the load had hit anybody—and nobody was in fact injured—he felt so wretched afterwards that he was unable to return to work as a crane operator. Donovan J ruled that he was entitled to damages. (See also *Galt v British Railways Board* (1983) 133 NLJ 870 and *Wigg v British Railways Board* (1986) 136 NLJ 446, both also mentioned in this context by Lord Oliver in *Alcock*.)

The above authorities were distinguished in *Hunter v British Coal* [1998] 2 All ER 97, which makes clear that even in these 'inadvertent agency' cases the requirement of proximity in time and space still applies. The plaintiff, a vehicle driver in a coal mine, accidentally struck a water hydrant whilst manoeuvring his vehicle, causing water to flow out. Unable to close up the hydrant valve, he went off in search of a hose-pipe to channel the escaping water safely away, leaving a fellow-employee, C, at the scene. When he was 30 metres away from the scene, the hydrant burst and he rushed to find a stop valve to shut the water off, which he managed to do after about 10 minutes. Whilst doing so, he heard a message over the tannoy that a man had been injured and, on his way back to the scene of the accident, he met a workmate who told him that it looked like C was dead. The plaintiff immediately thought that he was responsible and consequently suffered clinical depression, for which he sought damages. Although the accident occurred as a result of the defendants' negligence in failing to maintain the prescribed minimum vehicle clear-ances at the accident site, the Court of Appeal (Hobhouse LJ dissenting) held that the plaintiff was not entitled to damages as he had not been present at the scene at the time of the accident or come upon its aftermath; he had reacted only to what he was told. *Hunter* accordingly represents an attempt to limit the category of liability to unwitting agents of misfortune. (See also *Monk v PC Harrington Ltd* [2008] EWHC 1879 (QB), [2009] PIQR P3: no reasonable basis for claimant's belief that he was responsible for the accident.) Whether that category can be sustained at all must however be a matter of some doubt, especially in the light of the 'thus far and no further' approach of the House of Lords in *White*, though their Lordships subsequently declined to exclude the possibility of such claims when they were invited to do so in a later striking-out application (*W v Essex County Council* [2001] 2 AC 592).

IV. Stress

In *Alcock*, the House of Lords had emphasised the general requirement that psychiatric ill-ness should come about by shock. 'Psychiatric illness caused in other ways…,' said Lord Ackner, 'attracts no damages' (see [1992] 1 AC 310 at 400). His Lordship gave as examples depression arising from the experience of living without a loved one and stress-related ill-ness arising from the wayward conduct of a brain-damaged child or the strain of caring for an injured spouse (citing Brennan J in *Jaensch v Coffey* (1984) 155 CLR 549 at 569). In *Sion v Hampstead Health Authority* [1994] 5 Med LR 170, the Court of Appeal entertained an allegation of stress-related illness suffered by a father who had mounted a two-week-long vigil at the hospital bedside of his dying son. The court declined to hold the defendant health authority under a duty of care to the father as on the facts pleaded his illness had not been caused by a single shocking event (see also *Taylorson v Shieldness Produce Ltd* [1994] PIQR P329, but cf. *Walters v North Glamorgan NHS Trust* [2003] PIQR P16 where the Court of Appeal ruled that a 36-hour period beginning when the claimant's son suffered an epileptic fit and ending when he died in his mother's arms was a single horrifying event).

Lest it be thought that liability for stress is precluded altogether, however, it should be noted that Bingham LJ indicated in *Sion* that the requirement of a shock might not have applied to a claim by a patient, who could have been regarded as a 'primary victim' of the hospital's negligence. It seems best to avoid use of this problematic terminology in such cases, but it is nevertheless clear that a body of case law supports liability even for stress-related illness in a variety of contexts in which the defendant may be said to have assumed responsibility for the claimant's mental health.

Hatton v Sutherland [2002] EWCA Civ 76, [2002] 2 All ER 1

This was effectively a test case to determine the nature of the legal duty imposed on employers in respect of psychiatric illness through stress at work, and the circumstances in which a court may find that it was reasonably foreseeable to an employer that his employee might suffer such illness and that the employer was in breach of his duty. The Court of Appeal was faced with four conjoined appeals. The extract deals only with the general principles applicable to them and not with the individual cases.

Hale LJ

18. Several times while hearing these appeals we were invited to go back to first principles. Liability in negligence depends upon three inter-related requirements: the existence of a duty to take care; a failure to take the care which can reasonably be expected in the circumstances; and damage suffered as a result of that failure. These elements do not exist in separate compartments: the existence of the duty, for example, depends upon the type of harm suffered. Foreseeability of what might happen if care is not taken is relevant at each stage of the enquiry. Nevertheless, the traditional elements are always a useful tool of analysis, both in general and in particular cases.

Duty

19. The existence of a duty of care can be taken for granted. All employers have a duty to take reasonable care for the safety of their employees: to see that reasonable care is taken to provide them with a safe place of work, safe tools and equipment, and a safe system of working: see *Wilsons & Clyde Coal Co Ltd v English* [1938] AC 57. However, where psychiatric harm is suffered, the law distinguishes between primary and secondary victims. A primary victim is usually someone within the zone of foreseeable physical harm should the defendant fail to take reasonable care: see *Page v Smith* [1996] AC 155. A secondary victim is usually someone outside that zone: typically such a victim foreseeably suffers psychiatric harm through seeing, hearing or learning of physical harm tortiously inflicted upon others. There are additional control mechanisms to keep liability towards such people strictly within bounds: see *Alcock v Chief Constable of South Yorkshire Police* [1992] 1 AC 310. ...

20. In *Petch v Commissioners of Customs and Excise* [1993] 1 CR 789, CA, it was accepted that the ordinary principles of employers' liability applied to a claim for psychiatric illness arising from employment, although the claim failed. In the landmark case of *Walker v Northumberland County Council* [1995] 1 All ER 737, Colman J applied those same principles in upholding the claim. Both have recently been cited with approval in this Court in *Garrett v London Borough of Camden* [2001] EWCA Civ 395. Also in *White v Chief Constable of South Yorkshire Police* [1999] 2 AC 455, Lord Hoffmann stated, at p. 504, that

> The control mechanisms were plainly never intended to apply to all cases of psychiatric injury. They contemplate that the injury has been caused in consequence of death or injury suffered (or apprehended to have been suffered or as likely to be suffered) by someone else.

As to *Walker*, he commented, at p. 506, that:

> the employee was in no sense a secondary victim. His mental breakdown was caused by the strain of doing the work which his employer had required him to do.

21. In summary, therefore, claims for psychiatric injury fall into four different categories:

(1) tortious claims by primary victims: usually those within the foreseeable scope of physical injury, for example, the road accident victim in *Page v Smith* [1996] AC 155; some primary victims may not be at risk of physical harm, but at risk of foreseeable psychiatric harm because the circumstances are akin to those of primary victims in contract (see (3) below);

(2) tortious claims by secondary victims: those outside that zone who suffer as a result of harm to others, for example, the witnesses of the Hillsborough disaster in *Alcock v Chief Constable of South Yorkshire Police* [1992] 1 AC 310;

(3) contractual claims by primary victims: where the harm is the reasonably foreseeable product of specific breaches of a contractual duty of care towards a victim whose identity is known in advance, for example, the solicitors clients in *Cock v Swinfen* [1967] 1 WLR 457, CA, *McLoughlin v Grovers* [2001] EWCA Civ 1743, or the employees in *Petch v Commissioners of Customs and Excise* [1993] ICR 789, *Walker v Northumberland County Council* [1995] 1 All ER 737, *Garrett v London Borough of Camden* [2001] EWCA Civ 395, and in all the cases before us.

(4) contractual claims by secondary victims: where the harm is suffered as a result of harm to others, in the same way as secondary victims in tort, but there is also a contractual relationship with the defendant, as with the police officers in *White v Chief Constable of South Yorkshire Police* [1999] 2 AC 455.

22. There are, therefore, no special control mechanisms applying to claims for psychiatric (or physical) injury or illness arising from the stress of doing the work which the employee is required to do. But these claims do require particular care in determination, because they give rise to some difficult issues of foreseeability and causation and, we would add, identifying a relevant breach of duty.

Foreseeability

23. [T]he threshold question is whether this kind of harm to this particular employee was reasonably foreseeable. The question is not whether psychiatric injury is foreseeable in a person of ordinary fortitude. The employer's duty is owed to each individual employee, not to some as yet unidentified outsider: see *Paris v Stepney Borough Council* [1951] AC 367. The employer

knows who his employee is. It may be that he knows, as in *Paris*, or ought to know, of a particular vulnerability; but he may not. Because of the very nature of psychiatric disorder, as a sufficiently serious departure from normal or average psychological functioning to be labelled a disorder, it is bound to be harder to foresee than is physical injury. Shylock could not say of a mental disorder, If you prick us, do we not bleed? But it may be easier to foresee in a known individual than it is in the population at large . . .

24. However, are there some occupations which are so intrinsically stressful that resulting physical or psychological harm is always foreseeable? Mr Lewis [for one of the defendants] appeared to accept that this was so: he gave the examples of traffic police officers who regularly deal with gruesome accidents or child protection officers who regularly investigate unthinkable allegations of child abuse. . . . The notion that some occupations are in themselves dangerous to mental health is not borne out by the literature . . . : it is not the job but the interaction between the individual and the job which causes the harm. Stress is a subjective concept: the individual's perception that the pressures placed upon him are greater than he may be able to meet. Adverse reactions to stress are equally individual, ranging from minor physical symptoms to major mental illness.

25. All of this points to there being a single test: whether a harmful reaction to the pressures of the workplace is reasonably foreseeable in the individual employee concerned. Such a reaction will have two components: (1) an injury to health; which (2) is attributable to stress at work. The answer to the foreseeability question will therefore depend upon the inter-relationship between the particular characteristics of the employee concerned and the particular demands which the employer casts upon him. As was said in *McLoughlin v Grovers* [2001] EWCA Civ 1743, expert evidence may be helpful although it can never be determinative of what a reasonable employer should have foreseen. A number of factors are likely to be relevant.

26. These include the nature and extent of the work being done by the employee. Employers should be more alert to picking up signs from an employee who is being over-worked in an intellectually or emotionally demanding job than from an employee whose workload is no more than normal for the job or whose job is not particularly demanding for him or her. It will be easier to conclude that harm is foreseeable if the employer is putting pressure upon the individual employee which is in all the circumstances of the case unreasonable. Also relevant is whether there are signs that others doing the same work are under harmful levels of stress. There may be others who have already suffered injury to their health arising from their work. Or there may be an abnormal level of sickness and absence amongst others at the same grade or in the same department. But if there is no evidence of this, then the focus must turn to the individual.

27. More important are the signs from the employee himself. Here again, it is important to distinguish between signs of stress and signs of impending harm to health. Stress is merely the mechanism which may but usually does not lead to damage to health. *Walker* is an obvious illustration: Mr Walker was a highly conscientious and seriously overworked manager of a social work area office with a heavy and emotionally demanding case load of child abuse cases. Yet although he complained and asked for help and for extra leave, the judge held that his first mental breakdown was not foreseeable. There was, however, liability when he returned to work with a promise of extra help which did not materialise and experienced a second breakdown only a few months later. If the employee or his doctor makes it plain that unless something is done to help there is a clear risk of a breakdown in mental or physical health, then the employer will have to think what can be done about it.

28. Harm to health may sometimes be foreseeable without such an express warning. Factors to take into account would be frequent or prolonged absences from work which are

uncharacteristic for the person concerned; these could be for physical or psychological complaints; but there must also be good reason to think that the underlying cause is occupational stress rather than other factors; this could arise from the nature of the employee's work or from complaints made about it by the employee or from warnings given by the employee or others around him.

29. But when considering what the reasonable employer should make of the information which is available to him, from whatever source, what assumptions is he entitled to make about his employee and to what extent is he bound to probe further into what he is told? Unless he knows of some particular problem or vulnerability, an employer is usually entitled to assume that his employee is up to the normal pressures of the job. It is only if there is something specific about the job or the employee or the combination of the two that he has to think harder. But thinking harder does not necessarily mean that he has to make searching or intrusive enquiries. Generally he is entitled to take what he is told by or on behalf of the employee at face value. . . .

31. These then are the questions and the possible indications that harm was foreseeable in a particular case. But how strong should those indications be before the employer has a duty to act? Mr Hogarth [for one of the defendants] argued that only clear and unequivocal signs of an impending breakdown should suffice. That may be putting it too high. But in view of the many difficulties of knowing when and why a particular person will go over the edge from pressure to stress and from stress to injury to health, the indications must be plain enough for any reasonable employer to realise that he should do something about it.

COMMENTARY

One of the claimants successfully appealed to the House of Lords (*Barber v Somerset County Council* [2004] 1 WLR 1089), but the Law Lords unanimously approved the statements of legal principle and practical guidance in Hale LJ's judgment. A note of caution was struck by Lord Walker, however. He noted, at [65], that the judgment should not be read 'as having anything like statutory force', and stated: 'Every case will depend on its own facts'. The point is further made out by *Daw v Intel Incorporation (UK) Ltd* [2007] EWCA Civ 70, where the defendant employer sought to rely on their provision of a counselling service and medical assistance as discharging their duty of care, relying upon Hale LJ's statement ([2002] 2 All ER 1 at [43] (not in the extract)) that '[a]n employer who offers a confidential advice service, with referral to appropriate counselling or treatment services, is unlikely to be found in breach of duty'. The Court of Appeal reached a different conclusion on the facts, noting that the indications of impending breakdown made it plain that immediate management action was required. Pill LJ commented, at [45]: 'The reference to counselling services in *Hatton* does not make such services a panacea by which employers can discharge their duty of care in all cases.' (See also *Dickins v O2 plc* [2008] EWCA Civ 1144, [2009] IRLR 58, where *Daw* was applied.)

It had been accepted before *Hatton* that employers might owe a duty to take reasonable care to guard their employees from stress-related mental illness (see, e.g., *Petch v Commissioners of Customs and Excise* [1993] ICR 789; the first case to impose liability was *Walker v Northumberland County Council* [1995] 1 All ER 737, noted by Nolan (1995) 24 ILJ 280). One ambiguity about the present decision is whether the duty of care arises in all cases ('[t]he existence of a duty of care can be taken for granted': at [19]) or only exceptionally. The latter is suggested by Hale LJ's 'threshold question', at [23], of whether harm to the particular employee was reasonably foreseeable. The alternative interpretation is that the threshold question relates to the question of breach of duty: what Hale LJ is in effect saying is that the employer need normally take no special steps to fulfil his duty of care unless he knows of a risk to a particular employee. Whichever analysis is employed is unlikely to affect the outcome. What is more significant is the steep 'foreseeability' hurdle *Hatton* places in the way of an employee claiming for stress-related illness. The decision effectively insulates the employer from liability in the quite typical case where the employee will not admit to experiencing stress for fear of appearing unable to cope (*Pratley v Surrey County Council* [2004] ICR 159). Nevertheless, if stress-induced illness is foreseeable—for example, because of a previous breakdown—it is not necessarily contributory negligence for the employee not to voice his concerns that the job may again be becoming too much for him (*Young v Post Office* [2002] IRLR 660).

The decision leaves the law of employers' liability in a rather complicated state. Three situations must now be distinguished, according to whether the claimant's psychiatric injury results from (1) occupational stress (the employer owes a duty of care if the injury was foreseeable: *Hatton*), (2) shock from witnessing injury or death to another person (no duty of care in the absence of a close tie of love and affection: *White*), or (3) the foreseeable risk of physical harm (the claimant is a primary victim). The latter category is confirmed by *Donachie v Chief Constable of Greater Manchester* (2004) 148 SJLB 509 where, in the course of a dangerous covert operation, the claimant police officer was required to fix a tagging device to the underside of a suspect's car. Because the batteries were faulty, he had to make a total of nine trips to the vehicle before the device functioned, and he feared each time that he might be discovered and physically attacked. His stress resulted in clinical psychiatric injury. The Court of Appeal found that he was a primary victim because there had been a reasonable foreseeability of physical injury.

Melville v Home Office, sub nom. Hartman v South Essex Mental Health NHS Trust [2005] ICR 782 blurred the already fine line between the different categories. The claimant, a health care officer at the defendant's prison, was required as part of his duties to recover the bodies of prisoners who had committed suicide. In 17 years, he attended eight suicides. After the last of these—when he had helped cut down the body, remove a ligature and attempt a revival—he developed a stress-related illness. The trial judge found that psychiatric injury was reasonably foreseeable in the circumstances, and the Court of Appeal ruled that this was sufficient to establish a duty of care. It was immaterial that the stress was caused by a traumatic episode or episodes rather than day-to-day work. In effect, the Court of Appeal seems to have extended category (1), above, beyond cases of stress to cases of shock and so relieved the claimant employee of the requirement of proving a close tie of love and affection with the dead prisoners. If this is consistent with *White* (which remains to be seen), it can only be on the basis that the alleged breach of duty related not to the suicides in themselves but the failure to provide the claimant with counselling and other support after they had occurred. (Cf. *Leach v Chief Constable of Gloucestershire* [1999] 1 WLR 1421.)

Amongst the other anomalies to be found in this area are that an employer owes no duty of care for an employee's mental health in respect of the manner of the latter's dismissal from employment, as the jurisdiction of the employment tribunals in such matters is intended to be exclusive (*Johnson v Unisys Ltd* [2003] 1 AC 518). The duty may, however, arise in respect of disciplinary action short of dismissal (e.g. suspension: *Gogay v Hertfordshire County Council* [2000] IRLR 703) even where it leads ultimately to dismissal (*Eastwood v Magnox Electric plc* [2005] 1 AC 503). In the last-mentioned case, at [33], Lord Nicholls described the resulting distinctions as 'awkward and unfortunate' and recommended urgent legislative attention.

Relevance of Obligations under the Contract of Employment

If the employee has, under the contract of employment, undertaken an agreed amount of work, can the employer nonetheless breach the duty owed by requiring the employee to undertake that work? The issue did not arise directly in *Barber v Somerset County Council* [2004] 1 WLR 1089 but Lord Rodger observed, at [34]:

The contract of employment will usually regulate what is to happen if an employee becomes unable, due to illness or injury, to carry out his duties. There may be provision for a defined period on full pay, followed by a further defined period on reduced pay, followed by termination of the contract. At the end of the process the employer is free to make new arrangements...Whatever the position, however, the introduction of a tortious duty of reasonable care on the employer to provide assistance so that the employee can return to work and draw his normal pay, but do less than his full duties for an indefinite period, does not sit easily with such contractual arrangements. Nor does it seem likely to promote efficiency within the enterprise or department.

See also *Koehler v Cerebos (Australia) Ltd* (2005) 222 CLR 44, another case of occupational stress, where a majority of the High Court of Australia stated (obiter) at [29]: 'Insistence upon performance of a contract cannot be in breach of a duty of care.' For comment, see Lunney (2005) 2 UNELJ 75.

A Wider Principle of Assumption of Responsibility?

A number of commentators have proposed a principle of assumed responsibility as a means of rationalising the occupational stress cases and other cases falling outside the established categories of primary (narrowly defined) and secondary victims (see, e.g. *Markesinis & Deakin*, pp. 152–5). Such a principle would apply not only in the employment sphere, but also to other contractual relationships and even to non-contractual assumptions of responsibility. The claimant in such a case need not show either that he was physically imperilled or that he was proximate in time and space to a directly-perceived accident involving a 'primary victim' with whom he had close ties of love and affection; indeed there need not be any primary victim at all, in the narrow sense of the term. Many of the cases concern the doctor–patient relationship. A typical scenario is where a mother gives birth to a physically or mentally disabled baby as a consequence of negligence in her ante-natal care, and suffers psychiatric illness as a result of finding out the child's condition. The hospital undoubtedly owes a duty of care in treating the mother and can be held liable to her for both the physical and the psychiatric consequences of its negligent treatment. It is not necessary to show that the mother directly perceived her child's disability at the time of his delivery (*Farrell v Merton, Sutton and Wandsworth Health Authority* (2001) 57 BMLR 158). Whether a duty is also owed to the father of the child in such circumstances is open to more doubt (cf. *Sion v Hampstead Health Authority* [1994] 5 Med LR 170: no duty to father mounting vigil at dying child's bedside). Presumably, however, the duty to mother and (perhaps) father extends only to the immediate consequences of the treatment, and does not allow recovery for psychiatric illness suffered through the stress of caring for the disabled child. Query whether the recognition of a duty in the circumstances of *AB v Tameside & Glossop Health Authority* [1997] 8 Med LR 91 and *Allin v City & Hackney Health Authority*, both noted above, p. 349f, might be warranted on the basis of the defendant's assumption of responsibility for its patient's mental health. (But is it right that a mother should be able to claim damages from a doctor who negligently and inaccurately reports the death of her baby during childbirth, but not from a police officer guilty of the same error in reporting the baby's death in a car accident? See Jones (1997) 13 PN 111 at 113; Mullany (1998) 114 LQR 380 at 383.)

The doctrine of assumption of responsibility may also account for the duty owed by a school to protect its pupils from bullying (*Bradford-Smart v West Sussex County Council* [2002] EWCA Civ 7: no breach on the facts) and the like duty owed by employers to their employees (*Waters v Commissioner of Police of the Metropolis* [2000] 1 WLR 1607). Where a firm of solicitors undertakes a client's defence in criminal proceedings, it also appears to assume responsibility for his mental health and can (arguably) be held liable for psychiatric harm suffered after the firm's negligence results in his wrongful conviction (*McLoughlin v Grovers (A Firm)* [2001] EWCA Civ 1743). Another possible application of the principle is *Al-Kandari v J. R. Brown & Co* [1988] QB 665, where the defendant solicitors were held liable for the plaintiff's psychiatric illness resulting from (*inter alia*) the abduction of her children to Kuwait by her husband, the defendants' client. The defendants, who were representing the husband in custody proceedings, assumed responsibility to the plaintiff by agreeing to safeguard the husband's passport with a view to preventing precisely the events that occurred, but they negligently failed to do so. (This aspect of the case is brought out more clearly in the report of the first instance judgment: see [1987] QB 514.) The arguable duty owed by a local authority social services department to the foster family with whom it places a child in its care may also best be regarded as flowing from the former's assumption of responsibility to the latter (*W v Essex County Council* [2001] 2 AC 592, discussed p. 369, above).

In *Attia v British Gas* [1988] QB 304, the Court of Appeal accepted that a gas supplier might arguably owe a duty of care in respect of psychiatric injury suffered by a woman coming home to find that gas board employees, whilst attempting to install central heating, had caused an explosion and set the building on fire. This otherwise problematic decision might also be rationalised on the basis of the supplier's assumption of responsibility to the plaintiff in agreeing to carry out work on her home. (For an analysis of problems raised by the court's attempt to base the decision on principles of remoteness, see *Jones*, p. 173.)

Do you think it could be argued that an employer assumes a duty to avoid causing its employees psychiatric illness by exposing them to shocking events?

Stress-Related Illness Caused by the Fear of Developing Physical Illness

A separate category of cases—or perhaps a sub-category of the above—is where the claimant suffers a stress-related illness as a result of the fear of developing a physical illness, having been placed at risk of the latter by the defendant's negligence. In *Aston v Imperial Chemical Industries Group* (unreported, 21 May 1992; noted by Law Commission, p. 27 n. 124), Rose J awarded damages in respect of a depressive illness suffered by the plaintiff as a result of anxiety that exposure to carcinogenic fumes in his workplace might cause angiosarcoma of the liver, a usually fatal condition with a latency period of about 15 years.

Subsequently, in *Re Creutzfeldt-Jakob Disease Litigation* [1998] 41 BMLR 157, Morland J held that a group of plaintiffs who, being handicapped by dwarfism had been treated as children with the growth hormone HGH, were owed a duty of care by the Department of Health in respect of psychiatric illness caused by their becoming aware that their treatment was capable of infecting them with Creutzfeldt-Jacob Disease and hence that an unknown number of them might be incubating the disease. In a preliminary hearing on various points of law, his Lordship ruled that the plaintiffs could not be treated as primary victims in the *Page v Smith* sense (see Section III, above)—they feared not immediate physical injury but rather that at some time in the future they would be struck down by a ghastly, untreatable, terminal illness which would attack their brains—and that to treat them as such would in any case be contrary to public policy because it would open up a possibly huge number of claims arising out of the exposure of individuals to toxic substances such as asbestos or radioactive materials; this would make insurance difficult or impossible for producers, prescribers, and suppliers of such products and could inhibit them from warning members of the public of the danger to them. But Morland J was able to find a duty of care on the alternative, and narrower, basis that the relationship between the defendant and the recipients of HGH was one of close proximity, akin to that of doctor and patient. Subsequently, six members of the plaintiff group succeeded in recovering damages from the Health Department (*Andrews v Secretary of State for Health*, unreported, 19 June 1998).

In *Grieves v FT Everard & Sons Ltd* [2008] 1 AC 281, noted p. 356f above, the House of Lords agreed with Morland J's view that *Page v Smith* did not apply to cases of anxiety at possible future injury. *Grieves* was a case of clinical depression resulting from the claimant's fear, on discovering that he had asbestos fibres in his lungs, that he might in future develop a life-threatening or fatal disease. He brought an action for damages against his previous employers, who had negligently exposed him to the asbestos. The House of Lords explicitly followed the approach to employers' liability established by Hale LJ in *Hatton v Sutherland*, above. Though her judgment was concerned with occupational stress, it applied to any psychiatric injury caused by the employer's breach of duty. The threshold question was whether psychiatric injury was reasonably foreseeable in the particular employee. On the facts, the defendant employers were unlikely to have had specific knowledge of how the claimant might react to his discovery, long after he had left their employment, that he was at risk from asbestos-related disease. They were therefore entitled to assume that he was a person of ordinary fortitude, and there was no evidence from which it could be concluded that such a person might reasonably foreseeably suffer psychiatric injury in consequence of their negligence. The action therefore failed.

The Law Lords distinguished the *Creutzfeldt-Jakob Disease* case as Morland J there made a factual finding that the claimant's psychiatric injury was reasonably foreseeable in the circumstances. *Grieves v Everard* should not therefore be understood as ruling out liability altogether in 'fear of the future' cases, but only as an application on particular facts of the ordinary requirement of reasonable foreseeability of psychiatric injury. Nevertheless, it seems likely that the considerations that made the psychiatric injury unforeseeable in *Grieves* will also be present in the majority of cases, and successful claims will therefore be rare.

v. Evaluation and Reform

1. Criticisms of the Current Law

It is apparent from the earlier parts of this chapter that the English law of liability for psychiatric illness has attracted severe criticism. Almost everyone is agreed that the current state of the law is unsatisfactory. This, according to Stapleton, is the area of the law of tort where the 'silliest' rules now prevail (*op. cit.*, p. 95). Todd too finds that the law is 'in a dreadful mess' ((1999) 115 LQR 345 at 349). And for Jones, the result in practice is 'a long list of anomalies' ((1997) 13 PN 111 at 113). Even the judiciary has conceded that—as Lord Hoffmann put it in *White*—'the search for principle' in this area of the law has been 'called off'. The House of Lords in that case viewed the law as so far beyond judicial repair that the only sensible maxim to adopt was—in Lord Steyn's words—'thus far and no further' (p. 500):

> My Lords, the law on the recovery of compensation for pure psychiatric harm is a patchwork quilt of distinctions which are difficult to justify. There are two theoretical solutions. The first is to wipe out recovery in tort for pure psychiatric injury. . . . But that would be contrary to precedent and, in any event, highly controversial. Only Parliament could take such a step. The second solution is to abolish all the special limiting rules applicable to psychiatric harm. . . . Precedent rules out this course and, in any event, there are cogent policy considerations against such a bold innovation. In my view the only sensible general strategy for the courts is to say thus far and no further. The only prudent course is to treat the pragmatic categories as reflected in authoritative decisions such as *Alcock* and *Page v Smith* as settled for the time being but by and large to leave any expansion or development in this corner of the law to Parliament. In reality there are no refined analytical tools which will enable the courts to draw lines by way of compromise solution in a way which is coherent and morally defensible. It must be left to Parliament to undertake the task of radical law reform.

Some may wonder whether this is not rather a pusillanimous response given that it was the House of Lords itself that was primarily responsible for the mess it now finds itself in.

Many of the above criticisms are directed at the practicality and consistency of the legal principles in question, but there is also a significant debate as to whether the law should continue to attempt a balance between a limited right to recover damages in respect of psychiatric illness and the fear of opening the floodgates of liability. This effectively was the approach advocated by the Law Commission, whose reform proposals are set out in Sub-section (2), below. The Law Commission's approach should be contrasted with that of Mullany and Handford, on the one hand, and Stapleton, on the other, who take more extreme and opposing approaches to liability for psychiatric illness (see immediately below). All these analyses can be fruitfully read in the light of the more fundamental critique of the law advanced by two American feminist writers, also extracted in this Section.

P. Handford, *Mullany & Handford's Tort Liability for Psychiatric Damage*, 2nd edn. (Ryde, NSW: Law Book Co, 2006), paras 30.40 and 30.60

[T]he fact that an injury cannot always be seen by the naked eye does not mean that it is any less of a 'real' injury than those which involve the breaking of bones, the spilling of blood, the scarring of tissue or 'physical' pain. Indeed, on one view, the mental repercussions of trauma are more serious, more deserving of the law's attention than those of a physical nature. Mental conditions frequently persist long after organic injuries have disappeared. Broken bones knit, wounds heal often without scarring or permanent disability and those that do scar, although unsightly, leave less of a mark than scars on the mind. Physical pain usually subsides and often long before the psychological impact of distressing events disappears. The after-effects of trauma may never fully dissipate and may remain to haunt a person for the remainder of his or her life, forever eroding mental stability. . . . [A]s a general observation, an injured mind is far more difficult to nurse back to health than an injured body and is arguably more debilitating and disruptive of a greater number of aspects of human existence . . .

Wherever the consequences of a wrong call for redress it is incumbent upon the courts to create precedent irrespective of the by-product of increased litigation. Tortfeasors must be made to take full responsibility for their actions or inactions including full liability for all kinds of loss caused by their substandard conduct. Negligently caused trauma-induced psychiatric damage is not an independent intervening cause but flows in uninterrupted sequence from the defendant's lack of care and is a harm for which his or her responsibility to provide recompense does not diminish because of a potential frequency of occurrence. It is open to serious question, however, whether further liberalising of the law governing recovery for mental damage would in fact lead to the predicted increase in suits.

COMMENTARY

The authors contend that liability for psychiatric harm should be treated in the same way as physical injury, and the proximity requirements used to limit liability in this area should be abandoned. In most cases, the reasonable foreseeability of psychiatric illness should be enough to give rise to a duty of care, a position which the authors contend would not lead to a flood of litigation because the requirement that the illness be reasonably foreseeable is 'a considerable hurdle to surmount in itself' (para. 30.70). In the first edition of their book (1993) and in a number of subsequent commentaries, the authors together and separately subjected decisions in this area to strenuous and sustained criticism from this perspective (see, e.g. (1997) 113 LQR 410; (1998) 114 LQR 380; (1999) 115 LQR 30).

A similar approach is to be found in H. Teff, *Causing Psychiatric and Emotional Harm: Reshaping the Boundaries of Legal Liability* (Oxford: Hart, 2009). Amongst judicial approaches, the most similar to that of Mullany and Handford is to be found in Lord Bridge's speech in *McLoughlin v O'Brian*, extracted above. It should be noted that this can no longer be regarded as an authoritative statement of the law in this jurisdiction.

J. Stapleton, 'In Restraint of Tort', in P. Birks (ed.), *The Frontiers of Liability*, vol. 2 (Oxford: OUP, 1994)

[A]ppellate courts suspect, and with reason it seems to me, that once a general duty to avoid nervous shock was recognised, many more individuals would be recognised as presenting the relevant symptoms to their GPs. Recovery from grief is a complex and mysterious process. May it not be a major concern of judges that while the prospect of compensation for, say, a broken leg may inhibit recuperation to a minor degree, the prospect of compensation for grief would have a much more powerful disincentive to rehabilitation and one which medical evidence would find extremely difficult to unravel from the original condition? If a central factor in grief and depression is anger, might not the adversarial nature of legal process be especially counter-productive? Associated with this concern is the very real one of characterising the relevant actionable damage. We are told that pathological grief is compensatable... but not normal grief. Leaving aside the perplexing question of why this is so, we are still confronted by the possibility that with hindsight and in the context of a civil claim, medical opinion may define 'pathological' grief much more loosely than the law would find tolerable. After all, the boundary between normal and pathological grief is of virtually no significance for medical treatment.

So the concerns about recovery for nervous shock are real, but the available techniques for controlling it are not only artificial but bring the law into disrepute. That at present claims can turn on the requirement of 'close ties of love and affection' is guaranteed to produce outrage. Is it not a disreputable sight to see brothers of Hillsborough victims turned away because they had no more than brotherly love towards the victims?...

Some US jurisdictions who had once recognised a tort relating to privacy have now abolished it because it was felt that no reasonable boundaries for the cause of action could be found, and this was an embarrassment to the law. Should not our courts wipe out recovery for pure nervous shock on the same basis?

COMMENTARY

Stapleton's approach is an extreme one, and perhaps deliberately provocative. It is not easy to find commentators prepared to go quite as far as she does. But similar concerns that liability for psychiatric illness may have been treated too expansively are evident, for example in Atiyah, *The Damages Lottery* (Oxford: Hart, 1997), pp. 56–62.

The Law Commission noted in its subsequent report on *Liability for Psychiatric Illness* (extracted below) that 'medical and legal experts in the field... have impressed upon us how life-shattering psychiatric illness can be and how, in many instances, it can be more debilitating than physical injuries' (para. 1.9). Do you think Stapleton's approach gives adequate consideration to such evidence?

M. Chamallas with L. K. Kerber, 'Women, Mothers and the Law of Fright: A History' (1990) 88 Mich L Rev 814, p. 814

The law of torts values physical security and property more highly than emotional security and human relationships. This apparently gender-neutral hierarchy of values has privileged men, as the traditional owners and managers of property, and has burdened women, to whom the emotional work of maintaining human relationship has commonly been assigned. The law has often failed to compensate women for recurring harms—serious though they may be in the lives of women—for which there is no precise masculine analogue. This phenomenon is evident in the history of tort law's treatment of fright-based physical injuries, a type of claim historically brought more often by female plaintiffs. There are two paradigm cases of fright-based physical injury: the pregnant plaintiff who suffers a miscarriage or stillbirth as a result of being frightened and the mother who suffers nervous shock when she witnesses her child's injury or death. These claims were classified in the law as emotional harms and a number of special doctrinal obstacles were created to contain recovery in such cases.

COMMENTARY

The cases considered in this chapter show that emotional harm—at least in the modern law—cannot be regarded as a condition which affects women alone. But there is a strong argument that considerations of gender do indeed, as Chamallas and Kerber suggest, provide a historical explanation for the slow and reluctant recognition of psychiatric illness as worthy of compensation. The way such gender considerations operate is a complex matter, and a number of different views are possible, but one plausible account is that the typical domestic situation of women once made them especially prone to psychiatric illness, which was therefore regarded as a 'feminine' condition in contrast with the 'masculine' virtues of courage and fortitude which it was thought to undermine. Hence arose a tendency to regard psychiatric illness as arising from the victim's pre-existing susceptibility (see esp. *Bourhill v Young*, extracted above, p. 129). Other traces of stereotypical male attitudes towards women may also be evident in fears that those claiming in respect of psychiatric illness might be prone to exaggerate or to lie about their condition. And even the requirements for a successful psychiatric illness claim may be analysed in gender terms, for example the general requirement of a 'shock' which, by focusing upon a single causative event outside normal human experience, precludes consideration of the stresses and frustrations that are common to many women's experience of workplace and domestic environments.

2. Proposals for Reform

Liability for psychiatric illness arises in England exclusively as a matter of common law, but—as has been noted—there are growing calls for legislative reform. Whether reform of this nature, or indeed any reform at all, should be made to English law in this area was considered by the Law Commission, which examined the question of liability for psychiatric illness as part of its examination of the damages remedy undertaken with particular reference to personal injury litigation under its recent programmes of law reform (see Law Com. No. 234 (1995) and Law Com. No. 259 (1999)).

Law Commission, *Liability for Psychiatric Illness*, Report No. 249 (1998)

[After a lengthy consultation process and a thorough consideration of the question of liability for psychiatric illness, the Law Commission confined its proposals to the secondary victim scenario, as it was prepared to leave the law in other categories of case to be further developed by the courts as and when deemed necessary. It summarised its basic recommendation as follows:]

> We recommend that, where it is reasonably foreseeable that such a plaintiff might suffer psychiatric illness, the plaintiff's proximity to the scene of the 'accident', and the manner by which he or she learns of it, should not be used as criteria to restrict the claim. In addition, we make two recommendations that are of general application to psychiatric illness claims. First, the requirement that the psychiatric illness be induced by a shock should be abandoned. And secondly, where the plaintiff's psychiatric illness is suffered as a result of another person's death, injury or imperilment, it should not be an absolute bar to recovery that that person is the defendant him or herself.

[The factors which the Commission felt justified this approach to liability for psychiatric illness are considered in the extracts, below.]

After much deliberation, we . . . remain persuaded that at this point in time . . . the 'floodgates argument' . . . requires special policy limitations to be imposed over and above the test of reasonable foreseeability. In particular, we are concerned that the dividing line between what level of mental disturbance does and does not amount to a psychiatric illness is a matter of degree not kind and that the concept of psychiatric illness has widened significantly over the past few years. Our review of the relevant medical literature has led us to believe that the adoption of a simple foreseeability test would or could result in a significant increase in the number of claims which, at least at this point in time, would be unacceptable. This in turn might lead the courts to make use of policy considerations, concealed beneath the foreseeability test, in an attempt to restrict the number of successful claims. Such confusion could only result in an increased volume of litigation. While we accept that it is difficult to be sure that a move to a pure reasonable foreseeability test would open the floodgates of litigation, we believe that there is at least a significant risk of that consequence. It would be imprudent to take that risk when we can leave the courts free to develop the common law in the light of the effects of our more limited reforms. . . . Accordingly, we recommend that . . . special limitations over and above reasonable foreseeability should continue to be applied to claims for psychiatric illness where the defendant has injured or imperilled someone other than the plaintiff, and the plaintiff, as a result, has suffered psychiatric illness.

Having reached the conclusion that there should be special limitations over and above reasonable foreseeability, we need to consider whether all three *Alcock* proximity requirements need be maintained, and if not, whether the restrictions should focus on the relationship between the immediate victim and the plaintiff, or on the plaintiff's closeness to and means of perception of the accident. We believe that the imposition of all three proximity requirements is unduly restrictive, and that it is the last two limitations that have resulted in the most arbitrary decisions. How many hours after the accident the mother of an injured child manages to reach the hospital should not be the decisive factor in deciding whether the defendant may be liable for the mother's consequential psychiatric illness. We consider that so long as special control mechanisms over and above foreseeability are required in order to limit the potential number of claimants, the most acceptable method of achieving this is to restrict the claimants by reference to their connection with the immediate victim. Provided that the requirement for a close tie of love and affection between the plaintiff and the immediate victim is retained, the main floodgates objection of the possibility of many claims arising from a single event is limited. Furthermore, the advice we received from medical consultees supports the view that where there is a close tie of love and affection between the plaintiff and the immediate victim, the plaintiff's proximity to the accident or its aftermath is not always a relevant factor in determining his or her reaction to it.

COMMENTARY

The Commission explained its view of the 'floodgates' argument, which it regarded as the most convincing justification for a restrictive approach to liability for psychiatric illness (pp. 83–4, fn. 9):

The 'floodgates' argument may itself be subdivided into two distinct concerns: (i) the fear of a proliferation of claims from a single event (probably the argument's central force) and (ii) the possibility of
a mass of claims from a mass of separate events. Both possibilities give rise to the concern that such
a proliferation of claims would clog the court system and divert too many of society's resources into
compensating the victims of psychiatric illness at the expense of other equally or more deserving
plaintiffs. If the system fails to cope, the law will fall into disrepute and this would be a disservice to
those few who most deserve legal support. In addition, the first possibility raises objections that to
allow a mass of claims from a single event would place an undue burden on the defendant disproportionate to the negligent conduct.

Notwithstanding the fears expressed in this paragraph, the Law Commission was content to recommend a limited expansion in liability for psychiatric illness (as indicated in the extract above) even while accepting that this would lead to an increase in the number and total burden of personal injury claims. It speculated that, in relation to motor vehicle accidents, 'a reasonable assumption seems to be that our proposals would give rise to a 10 per cent increase in the number of personal injury claims' (para. 1.12), and that 'it is reasonable to estimate that our proposals would give rise to an increase in motor insurance premiums in the range of two to five per cent' (para. 1.13). Furthermore, the Commission conceded that the rise in other sectors of the insurance market, for example employers' liability, was likely to be higher (para. 1.13, fn. 37). Do you think that the public is willing to pay extra for its motor vehicle insurance, and extra also for products which are increased in price as a result of higher employers' liability insurance premiums, just in order to finance an increase in the scope of tort liability for psychiatric illness? (Would *you* be willing to pay extra?)

A few of the more specific recommendations made by the Law Commission should also be briefly considered.

(i) The Commission proposed that legislation should initially draw the line at cases where the loved one has in fact been killed, injured or imperilled by the defendant, and should not extend it to a case where the plaintiff reasonably believes that the loved one has been imperilled, etc. (para. 6.18). Would such a case give rise to liability at common law?

(ii) The Commission endorsed the idea of laying down by statute a fixed list of relationships of love and affection (including stable homosexual relationships), though without prej-
udice to the courts' ability to recognise that other relationships satisfied this requirement on the facts of individual cases (para. 6.26). What would be the advantages of a statutory list of this nature?

(iii) Although the Commission did not feel able to extend liability under its proposed legislation to include bystanders, it did not wish 'to be construed as impeding the judicial devel-
opment of liability to bystanders' (para. 7.15). How liability could be extended to bystanders without adopting the rejected criterion of reasonable foreseeability of psychiatric illness is not easy to see.

(iv) The Commission recommended that the requirement that the psychiatric illness be shock-induced be abandoned (para. 5.33). This would mean that a relative who suffers a psychiatric illness as a result of nursing the victim of an accident would be able to claim against the negligent tortfeasor. How this proposal would alter the law relating to stress-induced psychiatric illness more generally is not considered and is hard to predict.

Do you think that these changes would result in (1) a more coherent, and (2) a fairer approach to the recovery of damages for negligently inflicted psychiatric damage?

In May 2007, the government provisionally rejected the Law Commission's reform proposals in a Department of Constitutional Affairs (DCA) consultation paper, *The Law on Damages* (CP 9/07), considering it preferable to allow the courts to continue to develop the law in this area. In the government's view, the courts had interpreted the *Alcock* requirements 'in a flexible and sensitive way' (para. 89). Noting that medical knowledge of psychiatric illness was still developing, the consultation paper stated (*ibid.*):

It is difficult at this stage to see how legislation could successfully assimilate the differing perspectives and arguments in this complex area into a simple and coherent system which would improve upon the current principles established by the courts, without running the risk of imposing rigid requirements which are not readily able to accommodate developments in medical knowledge and jurisprudence, and without opening the way to speculative and inappropriate claims.

The consultation paper dismissed the Law Commission's idea of a statutory list of close relationships, which might allow undesirable claims by long-separated spouses or brothers and sisters who have lost touch. By implication, it also rejected the Law Commission's recommendation that proximity in time and space and proximity of perception should be abandoned as preconditions of liability to secondary victims. Relying exclusively on a test of close relationship would expand the class of potential claimants and lead to a significant increase in insurance premiums. For similar reasons, the consultation paper affirmed the law's existing requirement of shock, finding also that this serves a useful purpose in ensuring the causation test is met: 'Without shock the evidential complexities of the case increase and investigating it becomes more costly. It would be more difficult to establish whether the claimant's illness was directly caused by the act or omission in question, and not by some other intervening event' (para. 90). Another advantage of the shock requirement was that it offered closure to the negligent party by guarding against claims arising long after the event.

By contrast, in *Tame v New South Wales* (2002) 211 CLR 317, a majority of the High Court of Australia rejected the *Alcock* 'control mechanisms', and the distinction between primary and secondary victims, and adopted instead a simple test of reasonable foreseeability: ought the defendant to have foreseen that his conduct might result in psychiatric harm to the plaintiff? Whether *physical* injury was reasonably foreseeable was a quite separate matter, of no relevance to a claim for psychiatric injury. Applying the test of reasonable foreseeability might involve consideration of factors to which English law attached legal significance, e.g. the plaintiff's abnormal sensitivity and his closeness in time and space to an immediately traumatic event. But neither normal fortitude nor direct perception of a shocking event, or its immediate aftermath, was to be regarded as critical to the recognition of a duty of care under Australian law. Rigid restrictions of that nature 'operated in an arbitrary and capricious manner' and 'bring the law into disrepute' (at [190], per Gummow and Kirby JJ).

For comment on *Tame*, see Trindade (2003) 119 LQR 204. Note, however, that recovery for negligently inflicted psychiatric injury in most Australian jurisdictions is now governed by legislation (see, e.g., Civil Liability Act 2002 (NSW) Part 3). For comparison, see *van Soest v*

Residual Health Management Unit [2000] 1 NZLR 179, where the New Zealand Court of Appeal adopted the English approach.

Compare the government's general satisfaction with the approach taken by the English courts with the views expressed by the courts themselves (e.g. in *White v Chief Constable of S. Yorks*, above). Do *you* think the approach of the English courts has been satisfactory? If not, whose responsibility do you think it should be to develop the law? (Cf. Lord Steyn's 'thus far and no further approach' in *White*, expressly followed in *Rothwell v Chemical & Insulating Co Ltd* [2008] 1 AC 281 at [54] per Lord Hope and [95] per Lord Rodger.)

8 NEGLIGENCE: DUTY OF CARE— ECONOMIC LOSS

I. The Basic Exclusionary Rule

1. Introduction

According to Lord Oliver in *Murphy v Brentwood District Council* [1991] 1 AC 398 at 487, '[t]he infliction of physical injury to the person or property of another universally requires to be justified. The causing of economic loss does not.' In a modern market economy, financial interests are every day at risk from a variety of directions: trade competition (fair or unfair), strikes and industrial action, natural hazards, and so on. Liability in such contexts is already governed by a number of principles of limited scope. Of particular note here are the so-called 'economic torts' (which are not covered in this book). These deal with different forms of unlawful conduct in which there is an intention to cause economic loss to the claimant. Liability is restricted by the requirement that the defendant act unlawfully, for example by wrongfully procuring a breach of contract, by combining in a conspiracy, or by using intimidation (see *Clerk & Lindsell*, ch. 25, and *Oliphant*, ch. 29). Restrictions on the scope of liability recognised by these torts would be subverted if negligence were to play an increased role in this area, and the delicate balance that exists between competing interests in the fields of trade competition, labour relations, etc., might be upset.

So in English law the tort of negligence contents itself with a restrictive approach to liability for interference with trade and other purely economic interests. It adopts a general exclusionary rule towards pure economic losses, though it was accepted in the leading case of *Hedley Byrne & Co Ltd v Heller & Partners Ltd* [1964] AC 465 (extracted p. 408 below) that a duty to take care against such losses might arise if the defendant voluntarily assumes responsibility for the claimant's economic welfare. English law is not unique in taking this rather restrictive approach. German law also limits the scope of liability for the negligent infringement of purely economic interests. The BGB does not list economic interests amongst the protected rights (*Rechtsgüter*) specified in its general negligence liability section (823 I BGB), but it might have been open to the German courts to interpret the words in that section 'any other right' (*ein sonstiges Recht*) so as to include them. In fact, the courts interpreted that phrase narrowly, by and large excluding economic rights, although the 'right to an established and active business' (*Recht am eingerichteten und ausgeübten Gewerbebetrieb*) has been held to fall within the concept of 'other right'. Interesting questions arise as to the extent to which recognition of this right allows recovery in cases where English law excludes liability on the basis that the loss is purely economic (e.g. in the cable case scenario, considered below). French law by contrast takes a more relaxed view, and all sorts of economic losses are recoverable provided that they satisfy the tests of certainty and directness.

It is important to note that the reluctance to compensate applies only to losses that are purely economic. Of course, many actions in negligence are 'economic' in one sense or another. Even in a personal injury case, the claimant claims monetary compensation, while the award is calculated on the basis of not only the injury suffered by the claimant, but also its financial consequences. Such losses are not purely economic, because they stem from physical damage (i.e. personal injury or property damage) suffered by the claimant. Pure economic loss is loss that does not arise out of physical damage suffered by the claimant. The distinction between pure economic loss and loss which is consequential upon physical harm is considered further below (see especially the *Spartan Steel* case).

2. Case Law

The classic early authority for the rule that pure economic loss cannot generally be the subject of a claim in the tort of negligence is *Cattle v Stockton Waterworks Co* (1875) LR 10 QB 453. Blackburn J refused to allow a claim for financial losses arising in the following circumstances: the plaintiff, a contractor engaged in tunnelling on the land of a third party, was delayed in his work and put to additional expense when the tunnel was flooded by water which escaped from a leak in the defendant's main; the plaintiff failed to make the full profits that he expected from the contract. Shortly afterwards, the decision was approved by the House of Lords in its decision in *Simpson v Thompson* (1877) 3 App Cas 279.

With the rapid expansion of liability for negligence occasioned by *Donoghue v Stevenson*, it became possible to question the continuing authority of the decision in *Cattle*. See the following extract.

Spartan Steel and Alloys Ltd v Martin & Co Ltd [1973] QB 27

The plaintiffs manufactured stainless steel alloys at a factory which was directly supplied with electricity by a cable from a power station. The factory worked 24 hours a day. Continuous power was required to maintain the temperature in a furnace in which metal was melted. The defendants' employees, who were working on a near-by road, damaged the cable whilst using an excavating shovel. The electricity board shut off the power supply to the factory for 14½ hours until the cable was fixed. There was a danger that a 'melt' in the furnace might solidify and damage the furnace's lining, so the plaintiffs poured oxygen onto the melt and removed it. They claimed damages from the defendants in respect of: (1) a £368 reduction in the value of the melt which had been removed from the furnace; (2) the loss of a profit of £400 that they would have made from that melt had the electricity not been cut off; and (3) the loss of a profit of £1,767 on another four melts which they would have put into the furnace during the time that the electricity was interrupted. The defendants accepted that their employees had been negligent, but disputed the amount of their liability.

Lord Denning MR

At bottom I think the question of recovering economic loss is one of policy. Whenever the courts draw a line to mark out the bounds of duty, they do it as a matter of policy so as to limit the responsibility of the defendant. Whenever the courts set bounds to the damages recoverable—saying that they are, or are not, too remote—they do it as matter of policy so as to limit the liability of the defendant.

In many of the cases where economic loss has been held not to be recoverable, it has been put on the ground that the defendant was under no duty to the plaintiff. Thus where a person is injured in a road accident by the negligence of another, the negligent driver owes a duty to the injured man himself, but he owes no duty to the servant of the injured man: see *Best v Samuel Fox & Co Ltd* [1952] AC 716 at 731; nor to the master of the injured man: *Inland Revenue Comrs v Hambrook* [1956] 2 QB 656 at 660; nor to anyone else who suffers loss because he had a contract with the injured man: see *Simpson & Co v Thomson* (1877) 3 App Cas 279 at 289; nor indeed to anyone who only suffers economic loss on account of the accident: see *Kirkham v Boughey* [1958] 2 QB 338 at 341. Likewise, when property is damaged by the negligence of another, the negligent tortfeasor owes a duty to the owner or possessor of the chattel, but not to one who suffers loss only because he had a contract entitling him to use the chattel or giving him a right to receive it at some later date: see *Elliott Steam Tug Co v Shipping Controller* [1922] 1 KB 127 at 139 and *Margarine Union GmbH v Cambay Prince Steamship Co Ltd* [1969] 1 QB 219 at 251, 252.

In other cases, however, the defendant seems clearly to have been under a duty to the plaintiff, but the economic loss has not been recovered because it is too remote. Take the illustration given by Blackburn J in *Cattle v Stockton Waterworks Co* (1875) LR 10 QB 453 at 457: when water escapes from a reservoir and floods a coalmine where many men are working; those who had their tools or clothes destroyed could recover, but those who only lost their wages could not. Similarly, when the defendants' ship negligently sank a ship which was being towed by a tug, the owner of the tug lost his remuneration, but he could not recover it from the negligent ship although the same duty (of navigation with reasonable care) was owed to both tug and tow: see *Société Remorquage à Hélice v Bennetts* [1911] 1 KB 243 at 248. In such cases if the plaintiff or his property had been physically injured, he would have recovered; but, as he suffered only economic loss, he is held not entitled to recover. This is, I should think, because the loss is regarded by the law as too remote: see *King v Phillips* [1953] 1 QB 429 at 439, 440.

On the other hand, in the cases where economic loss by itself has been held to be recoverable, it is plain that there was a duty to the plaintiff and the loss was not too remote. Such as when one ship negligently runs down another ship, and damages it, with the result that the cargo has to be discharged and reloaded. The negligent ship was already under a duty to the cargo-owners; and they can recover the cost of discharging and reloading it, as it is not too remote: see *Morrison Steamship Co Ltd v Steamship Greystoke Castle* [1947] AC 265. Likewise, when a banker negligently gives a reference to one who acts on it, the duty is plain and the damage is not too remote: see *Hedley Byrne & Co Ltd v Heller & Partners Ltd* [1964] AC 465.

The more I think about these cases, the more difficult I find it to put each into its proper pigeon-hole. Sometimes I say: 'There was no duty.' In others I say: 'The damage was too remote.' So much so that I think the time has come to discard those tests which have proved so elusive. It seems to me better to consider the particular relationship in hand, and see whether or not, as a matter of policy, economic loss should be recoverable...

So I turn to the relationship in the present case. It is of common occurrence. The parties concerned are the electricity board who are under a statutory duty to maintain supplies of electricity in their district; the inhabitants of the district, including this factory, who are entitled by statute to a continuous supply of electricity for their use; and the contractors who dig up the road. Similar relationships occur with other statutory bodies, such as gas and water undertakings. The cable may be damaged by the negligence of the statutory undertaker, or by the negligence of the contractor, or by accident without any negligence by anyone; and the power may have to be cut off whilst the cable is repaired. Or the power may be cut off owing to a short-circuit in the power house; and so forth. If the cutting off of the supply causes economic loss to the consumers, should it as matter of policy be recoverable? And against whom?

The first consideration is the position of the statutory undertakers. If the board do not keep up the voltage or pressure of electricity, gas or water—or, likewise, if they shut it off for repairs—and thereby cause economic loss to their consumers, they are not liable in damages, not even if the cause of it is due to their own negligence. The only remedy (which is hardly ever pursued) is to prosecute the board before the justices. Such is the result of many cases, starting with a water board: *Atkinson v Newcastle & Gateshead Waterworks Co* (1877) LR 2 Ex D 441; going on to a gas board: *Clegg, Parkinson & Co v Earby Gas Co* [1896] 1 QB 592; and then to an electricity company: *Stevens v Aldershot Gas, Water and District Lighting Co* (1932) 31 LGR 48. In those cases the courts, looking at the legislative enactments, held that Parliament did not intend to expose the board to liability for damages to the inhabitants en masse . . . No distinction was made between economic loss and physical damage; and taken at their face value the reasoning would mean that the board was not liable for physical damage either. But there is another group of cases which go to show that, if the board, by their negligence in the conduct of their supply, cause direct physical damage to person or property, the cases seem to show that they are liable: see *Milnes v Huddersfield Corpn* (1886) 11 App Cas 511 at 530 per Lord Blackburn; *Midwood & Co Ltd v Manchester Corpn* [1905] 2 KB 597; *Heard v Brymbo Steel Co Ltd* [1947] KB 692 and *Hartley v Mayoh & Co* [1947] KB 692. But one thing is clear, the board have never been held liable for economic loss only. If such be the policy of the legislature in regard to electricity boards, it would seem right for the common law to adopt a similar policy in regard to contractors. If the electricity boards are not liable for economic loss due to negligence which results in the cutting off of the supply, nor should a contractor be liable.

The second consideration is the nature of the hazard, namely, the cutting of the supply of electricity. This is a hazard which we all run. It may be due to a short circuit, to a flash of lightning, to a tree falling on the wires, to an accidental cutting of the cable, or even to the negligence of someone or other. And when it does happen, it affects a multitude of persons; not as a rule by way of physical damage to them or their property, but by putting them to inconvenience, and sometimes to economic loss. The supply is usually restored in a few hours, so the economic loss is not very large. Such a hazard is regarded by most people as a thing they must put up with—without seeking compensation from anyone. Some there are who install a stand-by system. Others seek refuge by taking out an insurance policy against breakdown in the supply. But most people are content to take the risk on themselves. When the supply is cut off, they do not go running round to their solicitor. They do not try to find out whether it was anyone's fault. They just put up with it. They try to make up the economic loss by doing more work next day. This is a healthy attitude which the law should encourage.

The third consideration is this. If claims for economic loss were permitted for this particular hazard, there would be no end of claims. Some might be genuine, but many might be inflated, or even false. A machine might not have been in use anyway, but it would be easy to put it down to the cut in supply. It would be well-nigh impossible to check the claims. If there was economic loss on one day, did the applicant do his best to mitigate it by working harder next day? And so forth. Rather than expose claimants to such temptation and defendants to such hard labour—on comparatively small claims—it is better to disallow economic loss altogether, at any rate when it stands alone, independent of any physical damage.

The fourth consideration is that, in such a hazard as this, the risk of economic loss should be suffered by the whole community who suffer the losses—usually many but comparatively small losses—rather than on the one pair of shoulders, that is, on the contractor on whom the total of them, all added together, might be very heavy.

The fifth consideration is that the law provides for deserving cases. If the defendant is guilty of negligence which cuts off the electricity supply and causes actual physical damage to person or property, that physical damage can be recovered: see *Baker v Crow Carrying Co Ltd*, unreported, CA 1960, referred to by Buckley LJ in *SCM v Whittall* [1971] 1 QB 338 at 356, and also any economic loss truly consequential on the material damage: see *British Celanese Ltd v A H Hunt (Capacitors) Ltd* [1969] 1 WLR 959 and *SCM v Whittall* [1971] 1 QB 338. Such cases will be comparatively few. They will be readily capable of proof and will be easily checked. They should be and are admitted.

These considerations lead me to the conclusion that the plaintiffs should recover for the physical damage to the one melt (£368), and the loss of profit on that melt consequent thereon (£400); but not for the loss of profit on the four melts (£1,767), because that was economic loss independent of the physical damage. I would, therefore, allow the appeal and reduce the damages to £768.

Lawton LJ gave a separate judgment in which he concurred with Lord Denning MR. **Edmund-Davies LJ** dissented, holding that all foreseeable loss, including economic loss, that was directly attributable to the negligence ought to be recoverable.

Appeal allowed.

COMMENTARY

Although this case concerned economic loss caused as a consequence of damage to property owned by another, a similarly restrictive approach is taken where the economic loss is caused as a consequence of a personal injury suffered by a third party. For example, in *London Borough of Islington v University College London Hospital* [2005] 85 BMLR 171, the Court of Appeal held that the defendant hospital owed no duty to a local council that was required to provide residential care to a patient injured due to the hospital's negligence; Ouseley J noted that the case was similar to a business being deprived of the services of a negligently treated patient or of a negligently injured road user where no claim would lie. It seems unlikely that such a claim would succeed anywhere in the common law world, but certain civilian jurisdictions take a very different approach. In Italy, the famous *Meroni* decision of the Supreme Court (*Torino Calcio SpA v Romero*, Cass. civ., SU, 26.1.1971, no. 174) ruled that a football club could recover damages after its star player (Meroni) was killed in a car accident caused by the defendant's negligence. A similar claim had previously succeeded in France (*Football Club de Metz v Wiroth*, Colmar, Ch. dét. à Metz, 20 avril 1955). However, a majority of European jurisdictions would reject such a claim. See further M. Bussani and V. V. Palmer (eds), *Pure Economic Loss in Europe* (Cambridge: CUP, 2003), pp. 134–5 and 241–54. Cf. *West Bromwich Albion FC Ltd v El-Safty* [2007] PIQR P7: doctor owing no duty to football club in respect of the treatment of one of its players.

Liability in the 'cable case' scenario has been confirmed by the French courts on a number of occasions (see the cases extracted in *van Gerven*, pp. 198–9). In German law, where liability for pure economic loss is generally excluded, the same result has been reached as in *Spartan Steel*: the courts have held that there is no interference with the *Recht am Gewerbebetrieb* when production is stopped as a result of a power cut caused by damage to an electricity cable (BGHZ 29, 65, NJW, 479, extracted in *van Gerven*, pp. 187–8).

The loss suffered by the claimant in such cases may be classified as relational loss, in that it results from property damage or personal injury suffered by a third party (typically a person with whom the claimant is linked by contract). Where the contractual arrangements are such that the consequences of the physical harm fall substantially on the claimant, a case may be put for allowing an action to the claimant, even though the loss is purely economic. After all, the other party to the contract (who has the right to sue) has not suffered the substantial loss, and cannot under orthodox contractual principles recover for a loss suffered by someone else (cf. *The Albazero* [1977] AC 774; *Linden Gardens Trust Ltd v Lenesta Sludge Disposals Ltd* [1994] 1 AC 85; *Alfred McAlpine Construction Ltd v Panatown Ltd* [2001] 1 AC 518). The paradoxical position may arise that the person who has suffered the loss has no claim, while the person who has the claim has suffered no loss (cf. *White v Jones*, below).

There is little sign that English law is inclined to develop a new principle of liability in response to this problem (but see Robert Goff LJ's tentative formulation of a principle of 'transferred loss', related to the German (contractual) notion of *Drittschadensliquidation*, in *Leigh & Sillavan Ltd v Aliakmon Shipping Co Ltd* [1985] QB 350, CA, which was rejected when the case reached the House of Lords [1986] AC 785). Nevertheless, other Commonwealth courts, although they share English law's generally restrictive approach to pure economic losses, have shown a willingness to expand the frontiers of liability in this area. In *Canadian National Railway Co v Norsk Pacific Steamship Co* [1992] 1 SCR 1021, the Supreme Court of Canada recognised a claim for relational economic loss where the plaintiff railway company was deprived of the use of a railway bridge—which belonged to a third party with whom the plaintiff had negotiated a contractual licence—as the result of damage to the bridge caused when the defendant's boat was negligently driven into it. The majority of the court held that liability arose because the plaintiff was engaged in a joint venture with the owner of the bridge:

[W]here the plaintiff's operations are so closely allied to the operations of the party suffering physical damage and to its property (which—as damaged—causes the plaintiff's loss) that it can be considered a joint venturer with the owner of the property, the plaintiff can recover its economic loss even though the plaintiff has suffered no physical damage to its own property. To deny recovery in such circumstances would be to deny it to a person who for practical purposes is in the same position as if he or she owned the property physically damaged.

CNR v Norsk Pacific, per McLachlan J. See also *Caltex Oil (Australia) v The Dredge 'Willemstad'* (1975–6) 136 CLR 529, *Perre v Apand Pty Ltd* (1999) 198 CLR 180.

Do you think that English law should adopt such a principle?

3. Justifications for the Exclusionary Rule

Canadian National Railway Co v Norsk Pacific Steamship Co [1992] 1 SCR 1021 (Supreme Court of Canada)

The facts of this case are given in the commentary above.

McLachlan J

Are there practical reasons why the recovery of economic loss should be confined to cases where the plaintiff has sustained physical damage or injury or relied on a negligent misrepresentation? Will extension of recovery of economic loss to other situations open the floodgates of liability, prove so uncertain as to be unworkable, or have an adverse economic impact? Such questions are difficult to answer, but some assistance may be gained from looking at what has happened where the rule has been broadened and from examining the merits of the economic arguments urged in support of restricting recovery.

(1) The Comparative Evidence

The comparative historical perspective provides little support for the need for a rule which confines recovery of economic loss to cases where the plaintiff has suffered physical loss or has relied on a negligent misstatement. The civil law in Canada and abroad appears to function adequately without recourse to such a rule. In the common law jurisdictions of Canada, where the availability of damages for pure economic loss has been accepted for a decade and a half, the twin spectres of unlimited recovery and unworkable uncertainty have not materialised. And to the extent that recovery for pure economic loss has been allowed in the United States, it seems not to have provoked adverse consequences but rather to have satisfied the public demand for justice so essential to maintaining the vitality of the law of negligence.

(2) Economic Theory

The arguments advanced under this head proceed from the premise that a certain type of loss should not be seen in terms of fault but seen rather as the more or less inevitable by-product of desirable but inherently dangerous (or 'risky') activity. Viewing the activity thus, it is argued that it may well be just to distribute its costs among all who benefit from that activity, and conversely unfair to impose it upon individuals who (assuming human error to be the inevitable by-product of human activity) are viewed as the 'faultless' instruments causing the loss. This basis for administering losses has been variously described as 'collectivisation of losses' or 'loss distribution' . . . It arguably amounts to a rejection or diminution of the concept of personal fault on which our law of tort (and the civil law of delict) is based.

Three arguments are put forward: (1) the insurance argument; (2) the loss spreading argument; and (3) the 'contractual allocation of risk' argument. None of them, in my view, establishes that the extension of recovery granted by the courts in this case is unfair or inefficient.

The insurance argument says that the plaintiff is in a better position to predict economic loss consequent on an accident, and hence better able to obtain cheap insurance against the contingency. From a macro-economic point of view, this will result in an overall saving. The argument, however, depends on a number of questionable assumptions. As Bishop, 'Economic Loss in Tort' (1982) 2 OJLS 1 at p. 2, puts it:

> It is said that the victim, even when he sustains large losses, is the least cost insurer where financial loss is concerned. This argument must overcome two difficulties. First, the common law restriction of financial loss recovery reduces incentives to tortfeasors to take care. For example it is cheaper for a builder to dig without checking for the presence of gas mains or electricity cables. Such reduced care will, in the long run, result in more accidents. So, if the insurance argument is to be sustained, the victim must be not only the better insurer, but better by some margin so great that it justifies the losses from more frequent and more severe injury. Second, it seems doubtful that either victim or tortfeasor could in fact insure at reasonable cost in the insurance markets of the real world. There does exist 'key man' or business interruption insurance, but no general insurance against lost profit—a type of insurance that would suffer from extreme moral hazard problems. The price of market insurance will always include some cost for administration. Most firms will find the price too high to justify purchase. Usually the only insurance available will be self-insurance. Why should we assume that victims do that better than tortfeasors?

The loss spreading justification asserts that it is better for the economic well-being of society to spread the risk among many parties rather than place it on the shoulders of the tortfeasor.

Again, this argument is based on questionable assumptions. To quote Bishop, *supra*, at p. 2, once more:

> [This argument] is a variant of the insurance argument. The tortfeasor, for example a small construction firm, easily could be bankrupted by the claims, for example those arising from interrupted power supply. In such cases it is said that numerous small losses to victims are to be preferred to one large loss to the tortfeasor. The victims as a class are natural self-insurers of the loss. The tortfeasor would have to engage in expensive market transactions to insure. Perhaps this is so, but there are two points against it. First not only the question of justice or of efficient risk distribution are involved. Where losses are spread by relieving the tortfeasor of liability we can expect more accidents, and so more losses, to occur. Second, some of the victims may sustain large losses not small ones.

In any case, the loss spreading rationale cannot justify the numerous cases where *there is only one victim.* [Emphasis in original.]

A third argument focuses on the ability of persons who stand to suffer economic loss due to the damage to the property of another, to allocate the risk within their contracts effectively with property owners. The law of negligence has no business compensating such persons, it is argued, because it makes better economic sense for them to provide for the possibility of damage to the bridge by negotiating a term that in the event of failure the owner of the bridge would compensate them . . .

The 'contractual allocation of risk' argument rests on a number of important, but questionable assumptions. First, the argument assumes that all persons or business entities organise their affairs in accordance with the laws of economic efficiency, assigning liability to the 'least-cost risk avoider.' Second, it assumes that all parties to a transaction share an equality of bargaining power which will result in the effective allocation of risk. It is not considered that certain parties who control the situation (e.g. the owners of an indispensable bridge) may refuse to indemnify against the negligence of those over whom they have no control, or may demand such an exorbitant premium for this indemnification that it would be more cost-effective for the innocent victim to insure itself. Thirdly, it overlooks the historical centrality of personal fault to our concept of negligence or 'delict' and the role this may have in curbing negligent conduct and thus limiting the harm done to innocent parties, not all of whom are large enterprises capable of maximising their economic situation. Given the uncertainty of these premises, it is far from clear that the Court should deny recovery of pure economic loss on the basis of arguments based on allocation of risk.

(3) Summary of Pragmatic Considerations

I conclude that it has not been shown that the approach enunciated by this Court in *Kamloops* threatens to open the floodgates of indeterminate liability, leads to undue uncertainty, or causes unfair or inefficient economic allocation of resources. On the contrary, the *Kamloops* approach is arguably sensitive to these concerns. Moreover, should the courts in following this approach extend liability too far, it is open to the legislatures of this country to impose limits. There is no practical reason evident at this stage for the courts to retreat to the inflexibility of a rule that never countenances recovery of economic loss except where the plaintiff has suffered physical damage or injury or has relied on a negligent misrepresentation.

COMMENTARY

McLachlan J refers to the earlier decision of the Canadian Supreme Court in *Kamloops v Nielsen* [1984] 2 SCR 2. This case adopted as the law of Canada the two-stage approach to establishing the duty of care set out by Lord Wilberforce in *Anns v Merton London Borough Council* [1978] AC 728. Relying on this approach the Canadian Supreme Court for a time exhibited a willingness to go beyond the English authorities in allowing claims for pure economic loss. The cases extracted in Section II, below, illustrate this difference but it should be noted that the Supreme Court has in more recent cases been less willing to innovate (see Giliker, 'Revisiting pure economic loss; lessons to be learnt from the Supreme Court of Canada?' (2005) 25 LS 49; *Design Services Ltd v Canada* (2008) 293 DLR (4th) 437).

Is a court in a position to answer questions relating to insurance and loss spreading? In dissent, La Forest J considered the same factors but came to a different result on the facts, arguing that lawyers 'should inform themselves about fundamental matters of insurability'. Within the confines of private litigation is this a realistic expectation? Even if judges were prepared to undertake such analysis, doubts have been expressed over the availability of the necessary empirical data (Markesinis (1993) 109 LQR 5 at 10). As regards the utility of courts' attempts at comparative research and economic analysis, Weir offers the following, rather uncharitable view ('Errare Humanum Est', in Birks (ed.), *The Frontiers of Liability* (Oxford: OUP, 1994), vol. 2, 103 at 107):

It is fortunate that there are, or were, so many trees in that ex-dominion, for otherwise one might wonder at spending over 100 pages on futile exercises in comparative law and juvenile law and economics... What is quite clear is that no practitioner is aided in the slightest by the contrary disquisitions, more suitable to a law review—if one could get them published— than to the law reports.

Do you think Canadian practitioners were given much guidance by the decision in *Norsk* as to how future cases might be decided?

II. Defective Product Economic Loss

Claims involving the manufacture of defective goods and the construction of defective buildings have caused the courts particular problems. The duty of care formulated by Lord Atkin in *Donoghue v Stevenson* referred to foresight of physical injury or damage to property as a consequence of negligent behaviour. But if goods simply fail to work, there is no 'damage' on which to base a duty of care; the appropriate claim would seem to be in contract. The claimant's argument is that the goods are not of an acceptable quality, and quality is protected, if at all, through contractual warranties. A similar analysis would apply where a building was uninhabitable because of defective design or construction. Where is the damage on which to base a *Donoghue v Stevenson* duty of care? What if the goods or the building cause physical harm to themselves, for example the electrical appliance blows up or cracks start to appear in the walls of the building? On one view, there is little to distinguish such cases from those of pure unfitness for use. The basic complaint is that the owner's expectations in acquiring the goods or the building have been frustrated because he received something of lesser quality than he was expecting, and as a result paid more than the good or building was worth. Accordingly, the loss suffered is purely economic. Of course, it may be easier to tell that the good or building is of a lesser quality if its defectiveness becomes manifest (i.e. by blowing up or cracking) but this does not change the nature of the complaint. If the protection of expectations is properly seen as the preserve of the law of contract, should the owner be allowed to look beyond this for a remedy in the law of tort?

In two cases in the 1970s, the Court of Appeal and the House of Lords recognised claims for losses arising out of the defective construction of a building (see *Dutton v Bognor Regis Urban District Council* [1972] 1 QB 373; *Anns v Merton London Borough* [1978] AC 728). In *Anns*, a defect in the building's foundations caused subsidence, leading to the appearance of cracks in the building's walls. The House of Lords allowed a claim for the recovery of repair costs, Lord Wilberforce stating that this was necessary in order to avoid a 'present or imminent danger to the health or safety of the persons occupying it'. In his view, the plaintiff had suffered 'material physical damage'. A complicating feature of the case was that the plaintiff had brought proceedings not against the builder but against the local authority, which had the power under statute to supervise the building work. (For analysis of this aspect of the case, see p. 507, below.) The precise principle on which the House of Lords based its decision was notoriously unclear. Was it necessary to show an imminent danger to health or safety? If so, was this because the claim was against a public body exercising powers under a statute designed to protect health and safety? Or did this requirement have to be satisfied in every claim in respect of a defective building (even against the builder)? And on what basis did Lord Wilberforce conclude that there was 'material physical damage'? These issues, and indeed the very legitimacy of the liability recognised in *Anns*, were considered in the two more recent decisions of the House of Lords extracted below.

D & F Estates Ltd v Church Comrs for England [1989] AC 177

The plaintiffs were, respectively, the lessee and the occupiers of a flat in a building called Chelwood House which was owned by the first defendants. The building had been erected in 1963–5 by the third defendants (the builders) who had engaged a sub-contractor to carry out the necessary plastering work. The builders reasonably believed the sub-contractor to be skilled and competent but in fact the sub-contractor carried out the work negligently. In 1980, the plaintiffs found that the plaster in their flat was loose and brought an action against, *inter alia*, the builders claiming the cost of remedial work. The judge awarded the plaintiffs damages against the builders but the Court of Appeal reversed this decision on the grounds that, having employed a competent sub-contractor, the builders owed no further duty of care to the plaintiffs. The plaintiffs appealed to the House of Lords, where their Lordships considered a submission that the cost of repairing the defective plaster was not damage which the plaintiffs could recover in tort since it represented pure economic loss.

Lord Bridge of Harwich

[T]he liability of the builder of a permanent structure which is dangerously defective...can only arise if the defect remains hidden until the defective structure causes personal injury or damage to property other than the structure itself. If the defect is discovered before any damage is done, the loss sustained by the owner of the structure, who has to repair or demolish it to avoid a potential source of danger to third parties, would seem to be purely economic. Thus, if I acquire a property with a dangerously defective garden wall which is attributable to the bad workmanship of the original builder, it is difficult to see any basis in principle on which I can sustain an action in tort against the builder for the cost of either repairing or demolishing the wall. No physical damage has been caused. All that has happened is that the defect in the wall has been discovered in time to prevent damage occurring. I do not find it necessary for the purpose of deciding the present appeal to express any concluded view as to how far, if at all, the *ratio decidendi* of *Anns v Merton London Borough* [1978] AC 728 involves a departure from this principle establishing a new cause of action in negligence against a builder when the only damage alleged to have been suffered by the plaintiff is the discovery of a defect in the very structure which the builder erected.

My example of the garden wall, however, is that of a very simple structure. I can see that more difficult questions may arise in relation to a more complex structure like a dwelling house. One view would be that such a structure should be treated in law as a single indivisible unit. On this basis, if the unit becomes a potential source of danger when a hitherto hidden defect in construction manifests itself, the builder, as in the case of the garden wall, should not in principle be liable for the cost of remedying the defect...

However, I can see that it may well be arguable that in the case of complex structures, as indeed possibly in the case of complex chattels, one element of the structure should be regarded for the purpose of the application of the principles under discussion as distinct from another element, so that damage to one part of the structure caused by a hidden defect in another part may qualify to be treated as damage to 'other property', and whether the argument should prevail may depend on the circumstances of the case. It would be unwise and it is unnecessary for the purpose of deciding the present appeal to attempt to offer authoritative solutions to these difficult problems in the abstract...

In the instant case the only hidden defect was in the plaster. The only item pleaded as damage to other property was 'cost of cleaning carpets and other possessions damaged or dirtied by falling plaster; £50'. Once it appeared that the plaster was loose, any danger of personal injury or of further injury to other property could have been simply avoided by the timely removal of the defective plaster. The only function of plaster on walls and ceilings, unless it is itself elaborately decorative, is to serve as a smooth surface on which to place decorative paper or paint. Whatever case there may be for treating a defect in some part of the structure of a building as causing damage to 'other property' when some other part of the building is injuriously affected, as for example cracking in walls caused by defective foundations, it would seem to me entirely artificial to treat the plaster as distinct from the decorative surface placed on it...

It seems to me clear that the cost of replacing the defective plaster itself, either as carried out in 1980 or as intended to be carried out in future, was not an item of damage for which the builder of Chelwood House could possibly be made liable in negligence under the principle of *Donoghue v Stevenson* [1932] AC 562 or any legitimate development of that principle. To make him so liable would be to impose on him for the benefit of those with whom he had no contractual relationship the obligation of one who warranted the quality of the plaster as regards materials, workmanship and fitness for purpose. I am glad to reach the conclusion that this is not the law, if only for the reason that a conclusion to the opposite effect would mean that the courts, in developing the common law, had gone much farther than the legislature were prepared to go in 1972, after comprehensive examination of the subject by the Law Commission, in making builders liable for defects in the quality of their work to all who subsequently acquire interests in buildings they have erected. The statutory duty imposed by the 1972 Act was confined to dwelling houses and limited to defects appearing within six years. The common law duty, if it existed, could not be so confined or so limited. I cannot help feeling that consumer protection is an area of law where legislation is much better left to the legislators.

Lord Oliver of Aylmerton

My Lords, I have had the advantage of reading in draft the speech prepared by my noble and learned friend Lord Bridge, and I agree that the appeal should be dismissed for the reasons which he has given. In particular, I agree with his conclusion that, quite apart from the question of [the builder's] liability for the negligent performance by their sub-contractors of the duties under the plastering sub-contract, the cost of replacing the defective plaster would, in any event, be irrecoverable.

It is, I think, clear that the decision of this House in *Anns v Merton London Borough* [1978] AC 728 introduced, in relation to the construction of buildings, an entirely new type of product liability, if not, indeed, an entirely novel concept of the tort of negligence... In the first place, in no other context has it previously been suggested that a cause of action in tort arises in English law for the defective manufacture of an article which causes no injury other than injury to the defective article itself. If I buy a secondhand car to which there has been fitted a pneumatic tyre which, as a result of carelessness in manufacture, is dangerously defective and which bursts, causing injury to me or to the car, no doubt the negligent manufacturer is liable in tort on the ordinary application of *Donoghue v Stevenson*. But if the tyre bursts without causing any injury other than to itself or if I discover the defect before a burst occurs, I know of no principle on which I can claim to recover from the manufacturer in tort the cost of making good the defect which, in practice, could only be the cost of supplying and fitting a new tyre. That would be, in effect, to attach to goods a non-contractual warranty of fitness which would follow the goods into whosoever hands they came. Such a concept was suggested, obiter, by Lord Denning MR in *Dutton's* case [1972] 1 QB 373 at 396, but it was entirely unsupported by any authority and is, in my opinion, contrary to principle.

The proposition that damages are recoverable in tort for negligent manufacture when the only damage sustained is either an initial defect in or subsequent injury to the very thing that is manufactured is one which is peculiar to the construction of a building and is, I think, logically explicable only on the hypothesis suggested by my noble and learned friend Lord Bridge, that in the case of such a complicated structure the other constituent parts can be treated as separate items of property distinct from that portion of the whole which has given rise to the damage, for instance, in *Anns'* case, treating the defective foundations as something distinct from the remainder of the building. So regarded this would be no more than the ordinary application of the *Donoghue v Stevenson* principle. It is true that in such a case the damages would include, and in some cases might be restricted to, the costs of replacing or making good the defective part, but that would be because such remedial work would be essential to the repair of the property which had been damaged by it...

My Lords, I have to confess that the underlying logical basis for and the boundaries of the doctrine emerging from *Anns v Merton London Borough* are not entirely clear to me and it is in any event unnecessary for the purposes of the instant appeal to attempt a definitive exposition. This much at least seems clear: that in so far as the case is authority for the proposition that a builder responsible for the construction of the building is liable in tort at common law for damage occurring through his negligence to the very thing which he has constructed, such liability is limited directly to cases where the defect is one which threatens the health or safety of occupants or of third parties and (possibly) other property. In such a case, however, the damages recoverable are limited to expenses necessarily incurred in averting that danger. The case cannot, in my opinion, properly be adapted to support the recovery of damages for pure economic loss going beyond that, and for the reasons given by my noble and learned friend Lord Bridge, with whose analysis I respectfully agree, such loss is not in principle recoverable in tort unless the case can be brought within the principle of reliance established by *Hedley Byrne v Heller* [1964] AC 465. In the instant case the defective plaster caused no damage to the remainder of the building and in so far as it presented a risk of damage to other property or to the person of any occupant that was remediable simply by the process of removal. I agree, accordingly, for the reasons which my noble and learned friend Lord Bridge has given, that the cost of replacing the defective plaster is not an item for which the builder can be held liable in negligence. I too would dismiss the appeal.

Lord Ackner, **Lord Templeman** and **Lord Jauncey** concurred.

Appeal dismissed.

COMMENTARY

Perhaps one should not shed many tears for the plaintiffs' failure in this case. As Weir, 'Errare Humanum Est', in P. Birks (ed.), *The Frontiers of Liability*, vol. 2 (Oxford: OUP, 1994) 103 at 106 comments:

In D & F Estates . . . the plaintiffs, who, as it appeared, had got their London flat gratuitously from a property company in which they were interested, and were now living in the south of France, were complaining that the plaster was starting to fall off the walls to the risk of their persons(!) only fifteen years after the flat was completed. The trial judge awarded them a sum of over £89,000 plus interest. The principle which led to this was surely ripe for lopping.

The lopping began in the decision of the House of Lords, which affirmed that damage to a building attributable to its defective construction constitutes pure economic loss. As the action was brought against the builder, it was not strictly speaking necessary to consider whether their Lordships' earlier decision in *Anns* could still be maintained, although its position could well be described as perilous. The opportunity to consider *Anns* directly came shortly afterwards, in the next case extracted below.

Murphy v Brentwood District Council   [1991] 1 AC 398

The plaintiff was the purchaser of one of a pair of semi-detached houses in Brentwood. The house was built and sold by ABC Homes. Its foundations took the form of a concrete raft, whose design had been approved by the council on the recommendation of independent consulting engineers. Some ten or more years had passed when serious cracks began to appear in the walls of the house. After investigation, it transpired that the concrete raft had subsided differentially, causing the cracking. The plaintiff was unable to afford remedial work, which in any case would have been uneconomical, and so sold the house for some £35,000 less than its estimated worth—to a builder who was aware of the defects. The plaintiff (or his insurers) sued the council, whom the trial judge found had been negligent in considering the suitability of the design: their duty of care had not been discharged by acting on the advice of competent independent engineers.

Lord Keith of Kinkel

My Lords, this appeal raises directly the question whether *Anns v Merton London Borough* [1978] AC 728 was in all respects correctly decided . . .

In my opinion it must now be recognised that, although the damage in *Anns* was characterised as physical damage by Lord Wilberforce, it was purely economic loss. In *Sutherland Shire Council v Heyman* (1985) 60 ALR 1 at pp. 60–61 where, as observed above, the High Court of Australia declined to follow *Anns* when dealing with a claim against a local authority in respect of a defectively constructed house, Deane J said:

Nor is the respondents' claim in the present case for ordinary physical damage to themselves or their property. Their claim, as now crystallized, is not in respect of damage to the fabric of the house or to other property caused by collapse or subsidence of the house as a result of the inadequate foundations. It is for the loss or damage represented by the actual inadequacy of the foundations, that is to say, it is for the cost of remedying a structural defect in their property which already existed at the time when they acquired it. In *Anns v. Merton London Borough Council*, it was held by the House of Lords that a local government authority owed a relevant duty of care, in respect of inspection of the foundations of a building, to persons who subsequently became long term lessees (either as original lessees or as assignees) of parts of the building. Lord Wilberforce, in a speech with which three of the other four members of the House of Lords agreed, expressed the conclusion that the appropriate classification of damage sustained by the lessees by reason of the inadequacy of the foundations of the completed building was 'material, physical damage, and what is recoverable is the amount of expenditure necessary to restore the dwelling to a condition in which it is no longer a danger to the health or safety of persons occupying and possibly (depending on the circumstances) expenses arising from necessary displacement' (see [1978] AC 728 at 759). While, in a case where a subsequent purchaser or long term tenant reasonably elects to retain the premises and to reinforce the foundations, one possible measure of the damages involved in the actual inadequacy would (if such damages were recoverable) be that suggested by his Lordship, I respectfully disagree with the classification of the loss sustained in such circumstances as 'material, physical damage'. Whatever may be the position with respect to consequential damage to the fabric of the building or to other property caused by subsequent collapse or subsidence, the loss or injury involved in the actual inadequacy of the foundations cannot, in the case of a person who purchased or leased the property after the inadequacy existed but before it was known or manifest, properly be seen as ordinary physical or material damage. The only property which could be said to have been damaged in such a case is the building. The building itself could not be said to have been subjected to 'material, physical damage' by reason merely of the inadequacy of its foundations since the building never existed otherwise than with its foundations in that state. Moreover, even if the inadequacy of the foundations could be seen as material, physical damage to the building, it would be damage to property in which a future purchaser or tenant had no interest at all at the time when it occurred. Loss or injury could only be sustained by such a purchaser or tenant on or after the acquisition of the freehold or leasehold estate without knowledge of the faulty foundations. It is arguable that any such loss or injury should be seen as being sustained at the time of acquisition when, because of ignorance of the inadequacy of the foundations, a higher price is paid (or a higher rent is agreed to be paid) than is warranted by the intrinsic worth of the freehold or leasehold estate that is being acquired. Militating against that approach is the consideration that, for so long as the inadequacy of the foundations is neither known nor manifest, no identifiable loss has come home: if the purchaser or tenant sells the freehold or leasehold estate within that time, he or she will sustain no loss by reason of the inadequacy of the foundations. The alternative, and in my view preferable, approach is that any loss or injury involved in the actual inadequacy of the foundations is sustained only at the time when that inadequacy is first known or manifest. It is only then that the actual diminution in the market value of the premises occurs. On either approach, however, any loss involved in the actual inadequacy of the foundations by a person who acquires an interest in the premises after the building has been completed is merely economic in its nature.

I find myself in respectful agreement with the reasoning contained in this passage, which seems to me to be incontrovertible.

It being recognised that the nature of the loss held to be recoverable in *Anns* was pure economic loss, the next point for examination is whether the avoidance of loss of that nature fell within the scope of any duty of care owed to the plaintiffs by the local authority. On the basis of the law as it stood at the time of the decision the answer to that question must be in the negative. The right to recover for pure economic loss, not flowing from physical injury, did not then extend beyond the situation where the loss had been sustained through reliance on negligent misstatements, as in *Hedley Byrne v Heller* [1964] AC 465. There is room for the view that an exception is to be found in *Morrison Steamship Co v Greystoke Castle (cargo owners)* [1947]

AC 265. That case, which was decided by a narrow majority, may, however, be regarded as turning on specialties of maritime law concerned in the relationship of joint adventurers at sea. Further, though the purposes of the 1936 Act as regards securing compliance with building byelaws covered the avoidance of injury to the safety or health of inhabitants of houses and of members of the public generally, these purposes did not cover the avoidance of pure economic loss to owners of buildings (see *Governors of the Peabody Donation Fund v Sir Lindsay Parkinson & Co Ltd* [1985] AC 210 at 241). On analysis, the nature of the duty held by *Anns* to be incumbent on the local authority went very much further than a duty to take reasonable care to prevent injury to safety or health. The duty held to exist may be formulated as one to take reasonable care to avoid putting a future inhabitant owner of a house in a position in which he is threatened, by reason of a defect in the house, with avoidable physical injury to person or health and is obliged, in order to continue to occupy the house without suffering such injury, to expend money for the purpose of rectifying the defect.

The existence of a duty of that nature should not, in my opinion, be affirmed without a careful examination of the implications of such affirmation. To start with, if such a duty is incumbent on the local authority, a similar duty must necessarily be incumbent also on the builder of the house. If the builder of the house is to be so subject, there can be no grounds in logic or in principle for not extending liability on like grounds to the manufacturer of a chattel. That would open up an exceedingly wide field of claims, involving the introduction of something in the nature of a transmissible warranty of quality. The purchaser of an article who discovered that it suffered from a dangerous defect before that defect had caused any damage would be entitled to recover from the manufacturer the cost of rectifying the defect, and, presumably, if the article was not capable of economic repair, the amount of loss sustained through discarding it. Then it would be open to question whether there should not also be a right to recovery where the defect renders the article not dangerous but merely useless. The economic loss in either case would be the same. There would also be a problem where the defect causes the destruction of the article itself, without causing any personal injury or damage to other property. A similar problem could arise, if the *Anns* principle is to be treated as confined to real property, where a building collapses when unoccupied . . .

In *D & F Estates Ltd v Church Comrs for England* [1989] AC 177 both Lord Bridge and Lord Oliver expressed themselves as having difficulty in reconciling the decision in *Anns* with pre-existing principle and as being uncertain as to the nature and scope of such new principle as it introduced. Lord Bridge suggested that in the case of a complex structure such as a building one element of the structure might be regarded for *Donoghue v Stevenson* purposes as distinct from another element, so that damage to one part of the structure caused by a hidden defect in another part might qualify to be treated as damage to 'other property' (see [1989] AC 177 at 206). I think that it would be unrealistic to take this view as regards a building the whole of which had been erected and equipped by the same contractor. In that situation the whole package provided by the contractor would, in my opinion, fall to be regarded as one unit rendered unsound as such by a defect in the particular part. On the other hand, where, for example, the electric wiring had been installed by a sub-contractor and due to a defect caused by lack of care a fire occurred which destroyed the building, it might not be stretching ordinary principles too far to hold the electrical sub-contractor liable for the damage . . . But, even if Lord Bridge's theory were to be held acceptable, it would not seem to extend to the founding of liability on a local authority, considering that the purposes of the 1936 Act are concerned with averting danger to health and safety, not danger or damage to property. Further, it would not cover the situation which might arise through discovery, before any damage had occurred, of a defect likely to give rise to damage in the future.

Liability under the *Anns* decision is postulated on the existence of a present or imminent danger to health or safety. But, considering that the loss involved in incurring expenditure to avert the danger is pure economic loss, there would seem to be no logic in confining the remedy to cases where such danger exists. There is likewise no logic in confining it to cases where some damage (perhaps comparatively slight) has been caused to the building, but refusing it where the existence of the danger has come to light in some other way, for example through a structural survey which happens to have been carried out, or where the danger inherent in some particular component or material has been revealed through failure in some other building. Then there is the question whether the remedy is available where the defect is rectified, not in order to avert danger to an inhabitant occupier himself, but in order to enable an occupier, who may be a corporation, to continue to occupy the building through its employees without putting those employees at risk.

In my opinion it is clear that *Anns* did not proceed on any basis of established principle, but introduced a new species of liability governed by a principle indeterminate in character but having the potentiality of covering a wide range of situations, involving chattels as well as real property, in which it had never hitherto been thought that the law of negligence had any proper place...

In my opinion there can be no doubt that *Anns* has for long been widely regarded as an unsatisfactory decision. In relation to the scope of the duty owed by a local authority it proceeded on what must, with due respect to its source, be regarded as a somewhat superficial examination of principle and there has been extreme difficulty, highlighted most recently by the speeches in the *D & F Estates* case, in ascertaining on exactly what basis of principle it did proceed. I think it must now be recognised that it did not proceed on any basis of principle at all, but constituted a remarkable example of judicial legislation. It has engendered a vast spate of litigation, and each of the cases in the field which have reached this House has been distinguished. Others have been distinguished in the Court of Appeal. The result has been to keep the effect of the decision within reasonable bounds, but that has been achieved only by applying strictly the words of Lord Wilberforce and by refusing to accept the logical implications of the decision itself. These logical implications show that the case properly considered has potentiality for collision with long-established principles regarding liability in the tort of negligence for economic loss. There can be no doubt that to depart from the decision would re-establish a degree of certainty in this field of law which it has done a remarkable amount to upset.

So far as policy considerations are concerned, it is no doubt the case that extending the scope of the tort of negligence may tend to inhibit carelessness and improve standards of manufacture and construction. On the other hand, overkill may present its own disadvantages, as was remarked in *Rowling v Takaro Properties Ltd* [1988] AC 473 at 502. There may be room for the view that *Anns*-type liability will tend to encourage owners of buildings found to be dangerous to repair rather than run the risk of injury. The owner may, however, and perhaps quite often does, prefer to sell the building at its' diminished value, as happened in the present case.

It must, of course, be kept in mind that the decision has stood for some 13 years. On the other hand, it is not a decision of the type that is to a significant extent taken into account by citizens or indeed local authorities in ordering their affairs. No doubt its existence results in local authorities having to pay increased insurance premiums, but to be relieved of that necessity would be to their advantage, not to their detriment. To overrule it is unlikely to result in significantly increased insurance premiums for householders. It is perhaps of some significance that most litigation involving the decision consists in contests between insurance companies, as is largely the position in the present case. The decision is capable of being regarded as affording a measure of justice, but as against that the impossibility of finding any coherent and logically based doctrine behind it is calculated to put the law of negligence into a state of confusion defying rational analysis. It is also material that *Anns* has the effect of imposing on builders generally a liability going far beyond that which Parliament thought fit to impose on house builders alone by the Defective Premises Act 1972, a statute very material to the policy of the decision but not adverted to in it. There is much to be said for the view that in what is essentially a consumer protection field, as was observed by Lord Bridge in *D & F Estates Ltd v Church Comrs for England* [1989] AC 177 at 207, the precise extent and limits of the liabilities which in the public interest should be imposed on builders and local authorities are best left to the legislature.

My Lords, I would hold that *Anns* was wrongly decided as regards the scope of any private law duty of care resting on local authorities in relation to their function of taking steps to secure compliance with building byelaws or regulations and should be departed from . . .

My Lords, for these reasons I would allow the appeal.

Lord Bridge of Harwich

Dangerous Defects and Defects of Quality

If a manufacturer negligently puts into circulation a chattel containing a latent defect which renders it dangerous to persons or property, the manufacturer, on the well-known principles established by *Donoghue v Stevenson* [1932] AC 562 will be liable in tort for injury to persons or damage to property which the chattel causes. But if a manufacturer produces and sells a chattel which is merely defective in quality, even to the extent that it is valueless for the purpose for which it is intended, the manufacturer's liability at common law arises only under and by reference to the terms of any contract to which he is a party in relation to the chattel; the common law does not impose on him any liability in tort to persons to whom he owes no duty in contract but who, having acquired the chattel, suffer economic loss because the chattel is defective in quality. If a dangerous defect in a chattel is discovered before it causes any personal injury or damage to property, because the danger is now known and the chattel cannot be safely used unless the defect is repaired, the defect becomes merely a defect in quality. The chattel is either capable of repair at economic cost or it is worthless and must be scrapped. In either case the loss sustained by the owner or hirer of the chattel is purely economic. It is recoverable against any party who owes the user a relevant contractual duty. But it is not recoverable in tort in the absence of a special relationship of proximity imposing on the tortfeasor a duty of care to safeguard the plaintiff from economic loss. There is no such special relationship between the manufacturer of a chattel and a remote owner or hirer.

I believe that these principles are equally applicable to buildings. If a builder erects a structure containing a latent defect which renders it dangerous to persons or property, he will be liable in tort for injury to persons or damage to property resulting from that dangerous defect. But, if the defect becomes apparent before any injury or damage has been caused, the loss sustained by the building owner is purely economic. If the defect can be repaired at economic cost, that is the measure of the loss. If the building cannot be repaired, it may have to be abandoned as unfit for occupation and therefore valueless. These economic losses are recoverable if they flow from breach of a relevant contractual duty, but, here again, in the absence of a special relationship of proximity they are not recoverable in tort. The only qualification I would make to this is that, if a building stands so close to the boundary of the building owner's land that after discovery of the dangerous defect it remains a potential source of injury to persons or property on neighbouring land or on the highway, the building owner ought, in principle, to be entitled to recover in tort from the negligent builder the cost of obviating the danger, whether by repair or by demolition, so far as that cost is necessarily incurred in order to protect himself from potential liability to third parties . . .

The Complex Structure Theory

In my speech in the *D v F Estates* case [1989] AC 177 at 206–207 I mooted the possibility that in complex structures or complex chattels one part of a structure or chattel might, when it caused damage to another part of the same structure or chattel, be regarded in the law of tort as having caused damage to 'other property' for the purpose of the application of *Donoghue v Stevenson* principles. I expressed no opinion as to the validity of this theory, but put it forward for consideration as a possible ground on which the facts considered in *Anns* might be distinguishable from the facts which had to be considered in *D & F Estates* itself. I shall call this for convenience 'the complex structure theory' and it is, so far as I can see, only if and to the extent that this theory can be affirmed and applied that there can be any escape from the conclusions I have indicated above under the rubric 'Dangerous defects and defects of quality'.

The complex structure theory has, so far as I know, never been subjected to express and detailed examination in any English authority.

[His Lordship considered the 'extreme application of the complex structure theory treating each part of the entire structure as a separate item of property', and continued:] [S]uch an application of the theory seems to me quite unrealistic. The reality is that the structural elements in any building form a single indivisible unit of which the different parts are essentially interdependent. To the extent that there is any defect in one part of the structure it must to a greater or lesser degree necessarily affect all other parts of the structure. Therefore any defect in the structure is a defect in the quality of the whole and it is quite artificial, in order to impose a legal liability which the law would not otherwise impose, to treat a defect in an integral structure, so far as it weakens the structure, as a dangerous defect liable to cause damage to 'other property'.

A critical distinction must be drawn here between some part of a complex structure which is said to be a 'danger' only because it does not perform its proper function in sustaining the other parts and some distinct item incorporated in the structure which positively malfunctions so as to inflict positive damage on the structure in which it is incorporated. Thus, if a defective central heating boiler explodes and damages a house or defective electrical installation malfunctions and sets the house on fire, I see no reason to doubt that the owner of the house, if he can prove that the damage was due to the negligence of the boiler manufacturer in the one case or the electrical contractor in the other, can recover damages in tort on *Donoghue v Stevenson* principles. But the position in law is entirely different where, by reason of the inadequacy of the foundations of the building to support the weight of the superstructure, differential settlement and consequent cracking occurs. Here, once the first cracks appear, the structure as a whole is seen to be defective and the nature of the defect is known. Even if, contrary to my view, the initial damage could be regarded as damage to other property caused by a latent defect, once the defect is known the situation of the building owner is analogous to that of the car owner who discovers that the car has faulty brakes. He may have a house which, until repairs are effected, is unfit for habitation, but, subject to the reservation I have expressed with respect to ruinous buildings at or near the boundary of the owner's property, the building no longer represents a source of danger and as it deteriorates will only damage itself.

For these reasons the complex structure theory offers no escape from the conclusion that damage to a house itself which is attributable to a defect in the structure of the house is not recoverable in tort in *Donoghue v Stevenson* principles, but represents purely economic loss which is only recoverable in contract or in tort by reason of some special relationship of proximity which imposes on the tortfeasor a duty of care to protect against economic loss . . .

Imminent Danger to Health or Safety

A necessary element in the building owner's cause of action against the negligent local authority, which does not appear to have been contemplated in *Dutton* but which, it is said in *Anns*, must be present before the cause of action accrues, is that the state of the building is such that there is present or imminent danger to the health or safety of persons occupying it. Correspondingly the damages recoverable are said to include the amount of expenditure necessary to restore the building to a condition in which it is no longer such a danger, but presumably not any further expenditure incurred in any merely qualitative restoration. I find these features of the *Anns* doctrine very difficult to understand. The theoretical difficulty of reconciling this aspect of the doctrine with previously accepted legal principle was pointed out by Lord Oliver in *D & F Estates* [1989] AC 177 at 212–213. But apart from this there are, as it appears to me, two insuperable difficulties arising from the requirement of imminent danger to health or safety as an ingredient of the cause of action which lead to quite irrational and capricious consequences in the application of the *Anns* doctrine. The first difficulty will arise where the relevant defect in the building, when it is first discovered, is not a present or imminent danger to health or safety. What is the owner to do if he is advised that the building will gradually deteriorate, if not repaired, and will in due course become a danger to health and safety, but that the longer he waits to effect repairs the greater the cost will be? Must he spend £1,000 now on the necessary repairs with no redress against the local authority? Or is he entitled to wait until the building has so far deteriorated that he has a cause of action and then to recover from the local authority the £5,000 which the necessary repairs are now going to cost? I can find no answer to this conundrum. A second difficulty will arise where the latent defect is not discovered until it causes the sudden and total collapse of the building, which occurs when the building is temporarily unoccupied and causes no damage to property except to the building itself. The building is now no longer capable of occupation and hence cannot be a danger to health or safety. It seems a very strange result that the building owner should be without remedy in this situation if he would have been able to recover from the local authority the full cost of repairing the building if only the defect had been discovered before the building fell down.

Liability for Economic Loss

All these considerations lead inevitably to the conclusion that a building owner can only recover the cost of repairing a defective building on the ground of the authority's negligence in performing its statutory function of approving plans or inspecting buildings in the course of construction if the scope of the authority's duty of care is wide enough to embrace purely economic loss. The House has already held in *D & F Estates* that a builder, in the absence of any contractual duty or of a special relationship of proximity introducing the *Hedley Byrne* principle of reliance, owes no duty of care in tort in respect of the quality of his work. As I pointed out in *D & F Estates*, to hold that the builder owed such a duty of care to any person acquiring an interest in the product of the builder's work would be to impose on him the obligations of an indefinitely transmissible warranty of quality.

By s. 1 of the Defective Premises Act 1972 Parliament has in fact imposed on builders and others undertaking work in the provision of dwellings the obligations of a transmissible warranty of the quality of their work and of the fitness for habitation of the completed dwelling. But, besides being limited to dwellings, liability under that Act is subject to a limitation period of six years from the completion of the work and to the exclusion provided for by s. 2. It would be remarkable to find that similar obligations in the nature of a transmissible warranty of quality, applicable to buildings of every kind and subject to no such limitations or exclusions as are imposed by the 1972 Act, could be derived from the builder's common law duty of care or from the duty imposed by building byelaws or regulations. In *Anns* Lord Wilberforce expressed the opinion that a builder could be held liable for a breach of statutory duty in respect of buildings which do not comply with the byelaws. But he cannot, I think, have meant that the statutory obligation to build in conformity with the byelaws by itself gives rise to obligations in the nature of transmissible warranties of quality. If he did mean that, I must respectfully disagree. I find it impossible to suppose that anything less than clear express language such as is used in s. 1 of the 1972 Act would suffice to impose such a statutory obligation . . .

In *Dutton* [1972] 1 QB 373 at 397–398 Lord Denning MR said:

> [M]rs Dutton has suffered a grievous loss. The house fell down without any fault of hers. She is in no position herself to bear the loss. Who ought in justice to bear it? I should think those who were responsible. Who are they? In the first place, the builder was responsible. It was he who laid the foundations so badly that the house fell down. In the second place, the council's inspector was responsible. It was his job to examine the foundations to see if they would take the load of the house. He failed to do it properly. In the third place, the council should answer for his failure. They were entrusted by Parliament with the task of seeing that houses were properly built. They received public funds for the purpose. The very object was to protect purchasers and occupiers of houses. Yet, they failed to protect them. Their shoulders are broad enough to bear the loss.

These may be cogent reasons of social policy for imposing liability on the authority. But the shoulders of a public authority are only 'broad enough to bear the loss' because they are financed by the public at large. It is pre-eminently for the legislature to decide whether these policy reasons should be accepted as sufficient for imposing on the public the burden of providing compensation for private financial losses. If they do so decide, it is not difficult for them to say so.

I would allow the appeal.

Lord Oliver of Aylmerton

In the 13 years which have elapsed since the decision of this House in *Anns v Merton London Borough* [1978] AC 728 the anomalies which arise from its literal application and the logical difficulty in relating it to the previously established principles of the tort of negligence have become more and more apparent. This appeal and the appeal in *Dept of the Environment v Thomas Bates & Son Ltd* [1991] 1 AC 499 which was heard shortly before it, have highlighted some of the problems which *Anns* has created and underline the urgent need for it now to be re-examined.

In approaching such a re-examination there are a number of points to be made at the outset. Firstly, it has to be borne in mind that neither in *Anns* nor in *Dutton v Bognor Regis Urban District Council* [1972] 1 QB 373, which preceded it, was the liability of the local authority based on the proposition that the Public Health Act 1936 gave rise to an action by a private individual for breach of statutory duty of the type contemplated in *Cutler v Wandsworth Stadium Ltd* [1949] AC 398, a type of claim quite distinct from a claim in negligence (see *London Passenger Transport Board v Upson* [1949] AC 155 at 168 per Lord Wright). The duty of the local authority was, as Lord Wilberforce stressed in the course of his speech in *Anns* [1978] AC 728 at 758, the ordinary common law duty to take reasonable care, no more and no less. Secondly, in neither case was it possible to allege successfully that the plaintiffs had relied on the proper performance by the defendant of its Public Health Act duties so as to invoke the principles expounded in *Hedley Byrne & Co Ltd v Heller & Partners Ltd* [1964] AC 465. In the course of his speech in *Anns* [1978] AC 728 at 768–769 Lord Salmon was at pains to emphasise that the claim had nothing to do with reliance. Thirdly, the injury of which the plaintiffs complained in *Anns* was not 'caused' by the defendant authority in any accepted sense of the word. The complaint was not of what the defendant had done but of what it had not done. It had failed to prevent the builder of the flats from erecting a substandard structure . . .

Fourthly, although in neither case was the builder who had actually created the defect represented at the hearing, the fact that the claim was, in essence, one based on the failure of the defendant to prevent the infliction of tortious injury by the builder rendered it necessary to determine also the question of what, if any, liability lay on him. If the builder was under no obligation to the plaintiffs to take reasonable care to provide proper foundations it is difficult to see how the defendant authority could be liable for failing to prevent what was, *vis-à-vis* the plaintiffs, lawful conduct on his part save on the footing that the 1936 Act imposed an absolute statutory duty to ensure that no substandard building was erected. But, as already mentioned, the action was not one for breach of statutory duty. The liability of the local authority and that of the builder are not, therefore, logically separable.

Finally, despite the categorisation of the damage as 'material, physical damage' (see *Anns* [1978] AC 728 at 759 per Lord Wilberforce), it is, I think, incontestable on analysis that what the plaintiffs suffered was pure pecuniary loss and nothing more. If one asks, 'What were the damages to be awarded for?' clearly they were not to be awarded for injury to the health or person of the plaintiffs, for they had suffered none. But equally clearly, although the 'damage' was described, both in the Court of Appeal in *Dutton* and in this House in *Anns*, as physical or material damage, this simply does not withstand analysis. To begin with, it makes no sort of sense to accord a remedy where the defective nature of the structure has manifested itself by some physical symptom, such as a crack or a fractured pipe, but to deny it where the defect has been brought to light by, for instance, a structural survey in connection with a proposed sale. Moreover, the imminent danger to health or safety which was said to be the essential ground of the action was not the result of the physical manifestations which had appeared but of the inherently defective nature of the structure which they revealed. They were merely the outward signs of a deterioration resulting from the inherently defective condition with which the building had been brought into being from its inception and cannot properly be described as damage caused to the building in any accepted use of the word 'damage'.

In the speech of Lord Bridge and in my own speech in *D & F Estates Ltd v Church Comrs for England* [1989] AC 167 there was canvassed what has been called 'the complex structure theory'. This has been rightly criticised by academic writers, although I confess that I thought that both Lord Bridge and I had made it clear that it was a theory which was not embraced with any enthusiasm but was advanced as the only logically possible explanation of the categorisation of the damage in *Anns* as 'material, physical damage'. Lord Bridge has, in the course of his speech in the present case, amply demonstrated the artificiality of the theory and, for the reasons which he has given, it must be rejected as a viable explanation of the underlying basis for the decision in *Anns*. However that decision is analysed, therefore, it is in the end inescapable that the only damage for which compensation was to be awarded and which formed the essential foundation of the action was pecuniary loss and nothing more. The injury which the plaintiff suffers in such a case is that his consciousness of the possible injury to his own health or safety or that of others puts him in a position in which, in order to enable him either to go on living in the property or to exploit its financial potentiality without that risk, whether substantial or insubstantial, he has to expend money in making good the defects which have now become patent...

The fact is that the categorisation of the damage in *Anns* as 'material, physical damage', whilst, at first sight, lending to the decision some colour of consistency with the principle of *Donoghue v Stevenson*, has served to obscure not only the true nature of the claim but, as a result, the nature and scope of the duty on the breach of which the plaintiffs in that case were compelled to rely.

It does not, of course, at all follow as a matter of necessity from the mere fact that the only damage suffered by a plaintiff in an action for the tort of negligence is pecuniary or 'economic' that his claim is bound to fail...

The critical question, as was pointed out in the analysis of Brennan J in his judgment in *Sutherland Shire Council v Heyman* (1985) 60 ALR 1, is not the nature of the damage in itself, whether physical or pecuniary, but whether the scope of the duty of care in the circumstances of the case is such as to embrace damage of the kind which the plaintiff claims to have sustained (see *Caparo Industries plc v Dickman* [1990] 2 AC 605). The essential question which has to be asked in every case, given that damage which is the essential ingredient of the action has occurred, is whether the relationship between the plaintiff and the defendant is such, or, to use the favoured expression, whether it is of sufficient 'proximity', that it imposes on the latter a duty to take care to avoid or prevent that loss which has in fact been sustained. That the requisite degree of proximity may be established in circumstances in which the plaintiff's injury results from his reliance on a statement or advice on which he was entitled to rely and on which it was contemplated that he would be likely to rely is clear from *Hedley Byrne* and subsequent cases, but *Anns* was not such a case and neither is the instant case. It is not, however, necessarily to be assumed that the reliance cases form the only possible category of cases in which a duty to take reasonable care to avoid or present pecuniary loss can arise...

I frankly doubt whether, in searching for such limits [on the duty of care], the categorisation of the damage as 'material', 'physical', 'pecuniary', or 'economic' provides a particular useful contribution. Where it does, I think, serve a useful purpose is in identifying those cases in which it is necessary to search for and find something more than the mere reasonable foreseeability of damage which has occurred as providing the degree of 'proximity' necessary to support the action... The infliction of physical injury to the person or property of another universally requires to be justified. The causing of economic loss does not. If it is to be categorised as wrongful it is necessary to find some factor beyond the mere occurrence of the loss and the fact that its occurrence could be foreseen. Thus the categorisation of damage as economic serves at least the useful purpose of indicating that something more is required and it is one of the unfortunate features of *Anns* that it resulted initially in this essential distinction being lost sight of...

Lord Jauncey of Tullichettle considered in the course of his concurring speech whether the decision in *Anns* could be reconciled with the principle of *Donoghue v Stevenson* on the basis of the complex structure theory:

I agree with the views of my noble and learned friend Lord Bridge in this appeal that to apply the complex structure theory to a house so that each part of the entire structure is treated as a separate piece of property is quite unrealistic. A builder who builds a house from foundations upwards is creating a single integrated unit of which the individual components are interdependent. To treat the foundations as a piece of property separate from the walls or the floors is a wholly artificial exercise. If the foundations are inadequate the whole house is affected. Furthermore, if the complex structure theory is tenable there is no reason in principle why it should not also be applied to chattels consisting of integrated parts such as a ship or a piece of machinery. The consequences of such an application would be far reaching. It seems to me that the only context for the complex structure theory in the case of a building would be where one integral component of the structure was built by a separate contractor and where a defect in such a component had caused damage to other parts of the structure, e.g. a steel frame erected by a specialist contractor which failed to give adequate support to floors or walls. Defects in such ancillary equipment as central heating boilers or electrical installations would be subject to the normal *Donoghue v Stevenson* principle if such defects gave rise to damage to other parts of the building.

Lord Mackay, Lord Brandon and **Lord Ackner** concurred.

Appeal allowed.

COMMENTARY

The action in *Murphy* was against the local authority for failing to ensure that the builder constructed the house in accordance with local authority by-laws (the *Anns* action). The liability of the builder was not in issue, although it was accepted that the liability of the local authority could not be any more extensive than that of the builder. However, in a case heard together with *Murphy* (*Department of the Environment v Thomas Bates and Son Ltd* [1991] 1 AC 499), the House of Lords affirmed that a builder did not owe a duty of care to a remote purchaser in respect of pure economic loss suffered through the defective construction of a building, an unsurprising result given the decision in *D & F Estates*. This was followed, with reservations, by the Court of Appeal in *Bellefield Computer Services Ltd v E Turner & Sons* [2000] BLR 97. In this case a builder carelessly constructed a building so as to render it more likely to suffer more extensive fire damage than it otherwise would have if it had been constructed with due care, although the negligence did not increase the risk of a fire starting in the first place. Following the reasoning of *Murphy*, it was held that the builder was not liable for the additional damage caused to the building by fire (as this was irrecoverable economic loss) but was liable for the loss of the possessions in the building, a result which Schiemann LJ described as odd. Commenting on the case, Duncan Wallace (2000) 116 LQR 530 at 531 notes: 'the Court of Appeal obviously felt some embarrassment in explaining and justifying this particular consequence of the *Murphy* speeches, as well as the resulting judicial characterisation of what was in reality catastrophic physical fire damage as legally irrecoverable "pure economic loss"'.

The New Zealand courts, in contrast with *Murphy*, have imposed liability on the local authority without finding it necessary to consider the liability of the builder, on the basis that potential home buyers relied on councils (in the sense that they expected the council to carry out its functions carefully) to inspect building work in order to ensure it was within building by-laws (*Invercargill CC v Hamlin* [1994] 3 NZLR 513, affirmed by the Privy Council (see [1996] AC 624) on the basis that it was for the New Zealand courts to decide whether, as a matter of policy, it was appropriate to hold councils under a duty of care in respect of the inspection of building work). Note, though, that the New Zealand courts have now limited *Hamlin* to cases involving non-commercial property, commercial purchasers being seen as less vulnerable (*Te Mata Properties Ltd v Hastings District Council* [2009] 1 NZLR 460; *Queenstown Lakes District Council v Charterhall Trustees Ltd* [2009] 3 NZLR 786). Where it applies, the liability recognised in *Hamlin* extends not just to situations where the defect threatened injury to person or property but to standards of workmanship generally (i.e. to defectiveness, not just dangerousness). For comment on *Hamlin*, see Duncan Wallace (1995) 111 LQR 285 (New Zealand Court of Appeal), and Martin (1997) 60 MLR 94 and Duncan Wallace (1996) 112 LQR 369 (Privy Council).

Defective Premises Act 1972

Mr Murphy bought his newly-built home in 1970. If the house had been built a few years later, he might have benefited from the statutory claim introduced by the Defective Premises Act 1972. Section 1(1) of this Act provides that a person taking on work for or in connection with the provision of a dwelling owes a duty to the person for whom services are provided, and to every person who acquires an interest (legal or equitable) in the dwelling. Certain cases ('Approved Housing Schemes') were exempted from the Act (s. 2); the most significant of these was the scheme operated by the National House Building Council (NHBC). However, the NHBC has stopped submitting schemes for approval and it has been postulated that the Act now has a much wider field of operation (*Winfield & Jolowicz*, para. 9.38) although the number of reported cases dealing with s. 1 remains small. One reason may be the short limitation period: six years from the date of completion of the dwelling or the date on which rectification work is done to correct faults in the original dwelling (s. 1(5): see *Alderson v Beetham Organisation Ltd* [2003] 1 WLR 1686). Contrast the limitation period in respect of latent damage recoverable at common law: three years from the date at which the existence of a cause of action was reasonably discoverable, up to a maximum of 15 years from the date of the defendant's negligent act (Limitation Act 1980, ss. 14A and 14B).

The effect of s. 1 of the Defective Premises Act is to provide a statutory warranty of quality (to the 'fit for habitation' standard) for dwellings (commercial premises are outside the scope of the Act; cf. *Catlin Estates Ltd v Carter Jonas* [2005] EWHC 2315 (TCC), holding that a 'hunting lodge' could be a dwelling) which extends to the failure to carry out necessary work as well as carrying it out badly (*Andrews v Schooling* [1991] 1 WLR 783 at 792, per Beldam LJ). Liability is not strict but is based on a failure to act in a workmanlike or professional manner, which may be stricter in some ways than the negligence standard (*Winfield & Jolowicz*, para. 9.38 n. 83). On whom is the duty imposed? Section 1 refers to a person 'taking on work' in connection with the provision of a dwelling. This would include the builder, subcontractors, and any professional advisors involved in the provision of the dwelling (e.g. architects or surveyors; see *Bole v Huntsbuild Ltd* [2009] EWHC 483 (TCC)). Would a local authority be caught by virtue of its officers conducting inspections? (See *Sparham-Souter v Town & Country Developments (Essex) Ltd* [1976] QB 858.) However, the owner of a dwelling does not 'take on work' for the purposes of s. 1(1) merely by virtue of the fact that he has given instructions for work to be done, or has employed someone to do work (*Mirza v Bhandal*, unreported, QBD, 27 April 1999, Latham J). Nevertheless 'providers' or 'arrangers' for the provision of dwellings or installations might be caught by s. 1(4) if such activities are carried on in the course of a business. More generally, not everyone involved in the provision of the dwelling is subject to the duty in s. 1(1): a person employed on terms that the work is to be carried out in accordance with instructions given by another is generally taken to have discharged the duty imposed by s. 1(1) if the instructions have been followed (s. 1(2)).

The House of Lords in *Murphy* thought the existence of the Defective Premises Act 1972 was a factor against imposing a common law duty of a different scope. Do you agree? Should matters of consumer protection be left only to the legislature?

Complex Structures

The line between property damage and pure economic loss is not always easy to draw, as the above cases make clear. In *Aswan Engineering v Lupdine* [1987] 1 WLR 1, the claim was against a manufacturer of pails in which a waterproofing compound, Lupdine, had been stored. The pails, left out in the sun on a Kuwait dock, melted and the Lupdine was lost. If the pails and the Lupdine were treated as one product, the defective manufacture had not caused physical injury or property damage to anyone or anything else; hence the only loss was economic (i.e the value of the melted pails and the lost Lupdine). However, if the pails could be regarded as separate from the Lupdine, it could be said that their defective manufacture had damaged property (the Lupdine contained in them) and hence the owner could bring a claim for property damage. Although it was not necessary for the Court of Appeal to decide, Lloyd LJ indicated that he would consider the loss of the Lupdine as property damage whilst

Nicholls LJ took the view that it would be economic loss. The issue is of great practical importance given the differing conditions for establishing a duty of care between property damage and pure economic loss. How would the complex-structures argument recognised by members of the House of Lords in the above cases apply to such a case? Would the purchaser of a bottle of wine whose contents were ruined by a defective cork suffer property damage (because the cork had damaged the wine) or pure economic loss (because the 'product' included both the wine and cork so the defect only caused the bottle as a whole to lose value)?

In *Winnipeg Condominium Corporation No. 36 v Bird Construction Co* [1995] 1 SCR 85, La Forest J (delivering the judgment of the Supreme Court of Canada) after agreeing with Lord Bridge's criticism of the complex structure theory in relation to buildings, noted:

In cases involving the recoverability of economic loss in tort, it is preferable for the courts to weigh the relevant policy issues openly. Since the use of [the complex structure] theory serves mainly to circumvent and obscure the underlying policy questions, I reject the use of the 'complex structure' theory in cases involving the liability of contractors for the cost of repairing defective buildings.

Some of the policy considerations referred to by La Forest J are explored in the extracts below.

E. Quill, 'Consumer protection in respect of defective buildings' (2006) 14 Tort L Rev 105

There are two problems with [the reasoning in *Murphy*]. First of all, to say that a building is just a big product fails to recognise the greater practical and economic significance that building purchases entail, particularly in the case of the purchase of one's home. Second, and more importantly, the analogy overlooks the fact that tort law's protection against economic loss in the case of manufactured goods is not necessary, as the buyer's vulnerability has been largely addressed by consumer protection legislation. Manufactured goods are generally bought from retailers, with the built in protections for the consumer... [Conversely], if the average house buyer asked the seller to give an undertaking to accept responsibility for the economic cost of latent defects, the seller would simply refuse to sell and wait for another buyer...

The result in *Murphy* may be justified in England, as many persons are not vulnerable; the fact that an individual may be more vulnerable than the rest does not necessarily require an exception, though one may be desirable. The combination of statutory provisions and insurance arrangements may be considered to provide a sufficient, if imperfect, level of protection. Despite the fact that such an interpretation is plausible, it is submitted that the degree of vulnerability of homeowners and small business in England does still warrant the imposition of a duty and that the position adopted in *Murphy* is unsatisfactory.

Winnipeg Condominium Corporation No. 36 v Bird Construction Co [1995] 1 SCR 85 (Supreme Court of Canada)

This case raised the question whether a contractor responsible for the construction of a building can be held liable in negligence to a subsequent purchaser of the building, who is not in contractual privity with the contractor, for the cost of repairing defects in the building arising out of negligence in its construction. The court was asked to determine whether Canadian law should continue to follow the *Anns* approach, adopted by the court in *City of Kamloops v Nielsen* [1984] 2 SCR 2, or should follow the new approach of the House of Lords in *D & F Estates* and *Murphy*.

La Forest J delivered the judgment of the court

In my view, the reasonable likelihood that a defect in a building will cause injury to its inhabitants is ... sufficient to ground a contractor's duty in tort to subsequent purchasers of the building for the cost of repairing the defect if that defect is discovered prior to any injury and if it poses a real and substantial danger to the inhabitants of the building ... If a contractor can be held liable in tort where he or she constructs a building negligently and, as a result of that negligence, the building causes damage to persons or property, it follows that the contractor should also be held liable in cases where the dangerous defect is discovered and the owner of the building wishes to mitigate the danger by fixing the defect and putting the building back into a non-dangerous state. In both cases, the duty in tort serves to protect the bodily integrity and property interests of the inhabitants of the building ...

Apart from the logical force of holding contractors liable for the cost of repair of dangerous defects, there is also a strong underlying policy justification for imposing liability in these cases. Under the law as developed in *D & F Estates* and *Murphy*, the plaintiff who moves quickly and responsibly to fix a defect before it causes injury to persons or damage to property must do so at his or her own expense. By contrast, the plaintiff who, either intentionally or through neglect, allows a defect to develop into an accident may benefit at law from the costly and potentially tragic consequences. In my view, this legal doctrine is difficult to justify because it serves to encourage, rather than discourage, reckless and hazardous behaviour. Maintaining a bar against recoverability for the cost of repair of dangerous defects provides no incentive for plaintiffs to mitigate potential losses and tends to encourage economically inefficient behaviour. The Fourth District Court of Appeal for Florida in *Drexel Properties, Inc v Bay Colony Club Condominium, Inc* 406 So.2d 515 (1981), at p. 519, explained the problem in the following manner:

> Why should a buyer have to wait for a personal tragedy to occur in order to recover damages to remedy or repair defects? In the final analysis, the cost to the developer for a resulting tragedy could be far greater than the cost of remedying the condition.

Woodhouse J in *Bowen v Paramount Builders (Hamilton) Ltd* [1977] 1 NZLR 394 at 417, described the problem in similar terms:

> It would seem only common sense to take steps to avoid a serious loss by repairing a defect before it will cause physical damage; and rather extraordinary if the greater loss when the building falls down could be recovered from the careless builder but the cost of timely repairs could not.

Allowing recovery against contractors in tort for the cost of repair of dangerous defects thus serves an important preventative function by encouraging socially responsible behaviour ...

[N]o serious risk of indeterminate liability arises with respect to this tort duty. In the first place, there is no risk of liability to an indeterminate class because the potential class of claimants is limited to the very persons for whom the building is constructed: the inhabitants of the building. The fact that the class of claimants may include successors in title who have no contractual relationship with the contractors does not, in my view, render the class of potential claimants indeterminate. As noted by the New Jersey Supreme Court in *Aronsohn v Mandara*

(1984) 484 A2d 675 at 680, '[t]he contractor should not be relieved of liability for unworkman-like construction simply because of the fortuity that the property on which he did the construction has changed hands.'

Secondly, there is no risk of liability in an indeterminate amount because the amount of liability will always be limited by the reasonable cost of repairing the dangerous defect in the building and restoring that building to a non-dangerous state. Counsel for Bird advanced the argument that the cost of repairs claimed for averting a danger caused by a defect in construction could, in some cases, be disproportionate to the actual damage to persons or property that might be caused if that defect were not repaired. For example, he expressed concern that a given plaintiff could claim thousands of dollars in damage for a defect which, if left unrepaired, would cause only a few dollars damage to that plaintiff's other property. However, in my view, any danger of indeterminacy in damages is averted by the requirement that the defect for which the costs of repair are claimed must constitute a real and substantial danger to the inhabitants of the building, and the fact that the inhabitants of the building can only claim the reasonable cost of repairing the defect and mitigating the danger. The burden of proof will always fall on the plaintiff to demonstrate that there is a serious risk to safety, that the risk was caused by the contractor's negligence, and that the repairs are required to alleviate the risk.

Finally, there is little risk of liability for an indeterminate time because the contractor will only be liable for the cost of repair of dangerous defects during the useful life of the building. Practically speaking, I believe that the period in which the contractor may be exposed to liability for negligence will be much shorter than the full useful life of the building. With the passage of time, it will become increasingly difficult for owners of a building to prove at trial that any deterioration in the building is attributable to the initial negligence of the contractor and not simply to the inevitable wear and tear suffered by every building ...

COMMENTARY

It was not necessary for the Canadian Supreme Court to consider whether a builder would owe a duty in respect of non-dangerous defects, although, as Fleming (1995) 111 LQR 362 notes, some of the policy arguments used by La Forest J in support of liability apply equally to non-dangerous defects. The Australian High Court has held that builders owe a duty to remote purchasers in respect to non-dangerous defects (*Bryan v Maloney* (1995) 182 CLR 609) and it seems a similar position applies in New Zealand (*Rolls Royce New Zealand Ltd v Carter Holt Harvey Ltd* [2005] 1 NZLR 324 at [71]). In neither jurisdiction, however, does the duty extend to commercial property (*Woolcock Street Investments Pty Ltd v CDG Pty Ltd* (2004) 216 CLR 515; *Queenstown Lakes District Council v Charterhall Trustees Ltd* [2009] 3 NZLR 786) as the owner of commercial property is generally less vulnerable than the owner of a dwelling. This suggests that, in Australia and New Zealand, rather than depending on a bright-line division based on the use of the premises—a division that is somewhat artificial—the existence of the duty of care will in future depend on the particular vulnerability of the plaintiff *vis-à-vis* the builder/architect and much will depend on what steps the remote purchaser might have taken to protect himself (see Coveney (2004) TLJ 187). This consideration may also explain why the High Court in *Woolcock* left open the correctness of *Bryan v Maloney*; it may be that not every purchaser of dwelling is vulnerable in the sense that is necessary to create the duty of care. However, Todd, 'Policy Issues in Defective Property Cases' in J. Neyers, E. Chamberlain & S. Pitel (eds), *Emerging Issues in Tort Law* (Hart Publishing, 2007), argues that for vulnerability to work it must apply to a category of cases and not be at large in every case. He argues that commercial purchasers cannot sensibly be treated differently and that all remote purchasers 'are vulnerable to suffering loss through acquiring structures for long term use but with hidden defects' (p. 231). Alternatively, does the true distinction lie in the 'relative inability of the residential buyer to spread risk' whereas the commercial buyer 'has a clear ability to assess the assignment of risk in a normal commercial way, laying off the risk through pricing and spreading the risk through a port-folio of investments' (Partlett, 'Defective Structures and Economic loss in the United States', in J. Neyers, E. Chamberlain & S. Pitel, *op. cit.*, pp. 248–249). Given the difficulties with the distinction, is it preferable to determine the existence of a duty by reference to how danger-ous the defect might be? In support of the latter approach, see Grubb and Mullis, 'An Unfair Law for Dangerous Products: The Fall of *Anns*' (1991) Conv 225, who argue that it is the dangerous nature of the building that brings into play the policy arguments, such as deter-rence and loss distribution, in favour of imposing a duty of care.

Another part of *Murphy* that has proved unpalatable to Commonwealth courts is the use of reasoning applicable to chattels by way of analogy to realty. As La Forest J pointed out in *Winnipeg*, the idea that one can discard a house instead of repairing it smacked of unreality. Similarly, Mason CJ, Gaudron and Deane JJ in *Bryan* noted that the purchase of a house was likely to represent 'one of the most significant, and possibly the most significant, investment the subsequent owner will make during his or her lifetime'. If the reality is that the owner cannot discard the house and must live in it, what happens if/when the defect ultimately results in physical injury or property damage? La Forest J in *Winnipeg* seems to assume that such an owner could recover damages, but this is contrary to Lord Keith's view in *Murphy* that, although the ordinary *Donoghue v Stevenson* duty is owed in respect of physical injury or property damage, 'that principle is not apt to bring home liability towards an occupier who knows the full extent of the defect yet continues to occupy the building'. However, in *Targett v Torfaen Borough Council* [1992] 3 All ER 27 the defendant designed and built coun-cil flats, one of which was occupied by the plaintiff as a weekly tenant. Access to the flat was provided by two flights of stairs. The lower flight had no handrail nor was there any artificial light provided in the vicinity. The plaintiff was injured whilst descending the lower flight of stairs in darkness and in bad weather. The Court of Appeal rejected an argument, derived from *Murphy*, that because the plaintiff knew of the dangerous state of the stairs but contin-ued to occupy the premises, this barred his claim. Commenting on the effect of knowledge of a defect, Nicholls LJ noted:

[K]nowledge of the existence of a danger does not always enable a person to avoid the danger. In simple cases it does. In other cases, especially where buildings are concerned, it would be absurdly unrealistic to suggest that a person can always take steps to avoid a danger once he knows of its existence, and that if he does not do so he is the author of his own misfortune. Here, as elsewhere, the law seeks to be realistic. Hence the established principle . . . that knowledge or opportunity for inspection per se, and without regard to any consequences they may have in the circumstances, cannot be conclusive against the plaintiff. Knowledge, or opportunity for inspection, does not by itself always negative the duty of care or break the chain of causation. Whether it does so depends on all the circumstances. It will only do so when it is reasonable to expect the plaintiff to remove or avoid the danger, and unreasonable for him to run the risk of being injured by the danger.

Would a fairer result be to allow the claim but reduce the damages because the claimant was guilty of contributory negligence by remaining in the building after he knew of the exist-ence of the defects? (Note: in *Targett* the plaintiff's damages were in fact reduced by 25 per cent because of his contributory negligence in descending the stairs, not for his decision to remain in occupation of the premises.)

If the claimant *should* have known of the defect before it materialises and causes damage, can it still be regarded as latent? In *Pearson Education Ltd v Charter Partnership Ltd* [2007] EWCA Civ 130 the Court of Appeal doubted whether anything other than actual knowledge of the defect could lead to a denial of recovery, as opposed to a reduction for contributory negligence, if the defect materialised and caused damage. Although the case dealt with commercial premises, the reasoning is at least as applicable to domestic dwellings: would it be fair to deny recovery altogether to a claimant injured when her house collapsed as a result of a carelessly created latent defect because the defect might have been discovered if she had commissioned a building survey before inhabiting the property?

Thus the position has been reached where the superior courts of England and the Commonwealth have adopted at least three different approaches in respect to the liability of a builder to a subsequent purchaser for defects in a building. *D & F Estates* and *Murphy* (England) refuse to impose a duty in respect of such defects; *Winnipeg Condominium* (Canada) imposes a duty only in respect of dangerous defects; and *Bryan and Hamlin* (Australia and New Zealand) currently impose a duty in respect of at least some non-dangerous defects (although note the discussion of *Woolcock*, above). Which approach of the three do you find most convincing? Do you think that *Winnipeg* and *Bryan* can successfully meet the practical objections to the *Anns* approach raised by the House of Lords in *D & F Estates* and *Murphy*? For further discussion, see Quill, 'Consumer protection in respect of defective buildings' (2006) 14 Tort L Rev 195.

III. The *Hedley Byrne* Exception

There exists one major—although not unique—exception to the common law's general exclusion of liability in negligence for pure economic loss. A duty of care may arise in respect of such loss where the defendant voluntarily assumes responsibility towards the plaintiff. The foundations for this liability—which seems in some respects closer to liability in contract (also based on an assumption of responsibility) than liability in tort—were laid by the House of Lords in the case of *Hedley Byrne & Co Ltd v Heller & Partners Ltd* [1964] AC 465.

Although the *Hedley Byrne* principle now appears to extend beyond negligent misstatement (see Section IV), the case itself was concerned with this issue. While the law of contract developed rules for negligent misrepresentation inducing a contract, only a limited remedy (rescission) was provided, and then only where the misrepresentation actually resulted in a contract (see now Misrepresentation Act 1967, G. Treitel, *The Law of Contract*, 12th edn. (London: Sweet & Maxwell, 2007), ch. 9). Of course, parties already in a contractual relationship might owe a duty to be careful when providing statements to the other contracting party, and a breach of this obligation would result in an award of damages for economic loss. Outside this, liability for statements causing economic loss was thought to arise only in limited circumstances, namely where there was fraud or the parties were in a fiduciary relationship. The exception for fraud traced its history to *Pasley v Freeman* (1789) 3 TR 51 but the modern law was stated in *Derry v Peek* (1889) 14 App Cas 337. In this case the House of Lords considered the liability of company directors with respect to false statements in a prospectus. The cause of action brought against the directors was deceit, not negligence, and the House of Lords held that, in an action of deceit, the plaintiff must prove actual fraud in making the statement (i.e. that it was made with knowledge of its falsity or at least recklessness as to whether it was true or false). This remains the law today in the tort of deceit. However, for a time it was thought that the case laid down the rule that, in the absence of contract, an innocent but negligent misrepresentation could not give rise to liability. Indeed, Lord Bramwell in *Derry* had said (at 347). 'To found an action for damages there must be a contract and breach, or fraud.' However, in *Nocton v Lord Ashburton* [1914] AC 932 a solicitor was held liable in negligence for a non-fraudulent statement given to his client. Lord Haldane held that the fiduciary relationship between the parties imposed a duty on the solicitor. His Lordship argued that this was not inconsistent with *Derry*; as all that that case could be taken as deciding was that, on its facts, the relationship did not impose any duty on the directors to take care in respect of the statements in the prospectus (on which see Lobban, 'Nineteenth Century Frauds in Company Formation: *Derry v Peek* in Context' (1996) 112 LQR 287). Lord Haldane reiterated his view of *Derry* in *Robinson v National Bank of Scotland* [1916] SC (HL) 154 at 157:

> I think, as I said in *Nocton's* case, that an exaggerated view was taken by a good many people of the scope of the decision in *Derry v. Peek*. The whole of the doctrine as to fiduciary relationships, as to the duty of care arising from implied as well as express contracts, as to the duty of care arising from other special relationships which the courts may find to exist in particular cases, still remains, and I should be very sorry if any word fell from me which should suggest that the courts are in any way hampered in recognising that the duty of care may be established when such cases really occur.

However, by the time of *Hedley Byrne* the only special relationship that was recognised as giving rise to a duty to take care in respect of a statement was the fiduciary relationship. An example of this restrictive approach can be found in *Candler v Crane, Christmas & Co* [1951] 2 KB 164. The plaintiff was a potential investor in a company for which the defendants were the auditors. The plaintiff asked to see the company accounts before making his decision, and the managing director of the company asked the defendants to prepare the accounts and to show them to and discuss them with the plaintiff. After showing the accounts to his own accountant the plaintiff decided to invest in the company. In fact, the accounts were carelessly prepared, contained numerous false statements, and gave a wholly misleading picture of the state of the company, which was wound up within a year, the plaintiff losing the whole of his investment. By a majority of 2–1 the Court of Appeal held that, in the absence of fraud or of any contractual or fiduciary relationship between the parties, a false but careless statement gave rise to no liability. Denning LJ dissented, holding that the accountants owed a limited duty to any third person to whom they showed their accounts or to whom they knew that their clients were going to show them, when, to the knowledge of the accountants, that person would consider their accounts with a view to the investment of money or taking other action to his gain or detriment.

The restrictive approach represented by *Candler* was challenged before the House of Lords in *Hedley Byrne*.

Hedley Byrne & Co Ltd v Heller & Partners Ltd [1964] AC 465

The appellants, a firm of advertising agents, placed substantial orders for advertising time on television programmes and for advertising space in certain newspapers on behalf of a client, Easipower Ltd, on terms by which they became personally liable to the television and newspaper companies. After becoming doubtful about Easipower's creditworthiness, the appellants asked their bank (the National Provincial Bank) to telephone the respondents (Easipower

Ltd's bankers) to seek a credit reference. The reply came back: '[b]elieved to be respectably constituted and considered good for its normal business engagements' and that they 'would not undertake any commitments they are unable to fulfil.' In response to a subsequent written inquiry from the appellants asking whether the respondents considered Easipower Ltd 'trust-worthy, in the way of business, to the extent of £100,000 per annum', the respondents replied, in a letter marked 'CONFIDENTIAL. For your private use and without responsibility on the part of the bank or its officials', that Easipower Ltd was a 'respectably constituted company, consid-ered good for its ordinary business engagements'; the respondents warned, however: 'Your figures are larger than we are accustomed to see.' The appellants relied on these statements and as a result they lost over £17,000 when Easipower Ltd went into liquidation. They then sought to recover this loss from the respondents as damages on the ground that these replies were given negligently and in breach of the respondents' duty to exercise care in giving them. At first instance, McNair J gave judgment for the respondents on the ground that they owed no duty of care to the appellants. This judgment was affirmed by the Court of Appeal, which was bound by the authority of *Candler v Crane, Christmas & Co* [1951] 2 KB 164 but held in any case that it would be unreasonable to impose on a banker the obligation suggested.

Lord Reid

My Lords, this case raises the important question whether and in what circumstances a person can recover damages for loss suffered by reason of his having relied on an innocent but negli-gent misrepresentation . . .

Before coming to the main question of law it may be well to dispose of an argument that there was no sufficiently close relationship between these parties to give rise to any duty. It is said that the respondents did not know the precise purpose of the inquiries and did not even know whether National Provincial Bank Ltd wanted the information for its own use or for the use of a customer: they knew nothing of the appellants. I would reject that argument. They knew that the inquiry was in connection with an advertising contract, and it was at least probable that the information was wanted by the advertising contractors. It seems to me quite immaterial that they did not know who these contractors were: there is no suggestion of any speciality which could have influenced them in deciding whether to give information or in what form to give it. I shall therefore treat this as if it were a case where a negligent misrepresentation is made directly to the person seeking information, opinion or advice, and I shall not attempt to decide what kind or degree of proximity is necessary before there can be a duty owed by the defendant to the plaintiff.

The appellants' first argument was based on *Donoghue (or McAlister) v Stevenson*. That is a very important decision, but I do not think that it has any direct bearing on this case. That decision may encourage us to develop existing lines of authority, but it cannot entitle us to disregard them. Apart altogether from authority I would think that the law must treat negligent words differently from negligent acts. The law ought so far as possible to reflect the stand-ards of the reasonable man, and that is what *Donoghue (or McAlister) v Stevenson* sets out to do. The most obvious difference between negligent words and negligent acts is this. Quite careful people often express definite opinions on social or informal occasions, even when they see that others are likely to be influenced by them; and they often do that without taking that care which they would take if asked for their opinion professionally, or in a business connec-tion. The appellants agree that there can be no duty of care on such occasions, and we were referred to American and South African authorities where that is recognised, although their law appears to have gone much further than ours has yet done. But it is at least unusual casu-ally to put into circulation negligently-made articles which are dangerous. A man might give a friend a negligently-prepared bottle of home-made wine and his friend's guests might drink it with dire results; but it is by no means clear that those guests would have no action against the negligent manufacturer. Another obvious difference is that a negligently-made article will only cause one accident, and so it is not very difficult to find the necessary degree of proximity or neighbourhood between the negligent manufacturer and the person injured. But words can be broadcast with or without the consent or the foresight of the speaker or writer. It would be one thing to say that the speaker owes a duty to a limited class, but it would be going very far to say that he owes a duty to every ultimate 'consumer' who acts on those words to his detriment. It would be no use to say that a speaker or writer owes a duty, but can disclaim responsibility if he wants to. He, like the manufacturer, could make it part of a contract that he is not to be liable for his negligence: but that contract would not protect him in a question with a third party at least if the third party was unaware of it.

So it seems to me that there is good sense behind our present law that in general an innocent but negligent misrepresentation gives no cause of action. There must be something more than the mere misstatement. I therefore turn to the authorities to see what more is required. The most natural requirement would be that expressly or by implication from the circumstances the speaker or writer has undertaken some responsibility, and that appears to me not to conflict with any authority which is binding on this House. Where there is a contract there is no difficulty as regards the contracting parties: the question is whether there is a warranty. The refusal of English law to recognise any *jus quaesitum tertio* causes some difficulties, but they are not relevant here. Then there are cases where a person does not merely make a statement, but performs a gratuitous service. I do not intend to examine the cases about that, but at least they show that in some cases that person owes a duty of care apart from any contract, and to that extent they pave the way to holding that there can be a duty of care in making a statement of fact or opinion which is independent of contract...

[His Lordship considered *Derry v Peek*, *Nocton v Lord Ashburton* and *Robinson v National Bank of Scotland*, and, after referring to the extract from the latter set out in the text above, continued:] This passage makes it clear that Lord Haldane did not think that a duty to take care must be limited to cases of fiduciary relationship in the narrow sense of relationships which had been recognised by the Court of Chancery as being of a fiduciary character. He speaks of other special relationships, and I can see no logical stopping place short of all those relationships where it is plain that the party seeking information or advice was trusting the other to exercise such a degree of care as the circumstances required, where it was reasonable for him to do that, and where the other gave the information or advice when he knew or ought to have known that the inquirer was relying on him. I say 'ought to have known' because in questions of negligence we now apply the objective standard of what the reasonable man would have done.

A reasonable man, knowing that he was being trusted or that his skill and judgment were being relied on, would, I think, have three courses open to him. He could keep silent or decline to give the information or advice sought: or he could give an answer with a clear qualification that he accepted no responsibility for it or that it was given without that reflection or inquiry which a careful answer would require: or he could simply answer without any such qualification. If he chooses to adopt the last course he must, I think, be held to have accepted some responsibility for his answer being given carefully, or to have accepted a relationship with the inquirer which requires him to exercise such care as the circumstances require.

If that is right then it must follow that *Candler v Crane, Christmas & Co* was wrongly decided...

[His Lordship held that, on the facts, it would be difficult to decide what duty, beyond a duty of honesty, a banker would owe to the recipient of a credit reference relating to one of its customers, but found for the respondents on the basis that their disclaimers of responsibility showed that they never undertook any duty to exercise care in giving their replies.]

Lord Morris of Borth-y-Gest

Leaving aside cases where there is some contractual or fiduciary relationship there may be many situations in which one person voluntarily or gratuitously undertakes to do something for another person and becomes under a duty to exercise reasonable care...Apart from cases where there is some direct dealing, there may be cases where one person issues a document which should be the result of an exercise of the skill and judgment required by him in his calling and where he knows and intends that its accuracy will be relied on by another...

[His Lordship proceeded to discuss *Derry v Peek, Nocton v Ashburton* and other authorities, and continued:] The guidance which Lord Haldane gave in *Nocton v Ashburton* was repeated by him in his speech in *Robinson v National Bank of Scotland.* He clearly pointed out that *Derry v Peek* did not affect (a) the whole doctrine as to fiduciary relationships (b) the duty of care arising from implied as well as express contracts and (c) the duty of care arising from other special relationships which the courts may find to exist in particular cases.

My Lords, I consider that it follows and that it should now be regarded as settled that if someone possessed of a special skill undertakes, quite irrespective of contract, to apply that skill for the assistance of another person who relies on such skill, a duty of care will arise. The fact that the service is to be given by means of, or by the instrumentality of, words can make no difference. Furthermore if, in a sphere in which a person is so placed that others could reasonably rely on his judgment or his skill or on his ability to make careful inquiry, a person takes it on himself to give information or advice to, or allows his information or advice to be passed on to, another person who, as he knows or should know, will place reliance on it, then a duty of care will arise...

[I]n my judgment the bank in the present case, by the words which they employed, effectively disclaimed any assumption of a duty of care. They stated that they only responded to the inquiry on the basis that their reply was without responsibility. If the inquirers chose to receive and act upon the reply they cannot disregard the definite terms upon which it was given...

I would therefore dismiss the appeal.

Lord Devlin

Counsel for the respondents has given your Lordships three reasons why the appellants should not recover. The first is founded on a general statement of the law which, if true, is of immense effect. Its hypothesis is that there is no general duty not to make careless statements. No one challenges that hypothesis. There is no duty to be careful in speech, as there is a duty to be honest in speech. Nor indeed is there any general duty to be careful in action. The duty is limited to those who can establish some relationship of proximity such as was found to exist in *Donoghue v Stevenson.* A plaintiff cannot therefore recover for financial loss caused by a careless statement unless he can show that the maker of the statement was under a special duty to him to be careful. Counsel submits that this special duty must be brought under one of three categories. It must be contractual; or it must be fiduciary; or it must arise from the relationship of proximity, and the financial loss must flow from physical damage done to the person or the property of the plaintiff. The law is now settled, counsel submits, and these three categories are exhaustive. It was so decided in *Candler v Crane, Christmas & Co* [1951] 2 KB 164 and that decision, counsel submits, is right in principle and in accordance with earlier authorities...

A simple distinction between negligence in word and negligence in deed might leave the law defective but at least it would be intelligible. This is not, however, the distinction that is drawn in counsel for the respondents' argument and it is one which would be unworkable. A defendant who is given a car to overhaul and repair if necessary is liable to the injured driver (a) if he overhauls it and repairs it negligently and tells the driver that it is safe when it is not; (b) if he overhauls it and negligently finds it not to be in need of repair and tells the driver that it is safe when it is not; and (c) if he negligently omits to overhaul it at all and tells the driver that it is safe when it is not. It would be absurd in any of these cases to argue that the proximate cause of the driver's injury was not what the defendant did or failed to do but his negligent statement on the faith of which the driver drove the car and for which he could not recover. In this type of case where if there were a contract there would undoubtedly be a duty of service, it is not practicable to distinguish between the inspection or examination, the acts done or omitted to be done, and the advice or information given. So neither in this case nor in *Candler v Crane, Christmas & Co* (Denning LJ noted the point ([1951] 2 KB 164 at 179) when he gave the example of the analyst who negligently certifies food to be harmless) has counsel for the respondents argued that the distinction lies there.

This is why the distinction is now said to depend on whether financial loss is caused through physical injury or whether it is caused directly. The interposition of the physical injury is said to make a difference of principle. I can find neither logic nor common sense in this. If irrespective of contract, a doctor negligently advises a patient that he can safely pursue his occupation and he cannot and the patient's health suffers and he loses his livelihood, the patient has a remedy. But if the doctor negligently advises him that he cannot safely pursue his occupation when in fact he can and he loses his livelihood, there is said to be no remedy. Unless, of course, the patient was a private patient and the doctor accepted half a guinea for his trouble: then the patient can recover all [in contract]. I am bound to say, my Lords, that I think this to be nonsense. It is not the sort of nonsense that can arise even in the best system of law out of the need to draw nice distinctions between borderline cases. It arises, if it is the law, simply out of a refusal to make sense. The line is not drawn on any intelligible principle. It just happens to be the line which those who have been driven from the extreme assertion that negligent statements in the absence of contractual or fiduciary duty give no cause of action have in the course of their retreat so far reached...

It would be surprising if the sort of problem that is created by the facts of this case had never until recently arisen in English law. As a problem it is a by-product of the doctrine of consideration. If the respondents had made a nominal charge for the reference, the problem would not exist. If it were possible in English law to construct a contract without consideration, the problem would move at once out of the first and general phase into the particular; and the question would be, not whether on the facts of the case there was a special relationship, but whether on the facts of the case there was a contract.

The respondents in this case cannot deny that they were performing a service. Their sheet anchor is that they were performing it gratuitously and therefore no liability for its performance can arise. My Lords, in my opinion this is not the law. A promise given without consideration to perform a service cannot be enforced as a contract by the promisee; but if the service is in fact performed and done negligently, the promisee can recover in an action in tort...

[After considering cases where liability had been imposed for the performance of a voluntary act, and noting that there were examples of the liability extending to purely financial loss, his Lordship continued:] My Lords, it is true that this principle of law has not yet been clearly applied to a case where the service which the defendant undertakes to perform is or includes the obtaining and imparting of information. But I cannot see why it should not be: and if it had not been thought erroneously that *Derry v Peek* (1889) 14 App Cas 337 negatived any liability for negligent statements, I think that by now it probably would have been. It cannot matter whether the information consists of fact or of opinion or is a mixture of both, nor whether it was obtained as a result of special inquiries or comes direct from facts already in the defendant's possession or from his general store of professional knowledge. One cannot, as I have already endeavoured to show, distinguish in this respect between a duty to inquire and a duty to state.

I think, therefore, that there is ample authority to justify your lordships in saying now that the categories of special relationships, which may give rise to a duty to take care in word as well as in deed, are not limited to contractual relationships or to relationships of fiduciary duty, but include also relationships which in the words of Lord Shaw in *Nocton v Lord Ashburton* ([1914] AC 932 at 972) are 'equivalent to contract', that is, where there is an assumption of responsibility in circumstances in which, but for the absence of consideration, there would be a contract. Where there is an express undertaking, an express warranty as distinct from mere representation, there can be little difficulty. The difficulty arises in discerning those cases in which the undertaking is to be implied. In this respect the absence of consideration is not irrelevant. Payment for information or advice is very good evidence that it is being relied on and that the informer or adviser knows that it is. Where there is no consideration, it will be necessary to exercise greater care in distinguishing between social and professional relationships and between those which are of a contractual character and those which are not. It may often be material to consider whether the adviser is acting purely out of good nature or whether he is getting his reward in some indirect form. The service that a bank performs in giving a reference is not done simply out of a desire to assist commerce. It would discourage the customers of the bank if their deals fell through because the bank had refused to testify to their credit when it was good.

I have had the advantage of reading all the opinions prepared by your Lordships and of studying the terms which your Lordships have framed by way of definition of the sort of relationship which gives rise to a responsibility towards those who act on information or advice and so creates a duty of care towards them. I do not understand any of your Lordships to hold that it is a responsibility imposed by law on certain types of persons or in certain sorts of situations. It is a responsibility that is voluntarily accepted or undertaken either generally where a general relationship, such as that of solicitor and client or banker and customer, is created, or specifically in relation to a particular transaction. In the present case the appellants were not...the customers or potential customers of the bank. Responsibility can attach only to the single act, i.e., the giving of the reference, and only if the doing of that act implied a voluntary undertaking to assume responsibility. This is a point of great importance because it is, as I understand it, the foundation for the ground on which in the end the House dismisses the appeal. I do not think it possible to formulate with exactitude all the conditions under which the law will in a specific case imply a voluntary undertaking, any more than it is possible to formulate those in which the law will imply a contract. But in so far as your Lordships describe the circumstances in which an implication will ordinarily be drawn, I am prepared to adopt any one of your Lordships' statements as showing the general rule...

I shall...content myself with the proposition that wherever there is a relationship equivalent to contract there is a duty of care. Such a relationship may be either general or particular. Examples of a general relationship are those of solicitor and client and of banker and customer...There may well be others yet to be established. Where there is a general relationship of this sort it is unnecessary to do more than prove its existence and the duty follows. Where, as in the present case, what is relied on is a particular relationship created ad hoc, it will be necessary to examine the particular facts to see whether there is an express or implied undertaking of responsibility.

I regard this proposition as an application of the general conception of proximity. Cases may arise in the future in which a new and wider proposition, quite independent of any notion of contract, will be needed. There may, for example, be cases in which a statement is not supplied for the use of any particular person, any more than in *Donoghue v Stevenson* the ginger beer was supplied for consumption by any particular person; and it will then be necessary to return to the general conception of proximity and to see whether there can be evolved from it, as was done in *Donoghue v Stevenson*, a specific proposition to fit the case. When that has to be done, the speeches of your Lordships today...will afford good guidance as to what ought to be said. I prefer to see what shape such cases take before committing myself to any formulation, for I bear in mind Lord Atkin's warning...against placing unnecessary restrictions on the adaptability of English law. I have, I hope, made it clear that I take quite literally the dictum of Lord Macmillan, so often quoted from the same case, that ([1932] AC 562 at 619) 'the categories of negligence are never closed'. English law is wide enough to embrace any new category or proposition that exemplifies the principle of proximity.

Lord Pearce

The reason for some divergence between the law of negligence in word and that of negligence in act is clear. Negligence in word creates problems different from those of negligence in act. Words are more volatile than deeds. They travel fast and far afield. They are used without being expended and take effect in combination with innumerable facts and other words. Yet they are dangerous and can cause vast financial damage. How far they are relied on unchecked...must in many cases be a matter of doubt and difficulty. If the mere hearing or reading of words were held to create proximity, there might be no limit to the persons to whom the speaker or writer could be liable. Damage by negligent acts to persons or property on the other hand is more visible and obvious; its limits are more easily defined...

How wide the sphere of the duty of care in negligence is to be laid depends ultimately on the courts' assessment of the demands of society for protection from the carelessness of others. Economic protection has lagged behind protection in physical matters where there is injury to person and property. It may be that the size and the width of the range of possible claims has acted as a deterrent to extension of economic protection...

The true rule is that innocent misrepresentation per se gives no right to damages. If the misrepresentation was intended by the parties to form a warranty between two contracting parties, it gives on that ground a right to damages (*Heilbut, Symons & Co v Buckleton* [1913] AC 30). If an innocent misrepresentation is made between parties in a fiduciary relationship it may, on that ground, give a right to claim damages for negligence. There is also in my opinion a duty of care created by special relationships which, though not fiduciary, give rise to an assumption that care as well as honesty is demanded.

Was there such a special relationship in the present case as to impose on the respondents a duty of care to the appellants as the undisclosed principals for whom National Provincial Bank Ltd was making the inquiry? The answer to that question depends on the circumstances of the transaction. If, for instance, they disclosed a casual social approach to the inquiry no such special relationship or duty of care would be assumed (see *Fish v Kelly* (1864) 17 CBNS 194). To import such a duty the representation must normally, I think, concern a business or professional transaction whose nature makes clear the gravity of the inquiry and the importance and influence attached to the answer...A most important circumstance is the form of the inquiry and of the answer. Both were here plainly stated to be without liability. Counsel for the appellants argues that those words are not sufficiently precise to exclude liability for negligence. Nothing, however, except negligence could, in the facts of this case, create a liability (apart from fraud to which they cannot have been intended to refer and against which the words would be no protection since they would be part of the fraud). I do not, therefore, accept that, even if the parties were already in contractual or other special relationship, the words would give no immunity to a negligent answer. But in any event they clearly prevent a special relationship from arising. They are part of the material from which one deduces whether a duty of care and a liability for negligence was assumed. If both parties say expressly (in a case where neither is deliberately taking advantage of the other) that there shall be no liability, I do not find it possible to say that a liability was assumed...

I would, therefore, dismiss the appeal.

Appeal dismissed.

COMMENTARY

What is the basis of the *Hedley Byrne* liability? Two factors seem to have been required by their Lordships: an assumption of responsibility by the defendant and reasonable reliance by the plaintiff. These factors are not mutually exclusive, for one factor that may assist in showing an assumption of responsibility is knowledge that the information or advice will be relied upon. Although a few specific examples were given of relationships where the duty would arise (e.g. solicitor/client), the language of the speeches is very wide. Weir, 'Errare Humanum Est', in *Frontiers of Liability*, vol. 2 (Oxford: OUP, 1994) 103 at p. 105(n), has (rather uncharitably) stated:

Never has there been such a judicial jamboree as *Hedley Byrne* where one almost has the feeling that their lordships had been on a trip to Mount Olympus and perhaps smoked a joint on the bus. Something certainly went to their heads, presumably not the merits of the claim, which they dismissed.

Their Lordships were agreed that there were circumstances in which liability might arise in respect of pure economic loss suffered through reliance upon the negligent provision of information or advice. It is not clear, however, that they considered that a banker giving a reference in the form of a brief expression of opinion as to the creditworthiness of a customer thereby assumed a duty of care to the person requesting the reference. Subsequently, however, it has generally been taken for granted that a banker does indeed owe a duty of care in such circumstances (see *Mutual Life & Citizens Assurance Co Ltd v Evatt* [1971] AC 793). Stapleton, 'Duty of Care and Economic Loss: A Wider Agenda' (1991) 107 LQR 249 at p. 260 notes the plaintiff in *Hedley Byrne* had to overcome two hurdles: that against recovery for negligent words as opposed to negligent acts, and that against recovery of pure economic loss as opposed to loss connected with physical damage. She comments: 'With hindsight it is surprising how far the attention of the House of Lords was absorbed by the first question.' Lord Devlin could find 'neither logic nor common sense' (p. 517) in any distinction between pure economic loss and loss connected with physical damage, while Lord Hodson thought it was 'difficult to see why liability as such should depend on the nature of the damage' (p. 509). Only in the speech of Lord Pearce is there any analysis of the reasons why liability for pure economic loss might be restricted, and even that is very brief. Perhaps one should not be too critical of their Lordships. It is clear that any duty owed by a statement maker—whatever the nature of the loss—needs well-defined limits, a point illustrated by the recent decision of *Sutradhar (FC) v National Environment Research Council* [2006] UKHL 33. Here it was alleged the duty in respect of a negligent misstatement resulting in physical injury was owed to a large section of the population of Bangladesh(!), a proposition unanimously rejected by the House of Lords (see further Lunney (2006) 14 Tort L Rev 129, and p. 467, below).

The question of a *jus quaesitum tertio* (a third-party right under a contract), raised in the extracts above by Lord Reid, was considered by the Law Commission in its Report *Privity of Contract: Contracts for the Benefit of Third Parties*, Law Com. No. 242 (Cm. 3329, 1996). This report formed the basis for the Contracts (Rights of Third Parties) Act 1999 which provides a limited right for the third-party beneficiary to enforce a contract made for his benefit.

However, as Lord Reid noted, the problem in *Hedley Byrne* was that there was no contract at all; hence cases on this branch of the law were not relevant. However, in other contexts the privity rule can be seen to have been influential in encouraging courts to find a tortious remedy (see Section IV, below).

Clearly part of the business of a bank is giving advice on the creditworthiness or otherwise of its customers. Would a duty be owed where the defendant chose to provide information in a commercial setting even though the advice given did not form part of its core business? In *Mutual Life & Citizens Assurance Co Ltd v Evatt* [1971] AC 793 the plaintiff suffered economic loss after relying on advice requested from the defendant assurance company about the financial stability of one of its subsidiary companies. The majority of the Privy Council held that no duty of care was owed, the *Hedley Byrne* duty being limited to advisors who carry on the business or profession of giving advice of the kind sought and to advice given by them in the course of that business. Lords Reid and Morris (both of whom delivered speeches in *Hedley Byrne* itself) dissented, holding that all that was required was that the advice was given on a business occasion or in the course of business activities. The minority approach was favoured in *Esso Petroleum v Mardon* [1976] QB 801, and in *Spring v Guardian Assurance plc* [1995] 2 AC 296 at 320 Lord Goff noted that the decision had attracted serious criticism in 'light of the formidable dissenting opinion of Lord Reid and Lord Morris of Borth-y-Gest....' Thus an auctioneer can owe a duty to a potential bidder in respect of advice it proffers to that bidder about a lot coming up for auction even if this is not seen as its core business (see *Thomson v Christie Manson & Woods Limited* [2005] EWCA Civ 555, although no breach was established on the facts).

Lord Reid indicated that it is unlikely that one will be held to be under a duty when providing information in a social context. An example of when such a duty might arise is *Chaudhury v Prabhaker* [1989] 1 WLR 29. The plaintiff asked the first defendant, a friend of hers, to find her a used car. Although he was not a mechanic, he 'had had a lot to do with motor cars'. Despite her stipulation that the car should not have been in an accident, he negligently recommended a car that had been in accident and that was worthless. At trial the defendant conceded that he owed the plaintiff a duty of care, a concession thought to have been rightly made by a majority of the Court of Appeal, because the agency arrangement held to exist between the parties indicated that the occasion was not a social one (cf. May LJ, who thought that to impose a *Hedley Byrne* duty in this and similar situations would make social relations and responsibilities between friends unnecessarily hazardous).

A *Hedley Byrne* duty has been held to exist when the defendant's statement takes the form of a threat. In *Welton v North Cornwall District Council* [1997] 1 WLR 570 an environmental health officer of the defendant told the plaintiffs that unless certain alterations were made to their guest house (so as to meet statutory requirements) he would close the business down. In fact, the alterations were not required and the plaintiffs successfully sued to recover their wasted costs, the Court of Appeal holding that the statement fell within the *Hedley Byrne* principle. If *Hedley Byrne* creates a duty in respect of the provision of information and advice, can a threat be regarded as a form of information or advice (see Mullender (1999) 62 MLR 425)? (Is *Hedley Byrne* liability limited to the provision of information and advice?)

Apart from the traditional list of persons who give professional advice (e.g. solicitors, accountants, surveyors, engineers), the wide language of *Hedley Byrne* has been used to impose a duty on a range of other defendants such as public authorities (e.g. *Shaddock v Parramatta City Council* (1981) 150 CLR 225). The status of the defendant as a public authority exercising statutory functions should not be disregarded. In *Jain v Trent Strategic Health Authority* [2009] 1 AC 853 the House of Lords held that a local health authority, which had statutory responsibility for registering nursing homes, owed no duty of care to avoid causing economic loss to the proprietors of nursing homes. This was so even though the information provided by the defendant to the magistrate who cancelled the defendant's authority to run their nursing home (in an *ex parte* hearing—the defendants were not represented) was inaccurate and as a result of a slipshod investigation. Given that the purpose of the legislation requiring nursing homes to be registered was the protection of residents, the imposition of a duty in favour of others who might be adversely affected by the exercise of the power 'would or might inhibit the exercise of the statutory powers and be potentially adverse to the interests of the class of persons the powers were designed to benefit or protect' (per Lord Scott at [28]). For comment on *Jain*, see Bagshaw (2009) 17 TLJ 295. See also *Harris v Evans* [1998] 1 WLR 1285.

Can liability attach to representations made on a website? In *Patchett v Swimming Pool & Allied Trades Association Ltd* [2009] EWCA Civ 717, the claimants relied on information provided on the defendant's website to choose a contractor to build their swimming pool, which information was misleading. The Court of Appeal rejected an argument that 'special considerations' applied to representations made on a website but also made it clear that *Hedley Byrne* liability could arise in respect of such representations on the application of the usual principles. On the facts, the majority held that the website made it clear that the statements it contained were not to be relied upon without further enquiry, so no duty of care was owed. Given the virtually limitless number of people who can access a website, it may be difficult to find that a duty arises because there will be no way of limiting the class to whom the duty would be owed. This was overcome in *Patchett*; the website deliberately targeted those thinking of having a swimming pool built and the duty was owed only to that class (although, as noted, the claim failed for other reasons).

Do you think the House of Lords envisaged *Hedley Byrne* applying to this type of case?

IV. The Development of *Hedley Byrne* Liability

1. *Hedley Byrne* and the Supply of Information

The paradigm example of *Hedley Byrne* liability involves a two-party situation: A gives information or advice to B which B relies upon to his detriment. But what if A gives information to B, who passes it to C, and it is C who relies on it to his detriment. If A is liable to anyone who receives and relies on the information this may create a potential 'floodgates' problem. As Lord Reid pointed out in *Hedley Byrne*, 'words can be broadcast with or without the consent or the foresight of the speaker or writer. It would be one thing to say that the speaker owes a duty to a limited class, but it would be going very far to say that he owes a duty to every ultimate "consumer" who acts on those words to his detriment.' However, *Hedley Byrne* has been extended to impose a duty on the maker of a statement in favour of a third-party recipient of that information. The extension and its limits are considered in the extracts below.

Smith v Eric S Bush (A Firm); Harris and Another v Wyre Forest District Council [1990] 1 AC 831

The issue for the House of Lords in these appeals was whether a valuer owed a duty of care to the purchaser of a house in circumstances where the valuer had been instructed to carry out the valuation, not by the purchaser, but by the purchaser's mortgagee. In both cases the purchaser paid a fee to the mortgagee for the purpose of the having a valuation of the property carried out. In *Smith* the valuation was carried out by a third party, whilst in *Harris* it was undertaken by the mortgagee (the council) itself. In *Smith* the valuation was passed onto and was read by the purchaser; in *Harris* the purchaser did not read the valuation but assumed that, because the council was prepared to lend the money, the house must have been worth the proposed purchase price. In both cases the purchasers were aware of disclaimers of liability by the surveyors in relation to the surveys. In *Smith* the disclaimer was to the effect that neither the society nor its surveyor warranted that the report and valuation would be accurate and that the report and valuation would be supplied without any acceptance of responsibility, whilst in *Harris* it said that the valuation was confidential and was intended solely for the information of the local authority and that no responsibility whatsoever was implied or accepted by the local authority for the value or condition of the property by reason of the inspection and report. In both cases the purchasers bought the house without having an independent survey carried out, and in both cases the survey was carried out negligently resulting in economic loss to the purchasers. In *Smith* the plaintiff was successful at first instance and on appeal, whilst in *Harris* the plaintiff won at first instance but the decision was overturned by the Court of Appeal on the basis that the disclaimer prevented the council from owing a duty of care. The House of Lords dismissed the appeal in *Smith* and allowed the appeal in *Harris*. The extracts concern the question whether the valuer owed a duty of care to the purchasers. It should also be noted, however, that their Lordships also rejected the defence that the disclaimer prevented any duty of care that might otherwise have been owed from arising. It was held that, on the facts of the cases, the disclaimer clauses fell foul of the Unfair Contract Terms Act 1977 (see further p. 317, above).

Lord Templeman

These two appeals are based on allegations of negligence in circumstances which are akin to contract. Mr and Mrs Harris paid £22 to the council for a valuation. The council employed, and therefore paid, Mr Lee, for whose services as a valuer the council are vicariously liable. Mrs Smith paid £36.89 to the Abbey National for a report and valuation and the Abbey National paid the surveyors for the report and valuation. In each case the valuer knew or ought to have known that the purchaser would only contract to purchase the house if the valuation was satisfactory and that the purchaser might suffer injury or damage or both if the valuer did not exercise reasonable skill and care. In these circumstances I would expect the law to impose on the valuer a duty owed to the purchaser to exercise reasonable skill and care in carrying out the valuation.

In *Cann v Wilson* (1888) 39 Ch D 39, approved by this House in *Hedley Byrne & Co Ltd v Heller & Partners Ltd* [1964] AC 465, a valuer instructed by a mortgagor sent his report to the mortgagee, who made an advance in reliance on the valuation. The valuer was held liable in the tort of negligence to the mortgagee for failing to carry out the valuation with reasonable care and skill.

A valuer who values property as a security for a mortgage is liable either in contract or in tort to the mortgagee for any failure on the part of the valuer to exercise reasonable skill and care in the valuation. The valuer is liable in contract if he receives instructions from and is paid by the mortgagee. The valuer is liable in tort if he receives instructions from and is paid by the mortgagor but knows that the valuation is for the purpose of a mortgage and will be relied on by the mortgagee…

In the present appeals the relationship between the valuer and the purchaser is 'akin to contract'. The valuer knows that the consideration which he receives derives from the purchaser and is passed on by the mortgagee, and the valuer also knows that the valuation will determine whether or not the purchaser buys the house…

In the present proceedings by Mr and Mrs Harris the council accepted the application form and the valuation fee and chose to conduct their duty of valuing the house through Mr Lee. In the case of Mrs Smith the surveyors first accepted the valuation fee derived from Mrs Smith and undertook the duty of preparing a report which they knew would be shown to and relied on by Mrs Smith…

It was submitted by counsel for the council and Mr Lee that the valuation was prepared in fulfilment of the statutory duty imposed on the council by s. 43 of the Housing (Financial Provisions) Act 1958. Similarly, the valuation obtained by the Abbey National was essential to enable them to fulfil their statutory duty imposed by the Building Societies Act 1962. But in *Candler v Crane, Christmas & Co* [1951] 2 KB 164 the draft accounts were prepared for the company, which was compelled by statute to produce accounts.

In the present appeals the statutory duty of the council to value the house did not in my opinion prevent the council coming under a contractual or tortious duty to Mr and Mrs Harris, who were cognisant of the valuation and relied on the valuation. The contractual duty of a valuer to value a house for the Abbey National did not prevent the valuer coming under a tortious duty to Mrs Smith, who was furnished with a report of the valuer and relied on the report.

In general, I am of the opinion that in the absence of a disclaimer of liability the valuer who values a house for the purpose of a mortgage, knowing that the mortgagee will rely and the mortgagor will probably rely on the valuation, knowing that the purchaser mortgagor has in effect paid for the valuation, is under a duty to exercise reasonable skill and care and that duty is owed to both parties to the mortgage for which the valuation is made. Indeed, in both the appeals now under consideration the existence of such a dual duty is tacitly accepted and acknowledged because notices excluding liability for breach of the duty owed to the purchaser were drafted by the mortgagee and imposed on the purchaser…

Lord Griffiths

Counsel for the council [in the *Harris* case] and Mr Lee has submitted that they did not [sc. owe a duty in tort] because there was no voluntary assumption of responsibility on their part in respect of Mr Lee's inspection and report. He submits that *Yianni v Edwin Evans & Sons (a firm)* [1982] QB 438 was wrongly decided. That case was the first of a number of decisions, at first instance, in which surveyors instructed by mortgagees have been held liable to purchasers for negligent valuations. The facts were that the plaintiffs, who wished to buy a house at a price of £15,000, applied to a building society for a mortgage. The building society engaged a firm of valuers to value the property for which the plaintiffs had to pay. There was no disclaimer of liability although the mortgage application form advised the plaintiffs to obtain an independent survey. They did not do so because of the cost involved. The surveyors valued the property at £15,000 and assessed it as suitable for maximum lending. The building society offered the plaintiffs a maximum loan of £12,000 with which they purchased the property. There was serious damage to the house caused by subsidence which should have been discovered by the surveyors at the time of their inspection and it was admitted that the surveyors had been negligent.

In that case there was no disclaimer of liability and the valuer's report was not shown to the purchaser. Ignoring the disclaimer of liability, the facts are virtually indistinguishable from the present case unless it can be said that the fact that Mr Lee was an in-house valuer can make a difference when considering the existence of his duty of care to the purchaser. Park J said (at 454):

> I conclude that, in this case, the duty of care would arise if, on the evidence, I am satisfied that the defendants knew that their valuation of 1 Seymour Road, in so far as it stated that the property provided adequate security for an advance of £12,000, would be passed on to the plaintiffs, who . . . in the defendants' reasonable contemplation would place reliance on its correctness in making their decision to buy the house and mortgage it to the building society.

Finding both these conditions satisfied, Park J held the surveyors to be liable.

Counsel for the council and Mr Lee drew attention to the doubts expressed about the correctness of this decision by Kerr LJ in the course of his judgment in the Court of Appeal, and submitted, on the authority of *Hedley Byrne & Co Ltd v Heller & Partners Ltd* [1964] AC 465, that it was essential to found liability for a negligent misstatement that there had been 'a voluntary assumption of responsibility' on the part of the person giving the advice. I do not accept this submission and I do not think that voluntary assumption of responsibility is a helpful or realistic test for liability. It is true that reference is made in a number of the speeches in the *Hedley Byrne* case to the assumption of responsibility as a test of liability but it must be remembered that those speeches were made in the context of a case in which the central issue was whether a duty of care could arise when there had been an express disclaimer of responsibility for the accuracy of the advice. Obviously, if an adviser expressly assumes responsibility for his advice, a duty of care will arise, but such is extremely unlikely in the ordinary course of events. The House of Lords approved a duty of care being imposed on the facts in *Cann v Wilson* (1888) 39 Ch D 39 and in *Candler v Crane, Christmas & Co* [1951] 2 KB 164. But, if the surveyor in *Cann v Wilson* or the accountant in *Candler v Crane, Christmas & Co* had actually been asked if he was voluntarily assuming responsibility for his advice to the mortgagee or the purchaser of the shares, I have little doubt he would have replied: 'Certainly not. My responsibility is limited to the person who employs me.' The phrase 'assumption of responsibility' can only have any real meaning if it is understood as referring to the circumstances in which the law will deem the maker of the statement to have assumed responsibility to the person who acts on the advice . . .

The essential distinction between the present case and the situation being considered in the *Hedley Byrne* case and in the two earlier cases is that in those cases the advice was being given with the intention of persuading the recipient to act on it. In the present case the purpose of providing the report is to advise the mortgagee but it is given in circumstances in which it is highly probable that the purchaser will in fact act on its contents, although that was not the primary purpose of the report. I have had considerable doubts whether it is wise to increase the scope of the duty for negligent advice beyond the person directly intended by the giver of the advice to act on it to those whom he knows may do so . . .

I have come to the conclusion that *Yianni's* case was correctly decided. I have already given my view that the voluntary assumption of responsibility is unlikely to be a helpful or realistic test in most cases. I therefore return to the question in what circumstances should the law deem those who give advice to have assumed responsibility to the person who acts on the advice or, in other words, in what circumstances should a duty of care be owed by the adviser to those who act on his advice? I would answer: only if it is foreseeable that if the advice is negligent the recipient is likely to suffer damage, that there is a sufficiently proximate relationship between the parties and that it is just and reasonable to impose the liability. In the case of a surveyor valuing a small house for a building society or local authority, the application of these three criteria leads to the conclusion that he owes a duty of care to the purchaser. If the valuation is negligent and is relied on damage in the form of economic loss to the purchaser is obviously foreseeable. The necessary proximity arises from the surveyor's knowledge that the overwhelming probability is that the purchaser will rely on his valuation, the evidence was that surveyors knew that approximately 90% of purchasers did so, and the fact that the surveyor only obtains the work because the purchaser is willing to pay his fee. It is just and reasonable that the duty should be imposed for the advice is given in a professional as opposed to a social context and liability for breach of the duty will be limited both as to its extent and amount. The extent of the liability is limited to the purchaser of the house: I would not extend it to subsequent purchasers. The amount of the liability cannot be very great because it relates to a modest house. There is no question here of creating a liability of indeterminate amount to an indeterminate class. I would certainly wish to stress, that in cases where the advice has not been given for the specific purpose of the recipient acting on it, it should only be in cases when the adviser knows that there is a high degree of probability that some other identifiable person will act on the advice that a duty of care should be imposed. It would impose an intolerable burden on those who give advice in a professional or commercial context if they were to owe a duty not only to those to whom they give the advice but to any other person who might choose to act on it ...

I have already pointed out that the only real distinction between the present case and *Yianni*'s case is that the valuation was carried out by an in-house valuer. In my opinion this can make no difference. The valuer is discharging the duties of a professional man whether he is employed by the mortgagee or acting on his own account or is employed by a firm of independent surveyors. The essence of the case against him is that he as a professional man realised that the purchaser was relying on him to exercise proper skill and judgment in his profession and that it was reasonable and fair that the purchaser should do so. Mr Lee was in breach of his duty of care to the Harris's and the local authority, as his employers, are vicariously liable for that negligence.

Lord Jauncey of Tullichettle

There are a number of references in the speeches in the *Hedley Byrne* case to voluntary assumption of responsibility. Although in that case the respondent bankers gave the financial reference without payment, I do not understand that 'voluntary' was intended to be equiparated with 'gratuitous'. Rather does it refer to a situation in which the individual concerned, albeit under no obligation in law to assume responsibility, elected so to do. This is, I think, made clear by Lord Devlin's reference to the responsibility voluntarily undertaken by a solicitor to his client.

Here the building society had a statutory duty under s. 25 of the Building Societies Act 1962 to satisfy itself as to the adequacy of the security of any advance to be made and for that purpose to obtain 'a written report prepared and signed by a competent and prudent person who ... is experienced in the matters relevant to the determination of the value ...' (see s. 25(2)(a)). In pursuance of that duty the building society instructed the surveyors, who, by accepting these instructions, not only entered into contractual relations with the building society but also came under a duty in tort to exercise reasonable care in carrying out their survey and preparing their report. To that extent they were in no different position to that of any other professional person who has accepted instructions to act on behalf of a client. However, there were certain other factors present which must be taken into account. In the first place the surveyors were aware that their report would be made available to Mrs Smith. In the second place they were aware that she would probably rely on the contents of the report in deciding whether or not to proceed with the purchase of the house and that she would be unlikely to obtain an independent valuation. In the third place they knew that she had at the time of the mortgage application paid to the building society an inspection fee which would be used to defray their fee. In these circumstances would the surveyors in the absence of disclaimers of responsibility have owed a duty of care to Mrs Smith? . . .

The question must always be whether the particular facts disclose that there is a sufficiently proximate relationship between the provider of information and the person who has acted on that information to his detriment, such that the former owes a duty of care to the latter.

It is tempting to say that in this case the relationship between Mrs Smith and the surveyors was, in the words of Lord Shaw in *Nocton v Lord Ashburton* [1914] AC 932 at 972, quoted by Lord Devlin in *Hedley Byrne & Co Ltd v Heller & Partners Ltd* [1964] AC 465 at 528–529, 'equivalent to contract' inasmuch as she paid for the surveyors' report. However, I do not think that Lord Devlin, when he used those words, had in mind the sort of tripartite situation which obtained here, but rather was he considering a situation where the provider and receiver of information were in contact with one another either directly or through their agents, and where, but for the lack of payment, a contract would have existed between them. In the present case a contract existed between the building society and the surveyors who carried out their inspection and produced their report in pursuance of that contract. There was accordingly no room for a contract between Mrs Smith and the surveyors. I prefer to approach the matter by asking whether the facts disclose that the surveyors in inspecting and reporting must, but for the disclaimers, by reason of the proximate relationship between them, be deemed to have assumed responsibility towards Mrs Smith as well as to the building society who instructed them.

There can be only an affirmative answer to this question. The four critical facts are that the surveyors knew from the outset (1) that the report would be shown to Mrs Smith, (2) that Mrs Smith would probably rely on the valuation contained therein in deciding whether to buy the house without obtaining an independent valuation, (3) that if, in these circumstances, the valuation was, having regard to the actual condition of the house, excessive Mrs Smith would be likely to suffer loss and (4) that she had paid to the building society a sum to defray the surveyors' fee.

In the light of this knowledge the surveyors could have declined to act for the building society, but they chose to proceed. In these circumstances they must be taken not only to have assumed contractual obligations towards the building society but delictual [tortious] obligations towards Mrs Smith, whereby they became under a duty towards her to carry out their work with reasonable care and skill. It is critical to this conclusion that the surveyors knew that Mrs Smith would be likely to rely on the valuation without obtaining independent advice. In both *Candler v Crane, Christmas & Co* [1951] 2 KB 164 and *Hedley Byrne & Co Ltd v Heller & Partners Ltd* [1964] AC 465 the provider of the information was the obvious and most easily available, if not the only available, source of that information. It would not be difficult therefore to conclude that the person who sought such information was likely to rely on it. In the case of an intending mortgagor the position is very different since, financial considerations apart, there is likely to be available to him a wide choice of sources of information, to wit independent valuers to whom he can resort, in addition to the valuer acting for the mortgagee. I would not therefore conclude that the mere fact that a mortgagee's valuer knows that his valuation will be shown to an intending mortgagor of itself imposes on him a duty of care to the mortgagor. Knowledge, actual or implied, of the mortgagor's likely reliance on the valuation must be brought home to him. Such knowledge may be fairly readily implied in relation to a potential mortgagor seeking to enter the lower end of the housing market but non constat that such ready implication would arise in the case of a purchase of an expensive property whether residential or commercial . . .

I would only add three further matters in relation to this part of the case. In the first place the duty of care owed by the surveyors to Mrs Smith resulted from the proximate relationship between them arising in the circumstances hereinbefore described. Such duty of care was accordingly limited to Mrs Smith and would not extend to 'strangers' (to use the words of Denning LJ in *Candler v Crane, Christmas & Co* [1951] 2 KB 164 at 181) who might subsequently derive a real interest in the house from her. In the second place the fact that A is prepared to lend money to B on the security of property owned by or to be acquired by him cannot per se impose on A any duty of care to B. Much more is required. Were it otherwise a loan by A to B on the security of property, real or personal, would ipso facto amount to a warranty by A that the property was worth at least the sum lent. In the third place the sum sought by Mrs Smith as a mortgage was relatively small and represented only a small proportion of the purchase price. The house with all its defects was worth substantially more than that sum, and had the report merely stated that the house was adequate security for that sum Mrs Smith would have had no complaint. However, the report contained a 'mortgage valuation' of the house, which valuation wholly failed to reflect the structural defect. It is that valuation of which Mrs Smith is entitled to complain…

[His Lordship found it more difficult to hold that, in *Harris v Wyre Forest DC* the surveyor knew his report would be relied upon by the plaintiff but was not prepared to dissent on this point and allowed the appeal in that case.]

Lord Keith and **Lord Brandon** concurred.

Appeal in Smith v Eric S Bush *dismissed. Appeal in* Harris v Wyre Forest District Council *allowed.*

COMMENTARY

The difficulty in applying the *Hedley Byrne* principle to the facts of these cases is clear: the defendants did not make any representation to the plaintiffs at all. The survey was prepared for the building society and local authority respectively. At the very least, for the plaintiffs to succeed *Hedley Byrne* would have to be extended to situations where information was prepared for one party, passed on to another and then relied upon by that other to his detriment. Further, in *Harris* the plaintiff did not even see the survey. How could there have been any reliance?

For Lord Templeman, a duty was established because the relationship between the plaintiffs and defendants was 'akin' to contract. However, as Lord Jauncey points out, it is unlikely this was the type of situation envisaged by Lord Devlin when he used this term in *Hedley Byrne*. There, the parties were known to each other (through their agents) in circumstances where there was no contractual obligation to provide the information to anyone else. In *Smith* and *Harris* the plaintiff and defendant had no contract and one defendant was bound to provide the survey to a third party, the bank in *Smith*. Thus Lord Griffiths and Lord Jauncey held that the duty of care was established through a sufficiently proximate relationship based upon payment by the plaintiffs for the survey and knowledge by the defendants of the high likelihood that the plaintiffs would rely on the survey without obtaining any independent advice (more likely to be established where the purchase price of the property in question is low). Is this reasoning materially different from Lord Templeman's? (See further *Customs and Excise Commissioners v Barclays Bank plc*, extracted below.)

Kaye (1989) 52 MLR 841, noting that the valuer seems to owe a duty to both mortgagor and mortgagee, queries the position of the vendor who loses a sale when the surveyor negligently reports the existence of a fault that does not exist. The vendor is in just as proximate a relationship as the purchaser: he is known to the valuer who is aware that the vendor relies on the valuation to sell the house. If the surveyor is negligent and the purchase does not proceed, the vendor may well suffer loss, especially if there is a falling housing market. However, the vendor does not pay for the valuation. Should this be enough to prevent a duty of care from being owed?

What if a borrower fails to have his own survey done? Both Lords Griffiths and Jauncey indicated it was arguable that no duty would arise in respect of higher value properties, although why this is so is unclear. It might be because reliance in such circumstances is unreasonable, because a reasonable purchaser would conduct his own survey. At what price does this become necessary? Even if it was held to be unreasonable not to have one's own survey carried out, might this not go to contributory negligence rather than negativing the duty of care? (Cf. Harwood (1987) 50 MLR 841, who suggests that only in exceptional circumstances will a plea of contributory negligence be successful, because generally the purchaser should be able to place total reliance on the lender's survey. Both the purchaser and the lender invest a large amount of money on the security of the house, and a vital element is that the house is free from structural defects.) A more fundamental problem is that in some cases the interests of the purchaser and lender are not the same. The purchaser is interested in the valuation of the property *vis-à-vis* the purchase price. Conversely, the lender is interested in its value for the purpose of ensuring that, if the borrower (purchaser) cannot repay the loan, the property is of sufficient value to cover the loan. When the loan represents a significant proportion of the purchase price, these interests may converge. But where the loan represents a smaller proportion of the purchase price (e.g. 50 per cent) the purpose of the valuation is different. In these cases, is it acceptable to impose liability on the valuer?

One argument raised by the defendants was that, as the surveys were carried out to comply with statutory obligations imposed on the building society and the council, this precluded a duty of care being owed for another purpose. This argument was rejected by Lord Templeman, but in other contexts (see *Caparo*, below) the argument has had more success, and even where the purchase of houses has been involved it has had some success. In *Curran v NI Co-Ownership Housing Association* [1987] AC 718, the defendant association made an improvement grant to allow an extension to be added to a house. Before paying the grant the defendant had a statutory duty to be satisfied that the extension was built to a satisfactory standard. Some time after the extension was complete the property was sold to the plaintiff, and it became apparent that the extension had been defectively constructed and required rebuilding. The plaintiff sued to recover the economic loss associated with the rebuilding but the claim was struck out by the House of Lords. It was held that the purpose of the statutory duty was to see that public money was properly spent rather than to protect the recipient of the grant and any successors in title. Could it not be said that the purpose of the statutory duty in *Smith* was to protect the interests of building society savers? If so, was it legitimate to superimpose a common law duty to protect the interests of current or future owners?

In *Smith* and *Harris* the employer of the surveyors who carried out the work was sued, but in *Merrett v Babb* [2001] QB 1174 a majority of the Court of Appeal held that the surveyor who carried out the inspection of the property owed a duty of care to the prospective purchasers as an individual. For May LJ, '[t]he relevant relationship was that between the purchaser and the employed professional valuer and the nature of the valuer's employment is not relevant to that relationship'. However, this may not be so in every case. If the professional valuer had been a director of his employer company rather than an employee, the position might have been different, for in that situation the valuer would normally be seen as acting on behalf of the company and the liability would be solely that of the company (*Williams v Natural Life Health Foods Ltd* [1998] 1 WLR 830). Given that both are representing the company, why should the employee be worse off? (Cf. *Bradford & Bingley v Hayes*, unreported, QBD, 25 July 2001, where it was held a director of a company employed by the mortgagee did not assume a personal responsibility to the mortgagee.)

Valuers have been held liable to third parties in contexts other than the purchase of real property. In *Killick v PricewaterhouseCoopers* [2001] 1 Lloyd's Rep PN 18 the defendant was appointed by directors of a company to value the shares of the company for the purpose of determining the amount to be paid to the estate of a deceased shareholder who was required by the articles of association to sell his shares in the company. Neuberger J held that the defendant owed a duty of care to the executor of the shareholder, one reason being that the defendant knew the specific purpose of its appointment. If anything, this is a stronger case than *Smith* as the probability of the valuation being relied upon by the third party was 100 per cent (cf. *Raja v Austin Gray (A Firm)* [2003] 1 EGLR 91 where the claimant's ability to sue another party for loss caused by the allegedly negligent valuation precluded the valuer owing a duty to the claimant).

As the House of Lords was anxious to point out in *Smith v Bush*, however, that decision is not to be taken as imposing a general liability on information providers to third parties. This was made explicit in the following case.

Caparo Industries plc v Dickman [1990] 2 AC 605

The respondent company, Caparo, owned shares in another company, Fidelity. Shortly before the publication of Fidelity's audited accounts for the tax year ending 31 March 1984, Caparo started to buy shares in the company, and it proceeded to make a successful takeover bid after the accounts (which showed a £1.2 million pre-tax profit) were made public. It was later discovered that Fidelity had not made a profit during that tax year; in fact it had made a loss of £400,000. Caparo brought an action against Fidelity's auditors for the loss caused to them in paying an excessive price for Fidelity's shares, alleging that the auditors owed it a duty of care because they could foresee that a potential takeover bidder, or alternatively an existing shareholder, would rely on the accounts in order to make investment decisions about the level of shareholding in Fidelity. An application to strike out the claim as disclosing no cause of action was upheld by the trial judge, but the Court of Appeal allowed the appeal as far as it related to Caparo's claim in its capacity as an existing shareholder. The auditors appealed to the House of Lords.

Lord Bridge

The salient feature of all these cases [sc. where *Hedley Byrne* liability was imposed] is that the defendant giving advice or information was fully aware of the nature of the transaction which the plaintiff had in contemplation, knew that the advice or information would be communicated to him directly or indirectly and knew that it was very likely that the plaintiff would rely on that advice or information in deciding whether or not to engage in the transaction in contemplation. In these circumstances the defendant could clearly be expected, subject always to the effect of any disclaimer of responsibility, specifically to anticipate that the plaintiff would rely on the advice or information given by the defendant for the very purpose for which he did in the event rely on it. So also the plaintiff, subject again to the effect of any disclaimer, would in that situation reasonably suppose that he was entitled to rely on the advice or information communicated to him for the very purpose for which he required it. The situation is entirely different where a statement is put into more or less general circulation and may foreseeably be relied on by strangers to the maker of the statement for any one of a variety of different purposes which the maker of the statement has no specific reason to anticipate. To hold the maker of the statement to be under a duty of care in respect of the accuracy of the statement to all and sundry for any purpose for which they may choose to rely on it is not only to subject him, in the classic words of Cardozo CJ, to 'liability in an indeterminate amount for an indeterminate time to an indeterminate class' (see *Ultramares Corp v Touche* (1931) 255 NY 170 at 179), it is also to confer on the world at large a quite unwarranted entitlement to appropriate for their own purposes the benefit of the expert knowledge or professional expertise attributed to the maker of the statement. Hence, looking only at the circumstances of these decided cases where a duty of care in respect of negligent statements has been held to exist, I should expect to find that the 'limit or control mechanism . . . imposed on the liability of a wrongdoer towards those who have suffered economic damage in consequence of his negligence' (see the *Candlewood* case [1986] AC 1 at 25) rested on the necessity to prove, in this category of the tort of negligence, as an essential ingredient of the 'proximity' between the plaintiff and the defendant, that the defendant knew that his statement would be communicated to the plaintiff, either as an individual or as a member of an identifiable class, specifically in connection with a particular transaction or transactions of a particular kind (e.g. in a prospectus inviting investment) and that the plaintiff would be very likely to rely on it for the purpose of deciding whether or not to enter on that transaction or on a transaction of that kind . . .

These considerations amply justify the conclusion that auditors of a public company's accounts owe no duty of care to members of the public at large who rely on the accounts in deciding to buy shares in the company. If a duty of care were owed so widely, it is difficult to see any reason why it should not equally extend to all who rely on the accounts in relation to other dealings with a company such as lenders or merchants extending credit to the company. A claim that such a duty was owed by auditors to a bank lending to a company was emphatically and convincingly rejected by Millett J in *Al Saudi Banque v Clark Pixley (a firm)* [1990] Ch 313. The only support for an unlimited duty of care owed by auditors for the accuracy of their accounts to all who may foreseeably rely on them is to be found in some jurisdictions in the United States of America, where there are striking differences in the law in different states. In this jurisdiction I have no doubt that the creation of such an unlimited duty would be a legislative step which it would be for Parliament, not the courts, to take.

The main submissions for Caparo are that the necessary nexus of proximity between it and the auditors giving rise to a duty of care stems from (1) the pleaded circumstances indicating the vulnerability of Fidelity to a take-over bid and from the consequent probability that another company, such as Caparo, would rely on the audited accounts in deciding to launch a take-over bid or (2) the circumstance that Caparo was already a shareholder in Fidelity when it decided to launch its take-over bid in reliance on the accounts. In relation to the first of these two submissions, Caparo applied, in the course of the hearing, for leave to amend para. 16(2) of the statement of claim by adding the words 'or alternatively that it was highly probable that such persons would rely on the accounts for that purpose' . . .

[His Lordship then considered the position of auditors in relation to the shareholders of a public limited liability company arising from the relevant provisions of the Companies Act 1985, and continued:]

No doubt these provisions establish a relationship between the auditors and the shareholders of a company on which the shareholder is entitled to rely for the protection of his interest. But the crucial question concerns the extent of the shareholder's interest which the auditor has a duty to protect. The shareholders of a company have a collective interest in the company's proper management and in so far as a negligent failure of the auditor to report accurately on the state of the company's finances deprives the shareholders of the opportunity to exercise their powers in general meeting to call the directors to book and to ensure that errors in management are corrected, the shareholders ought to be entitled to a remedy. But in practice no problem arises in this regard since the interest of the shareholders in the proper management of the company's affairs is indistinguishable from the interest of the company itself and any loss suffered by the shareholders, e.g. by the negligent failure of the auditor to discover and expose a misappropriation of funds by a director of the company, will be recouped by a claim against the auditor in the name of the company, not by individual shareholders.

I find it difficult to visualise a situation arising in the real world in which the individual shareholder could claim to have sustained a loss in respect of his existing shareholding referable to the negligence of the auditor which could not be recouped by the company. But on this part of the case your Lordships were much pressed with the argument that such a loss might occur by a negligent undervaluation of the company's assets in the auditor's report relied on by the individual shareholder in deciding to sell his shares at an undervalue. The argument then runs thus. The shareholder, qua shareholder, is entitled to rely on the auditor's report as the basis of his investment decision to sell his existing shareholding. If he sells at an undervalue he is entitled to recover the loss from the auditor. There can be no distinction in law between the shareholder's investment decision to sell the shares he has or to buy additional shares. It follows, therefore, that the scope of the duty of care owed to him by the auditor extends to cover any loss sustained consequent on the purchase of additional shares in reliance on the auditor's negligent report.

I believe this argument to be fallacious. Assuming without deciding that a claim by a shareholder to recover a loss suffered by selling his shares at an undervalue attributable to an undervaluation of the company's assets in the auditor's report could be sustained at all, it would not be by reason of any reliance by the shareholder on the auditor's report in deciding to sell: the loss would be referable to the depreciatory effect of the report on the market value of the shares before ever the decision of the shareholder to sell was taken. A claim to recoup a loss alleged to flow from the purchase of overvalued shares, on the other hand, can only be sustained on the basis of the purchaser's reliance on the report. The specious equation of 'investment decisions' to sell or to buy as giving rise to parallel claims thus appears to me to be untenable. Moreover, the loss in the case of the sale would be of a loss of part of the value of the shareholder's existing holding, which, assuming a duty of care owed to individual shareholders, it might sensibly lie within the scope of the auditor's duty to protect. A loss, on the other hand, resulting from the purchase of additional shares would result from a wholly independent transaction having no connection with the existing shareholding.

I believe it is this last distinction which is of critical importance and which demonstrates the unsoundness of the conclusion reached by the majority of the Court of Appeal. It is never sufficient to ask simply whether A owes B a duty of care. It is always necessary to determine the scope of the duty by reference to the kind of damage from which A must take care to save B harmless:

> The question is always whether the defendant was under a duty to avoid or prevent that damage, but the actual nature of the damage suffered is relevant to the existence and extent of any duty to avoid or prevent it.

(See *Sutherland Shire Council v Heyman* (1985) 60 ALR 1 at 48, per Brennan J.)

Assuming for the purpose of the argument that the relationship between the auditor of a company and individual shareholders is of sufficient proximity to give rise to a duty of care, I do not understand how the scope of that duty can possibly extend beyond the protection of any individual shareholder from losses in the value of the shares which he holds. As a purchaser of additional shares in reliance on the auditor's report, he stands in no different position from any other investing member of the public to whom the auditor owes no duty.

Lord Oliver considered the purpose behind the statutory requirement for an audit, and continued:

[T]he history of the legislation is one of an increasing availability of information regarding the financial affairs of the company to those having an interest in its progress and stability. It cannot fairly be said that the purpose of making such information available is solely to assist those interested in attending general meetings of the company to an informed supervision and appraisal of the stewardship of the company's directors, for the requirement to supply audited accounts to, for instance, preference shareholders having no right to vote at general meetings and to debenture holders, cannot easily be attributed to any such purpose. Nevertheless, I do not, for my part, discern in the legislation any departure from what appears to me to be the original, central and primary purpose of these provisions, that is to say the informed exercise by those interested in the property of the company, whether as proprietors of shares in the company or as the holders of rights secured by a debenture trust deed, of such powers as are vested in them by virtue of their respective proprietary interests.

It is argued on behalf of the respondents (Caparo) that there is to be discerned in the legislation an additional or wider commercial purpose, namely that of enabling those to whom the accounts are addressed and circulated to make informed investment decisions, for instance by determining whether to dispose of their shares in the market or whether to apply any funds which they are individually able to command in seeking to purchase the shares of other shareholders. Of course, the provision of any information about the business and affairs of a trading company, whether it be contained in annual accounts or obtained from other sources, is capable of serving such a purpose just as it is capable of serving as the basis for the giving of financial advice to others, for arriving at a market price, for determining whether to extend credit to the company, or for the writing of financial articles in the press. Indeed, it is readily foreseeable by anyone who gives the matter any thought that it might well be relied on to a greater or lesser extent for all or any of such purposes. It is, of course, equally foreseeable that potential investors having no proprietary interest in the company, might well avail themselves of the information contained in a company's accounts published in the newspapers or culled from an inspection of the documents to be filed annually with the registrar of companies (which includes the audited accounts) in determining whether or not to acquire shares in the company. I find it difficult to believe, however, that the legislature, in enacting provisions clearly aimed primarily at the protection of the company and its informed control by the body of its proprietors, can have been inspired also by consideration for the public at large and investors in the market in particular...

The extension of the concept of negligence since the decision of this House in *Hedley Byrne & Co Ltd v Heller & Partners Ltd* [1964] AC 465 to cover cases of pure economic loss not resulting from physical damage has given rise to a considerable and as yet unsolved difficulty of definition. The opportunities for the infliction of pecuniary loss from the imperfect performance of everyday tasks on the proper performance of which people rely for regulating their affairs are illimitable and the effects are far reaching. A defective bottle of ginger beer may injure a single consumer but the damage stops there. A single statement may be repeated endlessly with or without the permission of its author and may be relied on in a different way by many different people. Thus the postulate of a simple duty to avoid any harm that is, with hindsight, reasonably capable of being foreseen becomes untenable without the imposition of some intelligible limits to keep the law of negligence within the bounds of common sense and practicality. Those limits have been found by the requirement of what has been called a 'relationship of proximity' between plaintiff and defendant and by the imposition of a further requirement that the attachment of liability for harm which has occurred be 'just and reasonable'. But, although the cases in which the courts have imposed or withheld liability are capable of an approximate categorisation, one looks in vain for some common denominator by which the existence of the essential relationship can be tested. Indeed, it is difficult to resist a conclusion that what have been treated as three separate requirements are, at least in most cases, in fact merely facets of the same thing, for in some cases the degree of foreseeability is such that it is from that alone that the requisite proximity can be deduced, whilst in others the absence of that essential relationship can most rationally be attributed simply to the court's view that it would not be fair and reasonable to hold the defendant responsible. 'Proximity' is, no doubt, a convenient expression so long as it is realised that it is no more than a label which embraces not a definable concept but merely a description of circumstances from which, pragmatically, the courts conclude that a duty of care exists . . .

Leaving this on one side, however, it is not easy to cull from the speeches in the *Hedley Byrne* case any clear attempt to define or classify the circumstances which give rise to the relationship of proximity on which the action depends and, indeed, Lord Hodson expressly stated (and I respectfully agree) that he did not think it possible to catalogue the special features which must be found to exist before the duty of care will arise in the given case (see [1964] AC 465 at 514). Lord Devlin is to the same effect (at 530). The nearest that one gets to the establishment of a criterion for the creation of a duty in the case of a negligent statement is the emphasis to be found in all the speeches on 'the voluntary assumption of responsibility' by the defendant. This is a convenient phrase but it is clear that it was not intended to be a test for the existence of the duty for, on analysis, it means no more than that the act of the defendant in making the statement or tendering the advice was voluntary and that the law attributes to it an assumption of responsibility if the statement or advice is inaccurate and is acted on. It tells us nothing about the circumstances from which such attribution arises . . .

[After considering the decision of the House of Lords in *Smith v Eric S Bush (A Firm); Harris v Wyre Forest DC*, his Lordship continued:] Thus *Smith v Eric S Bush*, although establishing beyond doubt that the law may attribute an assumption of responsibility quite regardless of the expressed intentions of the adviser, provides no support for the proposition that the relationship of proximity is to be extended beyond circumstances in which advice is tendered for the purpose of the particular transaction or type of transaction and the adviser knows or ought to know that it will be relied on by a particular person or class of persons in connection with that transaction. The judgment of Millett J in the recent case of *Al Saudi Banque v Clark Pixley (a firm)* [1990] Ch 313 (decided after the decision of the Court of Appeal in the instant case) contains an analysis of the decision of this House in *Smith v Eric S Bush* and concludes (and I agree) that it established a more stringent test of the requirements for proximity than that which had been applied by the Court of Appeal in the instant case . . .

My Lords, no decision of this House has gone further than *Smith v Eric S Bush* but your Lordships are asked by Caparo to widen the area of responsibility even beyond the limits to which it was extended by the Court of Appeal in this case and to find a relationship of proximity between the adviser and third parties to whose attention the advice may come in circumstances in which the reliance said to have given rise to the loss is strictly unrelated either to the intended recipient or to the purpose for which the advice was required. My Lords, I discern no pressing reason of policy which would require such an extension and there seems to me to be powerful reasons against it . . .

As I have already mentioned, it is almost always foreseeable that someone, somewhere and in some circumstances, may choose to alter his position on the faith of the accuracy of a statement or report which comes to his attention and it is always foreseeable that a report, even a confidential report, may come to be communicated to persons other than the original or intended recipient. To apply as a test of liability only the foreseeability of possible damage without some further control would be to create a liability wholly indefinite in area, duration and amount and would open up a limitless vista of uninsurable risk for the professional man . . .

In my judgment, accordingly, the purpose for which the auditors' certificate is made and published is that of providing those entitled to receive the report with information to enable them to exercise in conjunction those powers which their respective proprietary interests confer on them and not for the purposes of individual speculation with a view to profit. The same considerations as limit the existence of a duty of care also, in my judgment, limit the scope of the duty and I agree with O'Connor LJ that the duty of care is one owed to the shareholders as a body and not to individual shareholders.

To widen the scope of the duty to include loss caused to an individual by reliance on the accounts for a purpose for which they were not supplied and were not intended would be to extend it beyond the limits which are so far deducible from the decisions of this House. It is not, as I think, an extension which either logic requires or policy dictates and I, for my part, am not prepared to follow the majority of the Court of Appeal in making it. In relation to the purchase of shares of other shareholders in a company, whether in the open market or as a result of an offer made to all or a majority of the existing shareholders, I can see no sensible distinction, so far as a duty of care is concerned, between a potential purchaser who is, *vis-à-vis* the company, a total outsider and one who is already the holder of one or more shares.

Lord Roskill, **Lord Ackner** and **Lord Jauncey** delivered separate concurring opinions.

Appeal allowed.

COMMENTARY

Why did the plaintiffs win in *Smith* and *Harris* but lose in *Caparo*? The short answer is the pre-eminence given by the House of Lords to the purpose of the statement. In *Caparo* the auditors did not carry out the audit merely because the company felt it needed its accounts audited; rather, there was a statutory duty under the Companies Act 1985 for the company to appoint an auditor and produce audited accounts. The reason for this requirement was held to be the need to provide shareholders with information about the company's performance so that, if the shareholders thought it necessary, action could be taken at a general meeting of the company against those responsible for its management, the board of directors. However, the audited accounts were only provided to allow shareholders, as a body, to exercise this supervisory jurisdiction over the company. They were not provided to give potential investors information on which to make investment decisions, nor were they for the assistance of existing shareholders, as individuals, in making decisions about levels of shareholding in the company. This view of *Caparo* was recently affirmed in the controversial decision in *Stone & Rolls Ltd v Moore Stephens* [2009] 1 AC 1391 where a bare majority of the House of Lords held that an auditor owed no duty of care to an insolvent company where the auditor's negligence consisted of not detecting the fraud of the person running the company where the company was a 'one man company'. Although the decision was primarily influenced by the illegality defence (see Ch. 6), the majority were concerned that allowing an action to the company would (as it was insolvent) be solely in the creditors' interests, and that this would run counter to the limited duty auditors were held to owe under *Caparo*.

What was different about *Smith* and *Harris*? Although the statement was made to the building society and council it was made for the specific transaction that the plaintiffs were negotiating. In contrast, the purpose for which the audit was made in *Caparo* (as found by their Lordships: cf. Mullis and Oliphant (1991) 7 PN 22, 26) had nothing to do with the transaction for which it was relied upon. Note that the Companies Act 2006, Part 16 which introduced new statutory provisions for the audit of companies, does not appear to change this view as the primary duty of the auditor remains one that is linked to the proper performance of the company rather than the provision of financial information about the company to the general public.

The audit in *Caparo* was carried out to comply with the requirements of the Companies Act 1985, but it should not be thought that no financial investigation carried out by accountants under statute is capable of giving rise to a duty of care to anyone other than the subject of the audit. The key question remains the purpose behind the statutory requirement. In *Law Society v KPMG Peat Marwick* [2000] 1 WLR 1921 the Court of Appeal held that the defendant accountants owed a duty to the claimant in respect of a report on the activities of a certain firm of solicitors. Even though the solicitors paid for the report, it was prepared for the purpose of providing the Law Society with information enabling it to decide whether to exercise its regulatory powers, and of thereby protecting the contents of the Solicitors' Compensation Fund which the Law Society maintains to provide redress to the victims of solicitors' fraud. The duty was owed to the Law Society as trustee of the compensation fund, and extended to losses incurred by the fund as a result of pay-outs to the firm's defrauded clients.

Although *Smith v Bush* and *Caparo* can be distinguished on the 'purpose' basis, it is not an entirely satisfactory way of reconciling the results. No doubt the surveyors in *Smith* and *Harris*, if asked the purpose of the survey, would have said it was for the purpose of providing information to the building society and council so they could decide whether to lend the plaintiffs the funds to purchase the houses. In effect, the House of Lords deemed the survey to have an additional purpose, namely to provide information to a purchaser to allow him to decide whether to purchase a particular property. True, it was highly likely that purchasers would use the survey in that way, but given the reluctance of the House of Lords in *Caparo* to accept foreseeability as an appropriate basis on which to found a duty of care where the loss is purely economic it is doubtful whether this can be regarded as the key element of the duty of care. (Cf. Witting (2000) 20 OJLS 615 who argues that it is the statement maker's actual knowledge that the claimant will rely on the statement that requires him to act with reasonable care.) But what the plaintiffs in *Smith* and *Harris* did, and Caparo did not, was to pay for the service. There was no 'free-rider' problem in *Smith* and *Harris*; the plaintiffs had, effectively, bought the right to rely on the survey to the surveyor's knowledge. Conversely, Caparo, at least in its capacity as a potential investor, paid nothing for the audit. Furthermore, it was not an individual making one of the most important decisions of his or her life, but a commercial enterprise engaged in a profit-making exercise. As Weir [1990] CLJ 212 notes:

[Caparo] was not investing in Fidelity plc, it was buying it, taking it over. Caparo was a predator. Nor was Caparo exactly wet behind the ears. With a turnover of over £150 m. it is among the top 500 manufacturing companies in Britain. Its chairman, Mr Swarj Paul, chairs over twenty other companies. Allegedly the directors of Fidelity were fraudulent. Greed foiled by fraud is not quite maiden virtue rudely strumpeted, but it is hurtful all the same, and none the less so when the fraud is facilitated by negligence. But if Caparo were conned out of their booty, let them go against the vendors for fraud or breach of contract. Let not the predator turn and rend those who failed to catch the fraudster who succeeded in catching him. *Caveat praedator* is a sound and moral rule.

Of course, the vast majority of investors in Fidelity were not interested in taking it over but were interested in a sound investment. As such investors were unlikely to have the resources to undertake an independent assessment of Fidelity's financial position, did they have any choice but to rely on the audited accounts?

At the time of *Caparo*, many firms of accountants were partnerships, in which each partner was jointly and severally liable for the debts of the partnership. As the amount of money involved when auditing large company accounts may be huge, the potential liability is enormous if things go wrong. In 1995, the High Court found the accountancy firm, Binder Hamlyn, liable to pay £65 million in damages (reaching £105 million with interest and costs) in respect of an offhand remark allegedly delivered by one of the firm's audit partners at a meeting six years before the claim was brought (see *Daily Telegraph*, 7 December 1995). This figure was estimated to be in excess of the firm's liability insurance by £34 million, leaving each of its 120 partners to pay about £325,000 in order to cover the shortfall. Ultimately, before a scheduled appeal could be heard, Binder Hamlyn agreed to pay $86 million in an out-of-court settlement (see *Daily Telegraph*, 22 February 1997). Even these figures seem to be dwarfed by claims arising out of the collapse of the Bank of Credit and Commerce International in 1991: it was reported in 1998 that former BCCI auditors Pricewaterhouse Coopers and Ernst & Young were preparing to pay out up to $300 million in respect of their roles in the bank's collapse (see *Daily Telegraph*, 13 September 1998). As a result of concerns about excessive personal liabilities, the Government passed the Limited Liability Partnerships Act 2000. The Act creates a new kind of business entity—the limited liability partnership ('LLP')—which has a separate legal identity from its members, and it is that entity that is responsible for the debts of the LLP rather than the individual members. Accordingly, it is now possible for individual members of firms of accountants and solicitors to limit their personal liability to investors and shareholders in a way that was not possible at the time of *Caparo*. Moreover, the Companies Act 2006, ss. 534–538 now allows auditors to limit their liability to companies they audit, and s. 1157 of the Act allows a court in proceedings for negligence against an auditor to relieve him, either wholly or in part, from his liability on such terms as it thinks fit if the court hearing the case considers that the auditor may be liable but that he acted honestly and reasonably, and that having regard to all the circumstances of the case (including those connected with his appointment) he ought fairly to be excused. In light of these provisions do auditors continue to need the protection provided by *Caparo*?

The cases since *Caparo* have tended to define the purpose of the auditor's statement narrowly and consequently to deny the existence of a duty of care (see, e.g. *Al Nakib Investments (Jersey) Ltd v Longcroft* [1990] 1 WLR 1390; *James McNaughton Paper Group v Hicks Anderson* [1991] 2 QB 295; cf. *Morgan Crucible Co plc v Hill Samuel Bank Ltd* [1991] Ch 295). Unless the defendant knows in the most explicit terms that the information it is providing will be used by an identified third party for the purpose of making an investment decision, in circumstances where it is reasonable that the third party relies on that information without taking further advice—a rare combination of circumstances—no duty will be owed (see, e.g., *Precis (521) plc v William M Mercer Ltd* [2005] EWCA Civ 114; *Man Nutzfahrzeuge AG v Freightliner Ltd* [2008] 2 BCLC 22).

Other Jurisdictions

Some civil law jurisdictions have found accountants liable in circumstances similar to *Caparo* (see *van Gerven*, pp. 231–5, 241–2, and cf. European Commission Staff Working Paper: *Consultation on Auditor's Liability and its Impact on European Capital Markets*, Directorate General for Internal Market and Services (2007)). That French law reaches this conclusion is not surprising, as it does not utilise the duty concept to limit claims in negligence; once fault, causation, and damage have been established an action lies. The position in German law is more difficult. Liability for pure economic loss under the general negligence provision of the German civil code, §823 I BGB, is limited (see p. 379, above), but it has been possible to find auditors liable under §826 BGB which imposes a liability, covering pure economic loss, on anyone who intentionally causes harm to another in a manner *contra bonos mores*. This latter term has been defined as referring to behaviour that significantly offends 'the fundamental concepts of morally acceptable conduct towards persons with whom one is in a legal relationship'. Section 826 has also been interpreted to require a 'will to harm' on the part of the defendant. It might be thought these conditions would be difficult to satisfy in the case of an action by a lender who merely relies on negligently audited accounts, but it seems liability would arise in those circumstances. This is because careless or unconscionable conduct can satisfy the *contra bonos mores* requirement, and intent to harm can be inferred if it was conceivable on the part of the defendant that the statement could be used in negotiations with a provider of finance and could lead that person into taking a decision disadvantageous to him. This approach appears to equate intention of harm with foresight, and English courts have consistently refused to impose liability on this basis alone.

Other common law courts have reached decisions in line with *Caparo*. In *Esanda Finance Corporation Ltd v Peat Marwick Hungerfords* (1997) 188 CLR 241 the High Court of Australia held that an allegation that it was foreseeable to the auditors of a company that creditors and financiers of that company might rely on the audited accounts in deciding whether to enter into a particular financial transaction was insufficient to establish an arguable case for a duty of care. For a plaintiff to succeed it had to be shown that the defendant knew or ought to have known that the information would be communicated to the plaintiff for a purpose likely to lead the plaintiff to enter into a transaction of the kind entered into; and that the entry into the transaction was likely to be due to reliance on the information or advice. Shortly after *Esanda* was decided the Supreme Court of Canada also rejected the claims of shareholders and investors in a company against the auditor of that company, suggesting that only where the auditor knew (rather than could foresee) both the recipient of the information and the purpose for which it would be used would a duty of care be owed (*Hercules Management Ltd v Ernst & Young* [1997] 2 SCR 165). Further, as La Forest J agreed with the decision in *Caparo* as to the purpose of the statutory audit, the result would not differ depending upon whether the financial reports were relied upon in assessing the prospect of further investments or in evaluating existing investments, as in both cases the purpose to which the accounts were put were individual or personal investment decisions. This was not the purpose for which the accounts were prepared. In *Caparo* Lord Bridge had accepted that there may be a distinction between an investment decision to sell as a result of an audit which negligently undervalued company assets from a decision to buy as a result of an audit which negligently overvalued the company. However, as La Forest J points out, it is difficult to see why this distinction is justified: if the purpose of an audit is not to provide information to shareholders for investment decisions, the nature of the investment decision (i.e. whether to buy or sell) should be irrelevant. For comment on *Esanda* and *Hercules* see Phegan (1997) 5 TLJ 4.

It might be thought that the decision in *Caparo* heralded a similar era of limiting liability for professionals. The next sub-section, however, indicates how an expanded view of *Hedley Byrne* has opened up a new vista of negligence liability for professionals.

2. *Hedley Byrne* and the Provision of Services

Hedley Byrne was a case which concerned the provision of information or advice, and the concepts it utilised to establish a duty of care—assumption of responsibility and reliance—were suited to that situation. In different factual scenarios, the concepts may be more difficult to apply. In particular, the notion of reliance may prove problematic. In one sense everybody relies on everyone else in the conduct of daily life—the pedestrian relies on the motorist to drive carefully, the patron of a restaurant relies on the chef to cook carefully, etc.—but if this is what was meant by reliance the scope of *Hedley Byrne* liability would be almost limitless. Similarly, it is easier (although, as noted above, not always easy) to apply the notion of assumption of responsibility to the provision of information. When one chooses to provide information to another in circumstances where the provider knows that the other will take it seriously, it might meaningfully be said that the provider may be deemed to have assumed responsibility for that information. But can the same be said of choosing to act? Can a car driver be said to assume responsibility to pedestrians merely by choosing to drive?

Nonetheless, it has been clear for some time that *Hedley Byrne* liability may extend beyond the provision of information to the provision of services although, in light of *Customs and Excise Commissioners v Barclays Bank plc*, extracted below at p. 452, it may be that such liability is not based on *Hedley Byrne* at all. But there was certainly an argument for some kind of extension: the obvious case lies in the liability of professionals. It would be an odd result if a solicitor could be liable under *Hedley Byrne* for careless advice but not for carelessly drafting a document. Of course, the solicitor would also be liable in contract, so the practical effects of imposing liability in tort is to provide the claimant with a different limitation period (six years from the date of damage rather than six years from the date at which the contract was breached), and perhaps different rules as to damages. As has been seen in relation to information and advice, however, the difficulty lies in extending a remedy to persons who are adversely affected by the provision of a service performed by the defendant under a contract with another party. *Smith* and *Caparo* would suggest a restrictive approach to such claims, but in certain circumstances the House of Lords has allowed this type of action in relation to the negligent performance of professional services. It must be admitted, however, that the boundaries of this liability have yet to be definitely established.

Henderson v Merrett Syndicates Ltd [1995] 2 AC 145

The case arose out of the substantial losses suffered by the Lloyds Insurance Syndicates during the early 1990s. Members of certain Syndicates ('Names') brought actions against those responsible for the management of the Syndicates in both contract and tort, and a number of these actions were before the House of Lords on applications to have the actions struck out as disclosing no cause of action. Two of the many issues that were before the House were (1) whether the existence of a contract between the parties prevented the existence of a concurrent duty of care in tort between those parties, and (2) whether the Syndicate managers' owed a duty of care to the Names (of whom some had contracts with the managers and some did not). As regards (1) their Lordships accepted that there could be concurrent liability in contract and tort, although the tort duty could be modified by the terms of the contract between the parties. The extract focuses upon the second issue.

Lord Goff of Chieveley

My Lords, every person who wishes to become a Name at Lloyd's and who is not himself or herself an underwriting agent must appoint an underwriting agent to act on his or her behalf, pursuant to an underwriting agency agreement. Underwriting agents may act in one of three different capacities. (1) They may be members' agents, who (broadly speaking) advise Names on their choice of syndicates, place Names on the syndicates chosen by them, and give general advice to them. (2) They may be managing agents, who underwrite contracts of insurance at Lloyd's on behalf of the Names who are members of the syndicates under their management, and who reinsure contracts of insurance and pay claims. (3) They may be combined agents, who perform both the role of members' agents, and the role of managing agents in respect of the syndicates under their management.

Until 1990, the practical position was as follows. Each Name entered into one or more underwriting agency agreements with an underwriting agent, which was either a members' agent or a combined agent. Each underwriting agency agreement governed the relationship between the Name and the members' agent, or between the Name and the combined agent in so far as it acted as a members' agent. If however the Name became a member of a syndicate which was managed by the combined agent, the agreement also governed the relationship between the Name and the combined agent acting in its capacity of managing agent. In such a case the Name was known as a direct Name. If however the Name became a member of a syndicate which was managed by some other managing agent, the Name's underwriting agent (whether or not it was a combined agent) entered into a sub-agency agreement under which it appointed the managing agent its sub-agent to act as such in relation to the Name. In such a case the Name was known as an indirect Name...

The main argument advanced by the managing agents against the existence of a duty of care in tort was that the imposition of such a duty upon them was inconsistent with the contractual relationship between the parties. In the case of direct Names, where there was a direct contract between the Names and the managing agents, the argument was that the contract legislated exclusively for the relationship between the parties, and that a parallel duty of care in tort was therefore excluded by the contract. In the case of indirect Names, reliance was placed on the fact that there had been brought into existence a contractual chain, between Name and members' agent, and between members' agent and managing agent; and it was said that, by structuring their contractual relationship in this way, the indirect Names and the managing agents had deliberately excluded any direct responsibility, including any tortious duty of care, to the indirect Names by the managing agents. In particular, the argument ran, it was as a result not permissible for the Names to pray in aid, for limitation purposes, the more favourable time for accrual of a cause of action in tort. To do so, submitted the managing agents, would deprive them of their contractual expectations, and would avoid the policy of Parliament that there are different limitation regimes for contract and tort.

Such was the main argument advanced on behalf of the managing agents. Moreover, as appears from my summary of it, the argument is not precisely the same in the case of direct Names and indirect Names respectively. However, in any event, I think it desirable first to consider the principle upon which a duty of care in tort may in the present context be imposed upon the managing agents, assuming that to impose such a duty would not be inconsistent with the relevant contractual relationship. In considering this principle, I bear in mind in particular the separate submission of the managing agents that no such duty should be imposed, because the loss claimed by the Names is purely economic loss. However the identification of the principle is, in my opinion, relevant to the broader question of the impact of the relevant contract or contracts.

The Governing Principle

Even so, I can take this fairly shortly. I turn immediately to the decision of this House in *Hedley Byrne & Co Ltd v Heller & Partners Ltd*. There, as is of course well known, the question arose whether bankers could be held liable in tort in respect of the gratuitous provision of a negligently favourable reference for one of their customers, when they knew or ought to have known that the plaintiff would rely on their skill and judgment in furnishing the reference, and the plaintiff in fact relied upon it and in consequence suffered financial loss. Your Lordships' House held that, in principle, an action would lie in such circumstances in tort; but that, in the particular case, a duty of care was negatived by a disclaimer of responsibility under cover of which the reference was supplied.

The case has always been regarded as important in that it established that, in certain circumstances, a duty of care may exist in respect of words as well as deeds, and further that liability may arise in negligence in respect of pure economic loss which is not parasitic upon physical damage. But, perhaps more important for the future development of the law, and certainly more relevant for the purposes of the present case, is the principle upon which the decision was founded. The governing principles are perhaps now perceived to be most clearly stated in the speeches of Lord Morris of Borth-y-Gest (with whom Lord Hodson agreed) and of Lord Devlin . . .

[His Lordship quoted from these speeches and continued:] From these statements, and from their application in *Hedley Byrne*, we can derive some understanding of the breadth of the principle underlying the case. We can see that it rests upon a relationship between the parties, which may be general or specific to the particular transaction, and which may or may not be contractual in nature. All of their Lordships spoke in terms of one party having assumed or undertaken a responsibility towards the other. On this point, Lord Devlin spoke in particularly clear terms . . . Further, Lord Morris spoke of that party being possessed of a 'special skill' which he undertakes to 'apply for the assistance of another who relies upon such skill.' But the facts of *Hedley Byrne* itself, which was concerned with the liability of a banker to the recipient for negligence in the provision of a reference gratuitously supplied, show that the concept of a 'special skill' must be understood broadly, certainly broadly enough to include special knowledge. Again, though *Hedley Byrne* was concerned with the provision of information and advice, the example given by Lord Devlin of the relationship between solicitor and client, and his and Lord Morris's statements of principle, show that the principle extends beyond the provision of information and advice to include the performance of other services. It follows, of course, that although, in the case of the provision of information and advice, reliance upon it by the other party will be necessary to establish a cause of action (because otherwise the negligence will have no causative effect), nevertheless there may be other circumstances in which there will be the necessary reliance to give rise to the application of the principle. In particular, as cases concerned with solicitor and client demonstrate, where the plaintiff entrusts the defendant with the conduct of his affairs, in general or in particular, he may be held to have relied on the defendant to exercise due skill and care in such conduct.

In subsequent cases concerned with liability under the *Hedley Byrne* principle in respect of negligent misstatements, the question has frequently arisen whether the plaintiff falls within the category of persons to whom the maker of the statement owes a duty of care. In seeking to contain that category of persons within reasonable bounds, there has been some tendency on the part of the courts to criticise the concept of 'assumption of responsibility' as being 'unlikely to be a helpful or realistic test in most cases' (see *Smith v Eric S Bush* [1990] 1 AC 831, 864–865, per Lord Griffiths; and see also *Caparo Industries Plc v Dickman* [1990] 2 AC 605, 628, per Lord Roskill). However, at least in cases such as the present, in which the same problem does not arise, there seems to be no reason why recourse should not be had to the concept, which appears after all to have been adopted, in one form or another, by all of their Lordships in

Hedley Byrne... Furthermore, especially in a context concerned with a liability which may arise under a contract or in a situation 'equivalent to contract' it must be expected that an objective test will be applied when asking the question whether, in a particular case, responsibility should be held to have been assumed by the defendant to the plaintiff: see *Caparo Industries Plc v Dickman* [1990] 2 AC 605, 637, per Lord Oliver of Aylmerton. In addition, the concept provides its own explanation why there is no problem in cases of this kind about liability for pure economic loss; for if a person assumes responsibility to another in respect of certain services, there is no reason why he should not be liable in damages to that other in respect of economic loss which flows from the negligent performance of those services. It follows that, once the case is identified as falling within the *Hedley Byrne* principle, there should be no need to embark upon any further enquiry whether it is 'fair, just and reasonable' to impose liability for economic loss—a point which is, I consider, of some importance in the present case. The concept indicates too that in some circumstances, for example where the undertaking to furnish the relevant service is given on an informal occasion, there may be no assumption of responsibility; and likewise that an assumption of responsibility may be negatived by an appropriate disclaimer. I wish to add in parenthesis that, as Oliver J recognised in *Midland Bank Trust Co Ltd v Hett, Stubbs & Kemp* [1979] Ch 384, 416... an assumption of responsibility by, for example, a professional man may give rise to liability in respect of negligent omissions as much as negligent acts of commission, as for example when a solicitor assumes responsibility for business on behalf of his client and omits to take a certain step, such as the service of a document, which falls within the responsibility so assumed by him.

Lord Browne-Wilkinson

My Lords, I have read the speech of my noble and learned friend, Lord Goff of Chieveley, with which I am in complete agreement. I add a few words of my own on the relationship between the claim based on liability for negligence and the alternative claim advanced by the Names founded on breach of fiduciary duty.

The decision of this House in *Hedley Byrne & Co Ltd v Heller & Partners Ltd* was, to a substantial extent, founded on the earlier decision of this House in *Nocton v Lord Ashburton* [1914] AC 932. In that case, Lord Ashburton sought to be relieved from the consequences of having loaned money to, amongst others, his solicitor Nocton. Lord Ashburton's pleadings were based primarily on an allegation of fraud; in particular, there was no allegation on the pleadings either of breach of contract by Nocton or of negligence. The lower courts treated the case as being wholly dependent on proof of fraud. But in this House Nocton was held liable for breach of a fiduciary obligation owed by him as solicitor to his client. However, although the decision was based on breach of fiduciary duty, both Viscount Haldane LC and Lord Shaw expressed such fiduciary duty as being but one example of a wider general principle, viz., that a man who has voluntarily assumed to act on behalf of, or to advise, another in law assumes a duty to that other to act or to advise with care...

[His Lordship quoted from the speech of Viscount Haldane in *Nocton* and continued:] It was these passages from the speeches of Viscount Haldane LC, and others, which this House in *Hedley Byrne* took up and developed into the general principle there enunciated as explained by my noble and learned friend, Lord Goff of Chieveley.

This derivation from fiduciary duties of care of the principle of liability in negligence where a defendant has by his action assumed responsibility is illuminating in a number of ways. First, it demonstrates that the alternative claim put forward by the Names based on breach of fiduciary duty, although understandable, was misconceived. The liability of a fiduciary for the negligent transaction of his duties is not a separate head of liability but the paradigm of the general duty to act with care imposed by law on those who take it upon themselves to act for or advise others. Although the historical development of the rules of law and equity have, in the past, caused different labels to be stuck on different manifestations of the duty, in truth the duty of care imposed on bailees, carriers, trustees, directors, agents and others is the same duty: it arises from the circumstances in which the defendants were acting, not from their status or description. It is the fact that they have all assumed responsibility for the property or affairs of others which renders them liable for the careless performance of what they have undertaken to do, not the description of the trade or position which they hold. In my judgment, the duties which the managing agents have assumed to undertake in managing the insurance business of the Names brings them clearly into the category of those who are liable, whether fiduciaries or not, for any lack of care in the conduct of that management.

Secondly, in my judgment, the derivation of the general principle from fiduciary duties may be instructive as to the impact of any contractual relationship between the parties on the general duty of care which would otherwise apply. The phrase 'fiduciary duties' is a dangerous one, giving rise to a mistaken assumption that all fiduciaries owe the same duties in all circumstances. That is not the case. Although, so far as I am aware, every fiduciary is under a duty not to make a profit from his position (unless such profit is authorised), the fiduciary duties owed, for example, by an express trustee are not the same as those owed by an agent. Moreover, and more relevantly, the extent and nature of the fiduciary duties owed in any particular case fall to be determined by reference to any underlying contractual relationship between the parties. Thus, in the case of an agent employed under a contract, the scope of his fiduciary duties is determined by the terms of the underlying contract. Although an agent is, in the absence of contractual provision, in breach of his fiduciary duties if he acts for another who is in competition with his principal, if the contract under which he is acting authorises him so to do, the normal fiduciary duties are modified accordingly: see *Kelly v Cooper* [1993] AC 205, and the cases there cited. The existence of a contract does not exclude the co-existence of concurrent fiduciary duties (indeed, the contract may well be their source); but the contract can and does modify the extent and nature of the general duty that would otherwise arise.

In my judgment, this traditional approach of equity to fiduciary duties is instructive when considering the relationship between a contract and any duty of care arising under the *Hedley Byrne* principle (of which fiduciary duties of care are merely an example). The existence of an underlying contract (e.g. as between solicitor and client) does not automatically exclude the general duty of care which the law imposes on those who voluntarily assume to act for others. But the nature and terms of the contractual relationship between the parties will be determinative of the scope of the responsibility assumed and can, in some cases, exclude any assumption of legal responsibility to the plaintiff for whom the defendant has assumed to act. If the common law is not to become again manacled by 'clanking chains' (this time represented by causes, rather than forms, of action), it is in my judgment important not to exclude concepts of concurrent liability which the courts of equity have over the years handled without difficulty. I can see no good reason for holding that the existence of a contractual right is in all circumstances inconsistent with the co-existence of another tortious right, provided that it is understood that the agreement of the parties evidenced by the contract can modify and shape the tortious duties which, in the absence of contract, would be applicable.

Lord Keith, **Lord Mustill** and **Lord Nolan** agreed with Lord Goff.

Appeals dismissed.

COMMENTARY

The genesis of Lord Goff's analysis can be found in the earlier House of Lords' decision in *Spring v Guardian Assurance plc* [1995] 2 AC 296. The plaintiff sued his former employer with respect to a reference it had prepared. The defendant employer was required to provide a reference under the relevant rules of its regulatory body, but negligently prepared it, stating that the plaintiff was an unsuitable person to work in the industry. The result was that the plaintiff was unable to obtain further employment in the industry. Two arguments were raised against the plaintiff's claim: first, that the plaintiff had suffered only pure economic loss, which was not generally recoverable; and, secondly, that the imposition of a duty of care would be inconsistent with the defence of qualified privilege available to referees in the tort of defamation (which limited the referee's liability to circumstances where he acted maliciously: see p. 761, below). By a 4–1 majority the House of Lords allowed the claim. Leaving aside the qualified privilege point (which was rejected by the House of Lords), on what basis was the duty of care owed? Two of their Lordships went back to first principles, and found that the three requirements for a duty of care in *Caparo Industries plc v Dickman* had been satisfied. However, Lord Goff, with whom Lord Lowry agreed on this point, argued that a duty of care was owed according to the principles laid out in *Hedley Byrne*. It should be noted that, as traditionally understood, *Spring* was not a *Hedley Byrne* case. The defendant provided the plaintiff employee with no advice, nor did it make a representation to him. Rather, the reference was given to a third party, the future employer. Further, the plaintiff did not rely on the reference, at least not in the sense of using it to decide how he should act. Again, it was the future employer who relied on the reference in that sense. And the employer had no special skill or expertise in writing references nor did it hold itself out as possessing such skill. How then could Lord Goff find a duty based on *Hedley Byrne*?

In a judgment unaided by argument from counsel, Lord Goff redefined the scope of the *Hedley Byrne* exception. The basis of *Hedley Byrne* was an assumption of responsibility by the plaintiff to the defendant. This could occur where the plaintiff entrusted the conduct of his affairs to the other, relying on that other to exercise his best efforts on the plaintiff's behalf. His Lordship questioned whether any special skill was required, noting the powerful arguments in the minority speeches in *Mutual Life v Evatt* requiring only that the defendant was acting in a professional capacity, but ultimately he reserved his opinion on this issue. He was content to point out that the defendant in *Spring*, possessing special information about the plaintiff (his employment history), had been entrusted with the task of writing the plaintiff's reference, and was therefore under a duty to take care in performing that task. Furthermore, the fact that the defendant had to write the reference did not prevent an assumption of responsibly from arising.

As can be seen, this line of reasoning was taken up and expanded in *Henderson,* where it was endorsed by the other members of the House (see also *Williams v Natural Life Health Foods Ltd* [1998] 1 WLR 830). Expanding on *Spring,* Lord Goff made it clear that the liability under *Hedley Byrne* attached to the performance of services. It is not clear exactly what is meant by 'services' in this context. Lord Goff frequently uses the example of the solicitor/client relationship as the paradigm *Hedley Byrne* relationship, which suggests he was thinking of the old 'professions' (lawyers, doctors, accountants, engineers, surveyors), but in ordinary parlance the term has a wider meaning: a plumber or an electrician clearly performs a skilled service when doing his job. Further, the notion of entrusting the conduct of one's affairs to another sounds like something from the law of fiduciaries. However, a fiduciary's requirement to act carefully to avoid causing economic loss to the person in whose interest he is acting is, according to Lord Browne-Wilkinson, merely an example of the wider responsibility placed on those who have agreed to act in the interests of others. But in what sense had the managing agents agreed to act in the best interests of the indirect Names? Certainly there was no form of explicit entrustment by means of a contract; there was no contract between the indirect Names and the managing agents. It was foreseeable that if the managing agents acted negligently the indirect Names might suffer loss, but this cannot amount to entrustment unless a duty is to be imposed on those whose negligence might foreseeably cause pure economic loss. However, looking at the facts as a whole, it may not be stretching language too far to find an entrustment by the Names. The Names had little say in the form of the relationship with the members and managing agents. The Names signed up with a member's agent, who might or might not become their managing agents, and gave them complete discretion as to how the insurance syndicates of which they became part were managed. The Names had no choice; if they wanted to be involved, they had to abide by this system. Although there was no direct relationship between the managing agents and the indirect Names, the managing agents knew that they were in complete control over the success or otherwise of the Names' investment, and knew that the Names were relying on them to exercise care in the performance of this task. Even if there was no express entrusting, there was entrusting in fact, and it could thus be held that there had been an assumption of responsibility to the Names (cf. *Customs and Excise Commissioners v Barclays Bank plc*, extracted below, where several members of the House of Lords found some difficulty in seeing an assumption of responsibility in *Henderson*).

On the facts of *Henderson*, the indirect Names were not the only party to whom the managing agents had assumed responsibility. They had expressly assumed responsibility to the member's agents for the management of the syndicates under a contract. What if the indirect Names claimed that the managing agents owed them a duty in tort which went beyond that which was expressly assumed under the contact with the member's agents? Both Lord Goff and Lord Browne-Wilkinson accepted that the existence of a contract might affect the scope of any assumption of responsibility in tort of a party to that contract to a third party. That presented no problem on the facts of *Henderson*, as the responsibility assumed by the managing agents by contract to the member's agents and in tort to the indirect Names were of the same nature and extent.

Later cases have shown that it is not necessary that the assumption of responsibility in tort to the third party be even of same nature as that contained in the contract. In *Dean v Allin & Watts* [2001] 2 Lloyd's Rep 249 the Court of Appeal held that a solicitor had assumed a duty of care in tort to the lender even though his client (the person to whom the solicitor had contractually assumed responsibility) was the borrower. As both parties wanted the lender to have an effective security, it was possible to have duties owed in both contract and tort, although it was accepted that such a situation would be rare as the imposition of the tortious duty would normally be inconsistent with the contractual duty owed to the solicitor's client (as the general rule is that a solicitor owes no duty of care to a party with whom the client is negotiating a contract: *Gran Gelato v Richcliff (Group) Ltd* [1992] Ch 560).

In *Henderson*, Lord Goff considered that, once an assumption of responsibility had been found, it was no longer necessary to consider whether it was fair, just, and reasonable to impose a duty of care. Perhaps it would be better to say that a finding that one has 'assumed responsibility' to another is ultimately a question of law, and itself reflects considerations of fairness, justice and reasonableness (see e.g., *Andrew v Kounnis Freeman* [1999] 2 BCLC 641, 654–5 per Buxton LJ, and the speech of Lord Hoffmann in *Customs and Excise Commissioners v Barclays Bank plc*, extracted below, at [36]).

The Scope of *Hedley Byrne* after *Henderson*

It is clear from *Henderson* that an assumption of responsibility may be implied; in this sense it is like 'proximity', a statement of conclusion representing the court's view as to whether the defendant should be under a duty to the claimant in the circumstances of the case. But if, in fact, the assumption of responsibility is based upon an entrustment of the conduct of affairs from one party to another, it is difficult to see why the liability should be limited to professionals; we trust others to perform skilled services for us too. In *Junior Books v Vietchi* [1983] 1 AC 520 the pursuers were the owners of land on which a warehouse was to be constructed. They entered into a contract with the main contractor to build the warehouse, and instructed the main contractor to employ the defender, whose work they knew, as the flooring sub-contractor. Because of the defender's negligence the floor was defective and the pursuer suffered economic loss. A majority of the House of Lords allowed the claim but the reasoning, which was based on the two-stage *Anns* test, threatened to abolish the distinction between property damage and pure economic loss. With the retreat from *Anns* such a position became untenable and it was clear by the end of the 1980s that the decision was limited to its own facts. In *Murphy v Brentwood District Council* (above) Lord Keith suggested, without explanation, that the decision in *Junior Books* was an example of the *Hedley Byrne* principle but, as the principle was then understood, this rationalisation was dubious. However, after *Spring* and *Henderson* it is not so far-fetched to see the case as an example of a *Hedley Byrne* liability. The building owners did entrust the conduct of their affairs (the construction of the floor) to the sub-contractors by requiring that they be employed to build the floor. Conversely, the sub-contractors agreed to act knowing that reliance was being placed upon them. It is unlikely that Lord Goff was intending liability to arise in such circumstances, but on what basis could such a claim be denied? (See below.) Do you agree with Hedley [1995] CLJ 27 at 29 that 'a vague principle [assumption of responsibility] enunciated by Lord Reid is still a vague principle, and not a very useful one unless it can be sensibly applied by judges of far less eminence'.

Hedley Byrne and Concurrent Liability

The existence of a contract between the claimant and defendant, or between the claimant or defendant and another party, may affect *Hedley Byrne* liability in two main ways. The first, considered in *Henderson*, was the contract's effect upon the *Hedley Byrne* (tortious) duty of care. Does the presence of a contract exclude the possibility of a concurrent duty in tort? In the late 1970s, Oliver J reviewed the authorities and found that a solicitor owed a concurrent duty in contract and tort to his client (*Midland Bank Trust Co Ltd v Hett, Stubbs & Kemp* [1979] Ch 384). However, in *Tai Hing Cotton Mill Ltd v Liu Chong Hing Bank Ltd* [1986] AC 80, Lord Scarman, giving the judgment of the Privy Council, doubted that 'there was anything to the advantage of the law's development in searching for a liability in tort where the parties are in a contractual relationship'. Further, the Privy Council were not prepared to accept that the parties' mutual obligations in tort could be any greater than those assumed expressly or by necessary implication in their contract. The reasoning behind this is clear: where the parties have expressly set out the rights and obligations to be assumed under the contract, the law of tort has no business re-writing the bargain. But this does not answer the question whether a concurrent tortious duty, no more extensive than the contractual duty, may be owed between parties to a contract. This question was answered in the affirmative in *Henderson*, Lord Goff holding that:

[T]he law of tort is the general law, out of which the parties can, if they wish, contract; and, as Oliver J [in *Midland Bank*] demonstrated, the same assumption of responsibility may, and frequently does, occur in a contractual context. Approached as a matter of principle, therefore, it is right to attribute to that assumption of responsibility, together with its concomitant reliance, a tortious liability, and then to inquire whether or not that liability is excluded by the contract because the latter is inconsistent with it . . . [I]n the instant case liability can, and in my opinion should, be founded squarely on the principle established in *Hedley Byrne* itself, from which it follows that an assumption of responsibility coupled with the concomitant reliance may give rise to a tortious duty of care irrespective of whether there is a contractual relationship between the parties, and in consequence, unless his contract precludes him from doing so, the plaintiff, who has available to him concurrent remedies in contract and tort, may choose that remedy which appears to him to be the most advantageous.

Several points arise from this analysis. First, Lord Goff gives primacy to the tortious duty over the contractual duty. The liability under *Hedley Byrne* was based on the assumption of responsibility in tort, irrespective of whether there was also a contractual duty between the parties. However, in circumstances where the relevant relationship between the parties is brought about by the contract between them, it seems artificial to hold that the assumption of responsibility is nonetheless established by some other means. As the only relationship between the parties in such a case is the contract, the tort duty should be based on the relationship established by that contract. In these circumstances can the law of tort really be said to be the general law out of which parties may contract? Secondly, in some respects the imposition of a tort duty in these circumstances may actually exceed the bounds of contractual liability. Whittaker (1997) 17 LS 169 argues that all that is required for a *Hedley Byrne* duty, at least in the case of parties to an agreement, is an agreement on the part of a defendant to perform a service for the claimant, and actual or apparent possession of a skill in respect of that service. Such a wide approach circumvents the doctrine of consideration because liability rests only on an agreement (perhaps unsupported by consideration) to do something. In such circumstances any liability in tort is of necessity in excess of that in contract. There may also be other distinctions between remedies in tort and contract (e.g. in respect of limitation periods and contributory negligence rules), and it must be asked whether there is good reason for giving the claimant a free choice between causes of action when this may deprive the defendant of legal protections that would otherwise be available. Why, for instance, Whittaker asks, should those who perform services involving some special degree of skill be liable beyond the contractual limitation period? Such difficulties lead Whittaker to reject the wide *Hedley Byrne* principle espoused in *Henderson* in favour of an alternative ground of liability based on agency.

The existence of a contract may also have an effect on any tort duty owed even where the contract is between the claimant or defendant and a third party. If the parties to a complicated transaction have arranged it through a chain of contracts setting out the rights and responsibilities of the parties, should the law of tort intervene by holding that parties who owe each other no contractual duty nonetheless owe a tort duty? In *Simaan General Contracting Co v Pilkington Glass Ltd (No. 2)* [1988] QB 758 the plaintiff was the main contractor responsible for constructing a building in Abu Dhabi. The plaintiff sub-contracted part of the construction of the building (curtain-walling), one of the conditions being that a particular type of the defendant's glass was used. The defendant supplied glass which was the wrong colour, and it was ultimately rejected by the plaintiff with the result that neither it nor its sub-contractor were paid by the building owner. As Bingham LJ noted, the problem arose because the plaintiff, instead of suing its sub-contractor under contract, chose to sue the defendant, with whom it had no contract, in tort. Such a tort duty was recognised in the controversial case of *Junior Books v Veitchi* (above) but this was distinguished, Bingham LJ arguing that there was no basis on which the defendant could be said to have assumed a direct responsibility for the quality of the goods to the plaintiff. This was because 'such a responsibility is, I think, inconsistent with the structure of the contract the parties have chosen to make' (see also *Rolls Royce New Zealand Ltd v Carter Holt Harvey Ltd* [2005] 1 NZLR 324).

Given the above, it is not surprising that one of the arguments in *Henderson* against a duty of care being owed by the defendant managing agents to the indirect Names was that the contractual structure chosen by the parties militated against any such duty. The managing agents only assumed responsibility to the member's agents under their contracts. This was rejected by Lord Goff, who held that the assumption of responsibility to one party under a contract did not prevent a similar assumption to a non-party in respect of the services to be performed under that contract. However, his Lordship was quick to point out that such a case would be rare: 'in many cases in which a contractual chain comparable to that in the present case is constructed it may well prove to be inconsistent with an assumption of responsibility which has the effect of, so to speak, short circuiting the contractual structure so put in place by the parties'. It was argued above that *Junior Books v Veitchi* might possibly be justified on the basis of the wide *Hedley Byrne* principle set out in *Henderson*, but, as an example of a contractual structure which would prevent a duty of care from being owed, Lord Goff used the following example:

Let me take the analogy of the common case of an ordinary building contract, under which main contractors contract with the building owner for the construction of the relevant building, and the main contractor sub-contracts with sub-contractors or suppliers (often nominated by the building owner) for the performance of work or the supply of materials in accordance with standards and subject to terms established in the sub-contract . . . if the sub-contracted work or materials do not in the result conform to the required standard, it will not ordinarily be open to the building owner to sue the sub-contractor or supplier direct under the *Hedley Byrne* principle, claiming damages from him on the basis that he has been negligent in relation to the performance of his functions. For there is generally no assumption of responsibility by the sub-contractor or supplier direct to the building owner, the parties having so structured their relationship that it is inconsistent with any such assumption of responsibility . . . It is true that, in this connection, some difficulty has been created by the decision of your Lordships' House in *Junior Books Ltd v Veitchi Co Ltd* [1983] 1 AC 520. In my opinion, however, it is unnecessary for your Lordships to reconsider that decision for the purposes of the present appeal.

It is not made explicit why the facts of *Henderson* were so materially different from *Junior Books* as to warrant a different finding. The problem, as Hedley [1995] CLJ 27 points out, is 'how, precisely, do we tell when the parties' contracts are a definitive statement of all the rights their arrangements create? We can hardly ask what the parties would have been told had they consulted a lawyer, for any competent lawyer would surely have replied that the law was complex and uncertain.' Much will depend on the circumstances; thus in *Riyad Bank v Ahli United Bank plc* [2006] 2 Lloyd's Rep 292 the contractual structure represented the desire of a Saudi Arabian bank not to be directly linked to a Kuwait investment fund as it might deter Saudi investors and said nothing as to the obligations the parties assumed to each other in tort. Perhaps, then, one reason for distinguishing *Junior Books* was that in most building contracts the parties are free (within commercial constraints) to negotiate their own contracts, but for at least some of the indirect Names ignorance or carelessness may have prevented them from being in a position to negotiate any kind of contractual structure other than the one that was offered to them when they signed up. Assuming that this is a reason for the different result, is this a satisfactory ground of distinction?

What if A undertakes to perform a task under a contract with B which will benefit C (the *Henderson* scenario) but where C knows nothing of the contract between A and B and therefore places no reliance on it? Can A be held to have assumed responsibility to C if, through A's negligence, C does not receive the benefit he would otherwise have done. This problem is considered in the extract below.

White v Jones [1995] 2 AC 207

A solicitor was instructed to draw up a new will for the testator. The new will, unlike the old, benefited his two daughters. Due to the solicitor's negligence the new will had not been drafted by the time the testator died. An action was brought against the solicitor in negligence by the testator's daughters. The trial judge dismissed the claim on the basis that the solicitors owed no duty of care to the beneficiaries, but the Court of Appeal allowed an appeal, awarding each of the plaintiffs £9,000. The defendant appealed to the House of Lords.

Lord Goff

The Conceptual Difficulties

...It is right however that I should immediately summarise these conceptual difficulties [sc. arising from the claim]. They are as follows.

(1) First, the general rule is well established that a solicitor acting on behalf of a client owes a duty of care only to his client...

(2) A further reason is given which is said to reinforce the conclusion that no duty of care is owed by the solicitor to the beneficiary in tort. Here, it is suggested, is one of those situations in which a plaintiff is entitled to damages if, and only if, he can establish a breach of contract by the defendant. First, the plaintiff's claim is one for purely financial loss; and as a general rule, apart from cases of assumption of responsibility arising under the principle in *Hedley Byrne & Co Ltd v Heller & Partners Ltd* [1964] AC 465, no action will lie in respect of such loss in the tort of negligence. Furthermore, in particular, no claim will lie in tort for damages in respect of a mere loss of an expectation, as opposed to damages in respect of damage to an existing right or interest of the plaintiff. Such a claim falls within the exclusive zone of contractual liability; and it is contrary to principle that the law of tort should be allowed to invade that zone... The present case, it is suggested, falls within that exclusive zone. Here, it is impossible to frame the suggested duty except by reference to the contract between the solicitor and the testator—a contract to which the disappointed beneficiary is not a party, and from which, therefore, he can derive no rights. Second, the loss suffered by the disappointed beneficiary is not in reality a loss at all; it is, more accurately, a failure to obtain a benefit. All that has happened is that what is sometimes called a spes succesionis has failed to come to fruition. As a result, he has not become better off; but he is not made worse off. A claim in respect of such a loss of expectation falls, it is said, clearly within the exclusive zone of contractual liability.

(3) A third, and distinct, objection is that, if liability in tort was recognised in cases such as *Ross v Caunters* [1980] Ch 297, it would be impossible to place any sensible bounds to cases in which such recovery was allowed. In particular, the same liability should logically be imposed in cases where an *inter vivos* transaction was ineffective, and the defect was not discovered until the donor was no longer able to repair it...

[His Lordship noted a number of other conceptual problems, and continued:]

The Impulse to do Practical Justice

Before addressing the legal questions which lie at the heart of the present case, it is, I consider, desirable to identify the reasons of justice which prompt judges and academic writers to conclude, like Megarry V-C in *Ross v Caunters*, that a duty should be owed by the testator's solicitor to a disappointed beneficiary. The principal reasons are, I believe, as follows.

(1) In the forefront stands the extraordinary fact that, if such a duty is not recognised, the only persons who might have a valid claim (i.e. the testator and his estate) have suffered no loss, and the only person who has suffered a loss (i.e. the disappointed beneficiary) has no claim: see *Ross v Caunters* [1980] Ch 297 at 303 per Megarry V-C. It can therefore be said that, if the solicitor owes no duty to the intended beneficiaries, there is a lacuna in the law which needs to be filled. This I regard as being a point of cardinal importance in the present case.

(2) The injustice of denying such a remedy is reinforced if one considers the importance of legacies in a society which recognises (subject only to the incidence of inheritance tax, and statutory requirements for provision for near relatives) the right of citizens to leave their assets to whom they please, and in which, as a result, legacies can be of great importance to individual citizens, providing very often the only opportunity for a citizen to acquire a significant capital sum; or to inherit a house, so providing a secure roof over the heads of himself and his family; or to make special provision for his or her old age. In the course of the hearing before the Appellate Committee Mr Matheson (who was instructed by the Law Society to represent the appellant solicitors) placed before the Committee a schedule of claims of the character of that in the present case notified to the Solicitors' Indemnity Fund following the judgment of the Court of Appeal below. It is striking that, where the amount of the claim was known, it was, by today's standards, of a comparatively modest size. This perhaps indicates that it is where a testator instructs a small firm of solicitors that mistakes of this kind are most likely to occur, with the result that it tends to be people of modest means, who need the money so badly, who suffer.

(3) There is a sense in which the solicitors' profession cannot complain if such a liability may be imposed upon their members. If one of them has been negligent in such a way as to defeat his client's testamentary intentions, he must regard himself as very lucky indeed if the effect of the law is that he is not liable to pay damages in the ordinary way. It can involve no injustice to render him subject to such a liability, even if the damages are payable not to his client's estate for distribution to the disappointed beneficiary (which might have been the preferred solution) but direct to the disappointed beneficiary.

(4) That such a conclusion is required as a matter of justice is reinforced by consideration of the role played by solicitors in society. The point was well made by Cooke J in *Gartside v Sheffield Young & Ellis* [1983] NZLR 37 at 43, when he observed:

> To deny an effective remedy in a plain case would seem to imply a refusal to acknowledge the solicitor's professional role in the community. In practice the public relies on solicitors (or statutory officers with similar functions) to prepare effective wills.

The question therefore arises whether it is possible to give effect in law to the strong impulse for practical justice which is the fruit of the foregoing considerations. For this to be achieved, I respectfully agree with Nicholls V-C [in the Court of Appeal in *White*] when he said that the court will have to fashion 'an effective remedy for the solicitor's breach of his professional duty to his client' in such a way as to repair the injustice to the disappointed beneficiary (see [1993] 3 WLR 730 at 739).

The Tortious Solution

I therefore return to the law of tort for a solution to the problem. For the reasons I have already given, an ordinary action in tortious negligence on the lines proposed by Megarry V-C in *Ross v Caunters* must, with the greatest respect, be regarded as inappropriate, because it does not meet any of the conceptual problems which have been raised. Furthermore, for the reasons I have previously given, the *Hedley Byrne* principle cannot, in the absence of special circumstances, give rise on ordinary principles to an assumption of responsibility by the testator's solicitor towards an intended beneficiary. Even so, it seems to me that it is open to your Lordships' House, as in *Linden Gardens Trust Ltd v Lenesta Sludge Disposals Ltd* [1994] 1 AC 85, to fashion a remedy to fill a lacuna in the law and so prevent the injustice which would otherwise occur on the facts of cases such as the present. In the *Lenesta Sludge* case, as I have said, the House made available a remedy as a matter of law to solve the problem of transferred loss in the case before them. The present case is, if anything, *a fortiori*, since the nature of the transaction was such that, if the solicitors were negligent and their negligence did not come to light until after the death of the testator, there would be no remedy for the ensuing loss unless the intended beneficiary could claim. In my opinion, therefore, your Lordships' House should in cases such as these extend to the intended beneficiary a remedy under the *Hedley Byrne* principle by holding that the assumption of responsibility by the solicitor towards his client should be held in law to extend to the intended beneficiary who (as the solicitor can reasonably foresee) may, as a result of the solicitor's negligence, be deprived of his intended legacy in circumstances in which neither the testator nor his estate will have a remedy against the solicitor. Such liability will not of course arise in cases in which the defect in the will comes to light before the death of the testator, and the testator either leaves the will as it is or otherwise continues to exclude the previously intended beneficiary from the relevant benefit... That is therefore the solution which I would recommend to your Lordships.

Lord Browne-Wilkinson

My Lords, I have read the speech of my noble and learned friend, Lord Goff of Chieveley, and agree with him that this appeal should be dismissed. In particular, I agree that your Lordships should hold that the defendant solicitors were under a duty of care to the plaintiffs arising from an extension of the principle of assumption of responsibility explored in *Hedley Byrne & Co Ltd v Heller & Partners Ltd* [1964] AC 465. In my view, although the present case is not directly covered by the decided cases, it is legitimate to extend the law to the limited extent proposed using the incremental approach by way of analogy advocated in *Caparo Industries plc v Dickman* [1990] 2 AC 605...

The law of England does not impose any general duty of care to avoid negligent misstatements or to avoid causing pure economic loss even if economic damage to the plaintiff was foreseeable. However, such a duty of care will arise if there is a special relationship between the parties. Although the categories of cases in which such a special relationship can be held to exist are not closed, as yet only two categories have been identified, viz (1) where there is a fiduciary relationship and (2) where the defendant has voluntarily answered a question or tenders skilled advice or services in circumstances where he knows or ought to know that an identified plaintiff will rely on his answers or advice. In both these categories the special relationship is created by the defendant voluntarily assuming to act in the matter by involving himself in the plaintiff's affairs or by choosing to speak. If he does so assume to act or speak he is said to have assumed responsibility for carrying through the matter he has entered upon. In the words of Lord Reid in *Hedley Byrne v Heller* [1964] AC 465 at 486, he has 'accepted a relationship... which requires him to exercise such care as the circumstances require,' i.e. although the extent of the duty will vary from category to category, some duty of care arises from the special relationship. Such relationship can arise even though the defendant has acted in the plaintiff's affairs pursuant to a contract with a third party.

I turn then to apply those considerations to the case of a solicitor retained by a testator to draw a will in favour of an intended beneficiary. As a matter of contract, a solicitor owes a duty to the testator to use proper skill in the preparation and execution of the will and to act with due speed. But as the speech of Lord Goff demonstrates, that contractual obligation is of little utility. Breach by the solicitor of such contractual duty gives rise to no damage suffered by the testator or his estate; under our existing law of contract, the intended beneficiary, who has suffered the damage, has no cause of action on the contract.

Has the intended beneficiary a cause of action based on breach of a duty of care owed by the solicitor to the beneficiary? The answer to that question is dependent upon whether there is a special relationship between the solicitor and the intended beneficiary to which the law attaches a duty of care. In my judgment the case does not fall within either of the two categories of special relationships so far recognised. There is no fiduciary duty owed by the solicitor to the intended beneficiary. Although the solicitor has assumed to act in a matter closely touching the economic well-being of the intended beneficiary, the intended beneficiary will often be ignorant of that fact and cannot therefore have relied upon the solicitor.

However, it is clear that the law in this area has not ossified. Both Viscount Haldane LC [in *Nocton v Lord Ashburton* [1914] AC 932] and Lord Devlin [in *Hedley Byrne v Heller* [1964] AC 465] envisage that there might be other sets of circumstances in which it would be appropriate to find a special relationship giving rise to a duty of care. In *Caparo Industries plc v Dickman* [1990] 2 AC 605 at 618 Lord Bridge, quoting from Brennan J in *Sutherland Shire Council v Heyman* (1985) 60 ALR 1 at 43–44, recognised that the law will develop novel categories of negligence 'incrementally and by analogy with established categories'. In my judgment, this is a case where such development should take place since there is a close analogy with existing categories of special relationship giving rise to a duty of care to prevent economic loss.

The solicitor who accepts instructions to draw a will knows that the future economic welfare of the intended beneficiary is dependent upon his careful execution of the task. It is true that the intended beneficiary (being ignorant of the instructions) may not rely on the particular solicitor's actions. But ... in the case of a duty of care flowing from a fiduciary relationship liability is not dependent upon actual reliance by the plaintiff on the defendant's actions but on the fact that, as the fiduciary is well aware, the plaintiff's economic well-being is dependent upon the proper discharge by the fiduciary of his duty. Second, the solicitor by accepting the instructions has entered upon, and therefore assumed responsibility for, the task of procuring the execution of a skilfully drawn will knowing that the beneficiary is wholly dependent upon his carefully carrying out his function. That assumption of responsibility for the task is a feature of both the two categories of special relationship so far identified in the authorities. It is not to the point that the solicitor only entered on the task pursuant to a contract with the third party (i.e. the testator). There are therefore present many of the features which in the other categories of special relationship have been treated as sufficient to create a special relationship to which the law attaches a duty of care. In my judgment the analogy is close.

Moreover, there are more general factors which indicate that it is fair, just and reasonable to impose liability on the solicitor. Save in the case of those rash testators who make their own wills, the proper transmission of property from one generation to the next is dependent upon the due discharge by solicitors of their duties. Although in any particular case it may not be possible to demonstrate that the intended beneficiary relied upon the solicitor, society as a whole does rely on solicitors to carry out their will-making functions carefully. To my mind it would be unacceptable if, because of some technical rules of law, the wishes and expectations of testators and beneficiaries generally could be defeated by the negligent actions of solicitors without there being any redress. It is only just that the intended beneficiary should be able to recover the benefits which he would otherwise have received.

Further, negligence in the preparation and execution of a will has certain unique features. First, there can be no conflict of interest between the solicitor and client (the testator) and the intended beneficiary. There is therefore no objection to imposing on a solicitor a duty towards a third party there being no possible conflict of interest. Second, in transactions *inter vivos* the transaction takes immediate effect and the consequences of solicitors' negligence are immediately apparent. When discovered, they can either be rectified (by the parties) or damages recovered by the client. But in the case of a negligently drawn will, the will has no effect at all until the death. It will have been put away in the deed box not to surface again until the testator either wishes to vary it or dies. In the majority of cases the negligence will lie hidden until it takes effect on the death of the testator, i.e. at the very point in time when normally the error will become incapable of remedy.

In all these circumstances, I would hold that by accepting instructions to draw a will, a solicitor does come into a special relationship with those intended to benefit under it in consequence of which the law imposes a duty to the intended beneficiary to act with due expedition and care in relation to the task on which he has entered...

Lord Nolan delivered a separate speech in favour of dismissing the appeal. **Lord Mustill** and **Lord Keith**, dissenting, delivered speeches allowing the appeal.

Appeal dismissed.

COMMENTARY

Lord Mustill's dissenting speech is worthy of serious attention (although space could not be found to accommodate it here). The speech begins by questioning the assumptions which, he argues, underlie the plaintiffs' claims. One assumption was that there must be something wrong with the law if the plaintiffs did not succeed, which, in the circumstances, would require that the plaintiffs' disappointment should be relieved by an award of money and that the money should, if the law permits, come from the solicitor. Another assumption was that some form of action should be granted simply because the solicitor had been negligent. His Lordship found little to commend this view:

The purpose of the courts when recognising tortious acts and their consequences is to compensate those plaintiffs who suffer actionable breaches of duty, not to act as second-line disciplinary tribunals imposing punishment in the shape of damages.

Accordingly, the question of law was this: if A promises B to perform a service for B which B intends, and A knows, will confer a benefit on C if it is performed, does A owe to C in tort a duty to perform carefully that service? After considering the authorities (including *Hedley Byrne* and *Henderson*), his Lordship held that an essential element of the special relationship necessary for a *Hedley Byrne* duty to arise was 'mutuality'. This term seems to mean some kind of reciprocal dealings between the parties—satisfied, in *Hedley Byrne*, by the request of the credit reference by Hedley Byrne's bankers and the response by Heller & Partners. But on the facts of *White* this was not the case. There was no relationship at all, in any ordinary sense, between parties who were linked only by the fact that if the solicitor did his job (and if the testator executed the will and did not revoke it) a third party might be better off. Nor could the problem be solved by trying to find an assumption of responsibility by the solicitor to the beneficiary: 'The solicitor does of course undertake the task of preparing the will, in the sense of agreeing to take it on. But this is between himself and his client.' The solicitor undertook the task of drawing up a will which would in fact benefit the beneficiaries but he did not draw it up for the beneficiaries. It was prepared for the testator.

Equally important is his Lordship's unwillingness to acquiesce in the creation of a special pocket of tort liability for the particular situation in *White*. His Lordship accepted that a 'broad new type of claim may properly be met by a broad new type of rationalisation' but 'rationalisation there must be, and it does not conduce to the orderly development of the law, or to the certainty which practical convenience demands, if duties are simply conjured up as a matter of positive law, to answer the apparent justice of an individual case'. But, in his Lordship's view, there was nothing to distinguish a solicitor from a much wider category of persons, so that the reasoning which allowed the beneficiary to recover must also apply 'where A promises B for reward to perform a service for B, in circumstances where it is foreseeable that performance of the service with care will cause C to receive a benefit, and that failure to perform it may cause C not to receive that benefit'. This would go beyond anything the tort of negligence had ever recognised, and his Lordship could not discern principled reasoning which could lead to the recognition of such an extensive new area of potential liability.

On the facts of *White v Jones*, a mid-way solution may have been possible. The beneficiaries had had some contact with the solicitors such as might have satisfied the requirement of mutuality (if such a requirement was necessary). This appears to have influenced Lord Nolan's speech dismissing the appeal, but Lord Mustill felt such an approach was not open as the case had been argued as a choice between a general duty or no duty at all.

The Different Approaches of Lord Goff and Lord Browne-Wilkinson

For Lord Goff, the case could not be decided in favour of the plaintiff by applying *Hedley Byrne*, for the work had not been carried out for the beneficiary and in most cases (although perhaps not on the facts of *White*) there was no reliance by the beneficiary. To establish liability through a deemed assumption of responsibility is simply to impose liability 'according to the justice of the case', a course of action Lord Mustill found unacceptable. Not everyone agrees with Lord Goff's view that the adoption of this approach causes the conceptual difficulties 'to fade innocuously away' (Haydon [1995] CLJ 238, 240). Nonetheless, it is submitted that both Lord Goff and Lord Mustill are in agreement over the core requirements of *Hedley Byrne*.

Lord Browne-Wilkinson's approach is more complicated. For his Lordship, the case could be decided by the assumption of responsibility principle explored in *Hedley Byrne*. But *Hedley Byrne* was not the seminal case; rather, as the speeches in *Hedley Byrne* indicated, it was *Nocton v Lord Ashburton* [1914] AC 932—the case where Viscount Haldane had found a solicitor liable to his client on the basis of the 'special relationship' between them (in that case a fiduciary relationship). Given that a fiduciary relationship could be a 'special relationship' for the purpose of imposing a duty of care in respect of pure economic loss, this meant that neither mutuality nor reliance were required, for a negligent trustee was liable for economic loss even if the beneficiary had never dealt with the trustee or relied on him in any way.

There is some support for the view that reliance is not a necessary element of every special relationship. In the information and advice line of cases (e.g. *Hedley Byrne* itself) reliance is necessary to establish a cause of action, for if the claimant has not relied on the information it has not been causative of the loss. However, this does not mean that the special relationship is characterised by reliance, a point made by Lord Mustill in *White* (cf. Lord Goff, who in both *Henderson* and *White* appears to envisage some form of reliance as being necessary). However, neither Lord Goff nor Lord Mustill envisaged the *Hedley Byrne* special relationship arising in the absence of some form of reciprocal dealings. The difficulty with dispensing with this requirement is that it becomes difficult to limit those to whom one assumes responsibility (the hallmark of the special relationship). Lord Browne-Wilkinson held that it is the assumption of responsibility for the task that creates the special relationship, and Lord Nolan gave the following examples (at 293–4):

If the defendant drives his car on the highway, he implicitly assumes a responsibility towards other road users, and they in turn implicitly rely on him to discharge that responsibility. By taking his car on to the road, he holds himself out as a reasonably careful driver... In the same way, as it seems to me, a professional man or an artisan who undertakes to exercise his skill in a manner which, to his knowledge, may cause loss to others if carelessly performed, may thereby implicitly assume a legal responsibility towards them.

The problem with this approach is that it fails to identify to whom and for what damage the responsibility is assumed. It may not be difficult to say that a driver, by the mere act of driving, assumes a responsibility to drive carefully so as not to inflict physical injury on others, but can (or should) the same reasoning apply to economic loss or psychiatric injury? Lord Browne-Wilkinson's approach did not find favour with Gummow J in the High Court of Australia in *Hill v Van Erp* (1997) 188 CLR 159 (a case which also concerned the liability of a solicitor to a disappointed beneficiary; see also Barker, 'Unreliable Assumptions in the Law of Negligence' (1993) 109 LQR 461 at 474).

Apart from the liability based on the 'assumption of responsibility for the task', on what other grounds did Lord Browne-Wilkinson find a special relationship? His Lordship held that, as in the case of a fiduciary, the solicitor is aware that the plaintiff's economic well-being is dependent upon the proper discharge of his duty. This says little more than that it was foreseeable that the beneficiary would suffer loss if the solicitor was negligent, but it has never been accepted that a duty of care should be owed merely because economic loss was foreseeable. In any case, the analogy with fiduciaries in this context is unhelpful because, although a fiduciary may be liable for negligently caused foreseeable economic loss, it is not the *reason* the fiduciary is liable for such loss (see Weir (1995) 111 LQR 357, 360). Apart from the foresight of loss, Lord Browne-Wilkinson's other reasons for imposing a duty of care are based solely on policy grounds, the most significant being the importance of wills to the passing of property from one generation to the next. As Blake (1995–6) 6 KCLJ 101, 104 notes:

On the face of it, this appears to be a test based on foreseeability of harm and as such resembles the approach to duty of care in *Anns v Merton London Borough Council* [1978] AC 728. Like Lord Wilberforce in that case, Lord Browne-Wilkinson applied a 'two-stage' test: after finding a prima facie duty, he then considered the relevant policy factors, finding that it was 'fair, just and reasonable' that a duty be imposed.

Do you agree? See further Murphy [1996] CLJ 43, who argues that the appropriate basis of liability in *White v Jones* is a sufficiently proximate relationship in accordance with *Donoghue v Stevenson*, the foresight of damage and the fairness, justice, and reasonableness of imposing a liability being assumed by all their Lordships, and more generally *Customs and Excise Commissioners v Barclays Bank plc*, extracted below.

Concluding Reflections

It might be thought unfair to analyse the decision in *White* in too much detail, for it is clear that the majority were intending to create a remedy to deal with a specific situation. Responding to criticism of the 'assumption of responsibility' principle, Lord Steyn noted: 'Coherence must sometimes yield to practical justice' (*Williams v Natural Life Health Foods Ltd* [1998] 1 WLR 830 at 837). Other courts have also struggled to find any kind of principled reasoning in this type of case. In *Hill v Van Erp* (1997) 188 CLR 159 a beneficiary's spouse was negligently advised to witness the will, with the result (under Queensland law) that the beneficiary was prevented from inheriting. By a 4–1 majority the High Court of Australia held that a solicitor owed a duty of care to an intended beneficiary. None of the majority thought that *Hedley Byrne* could be used in these circumstances, and the decision is based on similar policy grounds to that of the majority in *White* as well as on the fact that allowing the claim presented no problems of indeterminate liability. McHugh J dissented, agreeing with Lord Mustill that positive duties could not be conjured up to meet the justice of a case. Further, his Honour argued:

> If the rule of law is to have any meaning, if judicial decisions are to be based on more than a judge's sense of justice, like cases must be decided alike and in accordance with a principle that transcends the immediate facts of the case.

For example, allowing the *White* claim but denying a claim by the *inter vivos* beneficiary deprived of a benefit through a solicitor's negligence—and Lords Goff and Browne-Wilkinson suggested that such a claim by an *inter vivos* beneficiary would fail—might offend not only a lawyer's sense of the rule of law but also a broad notion of corrective justice. Or it might not. If conclusive arguments as to liability are to be addressed in this way it is submitted there is much force in Lord Mustill's comment that such an approach 'does not conduce to the orderly development of the law, or to the certainty which practical convenience demands'. There is much to be said for the view that the remedy for the beneficiary, if there should be one, lies in other areas of law such as creating exceptions to the privity rule (see Whittaker (1996) OJLS 1; Lorenz and Markesinis (1993) 56 MLR 558).

v. *Hedley Byrne* and the Three-Stage *Caparo* Test

As we have seen, the first category of case in which a duty of care to avoid pure economic loss was recognised in English law involved negligently made statements (*Hedley Byrne v Heller*), and the analytical tool used to derive that duty—assumption of responsibility—was peculiarly suited to that situation. When later courts looked to expand liability for pure economic loss beyond this scenario, some judges recognised that this concept had its limitations and preferred to adopt incrementalism and the three-stage test set out (and applied) by the House of Lords in *Caparo Industries plc v Dickman*, extracted p. 137, above. Almost at the same time, other judges—most notably Lord Goff—sought to expand the scope of assumption of responsibility so that most, if not all, cases in which a duty of care for pure economic loss had been imposed could be justified on this basis. Lower courts reconciled these differing approaches by applying all of the different approaches and arguing that they should all lead to the same result; in effect they each operated as a check on the accuracy of the others (see, e.g., *Bank of Credit and Commerce International (Overseas) Ltd v Price Waterhouse (No. 2)* [1998] PNLR 564 at 582 per Neill LJ; *Merrett v Babb* [2001] QB 1174). C. and P. Mitchell have argued that this approach was an 'utterly unconvincing basis for imposing liability' as consistency of result was guaranteed only by 'manipulating the questions, so that each is effectively the same, or [rejecting] any answers that are inconsistent' (2005) 121 LQR 194 at 199. The different tests were considered by the House of Lords in the following extract.

Customs and Excise Commissioners v Barclays Bank plc
[2007] 1 AC 181

Customs and Excise (the claimant) was in the process of recovering debts owed to it by two companies and it obtained 'freezing' injunctions over the assets of the companies, including bank accounts the companies held with the defendant bank. (A freezing injunction prevents the assets which are the subject of the injunction from being dealt with so as to avoid them being dissipated by their owners in anticipation of judgment being entered against the owners.) Barclays was notified of the injunction but in breach of it carelessly failed to prevent payments out of the accounts with the result that Customs and Excise was unable to recover all of the debts owed to it. Customs and Excise brought an action in negligence and was successful in the Court of Appeal but their Lordships allowed an appeal, holding that the relationship between the parties did not impose a duty of care on Barclays in respect of Customs and Excise's pure economic losses. In the course of reaching this decision their Lordships discussed the relationship between the main approaches to establishing a duty of care in pure economic loss: the test of assumption of responsibility, the *Caparo* three-stage test, and the incremental test.

Lord Bingham

The Test of Tortious Liability in Negligence for Pure Financial Loss

4 The parties were agreed that the authorities disclose three tests which have been used in deciding whether a defendant sued as causing pure economic loss to a claimant owed him a duty of care in tort. The first is whether the defendant assumed responsibility for what he said and did vis-à-vis the claimant, or is to be treated by the law as having done so. The second is commonly known as the threefold test: whether loss to the claimant was a reasonably foreseeable consequence of what the defendant did or failed to do; whether the relationship between the parties was one of sufficient proximity; and whether in all the circumstances it is fair, just and reasonable to impose a duty of care on the defendant towards the claimant (what Kirby J in *Perre v Apand Pty Ltd* (1999) 198 CLR 180, para 259, succinctly labelled 'policy'). Third is the incremental test, based on the observation of Brennan J in *Sutherland Shire Council v Heyman* (1985) 157 CLR 424, 481, approved by Lord Bridge of Harwich in *Caparo Industries plc v Dickman* [1990] 2 AC 605, 618, that:

> It is preferable, in my view, that the law should develop novel categories of negligence incrementally and by analogy with established categories, rather than by a massive extension of a prima facie duty of care restrained only by indefinable 'considerations which ought to negative, or to reduce or limit the scope of the duty or the class of person to whom it is owed'.

Mr Brindle for the bank contended that the assumption of responsibility test was most appropriately applied to this case, and that if applied it showed that the bank owed no duty of care to the commissioners on the present facts. But if it was appropriate to apply either of the other tests the same result was achieved. Mr Sales for the commissioners submitted that the threefold test was appropriate here, and that if applied it showed that a duty of care was owed. But if it was appropriate to apply either of the other tests they showed the same thing.

[His Lordship cited the cases to which counsel for both sides had referred, and continued:]

These authorities yield many valuable insights, but they contain statements which cannot readily be reconciled. I intend no discourtesy to counsel in declining to embark on yet another exegesis of these well-known texts. I content myself at this stage with five general observations. First, there are cases in which one party can accurately be said to have assumed responsibility for what is said or done to another, the paradigm situation being a relationship having all the indicia of contract save consideration. *Hedley Byrne* would, but for the express disclaimer, have been such a case. *White v Jones* and *Henderson v Merrett Syndicates Ltd*, although the relationship was more remote, can be seen as analogous. Thus, like Colman J (whose methodology was commended by Paul Mitchell and Charles Mitchell, 'Negligence Liability for Pure Economic Loss' (2005) 121 LQR 194, 199), I think it is correct to regard an assumption of responsibility as a sufficient but not a necessary condition of liability, a first test which, if answered positively, may obviate the need for further inquiry. If answered negatively, further consideration is called for.

5 Secondly, however, it is clear that the assumption of responsibility test is to be applied objectively (*Henderson v Merrett Syndicates Ltd* [1994] 2 AC 145, 181) and is not answered by consideration of what the defendant thought or intended...The problem here is, as I see it, that the further this test is removed from the actions and intentions of the actual defendant, and the more notional the assumption of responsibility becomes, the less difference there is between this test and the threefold test.

6 Thirdly, the threefold test itself provides no straightforward answer to the vexed question whether or not, in a novel situation, a party owes a duty of care. In *Caparo Industries plc v Dickman* [1990] 2 AC 605, 618, Lord Bridge, having set out the ingredients of the threefold test, acknowledged as much:

> But it is implicit in the passages referred to that the concepts of proximity and fairness embodied in these additional ingredients are not susceptible of any such precise definition as would be necessary to give them utility as practical tests, but amount in effect to little more than convenient labels to attach to the features of different specific situations which, on a detailed examination of all the circumstances, the law recognises pragmatically as giving rise to a duty of care of a given scope. Whilst recognising, of course, the importance of the underlying general principles common to the whole field of negligence, I think the law has now moved in the direction of attaching greater significance to the more traditional categorisation of distinct and recognisable situations as guides to the existence, the scope and the limits of the varied duties of care which the law imposes...

7 Fourthly, I incline to agree with the view expressed by the Messrs Mitchell in their article cited above, p 199, that the incremental test is of little value as a test in itself, and is only helpful when used in combination with a test or principle which identifies the legally significant features of a situation. The closer the facts of the case in issue to those of a case in which a duty of care has been held to exist, the readier a court will be, on the approach of Brennan J adopted in *Caparo Industries plc v Dickman*, to find that there has been an assumption of responsibility or that the proximity and policy conditions of the threefold test are satisfied. The converse is also true.

8 Fifthly, it seems to me that the outcomes (or majority outcomes) of the leading cases cited above are in every or almost every instance sensible and just, irrespective of the test applied to achieve that outcome...

Lord Hoffmann

31 How does one determine whether a duty of care is owed? In cases of pure economic loss such as this, it is not sufficient that the bank ought reasonably to have foreseen that unless

they had proper systems in place and their employees took reasonable care to give effect to any freezing orders which came along, the beneficiaries of those orders might suffer loss. In the case of personal or physical injury, reasonable foreseeability of harm is usually enough, in accordance with the principle in *Donoghue v Stevenson* [1932] AC 562, to generate a duty of care. In the case of economic loss, something more is needed.

32 The Court of Appeal applied what it called the 'threefold test' proposed by Lord Bridge of Harwich in *Caparo Industries plc v Dickman* [1990] 2 AC 605, 617–618 . . .

33 Longmore LJ held that this test was satisfied. Foreseeability was conceded; service of the order created proximity (even though the bank 'may not be particularly willing to have a relationship to the commissioners': see para 30) and it was 'eminently fair, reasonable and just' that a bank should take care not to allow a defendant to flout the order. The order placed a burden on the bank but provided for the bank to be paid its reasonable charges for compliance. Peter Gibson LJ agreed: 'practical justice requires the recognition of such a duty': para 63. So did Lindsay J.

34 Mr Brindle, who appeared for the bank, said that this was the wrong approach. One should ask whether the bank had assumed responsibility for monitoring the account. As authority for applying this test, he relied upon Lord Goff of Chieveley's analysis in *Henderson v Merrett Syndicates Ltd* [1995] 2 AC 145, 180–181. In this case, he said, the bank never assumed responsibility. If anything, it had responsibility thrust upon it.

35 There is a tendency, which has been remarked upon by many judges, for phrases like 'proximate', 'fair, just and reasonable' and 'assumption of responsibility' to be used as slogans rather than practical guides to whether a duty should exist or not. These phrases are often illuminating but discrimination is needed to identify the factual situations in which they provide useful guidance. For example, in a case in which A provides information to C which he knows will be relied upon by D, it is useful to ask whether A assumed responsibility to D: *Hedley Byrne & Co Ltd v Heller & Partners Ltd* [1964] AC 465: *Smith v Eric S Bush* [1990] 1 AC 831. Likewise, in a case in which A provides information on behalf of B to C for the purpose of being relied upon by C, it is useful to ask whether A assumed responsibility to C for the information or was only discharging his duty to B: *Williams v Natural Life Health Foods Ltd* [1998] 1 WLR 830. Or in a case in which A provided information to B for the purpose of enabling him to make one kind of decision, it may be useful to ask whether he assumed responsibility for its use for a different kind of decision: *Caparo Industries plc v Dickman* [1990] 2 AC 605. In these cases in which the loss has been caused by the claimant's reliance on information provided by the defendant, it is critical to decide whether the defendant (rather than someone else) assumed responsibility for the accuracy of the information to the claimant (rather than to someone else) or for its use by the claimant for one purpose (rather than another). The answer does not depend upon what the defendant intended but, as in the case of contractual liability, upon what would reasonably be inferred from his conduct against the background of all the circumstances of the case. The purpose of the inquiry is to establish whether there was, in relation to the loss in question, the necessary relationship (or 'proximity') between the parties . . .

36 It is equally true to say that a sufficient relationship will be held to exist when it is fair, just and reasonable to do so. Because the question of whether a defendant has assumed responsibility is a legal inference to be drawn from his conduct against the background of all the circumstances of the case, it is by no means a simple question of fact. Questions of fairness and policy will enter into the decision and it may be more useful to try to identify these questions than simply to bandy terms like 'assumption of responsibility' and 'fair, just and reasonable' . . .

Lord Rodger of Earlsferry

48 Mr Brindle . . . argued that no one owed a duty of care to avoid causing financial harm to another unless he had voluntarily undertaken responsibility towards that other person. Here

Barclays had not undertaken any responsibility to the commissioners for the way in which they would freeze the companies' accounts. They had just been required to act due to the notification of the order. Mr Sales argued in reply that assumption of responsibility was not the only criterion for holding that someone owed a duty of care. It was just one factor to be taken into account. The correct approach was to adopt the so-called 'threefold test' and to ask whether the loss was reasonably foreseeable, whether the parties were in a relationship of proximity and whether it would be fair, just and reasonable that the defendant should owe a duty of care to the claimant. It is common ground that in this case the loss was reasonably foreseeable.

49 There is no doubt that some passages in speeches in your Lordships' House provide support for the view that voluntary assumption of responsibility is the touchstone of liability for pure economic loss.

[His Lordship considered a number of cases discussing voluntary assumption of responsibility and continued:]

51 Part of the function of appeal courts is to try to assist judges and practitioners by boiling down a mass of case law and distilling some shorter statement of the applicable law. The temptation to try to identify some compact underlying rule which can then be applied to solve all future cases is obvious. Mr Brindle submitted that in this area the House had identified such a rule in the need to find that the defendant had voluntarily assumed responsibility. But the unhappy experience with the rule so elegantly formulated by Lord Wilberforce in *Anns v Merton London Borough Council* [1978] AC 728, 751–752, suggests that appellate judges should follow the philosopher's advice to 'Seek simplicity, and distrust it'.

52 Therefore it is not surprising that there are cases in the books—notably *Ministry of Housing and Local Government v Sharp* [1970] 2 QB 223, approved by Lord Slynn of Hadley in *Spring v Guardian Assurance plc* [1995] 2 AC 296, 332f–g—which do not readily yield to analysis in terms of a voluntary assumption of responsibility, but where liability has none the less been held to exist. I see no reason to treat these cases as exceptions to some over-arching rule that there must be a voluntary assumption of responsibility before the law recognises a duty of care. Such a rule would inevitably lead to the concept of voluntary assumption of responsibility being stretched beyond its natural limits—which would in the long run undermine the very real value of the concept as a criterion of liability in the many cases where it is an appropriate guide. In any event, as the words which I have quoted from his speech in *Merrett Syndicates* make clear, Lord Goff himself recognised that, although it may be decisive in many situations, the presence or absence of a voluntary assumption of responsibility does not necessarily provide the answer in all cases...

53 In the absence of any single touchstone, the House finds itself in the familiar position, envisaged by Lord Bridge of Harwich in *Caparo Industries plc v Dickman* [1990] 2 AC 605, 618, where a court faced with a novel situation must apply the threefold test.

Lord Mance

82 The conceptual basis on which courts decide whether a duty of care exists in particular circumstances has been repeatedly examined. Three broad approaches have been suggested, involving consideration (a) whether there has been an assumption of responsibility, (b) whether a three-fold test of foreseeability, proximity and 'fairness, justice and reasonableness' has been satisfied or (c) whether the alleged duty would be 'incremental' to previous cases. Mr Michael Brindle for the bank argues that in cases of economic loss the only relevant question is whether there has been an 'assumption of responsibility'. Mr Philip Sales for the commissioners submits that the primary approach should be through the threefold test of foreseeability, proximity and 'fairness, justice and reasonableness' and that assumption of responsibility and incrementalism are no more than potentially relevant factors under that test.

83 All three approaches may often (though not inevitably) lead to the same result. Assumption of responsibility is on any view a core area of liability for economic loss. All three tests operate at a high level of abstraction. What matters is how and by reference to what lower-level factors they are interpreted in practice: see eg *Caparo Industries plc v Dickman* [1990] 2 AC 605, per Lord Bridge of Harwich, at pp 617–618, and Lord Oliver of Aylmerton, at p633b–d.

84 As to incrementalism, I note that the House's support for this approach in *Caparo* was given with reference to a passage in Brennan J's judgment in *Sutherland Shire Council v Heyman* (1985) 157 CLR 424, 481, where he was rejecting the House's approach in *Anns v Merton London Borough Council* [1978] AC 728, from which the House itself resiled five months after *Caparo* in *Murphy v Brentwood District Council* [1991] 1 AC 398 ... Incrementalism was therefore viewed as a corollary of the rejection, now uncontroversial, of any generalised liability for negligently caused economic loss, rather than as necessarily inconsistent with the development of novel categories of negligence. Having said that, caution and analogical reasoning are generally valuable accompaniments to judicial activity, and this is particularly true in the present area.

87 ... [I]t has been said on a number of occasions that it is artificial or unhelpful to insist on fitting all claims for breach of a duty of care to avoid economic loss within the conception of assumption of responsibility, and there are several cases involving economic loss where the threefold test and incrementalism have been preferred.

[His Lordship considered *Smith v Eric S Bush, Caparo Industries v Dickman, Spring v Guardian Assurance*, and *White v Jones*, and continued:]

93 This review of authority confirms that there is no single common denominator, even in cases of economic loss, by which liability may be determined. In my view the threefold test of foreseeability, proximity and fairness, justice and reasonableness provides a convenient general framework although it operates at a high level of abstraction. The concept of assumption of responsibility is particularly useful in the two core categories of case identified by Lord Browne-Wilkinson in *White v Jones* [extracted above] when it may effectively subsume all aspects of the threefold approach. But if all that is meant by voluntary assumption of responsibility is the voluntary assumption of responsibility for a task, rather than of liability towards the defendant, then questions of foreseeability, proximity and fairness, reasonableness and justice may become very relevant. In *White v Jones* itself there was no doubt that the solicitor had voluntarily undertaken responsibility for a task, but it was the very fact that he had done so for the testator, not the disappointed beneficiaries, that gave rise to the stark division of opinion in the House. Incrementalism operates as an important cross-check on any other approach.

94 The present cannot be regarded as a case of assumption of responsibility. The involuntary nature of the bank's involvement with the commissioners makes it impossible to regard the situation as one 'akin to contract'; it is also difficult in any meaningful sense to speak of the bank as having voluntarily assumed responsibility even for the task in relation to which it was allegedly negligent, let alone responsibility towards the commissioners for the task. In a very general sense any bank, indeed anyone carrying on any activity during the course of which they might have cause to hold the moneys or possessions of another, might be said to accept the risk that a third party might obtain a freezing order in respect of such moneys or possessions. But that is to assign to the concept of voluntary assumption of responsibility so wide a meaning as to deprive it of effective utility. Further, I do not consider that it can make any difference to the above analysis in the case of Brightstar if the bank's letter of 29 January 2001 was posted before the bank's error. The letter was itself written simply to reflect and acknowledge the legal obligation which the freezing order imposed on the bank. To analyse the situation (as Lord Denning MR did in *Z Ltd v A-Z and AA-LL* [1982] QB 558, 575a–d) in terms

of a request to freeze the account in consideration of payment of the relevant expenses is in my opinion artificial.

95 Mr Brindle thus submits that no duty of care on the bank can be recognised because the bank did not voluntarily undertake responsibility even for the task which it is now alleged negligently to have executed. But Mr Sales can point to cases where a duty of care has been recognised even though the defendant cannot realistically be said to have voluntarily undertaken the relevant task...

COMMENTARY

In *Customs and Excise*, the House of Lords attempted to reconcile three different approaches that, as we have seen, were used in earlier case law to determine the duty of care question: the 'assumption of responsibility' test, the three-stage test from *Caparo Industries v Dickman* and the 'incremental test'. In fact, as Lord Bingham pointed out, the 'incremental test' was not a separate test at all. The point was elaborated by P. and C. Mitchell (2005) 121 LQR 194, 199, when commenting on the Court of Appeal decision: 'Factual analogies and distinctions are not helpful in themselves; they are only helpful when used in combination with a test or principle which identifies the legally significant features of the situation.'

This left two possibilities for a general approach to the duty of care in cases of pure economic loss. The first, assumption of responsibility, derived from the case in which recovery for pure economic loss in negligence was first countenanced: *Hedley Byrne & Co v Heller & Partners*, extracted at p. 408, above. Whilst their Lordships in *Customs and Excise* accepted that answering the duty of care question by reference to this test might be suitable in some, perhaps even many, cases, it was clear that it could not be regarded as *the* test for duty of care in cases of pure economic loss. Rather, the role of assumption of responsibility seems to be as a means of satisfying the three-stage test, but not the only means. Given the difficulties with the concept which have been explored earlier in this chapter, it has been suggested that it adds little to the three-stage test and should be jettisoned (Barker, 'Wielding Occam's Razor: Pruning Strategies for Economic Loss' (2006) 26 OJLS 289) but this was not the route taken by the House of Lords in *Customs and Excise*.

So what general approach should now be taken to answering the duty question? It is implicit in several of their Lordships' speeches that 'assumption of responsibility' is a useful analytical tool where the defendant's negligence consists of carelessly supplying information or advice on which the claimant relies to his detriment; if the defendant can be said to have assumed responsibility for being careful in the supply of this information a duty of care will be owed. More difficult is where no assumption of responsibility is found: can the claimant argue that, even though there is no assumption of responsibility, a duty of care might nonetheless be found applying the three-stage test? Whilst their Lordships did not see assumption of responsibility as the general test for duty of care in cases of pure economic loss, it is less clear whether this reasoning applies to cases where the assumption of responsibility test has been identified as serving a useful function (e.g. negligent supply of advice or information) so that, if no assumption of responsibility is found, no duty could be found applying the three-stage test. The difficulty here is that, even if one accepts that the three-stage test might be satisfied in cases of the negligent supply of advice or information where there is no assumption of responsibility, the existing case law *has* tended to use assumption of responsibility as the sole determinant of duty in such cases, although the concept—arguably—has been stretched to breaking point in doing so (see *Hendersen v Merrett*; *White v Jones*, extracted earlier in this chapter). Given that, as Lord Hoffmann pointed out, questions of fairness and policy influence both a finding of an assumption of responsibility and the application of the three-stage test, would it be better to see assumption of responsibility and the three-stage test as mutually exclusive tests, each one applying to a particular kind of negligently caused economic loss?

We would argue that there is little to be gained by seeing assumption of responsibility and the three-stage test as completely independent tests. As Lord Bingham points out, the three-stage test provides no straightforward answer to the duty question, and if existing case law suggests that assumption of responsibility is an appropriate concept given the facts of the case (primarily the negligent provision of advice, and perhaps professional services), it should be used as a means of answering the questions posed by the *Caparo* test. But the converse should not apply: as was made clear in *Customs and Excise*, the failure to establish an assumption of responsibility, even in cases where it was previously used as the sole test, should not necessarily be decisive. Of course, in the vast majority of cases where assumption of responsibility has been used in the past—especially in what might be called simple *Hedley Byrne* cases (see Section III of this chapter)—it will make no difference to the result if claimants are allowed to try and establish a duty of care using the general *Caparo* three-stage test; the factors that prevented the existence of an assumption of responsibility will also prevent a duty of care arising under the three-stage test. In other cases—especially the extended *Hedley Byrne* cases (Section IV, above)—it could be argued that the three-stage test is a preferable explanation for the results of cases which were reached by applying a very wide concept of assumption of responsibility. And in some cases—of which *Ministry of Housing and Local Government v Sharp* [1970] 2 QB 223 perhaps provides an example—an assumption of responsibility, on any definition, is an inappropriate tool to determine the duty question, so if a duty is to be imposed it should be done under the three-stage test.

All of the cases described above were decided prior to *Customs and Excise* and reflect the different approaches to the duty question that confronted the House of Lords in *Customs and Excise*. However, as Lord Bingham noted, it is very unlikely that the results of any of these cases would have been decided differently if different tests had been applied, albeit that the approach to the duty of care might have been different in light of *Customs and Excise*. So why does it matter what concepts the court relies upon to determine whether or not there is a duty of care in respect of pure economic loss?

For further analysis, see Stanton, 'Professional negligence: duty of care methodology in the twenty-first century' (2006) 22 PN 134.

VI. The Duty of Care and Pure Economic Loss—Evaluation

As has been illustrated above, the current approach to the recovery of pure economic loss in negligence has its difficulties. Can the balance struck by the court between pro- and anti-liability cases be justified? In this final section, we first consider an economic analysis of the liability rules in this area which provides some support for the current approach, before introducing the debate between rights-based and policy-based critiques of the current law.

1. Economic Analysis and Negligent Misrepresentation

W. Bishop, 'Negligent Representation through Economists' Eyes' (1980) 96 LQR 360

One peculiarity of information, considered as an economic good, is that the person who produces it may not, and usually will not, be able to appropriate all the social benefit that flows from its production. The meaning and significance of this are best considered by means of an example. Suppose someone discovers air currents in the upper atmosphere which can be predicted easily. This information will be valuable to anyone flying an aircraft, as this knowledge will enable him to chart his flight path so as to minimise fuel costs. It is unlikely that the discoverer will be able to become rich through his discovery even though the discovery saves many millions of dollars in resources that would otherwise be wasted. First, he may not be able to convince the purchaser of its value without giving him the very information he is trying to sell. Second, even if he sells the information to one airline, then that airline can easily pass the information onto others, perhaps at some financial gain to itself. If it seeks to guard the information it will have to control closely its employees, see that they never change jobs, and so on. In general, information, once produced, can be reproduced to others at small cost. Even though the social benefit of the information is large the private benefit to the producer is small . . .

The typical market in economic theory is the market for goods. The producer of a good sells it to the user, appropriating to himself all, or substantially all, of the benefit of the good that his efforts brought into existence. Or as is said in economics, private benefit equals social benefit. If the producer must pay all of the social cost of producing the good, then he will produce it only so long as the (marginal) social cost of doing so equals the (marginal) social benefit.

Much of tort law is concerned with ensuring that the producer is faced with the full social costs of production. When these diverge from private cost they are called external costs of production, or externalities. Nuisance and negligence law is typically concerned to internalise to the producer these external costs. When this is done production will be optimal in quantity and price, in the sense that all those goods, and only those goods, will be produced whose marginal social benefit equals their marginal social costs of production.

The contrast with the information market is sharp. Here the market will fail to achieve the social optimum. This happens not because of an external cost but because of an external benefit; the market failure is not on the supply side but on the demand side. The information producer may be faced with the full social cost, but because he cannot cover those costs through the sale of the product to those who benefit he does not produce as much of the good as is socially optimal; indeed he may produce none at all.

The application of this analysis to liability for negligent misrepresentation is the following. Such a liability rule is an attempt to make the information provider confront the total social cost of his action. But if he cannot reap the total social benefit he will not produce enough, if any, information. If there were no liability rule and if the private costs of information production were small, the optimal amount might be produced—though the quality of the information would probably be lower than ideal. But if we augment the costs through liability we risk inducing producers to curtail production, leaving us worse off then before.

Economic analysis suggests the following approach to cases of negligent misrepresentation. Courts should in general apply ordinary rules of negligence. However, where the misrepresentation in question results from the production of valuable information there is prima facie case for more restricted liability. Liability should be restricted when (a) the information is of a type that is valuable to many potential users, (b) the producer of the information cannot capture in his prices the benefits flowing to all users of the information, and (c) the imposition of liability to all persons harmed would raise potential costs significantly enough to discourage information production altogether. When these three conditions are met the court should impose liability on the defendant in relation to a limited class only. This class should include all information users with whom the producer has a trading relationship, whether direct or indirect. The class can be extended beyond this, but such extension should be limited by the principle expressed in (c), that is it should not be extended so widely that potential defendants would be discouraged from engaging in the activity that generates the information.

COMMENTARY

Whether one is a disciple of the law and economics movement or not, this rationalisation for the present liability rules in relation to the recovery of pure economic loss goes some way towards explaining the results in the cases above. Bishop's analysis provides an account of why the floodgates concern—the fear of 'liability to an indeterminate class for an indeterminate time in an indeterminate amount' (*Ultramares Corporation v Touche* 174 NE 441 (1931) at 444, per Cardozo J)—is particularly weighty in this context. Lord Oliver, rejecting the existence of a duty of care in *Caparo*, argued:

To apply as a test of liability only the foreseeability of possible damage without some further control would be to create a liability wholly indefinite in area, duration and amount and would open up a limitless vista of uninsurable risk for the professional man.

It appears that his fear was that, if this new kind of uninsurable risk was opened, professionals would simply cease to provide the information in question, to the detriment of society as a whole.

In cases where liability has been found, economic analysis suggests that such concerns should not be present. Do the cases reflect this? Bishop argues that in *Hedley Byrne*, although the information provided by Heller & Partners may have been of interest to others, it was primarily given for a specific purpose in a non-public document; hence in reality it was not likely to be of benefit to a wide class. Conversely, Heller & Partners also received a benefit, but not in monetary terms. Rather, it retained the business of its customers who expected their bank to provide references as to their creditworthiness and who, if they valued this service sufficiently, would be prepared to have the cost of misinformation spread equally amongst them (through higher bank charges). The cost of a liability rule (the award of damages if the reference was negligent) could be offset against the benefit to the bank of retaining or gaining customers. Thus social cost would roughly equate with social benefit. What about *Smith v Bush* and *Caparo*? Although Bishop's article appeared before these cases were decided, his analysis also provides an explanation of their differing results. In *Smith*, the information (the survey) was effectively paid for by the plaintiff. It was of benefit to a very small class of persons—those interested in buying the house within a short period of the survey. Thus it was likely that the social benefit of the survey was recouped through the surveyor's fees (although there may have been a volume discount offered to the bank but in any event the possibility of regular work from the bank is itself of value to the surveyor). The situation was vastly different in *Caparo*. The information provided by the auditors was public and was of benefit to a wide variety of investors and shareholders. It was not possible for the total social benefit provided by the auditors to be recouped in fees; hence, according to Bishop's analysis, the House of Lords correctly limited the class to whom the auditors could be liable for financial loss (cf. *Esanda Finance Corporation Limited v Peat Marwick Hungerfords* (1997) 188 CLR 241, where McHugh J expressly considered the economic consequences of imposing a wide liability on auditors).

The same analysis may also be held to explain the difference between the majority and minority in *White v Jones*. The primary social benefit of making a will is to the beneficiaries and testator. For those who favoured allowing the beneficiaries' claim, the benefit provided to those parties could be adequately recouped by the solicitor's fees. For those against, there were two problems in terms of the above analysis. First, the solicitor cannot be said to recoup the benefit through the fees charged because, at the date the will is made, it may not be known what benefit the beneficiary will be receiving. As McHugh J stated in *Hill v Van Erp* (1997) 188 CLR 159 at 216, 'It does not seem reasonable that the solicitor who has received a small fee from a testator should be liable years after the event for many hundreds of thousands of dollars because a person with whom the solicitor has had no dealings has failed to secure a benefit.' The second, related point is that because of this liability the solicitor will either cease to provide such services, or will take out liability insurance (if possible), and as a result the cost of providing the service will increase. Neither solution results in the optimum level of service provision.

Of course, not everyone buys into the law and economics argument; almost nobody agrees on what level and cost of services is economically desirable and, as Cane (*Tort Law and Economic Interests*, 2nd edn. (Oxford: OUP, 1996), 178) points out: 'At the end of the day, courts have to choose to favour one party or the other: to be "pro-plaintiff" or "pro-defendant".' However, there is little doubt that, at least on a subconscious level, considerations of this kind have influenced the law's view as to recovery for pure economic loss. Depending on one's wider political views, this will be seen as either enlightened or regressive.

2. Rights-Based and Policy-Based Critiques of the Current Law

A. Beever, *Rediscovering the Law of Negligence* (Oxford: Hart, 2007) pp. 232–3

The Principled Approach

As noted above, in *Spartan Steel*, Edmund Davies LJ argued that the principled approach would allow for recovery of consequential loss and relational economic loss. In fact, however, that is not the case. The view involves a very fundamental error that arises because of what David Stevens and Jason Neyers regard as the greatest weakness of the common law: its remedial mentality ((1999) 37 Alberta Law Review 221, 227)…The focus of analysis is invariably on the question 'should the claimant recover?', with various policies being offered for different views. The prior question, 'does the claimant have a right that could ground recovery?', has gone

largely unasked. The problem with economic loss will be solved if we balance the copious prudence (ie policy) that the topic of economic loss has engendered with a little juris (ie strict legal
analysis). When we do so, we will see that we need not agree with David Ibbetson's lament that
there is nothing in the law of negligence 'to restrain the urge to move from the proposition that
a person has suffered loss from the negligence of another to the conception that the loss ought
to be compensated' ((2003) 26 NSWLJ 475, 488). This formulation overlooks the distinction
between factual losses that flow from the violation of a primary right and those that do not.

COMMENTARY

The rights-based approach advocated by Beever is defined in contradistinction to a loss-
based model, where the nature of the claimant's loss determines its recoverability. According
to R. Stevens, *Torts and Rights* (Oxford: OUP, 2007), pp. 20–1:

Economic loss whether deliberately or carelessly inflicted, is not, without more, actionable. On the
'loss-based' model this exclusionary rule is difficult to explain . . . The common law could start with
the assumption that we each have a right not to have loss inflicted upon us. It would then be necessary to carve out wide-ranging exceptions where this would be objectionable as a matter of policy.
This is not the common law's starting point. There is no 'exclusionary rule' for economic loss. The
common law's starting position is that the infliction of economic loss does not per se infringe any
right of the claimant. This is true of both intentionally and negligently inflicted economic loss. On
a rights-based model it is not the ocean of no-liability which requires mapping, but the isolated
islands of rights.

Although there is no inherent right of a claimant which can form the basis of a claim for economic loss, rights-based accounts of pure economic loss generally allow for recovery where,
as in *Hedley Byrne v Heller*, the defendant has assumed responsibility to the claimant so as to
create the necessary right. Outside of such situations (or any other situaton which can generate a primary right in the claimant to be protected against the infliction of pure economic
loss), there should be no recovery. In this way a major concern of rights-based approaches
to the law of negligence—to exclude various forms of what are loosely described as policy
arguments from legal analysis—is achieved (assuming that the identification of the relevant
rights does not involve any 'policy' concerns).

A leading advocate of the alternative 'policy' approach has been Jane Stapleton. In an
important article in 1991 ('Duty of Care and Economic Loss: A Wider Agenda' (1991) 107
LQR 249) she argued that the decisions of the House of Lords in economic loss cases (at that
time) depended not on a reasoned application of policy arguments to the facts of the individual case but upon a 'pockets' approach to liability. She identifies three pockets—negligent
misstatement (as in *Hedley Byrne*), dependence on property of a third party (as in *Spartan
Steel*) and defective property (as in *Murphy v Brentwood*). She argues that the success or
otherwise of a claim depends upon the pocket to which it is allocated. The consequence of
this approach is that, although there may be similar policy issues underlying particular
claims, the treatment of the policy issues varies depending on the pocket in question. An
example of this type of 'tail wagging the dog' scenario can be seen by comparing *D & F
Estates Ltd v Church Commissioners* [1989] AC 177, and *Smith v Eric S Bush* [1990] 1 AC 831,
both extracted above. Both cases dealt with a defect in property. In both cases there were no
concerns over multiple or indeterminate claims, nor was there any problem with the claims

being of an indeterminate amount. However, different results were reached because the cases were decided in different pockets, one under the more favourable (for the claimant) *Hedley Byrne* pocket and one under the no-recovery 'defect in quality' pocket. This produces illogical results, in that one may sue a surveyor in tort for negligently failing to detect a defect in a house which results in pure economic loss but not the builder responsible for creating it, even if the same type of loss is suffered. Accordingly, to avoid this situation, Stapleton suggests that the 'pockets' approach should be replaced with the following agenda of policy concerns:

(1) the absence or controllability of the threat of indeterminate liability;

(2) the inadequacy of alternative means of protection;

(3) that the area is not one more appropriate to Parliamentary action and;

(4) that a duty would not allow a circumvention of a positive arrangement regarding allocation of risk which had been accepted by the plaintiff

A slightly more structured, but similar, approach has recently been advocated by Giliker, 'Revisiting pure economic loss: lessons to be learnt from the Supreme Court of Canada' (2005) 25 LS 49. Drawing on the approach of the Canadian Supreme Court, Giliker suggests that claims for pure economic loss should be divided into a number of categories— including negligent misstatements, negligent performance of services, and defective products—for the purposes of identifying the policy factors relevant to each type of claim. This differs significantly from the 'pockets' approach criticised by Stapleton because the choice of category does not determine the outcome; rather it is the first stage of a process for determining whether a duty will be owed and the role of categories is to focus the courts' attention on why recovery should be limited by reference to the policy factors that are relevant to the category in question. (Cf. Witting, 'Duty of Care; An Analytical Approach' (2005) 25 OJLS 33.) We agree that, viewed in this way, categorisation can serve a valuable function.

In *Customs and Excise Commissioners v Barclays Bank plc* Lord Walker (at [71]) thought that there had been 'some modest progress' in the direction recommended by Stapleton's article; in fact the most tangible example of this is Lord Mance's speech in the same case. His Lordship recognised that the answer to the 'fair, just and reasonable' limb of the *Caparo* test required the court to consider 'relevant factors' which he identified as including indeterminate liability, the availability of adequate alternative protection for the claimant, the availability of insurance, and whether any duty imposed on the defendant in tort would be inconsistent with other duties it owed (in contract or under the general law). In the end, however, his Lordship decided against the claimant on none of these grounds but his approach to policy concerns is much more comprehensive than some earlier decisions of the House of Lords: for instance, although policy factor (4) was considered in *Henderson*, factors (1) and (2) were equally relevant but received scant if any attention. Although the number of potential claimants was determinate, the value of the claims were not because the defendants were liable for the Names' losses and (which was a key feature of the arrangement) each Name had unlimited liability. Similarly, the Names all had contracts with member's agents which provided an alternative means of protecting themselves, and the only reason the Names were suing in tort was to secure a more favourable limitation period. Do these factors suggest that a duty should not have been owed? Could the rights-based approach have produced the same result without the policy analysis recommended by Stapleton? (See Stevens, *op. cit.*, p. 184.)

The adoption of Stapleton's criteria would not relieve the court from the task of making difficult value judgements, and because of this one commentator has doubted their value: 'there is a world of difference between being able to select relevant policy factors for discussion in economic loss cases and finding within them appropriate guidance' (Witting, 'Duty of Care; An Analytical Approach' (2005) 25 OJLS 33 at 44). Whatever the merits of the criticism of Stapleton's approach advanced in rights-based accounts of liability for pure economic loss (forming part of a wider attack on the use of policy in the duty of care inquiry: see p. 143, above), there is evidence of Stapleton's approach being used (see Stanton, 'Decision-making in the tort of negligence in the House of Lords' (2007) Tort L Rev 93). If the kinds of policy concerns Stapleton advocates are to be considered, it is desirable that this be done explicitly so that the policy factors considered determinative by the court can be identified and a discussion at the policy level on the proper limits (if any) of the tort of negligence in the recovery of pure economic loss can take place. Whether such an approach—especially in the absence of some form of categorisation—provides the necessary degree of guidance to those who have to practise the law is a different matter. It may be that some uncertainty is worth the price. Arguing that the law is in fact developing new pockets (which provide some guidance), Stanton (above) comments:

Overt use of policy lays the House open to the charge that results are being driven by factors that are difficult to predict. However, the foundations of the law that is being developed would seem to be strong because the pockets are being built on the basis of policies suited to the particular function rather than being driven by principles set at a level of generality which pay no attention to the particular situation at issue.

For further discussion of the policy factors (including some of the above) said to be relevant in negligence actions for pure economic loss, see Stapleton, 'Duty of Care: Peripheral Parties and Alternative Opportunities for Deterrence' (1995) 111 LQR 301, and Stapleton, 'Duty of Care Factors: A Selection from the Judicial Menus', in P. Cane and J. Stapleton (eds), *The Law of Obligations* (Oxford: OUP, 1998).

NEGLIGENCE: DUTY OF CARE— OMISSIONS AND ACTS OF THIRD PARTIES

I. Acts and Omissions

The law has historically been reluctant to impose liability for omissions as opposed to positive acts. The duty to intervene to assist another person who is at risk of injury is of limited scope. A doctor coming across an accident victim lying injured on the road has no obligation to render assistance; a strong swimmer can with impunity ignore the cries for help of someone who is drowning at sea; and it is evidently quite unthinkable that there should be 'liability in negligence on the part of one who sees another about to walk over a cliff with his head in the air and forbears to shout a warning' (*Yuen Kun Yeu v Attorney General of Hong Kong* [1988] AC 175 at 192, per Lord Keith). In short, there is no duty to be a good Samaritan. A number of reasons have been put forward to account for this reluctance to impose liability for omissions, notable amongst them being the over-burdensome nature of duties of affirmative action and the unfairness of singling out one of countless people who 'did nothing' to help the claimant. The issue was fully considered by Lord Hoffmann and Lord Nicholls in the course of their speeches in *Stovin v Wise*, extracted below.

Stovin v Wise [1996] AC 923

The facts of this case, and additional extracts, are given at pp. 513 and 535, below.

Lord Hoffmann

There are sound reasons why omissions require different treatment from positive conduct. It is one thing for the law to say that a person who undertakes some activity shall take reasonable care not to cause damage to others. It is another thing for the law to require that a person who is doing nothing in particular shall take steps to prevent another from suffering harm from the acts of third parties . . . or natural causes. One can put the matter in political, moral or economic terms. In political terms it is less of an invasion of an individual's freedom for the law to require him to consider the safety of others in his actions than to impose upon him a duty to rescue or protect. A moral version of this point may be called the 'Why pick on me?' argument. A duty to prevent harm to others or to render assistance to a person in danger or distress may apply to a large and indeterminate class of people who happen to be able to do something. Why should one be held liable rather than another? In economic terms, the efficient allocation of resources usually requires an activity should bear its own costs. If it benefits from being able to impose some of its costs on other people (what economists call 'externalities') the market is distorted because the activity appears cheaper than it really is. So liability to pay compensation for loss caused by negligent conduct acts as a deterrent against increasing the cost of the activity to the community and reduces externalities. But there is no similar justification for requiring a person who is not doing anything to spend money on behalf of someone else. Except in special cases (such as marine salvage) English law does not reward someone who voluntarily confers a benefit on another. So there must be some special reason why he should have to put his hand in his pocket.

Lord Nicholls (dissenting)

The distinction between liability for acts and liability for omissions is well known. It is not free from controversy. In some cases the distinction is not clear cut. The categorisation may depend upon how broadly one looks when deciding whether the omission is a 'pure' omission or is part of a larger course of activity set in motion by the defendant. Failure to apply the handbrake when parking a vehicle is the classic illustration of the latter. Then the omission is the element which makes the activity negligent . . .

Despite the difficulties, the distinction is fundamentally sound in this area of the law. The distinction is based on a recognition that it is one matter to require a person to take care if he embarks on a course of conduct which may harm others. He must take care not to create a risk of danger. It is another matter to require a person, who is doing nothing, to take positive action to protect others from harm for which he was not responsible, and to hold him liable in damages if he fails to do so. The law has long recognised that liability can arise more readily in the first situation than the second. This is reasonable. In the second situation a person is being compelled to act, and to act for the benefit of another. There must be some special justification for imposing an obligation of this character. Compulsory altruism needs more justification than an obligation not to create dangers to others when acting for one's own purposes . . .

The classic example of the absence of a legal duty to take positive action is where a grown person stands by while a young child drowns in a shallow pool. Another instance is where a person watches a nearby pedestrian stroll into the path of an oncoming vehicle. In both instances the callous bystander can foresee serious injury if he does nothing. He does not control the source of the danger, but he has control of the means to avert a dreadful accident. The child or pedestrian is dependent on the bystander: the child is unable to save himself, and the pedestrian is unaware of his danger. The prospective injury is out of all proportion to the burden imposed by having to take preventive steps. All that would be called for is the simplest exertion or a warning shout.

Despite this, the recognised legal position is that the bystander does not owe the drowning child or the heedless pedestrian a duty to take steps to save him. Something more is required than being a bystander. There must be some additional reason why it is fair and reasonable that one person should be regarded as his brother's keeper and have legal obligations in that regard. When this additional reason exists, there is said to be sufficient proximity. That is the customary label.

COMMENTARY

Although Lord Nicholls was dissenting, his views on the correct general approach to the imposition of liability for omissions largely coincided with those of Lord Hoffmann. For an elegant and persuasive critique of Lord Hoffmann's justifications for the standard no-liability rule, see J. Kortmann, *Altruism in Private Law: Liability for Nonfeasance and* Negotiorum Gestio (Oxford: OUP, 2005), ch. 3.

In *Sutradhar v National Environment Research Council* [2006] UKHL 33, [2006] 4 All ER 490 the House of Lords restated the general rule in forcible terms. As part of its overseas aid programme, the British Government commissioned the British Geological Survey (BGS) to test the performance of deep irrigation wells in Bangladesh. The tests could identify the presence of a number of toxins in the water, but not the presence of arsenic, which the defendant did not consider at the time to be a potential problem. In fact, arsenic contamination of drinking water precipitated a major environmental disaster in Bangladesh, with between 35 million and 77 million of the country's 125 million inhabitants at risk. The claimant developed symptoms associated with arsenical poisoning after he began drinking from an irrigation well in an area in which the BGS had tested. He claimed damages on the basis that the BGS had breached its positive duty to test for arsenic. The House of Lords struck out the claim, which Lord Hoffmann described, at [2], as 'hopeless'. He elaborated, at [27]:

[T]he fact that one has expert knowledge does not in itself create a duty to the whole world to apply that knowledge in solving its problems . . . BGS therefore owed no positive duties to the government or people of Bangladesh to do anything. They can be liable only for the things they did . . . , not for what they did not do.

The House of Lords also struck out the claimant's alternative claim of negligent misrepresentation (considered at p. 415, above). See further Lunney (2006) 14 Tort L Rev 129.

The Distinction between Acts and Omissions

In the above extract from *Stovin v Wise*, Lord Nicholls raises the question of the differentiation of positive acts from omissions, commenting that '[i]n some cases the distinction is not clear cut'. In fact, the terms 'act' and 'omission' are at a purely linguistic level no more than labels that can be applied interchangeably to every instance of human conduct; the distinction does not reflect any deep, philosophical subdivision of human conduct into two essentially different types. The point is further elaborated by H. L. A. Hart and Tony Honoré (*Causation in the Law*, 2nd edn. (Oxford: Clarendon Press, 1985), pp. 138–9):

Human conduct can be described alternatively in terms of acts or omissions. 'A medical man who diagnoses a case of measles as a case of scarlet fever may be said to have omitted to make a correct diagnosis; he may equally well be said to have made an incorrect diagnosis' (Harnett v Bond [1924] 2 KB 517 at 541, per Bankes LJ). Sometimes it is more appropriate to describe the conduct as an omission; if there is a legal duty to do an act, and the subject has not done it, the legally relevant description will be in terms of an omission to perform the act in question. But the description of conduct as an omission may not imply any bodily movements by the person whose conduct is in question: e.g. if the description is: 'The defendant failed to inspect the electrical wiring.' Consequently those courts and writers who are impressed by 'setting in motion' as a prime instance of causation, and who further conclude that we can only set things in motion by ourselves making movements, find it difficult to understand how an omission to act can negative causal connection.

It is now thought, at least in England, that there is no special difficulty about omissions . . . In truth, no rational distinction can be drawn between the causal status of acts and omissions.

By this analysis the authors are able to undermine the claim which is occasionally made that it is only positive acts—'making things happen'—that can operate as causes, and hence give rise to liability, because 'doing nothing' can bring nothing about. In fact, omissions can be legally causative, at least where there is a duty to act.

It would be wrong to conclude, however, that no rational distinction can be drawn between acts and omissions in determining whether they give rise to liability. In the tort context, the terms 'act' and 'omission' are applied to reflect a common-sense distinction between 'making things worse' and 'failing to make things better'. Liability for the latter results in significantly greater restrictions on liberty of action than does liability for the former, for it requires the defendant, who must already ensure that his activities do not expose others to unreasonable risks, to sacrifice his pursuit of those activities—in some cases, to drop everything else—in the interests of another person. But even here it must be admitted that the distinction is only one of degree, and that different duties of affirmative action restrict liberty of action to different degrees. In which case, it is fair to ask why liability for a failure to act should not be imposed where the action required entails very little on the defendant's part but prevents the claimant suffering serious injury. (See further *Atiyah*, pp. 72–7; cf. Logie [1989] CLJ 115.)

Duties of Rescue: A Comparative Overview

English law recognises no duty of rescue in the absence of special circumstances (e.g. an undertaking to safeguard the person imperilled), though someone who actually undertakes a rescue is unquestionably liable if the rescue exposes the person at risk to a new or increased danger which materialises (see *Horsley v Maclaren* (1972) 22 DLR (3d) 545, applied in England in *Day v High Performance Sports Ltd* [2003] EWHC 197 (QB)). (It is pertinent to note here that, in the United States, concern lest potential tort liabilities should deter would-be rescuers has led to a majority of jurisdictions passing so-called 'Good Samaritan' statutes which recognise an immunity from suit in such cases (see *Prosser & Keeton*, p. 387).) But a number of other jurisdictions do impose affirmative duties of rescue. By Article 222–6 of the French *Code pénal*, criminal liability is imposed on 'anyone who wilfully refrains from helping and assisting a person in danger, when he could have done so or caused others to do so without risk to himself or third parties' (*van Gerven*, p. 281); where the danger materialises and injury results, breach of this duty is actionable in damages under the *Code civil*, which makes no explicit distinction between acts and omissions in its provisions on tortious liability. (Article 1383 states that liability arises not only from the defendant's 'act' but also from 'negligence or carelessness'.) For further comparative analysis, see Kortmann, *op. cit.*, ch. 4, and *van Dam*, para. 808.

A few United States jurisdictions have also made failure to perform so-called 'easy' rescues punishable in the criminal law, though it seems that no court has yet recognized that an injured person can bring a civil action for damages in such a case (for discussion, see Franklin, 'Vermont Requires Rescue: A Comment' (1972) 25 Stan L Rev 51). However, the American Law Institute's *Restatement Third, Torts: Liability for Physical and Emotional Harm* (2009), in a striking departure from previous Restatements, now provides (§ 38): 'When a statute requires an actor to act for the protection of another, the court may rely on the statute to decide that an affirmative duty exists and its scope.' It is contemplated that this might form the basis for a liability in tort for breach of a criminal law statute imposing a duty of easy rescue.

The common law's failure to recognise a duty of rescue has been criticised by a number of commentators. Finding the decisions which uphold this rule 'revolting to any moral sense', *Prosser & Keeton* comment: 'The remedy in such cases is left to the "higher law" and the "voice of conscience", which, in a wicked world, would seem to be singularly ineffective either to prevent the harm or to compensate the victim' (pp. 376, 375). A similar position is taken by Bender, 'A Feminist's Primer on Feminist Theory and Tort' (1988) 38 J Leg Ed 3, who works it (passim) into her feminist critique of the law:

Tort law needs to be more of a system of response and caring than it is now. Its focus should be on interdependence and collective responsibility rather than on individuality, and on safety and help for the injured rather than on 'reasonableness' and economic efficiency... [I]mplicit male norms have been used to skew legal analysis... Not only does 'reasonable person' still mean 'reasonable man'—'reason' and 'reasonableness' are gendered concepts as well. Gender distinctions have often been reinforced by dualistic attributions of reason and rationality to men, emotion and intuition (or instinct) to women... The 'no duty [to rescue]' rule is a consequence of a legal system devoid of care and responsiveness to the safety of others.

However, not all advocates of a duty of rescue would go so far as to endorse the degree of mutual obligation envisaged by Bender. A good example is Weinrib, 'The Case for a Duty to Rescue' (1981) 90 Yale LJ 247, who supports the imposition of a duty to rescue in cases of emergency when the rescuer can act without prejudice to himself, but rejects any more widely applicable duty of beneficence. He explains: 'The deadening of industry resulting from both reliance on beneficence and devotion to beneficence would in the long run be an evil greater than the countenancing of individual instances of unfulfilled needs or wants.' Weinrib's later work eschews such policy arguments, and he now conceives of the law's fundamental distinction between misfeasance and nonfeasance as inherent in the correlative structure of tort law: tort law corrects the injustice effected by the defendant doing something that is incompatible with a right of the claimant (see, e.g., 'Correlativity, Personality, and the Emerging Consensus on Corrective Justice' (2001) 2 Theoretical Inq L 107). There is no general duty of affirmative action because a person imperilled ordinarily has no right to expect another person to come to his aid. For further development of this basic idea in the context of English law, see *Beever*, chs 6 and 9; *Stevens*, 9ff.

II. Liability for Omissions

Despite the general principle excluding liability for omissions, liability may arise in certain exceptional circumstances. But no precise categorisation is possible of the various situations in which a duty of affirmative action is recognised. As Tony Honoré has written, the cases 'do not fall into any neat pattern... They seem not to derive from or be reducible to a single principle' ('Are Omission Less Culpable?', in P. Cane and J. Stapleton (eds), *Essays for Patrick Atiyah* (Oxford: OUP, 1991), p. 47). Nevertheless, there has been a tendency in the courts to attempt what Honoré asserts is impossible, namely to reduce the various examples of liability for omission to instances of a single general principle. A number of cases purport to use a test of reasonable foreseeability—or perhaps a high degree of foreseeability—as the criterion for imposing liability for a culpable omission. This approach cannot be supported. In the first place, the test of foreseeability—or probability, or whatever—is hopelessly vague, providing no real guidance as to when liability is imposed and when it is not. In addition, it fails to account for English law's failure to impose liability for failing to intervene even when it is obvious that serious harm will otherwise result (e.g. in Lord Nicholl's 'callous bystander' examples in *Stovin*, above).

An alternative, and it is submitted more fruitful approach, is to identify a number of loosely-defined circumstances giving rise to duties of affirmative action. Amongst these are:

- the defendant's creation of a source of danger, even if entirely without fault;
- the defendant's undertaking of responsibility for the claimant's welfare; and
- the defendant's occupation of an office or position of responsibility (e.g. as a parent or employer, or as the owner or occupier of land).

The cases below illustrate these broad general categories, though it should be noted that not infrequently the categories overlap and it is a combination of factors, not one individual factor, that accounts for the decision reached on the facts.

Capital & Counties plc v Hampshire County Council [1997] QB 1004

This was a consolidated appeal involving three separate actions.

In the *Hampshire* case, the defendant fire brigade attended a fire on the plaintiffs' premises, its cause apparently unknown, and the fire officer, Station Officer Mitchell, ordered the plaintiffs' sprinkler system to be turned off. That was held to have been a negligent mistake which had an adverse effect on restraining the fire which spread rapidly and eventually destroyed the whole building.

In the *London* case, the plaintiffs' industrial premises were showered with flaming debris following an explosion on nearby waste land; the explosion was set off deliberately by the second defendants, who were a company specialising in special effects for film and television. When the fire brigade run by the first defendants arrived at the scene of the explosion they satisfied themselves that all the fires there had been extinguished and left the scene without inspecting the plaintiffs' premises which were severely damaged when a fire broke out there later on. In the *West Yorkshire* case, the plaintiffs' chapel was destroyed by a fire (cause unknown) which the defendant fire authority had failed to extinguish. The plaintiffs alleged that this was attributable to the defendants' negligence, and breach of statutory duty, in failing to ensure that its fire hydrants were in working order and capable of providing an adequate water supply. Of the seven fire hydrants surrounding the chapel, four failed to work for one reason or another, and three were either never found, or found so late as to be of little use, as a result of inadequate signing. [For analysis of the breach of statutory duty point, see p. 610, below.]

The Court of Appeal, in a judgment delivered by Stuart-Smith LJ, first considered the question: 'Is there a common law duty on the fire brigade to answer calls to fires or to take reasonable care to so do?' His conclusion was that there were no considerations sufficient to give rise to such a duty of affirmative action (at 1030):

> In our judgment the fire brigade are not under a common law duty to answer the call for help and are not under a duty to take care to do so. If therefore they fail to turn up or fail to turn up in time because they have carelessly misunderstood the message, got lost on the way or run into a tree, they are not liable . . .

His Lordship then considered whether a duty of care might arise once the fire brigade had arrived on the scene and started to fight the fire.

Stuart-Smith LJ (delivering the judgment of the Court)

Does the fire brigade owe a duty of care to the owner of property on fire, or anyone else to whom the fire may spread, once they have arrived at the fire ground and started to fight the fire?

...Counsel for the plaintiffs in the *Hampshire* case submit that there are two approaches in principle which lead to the conclusion of liability in their case.

First it is...argued that Station Officer Mitchell's act of switching off the sprinklers was a positive act of misfeasance which foreseeably caused the fire to get out of control and spread and cause the loss of blocks B and C and part of block A which would not otherwise have been affected...By reason of the differing circumstances in each appeal this line of argument is only of direct assistance to the plaintiffs in the *Hampshire* case. The alternative ground upon which it is said that proximity will arise is where someone possessed of a special skill undertakes, quite irrespective of contract, to apply that skill for the assistance of another person who relies upon such skill, and there is direct and substantial reliance by the plaintiffs on the defendant's skill...

We turn to consider the first of these submissions. The peculiarity of fire brigades, together with other rescue services, such as ambulance or coastal rescue and protective services such as the police, is that they do not as a rule create the danger which causes injury to the plaintiff or loss to his property. For the most part they act in the context of a danger already created and damage already caused, whether by the forces of nature, or the acts of some third party or even of the plaintiff himself, and whether those acts are criminal, negligent or non-culpable.

But where the rescue/protective service itself by negligence creates the danger which caused the plaintiff's injury there is no doubt in our judgment the plaintiff can recover...The judge [in the *Hampshire* case] held that at the time the sprinkler systems were turned off, the fire was being contained, but that once they were turned off it rapidly went out of control, spreading to blocks B and C which had been deprived of their own sprinkler protection...[T]he defendants by their positive act exacerbated the fire so that it rapidly spread...

We now turn to consider the second submission made on behalf of all the plaintiffs that the requisite proximity exists. It involves the concept of assumption of responsibility by the fire brigade and particular reliance by the owner. As a general rule a sufficient relationship of proximity will exist when someone possessed of special skill undertakes to apply that skill for the assistance of another person who relies upon such skill and there is direct and substantial reliance by the plaintiff on the defendant's skill (see *Hedley Byrne & Co Ltd v Heller & Partners* [1964] AC 465 and *Henderson v Merrett Syndicates Ltd* [1995] 2 AC 145). There are many instances of this. The plaintiffs submit that that which is most closely analogous is that of doctor and patient or health authority and patient. There is no doubt that once the relationship of doctor and patient or hospital authority and admitted patient exists, the doctor or the hospital owe a duty to take reasonable care to effect a cure, not merely to prevent further harm. The undertaking is to use the special skills which the doctor and hospital authorities have to treat the patient...In *Cassidy v Ministry of Health* [1951] 2 KB 343 at 360 Denning LJ said:

> In my opinion, authorities who run a hospital, be they local authorities, government boards, or any other corporation, are in law under the self-same duty as the humblest doctor. Whenever they accept a patient for treatment, they must use reasonable care and skill to cure him of his ailment.

...[I]t is clear that no such duty of care exists, even though there may be close physical proximity, simply because one party is a doctor and the other has a medical problem which may be of interest to both...[W]e consider that [counsel for the defendants in the *Hampshire* case] is right when he submitted that the fire brigade's duty is owed the public at large to prevent the spread of fire and that this may involve a conflict between the interests of various owners of premises. It may be necessary to enter and cause damage to A's premises in order to tackle a fire which has started in B's. During the Great Fire of London the Duke of York had to blow up a number of houses not yet affected by fire, in order to make a fire break...

Plaintiffs' counsel argue that the provisions of sub-ss. (3) and (2) of s. 30 [of the Fire Services Act 1947] which confer on the senior fire brigade officer present sole charge and control of fire fighting operations and make it a criminal offence wilfully to obstruct or interfere with any member of a fire brigade engaged in fire fighting, establish a proximate relationship, once responsibility for fighting the fire is taken over by the brigade.

This argument has its attraction, particularly on the somewhat extreme facts of the *Hampshire* case...[T]he plaintiffs had two systems of fire fighting, one very effective in the form of automatic sprinklers, the other the manual fire-fighting capability of their employees. Station Officer Mitchell rendered the first ineffectual and ordered out of the building the plaintiffs' employees who were attempting to attack the fire.

But it seems to us that the statute imposes control of operations on the senior officer for the benefit of the public generally where there may be conflicting interests. By taking such control that officer is not to be seen as undertaking a voluntary assumption of responsibility to the owner of the premises on fire, whether or not the latter is in fact reliant upon it...

In our judgment, a fire brigade does not enter into a sufficiently proximate relationship with the owner or occupier of premises to come under a duty of care merely by attending at the fire ground and fighting the fire; this is so, even though the senior officer actually assumes control of the fire-fighting operation.

COMMENTARY

The plaintiffs failed in their argument that a fire brigade which took control of fire-fighting operations, and ordered others to stop their independent efforts to put out the blaze, thereby assumed responsibility to the owners of the premises to which they had been called. But, in the *Hampshire* case, the court was able to impose liability on the basis that there was a positive act of misfeasance which foreseeably caused the fire to get out of control. It was assumed in this case that it was the act of the defendant's fire officer which was negligent. What if the officer had acted reasonably at the time he had the sprinklers switched off, but subsequently realised the risk that the fire might spread and then did nothing about it? Another question: why could the act of ordering others to stop fighting a fire independently not constitute a 'positive act of misfeasance' sufficient to give rise to liability?

The Court of Appeal's approach is very reminiscent of that taken by the House of Lords in *East Suffolk Rivers Catchment Board v Kent* [1941] AC 74. In that case, a breach in a sea wall caused by a very high tide led to the flooding of the plaintiff-respondents' land. The defendant-appellants in the exercise of their statutory powers undertook the repair of the wall, but carried out the work so inefficiently that the repairs of the breach, which the evidence suggested should have taken only 14 days, continued for 178 days, prolonging the period during which the respondents' land was under water. The House of Lords (Lord Atkin dissenting) held that the catchment board had not assumed any responsibility to the landowner beyond its undoubted duty not to cause additional damage. Lord Porter explained (at 105):

where, as here, the damage was not caused by any positive act on the part of the appellants but was caused and would have occurred to the like extent if they had taken no steps at all, I cannot see that the loss which the respondents suffered was due to any breach of a duty owed by the appellants.

Their duty was to avoid causing damage, not either to prevent future damage due to causes for which they were not responsible or to shorten its incidence. The loss which the respondents suffered was due to the original breach, and the appellants' failure to close it merely allowed the damage to continue during the time which they took in mending the broken bank.

The question whether the existence of a statutory power to take action for the benefit of another person can ever create a duty to that person is considered further in Chapter 10.

Capital & Counties plc v Hampshire County Council was applied in *OLL Ltd v Secretary of State for Transport* [1997] 3 All ER 897, a tortfeasor's action for contribution, where May J struck out a claim against the coastguard which alleged that it was negligent in misleading independent rescuers as to the likely location of a group of children on a canoeing expedition who were adrift at sea. According to the judge, this was not a case like the *Hampshire* case (above) where the plaintiff had caused direct physical harm by his positive conduct actually at the scene. *Winfield & Jolowicz* finds the decision 'difficult' as the allegation was clearly that the defendants had made the children worse off by depriving them of the assistance of others, and poses the following question (para. 5–22, n. 28):

Suppose a passing motorist said that he would take an unconscious casualty to hospital and other people at the scene forbore to call an ambulance. Would he not be liable if he stopped for refreshments, whereby the patient died? Why should it matter that he intervenes 'at the scene'?

These decisions must now be considered in the light of *Kent v Griffiths*, below.

Kent v Griffiths [2001] QB 36

The claimant suffered an asthma attack and her doctor, attending at her home, telephoned the London Ambulance Service (LAS) for an ambulance to take the claimant immediately to hospital. The call was accepted but, for reasons which were never explained, the ambulance took some forty minutes to travel the 6½ miles to the claimant's home. While in the ambulance on the way to the hospital, the claimant suffered a respiratory arrest which resulted in permanent brain damage. In her subsequent action for damages against (amongst others) the ambulance service, the judge found that the ambulance could and should have arrived at the claimant's home some 14 minutes earlier and that, if it had done so, there was a high probability that the respiratory arrest would have been averted. He found that the ambulance service had breached its duty of care to the claimant and allowed her claim for damages. The ambulance service appealed.

Lord Woolf

There are obvious similarities between the facts of this case and . . . the *Capital & Counties* type of situation. The activities of the fire services are subject to a statutory framework, so are the functions of ambulance services. Section 3(1) of the National Health Service Act 1977 imposes on the Secretary of State a duty to provide, throughout England and Wales, to such extent as he considers necessary to meet all reasonable requirements, 'medical, dental, nursing and ambulance services': sections 1 and 3(1) of the National Health Service Act 1977. This duty is an exhortatory or target duty which does not create a statutory right, the breach of which can give rise to a private law right to damages. As the police and the fire services can be summoned by 999 calls so can the ambulance service, as in this case . . .

Here what was being provided was a health service. In the case of health services under the 1977 Act the conventional situation is that there is a duty of care. Why should the position of the ambulance staff be different from that of doctors or nurses? In addition the arguments based on public policy are much weaker in the case of the ambulance service than they are in the case of the police or the fire service. The police and fire services' primary obligation is to the public at large. In protecting a particular victim of crime, the police are performing their more general role of maintaining public order and reducing crime. In the case of fire the fire service will normally be concerned not only to protect a particular property where a fire breaks out but also to prevent fire spreading. In the case of both services, there is therefore a concern to protect the public generally. The emergency services that can be summoned by a 999 call do, in the majority of situations, broadly carry out a similar function. But in reality they can be very different. The ambulance service is part of the health service. Its care function includes transporting patients to and from hospital when the use of an ambulance for this purpose is desirable. It is therefore appropriate to regard the LAS as providing services of the category provided by hospitals and not as providing services equivalent to those rendered by the police or the fire service. Situations could arise where there is a conflict between the interests of a particular individual and the public at large. But, in the case of the ambulance service in this particular case, the only member of the public who could be adversely affected was the claimant. It was the claimant alone for whom the ambulance had been called.

Cases could arise where an ambulance is required to attend a scene of an accident in which a number of people need transporting to hospital. That could be said to be a different situation, but, as the numbers involved would be limited, I would not regard this as necessarily leading to a different result. The result would depend on the facts. I would be resistant to a suggestion that the ambulance service could be regarded as negligent because by an error of judgment a less seriously injured patient was transported to hospital leaving a more seriously injured patient at the scene who, as a result, suffered further injuries. In such a situation, on the facts, it is most unlikely that there would be conduct which could be properly regarded as negligent. The requirement to establish that there has been a lack of care provides the LAS with the necessary protection.

An important feature of this case is that there is no question of an ambulance not being available or of a conflict in priorities. Again I recognise that where what is being attacked is the allocation of resources, whether in the provision of sufficient ambulances or sufficient drivers or attendants, different considerations could apply. There then could be issues which are not suited for resolution by the courts. However, once there are available, both in the form of an ambulance and in the form of manpower, the resources to provide an ambulance on which there are no alternative demands, the ambulance service would be acting perversely 'in circumstances such as the present', if it did not make those resources available. Having decided to provide an ambulance an explanation is required to justify a failure to attend within reasonable time . . .

[T]here is no reason why there should not be liability if the arrival of the ambulance was delayed for no good reason. The acceptance of the call in this case established the duty of care.

Aldous and **Laws LJJ** agreed.

Appeal dismissed.

COMMENTARY

Do you agree with Lord Woolf that the fire and ambulance service scenarios are properly distinguished on the basis that the fire service, when responding to a call, is acting in pursuance of a public duty, whilst the ambulance service typically is not? This may have been true in *Kent*, where the ambulance was called for a particular individual, but cases will arise where the ambulance service has competing calls on its resources, for example a serious accident with a large number of casualties, not all of whom can be taken to hospital at once. Lord Woolf apparently thought that there would still be a duty in such a case, and that the conflicting pressures on the ambulance service would be relevant only to the question of breach. If the need to prove a lack of care would really provide the ambulance service with enough protection (against what?), why not adopt the same analysis with respect to the fire service?

Commenting on the tension between *Capital & Counties* and *Kent*, the editor of *Winfield & Jolowicz* argues (para. 5–28):

If there is to be a difference between the cases, it seems better to realise that it lies in the fact that the fire service is primarily concerned with saving property and that imposing liability would tend to enure for the benefit of subrogated fire insurers who have taken a premium to cover the risk, though that would hardly justify a different result where life was at risk from the fire.

Against this, it may be noted that the courts have generally been hostile to the idea that the likelihood of the claimant being insured should influence their decisions on liability (see p. 26f, above).

Cf. *Smith v Chief Constable of Sussex Police* [2008] UKHL 50, [2009] 1 AC 225 at [55], where Lord Bingham (dissenting), immediately after noting the decision in *Kent v Griffiths*, said of *Capital & Counties*: 'I would wish to reserve my opinion on its correctness in the light of later authority.'

Whether or not these cases can be reconciled, the Human Rights Act 1998 now provides an alternative remedy against the rescue services in some circumstances, and may in time persuade the courts to review the extent of their affirmative duties at common law. See further Chapter 10, below.

Lord Woolf noted that ambulance services were provided under statutory provisions the breach of which did not give rise to a private law right to damages, yet found that the ambulance service might be liable for common law negligence. This analysis must now be read in light of the House of Lords' decision in *Gorringe v Calderdale Metropolitan Borough Council* [2004] 1 WLR 1057, extracted in Chapter 10, where their Lordships held that no positive duty to act could be founded merely on the presence of statutory powers which, if exercised, might have prevented the damage to the claimant. The Law Commission has queried whether *Kent* can survive *Gorringe* (*Remedies Against Public Bodies: A Scoping Report* (2006), p. 12, fn. 11), but it appears to us that the outcome in *Kent* can be defended, even after *Gorringe*, on the basis that the ambulance service assumed responsibility for the claimant when it accepted the 999 call; this provides a basis other than the existence of the statutory powers for the imposition of the positive duty. But what if, after receiving the call, the operator had replied: 'Sorry, all our ambulances are busy today'? In such a case, there would arguably be no assumption of responsibility as the operator does not undertake to provide an ambulance at all. Or does the ambulance service assume responsibility when the operator picks up the phone, or even by virtue of its well-publicised participation in the emergency calls system? Consider how the different analyses might affect the ambulance service's liability in a case where the emergency calls system has broken down and callers are unable to get though. In such a case, even if there is no liability at common law, an alternative claim might now be possible under the Human Rights Act 1998: see p. 533f, below.

Is Reliance Necessary?

In *Kent*, the Court of Appeal found that the duty was established by the ambulance service's 'acceptance' of the 999 call (cf. the trial judge who thought the duty arose only on the allocation of an ambulance to the claimant). The judgment contains nothing to suggest that there had to be detrimental reliance upon this by the claimant or another person. In fact, the claimant's doctor gave evidence that, if she had been told that it would be 40 minutes before the ambulance arrived, she would probably have asked the claimant's husband to drive them to the hospital. But the Court of Appeal appears not to have attached any significance to this evidence and thus treated detrimental reliance on the assumption of responsibility as irrelevant. To quote *Winfield & Jolowicz* again, 'it seems that the result would have been the same even if the claimant had been in a remote place with no alternative means of transport' (para. 5–28).

Barrett v Ministry of Defence [1995] 1 WLR 1217

The deceased, a serving naval airman, got himself exceedingly drunk while celebrating a promotion on his remote Norwegian base, where drink prices were according to the judge 'astonishingly cheap'. Over the course of the evening, he had been served drinks at bars on the base, and been brought drinks by friends. He was found unconscious and a duty officer organised for him to be taken by stretcher to his room, but no one kept watch over the deceased to ensure that he was lying in a safe position. While unconscious, the deceased choked on his own vomit and died. A disciplinary inquiry subsequently revealed that outbreaks of drunkenness were common at the base, and the senior naval officer at the base admitted he had not fulfilled his responsibility, imposed by the Queen's Regulations for the Royal Navy, of discouraging drunkenness. The deceased's widow brought an action for damages on behalf of his estate and dependants. At trial, the judge found the defendant to have been negligent in tolerating excessive drinking at the base, but reduced the award of damages by one-quarter because of the deceased's contributory negligence. The defendant appealed against the award.

Beldam LJ

The judge said that the deceased was a heavy drinker introduced to a potentially dangerous situation. In these circumstances the judge held that it was foreseeable in this particular environment that the deceased would succumb to heavy intoxication. Although it was only in exceptional circumstances that a defendant could be fixed with a duty to take positive steps to protect a person of full age and capacity from his own weakness, he considered in the exceptional circumstances that arose in this case it was just and reasonable to impose a duty to take care on the defendant. He also held that the defendant was in breach of that duty because it failed to enforce the standards it itself set in matters of discipline...

The judge also held that once the deceased had collapsed, the defendant had assumed responsibility for him and had taken inadequate steps to care for him. No medical officer or medical attendant was informed and supervision of the deceased was wholly inadequate by the standards which the defendant's own officers accepted were necessary. The defendant does not challenge the judge's findings that it was in breach of duty to take care of the deceased once he had collapsed and it had assumed responsibility for him. The defendant's principal ground of appeal is that the judge was wrong to hold that it was under any duty to take care to see that the deceased, a mature man 30 years of age, did not consume so much alcohol that he became unconscious. If the deceased himself was to be treated as a responsible adult, he alone was to blame for his collapse. On this basis the judge's apportionment of liability was plainly wrong. Even if the judge's finding of this duty were to stand, the deceased ought to have been regarded as equally responsible for his own death . . .

In the present case the judge posed the question whether there was a duty at law to take reasonable steps to prevent the deceased becoming unconscious through alcohol abuse. He said his conclusion that there was such a duty was founded on the fact that: 'It was foreseeable in the environment in which the defendant grossly failed to enforce their regulations and standing orders that the deceased would succumb to heavy intoxication.' And in these circumstances it was just and reasonable to impose a duty.

The plaintiff argued for the extension of a duty to take care for the safety of the deceased from analogous categories of relationship in which an obligation to use reasonable care already existed. For example, employer and employee, pupil and schoolmaster, and occupier and visitor. It was said that the defendant's control over the environment in which the deceased was serving and the provision of duty-free liquor, coupled with the failure to enforce disciplinary rules and orders, were sufficient factors to render it fair, just and reasonable to extend the duty to take reasonable care found in the analogous circumstances. The characteristic which distinguishes those relationships is reliance expressed or implied in the relationship which the party to whom the duty is owed is entitled to place on the other party to make provision for his safety. I can see no reason why it should not be fair, just and reasonable for the law to leave a responsible adult to assume responsibility for his own actions in consuming alcoholic drink. No one is better placed to judge the amount that he can safely consume or to exercise control in his own interest as well as in the interest of others. To dilute self-responsibility and to blame one adult for another's lack of self-control is neither just nor reasonable and in the development of the law of negligence an increment too far.

Should the individual members of the senior rates' mess who bought rounds of drinks for a group of mess mates and the deceased each be held to have had a share in the responsibility for his death? Or should responsibility only devolve on two or three of them who bought the last rounds? In the course of argument Mr. Nice for the plaintiff experienced great difficulty in articulating the nature of the duty. Eventually he settled on two expositions. It was a duty owed by the defendant to any serviceman at this base in this environment to take into account group behaviour and arising from a duty to provide for the servicemen's accommodation and welfare there was a duty to take reasonable care to prevent drunkenness/drinking '(a) to a level which endangered his safety or (b) such as to render him unconscious.' The impracticality of the duty so defined is obvious. The level of drinking which endangers safety depends upon the behaviour of the person affected. The disinhibiting effects of even two or three drinks may on occasions cause normally sober and steady individuals to behave with nonchalant disregard for their own and others' welfare and safety.

The plaintiff placed reliance on *Crocker v Sundance Northwest Resorts Ltd* (1988) 51 DLR (4th) 321, a decision of the Supreme Court of Canada, and on another Canadian case, *Jordan House Ltd v Menow* (1973) 38 DLR (3d) 105. In the first case the defendant was held liable to an intoxicated plaintiff for permitting him to take part in a dangerous ski hill race which caused him to be injured. The defendant had taken the positive step of providing him with the equipment needed for the race knowing that he was in no fit state to take part. The plaintiff had consumed alcohol in the defendant's bars. Liability was based not on permitting him to drink in the bars but in permitting him to take part in the race. In the *Jordan House* case the plaintiff was a habitual customer of the defendant. He became intoxicated from drinking heavily. The defendant proprietor evicted him knowing he was unsteady and incapable in spite of the fact that he would have to cross a busy thoroughfare. The court held that these circumstances, including the fact that at the time he was evicted the plaintiff's relationship with the defendant was that of invitee/invitor, were sufficient to justify the imposition of a duty to take care for the safety of the customer. In each of these cases the court founded the imposition of a duty on factors additional to the mere provision of alcohol and the failure strictly to enforce provisions against drunkenness.

In the present case I would reverse the judge's finding that the defendant was under a duty to take reasonable care to prevent the deceased from abusing alcohol to the extent he did. Until he collapsed, I would hold that the deceased was in law alone responsible for his condition. Thereafter, when the defendant assumed responsibility for him, it accepts that the measures taken fell short of the standard reasonably to be expected. It did not summon medical assistance and its supervision of him was inadequate.

The final question is how far the deceased should be regarded as responsible for his death. The amount of alcohol he had consumed not only caused him to vomit, it deprived him of the spontaneous ability to protect his air passages after he had vomited. His fault was therefore a continuing and direct cause of his death. Moreover his lack of self-control in his own interest caused the defendant to have to assume responsibility for him. But for his fault, it would not have had to do so. How far in such circumstances is it just and equitable to regard the deceased as the author of his misfortune? The deceased involved the defendant in a situation in which it had to assume responsibility for his care and I would not regard it as just and equitable in such circumstances to be unduly critical of the defendant's fault. I consider a greater share of blame should rest upon the deceased than on the defendant and I would reduce the amount of the damages recoverable by the plaintiff by two-thirds, holding the defendant one-third to blame.

Saville and **Neill LJJ** agreed.

Appeal allowed.

COMMENTARY

The basis of the court's decision was the defendant's assumption of responsibility for the deceased's health and safety, and not its supply to him of dangerous quantities of drink. The result, it seems, would have been the same even if the drink had come from some other source. The duty presumably arose at the moment when the senior officer ordered that the deceased be taken to his room, though the Court of Appeal did not rule on this because the defendant did not challenge the judge's finding that responsibility had been assumed.

Barrett may be compared with *Jebson v Ministry of Defence* [2000] 1 WLR 2055, where the plaintiff soldier was injured whilst engaged in drunken frolicking. The injury was sustained after a night out on the town arranged by the plaintiff's camp commander, who had laid on transport to take the troops back to barracks. On the way, the plaintiff tried to climb onto the canvas roof of the lorry in which he was travelling but lost his footing and fell onto the road. The Court of Appeal found that the commander had impliedly undertaken responsibility for the safety of soldiers who he should have foreseen would be drunk and rowdy. It was therefore his duty to ensure they were properly supervised on their way back to their base. On the facts, there had been a breach of this duty as the commander had neglected even to put anyone formally in charge of the troops, though the plaintiff's damages were reduced by 75 per cent for contributory negligence. In contrast with *Barrett*, the plaintiff's injury was caused by his behaviour whilst drunk, and not simply by the effects of alcohol on his body. But it is doubtful that the result would have been any different if (say) he had drunk himself comatose whilst out on the town, got inadvertently left behind, and choked on his own vomit, for the commander appears to have assumed responsibility for the soldiers' well-being over the course of the entire evening.

The risks associated with alcohol are well-known and willingly confronted by imbibers. The Court of Appeal was obviously very concerned that imposing liability purely on the basis of the defendant's supply of the alcohol would undesirably dilute individual responsibility, a position which lead the High Court of Australia to deny that a licensed club owed a duty of care to its patrons to take care to prevent them from drinking to excess (*Cole v South Tweed Heads Rugby League Football Club* (2004) 217 CLR 469; see also *CAL No 14 Pty Ltd v Scott* [2009] HCA 47). In Canada, however, a contrary decision was reached in *Jordan House Ltd v Menow* (1973) 38 DLR (3rd) 105. The plaintiff was ejected from the defendant's hotel in a state of extreme inebriation and was struck by a vehicle as he made his way home on foot along the main highway. The Supreme Court found that the defendant had breached its duty of care towards him by continuing to serve him when he was intoxicated and turning him out onto the road when there was a probable risk of personal injury. (Cf. *Childs v Desormeaux* [2006] 1 SCR 641, distinguishing between commercial and social hosts in the context of liability to third parties: see p. 503, below.)

Commenting on the general reluctance of courts to recognise a duty to the intoxicated patron, Orr and Dale have argued ('Impaired judgements: Alcohol server liability and "personal responsibility" after *Cole v South Tweed Heads Rugby League Football Club Ltd*' (2005) 13 TLJ 103 at 122):

> The person who drinks heavily has, through rhetoric, been constructed not as partial victim of the industry that profits from him or her, but as the entire author of any misfortune he or she suffers, in essence an outlaw. This has occurred in the course of a political and judicial battle that has been heavily influenced by impressions about common morality. This battle can be summed up in one phrase: 'personal responsibility'.

Do you think it is right to characterise the drinker in this context as 'an outlaw'?

English law's reluctance to recognise a duty on the purveyors of alcohol may be contrasted with its approach to the supply of products which present dangers that are not obvious to ordinary people. It is well established, for example, that manufacturers must supply appropriate instructions and warnings with their products (*Vacwell v BDH* [1971] 1 QB 88). The liability for failure to warn can often be regarded as one for misfeasance rather than pure nonfeasance, as it is natural to treat the supply of the product and the failure to warn as two aspects of a single course of conduct. But a liability for nonfeasance proper may arise where a latent defect is discovered in a product after it has reached the consumer, for the discovery of the defect may create a new duty of affirmative action:

> [A] manufacturer's duty of care does not end when the goods are sold. A manufacturer who realises that omitting to warn past customers about something which might result in injury to them must take reasonable steps to attempt to warn them, however lacking in negligence he may have been at the time the goods were sold.

(*Hobbs (Farms) v Baxenden* [1992] 1 Lloyd's Rep 54 at 65, per Sir Michael Ogden QC; see also *Walton v British Leyland UK Ltd*, unreported, 2 July 1978; *Rivtow Marine Ltd v Washington Iron Works* [1974] SCR 1189.) The approach of the courts in such cases in fact reflects a broader principle of responsibility by which the *innocent* doing of harm or creation of a risk may give rise to a positive duty. The classic example is the motorist who without fault runs into another person: it is generally accepted that he has a duty to summon help, even though he was not to blame for the accident (see Honoré, *op. cit.*, p. 47).

Assumption of Responsibility: Further Analysis

Most frequently, duties of affirmative action are undertaken by contract, in which case liability may be concurrent in contract and tort (see *Henderson v Merrett Syndicates Ltd*, extracted above, p. 434). But a contractual undertaking may be sufficient to generate a duty of affirmative action towards a third party, as where a testator engages a solicitor to write a will in favour of certain beneficiaries (see *White v Jones*, extracted above, p. 444). An undertaking of responsibility may also, of course, arise wholly independently of contract, as where school authorities assume responsibility for the welfare of young children (see *Barnes v Hants CC* [1969] 1 WLR 1563). In many cases, the undertaking will be made by non-verbal conventions which 'are often unclear in their implications' (Honoré, *op. cit.*, p. 47) and the court will be left with the difficult task of determining precisely what the duty is. Honoré elaborates:

> A good example, important in practice, is that of a householder who allows someone, family, friend, or stranger, into his home for a cup of tea, or as a guest at a party, or for a short or longer visit. Opening the door and inviting in is significant, but what duty does it import if the visitor wants to stay on, or falls ill, or is reluctant to leave because of the weather, or has no alternative accommodation?

Honoré suggests that liability is likely to be restricted to those cases where the guest is rendered dependent upon the host, for example because of sudden and incapacitating illness.

It will usually be possible to infer an assumption of responsibility only in cases where there is an intention to benefit a small and clearly defined class. In *Sutradhar v National Environment Research Council*, noted p. 467, above, the Court of Appeal found it 'absurd' to suggest that the British Geological Survey, by undertaking testing of the wells, had assumed responsibility to a large part of the Bangladeshi population in relation to the safety of its water: see [2004] EWCA Civ 175, [2004] PNLR 30 at [24], per Kennedy LJ (affirmed without reference to this point by the House of Lords). Cf. *Watson v British Boxing Board of Control* [2001] QB 1134: boxing regulator assuming responsibility for the adequacy of emergency medical facilities for fighters in an approved title bout.

As noted above, there has been a tendency in English law to require proof of an undertaking by the defendant on a particular occasion, rather than resting a duty of affirmative action on some wider basis, such as the defendant's office or position of responsibility. On the facts of *Barrett*, there was nothing to be gained by investigating the possibility that the officer's mere occupation of a position of responsibility *vis-à-vis* the deceased might have been enough to give rise to a duty to take care of him. But what if the commanding officer, having come across the deceased in a comatose state, had simply ignored him? *Winfield & Jolowicz* (para. 5–25, n. 47) submit that on these facts the officer would have been bound to assume responsibility for the deceased, and this does indeed seem to accord with principle as it is generally accepted that employers owe a duty to take reasonable care of employees who are taken sick or injured while at work (*Kasapis v Laimos* [1959] 2 Lloyd's Rep 378 at 381, per Salmon J).

Another clear example of affirmative duties arising by virtue of the defendant's position of responsibility is in the case of hazards which arise on the defendant's land and pose danger to his neighbours.

Goldman v Hargrave [1967] 1 AC 645 (Privy Council)

The appellant was the owner and occupier of land adjacent to that of the respondents. On 25 February 1961, lightning struck a tall redgum tree standing 100 feet high in the centre of the appellant's land. It began to burn in a fork 84 feet from the ground. Early the next morning the appellant telephoned to the district fire officer and asked for a tree-feller to be sent. The tree was cut down about midday on the same day. Up to this time the appellant's conduct in relation to the fire was not open to criticism. But he then decided to let the tree burn itself out and took no further steps to prevent the fire spreading. It was found that he could have extinguished the fire by spraying it with water either that same evening or the following morning; this would have been the prudent way of proceeding. On 1 March the weather changed and strong gusts of wind caused the fire to revive and spread on to the respondents' adjoining property, causing extensive damage. The respondent failed at first instance in his action for damages, but succeeded before the High Court of Australia. The appellant appealed to the Privy Council.

Lord Wilberforce (delivering the opinion of the Privy Council)

[T]he case is not one where a person has brought a source of danger on to his land, nor one where an occupier has so used his property as to cause a danger to his neighbour. It is one where an occupier, faced with a hazard accidentally arising on his land, fails to act with reasonable prudence so as to remove the hazard. The issue is therefore whether in such a case the occupier is guilty of legal negligence, which involves the issue whether he is under a duty of care, and if so, what is the scope of that duty . . .

What then is the scope of an occupier's duty, with regard to his neighbour, as to hazards arising on his land? With the possible exception of hazard of fire, to which their Lordships will shortly revert, it is only in comparatively recent times that the law has recognised an occupier's duty as one of a more positive character than merely to abstain from creating, or adding to, a source of danger or annoyance. It was for long satisfied with the conception of separate or autonomous proprietors, each of which was entitled to exploit his territory in a 'natural' manner and none of whom was obliged to restrain or direct the operations of nature in the interest of avoiding harm to his neighbours . . .

A decision which, it can now be seen, marked a turning point in the law was that of *Job Edwards Ltd v Birmingham Navigations* [1924] 1 KB 341. The hazard in that case was a fire which originated in a refuse dump placed on land by the act of a third party. When the fire threatened to invade the neighbouring land, the owners of the latter, by agreement, entered and extinguished the fire at a cost of some £1,000. The issue in the action was whether the owners of the land, where the fire was, were liable to bear part of the cost. The Court of Appeal by a majority answered this question negatively, but Scrutton LJ's dissenting judgment contained the following passage (at pp. 357–8):

> There is a great deal to be said for the view that if a man finds a dangerous and artificial thing on his land, which he and those for whom he is responsible did not put there; if he knows that if left alone it will damage other persons; if by reasonable care he can render it harmless, as if by stamping on a fire just beginning from a trespasser's match he can extinguish it; that then if he does nothing, he has 'permitted it to continue', and becomes responsible for it. This would base the liability on negligence, and not on the duty of insuring damage from

a dangerous thing under *Rylands v Fletcher*. I appreciate that to get negligence you must have a duty to be careful, but I think on principle that a landowner has a duty to take reasonable care not to allow his land to remain a receptacle for a thing which may, if not rendered harmless, cause damage to his neighbours.

... In 1940 the dictum of Scrutton LJ passed into the law of England when it was approved by the House of Lords in *Sedleigh-Denfield v O'Callaghan* [1940] AC 880. Their Lordships need not cite from this case in any detail since it is now familiar law. It establishes the occupier's liability with regard to a hazard created on his land by a trespasser, of which he has knowledge, when he fails to take reasonable steps to remove it. It was clear in that case that the hazard could have been removed by what Viscount Maugham (at p. 895) described as the 'very simple step' of placing a grid in the proper place. The members of the House approved the passage just cited from Scrutton LJ's judgment and Viscount Maugham (at p. 893) and Lord Wright (at p. 910) also adopted the statement of the law in Salmond's *Law of Torts*, 5th edn., 1920, pp. 258–65:

> When a nuisance has been created by the act of a trespasser or otherwise without the act, authority, or permission of the occupier, the occupier is not responsible for that nuisance unless, with knowledge or means of knowledge of its existence, he suffers it to continue without taking reasonably prompt and efficient means for its abatement.

The appellant, inevitably, accepts the development, or statement, of the law which the *Sedleigh-Denfield* case contains—as it was accepted by the High Court of Australia. He seeks to establish, however, a distinction between the type of hazard which was there involved, namely one brought about by human agency such as the act of a trespasser, and one arising from natural causes, or Act of God. In relation to hazards of this kind it was submitted that an occupier is under no duty to remove or to diminish it, and that his liability only commences if and when by interference with it he negligently increases the risk or danger to his neighbour's property.

  Their Lordships would first observe, with regard to the suggested distinction, that it is well designed to introduce confusion into the law. As regards many hazardous conditions arising on land, it is impossible to determine how they arose—particularly is this the case as regards fires. If they are caused by human agency, the agent, unless detected *in flagrante delicto*, is hardly likely to confess his fault. And is the occupier, when faced with the initial stages of a fire, to ask himself whether the fire is accidental or man-made before he can decide on his duty? Is the neighbour, whose property is damaged, bound to prove the human origin of the fire? The proposition involves that if he cannot do so, however irresponsibly the occupier has acted, he must fail. The distinction is not only inconvenient, but also it lacks, in their Lordships' view, any logical foundation.

  Within the class of situations in which the occupier is himself without responsibility for the origin of the fire, one may ask in vain what relevant difference there is between a fire caused by a human agency such as a trespasser and one caused by Act of God or nature. A difference in degree—as to the potency of the agency—one can see but none that is in principle relevant to the occupier's duty to act. It was suggested as a logical basis for the distinction that in the case of a hazard originating in an act of man, an occupier who fails to deal with it can be said to be using his land in a manner detrimental to his neighbour and so to be within the classical field of responsibility in nuisance, whereas this cannot be said when the hazard originates without human action so long at least as the occupier merely abstains. The fallacy of this argument is that, as already explained, the basis of the occupier's liability lies not in the use of his land: in the absence of 'adoption' there is no such use: but in the neglect of action in the face of something which may damage his neighbour. To this, the suggested distinction is irrelevant.

Their Lordships advised that the appeal should be dismissed.

COMMENTARY

This is a very interesting case to contrast with *Capital & Counties plc v Hampshire CC*, above. Although the latter case decides that the fire service owes no duty of care to the owner or occupier of burning property simply by virtue of their attendance at the fire scene, *Goldman* makes it clear that the owner/occupier owes a duty to neighbours (in the ordinary sense) who are threatened by the fire. If the owner/occupier is prevented from fighting the fire by the attendance of the fire brigade, and the fire brigade fight the fire so negligently that it escapes onto neighbouring land, whom (if anyone) can the neighbour sue for damages?

The owner/occupier's liability seems to arise by virtue of the responsibility he assumes as an incident of his ownership or occupation of the land in question. The ownership or occupation of land should be regarded as a privilege, of benefit to the owner/occupier but carrying with it certain obligations, including that of ensuring that the land does not become an unreasonable source of danger to neighbours. This obligation often arises concurrently in the separate tort of private nuisance (see Ch. 12, below). But note that negligence may be the only possible claim where the claimant is not the owner of the land affected, or where the complaint is of personal injury or interference with some other interest which is not an interest in land. (These restrictions on the scope of liability in nuisance were recognised by the House of Lords in *Hunter v Canary Wharf* [1997] AC 655: see p. 663, below.) The same consideration underlies the occupier's affirmative duty to ensure that his land is reasonably safe for those coming onto it, whether as visitors or trespassers. This duty, recognised initially by the common law, is now governed by the Occupiers' Liability Acts of 1957 and 1984 (see Ch. 11.II, below).

The negligence liability of a landowner in respect of dangers created by trespassers, as opposed to natural hazards, is considered in *Smith v Littlewoods Organisation*, extracted below at p. 494.

It is now worth considering what other positions of responsibility besides that of the owner/occupier of land give rise to duties of affirmative action.

Other Offices and Positions of Responsibility

In fact, English law has tended to base liability in such case on an undertaking by which responsibility is assumed on a particular occasion, rather than on a general responsibility attaching to particular offices or positions. In the case of a doctor, for instance, it is clear that responsibility is generally limited to the doctor–patient relationship and does not arise simply because the doctor is in the best position to help the injured party. A doctor coming upon a person injured in the street is not obliged to act as a good Samaritan (see *Capital & Counties v Hampshire CC*, above; query if it would make a difference if a GP were requested to give urgent treatment to the victim of an accident or emergency in his practice area, which he would be required to give by his terms of service: see A. Grubb (ed.), *Principles of Medical Law*, 2nd edn. (Oxford: OUP, 2004), paras 5.30–36). However, doctors and nurses in a hospital casualty department may assume a duty of care by helping or advising a person who is seeking attention (*Barnett v Chelsea & Kensington Hospital Management Committee* [1969] 1 QB 428), and it may yet be held that, as a casualty ward is held out as a service to those requiring treatment in an emergency, there would be a duty to treat a person who collapses in the ward even if he has not yet seen a doctor or nurse. See further Williams, 'Medical Samaritans: Is there a Duty to Treat?' (2001) 21 OJLS 393.

Notwithstanding this reluctance to recognise general responsibilities arising out of offices or positions, there are perhaps some cases which can be classified under this heading (although they might equally involve implied undertakings on the part of the defendant). The position of occupiers *vis-à-vis* entrants on their premises and of employers *vis-à-vis* their employees has already been considered. Amongst other examples, perhaps the most notable is the duty of prison authorities to protect the health of those entrusted to their custody, even against self-inflicted injury. Of this, Lord Hoffmann stated in *Reeves v Commissioner of Police for the Metropolis* [2000] 1 AC 360 at 369 that '[t]he duty ... is a very unusual one, arising from the complete control which the police or prison authorities have over the prisoner, combined with the special danger of people in prison taking their own lives'. Substantiating the latter point, his Lordship explained that '[t]he risk of suicide is particularly high amongst prisoners on remand facing a new environment and an uncertain future' (at 366). It was immaterial that the deceased had been of sound mind. (In fact the existence of a duty of care was conceded in this case—rightly, as the majority of the House of Lords thought; see also *Kirkham v Chief Constable of Greater Manchester Police* [1990] 2 QB 283.) It appears, however, that the duty will not arise unless there is a clear risk that a particular prisoner will attempt suicide, for the police cannot be held responsible where an apparently run-of-the-mill drunk takes his own life after being arrested for disorderly conduct and placed in the cells to sober up (*Orange v Chief Constable of West Yorkshire Police* [2001] EWCA Civ 611, [2002] QB 347). This is entirely consistent with the jurisprudence of the European Court of Human Rights, which requires the prison authorities to intervene only where there is a 'real and immediate risk' of suicide (*Keenan v United Kingdom* (2001) 33 EHRR 913).

In *Secretary of State for the Home Department v Robb* [1995] Fam 127, it was held that prison authorities have no right to stop a prisoner from committing suicide by starving himself to death. How is this consistent with the decision in *Reeves* that there may be a duty to prevent a prisoner taking his own life? Perhaps it is because the duty in *Reeves* was to deprive the prisoner, so far as possible, of the means of taking his own life, rather than actually to use force against him. If so, what if a guard had gone into the cell while the prisoner was attempting to asphyxiate himself: would he have had the duty (or the right) to use force to stop him?

The question whether the position and responsibilities of local authorities and other public bodies are enough to generate a legal duty of affirmative action, breach of which will sound in damages, is considered in Chapter 10.

The Parent–Child Relationship

One situation in which we might expect to find a general responsibility for the welfare of another is in relation to the parent–child relationship. However, there is no clear English authority on the point, and courts in other common law jurisdictions have tended to limit the parent's responsibility to those particular occasions on which he or she has undertaken to care for the child (see further McIvor, 'Expelling the Myth of the Parental Duty to Rescue' (2000) 12 CFLQ 229). Hence, Barwick CJ has stated in the High Court of Australia (*Hahn v Conley* (1971) 126 CLR 276 at 283–4, following the decision of the New Zealand Court of Appeal in *McCallion v Dodd* [1966] NZLR 710):

whilst in particular situations and because of their nature or elements, there will be a duty on the person into whose care the child has been placed and accepted to take reasonable care to protect the child against foreseeable danger, there is no general duty of care in that respect imposed by the law upon a parent simply because of the blood relationship.

A critical concern in such cases has been that families might be threatened with financial ruin if a third party sued by an infant plaintiff were to seek contribution from the infant's parents as joint tortfeasors (see *McCallion v Dodd* [1966] NZLR 710 at 727, per Turner J). In the United States, such considerations resulted in the even more extreme response of the judicial recognition of a parental immunity against suits brought by their children (see, e.g., *Hewellette v George*, 68 Miss 703, 9 So 885 (1891)). However, in more recent times many courts have resiled from that position by refusing to recognise the immunity, abolishing it, or developing exceptions to it (see *Rousey v Rousey*, 528 A 2d 416 (DC App, 1987), see generally D. B. Dobbs, *The Law of Torts* (St Paul, Minn.: West, 2000). On the liability of parents to their children generally, see C. McIvor, *Third Party Liability in Tort* (Oxford: Hart, 2006), pp. 21–4, and, for a comparative European analysis, M. Martin Casals (ed.), *Children in Tort Law, Part II: Children as Victims* (Vienna: Springer, 2006).

Legislation aimed at protecting the welfare of children frequently allows children to be placed with foster parents or in other types of residential care. Should those responsible for the care of the children owe a duty to them if a parent in similar circumstances would not? See *A v Roman Catholic Archdiocese of Wellington* [2007] 1 NZLR 536 discussing whether duties of 'good parenting' should be imposed on such bodies where the plaintiff alleged, amongst other things, that she was deprived of a normal upbringing as a result of the defendant's breach of those duties. (Parents do not owe any equivalent duty: see *Barrett v Enfield London Borough Council* [2001] 2 AC 550 at 587, per Lord Hutton.)

III. Liability for the Acts of a Third Party

The question of liability for the acts of a third party raises similar considerations to those examined above. Indeed, often the complaint is actually of an omission, for example a failure to control a third party, or to prevent a dangerous situation from being sparked off by a third party. But not all third-party cases involve omissions. Sometimes the complaint is simply that the defendant provided the third party with the opportunity or the means to injure the claimant, and it is that conduct which is alleged to be negligent, regardless of whether the defendant unreasonably failed at some subsequent point of time to intervene to prevent the injury.

Such cases often raise the same objections to the imposition of liability as do 'pure' omissions cases. But there is also an additional difficulty: causation. The deliberate intervention of a third party generally 'breaks the chain of causation', and a grossly negligent intervening act will often do so as well. For this reason, considerations which may be sufficient to ground a duty of affirmative action in the pure omissions cases (e.g. the fact that the defendant's conduct, taken as a whole, has exposed the claimant to increased danger) may not warrant the imposition of liability in respect of injury caused by a third party. If a motorist without fault injures a pedestrian in a collision, there may be a duty to stop and render assistance, and the motorist may be held liable if he neglects the duty and the pedestrian suffers from exposure as a consequence. But it seems unlikely that the motorist could be held liable for theft of the pedestrian's wallet by an opportunistic pickpocket, even though this would not have occurred but for the failure to render assistance and even though the motorist had left the pedestrian exposed to a danger against which he was unable to defend himself.

Nevertheless, the law does impose liability for the acts of third parties in certain exceptional situations which are broadly similar to those where there is liability for pure omissions. The causation difficulty is met by recognising a special type of duty—a duty to control a third party, a duty to safeguard a dangerous thing, etc.—which allows for the compensation of injuries where there is a weaker form of causal connection than is usually required, for example where the defendant provides the means or opportunity for a third party to bring about the harm. The defendant's liability is not, strictly speaking, for causing the harm, but for occasioning it (see Hart and Honoré, *op. cit.*, pp. 194–204).

Home Office v Dorset Yacht Co [1970] AC 1004

A party of borstal trainees was working on Brownsea Island in Poole Harbour under the supervision and control of three borstal officers. During the night seven of the trainees escaped. It was alleged that at the time of the escape the officers had retired to bed, in breach of their instructions, leaving the trainees to their own devices. The escapees went aboard a yacht which they found nearby, set it in motion and caused it to collide with the plaintiffs' yacht which was moored in the vicinity. The yacht was damaged by the collision and subsequently by the conduct of the trainees when they boarded the vessel. The plaintiffs sued the Home Office for damages. Preliminary proceedings were initiated in order to determine whether the Home Office or the borstal officers owed a duty of care to the plaintiffs. It was admitted that the Home Office would be vicariously liable if an action lay against any of the officers. The Court of Appeal having found in favour of the plaintiffs, the Home Office appealed to the House of Lords.

Lord Reid

[I]t is said that the respondents must fail because there is a general principle that no person can be responsible for the acts of another who is not his servant or acting on his behalf. But here the ground of liability is not responsibility for the acts of the escaping trainees; it is liability for damage caused by the carelessness of these officers in the knowledge that their carelessness would probably result in the trainees causing damage of this kind. So the question is really one of remoteness of damage. And I must consider to what extent the law regards the acts of another person as breaking the chain of causation between the defendants' carelessness and the damage to the plaintiff.

There is an obvious difference between a case where all the links between the carelessness and the damage are inanimate so that, looking back after the event, it can be seen that the damage was in fact the inevitable result of the careless act or omission, and a case where one of the links is some human action. In the former case the damage was in fact caused by the careless conduct, however unforeseeable it may have been at the time that anything like this would happen. At one time the law was that unforeseeability was no defence (*Re Polemis and Furness, Whithy & Co Ltd* [1921] 3 KB 560). But the law now is that there is no liability unless the damage was of a kind which was foreseeable (*Overseas Tankship (UK) Ltd v Morts Dock & Engineering Co Ltd (The Wagon Mound)* [1961] AC 388).

On the other hand, if human action (other than an instinctive reaction) is one of the links in the chain, it cannot be said that, looking back, the damage was the inevitable result of the careless conduct. No one in practice accepts the possible philosophic view that everything that happens was predetermined. Yet it has never been the law that the intervention of human action always prevents the ultimate damage from being regarded as having been caused by the original carelessness. The convenient phrase *novus actus interveniens* denotes those cases where such action is regarded as breaking the chain and preventing the damage from being held to be caused by the careless conduct. But every day there are many cases where, although one of the connecting links is deliberate human action, the law has no difficulty in holding that the defendant's conduct caused the plaintiff loss.

> There are some propositions that...are...beyond question in connection with this class of case. One is that human action does not per se sever the connected sequence of acts. The mere fact that human action intervenes does not prevent the sufferer from saying that damages for injury due to that human action, as one of the elements in the sequence, is recoverable from the original wrongdoer.

(per Lord Wright in *Lord v Pacific Steam Navigation Co Ltd, The Oropesa* [1943] P 32 at 37).

What then is the dividing line? Is it foreseeability or is it such a degree of probability as warrants the conclusion that the intervening human conduct was the natural and probable result of what preceded it? There is a world of difference between the two. If I buy a ticket in a lottery or enter a football pool it is foreseeable that I may win a very large prize—some competitor must win it. But, whatever hopes gamblers may entertain, no one could say that winning such a prize is a natural and probable result of entering such a competition...

[W]here human action forms one of the links between the original wrongdoing of the defendant and the loss suffered by the plaintiff, that action must at least have been something very likely to happen if it is not to be regarded as *novus actus interveniens* breaking the chain of causation. I do not think that a mere foreseeable possibility is or should be sufficient, for then the intervening human action can more properly be regarded as a new cause than as a consequence of the original wrongdoing. But if the intervening action was likely to happen I do not think it can matter whether that action was innocent or tortious or criminal. Unfortunately tortious or criminal action by a third party is often the 'very kind of thing' which is likely to happen as a result of the wrongful or careless act of the defendant. And in the present case, on the facts which we must assume at this stage, I think that the taking of a boat by the escaping trainees and their unskilful navigation leading to damage to another vessel were the very kind of thing that these borstal officers ought to have seen to be likely.

There was an attempt to draw a distinction between loss caused to the plaintiff by failure to control an adult of full capacity and loss caused by failure to control a child or mental defective. As regards causation, no doubt it is easier to infer *novus actus interveniens* in the case of an adult but that seems to me to be the only distinction. In the present case on the assumed facts there would in my view be no *novus actus* when the trainees damaged the respondents' property and I would therefore hold that damage to have been caused by the borstal officers' negligence.

Lord Morris of Borth-y-Gest

[A] normal or even modest measure of prescience and prevision must have led any ordinary person, but rather specially an officer in charge, to realise that the boys might wish to escape and might use a yacht if one was near at hand to help them to do so. That is exactly what it is said that seven boys did. In my view, the officers must have appreciated that either in an escape attempt or by reason of some other prompting the boys might interfere with one of the yachts with consequent likelihood of doing some injury to it. The risk of such a happening was glaringly obvious. The possibilities of damage being done to one of the nearby yachts (assuming that they were nearby) were many and apparent. In that situation and in those circumstances I consider that a duty of care was owed by the officers to the owners of the nearby yachts. The principle expressed in Lord Atkin's classic words in his speech in *Donoghue v Stevenson* [1932] AC 562 at 580 would seem to be directly applicable.

Lord Pearson

It seems to me that this case ought to, and does, come within the *Donoghue v Stevenson* principle unless there is some sufficient reason for not applying the principle to this case. Therefore, one has to consider the suggested reasons for not applying the principle here.

Proximity or remoteness. As there is no evidence, one can only judge from the allegations in the statement of claim. It seems clear that there was sufficient proximity; there was geographical proximity and it was foreseeable that the damage was likely to occur unless some care was taken to prevent it. In other cases a difficult problem may arise as to how widely the 'neighbourhood' extends, but no such problem faces the respondents in this case.

Act of third party. In *Weld-Blundell v Stephens* [1920] AC 956 at 986 Lord Sumner said:

> In general (apart from special contracts and relations and the maxim *Respondeat superior*), even though A is in fault, he is not responsible for injury to C which B, a stranger to him, deliberately chooses to do.

In *Smith v Leurs* (1945) 70 CLR 256 at 261–262 Dixon J said:

> apart from vicarious responsibility, one man may be responsible to another for the harm done to the latter by a third person; he may be responsible on the ground that the act of the third person could not have taken place but for his own fault or breach of duty. There is more than one description of duty the breach of which may produce this consequence. For instance, it may be a duty of care in reference to things involving special danger. It may even be a duty of care with reference to the control of actions or conduct of the third person. It is, however, exceptional to find in the law a duty to control another's actions to prevent harm to strangers. The general rule is that one man is under no duty of controlling another to prevent his doing damage to a third. There are, however, special relations which are the source of a duty of this nature. It appears now to be recognised that it is incumbent upon a parent who maintains control over a young child to take reasonable care so to exercise that control as to avoid conduct on his part exposing the person or property of others to unreasonable danger. Parental control, where it exists, must be exercised with due care to prevent the child inflicting intentional damage on others or causing damage by conduct involving unreasonable risk of injury to others.

In my opinion, this case falls under the exception and not the rule, because there was a special relation. The borstal boys were under the control of the Home Office's officers, and control imports responsibility. The boys' interference with the boats appears to have been a direct result of the Home Office's officers' failure to exercise proper control and supervision. Problems may arise in other cases as to the responsibility of the Home Office's officers for acts done by borstal boys when they have completed their escape from control and are fully at large and acting independently. No such problem faces the respondents in this case.

Lord Diplock

The branch of English law which deals with civil wrongs abounds with instances of acts and, more particularly, of omissions which give rise to no legal liability in the doer or omitter for loss or damage sustained by others as a consequence of the act or omission, however reasonably or probably that loss or damage might have been anticipated. The very parable of the good Samaritan (Luke x, verse 30) which was evoked by Lord Atkin in *Donoghue v Stevenson* illustrates, in the conduct of the priest and of the Levite who passed by on the other side, an omission which was likely to have as its reasonable and probable consequence damage to the health of the victim of the thieves, but for which the priest and Levite would have incurred no civil liability in English law. Examples could be multiplied. One may cause loss to a trades-man by withdrawing one's custom although the goods which he supplies are entirely satisfac-tory . . . [O]ne need not warn . . . [one's neighbour] of a risk of physical danger to which he is about to expose himself unless there is some special relationship between one and him such as that of occupier of land and visitor; one may watch one's neighbour's goods being ruined by a thun-derstorm although the slightest effort on one's part could protect them from the rain and one may do so with impunity unless there is some special relationship between one and him such as that of bailor and bailee . . .

In the present appeal, too, the conduct of the Home Office which is called in question differs from the kind of conduct discussed in *Donoghue v Stevenson* in at least two special character-istics. First, the actual damage sustained by the respondents was the direct consequence of a tortious act done with conscious volition by a third party responsible in law for his own acts and this act was interposed between the act of the Home Office complained of and the sustension of damage by the respondents. Secondly, there are two separate 'neighbour relationships' of the Home Office involved, a relationship with the respondents and a relationship with the third party. These are capable of giving rise to conflicting duties of care. This appeal, therefore, also raises the lawyer's question 'Am I my brother's keeper'? A question which may also receive a restricted reply . . .

It is common knowledge, of which judicial notice may be taken, that borstal training often fails to achieve its purpose of reformation, and that trainees when they have ceased to be detained in custody revert to crime and commit tortious damage to the person and property of others. But so do criminals who have never been apprehended and criminals who have been released from custody on completion of their sentences or earlier pursuant to a statutory power to do so. The risk of sustaining damage from the tortious acts of criminals is shared by the public at large. It has never been recognised at common law as giving rise to any cause of action against anyone but the criminal himself. It would seem arbitrary and therefore unjust to single out for the special privilege of being able to recover compensation from the authorities responsible for the prevention of crime a person whose property was damaged by the tortious act of a criminal, merely because the damage to him happened to be caused by a criminal who had escaped from custody before completion of his sentence instead of by one who had been lawfully released or who had been put on probation or given a suspended sentence or who had never been previously apprehended at all. To give rise to a duty on the part of the custo-dian owed to a member of the public to take reasonable care to prevent a borstal trainee from escaping from his custody before completion of the trainee's sentence there should be some relationship between the custodian and the person to whom the duty is owed which exposes that person to a particular risk of damage in consequence of that escape which is different in its incidence from the general risk of damage from criminal acts of others which he shares with all members of the public.

What distinguishes a borstal trainee who has escaped from one who has been duly released from custody, is his liability to recapture, and the distinctive added risk which is a reasonably foreseeable consequence of a failure to exercise due care in preventing him from escaping is the likelihood that in order to elude pursuit immediately on the discovery of his absence the escaping trainee may steal or appropriate and damage property which is situated in the vicin-ity of the place of detention from which he has escaped.

So long as Parliament is content to leave the general risk of damage from criminal acts to lie where it falls without any remedy except against the criminal himself, the courts would be exceeding their limited function in developing the common law to meet changing conditions if they were to recognise a duty of care to prevent criminals escaping from penal custody owed to a wider category of members of the public than those whose property was exposed to an exceptional added risk by the adoption of a custodial system for young offenders which increased the likelihood of their escape unless due care was taken by those responsible for their custody.

I should therefore hold that any duty of a borstal officer to use reasonable care to prevent a borstal trainee from escaping from his custody was owed only to persons whom he could reasonably foresee had property situate in the vicinity of the place of detention of the detainee which the detainee was likely to steal or to appropriate and damage in the course of eluding immediate pursuit and recapture. Whether or not any person fell within this category would depend on the facts of the particular case including the previous criminal and escaping record of the individual trainee concerned and the nature of the place from which he escaped.

[On the facts of the present case, Lord Diplock agreed that the borstal officers did owe a duty of care to the plaintiff yacht club.]

Viscount Dilhorne (dissenting) stated that the absence of any authority for the duty alleged showed that no such duty in fact existed. He added: 'If there should be one, that is, in my view, a matter for the legislature and not for the courts.'

Appeal dismissed.

COMMENTARY

This case provides an excellent example of the way in which different judicial approaches can lead to the same result. Lord Reid relied upon considerations of foreseeability or probability as the key to the existence of a duty, but manipulated the degree of foreseeability/probability required in order to distinguish those cases where liability should be imposed from those where it should not. Lord Morris also focused on the foreseeability of the risk. By contrast, Lord Pearson (explicitly) and Lord Diplock (implicitly) relied upon considerations of proximity as the mechanism for limiting the scope of the defendant's liability in an appropriate case. Tension between these two approaches still exists in the current law, though they are unlikely to lead to different outcomes on the facts of individual cases.

Would the Home Office be liable for the loss occasioned by a burglary committed by a trainee on parole or a prisoner permitted to go out to attend a funeral? Lord Reid thought that there were two reasons why in the vast majority of cases there would be no liability (at 1032):

In the first place it would have to be shown that the decision to allow any such release was so unreasonable that it could not be regarded as a real exercise of discretion by the responsible officer who authorised the release. And secondly it would have to be shown that the commission of the offence was the natural and probable, as distinct from merely a foreseeable, result of the release—that there was no *novus actus interveniens.*

A comparable scenario arose in *K v Secretary of State for the Home Department* [2002] EWCA Civ 775. The claimant was raped by a foreign citizen, with a criminal record in this country, who had been detained by the Home Office pending deportation but released for unexplained reasons. She sued the Home Office for damages, but the Court of Appeal struck out her claim for lack of any relationship of proximity between her and the Home Office such as would create a duty of care. The defendant's mere knowledge that another person posed an especially grave risk of harm to the public at large was not enough to create the necessary proximity: 'A defendant does not become the world's insurer against the grave danger (where the danger is general) posed by a third agency, which he might control but does not, by virtue only of the fact that he appreciates that the danger exists' (at [29], per Laws LJ). The result is in accord with the view of McIvor, *Third Party Liability in Tort* (Oxford: Hart, 2006), who argues that the duty to control is limited to situations in which there is a very strong relationship of control between the 'responsible' defendant and the 'irresponsible' third party, the claimant comes within a narrowly defined class of potential victims, and the harm-causing conduct of the third party was highly foreseeable in the circumstances (p. 19).

'Control Imports Responsibility'

It had been established prior to the *Dorset Yacht* case that a school may be held liable to a third party injured by the foreseeable negligence of a pupil under its control. In *Carmarthenshire County Council v Lewis* [1955] AC 549, the deceased lorry driver lost his life when he was forced to swerve his vehicle in an effort to avoid a small boy and drove into a lamp post. The boy, David, aged about four, had strayed onto the busy main road from the grounds of a nursery school maintained by the appellants, the local education authority, after being left unattended in the classroom for about 10 minutes; during his teacher's absence he got out of the classroom and made his way out of the school playground through an unlocked gate. The deceased's widow successfully brought an action against the education authority in negligence but it was only in the House of Lords that it was held liable for its own negligence in failing to prevent the child escaping (rather than being vicariously liable for the negligence of the teacher). Although the leading speech of Lord Reid focused on the foreseeability of the chain of events that occurred, consistently with his approach in the *Dorset Yacht* case some years later, the modern approach is to limit the scope of any duty of care by reference to proximity and policy factors, and, viewed from this perspective, it is probably best to regard the case as resting on the school authority's assumption of responsibility for control of the child, which may be seen as creating a relationship of proximity with those who were foreseeably endangered by him. This responsibility can be seen as a counterpart to that which the authority assumes to the children themselves. The latter entails, amongst other things, a duty to provide assistance to any child who falls ill while at school and to prevent pupils from exposing themselves to the risk of accidental injury at the hands of third parties (e.g. if allowed to stray onto a busy main road: see *Barnes v Hants CC* [1969] 1 WLR 1563). The duty no doubt extends to protecting schoolchildren from deliberate acts (e.g. of a known paedophile who is seen wandering in school grounds). See further C. McIvor, *Third Party Liability in Tort* (Oxford: Hart, 2006), pp. 24–35, and, for comparative discussion, M. Martin Casals (ed.), *Children in Tort Law, Part I: Children as Tortfeasors* (Vienna: Springer, 2006).

The *Dorset Yacht* case goes beyond *Carmarthenshire County Council v Lewis* by recognising a liability for negligent failure to prevent intentional misconduct by a minor for whom the defendant has assumed responsibility, even though the minor is old enough to be held responsible for his actions himself. Since then, efforts have been made to extend the case's authority from the context of a custodial relationship to other relationships in which the essential ingredient of control is also alleged to be present. In *Hill v Chief Constable of West Yorks* [1989] AC 53, the House of Lords had to consider 'whether the individual members of a police force, in the course of carrying out their functions of controlling and keeping down the incidence of crime, owe a duty of care to individual members of the public who may suffer injury to person or property through the activities of criminals, such as to result in liability in damages, on the ground of negligence, to anyone who suffers such injury by reason of breach of that duty.' The action arose out of the murder of a young woman (whose mother sued as her personal representative) by the notorious serial killer, Peter Sutcliffe, known as the Yorkshire Ripper. Distinguishing the case before him from the *Dorset Yacht* case—on the basis that there was no special relationship between either the police and the killer or between the police and the victim—Lord Keith elaborated (at 62):

It is plain that vital characteristics which were present in the *Dorset Yacht* case and which led to the imposition of liability are here lacking. Sutcliffe was never in the custody of the police force. Miss Hill was one of a vast number of the female general public who might be at risk from his activities but was at no special distinctive risk in relation to them, unlike the owners of yachts moored off Brownsea Island in relation to the foreseeable conduct of the borstal boys...In the case of an escaped criminal his identity and description are known. In the instant case the identity of the wanted criminal was at the material time unknown and it is not averred that any full or clear description of him was ever available.

The House of Lords therefore concluded that the claim had to fail for want of proximity. Another reason for the decision was that it was not 'fair, just and reasonable' to recognise a claim in such circumstances: see Chapter 3.

The police do not, however, have a blanket immunity from liability. By analogy with the *Dorset Yacht* case, it seems that they may be held liable for damage caused in the course of a prisoner's escape from their custody. There may also be circumstances in which they make an undertaking to particular members of the public sufficient to warrant the imposition of liability should they perform that undertaking carelessly. An example is provided by *Swinney v Chief Constable of the Northumbria Police* [1997] QB 464, where the relevant undertaking was inferred from the police's encouragement of the plaintiffs to give information about criminal activities and thereby to place themselves in a position of potential danger from the perpetrators. The Court of Appeal ruled that it was at least arguably 'fair, just and reasonable' to recognise a duty of care, although the plaintiff in fact lost at the subsequent trial on the grounds that there had been no breach of that duty (see *Swinney v Chief Constable of Northumbria (No. 2)* (1999) 11 Admin LR 811). It has also been decided that one police officer owes a duty to take steps by way of assistance to a fellow officer who is attacked by an arrested person being held in police custody (*Costello v Chief Constable of Northumbria Police* [1999] ICR 730). In that case, the negligent officer had been in close attendance for the specific purpose of coming to the aid of the plaintiff if she needed help, so the basis of the decision may well have been the officer's assumption of responsibility for the safety for his colleague, rather than, for example, his general duty as a police officer. The Court of Appeal expressly reserved its judgment as to whether a police officer would owe the same duty to a member of the public who was attacked in similar circumstances.

In *Tarasoff v University of California*, 551 P 2d 334 (1976), the Supreme Court of California held that a psychologist, whose patient confided to him his intention to kill a particular woman, might have a duty to warn the woman of the risk to her life and could be held liable if his breach of that duty was a contributory cause of her death at the patient's hands. This precise scenario has not yet arisen in English law, though the assumed facts were somewhat similar in *Palmer v Tees Health Authority* [2000] PIQR P1. It was alleged that the defendant health authority was responsible for the abduction and murder of the claimant's four-year-old daughter by a psychiatric patient who had been discharged from the defendant's hospital the previous year; he remained an out-patient but had failed to attend his most recent appointment. The claimant contended that the defendant had been negligent in failing to recognise the risk that the man might commit serious offences against children, and consequently to take steps to reduce the risk, for example by keeping him in hospital. The Court of Appeal struck out the action on the basis of a lack of proximity. The defendant had not assumed any responsibility towards the victim, who had been just an unidentifiable member of the large class of those at risk. The court reserved its opinion as to whether there might be sufficient proximity where the victim was identified or identifiable in advance, but Pill LJ commented (p. 19):

I see force in the submission that the question whether the identity of a victim is known ought not to determine whether the proximity test is passed. It is forcefully argued that the difference between the threat 'I will kill X' and the threat 'I will kill the first bald-headed man I meet' ought not to determine whether a duty is placed upon a defendant, though it would obviously go to the extent of the duty and the measures necessary to discharge it.

The point did not, however, arise for decision on the facts of the case. Cf. *Jane Doe v Board of Commissioner of Police for Metropolitan Toronto* (1998) 160 DLR (4th) 697 where a Canadian judge held that police owed a duty of care to the victim of a rapist, the victim being a member of small and easily identifiable class of women at risk from the rapist. For comment, see Hoyano (1999) 62 MLR 912.

In *Mitchell v Glasgow City Council* [2009] UKHL 11, [2009] 1 AC 874 (noted by Mullender (2009) 125 LQR 384), the deceased was attacked and killed by his next-door neighbour in council accommodation following a prolonged period of hostile, aggressive and antisocial behaviour on the neighbour's part. The council had known of the matter for some considerable time, and had issued the neighbour with warnings over his conduct. After further antisocial behaviour, it summoned the neighbour to a meeting, where he was told he could face eviction. He lost his temper and became abusive. On leaving the meeting, he returned home and committed the fatal assault. The deceased's family brought an action for damages against the council, alleging that it should have informed the deceased of its meeting with the neighbour, warned him he was at risk, and alerted the police—none of which it had done. Rejecting the claim on the basis that the council owed the deceased no duty of care, the House of Lords accepted that (at [29], per Lord Hope):

as a general rule   a duty to warn another person that he is at risk of loss, injury or damage as the result of the criminal act of a third party will arise only where the person who is said to be under that duty has by his words or conduct assumed responsibility for the safety of the person who is at risk.

On the facts, there was no basis for saying that the council had assumed a responsibility to advise the deceased of the steps that it was taking, or in some other way had induced him to rely on its doing so. (See also *X and Y v Hounslow LBC* [2009] EWCA Civ 286, noted by Mullender [2009] CLJ 507.) As the Council knew of its tenant's history of aggression towards the deceased, and was responsible (culpably or not) for his outburst of anger on the occasion in question, was it justifiable for the House of Lords to conclude that the Council owed the deceased no duty of care?

Control of Land

The issue of a landowner's liability to a neighbouring landowner for damage caused by trespassers was raised before the House of Lords in the tort of private nuisance where liability was established if the defendant 'adopted' or 'continued' the nuisance (see *Sedleigh-Denfield v O'Callaghan* [1940] AC 880). In negligence, it was also established that a landowner owed a duty to protect neighbours from natural hazards arising on the land (see *Goldman v Hargrave*, above). But the issue of liability in negligence for harm to neighbours resulting from the entry of trespassers onto the defendant's land was not raised before the House of Lords until *Smith v Littlewoods Organisation Ltd* [1987] 1 AC 241, extracted below, although it had been addressed by the Court of Appeal in *P Perl (Exporters) Ltd v Camden London Borough* [1984] 1 QB 342 and *King v Liverpool City Council* [1986] 1 WLR 890; in neither case did the court find the defendant liable.

Smith v Littlewoods Organisation Ltd [1987] AC 241

The respondents purchased a cinema with a view to demolishing it and replacing it with a supermarket. Having taken possession of the cinema, they employed contractors to make site investigations and do some preliminary work on foundations, but thereafter the cinema was empty and unattended by the respondents or any of their employees. Within a period of two or three weeks, it appeared that the main building was no longer lockfast and was being regularly entered by unauthorised persons. Debris began to accumulate outside the cinema and on two occasions attempts to start fires inside and adjacent to the cinema were observed by a passer-by but neither the respondents nor the police were informed. A short time afterwards, a fire was started in the cinema which seriously damaged two adjoining properties, one of which had to be demolished. The appellants, the owners of the affected properties, claimed damages against the respondents on the ground that the damage to their properties had been caused by the respondents' negligence. The judge found the claims established and awarded the appellants damages, but this decision was reversed by the Inner House of the Court of Session in Scotland. The appellants appealed to the House of Lords.

Lord Brandon

The particular facts of the present case appear to me to raise two, and only two, questions, on the answers to which the determination of the appeals depends.

The first question is: what was the general duty owed by Littlewoods, as owners and occupiers of the disused cinema, to the appellants, as owners or occupiers of other buildings near to the cinema? The answer to that question is, in my view, that Littlewoods owed to the appellants a duty to exercise reasonable care to ensure that the cinema was not, and did not become, a source of danger to neighbouring buildings owned or occupied by the appellants.

The second question is whether that general duty encompassed a specific duty to exercise reasonable care to prevent young persons obtaining unlawful access to the cinema and, having done so, unlawfully setting it on fire. The answer to that question, in accordance with general principles governing alike the law of delict in Scotland and the law of negligence in England, must depend on whether the occurrence of such behaviour was reasonably foreseeable by Littlewoods. It should have been reasonably foreseeable by Littlewoods if they had known of the activities of young persons observed by certain individuals in the locality. But they did not know of such activities because the individuals concerned did not inform either Littlewoods or the police of them, nor did the police themselves observe them. In the absence of information about such activities, either from the individuals referred to or from the police, I am of opinion that the occurrence of the behaviour in question was not reasonably foreseeable by Littlewoods. I conclude, therefore, that the general duty of care owed by Littlewoods to the appellants did not encompass the specific duty referred to above.

For these reasons I would dismiss the appeals.

Lord Griffiths

My Lords, I regard these appeals as turning upon the evaluation and application of the particular facts of this case to a well-established duty and standard of care. I agree so fully with the statement and evaluation of the facts appearing in the speech of my noble and learned friend Lord Mackay, that I can state my own reasons for dismissing these appeals very shortly.

The duty of care owed by Littlewoods was to take reasonable care that the condition of the premises they occupied was not a source of danger to neighbouring property.

The standard of care required of them was that stated in general terms by Lord Radcliffe in *Bolton v Stone* [1951] AC 850 at 868–869 and expanded in more particularity by Lord Wilberforce in *Goldman v Hargrave* [1967] 1 AC 645 at 662–663 when dealing with a fire on premises caused by an outside agency...

Listening to the seductive way in which counsel for the appellants developed his argument on the facts step by step, as described by Lord Mackay, I was reminded of the fable of the prince who lost his kingdom but for the want of a nail for the shoe of his horse. A series of foreseeable possibilities were added one to another and, hey presto, there emerged at the end the probability of a fire against which Littlewoods should have guarded. But, my Lords, that is not the common sense of this matter.

The fire in this case was caused by the criminal activity of third parties on Littlewoods' premises. I do not say that there will never be circumstances in which the law will require an occupier of premises to take special precautions against such a contingency but they would surely have to be extreme indeed. It is common ground that only a 24-hour guard on these premises would have been likely to prevent this fire, and even that cannot be certain, such is the determination and ingenuity of young vandals.

There was nothing of an inherently dangerous nature stored in the premises, nor can I regard an empty cinema stripped of its equipment as likely to be any more alluring to vandals than any other recently vacated premises in the centre of a town. No message was received by Littlewoods from the local police, fire brigade or any neighbour that vandals were creating any danger on the premises. In short, so far as Littlewoods knew, there was nothing significantly different about these empty premises from the tens of thousands of such premises up and down the country. People do not mount 24-hour guards on empty properties and the law would impose an intolerable burden if it required them to do so save in the most exceptional circumstances. I find no such exceptional circumstances in this case and I would accordingly dismiss the appeals.

Lord Mackay of Clashfern

It is plain from the authorities that the fact that the damage, on which a claim is founded, was caused by a human agent quite independent of the person against whom a claim in negligence is made does not, of itself, preclude success of the claim, since breach of duty on the part of the person against whom the claim is made may also have played a part in causing the damage.

[His Lordship referred with approval to the speech of Lord Reid in the *Dorset Yacht* case, and held that the mere possibility of the third party's intervention was insufficient to establish a liability. He continued:]

It is true, as has been pointed out by Oliver LJ in *Lamb v Camden London Borough* [1981] QB 625 at 642, that human conduct is particularly unpredictable and that every society will have a sprinkling of people who behave most abnormally. The result of this consideration, in my opinion, is that, where the only possible source of the type of damage or injury which is in question is agency of a human being for whom the person against whom the claim is made has no responsibility, it may not be easy to find that as a reasonable person he was bound to anticipate that type of damage as a consequence of his act or omission. The more unpredictable the conduct in question, the less easy to affirm that any particular result from it is probable and in many circumstances the only way in which a judge could properly be persuaded to come to the conclusion that the result was not only possible but reasonably foreseeable as probable would be to convince him that, in the circumstances, it was highly likely. In this type of case a finding that the reasonable man should have anticipated the consequence of human action as just probable may not be a very frequent option. Unless the judge can be satisfied that the result of the human action is highly probable or very likely he may have to conclude that all that the reasonable man could say was that it was a mere possibility. Unless the needle that measures the probability of a particular result flowing from the conduct of a human agent is near the top of the scale it may be hard to conclude that it has risen sufficiently from the bottom to create the duty reasonably to foresee it.

In summary I conclude, in agreement with both counsel, that what the reasonable man is bound to foresee in a case involving injury or damage by independent human agency, just as in cases where such agency plays no part, is the probable consequences of his own act or omission, but that, in such a case, a clear basis will be required on which to assert that the injury or damage is more than a mere possibility.

[His Lordship dismissed the appeal on the basis that the appellants had not established a probability that the vacant property would be set on fire with consequent risk of damage to neighbouring premises.]

Lord Goff of Chieveley

[I]t is well recognised that there is no general duty of care to prevent third parties from causing such damage. The point is expressed very clearly in Hart and Honoré, *Causation in the Law*, 2nd edn., 1985, pp. 196–7, where the authors state:

> The law might acknowledge a general principle that, whenever the harmful conduct of another is reasonably foreseeable, it is our duty to take precautions against it . . . But, up to now, no legal system has gone so far as this . . .

The same point is made in Fleming, The *Law of Torts*, 6th ed., 1983, p. 200, where it is said: 'there is certainly no *general* duty to protect others against theft or loss.' I wish to add that no such general duty exists even between those who are neighbours in the sense of being occupiers of adjoining premises. There is no general duty on a householder that he should act as a watchdog, or that his house should act as a bastion, to protect his neighbour's house.

Why does the law not recognise a general duty of care to prevent others from suffering loss or damage caused by the deliberate wrongdoing of third parties? The fundamental reason is that the common law does not impose liability for what are called pure omissions . . . [C]arried to extremes, this proposition may be repugnant to modern thinking. It may therefore require one day to be reconsidered especially as it is said to provoke an 'invidious comparison with affirmative duties of good-neighbourliness in most countries outside the Common Law orbit' (see Fleming, *The Law of Torts*, 6th edn, 1983, p. 138). But it is of interest to observe that, even if we do follow the example of those countries, in all probability we will, like them, impose strict limits on any such affirmative duty as may be recognised. In one recent French decision, the condition was imposed that the danger to the claimant must be 'grave, imminent, constant . . . nécessitant une intervention immédiate', and that such an intervention must not involve any 'risque pour le prévenu ou pour un tiers': see Lawson and Markesinis, *Tortious Liability for Unintentional Harm in the Common Law and the Civil Law* (1982), vol. 1, pp. 74–75. The latter requirement is consistent with our own law, which likewise imposes limits on steps required to be taken by a person who is under an affirmative duty to prevent harm being caused by a source of danger which has arisen without his fault (see *Goldman v Hargrave* [1967] 1 AC 645), a point to which I shall return later. But the former requirement indicates that any affirmative duty to prevent deliberate wrongdoing by third parties, if recognised in English law, is likely to be strictly limited. I mention this because I think it important that we should realise that problems like that in the present case are unlikely to be solved by a simple abandonment of the common law's present strict approach to liability for pure omissions.

Another statement of principle, which has been much quoted, is the observation of Lord Sumner in *Weld-Blundell v Stephens* [1920] AC 956 at 986:

> In general . . . even though A is in fault, he is not responsible for injury to C which B, a stranger to him, deliberately chooses to do.

This dictum may be read as expressing the general idea that the voluntary act of another, independent of the defender's fault, is regarded as *a novus actus interveniens* which, to use the old metaphor, 'breaks the chain of causation'. But it also expresses a general perception that we ought not to be held responsible in law for the deliberate wrongdoing of others. Of course, if a duty of care is imposed to guard against deliberate wrongdoing by others, it can hardly be said that the harmful effects of such wrongdoing are not caused by such breach of duty. We are therefore thrown back to the duty of care. But one thing is clear, and that is that liability in negligence for harm caused by the deliberate wrongdoing of others cannot be founded simply on foreseeability that the pursuer will suffer loss or damage by reason of such wrongdoing. There is no such general principle. We have therefore to identify the circumstances in which such liability may be imposed.

That there are special circumstances in which a defender may be held responsible in law for injuries suffered by the pursuer through a third party's deliberate wrongdoing is not in doubt. For example, a duty of care may arise from a relationship between the parties which gives rise to an imposition or assumption of responsibility on or by the defender, as in *Stansbie v Troman* [1948] 2 KB 48, where such responsibility was held to arise from a contract. In that case a decorator, left alone on the premises by the householder's wife, was held liable when he went out leaving the door on the latch and a thief entered the house and stole property. Such responsibility might well be held to exist in other cases where there is no contract, as for example where a person left alone in a house has entered as a licensee of the occupier. Again, the defender may be vicariously liable for the third party's act; or he may be held liable as an occupier to a visitor on his land. Again, as appears from the dictum of Dixon J in *Smith v Leurs* (1945) 70 CLR 256 at 262, a duty may arise from a special relationship between the defender and the third party, by virtue of which the defender is responsible for controlling the third party: see, for example, *Home Office v Dorset Yacht Co Ltd*. More pertinently, in a case between adjoining occupiers of land, there may be liability in nuisance if one occupier causes or permits persons to gather on his land, and they impair his neighbour's enjoyment of his land. Indeed, even if such persons come onto his land as trespassers, the occupiers may, if they constitute a nuisance, be under an affirmative duty to abate the nuisance. As I pointed out in *P Perl (Exporters) Ltd v Camden London BC* [1984] QB 342 at 359, there may well be other cases.

These are all special cases. But there is a more general circumstance in which a defender may be held liable in negligence to the pursuer, although the immediate cause of the damage suffered by the pursuer is the deliberate wrongdoing of another. This may occur where the defender negligently causes or permits to be created a source of danger, and it is reasonably foreseeable that third parties may interfere with it and, sparking off the danger, thereby cause damage to persons in the position of the pursuer. The classic example of such a case is, perhaps, *Haynes v Harwood* [1935] 1 KB 146, where the defendant's carter left a horse-drawn van unattended in a crowded street and the horses bolted when a boy threw a stone at them.

A police officer who suffered injury in stopping the horses before they injured a woman and children was held to be entitled to recover damages from the defendant. There, of course, the defendant's servant had created a source of danger by leaving his horses unattended in a busy street. Many different things might have caused them to bolt, a sudden noise or movement, for example, or, as happened, the deliberate action of a mischievous boy. But all such events were examples of the very sort of thing which the defendant's servant ought reasonably to have foreseen and to have guarded against by taking appropriate precautions. In such a case, Lord Sumner's dictum in *Weld-Blundell v Stephens* [1920] AC 956 at 986 can have no application to exclude liability.

Haynes v Harwood was a case concerned with the creation of a source of danger in a public place. We are concerned in the present case with an allegation that the defenders should be held liable for the consequences of deliberate wrongdoing by others who were trespassers on the defenders' property. In such a case it may be said that the defenders are entitled to use their property as their own and so should not be held liable if, for example, trespassers interfere with dangerous things on their land. But this is, I consider, too sweeping a proposition. It is well established that an occupier of land may be liable to a trespasser who has suffered injury on his land; though in *British Rlys Board v Herrington* [1972] AC 877, in which the nature and scope of such liability was reconsidered by your Lordships' House, the standard of care so imposed on occupiers was drawn narrowly so as to take proper account of the rights of occupiers to enjoy the use of their land. It is, in my opinion, consistent with the existence of such liability that an occupier who negligently causes or permits a source of danger to be created on his land, and can reasonably foresee that third parties may trespass on his land and, interfering with the source of danger, may spark it off, thereby causing damage to the person or property of those in the vicinity, should be held liable to such a person for damage so caused to him. It is useful to take the example of a fire hazard, not only because that is the relevant hazard which is alleged to have existed in the present case, but also because of the intrinsically dangerous nature of fire hazards as regards neighbouring property. Let me give an example of circumstances in which an occupier of land might be held liable for damage so caused. Suppose that a person is deputed to buy a substantial quantity of fireworks for a village fireworks display on Guy Fawkes night. He stores them, as usual, in an unlocked garden shed abutting onto a neighbouring house. It is well known that he does this. Mischievous boys from the village enter as trespassers and, playing with the fireworks, cause a serious fire which spreads to and burns down the neighbouring house. Liability might well be imposed in such a case; for, having regard to the dangerous and tempting nature of fireworks, interference by naughty children was the very thing which, in the circumstances, the purchaser of the fireworks ought to have guarded against.

But liability should only be imposed under this principle in cases where the defender has negligently caused or permitted the creation of a source of danger on his land, and where it is foreseeable that third parties may trespass on his land and spark it off, thereby damaging the pursuer or his property. Moreover, it is not to be forgotten that, in ordinary households in this country, there are nowadays many things which might be described as possible sources of fire if interfered with by third parties, ranging from matches and firelighters to electric irons and gas cookers and even oil-fired central heating systems. These are commonplaces of modern life; and it would be quite wrong if householders were to be held liable in negligence for acting in a socially acceptable manner. No doubt the question whether liability should be imposed on defenders in a case where a source of danger on his land has been sparked off by the deliberate wrongdoing of a third party is a question to be decided on the facts of each case, and it would, I think, be wrong for your Lordships' House to anticipate the manner in which the law may develop; but I cannot help thinking that cases where liability will be so imposed are likely to be very rare.

There is another basis on which a defender may be held liable for damage to neighbouring property caused by a fire started on his (the defender's) property by the deliberate wrongdoing of a third party. This arises where he has knowledge or means of knowledge that a third party has created or is creating a risk of fire, or indeed has started a fire, on his premises, and then fails to take such steps as are reasonably open to him (in the limited sense explained by Lord Wilberforce in *Goldman v Hargrave* [1967] 1 AC 645 at 663–664) to prevent any such fire from damaging neighbouring property. If, for example, an occupier of property has knowledge, or means of knowledge, that intruders are in the habit of trespassing on his property and starting fires there, thereby creating a risk that fire may spread to and damage neighbouring property, a duty to take reasonable steps to prevent such damage may be held to fall on him. He could, for example, take reasonable steps to keep the intruders out. He could also inform the police; or he could warn his neighbours and invite their assistance. If the defender is a person of substantial means, for example a large public company, he might even be expected to employ some agency to keep a watch on the premises. What is reasonably required would, of course, depend on the particular facts of the case. I observe that in *Goldman v Hargrave* such liability was held to sound in nuisance; but it is difficult to believe that, in this respect, there can be any material distinction between liability in nuisance and liability in negligence . . .

Turning to the facts of the present case, I cannot see that the defenders should be held liable under either of these two possible heads of liability. First, I do not consider that the empty cinema could properly be described as an unusual danger in the nature of a fire hazard. As the Lord President (Lord Emslie) pointed out (1986 SLT 272 at 276):

> There was nothing about the building, so far as we know from the evidence, to suggest that it could easily be set alight.

This conclusion was, in my judgment, entirely justified on the evidence in the case; and it is, I consider, fatal to any allegation that the defenders should be held liable on the ground that they negligently caused or permitted the creation of an unusual source of danger in the nature of a fire hazard.

Nor can I see that the defenders should be held liable for having failed to take reasonable steps to abate a fire risk created by third parties on their property without their fault. If there was any such fire risk, they had no means of knowing that it existed. If anybody (for example, the police) considered that there was such a risk they could and should have contacted the defenders (a well-known public company, whose particulars were given on a notice outside the cinema) by telephone to warn them of the situation; but they did not do so. But in any event, on the evidence, the existence of such a risk was not established . . . I wish to emphasise that I do not think that the problem in these cases can be solved simply through the mechanism of foreseeability. When a duty is cast on a person to take precautions against the wrongdoing of third parties, the ordinary standard of foreseeability applies; and so the possibility of such wrongdoing does not have to be very great before liability is imposed. I do not myself subscribe to the opinion that liability for the wrongdoing of others is limited because of the unpredictability of human conduct. So, for example, in *Haynes v Harwood* [1935] 1 KB 146 liability was imposed although it cannot have been at all likely that a small boy would throw a stone at the horses left unattended in the public road, and in *Stansbie v Troman* [1948] 2 KB 48 liability was imposed although it cannot have been at all likely that a thief would take advantage of the fact that the defendant left the door on the latch while he was out. Per contra, there is at present no general duty at common law to prevent persons from harming others by their deliberate wrongdoing, however foreseeable such harm may be if the defender does not take steps to prevent it.

Of course, if persons trespass on the defender's property and the defender either knows or has the means of knowing that they are doing so and that in doing so they constitute a danger to neighbouring property, then the defender may be under an affirmative duty to take reasonable steps to exclude them, in the limited sense explained by Lord Wilberforce in *Goldman v Hargrave* [1967] 1 AC 645 at 663–4, but that is another matter. I incline to the opinion that this duty arises from the fact that the defender, as occupier, is in exclusive control of the premises on which the danger has arisen...

[T]o impose a general duty on occupiers to take reasonable care to prevent others from entering their property would impose an unreasonable burden on ordinary householders and an unreasonable curb on the ordinary enjoyment of their property.

Lord Keith agreed with both **Lord Mackay** and **Lord Goff**.

Appeal dismissed.

B. S. Markesinis, 'Negligence, Nuisance and Affirmative Duties of Action' (1989) 105 LQR 104

Five Law Lords delivered opinions of varying lengths in *Smith's* case. In Lord Brandon's view the case raised two and only two questions: (a) whether a general duty was owed by the defenders to the plaintiff to ensure that their premises did not become a source of danger and (b) whether 'the general duty encompassed a specific duty to exercise reasonable care to prevent young persons obtaining unlawful access to the cinema [the defenders' premises], and, having done so, unlawfully setting it on fire.' The terminology of 'general' and 'specific' duty may not be entirely recognisable in the academic discussions of the elements of the tort of negligence... However, it is arguable that when referring to a 'specific duty', Lord Brandon had in mind what is more commonly referred to as the element of 'careless breach of the duty', not least since it appears clear from his short opinion that the answer to this second question will vary from case to case and should thus not receive a blanket negative answer. Whatever interpretation one adopts, one thing seems reasonably clear: Lord Brandon was not opting for a blanket exclusion of liability through the denial of a notional duty of care...

[Markesinis considers the opinion of Lord Griffiths, whose reasoning he found substantially the same as Lord Brandon's, and then turns to the opinion of Lord Mackay LC.]

[T]he non-liability rule, based on what was reasonably foreseeable, could, in text-book terms, be translated to suggest that the damage was remote... Nevertheless, I suspect that the Lord Chancellor's insistence in *Smith's* case on what is reasonable on the facts of each case seems to point more towards the expected standard that must be attained by each defendant in the light of the likelihood of the occurrence of the harm. To put it differently, though the vague concept of foreseeability was frequently used in all these judgments [including those in *Lamb,* and *King*], what I think the Lord Chancellor was saying is that, in view of all the surrounding circumstances, the more likely it is that the harm will occur the more likely that an obligation will be imposed on the defendant to do something about it. In fact, at the end of his judgment, the Lord Chancellor summarises his views by saying that

> in my opinion *various factors* will be taken into account by the reasonable man in considering cases involving fire on the one hand and theft on the other but since this is the principle the precise weight to be given to these factors in any particular case will depend upon the circumstances... *I consider that much must depend on what the evidence shows is done by ordinary people in like circumstances to those in which the claim of breach of duty arises.* [Italics added by Markesinis.]

This, it is submitted, is not remoteness language but standard of care language in which the foreseeability of harm is just one of many factors that have to be weighed by the judge before determining the expected standard of care...

Be that as it may, what I think is important in this opinion is not whether the Lord Chancellor's terminology should, in text-book terms, be placed under the heading of careless breach of duty or remote damage but rather on the fact that recovery is denied to this plaintiff rather than to all plaintiffs in similar situations... [L]iability was *not denied generally* and in all cases through the use of the device of duty of care. Professor Fleming put it succinctly when he wrote that 'if the policy against recovery is *quite categorical, too insistent to be confided every time to the chance arbitrament of each individual trial judge or jury's speculations about "risk" or "cause"*, the rule in question is nowadays generally formulated as one of "no duty"' (*Law of Torts*, 7th edn, 1987, p. 126) [italics added by Markesinis]...

[T]he Lord Chancellor (and, at least, two of his colleagues) felt it was inappropriate to resort to the blunderbuss weapon of duty of care...

COMMENTARY

In *Smith v Littlewoods*, all the members of the House of Lords were keen to restrict the liability of owners and occupiers for harm caused to neighbouring property by trespassers on their land. But they sought to do so in different ways. Lord Brandon, Lord Griffiths and Lord Mackay seem (as Markesinis argues) to have conceded the existence of a duty of care, but to have ruled that there was no breach of that duty. Lord Goff, by way of contrast, clearly ruled that no duty of care ever arose on the facts. Lord Keith expressed his concurrence with the opinions of both Lord Mackay and Lord Goff, but did not advert at all to the significant differences in approach between them.

In *Stovin v Wise* [1996] AC 923 at 931, Lord Nicholls stated, obiter: 'In cases involving the use of land, proximity is found in the fact of occupation.' Which, if any, of the above speeches is consistent with that view?

Lord Goff's Approach

Lord Goff expressed particular concern that imposing a general duty of care on owners and occupiers of land would result in an unreasonable burden upon ordinary householders. In his view, it was 'less objectionable' that occupiers should themselves take steps to guard against theft and vandalism wherever this was possible, and should be left to bear such losses as did occur. He noted that, in the vast majority of cases, these losses would be covered by insurance. His approach favours defendants, as the existence of a duty is a question of law which can be raised as a preliminary issue and can therefore be resolved without the need to go to the expense of a full trial, as would be inevitable if such cases were to turn on the issue of breach (a question of fact and therefore not suitable for resolution in preliminary proceedings).

It is to be noted, however, that his Lordship accepted that there may be exceptional instances in which liability will arise, for example, where 'persons trespass on the defender's property and the defender either knows or has the means of knowing that they are doing so and that in doing so they constitute a danger to neighbouring property'. If having 'the means of knowing' can be read as a requirement that the defender ought to know, and if what a person ought to know is defined by what is foreseeable, might this not undermine Lord

Goff's basic assertion that 'there is no general duty to prevent third parties from causing damage to others, even though there is a high degree of foresight that this may occur'?

Lord Goff also recognised a 'general circumstance' in which liability for the acts of a third party might be imposed, namely, where the defendant is responsible for a source of danger which is foreseeably sparked off by a third party. He cited *Haynes v Harwood* [1935] 1 KB 146 (noted above, p. 300) as 'the classic example' of this type of case. His Lordship was at pains, however, to restrict the scope for arguments based on this authority, and he made it clear that items encountered in ordinary daily life would not be regarded as posing a special danger, even though it might be foreseeable that their use would involve the risk of harm. (Should rubble on a building site be regarded as a source of danger? See *Gabriel v Kirklees Metropolitan Council* [2004] EWCA Civ 345, [2004] Build LR 441.) A more particular circumstance in which a duty of affirmative action might arise was where an occupier knew or had the means of knowing that trespassers were deliberately and wrongfully lighting fires on his land. Following Lord Goff, the Court of Appeal imposed liability for breach of such a duty in *Clark Fixing Ltd v Dudley Metropolitan Borough Council* [2001] EWCA Civ 1898. The defendant council acquired property, the roof of which was shared with adjoining premises. Trespassers entered the defendant's premises, starting a fire which spread via the roof to the claimants' premises next door and caused considerable damage. Unlike *Smith*, the council was well aware that there had been previous intrusions and fires, the claimants having complained of such events on a number of occasions. The council was therefore under a duty to take reasonable precautions against the spread of fire, for example by removing all readily-moveable combustible material, which could have been achieved at trifling expense. The council had failed to do this and was therefore liable for its negligence.

The difference between Lord Goff's general and particular grounds for liability is illustrated by *Sandhu Menswear Co Ltd v Woolworths plc* [2006] EWHC 1299 (TCC). Here the defendants left a large amount of combustible material outside a storage unit in an industrial estate in circumstances where it was foreseeable that trespassers would have access to the material and might set fire to it. Counsel for the defendants argued that, as no previous fires had been lit, there was no knowledge of the risk of damage by fire (unlike *Clark Fixing*). Nonetheless a duty was held to exist: the combustible material was a source of danger which had been carelessly created by the defendant; hence liability could be imposed under Lord Goff's 'general circumstance' for liability for the acts of a third party.

Aside from fire, the case law suggests that the courts take a narrow view of what constitutes a source of danger. In *Topp v London Country Bus (South West) Ltd* [1993] 1 WLR 976, the Court Appeal, applying the analysis of Lord Goff in *Smith*, rejected a claim that a special danger arose from the presence of a minibus, unlocked and with its keys in the ignition, in the vicinity of a public house at around about closing time. The bus was driven off in dangerous fashion by persons unknown and was shortly afterwards involved in an accident in which the deceased was killed. It has been argued that the approach of the Court of Appeal is seriously flawed by its reliance upon the approach of Lord Goff in *Smith*, notwithstanding the greater degree of support in that decision for the more flexible approach of Lord Mackay (see Howarth, 'My Brother's Keeper? Liability for Acts of Third Parties' (1994) 14 LS 88)? However, in *Mitchell v Glasgow City Council* [2009] UKHL 11, [2009] 1 AC 874, the House of Lords stated a clear preference for Lord Goff over Lord Reid in this context (see especially at [20]–[21] per Lord Hope ('cases of this kind which arise from another's deliberate wrongdoing cannot be founded simply upon the degree of foreseeability... [S]omething more than foreseeability is required') and [56] per Lord Rodger). Lord Goff's approach has also been followed by the courts in Australia (see *Modbury Triangle Shopping Centre v Anzil* (2001) 205 CLR 254, noted by Fordham (2001) 117 LQR 178). Which approach do *you* prefer?

Liability for serving alcohol

Even if an occupier has control over a third party sufficient to impose a duty to act positively for some purposes, there may be other situations in which control of itself will not give rise to such a duty. The issue has arisen in relation to those who serve alcohol to third parties on their premises. We have previously discussed the liability of such persons to those who consume the alcohol (see p. 476ff above) but liability may also arise where a patron affected by alcohol consumed on the premises causes injury to another. In some common law jurisdictions, it is accepted that a commercial occupier owes a duty to act to prevent a patron—including an intoxicated patron—from causing injury to other persons on the premises (see, e.g., *Wagstaff v Haslam* [2007] NSWCA 28; *Adeels Palace Pty Ltd v Moubarak* [2009] HCA 48). Does the duty extend to those who might be injured when the patron leaves the premises (e.g. in a collision caused when the patron drives home drunk)? The Supreme Court of Canada has indicated that such a duty is owed by the occupier of commercial premises serving alcohol (*Stewart v Pettie* [1995] 1 SCR 131), but not by a 'social host' (*Childs v Desormeaux* [2006] 1 SCR 641), at least where he does not enhance the risk by (e.g.) serving an obviously drunk guest whom he knows is going to drive home. Although both commercial and social host have some control over the patron/guest, respect for the the latter's rights of autonomy militated against a duty being found: 'A person who accepts an invitation to attend a private party does not park his autonomy at the door. The guest remains responsible for his or her conduct' (*Childs*, at [45] per McLachlin CJ). For comment on *Childs*, see Malkin and Voon, 'Social host's responsibility for their intoxicated guests: Where courts fear to tread' (2007) 15 TLJ 62 at 68–76 and generally McIvor, *Third Party Liability in Tort* (Oxford: Hart, 2006), ch. 4.

Do you think the distinction between commercial and social occupiers justifies the difference in result in the two contexts?

10 NEGLIGENCE: DUTY OF CARE—PUBLIC BODIES

I. Introduction

It was established in *Mersey Docks and Harbour Board Trustees v Gibbs* (1866) LR 1 HL 93 that public bodies have no blanket immunity from liability in tort, clearing the way for damages actions against local government, the utilities, regulators, and the emergency services. The almost complete abolition of Crown immunity by the Crown Proceedings Act 1947 opened the door further, allowing claims against (*inter alia*) government departments, with damages awards to be met by the Treasury. Over time public bodies have become ever more attractive targets for negligence actions: their pockets are deep enough to bear substantial awards of damages, and the array of powers and duties under which they operate make them vulnerable to a wide variety of allegations of non-feasance. The courts—fearing the depletion of public funds, a detrimental impact upon the performance of public functions, and undue interference in matters of government—have responded by limiting the scope of the duties of care that public bodies owe.

In *X and Others (Minors) v Bedfordshire CC* [1995] 2 AC 633, Lord Browne-Wilkinson surveyed the various causes of action that could be relied upon against a public body. He listed three: common law negligence, breach of statutory duty (considered separately in Ch. 11.IV), and misfeasance in public office. (This last head of liability—not considered further in this book—is of limited scope, applying only to cases where a public official acts with the object of injuring the claimant, i.e. with 'targeted malice', or with the knowledge that there was no power to perform the act in question.) To the causes of action listed by Lord Browne-Wilkinson must now be added two more: breaches of European Union law amounting to so-called Euro-torts (see Ch. 11.V) and violation of the specific obligations placed on 'public authorities' by the Human Rights Act 1998, s. 6 (see below). But it is vitally important to realise that 'the careless performance of a statutory duty does not in itself give rise to any cause of action in the absence of either a statutory right of action…[including any action arising under EU law] or a common law duty of care' (*X v Bedfordshire CC*, at 732, per Lord Browne-Wilkinson).

The Human Rights Act (extracted at p. 28, above) creates a new statutory remedy against public authorities for violation of the specified Convention rights. Conduct which is unlawful under s. 6(1) on grounds of its incompatibility with a person's Convention rights may be the subject of proceedings under s. 7(1). Under s. 8(1), the court has the power to grant whatever remedy within its powers it considers 'just and appropriate', including the award of damages where this is necessary to afford 'just satisfaction' to the victim. It is not yet entirely clear how the statutory remedy will interact with that at common law, though it appears that a claimant's rights to compensation at common law may in some cases render it inappropriate to make any further award under s. 8 (see, e.g., *Marcic v Thames Water Utilities Ltd* [2002] 2 QB 929, a case in nuisance, reversed on other grounds: [2004] 2 AC 42). To that extent, the common law liability may be regarded as primary, and that under the statute as secondary. The s. 8 case law certainly suggests that the award of damages for violation of a Convention right will be rare. In 2006, the Department of Constitution Affairs, reviewing more than five years of the Act's operation, found only 3 cases in which damages had been awarded—and one of these was subsequently overturned: see *van Colle v Chief Constable of the Hertfordshire Police* [2006] 3 All ER 963 (QB), reversed [2008] UKHL 50, [2009] 1 AC 225. The further question of whether the legislation has or will have the indirect effect of promoting judicial reconsideration of the scope of the common law duties owed by public bodies is considered at p. 527ff, below.

Although we shall make periodic reference to the Human Rights Act and the jurisprudence of the European Court of Human Rights in the rest of this chapter, our main focus is the common law duty of care. The chapter is sub-divided so as to make clear that common law actions against public bodies may have both public and private law dimensions. No doubt, there are many cases in which such actions do not raise issues of a specifically public character (e.g. actions in respect of the dangerous workplace environment of a public-sector employer or negligent driving by a public employee). But a public dimension is exposed when the claim relates to grievances of a sort that are normally pursued by way of an application for judicial review under Civil Procedure Rules Part 54. Although Part 54, in the interests of efficient government, imposes a number of procedural restrictions on applications for judicial review (e.g. a very short limitation period of three months), the courts have allowed litigants to side-step these restrictions by bringing ordinary civil claims against a public body in cases where they seek to vindicate a *private right*, for example, the right to recover damages for harm caused in breach of a duty of care (see *Davy v Spelthorne Borough Council* [1984] AC 262). This is not to say, however, that such litigants can side-step *substantive* limitations on the scope of judicial review that have been developed in public law in order to safeguard the exercise of executive discretion. Such limitations reflect a concern with the proper separation of powers that appears equally applicable to the private law context. The question therefore arises of how it can be addressed within the framework of an action for negligence. Such problems of what Lord Nicholls has called 'the interface of public and private law obligation' (*Stovin v Wise* [1996] AC 923 at 928) are the concern of Section II, below.

The private law dimension of negligence actions against public bodies denotes the application of normal principles of negligence in the context of such claims. In considering the ordinary duty questions set out in *Caparo Industries v Dickman*, the court may find its analysis shaped by the special position occupied by the defendant: 'the question whether there is such a common law duty and if so its ambit, must be profoundly influenced by the statutory framework within which the acts complained of were done' (*X v Bedfordshire CC*, at 739, per Lord Browne-Wilkinson). For instance, the statutory framework under which the body operates may make it plausible to argue that there is a relationship of proximity between it and those whom the legislation is intended to benefit such as to give rise to affirmative obligations towards the latter (as argued—unsuccessfully—in *Gorringe v Calderdale MBC*, below). Alternatively, the need to protect and ensure value from public funds may outweigh those considerations of fairness, justice and reasonableness which would otherwise point to the imposition of a duty of care. These matters are considered further in Sections III and IV, below.

II. The Public Law Dimension

It would not be right to hold every decision made by a public body open to judicial scrutiny. Public bodies are frequently part of the political process and more appropriately held accountable by a variety of mechanisms ranging from the ballot box to the obligation to report to Parliament. As has been noted, the legality of their actions can be challenged in public law by applications for judicial review. They are frequently entrusted with the task of balancing broad concerns of social or economic policy, and the interests of different sections of the public, rather than with the determination of individual rights. Such matters are 'not of a kind which can be satisfactorily elicited by the adversary procedure and rules of evidence adopted in English courts of law or of which judges are suited by their training and experience to assess the probative value' (*Home Office v Dorset Yacht Co Ltd* [1970] AC 1004 at 1067, per Lord Diplock). See further Law Commission, *Remedies Against Public Bodies: A Scoping Report* (2006), paras 5.9–5.15 ('What is distinctive about the state as a party'); R. Stevens, *Torts and Rights* (2007), p. 308ff.

Over time English law has developed a number of mechanisms to deal with these concerns, but has yet properly to rationalise their application or their interrelationship. The most important ideas to be found in the case law are the concepts of: (1) *vires*, (2) discretion; (3) a policy, as opposed to operational, sphere; (4) justiciability; and (5) irrationality. The development of these ideas is outlined below.

Vires

One early suggestion was that liability should be tested by reference to whether the defendant's conduct was *ultra vires*. In *Home Office v Dorset Yacht Co Ltd* [1970] AC 1004 at 1067, Lord Diplock stated:

> The public law concept of ultra vires has replaced the civil law concept of negligence as the test of the legality, and consequently of the actionability, of acts or omissions of government departments or public authorities done in the exercise of a discretion conferred on them by Parliament....

This went too far. The mere fact that a public authority has been found to have acted *ultra vires* does not mean that consequential injury should be actionable. A finding of *ultra vires* does not necessarily entail a finding of fault (e.g. because it may denote only a non-culpable misconstruction of a statute); nor does it address the elements of foreseeability, proximity and fairness, justice and reasonableness which are necessary to give rise to a duty of care. More pertinently, a finding of *ultra vires* might have nothing at all to do with the substantive merits of the decision (e.g. where the defect is in the procedure by which a decision is reached), and the subject-matter of the case may remain entirely unsuitable for judicial resolution. Lord Diplock's reliance upon the concept of *ultra vires* to determine liability in the law of tort has subsequently been criticised (e.g. by Lord Browne-Wilkinson in *X v Bedfordshire CC*, below), and doubts have even been expressed about the utility of the concept in public law (see, e.g., Craig, 'Ultra Vires and the Foundations of Judicial Review' [1998] CLJ 63). It seems that, in the private law context, *ultra vires* is at best a redundant label applied to situations where the court has already decided to hold the defendant liable, and that it would be conducive to clarity to abandon use of the term.

Discretion

Another way of addressing the problems of the public–private interface, also evident in the *Dorset Yacht* case, has proved more durable. This was to ask whether the conduct in question fell within the ambit of a discretion conferred on the defendant by Parliament. In the *Dorset Yacht* case, Lord Reid explained (at 1031):

> Where Parliament confers a discretion . . . there may, and almost certainly will, be errors of judgment in exercising such a discretion and Parliament cannot have intended that members of the public should be entitled to sue in respect of such errors. But there must come a stage when the discretion is exercised so carelessly or unreasonably that there has been no real exercise of the discretion which Parliament has conferred. The person purporting to exercise his discretion has acted in abuse or excess of his power.

On the facts of the *Dorset Yacht* case, it was held that the carelessness of officers at an institution for young offenders (borstal) in leaving their charges unattended was indeed in excess of any discretion that had been conferred upon them. It would have been different, suggested Lord Pearson, '[i]f the defendants had, in the exercise of their discretion, released some of these boys, taking them on shore and putting them on trains or buses with tickets to their homes' (at 1053). The matter being a valid exercise of the defendants' discretion, no liability could arise.

The concept of discretion remains of vital significance in the case law on the liability of public bodies (see, especially, the extracts from *X v Bedfordshire CC*, below), but it is important to realise that discretion cannot be looked at in 'all-or-nothing' terms and used as a simple criterion for the imposition of a duty of care. Even putting aside the obvious objection that a claim involving no significant element of discretion must still satisfy the ordinary duty requirements set out in *Caparo v Dickman*, it must be acknowledged that there is no absolute distinction between discretionary and non-discretionary spheres; rather there is a sliding scale along which the nature of the discretion present varies considerably. The mere existence of some element of discretion is insufficient to preclude the imposition of a duty of care. As Lord Slynn observed in *Barrett v London Borough of Enfield* [2001] 2 AC 550 at 571:

> This, however, does not in my view mean that if an element of discretion is involved in an act being done subject to the exercise of the overriding statutory power, common law negligence is necessarily ruled out. Acts may be done pursuant and subsequent to the exercise of a discretion where a duty of care may exist—as has often been said even knocking a nail into a piece of wood involves the exercise of some choice or discretion and yet there may be a duty of care in the way it is done. Whether there is an element of discretion to do the act is thus not a complete test leading to the result that, if there is, a claim against an authority for what it actually does or fails to do must necessarily be ruled out . . .

Policy and Operational Spheres

Such considerations made it necessary for the courts to explicate further the way in which the existence of a statutory (or prerogative) discretion impacts upon the issue of civil liability. In *Anns v Merton LBC* [1978] AC 728 at 754, Lord Wilberforce made a famous attempt to link the concept of discretion with a distinction between *policy* (or planning) and *operational* spheres of a public body's activities:

> Most, indeed probably all, statutes relating to public authorities or public bodies, contain in them a large area of policy. The courts call this 'discretion', meaning that the decision is one for

the authority or body to make, and not for the courts. Many statutes, also, prescribe or at least pre-suppose the practical execution of policy decisions: a convenient description of this is to say that in addition to the area of policy or discretion, there is an operational area. Although this distinction between the policy area and the operational area is convenient, and illuminat-ing, it is probably a distinction of degree; many 'operational' powers or duties have in them some element of 'discretion'. It can safely be said that the more 'operational' a power or duty may be, the easier it is to superimpose on it a common law duty of care.

It is important to note that Lord Wilberforce was using the term 'policy' here in a special sense. He was not referring to the many various public policy concerns that are relevant in determining whether it is fair, just and reasonable to impose a duty of care, but merely identifying a particular sphere of a public body's activity. His idea was that, when a public body is acting in the policy sphere (e.g. in assessing budgetary priorities), the courts should refrain—wholly or in part—from interfering with their activities by subjecting them to a duty of care.

Justiciability

Lord Wilberforce's distinction between policy and operational spheres was subsequently considered by Lord Keith, delivering the advice of the Privy Council in the case of *Rowling v Takaro Properties Ltd* [1988] AC 473 at 501. His Lordship stated:

> [T]his distinction does not provide a touchstone of liability, but rather is expressive of the need to exclude altogether those cases in which the decision under attack is of such a kind that a question whether it has been made negligently is unsuitable for judicial resolution, of which notable examples are discretionary decisions on the allocation of scarce resources or the distribution of risks...If this is right, classification of the relevant decision as a policy or planning decision in this sense may exclude liability; but a conclusion that it does not fall within that category does not, in their Lordships' opinion, mean that a duty of care will necessarily exist.

There are three ideas here. First, the policy–operations distinction does not itself determine whether there is a duty of care; it is not 'a touchstone of liability'. It is only a way of filter-ing out claims which are unsuitable for judicial resolution. Even if the matter in question is operational, it does not follow that there is a duty of care. Secondly, underlying the distinc-tion lies the idea of 'suitability for judicial resolution' (which is conveniently expressed by the term 'justiciability'). The policy–operations dichotomy is the mechanism by which the justiciability of a particular case is determined. Lastly, examples of non-justiciable decisions are discretionary decisions on the allocation of scarce resources or the distribution of risks. (For instance, in the *Dorset Yacht* case, the Home Office's establishment of an open borstal policy, entailing an increased risk of escape and consequent injury to ordinary members of the public, was effectively regarded as non-justiciable, though this was not the language used: see [1970] AC 1004 at 1065, per Lord Diplock.) It is notable here that Lord Keith relies upon exemplification rather than setting out precise criteria for deciding upon a case's justi-ciability, and risks a certain degree of circularity by re-introducing the term 'discretionary'. It is submitted that this was inevitable, for there is no more fundamental notion to which ref-erence can be made at this point, and that the courts can only rely upon intuitive judgments as to whether a matter is 'discretionary', 'in the policy sphere' or 'non-justiciable'.

Irrationality

Subsequently, in the two cases extracted here, the courts have adopted a test of 'Wednesbury unreasonableness' (see Associated Provincial Picture Houses Ltd v Wednesbury Corp [1948] 1 KB 223) or 'irrationality' as a precondition of the liability of a public body. The interplay of this requirement with the other factors listed above is examined by Lord Browne-Wilkinson in the first of the two cases extracted below, X v Bedfordshire CC. His approach may be usefully compared with that of Lord Hoffmann in Stovin v Wise, and indeed with that of Lord Nicholls (dissenting), in the extract that follows.

X and Others (Minors) v Bedfordshire County Council [1995] 2 AC 633

The House of Lords was faced with five separate appeals raising the issue of the liability of a local authority for the careless performance of its statutory functions with regard to the protection of children who are at risk of child abuse (see especially Child Care Act 1980 and Children Act 1989) and the provision of suitable education to children with special needs (see Education Acts 1944 and 1981 and regulations made thereunder). For present purposes, it is sufficient merely to outline the facts of just one of the cases—the Bedfordshire case—where the allegation was that the local authority had failed to act expeditiously to put five children from the same family onto the child protection register and to take them into care. The children sought damages for their consequent ill-treatment and illness, neglect of their proper development, and impairment of their health, alleging both personal negligence on the part of the local authorities (the 'direct liability' issue) and negligence on the part of others for whom the local authorities were vicariously liable (the 'indirect liability' issue).

The facts of the other appeals are set out, with additional extracts, in Section III, below.

Lord Browne-Wilkinson

[S]tatutory duties now exist over such a wide range of diverse activities and take so many different forms that no one principle is capable of being formulated applicable to all cases. However, in my view it is possible in considering the problems raised by these particular appeals to identify certain points which are of significance.

(1) Co-existence of Statutory Duty and Common Law Duty of Care

It is clear that a common law duty of care may arise in the performance of statutory functions. But a broad distinction has to be drawn between: (a) cases in which it is alleged that the authority owes a duty of care in the manner in which it exercises a statutory discretion; and (b) cases in which a duty of care is alleged to arise from the manner in which the statutory duty has been implemented in practice.

An example of (a) in the educational field would be a decision whether or not to exercise a statutory discretion to close a school, being a decision which necessarily involves the exercise of a discretion. An example of (b) would be the actual running of a school pursuant to the statutory duties. In such latter case a common law duty to take reasonable care for the physical safety of the pupils will arise. The fact that the school is being run pursuant to a statutory duty is not necessarily incompatible with a common law duty of care arising from the proximate relationship between a school and the pupils it has agreed to accept. The distinction is between (a) taking care in exercising a statutory discretion whether or not to do an act and (b) having decided to do that act, taking care in the manner in which you do it.

(2) Discretion, Justiciability and the Policy/Operational Test

(a) Discretion

Most statutes which impose a statutory duty on local authorities confer on the authority a discretion as to the extent to which, and the methods by which, such statutory duty is to be performed. It is clear both in principle and from the decided cases that the local authority cannot be liable in damages for doing that which Parliament has authorised. Therefore if the decisions complained of fall within the ambit of such statutory discretion they cannot be actionable in common law. However, if the decision complained of is so unreasonable that it falls outside the ambit of the discretion conferred upon the local authority, there is no a priori reason for excluding all common law liability.

That this is the law is established by the decision in the *Dorset Yacht* case and by that part of the decision in *Anns v Merton London Borough* [1978] AC 728 which, so far as I am aware, has largely escaped criticism in later decisions...

[Lord Browne-Wilkinson referred to the dictum of Lord Reid set out above at p. 507, and continued:] Lord Diplock...took a rather different line, making it a condition precedent to any common law duty arising that the decision impugned should be shown to be ultra vires in the public law sense. For myself, I do not believe that it is either helpful or necessary to introduce public law concepts as to the validity of a decision into the question of liability at common law for negligence. In public law a decision can be ultra vires for reasons other than *Wednesbury* unreasonableness (e.g. breach of the rules of natural justice) which have no relevance to the question of negligence. Moreover, it leads, in my judgment mistakenly, to the contention that claims for damages for negligence in the exercise of statutory powers should for procedural purposes be classified as public law claims and therefore, under *O'Reilly v Mackman* [1983] 2 AC 237, should be brought in judicial review proceedings: see *Lonrho plc v Tebbit* [1992] 4 All ER 280. However, although I consider that the public law doctrine of ultra vires has, as such, no role to play in the subject under discussion, the remarks of Lord Diplock were plainly directed to the fact that the exercise of a statutory discretion cannot be impugned unless it is so unreasonable that it falls altogether outside the ambit of the statutory discretion....It follows that in seeking to establish that a local authority is liable at common law for negligence in the exercise of a discretion conferred by statute, the first requirement is to show that the decision was outside the ambit of the discretion altogether: if it was not, a local authority cannot itself be in breach of any duty of care owed to the plaintiff.

In deciding whether or not this requirement is satisfied, the court has to assess the relevant factors taken into account by the authority in exercising the discretion. Since what are under consideration are discretionary powers conferred on public bodies for public purposes the relevant factors will often include policy matters, for example social policy, the allocation of finite financial resources between the different calls made upon them or (as in the *Dorset Yacht* case) the balance between pursuing desirable social aims as against the risk to the public inherent in so doing. It is established that the courts cannot enter upon the assessment of such 'policy' matters. The difficulty is to identify in any particular case whether or not the decision in question is a 'policy' decision.

(b) Justiciability and the Policy/Operational Dichotomy...

[Lord Browne-Wilkinson quoted the passages from *Anns* and *Rowling* that are set out above at p. 507f, and continued:] From these authorities I understand the applicable principles to be as follows. Where Parliament has conferred a statutory discretion on a public authority, it is for that authority, not for the courts, to exercise the discretion: nothing which the authority does within the ambit of the discretion can be actionable at common law. If the decision complained of falls outside the statutory discretion, it *can* (but not necessarily will) give rise to common law liability. However, if the factors relevant to the exercise of the discretion include matters of policy, the court cannot adjudicate on such policy matters and therefore cannot reach the conclusion that the decision was outside the ambit of the statutory discretion. Therefore a common law duty of care in relation to the taking of decisions involving policy matters cannot exist.

(3) If Justiciable, the Ordinary Principles of Negligence Apply

If the plaintiff's complaint alleges carelessness, not in the taking of a discretionary decision to do some act, but in the practical manner in which that act has been performed (e.g. the running of a school) the question whether or not there is a common law duty of care falls to be decided by applying the usual principles, i.e. those laid down in *Caparo Industries plc v Dickman* [1990] 2 AC 605 at 617–18. Was the damage to the plaintiff reasonably foreseeable? Was the relationship between the plaintiff and the defendant sufficiently proximate? Is it just and reasonable to impose a duty of care? See *Rowling v Takaro Properties Ltd* and *Hill v Chief Constable of West Yorkshire* [1989] AC 53 . . .

THE ABUSE CASES . . .

Direct Common Law Duty of Care Owed by the Local Authorities . . .

[Lord Browne-Wilkinson noted that, of the two abuse cases, it was only in the *Bedfordshire* case that the issue of a direct duty owed by the defendant council arose. He continued:] In the *Bedfordshire* case Mr Jackson QC formulated the common law duty of care owed by the county council as being 'a duty to children in respect of whom they receive reports of neglect or ill-treatment to take reasonable care to protect such children'. The first question is whether the determination by the court of the question whether there has been a breach of that duty will involve unjusticiable policy questions. The alleged breaches of that duty relate for the most part to the failure to take reasonable practical steps, e.g. to remove the children, to allocate a suitable social worker or to make proper investigations. The assessment by the court of such allegations would not require the court to consider policy matters which are not justiciable. They do not necessarily involve any question of the allocation of resources or the determination of general policy. There are other allegations that investigation of which by a court might require the weighing of policy factors, e.g. allegations that the county council failed to provide a level of service appropriate to the plaintiffs' needs. If the case were to go to trial, the trial judge might have to rule out these issues as not being justiciable. But since some of the allegations are justiciable, it would not be right to strike out the whole claim on this ground. Next, do the allegations of breach of duty in the operational field all relate to decisions the power to make which Parliament has conferred on the local authority, i.e. are they all decisions within the ambit of the local authority's statutory discretion?

I strongly suspect that, if the case were to go to trial, it would eventually fail on this ground since, in essence, the complaint is that the local authority failed to take steps to remove the children from the care of their mother, i.e. negligently failed properly to exercise a discretion which Parliament has conferred on the local authority. But again, it would not be right to strike out the claim on this ground because it is possible that the plaintiffs might be able to demonstrate at trial that the decisions of the local authority were so unreasonable that no reasonable local authority could have reached them and therefore, for the reasons given by Lord Reid in *Home Office v Dorset Yacht Co Ltd* [1970] AC 1004 at 1031, fall outside the ambit of the discretion conferred by Parliament.

[Lord Browne-Wilkinson reached a similar conclusion *vis-à-vis* the various education cases. His Lordship's analysis of the application to the cases before him of 'the usual principles' laid down in *Caparo v Dickman* is extracted below at p. 518.]

COMMENTARY

Summarising the principles applicable in determining whether Bedfordshire County Council owed a direct duty to the five plaintiff children, Lord Browne-Wilkinson identified two separate questions to be addressed before applying the ordinary *Caparo* principles:

(a) Is the negligence relied upon negligence in the exercise of a statutory discretion involving policy considerations: if so the claim will fail pro tanto as being non-justiciable; (b) were the acts alleged to give rise to the cause of action within the ambit of the discretion conferred on the local authority ... ?

This approach is especially interesting because most decided cases tend to mix together the questions of discretion and policy/operations, and to see them as interchangeable mechanisms for addressing the underlying need to ensure an appropriate separation of judicial and executive spheres of decision-making. Here, by contrast, Lord Browne-Wilkinson appears to treat discretion as a separate concern, distinct from both the policy–operations distinction and justiciability. Why?

   One plausible answer is that Lord Browne-Wilkinson intended merely to emphasise that questions of the separation of powers arise not only at the duty stage but also in considering breach. In some circumstances, the case against a public body may involve allegations of negligence in respect of a policy matter that it is not the court's business to consider (e.g. whether an open borstal policy is right or wrong). In such a case, the court should simply rule that the matter is not justiciable and that it cannot recognise a duty of care; the case therefore fails at the threshold, before the court has even heard submissions as to the reasonableness of the policy in question. In other circumstances, the court might rule that a particular matter is justiciable, but still feel some reluctance to substitute its judgment for that of the defendant (e.g. because of the defendant's particular expertise or its position in the political process). Here, we may say that the matter in question is only partially-justiciable or, more conventionally, that it involves the exercise of the defendant's discretion; the question is really one of breach of duty. In *Barrett v London Borough of Enfield* [2001] 2 AC 550 at 591, Lord Hutton explained:

I wish to emphasise that the considerations relied on by the defendant on the issue of justiciability will be of relevance and importance when the trial judge comes to consider whether the plaintiff has established a breach of the duty to take reasonable care. The standard of care in negligence must be related to the nature of the duty to be performed and to the circumstances in which the defendant has to carry it out. Therefore the standard of care to be required of the defendant in this case in order to establish negligence at common law will have to be determined against the background that it is given discretions to exercise in a sphere involving difficult decisions ... [T]he trial judge, bearing in mind the room for differences of opinion as to the best course to adopt in a difficult field and that the discretion is to be exercised by the authority ... and not by the court, must be satisfied that the conduct complained of went beyond mere errors of judgment in the exercise of a discretion and constituted conduct which can be regarded as negligent.

According to Lord Browne-Wilkinson the test to be applied at this stage is that of *Wednesbury* unreasonableness (see *Associated Provincial Picture Houses Ltd v Wednesbury Corp* [1948] 1 KB 223): is the defendant's conduct so unreasonable that no reasonable public body would conduct itself in such a way. Such conduct may be characterised as 'irrational'. Essentially this is to treat the *Wednesbury* unreasonableness test as the criterion for breach of duty. It should not be thought, however, that the *Wednesbury* test is substituted for the ordinary test of negligence. In fact, the conventional principles of breach of duty are quite capable of acknowledging a discretionary sphere in the defendant's conduct (see especially *Bolam v Friern Hospital Management Committee* [1957] 1 WLR 582) and the *Wednesbury* test is best regarded as an application of ordinary principles of negligence to the discretionary activities of public bodies. Of course, the nature of the discretion involved in a public body's conduct is a matter of degree (depending upon the sphere of activity in question, the budgetary constraints under which it was acting, etc.). (Lord Browne-Wilkinson may perhaps be criticised for appearing to treat the boundaries of the discretionary field as too clear-cut.) As the nature of the discretion becomes more limited, the test of breach employed in actions against public bodies will more closely resemble that in ordinary actions against private individuals. It is perhaps only in cases where there is a significant strategic discretion that it is appropriate to address the question of breach of duty in *Wednesbury* terms.

Lord Browne-Wilkinson's approach to the special problems raised by actions against public bodies should be reconsidered after reading the next extract.

Stovin v Wise [1996] AC 923

The plaintiff, Mr Stovin, was injured when his motor cycle collided with a car driven by the defendant, Mrs Wise. The latter had emerged from a dangerous junction from which her view of approaching traffic was obstructed by a raised bank of earth adjacent to the road. The trial judge attributed 70 per cent of the blame for the accident to Mrs Wise, but he also found the local highway authority, Norfolk County Council, whom Mrs Wise had joined as a third party to the proceedings, to be 30 per cent to blame on account of its failure to render the junction less hazardous. The highway authority had in fact taken preliminary steps to have the obstructing bank removed. Although the authority had the statutory power to require landowners to remove dangerous obstructions to the view of highway users (under Highways Act 1980, s. 79), in this case it had decided to proceed on a voluntary basis and simply written to the owner of the land in question, seeking permission to do the work and offering to pay the cost. It received no response, and in the year or so prior to the plaintiff's accident it had failed to take any further action. The Court of Appeal dismissed the council's appeal. The council appealed to the House of Lords.

Lord Hoffmann

Policy and Operations

[T]he distinction between policy and operations is an inadequate tool with which to discover whether it is appropriate to impose a duty of care or not....There are at least two reasons why the distinction is inadequate. The first is that, as Lord Wilberforce himself pointed out, the distinction is often elusive. This is particularly true of powers to provide public benefits which involve the expenditure of money. Practically every decision about the provision of such benefits, no matter how trivial it may seem, affects the budget of the public authority in either timing or amount....But another reason is that even if the distinction is clear cut, leaving no element of discretion in the sense that it would be irrational (in the public law meaning of that word) for the public authority not to exercise its power, it does not follow that the law should superimpose a common law duty of care. This can be seen if one looks at cases in which a public authority has been under a statutory or common law *duty* to provide a service or other benefit for the public or a section of the public. In such cases there is no discretion, but the courts have nevertheless not been willing to hold that a member of the public who has suffered loss because the service was not provided to him should necessarily have a cause of action, either for breach of statutory duty or for negligence at common law....

[Lord Hoffmann stated that, in a case of the non-exercise of a statutory power, it was necessary to prove that 'it would in the circumstances have been irrational not to have exercised the power, so that there was in effect a public law duty to act'. He then sought to apply that condition to the present case:]

Duties of a Highway Authority

I will start by asking whether, in the light of what the council knew or ought to have known about the junction, it would have had a duty in public law to undertake the work. This requires that it would have been irrational not to exercise its discretion to do so. The trial judge did not address himself to this question. He thought it was sufficient that, as he put it, 'a decision had already been taken to deal with the situation' in which 'budgetary considerations were not a restraint'.

The fact that ... [council officers] had agreed to do the work does not show that it would have been unreasonable or irrational for the council not to have done it. That is simply a non sequitur. The Court of Appeal seems to have reasoned that the 'decision' to do the work disposed of any question of policy or discretion and left only the operational question of when the work should have been done. But this too seems to me fallacious. The timing of the work and the budgetary year in which the money is spent is surely as much a matter of discretion as the decision in principle to do it....

It seems to me, therefore, that the question of whether anything should be done about the junction was at all times firmly within the area of the council's discretion. As they were therefore not under a public law duty to do the work, the first condition for the imposition of a duty of care was not satisfied.

Lord Nicholls (dissenting)

[A]s the part played by broad discretionary considerations in the exercise of the power grows, the less readily will a common law duty be superimposed, and vice versa. At the discretionary edge of the spectrum will be powers whose nature and purpose make it difficult to envisage any likely circumstances where a common law duty, sounding in damages, could be superimposed. A local authority's powers to decide what schools there should be, and where, and of what type, may be an example of this. At the other edge of the spectrum will be powers where comparatively little extra may be needed to found a common law duty owed to a particular person or class of persons. A power to remove dangers from public places must be near this edge of the spectrum. A power to control air safety may be another example, as in *Swanson Estate v Canada* (1991) 80 DLR (4th) 741.

Some decisions since *Anns* have gone further and identified a 'no go' area for concurrent common law duties (see *Anns* [1978] AC 728 at 754, *Sutherland Shire Council v Heyman* (1985) 157 CLR 424 at 469 per Mason J, *Rowling v Takaro Properties Ltd* [1988] AC 473 at 501 and *X and ors (minors) v Bedfordshire CC* [1995] 2 AC 633 at 738). In practice the two approaches will usually reach the same conclusion. My preference is for the more open-ended approach. The exclusionary approach presupposes an identifiable boundary, between policy and other decisions, corresponding to a perceived impossibility for the court to handle policy decisions. But the boundary is elusive, because the distinction is artificial, and an area of blanket immunity seems undesirable and unnecessary. It is undesirable in principle that in respect of certain types of decisions the possibility of a concurrent common law duty should be absolutely barred, whatever the circumstances. An excluded zone is also unnecessary, because no statutory power is inherently immune from judicial review. This has not given rise to any insuperable difficulties in public law. Nor should it with claims in tort if, very exceptionally, a concurrent common law duty were held to exist in an area of broad policy. Courts are well able to recognise that reasonable people can reach widely differing conclusions when making decisions based on social, political or economic grounds (see e.g. *Nottinghamshire CC v Secretary of State for the Environment* [1986] AC 240). Similarly with competing demands for money. Indeed, the courts have recognised that sometimes it may be necessary in private law to look into competing demands for available money . . . [T]his is inherent in the very concept of a common law duty to take positive action. Thus, this feature does not of itself exclude the existence of a concurrent common law duty . . . .

Norfolk County Council acted in a way no reasonable authority would have done. If there is a common law duty, breach of the duty is not disputed. With knowledge of the danger the council decided to act. It then failed to proceed with reasonable diligence. The failure to proceed was not an exercise of discretion by the council. The council did not change its mind. The matter was overlooked. Given the decision to act, the only proper course open to the council was to proceed to implement the decision. Had the council acted as any reasonable authority would, that is what would have happened. The council failed to fulfil its public law obligations just as much as if it were in breach of a statutory duty.

Lord Goff and **Lord Jauncey** concurred with Lord Hoffmann. **Lord Slynn** concurred with the dissenting opinion of Lord Nicholls.

Appeal allowed.

COMMENTARY

Putting aside for the moment Lord Hoffmann's criticisms of the policy/operations distinction, there is a superficial similarity between his Lordship's approach and that of Lord Browne-Wilkinson in *X v Bedfordshire CC*. The test of irrationality is just another name for the test of *Wednesbury* unreasonableness. But a crucial difference is that Lord Browne-Wilkinson applied his test to the defendant's actual conduct (did it actually behave irrationally/so unreasonably that . . . ?) whereas Lord Hoffmann applied his to the conduct that plaintiff alleged the defendant ought to have engaged in (would it be irrational if the defendant failed to do this?). The difference between the two approaches is clear if one considers the facts of *Stovin*. While it was no doubt irrational for the council to overlook its previous decision to remove the obstruction, it does not follow—as Lord Nicholls seems to have thought—that it would have been irrational for it to do anything other than implement this decision (see Convery (1997) 60 MLR 559 at 567). It would, for instance, have been defensible for the council to go back on its earlier decision in the light of changed budgetary priorities. There might have been a public law duty to reconsider the matter, but this did not entail—even as a matter of public law—a duty to act.

Why should the courts not impose liability simply on the basis that the defendant body's conduct was in fact irrational and, on the balance of probabilities, if it had not acted irrationally it would have provided the protection the claimant wanted? Admittedly this would require the court to second-guess how the defendant would have acted on the hypothetical facts, but it would not strictly speaking entail the court's assumption of responsibility for the exercise of the discretion in question; the defendant's discretion would be undiminished. Even if the council had been held liable to Mr Stovin, it would still have been free to reconsider the question whether the obstruction should be removed, and a policy decision that it should not would be immune from attack in subsequent negligence litigation.

Another feature of Lord Hoffmann's use of the term 'irrationality' should be noted. Whereas Lord Browne-Wilkinson in *X v Bedfordshire CC* used it as a test of breach, Lord Hoffmann seems to treat it as going to the existence of a duty, a view tacitly affirmed by his speech in *Gorringe v Calderdale MBC* [2004] 1 WLR 1057. However, although the difference may be verbal rather than substantive, we would argue that it is conducive to clarity to follow Lord Browne-Wilkinson's usage.

For further comment on the case, see Convery (1997) 60 MLR 559; Harris (1997) 113 LQR 398; Hopkins [1996] CLJ 425; and Mullender (1997) 5 Tort L Rev 180.

The Policy–Operations Distinction

Despite Lord Hoffmann's antipathy towards the policy/operations distinction, it seems that his Lordship did treat the 'policy' element of the council's responsibility in this area as a relevant consideration (albeit not the sole determinant of the existence of a duty). He held that the local authority's decision not only whether to proceed with the work but also when and how it should be done raised budgetary questions and fell within the authority's unreviewable 'policy' discretion ('the court is not in a position to say what an appropriate standard of improvement would be. This must be a matter for the discretion of the authority'). This reasoning was thought unconvincing by an Australian judge in the subsequent case of *Romeo v Conservation Commission of the Northern Territory* (1998) 192 CLR 431: Kirby J accepted (at [140]) that '[v]irtually every suggested precaution, said to be necessary to prevent damage, has financial and economic implications, whether the defendant is a public authority or private individual', but observed that private individuals cannot generally escape liability by arguing the allocation of resources was a matter for their own determination; was there therefore any reason why public bodies should be able to do so? The obvious response, however, is that a private person may cease from acting altogether and so, if he acts at all, must spend the appropriate resources. But if a public body ceases to act, its decision would almost certainly be judicially reviewed because it has a public law obligation to provide a wide variety of services and cannot simply 'shut down' because of its liability costs.

Although the existence of the policy/operations distinction has been affirmed on many occasions, it has seldom been applied so as to rule out liability on the basis that there is no duty of care (perhaps because 'true' policy decisions, e.g. to operate an open borstal policy, never actually result in negligence actions). More frequently, the courts have assumed the existence of a duty but treated the policy or discretionary element in the defendant's conduct as militating against a finding of breach (see, e.g., *Allison v Corby District Council* [1980] RTR 111: discretionary decision as to the number of dog catchers to employ; no liability for road accident caused by stray dogs). But there have been a few cases where claims directed against policy decisions have been ruled out at the duty stage. In *Rigby v Chief Constable of Northamptonshire* [1985] 1 WLR 1242, for example, Taylor J ruled that a negligence action could not be used to challenge a police force's decision to continue its use of flammable CS gas even though a non-flammable alternative had become available. But on the facts he held that there was operational negligence in using the flammable gas without having adequate fire-fighting equipment nearby. In *West v Buckinghamshire County Council* (1985) 83 LGR 449, Caulfield J held that a decision not to mark a narrow and dangerous road with continuous double white lines, but instead to paint hazard lines on the road to allow motorists to overtake when safe to do so, was a policy decision in respect of which the council owed no duty of care. Similarly, the Department of Health owes no duty of care in devising strategies to counter disease or to disseminate relevant information to the public: see, for example, *Department of Health and Social Security v Kinnear* (1984) 134 NLJ 886 (policy of promoting widespread immunisation against whooping cough by injection of the pertussis vaccine); *Danns v Department of Health* (1995) 25 BMLR 121, noted by Kennedy (1996) 4 Med L Rev 324 (dissemination of newly-discovered information about the possibility of natural reversals of vasectomy procedures).

Can the Policy–Operations Distinction be Accommodated within the Ordinary Principles of Negligence?

Some commentators dispute whether it is necessary to introduce the policy/operations distinction as a separate factor going to the existence of a duty. According to Bailey and Bowman, 'The Policy/Operational Dichotomy—A Cuckoo in the Nest' [1986] CLJ 430, 'the policy/operational concept adds nothing of substance to what is already inherent within private law principles, but rather serves only to generate unnecessary confusion and so to divert attention away from those policy factors which require consideration in a negligence action' (p. 430). The authors elaborate:

[T]he range of mechanisms comprising the private law principles of negligence already provides full protection for the legitimate interests of public authorities. In particular, the principles governing breach of duty are likely to be appropriate for that purpose. But, according to Lord Wilberforce [in *Anns*], consideration of the policy/operational dichotomy is a preliminary to the establishment of a duty of care. If, therefore, the plaintiff seeks to bring an action in respect of harm arising out of a policy decision taken by a public authority, he must first demonstrate that the decision was ultra vires—for example, that it was so unreasonable that no reasonable authority could have made it. Thus, in such a case, the duty of care is only shown to exist once the circumstances demonstrating its breach have been established. While it may be going too far to say that this 'leaves the plaintiff in a logical limbo' (Seddon (1978) 9 FL Rev 326), it is certainly cumbrous and unattractive analytically.

Three comments may be made in response. First, abandoning the public law concept of *vires*, as advocated above, would enable the courts to keep duty and breach issues separate: the duty stage would focus upon the nature of the defendant's discretion (was it in a policy or operational sphere?) not upon its actual exercise; if the case is found to be justiciable, then the latter is appropriately considered at the breach stage (was the exercise of the discretion irrational?). Secondly, although the question of justiciability might well be subsumed under the 'ordinary' heading of fairness, justice and reasonableness in the *Caparo* scheme, it may be conducive to clarity to consider it separately as it raises questions relating to the separation of powers which are quite distinct from the policy arguments normally analysed under that heading. (It must be admitted, however, that such a separation may be impossible if it is the cumulative weight of the defendant's discretion added to other policy factors which 'tips the balance' against the plaintiff, as indeed seems to have been the case in X v *Bedfordshire CC*: see extracts below in Section III.) Lastly, although it would be possible to treat justiciability as something going only to breach of duty, it may be perceived as desirable to bring it in at the duty stage as well, for example, because it allows public defendants to challenge the existence of a duty in a striking-out application, without a full trial on the merits. (In X v *Bedfordshire CC*, however, Lord Browne-Wilkinson seems to have thought that such applications should succeed only in the clearest cases, for it is often only after the full facts are known that it is possible to place the defendant's conduct in either policy or operational sphere; but cf. *DHSS v Kinnear*, above.) Whether public defendants ought to have this opportunity—by the creation of what is effectively, as Lord Nicholls pointed out in *Stovin*, a judicial 'no go' area in respect of policy matters—is a matter of acute controversy which is never far from the surface in discussions of public authority liability.

For further analysis of these issues, see Bailey, 'Public authority liability in negligence: the continued search for coherence' (2006) 26 LS 155 at 164–71; and C. McIvor, *Third Party Liability in Tort* (Oxford: Hart, 2006), pp. 98–111. See also *Carty v Croydon London Borough Council* [2005] EWCA Civ 19, [2005] 1 WLR 2312.

III. The Private Law Dimension (i): Policy Reasons for Limiting the Liability of Public Bodies

If a claim overcomes the hurdle of justiciability, it must then be subjected to the ordinary duty of care principles set out in *Caparo v Dickman*. This may be termed the private law dimension of a claim against a public body. At this stage, the claim may run up against one of the generally recognised bars to the recognition of a duty of care. For example, the claim may relate to pure economic loss (see, e.g., *Murphy v Brentwood District Council* [1991] 1 AC 398; *Jain v Trent Strategic Health Authority* [2009] UKHL 4, [2009] 1 AC 853), or make an allegation of non-feasance rather than misfeasance (considered further in Section IV, below), or it may be that the defendant is acting in a quasi-judicial capacity (see *Yuen Kun Keu v Attorney General of Hong Kong* [1988] AC 175). In such circumstances, it may be held that there is no relationship of proximity between the parties and hence no duty of care. (*Aliter*, if the exceptional circumstances necessary to give rise to such a duty—even on the part of a private individual—are present: see, e.g., *Welton v North Cornwall District Council* [1997] 1 WLR 570.) But even if a relationship of proximity is presupposed, it may not be fair, just, and reasonable to recognise a duty of care. Concerns about (*inter alia*) the depletion of public funds have prompted the courts to allow public bodies (especially local authorities) a wide de facto immunity from suit in performing their statutory functions. As Lord Hoffmann has stated (*Stovin v Wise*, at 952):

> It is one thing to provide a service at the public expense. It is another to require the public to pay compensation when a failure to provide the service has resulted in loss. . . . To require payment of compensation increases the burden on public funds.

In the leading case of *X v Bedfordshire CC*, extracted below, Lord Browne-Wilkinson thoroughly reviewed the relevant considerations.

X and Others (Minors) v Bedfordshire County Council [1995] 2 AC 633

The basic nature of different appeals consolidated before the House of Lords was outlined above, at p. 509, where the facts of the *Bedforshire* case were also set out.

The other child abuse case was the *Newham* case. The allegation was that the local authority had acted unlawfully in taking the decision to remove the first plaintiff, a girl, from the second plaintiff, her mother, and her cohabiting partner. The local authority had reached this decision on the recommendation of the social worker and psychiatrist who had interviewed the girl, and had (erroneously) understood her to be referring to the partner when she spoke of her sexual abuse. In fact, the girl had merely identified the abuser as 'John', and had meant to refer to a cousin who had previously lived at the same address, rather than the partner, who shared the same first name. The mistake was subsequently discovered and the child returned to her mother. The child and mother both claimed that their enforced separation had caused them to suffer a psychiatric disorder diagnosed as anxiety neurosis. They sought damages relying upon the council's vicarious liability for the alleged negligence and breaches of statutory duty of the social worker and psychiatrist.

In both cases, the defendant authorities sought to strike out the claims on the basis that they disclosed no cause of action. The following extracts deal only with the negligence claims in the child abuse cases. The negligence claims in the education cases are considered at p. 525ff below. For breach of statutory duty, see Chapter 11.IV.

Lord Browne-Wilkinson having dealt with the questions of justiciability and discretion (see extracts, above, p. 509), proceeded to consider the ordinary requirements for liability in negligence.

Direct Common Law Duty of Care Owed by the Local Authorities...

I turn then to consider whether, in accordance with the ordinary principles laid down in *Caparo Industries plc v Dickman* [1990] 2 AC 605, the local authority in the *Bedfordshire* case owed a direct duty of care to the plaintiffs. The local authority accepts that they could foresee damage to the plaintiffs if they carried out their statutory duties negligently and that the relationship between the authority and the plaintiffs is sufficiently proximate. The third requirement laid down in *Caparo* is that it must be just and reasonable to impose a common law duty of care in all the circumstances. It was submitted that this third requirement is only applicable in cases where the plaintiff's claim is for pure economic loss and that it does not apply where, as in the child abuse cases, the claim is for physical damage. I reject this submission: although *Caparo* and many other of the more recent cases were decisions where only pure economic loss was claimed, the same basic principles apply to claims for physical damage and were applied in, for example, *Hill v Chief Constable of West Yorkshire* [1989] AC 53.

Is it, then, just and reasonable to superimpose a common law duty of care on the local authority in relation to the performance of its statutory duties to protect children? In my judgment it is not. Sir Thomas Bingham MR took the view, with which I agree, that the public policy consideration which has first claim on the loyalty of the law is that wrongs should be remedied and that very potent counter-considerations are required to override that policy (see [1994] 2 WLR 554 at 572). However, in my judgment there are such considerations in this case.

First, in my judgment a common law duty of care would cut across the whole statutory system set up for the protection of children at risk. As a result of the ministerial directions contained in the HMSO booklet *Working Together* the protection of such children is not the exclusive territory of the local authority's social services. The system is inter-disciplinary, involving the participation of the police, educational bodies, doctors and others. At all stages the system involves joint discussions, joint recommendations and joint decisions. The key organisation is the child protection conference, a multi-disciplinary body which decides whether to place the child on the child protection register. This procedure by way of joint action takes place, not merely because it is good practice, but because it is required by guidance having statutory force binding on the local authority. The guidance is extremely detailed and extensive: the current edition of *Working Together* runs to 126 pages. To introduce into such a system a common law duty of care enforceable against only one of the participant bodies would be manifestly unfair. To impose such liability on all the participant bodies would lead to almost impossible problems of disentangling as between the respective bodies the liability, both primary and by way of contribution, of each for reaching a decision found to be negligent.

Second, the task of the local authority and its servants in dealing with children at risk is extraordinarily delicate. Legislation requires the local authority to have regard not only to the physical well-being of the child but also to the advantages of not disrupting the child's family environment: see e.g. s. 17 of the 1989 Act. In one of the child abuse cases, the local authority is blamed for removing the child precipitately: in the other, for failing to remove the children from their mother. As the *Report of the Inquiry into Child Abuse in Cleveland 1987*, Cm 412 (the Cleveland Report) said (p. 244):

> It is a delicate and difficult line to tread between taking action too soon and not taking it soon enough. Social services whilst putting the needs of the child first must respect the rights of the parents; they also must work if possible with the parents for the benefit of the children. These parents themselves are often in need of help. Inevitably a degree of conflict develops between those objectives.

Next, if a liability in damages were to be imposed, it might well be that local authorities would adopt a more cautious and defensive approach to their duties. For example, as the Cleveland Report makes clear, on occasions the speedy decision to remove the child is sometimes vital. If the authority is to be made liable in damages for a negligent decision to remove a child (such negligence lying in the failure properly first to investigate the allegations) there would be a substantial temptation to postpone making such a decision until further inquiries have been made in the hope of getting more concrete facts. Not only would the child in fact being abused be prejudiced by such delay: the increased workload inherent in making such investigations would reduce the time available to deal with other cases and other children.

The relationship between the social worker and the child's parents is frequently one of conflict, the parent wishing to retain care of the child, the social worker having to consider whether to remove it. This is fertile ground in which to breed ill feeling and litigation, often hopeless, the cost of which both in terms of money and human resources will be diverted from the performance of the social service for which they were provided. The spectre of vexatious and costly litigation is often urged as a reason for not imposing a legal duty. But the circumstances surrounding cases of child abuse make the risk a very high one which cannot be ignored.

If there were no other remedy for maladministration of the statutory system for the protection of children, it would provide substantial argument for imposing a duty of care. But the statutory complaints procedures contained in s. 76 of the 1980 Act and the much fuller procedures now available under the 1989 Act provide a means to have grievances investigated, though not to recover compensation. Further, it was submitted (and not controverted) that the local authorities' ombudsman would have power to investigate cases such as these.

Finally, your Lordships' decision in *Caparo v Dickman* lays down that, in deciding whether to develop novel categories of negligence the court should proceed incrementally and by analogy with decided categories. We were not referred to any category of case in which a duty of care has been held to exist which is in any way analogous to the present cases. Here, for the first time, the plaintiffs are seeking to erect a common law duty of care in relation to the administration of a statutory social welfare scheme. Such a scheme is designed to protect weaker members of society (children) from harm done to them by others. The scheme involves the administrators in exercising discretions and powers which could not exist in the private sector and which in many cases bring them into conflict with those who, under the general law, are responsible for the child's welfare. To my mind, the nearest analogies are the cases where a common law duty of care has been sought to be imposed upon the police (in seeking to protect vulnerable members of society from wrongs done to them by others) or statutory regulators of financial dealings who are seeking to protect investors from dishonesty. In neither of those cases has it been thought appropriate to superimpose on the statutory regime a common law duty of care giving rise to a claim in damages for failure to protect the weak against the wrong-doer: see *Hill v Chief Constable of West Yorkshire* and *Yuen Kun-yeu v A-G of Hong Kong* [1988] AC 175. In the latter case, the Privy Council whilst not deciding the point said that there was much force in the argument that if the regulators had been held liable in that case the principles leading to such liability 'would surely be equally applicable to a wide range of regulatory agencies, not only in the financial field, but also, for example, to the factory inspectorate and social workers, to name only a few' (see [1988] AC 175 at 198).

In my judgment, the courts should proceed with great care before holding liable in negligence those who have been charged by Parliament with the task of protecting society from the wrong-doings of others.

[Lord Browne-Wilkinson proceeded to reject the plaintiffs' claims of vicarious liability, stating (*inter alia*) that 'the same considerations which have led me to the view that there is no direct duty of care owed by the local authorities apply with at least equal force to the question whether it would be just and reasonable to impose such a duty of care on the individual social workers and the psychiatrist.' He therefore dismissed both appeals]

Lord Jauncey delivered a short concurring opinion. **Lord Lane** and **Lord Ackner** concurred with Lord Browne-Wilkinson. **Lord Nolan** concurred with most of Lord Browne-Wilkinson's opinion but dissented on one matter, considered further below.

Appeals in the child abuse actions dismissed.

COMMENTARY

The primary grounds for the decision of the House of Lords that neither the council nor its employees owed the plaintiffs any duty of care was that recognition of such a duty would not be fair, just, and reasonable, but their Lordships also ruled out certain of the claims on somewhat narrower grounds (not considered in the extract). First, the psychiatrist in the *Newham* case was in any case protected from liability by a principle of witness immunity as, if evidence of abuse had been found, 'proceedings by the local authority for the protection of the child would ensue and...her findings would be the evidence on which those proceedings would be based' (per Lord Browne-Wilkinson). Investigations undertaken in these circumstances could not be made the basis of a subsequent claim in negligence, for example, because the threat of liability might deter the full and frank disclosure of information. Secondly, the House of Lords ruled (Lord Nolan dissenting) that the psychiatrist and social worker in the *Newham* case owed no duty of care to the child they interviewed (other than not themselves to injure her), or indeed to her mother, because they were retained by the local authority to advise the local authority, not the plaintiffs, and had therefore assumed responsibility only to the former. In Lord Browne-Wilkinson's view, the position of the employees was analogous to that of a doctor instructed by a life insurer whose duty was only to insurance company, not to the insured. This reasoning was applied by the Court of Appeal in the subsequent case of *Kapfunde v Abbey National plc* [1999] 1 ICR 1 (doctor advising employer about health of job applicants owed no duty to the latter).

For further analysis of the decision, see Cane (1996) 112 LQR 13; Fleming [1996] CLJ 29; and Lowry and Oughton (1996) 4 Tort L Rev 12.

Further Proceedings in the European Court of Human Rights

Both child abuse cases were subsequently taken to the European Court of Human Rights on the application of the unsuccessful plaintiffs in the domestic litigation. In *Z v United Kingdom* [2001] 2 FLR 612, arising out of the *Bedfordshire* case, the Court ruled unanimously that there had been a violation of the applicants' rights under Article 3 of the Convention (prohibition against torture and inhuman or degrading treatment). The state had a positive obligation to take measures to ensure that individuals within its jurisdiction—particularly children and other vulnerable persons—were not subjected to torture or inhuman or degrading treatment, even if administered by a private individual, provided the authorities knew or ought to have known of the ill-treatment in question. The applicants' neglect and abuse undoubtedly amounted to inhuman and degrading treatment, and was brought to the local authority's attention several years before it took the applicants into emergency care. On the facts, even allowing for the difficult and sensitive decisions which social services departments have to make, the local authority was guilty of a failure to take reasonable steps to protect the applicants' Article 3 rights. The Court also found, by way of consequence, that the absence of any mechanism for establishing such liability in domestic law constituted a violation of Article 13 of the Convention (right to an effective remedy).

In *TP v United Kingdom* [2001] 2 FLR 549, arising out of the *Newham* case, the Court found a violation of the applicants' rights under Article 8 of the Convention (right to respect for private and family life). The actual decision is rather complex, and it is important to note that it was not the child applicant's removal from her mother that was found to have contravened the Convention. Although this amounted to an interference with their right to respect for family life, it was justified under Article 8(2) as it was in accordance with the law, pursued a legitimate aim—being clearly aimed at protecting the 'health or morals' and the 'rights and freedoms' of the child—and could be regarded as necessary in a democratic society. The Court noted that there were strong suspicions that the child had been abused, and well-founded doubts about the mother's ability to protect her, and concluded that the mistaken identification of 'John' was not so serious a mistake as to render the decision to take her into care illegitimate. What did amount to a violation of the applicants' rights under Article 8, however, was the authority's behaviour *after* the child was taken into its care, for it did not disclose the transcript of the interview which induced it to take this drastic action until a year later. Although the authority had considered that disclosure would have posed a risk to the child's welfare, it should at the least have sought a judicial ruling on the question, and its failure to do so had prevented the mother from being adequately involved in decisions made about her daughter's care, violating both applicants' rights under Article 8. As in *Z v United Kingdom*, the failure to provide a remedy for violation of the applicants' substantive rights under the Convention amounted to a further violation of Article 13.

The Strasbourg Court's decisions are not binding in domestic law, but English courts are required by s. 2 of the Human Rights Act to take account of its jurisprudence in any proceedings in which a question arises in connection with a Convention right. In fact, even before the Act came into effect, there were signs that the courts were beginning to soften the hard-line approach of *X v Bedfordshire* CC (see *Barrett v London Borough of Enfield*, below). Whether the implementation of the Act was cause for further refinement of the common law principles in this area was subsequently considered by both the Court of Appeal and the House of Lords in *D v East Berkshire Community Health NHS Trust*, below.

Barrett v London Borough of Enfield [2001] 2 AC 550

The plaintiff had been in the care of the local authority between the ages of 10 months and 18 years. During that time he was moved nine times between different foster placements. He alleged that he had developed psychiatric illness as a result and this was due to the negligence of the local authority. His claim was struck out in the county court and the Court of Appeal dismissed his appeal, ruling that (1) the considerations of fairness, justice and reasonableness identified by Lord Browne-Wilkinson in *X v Bedfordshire CC* also applied to preclude any claim in negligence by a child who is placed by the local authority in an inappropriate foster home, and (2) the plaintiff's complaints were essentially about matters involving the local authority's exercise of discretion in the performance of its statutory responsibilities. The plaintiff appealed to the House of Lords. The extracts below deal only with the former point.

Lord Slynn

[I]n the *Bedfordshire* case, your Lordships' House accepted...that in considering the direct liability in common law of the local authorities, 'the public policy consideration which has first claim on the loyalty of the law is that wrongs should be remedied and that very potent counter considerations are required to overrule that policy.' Yet a number of policy considerations in those cases led to the conclusion that it would not be fair, just and reasonable (the third test in the *Caparo* case) to impose a duty of care on the local authorities. Lord Browne-Wilkinson in his speech attached importance in particular (i) to the multi-disciplinary Child Protection Conference involved in deciding whether a child should be placed on the Child Protection Register; (ii) to the balance involved in dealing with the 'extra-ordinarily delicate decisions' in having regard to the rights of the child, but also to the advantages of not disrupting the family environment; (iii) to the risk of the authority being over-cautious and defensive if it were subject to judicial decisions in a damages claim; (iv) to the fact that the statutory complaints procedure and the Ombudsman would allow complaints to be investigated; (v) to the fact that no analogous duty had been recognised before.

Whilst not casting doubt on the validity of these factors in the context of the investigations, or the steps which it was said should have been taken, in those cases of child abuse and neglect of educational needs, it does not seem to me that they necessarily have the same force separately or cumulatively in the present case. Thus, although once a child is in care, there may well be cooperation between different social welfare bodies, the responsibility is that of the local authority and its social and other professional staff. The decision to remove the child from its home is already taken and the authority has statutory powers in relation to the child which do not necessarily involve the exercise of the kind of discretion involved in taking a child from its family into care. As to the likelihood of an authority being over-cautious, I am of the same opinion as Evans LJ in the Court of Appeal in this case [1998] QB 367, 380:

> I would agree that what is said to be a 'policy' consideration, namely that imposing a duty of care might lead to defensive conduct on the part of the person concerned and might require him to spend time or resources on keeping full records or otherwise providing for self-justification, if called upon to do so, should normally be a factor of little, if any, weight. If the conduct in question is of a kind which can be measured against the standards of the reasonable man, placed as the defendant was, then I do not see why the law in the public interest should not require those standards to be observed.

Nor do I think that the remedies accepted to be available in the *Bedfordshire* case are likely to be as efficacious as the recognition by the court that a duty of care is or may be owed at common law. I agree with Sir Thomas Bingham MR in his dissenting judgment in the Court of Appeal in the *Bedfordshire* case, at p. 662G:—

> I cannot accept, as a general proposition, that the imposition of a duty of care makes no contribution to the maintenance of high standards.

In summary the *Bedfordshire* case establishes that decisions by local authorities whether or not to take a child into care with all the difficult aspects that involves and all the disruption which may come about are not ones which the courts will review by way of a claim for damages in negligence, though there may be other remedies by way of judicial review or through extra judicial routes such as the Ombudsman.

The question in the present case is different, since the child was taken into care; it is therefore necessary to consider whether any acts or omissions and if so what kind of acts or omissions can ground a claim in negligence. The fact that no completely analogous claim has been accepted by the courts previously points to the need for caution and the need to proceed 'incrementally' and 'by analogy with decided cases'. . . .

It is obvious from previous cases and indeed is self-evident that there is a real conflict between on the one hand the need to allow social welfare services exercising statutory powers to do their work in what they as experts consider is the best way in the interests first of the child, but also of the parents and of society, without an unduly inhibiting fear of litigation if something goes wrong, and on the other hand the desirability of providing a remedy in appropriate cases for harm done to a child through the acts or failure to act of such services.

It is no doubt right for the courts to restrain within reasonable bounds claims against public authorities exercising statutory powers in this social welfare context. It is equally important to set reasonable bounds to the immunity such public authorities can assert. . . .

On the basis that the *Bedfordshire* case does not conclude the present case in my view it is arguable that at least in respect of some matters alleged both individually and cumulatively a duty of care was owed and was broken. . . . Accordingly, I consider that this claim should not be struck out. This does not mean that I think that the appellant must or will win. He faces considerable difficulties, but . . . I consider that he is entitled to have these matters investigated and not to have them summarily dismissed. I would accordingly allow the appeal.

Lord Browne-Wilkinson and **Lord Hutton** delivered separate concurring speeches. **Lord Nolan** and **Lord Steyn** concurred with the three speeches of their brethren.

Appeal allowed.

COMMENTARY

This was the first in a trilogy of pre-Human Rights Act decisions, also including *W v Essex CC* [2001] 2 AC 592 and *Phelps v Hillingdon LBC* [2001] 2 AC 619, in which the House of Lords exhibited a rather sceptical attitude towards the policy arguments that had prevailed in *X v Bedfordshire CC*. The factual distinction between *Barrett* and the abuse cases in *X* was that the alleged negligence in *Barrett* was in the treatment of the plaintiff while in care, whereas in *X* it was in the decision whether to take the plaintiffs into care or not. Whether this really warranted the difference in result is open to question. At the time, it was possible to see the House of Lords as being much less ready than before to strike out claims on the basis that they disclosed no cause of action because of its concern that disposing of claims without a hearing on the merits would contravene the claimant's right to a trial under

Article 6 of the European Convention, as interpreted in *Osman v United Kingdom* [1999] 1 FLR 193 (see Ch. 3.III.1, above). In *Barrett*, Lord Browne-Wilkinson explicitly pointed to confusion about the *Osman* decision's effects as a reason for exercising the power of strike-out sparingly and only in obvious cases (at 560). However, we now know that *Osman* was based on a misunderstanding of English law (see p. 151ff, above), recognition of which perhaps accounts, to some extent, for the renewed willingness to strike out unfounded claims evident in House of Lords' decisions of more recent vintage than the trilogy currently under consideration. See, e.g., *D v East Berkshire*, extracted below.

W v Essex County Council

Shortly after its decision in *Barrett*, the House of Lords also declined to strike out claims against a local authority in respect of its child-welfare responsibilities in *W v Essex CC*. A couple applied to the defendant council to become full-time specialist adolescent foster carers. During and after the vetting process, they made it clear that they were not willing to accept a foster child who was known or suspected to be a sexual abuser as they had young children of their own. They were told that their wishes would be respected. With their agreement, the council placed with them a 15-year-old boy, G. In the following month, G systematically and persistently subjected each of the four young children in the household to physical and sexual abuse. The children sued the council for damages in respect of the assaults and consequential psychiatric damage, and the parents sued for post-traumatic shock on learning what had happened. They alleged that the council knew or had reasonable cause to suspect that G was an active sexual abuser, who had previously been cautioned for sexually abusing his own sister, and that the council's social worker had deliberately lied to the parents when specifically asked whether G was a sexual abuser. The first-instance judge declined to strike out the children's claims and there was no appeal against this decision. The House of Lords was concerned only with the claim by the parents, to whom it found the council did owe an arguable duty of care. Their Lordships made no attempt to reconcile this ruling with their previous decision in *X v Bedfordshire CC*, apparently viewing the two cases as self-evidently distinguishable. (For consideration of those aspects of the decision relating to liability for negligently-inflicted psychiatric illness, see p. 347, above.)

Phelps v Hillingdon London Borough Council

Here the House of Lords turned to an issue that had been left expressly unresolved in *X v Bedfordshire*. In that case, the two child abuse cases were heard alongside three further appeals which raised the issue of special educational provision. The basic questions of law were whether a local education authority (LEA) could be held directly or vicariously liable to a pupil whose special educational needs it failed to identify, or address through the provision of special schooling, or whose needs it misidentified, in consequence of which the pupil was required to attend a special school. The claimants alleged a variety of losses flowed from the defendant LEA's breach of duty, including the impairment of personal and intellectual development and the restriction of vocational opportunities. The House of Lords ruled that, for similar reasons as applied in the abuse cases, it would not be fair, just and reasonable to impose a duty on LEAs simply by reason of their statutory duties in this area. LEAs would escape liability even if 'grossly delinquent'. But their Lordships accepted that an LEA might arguably assume a duty of care by its provision of a specialist advisory service to children with educational difficulties, and that similar duties were also arguably assumed by the authorities' educational psychologists, and perhaps other members of their staff who held themselves out as having special skills. Lord Browne-Wilkinson explained, at 763–4, that the position of such employees was 'quite different from that of the doctor and social worker in the child abuse cases':

There is no potential conflict of duty between the professional's duties to the plaintiff and his duty to the educational authority. Nor is there any obvious conflict between the professional being under a duty of care to the plaintiff and the discharge by the authority of its statutory duties.

He stated, however, that the duty of care provisionally recognised might have to be limited or excluded if any such conflicts were to emerge at full trial of the issue.

The opportunity to resolve the matter following a full hearing on the evidence arose in *Phelps v Hillingdon*. In a group of conjoined appeals, the first-named plaintiff ('Pamela') sought damages for the negligence of the defendant council's educational psychologist in failing to diagnose her dyslexia when she was referred for testing by her school at the age of 11. As a result, she received inappropriate schooling for several years and her development suffered. Shortly before she left school at 16, she was privately diagnosed as dyslexic. She sought damages for the loss of earnings she would have been able to make if her learning difficulties had been properly identified and addressed, and for the cost of private tuition in the future. At trial, Garland J ruled that the educational psychologist's misdiagnosis had been negligent and found the defendant council vicariously liable. The Court of Appeal allowed the council's appeal on the basis that neither the council, nor its educational psychologist, owed Pamela a duty of care, Stuart-Smith LJ expressing concern that the refusal to exercise the power of strike-out in *X v Bedfordshire* had 'led to a proliferation of claims' against educational psychologists employed by local authorities: [1999] 1 WLR 500 at 516. Pamela appealed successfully to the House of Lords. The Law Lords ruled that an educational psychologist called in to advise on Pamela's assessment and future provision for her, in circumstances where it was clear that Pamela's parents and teachers would follow that advice, owed her a duty of care for whose breach the defendant LEA would be vicariously liable. Their Lordships were notably sceptical of the countervailing policy arguments relied upon by the defence. Lord Clyde, for example, stated (at 672):

I am not persuaded that the recognition of a liability upon employees of the education authority for damages for negligence in education would lead to a flood of claims, or even vexatious claims, which would overwhelm the school authorities, nor that it would add burdens and distractions to the already intensive life of teachers. Nor should it inspire some peculiarly defensive attitude in the performance of their professional responsibilities. On the contrary it may have the healthy effect of securing that high standards are sought and secured. If it is thought that there would only be a few claims and for that reason the duty should not be recognised, the answer must be that if there are only a few claims there is the less reason to refuse to allow them to be entertained. As regards the need for this remedy, even if there are alternative procedures by which some form of redress might be obtained, such as resort to judicial review, or to an ombudsman, or the adoption of such statutory procedures as are open to parents, which might achieve some correction of the situation for the future, it may only be through a claim for damages at common law that compensation for the damage done to the child may be secured for the past as well as the future.

Any fear of a flood of claims may be countered by the consideration that in order to get off the ground the claimant must be able to demonstrate that the standard of care fell short of that set by the *Bolam* test: *Bolam v Friern Hospital Management Committee* [1957] 1 WLR 582. That is deliberately and properly a high standard in recognition of the difficult nature of some decisions which those to whom the test applies require to make and of the room for genuine differences of view on the propriety of one course of action as against another.

The decision of the House of Lords was based on the LEA's vicarious liability for the negligence of its educational psychologist. As the House of Lords found for the claimant on this basis, it was not necessary to go on to consider the LEA's direct liability for breach of its personal duty towards the claimant (though, in one of the other appeals heard at the same time, the Lords ruled that the existence of a personal duty was at least arguable). It appears, in any case, that the Lords thought the policy arguments applying to the liability of the employed psychologist might differ from those applying to the LEA's personal liability. It was not convinced by the Court of Appeal's concern that recognition of the vicarious liability would circumvent the LEA's protection against direct claims. As public bodies can only act through individuals, many of whom will be employees, it will frequently be easier for the claimant to establish liability against the public body vicariously (assuming the employee commits a tort). In determining whether it is fair, just and reasonable to recognise a duty of care on the employee, the only relevant policy concerns are those affecting his or her relationship with the claimant, and not the full range of policy concerns that arise in considering the public body's direct liability. Of course, there may be circumstances in which those concerns are very similar, and preclude the imposition of a duty of care on the employee too (see, e.g., *D v East Berkshire*, below).

Although the analysis of the policy considerations in *Phelps* may not be logically inconsistent with the reasoning in *X v Bedfordshire*, a change of judicial tone was certainly apparent, inducing one commentator to applaud the House of Lords for 'a decisive move away from blanket exclusions of duties of care for public services' (Fairgrieve, 'Pushing Back the Boundaries of Public Authority Liability. Tort Law Enters the Classroom' [2002] PL 288 at 307). Whether this change of tone was to last will be considered after the following extracts.

For further (more critical) analysis of the decision, see Mullis, 'A rod for the hunch-backed teacher?' (2001) 13 CFLQ 331.

D v East Berkshire Community Health NHS Trust [2003] EWCA Civ 1151, [2004] QB 558 and [2005] UKHL 23, [2005] 2 AC 373

In three separate appeals, child welfare professionals (doctors and social workers) had made unfounded allegations of child abuse against one or both of the parents. In the *East Berkshire* case, the mother was accused of suffering from Munchausen Syndrome by Proxy and of having fabricated her son's medical history of severe allergic reactions. The boy was put on the social services 'at risk' register until, six months later, tests confirmed he was suffering from extensive and severe allergies. In the *Dewsbury* case, a girl suffered from an initially undiagnosed medical condition which produced discoloured patches on her skin. She was taken to hospital after she hurt herself in the genital area while riding her bicycle and, having regard to marks on her legs, the consultant paediatrician concluded that she had been sexually abused and informed social services; as a consequence, her father was denied access to her in hospital. Ten days later, the correct diagnosis was made and social services accepted that there was no question of abuse. In the *Oldham* case, an infant born with brittle bones was taken to hospital with a broken femur, which was classified as an 'inflicted injury'. The police and social services were informed, and a care order was granted, resulting in an eight-month period of separation from her parents until the correct diagnosis of brittle bones was made. In each case, parent or parents brought an action for damages in negligence. In the *Dewsbury* case, the child also claimed.

In the Court of Appeal, the welfare professionals were found to have owed a duty of care to the child (in the *Dewsbury* case) but not to any of the parents. Dealing with the duty to the child, the Court stated:

> 83 In so far as the position of a child is concerned, we have reached the firm conclusion that the decision in *X (Minors) v Bedfordshire County Council* [1995] 2 AC 633 cannot survive the Human Rights Act. Where child abuse is suspected the interests of the child are paramount: see section 1 of the Children Act 1989. Given the obligation of the local authority to respect a child's Convention rights, the recognition of a duty of care to the child on the part of those involved should not have a significantly adverse effect on the manner in which they perform their duties. In the context of suspected child abuse, breach of a duty of care in negligence will frequently also amount to a violation of article 3 or article 8. The difference, of course, is that those asserting that wrongful acts or omissions occurred before October 2000 will have no claim under the Human Rights Act 1998. This cannot, however, constitute a valid reason of policy for preserving a limitation of the common law duty of care which is not otherwise justified. On the contrary, the absence of an alternative remedy for children who were victims of abuse before October 2000 militates in favour of the recognition of a common law duty of care once the public policy reasons against this have lost their force.
>
> 84 It follows that it will no longer be legitimate to rule that, as a matter of law, no common law duty of care is owed to a child in relation to the investigation of suspected child abuse and the initiation and pursuit of care proceedings. It is possible that there will be factual situations where it is not fair, just or reasonable to impose a duty of care, but each case will fall to be determined on its individual facts.

There was no appeal to the House of Lords against this conclusion, and the Law Lords seem to have conceded its correctness (see, e.g., Lord Nicholls at [82]). Their Lordships' sole concern was the parents' appeal against the Court of Appeal's decision that the welfare professionals owed them no duty of care.

Lord Nicholls

70 There are two cardinal features in these cases. One feature is that a parent was suspected of having deliberately harmed his or her own child or having fabricated the child's medical condition. The other feature, which is to be assumed, is that the ensuing investigation by the doctors was conducted negligently. In consequence, the suspected parent's family life was disrupted, to greater or lesser extent, and the suspected parent suffered psychiatric injury.

71 It is the combination of these features which creates the difficult problem now before the House. In the ordinary course the interests of parent and child are congruent. This is not so where a parent wilfully harms his child. Then the parent is knowingly acting directly contrary to his parental responsibilities and to the best interests of his child. So the liability of doctors and social workers in these cases calls into consideration two countervailing interests, each of high social importance: the need to safeguard children from abuse by their own parents, and the need to protect parents from unnecessary interference with their family life.

72 The first of these interests involves protection of children as the victims of crime. Child abuse is criminal conduct of a particularly reprehensible character: children are highly vulnerable members of society. Child abuse is also a form of criminal conduct peculiarly hard to combat, because its existence is difficult to discover. Babies and young children are unable to complain, older children too frightened. If the source of the abuse is a parent, the child is at risk from his primary and natural protector within the privacy of his home. This both increases the risk of abuse and means that investigation necessitates intrusion into highly sensitive areas of family life, with the added complication that the parent who is responsible for the abuse will give a false account of the child's history.

73 The other, countervailing interest is the deep interest of the parent in his or her family life. Society sets much store by family life. Family life is to be guarded jealously. This is reflected in article 8 of the European Convention on Human Rights. Interference with family life requires cogent justification, for the sake of children and parents alike. So public authorities should, so far as possible, cooperate with the parents when making decisions about their children. Public authorities should disclose matters relied upon by them as justifying interference with family life. Parents should be involved in the decision-making process to whatever extent is appropriate to protect their interests adequately.

74 The question raised by these appeals is how these countervailing interests are best balanced when a parent is wrongly suspected of having abused his child. Public confidence in the child protection system can only be maintained if a proper balance is struck, avoiding unnecessary intrusion in families while protecting children at risk of significant harm . . . Clearly, health professionals must act in good faith. They must not act recklessly, that is, without caring whether an allegation of abuse is well founded or not. Acting recklessly is not acting in good faith. But are health professionals liable to the suspected parents if they fall short of the standards of skill and care expected of any reasonable professional in the circumstances? Are they exposed to claims by the parents for professional negligence? Put differently and more widely, what is the appropriate level of protection for a person erroneously suspected of child abuse? Should he be protected against professional negligence by those charged with protecting the child? Or only against lack of good faith? . . .

85 In my view the Court of Appeal reached the right conclusion on the issue arising in the present cases. Ultimately the factor which persuades me that, at common law, interference with family life does not justify according a suspected parent a higher level of protection than other suspected perpetrators is the factor conveniently labelled 'conflict of interest'. A doctor is obliged to act in the best interests of his patient. In these cases the child is his patient. The doctor is charged with the protection of the child, not with the protection of the parent. The best interests of a child and his parent normally march hand-in-hand. But when considering whether something does not feel 'quite right', a doctor must be able to act single-mindedly in the interests of the child. He ought not to have at the back of his mind an awareness that if his doubts about intentional injury or sexual abuse prove unfounded he may be exposed to claims by a distressed parent.

86 This is not to suggest doctors or other health professionals would be consciously swayed by this consideration. These professionals are surely made of sterner stuff. Doctors often owe duties to more than one person; for instance, a doctor may owe duties to his employer as well as his patient. But the seriousness of child abuse as a social problem demands that health professionals, acting in good faith in what they believe are the best interests of the child, should not be subject to potentially conflicting duties when deciding whether a child may have been abused, or when deciding whether their doubts should be communicated to others, or when deciding what further investigatory or protective steps should be taken. The duty they owe to the child in making these decisions should not be clouded by imposing a conflicting duty in favour of parents or others suspected of having abused the child.

87 This is not to say that the parents' interests should be disregarded or that the parents should be kept in the dark. The decisions being made by the health professionals closely affect the parents as well as the child. Health professionals are of course fully aware of this. They are also mindful of the importance of involving the parents in the decision-making process as fully as is compatible with the child's best interests. But it is quite a step from this to saying that the health professionals personally owe a suspected parent a duty sounding in damages.

88 The claimants sought to meet this 'conflict of interest' point by noting that the suggested duty owed to parents has the same content as the duty owed to the child: to exercise due skill and care in investigating the possibility of abuse. This response is not adequate. The time when the presence or absence of a conflict of interest matters is when the doctor is carrying out his investigation. At that time the doctor does not know whether there has been abuse by the parent. But he knows that when he is considering this possibility the interests of parent and child are diametrically opposed. The interests of the child are that the doctor should report any suspicions he may have and that he should carry out further investigation in consultation with other child care professionals. The interests of the parent do not favour either of these steps. This difference of interest in the outcome is an unsatisfactory basis for imposing a duty of care on a doctor in favour of a parent.

Lord Brown

137 There is always a temptation to say in all these cases that no one, whether a doctor concerned with possible child abuse, a witness or a prosecutor will ever in fact be held liable unless he has conducted himself manifestly unreasonably; it is unnecessary, therefore, to deny a duty of care, better rather to focus on the appropriate standard by which to judge whether it is breached. That, however, is to overlook two fundamental considerations: first, the insidious effect that his awareness of the proposed duty would have upon the mind and conduct of the doctor (subtly tending to the suppression of doubts and instincts which in the child's interests ought rather to be encouraged), and second, a consideration inevitably bound up with the first, the need to protect him against the risk of costly and vexing litigation, by no means invariably soundly based. This would seem to me a very real risk in the case of disgruntled parents wrongly suspected of abuse; all too readily they might suppose proceedings necessary to vindicate their reputation.

138 I...readily acknowledg[e]...the legitimate grievances of these particular appellants, against whom no suspicions whatever remain, sufferers from a presumed want of professional skill and care on the part of the doctors treating their children. It is they, I acknowledge, who are paying the price of the law's denial of a duty of care. But it is a price they pay in the interests of children generally. The well-being of innumerable children up and down the land depends crucially upon doctors and social workers concerned with their safety being subjected by the law to but a single duty: that of safeguarding the child's own welfare. It is that imperative which in my judgment must determine the outcome of these appeals.

Lord Bingham (dissenting)

33 ...It is hard to see how, in the present context, imposition of a duty of care towards parents could encourage healthcare professionals either to overlook signs of abuse which they should recognise or to draw inferences of abuse which the evidence did not justify. But it could help to instil a due sense of professional responsibility, and I see no reason for distinguishing between the child and the parent. To describe awareness of a legal duty as having an 'insidious effect' on the mind of a potential defendant is to undermine the foundation of the law of professional negligence...

37 It is important to be clear on the scope of the duty which the appellants seek to be allowed to try and establish as owed by the healthcare professionals. It is a duty not to cause harm to a parent foreseeably at risk of suffering harm by failing to exercise reasonable and proper care in the making of a diagnosis of child abuse. This is in substance, the appellants contend, the same duty as the healthcare professionals already owe to the child. The duty to the child is breached if signs of abuse are overlooked which a careful and thorough examination would identify, and the obvious risk then is that abuse which would otherwise be stopped is allowed to continue.

But this would be a breach of the duty if owed to a normal parent, whose interest would be the same. It would be no different if a parent were the abuser, since the duty of the healthcare professional is to serve the lawful and not the criminal interests of the parent; in any event, an undetected abuser could never be heard to complain. If a diagnosis of child abuse were made when the evidence did not warrant it (which is the factual premise of all three appeals) there would be a breach of duty to the child, with separation or disruption of the family as possible or likely consequences. But this would be a breach of the duty owed to the parents also, and the consequences are not suffered by the child alone...The appellants do not argue for a duty to serve any interest of the parents save their interest in a skilful and careful diagnosis of the medical condition of their child...

44 It is in my opinion clear...that far from presuming a conflict between the interests of child and parent the law generally presumes that they are consonant with each other or at any rate, if not consonant, not so dissonant that healthcare professionals should proceed without fully informing and consulting the parents. There are of course occasions when emergency action must be taken without informing the parents, and when information must for a time be withheld. But there is no reason why the occasional need for healthcare professionals to act in this way should displace a general rule that they should have close regard to the interests of the parents as people with, in the ordinary way, the closest concern for the welfare of their children.

Lord Rodger delivered a separate concurring speech. **Lord Steyn** concurred with all three majority speeches.

Appeal dismissed.

COMMENTARY

There is an interesting difference between the Court of Appeal's attitude towards the Human Rights Act's effect on the duty of care at common law, and the House of Lords'. The Court of Appeal viewed the Act's implementation as a factor *in favour of* the recognition of a common law duty of care, because it had changed the balance of the policy arguments considered under the third stage of the *Caparo* approach. The House of Lords, it seems, regarded the Act as *militating against* the recognition of new duties of care at common law, Lord Nicholls finding change of the established approach to duty issues to be 'unnecessary' because claims could be brought directly against public authorities under the Act where there was a breach of Convention rights (at [94]; by contrast, Lord Rodger, at [118], reserved his position on the matter). Implicitly criticising Lord Nicholls, Lord Bingham observed (at [50]):

[T]he question does arise whether the law of tort should evolve, analogically and incrementally, so as to fashion appropriate remedies to contemporary problems or whether it should remain essentially static, making only such changes as are forced upon it, leaving difficult and, in human terms, very important problems to be swept up by the Convention. I prefer evolution.

Lord Bingham returned to the theme in another dissenting opinion, in *Smith v Chief Constable of Sussex Police* [2008] UKHL 50, [2009] 1 AC 225 at [58], where he accepted that there was a strong case for developing the common law of negligence in the light of the Convention rights, and that, where a common law duty covers the same ground as a Convention right, it should, so far as practicable, develop in harmony with it. But the dominant view in the House of Lords was again that the possibility of a claim under the Human

Rights Act obviated the need for further development of the common law action (see especially [82] per Lord Hope and [136] per Lord Brown). For further analysis, see J. Steele, Damages in tort and under the Human Rights Act: remedial or functional separation? [2008] CLJ 606, and see p. 144ff, above.

The Court of Appeal's decision could well serve as the basis of a question in a legal general knowledge quiz: When is it possible for the Court of Appeal to overrule the House of Lords? Of course, the decision did not strictly speaking 'overrule' *X v Bedfordshire*, and accords with the established principle that it is open to any court to conclude that a decision of the House of Lords is inconsistent with intervening legislation (cf. McIvor's view that the Court of Appeal's analysis of the effects of the Act is 'highly questionable': (2006) 14 TLJ 205 at 206). Nevertheless, the outcome is certainly very striking. In *Kay v Lambeth London Borough Council* [2006] 2 AC 465 at [45], Lord Bingham said that the Court had been entitled to conclude that the decision of the House of Lords could not survive the implementation of the Human Rights Act, but he stressed that such a course would be permissible only in very exceptional cases.

Both the Court of Appeal and House of Lords decided that the welfare professionals owed no duty of care to the parents of children suspected of having been abused. To that extent, they can be seen to have resuscitated at least some of the policy arguments against recognition of a duty of care that had held sway in *X v Bedfordshire*. The crucial consideration here was the potential conflict of interests between child and parent. Recognising a duty to the latter might undermine the acknowledged duty to the former. Although the High Court of Australia reached the same conclusion for much the same reasons (*Sullivan v Moody* (2001) 207 CLR 562), their Lordships had earlier explicitly rejected the same argument in the comparable situation of the advocate in court (*Arthur J. S. Hall & Co (A Firm) v Simons* [2002] 1 AC 615) and, if the advocate's duty to his client is compatible with his overriding duty to the court, it is not clear why a different conclusion is warranted in relation to doctors and social workers. It should in any case be emphasised that the welfare professional's proposed duty was only to respect the *legitimate* interests of the parent, and not the criminal desires of the abuser (cf. Lord Bingham's comments at [37]). The parent can only reasonably expect the care professionals to investigate suspicious circumstances with care and skill, and to resolve the matter with due expedition if it transpires the suspicion was unfounded. Contrary to what Lord Nicholls appears to have believed, there is no question of the care professional owing the parent a duty to keep his suspicions to himself. In fact, the argument about conflicting duties seems ultimately to rest not on their strict incompatibility—because if there is a conflict the child's interests prevail—but on their potential effect psychologically: care professionals may be subconsciously induced to adopt detrimentally defensive practices. Such overkill arguments have also been rejected by the courts in other contexts: see, e.g., the extract from Lord Slynn's opinion in *Barrett*, above, and note Lord Reid's robust rejection of these concerns in the *Dorset Yacht* case [1970] AC 1004 at 1033: 'experience leads me to believe that Her Majesty's servants are made of sterner stuff.' (See also *D v E Berks*, at [33], per Lord Bingham, extracted above.) This again raises the question why such concerns should be given such weight here.

For further criticism of the majority approach, from opposed perspectives, see Bailey, 'Public authority liability in negligence: the continued search for coherence' (2006) 26 LS 155 at 176–82, and McIvor (2006) 14 TLJ 205 (who argues that the majority did not go far enough, and should have recognised that the policy arguments they relied upon precluded a duty even to the child). Additional extracts from the case may be found at p. 125, above.

Not Fair, Just and Reasonable to Impose a Duty: Other Cases

Policy arguments comparable to those relied upon in *X v Bedfordshire* and *D v East Berkshire* have also led to the denial of a duty of care in a variety of other circumstances. In *Elguzouli-Daf v Commissioner of Police for the Metropolis* [1995] QB 335, for example, the Court of Appeal rejected claims by remand prisoners held in custody for excessive periods of time as a result of the alleged negligence of the Crown Prosecution Service. The court held that the risk of defensive action by prosecutors, and the diversion of resources away from the CPS's discharge of its primary responsibilities, 'outweigh[ed] the dictates of individualised justice' (at 349, per Steyn LJ). For similar reasons, the Court of Appeal also dismissed an action for negligent detention by a Liberian asylum-seeker against the immigration authorities (see *W v Home Office* [1997] Imm AR 302, and see also *Harris v Evans* [1998] 1 WLR 1285: HSE inspector).

In *Jain v Trent Strategic Health Authority* [2009] UKHL 4, [2009] 1 AC 853 the claimants lost their nursing home business after the local health authority unreasonably made an ex parte, without notice application to a magistrate for cancellation of their statutorily required registration. By the time the claimants were able to present their side of the story, in the appeal hearing six months later, their business had suffered irreversible damage. They then lost their action for damages. The HRA was not effective at the relevant time, so the claimants had to rely on common law negligence. The Law Lords rejected their claim on the basis that the authority owed them no duty of care. Lord Scott (delivering the leading opinion) highlighted, amongst the considerations of policy that dictated this conclusion, the defendant's status as a public authority (at [28]):

[W]here action is taken by a state authority under statutory powers designed for the benefit or protection of a particular class of persons, a tortious duty of care will not be held to be owed by the state authority to others whose interests may be adversely affected by an exercise of the statutory power. The reason is that the imposition of such a duty would or might inhibit the exercise of the statutory powers and be potentially adverse to the interests of the class of persons the powers were designed to benefit or protect, thereby putting at risk the achievement of their statutory purpose...

Their Lordships repeatedly expressed their regret at the outcome, Lord Carswell noting (at [52]): 'Unhappily, improvements in procedure adopted in the future and changes in the law will not help the claimants. They will understandably feel aggrieved by the extent of the power entrusted to officials and the extent of its misuse in their case...' (See also Baroness Hale at [42]: 'a serious injustice...which deserved a remedy.') Is it right for the courts to declare their impotence in such cases, and to trust to the legislator to amend the law?

Perhaps the most notorious reliance on such arguments was by the House of Lords in the context of police investigations in *Hill v Chief Constable of West Yorkshire* [1989] AC 53, extracted at p. 143, above. It was the *Hill* reasoning that was the chief target for attack of the ECtHR in its decision in *Osman v United Kingdom*, which, as we have noted, threatened for a time to undermine English law's basic approach to the duty of care issues. Following the Strasbourg Court's acceptance that it had misunderstood the nature of the requirement of fairness, justice and reasonableness under the *Caparo* approach, the House of Lords took the opportunity to endorse the continued application of the *Hill* approach in *Brooks v Commissioner of Police of the Metropolis* [2005] UKHL 24, [2005] 1 WLR 1495 (noted p. 144, above). It may be observed, however, that in many of the circumstances in which the *Hill* reasoning would lead to the denial of any duty of care at common law, it will now be possible to bring a claim against the police under the Human Rights Act. In *Van Colle v Chief*

Constable of Hertfordshire [2008] UKHL 50, [2009] 1 AC 225, the House of Lords affirmed that the police, as a public authority under the Act, may have a positive obligation to take reasonable preventive measures to protect the Article 2, ECHR rights of an individual whose life they know or ought to know is at real and immediate risk as a result of the criminal acts of a third party. This aspect of the ECtHR's *Osman* decision survives. But the Law Lords emphasized that the test of real and immediate risk is not easily satisfied, the threshold being high (see also *In re Officer L* [2007] UKHL 36, [2007] 1 WLR 2135 at [20], per Lord Carswell). In *van Colle*, the deceased was murdered after reporting to the police that he had received telephone threats while scheduled to act as a prosecution witness at the trial of a minor criminal. A disciplinary tribunal found that the officer in charge of the case was guilty of not performing his duties conscientiously and diligently in respect of witness intimidation. But the House of Lords concluded unanimously that the warning signs in the case were very much less clear and obvious than those in *Osman* (itself a case where the risk was found not to have been real and immediate) and found that no liability under the Human Rights Act arose on the facts. For further consideration of the real and immediate risk test in the House of Lords, see *Savage v South Essex Partnership NHS Foundation Trust* [2008] UKHL 74, [2009] 1 AC 681 and *Mitchell v Glasgow City Council* [2009] UKHL 11, [2009] 1 AC 874.

Given the stringency of the requirements of the HRA claim, and the courts' evident disinclination to treat the Act as justifying any substantial modification in their approach to public authority liability at common law, it appears that the Act's implementation has done little to improve the prospects of obtaining damages of those injured by the careless exercise of statutory powers.

IV. The Private Law Dimension (ii): Statutory Responsibilities as a Source of Affirmative Duties

As the role of a public body is in many cases supervisory or regulatory, complaints made against it frequently relate to non-feasance rather than misfeasance (but not always: see, e.g., *M v Newham District Council* [1995] 2 AC 633). Notwithstanding the general reluctance of the courts to recognise duties of affirmative action, suits of this nature have been successful in circumstances where a private organisation or individual might equally have been liable (see, e.g., *Welton v North Cornwall District Council* [1997] 1 WLR 570). The most important question to arise, however, is whether the mere existence of a statutory duty or power is sufficient to give rise to a common law duty to act, even in circumstances in which a private individual would not be held legally responsible.

In *East Suffolk Rivers Catchment Board v Kent* [1941] AC 74, a majority of the House of Lords apparently answered this question in the negative, holding that a rivers authority repairing a breach in the sea wall could not be held liable for unnecessary delays in the work which prolonged the period during which the plaintiff's pasture land was flooded. The reason given was that it could not be said that the delay had caused the plaintiff any damage he would not have sustained had the authority done nothing. Lord Romer stated the principle to be applied in such cases in the following terms (at 102):

> Where a statutory authority is entrusted with a mere power it cannot be made liable for any damage sustained by a member of the public by reason of a failure to exercise that power. If in the exercise of their discretion they embark upon an execution of the power, the only duty they owe to any member of the public is not thereby to add to the damages that he would have suffered had they done nothing. So long as they exercise their discretion honestly, it is for them to determine the method by which and the time within which and the time during which the power shall be exercised; and they cannot be made liable, except to the extent that I have just mentioned, for any damage that would have been avoided had they exercised their discretion in a more reasonable way.

The question for the courts subsequently, metaphorically speaking, has been whether to make a breach in the *East Suffolk* wall.

The common law's principal challenge to the authority of the *East Suffolk* case was made by Lord Wilberforce in *Anns v Merton London Borough Council* [1978] AC 728. His Lordship held that the *East Suffolk* ruling could not be taken to preclude a finding that the statutory scheme under which a public body operated gave rise to a duty of care. In his opinion, the decision antedated the development of a generalised liability in respect of negligent conduct, which was only accepted some years after Lord Atkin's formulation of the neighbour principle in *Donoghue v Stevenson*. On the facts of *Anns*, this allowed the House of Lords to decide that a local authority, with statutory responsibility for inspecting building works in the interests of public health and safety, was liable to compensate lessees of a new block of flats who suffered loss as a result of the authority's negligent failure to inspect the property's foundations so as to ensure its structural soundness; it was necessary to repair the defective foundations, and cracks in the walls that they had caused, in order to protect the plaintiffs' health and safety. This result was especially controversial because the plaintiff's loss was purely economic—it arose from an inherent defect in the property—and *Anns* has since been overruled on this point (see *Murphy v Brentwood District Council* [1991] 1 AC 398). But the status of that aspect of the decision which is under consideration here has not yet been authoritatively determined, although the issue was raised again in the case of *Stovin v Wise* [1996] AC 923. In *Stovin*, Lord Hoffmann noted that until the decision in *Anns v Merton London Borough* [1978] AC 728 there was no authority for treating a statutory power as giving rise to a common law duty of care. After doubting Lord Wilberforce's explanation of *East Suffolk*, he continued (at 952–3):

> Whether a statutory duty gives rise to a private cause of action is a question of construction (see *Hague v Deputy Governor of Parkhurst Prison, Weldon v Home Office* [1992] 1 AC 58) [extracted p. 623, below]. It requires an examination of the policy of the statute to decide whether it was intended to confer a right to compensation for breach. Whether it can be relied upon to support the existence of a common law duty of care is not exactly a question of construction, because the cause of action does not arise out of the statute itself. But the policy of the statute is nevertheless a crucial factor in the decision....
>
> In the case of a mere statutory power, there is the further point that the legislature has chosen to confer a discretion rather than create a duty. Of course there may be cases in which Parliament has chosen to confer a power because the subject matter did not permit a duty to be stated with sufficient precision. It may nevertheless have contemplated that in circumstances in which it would be irrational not to exercise the power, a person who suffered loss because it had not been exercised, or not properly exercised, would be entitled to compensation.

I therefore do not say that a statutory 'may' can never give rise to a common law duty of care. I prefer to leave open the question of whether *Anns*' case was wrong to create any exception to Lord Romer's statement of principle in the *East Suffolk* case.

The issue came again before the House of Lords in the following case.

Gorringe v Calderdale Metropolitan Borough Council [2004] UKHL 15, [2004] 1 WLR 1057

The claimant was driving too fast for safety on an undulating country road. When she reached the crest of a rise, it appears that she saw a bus coming towards her in the opposite direction and, perhaps thinking that it was on her side of the road, braked sharply causing her wheels to lock and her car to skid head-on into the bus's path. She suffered very serious injuries and was never able subsequently to give an account of the accident. She brought an action for damages against the defendant council, the relevant highway authority, alleging that it ought to have painted the word 'SLOW' on the road surface on the rise towards the crest. She contended that this duty arose either under the Highways Act 1980, s. 41 (duty to maintain the highway), or at common law. In fact, the road had previously been marked with a 'SLOW' warning but that had disappeared, probably when the road was repaired seven or eight years prior to the accident. The claimant was successful at trial but the defendant council appealed successfully to the Court of Appeal [2002] RTR 446, which (by a majority) found that the council was not in breach of any duty to the claimant. The claimant appealed to the House of Lords. The extract deals only with the duty of care at common law.

Lord Brown

96 Section 39 of the Road Traffic Act 1988 imposes upon local authorities certain statutory duties, couched in the broadest of terms, designed to promote road safety and to prevent road accidents. It is Mrs Gorringe's case that in the discharge of those duties the respondent local authority (Calderdale) ought properly to have warned her of the dangers of the road ahead, in particular by painting a 'Slow' sign on the road surface. Although acquitted of all blame by the trial judge, Mrs Gorringe now accepts that she herself must be regarded as having approached the crest at a negligently fast speed. Assume, however, that a 'Slow' sign on the road would have protected her against her own negligence. Was Calderdale duty-bound to put it there and, if so, is a breach of such duty actionable in private law? These are the issues raised before your Lordships' House.

97 It is not suggested that Calderdale's section 39 duty is actionable as such in private law. In other words it is accepted that no claim could arise here for breach of statutory duty. What is suggested, however, is that a common law duty of care arises out of Calderdale's statutory duty, and that Calderdale would be liable in a private law claim for damages for breach of that duty.

98 The argument is founded principally on *Larner v Solihull Metropolitan Borough Council* [2001] RTR 469, in which the Court of Appeal, although rejecting the claim on the facts, contemplated that damages for breach of a common law duty of care would be recoverable for a local authority's failure to paint warning signs on the road, based upon a breach of its section 39 duty, provided always that the default complained of was not within the ambit of the authority's discretion (paras 13 and 15); provided, in other words, that the council could be shown to have acted irrationally, that being the suggested touchstone by which the breach of a public law duty gives rise to common law liability.

99 In deciding that a common law duty of care could arise, the court adopted the reasoning in favour of such a duty given by the minority of the House in *Stovin v Wise* [1996] AC 923, and in addition relied on a trilogy of decisions in your Lordships' House—*X (Minors) v Bedfordshire County Council* [1995] 2 AC 633, *Barrett v Enfield London Borough Council* [2001] 2 AC 550 and *Phelps v Hillingdon London Borough Council* [2001] 2 AC 619—in each of which a duty of care was held (at least arguably) to have arisen.

100 ...[T]he common law duty of care in those cases was found or suggested to have arisen not by reference to the existence of the respective authorities' statutory powers and duties but rather from the relationships in fact created between those authorities and the children for whom in differing ways they had assumed responsibility. I would add, moreover, this further distinction. Unless in those cases the court were to find the authority's various responsibilities capable of giving rise to a common law duty of care, those wronged children, themselves wholly blameless, would go uncompensated, however inadequately their interests had been safeguarded. In the highway context, by contrast, the claimant (or some other road user involved in the accident) will almost inevitably himself have been at fault. In these circumstances it seems to me entirely reasonable that the policy of the law should be to leave the liability for the accident on the road user who negligently caused it rather than look to the highway authority to protect him against his own wrong.

101 With regard to the physical state of the highway itself, of course, the legislation has since 1961 (Highways (Miscellaneous Provisions) Act) placed the responsibility for its maintenance upon the highway authority, a duty now found in section 41 of the Highways Act 1980, as amended... This duty, moreover, is actionable as such so as to give rise to a private law claim for damages. Road users, therefore, are entitled to rely upon the state of the road's surface and accordingly the primary liability for any loss resulting from a breach of the section 41 duty rests on the authority. Road users are not, however, entitled to rely upon the highway authority with regard to the various other hazards of road use. They are not entitled to suppose that their journeys will be free from these or that the need for care will generally be highlighted so as to protect them from their own negligence.

102 What I have said thus far is in the context of road accidents involving negligence on the part of at least one of the road users involved. But that is because I find it difficult to contemplate a case in which a road accident could occur without such negligence unless either (a) it results from the physical state of the road (in which case, as already explained, liability will in any event rest upon the highway authority), or (b) the highway authority will, irrespective of any particular statutory power or duty, be liable in a conventional common law negligence action for having enticed the motorist to his fate by some positive act. Assuming that the road user is not to be regarded as negligent, he must inevitably have been misled into ignoring whatever danger precipitated his accident. Although motorists are not entitled to be forewarned of the ordinary hazards of highway use, plainly they must not be trapped into danger. If, for example, an authority were to signal a one-way street but omit to put 'No Entry' signs at the other end, it might well be found liable, not because of any statutory power or duty to erect such signs but rather because it induced a perfectly careful motorist into the path of danger. Or assume road markings indicating where it is safe to overtake and where it is not and that by some crass mistake in the painting of these a motorist were to be ensnared into the path of an oncoming vehicle previously hidden in a blind spot ahead. That too would suggest to me misfeasance of the kind traditionally attracting tortious liability without the need to look for some statutory power or duty as its foundation. Such cases, however, may be expected to be few and far between...

103 There seems to me, therefore, no good reason for superimposing upon such general powers and duties as are conferred upon highway authorities a common law duty of care

in respect of their exercise. Nor does it seem to me that Parliament can have intended a private law liability in damages to flow from a public law failure in the exercise of the authority's powers or the discharge of its duties. Where with regard to highways Parliament does intend users to have a remedy for damages it says so…A maintenance obligation of this nature, moreover, lends itself to enforcement by way of private law action altogether more readily than a more general duty of care…One cannot over-maintain the fabric of the public highway. Warning overload, however, is all too easily imaginable. As it is, road users tend to discount such warnings as are implicit in the various speed limits and other cautionary signs to which they are subject. The currency would be debased still further were highway authorities, anxious to avoid lengthy and expensive litigation of the kind Calderdale has been subjected to here, to feel obliged to multiply its street signing still further.

104 It follows from all this that, sympathetic though inevitably one must feel towards someone as severely injured as Mrs Gorringe, she cannot look to Calderdale for any part of her loss. Its only duty towards her was to maintain the physical condition of the highway as it did and not to ensnare her into unforeseeable danger. On the trial judge's finding that she herself was blameless, one could have understood a further conclusion that she must necessarily therefore have been trapped into her fate by Calderdale's negligence. Once it is recognised, however, that the danger of driving as she did should have been obvious to her, as is now accepted, her claim must fail. Even if, contrary to the conclusions arrived at by the majority of the Court of Appeal, Calderdale failed in its public law duty under section 39, that gave rise to no corresponding breach of a duty of care actionable in private law.

Lord Steyn, **Lord Hoffmann**, **Lord Scott** and **Lord Rodger** delivered separate concurring opinions.

Appeal dismissed.

COMMENTARY

This decision continues the judicial fight-back against the perceived rise of a 'compensation culture', which so concerned the House of Lords in *Tomlinson v Congleton Borough Council*, extracted at pp. 32, 173 and 579. As in the earlier case, their Lordships clearly considered that the accident was essentially the claimant's own fault and that she should not be allowed to look to the defendant to protect her from her own wrong (see [100] above, and also at [8], per Lord Hoffmann).

The decision reasserts the restrictive approach to the superimposition of common law duties on a statutory framework that was evident in *Stovin v Wise* [1996] AC 923, where the leading majority speech was delivered by Lord Hoffmann, who also sat in *Gorringe*. Talking in *Stovin* of the omission to perform a statutory duty, Lord Hoffmann stated (at 952–3):

If such a duty does not give rise to a private right to sue for breach, it would be unusual if it nevertheless gave rise to a duty of care at common law which made the public authority liable to pay compensation for foreseeable loss caused by the duty not being performed. It will often be foreseeable that loss will result if, for example, a benefit or service is not provided. If the policy of the Act is not to create a statutory liability to pay compensation, the same policy should ordinarily exclude the existence of a common law duty of care.

In *Larner*, mentioned in the extract above, the Court of Appeal suggested that there might be 'circumstances of an exceptional nature where a common law liability can arise', provided the authority acted 'wholly unreasonably': [2001] RTR 469 at 475, per Lord Woolf. The claimant in the present case relied on that dictum, but Lord Hoffmann maintained his previous line, at [32]: 'I find it difficult to imagine a case in which a common law duty can be founded simply upon the failure (however irrational) to provide some benefit which a public authority has power (or a public law duty) to provide.' Referring to the same passage in Lord Hoffmann's opinion in *Stovin*, Lord Scott in *Gorringe*, at [71], expressed his agreement but added:

Indeed, I would be inclined to go further. In my opinion, if a statutory duty does not give rise to a private right to sue for breach, the duty cannot create a duty of care that would not have been owed at common law if the statute were not there.

In the intervening years, a number of House of Lords' decisions (notably *Barrett v Enfield London Borough Council*; *Phelps v Hillingdon London Borough Council* and *W v Essex County Council*) had given some reason to believe that a more expansive approach was coming to prevail. But these, we are now told, are to be regarded as turning upon the defendant's assumption of responsibility for the claimant's welfare, a factor that would give rise to a duty of care independently of the statutory context.

Another factor that might give rise to a common law duty of affirmative action independently of any statute is the defendant's creation of a source of danger. But the House of Lords did not consider that, in the present case, the failure to paint a 'SLOW' marking on the road amounted to the creation of a danger, though it accepted that there might be other, comparable cases where the contrary conclusion was warranted. Lord Brown gave as examples a 'crass mistake' in the painting of road markings indicating it was safe to overtake, and the signalling of a one-way street with no 'No Entry' signs at the other end; such mistakes might 'induce...a perfectly careful motorist into the path of danger'. However, their Lordships were notably unenthusiastic about the Court of Appeal's decision in favour of the claimant in *Bird v Pearce* [1979] RTR 369 where it considered that the local highway authority had negligently created a hazard by removing and failing to repaint give-way markings at a junction of roads. Quite why this decision so troubled the House of Lords is hard to fathom: surely a clear indication of who has priority at a road junction is one of the most basic expectations of modern road-users, and the absence of such markings an obvious source of danger even to careful drivers. *Bird* seems a far stronger case for liability than Lord Brown's example of a crass mistake in the painting of overtaking markings: all drivers know that, whether overtaking is permitted or not, they should only overtake if they have a clear view of the road ahead and sufficient time and space to do so.

v. Evaluation and Reform

Law Commission, *Administrative Redress: Public Bodies and the Citizen*, Consultation Paper No. 187 (2008)

3.118 The underlying rationale of the tort of negligence in all cases is to provide compensation for those who suffer loss as a result of the negligence of others. As a matter of basic principle, courts consider that this standard model applies equally whether the defendant is an individual or private organisation, or a public body.

3.119 At the same time, however, courts have come to accept that claims against public bodies frequently raise particular difficulties of their own. Where the defendant is a public body, the traditional goal of ensuring compensation must be weighed against competing public interest factors, which may for one reason or another militate *against* liability. Of particular concern has been the potential for state liability to expand uncontrollably. This is acutely apparent in cases where the claimant has been injured as an *indirect* result of a public body's conduct and where the injury has consisted of *pure economic loss* . . .

3.135 In private law, courts have employed the notion of proximity as a control mechanism for limiting a defendant's exposure to liability . . . It is thought that it would be undesirable if an individual could be held to owe a duty of care to a potentially very large class of persons and in respect of loss which is widely dispersed and indeterminate . . .

3.136 By contrast, it is not immediately apparent that these reasons apply with the same force where the defendant is a public body. By their very nature, public bodies come into contact with the general population on a daily basis. They frequently enjoy extensive legal powers in respect of large sections of society, who entrust them to discharge their public functions competently. State intervention, whether in providing public welfare or in regulating private enterprise, is pervasive and it can affect the most intimate aspects of citizens' lives. Moreover, the fact that public bodies typically act in the public interest is a ground for distinguishing them from private individuals, who may generally (within limits) pursue their own self-interest in relation to other citizens with whom they do not have any voluntary relationship. For these reasons, it may be that the notion of 'proximity' . . . is inapt, or simply superfluous, as a criterion for determining liability in the citizen/state context.

3.137 Case law demonstrates that reliance on 'proximity' as a formal pre-condition to establishing a duty of care leads to results which are inconsistent and unpredictable and in some cases unjust. For example, the Home Office may negligently release a dangerous offender into society who then commits a crime. It has been held that there is not sufficient 'proximity' between the victim and the Home Office to establish a duty of care (*K v Secretary of State for the Home Department* [2002] EWCA Civ 775, (2002) 152 NLJ 917). A similar problem may arise where police officers persistently neglect valid requests for special protection by a prosecution witness and that witness is subsequently murdered (*Van Colle v Chief Constable of Hertfordshire* [2007] EWCA Civ 325 at [9]) . . .

3.161 As was the case with the notion of proximity generally, the omissions rule does not appear to be particularly well suited to the context of state wrongdoing. First and foremost, the rationales for a general principle of no-liability [see Lord Hoffmann's analysis in *Stovin v Wise*, extracted p. 465, above] do not necessarily apply with the same force in citizen/state relationships as they do in relations between private individuals. The argument that a duty to act would curtail a defendant's autonomy disregards the fact that, where the defendant is a public body, its freedom of action is already restricted by the limits of the mandate conferred upon it by democratic processes. Similarly, the economic justification for the omissions principle seems inapt. Public bodies and officials are paid to perform certain services and it may even be economically more efficient for them to act than for society to support the claimant's injury. In simple terms, it is one thing to impose upon a stranger on the beach a duty to take care to save a drowning child; it is altogether different to impose such a duty upon a lifeguard employed by the local authority. Likewise, the moral argument seems misplaced in the context of state omissions. Often, the public body will be the only body with the necessary legal powers to take action to prevent the claimant from suffering harm . . .

3.163 . . . [A] further criticism of the omissions rule is that it is capable of producing particularly unfair results. Courts have become extremely reluctant to impose a duty of care . . . It seems harsh to apply such a blanket rule, regardless of how flagrant or ill-advised the omission by the public body and irrespective of the severity of the claimant's injury.

4.2 ...[T]he 'modified corrective justice' principle...suggests that where an aggrieved citizen cannot obtain just redress for substandard administrative action through alternative, non-court based mechanisms, they should be able to access the courts to obtain redress, within certain parameters...

4.3 These parameters are expressed as a package that attempts to balance the interests of aggrieved claimants against the danger that liability might create an undue burden on resources. The consequence of this is to modify the availability of damages in judicial review and create more certainly and predictability in the tortious liability of public bodies.

4.4 In judicial review, it is suggested that damages should be available as a remedy alongside the prerogative remedies where the administrative decision involved 'serious fault' and where the claimant suffers loss. This would essentially harmonise the system with that which already exists for a 'sufficiently serious' breach of EU law.

4.5 In tort, a similar 'serious fault' scheme would apply to the sphere of public action that can be described as 'truly public'. Action undertaken by public bodies that is not 'truly public' would be subject to the ordinary law of tort. It is not proposed that our suggested scheme would replace the current regime in areas such as medical negligence. Within the 'truly public' sphere the tortious standard of negligence would be replaced by a higher standard of 'serious fault'.

4.6 Within both of these schemes, potential liability would only be imposed where it could be demonstrated that the relevant legal regime 'conferred' a benefit on the claimant. Furthermore, the package would entail modifying the blanket rule on joint and several liability in this area of public body liability...

4.9 ...'[M]odified corrective justice'... is the principle on which to base the liability of public bodies in those residual cases that require the court's attention. To summarise...

(1) In general, the principle of corrective justice underpins the relationship between the state and individual claimants;

(2) However, in certain circumstances the normal principle of corrective justice needs to be modified. This is in order to take into account certain features of the relationship between the state and potential claimants;

(3) In relation to monetary compensation, the relationship between the state and an individual claimant has a different moral complexion to the relationship between private individual claimants;

(4) An individual's relationship with and expectations of the state are such that they should look first to non-monetary remedies against the state;

(5) However, where compensation is in issue, there is a moral case for limiting it to particularly serious conduct where the state is the respondent;

(6) This modification only applies where the state is undertaking 'truly public' activity. Therefore, it does not apply where the impugned activity could equally have been carried out by a private individual.

COMMENTARY

The Law Commission seems to have attempted to steer a middle course between the views of those who think that public body liability for negligence has already been extended too far, and is generally undesirable, and those who consider that such liability does not go far enough, and results in the arbitrary, anomalous and unwarranted exclusion of deserving claims. The risk for the Law Commission is that its attempt to find a compromise approach will satisfy no one.

Amongst those who support a restrictive approach to the negligence liability of public bodies, a number of divergent political philosophies can be identified, and it is important to be alert to the range of different opinions that can be described as broadly opposed to the expansion in the liabilities of public bodies. Some commentators espouse a rugged individualism which views any reliance upon public institutions, and above all attempts to sue them when things go wrong, as symptomatic of a decline in notions of personal responsibility; according to this view, everyone should look after their own interests through personal insurance (see, e.g., P. Atiyah, *The Damages Lottery* (Oxford: Hart, 1997)). Others, self-avowedly liberal, endorse notions of social responsibility but would keep them out of tort. As Howarth has written, 'the modern welfare state, on which falls the main burden of treating and supporting accident victims, is itself the main expression of social democracy, not the rules of private law. Tort law is not about the socialisation of risk ... but about the rights and duties of individuals' ('My brother's keeper? Liability for acts of third parties' (1994) 14 LS 88 at 89). A different argument, although one which is often combined with the liberal position just outlined, is purely pragmatic, pointing to the adverse effects on the discharge of public responsibilities that would result if public bodies were held to owe generalised duties of care. This is the argument that features most prominently in the law reports. In recent scholarship, a further argument—purportedly apolitical—has been advanced with considerable vigour: public bodies should not be liable for harm that is causally attributable to their carelessness unless the victim had a right to demand the body's exercise of reasonable care for his or her benefit, and, under the 'rule of law', rights against public bodies are generally no more extensive than those against private individuals (see, e.g., R. Stevens, *Torts and Rights* (2007), ch. 10; A. Beever, *Rediscovering the Law of Negligence* (2007), ch. 9).

A rival conception of the entitlements that individuals have against the state is to be found on the other side of the debate. T. Cornford, *Towards a Public Law of Tort* (Ashgate, 2008) argues that, where a duty arising in public law is intended to benefit particular persons, corrective justice demands that there should be a prima facie right to reparation for breach of that duty. Private persons are generally entitled to expect the state to conduct itself reasonably, though Cornford accepts that compensation may be withheld if its award would unduly affect the public interest or the interests of other citizens. A similar conception of the individual's private law rights against the state seems (at least implicitly) to underpin several other critical analyses of the courts' recognition of broad areas of 'no duty', which the authors consider tantamount to condoning public body inaction and carelessness (see, e.g., Harris (1997) 113 LQR 398 at 401, and for further critical comment *Conaghan & Mansell*, p. 44ff and McIvor, *op. cit.*, p. 135 ('an entirely misguided and overly restrictive approach')).

The Law Commission's own analysis is pragmatic rather than theoretical, and accepts the relevance of considerations which, in terms of the above debate, point in different directions. On the one hand, the Commission (para. 4.41ff) identifies an expansion in the negligence liabilities of public bodies in recent decades in such areas as educational negligence, the provision of protective care to vulnerable children, and the work of the emergency services. (Can you list cases illustrative of the expansion of liability in each of these areas?) On the other hand, it accepts that this expansion has occurred in piecemeal fashion, resulting in considerable legal uncertainty, and leaving a number of deserving claimants without a remedy. (What examples are advanced by the Law Commission in the extract above? In which cases, if any, do *you* think a deserving claim was rejected for insufficient reason?)

The Law Commission's Proposals for Reform

The Law Commission's proposal for reform of the system of private law redress for loss caused by administrative action (see generally Oliphant, *European Tort Law 2008*, 213f) is that the liability of public bodies for 'truly public' acts or omissions should be limited by a new requirement of 'serious fault', and restricted to situations where the underlying legislative scheme was intended to confer rights or benefits on the individual claimant. The intention is to expand the range of cases in which damages are potentially available—because the current limitations on liability leave a number of gaps—but at the same time to counteract any consequential increase in liability costs by raising the threshold of fault. The latter consideration also underpins the Commission's further recommendation that there should be a departure from the ordinary English rule of 'joint and several' liability by which any party liable in tort for the same damage may be ordered to compensate the victim in full, albeit with the right to seek contribution or indemnity from other responsible parties. It was felt that joint and several liability could operate harshly in the present context, as the state—always an attractive target for litigation because of its 'deep pockets'—would be left to bear the full cost of compensating the victim if other responsible parties were insolvent or could not be traced, even if its culpability was comparatively small (para. 4.64ff). The Law Commission's recommendation is that there should be a judicial discretion to apportion the liability of a public body for a truly public act or omission when this would be equitable in a given situation.

The Commission (para. 4.4) explicitly links its proposed requirements of 'serious fault' and 'intent to confer a benefit' with the European Court of Justice's approach to state liability following its decision in C-6/90, *Francovich v Italy* [1991] ECR I 5357. However, the ECJ test of 'sufficiently serious breach' seems to have been inadvertently transformed in adapting it to English law, becoming in the Law Commission's proposal a test of 'serious fault'. But the ECJ test does not necessarily entail fault as it is conceived in English law, even if the degree of fault exhibited is a relevant consideration in determining seriousness: *R v Secretary of State for Transport, ex parte Factortame Ltd (No 5)* [2000] 1 AC 524. At first glance, the Law Commission's proposal therefore seems rather more restrictive than the test on which it purports to be modelled.

The requirement of an intent to confer a benefit on the claimant is superficially similar to the existing requirement of the tort of breach of statutory duty that the statute was intended to confer a private right of action on the claimant (see Ch. 11.IV, below). But the Law Commission's proposed test is in fact somewhat more easily satisfied because Parliament may intend to benefit particular sections of society by the passage of particular legislative provisions without adverting at all to the question whether an action for damages should be allowed if there is a breach of duty. If the proposal is implemented, the separate tortious liability for breach of statutory duty would effectively become redundant in actions against public bodies, and the Consultation Paper in fact contemplates its abolition in that context, though not as regards breaches of health and safety legislation (para. 4.105).

The Law Commission's proposals have received a rather hostile reception from academic commentators, who have criticized a perceived lack of clarity and coherence in the key concepts of 'serious fault', 'truly public' and 'conferral of benefit', and object to the state setting itself above the citizen by excluding its liability for 'mere' negligence. The harsh judgement of one respected commentator is that the proposals are 'unprincipled and lacking in coherence': Cornford [2009] PL 70, 70. For further criticism, see Mullender (2009) 72 MLR 961. For comment on the lack of empirical evidence for the Law Commission's analysis, see Morgan (2009) 125 LQR 215.

Addendum: the Law Commission announced in May 2010 that, given the level of opposition to its proposals, it would not pursue reform of private law redress in respect of administrative action: *Administrative Redress: Public Bodies and the Citizen* (Law Com. No. 322, 2010).

Beyond Tort Law

Even if it is thought desirable that a public body should pay compensation for those adversely affected by its action, there is disagreement about whether an expansion of the law of negligence is the correct way to achieve this. The Law Commission's own view (para. 2.3f) is that the vast majority of complaints against public bodies are handled effectively without involving the civil courts, namely by internal redress mechanisms (e.g. formal complaint procedures), external non-court avenues of redress (e.g. public inquiries and tribunals) and the public sector ombudsmen. Only in a comparatively small number of 'residual' complaints is the involvement of the courts necessary—and many of these could be addressed in proceedings for judicial review if (as the Commission recommends: para. 4.31ff) damages are made available as a remedy. In similar vein, Bailey, 'Public authority liability in negligence: the continued search for coherence' (2006) 26 LS 155 at 162 writes:

> Apart from the law of tort, compensation for losses caused through the maladministration of a public authority may be paid on an ex gratia basis, commonly but not invariably following an adverse report by an ombudsman... By contrast with tort claims, it can be seen that such schemes are broader in scope, not being confined to claimants who suffered losses of a kind covered by tort law or to acts or omissions that would constitute breach of a legal duty. The transaction costs are likely to be much lower, especially where a factual basis for a claim has been established by an ombudsman's report... [G]iven the notoriously high administrative and legal costs in obtaining tort damages, this [approach] is likely to be more satisfactory as a method of securing compensation for the victims of maladministration than an expansion of the law of tort.

If this is accepted, should reform of the law in this area focus on eliminating *all* negligence claims against public bodies in favour of providing a general remedy for public maladministration by way of a statutory compensation scheme? See further C. Harlow, *State Liability: Tort Law and Beyond* (Oxford: OUP, 2004), and, for an Anglo-French comparison, D. Fairgrieve, *State Liability in Tort: A Comparative Law Study* (Oxford: OUP, 2003), ch. 8.

In conclusion, we may observe that the choice between the different possible permutations of liability, no liability, and alternative redress is necessarily personal. None of them can be demonstrated to be either right or wrong. But differences of opinion cannot be simply reduced to reflections of different political viewpoints because even commentators of similar political persuasions have widely divergent views as to the role that tort law ought to play in modern society and its relationship with other redress mechanisms, or simply believe that tort law should be entirely apolitical.

11 SPECIAL LIABILITY REGIMES

Although much of the law of tort is based upon the general principles of common law, there are a number of situations where special liability regimes have been created. These may usefully be contrasted with general negligence liability. The first regime to be considered is employers' liability, whose origins lie in the nineteenth century. The courts of that period, anxious to protect industry against claims by employees, recognised a defence of common employment which prevented an employer from being vicariously liable for an injury to one employee caused by the negligence of another. This rule effectively left the injured employee without a remedy (as the negligent employee was unlikely to be able to satisfy a judgment against him). However, more sympathetic courts began creating *non-delegable* duties owed by the employer to the employee. If the employee was injured by a breach of one of these duties, it no longer mattered whether the breach was by a fellow employee or not, because the duty was to see that care was taken. Although the defence of common employment was abolished in 1948, the special liability rules relating to employers remain part of the law of tort, and additional liabilities have also been imposed on employers by Parliament.

Two of the most important of the other special regimes concern the liability of occupiers to those coming onto their land (governed by the Occupiers' Liability Acts of 1957 and 1984) and liability in respect of defective products (governed by the Consumer Protection Act 1987). In both these areas Parliament has intervened to remedy perceived failings in the common law. The Occupiers' Liability Acts replaced the previous common law liability of occupiers, which was generally thought to need rationalisation. A different catalyst prompted the passing of the Consumer Protection Act 1987: a Directive from the European Community requiring uniformity in the product liability laws of member states forced the United Kingdom to legislate and to create a form of strict liability in the 1987 Act. The Act has not, however, replaced the common law, and it remains open to a claimant to sue in negligence or any other tort if its elements are satisfied. Although such actions will generally be more difficult to establish than the cause of action under the Act, there are some limitations on the statutory action so it is unlikely the common law liability in respect of defective products has been rendered completely redundant.

The final parts of this chapter consider the common law action for breach of statutory duty and the development of a similar liability for violations of European Union law. These liabilities differ from negligence liability in that the source of the defendant's duty is not the common law; the claimant's case is founded on a breach of a duty imposed on the defendant by Parliament (or the European Union, as the case may be). The claimant is thus able to invoke an alternative cause of action from that in negligence, perhaps to avail himself of a strict rather than a fault-based liability (depending upon the precise terms of the legislation in question) or to by-pass restrictions on the scope of the duty of care in negligence (although the claimant must still establish causation and damage). A major impetus for the creation of breach of statutory duty domestically lay in the restrictions placed on the liability of employers to employees, and many of the early actions arise out of statutory duties imposed on employers. However, statutory duties are now imposed in a wide variety of circumstances and on public as well as private defendants. While it is generally accepted that not *every* breach of a statutory duty can give rise to a successful claim against the party upon whom the duty is imposed, the difficulty has been in articulating a principle which separates those situations where an action may lie from those where it may not. The liability for violation of EU law rights is of much more recent development, and the principles are still being worked out by the European Court of Justice. It is with this developing liability for so-called 'Euro-torts' that the chapter closes.

I. Employers' Liability

1. Introduction

For much of the twentieth Century, workplace accidents generated more tort claims than any other type of accidents. The *Pearson Commission* (vol. II, table 11) estimated that in 1973 46 per cent of tort claims arose out of workplace injuries, and another 1.2 per cent arose out of industrial disease. With motor vehicle claims, they accounted for some 88 per cent of all tort claims. However, workplace injury rates have fallen rapidly since that time, partly because of structural changes in the UK economy (e.g. a shift from heavy industry to services). The latest official figures, supplied by the Compensation Recovery Unit (CRU), record about 87,000 employers' liability claims a year, out of a total of around 812,000 claims of personal injury, i.e. approximately 11 per cent of the total. Road accident claims are statistically much more significant now (approximately 77 per cent of all personal injury claims), but employers' liability claims remain second in the list. In recent years the number of workplace disease claims has been unusually high, sometimes much higher than the number of workplace accidents claims, largely because of the massive compensatory schemes set up for former miners suffering from vibration white finger and respiratory disease. The schemes ran from 1999–2004 and disposed of more than 750,000 claims (which are included in the CRU figures). Following the closure of the schemes, the number of workplace disease claims tailed off substantially. See further p. 947, below.

There are a number of sources of the employer's responsibility to an employee for accidental injury at work. First, there is vicarious liability for the torts of employees committed in the course of employment (see further Ch. 15). Secondly, a claim may be brought for breach of the employer's personal and non-delegable duty of care. This duty is in most respects governed by normal principles of the tort of negligence, but is distinctive on account of its *non-delegable* character: the employer cannot escape liability by engaging a competent person to ensure that the obligations owed personally to every employee are discharged. Lastly, there are various statutory duties (e.g. those arising under regulations issued pursuant to Health and Safety at Work Act 1974; the general duties under the Act itself do not give rise to civil liability: s. 47(1)). The statutes in question may expressly give rise to a claim for damages, or may alternatively be actionable under the common law principles governing civil liability for breach of statutory duty (see below). Claims under the last two heads, being claims for breach of personal duties, may arise even when it is not possible to point the finger of blame at any individual employee for whom the employer can be held vicariously liable (e.g. where the accident arises from a defect in the employer's organisational structures rather than from a particular negligent act; so too when an employee's negligent act is outside the course of employment).

These regimes are buttressed by the Employers' Liability (Compulsory Insurance) Act 1969 by which employers must compulsorily insure against their civil liabilities to their employees. The Act was introduced in order to remedy the situation in which employees injured in the course of their employment were awarded compensation against their employer by the courts, yet did not receive that compensation because their employer did not have the necessary resources (cf. compulsory third-party insurance for drivers of motor vehicles). Where an employer fails to take out the necessary insurance and is unable to meet a damages award, the injured employee has no remedy, for the only sanction is a criminal fine; it is not possible to claim damages for breach of the statutory duty against the recalcitrant directors of the company (see *Richardson v Pitt-Stanley* [1995] QB 123). For this reason, there have been calls—as yet unanswered—for the establishment and funding of an employers' liability insurance bureau to meet claims in such cases (see, e.g., Simpson (1972) 35 MLR 63).

In addition to a claim for damages, an injured employee may also have a claim for various social security benefits. The first workers' compensation scheme was introduced in 1897, guaranteeing employees injured in the course of employment a measure of compensation whether or not the employer had been at fault; the cost of compensation was initially borne by the employer (see by way of background P. Bartrip and S. Burman, *The Wounded Soldiers of Industry* (Oxford: Clarendon Press, 1983)). In 1911, the National Insurance Act provided for the payment of benefits—partially subsidised by the taxpayer—to the unemployed and those suffering from sickness not related to their employment. With the advent of the welfare state in 1948, both these schemes were integrated within it, the former as the Industrial Injuries Scheme. Initially the scheme was administered separately from the rest of the social security system, with its own fund, and accorded those injured at work considerably more generous treatment than the unemployed or those suffering from sickness that was not work-related. But benefits to those injured at work are no longer separately administered and the former 'industrial preference' has very largely disappeared except in cases of long-term incapacity, which may result in the award of disablement benefit on top of ordinary social security benefits (see further *Atiyah*, ch. 13). In other cases, those who are off-work because of a workplace injury make do with the same statutory sick pay that is available to those off work because of any injury or illness whatsoever.

(a) Historical Origins of Employers' Liability

Although claims of employers' liability are among the most common encountered in the modern law, in historical terms actions against employers were not recorded until comparatively recent times (well after liability in respect of road accidents, for example). The first recorded English case is *Priestley v Fowler* (1837) 3 M & W 1, 150 ER 1030, an action arising out of the plaintiff's injury in an accident caused by the coachman's overloading of the delivery van on which the plaintiff was riding on his employer's business. Lord Abinger CB apparently accepted that liability would arise where the employer was personally at fault, but found against the plaintiff on the grounds that he was better placed than his employer to know that the coach was unsafe and had willingly accepted the risk of injury. Lord Abinger warned that admitting such claims would increase employers' liabilities by 'an alarming extent' (at 5–6):

> If the owner of the carriage is therefore responsible for the sufficiency of his carriage to his servant, he is responsible for the negligence of his coach-maker, or his harness-maker, or his coachman. The footman, therefore, who rides behind the carriage, may have an action against his master for a defect in the carriage owing to the negligence of the coach-maker, or for a defect in the harness arising from the negligence of the harness-maker, or for drunkenness, neglect, or want of skill in the coachman; nor is there any reason why the principle should not, if applicable in this class of cases extend to many others. The master, for example, would be liable to the servant for the negligence of the chambermaid, for putting him into a damp bed; for that of the upholsterer, for sending in a crazy bedstead, whereby he was made to fall down while asleep and injure himself; for the negligence of the cook, in not properly cleaning the copper vessels used in the kitchen; of the butcher, in supplying the family with meat of a quality injurious to the health; of the builder, for a defect in the foundation of the house, whereby it fell, and injured both the master and the servant by the ruins.

His Lordship felt that '[t]he inconvenience, not to say the absurdity of these consequences' provided sufficient reason for dismissing the plaintiff's claim. These remarks were subsequently held to warrant the recognition of the defence of 'common employment' (see below), and guarded employers against the vast majority of claims (but see A. W. B. Simpson, 'A Case of First Impression: *Priestley v Fowler* (1837)' in *idem*, *Leading Cases in the Common Law* (Oxford: Clarendon Press, 1995), 128). For discussion of *Priestley* in the wider context of an employer's liability to his employees, see Stein, '*Priestley v Fowler* and the Emerging Tort of Negligence' (2003) 46 BCL Rev 689.

Various reasons for the comparatively late development of the law of employers' liability may be advanced. Simpson (*op. cit.*) notes that 'before suits against employers or statutory schemes of workmen's compensation came into vogue there were other mechanisms for dealing with such accidents [sc. accidents at work]. In particular there was the law of master and servant, and the poor law' (p. 113). He associates the rise of the tort action against the employer to the decline in these alternative mechanisms for the support of the injured employee. First, in the case of menial servants (who constituted a major part of the workforce), the employer's obligations to provide board, lodging and remuneration continued until the end of the term of employment even in the event of the servant's disability. Simpson explains (p. 113):

> In the pre-industrial world, the typical servant was the menial servant in husbandry, retained at the annual hirings for a term of one year . . . Menials received board and lodging as their principal remuneration, and modest money payment . . . The old law on such servants gave them an important, if short-term, protection against the consequences of an accident at work. It was explained in Dalton's *Countrey Justice* (5th ed., 1635):
>
>> If a servant retained for a yeere, happen within the time of his service to fall sicke, or to be hurt or lamed . . . by act of God, or in doing his Master's business, yet it seemeth the Master must not therefore put such servant away, nor abate any part of his wages for such time.

The newer industrial world, however, brought with it a change in the typical employment relationship. Simpson notes that menial servants were replaced by 'labourers' hired for the task, the day or the month, with the result that 'the protection afforded to the sick and injured amongst the working population was . . . reduced by changing employment practices' (p. 114). He submits that the first tort actions were therefore, 'in a sense, a move to fill a gap in a protection which had formerly existed' (p. 117).

Secondly, there was the role played by the Poor Law, the forerunner of the social security system. Simpson notes (p. 117):

In the early nineteenth century and before, it was the poor law which was the principal legal provision for the victims of serious accidents at work, not the law of tort. Given the cost of litigation, and the poverty of the working population, tort law was largely irrelevant.

Under the Poor Law, every parish had the obligation of providing relief to the poor (including the 'poor by casualty') settled within its boundaries. The relief could take a number of different forms: payment of medical expenses, provision of board and lodgings in a workhouse, and 'outdoor' relief to disabled people in their homes (e.g. payment of a weekly pension). In 1834, major reforms of the Poor Law were effected by a Poor Law Amendment Act 1834 which abolished outdoor relief, stipulating that relief was to be provided only in the workhouse. Simpson suggests that this reform, which made the receipt of Poor Law assistance depend upon acceptance of the disagreeable conditions of the workhouse, may have had something to do with the growing recourse to tort thereafter (p. 123).

(b) The Common Employment Doctrine

The first tort actions met the almost insuperable obstacle of the doctrine of common employment. The doctrine was not clearly stated in *Priestley v Fowler* (1837) 3 M & W 1, but in *Hutchinson v York, Newcastle and Berwick Ry* (1850) 5 Ex 343 Alderson B held the earlier case to have been decided on the basis that an employer is not in general liable to one employee for damage resulting from the negligence of another; the employer could only be liable for personal negligence (e.g. in failing to select competent staff). The doctrine was premised upon the assumption that '[w]hen the workman contracts to do work of any particular sort, he knows, or ought to know, to what risks he is exposing himself; he knows, if such be the nature of the risk, that want of care on the part of a fellow-workman may be injurious or fatal to him, and that against such want of care his employer cannot by possibility protect him' (*Bartonshill Coal Co v Reid* (1853) 3 Macq 266 (Sco) at 284, per Lord Cranworth). Together with the defences of *volenti non fit injuria* and contributory negligence (then a total defence to liability) it formed part of an 'unholy trinity' of doctrines whose effect was to curtail drastically the scope for successful actions by employees against their employer in respect of accidents in the workplace.

The harsh effects of the common employment rule were limited by the development of the employer's personal liability, both for breach of statutory duty (see *Groves v Lord Wimborne*, extracted below at p. 617) and for breach of the common law duty. The employee was presumed only to have accepted the risk of negligence of a fellow employee, not that of the employer, so a claim might be successful where the employer was in breach of duty (see, e.g., *Brydon v Stewart* (1855) 2 Macq 30). Admittedly, for some time it appeared that the employer could be liable only if personally guilty of some negligent conduct, as was held by the Court of Appeal in *Fenton v Denville* [1932] 2 KB 30. Such a rule would have greatly restricted the scope of employers' liability, for as *Winfield & Jolowicz* points out (para. 8–2), 'how can an employer be personally negligent unless he actually takes a hand in the work himself, a physical impossibility where the employer is not a human individual but, as…is now the general rule, a company with independent legal personality?' But *Fenton* was in any case overruled by the decision of the House of Lords in *Wilsons and Clyde Coal Co Ltd v English* [1938] AC 57, which held that the employer could be held responsible for the negligence of an agent entrusted with the performance of the employer's personal and non-delegable duty, on the basis that there are 'fundamental obligations of a contract of employment...for which employers are absolutely responsible' (at 78, per Lord Wright). It is hard to dissent from the view that this was 'a typical piece of judicial legislation, designed to mitigate the mischief of the doctrine of common employment' (Williams, 'Liability for Independent Contractors' [1956] CLJ 180 at 190).

Such developments coincided in point of time with the relaxation of the other two doctrines chiefly responsible for limiting the employer's liability to employees. Contributory negligence, a complete defence at common law, was made less effective by judicial development of the 'last chance' doctrine (see above, p. 301f) whereby employers remained liable if they could have intervened to prevent injury after the employee's careless act, and the nature of the defence was eventually changed by the Law Reform (Contributory Negligence) Act 1945 which made it only a partial answer to the employee's claim (see further Ch. 6.III). Meanwhile, the courts began to apply the defence of *volenti* less stringently, and with greater awareness of the economic imperatives that made workers risk life and limb; the fact that workers were aware of the dangerous conditions in which they worked was no longer held to signify their voluntary acceptance of the risk of consequent injury (see *Smith v Baker & Sons* [1890] AC 325).

It was apparent already by the time of *Wilsons and Clyde Coal* that the judicial mood was resolutely opposed to the common employment defence. For Lord Wright, it was an 'illogical' doctrine (at 79), mere 'dogma' which paid 'little regard to reality or to modern ideas of economics or industrial conditions' (at 80). But the doctrine had been affirmed by the highest appellate court (in *Bartonshill Coal Co v Reid* (1858) 3 Macq 266), and it could only be repealed by legislation, the House of Lords having no power at that time to depart from its previous decisions. The effects of the doctrine were limited by the Employers' Liability Act 1880, but it was only in 1948 that concerns as to the rule's fairness and workability led to its complete abolition by statute (Law Reform (Personal Injuries) Act 1948, s. 1). Nevertheless, even though the chief reason for its recognition has now disappeared, the idea of the employer's personal and non-delegable duty remains.

2. Employers' Liability Today

(a) The Different Heads of Duty

The leading modern authority on the employer's personal liability to an employee is the decision of the House of Lords in *Wilsons and Clyde Coal Co Ltd v English* [1938] AC 57. In that case, Lord Wright described the employer's obligation as 'threefold'—'the provision of a competent staff of men, adequate material, and a proper system and effective supervision' (at 78). In other authorities, different summaries of the various aspects of the obligation have been adopted, and very often a fourth head of obligation—the duty to provide a safe place of work—has been added, but such differences are only differences of emphasis, not substance. As has been well observed: 'It is no doubt convenient, when one is dealing with any particular case, to divide that duty into a number of categories; but for myself I prefer to consider the master's duty as one applicable in all circumstances, namely, to take reasonable care for the safety of his men...' (*Wilson v Tyneside Window Cleaning Co* [1958] 2 QB 110 at 124, per Parker LJ).

It has been authoritatively noted that '[t]he liability of an employer to his employees for negligence, either direct or vicarious, is not a separate tort with its own rules. It is an aspect of the general law of negligence' (*White v Chief Constable of South Yorkshire Police* [1999] 2 AC 455 at 506, per Lord Hoffmann). But, notwithstanding the general truth of this observation, the law of employer's liability still warrants special attention because the existence of an employment relationship shapes the application of normal principles of the law of negligence. In particular, the employment relationship may suffice to give rise to a duty of care that would not otherwise be owed. Despite the law's general reluctance to recognise liability for omissions, it seems that an employer owes a duty of affirmative action to an employee injured in the course of employment and in need of medical attention (*Kasapis v Laimos* [1959] 2 Lloyd's Rep 378). Furthermore, and again exceptionally, an employer may owe a duty to protect the economic interests of an employee, for example, in writing an employment reference (*Spring v Guardian Assurance* [1995] 2 AC 296) or in advising of the entitlement to exercise valuable pension options (*Scally v Southern Health and Social Services Board* [1992] 1 AC 294; but cf. *Reid v Rush & Tompkins Group plc* [1990] 1 WLR 212). And it may also be that certain limitations on the right to sue in respect of psychiatric illness are inapplicable where an action is brought for breach of the employer's personal duty, for example, in the case of occupational stress (see *Hatton v Sutherland*, extracted above, p. 363). Nevertheless, such liabilities are liabilities within the tort of negligence, and all the requirements of that tort must be established. It is not enough merely to point to the existence of an employment relationship in order to make out a duty of care, for it may well be the case that the employer's duty is owed only in respect of damage of a particular kind and not in respect of damage of the kind actually suffered by the claimant (see, e.g., *Reid* and *White*, above).

(b) The Non-Delegable Nature of the Employer's Duty

The crucial defining feature of the employer's duty is its personal and non-delegable nature. Lord Macmillan described it thus in the leading case (*Wilsons and Clyde Coal Co Ltd v English* [1938] AC 57 at 75):

> It remains the owner's obligation, and the agent whom the owner appoints to perform it performs it on the owner's behalf. The owner remains ... responsible for the negligence of the person whom he has appointed to perform his obligation for him, and cannot escape liability by merely proving that he has appointed a competent agent. If the owner's duty has not been performed, no matter how competent the agent selected by the owner to perform it for him, the owner is responsible.

So although the duty is described as 'non-delegable', this does not entail that the duty 'is incapable of being the subject of delegation, but only that the employer cannot escape liability if the duty has been delegated and then not properly performed' (*McDermid v Nash Dredging & Reclamation Co Ltd* [1987] AC 906 at 910, per Lord Hailsham). As Lord Wright stated in *Wilsons and Clyde Coal Co Ltd v English* (at 81), '[i]t is the obligation which is personal to him, and not the performance.' The employer takes the risk of negligence on the part of employees, even independent contractors, he appoints to perform his duties.

Employers may be liable for the negligence of their delegates without being personally at fault. Their duty is not only to take care personally, but also to ensure that care is taken by whomsoever they delegate the duty to. The liability is not, however, strict. It requires fault on the part of some person, whether the employer personally or the delegate engaged to do the task in question. Accordingly, liability cannot arise if both the employer and the delegate take all reasonable care. Thus, where the accident is caused by an 'inherent secret defect' in machinery, which could not have been discovered by the exercise of due skill and attention on the part of either the employer or the person engaged by him, this will negate any liability (*Weems v Mathieson* (1861) 4 Macq 215 at 222, per Lord Campbell LC).

Although the employer's duty is non-delegable, it is possible to *discharge* the duty in certain circumstances by entrusting its performance to an independent contractor (but not an employee). This difficult issue is further explored in the extracts below and the following commentaries.

Davie v New Merton Board Mills Ltd [1959] AC 604

The plaintiff, a maintenance fitter, was hammering out a metal key with the aid of a drift (a metal tool similar to a chisel) when, as he struck it with the hammer, a particle of metal flew off the head of the drift and into his eye, causing injuries. The drift, which had been provided for his use by his employers (the defendants), although apparently in good condition, was of excessive hardness and therefore, in the circumstances, a dangerous tool. It had been negligently manufactured by reputable makers, who had sold it in turn to a reputable firm of suppliers; they had sold it to the employers, whose system of maintenance and inspection was not at fault. The plaintiff claimed damages for negligence against his employers on the ground that they had supplied him with a defective tool. He succeeded at trial, but that decision was reversed by the Court of Appeal. He appealed to the House of Lords.

In the Court of Appeal [1958] 1 QB 210 at 236–7, Jenkins LJ (dissenting) had well summarised the argument in favour of liability in such cases:

> An employee has to use the tools provided by his employer and has no voice in the selection of the tools or as to the manufacturer or supplier from whom they are obtained. If he is injured through a defect in one of the tools provided by his employer, it is surely not unreasonable that the employer should be held liable if the defect was due to the negligent manufacture of the tool... Otherwise the employee might well be without a remedy. He would not know and might not be able to find out who the manufacturer was.

Viscount Simonds

It must... be shown wherein lay the want of reasonable care, and at once the question arises, for whose negligence, acts, I suppose, of omission and commission, the employer is liable in the long chain which ends with the supply by him of a tool to his workman but may begin with the delving of the raw material of manufacture in a distant continent. In the case before us the chain is long enough. The respondents were not guilty of any negligence nor was any servant or agent of theirs nor was the reputable firm who supplied the drifts, but at the end of the chain were the manufacturers. The respondents stood in no contractual relation to them: so little connection was there between them that it was long in dispute whether the fatal drift had been manufactured by them and delivered by them to the suppliers. But it is for their negligence in manufacture that the appellant would make the respondents liable... [S]uch a result... cannot commend itself to reason; for, if indeed it is the law, every man employing another and supplying him with tools for his job acts at his peril: if someone at some time has been careless, then, for any flaw in the tools, it is he who is responsible, be he himself ever so careful...

The employer, it was said, was under a duty to take reasonable care to supply his workmen with proper plant and machinery. It was assumed that this included tools such as drifts, and I, too, will, without deciding it, assume it. It was then said that the employer could not escape responsibility by employing a third party, however expert, to do his duty for him. So far, so good . . . But then comes the next step—but I would rather call it a jump, and a jump that would unhorse any rider. Therefore, it was said, the employer is responsible for the defect in goods that he buys in the market, if it can be shown that that defect was due to the want of skill or care on the part of anyone who was concerned in its manufacture. But, my Lords, by what use or misuse of language can the manufacturer be said to be a person to whom the employer delegated a duty which it was for him to perform? How can it be said that it was as the delegate or agent of the employer that the manufacturer failed to exhibit due skill and care? It is, to my mind, clear that he cannot . . .

Lord Reid observed that the manufacturers in the case before him 'cannot possibly be deemed to have been the agents or servants' of the respondent employers, and continued:

[A]n employer, besides being liable to his servant for injury caused by the negligence of his own servants, is in some cases liable in respect of the negligence of others. Where, then, is the line to be drawn? On the one hand it appears that an employer is liable for the negligence of an independent contractor whom he has engaged to carry out one of what have been described as his personal duties on his own premises and whose work might normally be done by the employer's own servant—at least if the negligent workmanship is discoverable by reasonable inspection. On the other hand for the reasons which I have given, I am of opinion that he is not liable for the negligence of the manufacturer of an article which he has bought, provided that he has been careful to deal with a seller of repute and has made any inspection which a reasonable employer would make. That leaves a wide sphere regarding which it is unnecessary, and it would, I think, be undesirable, to express any opinion here. Various criteria have been suggested, and it must be left for the further development of the law to determine which is correct. In my judgment this appeal should be dismissed.

Lord Morton, **Lord Tucker** and **Lord Keith** delivered separate concurring opinions.

Appeal dismissed.

COMMENTARY

The House of Lords left open the question of a special tool made to order by the manufacturer.

Hamson [1959] CLJ 157 suggests that this case indicates the House of Lords' preference for a tort-based approach, applying ordinary principles of vicarious liability, over a contractual solution imposing liability for non-performance of a specified task regardless of the employer's personal fault. (An employer cannot normally be vicariously liable for the fault of any person other than an employee.) In fact, employers' liability is normally regarded as arising concurrently in contract and tort, with the claimant left with the option between the two bases where it makes any difference to the claim (see *Matthews v Kuwait Bechtel Corp* [1959] QB 57, which appears to be supported by the decision of the House of Lords, in a different context, in *Henderson v Merrett Syndicates*, extracted at p. 434, above; cf. *Scally v Southern Health and Social Services Board* [1992] 1 AC 294, which suggests that the contract duty is primary, at least where the subject matter of the claim is loss of a valuable entitlement under the contract).

Davie may be contrasted with the decision in *Taylor v Rover Co Ltd* [1966] 1 WLR 1491, where the employer was held liable for failure to withdraw a tool (a chisel) after it had become broken and dangerous. What is the material difference between the two cases?

The Employer's Liability (Defective Equipment) Act 1969

The narrow *ratio decidendi* of the House of Lords in *Davie* has been effectively reversed by the Employer's Liability (Defective Equipment) Act 1969. Section 1(1) provides:

(1) Where after the commencement of this Act—

    (a) an employee suffers personal injury in the course of his employment in consequence of a defect in equipment provided by his employer for the purposes of the employer's business; and

    (b) the defect is attributable wholly or partly to the fault of a third party (whether identified or not),

the injury shall be deemed to be also attributable to negligence on the part of the employer (whether or not he is liable in respect of the injury apart from this subsection), but without prejudice to the law relating to contributory negligence and to any remedy by way of contribution or in contract or otherwise which is available to the employer in respect of the injury.

Section 1(2) renders void any agreement purporting to exclude or limit the liability under s. 1.

The effect of the statute is to deem the employer to be personally at fault for an employee's personal injury where the conditions in (a) and (b), above, are satisfied. Equipment is defined in the statute to include 'any plant and machinery, vehicle, aircraft and clothing'. 'Equipment' includes not only the tools used to work upon raw material but also the raw material itself (*Knowles v Liverpool City Council* [1993] 1 WLR 1428). It has been judicially determined that it also includes a 90,000-ton ship on which the employee in question was serving (*Coltman v Bibby Tankers Ltd* [1988] AC 276; the House of Lords rejected an argument that, as the ship was the plaintiff's workplace, it could not be 'equipment'). 'Fault' is defined to include any 'act or omission which gives rise to liability in tort' (s. 1(7)) and therefore seems to include the supply of a defective product under Part I of the Consumer Protection Act 1987. According to Lang, 'The Employers' Liability (Defective Equipment Act—Lion or Mouse' (1984) 47 MLR 48 at 53:

The decided cases suggest that the Act has not imposed a harsh burden upon the employer because the employer is rarely found liable under it. The problem of proving third party fault has been insurmountable for some plaintiffs and others have been unable to prove that their accident was caused by a defect in equipment.

See also the Provision and Use of Work Equipment Regulations (SI 1998/2306) which cover some of the same ground as the statute, although it appears that the definition of 'equipment' in reg. 2(1)—'any machinery, appliance, apparatus, tool or installation for use at work'—is narrower than under the Act.

Delegation Contrasted with Discharge

Although the effect of *Davie* has been reversed by statute in respect of defective equipment, the decision remains authority for a wider rule that an employer may in some circumstances *discharge* the personal duty, not merely delegate its performance, by entrusting its performance to some other person. In *Sumner v William Henderson & Sons Ltd* [1964] 1 QB 450 at 467, Phillimore J summarised *Davie* as providing that 'the employers, being under a duty to take reasonable care to provide a reasonably safe tool...had discharged that duty by buying one from a reputable supplier'; he added however (at 467–8) that '[t]he ratio of this decision is, I think, that on the facts the employers could not be said to have delegated their duty to the manufacturers, to whose negligence the latent defect was presumably due.' The criterion for determining whether the duty has been discharged rather than merely delegated remains obscure, however, and the cases are not all that easy to reconcile.

In *Sumner* (reversed on different grounds at [1963] 1 WLR 823), the plaintiff's wife had been killed in a fire in the department store in which she worked; the store was undergoing extension and modernisation, and it appeared that the fire resulted from a fault in the electrical cable that had been laid down. Addressing certain preliminary questions raised by the case, Phillimore J held (following *Davie*) that the employers could not be held liable for any fault on the part of the manufacturers of the cable, but (distinguishing *Davie*) that they could be held liable for the negligence of those supervising or carrying out the work, including the electrical contractors engaged to install the wiring; the contractors were acting as the employers' delegates. The case would have been decided differently if the fault had been in the cable they were installing rather than in their execution of that task.

Compare also the following case.

McDermid v Nash Dredging & Reclamation Co Ltd [1987] AC 906

The plaintiff lost his leg as a result of the negligence of the master of the vessel on which he was working, a Captain Sas. The vessel was not owned by his employer, Nash (the defendants) but by Nash's Dutch parent company, Stevin, for whom the defendants had instructed him to work. (In fact, the defendant company had been set up precisely for the purpose of procuring, and paying for, the services of the British staff engaged by the Dutch parent.) The plaintiff was directed to work on a dredger owned by Stevin, alongside which was tied a tug (the *Ina*). The accident occurred when, as the plaintiff tried to untie the tug from its mooring, Captain Sas moved the tug without waiting for the plaintiff to give the agreed signal by knocking twice on the side of the wheelhouse to indicate that the ropes were safely on board (the 'double knock system'). The plaintiff's leg was caught up in the ropes, resulting in his injuries.

Lord Hailsham of St Marylebone

The plaintiff's claim in the proceedings was based on the allegation, *inter alia*, of a 'non-delegable' duty resting on his employers to take reasonable care to provide a 'safe system of work': cf. *Wilsons & Clyde Coal Co Ltd v English* [1938] AC 57. The defendants did not, and could not, dispute the existence of such a duty of care, nor that it was 'non-delegable' in the special sense in which the phrase is used in this connection. This special sense does not involve the proposition that the duty cannot be delegated in the sense that it is incapable of being the subject of delegation, but only that the employer cannot escape liability if the duty has been delegated and then not properly performed. Equally the defendants could not and did not attempt to dispute that it would be a central and crucial feature of any safe system on the instant facts that it would prevent so far as possible the occurrence of such an accident as actually happened, viz. injury to the plaintiff as the result of the use of the *Ina*'s engine so as to move the *Ina* before both the ropes were clear of the dredger and stowed safely inboard and the plaintiff was in a position of safety.

Since such a system could easily have been designed and put in operation at the time of the accident in about half-a-dozen different ways, and since it is quite obvious that such a system would have prevented the accident had it been in operation, and since the duty to provide it was 'non-delegable' in the sense that the defendants cannot escape liability by claiming to have delegated performance of their duty, it is a little difficult to see what possible defence there could ever have been to these proceedings...

Although the duty of providing a safe system of work was 'non-delegable' in the special sense I have described, it had in fact been delegated on alternate shifts to Captain Sas and Captain Clifford in the circumstances I have described. In both cases the delegation covered, so far as can be ascertained, the whole operation of the *Ina*, the orders to the deckhand, the system of work to be followed and, since the skipper was at the wheel, the operation of the engine . . . [T]he defendants had delegated their duty to the plaintiff to Captain Sas, the duty had not been performed, and the defendants must pay for the breach of their 'non-delegable' obligation.

Lord Brandon of Oakbrook

A statement of the relevant principle of law can be divided into three parts. First, an employer owes to his employee a duty to exercise reasonable care to ensure that the system of work provided for him is a safe one. Secondly, the provision of a safe system of work has two aspects: (a) the devising of such a system and (b) the operation of it. Thirdly, the duty concerned has been described alternatively as either personal or non-delegable. The meaning of these expressions is not self-evident and needs explaining. The essential characteristic of the duty is that, if it is not performed, it is no defence for the employer to show that he delegated its performance to a person, whether his servant or not his servant, whom he reasonably believed to be competent to perform it. Despite such delegation the employer is liable for the non-performance of the duty.

   In the present case the relevant system of work in relation to the plaintiff was the system for unmooring the tug *Ina*. In the events which occurred the defendants delegated both the devising and the operating of such system to Captain Sas, who was not their servant. An essential feature of such system, if it was to be a safe one, was that Captain Sas would not work the tug's engines ahead or astern until he knew that the plaintiff had completed his work of unmooring the tug. The system which Captain Sas devised was one under which the plaintiff would let him know that he had completed that work by giving two knocks on the outside of the wheelhouse . . . [O]n the occasion of the plaintiff's accident, Captain Sas did not operate that system. He negligently failed to operate it in that he put the tug's engines astern at a time when the plaintiff had not given, and he, Captain Sas, could not therefore have heard, the pre-scribed signal of two knocks by the plaintiff on the outside of the wheelhouse. For this failure by Captain Sas to operate the system which he had devised, the defendants, as the plaintiff's employers, are personally, not vicariously, liable to him.

COMMENTARY

Liability here was based on the employer's non-delegable duty to provide a safe system of work. The decision broke new ground by imposing liability on the employer where there is a failure to use a system that was supposed to be used, rather than a failure to adopt any system at all. However, it is hard to distinguish cases where the breach of duty is the employer's, because the system was not operated, and those where the breach is exclusively the employee's, because the system was operated carelessly (see further McKendrick (1990) 53 MLR 770). In the present case, if the breach had been regarded as exclusively Captain Sas's then the plaintiff would have had to sue the Dutch parent company, Stevin, on the basis of vicarious liability.

   A plausible explanation of the decision is that, as the master of the tug was in charge of the plaintiff-employee's workplace, he could for that reason be regarded as the employer's delegate. Underlying the strict legal issues in the case was the question whether the plaintiff should be allowed to sue Nash under English law rather than having to sue Stevin under

Dutch law. Analogous questions have been raised in subsequent cases, but with divergent results.

In *Cook v Square D Ltd* [1992] ICR 262, the plaintiff was sent by his employers on a short-term assignment in Saudi Arabia where he was to commission a computer control system for premises occupied by a third party. While on the premises, he fell through a hole in the floor left by a tile that had been lifted out of position and injured his knee. The Court of Appeal, distinguishing *McDermid*, held that there was no delegation of the employers' duty at all: the employers had been satisfied that the occupiers of the site and the main contractors working there were both reliable companies and were aware of their responsibility for the safety of workers on site. According to Farquharson LJ, '[t]he suggestion that the home-based employers have any responsibility for the daily events of a site in Saudi Arabia has an air of unreality' (at 271). The court nevertheless accepted that there may be some circumstances where the employer has an obligation to inspect an overseas site (e.g. if a large number of employees were to work there or if the engagement was for a considerable period of time).

In *Johnson v Coventry Churchill International Ltd* [1992] 3 All ER 14, the plaintiff had been sent to work in West Germany by the defendant employers, an agency which recruited British personnel to work worldwide. Whilst engaged on a construction site, the plaintiff suffered injury when a rotten plank gave way under his weight as he entered the site by means of a makeshift bridge. J. W. Kay QC (sitting as a Deputy Judge of the High Court) held that there was a clear failure to provide a safe means of access to the plaintiff's place of employment as no adequate system of inspection was in place. The judge stated (at 22): 'I do not think that it is necessary for me to find that there was something that the defendants could have done themselves about it since the onus is on them to ensure a safe means of access and no steps were taken by them to that end.' A reason for placing a non-delegable duty on the employer was that 'the plaintiff...had, and could have had, no means of judging in advance the measure of safety in force at the place where he was sent to work. It was, therefore, incumbent on the defendants as his employers to ensure a safe system of work' (*ibid.*). No doubt a further material factor in the case was that the plaintiff could not have brought a claim against the owners of the site under German law, which had abolished employers' liability in return for very substantial workers' compensation benefits to which the plaintiff would not be entitled, at least after his return to the UK (noted by the judge at 25).

These two cases both deal with the duty to provide a safe place of work rather than a safe system, but there is no reason to distinguish them from *McDermid* on that basis. The difference of result as between the two cases suggests not merely that the nature of the non-delegable duty remains hard to grasp but also that there are deep-rooted divergences of opinion as to how extensive the employer's responsibility *ought* to be.

II. Occupiers' Liability

1. The Law pre-1957

Although the liability of occupiers has been regulated by statute since 1957, reference to the earlier law is required as the legislation incorporates some common law concepts. The common law of occupiers' liability was complicated and unsatisfactory and depended upon the classification of entrants onto the occupier's land into one of three, or possibly four, categories: the contractual entrant, the invitee, the licensee and the trespasser. This was necessary because the duty owed by the occupier varied depending on the status of the entrant (see Dixon J in the Australian case of *Lipman v Clendinnen* (1932) 46 CLR 550).

In *Robert Addie and Sons (Collieries) Ltd v Dumbreck* [1929] AC 358, Lord Hailsham LC described the duties owed to the various category of entrant as follows. The highest duty was owed to those persons who were present by the invitation of the occupier. Towards such persons the occupier had the duty of taking reasonable care that the premises were safe. In the case of licensees (express or implied) the duty was less stringent: the occupier had no duty to ensure that the premises were safe, but was bound not to create a trap or to allow to exist upon the premises any concealed danger which was not apparent to the visitor, but which was known—or ought to have been known—to the occupier. Towards the trespasser the occupier had no duty to take reasonable care for his protection or even to protect him from concealed danger. The trespasser came on to the premises at his own risk. An occupier in such a case was liable only where the injury was due to some wilful act involving something more than the absence of reasonable care, that is, some act done with the deliberate intention of doing harm to the trespasser, or at least some act done with reckless disregard to the presence of the trespasser.

Although Lord Hailsham described three types of entrant, his first category is probably an amalgam of two other categories: the contractual entrant (e.g. a hotel guest) and the invitee (a customer in a shop), and the occupier owed the duty of reasonable care to make the premises safe only to the contractual entrant. The status of the customer was discussed in *Indermaur v Dames* (1866) LR 1 CP 274 where Willes J noted that 'his protection does not depend upon the fact of a contract being entered into in the way of the shopkeeper's business during the stay of the customer, but upon the fact that the customer has come into the shop in pursuance of a tacit invitation given by the shopkeeper, with a view to business which concerns himself.' Such an entrant was entitled to the exercise of reasonable care by the occupier to prevent damage from unusual danger, of which the occupier knows or ought to know. The duty arose even though the invitee was aware of the danger and was not necessarily fulfilled by warning the entrant of the danger. It should be remembered that 'invitee' is a legal term of art; the entrant had to be on the occupier's premises for 'a purpose in which the occupier himself has some concern, a pecuniary, material or business interest' (per Dixon J in *Lipman*, above, p. 556). Even though one might invite a friend over for a social dinner, such a person would be a licensee, not an invitee, and would only be owed the lesser duty of care. But it was far better to be a licensee than a trespasser, for as the above extract shows, the trespasser received minimal protection: he could not be treated as an outlaw and deliberately or recklessly harmed, but beyond that no duty was owed.

One consequence of the lack of protection given to trespassers was that plaintiffs attempted to argue that they had an implied licence to be on the premises, and, as a licensee, were owed a higher duty of care. Whilst judges may not have felt especially sympathetic towards adult trespassers using this argument, the position was different for children who, as Lord Buckmaster put it in *Addie*, 'could know nothing of the law of trespass or licence' (although his Lordship's sympathy did not extend to actually allowing the plaintiff to recover in that case). A leading example of the more lenient approach shown to children is found in *Cooke v Midland Great Western Railway of Ireland* [1909] AC 229. A young child was injured when playing on some machinery on the defendant's land (on which he was trespassing). To get to the machinery the child entered the defendant's land through a gap in a fence (which, to the defendant's knowledge, other children did as well). An application to strike out the child's cause of action was dismissed, Lord MacNaughton noting that it did not seem unreasonable to hold that 'if they [the defendants] allow their property to be open to all comers, infants as well as children of maturer age, and place upon it a machine attractive to children and dangerous as a plaything, they may be responsible in damages to those who resort to it with their tacit permission, and who are unable, in consequence of their tender age, to take care of themselves.' This approach, known as the doctrine of allurement, had the effect of promoting the child to a licensee, with the result that the more extensive duty was owed and the chances of recovering increased.

2. The 1957 Act

The subtleties that were required to draw distinctions between the various classes of entrants, particularly licensees and invitees, provoked criticism of this branch of the law. Accordingly, it was referred to the Law Reform Committee in 1952 and a report was published in 1954 (*Third Report: Occupiers' Liability to Invitees, Licensees and Trespassers*). The main recommendations of the report were that the distinction between invitees and licensees be abolished and that the occupier owe the same duty to everyone on the premises with his permission. This duty was to take reasonable care to ensure that the premises were reasonably safe for use by the visitor for the purpose to which the invitation or permission related. The Committee argued that the distinction between invitees and licensees (together with the different duty the occupier owed to each) was artificial:

> A reasonable occupier of premises surely does not say to himself (for instance) 'These steps are dangerously slippery with frozen snow but they don't amount to a trap. I am expecting no visitors except Jones, who is coming to dinner. He is a mere licensee, and I need not do anything about the steps so far as he is concerned' ... Nor, on the other hand, does he say to himself 'I must clear the snow off the steps because Brown is coming to see me on business. He will be an invitee, and if he slips on the steps I may find myself liable to him in damages'. Surely the reasonable occupier's thought is more likely to be 'These steps are dangerous. I must clear the snow off them. Otherwise someone coming to my house may slip and get hurt.'

As a result of the Committee's report, Parliament passed the Occupiers' Liability Act 1957 which embodied the main recommendations made by the Committee.

Occupiers' Liability Act 1957

An Act to amend the law of England and Wales as to the liability of occupiers and others for injury or damage resulting to persons or goods lawfully on any land or other property from dangers due to the state of the property or to things done or omitted to be done there ...

1. PRELIMINARY
(1) The rules enacted by the two next following sections shall have effect, in place of the rules of the common law, to regulate the duty which an occupier of premises owes to his visitors in respect of dangers due to the state of the premises or to things done or omitted to be done on them.

(2) The rules so enacted shall regulate the nature of the duty imposed by law in consequence of a person's occupation or control of premises and of any invitation or permission he gives (or is to be treated as giving) to another to enter or use the premises, but they shall not alter the rules of the common law as to the persons on whom a duty is so imposed or to whom it is owed; and accordingly for the purpose of the rules so enacted the persons who are to be treated as an occupier and as his visitors are the same (subject to subsection (4) of this section) as the persons who would at common law be treated as an occupier and as his invitees or licensees.

(3) The rules so enacted in relation to an occupier of premises and his visitors shall also apply, in like manner and to the like extent as the principles applicable at common law to an occupier of premises and his invitees or licensees would apply, to regulate—
   (a) the obligations of a person occupying or having control over any fixed or moveable structure, including any vessel, vehicle or aircraft; and
   (b) the obligations of a person occupying or having control over any premises or structure in respect of damage to property, including the property of persons who are not themselves his visitors.

(4) A person entering any premises in exercise of rights conferred by virtue of—
   (a) section 2(1) of the Countryside and Rights of Way Act 2000, or
   (b) an access agreement or order under the National Parks and Access to the Countryside Act 1949,
is not, for the purposes of this Act, a visitor of the occupier of the premises.

2. EXTENT OF OCCUPIERS' ORDINARY DUTY

(1) An occupier of premises owes the same duty, the 'common duty of care', to all his visitors, except in so far as he is free to and does extend, restrict, modify or exclude his duty to any visitor or visitors by agreement or otherwise.

(2) The common duty of care is a duty to take such care as in all the circumstances of the case is reasonable to see that the visitor will be reasonably safe in using the premises for the purposes for which he is invited or permitted by the occupier to be there.

(3) The circumstances relevant for the present purpose include the degree of care, and of want of care, which would ordinarily be looked for in such a visitor, so that (for example) in proper cases—
   (a) an occupier must be prepared for children to be less careful than adults; and
   (b) an occupier may expect that a person, in the exercise of his calling, will appreciate and guard against any special risks ordinarily incident to it, so far as the occupier leaves him free to do so.

(4) In determining whether the occupier of premises has discharged the common duty of care to a visitor, regard is to be had to all the circumstances, so that (for example)—
   (a) where damage is caused to a visitor by a danger of which he had been warned by the occupier, the warning is not to be treated without more as absolving the occupier from liability, unless in all the circumstances it was enough to enable the visitor to be reasonably safe; and
   (b) where damage is caused to a visitor by a danger due to the faulty execution of any work of construction, maintenance or repair by an independent contractor employed by the occupier, the occupier is not to be treated without more as answerable for the danger if in all the circumstances he had acted reasonably in entrusting the work to

an independent contractor and had taken such steps (if any) as he reasonably ought in order to satisfy himself that the contractor was competent and that the work had been properly done.

(5) The common duty of care does not impose on an occupier any obligation to a visitor in respect of risks willingly accepted as his by the visitor (the question whether a risk was so accepted to be decided on the same principles as in other cases in which one person owes a duty of care to another).

(6) For the purposes of this section, persons who enter premises for any purpose in the exercise of a right conferred by law are to be treated as permitted by the occupier to be there for that purpose, whether they in fact have his permission or not.

3. EFFECT OF CONTRACT ON OCCUPIER'S LIABILITY TO THIRD PARTY

(1) Where an occupier of premises is bound by contract to permit persons who are strangers to the contract to enter or use the premises, the duty of care which he owes to them as his visitors cannot be restricted or excluded by that contract, but (subject to any provision of the contract to the contrary) shall include the duty to perform his obligations under the contract, whether undertaken for their protection or not, in so far as those obligations go beyond the obligations otherwise involved in that duty.

(2) A contract shall not by virtue of this section have the effect, unless it expressly so provides, of making an occupier who has taken all reasonable care answerable to strangers to the contract for dangers due to the faulty execution of any work of construction, maintenance or repair or other like operation by persons other than himself, his servants and persons acting under his direction and control.

(3) In this section 'stranger to the contract' means a person not for the time being entitled to the benefit of the contract as a party to it or as the successor by assignment or otherwise of a party to it, and accordingly includes a party to the contract who has ceased to be so entitled.

(4) Where by the terms or conditions governing any tenancy (including a statutory tenancy which does not in law amount to a tenancy) either the landlord or the tenant is bound, though not by contract, to permit persons to enter or use premises of which he is the occupier, this section shall apply as if the tenancy were a contract between the landlord and the tenant.

(5) This section, in so far as it prevents the common duty of care from being restricted or excluded, applies to contracts entered into and tenancies created before the commencement of this Act, as well as to those entered into or created after its commencement; but, in so far as it enlarges the duty owed by an occupier beyond the common duty of care, it shall have effect only in relation to obligations which are undertaken after that commencement or which are renewed by agreement (whether express or implied) after that commencement...

5. IMPLIED TERM IN CONTRACTS

(1) Where persons enter or use, or bring or send goods to, any premises in exercise of a right conferred by contract with a person occupying or having control of the premises, the duty he owes them in respect of dangers due to the state of the premises or to things done or omitted to be done on them, in so far as the duty depends on a term to be implied in the contract by reason of its conferring that right, shall be the common duty of care.

(2) The foregoing subsection shall apply to fixed and moveable structures as it applies to premises.

(3) This section does not affect the obligations imposed on a person by or by virtue of any contract for the hire of, or for the carriage for reward of persons or goods in, any vehicle, vessel, aircraft or other means of transport, or by virtue of any contract of bailment.

(4) This section does not apply to contracts entered into before the commencement of this Act.

COMMENTARY

As is made clear in s. 1, the Act replaces the common law rules as to an occupier's liability, but only to the extent set out in the section. Whether one is an 'occupier' or a 'visitor' is a question to be decided by application of the existing common law rules, a visitor being one who would have been classified as a contractual entrant, invitee or licensee. Thus the hotel guest, the customer of a shop and the dinner guest are all visitors under the 1957 Act. However, the Act does not eliminate the need to classify entrants completely, for s. 1 refers to visitors as those who would have been invitees or licensees under the common law. Trespassers are not visitors and are not subject to the Act, so the important distinction is now between visitors and non-visitors. In this respect the old cases dealing with the doctrine of allurement remain worthy of attention as they provide examples where apparently child trespassers may be regarded as licensees, making them visitors and hence entitled to receive the duty owed to visitors under the Act. Similarly, the Act says nothing of the duty owed to trespassers, although, as will be discussed below, their position has also been dealt with by legislation.

(a) Occupier

Wheat v E. Lacon & Co Ltd [1966] AC 552

The first defendants, who were brewers, owned a public house. By virtue of a contract with the first defendant, R and his wife were responsible for the management of the public house. The contract allowed the brewery to enter the premises to view the state of repair. It also allowed R and his wife to occupy the public house (including the first floor) although the agreement stated that this occupation did not create any tenancy nor give the manager any estate or interest in the land. The brewery, as a privilege, also allowed R's wife to take paid lodgers in the residential part of the public house. One of the methods of access from the ground floor to the first was a back staircase. In September 1958 plaintiff's husband (both the plaintiff and her husband were paying guests of R's wife) was found dead at the bottom of the back stairs. It appeared that he had fallen whilst attempting to get to the bar on the ground floor to buy some drinks. There was an electric light at the top of the staircase but there was no bulb in it at the time of the accident. There was also a handrail down the left-hand side of the staircase terminating directly above the third step. The plaintiff brought an action under the Fatal Accidents Acts 1846–1908, and the Law Reform (Miscellaneous Provisions) Act 1934, against the brewery, R, and R's wife for damages in respect of her husband's death, alleging negligence and breach of duty under the Occupiers' Liability Act, 1957. The plaintiff's claim against all three defendants was dismissed at first instance and an appeal as regards the brewery was dismissed before the Court of Appeal, a majority holding that the defendants were not in occupation. The plaintiff appealed to the House of Lords.

Lord Denning

In the Occupiers' Liability Act, 1957, the word 'occupier' is used in the same sense as was used in the common law cases on occupiers' liability for dangerous premises. It was simply a convenient word to denote a person who had a sufficient degree of control over premises to put him under a duty of care towards those who came lawfully on to the premises. Those persons were divided into two categories, invitees and licensees: and a higher duty was owed to invitees than to licensees. But by the year 1956 the distinction between invitees and licensees had been reduced to vanishing point. The duty of the occupier had become simply a duty to take reasonable care to see that the premises were reasonably safe for people coming lawfully on to them: and it made no difference whether they were invitees or licensees: see *Slater v Clay Cross Co Ltd* [1956] 2 QB 264. The Act of 1957 confirmed the process. It did away, once and for all, with invitees and licensees and classed them all as 'visitors'; and it put upon the occupier the same duty to all of them, namely, the common duty of care. This duty is simply a particular instance of the general duty of care which each man owes to his 'neighbour.' When Lord Esher first essayed a definition of this general duty, he used the occupiers' liability as an instance of it: see *Heaven v Pender* (1883) 11 QBD 503 and when Lord Atkin eventually formulated the general duty in acceptable terms, he, too, used occupiers' liability as an illustration: see *Donoghue v Stevenson* and particularly his reference to *Grote v Chester Railway Company* (1848) 2 Ex 251. Translating this general principle into its particular application to dangerous premises, it becomes simply this: wherever a person has a sufficient degree of control over premises that he ought to realise that any failure on his part to use care may result in injury to a person coming lawfully there, then he is an 'occupier' and the person coming lawfully there is his 'visitor': and the 'occupier' is under a duty to his 'visitor' to use reasonable care. In order to be an 'occupier' it is not necessary for a person to have entire control over the premises. He need not have exclusive occupation. Suffice it that he has some degree of control. He may share the control with others. Two or more may be 'occupiers.' And whenever this happens, each is under a duty to use care towards persons coming lawfully on to the premises, dependent on his degree of control. If each fails in his duty, each is liable to a visitor who is injured in consequence of his failure, but each may have a claim to contribution from the other.

In *Salmond on Torts*, 14th ed. (1965), p. 372, it is said that an 'occupier' is 'he who has the immediate supervision and control and the power of permitting or prohibiting the entry of other persons.' This definition was adopted by Roxburgh J in *Hartwell v Grayson, Rollo and Clover Docks Ltd* [1947] KB 901 and by Diplock LJ in the present case. There is no doubt that a person who fulfils that test is an 'occupier.' He is the person who says 'come in.' But I think that test is too narrow by far. There are other people who are 'occupiers,' even though they do not say 'come in.' If a person has any degree of control over the state of the premises it is enough. The position is best shown by examining the cases in four groups.

First, where a landlord let premises by demise to a tenant, he was regarded as parting with all control over them. He did not retain any degree of control, even though he had undertaken to repair the structure. Accordingly, he was held to be under no duty to any person coming lawfully on to the premises, save only to the tenant under the agreement to repair. In *Cavalier v Pope* [1906] AC 428 it was argued that the premises were under the control of the landlord because of his agreement to repair: but the House of Lords rejected that argument. That case has now been overruled by section 4 of the Act of 1957 to the extent therein mentioned.

Secondly, where an owner let floors or flats in a building to tenants, but did not demise the common staircase or the roof or some other parts, he was regarded as having retained control of all parts not demised by him. Accordingly, he was held to be under a duty in respect of those retained parts to all persons coming lawfully on to the premises. So he was held liable for a defective staircase in *Miller v Hancock* [1893] 2 QB 177; for the gutters in the roof of *Hargroves, Aronson & Co v Hartopp* [1905] 1 KB 472 and for the private balcony in *Sutcliffe v Clients Investment Co Ltd* [1924] 2 KB 746. The extent of the duty was held to be that owed to a licensee, and not to an invitee: see *Fairman v Perpetual Investment Building Society* [1923] AC 74; *Jacobs v London County Council* [1950] AC 361. Since the Act of 1957 the distinction between invitees and licensees has been abolished, and the extent of the duty is now simply the common duty of care. But the old cases still apply so as to show that the landlord is responsible for all parts not demised by him, on the ground that he is regarded as being sufficiently in control of them to impose on him a duty of care to all persons coming lawfully on to the premises.

Thirdly, where an owner did not let premises to a tenant but only licensed a person to occupy them on terms which did not amount to a demise, the owner still having the right to do repairs, he was regarded as being sufficiently in control of the structure to impose on him a duty towards all persons coming lawfully on to the premises. So he was held liable for a visitor who fell on the defective step to the front door in *Hawkins v Coulsdon and Purley UDC* [1954] 1 QB 319; and to the occupier's wife for the defective ceiling which fell on her in *Greene v Chelsea Borough Council* [1954] 2 QB 127. The extent of the duty was that owed to a licensee, but since the Act of 1957 the duty is the common duty of care to see that the structure is reasonably safe.

Fourthly, where an owner employed an independent contractor to do work on premises or a structure, the owner was usually still regarded as sufficiently in control of the place as to be under a duty towards all those who might lawfully come there. In some cases he might fulfil that duty by entrusting the work to the independent contractor: see *Haseldine v CA Daw & Son* [1941] 2 KB 343 and section 2(4) of the Act of 1957. In other cases he might only be able to fulfil it by exercising proper supervision himself over the contractor's work, using due diligence himself to prevent damage from unusual danger: see *Thomson v Cremin* [1956] 1 WLR 103n as explained by Lord Reid in *Davie v New Merton Board Mills Ltd* [1959] AC 604. But in addition to the owner, the courts regarded the independent contractor as himself being sufficiently in control of the place where he worked as to owe a duty of care towards all persons coming lawfully there. He was said to be an 'occupier' also: see *Hartwell's* case; but this is only a particular instance of his general duty of care: see *Billings (AC) & Sons Ltd v Riden* [1958] AC 240 per Lord Reid.

In the light of these cases, I ask myself whether the brewery company had a sufficient degree of control over the premises to put them under a duty to a visitor. Obviously they had complete control over the ground floor and were 'occupiers' of it. But I think that they had also sufficient control over the private portion. They had not let it out to Mr Richardson by a demise. They had only granted him a licence to occupy it, having a right themselves to do repairs. That left them with a residuary degree of control which was equivalent to that retained by the Chelsea Corporation in *Greene's* case. They were in my opinion 'an occupier' within the Act of 1957, Mr Richardson, who had a licence to occupy, had also a considerable degree of control. So had Mrs Richardson, who catered for summer guests. All three of them were, in my opinion, 'occupiers' of the private portion of the 'Golfer's Arms.' There is no difficulty in having more than one occupier at one and the same time, each of whom is under a duty of care to visitors . . .

Lord Morris

The conclusion I reach is that as regards the premises as a whole both Lacons and the manager were occupiers, but that by mutual arrangement Lacons would not (subject to certain overriding considerations) exercise control over some parts. They gave freedom to their manager to live in his home in privacy. They gave him freedom to furnish it as and how he chose. They gave him freedom to receive personal guests, and also to receive guests for reward. I think it follows that both Lacons and the Richardsons were 'occupiers' *vis-à-vis* Mr Wheat and his party. Both Lacons and the Richardsons owed Mr Wheat and his party a duty. The duty was the common duty of care. The measure and the content of that duty were not, however, necessarily the same in the case of Lacons and in the case of the Richardsons. The duty was to take such care as in all the circumstances of the case was reasonable to see that Mr Wheat and his party would be reasonably safe in using the premises as guests for reward. Lacons did not know that Mr Wheat and his party were to arrive but they had given permission to their manager to take guests, and the result was that Mr Wheat and his party were on the premises with Lacons' permission. The 'circumstances of the case' would, however, vary as between Lacons and the Richardsons. Thus, if after Mr Wheat and his party had arrived they had been ascending the main staircase and if it had collapsed and caused them injury a question would have arisen whether either Lacons or the Richardsons or any or all of them had been lacking in their duty. 'The circumstances of the case' in such a situation would have, or might have, been quite different so far as Lacons were concerned from what they would have been so far as the Richardsons were concerned. If, to take another possibility, the Wheats had entered a living-room of the Richardsons which had been fitted and equipped and furnished by the Richardsons and had suffered some mishap which arose from the state or condition of the equipment or furnishings 'the circumstances of the case' would have been, or might have been, quite different so far as the Richardsons were concerned from the circumstances so far as Lacons were concerned.

In the illustrations to which I have referred it might be or could be that there would be some failure on the part of Lacons to take care in regard to the staircase and no failure on the part of the Richardsons: so it might be or could be that there would be some failure on the part of the Richardsons in regard to some equipment or furnishing in a living-room and no failure on the part of Lacons.

It may, therefore, often be that the extent of the particular control which is exercised within the sphere of joint occupation will become a pointer as to the nature and extent of the duty which reasonably devolves upon a particular occupier...

[The House of Lords went on to dismiss the appeal on the basis that the brewery was not in breach of the common duty of care.]

COMMENTARY

It has been said that the terms 'occupied', 'occupier' and 'occupation' are not legal terms of art, with 'one single and precise legal meaning applicable in all circumstances' (*Graysim Holdings Limited v P & O Property Holdings Ltd* [1996] AC 329, 334 per Lord Nicholls). However, this does not mean that the terms bear the meaning they would in common parlance, for it could hardly be said in ordinary speech that the brewery 'occupied' the residential accommodation of its manager. Although the Richardsons were occupiers for the purpose of the Act, there may, as Lord Denning points out, be more than one occupier if each exhibits sufficient control. In this context, however, it is worth noting Lord Morris's comment that the extent of control may be relevant to the 'nature and extent' of the duty. Even though the level of control of the defendant was sufficient to make it an occupier under the Act, the nature of the control did not make it responsible for the failure to ensure a light bulb was fitted. Such day-to-day maintenance of the property was the job of the occupier in residence, the manager and his wife (albeit that on the facts they were found not to have neglected this responsibility).

As Lord Nicholls noted in *Grayshim Holdings* (above), the meaning of occupier varies with context: its meaning 'in the context of the Rent Acts, for instance, is not in all respects the same as in the context of the Occupiers' Liability Act 1957'. Accordingly, care should be taken in using cases from areas other than occupiers' liability for the purpose of deciding who is an occupier under the Act.

If Lacons had granted the pub manager a tenancy, not merely a contractual licence, the situation would have been governed by statute. As Lord Denning noted, at common law, the landlord was deemed to relinquish control by virtue of the lease and thus owed no duty to anyone (other than the tenant under the terms of the lease). It made no difference whether the lease imposed any obligation to maintain or repair (*Cavalier v Pope* [1906] AC 428). The immunity that this decision gave to landlords was partly abrogated by s. 4 of the 1957 Act (referred to by Lord Denning), but s. 4 has itself been repealed and replaced with s. 4 of the Defective Premises Act 1972, which provides in s. 4(1):

> Where premises are let under a tenancy which puts on the landlord an obligation to the tenant for the maintenance or repair of the premises the landlord owes to all persons who might reasonably be expected to be affected by defects in the state of the premises a duty to take such care as is reasonable in all the circumstance to see that they are reasonably safe from personal injury or from damage to their property caused by a relevant defect.

For a discussion of the effect of this section see *Winfield & Jolowicz*, para. 9–40.

(b) The Common Duty of Care

The occupier owes his lawful visitors the common duty of care, defined in s. 2(2) as being the care required to ensure that the visitor is reasonably safe in using the premises for the purpose for which he was invited or permitted to be on the premises. In *Fairchild v Glenhaven Funeral Services* [2002] 1 WLR 1052 the Court of Appeal, approving the speech of Lord Goff in *Ferguson v Welsh* [1987] 1 WLR 1553, held that s. 2 only related to the visitor's safety in using the *premises*. This is known as the 'occupancy' duty. It seems that the occupancy duty may encompass some activities carried out on the land as the second part of s. 1(1) relates to dangers created by 'things done or omitted to be done' on the premises. In *Tomlinson v Congleton Borough Council* [2004] 1 AC 46 this was interpreted by Lords Hoffmann and Hobhouse as meaning some activity conducted by the occupier, or by others with his consent, that creates a risk to persons on the premises (e.g. if shooting is taking place on the premises, or speedboats are allowed to go into an area where swimmers are present). Conversely, the Court of Appeal in *Fairchild* held that the common duty of care did not apply to an *activity* (unless such as to affect the state of the premises) carried on on the premises by a third party who was there with the consent of the occupier, although the occupier could be made liable by the application of ordinary common law principles if the appropriate conditions were satisfied.

The distinction between activities on the land which make an occupier liable under the Act and those that do not is not easy to draw and the cases are not always consistent. In *Revill v Newberry* [1996] QB 567, p. 576, in the context of the Occupiers' Liability Act 1984 the Court of Appeal has held that the legislation does not govern the liability of the occupier for his activities on the land, and in *Cunningham v Reading Football Club Ltd* [1992] PIQR

P141 a duty under both the Act and the common law was held to extend to taking care to ensure that the state of the premises was not such as to enable third parties, including other lawful entrants, to cause harm to visitors by ripping up lumps of concrete and using them as projectiles. As far as liability under the Act was concerned, was this not imposing liability for an activity of a third party who was on the land with the consent of the occupier? This lack of clarity is less important than it might seem at first glance for two reasons. First, it has been said that there may be 'many occasions when an occupier may be legally liable in negligence in respect of the activities which he permits or encourages on his land' (*Bottomley v Todmorden Cricket Club* [2003] EWCA Civ 1575, [2004] PIQR P18 at [42], per Brooke LJ) so that, even if the Act does not apply, the occupier may owe a duty at common law with respect to activities carried out on the land. Second, as Brooke LJ noted in the same paragraph, it is rarely necessary to draw a distinction between occupancy and activity duties as the requirements of the common duty of care under the Act are practically identical to the common law (see *Winfield & Jolowicz*, para. 9–3). The result is that even cases post-*Fairchild* do not always draw the distinction between occupancy and activity duties (see, e.g., *Maguire v Sefton Metropolitan Borough Council* [2006] EWCA Civ 316). Rather, the significance of the common duty of care created by the Act lies not in the distinction between occupancy and activity duties, but (as in the previous common law) in its imposition of a duty to act positively—a rare phenomenon in the law of tort—to protect the visitor.

A typical way of satisfying the common duty of care is to warn of risks associated with the premises. Although the usual risks against which the occupier must warn relate to the physical state of buildings and other structures, the duty extends to dangers present in the land itself (e.g. a hole in the ground hidden by overgrowth) or, indeed, on the land (see the unusual case of *Shorten v Grafton District Golf Club* [2000] NSWCA 58 (New South Wales Court of Appeal), where the defendant was held liable for its failure to warn that kangaroos present on the golf course might be dangerous if approached). However, recent cases have laid emphasis on the words 'dangers due to the state of the premises or to things done or omitted to be done on them' in s. 1(1) of the Act (substantially repeated in s. 1(1)(a) of the OLA 1984), and stressed that the relevant risk must be one that is associated with the land, rather than the use that the visitor makes of the land. Thus the risk of diving into water of unknown depth is not a risk associated with the state of the premises, but arises from the visitor's obviously dangerous activity (*Donoghue v Folkstone Properties Ltd* [2003] QB 1008; *Tomlinson v Congleton Borough Council* [2004] 1 AC 46). Likewise the risk of falling from an external fire escape if one choses to use it as a climbing frame (*Keown v Coventry Healthcare NHS Trust* [2006] 1 WLR 953). This approach gives rise to a number of questions. First, in the diving scenario, should it make any difference if, instead of hitting his head on the bottom of the lake, the claimant hits his head on an object that is protruding from the bottom? (See *Rhind v Astbury Water Park Ltd* [2004] EWCA Civ 756, where the relevant danger was found to be attributable to the state of the premises but the claim failed because the claimant was a trespasser and the defendant had no reason to know that the object was there.) Secondly, should the approach of the recent cases apply where the very purpose for which the occupier allows the visitor onto the land is to engage in an activity that may make the premises dangerous? For example, can the occupier of a ski resort avoid liability under the Act if a skier is injured by crashing into a tree by arguing that this is not a danger due to the state of the premises or to things done or omitted to be done on them, even if the risk could have been avoided by placing the ski-run in a different part of the land? (See, generally, Buckley, 'Occupiers' Liability in England and Canada' (2006) 35 Comm L World Rev 197.)

Given the close relationship between the duty of care at common law and the common duty of care under the Act, it should come as no surprise that the factors relevant to breach of duty at common law are also relevant to breach of the common duty of care, for example the gravity of the potential harm to the visitor, the cost of preventing that harm, the likelihood of the harm occurring and the utility of the defendant's occupation (see *Tomlinson v Congleton Borough Council* [2004] 1 AC 46 at [34], per Lord Hoffmann, and [80], per Lord Hobhouse). The purpose for which the visitor is on the premises remains relevant as the common duty of care is a duty to take reasonable care to see that the visitor will be reasonably safe in using the premises for the purposes for which he is invited or permitted by the occupier to be there. Thus a warning that the bathroom floor is slippery might exonerate the occupier *vis-à-vis* a dinner guest but may not do so for a hotel guest. However, the status of the entrant no longer determines the standard of care: it is simply another factor that is added to the breach of duty matrix. However, in determining whether there has been a breach of the common duty of care, s. 2(3) and (4) of the Act sets out a number of specific factors that, where applicable, must be considered.

(i) Children

The Act requires the occupier to take account of the fact that children are less careful than adults (s. 2(3)(a)). What may be sufficient for an adult visitor may be hopelessly inadequate for a child. For example, a written warning might place an adult on guard against a potential danger, but would be of little use in warning a toddler who cannot yet read. None the less, the occupier's duty is one of reasonable care, and it must be remembered that it is almost impossible to make premises completely safe for children. This is especially so where a child escapes momentarily from its parents; although such a scenario is foreseeable by the occupier, there may be nothing that can reasonably be done in such circumstances to protect the child (see, e.g., *Bourne Leisure Ltd v Marsden* [2009] EWCA Civ 671).

A particular problem for child claimants was illustrated in *Phipps v Rochester Corporation* [1955] 1 QB 450. The plaintiff, aged five, and his seven-year-old sister were walking across a large open space of grassland which was part of a building site being developed by the defendant. A deep trench, which would have been obvious to an adult, had been dug in the grassland by the defendant as part of the development. Whilst crossing the open space the plaintiff fell into the trench and broke his leg, and an action was brought against the defendant as occupier. The trial judge, Devlin J, accepted that the trench constituted a danger to a small child. In determining what steps the occupier should have taken, Devlin J commented (at 471):

> I think that it would be an unjustifiable restriction of the principle if one were to say that although the licensor may in determining the extent of his duty have regard to the fact that it is the habit, and also the duty, of prudent people to look after themselves, he may not in that determination have a similar regard to the fact that it is the habit, and also the duty, of prudent people to look after their little children. If he is entitled, in the absence of evidence to the contrary, to assume that parents will not normally allow their little children to go out unaccompanied, he can decide what he should do and consider what warnings are necessary on that basis.

Thus the occupier was not in breach: the risk was obvious and the occupier could assume that parents would not expose their children to this risk; it was not required, in Devlin J's words, to 'assume parental responsibility'. Although the case is pre-1957 the reasoning is equally applicable to the common duty of care: *Simkiss v Rhondda Borough Council* (1983) 81 LGR 460.

Phipps creates something of a dilemma for the claimant. To succeed it must be argued that the state of the land or premises was dangerous, for if it is not there is no breach of the common duty of care. But in cases like *Phipps*, where the parents allowed their children onto the land unaccompanied, the defendant can respond in two ways. First, it can be said that, if the parents thought it safe for their children to enter the land, the occupier is also entitled to think that it was safe and hence the common duty of care has not been breached. Conversely, if the parents did not think it safe to let the children onto the land unaccompanied, why were the children in fact let onto the land? In such case it might be held that the cause of the child's injury was the parent's or guardian's negligence; alternatively, if the occupier was held liable there seems no reason why he could not seek contribution from the parent under the Civil Liability (Contribution) Act 1978 (see *Winfield & Jolowicz*, para. 9–11). Although the mere fact of parenthood does not of itself create a duty of care (see *Hahn v Conley* (1971) 126 CLR 378; *Surtees v Kingston-upon-Thames Borough Council* [1991] 2 FLR 559) there is little doubt that somebody exercising parental control owes a duty to the child to take reasonable care not to expose the child to the risk of physical injury, the situation in *Phipps*.

However, the dilemma should not be overstated. If the danger is latent, even a prudent parent will not discover it, so the *Phipps* reasoning no longer applies. In addition, the dilemma facing the child claimant faces any claimant where the danger is patent: if the entrant knew of the danger but none the less entered any consequent injury might be deemed to be caused by the entrant's own action, or the defences of *volenti* or contributory negligence might apply. Of course, the problem in cases like *Phipps* is that the claimant child is not negligent: the claim fails because of the parent's negligence. *Markesinis & Deakin*, p. 354, argue that a parent's assessment of the danger should only be one factor in determining whether the occupier has exercised the appropriate level of care. Further, the authors argue that if this assessment was a factor in causing the child harm, the occupier's liability should only be reduced, not avoided. Do you agree?

(ii) Special Risks Associated with Particular Callings

In determining whether the common duty of care has been breached, the occupier does not have to warn persons having special skills as a result of their calling of risks associated with the exercise of those skills because such a person will appreciate and guard against any special risks ordinarily incident to that calling (s. 2(3)(b)). Two issues arise: first, what is a calling; and, secondly, what risks are associated with a particular calling? In the leading case of *Roles v Nathan* [1963] 1 WLR 1117 the plaintiffs were the widows of two chimney sweeps who had been overcome by carbon monoxide fumes whilst cleaning boiler flues. The deceased men had been warned a number of times of the dangers of poisoning from carbon monoxide gas and had been told to take precautions, but had ignored the advice given to them. Lord Denning MR rejected the widows' claims against the occupier:

> The householder can reasonably expect the sweep to take care of himself so far as any dangers from the flues are concerned. These chimney sweeps ought to have known that there might be dangerous fumes about and ought to have taken steps to guard against them . . . When a householder calls in a specialist to deal with a defective installation on the premises, he can reasonably expect the specialists to appreciate and guard against the dangers arising from the defect.

What constitutes a special risk associated with a particular calling is a question of fact to be decided in each case. In *Neame v Johnson*, unreported, 24 November 1992, the Court of Appeal held that the risk of falling over books or other material left on the floor of residential accommodation was one associated with being an ambulanceman. However, the fact that the state of the premises is a risk only to a person exercising a calling does not necessarily mean that it is ordinarily incidental to his work within the meaning of s. 2(3)(b). In *Williams v Department of the Environment*, QBD, 30 November 1981, Tudor Evans J held that the risk of injury from an exposed spindle in a boiler was not incidental to the calling of an industrial heating engineer employed to service the boiler, even though the spindle was unlikely to pose a risk to anyone else entering the area. The exposed spindle was 'simply part of the plaintiff's place of work which made it unsafe and with which he was not involved' (see also *Woollins v British Celanese Ltd* [1966] 1 KIR 438). However, if the calling involves the use of the premises in a way in which they would not normally be used, the risk associated with the special use is one associated with that calling. Dealing with a case involving the use of premises by an electrician, Jupp J commented in *West v T. Clarke Ltd*, QBD, 20 May 1982:

> Now, what of the occupiers? They are responsible for the safety of the premises, and when they invite people in they must take care that the premises are safe if used within the scope of the invitation. When an electrician is invited in, the same applies. It is for the occupiers to see that he can go about his business in safety so far as the premises are concerned, but there must come a time when the electrician ceases to be using the premises in an ordinary kind of way and begins to make use of them in a way which is ordinarily incident to his calling. At that point he ceases to rely on the occupier to keep him safe and free from risk. He has to rely on himself. When and where that point is reached is in my judgment a matter of fact and degree. I am quite clear that the point is not governed in the case of an electrician by being confined to dangers from electrical wirings and electrical circuits. It must include when going into a loft or roof space, making sure that the precise place from which he is going to work is safe. Just where that is will depend on the facts of each particular case.

(iii) Warnings

The common duty of care may be discharged by a warning, but s. 2(4)(a) limits this to situations where the warning was, in all the circumstances, enough to enable the visitor to be reasonably safe. The genesis of this sub-section lies in the pre-Act decision of the House of Lords in *London Graving Dock Co Ltd v Horton* [1951] AC 151. The plaintiff welder was injured when some staging on the ship on which he was working failed. He had complained of the dangerous state of the staging for the previous month but the defendant had done nothing to remedy the problem. It was accepted that the plaintiff was owed the duty of an invitee (a duty to warn of unusual dangers) and that the staging was an unusual danger, but, as he had full knowledge of that danger, a majority of the House of Lords held that the defendant was not in breach. This was so irrespective of whether the plaintiff could be said to have accepted the risk. The practical effect of this, as Lord Reid pointed out in a powerful dissent, was to equate knowledge of a risk with acceptance of the risk, a proposition which the majority accepted would have been incorrect if the plaintiff had been an employee of the defendant (see Ch. 6, and *Smith v Austin Lifts Ltd* [1959] 1 WLR 100 at 117, per Lord Denning). Lord MacDermott, also dissenting, gave the following example of the consequences of the majority approach:

> A, at the end of his day's work, repairs to the local railway station to get home. He goes to the ticket office by the usual and only means of approach. The roof overhead is in a dangerous state and bits of it are liable to fall at any moment. The railway company know of this and could readily avert the danger for those beneath by placing a temporary screen under the defective part. But all they do is to post a notice describing the danger in clear terms. A reads and understands this before he enters the perilous area, but hurries on in order to get his ticket and is hurt by a

piece of falling glass. He was not volens or careless. Yet, if the appellants are right, he was owed no duty by the company and has no redress.

My Lords, if the law confers that sort of immunity on occupiers of premises, it is, to my mind, inadequate and open to grave criticism...

Lord Denning in *Roles v Nathan* [1963] 1 WLR 1117 suggested the courts might ultimately have developed the law along the lines of s. 2(4)(a), although the only authority cited in support of this proposition was his own judgment in *Greene v Chelsea Borough Council* [1954] 2 QB 127, and there were subsequent cases applying *Horton*. The Act now makes the position clear. Whether the warning is sufficient to discharge the common duty of care imposed by s. 2(2) is a question of fact requiring a weighing of the relevant circumstances, including the reason for the visitor's presence on the premises, the nature of the danger, the knowledge of the visitor, and the practicability of the possible means of removing or reducing the risk. An example of the change made by the Act is given by Lord Denning in *Roles v Nathan* [1963] 1 WLR 1117 at 1124:

> Suppose for instance, that there was only one way of getting into and out of premises, and it was by a footbridge over a stream which was rotten and dangerous. According to *Horton's* case, the occupier could escape all liability to any visitor by putting up a notice: 'This bridge is dangerous,' even though there was no other way by which the visitor could get in or out, and he had no option but to go over the bridge. In such a case, section 2(4) makes it clear that the occupier would nowadays be liable. But if there were two footbridges, one of which was rotten, and the other safe a hundred yards away, the occupier could still escape liability, even today, by putting up a notice: 'Do not use this footbridge. It is dangerous. There is a safe one further upstream.' Such a warning is sufficient because it does enable the visitor to be reasonably safe.

Alternatively, there may be some situations where a simple notice will satisfy the requirements of the Act. (An example given by Lord MacDermott in *Horton* is a warning of dangers which lurk in navigable waters.)

Does an occupier need to warn of risks that are obvious? In *Darby v National Trust* [2001] EWCA Civ 189, the claimant's husband was killed in a drowning accident on the defendant's property. The Court of Appeal held that the failure of the defendant to erect signs saying 'Danger No Swimming' around one of the ponds on its property was not negligent: the risks to the claimant's husband associated with swimming in the pond were 'perfectly obvious', and any general notice advising visitors not to swim 'would have told [him] no more than he already knew.' In particular, the Court of Appeal was not prepared to accept that there was a different risk associated with swimming in the pond on the defendant's land than in swimming in the sea or any other open water. If a warning notice was required in one case, it was required in all, and, in the opinion of May LJ: 'it cannot be the duty of the owner of every stretch of coastline to have notices warning of the dangers of swimming in the sea.'

Should the position be any different if the swimmer was a trespasser? (See *Tomlinson v Congleton Borough Council* [2004] 1 AC 46, extracted below.)

(iv) Occupier's Use of Independent Contractors

Section 2(4)(b) provides that an occupier discharges the common duty of care in circumstances where:

(i) The breach was caused by the faulty execution of an act of construction, maintenance, or repair of an independent contractor;

(ii)   It was reasonable for the occupier to employ the contractor to undertake the task in question; and

(iii) The occupier took reasonable steps to ensure the contractor was competent and the work was properly done.

Where the independent contractor has been engaged to perform a task requiring the exercise of special skill, courts have normally found that the occupier can avail himself of s. 2(4)(b) even if the contractor has carried out the task negligently (assuming reasonable care has been taken in choosing the contractor in the first place).

Haseldine v Daw [1941] 2 KB 343

The plaintiff was injured when the lift in which he was riding malfunctioned and crashed to the ground. The plaintiff sued, amongst others, the landlord (who was the occupier of that part of the premises). The landlord had entered into a service contract for the lift with a competent firm of engineers and the lift had recently been serviced.

Scott LJ

The invitor is bound to take that kind of care which a reasonably prudent man in his place would take—neither more nor less. The landlord of a block of flats, as occupier of the lifts, does not profess as such to be either an electrical or, as in this case, a hydraulic engineer. Having no technical skill he cannot rely on his own judgment, and the duty of care towards his invitees requires him to obtain and follow good technical advice. If he did not do so, he would, indeed, be guilty of negligence. To hold him responsible for the misdeeds of his independent contractor would be to make him insure the safety of his lift.

Goddard LJ

Towards an invitee the occupier has the duty of taking care that the premises are reasonably safe. I need not quote the classic passage from the judgment of Willes J in *Indermaur v Dames* [above], but he there points out that whether reasonable care has been taken is to be determined as a matter of fact. It seems to me that, by employing a first class firm of lift engineers to make periodical inspections of the lift, to adjust it and to furnish reports upon it, the landlord did all that a reasonable man could do towards seeing that it was safe, especially when it is remembered that he also had the advantage of quarterly inspections by the insurance company's engineer. But it is argued that, if the engineers were negligent, it cannot be said that the occupier has discharged his duty. With this, I cannot agree. An occupier or any other person may have, either by contract or by law, such a degree of duty imposed on him that he cannot discharge it by employing a contractor to do work for him, but where the duty is to take care that the premises are safe I cannot see how it can be discharged better than by the employment of competent contractors. Indeed, one may well ask how otherwise could the duty be discharged?

COMMENTARY

In principle it is hard to fault this decision, as the landlord had no expertise in servicing lifts and took the only reasonable step open to it to ensure visitors were safe. However, on the facts it appears that the landlord knew that the lift had never been completely overhauled during its thirty-five years of operation, that the engineers had reported parts of its work-ings were badly worn and scoured, and that the engineers' preferred options were to replace the worn parts or to electrify the lift. Although the engineers did not suggest the lift was unsafe, could it have been argued these repairs and improvements should have been carried out (see *Dimitrelos v 14 Martin Place Pty Ltd* [2007] NSWCA 85 at [16] per Young CJ in Eq)? (One of the reasons they were not was because the landlord was 'disinclined to incur the expenditure'.) On the other hand it might seem harsh to require the occupier to 'second guess' an expert. As Salmon J said in a case involving negligence by an independent electrical contractor, 'I cannot think it incumbent upon them [the occupiers] to send one of their directors or servants to a polytechnic to take a course in electrical engineering and then attempt the rewiring themselves' (*Green v Fibreglass Ltd* [1958] 2 QB 245). The reasoning in *Haseldine* has been applied under the 1957 Act to relieve occupiers from liability in relation to electrical work carried out by an independent contractor (*Cook v Broderip* [1968] EG 128) and in respect of the negligence of a contractor responsible for the choice and installation of glass in a shop front-door (*Smith v Storey*, unreported, CA Civil Division, 26 June 1980).

It may have been difficult for the landlord to check if the lift had been properly serviced, but where the work is less skilled there may be an obligation on the occupier to ascertain if the work has been properly done. In *Woodward v Mayor of Hastings* [1945] KB 174 the plain-tiff was injured when he fell off an icy step on school premises. The step had been negligently left in an icy state by a cleaner. The Court of Appeal held that the cleaner was the agent of the defendant occupier and was liable on this basis, but that, even if she was not, the defendant was liable from the mere fact of the occupation of the premises. The defendant argued that as the task had been delegated to some competent person *Haseldine v Daw* absolved him from liability, but this was rejected, Du Parcq LJ memorably commenting that 'the craft of the charwoman may have its mysteries, but there is no esoteric quality in the nature of the work which the cleaning of a snow-covered step demands'. The obvious distinction between *Haseldine* and *Woodward* is the complexity of the delegated task: the more complex the task the more likely the occupier will satisfy the common duty of care by employing a compe-tent contractor, although the occupier might remain liable if the contractor's negligence was apparent even to a layperson. Not everyone has found this distinction satisfactory. In *Riverstone Meat Co Pty Ltd v Lancashire Shipping Co Ltd* [1961] AC 807 at 879, Lord Hodson thought that 'the distinction between the last two cases based on specialised work being necessary in the case of the repair of a lift and being unnecessary in the case of the cleaning of a school may have to be reconsidered'. However, his Lordship did not elaborate further and subsequent cases have implicitly adopted the distinction. In *Ferguson v Welsh* [1987] 1 WLR 1553 a majority of the House of Lords held that an occupier, either under the Act or at common law, was not normally required to inspect work done by an independent demoli-tion contractor to check if a safe system of work was in place. However, if the occupier knew that an unsafe system was in place it might be required to take action. Lord Goff differed from the majority on this point, arguing that mere knowledge was insufficient to make the occupier liable either under the Act or at common law as the occupier was not required to supervise activities on its land which did not relate to the safety of the premises, and this view was approved by the Court of Appeal in *Fairchild v Glenhaven Funeral Services* [2002] 1 WLR 1052. However, it is submitted that the majority approach still applies to the 'occu-pancy' duties of the occupier. Thus in the case of specialist independent contractors if, but only if, the occupier has reason to believe that work carried out by an independent contrac-tor has left the premises in a dangerous state, further inspection may be required.

In *Gwilliam v West Hertfordshire Hospital NHS Trust* [2003] QB 443, the 63-year-old claimant was injured whilst attempting to use a 'splat-wall', a process which involved leaping from a trampoline onto a Velcro wall. The splat-wall was provided by an independent contractor as part of a charity fair organised by the defendant occupier to raise funds, and it was due to the independent contractor's negligence that the claimant was injured. As the liability insurance of the independent contractor had expired, the claimant was unable to recover her full damages from him, and she sued the occupier for negligently failing to ensure that the independent contractor had adequate liability insurance. One member of the majority, Lord Woolf, held that s. 2(2) of the 1957 Act required an occupier to inquire as to the insurance position of the independent contractor, although on the facts the occupier had done so and the agreement had been made on the understanding insurance would be in place. Sedley LJ dissented on the question whether the duty should extend to checking the contractor's insurance position: if the occupier was liable on these facts why not the private person whose garden was used for a local fete where the visitor was injured by the negligence of an uninsured stallholder? It is submitted that the dissent of Sedley LJ is to be preferred. The majority of the Court of Appeal thought that merely receiving an affirmative reply from the independent contractor as to the existence of insurance was sufficient, but this provides little protection to the injured visitor. Conversely, if the duty is to have any substance it is unduly onerous on the occupier. Should the occupier, for example, really be required not only to inquire whether the contractor has taken out insurance but also to seek confirmation that the insurance policy remains in force throughout the duration of the work? Unsurprisingly, in *Naylor v Payling* [2004] EWCA Civ 560 the Court of Appeal held that there is no *general* requirement to check on the insurance position of an independent contractor; and more recently the Court of Appeal in *Glaister v Appelby-in-Westmoreland Town Council* [2009] EWCA Civ 1325 has expressed a preference for the reasoning of Sedley LJ in *Gwilliam*.

(v) Exclusion of Liability and Volenti

Section 2(1) of the Act allows an occupier—'in so far as he is free' to do so—to extend, restrict, modify or exclude his duty to a visitor by agreement or otherwise. The main restriction on an occupier's ability to exclude or limit liability is provided by the Unfair Contract Terms Act (UCTA) 1977 (which in s. 1(1)(c) provides that 'negligence' includes the breach of the common duty of care under the Occupiers' Liability Act 1957). The result is that the restrictions in s. 2 of UCTA apply, so that, in respect of business liability, the occupier cannot exclude liability for death or personal injury, and attempts to limit business liability for other types of damage are subject to a reasonableness requirement. Because of the change made by UCTA, care must be taken when looking at pre-UCTA cases which were necessarily decided on different principles (see, e.g., *Ashdown v Samuel Williams & Sons Ltd* [1957] 1 QB 409 and *White v Blackmore* [1972] 2 QB 651, extracted at p. 317, above. Attention should also be drawn to UCTA s. 1(3)(b), which recognises that, in certain circumstances, access to premises for recreational or educational purposes may fall outside the business purposes of the occupier and therefore beyond the scope of the Act (see p. 317, above).

Whether the attempt to exclude or restrict liability is effective (i.e. whether it forms part of the agreement between the parties, or if a notice, whether reasonable steps have been taken to bring the notice to the attention of the claimant) depends upon the application of the normal rules relating to these issues (see Ch. 6) and raises no problems specific to occupiers' liability.

Section 2(5) allows the occupier the defence of *volenti non fit injuria*. As the sub-section directs that whether a risk has been accepted is to be decided on the same principles applicable to the ordinary law of negligence it will not be discussed further here.

3. The 1984 Act

As noted above, at common law the trespasser received the least protection of any entrant on the occupier's premises. The minimal duty set out in *R   Addie & Sons (Collieries) Ltd v Dumbreck* [1929] AC 358 reflected a wider view that trespassers were wrongdoers and in one sense deserved what they got. Furthermore, to take precautions against uninvited guests was thought too onerous a burden to place on landowners. However, although the term 'trespasser' covered people whose claim might well be regarded as without merit, it also included those whose case was considerably stronger, for example, children. Dissatisfaction with the law, especially as it affected children, encouraged the courts to find implied licences so that children became lawful visitors. Also, where the injury was caused by the occupier's activities (rather than the state of the premises) a trespasser might recover on ordinary *Donoghue v Stevenson* principles. In *Videan v British Transport Commission* [1963] 2 QB 650 the Court of Appeal differed over whether the occupier owed a duty to a trespasser with respect to the state of the premises (the 'occupation' duty). Lord Denning accepted that the occupier's activity duty was based simply on foresight of the trespasser. If the presence of a trespasser could be foreseen a duty of care was owed at common law. However, the same principle did not apply 'where [the occupier] has done no work on the land: for then his liability is as occupier and nothing else'. Conversely, Pearson LJ saw no sound basis of principle for differentiating sharply between liability for the static condition of the land and liability for activities on the land. A duty of 'common humanity' was owed to the trespasser in respect of both activity and occupation duties. Although there was no consensus in the speeches, the latter position appears to have been adopted by the House of Lords in *British Railways Board v Herrington* [1972] AC 877. Lord Diplock defined the duty as follows:

> My Lords, I conclude therefore that there is no duty owed by an occupier to any trespasser unless he actually knows of the physical facts in relation to the state of his land or some activity carried out on it, which constitute a serious danger to persons on the land who are unaware of those facts. He is under no duty to any trespasser to make inspections or enquiries to ascertain whether there is any such danger. Where he does know of physical facts which a reasonable man would appreciate involved danger of serious injury to the trespasser his duty is to take reasonable steps to enable the trespasser to avoid the danger. What constitute reasonable steps will depend on the kind of trespasser to whom the duty is owed . . .

The duty established was a lesser duty than that under the 1957 Act, only being owed when a reasonable person, knowing the physical facts which the occupier actually knew, would appreciate that a trespasser's presence at the point and time of the danger was so likely that in all the circumstances it would be inhumane not to take appropriate steps to eliminate, reduce or warn of the danger. Whether it was inhumane not to warn or offer some protection would be judged objectively and depended on all the circumstances of the case, including (per Lord Diplock) the permanent or intermittent character of the danger; the severity of the injuries which it was likely to cause; in the case of children, the attractiveness to them of that which constituted the dangerous object or condition of the land; and the expense involved in giving effective warning of it to the kind of trespasser likely to be injured, in relation to the occupier's resources in money or in labour.

Subsequently, the issue was referred to the Law Commission, which published its *Report on Liability for Damage or Injury to Trespassers and Related Questions of Occupiers' Liability* (Law Com. No. 75) in 1976. The Commission felt that no clear principle emerged from *Herrington* because of the divergence between the speeches, and recommended legislation. This report formed the basis for the Occupiers' Liability Act 1984.

Occupiers' Liability Act 1984

An Act to amend the law of England and Wales as to the liability of persons as occupiers of premises for injury suffered by persons other than their visitors...

1. DUTY OF OCCUPIER TO PERSONS OTHER THAN HIS VISITORS

(1) The rules enacted by this section shall have effect, in place of the rules of the common law, to determine—

    (a) whether any duty is owed by a person as occupier of premises to persons other than his visitors in respect of any risk of their suffering injury on the premises by reason of any danger due to the state of the premises or to things done or omitted to be done on them; and

    (b) if so, what that duty is.

(2) For the purposes of this section, the persons who are to be treated respectively as an occupier of any premises (which, for those purposes, include any fixed or movable structure) and as his visitors are—

    (a) any person who owes in relation to the premises the duty referred to in section 2 of the Occupiers' Liability Act 1957 (the common duty of care), and

    (b) those who are his visitors for the purposes of that duty.

(3) An occupier of premises owes a duty to another (not being his visitor) in respect of any such risk as is referred to in subsection (1) above if—

    (a) he is aware of the danger or has reasonable grounds to believe that it exists;

    (b) he knows or has reasonable grounds to believe that the other is in the vicinity of the danger concerned or that he may come into the vicinity of the danger (in either case, whether the other has lawful authority for being in that vicinity or not); and

    (c) the risk is one against which, in all the circumstances of the case, he may reasonably be expected to offer the other some protection.

(4) Where, by virtue of this section, an occupier of premises owes a duty to another in respect of such a risk, the duty is to take such care as is reasonable in all the circumstances of the case to see that he does not suffer injury on the premises by reason of the danger concerned.

(5) Any duty owed by virtue of this section in respect of a risk may, in an appropriate case, be discharged by taking such steps as are reasonable in all the circumstances of the case to give warning of the danger concerned or to discourage persons from incurring the risk.

(6) No duty is owed by virtue of this section to any person in respect of risks willingly accepted as his by that person (the question whether a risk was so accepted to be decided on the same principles as in other cases in which one person owes a duty of care to another).

(6A) At any time when the right conferred by section 2(1) of the Countryside and Rights of Way Act 2000 is exercisable in relation to land which is access land for the purposes of Part I of that Act, an occupier of the land owes (subject to subsection (6C) below) no duty by virtue of this section to any person in respect of—

   (a) a risk resulting from the existence of any natural feature of the landscape, or any river, stream, ditch or pond whether or not a natural feature, or

   (b) a risk of that person suffering injury when passing over, under or through any wall, fence or gate, except by proper use of the gate or of a stile.

(6AA) Where the land is coastal margin for the purposes of Part 1 of that Act (including any land treated as coastal margin by virtue of s 16 of that Act) subsection (6A) has effect as if for paragraphs (a) and (b) of that subsection there were substituted 'a risk resulting from the existence of any physical feature (whether of the landscape or otherwise)'.

(6B) For the purposes of subsection (6A) above, any plant, shrub or tree, of whatever origin, is to be regarded as a natural feature of the landscape.

(6C) Subsection (6A) does not prevent an occupier from owing a duty by virtue of this section in respect of any risk where the danger concerned is due to anything done by the occupier—

   (a) with the intention of creating that risk, or

   (b) being reckless as to whether that risk is created.

(7) No duty is owed by virtue of this section to persons using the highway, and this section does not affect any duty owed to such persons.

(8) Where a person owes a duty by virtue of this section, he does not, by reason of any breach of the duty, incur any liability in respect of any loss of or damage to property.

(9) In this section—

   'highway' means any part of a highway other than a ferry or waterway;

   'injury' means anything resulting in death or personal injury, including any disease and any impairment of physical or mental condition; and

   'movable structure' includes any vessel, vehicle or aircraft.

1A. SPECIAL CONSIDERATIONS RELATING TO ACCESS LAND

In determining whether any, and if so what, duty is owed by virtue of section 1 by an occupier of land at any time when the right conferred by section 2(1) of the Countryside and Rights of Way Act 2000 is exercisable in relation to the land, regard is to be had, in particular, to—

   (a) the fact that the existence of that right ought not to place an undue burden (whether financial or otherwise) on the occupier,

   (b) the importance of maintaining the character of the countryside, including features of historic, traditional or archaeological interest, and

   (c) any relevant guidance given under section 20 of that Act.

COMMENTARY

Section 1(1) replaces any common law duty owed by the occupier to persons other than visitors with the duty provided by the Act. The terms 'occupier' and 'visitor' have the same meaning as in the 1957 Act. In *Revill v Newberry* [1996] QB 567 Neill LJ held that the 1984 Act imposed a duty on the occupier as an occupier; hence where the claim related to an activity of the occupier the ordinary common law of negligence would apply and the fact that the defendant was also an occupier was 'irrelevant'. However, it was accepted that the Act was 'very helpful' in defining the scope of the duty owed at common law; indeed Neill LJ applied the requirement in s. 1(3)(b) before finding the defendant liable. The logic of this approach has been questioned (see Weir [1996] CLJ 182, 183, who describes the above reasoning as an 'inconsequential farrago'), but the result is that the Act's main role, analogous to that of the 1957 Act, is to impose in limited circumstances a positive duty to act reasonably to ensure that the state of the premises is not a danger to trespassers.

The Existence of the Duty

The duty is imposed by s. 1(3), and roughly equates to the elements set out in Lord Diplock's speech in *Herrington*. Section 1(3)(a) and (b) contain a partly objective, partly subjective test, and, as in *Herrington*, there seems to be no requirement to carry out inspections of premises. In *Swain v Puri*, unreported, CA Civil Division, 4 July 1995, it was argued that s. 1(3)(b) should be construed as including a situation where the occupiers ought to have known that the trespasser might come into the vicinity of the danger. This was rejected by the Court of Appeal; according to Evans LJ what was required was 'actual knowledge including "shut-eye" knowledge either of the actual risk or of primary facts' from which the court might draw the necessary inference. By 'shut-eye' knowledge his Lordship meant knowledge which was 'equivalent to actual knowledge as a matter of law, and it may be equated...with an element of wilfulness though not with negligence alone'. Thus the occupier cannot close his eyes to the obvious, knowing that, if he did look, he would discover facts which would indicate the presence of trespassers. Conversely, constructive knowledge based on mere negligence in ascertaining the facts from which it could be inferred that trespassers were in the vicinity of the danger was not enough.

It might be thought that one fact that would assist in satisfying the section was that the occupier had taken precautions to prevent trespassers from coming into the vicinity of the danger. However, this was rejected in *White v City of St Albans*, unreported, CA Civil Division, 2 March 1990, on the basis that taking steps to prevent trespassers entering premises was no evidence that the occupier had knowledge that trespassers were in fact in the vicinity of the danger. Section 1(3)(b) also requires that the presence of the trespasser in the vicinity must be known to the occupier *at the time* when the trespass takes place. This was graphically illustrated in *Donoghue v Folkstone Properties Ltd* [2003] QB 1008 where the claimant dived into water in the early hours of a mid-winter day and hit his head on an underwater obstruction. Although the occupier knew that other people who were trespassing dived off the slipway, that was in the summer. The Court of Appeal held that the section required the occupier to know or have reasonable grounds to know of the presence of the trespasser, either individually or as a member of a class, in the vicinity of the danger at the relevant time. This was not the case for the claimant; the occupier had no reason to know of the presence of trespassers diving into the water late at night in mid-winter, even if it knew that other people trespassed at different times of the year; hence s. 1(3)(b) was not satisfied and no duty was owed under the 1984 Act. The result, as Lord Phillips MR noted (at [55]), is that the existence of a duty may vary between summer and winter, and even between times of the day.

Section 1(3)(c) seems to be objective, taking into account the same factors that are considered in deciding if there has been a breach of duty. There is undoubtedly an overlap between the considerations relevant to the existence of the duty in s. 1(3) and those relevant to breach of duty in s. 1(4) (e.g., the age of the trespasser will be relevant to both).

Is it appropriate for the occupier to take precautions against risks which are, or should be, obvious to the non-visitor? The following extract considers this issue.

Tomlinson v Congleton Borough Council [2004] 1 AC 46

The claimant was injured when he dived into a too shallow area of a lake, the lake being on the defendant's property. Although the defendant had put signs saying: 'Dangerous Water: No Swimming', many people, including the claimant, ignored the sign and continued to swim. Prior to the accident, the defendant had assessed swimming in the lake as a dangerous activity and had agreed that further steps should be taken to discourage swimming but the work—which would have included bulldozing the beach and planting bull rushes in its place—had not been carried out when the accident happened. The trial judge rejected the claim but an appeal was allowed by a majority of the Court of Appeal. The House of Lords unanimously allowed the defendant's appeal. One ground of their Lordships' decision—that there was no danger relating to the state of the premises—has been discussed above (p. 566). The extract deals with the question of whether the other conditions for liability had been satisfied. Although their Lordships (by a majority) thought the claimant was correctly classified as a trespasser, they also considered the position if he had been a lawful visitor under the 1957 Act.

Lord Hoffmann

The 1957 and 1984 acts contrasted

[38] In the case of the 1984 Act, there is the additional consideration that unless in all the circumstances it is reasonable to expect the occupier to do something, that is to say, to 'offer the other some protection', there is no duty at all. One may ask what difference there is between the case in which the claimant is a lawful visitor and there is in principle a duty under the 1957 Act but on the particular facts no duty to do anything, and the case in which he is a trespasser and there is on the particular facts no duty under the 1984 Act. Of course in such a case the result is the same. But Parliament has made it clear that in the case of a lawful visitor, one starts from the assumption that there is a duty whereas in the case of a trespasser one starts from the assumption that there is none.

The balance under the 1957 act

[39] My Lords, it will in the circumstances be convenient to consider first the question of what the position would have been if Mr Tomlinson had been a lawful visitor owed a duty under s 2(2) of the 1957 Act. Assume, therefore, that there had been no prohibition on swimming. What was the risk of serious injury? To some extent this depends upon what one regards as the relevant risk. As I have mentioned, the judge thought it was the risk of injury through diving while the Court of Appeal thought it was any kind of injury which could happen to people in the water. Although, as I have said, I am inclined to agree with the judge, I do not want to put the basis of my decision too narrowly. So I accept that we are concerned with the steps, if any, which should have been taken to prevent any kind of water accident. According to the Royal Society for the Prevention of Accidents, about 450 people drown while swimming in the United Kingdom every year (see *Darby v National Trust* [2001] PIQR P372 at 374). About 25–35 break their necks diving and no doubt others sustain less serious injuries. So there is obviously some degree of risk in swimming and diving, as there is in climbing, cycling, fell walking and many other such activities.

[40] I turn then to the cost of taking preventative measures. Ward LJ described it (£5,000) as 'not excessive'. Perhaps it was not, although the outlay has to be seen in the context of the

other items (rated 'essential' and 'highly desirable') in the borough council budget which had taken precedence over the destruction of the beaches for the previous two years.

[41] I do not however regard the financial cost as a significant item in the balancing exercise which the court has to undertake. There are two other related considerations which are far more important. The first is the social value of the activities which would have to be prohibited in order to reduce or eliminate the risk from swimming. And the second is the question of whether the council should be entitled to allow people of full capacity to decide for themselves whether to take the risk.

[42] The Court of Appeal made no reference at all to the social value of the activities which were to be prohibited. The majority of people who went to the beaches to sunbathe, paddle and play with their children were enjoying themselves in a way which gave them pleasure and caused no risk to themselves or anyone else. This must be something to be taken into account in deciding whether it was reasonable to expect the council to destroy the beaches.

[43] I have the impression that the Court of Appeal felt able to brush these matters aside because the council had already decided to do the work. But they were held liable for having failed to do so before Mr Tomlinson's accident and the question is therefore whether they were under a legal duty to do so. Ward LJ placed much emphasis upon the fact that the council had decided to destroy the beaches and that its officers thought that this was necessary to avoid being held liable for an accident to a swimmer. But the fact that the council's safety officers thought that the work was necessary does not show that there was a legal duty to do it. In *Darby's* case the claimant's husband was tragically drowned while swimming in a pond on the National Trust estate at Hardwick Hall. Miss Rebecca Kirkwood, the water and leisure safety consultant to the Royal Society for the Prevention of Accidents, gave uncontradicted evidence, which the judge accepted, that the pond was unsuitable for swimming because it was deep in the middle and the edges were uneven. The National Trust should have made it clear that swimming in the pond was not allowed and taken steps to enforce the prohibition. But May LJ said robustly that it was for the court, not Miss Kirkwood, to decide whether the Trust was under a legal duty to take such steps. There was no duty because the risks from swimming in the pond were perfectly obvious.

Free will

[44] The second consideration, namely the question of whether people should accept responsibility for the risks they choose to run, is the point made by Lord Phillips MR in *Donoghue v Folkestone Properties Ltd* [2003] 3 All ER 1101 at [53] and which I said was central to this appeal. Mr Tomlinson was freely and voluntarily undertaking an activity which inherently involved some risk. By contrast, Miss Bessie Stone, to whom the House of Lords held that no duty was owed, was innocently standing on the pavement outside her garden gate at 10 Beckenham Road, Cheetham when she was struck by a ball hit for six out of the Cheetham Cricket Club ground. She was certainly not engaging in any activity which involved an inherent risk of such injury. So compared with *Bolton v Stone*, this is an a fortiori case.

[45] I think it will be extremely rare for an occupier of land to be under a duty to prevent people from taking risks which are inherent in the activities they freely choose to undertake upon the land. If people want to climb mountains, go hang gliding or swim or dive in ponds or lakes, that is their affair. Of course the landowner may for his own reasons wish to prohibit such activities. He may think that they are a danger or inconvenience to himself or others. Or he may take a paternalist view and prefer people not to undertake risky activities on his land. He is entitled to impose such conditions, as the council did by prohibiting swimming. But the law does not require him to do so.

[46] My Lords, as will be clear from what I have just said, I think that there is an important question of freedom at stake. It is unjust that the harmless recreation of responsible parents

and children with buckets and spades on the beaches should be prohibited in order to comply with what is thought to be a legal duty to safeguard irresponsible visitors against dangers which are perfectly obvious. The fact that such people take no notice of warnings cannot create a duty to take other steps to protect them. I find it difficult to express with appropriate moderation my disagreement with the proposition of Sedley LJ ([2003] 3 All ER 1122 at [45]) that it is 'only where the risk is so obvious that the occupier can safely assume that nobody will take it that there will be no liability'. A duty to protect against obvious risks or self-inflicted harm exists only in cases in which there is no genuine and informed choice, or in the case of employees, or some lack of capacity, such as the inability of children to recognise danger (see *British Railways Board v Herrington* [1972] AC 877) or the despair of prisoners which may lead them to inflict injury on themselves (see *Reeves v Metropolitan Police Comr* [2000] 1 AC 360) ...

[50] My Lords, for these reasons I consider that even if swimming had not been prohibited and the council had owed a duty under s 2(2) of the 1957 Act, that duty would not have required them to take any steps to prevent Mr Tomlinson from diving or warning him against dangers which were perfectly obvious. If that is the case, then plainly there can have been no duty under the 1984 Act. The risk was not one against which he was entitled under s 1(3)(c) to protection. I would therefore allow the appeal and restore the decision of Jack J. It follows that the cross-appeal against the apportionment of damages must be dismissed.

Lord Hobhouse of Woodborough

[73]...The key is in the circumstances and what it is reasonable to expect of the occupier. The reference to warnings and discouragements in sub-s (5) and the use of the words 'some protection' in sub-s (3)(c) both demonstrate that the duty is not as onerous as Mr Tomlinson argues. Warnings can be disregarded (as was the case here); discouragements can be evaded; the trespasser may still be injured (or injure himself) while on the premises. There is no guarantee of safety any more than there is under the 1957 Act. The question remains what is it reasonable to expect the occupier to do for unauthorised trespassers on his land. The trespasser by avoiding getting the consent of the occupier, avoids having conditions or restrictions imposed upon his entry or behaviour once on the premises. By definition, the occupier cannot control the trespasser in the same way as he can control a visitor. The Acts both lay stress upon what is reasonable in all the circumstances. Such circumstances must be relevant to the relative duties owed under the two Acts.

[74] Returning to the facts of this case, what more was it reasonable to expect of the council beyond putting up the notices and issuing warnings and prohibitions?...[t]his is a case where, as held by the judge, all the relevant characteristics of this mere were already obvious to Mr Tomlinson. In these circumstances, no purpose was in fact served by the warning. It told Mr Tomlinson nothing he did not already know. (See *Staples v West Dorset DC* (1995) 93 LGR 536, *Whyte v Redland Aggregates Ltd* [1997] CA Transcript 2034, *Ratcliff v McConnell* [1999] 1 WLR 670, *Darby v National Trust* [2001] EWCA Civ 189, [2001] PIQR P372.) The location was not one from which one could dive into water from a height. There was a shallow gradually sloping sandy beach. The bather had to wade in and Mr Tomlinson knew exactly how deep the water was where he was standing with the water coming up to a little above his knees. Mr Tomlinson's case is so far from giving a cause of action under the statute that it is hard to discuss coherently the hypotheses upon which it depends. There was no danger; any danger did not arise from the state of the premises; any risk of striking the bottom from diving in such shallow water was obvious; Mr Tomlinson did not need to be warned against running that risk; it was not reasonable to expect the occupier to offer the claimant (or any other trespasser) any protection against that obvious risk...

COMMENTARY

Section 1(3)(c) of the 1984 requires that the risk be one that it is reasonable for the occupier to take steps to prevent before a duty arises. In *Tomlinson*, given the social utility of the use of the lake and the fact that the claimant had chosen to engage in an activity with an obvious risk, this was not satisfied. Both Lord Hoffmann and Lord Hobhouse were influenced by concerns that the law should not intervene so as to limit the autonomous right of an individual to engage in activities that carried an obvious degree of risk, especially where this would result in the elimination of a recreational facility which was used safely by the vast majority of visitors (the warning signs clearly being ineffective in this case). Their Lordships also made it clear that the result would have been the same if the claimant had been a visitor; the common duty of care did not require steps to be taken to prevent the claimant from undertaking an activity with obvious risks. Further extracts from the case may be found at pp. 32 and 173, above and note *Siddorn v Patel* [2007] EWHC 1248 (QB) where the risk of falling through a skylight if one chooses to dance on a roof was held not to fall within s. 1(1)(a) of the Act, a result consistent with *Tomlinson*.

A slightly different approach was taken by the majority of the High Court of Australia in *Vairy v Wyong Shire Council* (2005) 223 CLR 422 and *Mulligan v Coffs Harbour City Council* (2005) 223 CLR 486, where it was held that the obviousness of the risk that attached to the claimant's activity (diving into water of unknown depth) on the land was only one factor to consider in determining whether the occupier was required to take steps to prevent the risk from materialising although it might be determinative in particular cases. Although these cases were decided in a different context (in particular the liability of occupiers in the cases was based on common law, not statute) they reflect policy concerns similar to those influencing the House of Lords in *Tomlinson*.

The influence of *Tomlinson* has been felt beyond occupier's liability; the decision also applies to the requirement of breach of duty in negligence at common law (see p. 173, above), though that did not stop Parliament from reiterating its core message in s. 1 of the Compensation Act 2006 (see Ch. 4). Should the reasoning in *Tomlinson* apply to risks that arise other than in respect of the claimant's activity on the land? If an adult is trespassing on land on which there is a large, obvious but unfenced pit into which he falls, could the claim be met by arguing that the risk was obvious and that it was not reasonable, as required by s. 1(3)(c), to take steps to avoid it? Note that s. 1(3)(c) must be interpreted by reference to the individual claimant: depending on the circumstances, it may be reasonable to do nothing if the claimant is an adult but necessary to take positive action if he is a child.

For comment on *Tomlinson*, see Lunney (2003) 11 Tort L Rev 140, and Oliphant, in *European Tort Law 2003*, p. 132f.

The Standard of Care

Once these conditions are satisfied and the duty is owed, the standard of care imposed in s. 1(4) is based on reasonableness having regard to the circumstances of the case. The standard of care may be different under the 1984 Act from that under the common law, as under the *Herrington* approach the resources of the occupier were relevant in deciding what was reasonable. As *Winfield & Jolowicz*, para. 9–26 points out, the statutory standard seems wholly objective but at least one court has assumed that the discharge of the duty should take into account the resources of the occupier (see *Ratcliff v McConnell* [1999] 1 WLR 670). However, the nature of the trespass will have an impact on what is reasonable in the circumstances: burglars cannot expect the same protection as a child (cf. *Donoghue v Folkestone*

Properties [2003] QB 1008; *Young v Kent County Council* [2005] EWHC 1342 (QBD)). The standard is, however, one of reasonableness, and whilst child trespassers evoke greater sympathy than most the occupier is not an insurer of their safety. In *Platt v Liverpool City Council* [1997] CLY 4864, a child trespasser was killed and his friend injured when the house in which they were playing collapsed. It was accepted that s. 1(3) of the 1984 Act was satisfied but the Court of Appeal found no breach of the duty. Unoccupied council houses had their doors and windows covered with metal sheets and were inspected once a day to check the sheeting had not been removed. In addition, the property in question was surrounded by 'a corrugated metal 22-gauge fence, 8 feet high, secured on a timber frame and secured to wooden posts embedded in concrete. The corrugated metal sheeting was attached to the frame by 2-inch long nails with a screw thread which could not be removed without special tools'. Rejecting a suggestion that the council should have hired security guards, Kennedy LJ thought it 'simply absurd' to argue that the council had failed to exercise reasonable care.

Warnings

As is the case under the 1957 Act, the 1984 Act provides that a warning may be sufficient to discharge the duty if it provides reasonable notice of the danger. Where the trespassers anticipated by the occupier are children it will be difficult to show a notice is, of itself, sufficient but there is a better chance with adults. It may, however, be necessary to draw a distinction between notices which merely delimit the scope of an entrant's permission to be on the premises, and those which affirm the existence of a danger and warn of it. In *Westwood v Post Office* [1973] 1 QB 591 a notice outside a door stated: 'Only the authorised attendant is permitted to enter.' The notice related to lift machinery stored in the room, but the plaintiff's husband, who had no licence to enter the room, fell through a defective trapdoor and was killed. The Court of Appeal treated the notice as relevant both to the status of the deceased when entering the room and to the discharge of any duty owed to the deceased by the defendant. By entering the room contrary to the notice, the deceased was a trespasser as the notice would be understood as meaning 'keep out' by any intelligent person. Even so, a trespasser was owed the duty of common humanity under *Herrington*, but Lawton LJ could not see how the case could be brought under that principle because the defendant did not know that the deceased would use the lift motor room for an unauthorised purpose and in disregard of a plainly worded notice to keep out. To the extent that the case suggests the occupier's duty to trespassers may be satisfied by general prohibitions on entry upon premises, it is questionable. When the case reached the House of Lords on appeal ([1974] AC 1), Lord Kilbrandon noted:

> The notice said nothing about danger. On the contrary, its terms insinuated that the room was safe enough for the authorised attendant. It is perfectly possible, if not probable, that the notice was put up because the lift motor room was the place in which were kept those tools and spares for the safety of which the authorised attendant alone would be responsible to his employers; the notice may well have been so understood.

Although these comments related to whether the deceased had been guilty of any contributory negligence by entering the room with knowledge of the notice, they are equally applicable to attempts to discharge the duty owed to a trespasser by a warning notice. The notice did not draw attention to the particular danger which killed the deceased. As the 1984 Act requires that the warning be sufficient to enable a non-visitor to appreciate and avoid the risk, it should not now be open to an occupier to argue that the non-visitor could have avoided the danger merely by obeying an instruction to keep out. A notice which warns of a danger may however discharge the duty under the Act on the basis that telling the trespasser of the risk and 'leaving the ball in his court' was all that could reasonably be expected of the occupier.

A warning notice may also have the effect of triggering the defence of *volenti* which is expressly preserved by s. 1(6). In *Westwood v Post Office* (above) Lawton LJ held that the deceased had accepted the risk of any injury from the state of the premises when he entered the room with knowledge of the prohibition upon entry. This reasoning is very dubious: if the trespasser does not know of the risk and is not made aware of it by the warning, it is difficult to show it has been assumed. However, in *Ratcliff v McConnell* [1999] 1 WLR 670 a warning at the shallow end of a pool stating 'Deep end shallow dive' was one factor that led the Court of Appeal to reject the trespasser plaintiff's claim for damages for injury caused by diving in at the shallow end of the pool. The defendants took steps to keep the pool locked after hours, and the plaintiff knew that after hours access was prohibited. He also admitted that he had paid 'no regard' to the prohibition on access and was going to do what he wanted anyway. On these facts Stuart-Smith LJ (at 684) thought it 'quite plain' that the plaintiff was aware of the risk and willingly accepted it. In light of the decision of the House of Lords in *Tomlinson*, however, it is unlikely that the defence of *volenti* would now be needed: the presence of the pool is unlikely to be seen as a danger attributable to the state of the premises, and even if it is the obvious nature of the risk is such that it may be reasonable for the occupier to do nothing to guard against it (s. 1(3)(c)).

In *Scott v Associated British Ports*, unreported, CA Civil Divison, 22 November 2000, Simon Brown LJ argued: 'on certain facts a comparable duty would be owed by occupiers to trespassers who they know are consciously imperiling themselves on their land to that owed by police or prison officers to those known to be of suicidal tendencies'. Given that (1) trespassers are not compelled to come onto the land in the same way that prisoners must go to prison; and (2) occupiers have no control over trespassers whereas police and prison officers have a prisoner or detainee in custody, are the situations really analogous? And can Simon Brown LJ's reasoning survive *Tomlinson*?

Exclusion of Liability

Unlike the 1957 Act, there is no reference to excluding the duty under the 1984 Act. It seems UCTA would not apply to prevent any attempt to exclude the duty as UCTA only expressly refers to the exclusion of the common duty of care under the 1957 Act. The Law Commission Report on which the Act was based (*Report on Liability for Damage or Injury to Trespassers and Related Questions of Occupiers' Liability*, Law Com. No. 75) expressly provided for exclusion of duty by contract term or notice to the extent it was reasonable or fair but this was not included in the Act.

Jones, p. 324, suggests that the duty under the 1984 Act cannot be excluded, because the rationale for allowing the occupier to exclude the duty in the case of visitors (the conditional licence) does not apply to trespassers: if the visitor wants to come onto the occupier's premises the occupier is free to impose conditions, and if the visitor does not agree to the conditions he does not have to enter the premises at all. (This argument is now subject to the limitations on the exclusion of liability imposed by UCTA as regards the duty imposed by the 1957 Act.) However the same rationale cannot apply to trespassers as they never have any licence to be on the premises at all. Therefore, it might be argued that the duty owed to trespassers is an irreducible minimum and as a matter of public policy it should not be possible to exclude it. But, as *Jones* also notes, if the duty cannot be excluded, it would seem that the lawful visitor may be worse off than the trespasser, because the duty owed to the visitor can be excluded by the non-business occupier. Can this be what was intended?

If the duty under the 1984 Act may be excluded, is there any residual duty left? *R. Addie & Sons (Collieries) Ltd v Dumbreck* (above) affirms that the occupier has no licence to inflict physical injury upon the trespasser merely because he is a trespasser. But should the courts go further and insist that the common duty of humanity be owed?

Damage to Property

The Act does not apply to property damage, which is presumably governed by the common law. It is difficult to see how the duty of common humanity could extend to taking precautions to avoid property damage, although in *Tutton v Walter* [1986] QB 61 it was argued the plaintiff's bees, which foraged across land sprayed by the defendant with a poisonous chemical, were 'trespassing' and were hence owed the common duty of humanity. The trial judge decided that the categories of visitor and trespasser were inapt to be applied to the bees and the ordinary law of negligence was applicable, although it was also held that the same result would have been reached if the common duty of humanity was the relevant standard. Could an occupier be liable under the Act, or otherwise, if he knew his neighbour's dog frequently strayed onto his property and omitted to take reasonable precautions to ensure the dog's safety?

Non-Visitors Other than Trespassers

It should be remembered that not all non-visitors are trespassers. Those entering upon land pursuant to a public right of way are not trespassers but neither are they visitors, as they have no licence from the occupier to be on the land. Where a public right of way is maintainable at public expense as defined in the Highways Act 1980, a statutory duty similar to that of common law negligence is imposed on the local highway authority (Highways Act 1980, ss. 41, 58). Where this is not the case, s. 1(7) makes it clear that the 1984 Act creates no new duty on the occupier. This can lead to the unfortunate results. In *McGeown v Northern Ireland Housing Executive* [1995] 1 AC 233, the plaintiff failed in her claim for injuries she received when she tripped over a hole in a public footpath. As the footpath was not a highway maintainable at public expense, she was not a visitor under the 1957 Act, and as s. 1(7) did not apply to impose any duty on the occupier, the occupier was not liable for the maintenance of the footpath. The result of the case is that, apparently, no-one is responsible as a matter of private law for the upkeep of public rights of way not maintainable at public expense. If the occupier of land subject to a public right of way which he knows is constantly used by children discovers a bomb just below the surface, is he able to sit back and do nothing? Should the occupier owe the *Herrington* duty of common humanity? See Buckley [1984] Conv 413 at 415.

Whilst agreeing with the result, Lord Browne-Wilkinson suggested that not all persons exercising a public right of way fell outside the 1957 Act. For example, person using some parts of a shopping centre might be classified as invitees even though they might be entering onto the shopping centre in the exercise of a public right of way. According to his Lordship such a person would be owed the common duty of care under the 1957 Act, for if this was not the position, '[w]ho, other than the occupier, is to maintain these structures which are used for the occupier's own business reasons?' Certainly the result of *McGeown* is open to criticism although whether the solution is a return to the distinction between licensees and invitees is questionable.

If the housing estate had been built by the council rather than the Housing Executive it is very likely the path would have been a highway maintainable at public expense (see

Gulliksen v Pembrokeshire County Council [2003] QB 123). Why should such different results flow from the fortuitous choice of builder?

Countryside and Rights of Way Act 2000

A new class of non-visitors who are nonetheless not trespassers was created by the Countryside and Rights of Way Act 2000. The Act provides for general rights of access to 'access land' subject to complying with the conditions set out in s. 2. Amendments to the 1984 Act make it clear that it is this Act, and not the 1957 legislation, that applies to persons entering upon access land. However, the extent of the protection to be afforded occupiers in respect of claims by persons entering access land was a contentious issue when the Countryside and Rights of Way Bill was before Parliament. The resulting compromise is contained in ss. 1(6A) and 1A of the 1984 Act. First, no duty is owed under the 1984 Act in respect of natural features of the land, certain other features whether non-natural or not, and certain injuries resulting from walls, fences or gates. An exception is provided where the risk was created intentionally or recklessly. Secondly, where a duty may be owed, s. 1A directs any duty should not place an undue burden on the occupier and that the importance of maintaining the character of the countryside should be considered when determining what the discharge of any such duty requires. It is not entirely clear what s. 1A adds to the Act: the first part adds little to the breach question as set out in s. 1(4), and the second part would fall within the 'social utility' consideration of the breach enquiry in any event (see Ch. 4). More important is s. 1(6A), which effectively makes the occupier liable for only intentional or reckless conduct. However, although this liability was referred to in the House of Lords as 'trespass' (see Hansard, HL vol. 619 col. 990, 23 November 2000, Lord Whitty), it may be that the harm caused is insufficiently direct for this cause of action, and the existence of a tort covering intentional but indirectly caused harm must be considered doubtful after their Lordships' decision in *Wainwright v Home Office* [2004] 2 AC 406 (extracted p. 69, above). Another paradox of the 2000 Act is that those who abuse the privilege of access granted by s. 2 become trespassers. This may make them better off, in terms of the protection afforded by the sections of the 1984 Act applying to non-visitors generally, than being an entrant on land under the 2000 Act. The trespasser has the general protection of the 1984 Act but, at least for the conditions set out in s. 1(6A), the entrant under the 2000 Act is only protected from intentionally or recklessly inflicted harm, which was the common law position for trespassers that has now been changed. It is doubtful whether these protective provisions are really necessary; as *Winfield & Jolowicz* notes (para. 9–29), the reason for these provisions may have been to prevent any argument that the occupier owed a duty in respect of natural hazards encountered by people exercising their 'right to roam', but after *Tomlinson v Congleton Borough Council* (above) liability in these situations would be very rare indeed.

III. Product Liability

The law of tort has long provided a remedy for consumers injured (at least physically) by a defectively manufactured product. Although nineteenth-century cases worried over the imposition of a general tort liability on manufacturers in respect of defective products, liability in negligence has regularly been imposed on the manufacturer of products since the landmark decison of the House of Lords in *Donoghue v Stevenson* [1932] AC 562 (see Ch. 3). Across the Atlantic, however, courts in the United States were imposing a more exacting standard on product manufacturers—that of strict liability, that is, liability without fault. Admittedly, there are examples in English law where the negligence standard imposed on manufacturers seems to have been strict liability in all but name (see *Grant v Australian Knitting Mills*, Ch. 3) but none the less the theoretical liability of the manufacturer remained rooted in negligence. The failure of the tort system to provide compensation to the victims of thalidomide brought calls for a stricter liability, and the *Pearson Commission* recommended (para. 317) that strict liability be imposed on producers of defective products. However, it was not until the Council of the European Communities issued Directive 85/374/EEC requiring the harmonisation of product liability laws that the United Kingdom adopted a statutory form of strict liability for defective products.

1. Rationales for Strict Liability for Defective Products

Escola v Coca-Cola Bottling Co of Fresno (1944) 150 P 2d 436

The plaintiff was injured when a bottle of Coca-Cola exploded as she was putting it into a refrigerator. The manufacturer's potential negligence liability to a consumer had already been established in *MacPherson v Buick Motor Co*, 217 NY 382 (1916), the US equivalent of *Donoghue v Stevenson*, but the question remained whether the manufacturer faced any stricter liability. The extract is concerned with the appropriate basis of such a liability.

Traynor J

I concur in the judgment, but I believe the manufacturer's negligence should no longer be singled out as the basis of a plaintiff's right to recover in cases like the present one. In my opinion it should now be recognised that a manufacturer incurs an absolute liability when an article that he has placed on the market, knowing that it is to be used without inspection, proves to have a defect that causes injury to human beings. *MacPherson v Buick Motor Co* established the principle, recognised by this court, that irrespective of privity of contract, the manufacturer is responsible for an injury caused by such an article to any person who comes in lawful contact with it. In these cases the source of the manufacturer's liability was his negligence in the manufacturing process or in the inspection of component parts supplied by others. Even if there is no negligence, however, public policy demands that responsibility be fixed wherever it will most effectively reduce the hazards to life and health inherent in defective products that reach the market. It is evident that the manufacturer can anticipate some hazards and guard against the recurrence of others, as the public cannot. Those who suffer injury from defective products are unprepared to meet its consequences. The cost of injury and the loss of time or health may be an overwhelming misfortune to the person injured and a needless one, for the risk of injury can be insured by the manufacturer and distributed among the public as a cost of doing business. It is to the public interest to discourage the marketing of products having defects that are a menace to the public. If such products nevertheless find their way into the market it is to the public interest to place the responsibility for whatever injury they may cause upon the manufacturer, who, even if he is not negligent in the manufacture of the product, is responsible for its reaching the market.

Council Directive 85/374/EEC

Whereas approximation of the laws of the Member States concerning the liability of the producer for damage caused by the defectiveness of his products is necessary because the existing divergences may distort competition and affect the movement of goods within the common market and entail a differing degree of protection of the consumer against damage caused by a defective product to his health or property;

Whereas liability without fault on the part of the producer is the sole means of adequately solving the problem, peculiar to our age of increasing technicality, of a fair apportionment of the risks inherent in modern technological production...

COMMENTARY

The judgment in *Escola* reflects the view that the proper cost to the manufacturer of producing a product includes the cost of the damage that a defective product causes to those who use it, irrespective of the reason for the defect (the 'enterprise' basis for strict liability). It can also be argued that strict liability reduces the flow of defective products to the market and increases overall economic efficiency (the 'deterrence' basis of strict liability). An alternative basis has been suggested by Stapleton. She calls this 'moral enterprise liability': 'if, in seeking to secure financial profit, an enterprise causes certain types of loss, it should be legally obliged to pay compensation to the victim' (*Products Liability* (London: Butterworths, 1994), ch. 8.) The rationale of the European Directive is rather more complicated, however. The second of the two paragraphs extracted above from its recitals reveals, arguably, a moral basis for liability without fault, perhaps based (tacitly) on something like Stapleton's moral enterprise theory. But the first of the two paragraphs shows how the European initiative was shaped by the requirements of the single market and its requirement of the harmonisation of production costs as between member states. Although this is an economic rationale, it is a rather different economic rationale from that of deterrence theory in tort. It is clear from recent decisions of the European Court of Justice that it is this rationale that was the primary motivating force behind the Directive. In two cases in 2002 (Case C–52/00, *Commission v France* [2002] ECR I–3827, and Case C–154/00, *Commission v Greece* [2002] ECR I–3879) the Court held that member states could not impose a more stringent form of product liability than that allowed by the Directive (an approach that was affirmed in the more recent decision in Case C–402/03, *Skov AEg v Bilka Lavprisvarehus A/S* [2006] ECR I–199), and in Case C–183/00, *Sanchez v Medicina Asturiana SA* [2002] ECR I–3901 it was held that laws of the member states passed prior to the Directive could not be maintained if they imposed greater levels of consumer protection than that provided for by the Directive. If member states were allowed to have such laws the different level of consumer protection this would produce might distort competition between traders and impede the free movement of goods. (See further Case C–177/04, *Commission v France* [2006] ECR I–2461.) This reasoning suggests that *any* variation between the member states would potentially distort competition. However, the Directive expressly allowed for a number of derogations whereby individual member states were given a choice as to the form in which the Directive could be implemented (e.g. whether agricultural products should be included, whether a 'development risks' defence would be allowed, and what level of damages would be recoverable). At first glance such variations would seem to be contrary to the reasoning of the European Court of Justice in its recent cases. However, the Commission subsequently emphasised that the balance between the competing interests struck by the Directive included, amongst others, the presence of the development risks defence, and that at the time the Directive was adopted it intended to provide for limited harmonisation only (*Third Report on the Application of Directive 85/374 on Liability for Defective Products*, 2006, COM (2006) 496 final, p. 8). Viewed in this light, the decisions of the European Court of Justice can be seen, not as requiring complete harmonisation, but as ensuring that the compromise between the interests of claimants, manufacturers and their insurers represented by the Directive is enforced in all member states. This balance, of course, may change over time; hence the amendment to remove the derogation for agricultural products: see p. 597, below. For further analysis, see S. Whittaker, *Liability for Products: English Law, French Law, and European Harmonization* (Oxford: OUP, 2005), pp. 440–4 and 659–61.

The rationales of the Directive have not found universal support (see Stapleton (1986) 6 OJLS 392, who notes that problems with proving a causal link between the defect and the claimant's injury prevent the true cost of the defect being borne by the producer) so it is questionable whether uniform product liability laws will impose liability in as wide a category of case as was envisaged, especially in light of derogations from the Directive allowed to member states. None the less, the decision of *A v National Blood Authority* [2001] 3 All ER 289 demonstrates that, whilst the Directive may not have solved all of the difficulties for a claimant, it has established a cause of action which is qualitatively different from that of negligence. For criticism of the Directive, see Stapleton, *Products Liability* (London: Butterworths, 1994), ch. 9.

The Directive was implemented in the United Kingdom by the passage of the Consumer Protection Act 1987. However, as the Act is to be interpreted so as to achieve the objects of the Directive, the main Articles of the Directive are extracted first, followed by the 1987 Act. That the Directive remains important is graphically illustrated by the decision of Burton J, as agreed by counsel, in *A v National Blood Authority* [2001] 3 All ER 289 to use the text of the Directive rather than that of the Act to determine a claim for a defective product.

2. The Law

Council Directive 85/374/EEC

Article 1

The producer shall be liable for damage caused by a defect in his product.

Article 2

For the purpose of this Directive, 'product' means all movables even if incorporated into another movable or into an immovable. 'Product' includes electricity.

Article 3

1. 'Producer' means the manufacturer of a finished product, the producer of any raw material or the manufacturer of a component part and any person who, by putting his name, trade mark or other distinguishing feature on the product presents himself as its producer.

2. Without prejudice to the liability of the producer, any person who imports into the Community a product for sale, hire, leasing or any form of distribution in the course of his

business shall be deemed to be a producer within the meaning of this Directive and shall be responsible as a producer.

3. Where the producer of the product cannot be identified, each supplier of the product shall be treated as its producer unless he informs the injured person, within a reasonable time, of the identity of the producer or of the person who supplied him with the product. The same shall apply, in the case of an imported product, if this product does not indicate the identity of the importer referred to in paragraph 2, even if the name of the producer is indicated.

Article 4

The injured person shall be required to prove the damage, the defect and the causal relationship between defect and damage.

Article 5

Where, as a result of the provisions of this Directive, two or more persons are liable for the same damage, they shall be liable jointly and severally, without prejudice to the provisions of national law concerning the rights of contribution or recourse.

Article 6

1. A product is defective when it does not provide the safety which a person is entitled to expect, taking all circumstances into account, including:
   (a) the presentation of the product
   (b) the use to which it could reasonably be expected that the product would be put
   (c) the time when the product was put into circulation.

2. A product shall not be considered defective for the sole reason that a better product is subsequently put into circulation.

Article 7

The producer shall not be liable as a result of this Directive if he proves:

(a) that he did not put the product into circulation; or
(b) that, having regard to the circumstances, it is probable that the defect which caused the damage did not exist at the time when the product was put into circulation by him or that this defect came into being afterwards; or
(c) that the product was neither manufactured by him for sale or any form of distribution for economic purpose nor manufactured or distributed by him in the course of his business; or
(d) that the defect is due to compliance of the product with mandatory regulations issued by the public authorities; or
(e) that the state of scientific and technical knowledge at the time when he put the product into circulation was not such as to enable the existence of the defect to be discovered; or
(f) in the case of a manufacturer of a component, that the defect is attributable to the design of the product in which the component has been fitted or to the instructions given by the manufacturer of the product.

Article 8

1. Without prejudice to the provisions of national law concerning the right of contribution or recourse, the liability of the producer shall not be reduced when the damage is caused both by a defect in product and by the act or omission of a third party.

2. The liability of the producer may be reduced or disallowed when, having regard to all the circumstances, the damage is caused both by a defect in the product and by the fault of the injured person or any person for whom the injured person is responsible.

Article 9

For the purpose of Article 1, 'damage' means:

(a) damage caused by death or by personal injuries

(b) damage to, or destruction of, any item of property other than the defective product itself, with a lower threshold of 500 ECU, provided that the item of property:

    (i)   is of a type ordinarily intended for private use or consumption, and

    (ii) was used by the injured person mainly for his own private use or consumption.

This Article shall be without prejudice to national provisions relating to non-material damage...

Article 12

The liability of the producer arising from this Directive may not, in relation to the injured person, be limited or excluded by a provision limiting his liability or exempting him from liability...

Consumer Protection Act 1987

An Act to make provision with respect to the liability of persons for damage caused by defective products...

PART I

1. PURPOSE AND CONSTRUCTION OF PART I

(1) This Part shall have effect for the purpose of making such provision as is necessary in order to comply with the product liability Directive and shall be construed accordingly.

(2) In this Part, except in so far as the context otherwise requires—

    'dependant' and 'relative' have the same meanings as they have in, respectively, the Fatal Accidents Act 1976 and the Damages (Scotland) Act 1976:

    'producer', in relation to a product, means—

    (a) the person who manufactured it;

    (b) in the case of a substance which has not been manufactured but has been won or abstracted, the person who won or abstracted it;

    (c) in the case of a product which has not been manufactured, won or abstracted but essential characteristics of which are attributable to an industrial or other process having been carried out (for example, in relation to agricultural produce), the person who carried out that process;

    'product' means any goods or electricity and (subject to subsection (3) below) includes a product which is comprised in another product, whether by virtue of being a component part or raw material or otherwise; and

    'the product liability Directive' means the Directive of the Council of the European Communities, dated 25th July 1985, (No 85/374/EEC) on the approximation of the laws, regulations and administrative provisions of the member States concerning liability for defective products.

(3) For the purposes of this Part a person who supplies any product in which products are comprised, whether by virtue of being component parts or raw materials or otherwise, shall not

be treated by reason only of his supply of that product as supplying any of the products so comprised.

2. LIABILITY FOR DEFECTIVE PRODUCTS

(1) Subject to the following provisions of this Part, where any damage is caused wholly or partly by a defect in a product, every person to whom subsection (2) below applies shall be liable for the damage.

(2) This subsection applies to—
    (a) the producer of the product;
    (b) any person who, by putting his name on the product or using a trade mark or other distinguishing mark in relation to the product, has held himself out to be the producer of the product;
    (c) any person who has imported the product into a member State from a place outside the member States in order, in the course of any business of his, to supply it to another.

(3) Subject as aforesaid, where any damage is caused wholly or partly by a defect in a product, any person who supplied the product (whether to the person who suffered the damage, to the producer of any product in which the product in question is comprised or to any other person) shall be liable for the damage if—
    (a) the person who suffered the damage requests the supplier to identify one or more of the persons (whether still in existence or not) to whom subsection (2) above applies in relation to the product;
    (b) that request is made within a reasonable period after the damage occurs and at a time when it is not reasonably practicable for the person making the request to identify all those persons; and
    (c) the supplier fails, within a reasonable period after receiving the request, either to comply with the request or to identify the person who supplied the product to him . . .

(5) Where two or more persons are liable by virtue of this Part for the same damage, their liability shall be joint and several.

(6) This section shall be without prejudice to any liability arising otherwise than by virtue of this Part.

3. MEANING OF 'DEFECT'

(1) Subject to the following provisions of this section, there is a defect in a product for the purposes of this Part if the safety of the product is not such as persons generally are entitled to expect; and for those purposes 'safety', in relation to a product, shall include safety with respect to products comprised in that product and safety in the context of risks of damage to property, as well as in the context of risks of death or personal injury.

(2) In determining for the purposes of subsection (1) above what persons generally are entitled to expect in relation to a product all the circumstances shall be taken into account, including—
    (a) the manner in which, and purposes for which, the product has been marketed, its get-up, the use of any mark in relation to the product and any instructions for, or warnings with respect to, doing or refraining from doing anything with or in relation to the product;
    (b) what might reasonably be expected to be done with or in relation to the product; and

(c) the time when the product was supplied by its producer to another; and nothing in this section shall require a defect to be inferred from the fact alone that the safety of a product which is supplied after that time is greater than the safety of the product in question.

4. DEFENCES

(1) In any civil proceedings by virtue of this Part against any person ('the person proceeded against') in respect of a defect in a product it shall be a defence for him to show—

    (a) that the defect is attributable to compliance with any requirement imposed by or under any enactment or with any Community obligation; or

    (b) that the person proceeded against did not at any time supply the product to another; or

    (c) that the following conditions are satisfied, that is to say—

        (i) that the only supply of the product to another by the person proceeded against was otherwise than in the course of a business of that person's; and

        (ii) that section 2(2) above does not apply to that person or applies to him by virtue only of things done otherwise than with a view to profit; or

    (d) that the defect did not exist in the product at the relevant time; or

    (e) that the state of scientific and technical knowledge at the relevant time was not such that a producer of products of the same description as the product in question might be expected to have discovered the defect if it had existed in his products while they were under his control; or

    (f) that the defect—

        (i) constituted a defect in a product ('the subsequent product') in which the product in question had been comprised; and

        (ii) was wholly attributable to the design of the subsequent product or to compliance by the producer of the product in question with instructions given by the producer of the subsequent product.

(2) In this section 'the relevant time', in relation to electricity, means the time at which it was generated, being a time before it was transmitted or distributed, and in relation to any other product, means—

    (a) if the person proceeded against is a person to whom subsection (2) of section 2 above applies in relation to the product, the time when he supplied the product to another;

    (b) if that subsection does not apply to that person in relation to the product, the time when the product was last supplied by a person to whom that subsection does apply in relation to the product.

5. DAMAGE GIVING RISE TO LIABILITY

(1) Subject to the following provisions of this section, in this Part 'damage' means death or personal injury or any loss of or damage to any property (including land).

(2) A person shall not be liable under section 2 above in respect of any defect in a product for the loss of or any damage to the product itself or for the loss of or any damage to the whole or any part of any product which has been supplied with the product in question comprised in it.

(3) A person shall not be liable under section 2 above for any loss of or damage to any property which, at the time it is lost or damaged, is not—

    (a) of a description of property ordinarily intended for private use, occupation or consumption; and

(b) intended by the person suffering the loss or damage mainly for his own private use, occupation or consumption.

(4) No damages shall be awarded to any person by virtue of this Part in respect of any loss of or damage to any property if the amount which would fall to be so awarded to that person, apart from this subsection and any liability for interest, does not exceed £275.

(5) In determining for the purposes of this Part who has suffered any loss of or damage to property and when any such loss or damage occurred, the loss or damage shall be regarded as having occurred at the earliest time at which a person with an interest in the property had knowledge of the material facts about the loss or damage.

(6) For the purposes of subsection (5) above the material facts about any loss of or damage to any property are such facts about the loss or damage as would lead a reasonable person with an interest in the property to consider the loss or damage sufficiently serious to justify his instituting proceedings for damages against a defendant who did not dispute liability and was able to satisfy a judgment.

(7) For the purposes of subsection (5) above a person's knowledge includes knowledge which he might reasonably have been expected to acquire—
    (a) from facts observable or ascertainable by him; or
    (b) from facts ascertainable by him with the help of appropriate expert advice which it is reasonable for him to seek;
but a person shall not be taken by virtue of this subsection to have knowledge of a fact ascertainable by him only with the help of expert advice unless he has failed to take all reasonable steps to obtain (and, where appropriate, to act on) that advice...

6. APPLICATION OF CERTAIN ENACTMENTS

(1) Any damage for which a person is liable under section 2 above shall be deemed to have been caused—
    (a) for the purposes of the Fatal Accidents Act 1976, by that person's wrongful act, neglect or default...

(2) Where—
    (a) a person's death is caused wholly or partly by a defect in a product, or a person dies after suffering damage which has been so caused;
    (b) a request such as mentioned in paragraph (a) of subsection (3) of section 2 above is made to a supplier of the product by that person's personal representatives or, in the case of a person whose death is caused wholly or partly by the defect, by any dependant or relative of that person; and
    (c) the conditions specified in paragraphs (b) and (c) of that subsection are satisfied in relation to that request,
this Part shall have effect for the purposes of the Law Reform (Miscellaneous Provisions) Act 1934, the Fatal Accidents Act 1976 and the Damages (Scotland) Act 1976 as if liability of the supplier to that person under that subsection did not depend on that person having requested the supplier to identify certain persons or on the said conditions having been satisfied in relation to a request made by that person.

(3) Section 1 of the Congenital Disabilities (Civil Liability) Act 1976 shall have effect for the purposes of this Part as if—
    (a) a person were answerable to a child in respect of an occurrence caused wholly or partly by a defect in a product if he is or has been liable under section 2 above in

respect of any effect of the occurrence on a parent of the child, or would be so liable if the occurrence caused a parent of the child to suffer damage;

(b) the provisions of this Part relating to liability under section 2 above applied in relation to liability by virtue of paragraph (a) above under the said section 1; and

(c) subsection (6) of the said section 1 (exclusion of liability) were omitted.

(4) Where any damage is caused partly by a defect in a product and partly by the fault of the person suffering the damage, the Law Reform (Contributory Negligence) Act 1945 and section 5 of the Fatal Accidents Act 1976 (contributory negligence) shall have effect as if the defect were the fault of every person liable by virtue of this Part for the damage caused by the defect.

(5) In subsection (4) above 'fault' has the same meaning as in the said Act of 1945...

7. PROHIBITION ON EXCLUSIONS FROM LIABILITY

The liability of a person by virtue of this Part to a person who has suffered damage caused wholly or partly by a defect in a product, or to a dependant or relative of such a person, shall not be limited or excluded by any contract term, by any notice or by any other provision...

45. INTERPRETATION

(1) In this Act, except in so far as the context otherwise requires...

'business' includes a trade or profession and the activities of a professional or trade association or of a local authority or other public authority;

'goods' includes substances, growing crops and things comprised in land by virtue of being attached to it and any ship, aircraft or vehicle...

'modifications' includes additions, alterations and omissions, and cognate expressions shall be construed accordingly...

'personal injury' includes any disease and any other impairment of a person's physical or mental condition;

'premises' includes any place and any ship, aircraft or vehicle...

'substance' means any natural or artificial substance, whether in solid, liquid or gaseous form or in the form of a vapour, and includes substances that are comprised in or mixed with other goods;

'supply' and cognate expressions shall be construed in accordance with section 46 below;...

46. MEANING OF 'SUPPLY'

(1) Subject to the following provisions of this section, references in this Act to supplying goods shall be construed as references to doing any of the following, whether as principal or agent, that is to say—

(a) selling, hiring out or lending the goods;

(b) entering into a hire-purchase agreement to furnish the goods;

(c) the performance of any contract for work and materials to furnish the goods;

(d) providing the goods in exchange for any consideration other than money;

(e) providing the goods in or in connection with the performance of any statutory function; or

(f) giving the goods as a prize or otherwise making a gift of the goods;

and, in relation to gas or water, those references shall be construed as including references to providing the service by which the gas or water is made available for use...

(3) Subject to subsection (4) below, the performance of any contract by the erection of any building or structure on any land or by the carrying out of any other building works shall be treated for the purposes of this Act as a supply of goods in so far as, but only in so far as, it involves the provision of any goods to any person by means of their incorporation into the building, structure or works.

(4) Except for the purposes of, and in relation to, notices to warn, references in this Act to supplying goods shall not include references to supplying goods comprised in land where the supply is effected by the creation or disposal of an interest in the land...

(8) Where any goods have at any time been supplied by being hired out or lent to any person, neither a continuation or renewal of the hire or loan (whether on the same or different terms) nor any transaction for the transfer after that time of any interest in the goods to the person to whom they were hired or lent shall be treated for the purposes of this Act as a further supply of the goods to that person.

(9) A ship, aircraft or motor vehicle shall not be treated for the purposes of this Act as supplied to any person by reason only that services consisting in the carriage of goods or passengers in that ship, aircraft or vehicle, or in its use for any other purpose, are provided to that person in pursuance of an agreement relating to the use of the ship, aircraft or vehicle for a particular period or for particular voyages, flights or journeys.

COMMENTARY

In *A v National Blood Authority* [2001] 3 All ER 289 at 297, Burton J declined to engage in detailed interpretation of the Consumer Protection Act 1987, stating that 'the practical course was to go straight to the fount, the Directive itself'. Arnull [2001] Euro L Rev 213 comments:

That approach goes further than required by the case law of the Court of Justice. It could be taken to imply that, whatever the national implementing legislation may say, an English court will always give effect to the requirements of a directive. Such an outcome would be hard to reconcile with both the nature of directives and the approach of the Court of Justice, which has been careful to emphasise that it is only in cases of ambiguity that an interpretation consistent with Community law must be preferred.

In *A* itself, however, there was no real objection to going to 'the fount' as the implementing statute must, in so far as possible, be interpreted consistently with the Directive, and there was no argument that the Act's language precluded such an interpretation.

The Directive has been amended once, to ensure that agricultural produce was brought within its scope (see p. 597, below), but the European Commission has stated that no further reform needs to be contemplated at present (*Third Report on the Application of Directive 85/374 on Liability for Defective Products*, 2006, COM (2006) 496 final, p. 11).

Who May be Liable?

Section 2(2) of the Act provides a number of possible defendants: the first and most obvious is the producer (as defined in s. 1(2)) of the product. However, other possible defendants are created by s. 2(2). First, the own brander—someone who by putting his name on the product or using trade or other distinguishing marks holds himself out to be the producer of the product—can be liable. Whether this is so depends on the nature of the mark. Could one of the big supermarket chains qualify under this section in respect of products marketed under their own name? Does anyone really think Sainsburys' Strawberry Jam is produced by Sainsburys? Secondly, an importer (where the import is in the course of business and for the purpose of 'supply' as defined in s. 46) may be liable. Not every importer is liable; it is only the first importer into the EU. This section ensures that there will be a defendant within the EU. Usually, the mere supply of goods is not enough to attract the operation of the Act. However, if the three conditions of s. 2(3) are satisfied a supplier may be liable under the Act. However, if the supplier can identify any one of the persons considered above then no liability will attach, so it is essential for their own sakes that suppliers keep adequate records. However, the supplier must do more than simply deny that it is the producer; it must couple that with providing information about the producer or its supplier promptly and on its own initiative (Case C–358/08 *Aventis Pasteur v OB*, 2009 ECJ EUR-Lex Lexis 1103). Of course, suppliers may still be liable strictly under the terms of the contract and through any implied terms under the Sale of Goods legislation.

Meaning of Product

Liability only attaches in respect of products. 'Product' is defined in s. 1(2) as goods, a term which is itself defined in s. 45 to include 'substances, growing crops and things comprised in land by virtue of being attached to it and any ship, aircraft, or vehicle'. It also includes a product which is comprised in another product. A building is probably not a 'good' (*Winfield & Jolowicz*, para. 10–16; cf. *Jones*, p. 483) and therefore a builder is not liable, although the producers of defective components of a building may be. However, a builder might be liable under s. 2(3) if he is a 'supplier' of the relevant components. The Directive allowed member states to exclude agricultural products from the scheme of strict liability, and the United Kingdom did so unless such products had undergone an 'industrial process'. However, Council Directive 99/34 extended the Products Liability Directive to primary agricultural products by amending Article 2, and the United Kingdom implemented the Directive through the Consumer Protection Act (Product Liability) (Modification) Order 2000, SI 2000/2771. Given that agricultural products may be defective for reasons completely outside the control of the farmer (poor weather, pollution, natural disasters) does it seem fair to impose strict liability for his or her produce? (See O'Rourke (1999) 149 NLJ 1106; Hodges, 'Reform of the Product Liability Directive 1998 9' [1999] Consumer L Jnl 35–7.) The Commission, however, felt that the different rules as to liability for agricultural produce that were present in the member states distorted competition in the market for such produce and thus amendment was needed; it also thought that consumers were entitled to expect high levels of safety in agricultural produce and that the amendment would increase consumer confidence in the safety of agricultural products. Thus the producer of beef infected with BSE is now subjected to liability under the Act, irrespective of whether the beef had undergone an industrial process (which would have been a prerequisite to liability in the United Kingdom prior to the amendment).

Meaning of Defect

The touchstone of defectiveness is the public's legitimate expectation as to the safety of the product, not whether the producer took reasonable care to ensure the product's safety. But, although liability is not fault-based in that sense, doubts have been expressed as to the strictness of the liability for defects on the basis that the risk/utility comparison that underpins negligence may resurface in the assessment of a product's defectiveness. Where there are allegations about the safety of a particular pharmaceutical drug, for example, it has been argued that one can only assess defectiveness by engaging in a balancing exercise in which the drug's generally beneficial properties are weighed against its rare, harmful side-effects, having regard to how frequently they occur and how serious they are if they occur (see Newdick [1985] 101 LQR 405). The strictness of the liability, and the meaning of defect, received judicial consideration in the following case.

A v National Blood Authority [2001] 3 All ER 289

The claimants were infected with the Hepatitis C virus from blood transfusions organised by the defendant. The blood was collected from donors, and although it was known that there was a risk that such blood might be infected with the virus, it was impossible to avoid the risk because the virus had not yet been identified or because no tests available at the time could detect the presence of the virus. The claimants sued under the Consumer Protection Act 1987, arguing that the supply of blood to them was the supply of a defective product, and that this had caused them damage. The defendant alleged that the unavoidability of the risk was a factor to be considered in determining whether the product was defective.

Burton J

As to Article 6, the Claimants assert that, with the need for proof of negligence eliminated, consideration of the conduct of the producer, or of a reasonable or legitimately expectable producer, is inadmissible or irrelevant. Therefore questions of avoidability cannot and do not arise: what the Defendants could or should have done differently: whether there were any steps or precautions reasonably available: whether it was impossible to take any steps by way of prevention or avoidance, or impracticable or economically unreasonable. Such are not 'circumstances' falling to be considered within Article 6. Insofar as the risk was known to blood producers and the medical profession, it was not known to the public at large (save for those few patients who might ask their doctor, or read the occasional article about blood in a newspaper) and no risk that any percentage of transfused blood would be infected was accepted by them.

The Defendants assert that the risk was known to those who mattered, namely the medical profession, through whom blood was supplied. Avoiding the risk was impossible and unattainable, and it is not and cannot be legitimate to expect the unattainable. Avoidability or unavoidability is a circumstance to be taken into account within Article 6. The public did not and/or was not entitled to expect 100% clean blood. The most they could legitimately expect was that all legitimately expectable (reasonably available) precautions or in this case tests had been taken or carried out. The Claimants must therefore prove that they were legitimately entitled to expect more, and/or must disprove the unavoidability of the harmful characteristic. There would need to be an investigation as to whether it was impossible to avoid the risk and/or whether the producers had taken all legitimately expectable steps. Insofar as there was thus an investigation analogous to, or involving similar facts to, an investigation into negligence, it was not an investigation of negligence by the individual producer and was necessary and, because it was not an investigation of fault, permissible...

[Having considered the specific circumstances listed in Article 6, and accepted that the list was not exhaustive, Burton J continued:]

The dispute therefore is as to what further, if anything, falls to be considered within 'all circumstances'. There is no dispute between the parties... that consideration of the fault of the producer is excluded; but does consideration of 'all circumstances' include consideration of the conduct to be expected from the producer, the level of safety to be expected from a producer of that product? The parties agree that the starting point is the particular product with the harmful characteristic, and if its inherent nature and intended use (e.g. poison) are dangerous, then there may not need to be any further consideration, provided that injury resulted from that known danger. However, if the product was not intended to be dangerous, that is the harmful characteristic was not intended, by virtue of the intended use of the product, then there must be consideration of whether it was safe and the level of safety to be legitimately expected. At this stage, the Defendants assert that part of the investigation consists of what steps could have been taken by a producer to avoid that harmful characteristic. The Defendants assert that conduct is to be considered not by reference to identifying the individual producer's negligence, but by identifying and specifying the safety precautions that the public would or could reasonably expect from a producer of the product. The exercise is referred to as a balancing act; the more difficult it is to make safe, and the more beneficial the product, the less is expected, and vice versa, an issue being whether a producer has complied with the safety precautions reasonably to be expected...

The Claimants however assert that, given that it is common ground that the Article imposes liability irrespective of fault, the exercise of considering what could or should have been done by the producer is an impermissible and irrelevant exercise, which lets questions of fault back in by the back door...

Non-standard products

In any event, however, the Claimants make a separate case in relation to the blood products here in issue: namely that they are what is called in the United States 'rogue products' or 'lemons', and in Germany '*Ausreisser*'—escapees or 'off the road' products. These are products which are isolated or rare specimens which are different from the other products of a similar series, different from the products intended or desired by the producer...

[Burton J stated that he preferred to call such products 'non-standard', explaining:]

Thus a standard product is one which is and performs as the producer intends. A non-standard product is one which is different, obviously because it is deficient or inferior in terms of safety, from the standard product; and where it is the harmful characteristic or characteristics present in the non-standard product, but not in the standard product, which has or have caused the material injury or damage. Some Community jurisdictions in implementing the Directive have specifically provided that there will be liability for non-standard' products, i.e., that such will automatically be defective within Article 6: Italy and Spain have done so by express legislation...

Conclusions on Article 6

I do not consider it to be arguable that the consumer had an actual expectation that blood being supplied to him was not 100% clean, nor do I conclude that he had knowledge that it was, or was likely to be, infected with Hepatitis C. It is not seriously argued by the Defendants, notwithstanding some few newspaper cuttings which were referred to, that there was any public understanding or acceptance of the infection of transfused blood by Hepatitis C. Doctors and surgeons knew, but did not tell their patients unless asked, and were very rarely asked. It was certainly, in my judgment, not known and accepted by society that there was such a risk...

I do not consider that the legitimate expectation of the public at large is that legitimately expectable tests will have been carried out or precautions adopted. Their legitimate expectation is as to the safeness of the product (or not). The court will act as...the appointed representative of the public at large, but in my judgment it is impossible to inject into the consumer's legitimate expectation matters which would not by any stretch of the imagination be in his actual expectation. He will assume perhaps that there are tests, but his expectations will be as to the safeness of the blood. In my judgment it is as inappropriate to propose that the public should not 'expect the unattainable'—in the sense of precautions which are impossible—at least unless it is informed as to what is unattainable or impossible, as it is to reformulate the expectation as one that the producer will not have been negligent or will have taken all reasonable steps.

In this context I turn to consider what is intended to be included within 'all circumstances' in Article 6. I am satisfied that this means all *relevant* circumstances. It is quite plain to me that...the directive was intended to eliminate proof of fault or negligence. I am satisfied that this was not simply a legal consequence, but that it was also intended to make it easier for claimants to prove their case, such that not only would a consumer not have to prove that a producer did not take reasonable steps, or all reasonable steps, to comply with his duty of care, but also that the producer did not take all legitimately expectable steps either...I conclude therefore that avoidability is not one of the circumstances to be taken into account within Article 6....

[I]n my judgment, the infected bags of blood were non-standard products. I have already recorded that it does not seem to me to matter whether they would be categorised in US tort law as manufacturing or design defects. They were in any event different from the norm which the producer intended for use by the public...I do not accept that all the blood products were equally defective because all of them carried the risk. That is a very philosophical approach. It is one which would...be equally apt to a situation in which one tyre in one million was defective because of an inherent occasional blip in the strength of the rubber's raw material. The answer is that the test relates to the use of the blood bag. For, and as a result of, the intended use, 99 out of 100 bags would cause no injury and would not be infected, unlike the one hundredth.

Even in the case of standard products such as drugs, side-effects are to my mind only capable of being socially acceptable' if they are made known...But I am satisfied, as I have stated above, that the problem was not known to the consumer. However, in any event, I do not accept that the consumer expected, or was entitled to expect, that his bag of blood was defective even if (which I have concluded was not the case) he had any knowledge of any problem. I do not consider...that he was expecting or entitled to expect a form of Russian roulette. That would only arise if, contrary to my conclusion, the public took that as socially acceptable...For such knowledge and acceptance there would need to be at the very least publicity and probably express warnings, and even that might not...be sufficient.

Where, as here, there is a harmful characteristic in a *non-standard* product, a decision that it is defective is likely to be straightforward, and I can make my decision accordingly. However, the consequence of my conclusion is that 'avoidability' is also not in the basket of *circumstances*, even in respect of a harmful characteristic of a *standard* product. So I shall set out what I consider to be the structure for consideration under Article 6. It must be emphasised that safety and intended, or foreseeable, use are the lynchpins: and, leading on from these, what legitimate expectations there are of safety in relation to foreseeable use...

The first step must be to identify the harmful characteristic which caused the injury (Article 4). In order to establish that there is a defect in Article 6, the next step will be to conclude whether the product is standard or non-standard. This will be done (in the absence of admission by the producer) most easily by comparing the offending product with other products of the same type or series produced by that producer. If the respect in which it differs from the series includes the harmful characteristic, then it is, for the purpose of Article 6, non-standard. If it does not differ, or if the respect in which it differs does not include the harmful characteristic, but all the other products, albeit different, share the harmful characteristic, then it is to be treated as a standard product.

Non-standard products

The *circumstances* specified in Article 6 may obviously be relevant—the product may be a second—as well as the circumstances of supply. But it seems to me that the primary issue in relation to a non-standard product may be whether the public at large accepted the non-standard nature of the product—i.e. they accept that a proportion of the products is defective (as I have concluded they do not in this case). That, as discussed, is not of course the end of it, because the question is of legitimate expectation, and the court may conclude that the expectation of the public is too high or too low. But manifestly questions such as warnings and presentations will be in the forefront. However, I conclude that the following are not relevant: (i) avoidability of the harmful characteristic—i.e. impossibility or unavoidability in relation to precautionary measures; (ii) the impracticality, cost or difficulty of taking such measures; and (iii) the benefit to society or utility of the product (except in the context of whether—with *full information and proper knowledge*—the public does and ought to accept the risk) ...

Standard products

If a standard product is unsafe, it is likely to be so as a result of alleged error in design, or at any rate as a result of an allegedly flawed system. The harmful characteristic must be identified, if necessary with the assistance of experts. The question of presentation/time/circumstances of supply/social acceptability etc will arise as above. The sole question will be safety for the foreseeable use. If there are any comparable products on the market, then it will obviously be relevant to compare the offending product with those other products, so as to identify, compare and contrast the relevant features. There will obviously need to be a full understanding of how the product works—particularly if it is a new product ... so as to assess its safety for such use. Price is obviously a significant factor in legitimate expectation, and may well be material in the comparative process. But again, it seems to me there is no room in the basket for: (i) what the producer could have done differently; and (ii) whether the producer could or could not have done the same as the others did ...

COMMENTARY

Burton J was clearly at pains to prevent the Directive's 'defect liability' being so diluted that it became little more than liability for fault by a different name. But, in so doing, he makes the controversial move of limiting the range of circumstances which are taken to influence the public's legitimate expectations. Article 6 specifies that the safety which a person is entitled to expect of a product is to be assessed 'taking *all* circumstances into account' (emphasis added). Burton J rewrites this as 'taking all *relevant* circumstances into account', and excludes from consideration such factors as the care taken by the producer, the product's utility, and (most crucially on the present facts) the avoidability of the defect. His approach is criticised by Hodges (2001) 117 LQR 528 at 530:

It is respectfully suggested that the judge was wrong to conclude that the avoidability of the risk being eradicated was not, as a matter of law, a relevant Article 6 consideration. Indeed, the Directive explicitly states that *all* considerations are to be taken into account. It is surely necessary for the court to *evaluate and balance all* the circumstances in order to apply the Article 6 'expectation test'. In doing so, the court must decide how much weight to give to each circumstance. It might be that, as a matter of principle, the court would conclude that, since the primary purpose of the Directive is to improve consumer protection and provide for consumers to receive compensation for injuries caused by defective products through a liability mechanism which is intended to operate simply, as the judge stressed, relatively little weight should be given to the unavoidability circumstance and that the product was defective. But the opposite conclusion is equally arguable…

Along with many commentators (e.g. Goldberg, 'Paying for Bad Blood: Strict Product Liability After the Hepatitis C Litigation' (2002) 10 Med Law Rev 165), we believe that Burton J did indeed go too far in ruling out any reference to avoidability, etc., at all, though he was right not to treat the unavoidability of infection as automatically negating defectiveness. Such considerations should not be decisive but they may be entitled to some weight. In fact, it is clear that the courts on other occasions have taken account of the very factors that Burton J would have excluded altogether from the inquiry. In *Abouzaid v Mothercare (UK) Ltd, The Times*, 20 February 2001, the defendants were held liable under Part I of the Consumer Protection Act when the claimant was injured by the buckle on an elastic strap used to fasten one of their products. The claimant, a 12-year-old boy, let the strap slip from his fingers when the elastic was taut and the recoil caused the buckle to strike him in the eye. One factor that influenced the court in its finding that the product was defective was that the producer could have done more to prevent the accident, for example, by using a different method of fastening or giving an appropriate warning. In other words, the avoidability of the danger pointed towards the conclusion of defectiveness. Another instructive case is *Bogle v McDonald's Restaurants Ltd* [2002] EWHC 490. There the defendants were sued by a number of claimants who alleged that they had been scalded when hot drinks served in McDonald's restaurants were knocked over and spilt. The High Court dismissed the claims both in negligence and under the Consumer Protection Act. The latter claim involved two allegations of defectiveness: that the coffee was served too hot, and that the manner in which McDonald's served the coffee, having regard to the lids used on the cups, was dangerous to consumers. Field J held that McDonald's had met the legitimate expectations of consumers as to safety, and commented:

Persons generally know that if a hot drink is spilled onto someone, a serious scalding injury can result. They accordingly know that care must be taken to avoid such spills, especially if they are with young children. They expect precautions to be taken to guard against this risk but not to the point that they are denied the basic utility of being able to buy hot drinks to be consumed on the premises from a cup with the lid off.

Here, then, the utility of the product and the inevitability of the risk if the product was to have utility were factors which led the judge to conclude that the potentially-harmful characteristics (the heat at which the drinks were served, and the failure of the lid used on the coffee cups to prevent coffee from spilling if the cup was knocked over) did not amount to defects in the coffee. It is hard to imagine how he could have reached a sensible conclusion if those factors were excluded from his consideration.

Although the consumer expectation test worked to the benefit of the claimants in *A*, a very different result was reached in *Pollard v Tesco Stores Ltd* [2006] EWCA Civ 393. Here the question was whether a child-resistant screwtop cap could be said to be defective, the cap not conforming to the relevant British Design Standard. Dismissing the claim, Laws LJ noted that members of the public would not have the faintest idea to what safety standard the product they are buying has been designed; rather, if the claim was to succeed it would do so, in effect, by implying a contractual warranty as to the safety standard to which the product had been designed. Instead, Laws LJ held that the relevant expectation was that a child-resistant cap would be more difficult to open than an ordinary screwtop, and judged by this standard the product was not defective. The case raises the question of what evidence, if any, the court should use to determine the public expectation as to the product's safety. The simple answer is that, in most cases, the public expectation is that the product will be safe (unless modified by knowledge of likely product variation—see below). This works tolerably well for non-standard products, because a non-standard product is unlikely to meet the consumers' expectations of safety however that is measured. However, it becomes much more difficult where the allegation is that a standard product is defective; to say that consumers expect the product to be safe requires an assessment of *how* safe the standard product can be made. In this context, should the public's ignorance of what is possible be used to limit the meaning of defectiveness, especially where there is an accepted benchmark (the relevant design standard) that might be used to make that judgement? Note that what is important is the expectation of the public as a whole; if the members of the claimant's family (the claimant was a child) had known of the relevant safety standards it would have made no difference to the court's assessment. Note also that a recent EU Directive (2009/48/EC) dealing with the harmonisation of levels of safety of toys assumes that a toy that did not comply with the safety levels set by the Directive would render the producer liable under Directive 85/374 (see para. 45 of the recital). Although the reason for this conclusion is not given, it must be because the consumer's expectation of safety includes compliance with the standards set by the EU. Is this result consistent with *Pollard*?

If, as indicated above, public expectation as to the safety of a product might serve to limit the circumstances in which liability arises under the Act, would an action in negligence provide an alternative? In negligence, the defendant's conduct is judged objectively by reference to a reasonable producer; consumer expectations are not determinative of the reasonableness of the defendant's conduct. In theory at least, this might be a less demanding standard to meet in cases where consumer expectations as to safety are limited by the knowledge of consumers.

Standard and Non-Standard Products

In setting out the correct structure for considering questions under Article 6, Burton J identified two preliminary questions to be asked before applying the 'legitimate expectations' test. First, what is the harmful characteristic which caused the injury? Secondly, is the product standard or non-standard? The second question can only be addressed once the first is answered, and the harmful characteristic causing the injury identified, for a non-standard product is one where that characteristic is not present in the standard product (defined as 'one which is and performs as the producer intends').

The distinction between standard and non-standard products serves broadly the same purpose as that which is sometimes made between design defects and manufacturing defects (see *Markesinis & Deakin*, p. 714). It appears that Burton J preferred his terminology to side-step the question whether it could truly be said that a bag of infected blood had been defectively manufactured, or merely that it had been produced from defective material. In contrast to cases involving non-standard products, it will seldom be 'straightforward' to establish that a standard product is defective because the claimant must attack the design or make-up of the product line as a whole, and it seems that the producer can avoid liability by showing that any risks associated with the standard product are also inherent in similar products on the market. Demonstrating defectiveness in the case of a non-standard product will generally be easier, as it may be enough for the claimant to point to the presence of a harmful characteristic that does not exist in the standard product. However, Burton J decided that non-standard products are not automatically to be treated as defective, as he notes is the case in Italy and Spain where this is a matter of express legislation.

Do you think that consumers (and persons generally) are entitled to expect, as a barest minimum, that products will demonstrate the level of safety intended by the producer? If so, is this consistent with Burton J's approach in the *National Blood Authority* case?

Legitimate Product Variation?

In the *National Blood Authority* case, Burton J's classification of the infected blood as a non-standard product was not the end of the story. The learned judge considered that it was necessary to ask whether the risk that some batches of transfused blood would be infected was known to the public and socially acceptable. On the facts, he found that the risk was not generally known and therefore could not be regarded as socially acceptable. Agreeing that social acceptability is the correct question, Howells and Mildred (2002) 65 MLR 95 at 100 criticise Burton J for seeking to answer it within the framework of 'an arbitrary comparison between an obviously dangerous non-standard product and an evidently safe standard non-infected product'. The criticism is a little unfair, for Burton J makes it quite clear that categorisation of a product as non-standard does not lead automatically to a conclusion that it is defective. But it must be conceded that the point of the distinction becomes difficult to see if, however the product is classified, the same questions of social acceptability determine whether it is defective or not.

Still, even if classification of a product as 'standard' or 'non-standard' does not affect the basic nature of the inquiry, it may serve to bias it one way or the other. In particular, it seems it will be a rare case in which a non-standard product will satisfy the social-acceptability test: although the public may not *always* be entitled to expect that a product will reach them as the producer intended, they must surely be entitled to expect that *as a general rule*. One of those rare cases may be *Richardson v LRC Products Ltd* (2000) 59 BMLR 185. There it was alleged that the defendant's condom burst whilst the claimant was having sex with her husband and that she conceived as a result. Ian Kennedy J rejected the claim, though his precise reasoning is not entirely transparent. One interpretation of his judgment is that the condom, even if it could be proved that the rubber from which it was made had been damaged before it left the factory, was not defective because the public knows and accepts the risk that a small proportion of condoms will burst in the course of use, and expects users to take additional precautions if they desire 100 per cent protection from the risk of conception. But it may be that his Lordship simply found that the condom had not been damaged in the factory and that the fracture was caused entirely by the condom's misuse.

If the risk is not obvious, it may be assumed that consumers expect the standard product to be safe unless they have been warned (see *Worsley v Tambrands Ltd*, unreported, QBD, 3 December 1999, Ebsworth J, where the warnings provided in respect of the risk of toxic shock syndrome from the use of a tampon prevented a finding that the tampons were defective).

Can a product become defective through abuse or misuse? In the Scottish case of *Chadwick v Continental Tyres* [2008] ScotCS CSOH 24 it was held that a risk that resulted from *any* kind of foreseeable misuse was not sufficient to make a product defective; in the words of Lord Uist, at [29], such a conclusion would be 'patently irrational in the context of applying the public expectation test'. However, the public's expectation of safety might well include some degree of misuse of the product and in these cases a failure to warn of the risks associated with the misuse might render the product defective. (Cf. *Chadwick*, where counsel for the defender queried to whom a warning should be given about the risks associated with driving on overloaded and underinflated tyres.) Are there circumstances where more than a warning about the risk might be required? See *Palmer v Palmer* [2006] EWHC 1284 (QBD), where a device to turn inertia reel seatbelts into static seatbelts was held to be defective by virtue of product design and inadequate instructions. In these cases, how can the question of defectiveness be determined other than by considering avoidability?

Causation and Damage

A prerequisite to a claim under the Act is damage. Damage is defined in s. 5 as death or personal injury or any loss of or damage to property. Pure economic loss is not recoverable and accordingly loss to the value of the product itself is irrecoverable. However, difficulty is created by the words in s. 5(2) 'or for the loss of or any damage to the whole or any part of any product which has been supplied with the product in question comprised in it'. What of complex products? If a defective tyre is supplied with a new car, it would seem that the property damage to the car is irrecoverable, but if it was a substitute tyre, that is, supplied separately later on, then the damage to the car can be recovered. This seems an arbitrary distinction, although liability in the first case might arise under general negligence principles (on which see *Aswan Engineering Establishment Co v Lupdine Ltd* [1987] 1 WLR 1). Although the Act must be interpreted to give effect to the Directive, the Directive gives little guidance in this context, Article 9 defining damage as 'damage to, or destruction of, any item of property other than the defective product itself'. The key question remains what is the 'product' for this purpose?

Note also that claims for property damage are limited to property ordinarily intended for private use, occupation, and consumption and intended by the person suffering the loss or damage mainly for his own private use, occupation, or consumption. Both subjectively and objectively the property must be intended for use or used for a non-commercial purpose, the aim being to exclude the owner of business property. In addition, property damage claims are limited to amounts over £275. There is no upper limit on the amount recoverable although this was allowable by the Directive.

The defective product must cause the damage, and the normal rules relating to causation apply. For example, if one stands on a heater which is defective because of a wiring fault, and it collapses, the heater's defect did not cause the damage. Alternatively, such use may amount to contributory negligence and thus reduce any award of damages to the claimant (s. 6(4)). However, as was pointed out by the Court of Appeal in *Ide v ATB Sales* [2008] EWCA Civ 424, the claimant need only prove that the defect caused the damage; it is not necessary to show what caused the defect (as would be required in a negligence action).

Limitation

A claimant has three years to bring an action, from either the date on which the action accrued or, if later, the date of his knowledge (i.e., knowledge of the material facts giving rise to the cause of action). Note, however, the long-stop limitation period of ten years after the product was put into circulation by the defendant. Note that the court can usually override the statutory limitation period for personal injury claims in negligence under s. 33 Limitation Act 1980, but this does not apply to the ten-year period (see ss. 11A and 33 Limitation Act 1980). It is worth observing, however, that in certain limited circumstances a party can still be substituted as defendant after the ten-year period (see *Aventis Pasteur SA v OB*, 2009 ECJ EUR-Lex Lexis 1113).

Defences

Once a claimant can show damage attributable to a defect in a product for which the defendant is responsible under the Act, liability is strict. However, s. 4 provides a number of defences; liability is strict, not absolute. Most of the section is self-explanatory but a number of the paragraphs require comment. Section 4(1)(a) provides a defence where the defect is attributable to compliance with any requirement imposed by law. The defence relates to compliance, not minimum standards. A law which allowed a food producer to add an ingredient to certain foods would not fall within the section, although it would be relevant to whether the product was considered defective. Section 4(1)(c) provides a defence where the supply by the defendant was not in the course of business so that, for instance, the giver of a Christmas present is not liable for any defect in the present. It should be noted, however, that that the Court of Justice has held the Directive may still apply even where the activity in question has no economic or business purpose and the product is used in the course of a specific medical service which is financed entirely from public funds and for which the patient is not required to pay any consideration (see *Henning Veedfald v Arhus Amtskommune* [2001] ECR I–3569, above). In *A v National Blood Authority* [2001] 3 All ER 289 at 318 (decided before the above case) Burton J agreed with the opinion of the Advocate General in *Veedfald*—subsequently adopted by the Court—that there was no necessary reason why a public authority or a non-profit-making organisation should be in a different position (from a commercial producer) if the product is unsafe.

A recent decision of the Court of Appeal on s. 4(1)(d)—applying where the defect did not exist in the product at the time of the defendant's supply—suggests that this defence may be more important than previously thought. In *Piper v JRI (Manufacturing) Ltd* (2006) 92 BMLR 141, the defendant argued that, because of the steps it took in its manufacturing processes, the defect could not have existed in the product in question at the time of supply, and this was accepted as establishing the defence. This is an interesting decision. The defendant did not rely on evidence that the *specific* product had no defect; rather, it relied on its system for manufacturing the product generally as well as suggesting an alternative possibility for how the defect might have been caused. It should not be thought, however, that a manufacturer can satisfy the defence solely by pleading the infallibility of its manufacturing process; it is imperative that some other source of the defect be identified (as was the case in *Piper*). For example, if the defendant in *Grant v Australian Knitting Mills* (p. 117) had been sued under the Act, it is unlikely it could have relied on this defence even though its manufacturing process produced proportionally fewer defects than that in *Piper*; there was simply no alternative explanation for the excess sulphites in the undergarments other than that they were the result of the manufacturing process.

The most controversial defence is the 'development risks' defence in s. 4(1)(e), which applies to what Advocate General Tesauro describes in the case extracted below as 'risks present in production sectors in which an advance in technological and scientific knowledge may make a product appear defective *ex post*, whereas it was not regarded as such at the time when it was manufactured'. It was not obligatory for Member States to recognise this defence; the Directive made it optional. However, if recognised, its terms must accord with the Directive. The case extracted below considers whether s. 4(1)(e) of the Consumer Protection Act does in fact accord with Article 7 of the Directive, which described the defence as arising where 'the state of scientific and technical knowledge at the time when the producer put the product into circulation was not such as to enable the existence of the defect to be discovered'.

Case C–300/95 *Commission v United Kingdom* [1997] ECR I–2649

The European Commission argued that Article 7 of Directive 85/374/EEC required an objective assessment of the state of scientific and technical knowledge whereas the Act appeared to call for a subjective assessment by focusing on the conduct of the reasonable producer. It was argued that this had the effect of transforming the strict liability introduced by the Directive into a liability founded on negligence.

Opinion of Mr Advocate General Tesauro

It should first be observed that, since that provision refers solely to the 'scientific and technical knowledge' at the time when the product was marketed, it is not concerned with the practices and safety standards in use in the industrial sector in which the producer is operating. In other words, it has no bearing on the exclusion of the manufacturer from liability that no one in that particular class of manufacturer takes the measures necessary to eliminate the defect or prevent it from arising if such measures are capable of being adopted on the basis of the available knowledge.

Other matters which likewise are to be regarded as falling outside the scope of Article 7(e) are aspects relating to the practicability and expense of measures suitable for eliminating the defect from the product. Neither, from this point of view, can the fact that the producer did not appraise himself of the state of scientific and technical knowledge or does not keep up to date with developments in this area as disclosed in the specialist literature, be posited as having any relevance for the purposes of excluding liability on his part. I consider, in fact, that the producer's conduct should be assessed using the yardstick of the knowledge of an expert in the sector (eg if a chemist or a pharmacologist has to keep up to date with the characteristics of a given substance, similar knowledge will be required for present purposes of an industrialist producing pharmaceuticals containing the same substance).

Some additional considerations need to be explored, however, in order to tie down the concept 'state of knowledge'.

The progress of scientific culture does not develop linearly in so far as new studies and new discoveries may initially be criticised and regarded as unreliable by most of the scientific community, yet subsequently after the passage of time undergo an opposite process of 'beatification' whereby they are virtually unanimously endorsed. It is therefore quite possible that at the time when a given product is marketed, there will be isolated opinions to the effect that it is defective, whilst most academics do not take that view. The problem at this juncture is to determine whether in such a situation, that is to say, where there is a risk that is not certain and will be agreed to exist by all only ex post, the producer may still rely on the defence provided for in Article 7(e) of the Directive.

In my view, the answer to this question must be in the negative. In other words, the state of scientific knowledge cannot be identified with the views expressed by the majority of learned opinion, but with the most advanced level of research which has been carried out at a given time...

Where in the whole gamut of scientific opinion at a particular time there is also one isolated opinion (which, as the history of science shows, might become with the passage of time *opinio communis*) as to the potentially defective and/or hazardous nature of the product, the manufacturer is no longer faced with an unforeseeable risk, since, as such, it is outside the scope of the rules imposed by the directive.

The aspect which I have just been discussing is closely linked with the question of the availability of scientific and technical knowledge in the sense of the accessibility of the sum of knowledge at a given time to interested persons. It is undeniable that the circulation of information is affected by objective factors, such as, for example, its place or origin, the language in which it is given and the circulation of the journals in which it is published.

To be plain, there exist quite major differences in point of the speed in which it gets into circulation and the scale of its dissemination between a study of a researcher in a university in the United States published in an international English-language international journal and, to take an example given by the Commission, similar research carried out by an academic in Manchuria published in a local scientific journal in Chinese, which does not go outside the boundaries of the region.

In such a situation, it would be unrealistic and, I would say, unreasonable to take the view that the study published in Chinese has the same chances as the other of being known to a European product manufacturer. So, I do not consider that in such a case a producer could be held liable on the ground that at the time at which he put the product into circulation the brilliant Asian researcher had discovered the defect in it.

More generally, the 'state of knowledge' must be construed so as to include all data in the information circuit of the scientific community as a whole, bearing in mind, however, on the basis of a reasonableness test the actual opportunities for the information to circulate.

Having thus identified the scope of the Community provision, I consider that I am unable to share the Commission's proposition that there is an irremediable conflict between it and the national provision at issue. Indeed, there is no denying that the wording of s. 4(1)(e) of the Act contains an element of potential ambiguity: in so far as it refers to what might be expected of the producer, it could be interpreted more broadly that it should.

Notwithstanding this, I do not consider that the reference to the 'ability of the producer', despite its general nature, may or even must (necessarily) authorise interpretations contrary to the rationale and the aims of the directive.

In the first place, consideration of the producer is central not only to the rules of the directive taken as whole, but also to Article 7(e), which, although it does not mention him, is aimed at the producer himself, as the person having to discharge the burden of proof in order to avoid incurring liability. From this angle, the provision of the Act merely expresses in a clear way a concept which is implicit in the Community provision.

Secondly, the reference contained in the Act to the producer's ability to discover the defect is not sufficient to make the test which it lays down a subjective one. That reference can certainly be regarded, as the United Kingdom has argued, as an objectively verifiable and assessable parameter, which is in no way influenced by consideration of the actual subjective knowledge of the producer or by his organisational and economic requirements. By virtue of that parameter, it must therefore be proved, in order to exclude liability on the part of the producer, that it was impossible, in the light of the most advanced scientific and technical knowledge objectively and reasonably obtainable and available, to consider that the product was defective.

Judgment

Certain general observations can be made as to the wording of Article 7(e) of the directive.

First, as the Advocate General rightly observes...since that provision refers to 'scientific and technical knowledge at the time when [the producer] put the product into circulation', Article 7(e) is not specifically directed at the practices and safety standards in use in the industrial sector in which the producer is operating, but, unreservedly, at the state of scientific and technical knowledge, including the most advanced level of such knowledge, at the time when the product in question was put into circulation.

Second, the clause providing for the defence in question does not contemplate the state of knowledge of which the producer in question actually or subjectively was or could have been apprised, but the objective state of scientific and technical knowledge of which the producer is presumed to have been informed.

However, it is implicit in the wording of Article 7(e) that the relevant scientific and technical knowledge must have been accessible at the time when the product in question was put into circulation.

It follows that, in order to have a defence under Article 7(e) of the directive, the producer of a defective product must prove that the objective state of scientific and technical knowledge, including the most advanced level of such knowledge, at the time when the product in question was put into circulation was not such as to enable the existence of the defect to be discovered. Further, in order for the relevant scientific and technical knowledge to be successfully pleaded against the producer, that knowledge must have been accessible at the time when the product in question was put into circulation...

[T]he Commission has failed to make out its claim that the result intended by Article 7(e) of the directive would clearly not be achieved in the domestic legal order. First, s. 4(1)(e) of the Act places the burden of proof on the producer wishing to rely on the defence, as Art. 7 of the directive requires. Second, s 4(1)(e) places no restriction on the state and degree of scientific and technical knowledge at the material time which is to be taken into account. Third, its wording as such does not suggest, as the Commission alleges, that the availability of the defence depends on the subjective knowledge of a producer taking reasonable care in the light of the standard precautions taken in the industrial sector in question... Lastly, there is nothing in the material produced to the court to suggest that the courts in the United Kingdom, if called upon to interpret s. 4(1)(e), would not do so in the light of the wording and the purpose of the directive so as to achieve the result which it has in view.

COMMENTARY

For a discussion of the arguments over the meaning of Article 7 of the Directive and s. 4(1)(e) see Newdick [1988] 47 CLJ 455. He argues that 'knowledge' of a risk exists when 'the accumulation of information is such that a producer ought to take action to protect the consumer from danger'. However, the ECJ decision seems to entail that (1) the test in applying the development risks defence is whether the relevant information was 'accessible' to the producer at the time the product was supplied (or at least to an expert in the sector, to use the Advocate General's terminology), but (2) the information that is treated as relevant is not limited to that which is currently employed in the sector in question but includes the most advanced level of scientific and technical knowledge that is accessible (even if other experts disagree). This is because, at that time, the risk becomes foreseeable. A question remains as to what constitutes 'accessible' information. The Advocate General suggested that work published in Manchuria might not be accessible, but in *A v National Blood Authority* [2001] 3 All ER 289 at 326 Burton J (obiter) thought the 'Manchurian exception' should be limited to an unpublished document or unpublished research. Thus it may be necessary, for instance, for producers to employ powerful computerised databases to order to satisfy themselves as to the nature of scientific and technical knowledge relating to their products before putting them into circulation (see Mildred and Howells (1998) 61 MLR 570 at 572).

The ECJ decision has attracted criticism, both for the burden it imposes on producers in satisfying the defence (Hodges (1998) 61 MLR 560), and, conversely, for requiring that the risk information be 'accessible' (described as 'perplexing' and 'gratuitous and illogical': Mildred and Howells (1998) 61 MLR 570 at 572). It is undoubtedly true that the case imposes formidable hurdles before the defence can be relied upon, but can this be said to be inconsistent with the Directive's purpose? See further European Commission, *First Report on Council Directive on…Liability for Defective Products*, COM (95) 617 final, 13 December 1995.

Another point that has been clarified is that the defence relates to risks that could not have been foreseen, not to known risks about which nothing can be done. In *A v National Blood Authority* [2001] 3 All ER 289 Burton J held that a known but unavoidable risk in a product did not qualify for the Article 7(e) defence (on which s. 4(1)(e) is based), although if the risk was one that formed part of the legitimate expectations of consumers in relation to the product it might influence the decision on whether the product was defective. This approach is contrary to two decisions from other jurisdictions—one in the Netherlands (*Scholton v Sanquin Bloedvoorziening*, Rb. Amsterdam, 3 February 1999, NJ 1999, 621) and one in Australia (*Graham Barclay Oysters Pty Ltd v Ryan* (2001) 177 ALR 18, a case under Australian legislation virtually identical to the 1987 Act where the impossibility of taking remedial steps against a known risk was considered sufficient to found the defence). However, academic support can be found for Burton J's approach, questioning the correctness of the Netherlands court's decision (*van Dam*, 1410–12). Thus the result of Burton J's approach is that where a previously unknown risk becomes known (either through its previous occurrence or through extrapolation from accessible scientific or technical data), the s. 4(1)(e) defence can apply once and once only—when the presence of the risk first became apparent. A comparison here may be drawn with the well-known case of *Roe v Minister of Health* [1954] 2 QB 66, where it was alleged that the storage of vials of nupercaine in a phenol solution was careless. The action in negligence failed because it was not known that the vials could develop microscopic cracks, allowing the phenol to contaminate the nupercaine. Assuming that there was no accessible information pointing to the existence of the risk, the same result would be reached today under the Consumer Protection Act 1987 if the facts were repeated, but only in respect of the first time it was discovered that the vials could leak. In this sense the defendant under both the common law of negligence and the Consumer Protection Act 1987 is not to be judged with the benefit of hindsight.

On the importance of the development risks defence, see *Third Report from the Commission to the Council on the Application of Directive 85/374 on Liability for Defective Products*, COM (2006) 496 final, para. 3.3, and, more generally, R Goldberg, *Causation and Risk in the Law of Torts* (Oxford: Hart, 1999), ch. 7.

The Effectiveness of the Act

There have been relatively few cases decided under Part I of the Consumer Protection Act 1987. This picture may be misleading, as the Act may play a role in encouraging producers to settle claims, especially in multi-party actions alleging a defect in a product's basic design, where it had previously proved very difficult to establish negligence (see, e.g., Glaxo's £7 million settlement of claims relating to the drug Myodil in 1995). More likely, however, consumers will continue to seek redress from producers through non-legal avenues (e.g. informal mediation through customer services departments). If legal remedies are sought, simple contractual claims against the retailer may be seen as preferable, especially in cases where the amount involved is small, and this will generally be the only recourse where the purchaser only wants his money back on a product that simply does not work. Even if the producer is sought to be made legally liable, this may be done in negligence as well as under the Act, and the extent to which the Act provides a better bet than the general law of negligence is still open to doubt: although it might have been thought that the decision of Burton J in *A v National Blood Authority* [2001] 3 All ER 289 would encourage claims under the Act where there would be no parallel claim in negligence, more recent cases suggest that there may be little advantage to suing under the Act rather than in negligence.

The effectiveness of the Directive was reviewed for the third time by the European Commission at the end of 2006 (*Third Report from the Commission to the Council on the Application of Directive 85/374 on Liability for Defective Products*, COM (2006) 496 final) with no change recommended. The evidence before the Commission suggested that the Directive was perceived as positive and beneficial to consumers, and that many stakeholders were wary of major reform which would alter the balance between the competing interests that was struck by the Directive. Thus the suggestions of the 1999 Commission Green Paper on possible improvements to the Directive, which canvassed a wide range of issues including the burden of proof, development risks, mental injuries, the threshold to property damage, limitation periods and the financial limits of damage claims (*Liability for Defective Products*, COM (99) 396 final, 28 July 1999) seem unlikely to be taken any further, although the Commission has accepted that close and regular monitoring of these issues should continue to take place to ensure the Directive continues to operate in a satisfactory manner.

IV. Breach of Statutory Duty

1. Introduction

Breach of statutory duty is an independent tort, separate and distinct from the tort of negligence. The fact that the defendant has breached a statutory duty protecting the claimant's health or safety may well be relevant in a negligence case as powerful evidence of breach of the common law duty of care. And in certain other jurisdictions (e.g. in the US and Canada) breach of statutory duty *only* has this effect; it is referred to as 'statutory negligence' (see further Section 4, below). But in English law the statutory duty may give rise wholly independently to a cause of action of its own. As Lord Wright stated in *London Passenger Transport Board v Upson* [1949] AC 155 at 168, 'a claim for damages for breach of a statutory duty … is a specific common law right which is not to be confused with a claim for negligence'.

We are not concerned here with statutes which expressly advert to the question whether breach of obligations contained in them should be actionable in damages, whether so as to confirm the existence of a civil remedy or to rule it out. (The Occupiers' Liability Acts and the Consumer Protection Act 1987 are good examples of statutes which expressly recognise civil liability.) Our target is those statutes—the vast majority—that are silent on the issue. The question for the courts is how to determine whether breach of the provisions of such a statute—or of regulations issued under it—is actionable in damages. If breach is found to be actionable, then a subsidiary question arises: what standard of duty is imposed? This is a simple matter of statutory interpretation and need not be pursued further here, but it ought to be noted that many statutory duties have a strict or absolute character and can lead therefore to the imposition of liability even in the absence of fault. (For analysis of the terms 'absolute' and 'strict' liability, see *Allison v London Underground* [2008] EWCA Civ 71, [2008] ICR

719 at [31] per Smith LJ. As to the justification for liability on the employer without fault, see *Lewisham London Borough Council v Malcolm (Equality and Human Rights Commission intervening)* [2008] UKHL 43, [2008] 1 AC 1399 at [28] per Lord Scott: 'As between employer and employee it should be for the employer to ensure that the premises in which and the machinery with which his employees work are safe. The risk that there are unforeseeable dangers must be accepted by the employer.')

It was not until the second half of the nineteenth century that tort liability for breach of statutory duty received proper attention by the courts. Admittedly, there had been prior to that time occasional references to the issue by judges and treatise writers. In a famous passage in *Comyn's Digest*, for instance, there appears the bold and unqualified pronouncement that '[i]n every case where a statute enacts or prohibits a thing for the benefit of a person, he shall have a remedy upon the same statute for the thing enacted for his advantage, or for the recompense of a wrong done to him contrary to the said law' (*Com. Dig.*, 'Action upon Statute', F). But it was not until the proliferation of legislative regulation by the vigorous social planners of the Victorian era that civil liability for breach of statutory duty became a matter of urgent judicial attention. Some of the early cases took an expansive view of the liability (but cf. *Doe d. Murray, Bishop of Rochester v Bridges* (1831) B&Ad 847). In *Couch v Steel* (1854) 3 E & B 402, 23 LJ (QB) 121, the plaintiff, a sailor, fell ill while at sea. The ship, contrary to the statutory requirement, was not carrying appropriate medication and the plaintiff suffered avoidable injury to his health. His claim for damages succeeded before Lord Campbell CJ who, adverting to the passage in *Comyn's Digest* cited above, held that there was a right to sue for 'breach of a public duty', notwithstanding the existence of a criminal penalty for the wrong in question. But such liability was quickly reined in, no doubt as a result of fears that the bounds of civil liability would expand in pace with new legislative regulation, going far beyond the scope of the negligence liabilities of the time (see in particular *Atkinson v Newcastle Waterworks Co* (1877) 2 Ex D 441 and *Gorris v Scott* (1874) LR 9 Exch 125, both extracted below).

The principal context in which statutory tort liability succeeded in establishing itself was the workplace. As we have seen (Section I, above), the negligence liability of employers to their employees had been radically curtailed by an 'unholy trinity' of defences, namely *volenti*, contributory negligence (then a total defence) and common employment. By the end of the century, however, there was a widespread perception that the courts had gone too far in restricting liability, as was evident in the passage through Parliament of the Employers' Liability Act 1880 (allowing employees only very limited claims) and the Workmen's Compensation Act 1897, which foreshadowed the social security legislation of the twentieth century. It was against this background that the tort of statutory breach emerged as a way of overcoming the limitations of the action in negligence. In *Baddeley v Earl Granville* (1887) 19 QBD 423, the defence of *volenti* was ruled inapplicable to breach of statutory duty (see further *Wheeler v New Merton Board Mills* [1933] 2 KB 669; exceptionally, the defence may be raised where the employer is only placed in breach by the actions of the claimant or of another employee acting in tandem with the claimant: *ICI v Shatwell* [1965] AC 656). Then, in a crucial development the Court of Appeal accepted, first, that industrial safety legislation could give rise to private rights and, secondly, that it was not possible to raise the common employment defence in an action brought to enforce those rights (see *Groves v Lord Wimborne* [1898] 2 QB 402, extracted below). Had it not been for this rather unusual historical context, it may well be that English law would have developed only a doctrine of statutory negligence rather than a separate and distinct tort of breach of statutory duty (see *Markesinis & Deakin*, pp. 381–2).

2. The Modern Law: The Indicators of Parliamentary Intent

In the modern law, whether a breach of statutory duty gives rise to a private right of action for damages is assessed by reference to Parliament's intention in passing the legislation in question. In *X (Minors) v Bedfordshire County Council* [1995] 2 AC 633 at 731, Lord Browne-Wilkinson set out the essence of the English approach as follows:

> The basic proposition is that in the ordinary case a breach of statutory duty does not, by itself, give rise to any private law cause of action. However, a private law cause of action will arise if it can be shown, as a matter of construction of the statute, that the statutory duty was imposed for the protection of a limited class of the public and that Parliament intended to confer on members of that class a private right of action for breach of the duty.

This is a very clear statement that English law recognises no tort of careless performance of a statutory duty *per se*. An action against a body acting under a statutory framework must satisfy the requirements of the tort of breach of statutory duty, or alternatively those of the tort of negligence (see Ch. 10), unless there is an *express* statutory liability that can be relied upon (e.g. under the Human Rights Act 1998).

In determining Parliament's intention, the courts have traditionally made use of a number of 'indicators'. In the past, the classic point of departure was a dictum of Lord Tenterden in *Doe d. Murray, Bishop of Rochester v Bridges* (1831) B & Ad 847 at 859:

> [W]here an Act creates an obligation, and enforces the performance in a specified manner, we take it as a general rule that performance cannot be enforced in any other manner. If the obligation is created, but no mode of enforcing its performance is ordained, the common law may, in general, find a mode suited to the particular nature of the case.

In other words, the presence of an alternative means of enforcing the statutory duty gave rise to a presumption against the recognition of a private right of action. Conversely, its absence raised a presumption in favour. This basic starting point was confirmed by the House of Lords in *Lonrho Ltd v Shell Petroleum Co Ltd* [1982] AC 173, although Lord Diplock stated that the non-actionability of penal legislation was subject to certain exceptions, notably where the statute was passed to benefit a particular class of the public. However, the courts—perhaps motivated by a concern not to outflank the tort of negligence—subsequently moved towards a less schematised and more flexible approach and have begun to attach greater import-ance to other considerations, such as whether the duty is merely regulatory in character and whether it expresses only a vague political aspiration, for example, in the social welfare field; both these factors weigh heavily against the imposition of liability (see respectively *R v Deputy Governor of Parkhurst Prison, ex p. Hague* [1992] 1 AC 58 and *O'Rourke v Camden London Borough Council* [1998] AC 188, both extracted below). The courts no longer seem to take Lord Tenterden's simple propositions as their starting point, and it has become more and more difficult to identify any clear and workable test of whether breach of a particular statutory duty is actionable in damages. The cases defy easy categorisation, and perhaps all that is possible is to give examples of cases where a private law remedy is recognised and those where it is not. Indeed, such is the difficulty of identifying any intelligible principles in this area that Lord Denning has remarked—perhaps not entirely in jest—that '[t]he divid-ing line between the pro-cases and the contra-cases is so blurred and so ill-defined that you might as well toss a coin to decide it' (*Ex parte Island Records Ltd* [1978] 1 Ch 122 at 135).

Atkinson v Newcastle Waterworks Co (1877) 2 Ex D 441

The plaintiff brought an action for damages against a waterworks company for not keeping their pipes charged as required by the Waterworks Clauses Act 1847, whereby his premises situated within the area of the defendants' responsibility were burnt down. The plaintiff succeeded before the Court of Exchequer Chamber; the defendants appealed.

Section 42 of the Waterworks Clauses Act 1847 provided:

> The undertakers shall at all times keep charged with water, under such pressure as aforesaid [which by s. 35 was such pressure as would make the water reach the top storey of the highest houses within the area in question], all their pipes to which fire-plugs shall be fixed, unless prevented by frost, unusual drought, or other unavoidable cause or accident, or during necessary repairs, and shall allow all persons at all times to take and use such water for extinguishing fire, without making compensation for the same.

By s. 43, breach of that section was punishable by a fine of £10. Additionally, in defined certain circumstances the undertaker became liable to a forfeit of 40s to town commissioners and rate-payers affected by inadequate supply for every day during which the breach of duty continued.

Lord Cairns LC

[I]n my judgment the general scheme of these waterworks clauses, and of any Act in which they are incorporated, would appear to be this: A waterworks company, proposing to supply water to a town, apply to parliament for powers to take certain springs and land, and to charge rates for the supply of water, in consideration of which powers being granted them they enter into certain obligations. Besides general obligations to supply the town commissioners with water for public purposes, they enter into certain special obligations as to fire-plugs, viz., to keep the pipes connected with those plugs charged with water at a certain pressure, and to allow all persons—not any particular persons, or owners of particular houses, but all persons—at all times to take water for the purpose of extinguishing fire without making compensation for it. The object for which the water is in such case to be used is a public object, and to effect that object the company are willing to accept the obligation to allow any person to take any quantity of water gratuitously, and further to keep the pipes from which that water is to be taken charged at such a pressure that the water so taken may be most effectively employed.

That this creates a statutory duty no one can dispute, but the question is whether the creation of that duty gives a right of action for damages to an individual who, like the plaintiff, can aver that he had a house situate within the company's limits and near to one of their fire-plugs, that a fire broke out, that the pipes connected with the plug were not charged at the pressure required by the section, and that in consequence his house was burnt down. Now, a priori, it certainly appears a startling thing to say that a company undertaking to supply a town like Newcastle with water, would not only be willing to be put under this parliamentary duty to supply gratuitously for the purpose of extinguishing fire an unlimited quantity of water at a certain pressure, and to be subjected to penalties for the non-performance of that duty, but would further be willing in their contract with parliament to subject themselves to the liability to actions by any number of householders who might happen to have their houses burnt down in consequence; and it is, a priori, equally improbable that parliament would think it a necessary or reasonable bargain to make. In the one case the undertakers would know beforehand what they had to meet as the consequence of their neglect, they would come under definite penalties; in the other they would virtually become gratuitous insurers of the safety from fire, so far as water is capable of producing that safety, of all the houses within the district over which their powers were to extend.

It is, however, necessary to look at the 43rd section, which imposes the penalty for the breach of the duty in question. That section deals with four classes of neglect, the neglect to fix, maintain, or repair fire-plugs, the neglect to furnish the town commissioners with a sufficient supply of water for public purposes, the neglect to keep the pipes charged under the required pressure, and the neglect to furnish any owner or occupier with the supply of water to which he is entitled. For each of those four classes of neglect the company is visited with a penalty of £10. And in two of them, the second and fourth, the company is also to forfeit to the commissioners or the ratepayer aggrieved a further penalty of 40s a day for every day during which the neglect continues after notice in writing given to the company. Now, why is it that in some cases there is a penalty which is to go into the pocket of the persons injured, and not in the case of neglecting to keep the pipes fixed to the fire-plugs charged under the proper pressure? The reason is obvious. In the former cases it is convenient to give a penalty to the individual, in the latter case it is not. In the cases of the town commissioners and the owners or occupiers asking for and not getting their proper supply of water, you have a person or persons known and determined to whom the penalty may be given, but in the case of neglect to keep the pipes properly charged there is no particular person whom you can single out beforehand, and say that in the event of a breach, he is to be entitled to the penalty. In that case then the only guarantee taken by parliament for the fulfilment of the obligation, an obligation which has the appearance of being imposed for the benefit of the public, is what I may term the public penalty of £10. Apart, then, from authority, I should say, without hesitation, that it was no part of the scheme of this Act to create any duty which was to become the subject of an action at the suit of individuals, to create any right in individuals with a power of enforcing that right by action; but that its scheme was, having laid down certain duties, to provide guarantees for the due fulfilment of them, and where convenient to give the penalties, or some of them, to the persons injured, but, where not convenient so to do, there simply to impose public penalties, not by way of compensation, but as a security to the public for the due performance of the duty. To split up the 43rd section, and to say that in those cases in which a penalty is to go into the pocket of the individual injured there is to be no right of action, but that where no penalty is so given to the individual there is to be a right of action, is to violate the ordinary rule of construction. There being here in a certain number of cases a penalty which the plaintiff himself admits excludes the right of action, the conclusion is irresistible that in the remaining cases also in the same section the legislature intended to give no right of action.

[His Lordship proceeded to rule that there was no binding authority against this conclusion, distinguishing the decision in *Couch v Steel* (1854) 3 E & B 402, 23 LJ (QB) 121 (which he considered in any case to be questionable) on the basis that it concerned a public general Act of Parliament, rather than a private Act.]

Cockburn CJ and **Brett LJ** delivered short concurring judgments.

Appeal allowed.

COMMENTARY

This case marks the demise of the view advanced by Lord Campbell in *Crouch v Steel* that those protected by a penal statute could prima facie bring a civil action upon it. In its place, the Court of Appeal adopted a narrow 'construction' approach which required consideration of whether the statute was intended to give rise to private rights. Although Lord Cairns distinguished *Crouch* on the rather narrow grounds that it was not applicable to private Acts of Parliament, it became apparent that Lord Campbell's view could not be sustained even in relation to public Acts (see, e.g., *Phillips v Britannia Hygienic Laundry Co Ltd* [1923] 2 KB 832, extracted below). *Winfield & Jolowicz* explains (para. 7–3) that the new approach was thought necessary in light of the introduction of regulatory regimes in many areas in the course of the nineteenth century: 'With the vast increase in legislative activity, the old rule was perceived to carry the risk of liability wider than the legislature could have contemplated, particularly in relation to public authorities.'

Atkinson was distinguished in the later case of *Dawson v Bingley Urban District Council* [1911] 2 KB 149, where the Court of Appeal considered a claim for damages for breach of s. 66 of the Public Health Act 1875. By this section, every urban authority was required to cause fire-plugs to be provided and maintained, and to 'paint or mark on the buildings and walls within the streets, words or marks near to such fire-plugs to denote the situation thereof'. The defendants, a local authority, affixed to a wall in a street which was not repairable by the inhabitants at large a plate intended to indicate the position of a fire-plug in the water main and marked 'FP 22 ft 3 in'; in fact, a line drawn straight from the plate across the street for the required distance crossed the water main at a spot 6 feet 10 inches away from the place where the fire plug was inserted in the main. A fire broke out on the plaintiffs' premises, which were a short distance from the plug; the fire brigade were quickly in attendance, but there was considerable delay owing to their inability to find the exact position of the fire-plug. As a result of the delay, the fire grew larger and caused more damage than it would otherwise have done. The Court of Appeal upheld the claim, distinguishing *Atkinson* on two grounds: '(a) the defendants there were not a public body but a private company, so that the Act, in the words of Lord Cairns, ought to be regarded "not as an Act of public and general policy but rather in the nature of a private legislative bargain with a body of undertakers"... and (b) the Act in that case itself imposed remedies in the form of penalties...' (per Kennedy LJ at 159–60). The Public Health Act 1875 contained no specific provision for the recovery of penalties or any other remedy for infringement of s. 66. (See also *Read v Croydon Corporation* [1938] 4 All ER 631.)

The decision in *Atkinson* may be tacitly underpinned by a concern not to impose civil liability on a utility in respect of a failure to provide a public service for which it has assumed responsibility; affirmative duties of this nature are not readily recognised in the law of tort. This concern is equally strong at the present day: in *Capital & Counties plc v Hampshire County Council* [1997] QB 1004 (extracted p. 470, above), the Court of Appeal held that the fire brigade could not be held liable in either breach of statutory duty, distinguishing *Dawson*, above, or the common law of negligence in respect of its failure to put out a fire. Such cases are fundamentally different from the line of authorities dating from the mid-nineteenth century which impose liability on railway companies for breach of duties associated with level-crossing gatekeeping (see, e.g., *Fawcett v Work & N Midland Ry* (1851) 16 QB 610). Although these duties also arose from private legislative bargains with the railway companies, they may be regarded as an incident of the duty to take reasonable care in operating a railway, and hence the liability is more appropriately regarded as one for misfeasance rather than nonfeasance.

Groves v Lord Wimborne [1898] 2 QB 402

The plaintiff, a boy, was employed at the defendant's iron works in which he worked a steam winch with revolving cog-wheels. The cog-wheels were dangerous to a person working the winch unless fenced. There was evidence that there had originally been a guard or fence to the cog-wheels, but it had for some reason been removed, and there had been no fence to the wheels while the plaintiff was employed at the winch, a period of about six months. While working the winch, the plaintiff's right arm was caught by the cog-wheels, and was so badly injured that the forearm had to be amputated. He alleged that the defendant had been in breach of the statutory duty imposed upon him by the Factory and Workshop Act 1878, s. 5(3), a breach which (if proved) would be punishable under the terms of the same statute by fine (s. 82). The learned judge held that an action would not lie for breach of the statutory duty imposed by the Act but he asked the jury to assess the damages provisionally, which they did at the sum of £150. The judge entered judgment for the defendant. The plaintiff appealed.

A. L. Smith LJ

The Act in question, which followed numerous other Acts in pari materia, is not in the nature of a private legislative bargain between employers and workmen, as the learned judge seemed to think, but is a public Act passed in favour of the workers in factories and workshops to compel their employers to do certain things for their protection and benefit. The first question is what duty is imposed by that Act upon the occupiers of factories and workshops with regard to the fencing of machinery. By s. 5 it is enacted that 'with respect to the fencing of machinery the following provisions shall have effect.' Then by sub-s. 3 of the section, as amended by the Factory and Workshop Act, 1891, s. 6, sub-s. 2, 'All dangerous parts of the machinery, and every part of the mill gearing shall either be securely fenced, or be in such position or of such construction as to be equally safe to every person employed in the factory as it would be if it were securely fenced'; and by sub-s. 4, 'All fencing shall be constantly maintained in an efficient state while the parts required to be fenced are in motion or use for the purpose of any manufacturing process'; and 'a factory in which there is a contravention of this section shall be deemed not to be kept in conformity with this Act.'

In the present case it is admitted that machinery on the defendant's premises which came within these provisions was not fenced as required by the Act, and that injury was thereby occasioned to the plaintiff, a boy employed on the works. On proof of a breach of this statutory duty imposed on the defendant, and injury resulting to the plaintiff therefrom, prima facie the plaintiff has a good cause of action . . . Could It be doubted that, if s. 5 stood alone, and no fine were provided by the Act for contravention of its provisions, a person injured by a breach of the absolute and unqualified duty imposed by that section would have a cause of action in respect of that breach? Clearly it could not be doubted. That being so, unless it appears from the whole 'purview' of the Act, to use the language of Lord Cairns in the case of *Atkinson v Newcastle Waterworks Co* (1877) 2 Ex D 441, that it was the intention of the Legislature that the only remedy for breach of the statutory duty should be by proceeding for the fine imposed by s. 82, it follows that, upon proof of a breach of that duty by the employer and injury thereby occasioned to the workman, a cause of action is established.

The question therefore is whether the cause of action which prima facie is given by s. 5 is taken away by any provisions to be found in the remainder of the Act. It is said that the provisions of ss. 81, 82, and 86 have that effect, and that it appears thereby that the purview of the Act is that the only remedy, where a workman has been injured by a breach of the duty imposed by s. 5, shall be by proceeding before a court of summary jurisdiction for a fine under s. 82, which fine is not to exceed £100. In dealing with the question whether this was the intention of the Legislature, it is material, as Kelly CB pointed out in giving judgment in the case of *Gorris v Scott* (1874) LR 9 Ex 125, to consider for whose benefit the Act was passed, whether it was passed in the interests of the public at large or in those of a particular class of persons. The Act now in question, as I have said, was clearly passed in favour of workers employed in factories and workshops, and to compel their employers to perform certain statutory duties for their protection and benefit. It is to be observed in the first place that under the provisions of s. 82 not a penny of the fine necessarily goes to the person injured or his family. The provision is only that the whole or any part of it may be applied for the benefit of the injured person or his family, or otherwise, as a secretary of state determines. Again, if proceedings for the fine are taken before magistrates, upon what considerations are they to act in determining the amount of the fine? One matter to be considered clearly would be the character of the neglect to fence. This neglect might be either of a serious or of a venial character. Suppose that it was of the latter character, but a person was unfortunately killed or injured in consequence of it. What fine are the magistrates to impose? Are they to impose a fine of the same amount as if it were a flagrant case of neglect to fence? The first thing one would say that they would have to consider would be whether the offence was of a grave character or otherwise. It may be said that in determining the amount of the fine the character of the injury sustained by the workman would be considered, but I am not sure that that is the meaning of the section. It seems to me that the fine is inflicted by way of punishment of the employer for neglect of the duty imposed by the Act, and must be proportionate to the character of the offence. This consideration and the fact that whatever penalty the magistrates inflict does not necessarily go to the injured workman or his family lead me to the conclusion that it cannot have been the intention of the Legislature that the provision which imposes upon the employer a fine as a punishment for neglect of his statutory duty should take away the prima facie right of the workman to be fully compensated for injury occasioned to him by that neglect. Another observation which makes the matter still clearer arises from the fact that, having regard to the provisions of s. 87, it may not be the employer, presumably a person of means and capable of paying a substantial fine, who would have to pay the fine. Under that section the employer may be exempted from the penalty, and the fine may be imposed upon the actual offender, who may be a workman employed at weekly wages; and yet it is said that a fine payable by such a person is the only remedy given by the statute to the injured workman for breach by the occupier of the imperative statutory duty. I cannot read this statute in the manner in which it is sought to be read by the defendant. I think that s. 5 does give to the workman a right of action upon the statute for injury caused by a breach of the statutory duty thereby imposed, and that he is not relegated to the provisions for the imposition of a fine on the employer, or it may be a workman, as his sole remedy.

[His Lordship proceeded to rule also that the defence of common employment (subsequently abolished by Law Reform (Personal Injuries) Act 1948) did not apply to a claim for breach of statutory duty.]

Rigby and **Vaughan Williams LJJ** delivered separate concurring judgments.

Appeal allowed.

COMMENTARY

Cornish & Clark comment (p. 520):

The Court of Appeal's attitude in the atmosphere of 1898 is not hard to understand: the campaigns that had resulted, first in the Employers' Liability Act 1880 and then the Workmen's

Compensation Act 1897, had induced a somewhat more generous attitude to industrial accident claims, a change already manifest in the modification of *volenti non fit iniuria*.

This decision signalled the start of the rapid development of civil liability for breach of industrial safety legislation. Indeed, Glanville Williams has highlighted health and safety at work as 'well nigh the only area in which penal legislation has been held to create statutory torts', at least in the twentieth century (see 'The Effect of Penal Legislation in the Law of Tort' (1960) 23 MLR 233 at 244). In most other contexts the courts have effectively reversed the presumption of liability, in the absence of a clearly stated contrary intention, that A. L. Smith LJ makes here.

Very many different statutory provisions govern workplace safety, but a measure of order has been imposed on this area of the law by the Health and Safety at Work Act 1974 and the regulations introduced thereunder which have gradually superseded a number of the disparate obligations contained in different statutes. For example, the fencing obligation considered in *Groves* and contained in successive statutes up until Factories Act 1961, s. 14 has been repealed and replaced by an equivalent duty contained now in the Provision and Use of Work Equipment Regulations (SI 1998/2306), reg. 11). Although the Act expressly excludes civil liability for breach of the general duties that it imposes on employers (s. 47(1)), it states that breach of a duty imposed by health and safety regulations shall be actionable unless otherwise provided (s. 47(2)).

The scope for civil actions for breach of such regulations has been further increased by the development of a regime of workplace health and safety under EU law. Article 153 of the Treaty on the Functioning of the EU (ex Article 137 TEC) commits the EU to supporting member states in seeking 'improvements in particular of the working environment to protect workers' health and safety.' A 'framework' Directive on health and safety (EC 89/391) was adopted in 1989 and subsequently implemented in English law in the Management of Health and Safety at Work Regulations (SI 1992/2051, replaced by SI 1999/3242), followed by a number of 'daughter' Directives which were also implemented in English law as regulations under the 1974 Act (s. 15). Section 47(2) of the Act provides for a general presumption of actionability for health and safety regulations issued under it unless the contrary is expressly provided. It may be noted, as an example of such provision, that breach of a duty imposed on an employer or employee by the 'framework' regulations does not confer a right of action in any civil proceedings in so far as that duty applies for the protection of a person other than the employer and persons in his employment (SI 1999/3242, reg. 22, as amended).

Phillips v Britannia Hygienic Laundry Co Ltd [1923] 2 KB 832

By s. 6(1) of the Locomotives on Highways Act 1896, the Local Government Board was empowered to make regulations with respect to the use of light locomotives on highways, and their construction, and the conditions under which they could be used. Breach of any such regulation was punishable by fine (s. 7). Article II, cl. 6, of the Motor Cars (Use and Construction) Order 1904, made under the above section, provided: 'The motor car and all the fittings thereof shall be in such a condition as not to cause, or to be likely to cause, danger to any person on the motor car or on any highway.'

A lorry (considered to be both a 'light locomotive' and a 'motor car' within the statutory scheme) was involved in an accident on the highway when one of its axles broke and a wheel came off, damaging the plaintiff's vehicle. It was discovered that the axle had been in a dangerously defective condition but that this was not attributable to any fault on the part of the owners, who had recently sent the lorry to a competent firm of mechanics to be overhauled and repaired. The owner of the damaged vehicle brought an action against the owners of the lorry for a breach of Article II, cl. 6, of the Order. The county court's decision in favour of the plaintiff was reversed by the Divisional Court. The plaintiff appealed to the Court of Appeal.

Bankers LJ

In the case we are considering the statute creates an obligation and provides a remedy for its non-observance, and the question is whether the scope and language of the statute indicate that the general rule is to prevail so that the remedy provided is the only remedy, or whether an exception to that general rule is to be admitted . . .

If the appellant's contention is to prevail every one injured by a motor car which does not comply with the regulations has a right of action. There is no reason for differentiating between those who are injured as a legal consequence of a breach from those who are injured in fact irrespectively of the breach of the regulations. Take cl. 7 for example. That clause provides that a car must have lamps exhibiting a white light in front and a red light in the rear. According to the appellant's contention a foot passenger crossing in front of a motor car would have a right of action if injured without any negligence of the driver, merely because the car had no red light in the rear. That cannot have been the intention of the Legislature. The absence of a red light in the rear may concern the safety of the car itself, or it may be a wise police regulation for other vehicles overtaking it, but it cannot affect the safety of a foot passenger passing in front of the car. This seems to indicate that it is not the intention of the Act to confer a right of action on every person injured by a car which does not conform to the regulations and to confer this right even though the breach of the regulations has no effect on the injury of which he complains. The matter might have been more doubtful if cl. 6 had stood alone. It provides that the car and all its fittings 'shall be in such a condition as not to cause, or to be likely to cause, danger to any person on the motor car or on any highway.' We have not to consider the case of a person injured on the highway. The injury here was done to the appellant's van; and the appellant, a member of the public, claims a right of action as one of a class for whose benefit cl. 6 was introduced. He contends that the public using the highway is the class so favoured. I do not agree. In my view the public using the highway is not a class; it is itself the public and not a class of the public. The clause therefore was not passed for the benefit of a class or section of the public. It applies to the public generally, and it is one among many regulations for breach of which it cannot have been intended that a person aggrieved should have a civil remedy by way of action in addition to the more appropriate remedy provided, namely a fine. In my opinion therefore this case is not an exception to the general rule; that rule applies, and the appeal must be dismissed.

Atkin LJ

I am of the same opinion. This is an important question, and I have felt some doubt upon it, because it is clear that these regulations are in part designed to promote the safety of the public using highways. The question is whether they were intended to be enforced only by the special penalty attached to them in the Act. In my opinion, when an Act imposes a duty of commission or omission, the question whether a person aggrieved by a breach of the duty has a right of action depends on the intention of the Act. Was it intended to make the duty one which was owed to the party aggrieved as well as to the State, or was it a public duty only? That depends on the construction of the Act and the circumstances in which it was made and to which it relates. One question to be considered is, Does the Act contain reference to a remedy for breach of it? Prima facie if it does that is the only remedy. But that is not conclusive. The intention as disclosed by its scope and wording must still be regarded, and it may still be that, though the statute creates the duty and provides a penalty, the duty is nevertheless owed to individuals. Instances of this are *Groves v Lord Wimborne* [1898] 2 QB 402 and *Britannic Merthyr Coal Co v David* [1910] AC 74. To my mind . . . the question is not to be solved by considering whether or not the person aggrieved can bring himself within some special class of the community or whether he is some designated individual. The duty may be of such paramount importance that it is owed to all the public. It would be strange if a less important duty, which is owed to a section of the public, may be enforced by an action, while a more important duty owed to the public at large cannot. The right of action does not depend on whether a statutory commandment or prohibition is pronounced for the benefit of the public or for the benefit of a class. It may be conferred on any one who can bring himself within the benefit of the Act, including one who cannot be otherwise specified than as a person using the highway . . . Therefore the question is whether these regulations, viewed in the circumstances in which they were made and to which they relate, were intended to impose a duty which is a public duty only or whether they were intended, in addition to the public duty, to impose a duty enforceable by an individual aggrieved. I have come to the conclusion that the duty they were intended to impose was not a duty enforceable by individuals injured, but a public duty only, the sole remedy for which is the remedy provided by way of a fine. They impose obligations of various kinds, some are concerned more with the maintenance of the highway than with the safety of passengers; and they are of varying degrees of importance; yet for breach of any regulation a fine not exceeding £10 is the penalty. It is not likely that the Legislature, in empowering a department to make regulations for the use and construction of motor cars, permitted the department to impose new duties in favour of individuals and new causes of action for breach of them in addition to the obligations already well provided for and regulated by the common law of those who bring vehicles upon highways. In particular it is not likely that the Legislature intended by these means to impose on the owners of vehicles an absolute obligation to have them roadworthy in all events even in the absence of negligence. For these reasons I think the appeal should be dismissed.

Younger LJ also agreed.

Appeal dismissed.

COMMENTARY

The reasoning of Bankes LJ in particular is premised upon the classic approach whereby penal legislation gives rise to no private rights unless passed for the benefit of a particular class of the public. By insisting that road users were not a class of the public but the public itself (cf. *Roe v Sheffield City Council* [2003] EWCA Civ 1, [2004] QB 653: persons using the highway a sufficiently limited class), Bankers LJ was able to find that the basic presumption of non-actionability applied. Later cases have made it clear, however, that the mere fact that legislation benefits a particular class does not necessarily make it actionable in damages (see, e.g., *Hague* and *O'Rourke*, extracted below).

This decision may be usefully contrasted with *Groves v Lord Wimborne*. Why should industrial safety legislation give rise to a potential liability in damages while road safety legislation does not? *Atiyah* comments (p. 96):

Perhaps the court was influenced—consciously or unconsciously—by the fact that in 1923 it was still not compulsory to insure against third party liability, and it may have shrunk from imposing a form of liability without fault on individual motorists, who might not have had the resources to meet a judgment for damages. Had this issue arisen after compulsory insurance was introduced in 1930, the result might have been different.

London Passenger Transport Board v Upson [1949] AC 155 is a rare example of a case in which road safety regulations have been held to create a cause of action in tort. The duty in question was the obligation to approach a pedestrian crossing at such a speed as to enable the vehicle to stop. Although the obligation was strict in nature, breach would in the ordinary course of events give rise to a strong inference of negligence on the part of the driver, and it is perhaps this factor which distinguishes the case from *Phillips*; the presence of a latent defect in the vehicle does not give rise to the same inference of negligence. (As the claim in breach of statutory duty succeeded, it was not necessary to determine finally whether—for the purposes of the plaintiff's alternative claim in negligence—the driver had in fact been careless. The fact that he had the lights in his favour and his view obstructed by the presence of a taxicab unlawfully parked on the crossing produced at least some doubt on this issue.)

Another noteworthy decision is *Monk v Warbey* [1935] 1 KB 75. The plaintiff claimed damages for personal injuries sustained as the result of a collision with a car owned by the defendant. The car had been lent by the defendant to a third party without the benefit of a policy of insurance in respect of third party risks. This was an offence under s. 35(1) of the Road Traffic Act 1930 (see now Road Traffic Act 1988, s. 143), but the Court of Appeal held that it was also actionable in tort. The duty of motor vehicle owners not to allow their vehicle to be driven by an uninsured person was introduced for the very purpose of making provision for third parties who suffered injury through negligent driving in such circumstances. Yet, as Greer LJ commented, s. 35 'would indeed be no protection...if no civil remedy were available for a breach of the section' (at 80). The existence of a criminal liability would be 'a poor consolation to the injured person' (at 81). Nevertheless, the imposition of liability upon a party who, not having personally caused any physical damage, would owe no duty of care at common law has been described by Glanville Williams as 'an improper type of judicial invention' ((1960) 23 MLR 233 at 259). Whatever the truth of this claim, the need to protect the victim of negligence on the part of an uninsured driver has led the insurance industry (perhaps acting in order to forestall legislative intervention) to set up in 1946 a fund administered by a Motor Insurers' Bureau designed to provide compensation in such cases. It seems therefore no longer necessary to rely upon the remedy recognised in *Monk v Warbey*, which in any event is of no value when the defendant lacks the means to satisfy the damages award.

The Court of Appeal declined to apply *Monk v Warbey* in the related context of legislation requiring that employers take out insurance against liabilities to their employees. In *Richardson v Pitt-Stanley* [1995] QB 123, the plaintiff had been injured in a work accident for which his employer was liable; the employer went into liquidation and was unable to satisfy the judgment. What was more, the employer had failed to comply with its obligation to insure against liability imposed by the Employers' Liability (Compulsory Insurance) Act 1969. This Act made it a criminal offence to fail to insure; the criminal liability extended to any director of the company who was guilty of culpable neglect. The plaintiff brought an action against the directors for breach of the statutory duty, but the Court of Appeal held that no civil remedy arose. In the view of Stuart-Smith LJ, protection of the plaintiff's economic interests was not the sole purpose of the Act, which might equally be viewed as designed to protect the insured employer against the potentially disastrous consequences to its business of a heavy claim or loss. This reasoning was powerfully criticised in the dissenting judgment of Sir John Megaw (at 135):

> The purpose was to give protection to a particular class of individuals, the employees, to eliminate, or, at least reduce, the risk to an injured employee of finding that he was deprived of his lawful compensation because of the financial position of the employer. I am confident that it was no part of the purpose or intention of Parliament in enacting this legislation to confer a benefit or protection on the employer.

R v Deputy Governor of Parkhurst Prison, ex p. Hague [1992] 1 AC 58

The plaintiff claimed that he was unlawfully segregated from other prisoners without the appropriate authorisations and, in consequence, in breach of rule 43(2) of the Prison Rules 1964, and brought an action for damages relying on, *inter alia*, the tort of breach of statutory duty. For further extracts, see p. 77, above.

Lord Bridge

Mr Sedley [for the plaintiff] has constructed an elaborate argument resting on a premise which he describes as 'the ground rule' for ascertaining whether a plaintiff has a cause of action for breach of statutory duty. It all depends, he submits, on whether he belongs to a class which the statutory provision was intended to protect and has suffered a detriment in consequence of a breach of the duty of a kind from which the provision was intended to protect him. If so, then in the absence of any other specific provision in the statute, such as a criminal penalty, to enforce performance of the statutory duty, it necessarily follows, Mr Sedley submits, that the law affords a remedy in damages for its breach. Hence the question of statutory construction is not the broad question whether an intention to give a cause of action can be inferred from the provision in question read in its context, but the narrower question whether the provision is intended to protect the interests of a class of which the plaintiff is a member. This then leads on to the conclusion that certain provisions of the Prison Rules 1964, which were intended to protect the interests of prisoners, and in particular rule 43(2) which was intended to protect prisoners from unlawful segregation, must give rise to a cause of action in favour of any prisoner who suffers a detriment from a breach of the duty imposed.

I believe the fallacy in this argument is that it relies on authorities relating to statutory duties imposed for no other purpose than to protect various classes of person from the risk of personal injury to which they are exposed and seeks to apply certain dicta in those authorities to a totally different statutory context. Thus *Groves v Lord Wimborne* [1898] 2 QB 402 was concerned with the question whether a breach of the duty to fence dangerous machinery imposed by section 5(4) of the Factory and Workshop Act 1878 gave a cause of action to a workman thereby injured notwithstanding the criminal sanctions also imposed by the statute for breach of the duty...

[L]ike any other question of statutory construction, the question whether an enactment gives rise to a cause of action for breach of statutory duty is a question of ascertaining the intention of the legislature...I can find nothing in rule 43 or in any context that is relevant to the construction of rule 43 which would support the conclusion that it was intended to confer a right of action on an individual prisoner. The purpose of the rule, apart from the case of prisoners who need to be segregated in their own interests, is to give an obviously necessary power to segregate prisoners who are liable for any reason to disturb the orderly conduct of the prison generally. The rule is a purely preventive measure. The power is to be exercised only in accordance with the procedure prescribed by sub-rule (2). But where the power has been exercised in good faith, albeit that the procedure followed in authorising its exercise was not in conformity with rule 43(2), it is inconceivable that the legislature intended to confer a cause of action on the segregated prisoner.

Lord Jauncey

[I]t must always be a matter for consideration whether the legislature intended that private law rights of action should be conferred upon individuals in respect of breaches of the relevant statutory provision. The fact that a particular provision was intended to protect certain individuals is not of itself sufficient to confer private law rights of action upon them, something more is required to show that the legislature intended such conferment...

The [Prison] rules are wide-ranging in their scope covering a mass of matters relevant to the administration and good government of a prison. Many of these do not directly relate to prisoners and I do not consider that those which do were ever intended to confer private law rights in the event of a breach. The rules are regulatory in character, they provide a framework within which the prison regime operates but they are not intended to protect prisoners against loss, injury and damage nor to give them a right of action in respect thereof. I would only add that if a prisoner suffered in health as a result of segregation contrary to the rules he would in all probability have a right of action in negligence against the prison authorities. If, as in the case of Hague, he suffered no damage to health then a breach of the rules would not result in loss or injury of the kind which normally flows from a breach of statutory duty and which the statute is designed to prevent...

Finally, I should emphasise that the conclusion which I have reached on this part of the appeal does not leave a prisoner without a remedy if the rules are broken to his detriment. He may complain to the governor or board of visitors under rule 8(1) and in the event of a complaint to the latter a report may be made to the Secretary of State under section 6(3) of the Act. He may also challenge any administrative decision of the Secretary of State or the governor which he considers to contravene the provisions of the Act or the rules by judicial review proceedings. In the case of a continuing wrong done to him a prisoner could expect that a hearing in judicial review proceedings could be obtained with little delay. These public law remedies are additional to any private law remedies which would be available to him such as damages for misfeasance in public office, assault or negligence.

COMMENTARY

In this case and that following immediately below, the House of Lords was faced with statutory duties that were not reinforced by any penal sanction. Yet they declined to treat that fact as giving rise to a presumption of civil liability. These decisions mark a decisive move away from the classic approach of Lord Tenterden in *Doe d. Murray, Bishop of Rochester v Bridges* (1831) B & Ad 847. In its place, a much more varied set of considerations (e.g. the regulatory character of the statute and the availability of alternative remedies) are found to be relevant in determining Parliament's intent. The existence of alternative public law remedies was also a decisive indicator against recognition of a private right of action in another case of custodial detainment, *Cullen v Chief Constable of the Royal Ulster Constabulary* [2003] 1 WLR 1763.

O'Rourke v Camden London Borough Council [1998] AC 188

The plaintiff alleged in his statement of claim that, having just been released from prison, he had nowhere to live and he applied to the council for accommodation. Under Housing Act 1985, s. 62, local authorities were obliged, where they had reason to believe that an applicant for housing may be homeless, to 'make such inquiries as are necessary to satisfy themselves as to whether he is homeless . . .'. Pending a decision under s. 62, local authorities were further obliged under s. 63(1) to provide temporary accommodation if they had 'reason to believe that an applicant may be homeless and have a priority need . . .'. The plaintiff alleged that although the defendant council in the present case had agreed to make inquiries under s. 62 and had placed him in temporary hotel accommodation pending the outcome of these inquiries, it had wrongfully evicted him from the hotel after less than two weeks without offering him any other accommodation. He claimed damages for breach of statutory duty. At the start of proceedings in the county court before Judge Tibber, the council made a successful application to strike out the particulars of the claim as disclosing no reasonable cause of action. On the plaintiff's appeal, the Court of Appeal held that s. 63(1) created a private law duty sounding in damages and reinstated the claim for breach of statutory duty. The council appealed to the House of Lords.

Lord Hoffmann

The question is whether section 63(1) creates a duty to Mr O'Rourke which is actionable in tort. There is no doubt that, like several other provisions in Part III [sc. of the Act], it creates a duty which is enforceable by proceedings for judicial review. But whether it gives rise to a cause of action sounding in damages depends upon whether the Act shows a legislative intention to create such a remedy. In *X (Minors) v Bedfordshire County Council* [1995] 2 AC 633, 731, the principles were analysed by Lord Browne-Wilkinson in a speech with which the other members of the House agreed. He said that although there was no general rule by reference to which it could be decided that a statute created a private right of action, there were a number of 'indicators.' The indicator upon which Mr Drabble, who appeared for Mr O'Rourke, placed most reliance was the common sense proposition that a statute which appears intended for the protection of a limited class of people but provides no other remedy for breach should ordinarily be construed as intended to create a private right of action. Otherwise, as Lord Simonds said in *Cutler v Wandsworth Stadium Ltd* [1949] AC 398 at 407, 'the statute would be but a pious aspiration.'

Camden, on the other hand, says that although Part III does not expressly enact any remedy for breach, that does not mean that it would be toothless without an action for damages or an injunction in private law. It is enforceable in public law by individual homeless persons who have locus standi to bring proceedings for judicial review. Furthermore, there are certain contraindications which make it unlikely that Parliament intended to create private law rights of action.

The first is that the Act is a scheme of social welfare, intended to confer benefits at the public expense on grounds of public policy. Public money is spent on housing the homeless not merely for the private benefit of people who find themselves homeless but on grounds of general public interest: because, for example, proper housing means that people will be less likely to suffer illness, turn to crime or require the attention of other social services. The expenditure interacts with expenditure on other public services such as education, the National Health Service and even the police. It is not simply a private matter between the claimant and the housing authority. Accordingly, the fact that Parliament has provided for the expenditure of public money on benefits in kind such as housing the homeless does not necessarily mean that it intended cash payments to be made by way of damages to persons who, in breach of the housing authority's statutory duty, have unfortunately not received the benefits which they should have done...

A second contra-indication is that Part III of the Act of 1985 makes the existence of the duty to provide accommodation dependent upon a good deal of judgment on the part of the housing authority. The duty to inquire under section 62(1) arises if the housing authority 'have reason to believe' that the applicant may be homeless and the inquiries must be such as are 'necessary to satisfy themselves' as to whether he is homeless, whether he has a priority need and whether he became homeless intentionally. When the investigations are complete, the various duties under section 65 of the Act arise only if the authority are 'satisfied' that the applicant is homeless and the extent of those duties depends upon whether or not they are 'satisfied' as to two other matters, namely that he has a priority need and that he became homeless intentionally. If a duty does arise, the authority has a wide discretion in deciding how to provide accommodation and what kind of accommodation it will provide. The existence of all these discretions makes it unlikely that Parliament intended errors of judgment to give rise to an obligation to make financial reparation. Control by public law remedies would appear much more appropriate...

[While reserving his position on whether subsequent developments in judicial review procedure could be taken into account in this regard, his Lordship proceeded to consider the adequacy of public law remedies available for breach of the Housing Act 1977 at the time it was enacted:] [T]he existing procedure was in most cases adequate to provide a swift remedy for a homeless person complaining of breach of duty. Lord Diplock said in *O'Reilly v Mackman* [1983] 2 AC 237 at 281 that:

> as [the old] Order 53 was applied in practice, as soon as the application for leave had been made it provided a very speedy means, available in urgent cases within a matter of days rather than months, for determining whether a disputed decision was valid in law or not.

Accordingly there is in my view no reason to construe the Act of 1977 on the assumption that in the absence of a remedy in damages, it would at the time it was enacted have been no more than 'a pious aspiration.' The machinery for enforcing it was in place...

I would therefore hold that the breach of statutory duty of which the plaintiff complains gives rise to no cause of action in private law and I would allow the appeal and restore the order of Judge Tibber striking out the action.

Lord Goff, **Lord Mustill**, **Lord Nicholls** and **Lord Steyn** concurred.

Appeal allowed.

COMMENTARY

In this decision, the House of Lords overruled the decision of the Court of Appeal in *Thornton v Kirklees Metropolitan Borough Council* [1979] QB 626, which held that the forerunners of the provisions considered in the present case, contained in the Housing (Homeless Persons) Act 1977, *did* give rise to a private law remedy. The House of Lords had previously accepted the correctness of *Thornton* in *Cocks v Thanet District Council* [1983] 2 AC 286, but in *O'Rourke* their Lordships held that this had been obiter and incorrect. Nevertheless, the House of Lords in *O'Rourke* claimed to follow the authority of *Cocks*, which held that a council's failure to move the plaintiff and his family from temporary to permanent accommodation under the terms of the Housing Act was not actionable in damages. The decision in *Cocks* seems in fact to have been based on the narrower grounds that, as the most the court could do was to order the council to reconsider the plaintiff's case, the obligation to move him to permanent accommodation—which was conditional on a positive finding in his favour—had not yet come into being. (The current legislative provisions on housing for the homeless are to be found in Housing Act 1996, Part VII.)

In the course of his speech, Lord Hoffmann cited with approval the following dictum of Lord Browne-Wilkinson in *X (Minors) v Bedfordshire County Council* [1995] 2 AC 633 at 731–2:

Although regulatory or welfare legislation affecting a particular area of activity does in fact provide protection to those individuals particularly affected by that activity, the legislation is not to be treated as being passed for the benefit of those individuals but for the benefit of society in general.

In both *X v Bedfordshire CC* and *O'Rourke*, the question of whether the statute in question was passed for the benefit of a section of the public was apparently posed as a preliminary to *any* successful action for breach of statutory duty, rather than being used to warrant an exception to the general non-actionability of penal legislation (as was assumed to be its role in, e.g., *Groves v Lord Wimborne* and *Phillips v Britannia Laundry*, above). Whether this approach will be adopted outside the context of welfare legislation remains to be seen, but it is already evident that, combined with the obvious judicial readiness to characterise welfare legislation as designed to benefit the public at large rather than any section of it, it has greatly curtailed the scope for claims of breach of statutory duty in this area.

If the approach is applied generally to questions of policy or discretion, it may serve to protect public bodies from undue judicial interference with their activities in much the same way as does the requirement of 'justiciability' in the tort of negligence (see further Ch. 10). Commenting on the 'very antipathetic' attitude of the courts to the tort's application in this context, K. Stanton et al., *Statutory Torts* (London: Sweet & Maxwell, 2003), para. 14.004 states:

[T]he use of the construction approach in this way…, although it operates on a different set of criteria, is closely related to the controls which limit the use of negligence as a damages remedy against bodies which exercise statutory functions. The effective result in relation to both torts is that decisions as to the appropriate allocation of resources made in the exercise of a discretion conferred by statute rarely, if ever, give rise to claims for damages in private law proceedings. A public authority's responsibility for decisions made within discretion is essentially a political one and the primary method of challenging such decisions in the courts is to make an application for judicial review.

3. The Scope of Protection

Even if the statute in question does support a private law remedy, the claimant must in order to bring a claim fall within the scope of its protection, that is, must suffer an injury of the type that the statute was intended to guard against and be a member of the class that the statute was intended to benefit.

Gorris v Scott (1874) LR 9 Exch 125

The facts are stated in the judgment of Kelly CB.

Kelly CB

This is an action to recover damages for the loss of a number of sheep which the defendant, a shipowner, had contracted to carry, and which were washed overboard and lost by reason (as we must take it to be truly alleged) of the neglect to comply with a certain order made by the Privy Council, in pursuance of the Contagious Diseases (Animals) Act 1869. The Act was passed merely for sanitary purposes, in order to prevent animals in a state of infectious disease from communicating it to other animals with which they might come in contact. Under the authority of that Act, certain orders were made; amongst others, an order by which any ship bringing sheep or cattle from any foreign port to ports in Great Britain is to have the place occupied by such animals divided into pens of certain dimensions, and the floor of such pens furnished with battens or foot holds. The object of this order is to prevent animals from being overcrowded, and so brought into a condition in which the disease guarded against would be likely to be developed. This regulation has been neglected, and the question is, whether the loss, which we must assume to have been caused by that neglect, entitles the plaintiffs to maintain an action.

The argument of the defendant is, that the Act has imposed penalties to secure the observance of its provisions, and that, according to the general rule, the remedy prescribed by the statute must be pursued; that although, when penalties are imposed for the violation of a statutory duty, a person aggrieved by its violation may sometimes maintain an action for the damage so caused, that must be in cases where the object of the statute is to confer a benefit on individuals, and to protect them against the evil consequences which the statute was designed to prevent, and which have in fact ensued; but that if the object is not to protect individuals against the consequences which have in fact ensued, it is otherwise; that if, therefore, by reason of the precautions in question not having been taken, the plaintiffs had sustained that damage against which it was intended to secure them, an action would lie, but that when the damage is of such a nature as was not contemplated at all by the statute, and as to which it was not intended to confer any benefit on the plaintiffs, they cannot maintain an action founded on the neglect....

[I]f we could see that it was the object, or among the objects of this Act, that the owners of sheep and cattle coming from a foreign port should be protected by the means described against the danger of their property being washed overboard, or lost by the perils of the sea, the present action would be within the principle. But, looking at the Act, it is perfectly clear that its provisions were all enacted with a totally different view; there was no purpose, direct or indirect, to protect against such damage; but, as is recited in the preamble, the Act is directed against the possibility of sheep or cattle being exposed to disease on their way to this country. The preamble recites that 'it is expedient to confer on Her Majesty's most honourable Privy Council power to take such measures as may appear from time to time necessary to prevent the introduction into Great Britain of contagious or infectious diseases among cattle, sheep, or other animals, by prohibiting or regulating the importation of foreign animals,' and also to provide against the 'spreading' of such diseases in Great Britain. Then follow numerous sections directed entirely to this object. Then comes s. 75, which enacts that 'the Privy Council may from time to time make such orders as they think expedient for all or any of the following purposes.' What, then, are these purposes? They are 'for securing for animals brought by sea to ports in Great Britain a proper supply of food and water during the passage and on landing,' 'for protecting such animals from unnecessary suffering during the passage and on landing,' and so forth; all the purposes enumerated being calculated and directed to the prevention of disease, and none of them having any relation whatever to the danger of loss by the perils of the sea. That being so, if by reason of the default in question the plaintiffs' sheep had been overcrowded, or had been caused unnecessary suffering, and so had arrived in this country in a state of disease, I do not say that they might not have maintained this action. But the damage complained of here is something totally apart from the object of the Act of Parliament, and it is in accordance with all the authorities to say that the action is not maintainable.

Pigott, **Pollock** and **Amphlett BB** concurred.

COMMENTARY

Gorris was distinguished in *Donaghey v Boulton & Paul Ltd* [1968] AC 1. In that case, the House of Lords held that breach of regulations requiring the use of crawling boards on 'roofs…covered with fragile materials through which a person is liable to fall a distance of more than 10 feet' was actionable in damages even by a worker who fell, not through the fragile material, but through a hole in the roof. The House of Lords distinguished *Gorris* on the basis that the plaintiff had been injured in the kind of accident, namely a fall from the roof, at which the regulation in question was directed. Lord Reid explained (at 26):

It is one thing to say that if the damage suffered is of a kind totally different from that which it is the object of the regulation to prevent, there is no civil liability. But it is quite a different thing to say that civil liability is excluded because the damage, though precisely of the kind which the regulation was designed to prevent, happened in a way not contemplated by the maker of the regulation.

His Lordship thought that the principles were analogous to those of remoteness of damage in the tort of negligence where it is accepted that, provided that harm of the type that occurred was foreseeable, it is immaterial that the precise way in which the harm came about was not (see esp. *Hughes v Lord Advocate* [1963] AC 837).

A more restrictive approach is however evident in the so-called 'flying part' cases. In *Close v Steel Co of Wales Ltd* [1962] AC 367, for example, the House of Lords held that the duty to fence machinery under the Factories Acts was designed to prevent employees being caught up in moving parts, not to protect them from injury suffered when a part comes loose and flies off the machinery. Note however that the employer will still be liable if it was foreseeable that part of the machinery might fly off: *see Hindle v Birtwistle* [1897] 1 QB 192.

A more recent case where the scope of the intended protection was crucial is *Fytche v Wincanton Logistics plc* [2004] UKHL 31, [2004] 4 All ER 221. The House of Lords had there to determine whether the claimant milk-tanker driver's steel-toe-capped boots, supplied to him as personal protective equipment, were meant to protect not just from the risk that heavy milk churns might fall on his foot, but also against the risk of frostbite. During a spell of exceptionally wintry weather, his tanker had got stuck on an icy country road and he worked for three hours in sub-zero temperatures to dig it out. A tiny hole in one of the boots let in water and he suffered frostbite in his little toe. The House of Lords, by a majority of three to two, rejected his claim for damages for his employer's breach of the obligation to keep the boots in good repair under the Personal Protective Equipment at Work Regulations. The relevant provision had to be construed by reference to the risk or risks in respect of which the employer was required to supply personal protective equipment, and did not impose an absolute obligation on the employer to effect repairs which had nothing to do with the equipment's protective function. As the toecaps were to protect against the risk of impact injuries, and the claimant was not expected to do work which required him to have waterproof boots, the existence of a hole did not constitute a breach of the obligation to keep the boots in good repair.

Cf. the similar results that can be achieved in the tort of negligence by application of principles of remoteness of damage (see, e.g., *Bradford v Robinson Rentals Ltd* [1967] 1 WLR 337).

Hartley v Mayoh & Co [1954] 1 QB 383

Fire brigade officers summoned to a fire in factory premises asked the factory manager to direct them to the main electric switch in order to cut off all current to the premises. This, unknown to the manager, consisted of two small tumbler switches, which both he and the firemen ignored; but he directed them to other master switches which were switched off, and which would have effectively cut off all current to that part of the premises where the fire was, had not two wires been transposed at a point in the wiring system, that transposition being the responsibility of the area electricity authority. Accordingly the current remained in the wires throughout the circuit so long as the main switch was on. A fire officer was fatally electrocuted in the fire. In an action by his widow, Barry J held the electricity authority liable as to 90 per cent of the damages, and the occupiers of the factory liable for the remaining 10 per cent, both under the common law governing occupiers' liability and for breach of regulations issued under the Factories Act. The Court of Appeal dismissed the occupiers' appeal in relation to the liability at common law. The following extracts relate to the alternative liability for breach of statutory duty.

Singleton LJ

The Regulations for the Generation, Transformation, Distribution and Use of Electrical Energy in Premises under the Factory and Workshop Acts, 1901 and 1907, are preserved for present purposes by section 159 of the Factories Act, 1937. The power to make regulations now is given by section 60 of the Act of 1937: '(1) Where the Minister [of Labour, etc.,] is satisfied that any manufacture, machinery, plant, process, or description of manual labour, used in factories is of such a nature as to cause risk of bodily injury to persons employed, or any class of those persons, he may, subject to the provisions of this Act, make such special regulations as appear to him to be reasonably practicable and to meet the necessity of the case.'

It is to be observed that the power to make the regulations is given when the Minister is satisfied that the work is of such a nature as to cause risk of bodily injury to 'persons employed'. Those words embrace the amendment made by section 12 of the Factories Act, 1948, prior to which time the power to make the regulations was given if the Minister was satisfied that the manufacture, etc, was of such a nature as to cause risk of bodily injury to persons employed 'in connexion therewith' . . .

In my view Hartley was not one of the class of persons for whose benefit the regulations were made in that he was not a person employed. For that reason I do not think that an action for breach of statutory duty lies against the occupiers.

Jenkins and **Hodson LJJ** delivered separate concurring judgments.

Appeal dismissed on other grounds.

COMMENTARY

The meaning of the words 'person employed', which is a commonly used description of the class intended to benefit from industrial safety legislation, has been considered in a number of other cases. It has been held to include an employee of an independent contractor doing work in the factory in question (*Stanton Iron Works v Skipper* [1956] 1 QB 255, as explained by Lord Kilmuir LC in *Canadian Pacific v Bryers* [1958] AC 485) and indeed any person working in a factory, no matter who the employer (*Massey-Harris-Ferguson v Piper* [1956] 2 QB 396). It does not cover, however, an employee doing private work in a factory out of working hours (*Napieralski v Curtis (Contractors)* [1959] 1 WLR 835, or even an independent contractor doing work in the factory in person (*Herber v Harold Shaw* [1959] 2 QB 138).

Hartley may be compared with *Knapp v Railway Executive* [1949] 2 All ER 508 where it was held that the duty to keep the gates of a level-crossing in the proper position was passed in order to protect members of the public using the road, not the train driver.

4. Evaluation and Reform

The current approach to liability for breach of statutory duty is open to a number of criticisms. The judicial method of looking for indicators of Parliament's presumed intent has produced results that are arbitrary and inconsistent, and it is premised upon the fiction that Parliament has really turned its mind to the civil actionability of all the statutes it passes. If Parliament had actually done so, would it not have been easy for it also to have stated clearly what its intention was? More fundamentally, it may be questioned whether, given that there is already a generalised liability for negligence under *Donoghue v Stevenson*, it is really necessary to have a separate liability for breach of statutory duty. An alternative favoured by some commentators is to treat a breach of a statutory duty merely as 'statutory negligence', giving rise to liability only where there is a common law duty of care but providing in such cases prima facie evidence of a breach of that duty, or even amounting to 'negligence *per se*'.

E. Thayer, 'Public Wrong and Private Action' (1917) 24 Harv L Rev 317

It is common, at least in the case of statutes, to treat the question of construction as if it should ... include an inquiry into the probable purpose of the statute with reference to private individuals—whether it was enacted for their benefit and was intended to give them a right of action. But this sort of speculation as to unexpressed legislative intent is a dangerous business, permissible only within narrow limits; and the tendency to over-indulge it is responsible for much of the confusion in the law. Proper regard for the legislature includes the duty both to give full effect to its expressed purpose, and also to go no further. The legislature could, if it chose, have provided in terms that any one injured by a breach of the statute should have a remedy by civil action. Such a provision is familiar in criminal statutes. Its omission in this instance must therefore be treated as the deliberate choice of the legislature, and the court has no right to disregard it. On the other hand, the argument that the failure to give a private action bespeaks an intent that the statute shall have no effect on private rights has little weight. The legislature must be presumed to know the law, and if upon common law principles such a statute would affect private rights, it must have been passed in anticipation of that result. The legislature is to be credited with meaning just what it said—that the conduct forbidden is an offense against the public, and that the offender shall suffer certain specified penalties for his offense. Whether his offense shall have any other legal consequence has not been passed on one way or the other as a question of legislative intent, but is to be left to be determined by the rules of law. The true attitude of the courts, therefore, is to ascertain the legislature's expressed intent, to refrain from conjecture as to its unexpressed intent (except in so far as that inquiry is necessary in order to give effect to what is expressed), and then to consider the resulting situation in the light of the common law. If his crime does not increase the wrongdoer's civil responsibilities on common-law principles, without calling in aid supposed legislative intent, then it should not affect them at all...

The doctrine that a breach of the law is 'evidence of negligence' is in truth perplexing and difficult of comprehension...[T]o invite the jury [in modern English law, the judge] to consider when and to what extent it is reasonable to break the law is a strange thing. The prudent man, it seems, is a law-abiding person within limits, but he does not carry his respect for law to extremes. What tests or considerations are to guide the jury in determining when he may reasonably become lawless? The proposition that his breach of law is 'prima facie evidence' of negligence helps but little, for the very statement implies that the prima facie impropriety may be rebutted. If so, what will rebut it? The doctrine in any form puts the court in an unsuitable attitude toward the legislature...

[Thayer proceeds to argue in favour of the negligence *per se* approach, illustrating his argument by reference to a hypothetical ordinance making it a criminal offence to leave a horse unhitched on the highway:] The ordinance has foreclosed the question whether an unhitched horse is a dangerous thing, not because it was passed with any specific reference to civil suits, but because the state, through its legislative organs, has condemned the act of leaving him unhitched by reason of its tendency to bring about just such harm as this. This can only mean that the act is labelled 'dangerous'. It is an unjust reproach to our old friend the ordinary prudent man to suppose that he would do such a thing in the teeth of the ordinance. It would mean changing his nature, and giving over the very traits which brought him into existence. And when by so doing he caused the very harm which the ordinance aimed to prevent, he would be the first to admit that he should break the ordinance at his peril.

COMMENTARY

The statutory negligence approach can result in the imposition of liability only where the common law recognises a duty of care. Familiar limitations on the scope of the duty of care, for example, in respect of omissions or pure economic loss, may therefore preclude the imposition of liability for statutory negligence in appropriate cases. An example given by Thayer himself was of a statute requiring occupiers to remove snow and ice from the pavement outside their premises: if a pedestrian injured as a result of the occupier's failure to perform his duty should sue, 'he will make no headway by the aid of common-law principles' (p. 329).

One perceived advantage of the statutory negligence approach is that it reduces complexity by relying upon a single principle of liability, namely, negligence. Treating breach of statutory duty as a separate tort superimposes a second principle of liability for which there is no demonstrated need. Worse, it invites claimants to seek to side-step limitations on liability in negligence on the basis not of properly weighed policy arguments but of an entirely fictitious Parliamentary intent. Recent experience suggests that such claims are likely to meet with little success (see especially *X v Bedfordshire CC*, above) but the law should not even hold out the possibility of success and thereby encourage claimants to waste their time, money and effort. Of course, this is not to say that the boundaries of liability in negligence ought not themselves to be extended; only that they should not be circumvented by a spurious appeal to the legislative will.

Criticisms of the Negligence *per se* Approach

The negligence *per se* doctrine has been adopted in a number of US jurisdictions, but rejected in others (and also in Canada: see *The Queen in the Right of Canada v Saskatchewan Wheat Pool* [1983] 1 SCR 205). A number of criticisms of the doctrine can be made (see generally Morris, 'The Role of Criminal Statutes in Negligence Actions' (1949) 49 Col L Rev 21). First, it may result in the imposition of a very large liability in damages in respect of a very minor infringement of a statute, for which the penalty might only be a small fine. Secondly, it makes no distinction between criminal prohibitions aimed at dangerous conduct and those which deal not with health and safety but, for example, with questions of public order or good government. For this reason (amongst others) it may be necessary to fall back upon an investigation of Parliament's intent, with all the problems that entails, in order to determine the mischief at which the statute was aimed. Lastly, the doctrine may result in strict liability even in cases of unavoidable accident, depending upon the construction of the statute in question, yet it provides no principled justification for the imposition of liability without proof of fault; in any case, it seems likely that the specification of statutory duties in strict or absolute terms owes less to a general theory of strict liability than to legislative happenstance.

The perceived defects in the negligence *per se* approach have led a number of jurisdictions to treat breach of statutory duty only as evidence of negligence. This approach has the benefit of greater flexibility, and does not entail the imposition of liability in the absence of fault (as in the unavoidable accident cases considered above). Amongst its supporters on this side of the Atlantic stands the notable figure of Glanville Williams, 'The Effect of Penal Legislation in the Law of Tort' (1960) 23 MLR 233.

Can supporters of the 'evidence of negligence' approach meet Thayer's objection that the doctrine requires the court to treat a breach of the law as (at least, potentially) reasonable conduct?

An Alternative Approach: A New Rule of Statutory Interpretation

Responding to criticisms of the unsatisfactory nature of English law in this area, the Law Commission has suggested an alternative approach (*The Interpretation of Statutes*, Report No. 21, 1969, para. 38). To dispense with the need for the largely fictitious inquiry into Parliament's intent, a new rule of statutory interpretion should be adopted by legislation in the following terms:

Where any Act passed after this Act imposes or authorises the imposition of a duty, whether positive or negative and whether with or without a special remedy for its enforcement, it shall be presumed, unless express provision to the contrary is made, that a breach of the duty is intended to be actionable (subject to the defences and other incidents applying to actions for breach of statutory duty) at the suit of any person who sustains damage in consequence of the breach.

This clause was subsequently inserted in an Interpretation of Legislation Bill put before Parliament in 1980, but the bill was never enacted and it seems unlikely at present that the

Law Commission's proposal will ever be adopted. Among the objections that can be put to it are that the presumption envisaged might lead to the imposition of liability in circumstances that were simply unforeseen by Parliament, that it would do nothing to relieve the courts of the task of inquiring into Parliament's intent in order to determine under the rule in *Gorris v Scott* whether the claimant's case falls within the mischief at which the statute was aimed, and that it would in any case have no relevance to legislation already on the statute books, which would still have to be addressed by the application of common law principles (see further Buckley, 'Liability in Tort for Breach of Statutory Duty' (1984) 100 LQR 204 at 231–2).

v. Euro-Torts

The UK's membership of the European Union (previously Community) raises the question whether breaches of the EU Treaties or other EU laws are actionable in damages in the same way as claims in respect of breaches of domestic legislation. In *Garden Cottage Foods v Milk Marketing Board* [1984] AC 130 (an application for interlocutory relief), the House of Lords did indeed treat breach of a Treaty provision as at least arguably actionable in damages and rationalised the claim as one for breach of statutory duty. Considering allegedly unfair competitive practices by the defendant, contrary to Article 86 of the Treaty of Rome (now Article 102 of the Treaty on the Functioning of the EU), Lord Diplock stated (at 141):

> A breach of the duty imposed by article 86 not to abuse a dominant position in the common market or in a substantial part of it, can . . . be categorised in English law as a breach of statutory duty that is imposed not only for the purpose of promoting the general economic prosperity of the common market but also for the benefit of private individuals to whom loss or damage is caused by a breach of that duty.

See also *Sempra Metals Ltd v Inland Revenue Comrs* [2007] UKHL 34, [2008] 1 AC 561 at [69] per Lord Nicholls, at [162] per Lord Walker and at [225] per Lord Mance, dealing with freedom of establishment under Article 43 TEC (now Article 49 TFEU).

Such a cause of action may well be regarded as arising out of a breach of domestic legislation, as the European Communities Act 1972, s. 2 incorporates EU law into the UK's legal systems, but it is probably better regarded as a separate European tort with its own distinctive elements, as the question whether a particular EU law gives rise to private rights, and the grounds of liability, are ultimately for the European Court of Justice to decide (though it is to be treated as a claim for breach of statutory duty for the purposes of the domestic law of limitation: *R v Secretary of State for Transport, ex p. Factortame Ltd (No. 6)* [2001] 1 WLR 942). See further Stanton, 'New Forms of the Tort of Breach of Statutory Duty' (2004) 120 LQR 324 at 328–30.

The tort is premised upon a developing principle of liability in damages for the violation of EU rights. The basic (but not exclusive) source of EU rights is the doctrine of direct effect. An EU law has direct effect, that is, it creates rights which can be exercised by persons in their national courts, if it is precise, clear and unconditional (Case 8/81, *Becker v Finanzamt Münster-Innenstadt* [1982] ECR 53). Subject to this requirement, provisions of the Treaty of Rome have 'horizontal' direct effect (i.e. they can be relied upon by one private individual against another) but EU Directives take effect only 'vertically' (i.e. they can only be relied upon by an individual against the state: see *Duke v GEC Reliance* [1988] AC 618). Although the doctrine of vertical direct effect allows individuals to vindicate their rights only against infringement by the state, it should be noted that the concept of 'the state' is given a wide definition in EU law and extends to all organisations or bodies which are subject to the authority and control of the state or have special powers beyond those which result from the normal rules applicable to relations between individuals (see Case 188/90, *Foster v British Gas plc* [1990] ECR I–3133, para. 18).

It is a fundamental doctrine of EU law that there should be adequate and effective judicial protection for EU rights, that is, that individuals in the EU should be able to enforce such rights before their national courts, under the provisions of their national laws, and that where compensation is awarded it should be adequate in relation to the damage sustained (see Case 14/83, *Von Colson v Land Nordrhein-Westfalen* [1984] ECR 1891). The procedure by which EU rights are protected is ostensibly a matter within the autonomy of each member state (see Case 33/76, *Rewe-Zentral Finanz eG v Landwirtschaftskammer für das Saarland* [1976] ECR 1989). But this has not prevented the Court of Justice from ruling that the principle of adequate and effective protection may, at least on occasion, require national courts to impose a remedy of a particular sort, even where domestic law would not so permit (see Case C–213/89, *R v Secretary of State for Transport, ex p. Factortame Ltd* [1990] ECR I–2433).

It is against this background that the European Court of Justice's recognition of a principle of state liability, in Case 6/90, *Francovich v Italy* [1991] ECR I–5357, should be considered. The Court ruled that a member state could be held liable in damages for the non-implementation of a Directive to individuals who, as a result, were unable to exercise rights which the Directive was intended to secure. This ruling was crucial on the facts of the case, because the Directive in question was not directly effective and, in the absence of a claim directly against the state, the aggrieved applicants would have had no way of obtaining redress. (The Directive, which required member states to ensure payment of outstanding wages in the event of an employer's insolvency, clearly created rights in favour of employees, but it did not make clear who was to pay the claims, that is, against whom the right could be exercised.) The Court of Justice has subsequently confirmed the general scope of the *Francovich* principle by recognising state liability even where the relevant EU law does have direct effect (see Case C–46/93, *Brasserie du Pêcheur SA v Federal Republic of Germany* [1996] ECR I–1029), and by applying it not only to the non-implementation of a Directive but also to contraventions of EU law by legislative act and omission (see, respectively, Case C–48/93, *R v Secretary of State for Transport, ex p. Factortame Ltd* and Case C–46/93, *Brasserie du Pêcheur SA v Federal Republic of Germany* [1996] ECR I–1029), administrative action (Case C–5/94, *R v Ministry of Agriculture, Fisheries and Food, ex p. Hedley Lomas (Ireland)* [1996] ECR I–2553), and judicial decision by a national court of final appeal (Case C–224/01, *Köbler v Austria* [2003] ECR I–10239). The requirements of a successful claim were set out most clearly in *Brasserie du Pêcheur* (para. 74):

> [I]ndividuals suffering loss or injury ... are entitled to reparation where the rule of Community law breached is intended to confer rights on them, the breach is sufficiently serious and there is a direct causal link between the breach and the damage sustained by the individuals ...

The key requirement of a 'sufficiently serious' breach of the EU law obligation does not necessarily entail fault as it is conceived in English law, though the degree of fault exhibited may be a relevant consideration (see *R v Secretary of State for Transport, ex p. Factortame Ltd (No. 5)* [2000] 1 AC 524). This limitation, precluding compensation claims where the breach is insufficiently serious, is a key distinction between the Euro-tort and the English tort of breach of statutory duty, which has no equivalent restriction.

It has been argued that the Court of Justice's jurisprudence on state liability demonstrates the existence of a general principle of liability in damages for the violation of EU law rights, whether these arise by virtue of direct effect or otherwise. According to van Gerven, it represents 'the last step (as yet?)' in a long series of rulings aimed at giving full effect to Community law' ('Bridging the Unbridgeable: Community and National Tort Laws after *Francovich* and *Brasserie*' (1996) 45 ICLQ 507 at 516). Where it was originally left to domestic law to select the remedy appropriate for the vindication of EU rights, *Francovich* recognises that EU law may require an award of compensation where such rights are infringed. In other words, van Gerven submits, '[t]he remedy of compensation...should be seen as an essential element of the legal protection of the individual's Community rights' *(ibid.)*. See also *Courage v Crehan* [2001] ECR I–6297, discussed below.

Notwithstanding these developments, the English courts were slow to allow damages claims for breaches of EU law for fear that claimants might thereby side-step limitations on liability in domestic tort law. In *Bourgoin SA v Ministry of Agriculture* [1986] QB 716, the Court of Appeal rejected a claim for damages in respect of the UK's unlawful ban (subsequently rescinded) on the import of turkeys from France into the UK. The court accepted that the prohibition against quantitative restrictions on imports in Article 30 of the EC Treaty (now Article 34 TFEU) did give rise to rights in private individuals, but held that these were adequately protected by the remedy of judicial review, and did not require a right to damages for their effective protection. This reasoning no longer seems sustainable in view of the introduction of the *Francovich* principle of state liability, and it has been doubted in the House of Lords (*Kirklees Metropolitan Borough Council v Wickes Building Supplies Ltd* [1993] AC 227 at 281, per Lord Goff). But, as the next extract shows, the scope of Euro-tort liability may be limited in other ways.

Three Rivers District Council v Governor and Company of the Bank of England [2003] 2 AC 1

The plaintiffs included over 6,000 investors from all over the world who were depositors with United Kingdom branches of the Bank of Credit and Commerce International SA (BCCI). In July 1991, BCCI and its associated companies collapsed with a huge deficit, much of which resulted from fraud on a very large scale. The bank's principal place of business had been in London and responsibility for supervision of its activities in this country was borne by the Bank of England under the Banking Acts of 1979 and 1987. The plaintiffs, who alleged they had suffered losses as a result of the collapse, sued the Governor and Company of the Bank of England for damages for misfeasance in public office and breaches of the Community Banking Co-ordination Directive (77/780). The Directive required Member States to require certain credit institutions to obtain authorisation before commencing their activities and stated that the regulatory authority should grant such authorisation only if satisfied as to the institution's financial soundness, its repute and its experience. The UK subsequently implemented the Directive in the Banking Act 1979, which was later replaced and replaced by the Banking Act 1987. Section 1(4) of the new statute gave the Bank an immunity from liability in the discharge of its functions except in cases in which bad faith was shown. The plaintiffs argued that the immunity was an impermissible restriction of their rights under Community law. At first instance, Clarke J struck out the plaintiffs' claims as revealing no arguable cause of action. A majority of the Court of

Appeal rejected the plaintiffs' appeal (Auld LJ dissenting). The plaintiffs then made a further appeal to the House of Lords. The extract below deals only with the claim for infringement of the Directive under Community law.

Lord Hope

The appellants maintain that the Directive of 1977 was intended and designed to protect the savings of depositors. They say that, in order to achieve this purpose, it imposed certain well-defined Community law obligations on the competent authorities of Member States in relation to the authorisation and supervision of banks, and that it conferred on depositors and potential depositors corresponding Community law rights against the competent authorities to have these obligations fulfilled. That being so, their Community law rights under the Directive of 1977 must prevail over the requirement in national law to prove bad faith or dishonesty as a prerequisite of the tort of misfeasance in public office under the common law. And they must prevail over the Bank's right to seek exemption from liability under section 1(4) of the Banking Act 1987...[T]he appellants do not need to show that depositors were the only persons in whose favour obligations were imposed or on whom rights were conferred by the Directive. But...they must be able to demonstrate that the result to be achieved by the Directive entailed the grant of rights to depositors and potential depositors as well as to the credit institutions operating in several Member States whose activities were to be authorised and supervised by the competent authorities. A triangular or tripartite relationship is implied by this argument, between the competent authorities and the credit institutions on the one hand and the competent authorities and the depositors on the other. It is not too difficult to see, as the majority in the Court of Appeal observed, that the Directive conferred rights on the credit institutions which were affected by it. What the appellants have to do is to show that third parties to these arrangements, depositors and potential depositors, were also granted rights by the Directive...

Looking back at the Directive as a whole, the key to a proper understanding of its purpose and effect seems to me to lie in the fact that it was the first step in a process of harmonisation of provisions for the regulation of credit institutions carrying on business within the Community. It was about the removal of barriers to the right of establishment under Article 52 of the EC Treaty. It confined itself to imposing a number of minimum conditions and prohibitions on Member States as to the authorisation and supervision of credit institutions having their head offices in another Member State or having their head offices outside the Community. It was based upon an appreciation of the fact that credit institutions require regulation in order to protect savings. So any measures of harmonisation had to meet the twin requirements of protecting savings on the one hand and creating conditions of equal competition between credit institutions operating in more than one Member State on the other. It placed duties of co-operation on the competent authorities where a credit institution was operating in one or more Member State other than that in which its head office was situated. But it stopped short of prescribing any duties of supervision to be performed by the competent authority within each Member State. It is not possible to discover provisions which entail the granting of rights to individuals, as the granting of rights to individuals was not necessary to achieve the results which were intended to be achieved by the Directive.

For these reasons I am unable, with great respect, to agree with Auld LJ's conclusions that the Directive of 1977 imposed clearly defined obligations on Member States and on their regulatory bodies and that in doing so it gave rise to corresponding Community law rights in depositors to enforce those obligations by an action of damages...I would therefore dismiss the appeal on the Community law claim.

Lord Steyn, **Lord Hutton**, **Lord Hobhouse** and **Lord Millett** agreed with Lord Hope that the appeal on the Community law claim should be dismissed.

Appeal dismissed in part.

COMMENTARY

There are two main strands in Lord Hope's analysis. First, the Banking Directive's legislative basis in the Treaty lay in the competence to harmonise EU law so as to remove barriers to the right of establishment, to which the protection of depositors' savings was purely incidental. Secondly, the Directive did not in fact impose any duties of supervision on the regulatory authorities of member states, but only a discretion to supervise. Lord Hope rejected, at [80], Auld LJ's view in the Court of Appeal that the relevant provisions of the Directive, though expressed in merely permissive terms, should be read as impliedly creating a duty. The first strand of analysis requires qualification, for it is clear that a Directive can confer EU rights on individuals even if founded on a legislative competence limited to the harmonisation of EU laws (as in *Francovich*). But the gist of Lord Hope's reasoning has been confirmed by the European Court of Justice. Indeed, the Court seems to have gone rather further than the House of Lords, deciding in unrelated proceedings that even the Second Banking Directive (89/646/EC), which sets out a much more comprehensive supervisory regime, confers no right on individual depositors and therefore does not preclude national laws which prevent compensation claims against the supervisory authority (Case C–222/02, *Paul v Germany* [2004] ECR I–9425). It is to be hoped, however, that the next time such issues are raised in the English courts there will be a reference to the Court of Justice under Article 267 TFEU, for it must be questioned whether the objectives of the Directive were really so clear as to make this course of action unnecessary in the *Three Rivers* case, even if their Lordships' view was subsequently vindicated by the ECJ in *Paul v Germany*. (See also, in a different context, *Poole v HM Treasury* [2007] EWCA Civ 1021, [2008] Lloyd's Rep IR 134.)

Undoubtedly, a concern of the House of Lords in *Three Rivers* was that a contrary decision would circumvent restrictions on the liability of regulators that exist in English tort law (see, especially, *Yuen Kun-yeu v Attorney General of Hong Kong* [1988] 1 AC 175), exposing the Bank of England to an indeterminate and potentially enormous liability. Under EU law, as Lord Hope recognised, at [64], 'the potential width of the class of persons granted rights does not militate against the conclusion that the relevant...Directives were intended to create rights'. In fact, the Court of Justice has already held that various provisions dealing with consumer protection, employment rights, freedom of trade and the safeguarding of the environment are sufficiently clear and precise to confer rights on individual members of a broadly-defined class (see respectively Cases C–178–179/94 and 188–190/94, *Dillenkofer v Germany* [1996] ECR 1–4845, Case 152/84, *Marshall v Southampton and South West Hampshire Area Health Authority (Teaching)* [1986] ECR 723, Case 58/89, *Brasserie du Pêcheur and Commission v Germany* [1991] ECR 1–4983). Clearly, then, there is scope for damages claims to be brought in the domestic courts in each of these fields, as well as others which are subject to EU law regulation. An example is provided by *Byrne v Motor Insurers' Bureau* [2008] EWCA Civ 574, [2009] QB 66 where the Court of Appeal ruled that the United Kingdom had violated the claimant's rights under the Motor Insurance Directive in a sufficiently serious manner to give rise to liability in respect of a road traffic accident caused by an untraced driver by virtue of the Motor Insurers Bureau's application of a shorter limitation period than under general tort law to untraced driver claims, there being no provision for the suspension of limitation till a child victim reached adulthood. The claimant had been three at the date of the accident. See also *Spencer v Secretary of State for Work and Pensions; Moore v Secretary of State for Transport* [2008] EWCA Civ 750, [2009] QB 358.

Where an EU law does create private rights, can the action be brought against private individuals or organisations or only against the state? The ECJ affirmed in *Courage v Crehan* [2001] ECR I-6297 that an individual may be liable in an action for damages on the basis of the violation of an EU right founded directly on the text of the Treaty itself (specifically, Article 81 TEC (now Article 121 TFEU): prevention, restriction or distortion of competition). It has been suggested that this completes the circle uniting principles of State liability and the Union's own liability for damage caused by its institutions and servants (Article 340 TFEU) with the protection of EU law rights under the *von Colson* case, and so provides the opportunity for a more integrated approach to tort liability under EU law. See, e.g., van Gerven, 'Harmonization of Private Law: Do We Need it?' (2004) 41 CMLR 505, especially 522–3; Drake, 'Scope of Courage and the principle of "individual liability" for damages: further development of the principle of effective judicial protection by the Court of Justice' [2006] ELR 841. However, the *Courage* decision did not purport to be an application or extension of the liability in *Francovich*, and the ECJ has subsequently stated that, in the absence of EU rules governing the matter, it is for the domestic legal system of each Member State to prescribe the detailed rules governing compensation for harm caused by violation of the Community right, subject to the ordinary requirements of equivalence (the rules must not be less favourable than those governing domestic actions) and effectiveness: see C-295/04, *Manfredi v Lloyd Adriatico Assicurazioni SpA* [2006] ECR I-6619 at [64]. It is far from certain that the elements of the *Francovich* liability will be considered essential for claims brought under *Courage*, and it therefore seems premature to speak of a unified liability regime for violation of EU rights.

12 NUISANCE AND THE RULE IN *RYLANDS v FLETCHER*

One of the oldest actions known to the common law is the action for nuisance. Its foundation can be traced to the twelfth century, to the establishment of the Assize of Nuisance. The origins of the modern tort of nuisance are, however, found in the development of the action on the case for nuisance. As has been noted previously, this form of action required the claimant to show some damage before the cause of action was complete. The damage in the action on the case for nuisance was primarily damage to land, which included damage to things affixed to the land (e.g. trees or crops) as well as damage to the amenity value of the land (e.g. interference with the enjoyment of the land through sound, smell, vibrations, etc.). These two aspects of the interests protected by the tort of nuisance are explained in *St Helens Smelting Co v Tipping* (below); however, the protection of amenity interests should not confuse one into thinking that nuisance protects personal as opposed to proprietary or possessory interests in land, a point made clear by a majority of the House of Lords in *Hunter v Canary Wharf* [1997] AC 655 (below). Whether nuisance should be expanded to protect personal interests remains the subject of debate.

The nuisance action takes two forms in modern law: public and private nuisance. Most of this chapter is concerned with private nuisance. Public nuisance is a crime, the prosecution of which is usually left to public bodies acting under statutory powers. None the less, a private individual may sue for a public nuisance where he has suffered special damage, that is, damage over and above the damage suffered by the public at large. In other respects, however, public and private nuisance share common elements.

To succeed in an action for private nuisance, the claimant must establish that the defendant is using his land unreasonably. What constitutes a reasonable user of land is a question of fact, and is decided by weighing up the various factors considered below. Another question that arises is the question of fault. Does the finding that the defendant is liable for an unreasonable user of land mean that he is at fault? If so, what is the difference between negligence and nuisance?

A claimant in an action for nuisance can claim one of two remedies: damages or an injunction. When the claimant seeks an injunction, he is asking the court to stop that part of the defendant's conduct that amounts to a nuisance rather than to have the conduct stopped altogether. In deciding whether to accede to the claimant's request, can, or should, a court take into account the public benefit of the defendant's conduct? Policy arguments point both ways: if the activity benefits the public it is poor policy to stop it, but if an activity which amounts to a nuisance is allowed to continue the claimant's private right has been expropriated in the public interest without compensation. Perhaps the best compromise lies in town planning legislation: if the activity of the defendant satisfies planning requirements it should be immune from a nuisance action. Recent cases suggest this utilitarian view has not found favour, and the tension between the rugged individualism of the common law and the wider community considerations of planning and environmental law is clearly evident in the modern law of nuisance. Additional uncertainties have been created by the introduction of the Human Rights Act 1998; in particular, the relationship between the principles of common law nuisance and the right to respect for private and family life in Article 8 of the ECHR awaits authoritative judicial explanation.

I. Public and Private Nuisance

At the outset of any discussion of nuisance, it is important to distinguish between private and public nuisance. Private nuisance, which is a tort, protects an occupier's right to use and enjoy her land free from unreasonable interferences. Conversely, public nuisance is the description given to a broad principle of criminal liability. *Archbold: criminal pleading, evidence and practice* (2007 edn.) describes a person as guilty of a public nuisance if she commits an act not warranted by law, or omits to discharge a legal duty, where the effect of the act or omission is to endanger the life, health, property, morals, or comfort of the public or to obstruct the public in the exercise of rights common to all Her Majesty's subjects. As the Court of Appeal recently pointed out in *In re Corby Group Litigation* [2009] QB 335, the 'essences' of the two torts are quite different; in particular, the concern of public nuisance with conduct endangering the life, safety and health of the public gives it a potentially greater scope of application than private nuisance as it is not limited to conduct interfering with the enjoyment of land (e.g., in the protection of the environment; see Parpworth, 'Public Nuisance in the environmental context' (2009) 11 *Journal of Planning and Environmental Law* 1526).

Because of the public nature of the offence, public officers or bodies are primarily responsible for enforcement (e.g. the Attorney General, or local authorities under s. 222 of the Local Government Act 1972). Although the primary penalty for the offence (which is triable both summarily and on indictment) is a criminal fine, an injunction may be sought to prevent an activity which is ongoing.

Whilst the criminal aspects of public nuisance are beyond the scope of this book, it is important to recognise that the perpetrator of a public nuisance may incur some civil liability. A private individual who has suffered special damage over and above that suffered by the public generally as a result of a public nuisance may sue to recover damages for this loss. Although the matter is not free from doubt, a claimant will suffer special damage where 'the right he shares with others has been appreciably more affected by the defendant's behaviour' (*Markesinis & Deakin*, p. 553). For example, the obstruction of the highway interferes with the public right of a driver to use it, but the owner of commercial premises whose entrance is blocked by the obstruction might well suffer special damage beyond that of the ordinary driver. Further, even though a private individual, absent special damage, has no standing to commence proceedings in public nuisance, an application can be made to the Attorney General to grant permission (known as a fiat) to an individual to allow that individual to commence proceedings (known as relator proceedings; see further Bradley and Ewing, *Constitutional and Administrative Law*, 13th edn. (Harlow: Pearson, 2003, pp. 808–9).

The differences between private and public nuisance are considered further in the extract below.

Attorney General v PYA Quarries Ltd [1957] 2 QB 169

An injunction was granted against the defendant in respect of its quarrying operations. It made improvements to the system of blasting, and then appealed against the original order on the basis that the remaining dust and vibrations caused as a result of its operations did not warrant the continuance of the injunction. It was argued that the trial judge had not distinguished between private and public nuisance and that the dust and vibration only amounted to a private nuisance remediable in damages and not a public nuisance for which the Attorney General could seek an injunction. In the course of their judgments, Denning LJ and Romer LJ considered the difference between public and private nuisance.

Romer LJ

Before considering these contentions in any detail it would, I think, be convenient to consider the nature of a public nuisance as distinct from nuisances which are customarily described as 'private'.... It is, however, clear, in my opinion, that any nuisance is 'public' which materially affects the reasonable comfort and convenience of life of a class of Her Majesty's subjects. The sphere of the nuisance may be described generally as 'the neighbourhood'; but the question whether the local community within that sphere comprises a sufficient number of persons to constitute a class of the public is a question of fact in every case. It is not necessary, in my judgment, to prove that every member of the class has been injuriously affected; it is sufficient to show that a representative cross-section of the class has been so affected for an injunction to issue.

Denning LJ

The classic statement of the difference [between private and public nuisance] is that a public nuisance affects Her Majesty's subjects generally, whereas a private nuisance only affects particular individuals. But this does not help much. The question, 'When do a number of individuals become Her Majesty's subjects generally?' is as difficult to answer as the question 'When does a group of people become a crowd?' Everyone has his own views. Even the answer 'Two's company, three's a crowd' will not command the assent of those present unless they first agree on 'which two.' So here I decline to answer the question how many people are necessary to make up Her Majesty's subjects generally. I prefer to look to the reason of the thing and to say that a public nuisance is a nuisance which is so widespread in its range or so indiscriminate in its effect that it would not be reasonable to expect one person to take proceedings on his own responsibility to put a stop to it, but that it should be taken on the responsibility of the community at large.

   Take the blocking up of a public highway or the non-repair of it. It may be a footpath very little used except by one or two householders. Nevertheless, the obstruction affects everyone indiscriminately who may wish to walk along it. Take next a landowner who collects pestilential rubbish near a village or permits gypsies with filthy habits to encamp on the edge of a residential neighbourhood. The householders nearest to it suffer the most, but everyone in the neighbourhood suffers too. In such cases the Attorney-General can take proceedings for an injunction to restrain the nuisance: and when he does so he acts in defence of the public right, not for any sectional interest.... But when the nuisance is so concentrated that only two or three property owners are affected by it ... then they ought to take proceedings on their own account to stop it and not expect the community to do it for them....

   Applying this test, I am clearly of opinion that the nuisance by stones, vibration and dust in this case was at the date of the writ so widespread in its range and so indiscriminate in its effect that it was a public nuisance.

Appeal dismissed.

COMMENTARY

In *R v Rimmington; R v Goldstein* [2006] 1 AC 459 Lord Rodger doubted, at least in the criminal context, whether it was satisfactory to seek to identify a public nuisance by asking whether the nuisance was so widespread that it would not be reasonable to expect one person to take proceedings to put a stop to it. In his opinion, 'it has remained an essential characteristic of a public nuisance that it affects the community, members of the public as a whole, rather than merely individuals'. As the 'community' is not a legal entity, however, it is hard to see how damage to the community can be established independently of the number of people in that community who are affected. So how many members of the community must be affected to constitute a nuisance to the public as a whole? In *Gillingham Borough Council v Medway (Chatham) Dock Co Ltd* [1993] QB 343 the defendants had been granted planning permission by the plaintiff to operate a commercial port in the area formerly used as naval dockyards. As a consequence, the access road to the dock was used twenty-four hours a day, with the result that the residents of two nearby roads were adversely affected. It was conceded by the defendant's council that the conduct, if it was a nuisance, affected a sufficient number of people to be classed as a public nuisance. See also *East Dorset District Council v Eaglebeam Ltd* [2006] EWHC 2378 (QB) where a nuisance affecting a 'substantial' number of houses was held to a public nuisance.

A public nuisance is established when 'the reasonable comfort and convenience of life of a class of Her Majesty's subjects' are affected by the activity in question. It should be noted, however, that the same activity may give rise to a claim in private nuisance as interfering with each individual's use and enjoyment of his land. This is so even where the use and enjoyment of land is affected by conduct on the highway or land over which the general public has a right of access and even if a separate claim in public nuisance for special damage is available; as was pointed out in *Color Quest Ltd v Total Downstream UK plc* [2009] EWHC 540 (Comm) at [432], the claims in public and private nuisance are not mutually exclusive. In *Halsey v Esso Petroleum* [1961] 1 WLR 683 the plaintiff complained of, amongst other things, the noise that resulted from lorries entering and exiting the defendant's refinery. A substantial part of this noise occurred when the lorries were on a public road. Veale J held that the plaintiff had a claim for private nuisance even though part of the nuisance occurred on a public road. The plaintiff was not complaining of interference with his right to use the highway (a public right) but of interference with the use and enjoyment of his property; hence the conduct amounted to a private nuisance (see also *Attorney General v Gastonia Coaches* [1977] RTR 219). However, such interference may also amount to a public nuisance for which the claimant can sue—see *Halsey, Gastonia* (above), *Vanderpant v Mayfair Hotels* [1930] 1 Ch 138—so in practice it may not matter which cause of action the claimant uses to sue. (Note, however, that there may be some advantages in terms of a wider range of recoverable losses (including personal injury) and a different standing requirement by suing in public nuisance—see *Markesinis & Deakin*, p. 551.) There is authority, however, that the defendant must make some use of land to incur liability in private nuisance. In *Southport Corporation v Esso Petroleum* [1954] 2 QB 182 the defendant was responsible for the discharge of 400 tonnes of oil into the Ribble estuary, which caused damage to a part of the foreshore owned by the defendant. Denning LJ held that 'the discharge of oil was not a private nuisance, because it did not involve the use by the defendants of any land, but only of a ship at sea', a view concurred in by Lord Radcliffe when the case reached the House of Lords ([1956] AC 218 at 242). Cf. *Overseas Tankship (UK) Ltd v Miller Steamship Co (Wagon Mound No. 2)* [1967] 1 AC 617 for a successful claim in public nuisance arising out of the (mis)use of Sydney Harbour.

A good example of the differences between a claim for damages in public and private nuisance is *Tate & Lyle Industries v GLC* [1983] 2 AC 509. The defendants erected ferry terminals in the Thames, and, as a result, parts of the river bed silted up. The plaintiffs had built a jetty into the Thames, but, as a result of the silting, large vessels were unable to access the jetty, and the plaintiffs incurred expense in carrying out their own dredging operations. The plaintiffs' claim in negligence and private nuisance failed because a proprietor was not entitled to object to an alteration to the depth of the water that did not threaten to cause damage to his land, to interfere with his acknowledged riparian rights, or to cause a nuisance, but merely obstructed the public right of navigation. However, the plaintiffs succeeded in public nuisance because the defendant's activities had interfered with the public right of navigation enjoyed by all users of the river and, as the plaintiffs had suffered special damage (the cost of the dredging), the claim was successful (see also *Jan de Nul (UK) Ltd v NV Royale Belge* [2002] EWCA Civ 209).

II. Private Nuisance

1. Reasonable User

Although negligence involves liability to one's legal neighbours, it is the tort of nuisance that deals with liability to one's physical neighbours. Part of being a good neighbour involves tolerance, and the fact that one party uses land to the annoyance of another does not create civil liability. Liability in private nuisance arises only when the conduct of the defendant amounts to an unreasonable user of land in that it causes an unreasonable interference with the claimant's use of land. Whether or not there has been a nuisance is a question of fact, the court weighing several factors in the particular circumstances of the case and asking if the conduct interferes with the claimant's use of his land 'not merely according to the elegant and dainty habits of living but according to plain and sober notions among our people' (*Walter v Selfe* (1851) 4 De G & Sm 315 at 322, per Knight Bruce V-C).

Whether conduct amounts to an unreasonable user depends upon a number of factors the most important of which are the nature and extent of the damage suffered by the claimant, the locality where the alleged nuisance is committed, the duration of the nuisance, the use the claimant is making of his land and the purpose with which the defendant acts. However, courts have generally ignored the utilitarian argument that where the defendant's conduct is for the public benefit it cannot amount to a nuisance, the common law being slow to extinguish private rights in the public interest. The extracts below consider these factors.

(a) Public Benefit

> **Bamford v Turnley** (1862) 3 B&S 66; 122 ER 27
>
> The plaintiff complained that the defendant's use of his land (burning bricks) resulted in smoke and smell which affected the plaintiff in the enjoyment of his land. The defendant won at trial,

and the plaintiff sought a rule for the defendant to show cause why judgment should not be entered for the plaintiff (in modern parlance, appealed against the decision). The Court of Queen's Bench refused the rule, but it was granted in the Court of Exchequer Chamber. One argument before the court was that the defendant's activity was for the public benefit.

Bramwell B

[I]t is said that, temporary or permanent, it is lawful because it for the public benefit. Now, in the first place, that law to my mind is a bad one which, for the public benefit, inflicts loss on an individual without compensation. But further, with great respect, I think this consideration misapplied in this and in many other cases. The public consists of all the individuals of it, and a thing is only for the public benefit when it is productive of good to those individuals on the balance of loss and gain to all. So that if all the loss and all the gain were borne and received by one individual, he on the whole would be a gainer. But whenever this is the case—whenever a thing is for the public benefit, properly understood—the loss to the individuals of the public who lose will bear compensation out of the gains of those who gain. It is for the public benefit that there should be railways, but it would not be unless the gain of having the railway was sufficient to compensate the loss occasioned by the use of the land required for its site; and accordingly no one thinks it would be right to take an individual's land without compensation to make a railway. It is for the public benefit that trains should run, but not unless they pay their expenses. If one of those expenses is the burning down of a wood of such value that the railway owners would not run the train and burn down the wood if it were their own, neither is it for the public benefit they should if the wood is not their own. If, though the wood were their own, they still would find it compensated them to run trains at the cost of burning the wood, then they obviously ought to compensate the owner of such wood, not being themselves, if they burn it down in making their gains. So in like way in this case a money value indeed cannot easily be put on the plaintiff's loss, but it is equal to some number of pounds or pence, £10, £50, or what not: unless the defendant's profits are enough to compensate this, I deny that it is for the public benefit he should do what he has done; if they are, he ought to compensate.

COMMENTARY

Modern law-and-economics scholars could not have put the argument better than Bramwell B: to gauge the proper cost of an activity the injury caused to outsiders must be taken into account (see R. Coase, 'The Problem of Social Cost' (1960) 3 JLE 1–44). In economic terms, if net utility (social benefit) after the activity is undertaken is greater than that before it, the activity is economically desirable and should be undertaken; in Bramwellian terms, the activity is for the public benefit only if it is profitable after paying compensation to those injured by it. Whether Bramwell was advocating an embryonic law-and-economics approach to social cost may be questioned (see Simpson, *Leading Cases in the Common Law* (Oxford: OUP, 1995), p. 175), and in any case he was hardly the first judge to confront the dilemma between public benefit and private rights. In *Jones v Powell* (1629, extracted in Baker and Milsom, *Sources of English Legal History* (London: Butterworths, 1986), p. 601) the Court of King's Bench divided over whether fumes from a brewhouse which caused inconvenience and damage to a neighbour's property (some papers) was actionable, Whitelocke J noting that '. . . it is better that they [the plaintiff's papers] should be spoiled than that the common wealth stand in need of good liquor'. The issue was important, as brewed beverages were safer to drink than ordinary water, and although all the judges accepted this fact they divided on whether the activity should be carried out where it caused serious damage to a neighbour.

Although the authorities suggest that public benefit is not an absolute defence, it seems that it may be a consideration taken into account in determining the reasonableness of the defendant's use of land. As *Fleming*, p. 471, comments:

> Likewise, some consideration will be given to the fact that the offensive enterprise is essential and unavoidable in the particular locality, like a coal mine, quarry, or some public utility or service such as early morning milk delivery. This argument, however, must not be pushed too far. In particular, it should be remembered that we are here concerned with reciprocal rights and duties of private individuals, and a defendant cannot simply justify his infliction of great harm upon the plaintiff by urging that a greater benefit to the public at large has accrued from his conduct.

If private rights are to be extinguished in favour of the general public this has generally been thought to be a matter for Parliament (see Lindley LJ in *Shelfer v City of London Electric Lighting Company* [1895] 1 Ch 287 at 316), and much of the development of the railways, mentioned by Bramwell B, took place through private Acts of Parliament allowing for compulsory land acquisition with payment of compensation to those affected (Kostal, *Law and English Railway Capitalism 1825–1875* (Oxford: OUP, 1994), ch. 4; Simpson, *Victorian Law and the Industrial Spirit*, Selden Society Lecture 1994). For a more general discussion of the role of nuisance in mediating between public and private interests, see Brenner, 'Nuisance Law and the Industrial Revolution' (1974) 3 JLS 403; McLaren, 'Nuisance Law and the Industrial Revolution—Some Lessons from Social History' (1983) 3 OJLS 155; Pontin, 'Tort Law and Victorian Government Growth: The Historiographical Significance of Tort in the Shadow of Chemical Pollution and Factory Safety Regulation' (1998) 18 OJLS 661.

If public benefit cannot directly convert the defendant's conduct from being a nuisance into lawful activity, might it have an affect on the remedy to which the claimant is entitled? (See *Dennis v Ministry of Defence* [2003] EWHC 793, p. 680, below.)

(b) Locality

St Helen's Smelting Co v Tipping   (1865) 11 HL Cas 642

The plaintiff bought property in June 1860, and several months later the defendant began extensive smelting works on its property. The defendant's property was situated within a mile and a half of the plaintiff's. The plaintiff alleged that the fumes from the defendant's works had caused damage to trees and shrubs on the plaintiff's land. The jury found for the plaintiff, and the defendant challenged the direction given by the trial judge, Mellor J. Appeals to the Court of Exchequer Chamber and the House of Lords were dismissed. One issue for decision was whether an instruction to the jury that there was no liability in nuisance if the defendant's activity was carried on in a 'convenient' or 'suitable' place was correct in law.

Lord Westbury

My Lords, in matters of this description it appears to me that it is a very desirable thing to mark the difference between an action brought for a nuisance upon the ground that the alleged nuisance produces material injury to the property, and an action brought for a nuisance on the ground that the thing alleged to be a nuisance is productive of sensible personal discomfort. With regard to the latter, namely, the personal inconvenience and interference with one's enjoyment, one's quiet, one's personal freedom, anything that discomposes or injuriously affects the senses or the nerves, whether that may or may not be denominated a nuisance, must undoubtedly depend greatly on the circumstances of the place where the thing complained of actually occurs. If a man lives in a town, it is necessary that he should subject himself to the consequences of those operations of trade which may be carried on in his immediate locality, which are actually necessary for trade and commerce, and also for the enjoyment of property, and for the benefit of the inhabitants of the town and the public at large. If a man lives in a street where there are numerous shops, and a shop is opened next door to him, which is carried on in a fair and reasonable way, he has no ground for complaint, because to himself individually there may arise much discomfort from the trade carried on in that shop. But when an occupation is carried on by one person in the neighbourhood of another, and the result of that trade, or occupation, or business, is a material injury to property, then there unquestionably arises a very different consideration. I think, my Lords, that in a case of that description, the submission which is required from persons living in society to that amount of discomfort which may be necessary for the legitimate and free exercise of the trade of their neighbours, would not apply to circumstances the immediate result of which is sensible injury to the value of the property....

My Lords...the only ground upon which your Lordships are asked to set aside [the] verdict, and to direct a new trial, is this, that the whole neighbourhood where these copper smelting works were carried on, is a neighbourhood more or less devoted to manufacturing purposes of a similar kind.... My Lords, I apprehend that that is not the meaning of the word 'suitable', or the meaning of the word 'convenient', which has been used as applicable to the subject. The word 'suitable' unquestionably cannot carry with it this consequence, that a trade may be carried on in a particular locality, the consequences of which trade may be injury and destruction to the neighbouring property....

Lord Cranworth and **Lord Wensleydale** agreed with Lord Westbury.

Judgment of the Exchequer Chamber affirmed.

COMMENTARY

The contemporary importance of this case can be gauged from the fact that the House of Lords exercised their right to request the judges from the superior courts (Queens Bench, Common Pleas and Exchequer) to attend the hearing and to offer an opinion. This was only done for cases of public importance (for a related example, see *McNaghten*'s case (1843) 10 C & F 200). Six of them were able to attend (including two of the most eminent nineteenth-century judges, Willes and Blackburn) and, before Lord Westbury gave his speech, they advised that the direction given by Mellor J was good in law.

St Helen's sets out the important distinction between activities of a neighbour which cause 'material injury to property' (in which case the locality in which the activity is pursued is irrelevant) and those which cause 'sensible personal discomfort' (in which the locality is relevant). Because locality is considered in at least some cases, it can be seen that, as argued above, some form of public interest is considered, for a landowner must put up with inconveniences resulting from 'those operations of trade which may be carried on in his immediate locality, which are actually necessary for trade and commerce, and also for the enjoyment of property, and for the benefit of the inhabitants of the town and the public at large'. But this argument does not apply where the inconvenience is 'material damage to property', for such a result can never arise from a reasonable use of property. But what is material damage to property, and why should locality be less important in this case? Lord Westbury's attempt to explain the difference is unhelpful; both interference with amenity and damage to property cause 'sensible injury to the value of the property'. *Weir*, p. 428, whilst accepting the distinction between the types of damage, argues that it must mean physical damage to property and not mere economic loss, but other authors have been less enthusiastic about the distinction itself (see *Fleming*, p. 468; *Winfield & Jolowicz*, para. 14–7). In *Hunter v Canary Wharf Ltd* [1997] AC 655 it was affirmed that both material physical damage and loss of amenity amount to interference with property interests, and this would suggest that, in deciding whether conduct amounts to a nuisance, the same factors should be considered. If both are property interests, why should a lengthy exposure to obnoxious smells be treated differently from a similar length of exposure that causes material damage to property? Against this, it has been argued (Lee (2003) 119 LQR 298) that the distinction continues to play an important role in the law of nuisance. Where the claimant suffers physical property damage, such damage is actionable without the complex balancing exercise traditionally associated with private nuisance. Conversely, where the damage to the land is identified as amenity damage, this directs the court to undertake the balancing exercise, which will include the locality in which the defendant's activity is carried out.

Even where locality is to be taken into account, it is important to recognise that a defendant's use of land may amount to a nuisance even if it is a type of activity suitable for the area. The locality principle does not provide an immunity; it must be weighed up against other relevant factors. A good example of this balancing exercise is *Halsey v Esso Petroleum* (above) where Veale J said:

So far as the present case is concerned, liability for nuisance by harmful deposits could be established by proving damage by the deposits to the property in question, provided of course that the injury was not merely trivial. Negligence is not an ingredient of the cause of action, and the character of the neighbourhood is not a matter to be taken into consideration. On the other hand, nuisance by smell or noise is something to which no absolute standard can be applied. It is always a question of degree whether the interference with comfort or convenience is sufficiently serious to constitute a nuisance. The character of the neighbourhood is very relevant and all the relevant circumstances have to be taken into account. What might be a nuisance in one area is by no means necessarily so in another. In an urban area, everyone must put up with a certain amount of discomfort and annoyance from the activities of neighbours, and the law must strike a fair and reasonable balance between the right of the plaintiff on the one hand to the undisturbed enjoyment of his property, and the right of the defendant on the other hand to use his property for his own lawful enjoyment.

Similar sentiments were expressed by Thesiger LJ in *Sturges v Bridgeman* (1879) 11 Ch D 852 at 865: 'what would be a nuisance in Belgrave Square would not necessarily be so in Bermondsey'. A more modern example is provided by *Baxter v Camden London Borough Council (No. 2)* [2001] 1 AC 1 where the plaintiff complained of noise created by her upstairs neighbours, both being tenants of the defendant in a converted house. The action in nuisance failed because the noise was part of the ordinary use of premises and '[o]ccupiers of low cost, high density housing must be expected to tolerate higher levels of noise from their neighbours than others in more substantial and spacious premises' (as Tuckey LJ had put it in the Court of Appeal: [2001] QB 1 at 10; cf. *Sampson v Hodson-Pressinger* [1981] 3 All ER 710).

Of course, the character of a neighbourhood is assessed not only geographically but also temporally; conduct amounting to a nuisance in Belgravia might well also do so in

Bermondsey today because the character of a locality changes over time. Sometimes this change is incremental, but it may also be brought about through a deliberate town planning decision made by a local authority. If a claimant is complaining of conduct that has been authorised by a planning consent, one question that arises is whether the locality of the neighbourhood should be judged by reference to the locality before or after the relevant planning consent. Summarising earlier authority, Sir Andrew Morritt C in *Watson v Croft-Promo-Sport Ltd* [2009] EWCA Civ 15 confirmed (at [32]) that the implementation of planning permission may so alter the nature and character of the locality as to shift the standard of reasonable user which governs the question of nuisance or no nuisance. What conduct will have this effect is a question of fact but in *Wheeler v JJ Saunders* [1996] Ch 19 both Staughton and Ralph Gibson LJJ held that the planning permission in question (for the intensification of pig farming) did not change the character of the neighbourhood, and were concerned to see that planning permission was not to be equated with the defence of statutory authority (in which an activity is authorised by an Act of Parliament). If the locality is to be judged after the implementation of the planning permission, do you agree that '…if a major industrial facility is built in a previously residential area and is held to change the character of the neighbourhood in the process, the facility would, by its very presence, be providing itself with a defence against nuisance'? (See Tromans [1995] CLJ 496.) Ralph Gibson LJ in *Wheeler* was concerned that '[t]he court should be slow to acquiesce in the extinction of private rights without compensation as a result of administrative decisions which cannot be appealed and are difficult to challenge', but this may well be the practical effect of judging locality after a planning consent has been implemented.

(c) Sensitivity of Claimant's Use of Land

Robinson v Kilvert (1889) 41 Ch D 88

The plaintiff was the tenant of premises, let to him by the defendant landlords, which were used as a paper warehouse. The defendants retained the use of the cellar of the premises, and after the lease commenced they began a manufacturing process that required the air to be hot and dry. To achieve this the cellar was heated, with the result that the temperature of the floor above was raised to 80F. The heat dried the plaintiff's brown paper stored in the above premises and made it less valuable. One issue for the Court of Appeal was whether the plaintiff could succeed in an action for nuisance.

Cotton LJ

Now the heat is not excessive, it does not rise above 80° at the floor, and in the room itself it is not nearly so great. If a person does what in itself is noxious, or which interferes with the ordinary use and enjoyment of a neighbour's property, it is a nuisance. But no case has been cited where the doing of something not in itself noxious has been held a nuisance, unless it interferes with the ordinary enjoyment of life, or the ordinary use of property for the purposes of residence or business. It would, in my opinion, be wrong to say that the doing of something not in itself noxious is a nuisance because it does harm to some particular trade in the adjoining property, although it would not prejudicially affect any ordinary trade carried on there, and does not interfere with the ordinary enjoyment of life. Here it is shewn that ordinary paper would not be damaged by what the Defendants are doing, but only a particular kind of paper, and it is not shewn that there is heat such as to incommode the workpeople on the Plaintiff's premises. I am of opinion, therefore, that the Plaintiff is not entitled to relief on the ground that what the Defendants are doing is a nuisance.

Lopes LJ

I think the Plaintiff cannot complain of what is being done as a nuisance. A man who carries on an exceptionally delicate trade cannot complain because it is injured by his neighbour doing something lawful on his property, if it is something which would not injure anything but an exceptionally delicate trade.... In the present case the Defendants are not shewn to have done anything which would injure an ordinary trade, and cannot, in my opinion, be held liable on the ground of nuisance....

COMMENTARY

'A man cannot increase the liabilities of his neighbour by applying his own property to special uses, whether for business or pleasure' (*Eastern and South African Telegraph Company Ltd v Cape Town Tramways Companies Ltd* [1902] AC 381 at 393). Where the injury to the claimant is caused as a result of his especially sensitive activity, no claim will lie. Although this principle is entrenched in the law of nuisance, examples of it being used to deny a claimant a claim are rare. In *Heath v Mayor of Brighton* (1908) 98 LT 718 the vicar and trustees of a church sought an injunction to stop the noise emanating from the defendant's power station which was alleged to disturb the vicar's deliberations over his sermons, but as no-one else appeared to have been bothered the injunction was refused. Another example is *Bridlington Relay v Yorkshire Electricity Board* [1965] Ch 436 where the plaintiffs, whose business was providing a relay service for sound and television broadcasts, sought an injunction to prevent the defendants from operating a new power line they had erected because it interfered with the relay service. One of the grounds on which Buckley J refused the injunction was the 'exceptionally sensitive' nature of the plaintiff's business. Most recently, in *Network Rail Infrastructure Ltd v C. J. Morris* [2004] EWCA Civ 172 the Court of Appeal considered whether electro-magnetic interference to the sound of electric guitars in the claimant's recording studio, caused by the defendant's nearby signalling system, constituted a nuisance. One of the defendant's arguments was that the claimant's use of land was extra-sensitive. In the course of finding for the defendant, the Court of Appeal cast doubt on the existence of a separate limitation on liability for extra-sensitive uses, Buxton LJ noting that the rule was subsumed under the general requirement of the reasonableness of the defendant's use of land. Assuming the limitation still applied, the Court of Appeal divided over whether the claimant's use of land was in fact extra-sensitive. However, applying the broad notion of what was reasonable as between neighbours, the claim failed: as the interference was not reasonably foreseeable as a result of the defendant's conduct it could not amount to an unreasonable use of land. Is much gained by abandoning the rule and incorporating it into general notions of reasonableness between neighbours? In negligence, there is a generalised requirement to act with reasonable care, but this is usually further subdivided (e.g. to focus on the likelihood and seriousness of the potential harm: see Chapter 4, Section II above) to give the concept some content when applying it the facts of the case. Could 'sensitivity of the claimant's use of land' be seen in the same way with respect to 'reasonable user'?

A farmer used his land to produce organic vegetables. Could he sue his neighbour in private nuisance if the neighbour used genetically modified seed which cross-pollinates the farmer's crops and prevented him from claiming the produce as organic, or would the farmer's use of land be hypersensitive? Would answering the question be any easier if it were framed it terms of what was reasonable as between the parties as neighbours? (See *R v Secretary of State for the Environment, Transport and the Regions, ex p. Watson, The Times,* 31 August 1998, CA Civ.)

(d) Malice

Christie v Davey [1893] 1 Ch 316

The plaintiff family were the occupiers of one half of a semi-detached property. They were a musical family, and used the house for playing, practising and teaching music. This annoyed the defendant, their next door neighbour, who wrote in the following terms:

> During this week we have been much disturbed by what I at first thought were the howlings of your dog, and, knowing from experience that this sort of thing could not be helped, I put up with the annoyance. But, the noise recurring at a comparatively early hour this morning, I find I have been quite mistaken, and that it is the frantic effort of some one trying to sing with piano accompaniment, and during the day we are treated by way of variety to dreadful scrapings on a violin, with accompaniments. If the accompaniments are intended to drown the vocal shrieks or teased catgut vibrations, I can assure you it is a failure, for they do not. I am at last compelled to complain, for I cannot carry on my profession with this constant thump, thump, scrape, scrape, and shriek, shriek, constantly in my ears. It may be a pleasure or source of profit to you, but to me and mine it is a confounded nuisance and pecuniary loss, and, if allowed to continue, it must most seriously affect our health and comfort.

As the letter was ignored, the defendant commenced a series of noises in his house whenever the playing of music was going on in the plaintiffs' house—such as knocking on the party-wall, beating on trays, whistling, shrieking, and imitating what was being played in the plaintiffs' house. The plaintiffs sought an injunction against the defendant in respect of this conduct, and the defendant counter-claimed for an injunction against the plaintiffs. North J rejected the counter-claim but granted the plaintiffs their injunction.

North J

The result is that I think I am bound to interfere for the protection of the Plaintiffs. In my opinion the noises which were made in the Defendant's house were not of a legitimate kind. They were what, to use the language of Lord Selborne in *Gaunt v Fynney* (1873) LR 8 Ch App 8, 'ought to be regarded as excessive and unreasonable.' I am satisfied that they were made deliberately and maliciously for the purpose of annoying the Plaintiffs. If what has taken place had occurred between two sets of persons both perfectly innocent, I should have taken an entirely different view of the case. But I am persuaded that what was done by the Defendant was done only for the purpose of annoyance, and in my opinion it was not a legitimate use of the Defendant's house to use it for the purpose of vexing and annoying his neighbours. I am not satisfied with the Defendant's attempts to explain away the Plaintiffs' statements. This being so, I am bound to give the Plaintiffs the relief which they ask.

COMMENTARY

Not all malicious uses of property affect the legality of the use. In *Bradford Corporation v Pickles* [1895] AC 587 the unloveable (or, to those so-minded, the entrepreneurial) Pickles owned land which contained a spring that supplied water to one of the corporation's dams. As a consequence of some drainage work proposed by Pickles, the water feeding the spring was to be diverted, rendering the corporations' dam useless. Despite a finding by the trial judge that the purpose of the draining was not to allow Pickles to quarry stone (as he alleged) but was rather 'in order that the Plaintiffs may be driven to pay him not to work it', the Court of Appeal and House of Lords held that the Corporation was not entitled to an injunction to prevent the work from being carried out. Lord Halsbury LC held:

> If it was a lawful act, however ill the motive might be, he had a right to do it. If it was an unlawful act, however good his motive might be, he would have no right to do it. Motives and intentions in such a question as is now before your Lordships seem to me to be absolutely irrelevant.

Whatever the position may be as regards interference with water percolating under one's own land (*Pickles* has been applied in modern times—see *Stephens v Anglian Water Authority* [1987] 1 WLR 1381) it seems clear that malice does affect the decision as to whether noise amounts to an unreasonable user or not. In *Allen v Flood* [1898] AC 1, Lord Watson made it clear that no proprietor has an absolute right to create noises on his own land, because any right which the law gives him is qualified by the condition that it must not be exercised to the nuisance of his neighbours or of the public. This approach was adopted in *Hollywood Silver Fox Farm v Emmett* [1936] 1 All ER 825, where, because of a dispute between the plaintiff and defendant, the defendant instructed his son to fire bird-scaring cartridges as near as possible to the breeding pens of the plaintiff's silver foxes whilst remaining on the defendant's land. As a result, one vixen would not breed and another ate her cubs. Applying *Christie*, Macnaghten J held the plaintiff entitled to damages and an injunction for this loss, as the malice rendered the discharge of the firearm an unreasonable user of land. That noise was to be treated differently from water rights is also indicated by the decisions of North J, the trial judge in both *Christie* and *Pickles* who held that malice was relevant in *Christie* but irrelevant in *Pickles*.

Several attempts have been made to reconcile the decisions, none of which are entirely convincing. Perhaps the best explanation (rather than justification), suggested in *Winfield & Jolowicz*, para. 14–12, is that the right to make noise on one's land is relative, whilst the right to alter percolating water is absolute (at least prior to appropriation). Where a relative right is in issue it is appropriate to consider malice. The problem arises, in the absence of clear judicial authority, in defining what are relative rights (though it is clear, for example, that the rights to make noise and smells are relative: *Stubbs v Sayer*, Court of Appeal Civil Division, 8 November 1990). However, another explanation of the difference between the cases has been put forward by M. Taggart, *Private Property and Abuse of Rights in Victorian England* (Oxford: OUP, 2002), p. 189:

> Historically, nuisance cases, almost without exception, concern the spread of something—be it odours, noise, water, gunshots, or whatever—from one property to another so as to interfere unreasonably with the use and enjoyment of the latter property. What happened in *Pickles* was the prevention of something (there percolating water) which the neighbour had no right to receive escaping from one property to another. *Pickles* stands for the proposition that it is not tortious in such circumstances to deprive someone of emanations from your property, even if maliciously motivated.

Thus, as Taggart points out, when the House of Lords in *Hunter v Canary Wharf* [1997] AC 655 was asked whether the erection of a building which interfered with the plaintiff land-owner's television reception constituted a nuisance, it answered in the negative. As Lord Goff noted, actions for private nuisance generally lay in respect of emanations from the defendant's land, not for the erection of something on the defendant's land which interfered with the ability of the plaintiff to receive something on his land (cf. Lord Cooke, who thought the position might be different if the building was constructed maliciously with the intention of interfering with the use and enjoyment of the plaintiff's land). However, it is clear that one exception to the general rule lies in respect of conduct of an occupier that interferes with the flow of surface water in a stream or river to a neighbour's land. Such conduct may be actionable in nuisance even though there is no emanation from the defendant's land (see *Swan Fisheries Ltd v Holberton*, unreported, QBD, 14 December 1987). Accordingly, it remains our view that *Bradford Corporation v Pickles* is best explained by the nature of the defendant's right rather than by the lack of an emanation from the defendant's land.

At this point, the bemused student may derive pleasure (or sadness) from the knowledge that the reproachable (or admirable) motives of Edward Pickles, the cause of the doctrinal confusion in the law of nuisance outlined, did not allow him to prosper. According to reports given to A. W. B. Simpson, Pickles emigrated to Canada at the turn of the century, having spent his money in vain on elaborate underground workings (*Victorian Law and the Industrial Spirit*, Selden Society Lecture, 1995).

2. Nuisance, Negligence and Fault

(a) Nuisance and Fault

One of the more confusing issues in nuisance is whether it is a fault-based tort. The short answer to this question is that it depends, first, on what remedy is sought, and, secondly, on what is meant by fault. Most authors agree that where the claimant is seeking an injunction, the question of fault is irrelevant (*Cambridge Water v Eastern Counties Leather*, below). This is because at the time the case is brought, the defendant knows that his conduct is causing the claimant inconvenience, and the only question for the court is whether the inconvenience amounts to a nuisance for the purpose of preventing such conduct in the future. In such a case the defendant is clearly at 'fault' in the sense that, as soon as the claimant commences the action (at the latest), the defendant knows that his conduct will cause the claimant injury, but this is not sufficient to impose liability. The question is simply one of reasonable user, and the claimant may fail to convince the court that an injunction should be granted even though there is clearly fault in the sense above; conversely, the defendant may have acted carefully in using his land but this will not prevent an injunction being granted if the activity amounts to an unreasonable use of land.

More difficult is the question whether fault is required where the claimant seeks damages rather than an injunction, that is, looks for compensation for a past wrong rather than to prevent a wrong from continuing. In *Wagon Mound (No. 2)* [1967] AC 617, Lord Reid, when discussing liability in nuisance, made the following somewhat cryptic comments (at 639):

> It is quite true that negligence is not an essential element in nuisance. Nuisance is a term used to cover a wide variety of tortious acts and omissions, and in many negligence in the narrow

sense is not essential. An occupier may incur liability for the emission of noxious fumes or noise, although he has used the utmost care in building and using his premises. The amount of fumes or noise which he can lawfully emit is a question of degree, and he or his advisors may have miscalculated what can be justified. Or he may deliberately obstruct the highway adjoining his premises to a greater degree than is permissible hoping that no one will object. On the other hand the emission of fumes or noise or the obstruction of the adjoining highway may often be the result of pure negligence on his part: there are many cases . . . where precisely the same facts will establish liability both in nuisance and in negligence. And although negligence may not be necessary, fault of some kind is almost always necessary and fault generally involves foreseeability . . .

The fault requirement in nuisance is considered further in the extract below.

Cambridge Water Co Ltd v Eastern Counties Leather plc
[1994] 2 AC 264

The facts are not relevant for present purposes, but are set out with a further extract at p. 687, below.

Lord Goff

Foreseeability of Damage in Nuisance

It is, of course, axiomatic that in this field we must be on our guard, when considering liability for damages in nuisance, not to draw inapposite conclusions from cases concerned only with a claim for an injunction. This is because, where an injunction is claimed, its purpose is to restrain further action by the defendant which may interfere with the plaintiff's enjoyment of his land, and *ex hypothesi* the defendant must be aware, if and when an injunction is granted, that such interference may be caused by the act which he is restrained from committing. It follows that these cases provide no guidance on the question whether foreseeability of harm of the relevant type is a prerequisite of the recovery of damages for causing such harm to the plaintiff. In the present case, we are not concerned with liability in damages in respect of a nuisance which has arisen through natural causes, or by the act of a person for whose actions the defendant is not responsible, in which cases the applicable principles in nuisance have become closely associated with those applicable in negligence: see *Sedleigh-Denfield v O'Callagan* [1940] AC 880 and *Goldman v Hargrave* [1967] 1 AC 645. We are concerned with the liability of a person where a nuisance has been created by one for whose actions he is responsible. Here, as I have said, it is still the law that the fact that the defendant has taken all reasonable care will not of itself exonerate him from liability, the relevant control mechanism being found within the principle of reasonable user. But it by no means follows that the defendant should be held liable for damage of a type which he could not reasonably foresee; and the development of the law of negligence in the past sixty years points strongly towards a requirement that such foreseeability should be a prerequisite of liability in damages for nuisance, as it is of liability in negligence. For if a plaintiff is in ordinary circumstances only able to claim damages in respect of personal injuries where he can prove such foreseeability on the part of the defendant, it is difficult to see why, in common justice, he should be in a stronger position to claim damages for interference with the enjoyment of his land where the defendant was unable to foresee such damage. Moreover, this appears to have been the conclusion of the Privy Council in *The Wagon Mound (No 2), Overseas Tankship (UK) Ltd v Miller Steamship Co Pty Ltd* [1967] 1 AC 617. The facts of the case are too well known to require repetition, but they gave rise to a claim for damages arising from a public nuisance caused by a spillage of oil in Sydney Harbour. Lord Reid, who delivered the advice of the Privy Council, considered that, in the class of nuisance which included the case before the Board, foreseeability is an essential element in determining liability. He then continued at 640:

> It could not be right to discriminate between different cases of nuisance so as to make fore-seeability a necessary element in determining damages in those cases where it is a neces-sary element in determining liability, but not in others. So the choice is between it being a necessary element in all cases of nuisance or in none. In their Lordships' judgment the simi-larities between nuisance and other forms of tort to which *The Wagon Mound (No 1)* applies far outweigh any differences, and they must therefore hold that the judgment appealed from is wrong on this branch of the case. It is not sufficient that the injury suffered by the respondents' vessels was the direct result of the nuisance if that injury was in the relevant sense unforeseeable.

It is widely accepted that this conclusion, although not essential to the decision of the particu-lar case, has nevertheless settled the law to the effect that foreseeability of harm is indeed a prerequisite of the recovery of damages in private nuisance, as in the case of public nuisance. I refer in particular to the opinion expressed by Professor Fleming in his book on *Torts* (8th edn, 1992) pp 443–4. It is unnecessary in the present case to consider the precise nature of this principle; but it appears from Lord Reid's statement of the law that he regarded it essentially as one relating to remoteness of damage.

COMMENTARY

It is clear from Lord Goff's speech that a failure to take reasonable care in carrying out an activity on land is not necessary to establish liability in nuisance, and it seems likely that this is what Lord Reid was referring to when he referred to negligence 'in the narrow sense' not being required. This does not mean, however, that liability is unaffected by foreseeability. A defendant will only be liable for the reasonably foreseeable consequences of the unreason-able user. This might be construed as a form of fault-based liability. If the defendant can fore-see injurious consequences to his neighbour from carrying out an activity but goes ahead regardless, it is difficult to argue that the defendant is totally blameless. Of course, the law of nuisance allows the defendant to cause foreseeable harm to his neighbours if the use of the land is reasonable, but reasonable use is not reasonable care. If a reasonable miscalculation is made in assessing the level of harm allowed to be inflicted on neighbours this is irrelevant in nuisance, although highly relevant in negligence. Thus, although there are similarities (careless conduct might well give rise to liability in both negligence and nuisance, for there may be an absence of both reasonable care and reasonable use; conversely there is no liability in respect of unforeseeable consequences resulting from the negligence or nuisance) a case can be made for distinguishing the role of fault in the two torts. See also Buckley, *The Law of Nuisance*, 2nd edn. (London: Butterworths, 1996), pp. 18–22.

An alternative view is that there is really no difference between the fault requirement in negligence and that in nuisance, at least where damages are sought rather than an injunc-tion. A defendant who carries on an activity, however carefully, which in law amounts to a nuisance 'cannot be acquitted of negligence' (Williams and Hepple, *Foundations of the Law of Tort*, 2nd edn. (London: Butterworths, 1984), p. 126). So in *St Helen's Smelting Co v Tipping* the defendants were guilty of negligence not in the operation of their factory but in choosing the site on which the factory was operated. But if this argument is correct, the plaintiff's action (in both negligence and nuisance) would have failed if the defendants had shown they had exercised reasonable care in the choice of the site for their smelting works. Such an argument would be irrelevant in nuisance, although in practice it would be rare to find that a defendant had exercised reasonable care in the choice of site for a business if the operation of that business amounted to an unreasonable user of the land in the tort of nuisance.

(b) Fault and Nuisances Created by Third Parties

Thus far we have concentrated on nuisances created by the defendant. But there are a number of cases where the defendant has been held liable in respect of nuisances created on his land by the act of a third party. In this category of case the basis of liability in nuisance appears similar to that in negligence. It is important to remember, however, that what constitutes actionable damage differs between nuisance and negligence. Hence, although liability may be based on fault, conduct may be actionable only in nuisance where the damage suffered is interference with amenity. Where the claimant's damage could be recoverable in a negligence action, however, it seems that any liability in nuisance mirrors that in negligence. In the words of Lord Walker in *Transco plc v Stockport Metropolitan Borough Council* [2004] 2 AC 1 at [96], the territory of private nuisance 'overlaps with (indeed, is a sort of condominium with) that of negligence'. (Cf. McIvor, *Third Party Liability in Tort* (Oxford: Hart, 2006), p. 51.)

> ### *Sedleigh-Denfield v O'Callaghan* [1940] AC 880
>
> The defendants owned land on which a pipe had been built, the pipe taking away water from a ditch. It was constructed by the local authority without the defendants' knowledge, and so far as it extended onto the defendants' land it amounted to a trespass to land and the workers who constructed it were trespassers. It had been intended to protect the entrance to the pipe with a grate, and one had been provided, but instead of placing it where it would prevent debris from entering the pipe it was placed on top of it 'where it was completely useless'. The plaintiff was the owner of adjoining land which was flooded when the pipe became blocked by debris after a heavy rainstorm. It had been argued at first instance that the defendant had no knowledge of the pipe, but it was held by the House of Lords that as a member of the defendant order, Brother Dekker, had knowledge of the pipe it had to be assumed that the defendants had knowledge of it as well.
>
> #### Lord Atkin
>
> In this state of the facts, the legal position is not, I think, difficult to discover. For the purpose of ascertaining whether, as here, the plaintiff can establish a private nuisance, I think that nuisance is sufficiently defined as a wrongful interference with another's enjoyment of his land or premises by the use of land or premises either occupied—or, in some cases, owned—by oneself. The occupier or owner is not an insurer. There must be something more than the mere harm done to the neighbour's property to make the party responsible. Deliberate act or negligence is not an essential ingredient, but some degree of personal responsibility is required, which is connoted in my definition by the word 'use'. This conception is implicit in all the decisions which impose liability only where the defendant has 'caused or continued' the nuisance. We may eliminate, in this case, 'caused.' What is the meaning of 'continued'? In the context in

which it is used, 'continued' must indicate mere passive continuance. If a man uses on premises something which he finds there, and which itself causes a nuisance by noise, vibration, smell or fumes, he is himself, in continuing to bring into existence the noise, vibration, smell or fumes, causing a nuisance. Continuing, in this sense, and causing are the same thing. It seems to me clear that, if a man permits an offensive thing on his premises to continue to offend—that is, if he knows that it is operating offensively, is able to prevent it, and omits to prevent it—he is permitting the nuisance to continue. In other words, he is continuing it. The liability of an occupier has been carried so far that it appears to have been decided that, if he comes to occupy, say, as tenant, premises upon which there exists a nuisance caused by a previous occupier, he is responsible, even though he does not know that either the cause or the result is in existence....

In the present case, however, there is, as I have said, sufficient proof of the knowledge of the defendants both of the cause and of its probable effect. What is the legal result of the original cause being due to the act of a trespasser? In my opinion, the defendants clearly continued the nuisance, for they come clearly within the terms I have mentioned above. They knew the danger, they were able to prevent it, and they omitted to prevent it.

Lord Wright

In my opinion, for reasons which I shall briefly explain, I think that the appeal should succeed. If it were merely a question of the physical conditions, no one would question that a case of private nuisance was established. The interposition of the pipe as the means of carrying the water from the ditch in place of the former open watercourse was not in itself objectionable. The trouble was that no protecting grid was put in place, and there was nothing to prevent the pipe from getting choked. There was thus the risk of a flood, which might spread, as in fact happened, to the appellant's premises, causing damage which in the actual result was considerable....

[W]here, as here, a plaintiff is damaged by his land being flooded, the facts bring it well within the sphere of nuisance. Such a case has a certain similarity with those to which the rule of *Rylands v Fletcher* applies, but there are obvious differences in substance. There are, indeed, well-marked differences between the two juristic concepts. This case has, therefore, properly been treated as a case of nuisance. It has affinity also with a claim for negligence, because the trouble arose from the negligent filling of the grid. But the gist of the present action is the unreasonable and unjustified intervention by the defendant in the use of his land with the plaintiff's right to enjoy his property. Negligence, moreover, is not a necessary condition of a claim for nuisance. What is done may be done deliberately, and in good faith and in a genuine belief that it is justified. Negligence here is not an independent cause of action but is ancillary to the actual cause of action, which is nuisance....

[His Lordship considered some authorities where liability had not been imposed in public nuisance, and continued:] In these modern cases, the plaintiff failed because he did not establish that the defendant either knew or ought to have known [of the nuisance]. In the present case, it is, in my opinion, clear on the facts ... that the respondents, by their servant, knew, or at least ought to have known, of the nuisance. On the law, as I have accepted it, the respondents' responsibility would seem to follow.

Lord Romer

The question to be decided is whether the respondents can be held liable for the damage caused to the appellant by the floods that took place in April 1937, and in November 1937, which were without question due to the accumulation in the culvert of rubbish which would not have been there had a proper grid been provided in the respondents' ditch. My Lords, I should have thought that, consistently with well-established principles of law, this question only permitted of an answer in the affirmative. An owner or occupier of land must so use it that he does not thereby substantially interfere with the comfortable enjoyment of their land by his neighbours. The user of the ditch by the construction of the culvert was not, indeed, a user of their land by the respondents at all. It was the act of a trespasser. Nevertheless, the respondents continued thereafter to use the ditch for the purpose of draining their adjoining fields, without taking steps to ensure that the water did not accumulate therein, and, as a consequence, flood the appellant's premises. Such steps were well within their power. All that it was necessary to do was to provide a grid which would prevent the rubbish which fell into the ditch from passing into the culvert. In these circumstances, it seems to me that they committed a nuisance upon their land, for which they must be held responsible.

Lord Porter

It is clear that an occupier may be liable though (i) he is wholly blameless (ii) he is not only ignorant of the existence of the nuisance but also without means of detecting it, and (iii) he entered into occupation after the nuisance had come into existence . . . Such a liability is, I think, inconsistent with the contention that the occupier is not liable for the acts of a trespasser of which he has knowledge, though possibly it might be contended that he is responsible for the acts of his predecessor in title, but not for those of a trespasser. Such a contention, however, is, I think, unsound, and the true view is that the occupier of land is liable for a nuisance existing on his property to the extent that he can reasonably abate it, even though he neither created it nor received any benefit from it. It is enough if he permitted it to continue after he knew, or ought to have known, of its existence. To this extent, but to no greater extent, he must be proved to have adopted the act of the creator of the nuisance.

Finally, however, it was said that the respondents knew, it is true, of the absence of a grid in front of the pipe, but did not know, and had no reason for suspecting, that any trouble would ensue. Therefore, it was contended that they had no knowledge of the nuisance, and, indeed, that no nuisance existed, but only the potentiality of a nuisance—that is, the possibility that the pipe might become blocked and cause a flood on the appellant's land. In a sense, this is true. The nuisance is not the existence of the pipe unprotected by a grid, but the flooding of the appellant's garden, which flooding might be repeated at any time of severe rain.

The respondents, however, ought, I think, as reasonable persons, to have recognised the probability, or at least the possibility, of a flood occurring . . . Moreover, in the present case, the evidence shows that the appellant had no knowledge of, or reason to suspect, the existence of any trouble owing to the pipe. However, the respondents had, as I have indicated, or ought to have had, knowledge of the danger, and could have prevented the danger if they had acted reasonably. For this I think they were liable—not because they were negligent, though it may be that they were, but for nuisance, because, with knowledge that a state of things existed which might at any time give rise to a nuisance, they took no steps to remedy that state of affairs.

COMMENTARY

The House of Lords held the defendants liable because they had continued or adopted the nuisance. A nuisance was continued or adopted if the defendant had knowledge of the existence of a nuisance on his land and had failed to take reasonable steps to bring the nuisance to an end. Although there are passages in Lord Atkin's and Lord Wright's speeches which suggest there is an absolute duty to end the nuisance the better view is that only reasonable steps are required, and, given the ease of preventing the nuisance in *Sedleigh-Denfield*, their Lordships probably felt that there was a requirement to abate the nuisance.

Lord Wright's comments on the 'well-marked differences between the two juristic concepts' of nuisance and the liability under the rule in *Rylands v Fletcher* must now be read in light of Lord Goff's speech in *Cambridge Water Co v Eastern Counties Leather plc* [1994] 2 AC 264, extracted at p. 687, below.

Several issues arise out of *Sedleigh-Denfield*. The first is what was the nuisance—was it the existence of the pipe in its defective state or was it the flood? Or was the nuisance, in fact, the failure to act reasonably in not securing the grate? These issues, and the relationship between nuisance and negligence in this context, are considered in the extract below.

C. Gearty, 'The Place of Private Nuisance in a Modern Law of Torts' [1989] CLJ 214, 235–7

An occupier of land 'continued' a nuisance if 'with knowledge or presumed knowledge of its existence he failed to take any reasonable means to bring it to an end though with ample time to do so.' Lord Wright and Lord Romer expressly approved this analysis of the law. It is easy to apply where the nuisance is one which interferes with personal comfort: a trespasser sneaking onto D's land and building something from which noxious gases are emitted; an intruder dumping an old electronic device which causes a noise nuisance and so on. It also works fairly well where the trespasser creates a state of affairs which causes damage to neighbouring land—though here we have preferred to speak of negligence. In all of these situations, the idea of D continuing something that is an ongoing nuisance has meaning. Difficulty arises where physical damage to property is caused by a single isolated event. How can such an occurrence be regarded as a nuisance capable of being known before it happens?

The facts of *Sedleigh-Denfield* make this crystal clear. The pipe lying in the ditch without its grid was not a nuisance. It interfered with nobody's comfort. It caused no damage to anyone. It may have had the potential to be a nuisance, but then so does any radio before it is turned on or any leaking lake-side tank before it is filled with oil. Neither Viscount Maugham nor Lord Wright addressed this point. They simply assumed that there was a nuisance which, applying an objective test, the occupiers ought to have seen and ought to have done something about. Neither pinpointed what the nuisance actually was. Lord Romer attempted to draw a distinction between a potential and an actual nuisance:

> The respondents did not themselves create this potential nuisance [ie the pipe without the grid], and cannot therefore be held liable for its creation. But an occupier of land upon which a nuisance has been created by another person is liable if he 'continues' the nuisance ... I agree with my noble and learned friend upon the woolsack, whose opinion I have had the privilege of reading, that the occupier 'continues' a nuisance if with knowledge or presumed knowledge of its existence he fails to take any reasonable means to bring it to an end though with ample time to do so. Judging them by this criteria, the respondents clearly continued the potential nuisance created by [the trespasser].

The response to this last point could well be, so what? Occupiers are not liable in nuisance simply because they own empty factories which would be noisy if they were working.

The two remaining law lords were aware of the problem. Lord Porter observed that 'the nuisance [was] not the existence of the pipe unprotected by a grid but the flooding of the appellant's garden.' Lord Atkin agreed that it was not a nuisance though it could 'threaten to become' one. This reasoning forced their Lordships even further away from nuisance. Liability attached because the defendants 'ought…as reasonable persons to have recognised the probability, or at least the possibility of a flood occurring.' Lord Atkin noted that the facts were such that 'when the ditch was flowing in full stream an obstruction might reasonably be expected in the pipe, from which obstruction flooding of the plaintiff's ground might reasonably be expected to result.'

We may note a distinction here. Three of their Lordships attached the label 'nuisance' to whatever could be said, in retrospect, to have been the cause of the damage. The remaining two defined nuisance as the damage-causing event. Both approaches made liability dependent upon what D, as a reasonable landowner, ought to have seen and how he ought to have behaved. The extent of the harm to P—the traditional concern of nuisance—hardly mattered at all and, indeed, is very difficult to discern from the judgments in *Sedleigh-Denfield*. This was negligence pure and simple, confused by an ill-fitting and woolly disguise of nuisance. It seems that the only people who were not your neighbours in the *Donoghue v Stevenson* sense were those who actually were.

COMMENTARY

Sedleigh-Denfield raised two important issues—first, whether an occupier can be liable for a nuisance on his land created by the acts of a third party (considered by the House of Lords); and secondly, whether an isolated event can amount to a nuisance (not discussed in any detail). Gearty argues that in both situations any liability imposed in nuisance mirrors the liability that would be imposed in negligence (at least where property damage is the result). An example of this in the context of acts of third parties is *Smith v Littlewoods Corporation* (see p. 494, above) where the liability of the cinema owner was discussed entirely in terms of negligence. Would anything have been gained by arguing the case in nuisance?

One reason for the reliance on nuisance (as opposed to negligence) in *Sedleigh-Denfield* may have been the traditional reluctance of the common law of negligence to impose a duty to act positively to prevent harm to a third party. However, it has since been recognised that the occupier of land may owe a duty to act positively to prevent harm to his neighbour (see *Goldman v Hargrave,* below). As Lord Cooke said in *Delaware Mansions Ltd v Westminster City Council* [2002] 1 AC 321 at 333: 'The label nuisance or negligence is treated as of no real significance. In this field, I think, the concern of the common law lies in working out the fair and just content and incidents of a neighbour's duty rather than affixing a label and inferring the extent of the duty from it.'

Given these developments, what benefits might there be in arguing the case in nuisance rather than negligence if a similar case arose today? (Cf. Lee (2003) 119 LQR 298.)

The reasoning in *Sedleigh-Denfield* has been used to impose liability on occupiers for the actions of their predecessors in title (*Bybrook Barn Centre Ltd v Kent County Council* [2001] BLR 55; cf. *Marcic v Thames Water Utilities Ltd* [2004] 2 AC 42 for the position of sewerage undertakers), and to support the liability of a landowner in nuisance where a third party uses the defendant's land as a base from which to engage in activities off the defendant's land which interfere with the claimant's use and enjoyment of his land. In *Lippiatt v South Gloucestershire Council* [2000] QB 51 the plaintiffs alleged that travellers occupied the defendant's land from whence they trespassed onto the plaintiff's farms and caused a nuisance. The Court of Appeal refused to strike out the plaintiff's claim (see also *Winch v Mid Bedfordshire District Council* [2002] All ER (D) 380, where *Lippiatt* was applied to find the defendant council liable). Although (in the absence of authorisation of the activity by the landowner) liability would arise under the principles in *Sedleigh-Denfield* (and, as argued above, be fault-based), it would seem to arise only in nuisance in respect of any amenity damage (such damage not being actionable in negligence).

A similar fault-based liability is imposed where the alleged nuisance is constituted by an isolated escape. (That an isolated escape can constitute a private nuisance was recently affirmed in *Color Quest Ltd v Total Downstream UK plc* [2009] EWHC 540 (Comm).) In *British Celanese Ltd v Hunt* [1969] 1 WLR 959 the plaintiff and the defendant both operated factories in an industrial estate, the power to which was supplied by an electricity substation owned by a third party. The defendant was a manufacturer of electrical components, and for this purpose stored thin strips of metal on the ground. Because the strips were light they were liable to be blown about by the wind, and on one previous occasion the strips had been blown into the substation, which caused an electrical fault with a loss of power supply to the estate. The defendant was warned to store the strips more carefully, but three years later strips which had been stored outside blew into the substation, causing a loss of power which caused loss to the plaintiff. Amongst other grounds, the plaintiff claimed in nuisance, and Lawton J refused to strike out this claim. It was held that there was no bar that prevented an action in nuisance in respect of an isolated escape, and 'in this case, the alleged happening of December 7, 1964, was not the first escape: there is said to have been one in 1961'. The gist of the claim was that the method of storing the strips interfered with the beneficial enjoyment of the plaintiff's property, as the defendant knew it would. But it was not the storing of the strips that caused the interference but the escape, and the escape was only actionable because it was foreseeable from the method of storing the strips. Given that the strips had been blown into the substation previously and that the defendant had been warned to use more care, it is evident that the defendant was only liable in nuisance because the method of storing the strips was negligent. As in any negligence claim, the cause of action is only complete when the damage occurs, but it is only actionable because the damage has been caused carelessly. Thus the liability in nuisance appears to merge into that in negligence (see also *SCM (United Kingdom) Ltd v W. J. Whittal & Son Ltd* [1970] 1 WLR 1017; Gearty, *op. cit.*; Murphy, 'Rethinking Injunctions in Tort Law' (2007) 27 OJLS 509, 522). Again, however, the position may be different if the claimant is alleging interference with amenity damage. As Stanley Burnton J said in *Anglian Water Services Ltd v Crawshaw Robbins & Co Ltd* [2001] BLR 173: 'A single act which caused a stench to come onto a neighbour's land, for example by damaging a pipe carrying noxious gas, would constitute actionable nuisance ... I doubt if a bad smell would support a claim in negligence; it would in nuisance.' In these situations, although the claimant will still need to show an absence of reasonable care, it seems that the cause of action must be classified as nuisance and not negligence.

(c) Nuisance and Acts of Nature

If an occupier could be liable in respect of a nuisance created by a third party, would the same rule apply where the nuisance arose from an act of nature or the natural condition of the land? The attitude of the courts to this issue has not always been consistent. In *Lemmon v Webb* [1894] 3 Ch 1 and *Smith v Giddy* [1904] 2 KB 448 it was not doubted that an occupier of land on which trees grew whose branches overhung his neighbour's property had committed a nuisance, provided that some damage had occurred. However, an occupier who allowed thistles to grow on his land was not liable when the thistle seeds blew onto his neighbour's land, which resulted in a proliferation of thistles, Lord Coleridge CJ commenting '[t]here can be no duty as between adjoining occupiers to cut the thistles, which are the natural growth of the soil' (*Giles v Walker* (1890) 24 QBD 656).

The issue arose for decision in *Goldman v Hargrave* [1967] 1 AC 645. The plaintiff and defendant were neighbours, and, due to a lightning strike on the defendant's property a redgum tree caught fire and became a fire risk. Although the defendant took some steps to alleviate the risk these were inadequate and a fire started which spread to the plaintiff's property and caused severe property damage. Applying the principle in *Sedleigh-Denfield* the Privy Council held that the occupier of land owed a duty to his neighbour to remove any hazards, whether natural or man-made. The duty was based on the occupier's knowledge of the hazard and foresight of damage to his neighbour if he failed to act. The standard of care required of the occupier was what it was reasonable to expect of him in his circumstances, but because the duty to act was imposed on the occupier, the individual resources of the occupier were to be considered in assessing whether his response was reasonable. The Privy Council clearly felt that the liability, if any, arose in negligence:

> Their Lordships propose to deal with these issues as stated, without attempting to answer the disputable question whether if responsibility is established it should be brought under the heading of nuisance or placed in a separate category.... The present case is one where liability, if it exists, rests upon negligence and nothing else; whether it falls within or overlaps the boundaries of nuisance is a question of classification which need not here be resolved.

(See further Lunney, '*Goldman v Hargrave*' in C. Mitchell and P. Mitchell (eds.), *Landmark Cases in the Law of Tort* (Hart, 2010), ch. 8.)

The leading English case is *Leakey v National Trust* [1980] QB 485. The plaintiffs owned two houses which had been built at the base of a large mound (Burrow Mump) on the defendants' land. As a consequence of natural weathering parts of the mound had broken off and fallen onto the plaintiffs' land, and it was established that, by 1968 at the latest, the defendants were aware of this occurrence. In the summer of 1976 a large crack opened in the mound, but the defendants refused to take any remedial action on the basis that they were not responsible for any damage caused by a natural movement of land. A few weeks later a significant quantity of debris from the mound fell onto the plaintiffs' land and the plaintiffs sought an injunction requiring the defendants to abate the nuisance as well as damages. Both the trial judge and the Court of Appeal upheld the plaintiffs' claim in nuisance. Megaw LJ dealt with the argument that the proper cause of action was negligence and not nuisance as follows:

> The plaintiffs' claim is expressed in the pleadings to be founded in nuisance. There is no express reference to negligence in the statement of claim. But there is an allegation of a breach of duty, and the duty asserted is, in effect, a duty to take reasonable care to prevent part of the defendants' land from falling on to the plaintiffs' property. I should, for myself, regard that as being properly described as a claim in nuisance. But even if that were, technically, wrong, I do not think that the point could or should avail the defendants in this case. If it were to do so, it would be a regrettable modern instance of the forms of action successfully clanking their spectral chains; for there would be no conceivable prejudice to the defendants in this case that the word 'negligence' had not been expressly set out in the statement of claim.

The result of these cases is that where the alleged nuisance is caused by a natural occurrence an action may be commenced in either nuisance or negligence, but that liability will be determined according to principles applicable to the law of negligence. The cases since

Leakey have tended to describe the cause of action as nuisance but, at least where damage to property (as opposed to amenity damage) is claimed, it is in reality negligence, and nothing is gained by this tactic (see e.g. *Holbeck Hall Hotel Ltd v Scarborough Borough Council* [2000] QB 836 (defendant council liable in 'nuisance' for failing to take reasonable steps to prevent slippage and erosion of their land, with the result that at a later date part of the plaintiff's hotel fell into the sea); *Delaware Mansions Ltd v Westminster City Council* [2002] 1 AC 321 (liability for encroaching tree roots); cf. *Green v Lord Somerleyton* [2003] EWCA Civ 198 (duty owed to neighbouring landowner in respect of the natural flow of water from the defendant's land, but no liability on the facts because the defendant had acted reasonably)). The only exception, noted above, is where the damage which the claimant alleges is not sufficient to found an action in negligence but would be in nuisance.

3. The Nature of Private Nuisance

In *Malone v Laskey* [1907] 2 KB 141 the Court of Appeal held that only a person with a possessory or proprietary interest in the land alleged to be the subject of the nuisance could sue. This view was challenged by another Court of Appeal 85 years later in *Khorasandjian v Bush* [1993] QB 727, when such a limitation was described by Dillon LJ as 'ridiculous'. In this case the plaintiff sought an injunction against the harassing behaviour of the defendant, part of which constituted the harassment of the plaintiff where she lived (her parents' house). One ground on which the injunction was granted was that the conduct of the defendant constituted a private nuisance, the Court of Appeal accepting her occupation of her parents' house as providing sufficient standing. This development was considered in the case extracted below and required the House of Lords to consider the nature of the action in private nuisance.

Hunter and Others v Canary Wharf Ltd [1007] AC 655

Two appeals were heard by the House of Lords relating to alleged nuisances created during the construction and development of Canary Wharf in London. The appeals required the House of Lords to consider two issues: first, whether interference with television reception caused by the erection of a large tower block (the Canary Wharf Tower) amounted to an actionable nuisance; and secondly, who was able to bring a claim in nuisance. At first instance the judge held that the interference with the television reception was capable of amounting to nuisance, and that only those who had exclusive possession of land could claim in nuisance. On appeal, the Court of Appeal held the interference was not capable of amounting to a nuisance, but extended the class of potential plaintiffs in nuisance to those in occupation of property as a home. The House of Lords unanimously agreed with the Court of Appeal that no claim arose in respect of the interference with television reception, but by a 4–1 majority held that only those with exclusive possession of property had a right to sue in nuisance. The extracts deal with the latter aspect of their Lordships' judgment.

Lord Goff

The question therefore arises whether your Lordships should be persuaded to depart from established principle, and recognise such a right in others who are no more than mere licensees on the land. At the heart of this question lies a more fundamental question, which relates to the scope of the law of private nuisance. Here, I wish to draw attention to the fact that although, in the past, damages for personal injury have been recovered at least in actions of public nuisance, there is now developing a school of thought that the appropriate remedy for such claims as these should lie in our now fully developed law of negligence, and that personal injury claims should be altogether excluded from the domain of nuisance. The most forthright proponent of this approach has been Professor Newark in his article 'The Boundaries of Nuisance' (1949) 65 LQR 480.... Furthermore, it is now being suggested that claims in respect of physical damage to the land should also be excluded from private nuisance (see e.g. the article by Mr Conor Gearty 'The Place of Private Nuisance in a Modern Law of Torts' [1989] CLJ 214). In any event, it is right for present purposes to regard the typical cases of private nuisance as being those concerned with interference with the enjoyment of land and, as such, generally actionable only by a person with a right in the land. Characteristic examples of cases of this kind are those concerned with noise, vibrations, noxious smells and the like. The two appeals with which your Lordships are here concerned arise from actions of this character.

For private nuisances of this kind, the primary remedy is in most cases an injunction, which is sought to bring the nuisance to an end, and in most cases should swiftly achieve that objective. The right to bring such proceedings is, as the law stands, ordinarily vested in the person who has exclusive possession of the land. He or she is the person who will sue, if it is necessary to do so. Moreover he or she can, if thought appropriate, reach an agreement with the person creating the nuisance, either that it may continue for a certain period of time, possibly on the payment of a sum of money, or that it shall cease, again perhaps on certain terms including the time within which the cessation will take place. The former may well occur when an agreement is reached between neighbours about the circumstances in which one of them may carry out major repairs to his house which may affect the other's enjoyment of his property. An agreement of this kind was expressly contemplated by Fletcher Moulton LJ in his judgment in *Malone v Laskey* [1907] 2 KB 141 at 153. But the efficacy of arrangements such as these depends upon the existence of an identifiable person with whom the creator of the nuisance can deal for this purpose. If anybody who lived in the relevant property as a home had the right to sue, sensible arrangements such as these might in some cases no longer be practicable.

Moreover, any such departure from the established law on this subject, such as that adopted by the Court of Appeal in the present case, faces the problem of defining the category of persons who would have the right to sue. The Court of Appeal adopted the not easily identifiable category of those who have a 'substantial link' with the land, regarding a person who occupied the premises 'as a home' as having a sufficient link for this purpose. But who is to be included in this category? It was plainly intended to include husbands and wives, or partners, and their children, and even other relatives living with them. But is the category also to include the lodger upstairs, or the *au pair* girl or resident nurse caring for an invalid who makes her home in the house while she works there? If the latter, it seems strange that the category should not extend to include places where people work as well as places where they live, where nuisances such as noise can be just as unpleasant or distracting. In any event, the extension of the tort in this way would transform it from a tort to land into a tort to the person, in which damages could be recovered in respect of something less serious than personal injury and the criteria for liability were founded not upon negligence but upon striking a balance between the interests of neighbours in the use of their land. This is, in my opinion, not an acceptable way in which to develop the law.

It was suggested in the course of argument that at least the spouse of a husband or wife who, for example as freeholder or tenant, had exclusive possession of the matrimonial home should be entitled to sue in private nuisance. For the purposes of this submission, your Lordships were referred to the relevant legislation, notably the Matrimonial Homes Act 1983 and the Family Law Act 1996. I do not, however, consider it necessary to go through the statutory provisions. As I understand the position, it is as follows. If under the relevant legislation a spouse becomes entitled to possession of the matrimonial home or part of it, there is no reason why he or she should not be able to sue in private nuisance in the ordinary way. But I do not see how a spouse who has no interest in the matrimonial home has, simply by virtue of his or her cohabiting in the matrimonial home with his or her wife or husband whose freehold or leasehold property it is, a right to sue. No distinction can sensibly be drawn between such spouses and other cohabitees in the home, such as children, or grandparents. Nor do I see any great disadvantage flowing from this state of affairs. If a nuisance should occur, then the spouse who has an interest in the property can bring the necessary proceedings to bring the nuisance to an end, and can recover any damages in respect of the discomfort or inconvenience caused by the nuisance. Even if he or she is away from home, nowadays the necessary authority to commence proceedings for an injunction can usually be obtained by telephone. Moreover, if the other spouse suffers personal injury, including injury to health, he or she may, like anybody else, be able to recover damages in negligence. The only disadvantage is that the other spouse cannot bring an independent action in private nuisance for damages for discomfort or inconvenience....

Lord Lloyd of Berwick stated that the measure of damages in all cases of nuisance was the diminution in value of the land, and continued:

> If the occupier of land suffers personal injury as a result of inhaling the smoke, he may have a cause of action in negligence. But he does not have a cause of action in nuisance for his personal injury, nor for interference with his personal enjoyment. It follows that the quantum of damages in private nuisance does not depend on the number of those enjoying the land in question. It also follows that the only persons entitled to sue for loss in amenity value of the land are the owner or the occupier with the right to exclusive possession....

Lord Hoffmann

Up to about 20 years ago, no one would have had the slightest doubt about who could sue. Nuisance is a tort against land, including interests in land such as easements and profits. A plaintiff must therefore have an interest in the land affected by the nuisance....

But the concept of nuisance as a tort against land has recently been questioned by the decision of the Court of Appeal in *Khorasandjian v Bush* [1993] QB 727....

[His Lordship considered this case, and continued:] This reasoning, which is echoed in some academic writing and the Canadian case of *Motherwell v Motherwell* (1976) 73 DLR (3d) 62, which the Court of Appeal followed, is based upon a fundamental mistake about the remedy which the tort of nuisance provides. It arises, I think, out of a misapplication of an important distinction drawn by Lord Westbury LC in *St Helen's Smelting Co v Tipping* (1865) 11 HL Cas 642 at 650, 11 ER 1483 at 1486. In that case, the plaintiff bought a 1,300 acre estate in Lancashire. He complained that his hedges, trees and shrubs were being damaged by pollution from the defendants' copper smelting works a mile and a half away. The defendants said that the area was full of factories and chemical works and that if the plaintiff was entitled to complain, industry would be brought to a halt.

St Helen's Smelting Co v Tipping was a landmark case. It drew the line beyond which rural and landed England did not have to accept external costs imposed upon it by industrial pollution. But there has been, I think, some inclination to treat it as having divided nuisance into two torts, one of causing 'material injury to the property', such as flooding or depositing poisonous substances on crops, and the other of causing 'sensible personal discomfort', such as excessive noise or smells. In cases in the first category, there has never been any doubt that the remedy, whether by way of injunction or damages, is for causing damage to the land. It is plain that in such a case only a person with an interest in the land can sue. But there has been a tendency to regard cases in the second category as actions in respect of the discomfort or even personal injury which the plaintiff has suffered or is likely to suffer. On this view, the plaintiff's interest in the land becomes no more than a qualifying condition or springboard which entitles him to sue for injury to himself.

If this were the case, the need for the plaintiff to have an interest in land would indeed be hard to justify. . . . But the premise is quite mistaken. In the case of nuisances 'productive of sensible personal discomfort', the action is not for causing discomfort to the person but, as in the case of the first category, for causing injury to the land. True it is that the land has not suffered 'sensible' injury, but its utility has been diminished by the existence of the nuisance. It is for an unlawful threat to the utility of his land that the possessor or occupier is entitled to an injunction and it is for the diminution in such utility that he is entitled to compensation. . . .

There may of course be cases in which, in addition to damages for injury to his land, the owner or occupier is able to recover damages for consequential loss. He will, for example, be entitled to loss of profits which are the result of inability to use the land for the purposes of his business. Or if the land is flooded, he may also be able to recover damages for chattels or livestock lost as a result. But inconvenience, annoyance or even illness suffered by persons on land as a result of smells or dust are not damage consequential upon the injury to the land. It is rather the other way about: the injury to the amenity of the land consists in the fact that the persons on it are liable to suffer inconvenience, annoyance or illness.

It follows that damages for nuisance recoverable by the possessor or occupier may be affected by the size, commodiousness and value of his property but cannot be increased merely because more people are in occupation and therefore suffer greater collective discomfort. If more than one person has an interest in the property, the damages will have to be divided among them. If there are joint owners, they will be jointly entitled to the damages. If there is a reversioner and the nuisance has caused damage of a permanent character which affects the reversion, he will be entitled to damages according to his interest. But the damages cannot be increased by the fact that the interests in the land are divided; still less according to the number of persons residing on the premise. . . .

Once it is understood that nuisances 'productive of sensible personal discomfort' do not constitute a separate tort of causing discomfort to people but are merely part of a single tort of causing injury to land, the rule that the plaintiff must have an interest in the land falls into place as logical and, indeed, inevitable (see *St Helen's Smelting Co v Tipping* (1865) 11 HL Cas 642 at 650, 11 ER 1483 at 1486).

Is there any reason of policy why the rule should be abandoned? Once nuisance has escaped the bounds of being a tort against land, there seems no logic in compromise limitations, such as that proposed by the Court of Appeal in this case, requiring the plaintiff to have been residing on land as his or her home. This was recognised by the Court of Appeal in *Khorasandjian*'s case, where the injunction applied whether the plaintiff was at home or not. There is a good deal in this case and other writings about the need for the law to adapt to modern social conditions. But the development of the common law should be rational and coherent. It should not distort its principles and create anomalies merely as an expedient to fill a gap.

So far as the claim is for personal injury, it seems to me that the only appropriate cause of action is negligence. It would be anomalous if the rules for recovery of damages under this head were different according as to whether, for example, the plaintiff was at home or at work. It is true, as I have said, that the law of negligence gives no remedy for discomfort or distress which does not result in bodily or psychiatric illness. But this is a matter of general policy and I can see no logic in making an exception for cases in which the discomfort or distress was suffered at home rather than somewhere else.

Finally, there is the position of spouses. It is said to be contrary to modern ways of thinking that a wife should not be able to sue for interference with the enjoyment of the matrimonial home merely because she has no proprietary right in the property. To some extent, this argument is based upon the fallacy which I have already discussed, namely that the action in nuisance lies for inconvenience or annoyance caused to people who happen to be in possession or occupation of land. But so far as it is thought desirable that the wife should be able to sue for injury to a proprietary or possessory interest in the home, the answer, in my view, lies in the law of property, not the law of tort. The courts today will readily assume that a wife has acquired a beneficial interest in the matrimonial home. If so, she will be entitled to sue for damage to that interest. On the other hand, if she has no such interest, I think it would be wrong to create a quasi-proprietary interest only for the purposes of giving her *locus standi* to sue for nuisance. What would she be suing for? Mr Brennan QC, who appeared for the plaintiffs, drew our attention to the rights conferred on a wife with no proprietary interest by the Matrimonial Homes Act 1983. The effect of these provisions is that a spouse may, by virtue of an order of the court upon a break-up of the marriage, become entitled to exclusive possession of the home. If so, she will become entitled to sue for nuisance. Until then, her interest is analogous to a contingent reversion. It cannot be affected by a nuisance which merely damages the amenity of the property while she has no right to possession.

Lord Cooke of Thorndon

My Lords, the lineaments of the law of nuisance were established before the age of television and radio, motor transport and aviation, town and country planning, a 'crowded island', and a heightened public consciousness of the need to protect the environment. All these are now among the factors falling to be taken into account in evolving the law....

Private nuisance is commonly said to be an interference with the enjoyment of land and to be actionable by an occupier. But 'occupier' is an expression of varying meanings, as a perusal of legal dictionaries shows.... Where interference with an amenity of a home is in issue there is no a priori reason why the expression should not include, and it appears natural that it should include, anyone living there who has been exercising a continuing right to enjoyment of that amenity.... A temporary visitor, however, someone who is 'merely present in the house' (a phrase used by Fletcher Moulton LJ in *Malone v Laskey* [1907] 2 KB 141 at 154), would not enjoy occupancy of sufficiently substantial nature....

Malone's case, a case of personal injury from a falling bracket rather than an interference with amenities, is not directly in point, but it is to be noted that the wife of the subtenant's manager, who had been permitted by the subtenant to live in the premises with her husband, was dismissed by Gorell Barnes P as a person who had 'no right of occupation in the proper sense of the term' and by Fletcher Moulton LJ as being 'merely present' (see [1907] 2 KB 141 at 151). My Lords, whatever the acceptability of those descriptions 90 years ago, I can only agree with the Appellate Division of the Alberta Supreme Court in *Motherwell v Motherwell* (1976) 73 DLR (3d) 62 at 77, that they are 'rather light treatment of a wife, at least in today's society where she is no longer considered subservient to her husband'. Current statutes give effect to current perceptions by according spouses a special status in respect of the matrimonial home, as by enabling the court to make orders regarding occupation (see in England the Family Law Act 1996, ss 30 and 31). Although such provisions and orders thereunder do not of themselves confer proprietary rights, they support in relation to amenities the force and common sense of the words of Clement JA in *Motherwell v Motherwell* (at 78):

> Here we have a wife harassed in the matrimonial home. She has a status, a right to live there with her husband and children. I find it absurd to say that her occupancy of the matrimonial home is insufficient to found an action in nuisance.

As between spouses and *de facto* partners the question whether contributions in money or services give a proprietary equitable interest in a matrimonial home is a notoriously difficult one today, wrestled with throughout the common law world. Nuisance actions would seem better left free of the complication of this side issue.

The status of children living at home is different and perhaps more problematical but, on consideration, I am persuaded by the majority of the Court of Appeal in *Khorasandjian v Bush* [1993] QB 727 and the weight of North American jurisprudence to the view that they, too, should be entitled to relief for substantial and unlawful interference with the amenities of their home. Internationally the distinct interests of children are increasingly recognised. The United Nations Convention on the Rights of the Child (New York, 20 November 1989; TS 44 (1992); Cm 1976), ratified by the United Kingdom in 1991 and the most widely ratified human rights treaty in history, acknowledges children as fully-fledged beneficiaries of human rights. Article 16 declares *inter alia* that no child shall be subjected to unlawful interference with his or her home and that the child has the right to the protection of law against such interference. International standards such as this may be taken into account in shaping the common law.

The point just mentioned can be taken further. Article 16 of the Convention on the Rights of the Child adopts some of the language of art 12 of the Universal Declaration of Human Rights (Paris, 10 December 1948; UN TS 2 (1949); Cmd 7226) and art 8 of the European Convention for the Protection of Human Rights and Fundamental Freedoms (Rome, 4 November 1950; TS 71 (1953); Cmd 8969). These provisions are aimed, in part, at protecting the home and are construed to give protection against nuisances (see *Arrondelle v UK* (Application No 7889/77) (1982) 26 DR 5 (aircraft noise) and *Lopez Ostra v Spain* (1994) 20 EHRR 277 (fumes and smells from a waste treatment plant)). The protection is regarded as going beyond possession or property rights (see Harris, O'Boyle and Warbrick *Law of the European Convention on Human Rights* (1995), p 319). Again I think that this is a legitimate consideration in support of treating residence as an acceptable basis of standing at common law in the present class of case....

[His Lordship considered the position in other common law jurisdictions, and the views of academic writers, and continued:] My Lords, there is a maxim *communis error facit jus*. I have collected the foregoing references not to invoke it, however, but to suggest respectfully that on this hitherto unsettled issue the general trend of leading scholarly opinion need not be condemned as erroneous. Although hitherto the law of England on the point has not been settled by your Lordships' House, it is agreed on all hands that some link with the land is necessary for standing to sue in private nuisance. The precise nature of that link remains to be defined, partly because of the ambiguity of 'occupy' and its derivatives. In ordinary usage the verb can certainly include 'reside in', which is indeed the first meaning given in the *Concise Oxford Dictionary*.

In logic more than one answer can be given. Logically it is possible to say that the right to sue for interference with the amenities of a home should be confined to those with proprietary interests and licensees with exclusive possession. No less logically, the right can be accorded to all who live in the home. Which test should be adopted, that is to say which should be the governing principle, is a question of the policy of the law. It is a question not capable of being answered by analysis alone. All that analysis can do is expose the alternatives. Decisions such as *Malone*'s case do not attempt that kind of analysis, and in refraining from recognising that value judgements are involved they compare less than favourably with the approach of the present-day Court of Appeal in *Khorasandjian's* case and this case. The reason why I prefer the alternative advocated with unwonted vigour of expression by the doyen of living tort writers is that it gives better effect to widespread conceptions concerning the home and family.

Of course in this field, as in most others, there will be borderline cases and anomalies wherever the lines are drawn. Thus there are, for instance, the lodger and, as some of your Lordships note, the au pair girl (although she may not figure among the present plaintiffs). It would seem weak, though, to refrain from laying down a just rule for spouses and children on the ground that it is not easy to know where to draw the lines regarding other persons. Without being wedded to this solution, I am not persuaded that there is sufficient justification for disturbing the conclusion adopted by Pill LJ with the concurrence of Neill and Waite LJJ [in the present case]. Occupation of the property as a home is, to me, an acceptable criterion, consistent with the traditional concern for the sanctity of family life and the Englishman's home—which need not in this context include his workplace. As already mentioned, it is consistent also with international standards.

Other resident members of the family, including such *de facto* partners and lodgers as may on the particular facts fairly be considered as having a home in the premises, could therefore be allowed standing to complain of truly serious interference with the domestic amenities lawfully enjoyed by them. By contrast, the policy of the law need not extend to giving a remedy in nuisance to non-resident employees in commercial premises. The employer is responsible for their welfare. On this part of the case I have only to add that normally there should not be any difficulty about sensible compromises with the author of the nuisance. Members of a household impliedly authorise the householder to represent them in such matters . . .

P. Cane, 'What a Nuisance!' (1997) 113 LQR 515, 519–20

Torts and Causes of Action

Underlying much of the reasoning in *Hunter* is a certain approach to the structure of tort law. For at least 100 years, tort law has been seen as made up of what I have elsewhere dubbed 'a loose federation of causes of action' called 'torts'. Torts performed a similar function to that of the old forms of action. This can clearly be seen clearly in assertions by Lord Goff and Lord Hoffmann in *Hunter* to the effect that the Court of Appeal in *Khorasandjian v Bush* should not have attempted to develop the law in the direction they favoured by altering the elements of the tort of nuisance but, if at all, by developing a new tort of harassment. It can also be seen in the idea that damages for bodily and psychological injury and for property damage should be sought by suing not in the tort of nuisance but rather in the tort of negligence. Thinking about tort law in such formularistic terms may not always be helpful. For instance, if it be asked why compensation for personal injury or property damage should not be recoverable in a nuisance action, the answer might be (Lord Hoffmann at p. 706) that 'negligence [is] based on fault but protect[s] interests of many kinds' whereas 'liability in nuisance [is] strict but protects only interests in land'. This answer is unsatisfactory for at least three reasons: it apparently fails to take account of the centrality to the tort of nuisance of the fault-based concept of unreasonableness; secondly, it fails to explain why the basis of liability for amenity damage should be more favourable to claimants (assuming liability in nuisance to be strict in some sense) than the basis of liability for personal injury and property damage; and thirdly, it provides no explanation of why a party who suffers injury which would be actionable in nuisance if the party had the required standing, but who personally lacks standing to sue in nuisance, should be able to make a claim in negligence for personal injury and property damage but not for amenity damage. . . .

Central to *Hunter* was the question of when the law should compensate for loss of enjoyment of life. Should it only provide such compensation to victims of personal injury and to persons in exclusive occupation of land; or should the class of potential beneficiaries of such compensation be expanded? And should any liability to pay such compensation be strict or based on negligence or intention? Answers to such questions found by consideration of whether nuisance is a property tort or whether claims to such compensation should be framed in nuisance or negligence are likely to be at best oblique and at worst insensitive to the social importance of the issue as stake. The traditional division of the law into 'torts' is, at most, of expository value. To allow the preservation of the supposed conceptual integrity of this structure to influence the law's approach to social problems is to allow the tail to wag the dog....

COMMENTARY

As the extract from Cane illustrates, the decision in *Hunter* has not met with universal approval (see also O'Sullivan [1997] CLJ 483; Oliphant (1998) 6 Tort L Rev 21).

There is little doubt that, historically, the forbears of the modern tort of nuisance (the assize of nuisance and the action on the case) were concerned with the protection of interests in land (see Loengard, 'The Assize of Nuisance' [1978] CLJ 144; and more generally *Baker*, ch. 24). But should the historical tie to land law be retained? The majority in *Hunter* do consider whether there are policy grounds for expanding the role of nuisance but find no pressing case for such expansion. In particular, the concern which prompted the Court of Appeal in *Khorasandjian*, that of providing a remedy for the defendant's harassing behaviour, has been mitigated by the Protection from Harassment Act 1997 (see Ch. 2), and in any event Lord Hoffmann felt that the legal basis for prohibiting such conduct should be found in the law relating to intentional torts rather than nuisance. The extent to which courts have been prepared to expand and modify existing torts depends upon the court's view of the need for a remedy to be given in the circumstances of the case. Perhaps their Lordships did not think, on the facts, that the price of doctrinal uncertainty was worth paying to give these plaintiffs a remedy.

Even accepting that, generally, nuisance is a tort against land, the limits of this approach remain to be explored. Lord Hoffmann accepted that consequential damage (i.e. loss of profits, or any chattels or livestock damaged or destroyed as a result of the nuisance) could be recovered in the tort of nuisance. However, he refused to accept that 'inconvenience, annoyance or even illness' suffered by persons on land as a result of smells or dust was damage consequential upon the injury to the land; rather 'the injury to the amenity of the land consists in the fact that the persons on it are liable to suffer inconvenience, annoyance or illness'. But if nuisance consists of an interference with one's right to quiet enjoyment of land, this does not mean that the claimant has in fact suffered any inconvenience; indeed, the Court of Appeal has recently held that a claimant can only expect to receive nominal damages for interference with the amenity of land that is unoccupied (*Dobson v Thames Water Utilities* [2009] EWCA Civ 28; see further p. 671, below). Where there *is* actual inconvenience, it is perfectly possible to treat that inconvenience or illness as consequential upon the nuisance (see Oliphant (1998) 6 Tort L Rev 21). If this is correct, it would mean that a claimant whose property is exposed to dust as a result of a nuisance and who suffers a physical injury as a result would receive an award of damages greater than a claimant in the same position who suffers no physical injury. Of course, the injury to the land (the loss of the use of quiet enjoyment) is the same in both cases, but the physical injury is consequential to that injury, so why should damages not be awarded for it in the same way as if the nuisance had damaged the claimant's chattels? However, the House of Lords has recently affirmed that damages for death or personal injury are not recoverable in private nuisance (*Transco plc v*

Stockport Metropolitan Borough Council [2004] 2 AC 1; cf. *In re Corby Group Litigation* [2009] QB 335, holding that *Hunter* did not affect previous authority suggesting that damages for personal injury can be recovered in public nuisance).

As far as the claim was for personal injury in *Hunter*, Lord Hoffmann thought the appropriate action was negligence. Thus one who has no standing to sue in nuisance and who suffers a physical injury as a result of the defendant's nuisance cannot claim unless an action can be brought in negligence. Nor can he claim solely for the distress or discomfort resulting from the defendant's acts, even if caused negligently, for this is not actionable damage for the tort of negligence.

Cane asks why a party who suffers injury which would be actionable in nuisance if the party had the required standing, but who personally lacks standing to sue in nuisance, should be able to make a claim in negligence for personal injury and property damage but not for amenity damage? The simple answer is that the law has thus far not felt the need to extend the general duty imposed through the law of negligence not to inflict careless physical injury or property damage upon another to include a duty not to cause discomfort or distress. Conversely, the exalted status traditionally given to property rights in the common law means that anything that can be characterised as an interference with land is entitled to a greater level of protection. Of course, whether one thinks such a balance appropriate, especially in the modern era, is a different matter.

Whatever the limitations of the common law, the passage of the Human Rights Act 1998 provides an alternative, albeit limited, remedy for those without a proprietary or possessory interest in affected land who nonetheless reside there. If a public authority is responsible for interfering with a person's right to private and family life protected by Art 8 of the ECHR—and conduct that amounts to an interference with amenity for the purpose of a private nuisance action may well do so—an action will lie for breach of the public authority's obligations under s. 6 of the Human Rights Act. However, damages will only be awarded in such actions if it is necessary to afford just satisfaction to the claimant (see Human Rights Act 1998, s. 8). In *Dobson v Thames Water Utilities* [2009] EWCA Civ 28 the Court of Appeal held that one factor to be considered in determining whether an award of damages was necessary in that sense was whether those who had a proprietary or possessory interest in the land had recovered damages for the interference in an action for private nuisance. This was because the assessment of such awards would in some degree consider the effect on those who resided there. In *Dobson* the question was whether an award of damages in a private nuisance action to the parents of a child would prevent the child from recovering damages for breach of his Article 8 rights in an action under the Human Rights Act 1998. The Court of Appeal refused to go this far, holding that each case would need to be determined on its own facts, but indicated that in such a case it might well have this effect. The result is that, even if an action under the Human Rights Act for breach of Article 8 is available, it may be less attractive than suing in private nuisance as a damages award cannot be guaranteed. For comment on *Dobson*, see Tofaris [2009] CLJ 273.

More generally, is the limitation on the claim for amenity damage to those with a possessory or proprietary interest in land consistent with the right to private and family life protected by Article 8 of the ECHR? In *McKenna v British Aluminium Ltd* [2002] Env LR 30, a large number of residents adjoining the defendant's factory brought actions in nuisance for mental distress and physical harm against the defendant in respect of, amongst other things, the noise and emissions emanating from it. Although some of the claimants had a possessory or proprietary interest in the affected land, some of them were children who were merely permanent residents living in the properties. Neuberger J refused to strike out the claim, holding that it was at least arguable that, in light of the different legal landscape of the Human Rights Act, a court might depart from *Hunter v Canary Wharf* and relax the standing requirement to sue in private nuisance. He held:

> There is obviously a powerful case for saying that effect has not been properly given to Article 8.1 if a person with no interest in the home, but who has lived in the home for some time and had his enjoyment of the home interfered with, is at the mercy of the person who owns the home, as the only person who can bring proceedings . . . .

It should be remembered that the decision of Neuberger J was on a striking-out application, so it was only necessary that he find it arguable that the claimants had standing to sue in nuisance. It remains to be seen whether the need to provide a remedy for people in the position of the child claimants in *McKenna* for breach of their Article 8 rights will force a re-consideration of *Hunter v Canary Wharf* as far as standing to sue in nuisance is concerned. It is interesting to note that some of the disappointed plaintiffs in *Hunter* took their case to Strasbourg, where the European Commission of Human Rights found that Article 8 applied to all the plaintiffs, not just to those with a possessory or proprietary interest in land. However, the applicants' claim was unsuccessful as a balance had to be struck between the interests of the applicants as individuals and those of the community as a whole. Given that the interference did not affect the applicant's health, was for a limited time only, and resulted from a planning decision, the government convinced the Commission that the development met a pressing social need and was proportionate (see Commentary on *McKenna v British Aluminum Ltd* [2002] Env LR 30). Whether the interference with Article 8 rights could be justified as necessary in a case like *McKenna*, where the interference affected the health of the claimants, remains to be seen. If it cannot, it seems clear that all persons affected must be able to sue for breach of their Article 8 rights, not just those with a possessory or proprietary interest in the affected land. Where the interference is by a public authority an action may be possible under the Human Rights Act 1998 for a breach of the s. 6 obligation that a public authority act compatibly with the Convention (as in *Dobson*), but if this is not available it is certainly possible that the tort of nuisance could be expanded to fill this gap in the law. If it is, however, it is difficult to see how the tort could still be characterised as one that protects interests in land; one's interest in one's own privacy is clearly a personal, and not a proprietary, interest.

4. Defences

(a) Claimant Coming to the Nuisance

Miller v Jackson [1977] QB 966

The plaintiffs purchased a house which was adjacent to a small cricket ground. Cricket had been played at the ground since 1905, but the plaintiffs' house was only built in 1972. As a consequence of the proximity of the house to the ground cricket balls were hit into the plaintiffs' garden during the cricket season, some of which caused damage to the plaintiff's property. Despite the erection of a chain fence to a height of just under 15 feet, cricket balls continued to land on the plaintiffs' property. The cricket club offered to supply and fit a safety net over the garden, to pay for any damage or expenses, and to install unbreakable glass in the windows of the plaintiffs' house. The plaintiffs rejected these offers and commenced proceedings in negligence and nuisance, seeking damages and an injunction. It was conceded by the club that, as long as cricket was played on the ground, there was no way in which it could stop balls going into the plaintiffs' premises. The trial judge upheld the plaintiffs' claim and granted an injunction.

Lord Denning MR

In our present case, too, nuisance was pleaded as an alternative to negligence. The tort of nuisance in many cases overlaps the tort of negligence. The boundary lines were discussed in two adjoining cases in the Privy Council: *The Wagon Mound (No 2)* and *Goldman v Hargrave* ([1967] 1 AC 645 at 657). But there is at any rate one important distinction between them. It lies in the nature of the remedy sought. Is it damages? Or an injunction? If the plaintiff seeks a remedy in damages for injury done to him or his property, he can lay his claim either in negligence or in nuisance. But, if he seeks an injunction to stop the playing of cricket altogether, I think he must make his claim in nuisance. The books are full of cases where an injunction has been granted to restrain the continuance of a nuisance. But there is no case, so far as I know, where it has been granted so as to stop a man being negligent. At any rate in a case of this kind, where an occupier of a house or land seeks to restrain his neighbour from doing something on his own land, the only appropriate cause of action, on which to base the remedy of an injunction, is nuisance.... It is the very essence of a private nuisance that it is the unreasonable use by a man of his land to the detriment of his neighbour....

I would, therefore, adopt this test: is the use by the cricket club of this ground for playing cricket a reasonable use of it? To my mind it is a most reasonable use. Just consider the circumstances. For over 70 years the game of cricket has been played on this ground to the great benefit of the community as a whole, and to the injury of none. No one could suggest that it was a nuisance to the neighbouring owners simply because an enthusiastic batsman occasionally hit a ball out of the ground for six to the approval of the admiring onlookers. Then I would ask: does it suddenly become a nuisance because one of the neighbours chooses to build a house on the very edge of the ground, in such a position that it may well be struck by the ball on the rare occasion when there is a hit for six? To my mind the answer is plainly No. The building of the house does not convert the playing of cricket into a nuisance when it was not so before. If and insofar as any damage is caused to the house or anyone in it, it is because of the position in which it was built. Suppose that the house had not been built by a developer, but by a private owner. He would be in much the same position as the farmer who previously put his cows in the field. He could not complain if a batsman hit a six out of the ground and, by a million to one chance, it struck a cow or even the farmer himself. He would be in no better position than a spectator at Lord's or the Oval or at a motor rally. At any rate, even if he could claim damages for the loss of the cow or the injury, he could not get an injunction to stop the cricket. If the private owner could not get an injunction, neither should a developer or a purchaser from him....

In this case it is our task to balance the right of the cricket club to continue playing cricket on their cricket ground, as against the right of the householder not to be interfered with. On taking the balance, I would give priority to the right of the cricket club to continue playing cricket on the ground, as they have done for the last 70 years. It takes precedence over the right of the newcomer to sit in his garden undisturbed. After all he bought the house four years ago in mid-summer when the cricket season was at its height. He might have guessed that there was a risk that a hit for six might possibly land on his property. If he finds that he does not like it, he ought, when cricket is played, to sit in the other side of the house or in the front garden, or go out; or take advantage of the offers the club have made to him of fitting unbreakable glass, and so forth. Or, if he does not like that, he ought to sell his house and move elsewhere. I expect there are many who would gladly buy it in order to be near the cricket field and open space. At any rate he ought not to be allowed to stop cricket being played on this ground.

Geoffrey Lane LJ

Was there here a use by the defendants of their land involving an unreasonable interference with the plaintiffs' enjoyment of their land? There is here in effect no dispute that there has been and is likely to be in the future an interference with the plaintiffs' enjoyment of no 20 Brackenridge. The only question is whether it is unreasonable. It is a truism to say that this is a matter of degree. What that means is this. A balance has to be maintained between on the one hand the rights of the individual to enjoy his house and garden without the threat of damage and on the other hand the rights of the public in general or a neighbour to engage in lawful pastimes. Difficult questions may sometimes arise when the defendants' activities are offensive to the senses, for example by way of noise. Where, as here, the damage or potential damage is physical the answer is more simple. There is, subject to what appears hereafter, no excuse I can see which exonerates the defendants from liability in nuisance for what they have done or from what they threaten to do. It is true no one has yet been physically injured. That is probably due to a great extent to the fact that the householders in Brackenridge desert their gardens whilst cricket is in progress. The danger of injury is obvious and is not slight enough to be disregarded. There is here a real risk of serious injury.

There is, however, one obviously strong point in the defendants' favour. They or their predecessors have been playing cricket on this ground (and no doubt hitting sixes out of it) for 70 years or so. Can someone by building a house on the edge of the field in circumstances where it must have been obvious that balls might be hit over the fence, effectively stop cricket being played? Precedent apart, justice would seem to demand that the plaintiffs should be left to make the most of the site they have elected to occupy with all its obvious advantages and all its equally obvious disadvantages. It is pleasant to have an open space over which to look from your bedroom and sitting room windows, so far as it is possible to see over the concrete wall. Why should you complain of the obvious disadvantages which arise from the particular purpose to which the open space is being put? Put briefly, can the defendants take advantage of the fact that the plaintiffs have put themselves in such a position by coming to occupy a house on the edge of a small cricket field, with the result that what was not a nuisance in the past now becomes a nuisance? If the matter were *res integra*, I confess I should be inclined to find for the defendants. It does not seem just that a long-established activity, in itself innocuous, should be brought to an end because someone chooses to build a house nearby and so turn an innocent pastime into an actionable nuisance. Unfortunately, however, the question is not open. In *Sturges v Bridgman* this very problem arose. The defendant had carried on a confectionary shop with a noisy pestle and mortar for more than 20 years. Although it was noisy, it was far enough away from neighbouring premises not to cause trouble to anyone, until the plaintiff, who was a physician, built a consulting-room on his own land but immediately adjoining the confectionary shop. The noise and vibrations seriously interfered with the consulting-room and became a nuisance to the physician. The defendant contended that he had acquired the right either at common law or under the Prescription Act 1832 by uninterrupted use for more than 20 years to impose the inconvenience. It was held by the Court of Appeal, affirming the judgement of Jessel MR, that use such as this which was, prior to the construction of the consulting room, neither preventable nor actionable, could not found a prescriptive right. That decision involved the assumption, which so far as one can discover has never been questioned, that it is no answer to a claim in nuisance for the defendant to show that the plaintiff brought the trouble on his own head by building or coming to live in a house so close to the defendant's premises that he would inevitably be affected by the defendant's activities, where no one had been affected previously. See also *Bliss v Hall* (1838) 4 Bing NC 183. It may be that this rule works injustice, it may be that one would decide the matter differently in the absence of authority. But we are bound by the decision in *Sturges v Bridgman* and it is not for this court as I see it to alter a rule which has stood for so long.

Cumming-Bruce LJ agreed with Geoffrey Lane LJ that the cricket club's activities amounted to a nuisance but thought an injunction was an inappropriate remedy. **Lord Denning MR** agreed that, if, contrary to his judgment, the conduct did amount to a nuisance, an injunction should not be granted.

Appeal allowed.

COMMENTARY

One issue for the court in *Miller* was whether it was a defence to a nuisance action to argue that the plaintiff 'came to the nuisance'. The majority of the Court of Appeal (Lord Denning MR dissenting) applied *Sturges v Bridgman* (1879) 11 Ch 85 and held that the defendant's activity did amount to a nuisance despite its longevity. In *Sturges* it was held that the defendant's conduct amounted to a nuisance even though he had been carrying on his business as a confectioner for more than twenty years before the plaintiff set up his surgery next to him. The *Sturges* court recognised that this was a difficult problem but felt it was against public policy that the use and value of the adjoining land should be restricted and diminished 'by reason of the continuance of acts incapable of physical interruption, and which the law gives no power to prevent'.

Perhaps the plaintiff did not know of the disruptive nature of the defendant's trade in *Sturges*, but the same cannot be said where the alleged nuisance is self-evident. In *Leakey v National Trust* [1980] QB 485 Megaw LJ, whilst acknowledging that it was no defence to argue that the plaintiff came to the nuisance, held that it may be a defence to show that 'the plaintiffs, knowing of the danger to their property, by word or deed, had showed their willingness to accept that danger'. It was also accepted that where the facts would provide a defence of *volenti non fit injuria* they would also provide a defence in a case such as *Leakey*. Not too much should be read into these statements from *Leakey*: as argued above the basis of liability in *Leakey* is best seen as negligence and *volenti* has long been a defence to a negligence action. It is still the law that if the claimant, with knowledge of the defendant's activity, chooses to live in an area where he may be affected by that activity it is no defence to a nuisance action to argue that the claimant somehow consented to the nuisance. If the claimant complains of an interference with his amenity, however, the state of the surrounding area is clearly relevant. Although it is no defence to say that the claimant came to the nuisance, the claimant can only expect the amenity consistent with the locality, a point that was expressly made in *Sturges v Bridgman*.

If the defendant's conduct has amounted to a nuisance for twenty years a defence of prescription may be available (i.e. the defendant acquires a right to carry out the activity free from any liability in nuisance). However, it is not enough that the conduct is carried on for in excess of twenty years; it must constitute a nuisance for twenty years. In *Sturges v Bridgman* the defendant had carried out his operations as a confectioner for twenty years, but as the plaintiff had not lived next door for that period the conduct was not a nuisance for twenty years so the defence failed. In addition, the claimant must have knowledge that the defendant's conduct amounts to a nuisance (see *Liverpool Corporation v Coghill & Son Ltd* [1918] 1 Ch 307; *Barney v BP Truckstops Ltd*, Chancery Division, 19 January 1995—plaintiff's lack of knowledge of defendant's use of sewers for over twenty years prevented successful claim of a prescriptive right).

(b) Statutory Authority and Planning Permission

It has long been the case that no action lies for doing that which the legislature has authorised, if it be done without negligence, although it occasions damage; but an action does lie for doing that which the legislature has authorised, if it be done negligently (*Geddis v Proprietors of Bann Reservoirs* (1878) 3 App Cas 430 at 455 per Lord Blackburn). In *Allen v Gulf Oil Refining Limited* [1981] AC 1001 the defendant built and operated an oil refinery under the authority of the Gulf Oil Refining Act 1965. The plaintiff was one of a number of residents of the surrounding area who had been adversely affected by noxious odours, vibrations, and offensive noise levels emanating from the refinery, as well as alleging that she and members of her family lived in fear of explosion at the refinery. The defendant pleaded statutory authority, and the House of Lords by a majority held that the statute expressly or by necessary implication gave authority to construct and operate the refinery, and that this authority conferred on the defendant immunity from proceedings for any nuisance which might be the inevitable result of constructing a refinery on the land, however carefully sited, constructed and operated. The question in thus one of statutory construction. However, it should be noted that statutory authority is subject to review in accordance with human rights law; if the authorised activity interferes with a person's right to privacy under Article 8(1) it will be necessary for the government to justify it (see e.g. *Hatton v United Kingdom* (2003) 37 EHRR 28—introduction of new system of night flying over Heathrow Airport engaged Article 8 despite s. 76(1) of the Civil Aviation Act 1982 which prevented actions relating to aircraft noise if the flights were in accord with an approved scheme, but no breach found on the facts).

Does the grant of planning permission in respect of the defendant's activity by a local planning authority have the same effect as statutory authority? The issue was considered by the Court of Appeal in *Allen* [1980] QB 156, where both Lord Denning MR and Cumming Bruce LJ held that it did not. Cumming-Bruce LJ commented that the only jurisdiction a planning authority had to authorise nuisance, if any, was its power to permit the change of the character of a neighbourhood in relation to the comfort and convenience of the inhabitants. However, in *Gillingham Borough Council v Medway (Chatham) Dock Co Ltd* [1993] QB 343, a case involving the granting of planning permission for the defendant to operate a twenty-four-hour commercial wharf in an area that had formerly been part of the Chatham Royal Dockyard, Buckley J hinted that planning consents relating to major redevelopments that of necessity prejudiced some local inhabitants might act as a defence to subsequent private nuisance actions by those adversely affected. It is unclear whether Buckley J was intending to say anything more than that large-scale planning consents can affect liability in private nuisance by changing the character of the neighbourhood (see p. 648, above). If he was, later cases have rejected this approach. Any suggestion that planning authority in all cases amounts to statutory authority and hence provides a defence to a nuisance action was disapproved in *Wheeler v JJ Saunders* [1996] Ch 19. Moreover, when *Hunter v Canary*

Wharf was before the Court of Appeal, one argument before the court was that the planning permission under which the development of the docklands area in London took place
authorised any nuisance which arose from it. As in *Gillingham*, the planning permission
was granted as part of a major redevelopment of the area. Even in these circumstances, however, Pill LJ accepted *Gillingham* only in so far as it suggested that the changed character of
the neighbourhood was brought about by the planning permission. This has recently been
affirmed by the Court of Appeal in *Watson v Croft Promo-Sport Ltd* [2009] EWCA Civ 15,
Sir Andrew Morritt C rejecting the notion that there was any category of 'strategic planning
decisions' that operated in the same way as statutory authority. The result is that planning
permission is relevant, if at all, only to the locality in which the alleged nuisance is committed. Even in major redevelopments where the competing interests of developers and existing
residents can be expected to have been weighed, planning permission is not akin to statutory authority. The common law has traditionally been slow to sanction the appropriation of
private rights in the public interest. For comment on *Gillingham*, see Steele and Jewell (1993)
56 MLR 568, and more generally Crawford 'Public Law Rules over Private Law' [1992] J
Env L 251.

Where planning permission does change the character of the neighbourhood so that it
may be difficult to sustain a claim in nuisance, it is possible that an argument may be made
that the planning permission falls foul of Article 8 of the ECHR. However, although the
courts have acknowledged that planning decisions are not immune from review for compliance with Article 8, it is clear that proper compliance with planning procedures will in most
cases be sufficient to ensure Article 8 is not infringed (see *South Bucks District Council v
Porter* [2002] 1 WLR 1359; *Lough v First Secretary of State* [2004] 1 WLR 2557).

5. Remedies

A claimant in nuisance seeks the remedy of an injunction to prevent the nuisance from
continuing, or damages for any loss caused by the nuisance, or both. Where the nuisance
has caused damage to property, damages are assessed according to the normal principles
relating to this type of damage (generally the cost of either replacing or repairing the property, whichever is less). More difficult is the assessment of the damages for loss of amenity.
In *Bone v Searle* [1975] 1 WLR 797 the plaintiffs could not show that the foul smell from the
defendant's pig farm had caused a reduction in the capital value of their properties, even
though it did constitute a nuisance. In considering what damages the plaintiffs were entitled
to Stephenson LJ thought that there was 'some parallel' between damages for loss of amenity
in personal injury claims and the loss of amenity as a result of a nuisance. This approach was
rejected by Lord Hoffmann in *Hunter v Canary Wharf* [1997] AC 855 because the damage
to the utility of the land caused by the nuisance was unrelated to the plaintiff's personal
discomfort or distress (cf. *Lloyd v Symonds*, Court of Appeal Civil Division, 20 March 1998).
The analogy suggested by Lord Hoffmann was with awards made for loss of amenity in
breach of contract cases where the contract is for the satisfaction of a personal preference
(see *Jarvis v Swans Tours Ltd* [1973] QB 233; *Jackson v Horizon Holidays Ltd* [1975] 1 WLR
1468; *Ruxley Electronics and Construction Ltd v Forsyth* [1996] AC 344; *Farley v Skinner*
[2002] 2 AC 732). However, in *Dobson v Thames Water Utilities* [2009] EWCA Civ 28, the
Court of Appeal accepted that even though the gist of private nuisance consisted of an interference with land, the valuation of that interference in the case of loss of amenity should

consider 'the actual impact' and the 'actual experiences' of those in occupation of the property. It is not clear how this is consistent with *Hunter v Canary Wharf* where their Lordships explicitly stated that damages for loss of amenity should not be increased because more people are in occupation, The Court of Appeal argued that its approach could be justified by Lord Hoffmann's comment that the award could be increased by the 'size, commodious and value of the property' but these indicia relate to the land itself, not to those who occupy it. As Tofaris comments ([2009] CLJ 273, 274): 'simultaneously holding that damages for nuisance are not to be increased according to the number of household members inconvenienced by a particular intrusion and stating that their experience offers the best evidence as to the practical effect of that intrusion on amenity can lead to ambiguity'.

In 1854 the Common Law Procedure Act gave the common law courts a limited power to grant equitable relief, and in 1858 s. 2 of Lord Cairns's Act allowed the Court of Chancery, where an injunction was sought, 'to award damages to the party injured, either in addition to or in substitution for such injunction or specific performance', and this power was retained in the Judicature Acts. The following extract deals with the circumstances in which a court should exercise its discretion to award damages in lieu of an injunction.

Shelfer v City of London Electric Lighting Company [1895] 1 Ch 287

An electric lighting company erected powerful engines and other works on land near to a house which was subject to a lease. Owing to excavations for the foundations of the engines, and to vibration and noise from the working of them, structural injury was caused to the house, and annoyance and discomfort to the lessee. The lessee and the reversioners brought separate actions against the company for an injunction and damages in respect of the nuisance and injury. One issue for the court was when it should use its statutory power to award damages in lieu of an injunction. On the facts the Court of Appeal allowed an appeal against the trial judge's refusal to grant an injunction.

A. L. Smith LJ

Many Judges have stated, and I emphatically agree with them, that a person by committing a wrongful act (whether it be a public company for public purposes or a private individual) is not thereby entitled to ask the Court to sanction his doing so by purchasing his neighbour's rights, by assessing damages in that behalf, leaving his neighbour with the nuisance, or his lights dimmed, as the case may be.

In such cases the well-known rule is not to accede to the application, but to grant the injunction sought, for the plaintiff's legal right has been invaded, and he is prima facie entitled to an injunction.

There are, however, cases in which this rule may be relaxed, and in which damages may be awarded in substitution for an injunction as authorized by this section.

In any instance in which a case for an injunction has been made out, if the plaintiff by his acts or laches has disentitled himself to an injunction the Court may award damages in its place. So again, whether the case be for a mandatory injunction or to restrain a continuing nuisance, the appropriate remedy may be damages in lieu of an injunction, assuming a case for an injunction to be made out.

In my opinion, it may be stated as a good working rule that—

(1) If the injury to the plaintiff's legal rights is small,

(2) And is one which is capable of being estimated in money,

(3) And is one which can be adequately compensated by a small money payment,

(4) And the case is one in which it would be oppressive to the defendant to grant an injunction:—
then damages in substitution for an injunction may be given.

There may also be cases in which, though the four above-mentioned requirements exist, the defendant by his conduct, as, for instance, hurrying up his buildings so as if possible to avoid an injunction, or otherwise acting with a reckless disregard to the plaintiff's rights, has disentitled himself from asking that damages may be assessed in substitution for an injunction.

It is impossible to lay down any rule as to what, under the differing circumstances of each case, constitutes either a small injury, or one that can be estimated in money, or what is a small money payment, or an adequate compensation, or what would be oppressive to the defendant. This must be left to the good sense of the tribunal which deals with each case as it comes up for adjudication. For instance, an injury to the plaintiff's legal right to light to a window in a cottage represented by £15 might well be held to be not small but considerable; whereas a similar injury to a warehouse or other large building represented by ten times that amount might be held to be inconsiderable. Each case must be decided upon its own facts; but to escape the rule it must be brought within the exception.

COMMENTARY

Prior to the Judicature Acts an injunction could only be granted by the Court of Chancery, the injunction being an equitable remedy. The general practice of the courts prior to 1858 was stated by Lord Kingsdown, in the *Imperial Gas Light and Coke Company v Broadbent* (1859) 7 HLC 600 as follows:

The rule I take to be clearly this: if a plaintiff applies for an injunction to restrain a violation of a common law right, if either the existence of the right or the fact of its violation be disputed, he must establish that right at law but when he has established his right at law, I apprehend that unless there be something special in the case, he is entitled as of course to an injunction to prevent the recurrence of that violation.

However, *Shelfer* made it clear that the powers given to the court under Lord Cairns's Act did not change the pre-existing practice. Again, the courts' reluctance to countenance the compulsory appropriation of private rights is evident. Of course, *Shelfer* does not suggest that damages can never be awarded in lieu of an injunction, but it will be rare in nuisance cases. This is because before the defendant's conduct will be judged as a nuisance, it must be unreasonable—either causing property damage or causing a significant interference with amenity—and in those circumstances it is difficult to characterise the injury to the claimant's legal rights as small. However, as Millett LJ noted in *Jaggard v Sawyer* [1995] 1 WLR 269 at 288 (a case on restrictive covenants), 'the outcome of any particular case usually turns on the question: would it in all the circumstances be oppressive to the defendant to grant the injunction to which the plaintiff is prima facie entitled?' If the plaintiffs in *Hunter v Canary Wharf* had been able to establish that the interference with television reception caused by the Canary Wharf Tower amounted to a nuisance, could they have sought a mandatory injunction ordering it to be taken down? (Note though that an injunction granted in those circumstances would be a mandatory injunction where the cost to the defendant in complying with the injunction is a relevant factor—see *Redland Bricks v Morris* [1970] AC 652; for an example of *Shelfer* being applied in this context, see *Regan v Paul Properties Ltd* [2006] EWCA Civ 1391, [2007] Ch 135.)

However, it is not to be supposed that courts at any time have completely ignored the defendant's position in deciding whether the claimant should be granted an injunction. One technique used by judges in industrial Britain was formally to grant an injunction but suspend its operation for a period (Brenner (1974) 3 JLS 403; cf. McLaren (1983) 3 OJLS 155). More recently, it has been suggested that the public interest can be taken into account in a more explicit way. In *Miller v Jackson* (above) the claim for an injunction was refused because, even though a majority held the activity of the cricket club constituted a nuisance, Cumming-Bruce LJ held that 'the inhabitants of the village may not be deprived of their facilities for an innocent recreation which they have so long enjoyed on this ground'. However, the use of the public interest to restrain the grant of an injunction was rejected shortly afterwards in *Kennaway v Thompson* [1981] QB 88. The plaintiff owned a house next to a man-made lake on which the defendant conducted motor-boat races. The plaintiff successfully sought an injunction in the Court of Appeal, Lawton LJ expressly disapproving of the result in *Miller* (see also *Elliot v London Borough of Islington* [1991] 1 EGLR 167, *Rosling v Pinnegar*, unreported, CA Civil Division, 9 October 1998). None the less, the Court of Appeal did not ban the racing but reduced its frequency as well as limiting the number of boats and the noise they could make. It has been suggested that this amounted to a compromise, taking into account the public interest in motor-boat racing (Harris et al., *Remedies in Contract and Tort*, 2nd edn. (Cambridge: CUP, 2002), p. 483), but such an approach is not evident in the judgment of Lawton LJ who was more concerned about what would be a reasonable use by the defendant. Nor was it considered in *Watson v Croft Promo-Sport Ltd* [2009] EWCA Civ 15, where the Court of Appeal granted an injunction to restrain activities at the Croft Motor Circuit; although the defendant was allowed to continue some racing and associated activities, Sir Andrew Morritt C made it clear the public interest of the defendant's activity was relevant only in marginal cases where the damage to the claimant was minimal (which was not the case in *Watson*). Clearly the plaintiff/claimant in these cases had to put up with some noise, and it seems that the Court of Appeal was merely establishing the appropriate limit, although what is acceptable may vary depending upon whether the defendant was carrying out his activity before the plaintiff arrived or if the defendant has any control over the extent of the interference. In *Tetley v Chitty* [1986] 1 All ER 663 the defendant council let its land to a go-kart racing club which organised races on the land. The plaintiffs, who had been in occupation of their land prior to the lease, successfully obtained an injunction against the defendant prohibiting it from allowing any racing, one of the reasons being the lack of effective control over the organisation of the races.

A different approach to remedies may be required where the defendant is a public authority carrying out an activity in the public interest. In *Dennis v Ministry of Defence* [2003] EWHC 793 (QB) the claimant was the owner of a large country estate that adjoined the RAF base at Wittering. The base was used to train pilots to fly Harrier jet fighters (vertical take-off and landing aircraft). The training exercises required the aircraft to be flown at low altitude, and this produced a great deal of noise. The claimant claimed that the noise amounted to a nuisance, or, alternatively, infringed his privacy under Article 8 of the ECHR and his right to property under Article 1 of the First Protocol to the ECHR. In respect of the nuisance claim, the defendant argued that the public benefit attached to the activity prevented it from being characterised as a nuisance. Buckley J held that, whilst public benefit could not be used to justify conduct that would otherwise be a nuisance, it may be relevant to determining the remedy that should be granted. The decision was clearly influenced by two concerns:

(1) allowing the public interest to prevail might not have been consistent with a challenge to the same conduct (as a breach of Article 8's right to private and family life) under s. 7 of the Human Rights Act 1998; and (2) the difficulty that, if a nuisance was found, an injunction would have been the appropriate remedy because the conditions for the award of damage in lieu of an injunction, set out in *Shelfer*, would not have been met. By recognising that the public interest was relevant to the remedy that might be awarded, Buckley J allowed the activity to continue but effectively extended the circumstances—well beyond *Shelfer*—when damages could be granted in lieu of an injunction. Moreover, Buckley J thought his solution would satisfy the requirements of human rights law, where there were examples of compensation being paid to those individuals who suffered a disproportionate burden from an activity being carried out in the public interest. Similar sentiments were expressed by the Court of Appeal in *Marcic v Thames Water Utilities Ltd* [2002] QB 929 (noted by Buckley (2002) 118 LQR 508) but the decision was overturned by the House of Lords on the ground that the defendant, a sewerage undertaker, was regulated by a statutory scheme that provided a procedure for dealing with the claimant's complaint which was held to exclude alternative actions either in nuisance or under the Human Rights Act 1998 ([2004] 2 AC 42). Accordingly, *Dennis* stands as an isolated case which clearly departs from the previous authority of *Shelfer* and *Kennaway,* a departure than can be justified—if at all—by the concern to ensure that the result complied with human rights law. However, human rights law does not always require the payment of compensation to those who suffer disproportionately in the public interest (see e.g. *Hatton v United Kingdom* (2003) 37 EHRR 28) and it cannot be said that the remedy in nuisance would mirror precisely the remedy for breach of Article 8. (See the discussion of the Court of Appeal in *Dobson v Thames Water Utilities* [2009] EWCA Civ 28 at [37]–[46], and more generally Bagshaw (2004) 120 LQR 37, 41.) Perhaps *Dennis* is best regarded as a 'hard case making bad law' that does not change the ordinary rules relating to public benefit arguments in private nuisance.

6. Statutory Nuisances

Many public and private nuisances can today be remedied by a local authority issuing an abatement notice under the Environmental Protection Act 1990. Such a notice may be issued where a 'statutory nuisance' exists. Section 79(1) of the Act sets out a number of matters that may be deemed to be statutory nuisances provided they are in such a state or condition as to be prejudicial to health or a nuisance. The matters include the state of the premises, smoke, fumes/gases from private dwellings, industrial dust or pollution, accumulations and deposits, animals and noise. Where an abatement notice has been issued, the party to whom it is addressed commits an offence if it is not complied with, although there is provision for an appeal. In certain circumstances the local authority may abate the nuisance itself and recoup the cost from the appropriate person.

It should also be noted that there are now a large number of statutes relating to the environment regulating conduct which might amount to a nuisance. In addition to the Environmental Protection Act 1990, these include the Clean Air Act 1993, the Water Industry Act 1991, the Water Resources Act 1991 and the Noise and Statutory Nuisance Act 1993.

For further discussion see Buckley, *The Law of Nuisance*, 2nd edn. (London: Butterworths, 1996), Part III.

7. An Economic Justification for the Tort of Nuisance?

R. H. Coase, 'The Problem of Social Cost' (1960) 3 JLE 1

This paper is concerned with those actions of business firms which have harmful effects on others.... The economic analysis of such a situation has usually proceeded in terms of a divergence between the private and social product of the factory.... The conclusions to which this kind of analysis seems to have led most economists is that it would be desirable to make the owner of the factory liable for the damage caused to those injured by smoke; or to place a tax on the factory owner varying with the amount of smoke produced and equivalent in money terms to the damage it would cause; or finally, to exclude the factory from residential districts (and presumably from other areas in which the emission of smoke would have harmful effects on others).

The traditional approach has tended to obscure the nature of the choice that has to be made. The question is commonly thought of as one in which A inflicts harm on B and what has to be decided is, How should we restrain A, but this is wrong. We are dealing with a problem of a reciprocal nature. To avoid the harm to B would be to inflict harm on A. The real question that has to be decided is, Should A be allowed to harm B or should B be allowed to harm A? The problem is to avoid the more serious harm. I [have referred to] the case of a confectioner, the noise and vibrations from whose machinery disturbed a doctor in his work [*Sturges v Bridgeman*]. To avoid harming the doctor would be to inflict harm on the confectioner. The problem posed by this case was essentially whether it was worth while, as a result of restricting the methods of production which could be used by the confectioner, to secure more doctoring at the cost of a reduced supply of confectionery products....

[Coase goes on to argue that, in a world without transaction costs (put simply, the costs of making a bargain), the allocation of resources made by a business to activities that 'damage' a neighbour is optimal (i.e. economically efficient) regardless of whether the business is liable for the damage or not. This is because of the operation of the market, although he accepts that it is necessary to establish at the outset whether the business is liable for damage or not in order to facilitate the appropriate market transaction, but 'the ultimate result (which maximises the value of production) is independent of the legal position if the pricing system is assumed to work without cost'. He then provides an example:]

Let us first reconsider the case of *Sturges v Bridgman*.... The court's decision established that the doctor had the right to prevent the confectioner from using his machinery. But, of course, it would have been possible to modify the arrangements envisaged in the legal ruling by means of a bargain between the parties. The doctor would have been willing to waive his right and allow the machinery to continue in operation if the confectioner would have paid him a sum of money which was greater than the loss of income which he would suffer from having to move to a more costly or less convenient location, or (and this was suggested as a possibility) from having to build a separate wall which would deaden the noise and vibration. The confectioner would have been willing to do this if the amount he would have had to pay the doctor was less than the fall in income he would suffer if he had to change his mode of operation at this location, abandon his operation, or move his confectionery business to some other location. The solution of the problem depends essentially on whether the continued use of the machinery adds more to the confectioner's income than it subtracts from the doctor's. But now consider the situation if the confectioner had won the case. The confectioner would then have had the right to continue his noise—and vibration—generating machinery without having to pay anything to the doctor. The boot would have been on the other foot: the doctor would have had to pay the confectioner to induce him to stop using the machinery. If the doctor's income would have fallen more through the continuance of the use of this machinery than it added to the income of the confectioner, there would clearly be room for a bargain whereby the doctor paid the confectioner to stop using the machinery. That is to say, the circumstances in which it would not pay the confectioner to continue to use the machinery and to compensate the doctor for the losses that this would bring (if the doctor had the right to prevent the confectioner from using his machinery) would be those in which it would be in the interest of the doctor to make a payment to the confectioner which would induce him to discontinue the use of the machinery (if the confectioner had the right to operate the machinery).... With costless market transactions, the decision of the courts concerning liability for damage would be without effect on the allocation of resources. It was of course the view of the judges that they were affecting the working of the economic system—and in a desirable direction.... The judges' view that they were settling how the land was to be used would be true only in the case in which the costs of carrying out the necessary market transactions [between the doctor and confectioner] exceeded the gain which might be achieved by any arrangement of rights. And it would be desirable to preserve the areas (Wimpole Street...) for residential or professional use (by giving non-industrial users the right to stop the noise, vibration, smoke, etc., by injunction) only if the value of the additional residential facilities obtained was greater than the value of cakes [from the confectioner]... lost. But of this the judges seem to have been unaware...

[Coase then considers the position when the cost of market transactions are taken into account, and continues:] Of course, if market transactions were costless, all that matters (questions of equity apart) is that the rights of the various parties should be well defined and the results of legal actions easy to forecast. But as we have seen, the situation is quite different when market transactions are so costly as to make it difficult to change the arrangement of rights established by the law. In such cases the courts directly influence economic activity. It would therefore seem desirable that the courts should understand the economic consequences of their decisions and should, insofar as this is possible without creating too much uncertainty about the legal position itself, take these consequences into account when making their decisions...

A thorough examination of the presuppositions of the courts in trying such cases would be of great interest, but I have not been able to attempt it. Nevertheless, it is clear from a cursory study that the courts have often recognised the economic implications of their decisions and are aware (as many economists are not) of the reciprocal nature of the problem. Furthermore, from time to time, they take these economic implications into account, along with other factors, in arriving at their decisions...

The problem which we face in dealing with actions which have harmful effects is not simply one of restraining those responsible for the harm. What has to be decided is whether the gain from preventing the harm is greater than the loss which would be suffered elsewhere as a result of stopping the action which produced the harm. In a world in which there are costs of rearranging the rights established by the legal system, the courts, in cases relating to nuisance, are, in effect, making a decision on the economic problem and determining how resources are to be employed. It was argued that the courts are conscious of this and that they often make, although not always in a very explicit fashion, a comparison between what would be gained and what lost by preventing actions which have harmful effects...

A. W. B. Simpson, 'Victorian Judges and the Problem of Social Cost: *Tipping v St Helen's Smelting Company (1865)*', in *Leading Cases in the Common Law* (Oxford: OUP, 1995) pp. 164–7

The Problem of Social Cost

A remarkable article, 'The Problem of Social Cost', first appeared in 1960. It was the work of Professor Ronald H. Coase, the only member of a Faculty of Law ever to win a Nobel Prize. The problem he discussed is easy enough to grasp: what ought to be done about 'those actions of business firms which have harmful effects on others. The standard example is that of a factory, the smoke of which has harmful effects on those occupying neighbouring properties'. And since few uses of property have no effects on neighbours whatever, the problem is ubiquitous. In a sense it is plainly a legal problem—what ought the law to do about such cases? But it can also be seen in other ways—as an ethical problem for example—which raises questions of justice or fairness. To Coase, however, it is an economic problem—what solution is best economically? And, as we shall see, an economist's view of how the problem ought to be handled is very different from that of common lawyer....

Coase was predominantly concerned with the harmful effects of actions, with social costs, not with benefits. For example, a factory producing useful chemicals may, by emitting smoke, cause a great deal of harm to neighbours. If the factory owner does not have to pay for this harm, it may be in his self-interest to operate the factory. It can be operated profitably so long as these effects on neighbours ('externalities' in the language of economists) do not have to be taken into consideration. But, if these effects entered the equation, it might not be in the general interest that the factory be opened at all; it might do more harm than good....

Coase produces an even more radical argument. So far, we have assumed that it is the factory which causes the harm. But, from the viewpoint of an economist, this is a mistake. The question in cases of social cost is really a reciprocal one—who is to be allowed to harm whom? If the factory can emit smoke and not pay for the damage to the laundry next door, then the factory is harming the launderer. If the launderer, who chooses to hang out washing on a line, can recover compensation, then the laundry is harming the factory owner. Since someone is bound to be harmed (which Coase treats as the same thing as bearing a cost) the real question is how to minimise the harm. Coase sometimes writes as if he finds the whole notion of causing harm unintelligible. Since the smoke only harms the laundry if the launderer hangs it out, both parties cause the harm. Had President Kennedy not been in Dallas, he would never have been shot by Oswald or whoever; he and Oswald both caused the death. But Coase is really merely emphasizing the reciprocal nature of the problem of incompatible forms of land use. I suppose the same theory might, at the risk of seeming offensive, be applied to attempts to reclaim the night.

This point is linked to a further one—the factory owner and launderer, or whoever, can, whatever the state of the law on pollution, sort out their problems by making a contract. The launderer might, for example, pay the factory to relocate. Indeed, so Coase argues, if we lived in a world in which everyone behaved with economic rationality, and there were no costs or difficulties in making a bargain ('transaction costs', in the language of economists), the parties would reach an economically efficient solution. The law, or at least the law of tort, would have no function. This is true by definition. In the real world, in which hardly anyone behaves with economic rationality, and there are transaction costs, nothing whatever follows from this. But the idea has got around that Coase's observation, originally intended merely to highlight the importance of transaction costs in the real world, demonstrates that it is best to leave conflicts to be sorted out by the market rather than by government regulation. Of course it is possible to resolve conflicts of land use by private bargains. This is well illustrated in nineteenth-century case law, and was fully understood by the judges of the period. The trouble was, however, that the weakness of legal remedies provided little incentive on the part of polluters to enter into bargains. They did better by continuing to pollute....

It may well be that in some ideal world the Coasean way of approaching the problem of social cost is correct, and one which rationality dictates. But courts do not, of course, engage in any such cost benefit analysis, and a moment's consideration would suggest that, if they did, the case of *Tipping v St Helen's Smelting Company* would have occupied the trial courts for months, if not years, or at least until the money ran out. There is simply no limit to the amount of information which would be of potential relevance. Furthermore, a cost benefit analysis, applied to the circumstances of a particular case, will generate no general rule; it inevitably follows from Coase's economic theory that imposing liability will sometimes make the situation better, and sometimes worse. His thesis leads to the conclusion that, from an economist's point of view, general rules of tort liability are a mistake . . . .

The Coasean approach suggests that, in deciding the respective rights of Tipping and his neighbour, the court should investigate the economic consequences of a decision one way or the other, either at a particular level or at the level of a system, and go for the allocation which would best promote the national wealth. Courts neither do nor can do this; the idea is wholly at odds with the sort of system of private property we have, in which idiots can be the beneficiaries of gifts, nincompoops can inherit, and chinless wonders can acquire title to pheasants by shooting them. In allocating property rights, private law treats economic efficiency as quite irrelevant.

Coase has also argued that efficient solutions to problems of competing land use can, in principle, be achieved by private contract between the parties. If escaping the pollution was worth more to Tipping than to St Helen's Smelting Company, then he would, if rational, pay the company an appropriate sum to abate the nuisance; conversely the company might, if it was more profitable to continue production, have paid Tipping money to discharge the injunction. In ideal circumstances all we need is the market. No doubt in principle such things are possible, but in the real world people rarely behave with economic rationality, even if they have the least idea of what such rationality dictates; there are, in any event, powerful social limits to the market, and those who offer money to resolve quarrels run a serious risk of aggravating the situation. The story of the negotiations between Tipping and his neighbour illustrates both points. Quarrelling neighbours and common lawyers, engaged in a process of dispute resolution at the margins of a largely traditional system of property law, inhabit one world, which is real and untidy. Economists inhabit another world. Between them a gulf seems to be fixed.

COMMENTARY

One aspect of Coase's argument was that, in a market free from transaction costs, liability rules would make no ultimate difference to the parties' ability to negotiate an economically efficient solution. However, his main point (as acknowledged by Simpson) was that, in a world in which any activity imposes external costs, it should not automatically be assumed that government intervention to correct perceived imbalances in the operation of the market would be the efficient solution. However, even Coase accepted that law did play an important role in defining the limits within which the parties could bargain. The problem, as Simpson notes, is that the original boundary drawn by the law provided little incentive for the polluters to bargain. In *St Helens Smelting v Tipping*, for example, the copper smelting continued even after Tipping won damages. He managed to obtain an injunction from the Courts of Chancery (*Tipping v St Helen's Smelting Company* (1865) LR 1 Ch App 66) but, as Simpson (*Victorian Law and the Industrial Spirit*, Selden Society, 1995) notes, this only prohibited the factory from committing a nuisance. He finally managed to force the closure of the plant, which 'moved a few miles away'. In light of the weakness of the common law remedies and the recalcitrance of the polluting manufacturers, is it surprising that intervention by the state was increasingly seen as the appropriate means of curtailing pollution? For a view that the extent of government regulation was influenced by the perceived remedy offered by the tort of nuisance see Pontin, 'Tort Law and Victorian Government Growth: The Historiographical Significance of Tort in the Shadow of Chemical Pollution and Factory Safety Regulation' (1998) 18 OJLS 661.

Do you agree with Coase that the courts, albeit in a non-explicit manner, have been aware of the 'reciprocal' nature of the problem of social cost? In *Bradford Corporation v Pickles* (above) was total social gain increased by Pickles (who had no use for the water) denying the Corporation (who did) the use of the water? (See further M. Taggart, *Private Property and Abuse of Rights in Victorian England* (Oxford: OUP, 2002).) And is there any sugges-tion in the case cited by Coase (*Sturges v Bridgman*) that the courts paid any attention to the competing national interests in medicine or confectioning in reaching a decision? Even Posner, a leading proponent of the law-and-economics movement, has written: 'It is difficult to believe for example that the entire problem of pollution can be left to be sorted out by the market, or even by the market plus the common law of nuisance' (*Overcoming Law* (New Haven, Conn.: Harvard University Press, 1995), p. 414). For a more positive view of the value of Coase's theory in the context of environmental harm, see Campbell, 'Of Coase and Corn: A (sort of) Defence of Private Nuisance' (2000) 63 MLR 197 and, more generally, Ogus and Veljanovski, *Readings in the Economics of Law and Regulation* (Oxford: Clarendon Press, 1984) pp. 83–4.

III. The Rule in *Rylands v Fletcher*

We have seen above that the law of nuisance has occasionally been applied to isolated events causing damage to a neighbour's property. It was argued above that in such cases liability is more properly to be founded on the law of negligence rather than nuisance; however, an exception must be made for cases falling within the ambit of the rule in *Rylands v Fletcher*. Where there has been an escape of a dangerous thing in the course of a non-natural use of land, the occupier is liable for damage to another as a result of the escape. This is so irre-spective of whether the occupier has been at fault (i.e. it is a tort of strict liability). However, liability is not absolute; there are defences, and the defendant is only liable for the foreseeable consequences of the escape.

1. *Rylands v Fletcher*

Fletcher v Rylands (1866) LR 1 Exch 265

The defendants employed independent contractors to build a dam on land they occupied. Unbeknownst to them, the dam was constructed over five disused mine shafts, which led into the underground workings of an old mine. There was a connection between these workings and the workings of the plaintiff's mines. When the reservoir was filled the water burst into the shafts and flowed into the plaintiff's mines, and the plaintiff sought to recover damages.

Blackburn J

We think that the true rule of law is, that the person who for his own purposes brings on his lands and collects and keeps there anything likely to do mischief if it escapes, must keep it in at his peril, and, if he does not do so, is *prima facie* answerable for all the damage which is the natural consequence of its escape. He can excuse himself by shewing that the escape was owing to the plaintiff's default; or perhaps that the escape was the consequence of vis major, or the act of God; but as nothing of this sort exists here, it is unnecessary to inquire what excuse would be sufficient. The general rule, as above stated, seems on principle just. The person whose grass or corn is eaten down by the escaping cattle of his neighbour, or whose mine is flooded by the water from his neighbour's reservoir, or whose cellar is invaded by the filth of his neighbour's privy, or whose habitation is made unhealthy by the fumes and noisome vapours of his neighbour's alkali works, is damnified without any fault of his own; and it seems but reasonable and just that the neighbour, who has brought something on his own property which was not naturally there, harmless to others so long as it is confined to his own property, but which he knows to be mischievous if it gets on his neighbour's, should be obliged to make good the damage which ensues if he does not succeed in confining it to his own property. But for his act in bringing it there no mischief could have accrued, and it seems but just that he should at his peril keep it there so that no mischief may accrue, or answer for the natural and anticipated consequences. And upon authority, this we think is established to be the law whether the things so brought be beasts, or water, or filth, or stenches.

COMMENTARY

When the case went on appeal to the House of Lords (*Rylands v Fletcher* (1868) LR 3 HL 330), the decision of the Court of Exchequer Chamber was upheld. Lord Cairns drew a distinction between flooding which arose as a result of a natural use of the land and was caused by the forces of nature (which would not be actionable) and flooding as a result of a non-natural use of land (which would be). Whether there is a difference between something 'not naturally' on the land (the expression used by Blackburn J) and 'non-natural user' is doubtful, as Lord Cairns explained non-natural user as meaning 'that which in its natural condition was not in or upon it'. None the less, subsequent cases adopted the term 'non-natural use of land' and applied it in a way which was more restrictive than Blackburn J's original formulation.

The subject of damage caused by the failure of dams was very topical in the early 1860s. In March 1864 the Bradfield Reservoir of the Sheffield Waterworks Company failed, inundating the Loxley valley and flooding parts of Sheffield to a depth of nine feet. At least 238 people were killed. On the relationship between contemporaneous dam disasters and the decision in *Rylands* see Simpson, 'Bursting Reservoirs and Victorian Tort Law: *Rylands and Horrocks v Fletcher* (1868)' in *Leading Cases in the Common Law* (Oxford: OUP, 1995). Another historical aside of interest is the identity of the third law lord who decided the case alongside Lords Cairns and Cranworth, who appears to have been the Bishop of Armagh, the practice of the time being to call on lay lords to make up a quorum where necessary—see Heuston (1970) 86 LQR 160; Yale (1970) 86 LQR 311.

(a) Nuisance and *Rylands v Fletcher*

Cambridge Water Co v Eastern Counties Leather plc [1994] 2 AC 264

In the course of operating its tannery the defendant used a chemical (PCE), some of which was spilt onto the floor of its factory. Over a period of time the PCE which had been spilt seeped through the ground and was carried (and was still being carried at the date of trial) by way of an underground water-flow to the plaintiff's borehole several miles away. This resulted in the water from the borehole becoming polluted with the chemical to an extent that it failed to satisfy the minimum health requirements for drinking water, and the plaintiff was forced to find an alternative supply of water. The plaintiff sued the defendant in negligence, nuisance, and under *Rylands v Fletcher* for the cost of developing the alternative source of water. The claims were dismissed at first instance, the trial judge holding that the negligence and nuisance claims failed because the type or kind of harm suffered by the plaintiff was not foreseeable, and that the use of land was not 'non-natural' for the purposes of *Rylands v Fletcher*. The Court of Appeal rejected the plaintiff's appeal against the decision on *Rylands v Fletcher* but allowed its appeal in respect of the tort of nuisance (for reasons we need not consider further here). The House of Lords reversed the decision on nuisance and also rejected the claim based on *Rylands*, holding that, as in negligence and nuisance, the type or kind of harm suffered as a result of the escape must be reasonably foreseeable.

Lord Goff

Nuisance and the Rule in *Rylands v Fletcher*

In order to consider the question in the present case in its proper legal context, it is desirable to look at the nature of liability in a case such as the present in relation both to the law of nuisance and the rule in *Rylands v Fletcher*, and for that purpose to consider the relationship between the two heads of liability.

I begin with the law of nuisance. Our modern understanding of the nature and scope of the law of nuisance was much enhanced by Professor Newark's seminal article on 'The Boundaries of Nuisance' (1949) 65 LQR 480. The article is avowedly a historical analysis, in that it traces the nature of the tort of nuisance to its origins, and demonstrates how the original view of nuisance as a tort to land (or more accurately, to accommodate interference with servitudes, a tort directed against the plaintiff's enjoyment of rights over land) became distorted as the tort was extended to embrace claims for personal injuries, even where the plaintiff's injury did not occur while using land in his occupation. In Professor Newark's opinion (p. 487), this development produced adverse effects, viz., that liability which should have arisen only under the law of negligence was allowed under the law of nuisance which historically was a tort of strict liability; and that there was a tendency for 'cross-infection to take place, and notions of negligence began to make an appearance in the realm of nuisance proper.' But in addition, Professor Newark considered, at pp. 487–488, it contributed to a misappreciation of the decision in *Rylands v Fletcher*:

> This case is generally regarded as an important landmark—indeed, a turning point—in the law of tort; but an examination of the judgments shows that those who decided it were quite unconscious of any revolutionary or reactionary principles implicit in the decision. They thought of it as calling for no more than a restatement of settled principles, and Lord Cairns went so far as to describe those principles as 'extremely simple.' And in fact the main principle involved was extremely simple, being no more than the principle that negligence is not an element in the tort of nuisance. It is true that Blackburn J. in his great judgment in the Exchequer Chamber never once used the word 'nuisance,' but three times he cited the case of fumes escaping from an alkali works—a clear case of nuisance—as an instance of liability under the rule which he was laying down. Equally it is true that in 1866 there were a number of cases in the reports suggesting that persons who controlled dangerous things were under a strict duty to take care, but as none of these cases had anything to do with nuisance Blackburn J. did not refer to them.

But the profession as a whole, whose conceptions of the boundaries of nuisance were now becoming fogged, failed to see in *Rylands v Fletcher* a simple case of nuisance. They regarded it as an exceptional case—and the Rule in *Rylands v Fletcher* as a generalisation of exceptional cases, where liability was to be strict on account of 'the magnitude of danger, coupled with the difficulty of proving negligence' [Pollock, *Law of Torts*, (14th edn., 1939), p. 386] rather than on account of the nature of the plaintiff's interest which was invaded. They therefore jumped rashly to two conclusions: firstly, that the Rule in *Rylands v Fletcher* could be extended beyond the case of neighbouring occupiers; and secondly, that the Rule could be used to afford a remedy in cases of personal injury. Both these conclusions were stoutly denied by Lord Macmillan in *Read v Lyons* [1947] AC 156, but it remains to be seen whether the House of Lords will support his opinion when the precise point comes up for decision.

We are not concerned in the present case with the problem of personal injuries, but we are concerned with the scope of liability in nuisance and in *Rylands v Fletcher*. In my opinion it is right to take as our starting point the fact that, as Professor Newark considered, *Rylands v Fletcher* was indeed not regarded by Blackburn J as a revolutionary decision: see, e.g., his observations in *Ross v Fedden* (1872) 26 LT 966, 968. He believed himself not to be creating new law, but to be stating existing law, on the basis of existing authority; and, as is apparent from his judgment, he was concerned in particular with the situation where the defendant collects things upon his land which are likely to do mischief if they escape, in which event the defendant will be strictly liable for damage resulting from any such escape. It follows that the essential basis of liability was the collection by the defendant of such things upon his land; and the consequence was a strict liability in the event of damage caused by their escape, even if the escape was an isolated event. Seen in its context, there is no reason to suppose that Blackburn J intended to create a liability any more strict than that created by the law of nuisance; but even so he must have intended that, in the circumstances specified by him, there should be liability for damage resulting from an isolated escape.

Of course, although liability for nuisance has generally been regarded as strict, at least in the case of a defendant who has been responsible for the creation of a nuisance, even so that liability has been kept under control by the principle of reasonable user—the principle of give and take as between neighbouring occupiers of land, under which 'those acts necessary for the common and ordinary use and occupation of land and houses may be done, if conveniently done, without subjecting those who do them to an action:' see *Bamford v Turnley* (1862) 3 B & S 62, 83, per Bramwell B. The effect is that, if the user is reasonable, the defendant will not be liable for consequent harm to his neighbour's enjoyment of his land; but if the user is not reasonable, the defendant will be liable, even though he may have exercised reasonable care and skill to avoid it. Strikingly, a comparable principle has developed which limits liability under the rule in *Rylands v Fletcher*. This is the principle of natural use of the land. I shall have to consider the principle at a later stage in this judgment. The most authoritative statement of the principle is now to be found in the advice of the Privy Council delivered by Lord Moulton in *Rickards v Lothian* [1913] AC 263, 280, when he said of the rule in *Rylands v Fletcher*:

> It is not every use to which land is put that brings into play that principle. It must be some special use bringing with it increased danger to others, and must not merely be the ordinary use of the land or such a use as is proper for the general benefit of the community.

It is not necessary for me to identify precise differences which may be drawn between this principle, and the principle of reasonable user as applied in the law of nuisance. It is enough for present purposes that I should draw attention to a similarity of function. The effect of this principle is that, where it applies, there will be no liability under the rule in *Rylands v Fletcher*; but that where it does not apply, i.e. where there is a non-natural use, the defendant will be liable for harm caused to the plaintiff by the escape, notwithstanding that he has exercised all reasonable care and skill to prevent the escape from occurring.

COMMENTARY

According to Lord Goff, the historical genesis of the rule in *Rylands v Fletcher* was in the tort of nuisance, with *Rylands* being a particular application of that tort to isolated escapes. This view has subsequently been accepted by the House of Lords (*Transco plc v Stockport Metropolitan Borough Council* [2004] 2 AC 1). However, academic commentators have been less convinced that *Rylands* can be explained in this way, arguing that *Rylands* derives from a general (if vague) principle of the medieval legal system of strict liability for causing harm. This was quite different from private nuisance which was intimately connected to the protection of rights in land (see *Hunter v Canary Wharf*, above). Murphy (2004) 24 OJLS 643 and Nolan (2005) 121 LQR 421 agree with Lord Goff that *Rylands* applies only to isolated escapes. However, the *Cambridge Water* case itself suggests, to the contrary, that the rule in *Rylands v Fletcher* is capable of applying to an escape that occurs over a period of time. In *Cambridge Water*, the escape of the chemical could hardly be described as isolated: it resulted from the defendant's work practices which were repeated over a long period of time. If an isolated escape is not necessary, how then is *Rylands v Fletcher* to be distinguished from nuisance? The conventional answer is to say that the conditions for liability differ. Nuisance requires an unreasonable use of land, whilst *Rylands v Fletcher* requires a non-natural use of land. As Nolan (2005) 121 LQR 421, 434–5 comments:

The unreasonable user issue is ultimately concerned with whether or not the interference with the claimant's land is tolerable, so the focus is not so much on the nature of the defendant's activity—though this is a factor to be considered—but on whether the resulting discomfort or inconvenience is something which the claimant can, in all the circumstances, be expected to put up with. The non-natural use concept is quite different, for here the focus is not on the harm to the claimant, or even a balancing of the two parties' interests, but simply on the nature of the defendant's activity.

Given, however, that *Rylands* is now seen as a subset of nuisance, this distinction does not explain *why* the *Rylands* subset should have a separate, and more restrictive, condition of liability than for an ordinary nuisance action. One possible explanation is that the courts wish to confine the stricter liability under *Rylands* within narrower bounds than apply to nuisance proper: if the defendant is to be held liable whether or not his use of land was reasonable, there must be some other exceptional feature of his use of land that justifies the liability. Thus the defendant is only liable for a non-natural user. As Lord Hoffmann pointed out in *Transco*, it is tempting to see in this idea the beginnings of a theory of 'enterprise liability'—a policy of requiring the 'costs' of a non-natural enterprise on land to be internalised (by making the party responsible for the enterprise liable for damage caused to others by the materialisation of risks created by that enterprise). It seems unlikely, however, that this was the motivation for the decision in *Rylands* itself (see Oliphant, 'Rylands v Fletcher and the Emergence of Enterprise Liability in the Common Law' in Koziol and Steininger, *European Tort Law 2004*), and, in contrast to jurisdictions in the United States, it has not developed into a general theory of liability for extra-hazardous activities. An attempt to extend *Rylands* in this way was rejected by Lord Goff in *Cambridge Water* on a number of grounds, perhaps the most telling being the failure of the Law Commission to recommend any proposals to implement strict liability for ultra-hazardous or especially dangerous activities (see Law Commission, *Civil Liability for Dangerous Things and Activities*, 1970, Law Com. No. 32). Neither did it matter that the damage caused was to the environment; increasing recognition of environmental problems together with national and international legislation made the extension of a common law remedy to cover this kind of damage less pressing. In the later case of *Transco*, Lord Bingham found Lord Goff's reason for refusing to extend *Rylands* 'compelling', such an extension being for Parliament rather than the courts.

As the orthodoxy is now that nuisance and *Rylands* are linked, it was not surprising that the House of Lords in *Cambridge Water* held that liability under *Rylands v Fletcher*, as in nuisance, only arises where the damage suffered by the claimant was foreseeable. But, this does not mean that the manner of the escape must be foreseeable; as Lord Hoffmann makes clear in *Transco*, the key question under *Rylands* is whether a defendant should be liable for an escape that was not intentional or reasonably foreseeable. The real test is whether, if there was an escape, the damage suffered by the claimant would have been of a type or kind that was a reasonably foreseeable consequence of the escape (see Cross [1995] 111 LQR 445). There may be escapes which give rise to specific defences (Act of God, acts of strangers) but generally it is irrelevant whether the escape was foreseeable or not. However, the requirement that the damage be foreseeable prevented the plaintiff's claim from succeeding in *Cambridge Water*: although some damage from the spillage of PCE might be imagined, the damage to the plaintiff's borehole could not. The plaintiff also argued that, even if the damage was unforeseeable at the time of the spillage, it was clearly foreseeable at the date of the trial; hence it sought to make the defendant liable in nuisance or *Rylands* for the continuing escapes. This was also rejected by Lord Goff. As the defendant could not foresee the damage at the date of the spillage it should not be strictly liable for damage which became foreseeable at a later date when it could do nothing to prevent the damage from continuing to occur. His Lordship thought that in these circumstances the defendant's liability for this 'historic pollution' should be no greater than that under the tort of negligence or under *Leakey v National Trust* (above). For criticism of this aspect of the decision see Wilkinson (1994) 57 MLR 799. As Wilkinson points out, if the subjective standard of *Leakey* is applied to such situations, well-off defendants may be hard pressed to convince courts that they have done enough to prevent the pollution from continuing.

If *Rylands v Fletcher* is simply a subset of the tort of nuisance, rules as to standing and damages should be the same for both, and this was affirmed by their Lordships in *Transco*. Thus only a person who has a possessory or proprietary interest in land should be able to sue. In *Transco*, their Lordships accepted that established statement of the standing requirement but were prepared, obiter, to extend it to cover the beneficiary of an easement over the affected land. The link with nuisance also suggests that an action lies only for damage to property interests (although some consequential damage might also be recovered: see above). As a consequence, their Lordships in *Transco* accepted the obiter view of Lord Macmillan in *Read v Lyons* [1947] AC 156 that liability under *Rylands v Fletcher* did not extend to personal injury because 'as the law now stands an allegation of negligence is in general essential to the relevancy of an action of reparation for personal injuries'. It has also been suggested that pure economic loss might be recoverable under *Rylands* if it was a sufficiently direct result of the escape (*Ryeford Homes v Sevenoaks District Council* [1989] Con LR 75) but this must also be read in light of *Hunter*. Thus economic loss which is consequential upon damage to a proprietary interest may be recoverable but economic loss standing on its own should not. This is easier to state in theory than in practice. An escape that interferes with one's amenity in land (e.g. by leaving a foul smell) should, following *Hunter*, be actionable, and if the interference affects the value of the property this will be recoverable as consequential damage. However, as (1) the only escapes likely to be sued upon are those which have consequences sufficiently serious as to cause a reduction in value of the property; and (2) a convenient way of assessing the award for interference with amenity is to measure the reduction in value caused by the interference, it becomes difficult, if not impossible, to distinguish the award of damages as compensating a proprietary interest rather than the underlying economic loss.

(b) Escape

In *Read v J. Lyons & Company Ltd* [1947] AC 156 the plaintiff, an inspector of munitions, had been injured when a high explosive shell exploded whilst being manufactured at the defendant's factory. As no negligence was alleged against the defendant the plaintiff sought damages relying on *Rylands v Fletcher*, but the House of Lords rejected the claim because there had been no 'escape'. According to Viscount Simon (at 168), '"escape", for the purpose of applying the proposition in *Rylands v Fletcher* means escape from a place where the defendant has occupation of or control over to a place which is outside his occupation or control'. This reasoning meant that if the plaintiff had been injured by the explosion when just outside the factory gates she might have been able to recover, whilst denied a remedy if injured just prior to leaving the factory. Lord Porter admitted there was force in this criticism of their Lordship's decision but held the limitation was justified as the liability under *Rylands* was an exception to the general rule of fault-based liability and hence should be restricted, a view which was accepted by Lord Scott (at [77]) in *Transco*.

(c) Dangerous Things

Almost anything can be a dangerous thing which has escaped for the purpose of a *Rylands v Fletcher* action. *Winfield & Jolowicz* (para. 15–6) list the following examples from the cases: fire, gas, explosions, electricity, oil, noxious fumes, colliery spoil, rusty wire from a decayed fence, vibrations, poisonous vegetation, a flag pole, and a chair-o-plane in a fair ground. Perhaps the most remarkable case is *Attorney General v Corke* [1933] Ch 89 where the accumulation of a group of itinerant travellers satisfied the requirement, Bennett J holding that persons whose homes were in caravans moving about from place to place 'have habits of life many of which are offensive to those who have fixed homes, and when collected together in large numbers, on a comparatively small parcel of land, such persons would be expected by reasonable people to do the kind of things which have been complained of in this action and of which proof has been given'. It is questionable whether Blackburn J had noxious persons in mind when giving his judgment, and subsequent cases have founded liability in such circumstances on nuisance rather than *Rylands v Fletcher* (*Smith v Scott* [1973] Ch 314; *Lippiatt v South Gloucestshire Council* [2000] 2 QB 5).

As is made clear in Lord Bingham's speech in *Transco*, below, the question of whether the thing brought onto land is dangerous is inextricably linked to the defendant's use of the land; thus water can be a dangerous thing if stored in a dam (*Rylands*) but not if brought onto land as part of the domestic supply of water to premises (*Rickards v Lothian* [1913] AC 263; *Transco*, below).

(d) Non-Natural Use of Land

Although it is far from certain what uses will constitute non-natural uses, it is clear that Blackburn J's original pronouncement of things 'not naturally' on the land has not been followed: as Lord Uthwatt stated in *Read v Lyons* [1947] AC 156, natural does not mean primitive. In *Rickards v Lothian* [1913] AC 263 at 280 Lord Moulton defined the term as meaning a special use bringing with it increased danger to others, not merely the ordinary use of the land or such a use as was proper for the general benefit of the community. Although the idea that a non-natural use should be judged by reference to the value of the activity to the community as a whole was rejected by Lord Goff in *Cambridge Water*, Lord Moulton's definition, and the question of non-natural use generally, was considered by the House of Lords in *Transco plc v Stockport Metropolitan Borough Council* [2004] 2 AC 1, extracted below.

Transco plc v Stockport Metropolitan Borough Council [2004] 2 AC 1

The defendant council was responsible for laying a water pipe to supply water to a tower block of housing also owned by it. Without fault on the part of the defendant, the pipe broke and a considerable volume of water was released, one consequence of which was that the embankment through which the claimant's gas pipe ran collapsed and the claimant was required to undertake urgent repairs to ensure the gas pipe would not crack. The claimant successfully sued under *Rylands* at first instance but was unsuccessful before the Court of Appeal. The House of Lords dismissed an appeal, the primary ground being that the defendant's use of land was not a non-natural use.

Lord Bingham

10 It has from the beginning been a necessary condition of liability under the rule in *Rylands v Fletcher* that the thing which the defendant has brought on his land should be 'something which ... will naturally do mischief if it escape out of his land' (LR 1 Ex 265, 279 per Blackburn J), 'something dangerous ...', 'anything likely to do mischief if it escapes', 'something ... harmless to others so long as it is confined to his own property, but which he knows to be mischievous if it gets on his neighbour's' (p 280), 'anything which, if it should escape, may cause damage to his neighbour' (LR 3 HL 330, 340, per Lord Cranworth). The practical problem is of course to decide whether in any given case the thing which has escaped satisfies this mischief or danger test, a problem exacerbated by the fact that many things not ordinarily regarded as sources of mischief or danger may none the less be capable of proving to be such if they escape. I do not think this condition can be viewed in complete isolation from the non-natural user condition to which I shall shortly turn, but I think the cases decided by the House give a valuable pointer. In *Rylands v Fletcher* itself the courts were dealing with what Lord Cranworth (LR 3 HL 330, 342) called 'a large accumulated mass of water' stored up in a reservoir, and I have touched on the historical context of the decision in paragraph 3(3) above. *Rainham Chemical Works* [1921] 2 AC 465, 471, involved the storage of chemicals, for the purpose of making munitions, which 'exploded with terrific violence'. In *Attorney General v Cory Bros & Co Ltd* [1921] 1 AC 521, 525, 530, 534, 536, the landslide in question was of what counsel described as an 'enormous mass of rubbish', some 500,000 tons of mineral waste tipped on a steep hillside. In *Cambridge Water*

[1994] 2 AC 264 the industrial solvents being used by the tannery were bound to cause mischief in the event, unforeseen on the facts that they percolated down to the water table. These cases are in sharp contrast with those arising out of escape from a domestic water supply (such as *Carstairs v Taylor* (1871) LR 6 Ex 217, *Ross v Fedden* (1872) 26 LT 966 or *Anderson v Oppenheimer* (1880) 5 QBD 602) which, although decided on other grounds, would seem to me to fail the mischief or danger test. Bearing in mind the historical origin of the rule, and also that its effect is to impose liability in the absence of negligence for an isolated occurrence, I do not think the mischief or danger test should be at all easily satisfied. It must be shown that the defendant has done something which he recognised, or judged by the standards appropriate at the relevant place and time, he ought reasonably to have recognised, as giving rise to an exceptionally high risk of danger or mischief if there should be an escape, however unlikely an escape may have been thought to be.

11 No ingredient of *Rylands v Fletcher* liability has provoked more discussion than the requirement of Blackburn J (LR 1 Ex 265, 280) that the thing brought on to the defendant's land should be something 'not naturally there', an expression elaborated by Lord Cairns (LR 3 HL 330, 339) when he referred to the putting of land to a 'non-natural use': see Stallybrass, 'Dangerous Things and the Non-Natural User of Land' (1929) 3 CLJ 376–397; Goodhart, 'Liability for Things Naturally on the Land' (1932) 4 CLJ 13–33; Newark, 'Non-Natural User and Rylands v Fletcher' (1961) 24 MLR 557–571; Williams, 'Non-Natural Use of Land' [1973] CLJ 310–322; Weir, 'Rylands v Fletcher Reconsidered' [1994] CLJ 216. Read literally, the expressions used by Blackburn J and Lord Cairns might be thought to exclude nothing which has reached the land otherwise than through operation of the laws of nature. But such an interpretation has been fairly described as 'redolent of a different age' (*Cambridge Water* [1994] 2 AC 264, 308), and in *Read v J Lyons & Co Ltd* [1947] AC 156, 169, 176, 187 and *Cambridge Water*, at p 308, the House gave its imprimatur to Lord Moulton's statement, giving the advice of the Privy Council in *Rickards v Lothian* [1913] AC 263, 280:

> It is not every use to which land is put that brings into play that principle. It must be some special use bringing with it increased danger to others, and must not merely be the ordinary use of the land or such a use as is proper for the general benefit of the community.

I think it clear that ordinary user is a preferable test to natural user, making it clear that the rule in *Rylands v Fletcher* is engaged only where the defendant's use is shown to be extraordinary and unusual. This is not a test to be inflexibly applied: a use may be extraordinary and unusual at one time or in one place but not so at another time or in another place (although I would question whether, even in wartime, the manufacture of explosives could ever be regarded as an ordinary user of land, as contemplated by Viscount Simon, Lord Macmillan, Lord Porter and Lord Uthwatt in *Read v J Lyons & Co Ltd* [1947] AC 156, 169–170, 174, 176–177, 186–187). I also doubt whether a test of reasonable user is helpful, since a user may well be quite out of the ordinary but not unreasonable, as was that of *Rylands*, *Rainham Chemical Works* or the tannery in *Cambridge Water*. Again, as it seems to me, the question is whether the defendant has done something which he recognises, or ought to recognise, as being quite out of the ordinary in the place and at the time when he does it. In answering that question, I respectfully think that little help is gained (and unnecessary confusion perhaps caused) by considering whether the use is proper for the general benefit of the community. In *Rickards v Lothian* itself, the claim arose because the outflow from a wash-basin on the top floor of premises was maliciously blocked and the tap left running, with the result that damage was caused to stock on a floor below: not surprisingly, the provision of a domestic water supply to the premises was held to be a wholly ordinary use of the land. An occupier of land who can show that another occupier of land has brought or kept on his land an exceptionally dangerous or mischievous thing in extraordinary or unusual circumstances is in my opinion entitled to recover compensation from that occupier for any damage caused to his property interest by the escape of that thing, subject to defences of Act of God or of a stranger, without the need to prove negligence.

Lord Hoffmann

44 It remains, however, if not to rationalise the law of England, at least to introduce greater certainty into the concept of natural user which is in issue in this case. In order to do so, I think it must be frankly acknowledged that little assistance can be obtained from the kinds of user which Lord Cairns must be assumed to have regarded as 'non-natural' in *Rylands v Fletcher* itself. They are, as Lord Goff of Chieveley said in the *Cambridge Water* case [1994] 2 AC 264, 308, 'redolent of a different age'. So nothing can be made of the anomaly that one of the illustrations of the rule given by Blackburn J is cattle trespass. Whatever Blackburn J and Lord Cairns may have meant by 'natural', the law was set on a different course by the opinion of Lord Moulton in *Rickards v Lothian* [1913] AC 263 and the question of what is a natural use of land or, (the converse) a use creating an increased risk, must be judged by contemporary standards.

45 Two features of contemporary society seem to me to be relevant. First, the extension of statutory regulation to a number of activities, such as discharge of water (section 209 of the Water Industry Act 1991) pollution by the escape of waste (section 73(6) of the Environmental Protection Act 1990) and radioactive matter (section 7 of the Nuclear Installations Act 1965). It may have to be considered whether these and similar provisions create an exhaustive code of liability for a particular form of escape which excludes the rule in *Rylands v Fletcher*.

46 Secondly, so far as the rule does have a residuary role to play, it must be borne in mind that it is concerned only with damage to property and that insurance against various forms of damage to property is extremely common. A useful guide in deciding whether the risk has been created by a 'non-natural' user of land is therefore to ask whether the damage which eventuated was something against which the occupier could reasonably be expected to have insured himself. Property insurance is relatively cheap and accessible; in my opinion people should be encouraged to insure their own property rather than seek to transfer the risk to others by means of litigation, with the heavy transactional costs which that involves. The present substantial litigation over £100,000 should be a warning to anyone seeking to rely on an esoteric cause of action to shift a commonplace insured risk.

47 In the present case, I am willing to assume that if the risk arose from a 'non-natural user' of the council's land, all the other elements of the tort were satisfied. Transco complains of expense having to be undertaken to avoid damage to its gas pipe; I am willing to assume that if damage to the pipe would have been actionable, the expense incurred in avoiding that damage would have been recoverable. I am also willing to assume that Transco's easement which entitled it to maintain its pipe in the embankment and receive support from the soil was a sufficient proprietary interest to enable it to sue in nuisance and therefore, by analogy, under the rule in *Rylands v Fletcher*. Although the council, as owner of Hollow End Towers, was no doubt under a statutory duty to provide its occupiers with water, it had no statutory duty or authority to build that particular tower block and it is therefore not suggested that the pipe was laid pursuant to statutory powers so as to exclude the rule. So the question is whether the risk came within the rule.

48 The damage which eventuated was subsidence beneath a gas main: a form of risk against which no rational owner of a gas main would fail to insure. The casualty was caused by the escape of water from the council's land. But the source was a perfectly normal item of plumbing. The pipe was, it is true, considerably larger than the ordinary domestic size. But it was smaller than a water main. It was installed to serve the occupiers of the council's high rise flats; not strictly speaking a commercial purpose, but not a private one either.

49 In my opinion the Court of Appeal was right to say that it was not a 'non-natural' user of land. I am influenced by two matters. First, there is no evidence that it created a greater risk than is normally associated with domestic or commercial plumbing. True, the pipe was larger. But whether that involved greater risk depends upon its specification. One cannot simply assume that the larger the pipe, the greater the risk of fracture or the greater the quantity of water likely to be discharged. I agree with my noble and learned friend, Lord Bingham of Cornhill, that the criterion of exceptional risk must be taken seriously and creates a high threshold for a claimant to surmount. Secondly, I think that the risk of damage to property caused by leaking water is one against which most people can and do commonly insure. This is, as I have said, particularly true of Transco, which can be expected to have insured against any form of damage to its pipe. It would be a very strange result if Transco were entitled to recover against the council when it would not have been entitled to recover against the water authority for similar damage emanating from its high-pressure main [because the authority had a specific statutory immunity].

Lord Scott

85 Just as in *Cambridge Water* the House found it impossible to regard the storage of chemicals in substantial quantities as a natural or ordinary use of land so, in the present case, it is in my opinion equally impossible to regard the supply by the council of water to the block of flats as anything other than a natural or ordinary use.

86 Indeed, the council was under a statutory obligation to provide a suitable supply of water for domestic purposes to the occupiers of the 66 flats. Nobody has suggested that the means by which the council did so could have been satisfactorily achieved by some other practicable method which would have carried with it a lesser risk of serious flood . . .

[His Lordship considered authorities on statutory authority and *Rylands*, and continued:]

88 These principles regarding statutory authority and immunity from action are not directly applicable in the present case. There was no specific statutory authority for the council to build the block of flats. But it had a statutory function in regard to housing and the building of the block of flats was in discharge of that statutory function. There was no specific statutory authority for the council to lay the supply pipe where it did in order to provide a water supply to the block of flats. But it did have a statutory duty by some suitable means or other to provide a supply of water for domestic purposes to the flats and no one has suggested that the laying of the supply pipe was not a proper discharge of that duty. In these circumstances the remarks of Lord Wilberforce [in *Allen v Gulf Oil Refining Ltd* [1981] AC 1001, 1011], although not directly applicable, are in my opinion highly relevant to the question whether the laying and maintaining by the council of the supply pipe was, for *Rylands v Fletcher* purposes, a 'natural' or 'ordinary' use of its land so as to exempt it from liability resulting therefrom in the absence of negligence.

89 Before answering that question it is, I think, worth reflecting on why it is that an activity authorised, or required, by statute to be carried on will not, in the absence of negligence, expose the actor to strict liability in nuisance or under the rule in *Rylands v Fletcher*. The reason, in my opinion, is that members of the public are expected to put up with any adverse side-effects of such an activity provided always that it is carried on with due care. The use of the land for carrying on the activity cannot be characterised as unreasonable if it has been authorised or required by statute. Viewed against the fact of the statutory authority, the user is a natural and ordinary use of the land. This approach applies in my opinion, to the present case. The council had no alternative, given its statutory obligations to the occupiers

of the flats, but to lay on a water supply. Strict liability cannot be attached to it for having done so.

Lord Hobhouse and **Lord Walker** delivered speeches dismissing the appeal.

COMMENTARY

Although their Lordships agreed with Lord Goff that non-natural use should not be assessed by reference to the value of the community as a whole (see, especially, Lord Walker at [105]), they affirmed that the first part of Lord Moulton's formulation should be accepted. Their Lordships held that the question was whether the use was ordinary, and this depended on the risks that the use created. All of their Lordships noted that this requirement imposed a high threshold; Lord Bingham said the use must be extraordinary and unusual, Lord Hoffmann that the risk created must be exceptional, and Lord Walker held that it was the extraordinary risk to neighbouring property if an escape occurred which made the use special (hence not ordinary) for the purpose of *Rylands*. On the facts of *Transco*, even though the water pipe was larger than an ordinary domestic water pipe (because it was supplying a residential tower block), the supply of water to domestic property was clearly an ordinary use of land. Conversely, in *Cambridge Water* (above) Lord Goff, obiter, stated (at 309) that the 'storage of substantial quantities of chemicals on industrial premises should be regarded as an almost classic case of non-natural use'. If the storage of chemicals on land was almost the classic case of non-natural user, one might think that the manufacture of explosives was obviously so, yet the House of Lords, also obiter, in *Read v Lyons* suggested that—at least in wartime—such might not be the case. However, the rejection of a 'general community benefit' component in the test of ordinary use led Lord Bingham and Lord Walker in *Transco* to doubt Lord Macmillan's dicta; Lord Walker (at [105]) thought a munitions factory another classic example of non-natural use.

Alone amongst their Lordships, Lord Hoffmann thought that risks of property damage against which first party insurance was frequently taken out by occupiers would not qualify as risks that would characterise a use as non-natural. If the frequency of insurance varies according to the type of occupier of the land (e.g. private dwelling or council-run playground), does this mean that a finding of non-natural use will vary depending on the fortuitous circumstance of which occupier is affected? See Bagshaw (2004) 120 LQR 388, 390.

The equation of non-natural with non-ordinary use significantly limits the range of uses that may attract liability. For example, it may be an ordinary use of land to build a road over it but could it be described as natural? Further, an additional hurdle is added in that the non-ordinary use must bring an exceptional danger to others. Whether the use would bring an increased danger to others would depend, amongst other things, on the foreseeable consequences of the use and the likelihood of the escape, factors that would normally be considered in a negligence action. Along these lines, Williams [1973] CLJ 310 argued that the non-natural use test is akin to unreasonable risk of harm in negligence. One balances the magnitude of the risk against the public benefit of the use, and if the risk is too great, the use can be categorised as creating an unreasonable risk of harm or a non-natural use, depending on whether the action is brought in negligence or under *Rylands*. The greater the risk associated with the use, the more precautions that must be taken so liability approaches strict liability in the case of uses that carry with them great risks, a point that was made by Lord

Macmillan in *Read v Lyons* when denying that the explosives manufacturer was under any absolute duty. In *Burnie Port Authority v General Jones Pty Ltd* (1994) 179 CLR 520 the analogy with negligence was thought sufficiently convincing by a majority of the High Court of Australia to hold that *Rylands v Fletcher* had been subsumed within the general law of negligence. The majority felt that the use of terms such as 'special' or 'not ordinary' use 'goes a long way to depriving the requirement of "non-natural" use of objective content'. None of their Lordships in *Transco*, however, felt that *Rylands* could be assimilated within negligence; Lord Walker thought (at [109]) that the undesirable result might be to stretch the law of negligence so as to exact a degree of care so stringent as to amount practically to a guarantee of safety. Moreover, as McHugh J (dissenting) pointed out in *Burnie* (at 589):

> [I]n determining the issue of non-natural use, factors that would be decisive on an issue of negligence will frequently be of only marginal relevance on the issue of non-natural use. Often, they will be irrelevant to the latter issue. In determining whether a use of land is natural, the court does not look at all the particular circumstances of the individual occupier but whether, in the time, place, and circumstances of the particular community, the character of the use of the land by that occupier constitutes a non-natural use. Thus, in the classic *Rylands v Fletcher* situation, land is used for a non-natural purpose even though the particular amount of water stored is small and the walls of the reservoir are thick and high. Similarly, burning a domestic fire to warm a room does not constitute a non-natural use of the premises because the fire has no guard and is left unattended. Non-natural use of land is a different concept from the negligent use of the land.

For discussion of the *Burnie Port* decision, see Heuston and Buckley (1994) 110 LQR 506; Lunney (1994–5) 5 KCLJ 133 and, more generally, Newark (1961) 24 MLR 557, and for a valuable comparative discussion of *Transco* (in the context of European civil law jurisdictions) see Willem van Boom, 'Some Remarks on the Decline of *Rylands v Fletcher* and the Disparity of European Strict Liability Regimes' [2005] ZEuP 618–37.

(e) Defences

Rickards v Lothian [1913] AC 263

The plaintiff was the lessee of part of the second floor of a building owned by the defendant. As a result of a tap being left on in the top floor lavatory water overflowed and damaged some of the plaintiff's stock on the second floor. The jury at the trial found that the act of turning on the tap was the 'malicious act of some person'. One issue for the Privy Council was the effect of this finding on a *Rylands v Fletcher* action.

Lord Moulton (delivering the opinion of the Privy Council)

It will be seen that Blackburn J, with characteristic carefulness, indicates that exceptions to the general rule may arise where the escape is in consequence of *vis major*, or the act of God, but declines to deal further with that question because it was unnecessary for the decision of the case then before him. A few years later the question of law thus left undecided in *Fletcher v Rylands* came up for decision in a case arising out of somewhat similar circumstances. The defendant in *Nichols v Marsland* (1876) 2 Ex D 1 had formed on her land certain ornamental pools which contained large quantities of water. A sudden and unprecedented rainfall occurred, giving rise to a flood of such magnitude that the jury found that it could not reasonably have been anticipated. This flood caused the lakes to burst their dams, and the plaintiff's adjoining lands were flooded. The jury found that there was no negligence in the construction or maintenance of the lakes. But they also found that if such a flood could have been anticipated the dams might have been so constructed that the flooding would have been prevented. Upon these findings the judge at the trial directed a verdict for the plaintiff, but gave leave to move to enter a verdict for the defendant. On the argument of the rule the Court of Exchequer directed the verdict to be entered for the defendant, and on appeal to the Exchequer Chamber that judgment was unanimously affirmed.

The judgment of the Court of Exchequer Chamber (Cockburn CJ, James and Mellish LJJ, and Baggallay JA) was read by Mellish LJ. After pointing out that the facts of the case rendered it necessary to decide the point left undecided in *Fletcher v Rylands*, he proceeds to lay down the law thereupon in the following language:

> If, indeed, the damages were occasioned by the act of the party without more—as where a man accumulates water on his own land, but, owing to the peculiar nature or condition of the soil, the water escapes and does damage to his neighbour—the case of *Rylands v Fletcher* establishes that he must be held liable. The accumulation of water in a reservoir is not in itself wrongful; but the making it and suffering the water to escape, if damage ensue, constitutes a wrong. But the present case is distinguished from that of *Rylands v Fletcher* in this, that it is not the act of the defendant in keeping this reservoir, an act in itself lawful, which alone leads to the escape of the water, and so renders wrongful that which but for such escape would have been lawful. It is the supervening vis major of the water caused by the flood, which, superadded to the water in the reservoir (which of itself would have been innocuous), caused the disaster. A defendant cannot, in our opinion, be properly said to have caused or allowed the water to escape, if the act of God or the Queen's enemies was the real cause of its escaping without any fault on the part of the defendant. If a reservoir was destroyed by an earthquake, or the Queen's enemies destroyed it in conducting some warlike operation, it would be contrary to all reason and justice to hold the owner of the reservoir liable for any damage that might be done by the escape of the water. We are of opinion therefore that the defendant was entitled to excuse herself by proving that the water escaped through the act of God.

Their Lordships are of opinion that all that is there laid down as to a case where the escape is due to 'vis major or the King's enemies' applies equally to a case where it is due to the malicious act of a third person, if indeed that case is not actually included in the above phrase. To follow the language of the judgment just recited—a defendant cannot in their Lordships' opinion be properly said to have caused or allowed the water to escape if the malicious act of a third person was the real cause of its escaping without any fault on the part of the defendant...

Appeal allowed.

COMMENTARY

As indicated in the extract above, Blackburn J in *Rylands v Fletcher* itself suggested that a number of defences could be relied upon. Nolan (2005) 121 LQR 421, 430 notes that the suggested defences go to establishing that the cause of the claimant's damage was not the act of the defendant, thereby reinforcing the view that liability under *Rylands* derives from older notions of strict liability where the defendant could avoid liability only by showing that the damage was not caused by the defendant (see also Ibbetson, *An Historical Introduction to the Law of Obligations* (Oxford: OUP, 1999), pp. 57–63). One defence specifically mentioned by

Blackburn J is Act of God, described in *Tennent v Earl of Glasgow* (1864) 2 M (HL) 22, 26–7 as an escape caused directly by natural causes without human intervention in circumstances in which no human foresight can provide against and of which human prudence is not bound to recognise the possibility. There are some examples of the defence succeeding—*Nichols v Marsland* is mentioned in the extract—but in *Greenock Corporation v Caledonian Railway* [1917] AC 556 the House of Lords criticised the use of the defence in *Nichols* and in modern times the defence will rarely, if ever, be successful, for with increasing knowledge the limits on the foreseeable have increased dramatically.

If the escape is caused by the deliberate act of a third party, then a defence may be available, as was the case in *Rickards*. But who is a third party for these purposes? In *Perry v Kendricks Transport Ltd* [1956] 1 WLR 85 the plaintiff, a boy of 10, was injured when the petrol tank of a disused coach parked on the defendants' land exploded. The petrol tank had been drained and the cap secured. As the plaintiff approached the coach he saw two other small boys near the coach and as he drew alongside the vehicle these boys jumped away and there was an explosion. The trial judge found that the cap of the tank had been removed that day by persons unknown and that one of the two boys had thrown a lighted match into the tank, causing the fumes to ignite. The trial judge dismissed a claim in negligence, and the plaintiff appealed, arguing a cause of action based on *Rylands v Fletcher*, but the Court of Appeal held that the act of the boys was the act of a stranger. According to Jenkins LJ (at 91), a stranger was someone over whom the occupier had no control, and in such cases it would be wrong to see the accumulation of the dangerous thing or the conduct of the occupier or persons on the land with his consent as the cause of the accident. It was accepted that the act of a trespasser child might not amount to a defence 'if it was a reasonable and probable consequence of their [the occupiers'] action, which they ought to have foreseen, that children might meddle with the dangerous thing and cause it to escape'. In this case the escape would be brought about by the defendants' negligence in dealing with the dangerous thing, but once that point was reached 'the claim based on *Rylands v Fletcher* merges into the claim in negligence: for if such a state of affairs could be made out, then it would no longer be necessary for the plaintiff to rely on *Rylands v Fletcher* at all. He could rely simply on the defendants' negligence.'

Thus two questions must be answered in ascertaining whether this defence applies. First, is the person responsible for the escape a stranger? Secondly, if so, could the act of the stranger be anticipated and steps taken to prevent it? A trespasser is clearly a stranger, but what about guests of the occupier? *Winfield & Jolowicz*, para. 15.15 suggests that licensees or guests of the occupier are not strangers unless the act is wholly alien to the invitation. If the act is found to be the act of the stranger, the liability, if any, is in negligence. 'By means of a defence of act of a stranger the basis of liability is shifted from the creation of a risk to responsibility for culpable failure to control the risk' (*Winfield & Jolowicz*, para. 15.15).

Other defences also apply: statutory authority, *volenti non fit injuria*, and contributory negligence, and for further discussion see generally *Winfield & Jolowicz*, paras 15-12–15-18; *Salmond & Heuston*, pp. 315–20; *Street*, pp. 478–83.

(f) The Future of *Rylands v Fletcher*

In *Transco*, one question for the House of Lords was whether there remained any point in continuing to recognise whatever cause of action *Rylands* had established. As noted above, in *Burnie Port Authority v General Jones Pty Ltd* (1994) 179 CLR 520 a majority of the High

Court of Australia incorporated the rule within the tort of negligence. Conversely, given its close relationship to nuisance, it might be thought desirable formally to incorporate it within that tort. However, all five members of the House of Lords in *Transco* rejected arguments that the rule should no longer have a separate existence, albeit with different degrees of enthusiasm. Thus for Lord Hoffmann the primary reason for retaining the rule was that, given its longevity and Lord Goff's apparent acceptance of it in *Cambridge Water*, it would go beyond the judicial function now to abolish it. Other of their Lordships were more positive. Lord Walker noted (at [99]) that, although its scope for operation had been restricted (and perhaps severely restricted) by the growth of statutory regulation of hazardous activities and the continuing development of the law of negligence, it would be premature to conclude that the principle was for practical purposes obsolete. And Lord Bingham stated (at [6]): 'there is in my opinion a category of case, however small it may be, in which it seems just to impose liability even in the absence of fault'. He considered that the *Cambridge Water* case, had there been foreseeability of damage, fell within that category.

The question remains, however, as to why a particular aspect of what is seen as the law of private nuisance should be the subject of a special liability regime. As Lord Hoffmann said in *Transco* (at [41]): 'It is hard to find any rational principle which explains the rule and its exceptions.' Academic commentators have divided over whether the rule in its current form should be retained. Nolan (2005) 121 LQR 421 argues it should be abolished whilst Murphy (2004) 24 OJLS 643, 669 maintains the rule serves as a 'useful residual mechanism for securing environmental protection by individuals affected by harmful escapes from polluting heavyweight industrialists.' The matter, however, may be somewhat moot; as several of their Lordships noted in *Transco*, there have been no reported cases successfully relying on the rule since the Second World War (although there have been examples of the fire variant of *Rylands*; see below), and the decision in *Transco* does not suggest the likelihood of many successful actions. (But note the recent decision in *Color Quest Ltd v Total Downstream UK plc* [2009] EWHC 540 (Comm), a case arising out of massive explosions at an oil storage depot (Buncefield) in 2005, where liability to some claimants under the rule in *Rylands v Fletcher* was admitted by the defendants). Bagshaw (2004) 120 LQR 388, 392 is surely right when noting that the main effect of the imperfections of the rule 'will probably be to challenge law students and textbook writers'.

2. *Rylands v Fletcher* and Liability for Fire

At various times throughout the history of the common law it has been posited that an occupier is liable for the spread of fire from his land, at least where it was lit by himself or by someone on the land with his permission (see for example *Beaulieu v Finglam* (1401), *Anon* (1584) in Baker and Milsom, *Sources of English Legal History* (London: Butterworths, 1986), pp. 557–9). It is doubtful whether this was ever the case, as in most cases the issue presented for decision was whether there had been negligence in tending the fire (Arnold, *Introduction to the Selden Society* Vol. 100 (1984), pp. lxviii–lxx). By the end of the seventeenth century it was clear that no strict liability attached to an occupier where the fire was started or was spread by the act of a stranger or through an act of nature (*Turberville v Stamp* (1697) 1 Ld Raym 264, 91 ER 1072). Indeed, the current position in England is that, as far as there is any special liability relating only to fires, an occupier is liable for the damage caused by the spread of a fire started on his land where there is negligence, either by the occupier or by someone on the land with his leave and licence (*H. & N. Emanuel v Greater London Council* [1971] 2 All ER 835; *Ribee v Norrie* [2001] L & TR 23). This view, which effectively imposes a non-delegable duty of care in respect of fires lit on the occupier's land, makes negligence the touchstone of liability, albeit not necessarily the occupier's negligence. As well, in addition to the common law, the Fires Prevention (Metropolis) Act 1774 (which applies generally) in s. 86 provides that no action shall be maintainable against an occupier for a fire which begins accidentally.

However, even if there is no special rule of strict liability relating to damage caused by fire, can the general rule in *Rylands v Fletcher* be applied to the spread of fire so as to impose strict liability? This issue was not directly for decision in *Emanuel*, although Lord Denning MR thought the principle he espoused was the basis for any form of strict liability for fire. One obstacle to using *Rylands* for liability for fire might be thought to be the 1774 Act. One argument against this was provided in *Filliter v Phippard* (1847) 11 QB 347, where it was held that the Act applied only to fires produced by mere chance or incapable of being traced to any cause. Thus a fire begun intentionally or negligently would not be covered. A different rationale for excluding the operation of the 1774 Act from *Rylands* claims was provided by Judge Thornton QC in *Johnson (Trading as Johnson Butchers) v BJW Property Developments Ltd* [2002] 3 All ER 574. In this case it was held that the key question in determining whether the 1774 Act was applicable was whether the escape of the fire was an accident, not whether the original fire was started accidently. In the context of a *Rylands* claim, as the escape of the fire must, by definition, have occurred following a non-natural use of the land, it was not 'accidental' within the meaning of the 1774 Act (see also *LMS International Ltd v Styrene Packaging and Insulation Ltd* [2006] Build LR 50, where this approach was approved).

What else might be required for *Rylands v Fletcher* to apply to escapes of fire? The rule normally requires a dangerous thing brought upon land to escape; hence before liability could attach a fire (the dangerous thing) should be brought onto land and escape. However, in *Musgrove v Pandelis* [1919] 2 KB 43 the Court of Appeal appears to have modified the rule in the context of fires. In that case, the defendant occupied a garage in which he parked his car, the plaintiff owning the remainder of the building. The defendant employed a chauffeur, and on one occasion when he was attempting to start the car it caught fire. The fire could have been controlled by simply turning off the petrol tap immediately, but the chauffeur negligently first went to find a cloth with which to turn it off, and by the time he returned the fire was too intense for him to perform this operation. The liability of the defendant, however, was not based on his responsibility for his servant's act (as in the *Emanuel* case above) but on *Rylands v Fletcher*. The Court of Appeal affirmed the trial judge, holding that the 1774 Act did not apply where liability arose under the rule in *Rylands v Fletcher*. Liability seems to have been based on the fact that the car was dangerous because (1) it might catch fire; and (2) that fire might spread. The Court of Appeal also held that 'fire' in the 1774 Act referred to the fire that caused the damage; in *Musgrove* that was deemed to be the fire that arose from the negligent failure to close the fuel tap, not the original unexplained fire.

Later cases have doubted the correctness of *Musgrove*. In *Collingwood v Home & Colonial Stores Ltd* [1936] 3 All ER 200, Romer LJ thought that it would be desirable if the House of Lords considered the reasoning of the case as far as it was based on *Rylands*. If it was not based on *Rylands*, Romer LJ thought it must be based on a wider principle which required acceptance of the propositions that (1) a motor car was a dangerous thing to bring onto land; and (2) this was not an ordinary and proper use of the land. This wider principle was expounded by MacKenna J in *Mason v Levy Auto Parts* [1967] 2 QB 530 (and applied in *LMS*

International Ltd v Styrene Packaging and Insulation Ltd [2006] Build LR 50) as consisting of three steps:

(i)   the defendant brought onto his land things likely to catch fire, and kept them there in such conditions that, if they did ignite, the fire would be likely to spread to the plaintiff's land;

(ii) the defendant did so in the course of a non-natural use of land;

(iii) the thing ignited and the fire spread.

Although bound by precedent to follow the case, MacKenna J also expressed doubt as to the correctness of the holding in *Musgrove* that the 1774 Act did not apply to fires falling under this hybrid of *Rylands* liability. However, in *Coxhill v Forward*, unreported, QBD, 19 March 1986, McNeill J agreed with *Musgrove*, stating: 'I do not think that the escape of what an occupier is bound to keep in at his peril—in effect as an insurer—can when it escapes properly be regarded as [an] "accidental" escape, even if it is fire' (see also *Johnson (Trading as Johnson Butchers) v BJW Property Developments Ltd* [2002] 3 All ER 574; *LMS International Ltd v Styrene Packaging and Insulation Ltd* [2006] Build LR 50, above).

The problem with the application of *Rylands v Fletcher* to fires is that it equates the dangerous thing brought onto the land with the fire that escapes. Conventional liability under *Rylands* is for things which would be dangerous if they escaped, not things dangerous if they caught fire. But if it does extend to things dangerous if they caught fire, the scope of liability is greatly expanded, for a great many things can catch fire and almost all of them are dangerous if they do so. However, liability can be controlled by the requirement of a non-natural use of land although it seems the term has a particular meaning in this context. For example, imagine two warehouses, one which stores paper, and one flammable and poisonous chemicals. Although both examples would satisfy (i) above, it is arguable that only the storage of poisonous chemicals would amount to a non-natural use because of the risks, *over and above the risk of the chemicals catching fire*, attached to the use of land for storing dangerous chemicals. It must be admitted, however, that this distinction does not always appear in the cases; thus in *LMS International Ltd v Styrene Packaging and Insulation Ltd* [2006] Build LR 50 the risk that made the use non-natural appears to be the risk of polystyrene stored on the premises catching fire and the fire spreading to adjoining premises. If this is the correct approach, it becomes difficult to see how the non-natural use element in (ii) is any different from the requirements of (i); in both the question is simply the risk of fire that is created by the defendant's use. It also becomes difficult to see why uses that give rise to potentially high fire risks—such as warehouses filled with paper—cannot be categorised as non-natural uses. Perhaps the problem lies in the potentially wide scope of liability of the fire variant of *Rylands*; it is hard to disagree with the proposition that by imposing strict liability in the form of *Rylands* on things likely to catch fire without allowing a defence under the 1774 Act, 'the Court of Appeal [in *Musgrove*] went very far' (per MacKenna J in *Mason* at 541). The best solution may be simply to reject the fire variant of *Rylands*, leaving the claimant to remedies in negligence and under the special rules that apply to fire cases generally.

For a discussion of the peculiarities of liability for the escape of fire see Ogus [1969] CLJ 104.

13 DEFAMATION

1. Introduction

No area of the law excites more interest, or controversy, than the law of defamation (i.e. libel and slander), considered here, and privacy, considered in Ch. 14 below. The combination of celebrity litigants, gossipy tittle-tattle, and frequently salacious allegations often results in front-page coverage in the popular press. And beneath this surface-level appeal lie matters of deeper concern, relating to the appropriate balance to be struck between freedom of expression (particularly in the news media) and individual interests in reputation and private information. With the implementation of the Human Rights Act 1998, the courts are now required to conduct the necessary balancing exercise within the framework of rights recognised by the European Convention on Human Rights, particularly Article 8 (right to private life, which encompasses the right to reputation) and Article 10 (right to freedom of expression), but the same approach is evident even in decisions from before the Act came into effect.

A defamatory statement is one which impugns another person's reputation or adversely affects his or her standing in the community. Defamation takes two forms: *libel*, referring to publications that are in permanent form or that are broadcast on stage or screen or over the airwaves; and *slander*, referring to publications in transient form (e.g. casual conversations). As a general rule, slander, unlike libel, only gives rise to liability if it results in consequential loss ('special damage'). A defamatory statement is actionable without proof of its falsity, but the defendant has a complete defence of *justification* if he or she succeeds in demonstrating its truth; the publication of true statements, whether or not it is in the public interest, cannot generally amount to defamation. Other defences are also available to the defendant in a defamation action, for example, that the statement was *fair comment on a matter of public interest* or that it was made to an interested party in performance of a duty or protection of an interest (on which occasions, a defence of *privilege* may arise). As for remedies, a claimant who *learns* of the prospective publication of defamatory material may seek an *interim injunction* (sometimes known as a 'gagging order') to prevent the publisher from going ahead; the interim injunction, if awarded, will last until such time as there is a full trial of the case. If the publication has already taken place, the claimant will at trial inevitably seek, in addition to a *permanent injunction, damages* for injury to reputation and for any consequential economic loss; in some cases, *exemplary damages* may be awarded.

II. Libel and Slander

1. The Distinction between Libel and Slander

English law divides defamatory statements into two classes—libels and slanders—and requires, with certain exceptions, that 'special damage' be proved in relation to the latter. The distinction has historical origins, stretching back to the early days of the tort in the sixteenth and seventeenth centuries. (See W. S. Holdsworth, *History of English Law*, vol. VIII, 2nd edn. (1937), p. 361f; Kaye, 'Libel and Slander—Two Torts or One?' (1975) 91 LQR 524; *Mitchell*, ch. 1.) Since the seventeenth century, written statements have been actionable without proof of special damage, the reasoning being that the fact of writing demonstrated particular malice (*King v Lake* (1667) 1 Hardres 470). Although this may suggest a distinction between libel and slander based on the difference between written and oral statements, defamation need not take the form of words and it has become necessary to determine whether visual images and gestures constitute libel or slander. The development of modern methods of communication (e.g. in the areas of film, television, telephone and sound recording) further complicated the matter. In some areas, statute has come to the common law's aid. Defamatory words, pictures, visual images and gestures on radio or television or any other 'programme service' are to be treated as libels by s. 166 of the Broadcasting Act 1990. In addition, 'the publication of [defamatory] words in the course of a performance of a play' is, by s. 4(1) of the Theatres Act 1968, also treated as libel.

When it comes to other ways of communicating meaning, we have to turn to the common law. Here it seems that the test is one that looks to the permanence or transience of the 'statement'. In *Monson v Tussauds Ltd* [1894] 1 QB 671 at 692, Lopes LJ stated:

> Libels are generally in writing or printing, but this is not necessary; the defamatory matter may be conveyed in some other permanent form. For instance, a statue, a caricature, an effigy, chalk-marks on a wall, signs or pictures may constitute a libel.

This definition of libel covered the facts of the case before the Court of Appeal, in which a waxworks model of the plaintiff was placed in an exhibition in the same room as a number of actual or alleged murderers and next to the Chamber of Horrors; the plaintiff had recently been tried for murder but the case against him had been 'not proven' (a special Scottish verdict implying neither guilt nor innocence). A later case, *Youssopoff v Metro-Goldwyn-Mayer Pictures Ltd* (1934) 50 TLR 581, suggests, however, a modified version of this test, by which it is necessary to show not only that the communication is permanent but also that it is visible.

Youssopoff v Metro-Goldwyn-Mayer Pictures Ltd (1934) 50 TLR 581

The plaintiff sued for libel in relation to suggestions in the film, *Rasputin, the Mad Monk*, that she (called Princess Natasha in the film) had been seduced by the eponymous figure of Rasputin. The jury found for the plaintiff and awarded her £25,000 damages. The defendants appealed.

> **Slesser LJ**
>
> This action is one of libel and raises at the outset an interesting and difficult problem which, I believe, to be a novel problem, whether the product of the combined photographic and talking instrument which produces these modern films does, if it throws upon the screen and impresses upon the ear defamatory matter, produce that which can be complained of as libel or slander.
>
> In my view, this action…was properly framed in libel. There can be no doubt that, so far as the photographic part of the exhibition is concerned, that is a permanent matter to be seen by the eye, and is the proper subject of an action for libel, if defamatory. I regard the speech which is synchronized with the photographic reproduction and forms part of one complex, common exhibition as an ancillary circumstance, part of the surroundings explaining that which is to be seen…
>
> **Scrutton LJ** and **Greer LJ** delivered separate concurring judgments.
>
> *Appeal dismissed.*

COMMENTARY

Slesser LJ held that the film pictures, being 'a permanent matter to be seen by the eye' could be regarded as libels. He also found the speech to be libel, but not simply because it too was permanent: in his view, it amounted to libel only because it was 'part of one complex, common exhibition'. To him, it was because the sound recording was 'ancillary' to the visual image that it could be regarded as libel rather than slander: it was 'an ancillary circumstance…explaining that which is to be seen'.

Where a sound recording exists independently of any visual image, Slesser LJ's reasoning suggests that the liability would arise only in slander. This would mean that defamatory statements contained in voicemails, etc., would in general be actionable only on proof of special damage. But this view may be too narrow. Certainly, a number of statutes imply that the correct test is simply whether the communication was 'in permanent form' (see, e.g., Theatres Act 1968, s. 4(1): 'the publication of words in the course of a performance of a play shall…be treated as publication in permanent form'; see also Broadcasting Act 1990, s. 166).

It is suggested therefore that permanence is the real test of a libel, as was assumed by Lopes LJ in *Monson v Tussauds*. No doubt the test of permanence will lead to distinctions of degree: while Lopes LJ considered that chalk-marks on a wall might constitute a libel, what about words on a computer-screen (not saved) or sky-writing by an aeroplane?

A libellous statement retains its status as a libel even when it is read aloud. This was decided by the Court of Appeal in *Forrester v Tyrrell* (1893) 9 TLR 257, in which a person reading aloud from a defamatory letter was held to be liable in libel rather than slander; it was immaterial that he had not handed the letter around. It seems the rule will not apply when the libel is merely repeated rather than read out.

2. Slander: General Requirement of Special Damage

Libel is actionable *per se*, whereas slander generally requires proof of actual injury ('special damage'). What amounts to actual injury? Mere loss of reputation is insufficient. So too is the loss of the society of friends. However, if the claimant has lost out on the hospitality of friends, that would amount to material loss (see *Moore v Meagher* (1807) 1 Taunt 39; *Davies v Solomon* (1871) LR 7 QB 112). More obvious examples are where the claimant loses his job or suffers diminished trading profits as a result of the slander.

Why liability for slander should be restricted in a way that libel is not has never been wholly convincingly explained. In the seventeenth century, Hale CB suggested that words written and published contained 'more malice'—perhaps we should say 'deliberation'—than words spoken (*King v Lake* (1667) Hardres 470 at 471; but cf. Kaye (1975) 91 LQR 531–2, and *Mitchell*, pp. 4–6), and another judge, speaking of the 'diffusive' effect of a libel in a public newspaper (*Harman v Delany* (1731) 2 Strange 898, Fitzgibbon 253), apparently had it in mind that libels were more easily communicated to the public at large. Subsequent judges and commentators have treated such reasoning with scepticism, but there is no doubt that the distinction is firmly entrenched in the law.

Thorley v Lord Kerry (1812) 4 Taunton 355, 128 ER 367

The facts are not material for present purposes.

Barnewall for the Plaintiff... denied that there was any solid ground, either in authority or principle, for the distinction supposed to have prevailed in some cases, that certain words are actionable when written, which are not actionable when spoken... The reason assigned, that the printing or writing indicates a greater degree of malice than mere speaking, is a bad one; for it is not the object of an action at law to punish moral turpitude, but to compensate a civil injury: the compensation must be proportionate to the measure of the damage sustained; but it cannot be said that publication of written slander is in all cases attended with a greater damage than spoken slander, for if a Defendant speaks words to an hundred persons assembled, he disseminates the slander and increases the damage an hundred-fold as much as if he only wrote it in a letter to one.

Mansfield CJ

[F]or myself, after having heard it extremely well argued, and especially, in this case, by Mr. Barnewall, I cannot, upon principle, make any difference between words written and words spoken, as to the right which arises on them of bringing an action. For the Plaintiff... it has been truly urged, that in the old books and abridgments no distinction is taken between words written and spoken. But the distinction has been made between written and spoken slander as far back as Charles the Second's time, and the difference has been recognized by the Courts for at least a century back.... [T]he law gives a very ample field for retribution by action for words spoken in the cases of special damage, of words spoken of a man in his trade or profession, of a man in office, of a magistrate or officer; for all these an action lies. But for mere general abuse spoken, no action lies.

In the arguments both of the judges and counsel, in almost all the cases in which the question has been, whether what is contained in a writing is the subject of an action or not, it has been considered, whether the words, if spoken, would maintain an action. It is curious that they have also adverted to the question, whether it tends to produce a breach of the peace: but that is wholly irrelevant, and is no ground for recovering damages. So it has been argued that writing shews more deliberate malignity; but the same answer suffices, that the action is not maintainable upon the ground of the malignity, but for the damage sustained. So, it is argued that written scandal is more generally diffused than words spoken, and is therefore actionable; but an assertion made in a public place, as upon the Royal Exchange, concerning a merchant in London, may be much more extensively diffused than a few printed papers dispersed, or a private letter: it is true that a newspaper may be very generally read, but that is all casual. . . .

The tendency of the libel to provoke a breach of the peace, or the degree of malignity which actuates the writer has nothing to do with the question. If the matter were for the first time to be decided at this day, I should have no hesitation in saying, that no action could be maintained for written scandal which could not be maintained for the words if they had been spoken.

COMMENTARY

Mansfield CJ found no principled justification for the distinction between libel and slander but felt compelled to accept it by weight of precedent. Judicial reconsideration now seems unlikely, but legislative reform remains possible. The question whether libel should be differentiated from slander has twice been raised in official reports. The Porter Committee (*Report of the Committee on the Law of Defamation*, 1948, Cmd. 7536, paras 38, 40) favoured retention of the distinction:

Slander is often trivial, not infrequently good-tempered and harmless, and in that form commonly enough a topic of conversation. If all slander were actionable *per se*, the scope for trivial but costly litigation might be enormously increased. So far as slander in ordinary conversation is concerned, it is not normally taken seriously by speaker or listener, and, in the great majority of cases, does little or no harm . . . [A] change in the law in England and Wales at the present date would, we think, be likely to encourage frivolous actions.

The Faulks Committee (*Report of the Committee on Defamation*, 1975, Cmnd. 5909), however, considered this last fear to be 'unfounded', partly because words spoken by way of vulgar abuse or merely as a joke would remain non-actionable, while the expense of litigation was a powerful disincentive to would-be litigants who, even if successful, might find their irrecoverable costs burdensome (paras 87–9). In Faulks's view (para. 86):

The distinction between libel and slander is entirely attributable to historical accident, but for which it would never have come into being. It represents one of the few spheres (if not the only one) in which the forms of action continue to rule us from the grave. It renders this part of the law unreasonable and unnecessarily complicated and refined, carrying a host of rules and exceptions, derived partly from precedent and partly from statute, which are illogical, difficult to learn, and in certain applications, to it must be added, unjust.

The committee recommended that the distinction between libel and slander be abolished and that slander be assimilated to libel (para. 91). As will already be apparent, the recommendation was never implemented.

Slanders Actionable *Per Se*

There are four exceptions to the rule that slander requires actual injury to be proved. In these cases slander may be said to be actionable *per se*.

(i) Imputation of Criminal Conduct

Where the defendant imputes to the claimant criminal conduct punishable with imprison-ment, the slander is actionable without proof of damage. The leading case is *Gray v Jones* [1939] 1 All ER 795 in which the defendant said to the plaintiff, 'you are a convicted person. I will not have you here.' It was irrelevant in this case that the plaintiff, against whom the allegation was that he *had been* convicted, was not put in jeopardy of any further prosecu-tion as (according to Atkinson J) the reason for the rule was that the misconduct alleged was so serious that other people were likely to shun the plaintiff and exclude him from their society. However, spoken words which convey a mere suspicion that the claimant has com-mitted a crime punishable by imprisonment will not support an action without proof of special damage (*Simmons v Mitchell* (1880) 6 App Cas 156, PC).

(ii) Imputation of Certain Contagious Diseases

Words which impute that the claimant is suffering from a serious contagious or infectious disease are actionable *per se*. In the leading case, the allegation '[h]e has got that damned pox from going to that woman on the Derby road' was held to warrant the award of £50 without proof of special damage, a sexually-transmitted venereal disease falling within the excep-tion (*Bloodworth v Gray* (1844) 7 Man & G 334). Orally accusing a person of having AIDS would similarly be actionable without proof of damage, but an oral accusation of insanity would not (not infectious), and neither would an oral accusation that the claimant had a cold (not serious).

(iii) Imputation of Unchastity

By Slander of Women Act 1891, s. 1, 'words spoken or published . . . which impute unchastity or adultery to any woman or girl shall not require special damage to render them action-able'. A woman having sex out of marriage may once have been considered unchaste, but standards of sexual morality have changed and it is doubtful that she would be so consid-ered today. Falsely calling a woman unchaste, according to Asquith LJ (*Kerr v Kennedy* [1942] 1 KB 409 at 411), 'is calculated both to bring her into social disfavour and, as the phrase runs, to damage her prospects in the marriage market and thereby her finances'. There is no equivalent provision for men. Do you think, therefore, that the law impliedly endorses the view that a woman who sleeps around is a 'slag', while a man who does the same is a 'stud'?

(iv) Imputation of Unfitness in Business

By s. 2 of the Defamation Act 1952, 'words calculated to disparage the plaintiff in any office, profession, calling, trade or business' are actionable without proof of actual injury. At common law it appeared to be the case that this exception only applied where the words were directed against the plaintiff 'in the way of' his profession or calling, etc. Thus, accusations of sexual misconduct by a schoolmaster with the caretaker's wife were not actionable, at least where there was no allegation that this would lower his profes-sional reputation (*Jones v Jones* [1916] 2 AC 481; *aliter*, presumably, if the misconduct was alleged to have been with a pupil). This requirement was abolished by the legislation referred to above, which makes it clear that such statements are actionable *per se* 'whether or not the words are spoken of the plaintiff in the way of his office, profession, calling, trade or business'.

III. Defamation: Elements of the Cause of Action

1. The Statement must be Defamatory

(a) Basic Definition of 'Defamatory'

A defamatory statement is one which injures a person's reputation. A harmful statement which does not impugn the claimant's reputation may yet be actionable under the independent tort of malicious falsehood (e.g. 'Smith told me he isn't coming to market today. Let me sell you my cattle instead'). The traditional test as to whether or not a statement is defamatory is to ask whether the words complained of were 'calculated to injure the reputation of another by exposing him to hatred, contempt, or ridicule' (*Parmiter v Coupland* (1840) 6 M & W 105 at 108, per Parke B). But Lord Atkin in *Sim v Stretch* (1936) 52 TLR 669 at 671 suggested a broader test:

> [T]he conventional phrase exposing the plaintiff to 'hatred, ridicule or contempt' is probably too narrow . . . I do not intend to ask your Lordships to lay down a formal definition, but after collating the opinions of many authorities I propose in the present case the test: would the words tend to lower the plaintiff in the estimation of right-thinking members of society generally?

Lord Atkin's test was not intended to be exhaustive. In a number of cases, a statement which adversely affects a person's standing in the community may be defamatory even though it does not lower the general estimation of that person's worth (e.g. imputations of disease or insolvency). A number of verbal formulations have been suggested, for example, that the words tend to make right-thinking people shun or avoid the claimant (*Villers v Monsley* (1769) 2 Wils 403) or tend to exclude him from society.

The law looks only to the *tendency* of the defendant's words, so liability can arise even if the words are not believed. However, allegations which no reasonable person would believe are not actionable (see *Loukas v Young* [1968] 2 NSWR 549: allegations of witchcraft). The words must always be considered in the precise circumstances and context of their publication, and what may be defamatory of one person is not necessarily defamatory of another (cf. *Palmer v Boyer* (1594) Cro Eliz 342: barrister alleged to know 'as much law as a jackanapes'; surely not defamatory of a lay person—but what of a first-year law student?). Whether particular words are defamatory is a question of fact, not law; hence previous decisions are not binding authority and cannot act as anything more than a guide to the case at hand, all the more so given possible variations in the circumstances and context of publication. As the question of defamatory meaning is one of fact, it is for the jury to decide, although the court must address the threshold question of whether the words are *capable* of bearing a defamatory meaning, which is a question of law.

The statement need not be in words. A picture, as the saying goes, is worth a thousand words. A visual image acquires its meaning from its context, and in particular from its juxtaposition with other images or with verbal expressions. In *Monson v Tussauds Ltd* [1894] 1 QB 671 it was held that a waxworks model of the plaintiff carried a defamatory meaning arising out of its placement in the defendants' exhibition in the same room as a number of actual or alleged murderers and next to the Chamber of Horrors. The plaintiff had been tried for murder but the case against him had been 'not proven'. This was held to be an actionable libel.

A defamatory allegation must strike at the claimant's reputation; insults and jokes may merely bruise the ego rather than lower a person's estimation in the eyes of others. (Insults of a racial or sexual nature may give rise to a claim in an employment tribunal under the Sex Discrimination Act 1975 or Race Relations Act 1976 as in, for example, *Insitu Cleaning Co Ltd v Heads* [1995] IRLR 4: 'Hello, big tits'.) It has been observed that 'exhibitions of bad manners or discourtesy' ought not to be 'placed on the same level as attacks on character'; they are not actionable wrongs (*Sim v Stretch* (1936) 52 TLR 669 at 672, per Lord Atkin). Nevertheless, '[t]he writing and publishing of anything which renders a man ridiculous is actionable' (*Villiers v Monsley* (1769) 1 Bos & P 331), and it has been observed that 'no one can cast about firebrands and death, and then escape from being responsible by saying he was in sport' (*Capital and Counties Bank v Henty* (1882) 7 App Cas 741 at 772, per Lord Blackburn). Holding a person up as a figure of fun may be defamatory of him because it affects in an adverse manner the attitude of other people towards him; however, it is a question of fact in every case whether banter or 'ribbing' goes beyond a joke and amounts to ridicule of such an extent that the claimant's reputation is damaged.

Berkoff v Burchill [1996] 4 All ER 1008

Julie Burchill, a well-known journalist, had twice made throw-away remarks about Stephen Berkoff, the actor and film-director, in film reviews in the *Sunday Times*. She had said, first, that 'film directors, from Hitchcock to Berkoff, are notoriously hideous-looking people'; then, in a review of *Mary Shelley's Frankenstein*, had written:

> The Creature is . . . rejected in disgust when it comes out scarred and primeval. It's a very new look for the Creature—no bolts in the neck or flat-top hairdo—and I think it works; it's a lot like Stephen Berkoff, only marginally better-looking.

The case came to the Court of Appeal on a preliminary issue, namely, whether (as the trial judge had found) the alleged implication of these words—that the plaintiff was 'hideously ugly'—was capable in law of being defamatory.

Neill LJ

[W]ords may be defamatory, even though they neither impute disgraceful conduct to the plaintiff nor any lack of skill or efficiency in the conduct of his trade or business or professional activity, if they hold him up to contempt, scorn or ridicule or tend to exclude him from society. On the other hand, insults which do not diminish a man's standing among other people do not found an action for libel or slander. The exact borderline may often be difficult to define.

The case for Mr Berkoff is that the charge that he is 'hideously ugly' exposes him to ridicule, and/or alternatively, will cause him to be shunned or avoided. . . . In his helpful submissions on behalf of the defendants, Mr Price QC rightly underlined the central characteristic of an action for defamation as being a remedy for publications which damage a person's reputation. But the word 'reputation', by its association with phrases such as 'business reputation', 'professional reputation' or 'reputation for honesty', may obscure the fact that in this context the word is to be interpreted in a broad sense as comprehending all aspects of a person's standing in the community. A man who is held up as a figure of fun may be defeated in his claim for damages by, for example, a plea of fair comment, or, if he succeeds on liability, the compensation which he receives from a jury may be very small. But nevertheless, the publication of which he complains may be defamatory of him because it affects in an adverse manner the attitude of other people towards him....

It is trite law that the meaning of words in a libel action is determined by the reaction of the ordinary reader and not by the intention of the publisher, but the perceived intention of the publisher may colour the meaning. In the present case it would, in my view, be open to a jury to conclude that in the context the remarks about Mr Berkoff gave the impression that he was not merely physically unattractive in appearance but actually repulsive. It seems to me that to say this of someone in the public eye who makes his living, in part at least, as an actor, is capable of lowering his standing in the estimation of the public and of making him an object of ridicule.

Phillips LJ

In almost every case in the books, words which have been held to be defamatory have been words which have denigrated the character or personality of the plaintiff, not the corporeal envelope housing that personality. The law of defamation protects reputation, and reputation is not generally dependent upon physical appearance. Exceptionally there has been a handful of cases where words have been held defamatory, notwithstanding that they do not attack character or personality....

'Shun or avoid'

It is not easy to find the touchstone by which to judge whether words are defamatory which tend to make other persons shun or avoid the plaintiff, but it is axiomatic that the words must relate to an attribute of the plaintiff in respect of which hearsay alone is enough to provoke this reaction. That was once true of a statement that a woman had been raped and would still be true of a statement that a person has a serious infectious or contagious disease, or is physically unwholesome or is mentally deranged. There is precedent for holding all such statements defamatory. There is, however, with one possible exception, no precedent for holding it defamatory to describe a person as ugly. In my judgment, such a statement differs in principle from those statements about a person's physical condition which have been held to be defamatory. Those statements have, in every case, been allegations of fact—illness, madness, filthiness or defilement. Hearsay factual statements about a person's physical condition can clearly be capable of causing those who hear or read them to avoid the subject of them. In contrast, a statement that a person is ugly, or hideously ugly, is a statement of subjective appreciation of that individual's features. To a degree both beauty and ugliness are in the eye of the beholder. It is, perhaps, just possible to think of a right minded person shunning one of his fellow men because of a subjective distaste for his features. What I find impossible to accept is that a right minded person would shun another merely because a third party had expressed distaste for that other person's features.

Ridicule

The class of cases where it has been held defamatory, or potentially defamatory, to damage a plaintiff's reputation by exposing him to ridicule is too elusive to encapsulate in any definition.... Where the issue is whether words have damaged a plaintiff's reputation by exposing him to ridicule, that question cannot be answered simply by considering whether the natural and ordinary meaning of the words used is defamatory per se. The question has to be considered in the light of the actual words used and the circumstance in which they are used. There are many ways of indicating that a person is hideously ugly, ranging from a simple statement of opinion to that effect, which I feel could never be defamatory, to words plainly intended to convey that message by way of ridicule. The words used in this case fall into the latter category. Whether they have exposed the plaintiff to ridicule to the extent that his reputation has been damaged must be answered by the jury. The preliminary point raised by the defendants cannot be answered in the affirmative and this appeal should be dismissed.

Millett LJ (dissenting)

Many a true word is spoken in jest. Many a false one too. But chaff and banter are not defamatory, and even serious imputations are not actionable if no one would take them to be meant seriously. . . .

Mr Berkoff is a director, actor and writer. Physical beauty is not a qualification for a director or writer. Mr Berkoff does not plead that he plays romantic leads or that the words complained of impugn his professional ability. In any case, I do not think that it can be defamatory to say of an actor that he is unsuitable to play particular roles. How then can the words complained of injure Mr Berkoff's reputation? They are an attack on his appearance, not on his reputation. It is submitted on his behalf that they would cause people 'to shun and avoid him' and would 'bring him into ridicule'. . . .

The cases in which words have been held to be defamatory because they would cause the plaintiff to be shunned or avoided, or 'cut off from society', have hitherto been confined to allegations that he suffers from leprosy or the plague or the itch or is noisome and smelly (see *Villers v Monsley* (1769) 2 Wils 403, 95 ER 886). I agree with Phillips LJ and for the reasons which he gives that an allegation of ugliness is not of that character. It is a common experience that ugly people have satisfactory social lives—Boris Karloff is not known to have been a recluse—and it is a popular belief for the truth of which I am unable to vouch that ugly men are particularly attractive to women.

I have no doubt that the words complained of were intended to ridicule Mr Berkoff, but I do not think that they made him look ridiculous or lowered his reputation in the eyes of ordinary people. . . .

The line between mockery and defamation may sometimes be difficult to draw. When it is, it should be left to the jury to draw it. . . . I am not persuaded that the present case could properly be put on the wrong side of the line. A decision that it is an actionable wrong to describe a man as 'hideously ugly' would be an unwarranted restriction on free speech. And if a bald statement to this effect would not be capable of being defamatory, I do not see how a humorously exaggerated observation to the like effect could be. People must be allowed to poke fun at one another without fear of litigation. It is one thing to ridicule a man; it is another to expose him to ridicule. Miss Burchill made a cheap joke at Mr Berkoff's expense; she may thereby have demeaned herself, but I do not believe that she defamed Mr Berkoff.

Appeal dismissed.

COMMENTARY

The previous authority on allegations of ugliness, referred to by Phillips LJ in the extract above, was *Winyard v Tatler Publishing Co Ltd* (1991) *Independent*, 16 August. In that case an allegation that the plaintiff, a beauty therapist, was an 'international boot' was said to mean, *inter alia*, that she was 'an ugly harridan'. In his judgment in the Court of Appeal, Staughton LJ referred to the judge's ruling:

It may well be that in some cases to say that a woman is old and ugly, or haggard, would do no more than cause injury to her feelings, and would not affect her character or reputation. But the judge evidently felt that a different view might be taken if she was a beauty therapist. It is not, apparently, that she would have failed to exercise her skills in preserving her own appearance, but that others might not wish her to be in charge of their treatment. I entirely agree with the judge's ruling on this point....

A joke will not lower a person's reputation if it is not meant to be treated seriously (e.g. as indicating a truly held view). *In Charleston v News Group Newspapers Ltd* [1995] 2 AC 65, the House of Lords considered a mock exposé on the front page of the *News of the World* in which the plaintiffs—Harold and Madge in the popular soap opera *Neighbours*—were pictured naked but for bondage gear and apparently engaged in sexual intercourse or sodomy; the headline read 'Strewth! What's Harold up to with our Madge? Porn Shocker for Neighbours Stars'. However, the captions on the pictures and the text of the article made it clear that the images were computer-generated: the actors were 'the unwitting stars of a sordid computer game' in which their faces were superimposed without their knowledge or consent on the bodies of real porn models. 'The remainder of the article', Lord Bridge noted (at 69), 'castigate[d] the makers of the "sordid computer game" in a tone of self-righteous indignation which contrast[ed] oddly with the prominence given to the main photograph'. His Lordship accepted that the publication must have been 'deeply offensive and insulting' to the plaintiffs, but held that it was not defamatory. The publication had to be read as a whole, and the headline and pictures considered in isolation could not give rise to liability; it was necessary always to consider whether the text of the article was sufficient to 'neutralise' the libellous implication of the headline, even though many readers might take note only of the latter. (For comment, see Prescott, 'Libel and Pornography' (1995) 58 MLR 752.)

Defamatory Statements: Other Examples

Numerous other examples of defamatory statements may be given. Imputations of criminal conduct are generally actionable, albeit that to say that someone has committed a parking offence or a minor speeding violation is unlikely to be regarded as defamatory. An allegation that the claimant has committed a civil wrong may also give rise to a cause of action, at least if the civil liability entails fault on the part of the wrongdoer (*Groom v Crocker* [1939] 1 KB 194: negligence relating to road traffic accident). And someone who is accused of morally disreputable behaviour also has a prima facie action for defamation (*Austin v Culpepper* (1684) 2 Show 313: 'dishonesty'; *MacLaren v Robertson* (1859) 21 D 183: 'liar'). Matters pertaining to sexual behaviour may be more problematic, especially as social attitudes here are liable to change very significantly with the passage of time. At the beginning of the century it was held that an allegation that a woman had had a child out of wedlock could be defamatory (*Chattell v Daily Mail* (1901) 18 TLR 165), but it is doubtful that to say the same now would be an actionable defamation. Imputations of homosexuality have on several occasions been found to be defamatory (see *Gatley*, para. 2.20), and, even if opinion about homosexuality has changed considerably over the years, it was accepted as recently as *Cruise v Express Newspapers plc* [1999] QB 931 that calling a married man 'gay' was capable of being defamatory. (Should saying the same of a single man, or woman, be treated differently?) Turning to matters financial, to say that someone is insolvent may well be actionable, because it will stop others trading with him, but merely to say that someone owes money gives rise to no right to sue, as that 'is true of every house-holder...on most days of the month' (*Wolfenden v Giles* (1892) 2 Br Col R 284 at 284, per Begbie CJ). Remarks made about a person's race give rise to issues of particular sensitivity. At various times, it has been held defamatory to describe an individual as German or as an 'international Jew financier', but special factors probably account for the result of these cases (see respectively *Slazenger Ltd v Gibbs* (1916) 33

TLR 35: 'German'—during World War I; *Camrose v Action Press, The Times*, 14–16 October 1937: 'international Jew financier'—*Gatley*, para. 2.16n suggests that the case turned on an imputation of disloyalty). Even in the middle of this century, courts in the American South held it defamatory to state that a white person was black (see, e.g., *Natchez Times v Dunigan*, 72 So 2d 681 (Miss. 1954)), but this was probably never the law in England (see *Hoare v Silverlock* (1848) 12 QB 630 at 632). In any case, here as elsewhere standards of right-thinking opinion have been subject to considerable changes over the course of time; indeed, it has more recently been held in the United States that it was defamatory of a corporation to state, at the time of apartheid, that it had had dealings with the government of South Africa (*Southern Air Transport Inc v American Broadcasting Co*, 877 F 2d 1010 (US App DC, 1989)).

Allegations of misfortune stand in a separate category. An allegation that a woman has been raped does not reflect upon her moral credit but it may yet be defamatory. The Court of Appeal in *Youssoupoff v Metro-Goldwyn-Mayer Pictures Ltd* (above) so held in respect of an allegation that the plaintiff had been seduced or raped by Rasputin, 'the Mad Monk'. Although it might be thought that the only emotion engendered by rape would be pity, the court felt that the reality of the situation was that the words tended 'to make the plaintiff be shunned and avoided and that without any moral discredit on her part' (at 587, per Slesser LJ). Perhaps the court had it in mind that people generally might try to avoid the plaintiff from embarrassment or some similar emotion. In like vein, we can suggest that to call someone 'insane', or to say that they suffer from at least some types of disease, may also be defamatory (as is presupposed by the rule that slanders imputing a serious contagious disease are actionable *per se*). But, as *Berkoff v Burchill* (above) suggests, it is doubtful whether an allegation that a person is ugly can be treated in the same way; if actionable, it should only be on the basis that it exposes the claimant to ridicule.

(b) The Standard of Opinion

'To write or say of a man something that will disparage him in the eyes of a particular section of the community but will not affect his reputation in the eyes of the average right-thinking man is not actionable within the law of defamation' (*Tolley v Fry* [1930] 1 KB 467 at 479, per Greer LJ). In a defamation action, the court must inquire into the beliefs of 'right-thinking' members of society: the question asked is whether the right-thinking person would construe the words in their ordinary meaning as lowering the reputation of the claimant. The courts accordingly inquire as to what people *should* think, not as to what they actually think. No doubt this varies over the course of time (see above), but there are certain constants, for example, in relation to allegations that the claimant has given information about the commission of a crime to the police.

Byrne v Deane [1937] 1 KB 818

Automatic gambling machines ('diddler machines'), which were kept illegally on the premises of a golf club of which the defendants were proprietors, were removed by the police after someone had informed them of the machines' presence. A verse appeared soon afterwards on some sheets of paper which were put up on the walls of the club. In a punning reference to the plaintiff, the last two lines of the verse read, but 'he who gave the game away, may he byrnn in hell and rue the day'. The issue for the Court of Appeal was whether the trial judge had been correct to leave to the jury the question whether the words were defamatory, in the sense that they meant that the plaintiff was 'guilty of underhand disloyalty' to his fellow members and should be ostracised by them. The defendants admitted that they had seen the notice on the wall, but denied having written it or put it there.

Slesser LJ

Now, in my view, to say or to allege of a man—and for this purpose . . . it does not matter whether the allegation is true or is not true—that he has reported certain acts, wrongful in law, to the police, cannot possibly be said to be defamatory of him in the minds of the general public.

We have to consider in this connection the *arbitrium boni*, the view which would be taken by the ordinary good and worthy subject of the King, and I have assigned to myself no other criterion than what a good and worthy subject of the King would think of some person of whom it had been said that he had put the law into motion against wrongdoers, in considering that such a good and worthy subject would not consider such an allegation in itself to be defamatory . . . .

[I]t has been argued here that these words in the present case cannot really be said to be defamatory because in substance the crime which it is suggested in the libel that this gentleman is endeavouring to prevent is really of so trivial a character, and one which is so popular with the mass of the people, that to prevent an innocent indulgence in the use of these machines, which have been described as 'diddlers' and also as 'fruit' machines, is not preventing a crime, the whole thing is so trivial, and that the real substance of the case is the dislike and animosity which must be created in the minds of his fellow members of the club against the plaintiff. I find it quite impossible, speaking for myself, to draw a distinction between one crime and another in this particular. In no case as it seems to me can it be said that merely to say of a man that he has given information which will result in the ending of a criminal act is in itself defamatory where he is doing no more than reporting to the police that which if known by the police might well end in the discovery of an illegal act and its suppression.

Greene LJ

If the allegation that he reported the matter to the police is not defamatory, in my judgment the allegation that in reporting the matter to the police he was guilty of disloyalty cannot be defamatory.

If that be right, the matter resolves itself into this: Are words capable of a defamatory meaning which say of the plaintiff that he reported to the police that on the club premises of which he was a member a criminal offence was being habitually committed? Now, it is said that the ordinary sense of society would say of a man who had done that in the case of this particular criminal offence that he had behaved in a disloyal and underhand fashion. It is said that this particular offence is one which can be looked at with an indulgent eye, and that there is something dishonourable in setting in motion the constitutional machinery provided in this country for the suppression of crime. I myself find it embarrassing to take into consideration questions of the way in which members of clubs might regard such an action. It seems to me that no distinction can be drawn between various categories of crime. I suggested in the course of the argument the case where members of a club were habitually engaged in having cock-fights conducted on the club premises, and I asked the question whether to say of a man that he had reported that to the police would be defamatory, and the answer that I got was not to my mind a satisfactory one. But to take the matter further: supposing in the club the members were engaged in habitually defrauding guests at cards, could it be said to be defamatory if a member of the club reported that to the police? and so on. It seems to me that if the argument is to be accepted it would involve the Court in this position: that it would have to differentiate between different kinds of crime and put in one category crimes which are of so bad a character as to call for universal reprobation even among the more easy-minded, and in another category crimes which many people think are stupid and ought never to have been made crimes at all.

It seems to me that, whatever may be the view of individuals on matters of that kind, this Court cannot draw a distinction of that description. In point of fact it may very well be that the Legislature in its wisdom has made into a crime something which the public conscience of many persons in this country does not consider involves any sort of moral reprobation; but this Court it seems to me cannot be concerned with considerations of that kind, and in my judgment to say of a man that he has put in motion the proper machinery for suppressing crime is a thing which cannot on the face of it be defamatory.

Greer LJ dissented.

Appeal allowed.

COMMENTARY

In *Mawe v Pigott* (1869) Ir R 4 CL 54 at 62, Lawson J stated: 'The very circumstances which will make a person be regarded with disfavour by the criminal classes will raise his character in the estimation of right-thinking men. We can only regard the estimation in which a man is held by society generally.' A contrasting (non-criminal) case is *Myroft v Sleight* (1921) 90 LJKB 883: McCardie J accepted that 'it would not be defamatory merely to say of an ordinary trade unionist . . . that he had openly continued at work in spite of the orders of his union', but on the facts of the case it was possible to find a separate imputation of disloyalty or hypocrisy which was in fact defamatory. (The plaintiff, who had voted in favour of strike action, was alleged to have asked his employer to let him continue working.) For another example of an implied imputation of hypocrisy, *see Shah v Akram* (1981) 79 LS Gaz 814 (allegation that a Muslim had insulted the Prophet).

Is the true rule of law from such cases that the courts cannot have regard to the opinion of a limited class of people like the members of a club or a union, or that it can only have regard to the opinions of 'right-thinking people'? Or is it a mixture of both? Compare the American approach: do the words hurt the plaintiff's standing with 'a considerable and respectable class in her community' (*Peck v Tribune Clo*, 214 US 185 (1909); supported by *Gatley*, para. 2.12 on the basis that 'the English test is arguably based upon the assumption of a consensus of moral opinion in society which, if it ever existed, has now passed away').

Reputation in an Illegal Calling or Activity

'The law does not regard a reputation illegally attained as proper to be protected' (*Wilkinson v Sporting Life* (1933) 49 CLR 365 at 379, per Evatt J). The case concerned an allegation that the plaintiff intended to cheat the public in the course of his undeniably illegal betting business. Despite the general rule just quoted, this allegation was found to be defamatory because the imputation of dishonesty tended to lower the plaintiff's estimation *as a person*, not merely as the practitioner of illegal activities.

(c) Meaning and the Question of Innuendo

In deciding whether or not the words used are in fact defamatory the jury is asked first to consider the meaning of the words in their 'natural and ordinary' sense. In some cases, however, the claimant may allege an 'innuendo' meaning. A *false or popular innuendo* is where the words bear a meaning that is not their literal meaning but instead constitutes an inference or implication from the words themselves. The question is whether a reasonable reader might 'read between the lines' (see *Lewis v Daily Telegraph* [1964] AC 234, extracted below). In such cases, the natural and ordinary meaning of the words is not their literal but their inferential meaning. A *true or legal innuendo*, by contrast, involves something more than reading between the lines. There is a true innuendo wherever the claimant argues that facts or circumstances which are not apparent from the words themselves ('extrinsic evidence') give those words a meaning they would not ordinarily have. A good illustration of a true innuendo can be seen in the case of *Cassidy v Daily Mirror Newspapers Ltd* [1929] 2 KB 331, also extracted below.

Lewis v Daily Telegraph [1964] AC 234

Details of a police investigation into the affairs of a large public company, Rubber Improvements Ltd, were leaked to the *Daily Telegraph*, which put a piece on the story on its front pages:

INQUIRY ON FIRM BY CITY POLICE

> Officers of the City of London Fraud Squad are inquiring to the affairs of Rubber Improvement Ltd and its subsidiary companies. The investigation was requested after criticisms of the chairman's statement and the accounts by a shareholder at the recent company meeting. The chairman of the company . . . is Mr John Lewis, former Socialist MP for Bolton.

A similar piece appeared in the *Daily Mail*. Lewis and his companies were subsequently absolved of all allegations of impropriety, and they issued writs against the proprietors of the two newspapers alleging that '[b]y the said words the defendants meant and were understood to mean that the affairs of the plaintiffs and/or its subsidiaries were conducted fraudulently or dishonestly or in such a way that the police suspected that their affairs were so conducted'. The defendants denied this, arguing that there were no grounds for imagining that reasonable readers would treat it as doing anything more than convey (accurate) information about the inquiry. The plaintiffs succeeded against both newspapers in separate trials, but, in a consolidated appeal, the Court of Appeal ruled that the judges had erred in leaving the cases to the jury. The plaintiffs appealed to the House of Lords.

Lord Reid

The essence of the controversy between the parties is that the appellants maintain that these passages are capable of meaning that they were guilty of fraud. The respondents deny this: they admit that the paragraphs are libellous but maintain that the juries ought to have been directed that they are not capable of the meaning which the appellants attribute to them. The learned judge directed the juries in such a way as to leave it open to them to accept the appellants' contention, and it is obvious from the amounts of damages awarded that the juries must have done this.

The gist of the two paragraphs is that the police, the City Fraud Squad, were inquiring into the appellants' affairs. There is no doubt that in actions for libel the question is what the words would convey to the ordinary man: it is not one of construction in the legal sense. The ordinary man does not live in an ivory tower and he is not inhibited by a knowledge of the rules of construction. So he can and does read between the lines in the light of his general knowledge and experience of worldly affairs. I leave aside questions of innuendo where the reader has some special knowledge which might lead him to attribute a meaning to the words not apparent to those who do not have that knowledge. That only arises indirectly in this case...

What the ordinary man would infer without special knowledge has generally been called the natural and ordinary meaning of the words. But that expression is rather misleading in that it conceals the fact that there are two elements in it. Sometimes it is not necessary to go beyond the words themselves, as where the plaintiff has been called a thief or a murderer. But more often the sting is not so much in the words themselves as in what the ordinary man will infer from them, and that is also regarded as part of their natural and ordinary meaning. Here there would be nothing libellous in saying that an inquiry into the appellants' affairs was proceeding: the inquiry might be by a statistician or other expert. The sting is in inferences drawn from the fact that it is the fraud squad which is making the inquiry. What those inferences should be is ultimately a question for the jury, but the trial judge has an important duty to perform....

In this case it is, I think, sufficient to put the test in this way. Ordinary men and women have different temperaments and outlooks. Some are unusually suspicious and some are unusually naive. One must try to envisage people between these two extremes and see what is the most damaging meaning they would put on the words in question. So let me suppose a number of ordinary people discussing one of these paragraphs which they had read in the newspaper. No doubt one of them might say—'Oh, if the fraud squad are after these people you can take it they are guilty.' But I would expect the others to turn on him, if he did say that, with such remarks as—'Be fair. This is not a police state. No doubt their affairs are in a mess or the police would not be interested. But that could be because Lewis or the cashier has been very stupid or careless. We really must not jump to conclusions. The police are fair and know their job and we shall know soon enough if there is anything in it. Wait till we see if they charge him. I wouldn't trust him until this is cleared up, but it is another thing to condemn him unheard.'

What the ordinary man, not avid for scandal, would read into the words complained of must be a matter of impression. I can only say that I do not think that he would infer guilt of fraud merely because an inquiry is on foot. And, if that is so, then it is the duty of the trial judge to direct the jury that it is for them to determine the meaning of the paragraph but that they must not hold it to impute guilt of fraud because as a matter of law the paragraph is not capable of having that meaning. So there was here, in my opinion, misdirection of the two juries sufficiently serious to require that there must be new trials.

Lord Hodson

Whether the words are capable of defamatory meaning is for the judge, and where the words, whether on the face of them they are or are not innocent in themselves, bear a defamatory or more defamatory meaning because of extraneous facts known to those to whom the libel has been published, it is the duty of the judge to rule whether there is evidence of such extraneous facts fit to be left to the jury.

It is in conjunction with secondary meanings that much of the difficulty surrounding the law of libel exists. These secondary meanings are covered by the word 'innuendo', which signifies pointing out what and who is meant by the words complained of....The first subdivision of the innuendo has lately been called the false innuendo as it is no more than an elaboration or embroidering of the words used without proof of extraneous facts. The true innuendo is that which depends on extraneous facts which the plaintiff has to prove in order to give the words the secondary meaning of which he complains....

There is one cause of action based on the words in their natural and ordinary meaning and another based on the words in such meaning as may be alleged in a true innuendo, but not a third cause of action based on the false innuendo...

Lord Morris of Borth-y-Gest (dissenting)

My Lords, a reasonable reader will probably be a fair-minded reader. The fair-minded reader would assume that a responsible newspaper would also be fair. If there was some private police inquiry in progress, the purpose of which was to ascertain whether or not there had been fraud or dishonesty, what possible justification could there be for proclaiming this far and wide to all the readers of a newspaper? If confidential information was received to the effect that there was a police inquiry, on what basis could the publishing of such information be warranted?...If there was a police inquiry by a 'Fraud Squad' which might result in the conclusion that any suspicion of fraud or dishonesty was wholly unwarranted, how manifestly unfair it would be to make public mention of the inquiry. What purpose could there be in doing so? With these thoughts and questions in his mind, a reasonable reader might well consider that no responsible newspaper would dare to publish, or would be so cruel as to publish, the words in question unless the confidential information, which in some manner they had obtained, was not information merely to the effect that there was some kind of inquiry in progress but was information to the effect that there was fraud or dishonesty. Some reasonable readers might therefore think that the words conveyed the meaning that there must have been fraud or dishonesty.

Lord Devlin delivered a separate concurring speech. **Lord Tucker** concurred with the speech of Lord Reid.

Appeal dismissed. Retrial ordered.

COMMENTARY

Disputes as to what meanings an allegedly defamatory statement can bear often form a major part of the pre-trial 'jockeying for position' between the parties which is a feature of many of the cases in this area. In considering the case law, it must always be remembered that trial of defamation actions is normally by jury, in contrast with most other actions in tort, including all actions for personal injury, which are heard by a judge sitting alone. It has been necessary, therefore, to develop rules to divide responsibility for the decision of different issues as between judge and jury, and this has led to a great deal of technicality—'technicalities beyond belief', according to Lord Denning (*What Next in the Law*, p. 179). According to Lord Donaldson MR, 'practice and procedure...in...claims for defamation is the last refuge of complexity and technicality in the law' (*Singh v Gillard* (1988) 138 NLJ 144 at 144). Because the determination of what allegations and evidence can be put in front of the jury is crucial, a whole succession of preliminary points may be taken as each side attempts to define the legal and factual issues in the way most favourable to itself. The result is that the process of pleading in a defamation action has come to resemble, according to one judge, an 'artificial minuet' (*Polly Peck (Holdings) plc v Trelford* [1986] 1 QB 1000 at 1020, per O'Connor LJ).

The present case shows that the 'dance' may continue even after full trial. In many of the appellate decisions extracted here, one side or other (here, the defendant) is arguing that the wrong issues were put to the jury. Here, it seems the defendants were aggrieved that their defence of truth was undermined because the jury might have construed the allegation to be that the plaintiffs were guilty of fraud, and not merely that they were suspected of it, even on reasonable grounds. Naturally, this might also have inflated the damages awarded. The defendants won before the Lords, and so were entitled to another trial, before a different jury, in which they could raise their defence again.

Meaning and Justification

As will have become apparent, there is an intrinsic link between questions of meaning and the defence of justification or truth (see further Section IV.1, below). A defendant pleading justification must prove the truth of each of the meanings the claimant is able to attribute to the words. In *Lewis*, the burden for the defendant at the retrial would have been to prove that the plaintiff had been reasonably suspected of guilt (but not that he was in fact guilty, as that was not what the defendant had alleged). In order to do so, he would now have to identify particular conduct on the part of the plaintiff giving rise to such a suspicion (see *Shah v Standard Chartered Bank* [1999] QB 241).

Innuendoes

In the course of his concurring speech in *Lewis*, above, Lord Devlin (at 278) gave the following explanation of a true innuendo:

> a derogatory implication...might not be detected at all, except by a person who was already in possession of some specific information. Thus, to say of a man that he was seen to enter a named house would contain a derogatory implication for anyone who knew that that house was a brothel but not for anyone who did not...

Where the claimant alleges a true innuendo, he must particularise in his statement of case the facts and matters which he relies upon in support of the extended meaning. As a matter of pleading, the approach recommended by the House of Lords in *Lewis* was for the claimant to set out in one paragraph of the statement of case the actual words used, in a second paragraph to set out any inferential (i.e. false innuendo) meanings allegedly to be derived from those words, and in a third paragraph to set out any secondary (i.e. true innuendo) meaning allegedly acquired by the words when read in the light of special facts, not apparent from the words themselves, alongside particulars of the special facts.

As the extract from Lord Hodson's speech makes clear, a single publication may give rise to more than one cause of action: one in respect of the ordinary meaning of the words; another in respect of each true innuendo arising from the words. What significance does this have in practice? Why does a false innuendo not give rise to a separate cause of action?

Defamatory Meaning Unknown to the Defendant

The intention of the defendant in making the statement is wholly irrelevant, so the lack of any intention to defame is no defence if the words would be understood as defamatory by those to whom they were communicated. As the following extract shows, this applies even in the case of a true innuendo where the defendant does not know the facts which made an apparently innocent statement defamatory.

Cassidy v Daily Mirror Newspapers Ltd [1929] 2 KB 331

The defendants published a photograph taken of Kettering Cassidy, also known as Michael Corrigan, and a woman. Cassidy, perhaps given to fantasy (he described himself as having been a General in the Mexican army), told a press photographer that he was going to marry the woman, and the photograph appeared above the words: 'Mr M. Corrigan, the race horse owner, and Miss [name omitted], whose engagement has been announced.' The action was brought by Mrs Cassidy, Cassidy's lawful wife. Although they lived apart Cassidy occasionally visited her. She argued that the words and picture were capable of meaning that 'Corrigan' was a single man and that, therefore, she was living in immoral co-habitation with him and only masquerading as his wife. At the trial, three of her acquaintances testified that they had in fact believed this on seeing the publication. The judge directed the jury to consider whether the publication was capable of conveying a meaning defamatory of the plaintiff to reasonably-minded people who knew the circumstances. The jury returned a verdict for the plaintiff for £500. The defendants appealed.

Scrutton LJ

[T]he alleged libel does not mention the plaintiff, but I think it is clear that words published about A may indirectly be defamatory of B. For instance, 'A is illegitimate.' To persons who know the parents those words may be defamatory of the parents. Or again, 'A has given way to drink; it is unfortunately hereditary'; to persons who know A's parents these words may be defamatory. Or 'A holds a D. Litt. degree of the University at X, the only one awarded.' To persons who know B, who habitually describes himself (and rightly so) as 'D. Litt. of X,' these words may be capable of a defamatory meaning. Similarly, to say that A is a single man or a bachelor may be capable of a defamatory meaning if published to persons who know a lady who passes as Mrs. A and whom A visits....

I do not agree with some dicta to the effect that if words are capable of several meanings, some defamatory and some innocent, they should not be left to the jury. I agree with the view expressed arguendo by Sir Montague Smith in the case of *Simmons v Mitchell* (1880) 6 App Cas 156, 158: 'The judge must decide if the words are reasonably capable of two meanings; if he so decide, the jury must determine which of the two meanings was intended;' and by 'intended' I understand that a man is liable for the reasonable inferences to be drawn from the words he used, whether he foresaw them or not, and that if he scatters two-edged and ambiguous statements broadcast, without knowing or making inquiry about facts material to the statements he makes and the inferences which may be drawn from them, he must be liable to persons who, knowing those facts, draw reasonable inferences from the words he publishes.

In my view the words published were capable of the meaning 'Corrigan is a single man,' and were published to people who knew the plaintiff professed to be married to Corrigan; it was for the jury to say whether those people could reasonably draw the inference that the so-called Mrs. Corrigan was in fact living in immoral cohabitation with Corrigan, and I do not think their finding should be interfered with.

But the second point taken was that the defendants could not be liable for the inference drawn, because they did not know the facts which enabled some persons to whom the libel was published, to draw an inference defamatory of the plaintiff.... In my view, ... it is impossible for the person publishing a statement which, to those who know certain facts, is capable of a defamatory meaning in regard to A, to defend himself by saying: 'I never heard of A and did not mean to injure him.' If he publishes words reasonably capable of being read as relating directly or indirectly to A and, to those who know the facts about A, capable of a defamatory meaning, he must take the consequences of the defamatory inferences reasonably drawn from his words.

It is said that this decision would seriously interfere with the reasonable conduct of newspapers. I do not agree. If publishers of newspapers, who have no more rights than private persons, publish statements which may be defamatory of other people, without inquiry as to their truth, in order to make their paper attractive, they must take the consequences, if on subsequent inquiry, their statements are found to be untrue or capable of defamatory and unjustifiable inferences. No one could contend that 'M. Corrigan, General in the Mexican Army,' was 'a source in whom we have full confidence.' To publish statements first and inquire into their truth afterwards, may seem attractive and up to date. Only to publish after inquiry may be slow, but at any rate it would lead to accuracy and reliability.

Russell LJ

Liability for libel does not depend on the intention of the defamer; but on the fact of defamation. . . . From a business point of view no doubt it may pay them [sc. the defendants] not to spend time or money in making inquiries, or verifying statements before publication; but if they had not made a false statement they would not now be suffering in damages. They are paying a price for their methods of business. . . .

Greer LJ (dissenting)

If the decision of my brethren in this case is right, it would be right to say that I could be successfully sued for damages for libel if, having been introduced to two apparently respectable people as persons engaged to be married, I repeated that statement in a letter to a friend, on the ground that my words meant that a lady totally unknown to me, who was in fact the wife of the man, was not his wife and was living in immoral intercourse with him. It seems to me wholly unreasonable to hold that my words could be construed as meaning anything of the kind, and wholly unjust that I should be made to pay damages because some unduly suspicious person drew an inference from the fact I stated, which was derogatory to the woman in question—and I am afraid that for the future people will have to walk with wary steps through life and hesitate a long time before they accept the assertion of any one whom they have known as a bachelor, that he is in truth a single man.

Appeal dismissed.

COMMENTARY

The Court of Appeal regarded itself as bound by the decision of the House of Lords in *E Hulton & Co v Jones*, extracted below. In 1952, the Porter Committee (Cmd. 7536) considered that holding defendants liable in such circumstances, without regard to whether or not they had exercised reasonable care, was liable to produce injustice. It recommended the introduction of a new statutory defence in cases of 'unintentional defamation' where the defendant could prove that he had taken reasonable care not to defame the plaintiff. In the Committee's view, a defendant relying upon the defence should have to take steps to clear the plaintiff's reputation by publishing a correction and an apology, whose form, in event of dispute, would be settled by the court. The defence was implemented, broadly in line with the Committee's recommendations, by Defamation Act 1952, s. 4. The most recent version of the defence appears in Defamation Act 1996, s. 2 (extracted below, p. 764).

2. The Statement must Refer to the Claimant

(a) General

'It is an essential element of the cause of action in defamation that the words complained of should be published "of the plaintiff"' (*Knuppfer v London Express* [1944] AC 116 at 120, per Viscount Simon LC). This is the requirement of reference to the claimant: the claimant must be identified as the person defamed. The claimant may be identified by name, description, pun (consider *Byrne v Deane*, above) or any reasonable inference. It is not necessary that there should be any 'peg or pointer' in the defamatory words, but only that reasonable people might understand the words as referring to the claimant. Furthermore, 'words published about A may indirectly be defamatory of B' (*Cassidy v Daily Mirror Newspapers Ltd* [1929] 2 KB 331 at 338–9, per Scrutton LJ), so a statement that A is a single man or a bachelor may be capable of a defamatory meaning if published to persons who know a woman who passes as Mrs A and whom A visits (as in *Cassidy*, above). As with the question of defamatory meaning, it is not necessary that the defendant intended to refer to the claimant. The question is not who was *meant* but who was *hit* (*E Hulton & Co v Jones* [1910] AC 20 at 22, per Lord Loreburn LC, *arguendo*). It is irrelevant that the defendant did not intend to refer to any real person but was talking instead about a fictional character (see *Hulton*, extracted below) or even that he intended to refer to another person of whom the words were true (*Newstead v London Express Newspaper Ltd* [1940] 1 KB 3). To this extent, defamation is a tort of strict liability.

E. Hulton & Co v Jones [1910] AC 20

Artemus Jones, a barrister, brought an action against the defendants in respect of a newspaper article which he claimed referred to him; he had previously contributed pieces to the newspaper in question. The article referred to 'Artemus Jones' a church warden in Peckham and cast imputations on his moral behaviour at a motor festival in Dieppe ('There is Artemus Jones with a woman who is not his wife, who must be, you know—the other thing!'). The defendants argued they had never intended the article to refer to the 'real' Artemus Jones but instead had intended to create a fictitious character whom they had given a 'fancy name'. After the plaintiff had succeeded at trial, the defendants appealed to the Court of Appeal and then to the House of Lords.

Lord Loreburn

My Lords, I think this appeal must be dismissed. A question in regard to the law of libel has been raised which does not seem to me to be entitled to the support of your Lordships. Libel is a tortious act. What does the tort consist in? It consists in using language which others knowing the circumstances would reasonably think to be defamatory of the person complaining of and injured by it. A person charged with libel cannot defend himself by shewing that he intended in his own breast not to defame, or that he intended not to defame the plaintiff, if in fact he did both. He has none the less imputed something disgraceful and has none the less injured the plaintiff. A man in good faith may publish a libel believing it to be true, and it may be found by the jury that he acted in good faith believing it to be true, and reasonably believing it to be true, but that in fact the statement was false. Under those circumstances he has no defence to the action, however excellent his intention. If the intention of the writer be immaterial in considering whether the matter written is defamatory, I do not see why it need be relevant in considering whether it is defamatory of the plaintiff. The writing, according to the old form, must be malicious, and it must be of and concerning the plaintiff. Just as the defendant could not excuse himself from malice by proving that he wrote it in the most benevolent spirit, so he cannot shew that the libel was not of and concerning the plaintiff by proving that he never heard of the plaintiff. His intention in both respects equally is inferred from what he did. His remedy is to abstain from defamatory words...

The damages are certainly heavy, but I think your Lordships ought to remember...that the jury were entitled to think, in the absence of proof satisfactory to them (and they were the judges of it), that some ingredient of recklessness, or more than recklessness, entered into the writing and the publication of this article, especially as Mr Jones, the plaintiff, had been employed on this very newspaper, and his name was well known in the paper and also well known in the district in which the paper circulated.

Lord Atkinson, **Lord Gorell** and **Lord Shaw of Dunfermline** concurred.

Appeal dismissed.

COMMENTARY

Hulton has been described as 'the most famous case in the law of libel' and also 'the most controversial' (Lord Denning, *What Next in the Law* (London: Butterworths, 1982), p. 173). It would certainly seem very unfair that an author should be held liable in defamation just because a real-life person happened to share the name of one of the author's less attractive creations. However, this is unlikely to be the result of the decision. The jury must always be satisfied that the words could reasonably be understood as referring to the claimant. Perhaps what swayed the jury in this case was evidence revealed in cross-examination that the writer of the piece had actually had a previous run-in with the plaintiff, which substantially undermined his claim that his use of the name was pure coincidence (see Mitchell, 'Artemus Jones and the Press Club' (1999) 20 J Leg His 64).

Negative Checking

In order to avoid liability under this principle, producers of film, television, and radio fiction now habitually engage in a practice known as 'negative checking' by which attempts are made to ensure that characters cannot be coincidentally confused with real-life figures (see *Barendt*, pp. 114–15). During the making of the TV series *Inspector Morse*, for example, the programme-makers checked with Thames Valley police to make sure there could be no confusion between real-life and fictional officers (p. 115n). *Barendt* comments (p. 195):

Arguably, it is bizarre to require broadcasters to go to the lengths they do to minimize the chance of liability for unintentional defamation. Negative checking of reference books and lists of addresses surely goes beyond the taking of reasonable precautions required in other areas of the law. Other media outlets do not have the time or the facilities to engage in this burdensome activity.

Bona Fide News Reports

The rule in *Hulton v Jones* was subsequently applied to bona fide news reporting (with what Lord Denning, *op. cit.*, considered 'an equally absurd result': p. 177). In *Morgan v Odhams Press Ltd* [1971] 1 WLR 1239, the defendants had published an article which stated that a certain woman had been kidnapped by a dog-doping gang. The woman had in fact been staying voluntarily with the plaintiff around this time. At trial, the plaintiff produced several witnesses who said that they thought that the article referred to him, and the jury returned a verdict in his favour. By a majority, the House of Lords held that the trial judge had been correct to leave the matter to the jury. It was immaterial that a close reading of the article would have made it clear that it could not refer to the plaintiff, as the ordinary reader does not read a newspaper article with the care with which a lawyer would read an important legal document, but may read it quickly in order to get a general impression.

Words True of their Intended Target

The difficulty facing news editors and other publishers is compounded by the rule that words true of their intended target may nevertheless be—wholly unforeseeably—defamatory of another. In *Newstead v London Express Newspaper Ltd* [1940] 1 KB 377, the *Daily Express* had described the prisoner in a trial for bigamy as 'Harold Newstead, thirty-year-old Camberwell man'. The plaintiff coincidentally fitted that description and was allowed to recover. The Court of Appeal applied *Hulton*, and held that the fact that the defendant had taken all due care was quite irrelevant. However, although Newstead won on the law before the Court of Appeal, the court declined to interfere with the jury's assessment of damages at a mere one farthing. (Perhaps this tells us something about the jury's view of this particular legal principle.)

Ability to Make Offer of Amends

In cases of this type, as in cases of unknown defamatory meaning (above), defendants may be able protect themselves by making an offer of amends under Defamation Act 1996, s. 2. This applies, *inter alia*, to publications in which the defendant neither knew nor had reason to know that the statement referred to the claimant or was likely to be so understood. The provision requires defendants to offer to print a correction and apology, and to pay such compensation and costs as are agreed or determined by the court. An advantage for defendants is that such compensation is assessed, in default of agreement, by a judge rather than a jury. See further Section IV.4, below.

Effect of the Human Rights Act

In *O'Shea v MGN Ltd* [2001] EMLR 40, the claimant complained of an advertisement appearing in the *Sunday Mirror* on behalf of an adult internet service. The advertisement included a photograph of a glamour model who closely resembled the claimant. The claimant alleged that the advertisement meant that she was appearing or performing on a highly pornographic website containing material of an explicit, indecent and lewd nature and had shamelessly agreed to promote the website and her appearance on it in a national newspaper. The claimant pleaded that a number of persons had identified her with the photograph. The defendant applied for summary judgment. Morland J accepted that a jury might reasonably have concluded that the claimant was the person referred to in the publication, but granted the application on the basis that it would be contrary to Article 10 of the European Convention on Human Rights to impose strict liability for inadvertent defamatory reference to a claimant as a result of identification from a photograph of somebody else of similar appearance. The strict liability rule represented an interference with the Convention right to freedom of expression, and there was no pressing social need for such interference such as would justify it under Article 10(2):

> The fact that in over a century no claim has been made in respect of a libel in respect of a 'look-alike' picture is an indication that there is no pressing social need for the application of the strict liability principle for the protection of the reputation of the 'look-alike'. . . . [M]y judgment is that the strict liability principle should not cover the 'look-alike' situation. To allow it to do so would be an unjustifiable interference with the vital right of freedom of expression disproportionate to the legitimate aim of protecting the reputations of 'look-alikes' and contrary to Article 10 of the Convention.

Morland J noted, at [33], that Defamation Act 1996, s. 2 did not substantially mitigate the strictness of the liability because it did not create a 'true' defence, for '[t]he blameless publisher has not only to make and publish a correction and apology but also to offer compensation'.

The *O'Shea* case indicates the potentially transformative effect of the Human Rights Act on the law of defamation, though it must be questioned whether the potential will ever be fully realised. There seems as yet to be no judicial appetite for reappraising the basic rule in *Hulton v Jones*. Whether the *O'Shea* decision will itself survive scrutiny by the appellate courts is open to some considerable doubt.

(b) Group Defamation

Where words are spoken of a group of people, proof that the article refers to an individual member of that group, is likely to be difficult. The classic example is the statement that 'all lawyers are thieves', which it has been said gives rise to no cause of action on the part of any individual lawyer (*Eastwood v Holmes* (1858) 1 F & F 347). However, there is no special rule precluding liability in all cases of group or class defamation.

Knuppfer v London Express Newspapers [1944] AC 116

The case arose out of a newspaper article, published at the time of World War II. The article claimed that a political party formed by émigrés from the Soviet Union, the 'Young Russians', consisted of 'quislings' with whom Hitler intended to establish a pro-German movement within the Soviet Union. The party, which the article stated was established in France and the United States, was alleged to be 'a minute body professing a pure Fascist ideology'; the article also claimed that 'Hitler intends to nominate a puppet fuehrer from their ranks to replace the Soviet national leaders of the Kremlin, and establish a reactionary totalitarian serf State...'. It concluded: 'The vast majority of Russian emigrés repudiate these people, but Hitler is accustomed to find instruments among the despised dregs of every community.' The plaintiff, a Russian resident in London who was head of the British branch of the Young Russia party, brought an action against the defendants for damages for libel, setting out the above words in his statement of claim, and alleging that they had been falsely and maliciously published of him by the defendants. The defendants denied that the words were reasonably capable of being understood to refer to the plaintiff. The total membership of the Young Russia Party worldwide was about 2,000 but the British branch comprised only twenty-four members. Four witnesses who were acquainted with the plaintiff testified that they thought of him when they read the article. The plaintiff won at trial, but lost before the Court of Appeal. He appealed to the House of Lords.

Viscount Simon LC

In the words complained of in this case there is no specific mention of the appellant from beginning to end, and the only countries in which it is stated that this group of emigrés is established are France and the United States.... The words make allegations of a defamatory character about a body of persons—some thousands in number—who belong to a society whose members are to be found in many countries...

Where the plaintiff is not named, the test which decides whether the words used refer to him is the question whether the words are such as would reasonably lead persons acquainted with the plaintiff to believe that he was the person referred to. There are cases in which the language used in reference to a limited class may be reasonably understood to refer to every member of the class, in which case every member may have a cause of action. A good example is *Browne v DC Thomson & Co*, 1912 SC 359, where a newspaper article stated in Queenstown 'instructions were issued by the Roman Catholic religious authorities that all Protestant shop assistants were to be discharged,' and where seven pursuers who averred that they were the sole persons who exercised religious authority in the name and on behalf of the Roman Catholic Church in Queenstown were held entitled to sue for libel as being individually defamed. . . . In the present case, however, the appellant rejected the view that every member of the Young Russia Group could bring his own action on the words complained of, and relied on his own prominence or representative character in the movement as establishing that the words referred to himself. There is, however, nothing in the words which refers to one member of the group rather than another. *Le Fanu v Malcolmson* (1848) 1 HLC 637 was, it is true, a decision of this House in which Lord Cottenham LC and Lord Campbell held that the verdict of a jury awarding damages to the owners of a factory in the county of Waterford against the proprietor of a newspaper published in that county could be upheld notwithstanding that the letterpress, in the course of denouncing the alleged cruelty with which factory operatives were treated, did not specifically refer to the plaintiff's factory. It appears, however, in that case that there were circumstances, such as the location of the factory, which enabled the jurors to identify the plaintiff's factory as the factory pointed at. . . . It will be observed that *Le Fanu v Malcolmson* was a case where there were facts pointing to the particular factory which was meant to be referred to though the article spoke in more general terms of a factory in Waterford. In the present case the statement complained of is not made concerning a particular individual, whether named or unnamed, but concerning a group of people spread over several countries and including considerable numbers. No facts were proved in evidence which could identify the appellant as the person individually referred to. Witnesses called for the appellant were asked the carefully framed question: 'To whom did your mind go when you read that article?' and they not unnaturally replied by pointing to the appellant himself, but that is because they happened to know the appellant as the leading member of the society in this country and not because there is anything in the article itself which ought to suggest even to his friends that he is referred to as an individual.

Lord Atkin in a short concurring opinion, warned against over-complicating the law in this area:

I venture to think that it is a mistake to lay down a rule as to libel on a class, and then qualify it with exceptions. The only relevant rule is that in order to be actionable the defamatory words must be understood to be published of and concerning the plaintiff. It is irrelevant that the words are published of two or more persons if they are proved to be published of him, and it is irrelevant that the two or more persons are called by some generic or class name. There can be no law that a defamatory statement made of a firm, or trustees, or the tenants of a particular building is not actionable, if the words would reasonably be understood as published of each member of the firm or each trustee or each tenant. The reason why a libel published of a large or indeterminate number of persons described by some general name generally fails to be actionable is the difficulty of establishing that the plaintiff was, in fact, included in the defamatory statement, for the habit of making unfounded generalizations is ingrained in ill-educated or vulgar minds, or the words are occasionally intended to be a facetious exaggeration. Even in such cases words may be used which enable the plaintiff to prove that the words complained of were intended to be published of each member of the group, or, at any rate, of himself.

Lord Thankerton and **Lord Russell of Killowen** concurred.

Appeal dismissed.

COMMENTARY

The principles set out by Viscount Simon LC were applied in *Aspro Travel Ltd v Owners Abroad Group* [1996] 1 WLR 132. In that case the Court of Appeal accepted, for the purposes of determining a preliminary issue, that a defamatory statement about the conduct of the affairs of a small family company could be understood as referring to each of the company directors. See also *Riches v News Group Newspapers* [1986] QB 256 (11 members of 'the Banbury CID' defamed individually). In which of Viscount Simon's two categories did these cases fall?

How was it that the plaintiff was able to succeed in *Le Fanu v Malcolmson*, mentioned by Viscount Simon in the extract, even though the allegations did not refer to each and every member of the class mentioned in the offending newspaper article (factory-owners in the county of Waterford)?

3. The Statement must be Published

The law of defamation is concerned with the protection of people's reputation in the eyes of their fellows. Accordingly, it is a requirement of an action in defamation that the words complained of be published to a person other than the person impugned. 'Publication' here means no more than 'communication', even to a single person, and a publisher is any person who communicates a defamatory meaning to a third party. A statement may be published in an almost infinite variety of ways, for example, in the course of a conversation, by letter, in a newspaper or book, or by broadcast transmission. Publication may be by omission, for example, a failure to remove graffiti scrawled on the walls of one's property (cf. *Byrne v Deane* [1937] 1 KB 818; unless removing the graffiti would require great trouble and expense: see p. 838, per Greene LJ), and in some circumstances a person may by conduct impliedly associate himself with words which cannot be shown to have been written or uttered by him (*Hird v Wood* (1894) 38 Sol J 234: man's sitting near placard and pointing at it with his finger held to be a publication). It has long been established, by exception to the general rule, that communication to the defendant's spouse is no publication (*Wennhak v Morgan* (1880) 20 QBD 637), though communication to *the claimant's* spouse *can* give rise to liability (*Theaker v Richardson* [1962] 1 WLR 151).

Every repetition of a defamatory statement is a new publication and creates a fresh cause of action in the person defamed. The publication must be made to a person capable of understanding the defamatory meaning. Where, for example, the statement is not defamatory on its face, but only when considered in the light of extrinsic evidence, the hearer must know of the extrinsic facts which make the statement defamatory (see *Cassidy*, above). Similarly, if a defamatory statement is written in a foreign language the recipient must be able to understand it. It is not necessary for the claimant to prove that the publication was intentionally made, but only that it was the natural and probable consequence of his actions.

Huth v Huth [1915] 3 KB 32

A man sent to his wife a letter which was defamatory of her and their children. It was opened and read by the butler. At the time, a wife was unable to sue her husband in tort, so the action was brought by the children. At first instance, the jury returned a verdict in favour of the defendant. The plaintiffs appealed to the Court of Appeal, which considered the question whether evidence that the butler had opened and read the letter was evidence of publication to a third party.

Lord Reading CJ

[I]t is no part of a butler's duty to open letters that come to the house of his master or mistress addressed to the master or mistress. . . . No one can help a man's curiosity being excited, but it does not justify him in opening a letter, and it could not make the defendant liable for the publication to the butler of the contents of the envelope . . .

Swinfen Eady LJ and **Bray J** agreed.

Appeal dismissed.

COMMENTARY

In *Huth v Huth*, the correspondence was contained in an (unsealed) envelope. It appears that a different rule applies where it is conveyed by way of a postcard which is not enclosed in an envelope. According to the so-called 'postcard rule', the words are presumed to be published to every person through whose hands the card passes: see *Oliphant*, para. 25.83.

In *Theaker v Richardson* [1962] 1 WLR 151 the defendant wrote a defamatory letter to the plaintiff who was a married woman. The letter, which was addressed to the plaintiff, was contained in a manila envelope similar to the kind used for distributing election addresses. The plaintiff's husband opened the envelope thinking (he said) that it was an election address. At the trial the jury found there had been a publication of a defamatory statement and awarded damages to the plaintiff. On appeal to the Court of Appeal, Pearson LJ stated (at 161) that the question that should be asked was, '[Was] his (i.e. the recipient's) conduct so unusual, out of the ordinary and not reasonably to be anticipated, or was it something which could quite easily and naturally happen in the ordinary course of events?' This was pre-eminently a jury question and as the jury had decided that the opening of the letter by the husband was something that could quite easily happen in the ordinary course of events the Court of Appeal would not interfere with their decision.

By Defamation Act 1996, s. 1, a special defence now applies to mere *distributors* of defamatory material, provided certain conditions are met. See further Section IV.5, below.

Repetition of Defamatory Statements

The originator of a defamatory statement may be liable not only for its republication with his authorisation, which gives rise to a second cause of action against him, but also for a third party's unauthorised but foreseeable repetition of allegations contained within the original publication. Here, there is only one cause of action, and the repetition of the allegations by the third party goes only to the question of damages. In *Slipper v British Broadcasting Corporation* [1991] 1 QB 283, the plaintiff, a retired police officer, had been the subject of a television programme about attempts to bring the escaped 'Great Train Robber', Ronnie Biggs, back to Britain from Brazil. The plaintiff alleged that the programme portrayed him as an 'incompetent buffoon'. The defendant television company had shown a preview of the programme to an audience of the press and television journalists prior to its broadcast to the public at large. As a result of the preview a number of reviews appeared in newspapers and magazines repeating the defamatory sting of the programme. The plaintiff claimed that passages from several specified newspaper reviews which repeated the allegedly defamatory sting of the film should be taken into account in the assessment of general damages. The defendants applied to have the parts of the claim based on the repetition of the libel struck out. They argued that defendants in a libel action are not liable for the repetition of the libel by a third party who was not their agent unless the third party was authorised to do so, it was intended that the third party do so, or the third party was morally bound to do so. The Court of Appeal rejected the defendant's argument that the repetition of a libel was only actionable in these limited circumstances, Slade LJ adopting a test of whether the repetition was reasonably foreseeable. In *McManus v Beckham* [2002] 1 WLR 2982 Waller LJ thought that the use of the term 'reasonable foreseeability' was 'dangerous' and that there could be situations where the originator of a defamatory statement would not be liable for its foreseeable repetition. But he conceded that it might not be necessary to show that the defendant was actually aware of the risk of repetition, provided a reasonable person would have recognised the risk as significant.

The Court of Appeal was there concerned with an action for slander against the pop-star, Victoria Beckham, wife of the footballer, David Beckham. Whilst in the claimants' shop, which sold celebrity memorabilia, she claimed that an autograph that purported to be her husband's was a fake and said to customers in the shop: 'Excuse me but do not buy any autographs from this shop, they are all fakes. This is not my husband's signature out there.' The incident was later described in a number of press reports. In a preliminary hearing, the question for the Court of Appeal was whether to strike out that part of the statement of claim relating to the stories in the press and the loss which the claimants alleged their business had suffered as a result of the stories. The court denied the striking-out application. Although Waller LJ stated that it was best in such cases not to use a test of foreseeability, Laws LJ considered that this was still the underlying issue, though he conceded that the term might usefully be avoided in the interests of clarity and the jury instructed in more explicit terms. Clarke LJ stated that he saw no disagreement between his two colleagues and concurred with them both.

Publication on the Internet

Every time an internet user accesses defamatory material posted on a website or stored in an electronic archive, there is a fresh publication giving rise to a new cause of action against the publisher (see, respectively, *Godfrey v Demon Internet Ltd* [2001] QB 201 and *Loutchansky v Times Newspapers Ltd (No. 2)* [2001] EWCA Civ 1805, [2002] QB 783). But who is the publisher of defamatory material posted on the internet? The author, of course—but what about the internet service provider (ISP) hosting the website, or even the moderator of a bulletin board or chat room? In *Bunt v Tilley* [2007] 1 WLR 1243 at [23] and [36], Eady J stated:

[F]or a person to be held responsible there must be knowing involvement in the process of publication of *the relevant words*. It is not enough that a person merely plays a passive instrumental role in the process...[A]n ISP which performs no more than a passive role in facilitating postings on the Internet cannot be deemed to be a publisher at common law.

An ISP was no more the publisher of defamatory material passing through its server without its knowledge than a telephone company would be the publisher of a defamatory call, or the postal services of a defamatory letter. In the usual case, 'ISPs do not participate in the process of publication as such but merely act as facilitators... They provide a means of transmitting communications without in any way participating in them' (at [9]). Exceptionally, however, the ISP could be held liable at common law if it had been notified of a defamatory posting and so rendered responsible for publication from that moment onwards (as in *Godfrey v Demon*, above). In such a case, the ISP might be able to rely upon a defence as a mere 'distributor' of the material in question (see Section IV.5, below), but a facilitator is not a publisher at all, and so has no need of a defence.

Since August 2002, the ISP has also been entitled to rely on the defences that it was the 'mere conduit' for the transmission of the defamatory material, that the transmission of the material resulted from automatic 'caching', and that it was merely hosting material which it did not know, and had no reason to know, was unlawful (Electronic Commerce (EC Directive) Regulations 2002, regs. 17–19).

Archival Material

In *Loutchansky v Times Newspapers Ltd (No. 2)* [2002] QB 783, the defendant newspaper argued that the court should adopt the 'single publication rule' that applies in several jurisdictions in the United States, whereby an article stored in their archive would be published once and for all at the time of its initial posting, and would give rise to only one cause of action no matter how many times it was accessed. On this basis, the claim against them was out of time as the article in question had first been put in the archive more than a year before proceedings were initiated. In support of this argument, the defendant newspaper relied on the court's duty under s. 6 of the Human Rights Act to develop the law compatibly with (*inter alia*) Article 10 of the European Convention, even if this meant departing from an established rule of English law. The Court of Appeal rejected the argument. There was no reason to believe that that the traditional 'multiple publication' rule was inconsistent with the right to freedom of expression under the Convention. The orthodox rule did not have a 'chilling effect' going beyond what was necessary and proportionate in a democratic society for the protection of reputation. Although the maintenance of archives, whether in hard copy or on the internet, had some social utility, it represented a comparatively insignificant aspect of freedom of expression. In any case, the law of defamation would not necessarily inhibit the responsible maintenance of archives, because attaching an appropriate notice to archive material which was or could be defamatory, so as to warn against treating it as the truth, would normally remove any defamatory sting. The court accepted that permitting an action to be based on the accessing of archive material long after its general publication could be seen to be at odds with some of the reasons for the introduction of a twelve-month limitation period for defamation, but it considered that the scale of the new publication and the injury resulting from it was likely to be modest when compared with the original publication. There was therefore no warrant for radically changing the law of defamation in the manner suggested.

In *Times Newspapers Ltd v United Kingdom* [2009] EMLR 14, the European Court of Human Rights found no breach of Article 10 of the Convention (freedom of expression) in the *Loutchansky* decision. Agreeing with the Court of Appeal, the ECtHR stated, at [47], that the requirement to publish an appropriate qualification to the archived article where libel proceedings were initiated in respect of the version in print was not a disproportionate interference with the right to freedom of expression. The ECtHR ruled, at [48], that no question of a potentially ceaseless liability for defamation arose on the facts, as the libel claim regarding the archive was brought while proceedings regarding the print version were underway, but it cautioned that 'libel proceedings brought against a newspaper after a significant lapse of time may well, in the absence of exceptional circumstances, give rise to a disproportionate interference with press freedom under Article 10.'

See also *Gutnick v Dow Jones & Co Inc* (2002) 210 CLR 575, where the High Court of Australia affirmed the multiple publication rule in a case in which it upheld an Australian businessman's entitlement to sue in Australia in respect of an internet article uploaded in the United States, some of the recorded 'hits' having been in Australia.

At time of writing, the multiple publication rule was the subject of a Ministry of Justice consultation exercise (see Ministry of Justice, *Defamation and the internet: the multiple publication rule*, CP20/09, 2009). One option being considered, as an alternative to introducing a single publication rule, is to extend the defence of qualified privilege to publications on online archives outside the one-year limitation period for the initial publication, unless the publisher refuses or neglects to update the electronic version, on request, with a reasonable letter or statement by the claimant by way of explanation or contradiction. In early 2010, a Parliamentary committee recommended that the Government should introduce a one-year limitation period on actions brought in respect of publications on the internet (House of Commons Culture, Media and Sport Committee, *Press Standards, Privacy and Libel*, HC (2009–10) 362-I, para. 230). The limitation period should be extended if the claimant could not reasonably have been aware of the publication's existence. After the expiry of the limitation period, the claimant would be debarred from recovering damages in respect of the publication but would be entitled to obtain a court order to correct any defamatory statement.

IV. Defamation: Defences

A number of the general defences to liability in tort also apply in relation to actions in defamation (e.g. consent, on which see *Monson v Tussauds Ltd* [1894] 1 QB 671) but here the focus is upon those defences which are peculiar to that cause of action: (1) justification, (2) fair comment on a matter of public interest, (3) privilege (both absolute and qualified), (4) offer of amends and (5) innocent dissemination.

1. Justification

A defendant may 'justify' a defamatory allegation by proving its truth in all material respects. Defamatory statements are presumed to be false and the burden of proving their truth lies on the defendant, contrary to the law's general approach of placing the burden of establishing the principal elements of the cause of action on the claimant. Truth is an absolute defence whatever the defendant's motive, save where publication is contrary to the Rehabilitation of Offenders Act 1974 (see below). It is immaterial that the defendant acted maliciously in a deliberate effort to harm the claimant. Conversely, if the statement should turn out to be false, it is no defence that the defendant took all reasonable steps to establish its veracity. It is equally irrelevant whether or not the publication was in the public interest, for the English law of defamation is concerned only with false imputations against a person's reputation, not with unwarranted invasions of privacy.

The test is whether the allegation is 'true in substance and in fact' (*Sutherland v Stopes* [1925] AC 47), so minor inaccuracies do not preclude the defence. According to the classic dictum of Burrough J in *Edwards v Bell* (1824) 1 Bing 403 at 409:

> It is sufficient if the substance of the libellous statement be justified … As much must be justified as meets the sting of the charge, and if anything be contained in a charge which does not add to the sting of it, that need not be justified.

What constitutes the 'sting' of a particular defamatory publication may, however, be a matter of considerable dispute between the parties.

Grobbelaar v News Group Newspapers Ltd [2002] 1 WLR 3024

The claimant, Bruce Grobbelaar, was a well-known footballer who played in goal for Liverpool FC for several years in the 1980s and early 1990s, and then for Southampton FC. In 1994, one of his associates, V, told a journalist working for the defendants' newspaper, *The Sun*, that Grobbelaar had received money for fixing the result of matches in which he was playing. V alleged that the money came from a betting syndicate in South East Asia. He was paid for his story. Seeking corroboration, *The Sun* covertly video- and sound-recorded a series of meetings between Grobbelaar and their informant. During these meetings, Grobbelaar confessed to having taken money for losing matches in the past and took £2,000 offered by V in return for fixing matches in the future. In November 1994, Grobbelaar was confronted with the allegations of match-fixing by *Sun* reporters and photographers. He denied any wrongdoing. The next day, *The Sun* printed a front-page exclusive under the headline 'Grobbelaar took bribes to fix games'. In subsequent daily issues, *The Sun* gave massive and relentless coverage to the story. Soon afterwards, Grobbelaar issued a writ against the defendant publishers, claiming damages for defamation. He denied he had dishonestly taken bribes or sought to fix the result of games in which he was playing. Before his action could proceed, however, Grobbelaar was arrested by the police in connection with the allegations made by *The Sun* and charged with criminal conspiracy and acceptance of a bribe. He stood trial twice on these charges. At the first trial, the jury could not agree on either count. At his subsequent retrial, the jury unanimously acquitted Grobbelaar of conspiracy, but could not agree on the count of bribe-taking. The prosecution declined to pursue the charge further and the judge directed a verdict of not guilty. Subsequently, Grobbelaar pleaded guilty to a disciplinary charge of assisting in betting brought against him by the Football Association. In his resumed defamation action, however, he was awarded £85,000 in compensatory damages at trial, where the defendants' main defence was justification. The Court of Appeal overturned the award on the basis that the jury's verdict was perverse. The defendants appealed to the House of Lords.

Lord Hobhouse

This is a case where there is an agreed natural and ordinary meaning of the libellous publications:

> The Plaintiff, (a) having dishonestly taken bribes, had fixed or attempted to fix the result of games of football in which he had played, and (b) had dishonestly taken bribes with a view to fixing the result of games in which he would be playing.

[I]n each limb, the agreed meaning contained two aspects: one was fixing, or attempting to fix, or intending to fix, the result of football matches in which the plaintiff was playing and the other was the dishonest taking of bribes to do so. The plaintiff had pleaded the whole of the published material and the defendants had abandoned any reliance upon s.5 of the Defamation Act 1952. It was therefore for the jury to decide where the sting of the defamatory statements lay and to decide whether the defendants had proved that it was in substance true—i.e. substantially justified.

But there was a complication: although the parties had agreed the meaning of the defamatory publications, they were not, anyway by the closing stages of the trial, agreeing about where the sting of the libel lay. The plaintiff had argued throughout that it lay in the allegation that he had deliberately fixed or 'thrown' matches and was prepared to do so again. The defendants by the end of the trial were arguing that the sting lay simply in the statement that he had taken bribes. The reason for this development was, so far as the defendants were concerned, not far to seek. In their pleading, they pleaded the defence of justification but they alleged that there was only one match where the plaintiff had deliberately let in a goal: Coventry City v Southampton, September 24, 1994. At the trial the plaintiff had made a positive case that he had never deliberately let in any goal, that he had never attempted to and that he never would. He not only gave evidence to that effect himself but relied upon film evidence of the games in which he had played and the unimpeached expert evidence [of various former footballers]. . . . The defendants called no evidence to contradict this part of the plaintiff's case. The defendants were therefore inevitably going to fail on the issue of justification unless they could persuade the jury that the sting lay in the taking of bribes rather than in the fixing of the result of matches and willingness to do so again.

The defendants failed in this endeavour and it is not difficult to see why. This was a trial by jury: the relevant issues were for the jury to decide. The assessment of the jurors would be closer to that of the football fans, who go to football matches and who would be outraged by the idea that one of their footballing heroes was only pretending to play and the match which they had paid to watch was only a charade, than it would be to that of others, like lawyers, who would be outraged by the taking of bribes whether or not accompanied by the deception of the would-be briber. The plaintiff's view of the sting of the libel was amply supported by the way in which the newspaper had itself presented the story to its readers . . .

Under these circumstances, the jury could not be criticised for taking the view that the sting was the accusation of match fixing. Even standing alone, it was a very serious accusation to make against a professional footballer and, if true, completely destructive of his reputation as a professional footballer. A goalkeeper who deliberately lets in goals *is* betraying the fans and reducing the game to a sham. For myself, I would have been surprised if the jury had come to any other verdict on the justification issue . . .

[His Lordship ruled that the appeal should be allowed and the verdict of the jury restored, but stated that the sum awarded as damages was excessive and should be reduced to £1.]

Lord Bingham, **Lord Millett** and **Lord Scott** delivered separate speeches in favour of the same outcome. **Lord Steyn** dissented.

Appeal allowed, but an award of damages of £1 substituted for the original award.

COMMENTARY

Whether a defendant draws the sting of an allegation depends on what the jury considers the allegation's 'gravamen' or 'real thrust'. Every case turns on its own facts. In *Alexander v North Eastern Railway Co* (1865) 6 B & S 340, 122 ER 1221 the defendants had published at their stations a notice which stated that the plaintiff had been caught riding without a valid ticket and had refused to pay the fare, and had subsequently been convicted by the magistrates, who sentenced him to pay a fine of £1 (plus costs) or suffer three weeks' imprisonment. In fact, the plaintiff had only been sentenced to fourteen days' imprisonment in default of payment of the fine. The plaintiff complained of the overstatement whose effect, he argued, was to make his offence appear more reprehensible than the justices had deemed it. The jury found for the defendants. But there was a different conclusion in a rather similar case decided shortly afterwards. In *Gwynn v SE Railway* (1868) 18 LT 738, the allegation was that the plaintiff was sentenced to a fine of 1s or to three days' imprisonment 'with hard labour' in default for travelling without a ticket. In fact, the allegation of hard labour was false. The jury found for the plaintiff and awarded damages of £250. It seems that the words must, in the opinion of the jury, have produced a wholly false impression of the gravity of the offence committed (see *Gatley*, para. 11.10). See also *Weaver v Lloyd* (1824) 1 B & C 678, 130 ER 162 (allegations of various acts of cruelty to a horse; the Court of King's Bench stated that 'the statement that [the plaintiff] knocked out the horse's eye imputed a much greater degree of cruelty than a charge of beating him on other parts of the body' (at 679)).

One difficult question of construction that often arises is whether particular words carry an imputation of specific or general misconduct. Allegations of general bad conduct are not justified by proof of a single instance of bad behaviour, so to call a person a 'libellous journalist' is not justified by proof of a libel verdict against him on a single occasion (*Wakley v Cooke* (1849) 4 Exch 511). Conversely, a statement alleging that the claimant did a specific thing cannot be justified by evidence of other conduct on his part. In *Bookbinder v Tebbit* [1989] 1 WLR 640 where the defendant, chairman of the Conservative Party, had alleged at a public meeting that the plaintiff, leader of a Labour-controlled council, had squandered £50,000 of public money in printing the caption 'Support Nuclear Free Zones' on all its school stationery, the Court of Appeal held that it was not possible to justify that allegation by pointing to other alleged instances of squandering public funds. But, in *Williams v Reason* [1988] 1 WLR 96 a newspaper article containing an allegation that the plaintiff had, in breach of the code of conduct governing amateur rugby players, written a book for financial gain was held capable of bearing the wider meaning of a charge of 'shamateurism', and evidence that he had accepted 'boot money' was admissible by way of justification. In such matters, it is not possible to give any guidance more specific than that the meaning of the words complained of must always be assessed in the light of the publication as a whole, and the precise context and circumstances of its communication.

As the *Grobbelaar* case illustrates, the defence of justification fails if the defendant merely proves the partial truth of the defamatory statement, but the proven facts may be taken into account in determining the level of damages. See further p. 774ff, below.

Multiple Allegations

Where the defendant makes multiple allegations against the claimant, the first question to ask is whether the allegations share a common sting or convey separate and distinct imputations. In the former case, the common sting may be justified notwithstanding the defendant's failure to prove the truth of every specific allegation in the publication. Indeed the defendant may be able to make out the defence by proving the truth of allegations contained in the publication even though the claimant has chosen not to rely on these—but rather on other allegations which the defendant cannot prove—in his claim form (*Polly Peck (Holdings) plc v Trelford* [1986] 1 QB 1000). The principle was applied in *Khashoggi v IPC Magazines Ltd* [1986] 1 WLR 1412. Mrs Soraya Khashoggi was featured in an article in *Woman's Own* headed 'What makes you divorce the richest man in the world'. The article contained what Lord Donaldson described as a highly-coloured account of her marriage to the international arms dealer which, in the view of his Lordship, was 'capable of carrying the meaning that she was a lady of considerable sexual enthusiasm'. In the article was an allegation that the last straw for her husband was an affair that she was having with a friend, the unnamed President of a nation state. At an interim hearing, the Court of Appeal held that the defendants were entitled to raise a '*Polly Peck* form of justification' on the basis that the sting of the article was promiscuity generally and it was not in the circumstances more defamatory to allege an extra-marital affair with one person rather than another; the defendants might adduce evidence to justify that common sting even though they might not be able to prove the particular affair complained of. (The immediate significance of this ruling was that the defendants, simply by pleading a possible defence of justification, were able to resist the plaintiff's attempt to win an interim injunction against publication under the rule in *Bonnard v Perryman* [1891] 2 Ch 269: see p. Section V.2(b), below.)

In the latter case—where the words contain two or more distinct charges—the basic rule is that the defence of justification, if it is to succeed, must address each of the meanings attributed to the words by the jury. However, a statutory analogue to the common law's 'sting' doctrine (which applies only to a single defamatory charge) has been introduced in this context. Defamation Act 1952, s. 5 provides:

In an action for libel or slander in respect of words containing two or more distinct charges against the plaintiff, a defence of justification shall not fail by reason only that the truth of every charge is not proved if the words not proved to be true do not materially injure the plaintiff's reputation having regard to the truth of the remaining charges.

In *Robson v News Group Newspapers* [1996] CLY 5660, an unproven allegation that the defendant had defrauded the Department of Social Security was held not to materially injure the plaintiff's reputation having regard to the effect of the true allegation that he had been convicted of a £4 million mortgage fraud.

The 'Rumour' Doctrine

Where the defendant reports another person's beliefs or suspicions, his words may be treated as direct statements relating to the subject-matter to which the other was referring, and he can rely upon the defence of justification only if he shows that the underlying facts are true ('*Truth*' *(NZ) Ltd v Holloway* [1960] 1 WLR 997). It is no defence that the defendant was merely repeating what he had been told (*Stern v Piper* [1997] QB 123 at 128, per Hirst LJ), for '[i]f one repeats a rumour one adds one's own authority to it and implies that it is well founded, that is to say, that it is true' (*Lewis v Daily Telegraph* [1964] AC 234 at 275, per Lord Hodson). Nevertheless, in *Aspro Travel Ltd v Owners Abroad Group* [1996] 1 WLR 132 the Court of Appeal accepted that there might be 'circumstances in which the existence of a rumour entitles a person to repeat that rumour even before he satisfies himself that the rumour is true and that in such circumstances it is possible to plead in justification that there were in truth such rumours' (at 140, per Schiemann LJ). In what circumstances might this be so? If the question is whether the circumstances warranted repetition of the rumour, would it be better to treat this as a matter of qualified privilege so that the defendant's motives can be taken into account? (See Section IV.3(b), below.)

The key question in all such cases is how the defendant's words are to be construed. A statement that a person is under suspicion is not necessarily an affirmation of his guilt, but it usually implies that there are reasonable grounds for suspicion (*Lewis v Daily Telegraph* [1964] AC 234 at 275, per Lord Hodson). If so, the defendant can rely on justification only if he can prove that the claimant in fact acted in such a way as to cause a reasonable observer to be suspicious (*Shah v Standard Chartered Bank* [1998] 4 All ER 155). Where the defendant reports the issuing of a writ against the claimant, indicating what the claimant is alleged to have done wrong, the jury must ascertain the report's true meaning before it can be determined whether or not the issuing of the writ itself amounts to justification (*Cadam v Beaverbrook Newspapers Ltd* [1959] 1 QB 413). In *Stem v Piper* [1997] QB 123, however, the Court of Appeal struck out a defence of justification where the defendant's newspaper had quoted from a witness statement which was to be relied upon in debt proceedings against the plaintiff. It was not enough that the allegations in question had indeed been taken from a witness statement as they were still essentially hearsay. The court attached particular importance to the one-sidedness of the report and the undesirability of private court documents being disseminated to the public at large.

Allegations of Criminal Conduct

If the charge is that the claimant is guilty of a criminal offence, the defendant need only point to the fact of the claimant's conviction for the offence by way of justification: conviction is conclusive evidence that the claimant has in fact committed it (Civil Evidence Act 1968, s. 13). However, the public interest in the rehabilitation of offenders has led to the introduction of a statutory provision to the effect that one who maliciously publishes details of a 'spent' conviction cannot rely upon the defence of justification (Rehabilitation of Offenders Act 1974, s. 8; a conviction becomes spent, except in the case of very serious criminal conduct, by the lapse of a period of time whose length is determined by the heaviness of the sentence imposed). The potential liability of the person who maliciously publishes true details of a spent conviction is the one (rather limited) exception to the rule that truth is a total defence to an action in defamation.

2. Fair Comment on a Matter of Public Interest

The defence of fair comment on a matter of public interest is, like justification, a complete defence to an action for defamation. Of all defences to an action in defamation, it has been described as 'the most useful to the media' (*Barendt*, p. 10), though it now probably ranks second in importance to the defence of 'media privilege' (see Section 3(b), below). According to Scott LJ, 'the right of "fair comment"…is one of the fundamental rights of free speech and writing which are so dear to the British nation, and it is of vital importance to the rule of law on which we depend for our personal freedom that the courts should preserve the right of "fair comment" undiminished and unimpaired' (*Lyon v Daily Telegraph* [1943] KB 746 at 753). Unlike the defence of (qualified) privilege, the defence is not limited to those who have a duty to publish the imputations in question (or an interest in so doing); any person is at liberty to comment upon a matter of public interest. However, the defence only applies to expressions of opinion, not to statements of fact.

London Artists v Littler [1969] 2 QB 375

The defendant, an impresario, wrote and published at a press conference a letter suggesting that the plaintiffs, variously involved in the Grade entertainment organisation, including its co-founder Lew Grade, had taken part in what appeared to be a plot to force the end of the run of a successful play, *The Right Honourable Gentleman*, which the defendant was producing at Her

Majesty's Theatre. The defendant alleged that the first plaintiffs, theatrical agents, had written on behalf of four leading players in the cast (Anthony Quayle, Coral Browne, Anna Massey and Corin Redgrave) giving identical notices to leave the cast. Such a coincidence of players' notices 'was almost unprecedented in the theatre world. It was likely to bring *The Right Honourable Gentleman* to a full stop' (at 388, per Lord Denning MR). The defendant had previously been informed that the Grade organisation wished to transfer to Her Majesty's (which was owned by one of the Grade companies) another play that was showing elsewhere in a Grade theatre.

In actions against the defendant for libel, he pleaded justification, fair comment on a matter of public interest, and qualified privilege. At the close of the plaintiffs' evidence, the plea of justification was withdrawn as it became apparent that the players had withdrawn for various reasons unconnected with the Grade organisation's plan to transfer a new play to Her Majesty's Theatre. The judge held, *inter alia*, that the plea of fair comment failed because the matter was not one of public interest and that the publication to the press was not privileged. Only the issue of damages was left to the jury, who awarded modest sums. The defendant appealed on the ground that the judge was wrong in shutting out the defence of fair comment from the jury.

Lord Denning MR

Three points arise on the defence of fair comment. First, was the comment made on a matter of public interest? The judge ruled that it was not. I cannot agree with him. There is no definition in the books as to what is a matter of public interest. All we are given is a list of examples, coupled with the statement that it is for the judge and not for the jury. I would not myself confine it within narrow limits. Whenever a matter is such as to affect people at large, so that they may be legitimately interested in, or concerned at, what is going on; or what may happen to them or to others; then it is a matter of public interest on which everyone is entitled to make fair comment. A good example is *South Hetton Coal Co v North-Eastern News Association* [1894] 1 QB 133. A colliery company owned most of the cottages in the village. It was held that the sanitary condition of those cottages—or rather their insanitary condition—was a matter of public interest. Lord Esher MR, said at p. 140, that it was 'a matter of public interest that the conduct of the employers should be criticised.' There the public were legitimately concerned. Here the public are legitimately interested. Many people are interested in what happens in the theatre. The stars welcome publicity. They want to be put at the top of the bill. Producers wish it too. They like the house to be full. The comings and goings of performers are noticed everywhere. When three top stars and a satellite all give notice to leave at the same time—thus putting a successful play in peril—it is to my mind a matter of public interest in which everyone, Press and all, are entitled to comment freely.

The second point is whether the allegation of a 'plot' was a fact which the defendant had to prove to be true, or was it only comment? In order to be fair, the commentator must get his basic facts right. The basic facts are those which go to the pith and substance of the matter: see *Cunningham-Howie v Dimbleby* [1951] 1 KB 360, 364. They are the facts on which the comments are based or from which the inferences are drawn—as distinct from the comments or inferences themselves. The commentator need not set out in his original article all the basic facts: see *Kemsley v Foot* [1952] AC 345; but he must get them right and be ready to prove them to be true. He must indeed afterwards in legal proceedings, when asked, give particulars of the basic facts: see *Burton v Board* [1929] 1 KB 301; but he need not give particulars of the comments or the inferences to be drawn from those facts. If in his original article he sets out basic facts which are themselves defamatory of the plaintiff, then he must prove them to be true: and this is the case just as much after section 6 of the Defamation Act, 1952, as it was before. It was so held by the New Zealand Court of Appeal in *Truth (NZ) Ltd v Avery* [1959] NZLR 274, which was accepted by this court in *Broadway Approvals Ltd v Odhams Press Ltd* [1965] 1 WLR 805. It is indeed the whole difference between a plea of fair comment and a plea of justification. In fair comment he need only prove the basic facts to be true. In justification he must prove also that the comments and inferences are true also.

So I turn to ask what were the basic facts in this case? In the particulars . . . Mr Emile Littler set out very many facts which conveyed no clear picture. But, putting them together, it appears that he was relying on three basic facts. First, that the owners wanted to get *The Right Honourable Gentleman* out of Her Majesty's Theatre. Second, that the stars and satellite all gave notice by the same agents at the same time in the same form. Third, that there was a plot between the owners and the stars (through the Grade Organisation) to bring to an end the run of *The Right Honourable Gentleman*. Mr Emile Littler proved the first two basic facts, but did not prove the third. He failed to prove a plot and had to withdraw the allegation. That put him in a quandary on fair comment. He could not prove one of the basic facts. So he turned right about. He then submitted that the allegation of a 'plot' was not a fact at all but only a comment. In my view that submission cannot be sustained, and for these reasons: In the first place, Mr Emile Littler in his pleadings treated the 'plot' as a statement of fact, and I do not think we should look with favour on such a complete turnabout in the middle of the case. In the second place, Mr Emile Littler in his evidence said it was a statement of fact. He was asked:

> What was said in the letters was deliberately intended by you to be said. That is right, is it not? (A.) It was a statement of fact. (Q.) What you believed to be a fact?

He answered 'Yes.' In the third place, on a fair reading of the whole letter . . . I think that the allegation of a plot was a statement of fact. The first paragraph runs in guarded language, 'it appears'; and the fifth paragraph says 'in other words'; but the last paragraph speaks of 'the combined effort.' Reading the letter as a whole, I have no doubt that it stated as a fact that there was a plot between the plaintiffs to bring down a chopper on the head of *The Right Honourable Gentleman*.

Mr Duncan [for the defendant] submitted, however, that the question whether the statement was a statement of fact or comment should have been left to the jury. He would be right if it was reasonably capable of being considered as comment. That is clear from many of the cases, finishing with the judgment of the Privy Council in *Jones v Skelton* [1963] 1 WLR 1362. But for the three reasons which I have given, I do not think the statement of a 'plot' was reasonably capable of being considered as comment. It was a statement of fact which was itself defamatory of the plaintiffs. The defendant, in order to succeed, had to prove it to be true. He failed to do so, and along with it went the defence of fair comment.

In case, however, I am wrong about this and it could be regarded as comment, then I turn to the third point, which is this: were there any facts on which a fair minded man might honestly make such a comment? I take it to be settled law that, in order for the defence of fair comment to be left to the jury, there must at least be a sufficient basis of fact to warrant the comment, in this sense, that a fair minded man might on those facts honestly hold that opinion. There is no need for the defendant to prove that his opinion was correct or one with which the jury agree. He is entitled to the defence of fair comment unless it can be said: 'No fair minded man could honestly hold that opinion'; see what Buckley LJ said in *Peter Walker & Son Ltd v Hodgson* [1909] 1 KB 239, 253.

In this case I am sure that Mr Emile Littler acted honestly and in good faith. He honestly thought that there was a plot to bring to a stop the run of *The Right Honourable Gentleman*. He was himself so convinced of it that he took the extreme step of telling it to the world. But I fear that he went beyond the bounds of a fair minded man. He jumped too hastily to his conclusion. He ought not to have been so precipitate. He ought to have made inquiries.... By jumping so quickly to a conclusion Mr Emile Littler came at odds with the law. He made a public condemnation not only of the artistes themselves but of Associated Television and the agents, London Artists, Mr Lew Grade and the Grade Organisation. The judge held that in alleging that all those were parties to a plot he was making an imputation without any basis of fact to support it. I think the judge was quite right in so holding and in not leaving it to the jury.

In the upshot it comes to this: the fate of *The Right Honourable Gentleman* was a matter of public interest. Mr Emile Littler was fully entitled to comment on it as long as his comment was fair and honest. He was entitled to give his views to the public through the press. But I think he went beyond the bounds of fair comment. He was carried away by his feelings at the moment. He did not wait long enough to check the facts and to get them right. He had no defence except as to damages: and on that he did well. I would dismiss this appeal.

Edmund Davies LJ and **Widgery LJ** delivered separate concurring judgments.

Appeal dismissed.

COMMENTARY

The requirements of the defence are considered in more detail in the following paragraphs, set out under four sub-headings rather than Lord Denning's three, with a further heading addressing the relevance of malice.

(a) Public Interest

In the extracted case, Lord Denning emphasised that the test was not solely whether the public was legitimately concerned in the matter in question but whether the public was legitimately interested. Matters of public interest therefore include comings and goings in the theatre. However, Edmund Davies LJ indicated his view that a statement that 'Mr Anthony Quayle had turned Buddhist' would not be a matter of public interest as it was 'unconnected with [his] public career' (at 394). Given the ever-increasing cult of celebrity in today's world, do you think that his Lordship's opinion would hold good in the present day?

(b) Comment rather than Fact

The defendant's allegations must appear as a comment rather than as a statement of fact. There is no defence of fair *information* on a matter of public interest. Writing extra-judicially, Lord Denning has observed: 'In many cases...the newspapers are not able to rely on "fair comment" because they cannot prove that the facts stated are true. Where this is the case, there is sometimes a need for the newspapers to be granted a privilege—a qualified privilege—for them to give fair information to the public when it is in the public interest for them to do so' (Lord Denning, *What Next in the Law* (London: Butterworths, 1982), p. 188). The extent to which the modern defence of qualified privilege does in fact perform this role is considered below.

The distinction between fact and comment depends not just upon the content of the allegations but also on their context, and the manner of their expression. It will be clear that words are expressed as comment if they are placed alongside statements of (proven) fact or prefaced by words like 'it seems'. As *Winfield & Jolowicz* states (para. 12–32):

> To say that 'A is a disgrace to human nature' is an allegation of fact. But if the words were, 'A murdered his father and is therefore a disgrace to human nature,' the latter words are clearly a comment on the former.

In *Telnikoff v Matusevich* [1991] 2 AC 343, the House of Lords considered the precise context in which the words in question had to be analysed. In the view of the majority, words contained in one publication had to be considered solely in the context of that publication; they could not be looked at in the context of other publications upon which the defendant claimed to comment. The defendant, a Russian Jew and radio broadcaster, wrote a letter to the *Daily Telegraph* in which he complained about an article by the plaintiff. This article had been critical of the high proportion of employees of the BBC Russian Service who came from Soviet minority groups. In his response, the defendant quoted from the article and said that the plaintiff advocated a blood test for new employees and dismissal for ethnically alien staff. Lord Keith said the question of whether the words were comment or fact should be assessed without taking into account the contents of the plaintiff's article. As the allegations were stated baldly, without the insertion of words like 'in effect', they could only be regarded as statements of fact.

Lord Ackner dissented on the basis that the decision would act as a significant deterrent to the publication of readers' letters and impose a difficult burden on editors. Lord Denning has also expressed concern at the impact of the law of defamation upon the publication of readers' letters: 'When a citizen is troubled by things going wrong, he should be free to "write to the newspaper": and the newspaper should be free to publish his letter. It is often the only way to get things put right' (*Slim v Daily Telegraph* [1968] 2 QB 157 at 170). A survey of regional newspaper editors published in 1997 revealed their view that the letters' page carried, with the exception of reports of local crime and court cases, the most significant libel risks of all sections of their newspapers (exceeding even the risks involved in the reporting of political and business/financial matters: *Barendt*, pp. 90–1).

(c) Basis of Truth

Once it has been established that the words in question are comment, the court must ask if that comment has a basis of truth. Although Lord Denning in the extract above dealt with this as an aspect of the distinction between comment and fact, it seems conducive to greater clarity to deal with it separately. At common law, the defendant was required to establish the truth of each and every factual matter upon which the publication purported to comment. But, by virtue of Defamation Act 1952, s. 6, the defendant need no longer prove that every factual allegation is true, so long as such allegations as are proved to be true form a sufficient basis for his comment. The relevant provision states:

> [I]n an action for libel or slander in respect of words consisting partly of allegations of fact and partly of expression of opinion, a defence of fair comment shall not fail by reason only that the truth of every allegation of fact is not proved if the expression of the opinion is fair comment having regard to such of the facts alleged or referred to in the words complained of as are proved.

The substratum of truth underlying the comment must be clearly indicated in the publication; however, the facts need not be set out in full by the defendant. This was affirmed by the House of Lords in *Kemsley v Foot* [1952] AC 345 in which Michael Foot, writing in *Tribune*, had described an article in the *Evening Standard* as 'the foulest piece of journalism appearing in this country for many a year'. The piece appeared under the headline 'Lower than Kemsley'. Lord Kemsley, the proprietor of rival newspapers, sued for defamation. The House of Lords held that the reference to Kemsley sufficiently indicated the facts on which Foot had commented. Lord Porter explained that the defendants could say (p. 357):

We have pointed to your Press. It is widely read. Your readers will, and the public generally can, know at what our criticism is directed. It is not bare comment. It is comment on a well-known matter...

(d) Fairness

The test of fairness is 'would any honest man, however prejudiced he might be, or however exaggerated or obstinate his views, have written this criticism' (*Turner v Metro-Goldwyn-Mayer* [1950] 1 All ER 449 at 461, per Lord Porter). The defence thus protects the 'crank' as well as those commenting intelligently on matters of public concern. (For this reason, the defence has been aptly re-christened the defence of *honest opinion* in New Zealand.) The defendant need not go on to satisfy the further test that the comment represented his own honest opinion; this bears only upon the issue of malice (see *Telnikoff v Matusevich* [1991] 2 AC 343). To adopt such a test would place editors of newspapers, current affairs programmes, etc., in an impossible position given the varied range of opinions held by journalists and correspondents which are—quite legitimately—expressed even within a single edition of a newspaper or current affairs programme.

In the above extract, it seems likely that Lord Denning went too far in his obiter dicta to the effect that a person who jumped too quickly to the wrong conclusion could not be regarded as acting fairly. If this were true, the protection afforded by the defence to the crank and the crackpot would prove illusory. In fact, in *Reynolds v Times Newspapers Ltd* [2001] 2 AC 127 at 193, Lord Nicholls noted that the latitude applied in determining whether a comment was fair was so extensive that 'time has come to recognise that in this context the epithet "fair" is now meaningless and misleading'.

(e) Malice

The defence of fair comment is rebutted by proof that the defendant made the comment with malice. In this context, 'the only touchstone is that of honesty' and malice is not established by evidence that the defendant was prompted by the dominant motive of injuring the claimant (*Branson v Bower* [2002] QB 737 at [7]–[8], per Eady J). By contrast, malice may be established by evidence of improper motive in relation to the defence of qualified privilege. See further Section IV.3(d), below.

3. Privilege

In certain situations, the law's concern for free discourse outweighs the need to protect personal reputations. An *absolute privilege* arises where the occasion demands utter freedom in the communication of views and information (e.g. in Parliament or in a court of law). A *qualified privilege* arises where the need for such freedom is not quite so great but nevertheless warrants some protection from the threat of litigation that is not allowed on non-privileged occasions. The reason why the privilege is described as qualified in these situations is that its effectiveness is conditional upon its bona fide exercise in the absence of malice: if the claimant can prove that the defendant was actuated by malice, the privilege is withdrawn. By way of contrast, an absolute privilege is effective no matter what the defendant's motivation.

(a) Absolute Privilege

The principle examples of absolute privilege are:

(i)   statements in Parliament (Bill of Rights 1688), but note that by Defamation Act 1996, s. 13 an MP may waive the privilege if he or she so desires, e.g. so as to pursue an action which the publisher seeks to defend by reference to proceedings in Parliament: see *Hamilton v Al Fayed* [2001] AC 395;

(ii) reports, etc., ordered to be published by Parliament (Parliamentary Papers Act 1840 s. 1);

(iii) statements made in the course of, or for the purpose of, judicial proceedings (including proceedings before tribunals), including the initial complaint made by a purported victim of crime to the police, even if no prosecution ensues: see *Westcott v Westcott* [2009] QB 407. (Where prosecution does ensue, however, there may be liability in the separate tort of malicious prosecution—provided the complainant was actively instrumental in setting the law in motion against the claimant and acted with malice.)

(iv) fair and accurate contemporaneous reports of judicial proceedings in the United Kingdom, before the European Courts or any international criminal tribunal set up by the UN (Defamation Act 1996 s. 14);

(v)   communications made by a minister or other officer of state to another in the course of his official duty (*Chatterton v Secretary of State for India* [1895] 2 QB 189).

In *A v United Kingdom* (2003) 36 EHRR 51, the European Court of Human Rights rejected a challenge to the absolute privilege applying to statements in Parliament. The privilege violated neither the right to respect to private life (Article 8) of the applicant, named in Parliament by her MP as a 'neighbour from hell', nor her right of access to a court (Article 6). It pursued the legitimate aim of protecting free parliamentary speech and could not be regarded as a disproportionate restriction on the applicant's rights.

(b) Qualified Privilege at Common Law

Reynolds v Times Newspapers Ltd [2001] 2 AC 127

The plaintiff, Albert Reynolds, was Taoiseach (Prime Minister) of Ireland from 1992 to 1994. His government collapsed as a result of a dispute about the appointment of the then Attorney-General (who under the Irish Constitution acts as an impartial legal adviser to the government) to the office of President of the High Court. The Labour Party opposed the appointment because of concerns about the failure of the Attorney-General's office to answer a request for the extradition of a Roman Catholic priest wanted by the Royal Ulster Constabulary on charges of sexual abuse of children in Northern Ireland. Further doubts as to the Attorney-General's suitability for judicial office were raised when it emerged that he had given false information about the handling of similar cases in the past. This false information was repeated by the plaintiff both in Cabinet and before the Dáil (the Irish Parliament). It was subsequently questioned whether the plaintiff realised that the information was false at the time he made these statements. As the political controversy mounted, the Labour Party withdrew its support from the coalition government and the plaintiff resigned his office as Taoiseach. The former Attorney-General also resigned his office as President of the High Court.

The plaintiff sought damages for defamation in respect of an article published in the issue of *The Sunday Times* under the heading 'Goodbye gombeen man', with the subsidiary headline: 'Why a fib too far proved fatal for the political career of Ireland's ... Mr Fixit.' The defendants were the newspaper's editor and publisher, and the journalist who wrote the piece (a Mr Ruddock). The plaintiff asserted that the words complained of in their natural and ordinary meaning meant and were understood to mean that the plaintiff had deliberately and dishonestly misled the Dáil and his cabinet colleagues in connection with the affair. The defendants were found liable at trial, but the plaintiff was awarded only contemptuous damages. (In the House of Lords, it was suggested in argument that this might have been because the jury had been made aware that the plaintiff had not sued in respect of similar stories published in Ireland by Irish newspapers). On appeal by the plaintiff, the Court of Appeal found that the judge had misdirected the jury in various respects which are not material for present purposes, and accordingly set aside the judgment of the court below and ordered a new trial. At the same time, it ruled that the defendants would not be entitled to rely upon a defence of qualified privilege at the re-trial because the nature, status and source of the story, and the circumstances of the publication, were not such as to give rise to a defence of qualified privilege, for example, because the defendants failed to record the plaintiff's own account of his conduct as given to the Dáil (in which he denied deliberate misinformation). The defendants appealed to the House of Lords where they argued that the House should recognise a new category of qualified privilege applying in all circumstances to the media's reporting of political issues.

Lord Nicholls of Birkenhead

There are occasions when the person to whom a statement is made has a special interest in learning the honestly held views of another person, even if those views are defamatory of someone else and cannot be proved to be true. When the interest is of sufficient importance to outweigh the need to protect reputation, the occasion is regarded as privileged. Sometimes the need for uninhibited expression is of such a high order that the occasion attracts absolute privilege, as with statements made by judges or advocates or witnesses in the course of judicial proceedings. More usually, the privilege is qualified in that it can be defeated if the plaintiff proves the defendant was actuated by malice ...

Over the years the courts have held that many common form situations are privileged. Classic instances are employment references, and complaints made or information given to the police or appropriate authorities regarding suspected crimes. The courts have always emphasised that the categories established by the authorities are not exhaustive. The list is not closed. The established categories are no more than applications, in particular circumstances, of the underlying principle of public policy. The underlying principle is conventionally stated in words to the effect that there must exist between the maker of the statement and the recipient some duty or interest in the making of the communication. Lord Atkinson's dictum, in *Adam v Ward* [1917] AC 309, 334, is much quoted:

> a privileged occasion is . . . an occasion where the person who makes a communication has an interest or a duty, legal, social, or moral, to make it to the person to whom it is made, and the person to whom it is so made has a corresponding interest or duty to receive it. This reciprocity is essential.

The requirement that both the maker of the statement and the recipient must have an interest or duty draws attention to the need to have regard to the position of both parties when deciding whether an occasion is privileged. But this should not be allowed to obscure the rationale of the underlying public interest on which privilege is founded. The essence of this defence lies in the law's recognition of the need, in the public interest, for a particular recipient to receive frank and uninhibited communication of particular information from a particular source. That is the end the law is concerned to attain. The protection afforded to the maker of the statement is the means by which the law seeks to achieve that end. Thus the court has to assess whether, in the public interest, the publication should be protected in the absence of malice.

In determining whether an occasion is regarded as privileged the court has regard to all the circumstances: see, for example, the explicit statement of Lord Buckmaster LC in *London Association for Protection of Trade v Greenlands Ltd* [1916] 2 AC 15, 23 ('every circumstance associated with the origin and publication of the defamatory matter'). And circumstances must be viewed with today's eyes. The circumstances in which the public interest requires a communication to be protected in the absence of malice depend upon current social conditions. The requirements at the close of the twentieth century may not be the same as those of earlier centuries or earlier decades of this century.

Privilege and Publication to the World at Large

Frequently a privileged occasion encompasses publication to one person only or to a limited group of people. Publication more widely, to persons who lack the requisite interest in receiving the information, is not privileged. But the common law has recognised there are occasions when the public interest requires that publication to the world at large should be privileged. In *Cox v Feeney* (1863) 4 F&F 13, 19, Cockburn CJ approved an earlier statement by Lord Tenterden CJ that 'a man has a right to publish, for the purpose of giving the public information, that which it is proper for the public to know'. Whether the public interest so requires depends upon an evaluation of the particular information in the circumstances of its publication. Through the cases runs the strain that, when determining whether the public at large had a right to know the particular information, the court has regard to all the circumstances. The court is concerned to assess whether the information was of sufficient value to the public that, in the public interest, it should be protected by privilege in the absence of malice.

This issue has arisen several times in the context of newspapers discharging their important function of reporting matters of public importance . . .

A New Category of Privileged Subject-Matter?

I turn to the appellants' submissions. The newspaper seeks the incremental development of the common law by the creation of a new category of occasion when privilege derives from the subject-matter alone: political information. Political information can be broadly defined . . . as information, opinion and arguments concerning government and political matters that affect the people of the United Kingdom. Malice apart, publication of political information should be privileged regardless of the status and source of the material and the circumstances of the publication. The newspaper submitted that the contrary view requires the court to assess the public interest value of a publication, taking these matters into account. Such an approach would involve an unpredictable outcome. Moreover, it would put the judge in a position which in a free society ought to be occupied by the editor. Such paternalism would effectively give the court an undesirable and invidious role as a censor or licensing body.

These are powerful arguments, but I do not accept the conclusion for which the newspaper contended. My reasons appear from what is set out below.

My starting point is freedom of expression. The high importance of freedom to impart and receive information and ideas has been stated so often and so eloquently that this point calls for no elaboration in this case. At a pragmatic level, freedom to disseminate and receive information on political matters is essential to the proper functioning of the system of parliamentary democracy cherished in this country. This freedom enables those who elect representatives to Parliament to make an informed choice, regarding individuals as well as policies, and those elected to make informed decisions. Freedom of expression will shortly be buttressed by statutory requirements. Under section 12 of the Human Rights Act 1998, expected to come into force in October 2000, the court is required, in relevant cases, to have particular regard to the importance of the right to freedom of expression. The common law is to be developed and applied in a manner consistent with article 10 of the European Convention for the Protection of Human Rights and Fundamental Freedoms (Cmd. 8969), and the court must take into account relevant decisions of the European Court of Human Rights (sections 6 and 2). To be justified, any curtailment of freedom of expression must be convincingly established by a compelling countervailing consideration, and the means employed must be proportionate to the end sought to be achieved.

Likewise, there is no need to elaborate on the importance of the role discharged by the media in the expression and communication of information and comment on political matters. It is through the mass media that most people today obtain their information on political matters. Without freedom of expression by the media, freedom of expression would be a hollow concept. The interest of a democratic society in ensuring a free press weighs heavily in the balance in deciding whether any curtailment of this freedom bears a reasonable relationship to the purpose of the curtailment. In this regard it should be kept in mind that one of the contemporary functions of the media is investigative journalism. This activity, as much as the traditional activities of reporting and commenting, is part of the vital role of the press and the media generally.

Reputation is an integral and important part of the dignity of the individual. It also forms the basis of many decisions in a democratic society which are fundamental to its well-being: whom to employ or work for, whom to promote, whom to do business with or to vote for. Once besmirched by an unfounded allegation in a national newspaper, a reputation can be damaged for ever, especially if there is no opportunity to vindicate one's reputation. When this happens, society as well as the individual is the loser. For it should not be supposed that protection of reputation is a matter of importance only to the affected individual and his family. Protection of reputation is conducive to the public good. It is in the public interest that the reputation of public figures should not be debased falsely. In the political field, in order to make an informed choice, the electorate needs to be able to identify the good as well as the bad. Consistently with these considerations, human rights conventions recognise that freedom of expression is not an absolute right. Its exercise may be subject to such restrictions as are prescribed by law and are necessary in a democratic society for the protection of the reputations of others.

The crux of this appeal, therefore, lies in identifying the restrictions which are fairly and reasonably necessary for the protection of reputation. Leaving aside the exceptional cases which attract absolute privilege, the common law denies protection to defamatory statements, whether of comment or fact, proved to be actuated by malice.... This common law limitation on freedom of speech passes the 'necessary' test with flying colours. This is an acceptable limitation. Freedom of speech does not embrace freedom to make defamatory statements out of personal spite or without having a positive belief in their truth.

In the case of statements of opinion on matters of public interest, that is the limit of what is necessary for protection of reputation. Readers and viewers and listeners can make up their own minds on whether they agree or disagree with defamatory statements which are recognisable as comment and which, expressly or implicitly, indicate in general terms the facts on which they are based.

With defamatory imputations of fact the position is different and more difficult. Those who read or hear such allegations are unlikely to have any means of knowing whether they are true or not. In respect of such imputations, a plaintiff's ability to obtain a remedy if he can prove malice is not normally a sufficient safeguard. Malice is notoriously difficult to prove. If a newspaper is understandably unwilling to disclose its sources, a plaintiff can be deprived of the material necessary to prove, or even allege, that the newspaper acted recklessly in publishing as it did without further verification. Thus, in the absence of any additional safeguard for reputation, a newspaper, anxious to be first with a 'scoop', would in practice be free to publish seriously defamatory misstatements of fact based on the slenderest of materials. Unless the paper chose later to withdraw the allegations, the politician thus defamed would have no means of clearing his name, and the public would have no means of knowing where the truth lay. Some further protection for reputation is needed if this can be achieved without a disproportionate incursion into freedom of expression.

This is a difficult problem. No answer is perfect. Every solution has its own advantages and disadvantages. Depending on local conditions, such as legal procedures and the traditions and power of the press, the solution preferred in one country may not be best suited to another country. The appellant newspaper commends reliance upon the ethics of professional journalism. The decision should be left to the editor of the newspaper. Unfortunately, in the United Kingdom this would not generally be thought to provide a sufficient safeguard. In saying this I am not referring to mistaken decisions. From time to time mistakes are bound to occur, even in the best regulated circles. Making every allowance for this, the sad reality is that the overall handling of these matters by the national press, with its own commercial interests to serve, does not always command general confidence.

As highlighted by the Court of Appeal judgment in the present case, the common law solution is for the court to have regard to all the circumstances when deciding whether the publication of particular material was privileged because of its value to the public. Its value to the public depends upon its quality as well as its subject-matter. This solution has the merit of elasticity. As observed by the Court of Appeal, this principle can be applied appropriately to the particular circumstances of individual cases in their infinite variety. It can be applied appropriately to all information published by a newspaper, whatever its source or origin.

Hand in hand with this advantage goes the disadvantage of an element of unpredictability and uncertainty. The outcome of a court decision, it was suggested, cannot always be predicted with certainty when the newspaper is deciding whether to publish a story. To an extent this is a valid criticism. A degree of uncertainty in borderline cases is inevitable. This uncertainty, coupled with the expense of court proceedings, may 'chill' the publication of true statements of fact as well as those which are untrue. The chill factor is perhaps felt more keenly by the regional press, book publishers and broadcasters than the national press. However, the extent of this uncertainty should not be exaggerated. With the enunciation of some guidelines by the court, any practical problems should be manageable. The common law does not seek to set a higher standard than that of responsible journalism, a standard the media themselves espouse. An incursion into press freedom which goes no further than this would not seem to be excessive or disproportionate. The investigative journalist has adequate protection. The contrary approach, which would involve no objective check on the media, drew a pertinent comment from Tipping J in *Lange v Atkinson* [1998] 3 NZLR 424, 477:

> It could be seen as rather ironical that whereas almost all sectors of society, and all other occupations and professions have duties to take reasonable care, and are accountable in one form or another if they are careless, the news media whose power and capacity to cause harm and distress are considerable if that power is not responsibly used, are not liable in negligence, and what is more, can claim qualified privilege even if they are negligent. It may be asked whether the public interest in freedom of expression is so great that the accountability which society requires of others, should not also to this extent be required of the news media.

The common law approach does mean that it is an outside body, that is, some one other than the newspaper itself, which decides whether an occasion is privileged. This is bound to be so, if the decision of the press itself is not to be determinative of the propriety of publishing the particular material. The court has the advantage of being impartial, independent of government, and accustomed to deciding disputed issues of fact and whether an occasion is privileged. No one has suggested that some other institution would be better suited for this task.

For the newspaper, Lord Lester's fall-back position was that qualified privilege should be available for political discussion unless the plaintiff proved the newspaper failed to exercise reasonable care. One difficulty with this suggestion is that it would seem to leave a newspaper open to publish a serious allegation which it had been wholly unable to verify. Depending on the circumstances, that might be most unsatisfactory. This difficulty would be removed if, as also canvassed by Lord Lester, the suggested limitation was stated more broadly, and qualified privilege was excluded if the plaintiff proved that the newspaper's conduct in making the publication was unreasonable. Whether this test would differ substantially from the common law test is a moot point. There seems to be no significant practical difference between looking at all the circumstances to decide if a publication attracts privilege, and looking at all the circumstances to see if an acknowledged privilege is defeated.

I have been more troubled by Lord Lester's suggested shift in the burden of proof. Placing the burden of proof on the plaintiff would be a reminder that the starting point today is freedom of expression and limitations on this freedom are exceptions. That has attraction. But if this shift of the onus were applied generally, it would turn the law of qualified privilege upside down. The repercussions of such a far-reaching change were not canvassed before your Lordships. If this change were applied only to political information, the distinction would lack a coherent rationale. There are other subjects of serious public concern. On balance I favour leaving the onus in its traditional place, on him who asserts the privilege, for two practical reasons. A newspaper will know much more of the facts leading up to publication. The burden of proof will seldom, if ever, be decisive on this issue.

For Mr Reynolds, Mr Caldecott submitted that in the context of political speech a report which 'failed to report the other side' should always fail the common law test and, further, that there should be a burden on the newspaper to establish a cogent reason why it should be excused from proving the truth of the assertion. I cannot accept either of these suggested requirements. Failure to report the plaintiff's explanation is a factor to be taken into account. Depending upon the circumstances, it may be a weighty factor. But it should not be elevated into a rigid rule of law. As to the second requirement, it is not clear to what extent, and in what respects, this suggestion covers ground different from the ground already covered by the common law principle . . .

Conclusion

My conclusion is that the established common law approach to misstatements of fact remains essentially sound. The common law should not develop 'political information' as a new 'subject-matter' category of qualified privilege, whereby the publication of all such information would attract qualified privilege, whatever the circumstances. That would not provide adequate protection for reputation. Moreover, it would be unsound in principle to distinguish political discussion from discussion of other matters of serious public concern. The elasticity of the common law principle enables interference with freedom of speech to be confined to what is necessary in the circumstances of the case. This elasticity enables the court to give appropriate weight, in today's conditions, to the importance of freedom of expression by the media on all matters of public concern.

Depending on the circumstances, the matters to be taken into account include the following. The comments are illustrative only.

1. The seriousness of the allegation. The more serious the charge, the more the public is misinformed and the individual harmed, if the allegation is not true.

2. The nature of the information, and the extent to which the subject-matter is a matter of public concern.

3. The source of the information. Some informants have no direct knowledge of the events. Some have their own axes to grind, or are being paid for their stories.

4. The steps taken to verify the information.

5. The status of the information. The allegation may have already been the subject of an investigation which commands respect.

6. The urgency of the matter. News is often a perishable commodity.

7. Whether comment was sought from the plaintiff. He may have information others do not possess or have not disclosed. An approach to the plaintiff will not always be necessary.

8. Whether the article contained the gist of the plaintiff's side of the story.

9. The tone of the article. A newspaper can raise queries or call for an investigation. It need not adopt allegations as statements of fact.

10. The circumstances of the publication, including the timing.

This list is not exhaustive. The weight to be given to these and any other relevant factors will vary from case to case. Any disputes of primary fact will be a matter for the jury, if there is one. The decision on whether, having regard to the admitted or proved facts, the publication was subject to qualified privilege is a matter for the judge. This is the established practice and seems sound. A balancing operation is better carried out by a judge in a reasoned judgment than by a jury. Over time, a valuable corpus of case law will be built up.

In general, a newspaper's unwillingness to disclose the identity of its sources should not weigh against it. Further, it should always be remembered that journalists act without the benefit of the clear light of hindsight. Matters which are obvious in retrospect may have been far from clear in the heat of the moment. Above all, the court should have particular regard to the importance of freedom of expression. The press discharges vital functions as a bloodhound as well as a watchdog. The court should be slow to conclude that a publication was not in the public interest and, therefore, the public had no right to know, especially when the information is in the field of political discussion. Any lingering doubts should be resolved in favour of publication.

Privilege and the Facts of this Case...

In the exercise of its discretion the Court of Appeal decided to rule on the issue of qualified privilege, rather than leave this matter to be dealt with by the trial judge at the re-trial. I can see no sufficient ground for interfering with that decision...[T]he facts relied upon by Mr Reynolds before the judge were clear and undisputed. A most telling criticism of the article is the failure to mention Mr Reynolds' own explanation to the Dáil. Mr Ruddock omitted this from the article because he rejected Mr Reynolds' version of the events and concluded that Mr Reynolds had been deliberately misleading. It goes without saying that a journalist is entitled and bound to reach his own conclusions and to express them honestly and fearlessly. He is entitled to dis-believe and refute explanations given. But this cannot be a good reason for omitting, from a hard-hitting article making serious allegations against a named individual, all mention of that person's own explanation. Particularly so, when the press offices had told Mr Ruddock that Mr Reynolds was not giving interviews but would be saying all he had to say in the Dáil. His statement in the Dáil was his answer to the allegations....By omitting Mr Reynolds' explan-ation English readers were left to suppose that, so far, Mr Reynolds had offered no explanation. Further, it is elementary fairness that, in the normal course, a serious charge should be accom-panied by the gist of any explanation already given. An article which fails to do so faces an uphill task in claiming privilege if the allegation proves to be false and the unreported explanation proves to be true.

Was the information in the *Sunday Times* article information the public was entitled to know? The subject matter was undoubtedly of public concern in this country. However, these seri-ous allegations by the newspaper, presented as statements of fact but shorn of all mention of Mr Reynolds' considered explanation, were not information the public had a right to know. I agree with the Court of Appeal this was not a publication which should in the public interest be protected by privilege in the absence of proof of malice....I would dismiss this appeal.

Lord Cooke of Thorndon and **Lord Hobhouse of Woodborough**, in the course of separate concurring speeches, expressed their full agreement with Lord Nicholls. **Lord Steyn** and **Lord Hope of Craighead** dissented.

Appeal dismissed.

COMMENTARY

Of the two members of the minority, only Lord Hope can be said to have dissented from the majority's approach to the basic question of principle. Lord Steyn disagreed with his brethren only because he thought that, given the pre-existing state of the authorities, the defendants had not had adequate notice of the need to give their view of the circumstances of the publication and ought to be allowed another opportunity to put the question of privilege before the trial court. The majority disagreed, finding that all relevant matters had been fully aired at trial; Lord Cooke of Thorndon commented that 'the defendants have had their day in court—indeed many days in three courts'.

The basis for Lord Hope's dissent was that questions such as whether the defendants had printed the plaintiff's side of the story were relevant only to the question of malice, and not to the question whether the occasion was privileged in the first place. Addressing this point, Lord Cooke admitted that there was indeed support for such a proposition in certain earlier authorities where the publication in question was to a very limited class; in such cases, it might not be necessary to advert specifically to the wider circumstances of the publication (e.g. the steps taken by the defendant to insure the information was accurate). But his Lordship ruled (at 225) that the defence's extension to publications made to the world at large meant that '*all* the circumstances of the case at hand, including the precautions taken by the defendant to ensure accuracy of fact, should be open to scrutiny'. The increase in the scope of the defence had to be balanced by the introduction of a mechanism for preventing abuse. His Lordship noted (at 219):

Although investigative reporting can be of public benefit, the commercial motivation of the press and other sections of the media can create a temptation, not always resisted, to exaggerate, distort or otherwise unfairly represent alleged facts in order to excite the interest of readers, viewers or listeners.

Do you think that the decision of the House of Lords in *Reynolds* undermines the defence of qualified privilege by substituting negligence for malice as the test of whether a privilege is misused?

Other Jurisdictions

The House of Lords in *Reynolds* was satisfied that its approach was consistent with European human rights law as set out in the leading case of *Lingens v Austria* (1986) 8 EHRR 407 (see further p. 783, below). Their Lordships also noted the approaches taken in this area by the courts in certain other jurisdictions. In *Lange v Australian Broadcasting Corporation* (1997) 189 CLR 520, the High Court of Australia had allowed a qualified privilege in respect of political speech subject to a requirement of reasonable care. It would be for the defendant to prove that he had taken reasonable care in respect of the publication. Although the Australian court's approach bore some similarity to that of the House of Lords in *Reynolds*, Lord Steyn felt that 'such a development would involve a radical re-writing of our law of defamation' and was not 'a satisfactory way of redressing the imbalance between freedom of speech and defamation in England'. Elaborating, Lord Cooke felt that there was 'at least some difference of emphasis' between the two approaches. He felt that '[a] major expansion of the privilege, such as may have been achieved in Australia, shifts the focus of political defamation to the conduct of the defendant' and would detract from the law's primary purpose of enabling claimants to clear their names. He concluded: 'If the Australian solution has disadvantages, they may lie in this change of focus and in the singling out of politicians as acceptable targets of falsehood.'

A more radical solution to the problem of political reporting was adopted by the Court of Appeal of New Zealand in *Lange v Atkinson* [1998] 3 NZLR 424. The court recognised a 'generic' defence of political free speech applying to statements directly concerning the functioning of representative government, including statements about the performance of specific individuals in elected public office, with the reasonableness of the publication relevant only to the question of malice, not the existence of the privilege. An appeal from this decision was heard by the Privy Council a week before the same panel of judges heard the appeal in *Reynolds*. The judgment of the Privy Council was that *Lange* should be reconsidered by the New Zealand Court of Appeal in the light of the views expressed in *Reynolds*, especially as to the need for at least some check on the ability of the news media to publish stories about political figures which could not be shown to have been actuated by malice. The Privy Council accepted that, in the light of the different circumstances of the two countries, it would still be open to the New Zealand court to reach a conclusion at variance with that reached in *Reynolds*, though they did not advocate such a result (*Lange v Atkinson* [2000] 1

NZLR 257). In *Lange v Atkinson (No. 2)* [2000] 3 NZLR 385, the New Zealand Court of Appeal reaffirmed its earlier decision, finding that the approach in *Reynolds* was likely to have 'undesirable' consequences: by introducing new uncertainty into the law, it increased the 'chilling effect' on the media, and at the same time it reduced the vital role of the jury in freedom of speech cases, it being the jury's task to rule on malice but the judge's to decide whether an occasion is privileged.

In Canada, the Supreme Court has recently adopted a new defence of responsible communication on matters of public interest that bears a considerable similarity to the defence of *Reynolds* privilege (*Grant v Torstar Corp*, 2009 SCC 61). However, the Court stated that the defence was distinct from qualified privilege, which was to be left intact in its traditional form (at [95], per McLachlin CJ). The case concerned a newspaper article, but the Court expressly denied that the defence was limited to media publications (see further in the Commentary under *Jameel*).

Another possible approach—considered by the House of Lords in *Reynolds*, although it was not argued by either party that the defence should be recognised in English law—is the 'public figure' defence adopted in the United States. See further p. 786f, below.

Jameel v Wall Street Journal Europe Sprl [2007] 1 AC 359

Five months after the devastating terrorist attacks on New York and Washington of 11 September 2001, the defendant's newspaper published an article about investigations into terrorist funding being conducted by the banking authorities in Saudi Arabia at the request of US law enforcement agencies. The article referred to a group of companies of which the first claimant was president and the second claimant was a part. A jury found that it was defamatory of them in suggesting (at a minimum) that there were reasonable grounds to investigate their involvement in the witting or unwitting funnelling of funds to terrorist organisations. The article stated that the companies 'couldn't be reached for comment'; in fact, the author had spoken to an employee the day before publication, but the employee had no authority to make a statement and asked for publication to be delayed for 24 hours so that the first claimant, who was overseas, could be contacted. The journalist declined the request. In the claimants' action for damages, the newspaper did not attempt to prove the truth of the defamatory imputation, but sought to strike out the action on the basis of *Reynolds* privilege. (The newspaper's alternative argument that a trading corporation was not entitled to sue for libel without pleading or proving special damage is considered at p. 785, below.) The striking-out application failed before Eady J and the Court of Appeal, which found that the newspaper had failed the test of responsible journalism because it had not delayed publication to allow the first claimant the opportunity to comment. The newspaper appealed to the House of Lords.

Lord Bingham

28 The decision of the House in *Reynolds v Times Newspapers Ltd* [2001] 2 AC 127 built on the traditional foundations of qualified privilege but carried the law forward in a way which gave much greater weight than the earlier law had done to the value of informed public debate of significant public issues. Both these aspects are, I think, important in understanding the decision.

29 Underlying the development of qualified privilege was the requirement of a reciprocal duty and interest between the publisher and the recipient of the statement in question... [W]here a publication related to a matter of public interest, it was accepted that the reciprocal

duty and interest could be found even where publication was by a newspaper to a section of the public or the public at large...

30 I do not understand the House to have rejected the duty/interest approach...But Lord Nicholls, at p 197, considered that matters relating to the nature and source of the information were matters to be taken into account in determining whether the duty-interest test was satisfied or, as he preferred to say 'in a simpler and more direct way, whether the public was entitled to know the particular information'.

31 The necessary precondition of reliance on qualified privilege in this context is that the matter published should be one of public interest. In the present case the subject matter of the article complained of was of undoubted public interest. But that is not always, perhaps not usually, so. It has been repeatedly and rightly said that what engages the interest of the public may not be material which engages the public interest.

32 Qualified privilege as a live issue only arises where a statement is defamatory and untrue. It was in this context, and assuming the matter to be one of public interest, that Lord Nicholls proposed, at p 202, a test of responsible journalism, a test repeated in *Bonnick v Morris* [2003] 1 AC 300 at 309. The rationale of this test is, as I understand, that there is no duty to publish and the public have no interest to read material which the publisher has not taken reasonable steps to verify. As Lord Hobhouse observed with characteristic pungency, at p 238, 'No public interest is served by publishing or communicating misinformation.' But the publisher is protected if he has taken such steps as a responsible journalist would take to try and ensure that what is published is accurate and fit for publication.

33 Lord Nicholls, at p 205, listed certain matters which might be taken into account in deciding whether the test of responsible journalism was satisfied. He intended these as pointers which might be more or less indicative, depending on the circumstances of a particular case, and not, I feel sure, as a series of hurdles to be negotiated by a publisher before he could successfully rely on qualified privilege. Lord Nicholls recognised, at pp 202–203, inevitably as I think, that it had to be a body other than the publisher, namely the court, which decided whether a publication was protected by qualified privilege. But this does not mean that the editorial decisions and judgments made at the time, without the knowledge of falsity which is a benefit of hindsight, are irrelevant. Weight should ordinarily be given to the professional judgment of an editor or journalist in the absence of some indication that it was made in a casual, cavalier, slipshod or careless manner.

34 Some misunderstanding may perhaps have been engendered by Lord Nicholls's references, at pp 195, 197, to 'the particular information'. It is of course true that the defence of qualified privilege must be considered with reference to the particular publication complained of as defamatory, and where a whole article or story is complained of no difficulty arises. But difficulty can arise where the complaint relates to one particular ingredient of a composite story, since it is then open to a plaintiff to contend, as in the present case, that the article could have been published without inclusion of the particular ingredient complained of. This may, in some instances, be a valid point. But consideration should be given to the thrust of the article which the publisher has published. If the thrust of the article is true, and the public interest condition is satisfied, the inclusion of an inaccurate fact may not have the same appearance of irresponsibility as it might if the whole thrust of the article is untrue.

35 These principles must be applied to the present case...The Court of Appeal upheld the judge's denial of *Reynolds* privilege on a single ground...: that the newspaper had failed to delay publication of the respondents' names without waiting long enough for the respondents to comment. This seems to me, with respect, to be a very narrow ground on which to deny the privilege, and the ruling subverts the liberalising intention of the *Reynolds* decision.

The subject matter was of great public interest, in the strictest sense. The article was written by an experienced specialist reporter and approved by senior staff on the newspaper...who themselves sought to verify its contents. The article was unsensational in tone and (apparently) factual in content. The respondents' response was sought, although at a late stage, and the newspaper's inability to obtain a comment recorded. It is very unlikely that a comment, if obtained, would have been revealing, since even if the respondents' accounts were being monitored it was unlikely that they would know. It might be thought that this was the sort of neutral, investigative journalism which *Reynolds* privilege exists to protect. I would accordingly allow the appeal and set aside the Court of Appeal judgment.

Lord Hoffmann

43 The newspaper's principal defence was based on *Reynolds v Times Newspapers Ltd* [2001] 2 AC 127. It is called in the trade '*Reynolds* privilege' but the use of the term privilege, although historically accurate, may be misleading. A defence of privilege in the usual sense is available when the defamatory statement was published on a privileged occasion and can be defeated only by showing that the privilege was abused...

46 Although Lord Nicholls uses the word 'privilege', it is clearly not being used in the old sense. It is the material which is privileged, not the occasion on which it is published. There is no question of the privilege being defeated by proof of malice because the propriety of the conduct of the defendant is built into the conditions under which the material is privileged. The burden is upon the defendant to prove that those conditions are satisfied. I therefore agree with the opinion of the Court of Appeal in *Loutchansky v Times Newspapers Ltd (Nos 2–5)* [2002] QB 783 at 806 that '*Reynolds* privilege' is 'a different jurisprudential creature from the traditional form of privilege from which it sprang'. It might more appropriately be called the *Reynolds* public interest defence rather than privilege...

50 In answering the question of public interest, I do not think it helpful to apply the classic test for the existence of a privileged occasion and ask whether there was a duty to communicate the information and an interest in receiving it. The *Reynolds* defence was developed from the traditional form of privilege by a generalisation that in matters of public interest, there can be said to be a professional duty on the part of journalists to impart the information and an interest in the public in receiving it. The House having made this generalisation, it should in my opinion be regarded as a proposition of law and not decided each time as a question of fact. If the publication is in the public interest, the duty and interest are taken to exist...

53 If the publication, including the defamatory statement, passes the public interest test, the inquiry then shifts to whether the steps taken to gather and publish the information were responsible and fair...

55 In this case, Eady J said that the concept of 'responsible journalism' was too vague. It was, he said, 'subjective'...But the standard of responsible journalism is as objective and no more vague than standards such as 'reasonable care' which are regularly used in other branches of law. Greater certainty in its application is attained in two ways. First, as Lord Nicholls said, a body of illustrative case law builds up. Secondly, just as the standard of reasonable care in particular areas, such as driving a vehicle, is made more concrete by extra-statutory codes of behaviour like the Highway Code, so the standard of responsible journalism is made more specific by the Code of Practice which has been adopted by the newspapers and ratified by the Press Complaints Commission. This too, while not binding upon the courts, can provide valuable guidance.

Lord Scott referred to Lord Atkinson's famous statement of the law in *Adam v Ward* [1917] AC 309 at 334, quoted at p. 746, above, and continued:

129 My Lords, however accurate Lord Atkinson's statement of law may be where the defamatory communication has been made to a relatively limited number of people, it does not, as it seems to me, cater for the role of the press, at the end of the 20th century and the beginning of the 21st, in reporting on matters of public importance. Newspapers address their contents to the public at large. Some, like the 'Wall Street Journal Europe', have an international readership, but the relationship between a newspaper and the members of the public who choose to read it is essentially the same, whether the readership be international or local. The publication is to the public at large. To insist on a reciprocity of duty and interest between the publisher of a newspaper and the reader of the newspaper, who may be in New York, London, Rome, or anywhere, either makes the requirement of reciprocity meaningless or deprives any defamatory statement in the paper, no matter how important as a matter of public interest the content of the statement may be, of the possibility of the protection of qualified privilege. It was this undesirable rigidity of the law of qualified privilege that, to my mind, the seminal judgment of Lord Nicholls of Birkenhead in the *Reynolds* case [2001] 2 AC 127 was designed to meet.

130 Lord Nicholls did not turn his back on the reciprocal duty/interest test for qualified privilege. Instead he moulded the test so as to cater for the publication of information that the public as a whole, as opposed to a specific individual or individuals, was entitled to know...

135 ...I would not myself accept the conclusion that *Reynolds* privilege is 'a different jurisprudential creature' from traditional qualified privilege.

Baroness Hale

146 It should by now be entirely clear that the *Reynolds* defence is a 'different jurisprudential creature' from the law of privilege, although it is a natural development of that law. It springs from the general obligation of the press, media and other publishers to communicate important information upon matters of general public interest and the general right of the public to receive such information. It is not helpful to analyse the particular case in terms of a specific duty and a specific right to know. That can, as experience since *Reynolds* has shown, very easily lead to a narrow and rigid approach which defeats its object. In truth, it is a defence of publication in the public interest...

Lord Hope delivered a separate concurring opinion.

Appeal allowed.

COMMENTARY

As is apparent from the extracts, there was disagreement between the Law Lords as to the jurisprudential nature of *Reynolds* privilege: was it simply a development of the established defence of qualified privilege, or a new and separate defence? If the latter interpretation prevails, that would mean that a different rule applies to communications to the public at large on matters of public interest from that applicable to conventionally privileged situations. One crucial issue is whether the *Reynolds* test of 'responsibility' is to be applied to the latter class of publications. In *Keams v General Council of the Bar* [2003] 1 WLR 1357, the Court of Appeal ruled that it was not. The Bar Council wrote to all heads of chambers and senior clerks/practice managers in the light of concerns expressed by a Bar member about the claimants who, he said, were seeking to instruct barristers directly even though they were not in fact solicitors. The letter stated that the claimants were not solicitors and should not be dealt with on their standard terms of business. In fact, the claimants were solicitors.

It was assumed for the purposes of the hearing that the Bar Council had made no effort to verify the information it had sent out. The Court of Appeal ruled that this was not fatal to the defence. The steps taken to verify the information were relevant in deciding whether a *Reynolds* privilege arose in respect of a media publication to the general public, but not where there was an existing and established relationship—such as that between the Bar Council and Bar members—which plainly required the flow of free and frank communications in both directions. It must be said that it seems right to confine the scope of *Reynolds* in this way—not least, because there might be an undue 'chilling effect' upon free speech on those occasions to which qualified privilege has traditionally attached if the privilege were to be withdrawn simply because the defendant was irresponsible.

In *Kearns*, the Court of Appeal considered that the *Reynolds* defence was confined to media publications, but the Privy Council in *Seaga v Harper* [2009] 1 AC 1, an appeal from Jamaica, stated that it could see no valid reason why the defence should not extend to 'publications made by any person who publishes material of public interest in any medium', so long as it was 'responsible' in the sense intended by Lord Nicholls. (See also *Jameel*, at [54] per Lord Hoffmann; *Grant v Torstar Corp.*, at [96] per McLachlin CJ.)

The Standard of Responsible Journalism

In *Reynolds*, Lord Nicholls listed ten factors that might be taken into account in applying the test of responsible journalism. On the facts, the House of Lords concluded that the defendants had failed to meet the standard, attaching most significance to their failure to give the claimant's side of the story (Lord Nicholls' eighth factor) though there was no rigid rule of law that such an omission meant that the publication was unprivileged.

The test of responsible journalism was subsequently considered on a number of occasions. In *Grobbelaar v News Group Newspapers Ltd* [2001] 2 All ER 437, for example, the Court of Appeal concluded that the defence of qualified privilege was not applicable to what was a sensational newspaper exposé unambiguously asserting the criminal guilt of its subject. (The facts of the case are given at p. 734, above, but note that the issue of qualified privilege was not appealed to the House of Lords.) The decisive consideration was the *tone* of the publication (Lord Nicholls' ninth factor). It was, according to Simon Brown LJ, absurd to suggest that newspapers would be discouraged from pursuing their investigatory role by such a ruling, particularly bearing in mind the obvious commercial benefits derived from sensationalist journalism. In fact, to allow the defence in such circumstances would give rise to the altogether greater risk that exposés would become even more sensational. (See also *Galloway v Telegraph Group Ltd* [2006] EMLR 11.)

In *Jameel*, the House of Lords criticised some of the post-*Reynolds* decisions for raising the standard of responsible journalism too high. Lord Nicholls' ten factors were not tests which each allegation contained in a journalistic story had to pass, but only illustrative of the considerations relevant in determining, by reference to the story as a whole, whether or not the journalism was responsible. On the facts, the failure to include the claimant's side of the story (Lord Nicholls' eighth factor) was not fatal to the defence even though delaying publication by 24 hours would have given the claimant the opportunity to comment. The newspaper had taken adequate steps to verify its story, and it was unlikely that the claimant would have made any comment that would have made a difference to what was published. It was the very nature of covert surveillance that its target was unaware of what was going on.

In applying the test, it may be relevant to ask whether the defendant could reasonably have attributed some non-defamatory meaning to the words in question, even in a case where they are subsequently found to be defamatory by the tribunal of fact. A journalist's failure to make further inquiries after an anonymous tip-off, or to include the claimant's side of the story, would surely constitute irresponsible journalism where he *expressly* alleged the claimant to have done something wrong, but would not necessarily do so where the defamatory imputation arose only by implication (*Bonnick v Morris* [2003] 1 AC 300, PC).

'Conventional' Qualified Privilege

As already noted, the conventional defence of qualified privilege depends on a reciprocity of duty or interest as between the defendant and the person to whom the statement is published. The determination of whether a duty to communicate exists is a question solely for the judge. The opinion of the maker of the statement is not relevant: honest belief in the existence of a duty cannot create a duty to communicate. The duty need not be legal; a moral or social duty will suffice. The classic statement of the relevant principles is that of Lindley LJ in *Stuart v Bell* [1891] 2 QB 341 at 350:

> [T]he question of moral or social duty being for the judge, each judge must decide it as best he can for himself. I take moral or social duty to mean a duty recognized by English people of ordinary intelligence and moral principle, but at the same time not a duty enforceable by legal proceedings, whether civil or criminal.

A duty to communicate may arise from another person's request for information, at least where that person has an interest in the matter under consideration (e.g. in the case of an employment reference). But a request is not necessary, and it has been found for instance that a close relative is justified in writing an unsolicited letter of warning to a widow who is engaged to be married to a man he considers an unprincipled trickster, provided he acts in good faith (*Todd v Hawkins* (1837) 8 C & P 88).

It is well established that the existence of an *interest* in communicating may also be sufficient to raise the privilege. For instance, it is enough that the defendant is responding reasonably after being subjected to a verbal attack. As Lord Oaksey explained in *Turner v Metro-Goldwyn-Mayer Pictures Ltd* [1950] 1 All ER 449 at 470:

> [T]here is . . . an analogy between the criminal law of self defence and a man's right to defend himself against written or verbal [sic] attacks. In both cases he is entitled . . . to defend himself effectively, and he only loses the protection of the law if he goes beyond defence and proceeds to offence.

Accordingly, a person defamed in a newspaper has a right to respond via the letters' page, even if this involves impugning the reputation of the person making the attack or a third party with whom the claimant has been confused (see *Watts v Times Newspapers Ltd* [1997] QB 650).

It is also considered that officers of a company have a common interest in communicating to each other information about matters affecting the company's business (see *Watt v Longsdon* [1930] 1 KB 130, noted below).

Excess of Privilege

In the conventional form of the defence, even if a reciprocal duty or interest arises, publication beyond the class of interested parties will be regarded as being in excess of privilege. Complaints, grievances and allegations of wrongdoing must be addressed to the proper authorities (e.g., in the case of complaints against a firm of solicitors, the Law Society or Ministry of Justice: see *Beach v Freeson* [1972] 1 QB 14) and must generally be investigated before being circulated to a wider class of person. In *De Buse v McCarthy* [1942] 1 KB 156, it was accepted that a local council had an interest in receiving a report from one of its committees which stated that certain council employees were suspected of the theft of petrol from a council depot. But the privilege did not extend to the publication of the employees' names and the suspicions against them in notices setting out the agenda for the meeting which were sent to and posted in public libraries. Ratepayers could not be regarded as interested in the domestic deliberations of the council before they had resulted in practical action or resolution; nor could the council have a duty or interest to tell ratepayers of their mere suspicions. This case may be regarded as a forerunner of the *Reynolds* decision, being an early example of a decision that the defence should be denied to a defendant in view of the circumstances of publication.

In the celebrated case of *Watt v Longsdon* [1930] 1 KB 130, the defendant, the director of a company, received a letter from an employee making allegations of immorality, drunkenness and dishonesty on the part of the plaintiff, who was the managing director of the company abroad. Without obtaining any corroboration of the contents of the letter, and without communicating with the plaintiff, the defendant showed the letter first to the chairman of the board of directors and then to the plaintiff's wife. The allegations in the letter were unfounded, but the defendant believed them to be true. The Court of Appeal held that the communication to the chairman of the board of directors was privileged but that the communication to the wife was not. The court emphasised that there was no general rule applicable in such cases, Scrutton LJ commenting (at 150):

It cannot, on the one hand, be the duty even of a friend to communicate all the gossip the friend hears at men's clubs or women's bridge parties to one of the spouses affected. On the other hand, most men would hold that it was the moral duty of a doctor who attended his sister in law, and believed her to be suffering from a miscarriage, for which an absent husband could not be responsible, to communicate that fact to his wife and the husband.

In what circumstances (if any) do you think it would be appropriate to tell the spouse of your business colleague about your colleague's suspected infidelity?

(c) Qualified Privilege under Statute

In addition to qualified privilege at common law, the defence may also arise under statute. The Defamation Act 1996 accords a qualified privilege to the reporting, for example, by newspapers or on the television or radio news, of various matters of record, including foreign parliamentary or judicial proceedings, statements issued on behalf of government departments, and the conduct of public meetings.

Defamation Act 1996

15. REPORTS, &C, PROTECTED BY QUALIFIED PRIVILEGE

(1) The publication of any report or other statement mentioned in Schedule 1 to this Act is privileged unless the publication is shown to be made with malice, subject as follows.

(2) In defamation proceedings in respect of the publication of a report or other statement mentioned in Part II of that Schedule, there is no defence under this section if the plaintiff shows that the defendant—
    (a) was requested by him to publish in a suitable manner a reasonable letter or statement by way of explanation or contradiction, and
    (b) refused or neglected to do so.

> For this purpose 'in a suitable manner' means in the same manner as the publication complained of or in a manner that is adequate and reasonable in the circumstances.
>
> (3) This section does not apply to the publication to the public, or a section of the public, of matter which is not of public concern and the publication of which is not for the public benefit.
>
> (4) Nothing in this section shall be construed
>> (a) as protecting the publication of matter the publication of which is prohibited by law, or
>> (b) as limiting or abridging any privilege subsisting apart from this section.

COMMENTARY

This provision of the Defamation Act 1996 is the latest restatement of statutory principles governing qualified privilege which date back to the Law of Libel Amendment Act 1888. Under the current Act, the defence is no longer limited to *newspaper* reports (cf. Defamation Act 1952, s. 7).

Schedule 1 to the Act lists the reports and statements referred to in s. 15(1) under two headings. In Part I, there are various statements having 'qualified privilege without explanation or contradiction', meaning that there is no obligation on a defendant wishing to rely upon this defence to publish an explanation or qualification of the words in question if requested to do so by the claimant. The most important examples of such statements are fair and accurate reports of the proceedings of legislatures, courts, governmental inquiries, and international organisations held in public anywhere in the world. Part I also applies to fair and accurate copies of or extracts from matter published by or on the authority of a government, legislature, international organisation or international conference anywhere in the world. The statements covered by Part II are 'privileged subject to explanation or contradiction'. If a defendant fails to publish in a suitable manner a reasonable letter or statement by way of explanation or contradiction of the defamatory words, as requested by the claimant, then the privilege is lost (s. 15(2)). Amongst the most important examples under this heading are fair and accurate reports of the proceedings of public meetings held in any EU state, general meetings of any UK public company and public sittings of tribunals, boards, committees, etc., acting under statutory powers. A press conference to which only journalists are invited is nevertheless a public meeting because the manifest intention is to communicate the proceedings to a wider public (*McCarten Turkington Breen v Times Newspapers* [2001] 2 AC 277). Part II of the Schedule also includes fair and accurate reports of decisions by associations in the fields of the arts and sciences, religion and charity, trade and industry, and games and sports. (Consider for instance the news reporting of a finding that a sports competitor had failed a drug test.) Covered as well are fair and accurate copies of or extracts from 'a notice or other matter issued for the information of the public' by the government (or by the EU authorities or another member state). It should be noted that the protection thereby offered to journalists is limited to the reporting of official information, and does not extend to assumptions, inferences and speculations confirmed or provoked by such information: '[t]hat would be to accord to investigative journalism the protection provided for reporting of official information' (*Blackshaw v Lord* [1984] QB 1 at 24, per Stephenson LJ). In the judgment just noted, Stephenson LJ also doubted whether information was *issued* if it was 'painfully extracted by journalists, like a tooth . . . from the mouth of an unwilling officer' (at 23–4), although he accepted that answers to questions put over the telephone might well be covered.

(d) Malice

Malice defeats the defences of both fair comment and qualified privilege, though the applicable principles vary as between the two defences as improper motive constitutes malice only for qualified privilege, not fair comment (see p. 743, above). In neither defence, however, is malice to be equated with hostility or ill-will; a simple lack of honest belief in the truth of what is being said will suffice.

Horrocks v Lowe [1975] AC 135

At a meeting of the Bolton Borough Council in November 1969, the defendant, Alderman Lowe, made a speech accusing the plaintiff, Councillor Horrocks, of misleading the Management and Finance Committee of the council in respect of a property-related dispute involving Bolton Corporation and a property development company of which the plaintiff was chairman. The defendant—who believed in any case that the plaintiff should not be a member of the committee in view of the danger of conflicts of interest arising in connection with the plaintiff's many property interests in the area—called for the plaintiff's removal from the committee. The plaintiff brought an action for slander. The defendant did not seek to justify the expressions he had used but relied on the defence of qualified privilege. It was not disputed that the words were spoken on a privileged occasion, but the plaintiff alleged that the privilege was defeated by malice on the defendant's part. At trial, Stirling J found that the defendant honestly believed everything he had said but concluded that his anxiety to have the plaintiff removed from the committee had caused him to act with 'gross and unreasoning prejudice'. On appeal to the Court of Appeal, the defendant successfully argued that his belief that everything he said was true made it impossible as a matter of law to find that he was actuated by malice. The plaintiff appealed to the House of Lords.

Lord Diplock

The public interest that the law should provide an effective means whereby a man can vindicate his reputation against calumny has nevertheless to be accommodated to the competing public interest in permitting men to communicate frankly and freely with one another about matters in respect of which the law recognises that they have a duty to perform or an interest to protect in doing so. What is published in good faith on matters of these kinds is published on a privileged occasion. It is not actionable even though it be defamatory and turns out to be untrue. With some exceptions which are irrelevant to the instant appeal, the privilege is not absolute but qualified. It is lost if the occasion which gives rise to it is misused. For in all cases of qualified privilege there is some special reason of public policy why the law accords immunity from suit—the existence of some public or private duty, whether legal or moral, on the part of the maker of the defamatory statement which justifies his communicating it or of some interest of his own which he is entitled to protect by doing so. If he uses the occasion for some other reason he loses the protection of the privilege.

So, the motive with which the defendant on a privileged occasion made a statement defamatory of the plaintiff becomes crucial. The protection might, however, be illusory if the onus lay on him to prove that he was actuated solely by a sense of the relevant duty or a desire to protect the relevant interest. So he is entitled to be protected by the privilege unless some other dominant and improper motive on his part is proved. 'Express malice' is the term of art descriptive of such a motive. Broadly speaking, it means malice in the popular sense of a desire to injure the person who is defamed and this is generally the motive which the plaintiff sets out to prove. But to destroy the privilege the desire to injure must be the dominant motive for the defamatory publication; knowledge that it will have that effect is not enough if the defendant is nevertheless acting in accordance with a sense of duty or in bona fide protection of his own legitimate interests.

The motive with which a person published defamatory matter can only be inferred from what he did or said or knew. If it be proved that he did not believe that what he published was true this is generally conclusive evidence of express malice, for no sense of duty or desire to protect his own legitimate interests can justify a man in telling deliberate and injurious falsehoods about another, save in the exceptional case where a person may be under a duty to pass on, without endorsing, defamatory reports made by some other person.

Apart from those exceptional cases, what is required on the part of the defamer to entitle him to the protection of the privilege is positive belief in the truth of what he published or, as it is generally though tautologously termed, 'honest belief.' If he publishes untrue defamatory matter recklessly, without considering or caring whether it be true or not, he is in this, as in other branches of the law, treated as if he knew it to be false. But indifference to the truth of what he publishes is not to be equated with carelessness, impulsiveness or irrationality in arriving at a positive belief that it is true. The freedom of speech protected by the law of qualified privilege may be availed of by all sorts and conditions of men. In affording to them immunity from suit if they have acted in good faith in compliance with a legal or moral duty or in protection of a legitimate interest the law must take them as it finds them. In ordinary life it is rare indeed for people to form their beliefs by a process of logical deduction from facts ascertained by a rigorous search for all available evidence and a judicious assessment of its probative value. In greater or in less degree according to their temperaments, their training, their intelligence, they are swayed by prejudice, rely on intuition instead of reasoning, leap to conclusions on inadequate evidence and fail to recognise the cogency of material which might cast doubt on the validity of the conclusions they reach. But despite the imperfection of the mental process by which the belief is arrived at It may still be 'honest,' that is, a positive belief that the conclusions they have reached are true. The law demands no more.

Even a positive belief in the truth of what is published on a privileged occasion—which is presumed unless the contrary is proved—may not be sufficient to negative express malice if it can be proved that the defendant misused the occasion for some purpose other than that for which the privilege is accorded by the law. The commonest case is where the dominant motive which actuates the defendant is not a desire to perform the relevant duty or to protect the relevant interest, but to give vent to his personal spite or ill will towards the person he defames. If this be proved, then even positive belief in the truth of what is published will not enable the defamer to avail himself of the protection of the privilege to which he would otherwise have been entitled. There may be instances of improper motives which destroy the privilege apart from personal spite. A defendant's dominant motive may have been to obtain some private advantage unconnected with the duty or the interest which constitutes the reason for the privilege. If so, he loses the benefit of the privilege despite his positive belief that what he said or wrote was true.

Judges and juries should, however, be very slow to draw the inference that a defendant was so far actuated by improper motives as to deprive him of the protection of the privilege unless they are satisfied that he did not believe that what he said or wrote was true or that he was indifferent to its truth or falsity. The motives with which human beings act are mixed. They find it difficult to hate the sin but love the sinner. Qualified privilege would be illusory, and the public interest that it is meant to serve defeated, if the protection which it affords were lost merely because a person, although acting in compliance with a duty or in protection of a legitimate interest, disliked the person whom he defamed or was indignant at what he believed to be that person's conduct and welcomed the opportunity of exposing it. It is only where his desire to comply with the relevant duty or to protect the relevant interest plays no significant part in his motives for publishing what he believes to be true that 'express malice' can properly be found . . . .

My Lords, what is said by members of a local council at meetings of the council or of any of its committees is spoken on a privileged occasion. The reason for the privilege is that those who represent the local government electors should be able to speak freely and frankly, boldly and bluntly, on any matter which they believe affects the interests or welfare of the inhabitants. They may be swayed by strong political prejudice, they may be obstinate and pig-headed, stupid and obtuse; but they were chosen by the electors to speak their minds on matters of local concern and so long as they do so honestly they run no risk of liability for defamation of those who are the subjects of their criticism.

In the instant case Mr Lowe's speech at the meeting of the Bolton Borough Council was upon matters which were undoubtedly of local concern. With one minor exception, the only facts relied upon as evidence from which express malice was to be inferred had reference to the contents of the speech itself, the circumstances in which the meeting of the council was held and the material relating to the subject matter of Mr Lowe's speech which was within his actual knowledge or available to him on inquiry. The one exception was his failure to apologise to Mr Horrocks when asked to do so two days later. A refusal to apologise is at best but tenuous evidence of malice, for it is consistent with a continuing belief in the truth of what one has said. Stirling J found it to be so in the case of Mr Lowe . . .

However prejudiced the judge thought Mr Lowe to be, however irrational in leaping to conclusions unfavourable to Mr Horrocks, this crucial finding of Mr Lowe's belief in the truth of what he said upon that privileged occasion entitles him to succeed in his defence of privilege. The Court of Appeal so held. I would myself do likewise and dismiss this appeal.

Lord Wilberforce, **Lord Hodson** and **Lord Kilbrandon** concurred with Lord Diplock. **Viscount Dilhorne** delivered a separate concurring opinion.

Appeal dismissed.

COMMENTARY

In the Court of Appeal [1972] 1 WLR 1625 at 1630, Lord Denning MR summarised his approach in the following maxim: 'So long as they are honest, they go clear.' Is this an adequate statement of the law?

In the above extract, Lord Diplock provides the classic statement of the principles governing the role of malice where there is a defence of qualified privilege. In short, malice can be established either by the defendant's lack of honest belief in the truth of the defamatory statement or by the presence of a dominant improper motive on the defendant's part (e.g. a desire to injure the claimant). In a case where the defendant positively believes in the truth of the defamatory statement, the courts will be slow to find that he was predominantly actuated by an improper motive. As Lord Diplock notes in a passage omitted from the extract, evidence of improper motive may be derived from either the defendant's conduct on other occasions or his incorporation of irrelevant defamatory matter in the communication in question. Irrelevant material might logically be said to fall altogether outside the privilege, but the law recognises that ordinary persons vary in their ability to identify what is logically relevant, and therefore that 'the protection afforded by the privilege would be illusory if it were lost in respect of any defamatory matter which upon logical analysis could be shown to be irrelevant to the fulfilment of a duty or the protection of the right upon which the privilege was founded' (at 151).

Effect of Malice by a Co-Defendant

Where there are several co-defendants, proof of malice against one does not deprive others who did not themselves act maliciously of the defence: *Eggar v Viscount Chelmsford* [1965] 1 QB 248.

4. Offers of Amends

At common law, liability in defamation is in most respects strict. It is no defence that the defendant did not intend to defame the claimant, nor even that he had no cause reasonably to foresee that the words published might defame the claimant (see, e.g., *Cassidy v Daily Mirror Newspapers Ltd* [1929] 2 KB 331, p. 721, above). The harshness of these principles has been mitigated by statute, which provides a mechanism for a defendant who has 'innocently' defamed another person to make an offer of amends which, in certain circumstances, acts as a defence against defamation proceedings.

Defamation Act 1996

2. OFFER TO MAKE AMENDS

(1) A person who has published a statement alleged to be defamatory of another may offer to make amends under this section.

(2) The offer may be in relation to the statement generally or in relation to a specific defamatory meaning which the person making the offer accepts that the statement conveys ('a qualified offer').

(3) An offer to make amends—
    (a) must be in writing,
    (b) must be expressed to be an offer to make amends under section 2 of the Defamation Act 1996, and
    (c) must state whether it is a qualified offer and, if so, set out the defamatory meaning in relation to which it is made.

(4) An offer to make amends under this section is an offer—
    (a) to make a suitable correction of the statement complained of and a sufficient apology to the aggrieved party,

(b) to publish the correction and apology in a manner that is reasonable and practicable in the circumstances, and

(c) to pay to the aggrieved party such compensation (if any), and such costs, as may be agreed or determined to be payable.

The fact that the offer is accompanied by an offer to take specific steps does not affect the fact that an offer to make amends under this section is an offer to do all the things mentioned in paragraphs (a) to (c)....

3. ACCEPTING AN OFFER TO MAKE AMENDS

(1) If an offer to make amends under section 2 is accepted by the aggrieved party, the following provisions apply.

(2) The party accepting the offer may not bring or continue defamation proceedings in respect of the publication concerned against the person making the offer, but he is entitled to enforce the offer to make amends, as follows.

(3) If the parties agree on the steps to be taken in fulfilment of the offer, the aggrieved party may apply to the court for an order that the other party fulfil his offer by taking the steps agreed.

(4) If the parties do not agree on the steps to be taken by way of correction, apology and publication, the party who made the offer may take such steps as he thinks appropriate, and may in particular—

(a) make the correction and apology by a statement in open court in terms approved by the court, and

(b) give an undertaking to the court as to the manner of their publication.

(5) If the parties do not agree on the amount to be paid by way of compensation, it shall be determined by the court on the same principles as damages in defamation proceedings. The court shall take account of any steps taken in fulfilment of the offer and (so far as not agreed between the parties) of the suitability of the correction, the sufficiency of the apology and whether the manner of their publication was reasonable in the circumstances, and may reduce or increase the amount of compensation accordingly.

(6) If the parties do not agree on the amount to be paid by way of costs, it shall be determined by the court on the same principles as costs awarded in court proceedings....

(10) Proceedings under this section shall be heard and determined without a jury.

4. FAILURE TO ACCEPT OFFER TO MAKE AMENDS

(1) If an offer to make amends under section 2, duly made and not withdrawn, is not accepted by the aggrieved party, the following provisions apply.

(2) The fact that the offer was made is a defence (subject to subsection (3)) to defamation proceedings in respect of the publication in question by that party against the person making the offer. A qualified offer is only a defence in respect of the meaning to which the offer related.

(3) There is no such defence if the person by whom the offer was made knew or had reason to believe that the statement complained of—

(a) referred to the aggrieved party or was likely to be understood as referring to him, and

(b) was both false and defamatory of that party; but it shall be presumed until the contrary is shown that he did not know and had no reason to believe that was the case.

(4) The person who made the offer need not rely on it by way of defence, but if he does he may not rely on any other defence. If the offer was a qualified offer, this applies only in respect of the meaning to which the offer related.

(5) The offer may be relied on in mitigation of damages whether or not it was relied on as a defence.

COMMENTARY

These provisions replace those which previously regulated the defence of offer of amends under Defamation Act 1952, s. 4. The earlier provisions were very rarely used as they were unattractive to defendants—being complex, limited in scope, and difficult to comply with—and to plaintiffs, to whom they gave no right to compensation. The Neill Committee—in whose *Report on Practice and Procedure in Defamation*, 1991, the provisions of the new Act originate—stated (at para. VII.17) that it was:

unsatisfactory that defendants should have a defence available, based on their reasonable behaviour after publication, which would leave the plaintiff with no compensation at all, in respect of hurt feelings or injury to reputation, to take account of what was *ex hypothesi* a defamation... [W]e see no overriding public interest in depriving plaintiffs of all compensation merely because the defendants have seen the error of their ways.

Does this beg the question of whether the person whose reputation has been injured by an innocent statement has truly been defamed? If the defendant is 'innocent', could it be said that the claimant has suffered *damnum absque iniuria* (harm but no legal injury)?

The effect of the provisions is (1) to create a formal mechanism for the consensual resolution of defamation disputes, with provision for judicial determination of appropriate compensation, etc., in default of agreement between the parties, and (2) to allow a defence to an 'innocent' defamer whose offer of amends is rejected by the person defamed. Defamation claimants will lose the right to compensation if they reject a valid offer of amends, unless they are able to prove that the publication was culpable in the sense that the defendant knew or had reason to know that the statement both referred to the claimant or was likely to be so understood, and was false and defamatory of the claimant (s. 4(3)). There is no culpability in this sense unless the defendant is at least aware of facts from which he ought to have formed the relevant knowledge; negligent ignorance of such facts is not enough (*Milne v Express Newspapers Ltd* [2005] 1 WLR 772). If the offer of amends is validly made, the claimant should therefore accept it; it then falls to determine what steps should be taken in fulfilment of the offer. As regards this latter matter, the offer of amends commits the defendant to make a suitable correction and a sufficient apology, and to publish the correction and apology in a reasonable and practicable manner. It also commits the defendant to pay compensation which is assessed by the court on the same principles as damages in defamation proceedings, plus costs, unless the parties agree the relevant figures themselves. If the claimant is not satisfied with the correction or apology offered by the defendant, or the manner of their publication, this can be taken into account by the court in the assessment of compensation.

In one key respect the new provisions are of broader scope than those under Defamation Act 1952, s. 4. The defence now seems to cover the case where the statement is known to refer to the claimant and to be defamatory of him, but is reasonably believed to be true (e.g. where an investigative journalist researches a story to the best of his ability and has made every reasonable effort to verify the defamatory allegations included in it).

As the offer-of-amends machinery requires the defendant to accept a liability to pay compensation assessed on the same basis as damages in defamation, why should the defendant want to make use of it? (See p. 726, above.)

5. Innocent Dissemination

Every person responsible for the publication of a defamatory statement is at risk of liability. An action may be brought, for instance, not only against the author of a defamatory newspaper article, but also against the paper's editor and proprietor, and even its printer and distributor, and the retail outlets in which it is sold. At common law, a defence developed—termed 'innocent dissemination'—in respect of those who merely played a subsidiary part in the publication of defamatory material, provided they did not know, and had no reason to believe, that the publication in question contained any defamatory material at all (see *Vizetelly v Mudie's Select Library Ltd* [1900] 2 QB 170; in fact, the defence failed on the facts of this case because the defendants, a circulating library, had overlooked a publisher's request that the offending newspaper be returned in view of its defamatory contents). The defence has now been put in statutory form in Defamation Act 1996, s. 1, though apparently without abolishing the common law defence.

Defamation Act 1996

1. RESPONSIBILITY FOR PUBLICATION

(1) In defamation proceedings a person has a defence if he shows that—
   (a) he was not the author, editor or publisher of the statement complained of,
   (b) he took reasonable care in relation to its publication, and
   (c) he did not know, and had no reason to believe, that what he did caused or contributed to the publication of a defamatory statement.

(2) For this purpose 'author', 'editor' and 'publisher' have the following meanings, which are further explained in subsection (3)—

   'author' means the originator of the statement, but does not include a person who did not intend that his statement be published at all;

   'editor' means a person having editorial or equivalent responsibility for the content of the statement or the decision to publish it; and

   'publisher' means a commercial publisher, that is, a person whose business is issuing material to the public, or a section of the public, who issues material containing the statement in the course of that business.

(3) A person shall not be considered the author, editor or publisher of a statement if he is only involved—
   (a) in printing, producing, distributing or selling printed material containing the statement;

(b) in processing, making copies of, distributing, exhibiting or selling a film or sound recording (as defined in Part I of the Copyright, Designs and Patents Act 1988) containing the statement;

(c) in processing, making copies of, distributing or selling any electronic medium in or on which the statement is recorded, or in operating or providing any equipment, system or service by means of which the statement is retrieved, copied, distributed or made available in electronic form;

(d) as the broadcaster of a live programme containing the statement in circumstances in which he has no effective control over the maker of the statement;

(e) as the operator of or provider of access to a communications system by means of which the statement is transmitted, or made available, by a person over whom he has no effective control.

In a case not within paragraphs (a) to (e) the court may have regard to those provisions by way of analogy in deciding whether a person is to be considered the author, editor or publisher of a statement.

(4) Employees or agents of an author, editor or publisher are in the same position as their employer or principal to the extent that they are responsible for the content of the statement or the decision to publish it.

(5) In determining for the purposes of this section whether a person took reasonable care, or had reason to believe that what he did caused or contributed to the publication of a defamatory statement, regard shall be had to—

(a) the extent of his responsibility for the content of the statement or the decision to publish it,

(b) the nature or circumstances of the publication, and

(c) the previous conduct or character of the author, editor or publisher.

COMMENTARY

The object of this provision is to allow a defence to the merely mechanical distributors of defamatory material, provided that they have no reason to believe that their conduct might contribute to the publication of a defamatory statement. The defence applies to those other than the 'author, editor or [commercial] publisher' of the statement. It covers those involved only in the printing, distributing and selling of printed material, and the broadcaster of a live programme where there is no 'effective control' over what is said. A party who acts merely as the passive medium for publication (e.g. the postal service) is not a publisher at all and so, strictly speaking, has no need of a specific defence (see *Bunt v Tilley* [2007] 1 WLR 1243, considered at p. 731, above).

The statutory defence's principal limitation is that, perhaps unlike the common law defence, it does not operate where the disseminator knows the material is defamatory but reasonably believes that it is true (see Milmo (1996) NLJ 222). In fact, the practice has developed of putting distributors, etc., 'on notice' of the risk that defamatory material may be contained in certain publications and requesting that the 'offending' publications be withdrawn. This has proved to be a very effective tactic to be deployed on the part of those anxious to prevent the widespread circulation of defamatory allegations about themselves. As *Barendt* remarks (p. 9): 'in comparison with writers and editors, committed to the truth of their book or paper and freedom of expression, distributors are much less likely to attempt to defend libel actions for reasons of principle'. If a distributor, etc., should continue to publish defamatory material after being given due warning of its content, he loses the benefit of the defence under s. 1 (*see Godfrey v Demon Internet Ltd* [1999] 4 All ER 342: internet service provider's failure to remove defamatory posting from its newsgroup after requested to do so).

v. Remedies

1. Damages

In the case of libel and slander actionable *per se*, injury to reputation is presumed to flow from the publication of defamatory material and the claimant is entitled to damages 'at large'. This signifies that the assessment of damages depends almost entirely on the facts of the individual case; unlike the law of personal injury, the sheer variety of circumstances arising in different cases has precluded the development of a tariff-based system for the valuation of losses of reputation. The award reflects not only the claimant's loss of reputation but also injury to his or her feelings; like loss of reputation, this is generally presumed to result from the defamation and need not be specially pleaded. The element in respect of injury to feelings may be particularly important where the claimant's loss of reputation is insignificant, for example, because no one believed the defendant's allegations (see *Fielding v Variety Incorporated* [1967] 2 QB 841). Where the defamatory allegations relate to the claimant's business activities, an award may also be made for general loss of business profits or specific losses arising from particular contracts. Every award should reflect the seriousness of the charge, the extent of the publication, and the nature of the defendant's conduct both in publishing the defamation and subsequently. An apology and retraction will generally be taken into account in mitigation of damages, but they do not necessarily preclude the award of substantial damages. (Save under the new summary procedure introduced by Defamation Act 1996, s. 9, the court has no power to order the defendant to issue an apology or correction; but cf. s. 15 of the Act.) Conversely the defendant's persistence in an unfounded defence of justification may serve to increase the distress suffered by the claimant as a result of the defamation and hence the size of the award. The award of damages will also reflect the nature of the claimant's reputation (see *Pamplin v Express Newspapers Ltd (No. 2)* [1988] 1 WLR 116, extracted below), as well as other features of the claimant's conduct (e.g. whether he or she was guilty of provocation: see *Watts v Fraser* (1835) 1 M & Rob 449).

Defamation is one of the few areas of law in which awards of exemplary (or punitive) damages are relatively common. See further Ch. 16.II.3, below.

The assessment of damages is a matter for the jury (or a judge sitting alone). The extent to which the judge may offer guidance to the jury on the assessment of damages is considered in the extract following immediately below.

John v MGN Ltd [1997] QB 586

An article in the *Sunday Mirror* alleged that Elton John, the well-known musician and entertainer, was 'hooked on a bizarre new diet which doctors have warned could kill'. According to the story, 'Elton's diet of death' involved him in chewing but not swallowing food; the story asserted that he had been observed at a Hollywood Christmas party spitting chewed food into a napkin. The article quoted medical opinion to the effect that John was suffering from a form of bulimia, from which it was admitted that he had suffered in the past. John sued the defendants, proprietors of the *Sunday Mirror* for damages (including exemplary damages). The judge ruled that there was sufficient evidence to place before the jury on the issue of exemplary damages. The jury found in the plaintiff's favour, awarding him £75,000 by way of compensatory damages and £275,000 by way of exemplary damages.

Sir Thomas Bingham MR delivered the judgment of the Court of Appeal

The principles of law relating to damages in defamation

Introduction

It is standard practice for plaintiffs in defamation actions to claim damages and also an injunction against repetition of the publication complained of. If the action is compromised, the defendant ordinarily undertakes not to repeat the publication. If the action goes to trial and the plaintiff wins and recovers damages, the defendant ordinarily undertakes not to repeat the publication and if he is unwilling to give that undertaking an injunction restraining him from further publication will usually be granted. But it is the award of damages, not the grant of an injunction (in lieu of an undertaking), which is the primary remedy which the law provides on proof of this tort, both because, save in exceptional cases, the grant of an injunction in practice follows and is dependent on success in recovering damages, and also because an injunction, while giving the plaintiff protection against repetition in future, gives him no redress for what has happened in the past. It is to an award of damages that a plaintiff must look for redress, and the principles governing awards of damages are accordingly of fundamental importance in ensuring that justice is done to plaintiffs and defendants and that account is taken of such public interests as may be involved.

Compensatory damages

The successful plaintiff in a defamation action is entitled to recover, as general compensatory damages, such sum as will compensate him for the wrong he has suffered. That sum must compensate him for the damage to his reputation; vindicate his good name; and take account of the distress, hurt and humiliation which the defamatory publication has caused. In assessing the appropriate damages for injury to reputation the most important factor is the gravity of the libel; the more closely it touches the plaintiff's personal integrity, professional reputation, honour, courage, loyalty and the core attributes of his personality, the more serious it is likely to be. The extent of publication is also very relevant: a libel published to millions has a greater potential to cause damage than a libel published to a handful of people. A successful plaintiff may properly look to an award of damages to vindicate his reputation: but the significance of this is much greater in a case where the defendant asserts the truth of the libel and refuses any retraction or apology than in a case where the defendant acknowledges the falsity of what was published and publicly expresses regret that the libellous publication took place. It is well established that compensatory damages may and should compensate for additional injury caused to the plaintiff's feelings by the defendant's conduct of the action, as when he persists in an unfounded assertion that the publication was true, or refuses to apologise, or cross-examines the plaintiff in a wounding or insulting way. Although the plaintiff has been referred to as 'he' all this of course applies to women just as much as men.

There could never be any precise, arithmetical formula to govern the assessment of general damages in defamation, but if such cases were routinely tried by judges sitting alone there would no doubt emerge a more or less coherent framework of awards which would, while recognising the particular features of particular cases, ensure that broadly comparable cases led to broadly comparable awards. This is what has happened in the field of personal injuries since these ceased to be the subject of trial by jury and became in practice the exclusive preserve of judges. There may be even greater factual diversity in defamation than in personal injury cases, but this is something of which the framework would take account.

The survival of jury trial in defamation actions has inhibited a similar development in this field. Respect for the constitutional role of the jury in such actions, and judicial reluctance to intrude into the area of decision-making reserved to the jury, have traditionally led judges presiding over defamation trials with juries to confine their jury directions to a statement of general principles, eschewing any specific guidance on the appropriate level of general damages in the particular case. While some distinguished judges (for example, Diplock LJ in *McCarey v Associated Newspapers Ltd (No 2)* [1965] 2 QB 86, 109) have considered that juries should be informed in broad terms of the conventional level of awards for personal injuries, not by way of analogy but as a check on the reasonableness of an award which the jury are considering, this has not been an authoritative view: see *Broome v Cassell & Co Ltd* [1972] AC 1027, 1071. Even in the rare case when a personal injury claim was to be tried by a jury it was thought inappropriate that a jury should be informed of the conventional level of awards (*Ward v James* [1966] 1 QB 273, 302), a striking departure from the modern practice when judges are sitting alone.

Whatever the theoretical attractions of this approach, its practical disadvantages have become ever more manifest. A series of jury awards in sums wildly disproportionate to any damage conceivably suffered by the plaintiff has given rise to serious and justified criticism of the procedures leading to such awards. This has not been the fault of the juries. Judges, as they were bound to do, confined themselves to broad directions of general principle, coupled with injunctions to the jury to be reasonable. But they gave no guidance on what might be thought reasonable or unreasonable, and it is not altogether surprising that juries lacked an instinctive sense of where to pitch their awards. They were in the position of sheep loosed on an unfenced common, with no shepherd.

While the Court of Appeal reaffirmed the fundamental soundness of the traditional approach in *Sutcliffe v Pressdram Ltd* [1991] 1 QB 153, the court did in that case recommend trial judges to draw the attention of juries to the purchasing power of the award they were minded to make, and of the income it would produce. . . . This was thereafter done, and juries were reminded of the cost of buying a motor car, or a holiday, or a house. But judges were still constrained by authority from steering the jury towards any particular level of award.

Following enactment of section 8(2) of the Courts and Legal Services Act 1990 and the introduction of RSC, Ord 59, r 11(4) in its present form [see now CPR r. 52.10(3)] the Court of Appeal was for the first time empowered, on allowing an appeal against a jury's award of damages, to substitute for the sum awarded by the jury such sum as might appear to the court to be proper. . . .

Any legal process should yield a successful plaintiff appropriate compensation, that is, compensation which is neither too much nor too little. That is so whether the award is made by judge or jury. No other result can be accepted as just. But there is continuing evidence of libel awards in sums which appear so large as to bear no relation to the ordinary values of life. This is most obviously unjust to defendants. But it serves no public purpose to encourage plaintiffs to regard a successful libel action, risky though the process undoubtedly is, as a road to untaxed riches. Nor is it healthy if any legal process fails to command the respect of lawyer and layman alike, as is regrettably true of the assessment of damages by libel juries. We are persuaded by the arguments we have heard that the subject should be reconsidered. This is not a field in which we are bound by previous authority (*Sutcliffe v Pressdram Ltd* [1991] 1 QB 153, 178) but it is necessary for us to review the arguments which have found favour in the past.

In considering the criticisms of the present lack of guidance which is given to juries on the issue of compensatory damages we have examined four possible changes in the present practice: (a) Reference to awards by other juries in comparable actions for defamation. (b) Reference to awards approved by the Court of Appeal or substituted by the Court of Appeal in accordance with RSC, Ord 59, r 11(4). (c) Reference to the scale of damages awarded in actions for personal injuries. (d) Submissions by counsel as to the appropriate award coupled with some guidance by the judge as to the appropriate bracket.

Other awards in actions for defamation

We wholly agree with the ruling in the *Rantzen* case (*Rantzen v Mirror Group Newspapers (1986) Ltd* [1994] QB 670) that juries should not at present be reminded of previous libel awards by juries. Those awards will have been made in the absence of specific guidance by the judge and may themselves be very unreliable markers.

The position may change in the future if the additional guidance which we propose later in this judgment is given and proves to be successful. As was pointed out in the course of argument, however, comparison with other awards is very difficult because the circumstances of each libel are almost bound to be unique. Furthermore, the corpus of such awards will be likely to become unwieldy and time would be expended on the respective parties pointing to features which were either similar or dissimilar in the other cases.

Awards approved or substituted by the Court of Appeal

We agree with the ruling in the *Rantzen* case that reference may be made to awards approved or made by the Court of Appeal. As and when a framework of awards is established this will provide a valuable pointer to the appropriate level of award in the particular case. But it is plain that such a framework will not be established quickly. . . . It is true that awards in this category are subject to the same objection that time can be spent by the parties on pointing to similarties and differences. But, if used with discretion, awards which have been subjected to scrutiny in the Court of Appeal should be able to provide some guidance to a jury called upon to fix an award in a later case.

Reference to damages in actions for personal injuries

In *Broome v Cassell & Co Ltd* [1972] AC 1027 at 1071–1072, Lord Hailsham of St Marylebone LC gave his reason for rejecting comparison with awards of damages for personal injuries. He said:

> In actions of defamation and in any other actions where damages for loss of reputation are involved, the principle of restitutio in integrum has necessarily an even more highly subjective element. Such actions involve a money award which may put the plaintiff in a purely financial sense in a much stronger position than he was before the wrong. Not merely can he recover the estimated sum of his past and future losses, but, in case the libel, driven underground, emerges from its lurking place at some future date, he must be able to point to a sum awarded by a jury sufficient to convince a by-stander of the baselessness of the charge. . . . This is why it is not necessarily fair to compare awards of damages in this field with damages for personal injuries. Quite obviously, the award must include factors for injury to the feelings, the anxiety and uncertainty undergone in the litigation, the absence of apology, or the reaffirmation of the truth of the matters complained of, or the malice of the defendant. The bad conduct of the plaintiff himself may also enter into the matter. . . .

This reasoning would weigh strongly against any attempt to equiparate damages for personal injuries and damages for defamation. It would not weigh so heavily, if at all, against reference to conventional levels of award for personal injuries as a check on the reasonableness of a proposed award of damages for defamation . . . .

It has often and rightly been said that there can be no precise correlation between a personal injury and a sum of money. The same is true, perhaps even more true, of injury to reputation. There is force in the argument that to permit reference in libel cases to conventional levels of award in personal injury cases is simply to admit yet another incommensurable into the field of consideration. There is also weight in the argument, often heard, that conventional levels of award in personal injury cases are too low, and therefore provide an uncertain guide. But these awards would not be relied on as any exact guide, and of course there can be no precise correlation between loss of a limb, or of sight, or quadriplegia, and damage to reputation. But . . . juries may properly be asked to consider whether the injury to his reputation of which the plaintiff complains should fairly justify any greater compensation. The conventional compensatory scales in personal injury cases must be taken to represent fair compensation in such cases unless and until those scales are amended by the courts or by Parliament. It is in our view offensive to public opinion, and rightly so, that a defamation plaintiff should recover damages for injury to reputation greater, perhaps by a significant factor, than if that same plaintiff had been rendered a helpless cripple or an insensate vegetable. The time has in our view come when judges, and counsel, should be free to draw the attention of juries to these comparisons.

Reference to an appropriate award and an appropriate bracket

It has been the invariable practice in the past that neither counsel nor the judge may make any suggestion to the jury as to what would be an appropriate award. . . . We have come to the conclusion, however, that the reasons which have been given for prohibiting any reference to figures are unconvincing. Indeed, far from developing into an auction (and we do not see how it could), the process of mentioning figures would in our view induce a mood of realism on both sides.

In personal injury actions it is now commonplace for the advocates on both sides to address the judge in some detail on the quantum of the appropriate award. Any apprehension that the judge might receive a coded message as to the amount of any payment into court has not to our knowledge been realised. The judge is not in any way bound by the bracket suggested, but he finds it helpful as a check on his own provisional assessment. We can for our part see no reason why the parties' respective counsel in a libel action should not indicate to the jury the level of award which they respectively contend to be appropriate, nor why the judge in directing the jury should not give a similar indication. The plaintiff will not wish the jury to think that his main object is to make money rather than clear his name. The defendant will not wish to add insult to injury by underrating the seriousness of the libel. So we think the figures suggested by responsible counsel are likely to reflect the upper and lower bounds of a realistic bracket. The jury must of course make up their own mind and must be directed to do so. They will not be bound by the submission of counsel or the indication of the judge. If the jury make an award outside the upper or lower bounds of any bracket indicated and such award is the subject of appeal, real weight must be given to the possibility that their judgment is to be preferred to that of the judge.

The modest but important changes of practice described above would not in our view undermine the enduring constitutional position of the libel jury. Historically, the significance of the libel jury has lain not in their role of assessing damages but in their role of deciding whether the publication complained of is a libel or no. The changes which we favour will, in our opinion, buttress the constitutional role of the libel jury by rendering their proceedings more rational and so more acceptable to public opinion.

[Applying these principles to the facts of the present case, the court ruled:

(a) Although there was some force in certain criticisms made of the judge's summing up, it was impossible to say that they amounted to misdirections which caused injustice: 'the summing up on compensatory damages was sufficient within the existing guidelines to give the jury the help they needed.'

(b) The award of £75,000 by way of compensatory damages was excessive—'Though the article was false, offensive and distressing it did not attack his personal integrity or damage his reputation as an artist'—and a figure of £25,000 should be substituted.

(c) The award of purely compensatory damages was not sufficient to punish the newspaper and deter it and others—'we do not think that this sum adequately reflects the gravity of the newspaper's conduct, or that it would deter it or other national newspapers of a similar character from such conduct in future'—and so the award of exemplary damages was warranted; however the jury's award of £275,000, making a grand total of £350,000, was 'manifestly excessive' and the lesser sum of £50,000 exemplary damages should be substituted, making a grand total of damages under both headings of £75,000.]

Appeal allowed in part.

COMMENTARY

The Court of Appeal's ability to fix the appropriate level of award is an important weapon against excessive and anomalous jury awards of damages, but it has not been frequently employed. At the time of writing, it seems that the power to intervene in this way (under s. 8(2) of the 1990 Act) has been exercised in only four cases other than *John* itself (see *Gorman v Mudd*, unreported, 15 October 1992, *Rantzen v Mirror Group Newspapers (1986) Ltd* [1994] QB 670; *Smith v Houston,* unreported, 16 December 1993; *Jones v Pollard* [1997] EMLR 233; cf. the Court of Appeal's refusal to interfere with the jury award in *Kiam v Neil (No. 2)* [1996] EMLR 493 and *Kiam v MGN Ltd* [2003] QB 281). Nevertheless, there is now considerably greater scope for overturning an excessive or inadequate jury award of damages than before the 1990 Act, when the test was whether the damages were so excessive as to be 'divorced from reality': *McCarey v Associated Newspapers Ltd (No. 2)* [1965] 2 QB 86 at 111, per Willmer LJ.

In *John*, the Court of Appeal clearly recognised the need for some means of moderating jury awards directly, rather than simply intervening on appeal. Its approach may be seen as favouring prevention rather than cure. What mechanisms did the Court of Appeal endorse? (Cf. *The Gleaner Co Ltd v Abrahams* [2003] UKPC 55, [2004] 1 AC 628 at [50]–[56], per Lord Hoffmann.)

Mitchell (1997–8) 8 KCLJ 107, 109 comments: 'Given that the gist of *John* is to persuade juries to decide damages as if they were judges, why not get judges to do it instead?' However, the Law Commission thought that, in light of the *John* decision (which it welcomed), it was not necessary to recommend that damages be assessed by a judge rather than a jury (*Damages for Personal Injury: Non-Pecuniary Loss* (1999) Law Com. No. 257, paras 4.14–23).

Pamplin v Express Newspapers Ltd (No. 2) [1988] 1 WLR 116

Relying on the rule that a person under the age of ten cannot be held liable for a criminal offence, the plaintiff registered his car in the name of his young son as part of a scheme for avoiding payment of parking fines. (In a similar scheme, the plaintiff's son also became the owner of the family television set.) He was subsequently prosecuted and convicted for failing to give information about the identity of the person driving the car at a time when it was illegally parked. The plaintiff claimed that he was merely trying to draw attention to a loophole in the law. A critical article and leader column in the *Sunday Express* labelled him a 'slippery unscrupulous spiv'; the plaintiff alleged them to mean that he was 'a thoroughly idle, wicked and unprincipled individual, making money by shady and dishonest practices, who was prepared to convert his son into a similar state of depravity and who was to be abhorred and found repugnant by all reasonable people'. The defendant pleaded justification and fair comment. The plaintiff accepted the truth of many of the allegations against him but argued that calling him a 'spiv' was 'over the top'. The jury found that the plaintiff had been defamed, rejecting the defences of justification and fair comment, but awarded him only one half-penny damages.

The plaintiff appealed on the grounds, *inter alia*, that the judge had misdirected the jury in telling them that they could take account, in mitigation of damages, of specific acts of misconduct which had been relied on by the defendants as part of their unsuccessful defence of justification.

Neill LJ

In considering what evidence can be used in mitigation of damages it is necessary to draw a distinction between evidence which is put forward to show that the plaintiff is a man of bad reputation and evidence which is already before the court on some other issue. Evidence which relates solely to the plaintiff's bad reputation and which is used to support an argument that he should receive a smaller sum by way of damages than a person of unblemished reputation is governed by the following general rules. (a) Subject to (b), the evidence must be evidence of the plaintiff's general reputation and may not relate to specific acts of misconduct. Furthermore, it seems clear that the evidence must relate to the relevant area or sector of the plaintiff's reputation. (b) Notwithstanding the general rule in (a), evidence can be given of any relevant criminal conviction recorded against the plaintiff. The basis for allowing evidence of previous convictions was explained by Lord Denning MR in *Goody v Odhams Press Ltd* [1967] 1 QB 333, 340:

> previous convictions...are the raw material upon which bad reputation is built up. They have taken place in open court. They are matters of public knowledge. They are accepted by people generally as giving the best guide to his reputation and standing. They must of course be relevant, in this sense, that they must be convictions in the relevant sector of his life and have taken place within a relevant period such as to affect his current reputation.

(c) The evidence must be evidence of the plaintiff's reputation at the date of the publication of the words complained of...

So much for evidence which is directed solely to establishing the plaintiff's previous bad reputation. But a defendant is also entitled to rely in mitigation of damages on any other evidence which is properly before the court and jury. This other evidence can include evidence which has been primarily directed to, for example, a plea of justification or fair comment...

There may be many cases...where a defendant who puts forward a defence of justification will be unable to prove sufficient facts to establish the defence at common law and will also be unable to bring himself within the statutory extension of the defence contained in section 5 of the Defamation Act 1952. Nevertheless the defendant may be able to rely on such facts as he has proved to reduce the damages, perhaps almost to vanishing point. Thus a defence of partial justification, though it may not prevent the plaintiff from succeeding on the issue of liability, may be of great importance on the issue of damages.

Oliver LJ

At the trial before Bristow J...[t]he plaintiff was compelled to admit to the appropriateness of the adjectives 'slippery' and 'unscrupulous' as regards some of his behaviour. He openly confessed to having told lies. What he objected to was not the use of these adjectives but the application to him of the word 'spiv'. The jury, although they rejected the pleas of fair comment and justification as regards this particular description, had to consider and quantify the loss of reputation suffered as a result. This was a man who had achieved, and deliberately achieved, the widest notoriety as the inventor of a thoroughly disreputable scheme for avoiding payment for which he was responsible. It was a scheme which involved using a six-year-old boy, tutoring him in a slick and unscrupulous device to circumvent the law and exposing him to the full glare of publicity. It was a scheme of which the plaintiff openly boasted and one which he was, without protest or denial, reported to be employing for avoiding other payments due from him. The jury were entitled to ask themselves the question whether, even assuming that the word 'spiv' may not have been wholly apposite, its use could be said to have caused any real damage to the reputation of a man who, by his openly avowed actions, had forfeited any right to be regarded as of good general reputation. For my part, I find the verdict one which, given this background, a jury could quite properly reach, for a man who openly and avowedly behaves like a rascal suffers little further damage to his already sullied reputation by being categorised as a rascal of a slightly different type...

Purchas LJ delivered a separate concurring judgment.

Appeal dismissed.

COMMENTARY

The case illustrates the rule that damages can be reduced if the claimant does not enjoy a good reputation. Although general evidence of bad reputation is admissible (*Scott v Sampson* (1882) 8 QBD 491), evidence of particular conduct has traditionally been regarded as inadmissible. But the defendant can get round this general prohibition in some cases by framing his defence of justification or fair comment so as to allow the jury to hear of the conduct in question anyway. In *Pamplin*, the plaintiff's reputation was already low as a result of the wide-spread press coverage of his activities, and the jury was entitled to take this into account in the assessment of damages. It was also entitled to take into account matters properly pleaded by way of justification and either admitted by the plaintiff or found to be true, even if this did not draw the full sting of the defamatory articles. As the plaintiff had admitted that many of the factual details were true—admitted indeed that his conduct had been 'slippery and unscrupulous'—this 'partial justification' could properly be taken into account in the assessment of damages by the jury. Another case of partial justification is *Grobbelaar v News Group Newspapers Ltd*, extracted p. 734 above, where the House of Lords awarded the claimant damages of only £1 in view of the proven allegations of corruption made against him by the defendant newspaper.

The basic prohibition against evidence of specific conduct, other than that properly pleaded by way of a defence, was qualified by the Court of Appeal in *Burstein v Times Newspapers Ltd* [2001] 1 WLR 579. The claimant, a composer of tonal classical musical, was accused of having organised hecklers to wreck performances of modernist atonal music. In fact, though he had been a member of a group called 'The Hecklers' which opposed modernist atonal music, he had only ever booed (on a single occasion) after the end of the performance. There was therefore no plausible defence of justification, and fair comment was not available either as the relevant statement was clearly one of fact. The trial judge ruled that evidence of the claimant's membership of The Hecklers and his booing of a perform-ance was inadmissible, even in mitigation of damages, and the jury awarded the claimant £8,000. The Court of Appeal found that the evidence should have been admitted in court, rather than leaving the jury to assess the damages 'in blinkers'. Though there should be no 'roving inquiry' into the claimant's life, the jury ought to be able to hear 'directly relevant background context'. On the facts, however, the Court of Appeal was not satisfied that the jury, even if it had heard the further evidence, would have assessed damages at any less than £8,000, and affirmed the initial award.

The rule seems clear enough, though it may be a difficult matter to draw the line between directly relevant and irrelevant (or only indirectly relevant) background in individual cases. A subsequent decision, *Turner v News Group Newspapers* [2006] 1 WLR 3469, illus-trates the breadth of the principles. The claimant complained of the (untrue) allegation that he had pressurised his then wife into having sex with strangers at a 'swingers' club. The defendant sought to introduce evidence in mitigation of damages, and raised a '*Burstein* plea' which the Court of Appeal accepted in respect of (1) evidence that the claimant and his then wife had visited a private-members club on 'fetish nights' (relevant to the assess-ment of the claimant's injury to feelings), and (2) evidence that the claimant had previ-ously publicised the failure of his marriage to her—'a page 3 model'—in the tabloid press (relevant to the assessment of his distress at the defendant's infringement of his privacy). It was immaterial that the evidence related not to the defamatory allegation itself but to the injury the claimant alleged that it had caused. The court also ruled in favour of the admis-sibility of evidence that the claimant had acted as his then wife's agent in arranging for her to be photographed in pornographic poses with a view to publication in 'top shelf' maga-zines: this fact was widely known within the circle of those who would have understood the defamatory reference to him, and was therefore a matter of 'general reputation' which was admissible irrespective of *Burstein*.

For further consideration of the *Burstein* plea, see *Warren v Random House Group Ltd* [2009] QB 600.

2. Injunctions

(a) General

Although the jurisdiction to grant the claimant an injunction to prevent the publication or republication of a libel arose some considerable time after the courts established the liability of a defamer to pay damages, in certain respects it can be regarded as the more important remedy, for it serves to preserve the claimant's reputation intact, not merely to compen-sate for its loss (but cf. the view of Sir Thomas Bingham MR in *John v MGN Ltd*, extracted above). Injunctions can be awarded not only to prevent the republication of a defamation that has previously been published, but also in advance of publication, in order to prevent an anticipated publication. In the latter circumstances, the injunction is described as *quia timet* ('because he or she fears [sc. the publication of defamatory material]').

Where the defendant has already published the defamatory words, the court will normally grant an injunction wherever it is satisfied that the words are injurious to the claimant and there is reason to fear further publication. Where the defendant has not yet published the defamation, it seems that (according to general principle) a *quia timet* injunction may be awarded if there is 'a very strong probability' that the defendant will cause 'grave damage' to the claimant in the future (*Morris v Redland Bricks Ltd* [1970] AC 652).

(b) Interim Injunctions

In the general law, the question whether an interim (previously, 'interlocutory') injunction should be awarded is determined according to the principles laid down by the House of Lords in *American Cyanamid Co v Ethicon Ltd* [1975] AC 396. But the special considerations raised by the law of defamation have long been held to warrant the special treatment of cases in which the claimant seeks to prevent the defendant from publishing defamatory allegations about him pending full trial in front of a jury (see *Bonnard v Perryman*, extracted below).

Bonnard v Perryman [1891] 2 Ch 269

The *Financial Observer* of 7 February 1891 printed a story about the plaintiffs under the headline: 'The Fletcher Mills of Providence, Rhode Island…A Jews' Den.' The article accused them of 'shady' business deals and of associating with another person who was described as a swindler, and questioned how they could carry on business without any apparent means of financial support. It listed the names of a number of Jewish businessmen with whom the plaintiffs, who were stated to be Jews, had dealt. The article urged its readers to 'think twice' before investing in the plaintiffs' business.

The plaintiffs sued for libel, and sought in addition to damages an injunction to restrain the defendants—respectively, the publisher, proprietor, and editor of the newspaper, and its printer—from communicating to any person any copy of the article in question, and from publishing any statement imputing to the plaintiffs fraudulent or dishonest conduct in connection with their business dealings. The plaintiffs gave affidavit evidence that the statements in the article were untrue, and denied specifically that they had any Jewish blood in them. In the present proceedings, they sought an interlocutory injunction in the terms described above pending full trial of the action in front of a jury. The first defendant resisted this application, and relied upon an affidavit in which he swore that all the allegations in the article were true, and stated: 'I shall be able to prove the same at the trial of this action by subpoenaing witnesses and by cross-examination of the Plaintiffs, and by other evidence which I cannot, and which I submit I ought not to have to, produce on an interlocutory application.' North J granted an interlocutory injunction. The defendants appealed.

Lord Coleridge CJ read the following judgment, in which **Lord Esher MR** and **Lindley**, **Bowen** and **Lopes LJJ** concurred:

[I]t is obvious that the subject-matter of an action for defamation is so special as to require exceptional caution in exercising the jurisdiction to interfere by injunction before the trial of an action to prevent an anticipated wrong. The right of free speech is one which it is for the public interest that individuals should possess, and, indeed, that they should exercise without impediment, so long as no wrongful act is done; and, unless an alleged libel is untrue, there is no wrong committed; but, on the contrary, often a very wholesome act is performed in the publication and repetition of an alleged libel. Until it is clear that an alleged libel is untrue, it is not clear that any right at all has been infringed; and the importance of leaving free speech unfettered is a strong reason in cases of libel for dealing most cautiously and warily with the granting of interim injunctions. We entirely approve of, and desire to adopt as our own, the language of Lord Esher MR, in *Coulson v Coulson* (1887) 3 TLR 846:

> To justify the Court in granting an interim injunction it must come to a decision upon the question of libel or no libel, before the jury have decided whether it was a libel or not. Therefore the jurisdiction was of a delicate nature. It ought only to be exercised in the clearest cases, where any jury would say that the matter complained of was libellous, and where, if the jury did not so find, the Court would set aside the verdict as unreasonable.

In the particular case before us, indeed, the libellous character of the publication is beyond dispute, but the effect of it upon the Defendant can be finally disposed of only by a jury, and we cannot feel sure that the defence of justification is one which, on the facts which may be before them, the jury may find to be wholly unfounded; nor can we tell what may be the damages recoverable. Moreover, the decision at the hearing may turn upon the question of the general character of the Plaintiffs; and this is a point which can rarely be investigated satisfactorily upon affidavit before the trial—on which further it is not desirable that the Court should express an opinion before the trial. Otherwise, an injunction might be granted before the trial in a case in which at the trial nothing but nominal damages, if so much, could be obtained. Upon the whole we think, with great deference to North J, that it is wiser in this case, as it generally and in all but exceptional cases must be, to abstain from interference until the trial and determination of the plea of justification. The appeal, therefore, must be allowed....

Kay LJ (dissenting)

[A]ccording to the ordinary practice, the Court should be actuated in granting or refusing the injunction by the consideration of what is commonly termed the balance of convenience and inconvenience. To which side in this case does that balance incline? If this injunction be continued in the whole or in part, it will not prevent the Defendant from protecting the public by any other statements he can legitimately make against the Plaintiffs; it will only prevent him from repeating this particular allegation. Even if at the trial the Defendant should be able to adduce evidence shewing that the Plaintiffs' denial of their association with the person described as a swindler is untrue, it is impossible to conceive that the Defendant can be damnified by being restrained meanwhile from repeating it. On the other hand, I can easily believe that this statement, if repeated, as the Defendant admits he intends to do in the interval before the trial, may occasion very great injury, if not ruin, to the Plaintiffs. If it should turn out at the trial of the action that the Plaintiffs' denial on this point is true, and that the Defendant's allegation is false, an irreparable injury may have been done to the Plaintiffs by denying them this relief by interim injunction. I think the true result of the affidavit evidence is, that the Defendant has a suspicion of the Plaintiffs' connection with the person whom he so defames, for which he is not able to allege any substantial foundation. For these reasons I should have granted the injunction, at least as to this part of the libel, and I should have been glad if the Court of Appeal had been prepared to sustain it.

Appeal allowed.

COMMENTARY

The special rules applicable in defamation should be contrasted with the rules generally applicable elsewhere in the law. Under the *American Cyanamid* principles, an interim injunction will be awarded where the claimant proves that (1) there is a serious question to be tried (but not necessarily a prima facie case) and (2) the balance of convenience favours the award of an injunction. In addition, the claimant may have to make an 'undertaking to pay damages to the defendant for any loss sustained by reason of the injunction if it should be held at the trial that the plaintiff had not been entitled to restrain the defendant from doing what he was threatening to do' (see [1975] AC 396 at 406, per Lord Diplock).

It has been held that the restatement by the House of Lords of the principles governing the award of interim injunctions in the *American Cyanamid* case did not affect the continued application of the rule of *Bonnard v Perryman*: see *J Trevor & Sons v Solomon* (1977) 248 EG 779; *Herbage v Pressdram Ltd* [1984] 1 WLR 1160. The rule against the award of an interim injunction also applies where the defendant pleads some other defence—see *Quartz Hill Consolidated Mining Co v Beal* (1882) 20 Ch D 501 (qualified privilege); *Fraser v Evans* [1969] 1 QB 349 at 360, per Lord Denning MR (fair comment)—unless the defendant was clearly actuated by malice (*Harakas v Baltic Mercantile and Shipping Exchange Ltd* [1982] 1 WLR 958 at 960, per Lord Denning MR). Do you think that the rule in *Bonnard v Perryman* adequately acknowledges the claimant's interest in an unsullied reputation, given especially the prevalence of the sentiment 'no smoke without fire'?

The jurisdiction to award an interim injunction 'ought only to be exercised in the clearest cases' (*Coulson v Coulson* (1887) 3 TLR 846). Hence it must be 'unarguable' that the statement is defamatory: see further *Kaye v Robertson* [1991] FSR 62 (inference that actor was lowered by a claim that he had given an 'exclusive' interview to a very low-brow newspaper was perhaps capable of being defamatory, but it was not unarguably defamatory).

Section 12 of the Human Rights Act directs the court to have regard to the Convention right to freedom of speech when considering the grant of any relief that might affect its exercise. Section 12(3) further specifies that, where injunctive relief is sought so as to restrain publication before trial, it is not to be granted 'unless the court is satisfied that the applicant is likely to establish that publication should not be allowed'. The 'likely' criterion was intended to set a minimum requirement for the grant of interim injunctive relief where questions of free speech are at issue, whatever the cause of action, but does not water down the more substantial protection already provided in defamation actions by the rule in *Bonnard v Perryman* (*Greene v Associated Newspapers Ltd* [2005] QB 972).

VI. Defamation, Free Speech and the Press

The question of whether English law strikes the correct balance between concerns of free speech and the protection of reputations may now be considered. Although English law has not in the past allowed direct reliance on the European Convention of Human Rights, judges have expressed themselves satisfied that the law of defamation accords with the rights recognised therein, for example, in respect of the unqualified right to criticise a political body (see *Derbyshire County Council v Times Newspapers* [1993] AC 534, extracted below). With the implementation of the Human Rights Act 1998, however, the courts arguably have a positive obligation to develop the common law in accordance with the Convention rights.

In *Reynolds v Times Newspapers* [2001] 2 AC 127 (extracted above), the House of Lords considered whether, with the coming into effect of this legislation imminent, it was appropriate to recognise a new defence to defamation liability related to the 'public figure' defence developed by the US Supreme Court in its decision in *New York Times Co v Sullivan*, 376 US 254 (1964), extracted below. A relevant consideration in addressing such questions is the extent of the 'chilling effect' of the law of defamation on the reporting of the news by different segments of the media (see the extract from *Barendt*, below).

E. Barendt et al., *Libel and the Media: The Chilling Effect* (Oxford: Clarendon Press, 1997)

[The authors consider whether defamation law has had a 'chilling effect' on the media, with the result that there is undue restriction on the media's freedom to publish material of real public interest. After a survey involving consultation with in-house media lawyers, media lawyers in independent practice, and journalists, broadcasters, etc., the authors conclude:]

We believe that our investigation of the impact of defamation law on various media has demonstrated clearly that the chilling effect in this area genuinely does exist and significantly restricts what the public is able to read and hear...[H]owever, our findings have led us to the conclusion that, whilst the idea of the chilling effect is entirely valid, it requires some reformulation to reflect fully the complexity of the ways in which its pernicious effects are actually brought about.

The most obvious manifestation, which may be called the *direct* chilling effect, occurs when articles, books or programmes are specifically changed in the light of legal considerations. Most often perhaps this takes the form of omission of material the author believes to be true but cannot establish to the extent judged sufficient to avoid an unacceptable risk of legal action and an award of damages. This produces the attitude exemplified by most magazine editors and publishers · 'if in doubt, strike it out'. 'Doubt' here, it should be emphasized, relates to their ability to present a legally sustainable defence, not to the editor's view of the validity of the story...[T]he impact of the directly chilling effect is not at all uniform. Different media experience it with notably different force...[I]t bears far more heavily on book publishers, broadcasters, and the regional press than on the national press, where its impact seems relatively minor.

However, there is another, deeper, and subtler way in which libel inhibits media publication. This may be called the *structural* [or *indirect*] chilling effect. It is not manifest through alteration or cancellation of a specific article, programme or book. Rather it functions in a preventive manner: preventing the creation of certain material. Particular organisations and individuals are considered taboo because of the libel risk; certain subjects are treated as off-limits, minefields into which it is too dangerous to stray. [Amongst the 'no-go areas' the authors identify are: investigations of deaths in police custody, exploitative employment practices by various large companies operating in the UK, and bribery or other corrupt practices by British companies bidding for overseas contracts.] Nothing is edited to lessen libel risk because nothing is written in the first place...[I]n this respect, unlike the direct chilling effect, there is no indication that the national press is any less affected....

A secondary form of structural chilling effect may be discerned, if less clearly. It is best encapsulated by the remark of a journalist on a national broadsheet...who suggested that the libel laws had made the British press more 'polemical'—by which he meant the antithesis of factually-orientated—than it otherwise might be. If true, this is a good example of the functional application of legal rules as understood, by those who operate under them. The key point is that, whilst the defence of justification in effect requires proof of the truth of any seriously discreditable allegation, that of fair comment is a little more generous from the point of view of the media . . .

COMMENTARY

Clearly, the so-called 'chilling effect' is unobjectionable in so far as it protects deserved reputations against unwarranted attack. But concern has been expressed for a number of years that the English law of defamation is too harsh in its operation—and that it costs too much to defend a claim even when a good defence is available—with the result that it unduly interferes with the reporting of the news by the media, and acts as a shield which can be manipulated by the rich and powerful in order to deflect attention away from shady business deals and intrigue. One name often mentioned in this context is that of the late media tycoon, Robert Maxwell. At the time of his death in 1991, there were reported to be more than 100 libel writs outstanding in his name (see *Weir*, p. 561). The *Independent's* obituary writer described him as a 'liar, a cheat and a bully [who] did more than any other individual to pervert the British law of libel' (quoted in T. Bower, *Maxwell: The Outsider* (London: Mandarin, 1991), p. 575).

The passage of the Human Rights Act 1998, which requires the courts in appropriate cases to have regard to the right to free speech in the European Convention of Human Rights, may serve to redress the balance to some degree.

European Convention for the Protection of Human Rights and Fundamental Freedoms

Article 10

Freedom of Expression

(1) Everyone has the right to freedom of expression. This right shall include freedom to hold opinions and to receive and impart information and ideas without interference by public authority and regardless of frontiers. This article shall not prevent States from requiring the licensing of broadcasting, television or cinema enterprises.

(2) The exercise of these freedoms, since it carries with it duties and responsibilities, may be subject to such formalities, conditions, restrictions or penalties as are prescribed by law and are necessary in a democratic society, in the interests of national security, territorial integrity or public safety, for the prevention of disorder or crime, for the protection of health or morals, for the protection of the reputation or rights of others, for preventing the disclosure of information received in confidence, or for maintaining the authority and impartiality of the judiciary.

COMMENTARY

The Convention allows restrictions on the right to free speech which are 'prescribed by law' and 'necessary in a democratic society'. As regards the latter requirement, a pressing 'social need' must be 'convincingly established' (*Weber v Switzerland* (1990) 12 EHRR 508). In the leading case of *Lingens v Austria* (1986) 8 EHRR 407, the European Court of Human Rights ruled that Austrian law violated Article 10 by allowing the Austrian Chancellor to bring a private prosecution for criminal defamation against a magazine publisher who had published allegations that the Chancellor had protected former members of the Nazi SS for political reasons. The court stated, at [41]:

Whilst the press must not overstep the bounds set, *inter alia*, for the 'protection of the reputation of others', it is nevertheless incumbent on it to impart information and ideas on political issues just as on those in other areas of public interest. Not only does the press have the task of imparting such information and ideas: the public also has a right to receive them...More generally, freedom of political debate is at the very core of the concept of a democratic society which prevails throughout the Convention. The limits of acceptable criticism are accordingly wider as such than as regards a private individual.

The Convention is also important in areas not directly raising questions of press freedom. In *Tolstoy Miloslavsky v United Kingdom* (1995) 20 EHRR 442, the court accepted that jury awards of damages for defamation were 'prescribed by law' as required by Article 10, and that the need for flexibility in individual cases was reason enough for the lack of any requirement to give reasons for such awards. But the court found that the award of £1.5 million in damages in that case, in conjunction with the Court of Appeal's inability at the time to review disproportionately large awards, constituted breaches of Article 10 (but see now *John v MGM*, above). The award was the highest ever in a defamation action in this country. (The defendant had accused the plaintiff of a war crime.)

Derbyshire County Council v Times Newspapers [1993] AC 534

The Sunday Times printed articles in successive editions concerning share deals involving the superannuation fund of Derbyshire County Council. The articles were headed 'Revealed: Socialist tycoon's deals with a Labour chief...Bizarre deals of a council leader and the media tycoon' and 'Council share deals under scrutiny'. The council leader was David Bookbinder; the 'media tycoon' was Owen Oyston. The articles questioned the propriety of certain investments made by the council of money in its superannuation fund in various deals with Oyston or companies controlled by him. Following the publication, actions of damages for libel were brought against the publishers of *The Sunday Times*, its editor, and the two journalists who wrote the articles, by Derbyshire County Council and Bookbinder. (Another action brought by Oyston was settled by an apology and the payment of damages and costs.)

Lord Keith

There are...features of a local authority which may be regarded as distinguishing it from other types of corporation, whether trading or non-trading. The most important of these features is that it is a governmental body. Further, it is a democratically elected body, the electoral process nowadays being conducted almost exclusively on party political lines. It is of the highest public importance that a democratically elected governmental body, or indeed any governmental body, should be open to uninhibited public criticism. The threat of a civil action for defamation must inevitably have an inhibiting effect on freedom of speech. In *City of Chicago v Tribune Co* (1923) 139 NE 86 the Supreme Court of Illinois held that the city could not maintain an action of damages for libel. Thompson CJ said, at p. 90:

> The fundamental right of freedom of speech is involved in this litigation, and not merely the right of liberty of the press. If this action can be maintained against a newspaper it can

be maintained against every private citizen who ventures to criticise the ministers who are temporarily conducting the affairs of his government. Where any person by speech or writing seeks to persuade others to violate existing law or to overthrow by force or other unlawful means the existing government, he may be punished... but all other utterances or publications against the government must be considered absolutely privileged. While in the early history of the struggle for freedom of speech the restrictions were enforced by criminal prosecutions, it is clear that a civil action is as great, if not a greater, restriction than a criminal prosecution. If the right to criticise the government is a privilege which, with the exceptions above enumerated, cannot be restricted, then all civil as well as criminal actions are forbidden. A despotic or corrupt government can more easily stifle opposition by a series of civil actions than by criminal prosecutions...

After giving a number of reasons for this, he said, at p. 90:

It follows, therefore, that every citizen has a right to criticise an inefficient or corrupt government without fear of civil as well as criminal prosecution. This absolute privilege is founded on the principle that it is advantageous for the public interest that the citizen should not be in any way fettered in his statements, and where the public service or due administration of justice is involved he shall have the right to speak his mind freely.

These propositions were endorsed by the Supreme Court of the United States in *New York Times Co v Sullivan* (1964) 376 US 254, 277. While these decisions were related most directly to the provisions of the American Constitution concerned with securing freedom of speech, the public interest considerations which underlaid them are no less valid in this country. What has been described as 'the chilling effect' induced by the threat of civil actions for libel is very important. Quite often the facts which would justify a defamatory publication are known to be true, but admissible evidence capable of proving those facts is not available. This may prevent the publication of matters which it is very desirable to make public...

I regard it as right for this House to lay down that not only is there no public interest favouring the right of organs of government, whether central or local, to sue for libel, but that it is contrary to the public interest that they should have it. It is contrary to the public interest because to admit such actions would place an undesirable fetter on freedom of speech...

In the case of a local authority temporarily under the control of one political party or another it is difficult to say that the local authority as such has any reputation of its own. Reputation in the eyes of the public is more likely to attach itself to the controlling political party, and with a change in that party the reputation itself will change. A publication attacking the activities of the authority will necessarily be an attack on the body of councillors which represents the controlling party, or on the executives who carry on the day to day management of its affairs. If the individual reputation of any of these is wrongly impaired by the publication any of these can himself bring proceedings for defamation. Further, it is open to the controlling body to defend itself by public utterances and in debate in the council chamber.

The conclusion must be, in my opinion, that under the common law of England a local authority does not have the right to maintain an action of damages for defamation. That was the conclusion reached by the Court of Appeal, which did so principally by reference to Article 10 of the European Convention for the Protection of Human Rights and Fundamental Freedoms (1953) (Cmd 8969), to which the United Kingdom has adhered but which has not been enacted into domestic law...

My Lords, I have reached my conclusion upon the common law of England without finding any need to rely upon the European Convention. My noble and learned friend, Lord Goff of Chieveley, in *Attorney General v Guardian Newspapers Ltd (No 2)* [1990] 1 AC 109, 283–284, expressed the opinion that in the field of freedom of speech there was no difference in principle between English law on the subject and Article 10 of the Convention. I agree, and can only add that I find it satisfactory to be able to conclude that the common law of England is consistent with the obligations assumed by the Crown under the Treaty in this particular field.

For these reasons I would dismiss the appeal...

Lord Griffiths, **Lord Goff**, **Lord Browne-Wilkinson** and **Lord Woolf** concurred with Lord Keith.

Appeal dismissed.

COMMENTARY

In *British Coal Corporation v National Union of Mineworkers*, unreported, QBD, 28 June 1996 the plaintiff, British Coal (previously the National Coal Board), sued over allegations in the magazine *Yorkshire Miner* that they had 'stolen' £450 million from the mineworkers' pension fund. French J held that the *Derbyshire* reasoning was not confined to democratically elected governmental bodies. His Lordship found that it was equally applicable to the case before him, commenting: 'the provisions of the relevant statues show how close is the control exerted by or on behalf of the minister, himself a member of a democratically elected government, over the activities of... the British Coal Corporation'. The same principle has also been applied to a political party: *Goldsmith v Bhoyrul* [1998] QB 459 (Buckley J).

The House of Lords' decision in the *Derbyshire* case came before the passage of the Human Rights Act 1998, although their Lordships were satisfied that the relevant provisions of English law were entirely consistent with the requirements of the European Convention of Human Rights (see also the *John* and *Reynolds* cases). It may therefore be questioned whether the implementation of the Act will produce any significant changes in the law in this area. Arguments have been addressed to the courts on numerous occasions to the effect that a particular rule of the law of defamation is inconsistent with the Convention right to free speech (see, e.g., *Loutchansky v Times Newspapers Ltd (No. 2)*, p. 732, above), but there are only very few examples of a court departing from established defamation principle on the basis of arguments under the Human Rights Act (see, e.g., *O'Shea v MGN Ltd*, noted p. 726, above; *Culnane v Morris* [2006] 1 WLR 2880).

In *Jameel v Wall Street Journal Europe Sprl*, extracted p. 753, above, one of the arguments before the House of Lords was that the Human Rights Act required a modification to the established approach to libel actions brought by trading corporations so as to introduce a requirement of actual, as opposed to presumed, damage. The argument attracted support from Lord Hoffmann and Baroness Hale, the latter stating, at [158]:

[S]uch a requirement would achieve a proper balance between the right of a company to protect its reputation and the right of the press and public to be critical of it. These days, the dividing line between governmental and non-governmental organisations is increasingly difficult to draw. The power wielded by the major multi-national corporations is enormous and growing. The freedom to criticise them may be at least as important in a democratic society as the freedom to criticise the government.

But a majority of the House of Lords took a different view, finding that the established approach was not inconsistent with the Convention right to freedom of expression because (at [19], per Lord Bingham):

[A]s the text of article 10 itself makes plain, the right guaranteed by the article is not unqualified. The right may be circumscribed by restrictions prescribed by law and necessary and proportionate if directed to certain ends, one of which is the protection of the reputation or rights of others. Thus a national libel law may, consistently with article 10, restrain the publication of defamatory material.

Lord Bingham stated, at [21], that he considered the chilling effect of the existing rule to have been exaggerated, noting that a company's directors and individuals would in any case be free to sue as personal plaintiffs, and the additional chilling effect resulting from the possibility of a claim by the company was therefore unlikely to be significant.

The general reluctance of the English courts to innovate in the interests of free speech may be contrasted with the greater boldness shown by the courts in the United States, as exemplified by the decision of the Supreme Court in the famous case of *New York Times v Sullivan*, extracted below.

New York Times Co v Sullivan, 376 US 254 (1964), United States Supreme Court

The *New York Times* published a full-page advertisement on behalf of the Committee to Defend Martin Luther King. At the bottom of the advertisement appeared the names of a number of alleged signatories, including those of the *New York Times's* co-defendants. The advertisement protested at a 'wave of terror' against persons of colour involved in peaceful human rights demonstrations in the South of the United States, and detailed *inter alia* a number of incidents which had occurred in Montgomery, the capital of Alabama. The plaintiff was one of three elected commissioners in the city and was in charge of the city police department. He sued for defamation. The question for the Court was whether defamation law in Alabama was consistent with the Constitutional right to free speech.

Brennan J

Under Alabama law as applied in this case, a publication is 'libelous per se' if the words 'tend to injure a person ..., in his reputation'. . . . The question before us is whether this rule of liability, as applied to an action brought by a public official against critics of his official conduct, abridges the freedom of speech and of the press that is guaranteed by the First and Fourteenth Amendments.

Respondent relied heavily . . . on statements of this Court to the effect that the Constitution does not protect libelous publications. Those statements do not foreclose our inquiry here. None of the cases sustained the use of libel laws to impose sanctions upon expression critical of the official conduct of public officials . . . [L]ibel can claim no talismanic immunity from constitutional limitations. It must be measured by standards that satisfy the First Amendment.

The general proposition that freedom of expression upon public questions is secured by the First Amendment has long been settled by our decisions. . . . Thus we consider this case against the background of a profound national commitment to the principle that debate on public issues should be uninhibited, robust and wide-open, and that it may well include vehement, caustic, and sometime unpleasantly sharp attacks on government and public officials. . . . The present advertisement, as an expression of grievance and protest on one of the major public issues of our time, would seem clearly to qualify for the constitutional protection. The question is whether it forfeits that protection by the falsity of some of its factual statements and by its alleged defamation of respondent . . .

The constitutional guarantees require, we think, a federal rule that prohibits a public official from recovering damages for a defamatory falsehood relating to his official conduct unless he proves that the statement was made with 'actual malice'—that is, with knowledge that it was false or with reckless disregard of whether it was false or not.

COMMENTARY

In the United States (unlike England) it is generally necessary for a defamation claimant to prove fault on the part of the defendant. In *Sullivan*, the court substituted a requirement of 'actual malice' for the normal requirement of fault in cases involving the conduct of public figures. It went on to hold that there was insufficient evidence of such malice on the part of any of the defendants to support a judgment for the plaintiff-respondent. The burden of proof was to demonstrate malice with 'convincing clarity'. It was subsequently held that a defendant's 'serious doubts as to the truth of his publication' would be regarded as a species of malice (*St Amant v Thompson*, 390 US 727 (1968)). For further analysis, see *Markesinis & Deakin*, pp. 869–73. A detailed account of the background to and impact of *Sullivan* is to be found in A. Lewis, *Make No Law* (New York: Vintage Books, 1991).

The question whether a rule similar to that of *New York Times v Sullivan* should be introduced into English law was considered by both the Faulks and Neill Committees on Defamation (see *Report on Defamation*, Cmnd. 5909, 1975; *Report on Practice and Procedure in Defamation*, 1991). On both occasions, such a reform was considered undesirable. The Neill Committee commented (at 164–5):

Standards of care and accuracy in the press are, in our view, not such as to give any confidence that a *'Sullivan'* defence would be treated responsibly. It would mean, in effect, that newspapers could publish more or less what they liked, provided they were honest, if their subject happened to be within the definition of a 'public figure'. We think this would lead to great injustice. Furthermore, it would be quite contrary to the tradition of our common law that citizens are not divided into different classes. What matters is the subject matter of the publication and how it is treated, rather than who happens to be the subject of the allegations. In our view the media are adequately protected by the defences of justification and fair comment at the moment, and it is salutary that these defences are available to them only if they have got their facts substantially correct.

In *Reynolds v Times Newspapers* (extracted p 744, above), the House of Lords indicated that it did not consider the *Sullivan* defence suited to English conditions (though it was not required to rule on the question). In particular, their Lordships noted that US law on the disclosure of newspaper sources made it easier for public figures to protect their reputations by proving actual malice than it would be in England, where the Contempt of Court Act 1981, s. 10 prohibits the courts from requiring disclosure of journalistic sources unless satisfied that disclosure is necessary in (*inter alia*) the interests of justice. As Lord Hobhouse remarked, in the United States '[t]he trade-off for the more extensive defence has been the requirement of full disclosure by way of extensive and onerous pretrial discovery.'

Is the more limited protection recognised by the House of Lords in the *Reynolds* case by way of the defence of qualified privilege adequate in English conditions? Could it not be argued that exposure to unfettered public scrutiny is simply part of the price of becoming a public figure? What would be the practical effect on the conduct of current and potential public figures of the introduction of a *Sullivan*-style defence. (Would it, for instance, serve to deter qualified persons from standing for public office?)

14 PRIVACY

1. Introduction

European Convention for the Protection of Human Rights and Fundamental Freedoms

Article 8

Right to respect for private and family life

(1) Everyone has the right to respect for his private and family life, his home and his correspondence.

(2) There shall be no interference by a public authority with the exercise of this right except such as is in accordance with law and is necessary in a democratic society in the interests of national security, public safety, or the economic well-being of the country, for the prevention of disorder or crime, for the protection of health or morals, or for the protection of the rights and freedoms of others.

The right of privacy under Article 8 of the European Convention was incorporated into English law by the Human Rights Act 1998, but English law as yet recognises no tort of invasion of privacy as such. Admittedly, a number of specific torts protect particular aspects of privacy, but this protection may be regarded as haphazard, incidental and incomplete. Indeed the courts have adopted something of a scatter-gun approach, well-illustrated by *Kaye v Robertson* [1991] FSR 62 (extracted below), whereby a number of causes of action are fired at a problematic case in the hope that one might hit the target. The English judiciary has been almost entirely immune to the persuasive advocacy of a general privacy tort by judges and commentators in the United States, notably Warren and Brandeis in a famous article in the *Harvard Law Review* (extracted below). Recent decisions, however, have seen substantial developments in the protection given to particular privacy interests, above all by adapting the law of breach of confidence to provide a remedy against the unauthorised disclosure of personal information (see Section II, below).

S. Warren and L. Brandeis, 'The Right to Privacy' (1890) 4 Harv L Rev 193

That the individual shall have full protection in person and in property is a principle as old as the common law; but it has been found necessary from time to time to define anew the exact nature and extent of such protection. Political, social, and economic changes entail the recognition of new rights, and the common law, in its eternal youth, grows to meet the demands of society. Thus, in very early times, the law gave a remedy only for physical interference with life and property, for trespasses *vi et armis*. Then the 'right to life' served only to protect the subject from battery in its various forms; liberty meant freedom from actual restraint; and the right to property secured to the individual his lands and his cattle. Later, there came a recognition of man's spiritual nature, of his feelings and his intellect. Gradually the scope of these legal rights broadened; and now the right to life has come to mean the right to enjoy life—the right to be let alone; the right to liberty secures the exercise of extensive civil privileges; and the term 'property' has grown to comprise every form of possession—intangible as well as tangible . . .

Recent inventions and business methods call attention to the next step which must be taken for the protection of the person, and for securing to the individual what Judge Cooley calls the right 'to be let alone' (*Cooley on Torts*, 2nd edn. (1888), p. 29). Instantaneous photographs and newspaper enterprise have invaded the sacred precincts of private and domestic life; and numerous mechanical devices threaten to make good the prediction that 'what is whispered in the closet shall be proclaimed from the house-tops.' For years there has been a feeling that the law must afford some remedy for the unauthorized circulation of portraits of private persons; and the evil of the invasion of privacy by newspapers, long keenly felt, has been but recently discussed . . .

Of the desirability—indeed of the necessity—of some such protection, there can, it is believed, be no doubt. The press is overstepping in every direction the obvious bounds of propriety and of decency. Gossip is no longer the resource of the idle and of the vicious, but has become a trade, which is pursued with industry as well as effrontery. . . . The intensity and complexity of life, attendant upon advancing civilization, have rendered necessary some retreat from the world, and man, under the refining influence of culture, has become more sensitive to publicity, so that solitude and privacy have become more essential to the individual; but modern enterprise and invention have, through invasions upon his privacy, subjected him to mental pain and distress, far greater than could be inflicted by mere bodily injury. . . . It is our purpose to consider whether the existing law affords a principle which can properly be invoked to protect the privacy of the individual; and, if it does, what the nature and extent of such protection is . . .

[Having considered, and rejected, the possibility that the law of defamation might provide such a principle, the authors continue:]

[T]he legal doctrines relating to infractions of what is ordinarily termed the common-law right to intellectual and artistic property are, it is believed, but instances and applications of a general right to privacy, which properly understood afford a remedy for the evils under consideration.

The common law secures to each individual the right of determining, ordinarily, to what extent his thoughts, sentiments, and emotions shall be communicated to others. . . . The existence of this right does not depend upon the particular method of expression adopted. It is immaterial whether it be by word or by signs, in painting, by sculpture, or in music. Neither does the existence of the right depend upon the nature or value of the thought or emotion, nor upon the excellence of the means of expression. The same protection is accorded to a casual letter or an entry in a diary and to the most valuable poem or essay, to a botch or daub and a masterpiece. In every such case the individual is entitled to decide whether that which is his shall be given to the public. No other has the right to publish his productions in any form, without his consent. . . . The right is lost only when the author himself communicates his production to the public—in other words, publishes it. It is entirely independent of the copyright laws, and their extension into the domain of art. The aim of those statutes is to secure to the author, composer, or artist the entire profits arising from his publication; but the common-law protection enables him to control absolutely the act of publication, and in the exercise of his own discretion, to decide whether there shall be any publication at all . . .

What is the nature, the basis of this right to prevent the publication of manuscripts or works of art? It is stated to be the enforcement of a right of property; and no difficulty arises in accepting this view, so long as we have only to deal with the reproduction of literary and artistic compositions. They certainly possess many of the attributes of ordinary property: they are transferable; they have a value; and publication or reproduction is a use by which that value is realized. But where the value of the production is found not in the right to take the profits arising from publication, but in peace of mind or the relief afforded by the ability to prevent any publication at all, it is difficult to regard the right as one of property, in the common acceptation of that term. A man records in a letter to his son, or in his diary, that he did not dine with his wife on a certain day. No one into whose hands those papers fall could publish them to the world, even if possession of the documents had been obtained rightfully; and the prohibition would not be confined to the publication of a copy of a letter itself, or of the diary entry; the restraint extends also to a publication of the contents. What is the thing protected? Surely, not the intellectual act of recording the fact that the husband did not dine with his wife, but that fact itself. It is not the intellectual product, but the domestic occurrence . . .

Although the courts have asserted that they rested their decisions on the narrow grounds of protection to property, yet there are recognitions of a more liberal doctrine. Thus in the case of *Prince Albert v Strange* (1849) 1 McN & G 23 . . . the opinions of both the Vice-Chancellor and of the Lord Chancellor, on appeal, show a more or less clearly defined perception of a principle broader than those which were mainly discussed, and on which they both placed their chief reliance . . .

These considerations lead to the conclusion that the protection afforded to thoughts, sentiments, and emotions, expressed through the medium of writing or of the arts, so far as it consists in preventing publication, is merely an instance of the enforcement of the more general right of the individual to be let alone. It is like the right not to be assaulted or beaten, the right not to be imprisoned, the right not to be maliciously prosecuted, the right not to be defamed. In each of these rights, as indeed in all other rights recognised by the law, there inheres the quality of being owned or possessed—and (as that is the distinguishing attribute of property) there may be some propriety in speaking of those rights as property. But, obviously, they bear little resemblance to what is ordinarily comprehended under that term. The principle which protects personal writings and all other personal productions, not against theft and physical appropriation, but against publication in any form, is in reality not the principle of private property, but that of an inviolate personality . . .

It should be stated that, in some instances where protection has been afforded against wrongful publication, the jurisdiction has been asserted, not on the ground of property, or at least not wholly on that ground, but upon the grounds of an alleged breach of an implied contract or of a trust or confidence . . .

[T]he courts, in searching for some principle upon which the publication of private letters could be enjoined, naturally came upon the ideas of breach of confidence, and of an implied contract; but it required little consideration to discern that this would not support the court in granting a remedy against a stranger; and so the theory of property in the contents of letters was adopted . . .

We must . . . conclude that the rights, so protected, whatever their exact nature, are not rights arising from contract or from special trust, but are rights against the world; and, as above stated, the principle which has been applied to protect these rights is in reality not the principle of private property, unless that word be used in an extended and unusual sense. The principle which protects personal writings and any other productions of the intellect or of the emotions, is the right to privacy, and the law has no new principle to formulate when it extends this protection to the personal appearance, sayings, acts and to personal relations, domestic or otherwise.

COMMENTARY

No later writers have pleaded the case for a right to privacy and a remedy for its violation more eloquently than Warren and Brandeis. Their advocacy was instrumental in the development of liability for breach of privacy throughout the United States; and all on the basis of a creative interpretation of *English* authorities, notably *Albert v Strange* (1849) 1 McN & G 23.

Albert v Strange

Albert v Strange involved the unauthorised copying of etchings made by Queen Victoria and her husband for their private amusement. The etchings, which represented Victoria and Albert's children and other subjects of personal interest, had been kept privately by the Royal Family, although a few copies had been given to friends. The plates of the etchings were entrusted to a printer in Windsor for him to make further impressions. One of his employees made unauthorised copies which were sold to the defendant. The defendant proposed to exhibit them and publish a catalogue with their descriptions, but Prince Albert succeeded in getting an injunction to prevent both the exhibition and the publication of the catalogue. Lord Cottenham LC accepted that it was justified on the grounds of both the enforcement of the Prince's property right and the employee's breach of confidence.

In the extract above, Warren and Brandeis argue that the real basis of the decision in *Albert v Strange* was not the enforcement of property rights (as stated by the court) but the protection of privacy. In their view, there could be no other explanation for the fact that the rule prevented not only the reproduction of the etchings made by the plaintiff and Queen Victoria but also the publication of any description of them: the former would be a copyright infringement under the law of intellectual property, but the latter is only explicable as the protection of the right to privacy. On this basis Warren and Brandeis argued that the right to privacy was already recognised in the common law and could therefore be applied by analogy to novel situations without the need for (judicial) legislation. The English courts, however, were resistant to the idea that there was a general right to privacy whose invasion was actionable in damages, and continued to look on an ad-hoc basis for established causes of action that might provide incidental protection against intrusions into the claimant's private sphere, as in the next extract below.

Kaye v Robertson [1991] FSR 62

The well-known actor Gorden Kaye, star of the television series *Allo!, Allo!*, was injured whilst driving his car when a piece of wood was detached from an advertising hoarding by gale-force winds and smashed through the vehicle's windscreen. He suffered very serious injuries to his head and brain and was taken to hospital, where he was put on a life-support machine and then in intensive care; he subsequently recovered sufficiently to be moved into a private room. At a time at which the actor was still in no fit condition to be interviewed, a journalist and photographer from the *Sunday Sport* newspaper gained access to Kaye's private room (ignoring notices which made it clear that they were not allowed to be there) and attempted to conduct an interview with him. The photographer took pictures which showed (*inter alia*) the substantial scarring on the actor's head. An interim application was made on the actor's behalf for injunctions to prevent the *Sunday Sport* from publishing an article (of which the actor's advisers had seen a draft) which claimed that Kaye had agreed to give an exclusive interview to the paper. Injunctions in the terms requested were granted by Potter J. The defendants, editor and publishers of the paper, appealed to the Court of Appeal.

Glidewell LJ

It is well-known that in English law there is no right to privacy, and accordingly there is no right of action for breach of a person's privacy. The facts of the present case are a graphic illustration of the desirability of Parliament considering whether and in what circumstances statutory provision can be made to protect the privacy of individuals.

In the absence of such a right, the plaintiff's advisers have sought to base their claim to injunctions upon other well-established rights of action. These are:

1. Libel

2. Malicious falsehood

3. Trespass to the person

4. Passing off.

The appeal canvassed all four rights of action, and it is necessary to deal with each in turn.

1. Libel

The basis of the plaintiff's case under this head is that the article as originally written clearly implied that Mr Kaye consented to give the first 'exclusive' interview to *Sunday Sport*, and to be photographed by their photographer. This was untrue: Mr Kaye was in no fit condition to give any informed consent, and such consent as he may appear to have given was, and should have been known by *Sunday Sport's* representative to be, of no effect. The implication in the article would have the effect of lowering Mr Kaye in the esteem of right-thinking people, and was thus defamatory.

The plaintiff's case is based on the well-known decision in *Tolley v J S Fry & Sons Ltd* [1931] AC 333. Mr Tolley was a well-known amateur golfer. Without his consent, Fry published an advertisement which consisted of a caricature of the plaintiff with a caddie, each with a packet of Fry's chocolate protruding from his pocket. The caricature was accompanied by doggerel verse which used Mr Tolley's name and extolled the virtues of the chocolate. The plaintiff alleged that the advertisement implied that he had received payment for the advertisement, which would damage his reputation as an amateur player. The judge at the trial ruled that the advertisement was capable of being defamatory, and on appeal the House of Lords upheld this ruling.

It seems that an analogy with *Tolley v Fry* was the main plank of Potter J's decision to grant injunctions in this case.

Mr Milmo for the defendants submits that, assuming that the article was capable of having the meaning alleged, this would not be a sufficient basis for interlocutory relief. In *William Coulson & Sons v James Coulson & Co* [1887] 3 TLR 46, this court held that, though the High Court has jurisdiction to grant an interim injunction before the trial of a libel action, it is a jurisdiction to be exercised only sparingly. . . . This is still the rule in actions for defamation, despite the decision of the House of Lords in *American Cyanamid Co v Ethicon Ltd* [1975] AC 396 in relation to interim injunctions generally . . .

Mr Milmo submits that on the evidence we cannot be confident that any jury would inevitably decide that the implication that Mr Kaye had consented to give his first interview to *Sunday Sport* was libellous. Accordingly, we ought not to grant interlocutory relief on this ground. It is in my view certainly arguable that the intended article would be libellous, on the authority of *Tolley v Fry*. I think that a jury would probably find that Mr Kaye had been libelled, but I cannot say that such a conclusion is inevitable. It follows that I agree with Mr Milmo's submission and in this respect I disagree with the learned judge; I therefore would not base an injunction on a right of action for libel.

2. Malicious Falsehood

The essentials of this tort are that the defendant has published about the plaintiff words which are false, that they were published maliciously, and that special damage has followed as the direct and natural result of their publication. As to special damage, the effect of section 3(1) of the Defamation Act 1952 is that it is sufficient if the words published in writing are calculated to cause pecuniary damage to the plaintiff. Malice will be inferred if it be proved that the words were calculated to produce damage and that the defendant knew when he published the words that they were false or was reckless as to whether they were false or not.

The test in *Coulson v Coulson* (supra) applies to interlocutory injunctions in actions for malicious falsehood as it does in actions for defamation. However, in relation to this action, the test applies only to the requirement that the plaintiff must show that the words were false. In the present case I have no doubt that any jury which did not find that the clear implication from the words contained in the defendants' draft article were false would be making a totally unreasonable finding. Thus the test is satisfied in relation to this cause of action.

As to malice I equally have no doubt from the evidence, including the transcript of the tape-recording of the 'interview' with Mr Kaye in his hospital room which we have read, that it was quite apparent to the reporter and photographer from *Sunday Sport* that Mr Kaye was in no condition to give any informed consent to their interviewing or photographing him. Moreover, even if the journalists had been in any doubt about Mr Kaye's fitness to give his consent, Mr Robertson could not have entertained any such doubt after he read the affidavit sworn on behalf of Mr Kaye in these proceedings. Any subsequent publication of the falsehood would therefore inevitably be malicious.

As to damage, I have already recorded that Mr Robertson appreciated that Mr Kaye's story was one for which other newspapers would be willing to pay 'large sums of money.' It needs little imagination to appreciate that whichever journal secured the first interview with Mr Kaye would be willing to pay the most. Mr Kaye thus has a potentially valuable right to sell the story of his accident and his recovery when he is fit enough to tell it. If the defendants are able to publish the article they proposed, or one anything like it, the value of this right would in my view be seriously lessened, and Mr Kaye's story thereafter be worth much less to him.

I have considered whether damages would be an adequate remedy in these circumstances. They would inevitably be difficult to calculate, would also follow some time after the event, and in my view would in no way be adequate. It thus follows that in my opinion all the preconditions to the grant of an interlocutory injunction in respect of this cause of action are made out. I will return later to what I consider to be the appropriate form of injunction.

3. Trespass to the Person

It is strictly unnecessary to consider this cause of action in the light of the view I have expressed about malicious falsehood. However, I will set out my view shortly. The plaintiff's case in relation to this cause of action is that the taking of the flashlight photographs may well have caused distress to Mr Kaye and set back his recovery, and thus caused him injury. In this sense it can be said to be a battery. Mr Caldecott, for Mr Kaye, could not refer us to any authority in which the taking of a photograph or indeed the flashing of a light had been held to be a battery. Nevertheless I am prepared to accept that it may well be the case that if a bright light is deliberately shone into another person's eyes and injures his sight, or damages him in some other way, this may be in law a battery. But in my view the necessary effects are not established by the evidence in this case. Though there must have been an obvious risk that any disturbance to Mr Kaye would set back his recovery, there is no evidence that the taking of the photographs did in fact cause him any damage.

Moreover, the injunction sought in relation to this head of action would not be intended to prevent another anticipated battery, since none was anticipated. The intention here is to prevent the defendants from profiting from the taking of the photographs, i.e. from their own trespass. Attractive though this argument may appear to be, I cannot find as a matter of law that an injunction should be granted in these circumstances. Accordingly I would not base an injunction on this cause of action.

4. Passing Off

Mr Caldecott submits (though in this case not with any great vigour) that the essentials of the tort of passing off, as laid down by the speeches in the House of Lords in *E Warnink BV v J Townend & Sons (Hull) Ltd* [1979] AC 731, are satisfied here. I only need say shortly that in my view they are not. I think that the plaintiff is not in the position of a trader in relation to his interest in his story about his accident and his recovery, and thus fails from the start to have a right of action under this head.

Bingham LJ

This case ... highlights, yet again, the failure of both the common law of England and statute to protect in an effective way the personal privacy of individual citizen. ... If ever a person has a right to be let alone by strangers with no public interest to pursue, it must surely be when he lies in a hospital bed recovering from brain surgery and in no more than partial command of his faculties. It is this invasion of privacy which underlies the plaintiff's complaint. Yet it alone, however gross, does not entitle him to relief in English law ...

[A] cause of action in malicious falsehood exists, but even that obliges us to limit the relief we can grant in a way which would not bind us if the plaintiff's cause of action arose from the invasion of privacy of which, fundamentally, he complains. We cannot give the plaintiff the breadth of protection which I would, for my part, wish.

Leggatt LJ

We do not need a First Amendment to preserve the freedom of the press, but the abuse of that freedom can be ensured only by the enforcement of a right to privacy. This right has so long been disregarded here that it can be recognised now only by the legislature. Especially since there is available in the United States a wealth of experience of the enforcement of this right both at common law and also under statute, it is to be hoped that the making good of this signal shortcoming in our law will not be long delayed.

Appeal allowed in part. Injunctions varied.

COMMENTARY

Kaye was granted an injunction to restrain publication of the malicious falsehood. Note the limited utility of this remedy (remarked upon by Bingham LJ): it allowed the publication of the story and certain less objectionable photographs provided that it was not claimed that the plaintiff had given his consent. The story eventually ran with a photograph of the actor lying asleep in bed.

What was the interest that the plaintiff was seeking to protect? Surely it was his interest in keeping his personal space inviolate and the details of his personal circumstances out of the public eye. By allowing him a remedy only in the tort of malicious falsehood, however, the law of the day made it appear that his principal concern was in the commercial exploitation of his situation.

As already noted, the American law of privacy is much more developed than that in England. It seems, for instance, that an American equivalent of Gorden Kaye would have an effective remedy against the intrusion of journalists and press photographers: in *Barber v Time Inc,* 159 SW 2d 291 (1942), the publication of the plaintiff's photograph, taken without consent whilst she was confined to a hospital bed, was held to be an invasion of a private right for which she was entitled to damages.

The case for a new tort was first given official consideration in England by the Younger Committee in 1972 (*Report on Privacy*, Cmnd. 5012). In fact, the committee came out against the recognition of a general right to privacy, regarding such a concept as 'ill-defined and unstable'. But it did recommend the creation of a set of new criminal offences and tortious liabilities (amongst the latter were a tort of unlawful surveillance by means of a technical device and a tort of disclosure or other use of information unlawfully acquired). The proposed new tortious liabilities were not implemented. Subsequently, Sir David Calcutt in his *Review of Press Self-Regulation* (1993, Cmnd. 2135) recommended that the case for a new statutory tort be reconsidered. Though the (Conservative) government of the day declined to do this, the Labour government elected in 1997 had the right to privacy very much in the forefront of its mind when it brought forward the legislation that became the Human Rights Act 1998. As already noted, the right to private life is one of the Convention rights (Article 8, ECHR) incorporated into English law under the Act. *Kaye v Robertson* was decided before the Act's implementation, and it fell to the House of Lords in *Wainwright v Home Office*, below, to determine the Act's effect on the judicial remedies available for the invasion of privacy.

Wainwright v Home Office [2004] 2 AC 406

The claimants, a mother and her son, were subjected to strip searches on a prison visit to see the first claimant's son and the second claimant's half-brother, O'Neill. The prison authorities suspected that O'Neill was dealing in drugs in the prison and required all visitors who wanted an open visit with him to submit to a strip search. It was subsequently found that the searches of the claimants were conducted in breach of the prison's own rules. The claimants sought damages for (amongst other things) the invasion of their privacy, and succeeded in the County Court. The Court of Appeal allowed the defendant's appeal, and the claimants took their case to the House of Lords. (Other aspects of the decision are considered at p. 69, above.)

Lord Hoffmann

15 My Lords, let us first consider the proposed tort of invasion of privacy. Since the famous article by Warren and Brandeis ('The Right to Privacy' (1890) 4 Harvard LR 193) the question of whether such a tort exists, or should exist, has been much debated in common law jurisdictions. Warren and Brandeis suggested that one could generalise certain cases on defamation, breach of copyright in unpublished letters, trade secrets and breach of confidence as all based upon the protection of a common value which they called privacy or, following Judge Cooley (*Cooley on Torts*, 2nd edn. (1888), p. 29) 'the right to be let alone'. They said that identifying this common element should enable the courts to declare the existence of a general principle which protected a person's appearance, sayings, acts and personal relations from being exposed in public.

16 Courts in the United States were receptive to this proposal and a jurisprudence of privacy began to develop. It became apparent, however, that the developments could not be contained within a single principle; not, at any rate, one with greater explanatory power than the

proposition that it was based upon the protection of a value which could be described as privacy. Dean Prosser, in his work on *The Law of Torts*, 4th edn. (1971), p. 804, said that:

> What has emerged is no very simple matter...it is not one tort, but a complex of four. To date the law of privacy comprises four distinct kinds of invasion of four different interests of the plaintiff, which are tied together by the common name, but otherwise have almost nothing in common except that each represents an interference with the right of the plaintiff 'to be let alone'.

17 Dean Prosser's taxonomy divided the subject into (1) intrusion upon the plaintiff's physical solitude or seclusion (including unlawful searches, telephone tapping, long-distance photography and telephone harassment) (2) public disclosure of private facts and (3) publicity putting the plaintiff in a false light and (4) appropriation, for the defendant's advantage, of the plaintiff's name or likeness. These, he said, at p. 814, had different elements and were subject to different defences.

18 The need in the United States to break down the concept of 'invasion of privacy' into a number of loosely-linked torts must cast doubt upon the value of any high-level generalisation which can perform a useful function in enabling one to deduce the rule to be applied in a concrete case. English law has so far been unwilling, perhaps unable, to formulate any such high-level principle. There are a number of common law and statutory remedies of which it may be said that one at least of the underlying values they protect is a right of privacy...Common law torts include trespass, nuisance, defamation and malicious falsehood; there is the equitable action for breach of confidence and statutory remedies under the Protection from Harassment Act 1997 and the Data Protection Act 1998. There are also extra-legal remedies under Codes of Practice applicable to broadcasters and newspapers. But there are gaps; cases in which the courts have considered that an invasion of privacy deserves a remedy which the existing law does not offer. Sometimes the perceived gap can be filled by judicious development of an existing principle. The law of breach of confidence has in recent years undergone such a process...On the other hand, an attempt to create a tort of telephone harassment by a radical change in the basis of the action for private nuisance in *Khorasandjian v Bush* [1993] QB 727 was held by the House of Lords in *Hunter v Canary Wharf Ltd* [1997] AC 655 to be a step too far. The gap was filled by the 1997 Act.

19 What the courts have so far refused to do is to formulate a general principle of 'invasion of privacy' (I use the quotation marks to signify doubt about what in such a context the expression would mean) from which the conditions of liability in the particular case can be deduced...

31 There seems to me a great difference between identifying privacy as a value which underlies the existence of a rule of law (and may point the direction in which the law should develop) and privacy as a principle of law in itself. The English common law is familiar with the notion of underlying values—principles only in the broadest sense—which direct its development. A famous example is *Derbyshire County Council v Times Newspapers Ltd* [1993] AC 534, in which freedom of speech was the underlying value which supported the decision to lay down the specific rule that a local authority could not sue for libel. But no one has suggested that freedom of speech is in itself a legal principle which is capable of sufficient definition to enable one to deduce specific rules to be applied in concrete cases. That is not the way the common law works.

32 Nor is there anything in the jurisprudence of the European Court of Human Rights which suggests that the adoption of some high level principle of privacy is necessary to comply with article 8 of the Convention. The European Court is concerned only with whether English law provides an adequate remedy in a specific case in which it considers that there has been an invasion of privacy contrary to article 8(1) and not justifiable under article 8(2). So in *Earl Spencer v*

United Kingdom (1998) 25 EHRR CD105 it was satisfied that the action for breach of confidence provided an adequate remedy for the Spencers' complaint and looked no further into the rest of the armoury of remedies available to the victims of other invasions of privacy. Likewise, in *Peck v United Kingdom* (2003) 36 EHRR 719 the court expressed some impatience, at paragraph 103, at being given a tour d'horizon of the remedies provided and to be provided by English law to deal with every imaginable kind of invasion of privacy. It was concerned with whether Mr Peck (who had been filmed in embarrassing circumstances by a CCTV camera) had an adequate remedy when the film was widely published by the media. It came to the conclusion that he did not.

33 Counsel for the Wainwrights relied upon *Peck's* case as demonstrating the need for a general tort of invasion of privacy. But in my opinion it shows no more than the need, in English law, for a system of control of the use of film from CCTV cameras which shows greater sensitivity to the feelings of people who happen to have been caught by the lens...[T]his is an area which requires a detailed approach which can be achieved only by legislation rather than the broad brush of common law principle.

34 Furthermore, the coming into force of the Human Rights Act 1998 weakens the argument for saying that a general tort of invasion of privacy is needed to fill gaps in the existing remedies. Sections 6 and 7 of the Act are in themselves substantial gap fillers; if it is indeed the case that a person's rights under article 8 have been infringed by a public authority, he will have a statutory remedy. The creation of a general tort will...pre-empt the controversial question of the extent, if any, to which the Convention requires the state to provide remedies for invasions of privacy by persons who are not public authorities...

[Lord Hoffmann proceeded to consider, and reject, a possible liability under *Wilkinson v Downton* (see extracts at p. 69, above), before returning to the matter of the claimants' Convention rights:]

48 Counsel for the Wainwrights submit that unless the law is extended to create a tort which covers the facts of the present case, it is inevitable that the European Court of Human Rights will find that the United Kingdom was in breach of its Convention obligation to provide a remedy for infringements of Convention rights. In addition to a breach of article 8, they say that the prison officers infringed their Convention right under article 3 not to be subjected to degrading treatment.

49 I have no doubt that there was no infringement of article 3. The conduct of the searches came nowhere near the degree of humiliation which has been held by the European Court of Human Rights to be degrading treatment...

50 In the present case, the judge found that the prison officers acted in good faith and that there had been no more than 'sloppiness' in the failures to comply with the rules. The prison officers did not wish to humiliate the claimants...

51 Article 8 is more difficult. Buxton LJ thought [2002] QB 1334 at [62], that the Wainwrights would have had a strong case for relief under section 7 if the 1998 Act had been in force. Speaking for myself, I am not so sure. Although article 8 guarantees a right of privacy, I do not think that it treats that right as having been invaded and requiring a remedy in damages, irrespective of whether the defendant acted intentionally, negligently or accidentally. It is one thing to wander carelessly into the wrong hotel bedroom and another to hide in the wardrobe to take photographs. Article 8 may justify a monetary remedy for an intentional invasion of privacy by a public authority, even if no damage is suffered other than distress for which damages are not ordinarily recoverable. It does not follow that a merely negligent act should, contrary to general principle, give rise to a claim for damages for distress because it affects privacy rather than some other interest like bodily safety: compare *Hicks v Chief Constable of South Yorkshire Police* [1992] 2 All ER 65.

52 Be that as it may, a finding that there was a breach of article 8 will only demonstrate that there was a gap in the English remedies for invasion of privacy which has since been filled by sections 6 and 7 of the 1998 Act. It does not require that the courts should provide an alternative remedy which distorts the principles of the common law.

53 I would therefore dismiss the appeal.

Lord Bingham, **Lord Hope**, **Lord Hutton** and **Lord Scott** concurred.

Appeal dismissed.

COMMENTARY

For Lord Hoffmann, the right of privacy was a *value* underlying the law but not a *principle* susceptible of direct application to individual claims. As he noted, even in the United States, where the principle is accepted, liability for invasion of privacy had to be broken down into a set of loosely-linked and much narrower torts to provide adequate guidance on specific facts. (The four types of invasion of privacy identified by Prosser, summarised by Lord Hoffmann in the extract, are now to be found in the US *Restatement of the Law of Torts*, 2d, 1977, § 652A.) His Lordship's antipathy towards a 'high level' privacy principle has been shared by a number of commentators, e.g. Wacks, who has argued: ' "Privacy" has become as nebulous a concept as "happiness" or "security". Except as a general abstraction of an underlying value, it should not be used as a means to describe a legal right...' ('The Poverty of "Privacy"' (1980) 96 LQR 73).

Protection of Privacy Interests by Way of Specific Torts

English law, then, remains committed to the 'scatter-gun' approach exemplified by *Kaye v Robertson*, and requires the claimant to make up for the lack of any general privacy tort by pleading as many specific torts as might plausibly provide a remedy on the facts. The protection offered by a selection of different torts is considered briefly below (see also Seipp, 'English Judicial Recognition of a Right to Privacy' (1983) 3 OJLS 325), before we turn, in Section 2 below, to recent developments in the law relating to the disclosure of private information.

(i) Trespass to the Person and the Rule in *Wilkinson v Downton*

Various torts protect against the intentional infringement of rights over one's body. Assault and battery protect bodily integrity; false imprisonment protects personal liberty. The rule in *Wilkinson v Downton* [1897] 2 QB 57 has been invoked as a remedy against harassment (see *Khorasandjian v Bush* [1993] QB 727), although Parliament has gone further still by introducing a statutory liability under the Protection from Harassment Act 1997. The Act allows the imposition of liability where the claimant merely suffers upset, humiliation, alarm or distress, but it is doubtful that the common law liability goes so far. In *Wainwright*, at [46], Lord Hoffmann suggested that the Act's requirement of 'a course of conduct' demonstrated Parliament's desire to adopt a cautious approach in this area, and that the common law might be advised to show similar caution, but the matter did not arise for final decision because the claimants could not show intention on the facts. The matter is given further consideration in Chapter 2.V, and is not pursued further here.

(ii) Trespass to Land and Nuisance

'An Englishman's home is his castle', and the torts of trespass to land and nuisance provide substantial protection of every person's interest in being left alone while on his or her land. A *trespass to land* is an unauthorised entry onto land possessed by another person. Photographers hiding in the bushes of one's land commit the tort of trespass, as do surveillance experts who enter to install a bugging device in the premises. However, the protection provided by the tort of trespass to land suffers from two major limitations. First, it only applies to physical invasions of land possessed by the claimant, not to physical invasions of land not possessed but only used by him (see *White v Bayley* (1861) 10 CB (NS) 227). Hence, no claim in trespass can be brought by a lodger living in another's house, a guest staying in a hotel bedroom or a patient in a hospital ward. Secondly, trespass does not apply to simple spying upon the claimant's land from neighbouring property or indeed from the skies. In *Baron Bernstein of Leigh v Skyviews Ltd* [1978] QB 479, Griffiths J held that an aeroplane used to take aerial photographs of the estate of Lord Bernstein of Leigh, former owner of the Granada TV channel, did not trespass on his land; the judge ruled that a landowner's rights are limited 'to such a height as is necessary for the ordinary use and enjoyment of his land'. (Cf. *Anchor Brewhouse Developments Ltd v Berkley House (Docklands Developments) Ltd* (1987) 38 BLR 82.)

A number of cases falling outside the scope of trespass may nevertheless give rise to liability in the tort of *private nuisance*. Nuisance covers a number of interferences with a person's use or enjoyment of land, ranging from persistent telephoning (*Khorasandjian v Bush*, above) to 'watching and besetting' (*Thomas v NUM* [1986] Ch 20; could this perhaps cover the encampment of journalists outside the claimant's house?). In *Baron Bernstein of Leigh v Skyviews Ltd*, Griffiths J considered the potential liability in nuisance of those photographing activities on neighbouring land (at 489):

[N]o court would regard the taking of a single photograph as an actionable nuisance. But if the circumstances were such that a plaintiff was subjected to the harassment of constant surveillance of his house from the air, accompanied by the photographing of his every activity, I am far from saying that the court would not regard such a monstrous invasion of his privacy as an actionable nuisance for which they would give relief.

A very significant limitation on the protection provided by this tort is that nuisance is actionable only by a person with an interest in the land affected, and not by that person's spouse, children or house guests. *Khorasandjian v Bush* had (controversially) gone the other way on this, as noted by Lord Hoffmann at [18] above, but was overruled by the House of Lords in *Hunter v Canary Wharf* [1997] AC 655.

(iii) Defamation

Although the tort of defamation protects an interest in 'personality', the interest that it protects (reputation) is very different from the interest in privacy. Under defamation law, a defendant has a complete defence of justification if the words in question are shown to be substantially true; there is no need to demonstrate that their publication was in the public interest. This effectively undermines any potential that the law of defamation might have had for ensuring the secrecy of private information. The tort of defamation does, it must be admitted, provide some protection of privacy where the claimant is portrayed in a 'false light' (as in *Tolley v J S Fry & Sons Ltd*, discussed in the extract from *Kaye v Robertson*, above), and to that extent prevents others from appropriating a person's name, image or likeness (which is one of the privacy interests listed by Prosser and in the US *Restatement of*

Torts, 2d: see above). But it is arguable that this is primarily a public commercial matter, not a matter of personal privacy, for in many cases the complaint is that the defendant's conduct has served to reduce the claimant's market value and thereby prevented the claimant from himself profiting to the utmost extent from the commercial exploitation of his name, image or likeness.

II. Privacy, Confidence and Human Rights

When people talk of privacy, they are usually talking about what the Younger Committee termed 'privacy of information, that is the right to determine for oneself how and to what extent information about oneself is communicated to others' (*Report of the Committee on Privacy*, 1972, Cmnd. 5012, p. 10). Although the courts have been unwilling to develop a new, general privacy tort, the law of liability for the unauthorised disclosure of private information has moved forward very rapidly in recent years. Strikingly, the courts have expanded the frontiers of liability here with little express reliance upon the Human Rights Act 1998, which has tended to be used as a supporting reason for the changes, rather than their primary cause, and have preferred to present the process as the natural development of existing principles of the law of confidence.

Campbell v MGN Ltd [2004] UKHL 22, [2004] 2 AC 457

Naomi Campbell, the famous fashion model, brought proceedings for damages against the defendant newspaper which she alleged had, acting on a tip-off, unlawfully published confidential information about her drug addiction and the therapy she had undergone for it with Narcotics Anonymous, with photographs of her in the street as she left a therapy session. The newspaper defended the action on the basis that it was in the public interest for it to correct the claimant's own untruthful public statements that she did not take drugs. The claimant conceded that the newspaper was entitled to publish the fact that she was a drug addict and receiving treatment for her addiction, but claimed damages in respect of further information the paper disclosed about her therapy sessions as well as the photographs it published. She succeeded before Morland J, but the Court of Appeal [2003] QB 633 ruled that the public interest which entitled the newspaper to inform its readers about the claimant's drug addiction and its treatment extended to its publication of details of her treatment. That information was justified by the need to give the story credibility, and journalists had to be given 'reasonable latitude' as to the manner in which they disclosed information in which the public was legitimately interested. Furthermore, the supporting photographs were of the claimant in the street as she was leaving a therapy session and did not convey information that was confidential. The claimant appealed to the House of Lords.

Lord Nicholls (dissenting)

Breach of Confidence: Misuse of Private Information

11 In this country, unlike the United States of America, there is no over-arching, all-embracing cause of action for 'invasion of privacy': see *Wainwright v Home Office* [2004] AC 406. But protection of various aspects of privacy is a fast developing area of the law . . . In this country development of the law has been spurred by enactment of the Human Rights Act 1998.

12 The present case concerns one aspect of invasion of privacy: wrongful disclosure of private information. The case involves the familiar competition between freedom of expression and respect for an individual's privacy. Both are vitally important rights. Neither has precedence over the other. The importance of freedom of expression has been stressed often and eloquently, the importance of privacy less so. But it, too, lies at the heart of liberty in a modern state. A proper degree of privacy is essential for the well-being and development of an individual. And restraints imposed on government to pry into the lives of the citizen go to the essence of a democratic state: see La Forest J in *R v Dyment* [1988] 2 SCR 417, 426.

13 The common law or, more precisely, courts of equity have long afforded protection to the wrongful use of private information by means of the cause of action which became known as breach of confidence. A breach of confidence was restrained as a form of unconscionable conduct, akin to a breach of trust. Today this nomenclature is misleading. The breach of confidence label harks back to the time when the cause of action was based on improper use of information disclosed by one person to another in confidence. To attract protection the information had to be of a confidential nature. But the gist of the cause of action was that information of this character had been disclosed by one person to another in circumstances 'importing an obligation of confidence' even though no contract of non-disclosure existed: see the classic exposition by Megarry J in *Coco v A N Clark (Engineers) Ltd* [1969] RPC 41, 47–48. The confidence referred to in the phrase 'breach of confidence' was the confidence arising out of a confidential relationship.

14 This cause of action has now firmly shaken off the limiting constraint of the need for an initial confidential relationship. In doing so it has changed its nature. In this country this development was recognised clearly in the judgment of Lord Goff of Chieveley in *Attorney General v Guardian Newspapers Ltd (No 2)* [1990] 1 AC 109, 281. Now the law imposes a 'duty of confidence' whenever a person receives information he knows or ought to know is fairly and reasonably to be regarded as confidential. Even this formulation is awkward. The continuing use of the phrase 'duty of confidence' and the description of the information as 'confidential' is not altogether comfortable. Information about an individual's private life would not, in ordinary usage, be called 'confidential'. The more natural description today is that such information is private. The essence of the tort is better encapsulated now as misuse of private information.

15 In the case of individuals this tort, however labelled, affords respect for one aspect of an individual's privacy. That is the value underlying this cause of action. An individual's privacy can be invaded in ways not involving publication of information. Strip searches are an example. The extent to which the common law as developed thus far in this country protects other forms of invasion of privacy is not a matter arising in the present case. It does not arise because, although pleaded more widely, Miss Campbell's common law claim was throughout presented in court exclusively on the basis of breach of confidence, that is, the wrongful *publication* by the 'Mirror' of private *information*.

16 The European Convention on Human Rights, and the Strasbourg jurisprudence, have undoubtedly had a significant influence in this area of the common law for some years. The provisions of article 8, concerning respect for private and family life, and article 10, concerning freedom of expression, and the interaction of these two articles, have prompted the courts of this country to identify more clearly the different factors involved in cases where one or other of these two interests is present. Where both are present the courts are increasingly explicit in evaluating the competing considerations involved. When identifying and evaluating these factors the courts, including your Lordships' House, have tested the common law against the values encapsulated in these two articles. The development of the common law has been in harmony with these articles of the Convention: see, for instance, *Reynolds v Times Newspapers Ltd* [2001] 2 AC 127, 203–204.

17 The time has come to recognise that the values enshrined in articles 8 and 10 are now part of the cause of action for breach of confidence. As Lord Woolf CJ has said, the courts have been able to achieve this result by absorbing the rights protected by articles 8 and 10 into this cause of action: *A v B plc* [2003] QB 195 at [4]. Further, it should now be recognised that for this purpose these values are of general application. The values embodied in articles 8 and 10 are as much applicable in disputes between individuals or between an individual and a non-governmental body such as a newspaper as they are in disputes between individuals and a public authority.

18 In reaching this conclusion it is not necessary to pursue the controversial question whether the European Convention itself has this wider effect. Nor is it necessary to decide whether the duty imposed on courts by section 6 of the Human Rights Act 1998 extends to questions of substantive law as distinct from questions of practice and procedure. It is suf-ficient to recognise that the values underlying articles 8 and 10 are not confined to disputes between individuals and public authorities. This approach has been adopted by the courts in several recent decisions, reported and unreported, where individuals have complained of press intrusion...

19 In applying this approach, and giving effect to the values protected by article 8, courts will often be aided by adopting the structure of article 8 in the same way as they now habitually apply the Strasbourg court's approach to article 10 when resolving questions concerning free-dom of expression. Articles 8 and 10 call for a more explicit analysis of competing considera-tions than the three traditional requirements of the cause of action for breach of confidence identified in *Coco v A N Clark (Engineers) Ltd* [1969] RPC 41.

20 I should take this a little further on one point. Article 8(1) recognises the need to respect private and family life. Article 8(2) recognises there are occasions when intrusion into private and family life may be justified. One of these is where the intrusion is necessary for the protec-tion of the rights and freedoms of others. Article 10(1) recognises the importance of freedom of expression. But article 10(2), like article 8(2), recognises there are occasions when protection of the rights of others may make it necessary for freedom of expression to give way. When both these articles are engaged a difficult question of proportionality may arise. This question is distinct from the initial question of whether the published information engaged article 8 at all by being within the sphere of the complainant's private or family life.

21 Accordingly, in deciding what was the ambit of an individual's 'private life' in particular circumstances courts need to be on guard against using as a touchstone a test which brings into account considerations which should more properly be considered at the later stage of proportionality. Essentially the touchstone of private life is whether in respect of the disclosed facts the person in question had a reasonable expectation of privacy.

22 Different forms of words, usually to much the same effect, have been suggested from time to time. The American Law Institute, *Restatement of the Law, Torts*, 2d (1977), sec-tion 652D, uses the formulation of disclosure of matter which 'would be highly offensive to a reasonable person'. In *Australian Broadcasting Corpn v Lenah Game Meats Pty Ltd* (2001) 208 CLR 199 at [42], Gleeson CJ used words, widely quoted, having a similar meaning. This particular formulation should be used with care, for two reasons. First, the 'highly offensive' phrase is suggestive of a stricter test of private information than a reasonable expectation of privacy. Second, the 'highly offensive' formulation can all too easily bring into account, when deciding whether the disclosed information was private, considerations which go more properly to issues of proportionality; for instance, the degree of intrusion into private life, and the extent to which publication was a matter of proper public concern. This could be a recipe for confusion.

The Present Case

23 I turn to the present case and consider first whether the information whose disclosure is in dispute was private. Mr Caldecott [for the claimant] placed the information published by the newspaper into five categories: (1) the fact of Miss Campbell's drug addiction; (2) the fact that she was receiving treatment; (3) the fact that she was receiving treatment at Narcotics Anonymous; (4) the details of the treatment—how long she had been attending meetings, how often she went, how she was treated within the sessions themselves, the extent of her commitment, and the nature of her entrance on the specific occasion; and (5) the visual portrayal of her leaving a specific meeting with other addicts.

24 It was common ground between the parties that in the ordinary course the information in all five categories would attract the protection of article 8. But Mr Caldecott recognised that, as he put it, Miss Campbell's 'public lies' precluded her from claiming protection for categories (1) and (2). When talking to the media Miss Campbell went out of her way to say that, unlike many fashion models, she did not take drugs. By repeatedly making these assertions in public Miss Campbell could no longer have a reasonable expectation that this aspect of her life should be private. Public disclosure that, contrary to her assertions, she did in fact take drugs and had a serious drug problem for which she was being treated was not disclosure of private information. As the Court of Appeal noted, where a public figure chooses to present a false image and make untrue pronouncements about his or her life, the press will normally be entitled to put the record straight: [2003] QB 633, 658. Thus the area of dispute at the trial concerned the other three categories of information.

25 Of these three categories I shall consider first the information in categories (3) and (4), concerning Miss Campbell's attendance at Narcotics Anonymous meetings. In this regard it is important to note this is a highly unusual case. On any view of the matter, this information related closely to the fact, which admittedly could be published, that Miss Campbell was receiving treatment for drug addiction. Thus when considering whether Miss Campbell had a reasonable expectation of privacy in respect of information relating to her attendance at Narcotics Anonymous meetings the relevant question can be framed along the following lines: Miss Campbell having put her addiction and treatment into the public domain, did the further information relating to her attendance at Narcotics Anonymous meetings retain its character of private information sufficiently to engage the protection afforded by article 8?

26 I doubt whether it did. Treatment by attendance at Narcotics Anonymous meetings is a form of therapy for drug addiction which is well known, widely used and much respected. Disclosure that Miss Campbell had opted for this form of treatment was not a disclosure of any more significance than saying that a person who has fractured a limb has his limb in plaster or that a person suffering from cancer is undergoing a course of chemotherapy. Given the extent of the information, otherwise of a highly private character, which admittedly could properly be disclosed, the additional information was of such an unremarkable and consequential nature that to divide the one from the other would be to apply altogether too fine a toothcomb. Human rights are concerned with substance, not with such fine distinctions.

27 For the same reason I doubt whether the brief details of how long Miss Campbell had been undergoing treatment, and how often she attended meetings, stand differently. The brief reference to the way she was treated at the meetings did no more than spell out and apply to Miss Campbell common knowledge of how Narcotics Anonymous meetings are conducted.

28 But I would not wish to found my conclusion solely on this point. I prefer to proceed to the next stage and consider how the tension between privacy and freedom of expression should be resolved in this case, on the assumption that the information regarding Miss Campbell's attendance at Narcotics Anonymous meetings retained its private character. At this stage I

consider Miss Campbell's claim must fail. I can state my reason very shortly. On the one hand, publication of this information in the unusual circumstances of this case represents, at most, an intrusion into Miss Campbell's private life to a comparatively minor degree. On the other hand, non-publication of this information would have robbed a legitimate and sympathetic newspaper story of attendant detail which added colour and conviction. This information was published in order to demonstrate Miss Campbell's commitment to tackling her drug problem. The balance ought not to be held at a point which would preclude, in this case, a degree of journalistic latitude in respect of information published for this purpose.

29 It is at this point I respectfully consider Morland J fell into error. Having held that the details of Miss Campbell's attendance at Narcotics Anonymous had the necessary quality of confidentiality, the judge seems to have put nothing into the scales under article 10 when striking the balance between articles 8 and 10. This was a misdirection. The need to be free to disseminate information regarding Miss Campbell's drug addiction is of a lower order than the need for freedom to disseminate information on some other subjects such as political information. The degree of latitude reasonably to be accorded to journalists is correspondingly reduced, but it is not excluded altogether.

30 There remains category (5): the photographs taken covertly of Miss Campbell in the road outside the building she was attending for a meeting of Narcotics Anonymous. I say at once that I wholly understand why Miss Campbell felt she was being hounded by the 'Mirror'. I understand also that this could be deeply distressing, even damaging, to a person whose health was still fragile. But this is not the subject of complaint. Miss Campbell, expressly, makes no complaint about the taking of the photographs. She does not assert that the taking of the photographs was itself an invasion of privacy which attracts a legal remedy. The complaint regarding the photographs is of precisely the same character as the nature of the complaints regarding the text of the articles: the information conveyed by the photographs was private information. Thus the fact that the photographs were taken surreptitiously adds nothing to the only complaint being made.

31 In general photographs of people contain more information than textual description. That is why they are more vivid. That is why they are worth a thousand words. But the pictorial information in the photographs illustrating the offending article of 1 February 2001 added nothing of an essentially private nature. They showed nothing untoward. They conveyed no private information beyond that discussed in the article. The group photograph showed Miss Campbell in the street exchanging warm greetings with others on the doorstep of a building. There was nothing undignified or distrait about her appearance. The same is true of the smaller picture on the front page. Until spotted by counsel in the course of preparing the case for oral argument in your Lordships' House no one seems to have noticed that a sharp eye could just about make out the name of the café on the advertising board on the pavement.

32 For these reasons and those given by my noble and learned friend, Lord Hoffmann, I agree with the Court of Appeal that Miss Campbell's claim fails...

Lord Hoffmann (dissenting)

36 My Lords, the House is divided as to the outcome of this appeal, but the difference of opinion relates to a very narrow point which arises on the unusual facts of this case. The facts are unusual because the plaintiff is a public figure who had made very public false statements about a matter in respect of which even a public figure would ordinarily be entitled to privacy, namely her use of drugs. It was these falsehoods which, as was conceded, made it justifiable, for a newspaper to report the fact that she was addicted. The division of opinion is whether in doing so the newspaper went too far in publishing associated facts about her private life. But the importance of this case lies in the statements of general principle on the way in which the

law should strike a balance between the right to privacy and the right to freedom of expression, on which the House is unanimous. The principles are expressed in varying language but speaking for myself I can see no significant differences...

49...Until the Human Rights Act 1998 came into force, there was no equivalent in English domestic law of article 8 of the European Convention or the equivalent articles in other international human rights instruments which guarantee rights of privacy. So the courts of the United Kingdom did not have to decide what such guarantees meant. Even now that the equivalent of article 8 has been enacted as part of English law, it is not directly concerned with the protection of privacy against private persons or corporations. It is, by virtue of section 6 of the 1998 Act, a guarantee of privacy only against public authorities. Although the Convention, as an international instrument, may impose upon the United Kingdom an obligation to take some steps (whether by statute or otherwise) to protect rights of privacy against invasion by private individuals, it does not follow that such an obligation would have any counterpart in domestic law.

50 What human rights law has done is to identify private information as something worth protecting as an aspect of human autonomy and dignity. And this recognition has raised inescapably the question of why it should be worth protecting against the state but not against a private person. There may of course be justifications for the publication of private information by private persons which would not be available to the state—I have particularly in mind the position of the media, to which I shall return in a moment—but I can see no logical ground for saying that a person should have less protection against a private individual than he would have against the state for the publication of personal information for which there is no justification. Nor, it appears, have any of the other judges who have considered the matter.

51 The result of these developments has been a shift in the centre of gravity of the action for breach of confidence when it is used as a remedy for the unjustified publication of personal information. It recognises that the incremental changes to which I have referred do not merely extend the duties arising traditionally from a relationship of trust and confidence to a wider range of people. As Sedley LJ observed in a perceptive passage in his judgment in *Douglas v Hello! Ltd* [2001] QB 967 at 1001, the new approach takes a different view of the underlying value which the law protects. Instead of the cause of action being based upon the duty of good faith applicable to confidential personal information and trade secrets alike, it focuses upon the protection of human autonomy and dignity—the right to control the dissemination of information about one's private life and the right to the esteem and respect of other people.

[Lord Hoffmann agreed with Lord Nicholls that the appeal should be dismissed, giving similar reasons.]

Baroness Hale

147 I start...from the fact—indeed, it is common ground—that *all* of the information about Miss Campbell's addiction and attendance at NA which was revealed in the 'Daily Mirror' article was both private and confidential, because it related to an important aspect of Miss Campbell's physical and mental health and the treatment she was receiving for it. It had also been received from an insider in breach of confidence. That simple fact has been obscured by the concession properly made on her behalf that the newspaper's countervailing freedom of expression did serve to justify the publication of some of this information. But the starting point must be that it was all private and its publication required specific justification.

148 What was the nature of the freedom of expression which was being asserted on the other side? There are undoubtedly different types of speech, just as there are different types of private information, some of which are more deserving of protection in a democratic society than others. Top of the list is political speech. The free exchange of information and ideas on

matters relevant to the organisation of the economic, social and political life of the country is crucial to any democracy. Without this, it can scarcely be called a democracy at all. This includes revealing information about public figures, especially those in elective office, which would otherwise be private but is relevant to their participation in public life. Intellectual and educational speech and expression are also important in a democracy, not least because they enable the development of individuals' potential to play a full part in society and in our democratic life. Artistic speech and expression is important for similar reasons, in fostering both individual originality and creativity and the free-thinking and dynamic society we so much value. No doubt there are other kinds of speech and expression for which similar claims can be made.

149 But it is difficult to make such claims on behalf of the publication with which we are concerned here. The political and social life of the community, and the intellectual, artistic or personal development of individuals, are not obviously assisted by pouring over the intimate details of a fashion model's private life. However, there is one way in which the article could be said to be educational. The editor had considered running a highly critical piece, adding the new information to the not inconsiderable list of Miss Campbell's faults and follies detailed in the article, emphasising the lies and hypocrisy it revealed. Instead he chose to run a sympathetic piece, still listing her faults and follies, but setting them in the context of her now-revealed addiction and her even more important efforts to overcome it. Newspaper and magazines often carry such pieces and they may well have a beneficial educational effect.

150 The crucial difference here is that such pieces are normally run with the co-operation of those involved. Private people are not identified without their consent. It is taken for granted that this is otherwise confidential information. The editor did offer Miss Campbell the opportunity of being involved with the story but this was refused. Her evidence suggests that she was concerned for the other people in the group. What entitled him to reveal this private information about her without her consent?

151 The answer which she herself accepts is that she had presented herself to the public as someone who was not involved in drugs. It would have been a very good thing if she were not. If other young women do see her as someone to be admired and emulated, then it is all to the good if she is not addicted to narcotic substances. It might be questioned why, if a role model has adopted a stance which all would agree is beneficial rather than detrimental to society, it is so important to reveal that she has feet of clay. But the possession and use of illegal drugs is a criminal offence and a matter of serious public concern. The press must be free to expose the truth and put the record straight.

152 That consideration justified the publication of the fact that, contrary to her previous statements, Miss Campbell had been involved with illegal drugs. It also justified publication of the fact that she was trying to do something about it by seeking treatment. It was not necessary for those purposes to publish any further information, especially if this might jeopardise the continued success of that treatment.

153 The further information includes the fact that she was attending Narcotics Anonymous meetings, the fact that she had been doing so for some time, and with some regularity, and the photographs of her either arriving at or leaving the premises where meetings took place. All of these things are inter-related with one another and with the effect which revealing them might have upon her. Revealing that she was attending Narcotics Anonymous enabled the paper to print the headline 'Naomi: I am a drug addict', not because she had said so to the paper but because it could assume that she had said this or something like it in a meeting. It also enabled the paper to talk about the meetings and how she was treated there, in a way which made it look as if the information came from someone who had been there with her, even if it simply came from general knowledge of how these meetings work. This all contributed to the

sense of betrayal by someone close to her of which she spoke and which destroyed the value of Narcotics Anonymous as a safe haven for her.

154 Publishing the photographs contributed both to the revelation and to the harm that it might do. By themselves, they are not objectionable. Unlike France and Quebec, in this country we do not recognise a right to one's own image: cf *Aubry v Éditions Vice-Versa Inc* [1998] 1 SCR 591. We have not so far held that the mere fact of covert photography is sufficient to make the information contained in the photograph confidential. The activity photographed must be private. If this had been, and had been presented as, a picture of Naomi Campbell going about her business in a public street, there could have been no complaint. She makes a substantial part of her living out of being photographed looking stunning in designer clothing. Readers will obviously be interested to see how she looks if and when she pops out to the shops for a bottle of milk. There is nothing essentially private about that information nor can it be expected to damage her private life. It may not be a high order of freedom of speech but there is nothing to justify interfering with it . . .

155 But here the accompanying text made it plain that these photographs were different. They showed her coming either to or from the NA meeting. They showed her in the company of others, some of whom were undoubtedly part of the group. They showed the place where the meeting was taking place, which will have been entirely recognisable to anyone who knew the locality. A picture is 'worth a thousand words' because it adds to the impact of what the words convey; but it also adds to the information given in those words. If nothing else, it tells the reader what everyone looked like; in this case it also told the reader what the place looked like. In context, it also added to the potential harm, by making her think that she was being followed or betrayed, and deterring her from going back to the same place again.

156 There was no need to do this. The editor accepted that even without the photographs, it would have been a front page story. He had his basic information and he had his quotes. There is no shortage of photographs with which to illustrate and brighten up a story about Naomi Campbell. No doubt some of those available are less flattering than others, so that if he had wanted to run a hostile piece he could have done so. The fact that it was a sympathetic story is neither here nor there. The way in which he chose to present the information he was entitled to reveal was entirely a matter for him. The photographs would have been useful in proving the truth of the story had this been challenged, but there was no need to publish them for this purpose. The credibility of the story with the public would stand or fall with the credibility of 'Mirror' stories generally.

157 The weight to be attached to these various considerations is a matter of fact and degree. Not every statement about a person's health will carry the badge of confidentiality or risk doing harm to that person's physical or moral integrity. The privacy interest in the fact that a public figure has a cold or a broken leg is unlikely to be strong enough to justify restricting the press's freedom to report it. What harm could it possibly do? Sometimes there will be other justifications for publishing, especially where the information is relevant to the capacity of a public figure to do the job. But that is not this case and in this case there was, as the judge found, a risk that publication would do harm. The risk of harm is what matters at this stage, rather than the proof that actual harm has occurred. People trying to recover from drug addiction need considerable dedication and commitment, along with constant reinforcement from those around them. That is why organisations like Narcotics Anonymous were set up and why they can do so much good. Blundering in when matters are acknowledged to be at a 'fragile' stage may do great harm.

158 The trial judge was well placed to assess these matters. He could tell whether the impact of the story on her was serious or trivial. The fact that the story had been published at all was bound to cause distress and possibly interfere with her progress. But he was best placed to

judge whether the additional information and the photographs had added significantly both to the distress and the potential harm. He accepted her evidence that it had done so. He could also tell how serious an interference with press freedom it would have been to publish the essential parts of the story without the additional material and how difficult a decision this would have been for an editor who had been told that it was a medical matter and that it would be morally wrong to publish it.

159 The judge was also obliged by section 12(4)(b) of the 1998 Act, not only to have particular regard to the importance of the Convention right to freedom of expression, but also to any relevant privacy code. The Press Complaints Commission Code of Practice supports rather than undermines the conclusion he reached:

> 3. *Privacy
> (i) Everyone is entitled to respect for his or her private and family life, home, health and correspondence. A publication will be expected to justify intrusions into any individual's private life without consent. (ii) The use of long lens photography to take pictures of people in private places without their consent is unacceptable. Note—Private places are public or private property where there is a reasonable expectation of privacy.

> The public interest
> There may be exceptions to the clauses marked * where they can be demonstrated to be in the public interest.
> 1. The public interest includes: (i) Detecting or exposing crime or a serious misdemeanour. (ii) Protecting public health and safety. (iii) Preventing the public from being misled by some statement or action of an individual or organisation…

This would appear to expect almost exactly the exercise conducted above and to lead to the same conclusion as the judge.

160 I would therefore allow this appeal and restore the order of the judge.

Lord Hope and **Lord Carswell** delivered separate opinions allowing the appeal for reasons similar to Baroness Hale's.

Appeal allowed.

COMMENTARY

This was first occasion on which the House of Lords provided explicit protection for a claimant's right to informational privacy, and it did so by adapting the established equitable remedy for breach of confidence. The development was widely-anticipated (see, e.g., Phillipson, 'Transforming Breach of Confidence? Towards a Common Law Right of Privacy under the Human Rights Act' (2003) 66 MLR 726) and all members of the House accepted that the remedy could be employed to protect private information even when it had not been acquired in the course of a confidential relationship. Lord Nicholls and Lord Hoffmann dissented on the ultimate disposition of the appeal, but their opinions contain some of the most useful analysis of the general principles to be applied. Significantly, Lord Nicholls had no qualms about describing the liability as a species of 'tort', despite its origins in equity, though he was the only member of the House of Lords to use that terminology. The tort terminology has been picked up, however, in more recent cases (see, e.g., *McKennitt v Ash* [2008] QB 73).

Do you think that the gist of the claimant's complaint was the information published about her or the fact that the newspaper was hounding her when she needed to be left alone to recover? If the latter, does the decision of the House of Lords mark a step in the direction of greater protection for privacy in general rather than just private information?

Privacy or Confidence?

Legal obligations of confidentiality have been recognised since at least the early nineteenth century (see, e.g., *Abernethy v Hutchinson* (1824) 1 H & Tw 28; *Prince Albert v Strange* (1849) 1 McN & G 23). In the modern law, three requirements must be satisfied if an action for breach of confidence is to succeed (see *Coco v A N Clark (Engineers) Ltd* [1969] RPC 41): (1) the information must 'have the necessary element of confidence about it' (i.e. it must not be in the public domain); (2) the defendant must be under 'an obligation of confidence'; and (3) the defendant must make 'unauthorised use' of the information. Many of the cases involve trade or government secrets, but the availability of this action in respect of personal confidences was never in question (see, e.g., *Duchess of Argyll v Duke of Argyll* [1967] Ch 302: marital secrets). The key requirement of an obligation of confidence was traditionally thought to entail some form of relationship between the parties, e.g. doctor/patient, solicitor/client, or at least an acceptance of the information on the (explicit or implicit) basis that it would be kept secret. Gradually the requirement was watered down. An obligation of confidence could be found to arise on the basis that improper means were employed in order to acquire the information in question, e.g. where a person trespassed to place a 'bug' in the claimant's home (*Francome v News Group Newspapers Ltd* [1984] 1 WLR 892). In a well-known dictum, Lord Goff went further, suggesting that an obligation of confidence might arise purely on the basis of the confidential character of the information, irrespective of the means by which it was acquired, e.g. in 'certain situations, beloved of law teachers, where an obviously confidential document is wafted by an electric fan out of a window into a crowded street, or where an obviously confidential document, such as a private diary, is dropped in a public place, and is then picked up by a passer-by' (*AG v Guardian Newspapers (No 2)* [1990] 1 AC 109 at 282).

In *Campbell v MGN Ltd*, the House of Lords confirmed this development, made clear that the fundamental question was whether the information was 'private' rather than 'confidential', and established a different framework for dealing with the private information cases, which was to proceed by direct reference to the rights under Articles 8 and 10, ECHR rather than the three requirements laid down by *Coco v Clark*. In effect, there are now two torts where previously there was one: one dealing with confidences (especially commercial confidences), in which the three requirements in *Coco v Clark* are applied; the other dealing with private information through the framework of the Convention rights. However, the two torts can on occasion be entangled. Information can be both private and subject to an obligation of confidence. In such a case, it seems unlikely that the court would embark upon two separate analyses—one in terms of the three requirements in *Coco v Clark*, the other in terms of the Convention rights—rather than simply treating the relationship of confidence as relevant to the claimant's expectation of privacy. Whether information is private depends on 'an interdependent amalgam of circumstances', including, for example, 'the nature of the information, the form in which it is conveyed and the fact that the person disclosing it was in a confidential relationship with the person to whom it relates' (*HRH Prince of Wales v Associated Newspapers Ltd* [2008] Ch 57 at [36], per Lord Phillips MR; see further *McKennitt v Ash* [2008] QB 73 and *Browne v Associated Newspapers Ltd* [2008] QB 103). In practice, the three-stage *Coco v Clark* analysis will probably be confined to cases of commercial confidence.

A further complication is that what is private to one person may have commercial value as a secret to another. The long-running legal saga of celebrity couple, Michael Douglas and Catharine Zeta-Jones, and *Hello!* magazine provides an illuminating case in point. The film stars sold *OK!* magazine the exclusive right to publish photographs of their wedding for a fee of £1 million, retaining a right of veto. They undertook to use their best efforts to ensure that no other media had access to the wedding and to prevent guests or anyone else present from taking photographs. All guests received with their invitation a separate notice stating, 'We would appreciate no photography or video devices at the ceremony or reception', and were visually checked for cameras on arrival, and all staff for the wedding were engaged on terms that no photographs be taken. A couple of days after the wedding, it came to the claimants' attention that *Hello!* magazine was planning to publish photographs of the wedding which, it later transpired, had been taken by a freelance photographer who had infiltrated the reception and taken pictures surreptitiously. The claimants failed in their application for an interim injunction to prevent the publication until trial of their action for breach of confidence, on the basis that they had been willing to trade their privacy for financial reward anyway (*Douglas v Hello! Ltd* [2001] 1 FLR 982), but they succeeded in their claim for damages at the subsequent trial (*Douglas v Hello! Ltd* [2003] 3 All ER 996). The photographs had interfered with their residual area of privacy, i.e. that which they retained even after selling the photographic rights to the wedding to *Hello!*, though this reduced the damages they were entitled to recover (£15,000). Their co-claimants, *OK!* magazine, were awarded in excess of £1 million for loss of profit resulting from *Hello!*'s 'spoiler'. The Court of Appeal overturned the award in favour of *OK!* on the basis that the magazine had no rights over the Douglases' residual area of privacy (*Douglas v Hello! Ltd (No. 3)* [2006] QB 125) but the House of Lords subsequently restored the trial judge's decision (*sub nom. OBG Ltd v Allan* [2008] 1 AC 1). *OK!* had no claim to privacy under Article 8, ECHR; neither could it make a claim that was parasitic upon the Douglases' right to privacy. But that was irrelevant. *OK!*'s claim was for the wrongful disclosure of commercially confidential information which was controlled by the Douglases and which the Douglases had licensed *OK!* to use. The magazine had paid £1 million for the benefit of the obligation of confidence imposed on the wedding guests and there was no reason of principle or policy why it should not be entitled to enforce that obligation. The decision shows that rights over information may arise, independently but simultaneously, on account of both its private and its confidential character. The right to keep information private cannot be sold on, as it is by its nature personal, but this does not preclude the commercial sale of the right to enforce a confidence.

'A Reasonable Expectation of Privacy'

According to Lord Nicholls, the test of whether information is private is—somewhat circularly—whether its subject has a reasonable expectation of privacy. Lord Nicholls preferred this formulation to the alternatives he considered at [22], e.g. whether disclosure of the information would be considered 'highly offensive' (the latter adopted only by Lord Hope of the Law Lords sitting in *Campbell*: see [92]). The test of substantial offence tended to blur the distinction between two distinct questions: what is private and when is publication of private facts wrongful? In truth, the ultimate focus should be on neither the nature and circumstances of the publication, nor the quality of the information itself, but on the claimant's expectations in relation to the information. What is private in respect of an ordinary member of the public, who has never courted publicity, might well not be private in respect of a contestant in a Big Brother-style reality TV show who knowingly submits to 24-hour-a-day surveillance.

Lord Nicholls' version of the test—whether the claimant had a reasonable expectation of privacy—differs from that advanced elsewhere, e.g. in Baroness Hale's speech at [134] (not extracted) where the test is whether *the person publishing the information* knows or ought to know there is a reasonable expectation of privacy (or confidence). Moreham ('Privacy in the common law: a doctrinal and theoretical analysis' (2005) 121 LQR 628 at 648) prefers the latter version of the test, mainly because it would be too harsh to hold a person liable for the disclosure of apparently innocuous information about which he could not be expected to know that the claimant was unusually sensitive. But do such concerns not go to the separate question of whether the interference with the claimant's privacy was wrongful on the facts, rather than to the matter of privacy in itself? It seems unnecessarily complicated to adopt a rule which would allow information about A to be classified as private when B seeks to publish it, but not when C seeks to do so. In any case, it is Lord Nicholls' claimant-centred version of the test that has been adopted in subsequent authorities (see, e.g., *Murray v Express Newspapers plc* [2009] Ch 481 at [35], though the Court of Appeal also stated at [28] that Baroness Hale's approach was 'the same' as Lord Nicholls').

Moreham further argues that an analysis in terms of *desires* is preferable to one based on *expectations* (p. 647):

> [E]xpectations…suggests that liability depends on whether privacy is likely to be respected in a particular situation, rather than on whether it should be respected in that situation…On this approach (which could easily be adopted on the current formulation of the English 'reasonable expectation' test), whether or not there is a breach of privacy is determined by reference to the practices of privacy interferers *themselves*—once an intrusive practice becomes sufficiently widespread…then claimants will have no action for breach of privacy if it occurs. There therefore seems to be a strong argument for shifting the focus of the English privacy action away from the claimant's expectations of privacy and on to his or her *desires*.

We agree with the underlying sentiment, but do not think it is necessary as yet to drop the terminology 'reasonable expectation of privacy', provided it is remembered that the question is what degree of privacy the claimant is entitled to expect that the law will protect, rather than whether he reasonably expects others in fact to respect his privacy.

Publication of Private Information Justified

As Lord Nicholls notes, the structure of the Convention right to privacy (Article 8, ECHR) acknowledges that intrusions into a person's private life may sometimes be justified. It is therefore necessary to adopt a two-stage process by which one asks, first, whether there was an interference with the claimant's private life, and, secondly, whether the interference was justified, e.g. in the interests of free speech. The latter question may well require a balancing of the competing rights under Articles 8 and 10 of the Convention. Neither right has priority over the other. 'The question', as Lord Hoffmann put it, at [55], 'is rather the extent to which it is *necessary* to qualify the one right in order to protect the underlying value which is protected by the other. And the extent of the qualification must be proportionate to the need.'

This two-stage analysis dispenses with the need to apply the specific defences that have been recognised in the law of breach of confidence (e.g. immorality or other iniquity, and public interest), further demonstrating the independent nature of the cause of action for wrongful disclosure of private information. However, although the structure of the inquiry may be different, the underlying issues of substance are the same. In *X v Y* [1988] 2 All ER

648, for example, the issue was whether the newspaper publication of the names of NHS doctors who had contracted AIDS fell under the public interest defence recognised in the law of breach of confidence. The court was required to weigh the public interests in a free press and an informed public debate against that in the confidentiality of hospital records, especially those concerning the victims of AIDS. On the facts, the latter prevailed, Rose J attaching importance to the consideration that there was already a wide-ranging debate about AIDS generally and its effect on doctors, which would not be materially advanced by disclosure of the doctors' identities. Like *Campbell*, the case involved the disclosure of personal medical history. But Baroness Hale said in *Campbell*, at [157] above, that the fact that someone was suffering from a cold or had a broken leg was unlikely to be considered to be so private that the press would be unable to report it. What is the difference between AIDS and a drug dependency, on the one hand, and a cold and a broken leg, on the other?

In the new law of privacy, as under the old law of confidence, the exposure of iniquity can justify what would otherwise be an unlawful intrusion into personal affairs. In *Campbell*, it was accepted that the newspaper had the right, in the wider public interest, to correct the claimant's misrepresentations about her past drug use. The divergence of view as between majority and minority Law Lords was over the extent of the latitude given to the newspaper in so doing, and, in particular, whether it should be able to support its story with a picture of the claimant in the street on leaving her Narcotics Anonymous therapy session. For Lord Hope, at [121], it was the photographs that tipped the balance in the claimant's favour. In the extracts, do you prefer the reasoning on this issue of Lord Nicholls, at [30]–[31], or Baroness Hale, at [154]–[159]?

The issue of iniquity very frequently arises in the context of media exposés of celebrities' sexual indiscretions. Extra-marital affairs are not protected to the same extent as relations between married couples. In *Theakston v MGN Ltd* [2002] EMLR 398 at [60], Ouseley J suggested there was a spectrum of sexual relationships attracting different degrees of protection:

Sexual relations within marriage at home would be at one end of the range or matrix of circumstances to be protected from most forms of disclosure; a one night stand with a recent acquaintance in a hotel bedroom might very well be protected from press publicity. A transitory engagement in a brothel is yet further away.

The judge declined to grant an injunction to prevent verbal descriptions of activities in which the claimant (a radio and television presenter) had engaged in a brothel, but awarded an injunction against the publication of photographs taken inside the premises as this would have been particularly intrusive and humiliating; additionally, the photographs had been taken for the purposes of blackmail and printing them would constitute a breach of the Press Complaints Commission Code of Practice.

Ouseley J's dictum was approved by the Court of Appeal in *A v B plc* [2003] QB 195, where a Premiership footballer was found to be entitled to only a 'very modest' degree of confidentiality in respect of transient, extra-marital relationships he had pursued with two women, one of whom now wished to sell her story to the defendant newspaper. The footballer failed in his application for an interim injunction preventing publication of the story pending trial, and was left to his remedy (if any) in damages.

In *Mosley v News Group Newspapers Ltd* [2008] EMLR 20. Eady J found that a reasonable expectation of privacy arose in respect of a sado-masochistic sex party involving the claimant (president of the governing body of Formula I motor racing) and five professional dominatrices. On the facts, this outweighed the defendant's interest in publishing the story, with accompanying photographs and video. The judge stated, at [127]: 'it is not . . . for the media to expose sexual conduct which does not involve any significant breach of the criminal law'. It made no difference that the claimant's activities were adulterous and might be regarded by some as perverted. Do you think this decision is consistent with *Theakston* and *A v B* above?

Cf. *Browne v Associated Newspapers Ltd* [2008] QB 103, where the Court of Appeal upheld the *Mail on Sunday*'s right to publish details of a homosexual relationship involving the chief executive of the oil company BP because other allegations in the newspaper's story (e.g. that the executive had misused BP's resources to benefit his partner and had revealed business secrets to him) would make no sense without publication of the nature of the relationship.

Privacy in Public Places

A particularly interesting question is whether one can have a reasonable expectation of privacy in a public place (see Moreham, 'Privacy in Public Places' [2006] CLJ 606). In *von Hannover v Germany*, Application No. 59320/00 (2005) 40 EHRR 1, the ECtHR ruled that Princess Caroline of Monaco was entitled to protection against the publication of photographs showing her going about her daily life in public places. There was a zone of a person's interaction with others, even in a public context, that fell within the scope of 'private life' (para. 50). Even though the intrusion into this area, on the facts, was by non-state actors, Article 8 did not merely compel the state to abstain from arbitrary interference with individuals' private lives, but also to take positive measures to secure respect for private life even in the sphere of relations between individuals, e.g. by protecting a person's picture against abuse by others (para. 57). This protection of private life had to be balanced against the freedom of expression guaranteed by Article 10 of the Convention, and, in particular, the essential role played by the press in a democratic society (para. 58), but the sole purpose of the photographs in question was to satisfy the curiosity of a particular readership and their publication did not contribute to any debate of general interest to society (para. 65). 'In these conditions', said the Court, 'freedom of expression calls for a narrower interpretation' (para. 66). The Court concluded:

[T]he public does not have a legitimate interest in knowing where the applicant is and how she behaves generally in her private life even if she appears in places that cannot always be described as secluded and despite the fact that she is well known to the public. Even if such a public interest exists, as does a commercial interest of the magazines in publishing these photos and these articles, in the instant case those interests must, in the Court's view, yield to the applicant's right to the effective protection of her private life.

A different conclusion was reached by the New Zealand Court of Appeal in *Hosking v Runting* [2005] NZLR 1, where the claimants' 18-month-old twins had been photographed in the street, being pushed in a stroller by their mother, who had previously been married to a well-known broadcaster, the twins' father. The court accepted (by a majority) that the law of New Zealand recognises a freestanding tort of invasion of privacy, but found that the photographs of the twins did not publicise any fact in respect of which there could be a reasonable expectation of privacy. Their birth, current age and other facts were matters of public record. The photographs were taken in a public place. And there was no evidence that their publication would be harmful to the twins either physically or emotionally.

In *Campbell v MGN*, at [154], Baroness Hale commented that there might be public interest in photographs of Naomi Campbell as she was popping out for a pint of milk. In *John v Associated Newspapers* [2006] EWHC 1611, Eady J considered this dictum on an application for an interim injunction to prevent publication of an innocuous photograph taken of the pop star Elton John in the street. Refusing the application, the judge noted that the photo-graph revealed nothing about the claimant's health or his social or sexual relationships, and it was not taken in circumstances involving harassment; the case was therefore akin to the Naomi Campbell pint of milk example. In *Murray v Express Newspapers plc* [2009] Ch 481, however, the Court of Appeal refused to strike out a claim for damages brought on behalf of the 19-month-old child of *Harry Potter* author, J. K. Rowling, in respect of the publication of a photograph of the child accompanied by its parents in a public street. The Court of Appeal rejected the proposition that routine acts such a visit to a shop or a ride on a bus could not attract a reasonable expectation of privacy. In its view, everything depended on the circum-stances. In the case at hand, the claimant's age was decisive; it was the courts' responsibility to protect children from intrusive media attention. *Hosking v Runting* could not be assumed to accord with English law.

In *OBG Ltd v Allan* [2007] UKHL 21 at [293], Lord Walker observed: 'under English law it is not possible for a celebrity to claim a monopoly in his or her image, as if it were a trade-mark or brand. Nor can anyone (whether celebrity or nonentity) complain simply of being photographed. There must be something more.' Is this an accurate statement of English law. What was the 'something more' in the cases of *Campbell v MGN*, *Murray v Express Newspapers* and *Theakston v MGN* (noted p. 812, above)?

What if the claimant is not a celebrity? In *Peck v United Kingdom*, Application No. 44647/98 (2003) 36 EHRR 41, the applicant, suffering from depression, was filmed by closed circuit television (CCTV) cameras as he walked around his local town centre with a large kitchen knife in his hands; still on camera, he then attempted suicide by cutting his wrists. The police, notified by the CCTV operator, arrived shortly afterwards and gave him medical assistance. Some time later, the council, which owned the footage, included still images from it in a press release about the ways in which CCTV could help the police to prevent crime. The images were printed in local newspapers. The council also provided footage of the inci-dent to local and national TV stations, which broadcast it with the applicant still recognis-able even though his face was masked. On these facts, the ECtHR found that the council's disclosure of the film and images from it constituted an interference with the applicant's private life. Though it pursued the legitimate aim of public safety, the prevention of disorder of crime, and the protection of the rights of others, the disclosure entailed a disproportion-ate interference with the applicant's private life and was therefore unjustified. It also found that the lack of an effective remedy for the interference against the newspapers and TV stations constituted a further violation of the Convention, under Article 13. At the relevant time (pre-*Campbell*), it was unlikely that a claim of breach of confidence would succeed, as the images seemed to lack the necessary quality of confidence and there seemed to be no circumstances importing an obligation of confidence.

After *Campbell*, do you think that the English courts would be able to find that, on such facts, there had been a wrongful disclosure of private information sounding in damages? Consider also what remedies might be available, against whom, under the Human Rights Act 1998 (passed only after the events in *Peck* had taken place).

The Human Rights Act and the European Convention

Under the Human Rights Act 1998, s. 2(1) the courts are required to have regard to relevant decisions of the ECtHR in determining any question arising in connection with a Convention right. But they are not bound by decisions of that court. Furthermore, even though the Act has, in one sense, incorporated the Convention rights into English law, it only provides an express remedy in the case of their violation by a public authority (see, e.g., Lord Hoffmann in *Campbell* at [49], above). So it is not immediately apparent how the Convention rights, including the right to privacy and indeed the right to freedom of expression, are relevant in actions between private parties.

One possible answer is that the Human Rights Act has a 'horizontal' effect because the courts, as they fall under the definition of public authority in s. 6(3) of the Act, are subject to the basic obligation to act compatibly with the Convention rights that is imposed on public authorities by s. 6(1). But in *Campbell*, Lord Nicholls said, at [18] above, that he was not going to deal with the question whether the obligation on the courts extended to matters of substantive law as distinct from questions of practice and procedure, while Lord Hoffmann, at [49]–[51] above, thought that the Act's 'subtle' effect was to make the courts question why privacy should be worth protection against the state and not a private person, and then embark on the development of existing (general) principles so as to address that anomaly. In fact, only Baroness Hale seems to have positively embraced the argument of horizontal effect, stating in [132], not quoted above, that '[t]he 1998 Act does not create any new cause of action between private persons. But if there is a relevant cause of action applicable, the court as a public authority must act compatibly with both parties' Convention rights.' Whether this view will command majority acceptance in future is uncertain. For now, there remains considerable force in Morgan's criticism ((2004) 120 LQR 563 at 564) that the 'persistent judicial failure to engage with the horizontal effect issue' is 'the fundamental problem with the privacy case law since October 2000' (the date on which the Human Rights Act came into force).

An alternative explanation is that English law has always recognised the fundamental values of privacy and free speech, and now just happens to find it convenient to address questions relating to them by reference to Articles 8 and 10 of the European Convention. On this view, the passage of the Human Rights Act is essentially coincidental.

What do you think is the best explanation of why the English courts have, in recent years, radically remoulded the established action for breach of confidence so as to provide a remedy for the wrongful disclosure of private information? Do you think they have struck an appropriate balance between the right of the individual to keep personal information private and the right of the press to publish matters of public interest? For discussion, see Culture, Media and Sport Committee, *Press Standards, Privacy and Libel*, HC (2009–10) 362-I, which found that '[t]he high costs of litigation combined with the legal uncertainty, owing to the small amount of case law, undoubtedly discourages the media from contesting privacy cases' (para. 62), but concluded that 'for now matters relating to privacy should continue to be determined according to common law, and the flexibility that permits, rather than set down in statute' (para. 67).

By contrast, a statutory cause of action for invasion of privacy has recently been proposed in Australia (see Australian Law Reform Commission, *For Your Information: Australian Privacy Law and Practice*, Report No. 108 (2009), ch. 74: 'serious invasion of privacy'). Cf. New Zealand Law Commission, *Invasion of Privacy: Penalties and Remedies*, Report 113 (2010), ch. 7, recommending that the tort of invasion of privacy should be left to develop at common law.

15 VICARIOUS LIABILITY

This chapter is concerned with the circumstances in which one party may be held liable for the tort of another. Generally this liability may be described as secondary liability. Several legal mechanisms have been used to achieve this result—the law of agency, the imposition of what is described as a 'non-delegable' duty of care, and vicarious liability. Vicarious liability can be regarded as the most significant of the three devices mentioned above, although similarities exist between the three.

Generally, the law of vicarious liability operates so as to impose liability on an employer, but several conditions must be satisfied. An employer (or in older authorities, the master) will be vicariously liable for the acts of his employee (servant); thus a contract of employment (alternatively known as a contract of service) is a pre-requisite to liability. Further, the employer is not liable for every act of the employee but only for acts that are committed in the course of the employee's employment. And although the matter is not free from doubt, the better view is that the employee must commit a wrong in the course of employment; if the employee is not liable neither is the employer (*Majrowski v Guy's & St Thomas's NHS Trust* [2007] 1 AC 224; cf. Stevens (2007) 123 LQR 30 and *London Drugs v Kuehne & Nagel International* [1992] 3 SCR 299, per La Forest J (Supreme Court of Canada)). Once this is accepted, whether the employee commits a tort or not is decided by the general law of tort and raises no particular problems in this context; hence it will not be discussed further in this chapter.

I. Development of and Justification for Vicarious Liability

Reedie v The London & North Western Railway Company (1849) 4 Exch 244, 154 ER 1201

The facts are not relevant to the extract.

Rolfe B

The liability of anyone, other than the party actually guilty of any wrongful act, proceeds on the maxim '*Qui facit per alium facit per se*' [He who does anything by another does it by himself]. The party employing has the selection of the party employed, and it is reasonable that he who has made choice of an unskilled or careless person to execute his orders, should be responsible for any injury resulting from the want of skill or want of care of the person employed; but neither the principle of the rule, nor the rule itself, can apply to a case where the party sought to be charged does not stand in the character of employer to the party by whose negligent act the injury has been occasioned. If the defendants had employed a contractor, carrying on an independent business, to repair their engines or carriages, and the contractor's workmen had negligently caused a heavy piece of iron to fall on a bystander, it would appear a strange doctrine to hold that the defendants were responsible.

COMMENTARY

A more modern restatement of a similar theme was made by Rix LJ in *Viasystems (Tyneside) Ltd v Thermal Transfer (Northern) Ltd* [2006] QB 510, 529; liability was imposed on the employer on the basis that 'those who set in motion and profit from the activities of their employees should compensate those who are injured by such activities even when performed negligently'. Are you convinced by these rationales? Alternatively, can the employer be said to be the cause, and therefore legally responsible, for the employee's tort? If this is so, why would it be any more of a 'strange' doctrine to hold that the defendants were liable for the negligence of the independent contractor?

Glanville Williams, 'Vicarious Liability and the Master's Indemnity' (1957) 20 MLR 220

Then there is the idea...that the master is a cause of the mischief, or has set a noxious instrument in motion. In itself this is true. The master is a cause in the factual sense, for if he had not employed the servant to do the particular work the harm would not have happened. The servant might have been doing mischief elsewhere and to some other victim. However, it is a very primitive notion that a person must be responsible for harm merely because he is its cause. Causation plus fault is accepted to be enough, but not causation alone. What element in the master-servant situation is there to replace personal fault as an intelligible ground of liability?

[After considering and dismissing other possible justifications for the master's liability, he continued:]

What other theory is there? Well, there is the purely cynical theory that the master is liable because he has a purse worth opening. The master is frequently rich, and he is usually insured—two arguments that might be used by any burglar, if he ever troubled to justify his thefts. The strange thing is to find them put forward by judges of eminence....Whatever (one may ask) can have put this extraordinary idea into judges' heads, that the mere possession of wealth is enough to justify the imposition of legal liability for a wrong? Obviously there is something missing from the dicta. There must be some fact to create liability, and not merely the fact of being a master. If so, we have another unprovable principle of natural justice: that masters ought to pay because they belong to the class of masters. One can manufacture eternal principles of natural justice of this sort without limit...

However distasteful the theory may be, we have to admit that vicarious liability owes its explanation, if not its justification, to the search for a solvent defendant.

P. S. Atiyah, *Vicarious Liability* (London: Butterworths, 1967)

Modern Theories in Justification of Vicarious Liability

The most widely held view among modern American writers is that vicarious liability is justified by the principle of loss-distribution. In the great majority of cases an employer who has to pay damages for the torts of his servants does not in fact have to meet these liabilities out of his own pocket. The cost of the liabilities is distributed over a large section of the community, and spread over some period of time. This occurs partly because of the practice of insurance, and partly because most employers are anyhow not individuals but corporations. Where the employer insures against his legal liabilities he will charge the cost of insurance to the goods or services which he produces. In general this cost will be passed on by the employer in the form of higher prices to the consumer. The consumer himself may also be able to play his part in spreading the cost in his turn, because not all consumers are themselves individuals. Business enterprises are usually consumers in the sense that they purchase other people's products and services as well as supply products and services themselves. In this way the cost of tort liabilities is spread very thinly over a substantial part of the public. It is, moreover, spread out over a period of time. As a rule no single individual has to put his hand into his pocket to pay out any large sum at any one moment. To be sure the company will have to pay its insurance premium, but the company can arrange its internal accounts so as to spread this cost over the year's activities. And, insofar as the cost of the premium is passed on in higher costs the consumer pays this element of cost every time he purchases the company's products or services.

Even where an enterprise does not insure (and, as pointed out above, some large enterprises will find it more economical to act as self-insurers) or where the enterprise is unable to pass the extra costs on wholly in the form of higher charges, e.g., because competition is too fierce, there will still be a considerable degree of loss distribution. But in this case the cost instead of being distributed wholly or principally amongst the consumers of the company's products, may be distributed amongst those who, in a commercial sense, constitute the enterprise itself, i.e. the shareholders and staff and employees of the enterprise. Shareholders may receive a slightly lower dividend and employees may receive a smaller wage increase. In practice, of course, these two methods of distribution will both occur, and it will scarcely be possible to allocate part of the cost, even notionally, to one class rather than the other. Inevitably, so many factors will enter into management decisions as to the proper price at which to sell the products of the company, that it will be impossible to isolate the (relatively minor) cost arising from insurance against tort liabilities. It is safe to say, therefore, that in practice these costs will be distributed both internally and externally in the great majority of cases...

But acknowledging the truth of this [that the selection of one form of loss distribution mechanism over another involves value judgments], it seems that in general the policy of placing the liability for the torts of servants on their employers is broadly a sound one. It is sound simply because, by and large, it is the most convenient and efficient way of ensuring that persons injured in the course of business enterprises do not go uncompensated. Of course if all workmen insured themselves against third-party risks, and if wages and salaries were slightly increased in order to enable workmen to do this, we could get on pretty well without vicarious liability at all. But this would not be so efficient or convenient a way of doing things simply because it would involve an enormous number of insurance policies instead of relatively few, with a consequent increase in insurance costs. Further, there would inevitably be a number of defaulters, even if such insurance were made compulsory by law—and this itself would of course cost money in enforcement.

Whether this is the most equitable way of distributing the risks created by business enterprises is a different and more difficult question which in the last resort depends on value judgments...

Bazley v Curry (1999) 174 DLR (4th) 45 (Supreme Court of Canada)

The defendant, a non-profit organisation, operated two residential care facilities for the treatment of emotionally troubled children. As it acted in place of the children's parents, it was responsible for all aspects of life for the children it cared for, from general supervision to intimate duties like bathing and tucking in at bedtime. Unknown to the defendant and without carelessness on its part, it hired a paedophile as an employee to work in one of its homes. It was later discovered that the paedophile had abused some of the children, and an action was brought against the defendant alleging it was vicariously liable for the damage caused to the children as a result of the actions of the employee.

McLachlin J

Fleming [*The Law of Torts* (9th edn, 1998)] has identified [the] policies lying at the heart of vicarious liability. In his view, two fundamental concerns underlie the imposition of vicarious liability: (1) provision of a just and practical remedy for the harm; and (2) deterrence of future harm. While different formulations of the policy interests at stake may be made (for example, loss internalization is a hybrid of the two), I believe that these two ideas usefully embrace the main policy considerations that have been advanced.

First and foremost is the concern to provide a just and practical remedy to people who suffer as a consequence of wrongs perpetrated by an employee. Fleming expresses this succinctly (at p. 410): 'a person who employs others to advance his own economic interest should in fairness be placed under a corresponding liability for losses incurred in the course of the enterprise'. The idea that the person who introduces a risk incurs a duty to those who may be injured lies at the heart of tort law. As Cardozo CJ stated in *Palsgraf v. Long Island Railway Co*, 162 NE 99 (NY 1928), at 100, '[t]he risk reasonably to be perceived defines the duty to be obeyed, and risk imports relation; it is risk to another or to others within the range of apprehension.' This principle of fairness applies to the employment enterprise and hence to the issue of vicarious liability. While charitable enterprises may not employ people to advance their economic interests, other factors, discussed below, make it fair that they should bear the burden of providing a just and practical remedy for wrongs perpetrated by their employees. This policy interest embraces a number of subsidiary goals. The first is the goal of effective compensation. 'One of the most important social goals served by vicarious liability is victim compensation. Vicarious liability improves the chances that the victim can recover the judgment from a solvent defendant' (B. Feldthusen, 'Vicarious Liability for Sexual Torts', in *Torts Tomorrow* (1998), 221, p. 224.) Or to quote Fleming, the master is 'a more promising source of recompense than his servant who is apt to be a man of straw' (p. 410).

However, effective compensation must also be fair, in the sense that it must seem just to place liability for the wrong on the employer. Vicarious liability is arguably fair in this sense. The employer puts in the community an enterprise which carries with it certain risks. When those risks materialize and cause injury to a member of the public despite the employer's reasonable efforts, it is fair that the person or organization that creates the enterprise and hence the risk should bear the loss. This accords with the notion that it is right and just that the person who creates a risk bears the loss when the risk ripens into harm. While the fairness of this proposition is capable of standing alone, it is buttressed by the fact that the employer is often in the best position to spread the losses through mechanisms like insurance and higher prices, thus minimizing the dislocative effect of the tort within society. 'Vicarious liability has the broader function of transferring to the enterprise itself the risks created by the activity performed by its agents' (*London Drugs*, per La Forest J., at 339).

The second major policy consideration underlying vicarious liability is deterrence of future harm. Fixing the employer with responsibility for the employee's wrongful act, even where the employer is not negligent, may have a deterrent effect. Employers are often in a position to reduce accidents and intentional wrongs by efficient organization and supervision. Failure to take such measures may not suffice to establish a case of tortious negligence directly against the employer. Perhaps the harm cannot be shown to have been foreseeable under negligence law. Perhaps the employer can avail itself of the defence of compliance with the industry standard. Or perhaps the employer, while complying with the standard of reasonable care, was not as scrupulously diligent as it might feasibly have been. As Wilkinson J. explained in the companion appeal's trial judgment:

> If the scourge of sexual predation is to be stamped out, or at least controlled, there must be powerful motivation acting upon those who control institutions engaged in the care, protection and nurturing of children. That motivation will not in my view be sufficiently supplied by the likelihood of liability in negligence. In many cases evidence will be lacking or have long since disappeared. The proof of appropriate standards is a difficult and uneven matter.

I agree. Beyond the narrow band of employer conduct that attracts direct liability in negligence lies a vast area where imaginative and efficient administration and supervision can reduce the risk that the employer has introduced into the community. Holding the employer vicariously liable for the wrongs of its employee may encourage the employer to take such steps, and hence, reduce the risk of future harm. A related consideration raised by Fleming is that by holding the employer liable, 'the law furnishes an incentive to discipline servants guilty of wrongdoing' (p. 410).

The policy grounds supporting the imposition of vicarious liability—fair compensation and deterrence—are related. The policy consideration of deterrence is linked to the policy consideration of fair compensation based on the employer's introduction or enhancement of a risk. The introduction of the enterprise into the community with its attendant risk, in turn, implies the possibility of managing the risk to minimize the costs of the harm that may flow from it. Policy considerations relating to the fair allocation of loss to risk-creating enterprises and the deterrence of harms tend to support the imposition of vicarious liability on employers. But, as Fleming notes, there often exists a countervailing concern. At one time the law held masters responsible for *all* wrongs committed by servants. Later, that policy was abandoned as too harsh in a complex commercial society where masters might not be in a position to supervise their servants closely. Servants may commit acts, even on working premises and during working hours, which are so unconnected with the employment that it would seem unreasonable to fix an employer with responsibility for them. For example, if a man assaults his wife's lover (who coincidentally happens to be a co-worker) in the employees' lounge at work, few would argue that the employer should be held responsible. Similarly, an employer would not be liable for the harm caused by a security guard who decides to commit arson for his or her own amusement: see, e.g., *Plains Engineering Ltd v Barnes Security Services Ltd* (1987) 43 CCLT 129 (Alta. QB). On further analysis, however, this apparently negative policy consideration of when liability would be appropriate is revealed as nothing more than the absence of the twin policies of fair compensation and deterrence that justify vicarious liability. A wrong that is only coincidentally linked to the activity of the employer and duties of the employee cannot justify the imposition of vicarious liability on the employer. To impose vicarious liability on the employer for such a wrong does not respond to common sense notions of fairness. Nor does it serve to deter future harms. Because the wrong is essentially independent of the employment situation, there is little the employer could have done to prevent it. Where vicarious liability is not closely and materially related to a risk introduced or enhanced by the employer, it serves no deterrent purpose, and relegates the employer to the status of an involuntary insurer. I conclude that a meaningful articulation of when vicarious liability should follow in new situations ought to be animated by the twin policy goals of fair compensation and deterrence that underlie the doctrine, rather than by artificial or semantic distinctions.

COMMENTARY

Although the matter is not free from doubt, the better view today is that the employer's liability for the tort of an employee is truly vicarious and does not rest on any primary liability (see below; Atiyah, above, p. 10; *Winfield & Jolowicz*, para. 20–1; *Salmond & Heuston*, pp. 431–4). An employer may have a primary liability in respect of a non-delegable duty, but, as the current editor of *Winfield & Jolowicz*, para. 20–1, points out, that would be so irrespective of whether there was any employer–employee relationship present on the facts. If this was the basis of the employer's liability there would be no point in considering whether there was an employer–employee relationship but, as this is an essential element of establishing vicarious liability, this must be because a different liability attaches to the employer because of this relationship.

Some of the traditional reasons in support of vicarious liability are also listed by Atiyah in his book: (1) control of the employee by the employer; (2) as the employer benefits from the employee's work the employer should also bear any burdens from that work; and (3) the employer has the choice of choosing the employee. These three, along with other possible justifications, are rejected in favour of the economic rationale for vicarious liability set out in the extract above. Glanville Williams (above) described this form of loss distribution as a form of social insurance and argued it was the most persuasive justification for vicarious liability, and the one that best fitted the existing law (in 1957). Whilst this argument also appealed to the Canadian Supreme Court in *Bazley v Curry*, another ground—deterrence—was also thought to justify the doctrine. As the employer creates a risk by conducting his enterprise and employing the employee, vicarious liability promotes conduct which minimises these risks. Of course, it might be argued that this is exactly what the law of negligence does, but the Supreme Court thought that the requirement to exercise reasonable care may not provide the desired level of risk management. But not every risk which manifests itself makes the employer liable; hence McLachlin J's exclusion of the assault at work. As Giliker (2002) 65 MLR 269 at 278 argues: 'More importantly, by adopting a test of risk, liability may be justified in terms of the *level* of risk created by the tortfeasor's employment'. Thus, although there was *some* risk that an employee might assault his wife's lover, it was not such as to make it socially desirable that the loss to the wife's lover should be imposed on the employer and spread through insurance. Some authors have gone further, arguing that in cases of intentional wrongdoing (see Section III.4 below) the employer should only be vicariously liable if they enhanced the risk by failing to take steps to stop the risk of the employee acting as he did (see Townshend-Smith (2000) 8 Tort L Rev 108; Yap, 'Enlisting close connections: a matter of course for vicarious liability?' (2008) 28 LS 197). If this is approach is taken, however, it is hard to see how the liability of the employer is vicarious; the employer is *directly* liable for failing to take reasonable steps to prevent the occurrence of a foreseeable risk.

Even if 'an employer ought to be liable for a tort which can fairly be regarded as a reasonably incidental risk to the type of business being carried on' (*Gravil v Carroll* [2008] EWCA Civ 689 at [21]), the *level* of risk which justifies this conclusion will vary, and to that extent it may be considered as simply another example of Professor Atiyah's observation that the *equity* of imposing vicarious liability lies in value judgements. Although the explicit policy-based approach to vicarious liability applied in *Bazley* has not been adopted in England, it is clear from the decision of the House of Lords in *Lister v Hesley Hall Ltd* [2002] 1 AC 215 (extracted at p. 844, below) that the rationales for the doctrine set out in *Bazley* are accepted as applicable in English courts. (See *Gravil v Carroll* [2008] EWCA Civ 689.)

II. The Employer–Employee Relationship

As noted above, a pre-requisite of vicarious liability is an employer–employee relationship between the party committing the wrong and the party who is alleged to be liable for that wrong. The question whether a person is employed under a contract of service (employee) or a contract for services (independent contractor) has to be decided in many contexts, and most of the authorities cited below are not concerned with the question of vicarious liability. Whether the employer–employee relationship is an absolute (if found to exist for one purpose it exists for all) or is relative is not entirely clear, but the latter view is preferable. There seems no reason why the same policy concerns that underlie decisions over whether a person is an employee for tax or social security purposes should apply to whether that person's tort should render another vicariously liable for it, though the cases in one area may no doubt serve as a guide in another. With that rider in mind, the student should look to the following cases for guidance.

Market Investigations v Minister of Social Security [1969] 2 QB 173

The issue for the court was whether, for the purposes of assessing national insurance contributions, a person employed on a series of short-term contracts by a company to carry out interviews was employed under contracts of service or contracts for services. The Department had held that she was an employee. The contracts provided that, in consideration for a fixed remuneration, the person would provide their own work and skill in the performance of a service for the company. The company could specify who was to be interviewed, the questions to be asked, the order in which questions should be asked and recorded, how answers were to be recorded and how the person should probe for answers. The person could be required to attend at the company's office for a short period to see a supervisor. Within the period specified for completion of a survey, however, the person was normally free to choose when to work, could undertake similar work for other organisations, and could not be moved by the company from the area in which the person had agreed to work. When working in the field the supervisor would have no means of getting in touch with the person, and the company's officers were of the opinion that the person could not be dismissed in the middle of a survey. No provision was made in the agreements for time off, sick pay or holidays.

Cooke J

The authorities on the distinction between a contract of service and a contract for services have been extensively reviewed in a number of recent cases, and in particular I refer to the judgment of Mocatta J in *Whittaker v Minister of Pensions and National Insurance* [1967] 1 QB 156, and the judgment of MacKenna J in *Ready Mixed Concrete (South East) v Minister of Pensions and National Insurance* [1968] 2 QB 497. With these and other recent decisions before me, I do not myself propose to embark on a lengthy review of the authorities. I begin by pointing out that the first condition which must be fulfilled in order that a contract may be classified as a contract of service is that stated by MacKenna J in the *Ready Mixed Concrete* case, namely that A agrees that, in consideration of some form of remuneration, he will provide his own work and skill in the performance of some service for B. The fact that this condition is fulfilled is not, however, sufficient. Further tests must be applied to determine whether the nature and provisions of the contract as a whole are consistent or inconsistent with its being a contract of service.

I think it is fair to say that there was at one time a school of thought according to which the extent and degree of the control which B was entitled to exercise over A in the performance of the work would be a decisive factor. However, it has for long been apparent that an analysis of the extent and degree of such control is not in itself decisive. Thus in *Collins v Hertfordshire County Council* [1947] KB 598 it had been suggested that the distinguishing feature of a contract of service is that the master can not only order or require what is to be done but also how it shall be done. The inadequacy of this test was pointed out by Somervell LJ in *Cassidy v Ministry of Health* [1951] 2 KB 343 at 352 when he referred to the case of a certified master of a ship. The master may be employed by the owners under what is clearly a contract of service, and yet the owners have no power to tell him how to navigate his ship. As Lord Parker CJ pointed out in *Morren v Swinton and Pendlebury Borough Council* [1965] 1 WLR 576 at 582, when one is dealing with a professional man, or a man of some particular skill and experience, there can be no question of an employer telling him how to do the work; therefore the absence of control and direction in that sense can be of little, if any, use as a test.

Cases such as *Morren's case* ([1965] 1 WLR 576) illustrate how a contract of service may exist even though the control does not extend to prescribing how the work shall be done. On the other hand, there may be cases when one who engages another to do work may reserve to himself full control over how the work is to be done, but nevertheless the contract is not a contract of service. A good example is *Queensland Stations Pty v Federal Comr of Taxation* (1945), 70 CLR 539 at p 552, the 'drover' case, when Dixon J said:

> In considering the facts it is a mistake to treat as decisive a reservation of control over the manner in which the droving is performed and the cattle are handled. For instance, in the present case the circumstance that the drover agrees to obey and carry out all lawful instructions cannot outweigh the countervailing considerations which are found in the employment by him of servants of his own, the provision of horses, equipment, plant, rations, and a remuneration at a rate per head delivered.

If control is not a decisive test, what then are the other considerations which are relevant? No comprehensive answer has been given to this question, but assistance is to be found in a number of cases.

In *Montreal Locomotive Works v Montreal and A–G for Canada* [1947] 1 DLR 161 at p 169, Lord Wright said this:

> In earlier cases a single test, such as the presence or absence of control, was often relied on to determine whether the case was one of master and servant, mostly in order to decide

issues of tortious liability on the part of the master or superior. In the more complex conditions of modern industry, more complicated tests have often to be applied. It has been suggested that a fourfold test would in some cases be more appropriate, a complex involving (i) control; (ii) ownership of the tools; (iii) chance of profit; (iv) risk of loss. Control in itself is not always conclusive. Thus the master of a chartered vessel is generally the employee of the shipowner though the charterer can direct the employment of the vessel. Again the law often limits the employer's right to interfere with the employee's conduct, as also do trade union regulations. In many cases the question can only be settled by examining the whole of the various elements which constitute the relationship between the parties. In this way it is in some cases possible to decide the issue by raising as the crucial question whose business is it, or in other words by asking whether the party is carrying on the business, in the sense of carrying it on for himself or on his own behalf and not merely for a superior.

In *Bank voor Handel en Scheepvaart NV v Slatford* [1953] 1 QB 248 at p. 295, Denning LJ said:

> . . . the test of being a servant does not rest nowadays on submission to orders. It depends on whether the person is part and parcel of the organisation. . . .

In *US v Silk* (1946) 331 US 704 the question was whether certain men were 'employees' within the meaning of that word in the Social Security Act 1935. The judges of the [United States] Supreme Court decided that the test to be applied was not 'power of control, whether exercised or not, over the manner of performing service to the undertaking', but whether the men were employees 'as a matter of economic reality'.

The observations of Lord Wright, of Denning LJ and of the judges of the Supreme Court in the USA suggest that the fundamental test to be applied is this: 'Is the person who has engaged himself to perform these services performing them as a person in business on his own account?'. If the answer to that question is 'yes', then the contract is a contract for services. If the answer is 'no' then the contract is a contract of service. No exhaustive list has been compiled and perhaps no exhaustive list can be compiled of considerations which are relevant in determining that question, nor can strict rules be laid down as to the relative weight which the various considerations should carry in particular cases. The most that can be said is that control will no doubt always have to be considered, although it can no longer be regarded as the sole determining factor; and that factors, which may be of importance, are such matters as whether the man performing the services provides his own equipment, whether he hires his own helpers, what degree of financial risk he takes, what degree of responsibility for investment and management he has, and whether and how far he has an opportunity of profiting from sound management in the performance of his task. The application of the general test may be easier in a case where the person who engages himself to perform the services does so in the course of an already established business of his own; but this factor is not decisive, and a person who engages himself to perform services for another may well be an independent contractor even though he has not entered into the contract in the course of an existing business carried on by him . . .

[Cooke J considered the contract in question and continued:]

It is apparent that the control which the company had the right to exercise in this case was very extensive indeed. It was in my view so extensive as to be entirely consistent with Mrs Irving's being employed under a contract of service. The fact that Mrs Irving had a limited discretion when she should do the work was not in my view inconsistent with the existence of a contract of service. For examples of a servant having such a discretion, see *Hobbs v Royal Arsenal Co-operative Society Ltd* (1930) 23 BWCC 254 and *Amalgamated Engineering Union v*

Minister of Pensions and National Insurance [1963] 1 WLR 441. Nor is there anything inconsistent with the existence of a contract of service in the fact that Mrs Irving was free to work for others during the relevant period. It is by no means a necessary incident of a contract of service that the servant is prohibited from serving any other employer. Again, there is nothing inconsistent with the existence of a contract of service in the master having no right to alter the place or area within which the servant has agreed to work. So far as concerns practical limitations on a master's power to give instructions to his servant, there must be many cases when such practical limitations exist. For example, a chauffeur in the service of a car hire company may, in the absence of radio communication, be out of reach of instructions for long periods…

[Cooke J went on to hold that there were no provisions of the contract, which, when considered as a whole, were inconsistent with a contract of service.]

Appeal dismissed.

R. Kidner, 'Vicarious Liability: For Whom Should the "Employer" be Liable?' (1995) 15 LS 47

It is suggested that the following in some mix or other are appropriate for the question [who is an employer] in so far as it relates to vicarious liability.

(1) Control by the 'employer' of the 'employee'. Traditionally this has meant asking whether the employer can control not only what is done but also how it is done. This makes little sense and the variant of asking whether the employer has the legal right to control is merely circular. Rather this factor should look at the degree of managerial control which is exercised over the activity and this may depend on how far a person is integrated into the organisation of the enterprise. At the one end of the spectrum a contractor will merely be asked to achieve an end result, or more ambiguously the specification of that end result may be so detailed as to amount to detailed control over how that result is to be achieved. At the other end of the spectrum is the person who is actually controlled in every detail of how things are to be done. Another way to look at the control test is to examine the degree to which the 'employee' is accountable to the employer: in other words to what extent is he subject to the managerial procedures of the employer in relation to such matters as quality of work, performance, productivity etc?

(2) Control by the contractor of himself. This is not about the Mr Newall who took no orders from anybody [see *Mersey Docks and Harbour Board v Coggins & Griffith* [1947] AC 1] but is rather an element of the entrepreneur test and involves looking at how the contractor arranges his work, his use of assets, his payment etc.

(3) The organisation test (in the first sense of how central the activity is to the enterprise). This involves the question, how far the activity is a central part of the employer's business from the point of view of the objectives of that business. This element flows from the need to establish who it is that is engaging in the activity and the more relevant the activity is to the fundamental objectives of the business the more appropriate it is to apply the risk to the business.

(4) The integration test (i.e. organisation test in the second sense of whether the activity is integrated into the organisational structure of the enterprise). This also looks at the traditional test of whether the function is being provided for the business or by the business and is also part of the entrepreneur test for it asks whether the activity is part of the enterprise's organisation or of some other organisation. A service may be absolutely essential to the business or wholly peripheral to it, but if it is being provided by what is in effect a separate business it

would be inappropriate to apply the risk to the enterprise. It is a factor of both who is engaging in the activity and also who stands to gain or lose from it.

(5) Is the person in business on his own account (the entrepreneur test)? This is not really a separate test as it is intimately involved in the other four, but it needs to be highlighted so that the burden of proof is right. For the purposes of vicarious liability a person should not be regarded as an independent contractor simply because according to the technical require-ments of employment law he is not an employee. Rather it needs to be established that he is actually behaving as an entrepreneur and is taking the appropriate risks and has the possibility of resulting profits. Thus even if a person's activity is peripheral to the enterprise and even if he is not for managerial purposes regarded as part of the organisation, a person could still be regarded as an employee if it is clear that in relation to that business he is not acting as an entrepreneur. Agency workers would be an example.

The function of this article has been to argue that those for whom an 'employer' should be vicariously liable should not be restricted by recent approaches in employment law and tort law needs to be able to take account of new forms of employment. The point is not that the relation-ship between employer and employee should be defined totally differently in the two areas of law, but that because of the objectives to be achieved the emphasis needs to be different...

The change can only be achieved if it is admitted that the term 'employee' can have different meanings for different purposes: however it is not being argued that vicarious liability should jettison the concept of employment as the governing relationship, but rather that the core of the concept should remain, subject to different interpretation and emphasis in light of different objectives. In looking at these objectives vicarious liability should have greater regard for the role of the 'contractor' within the organisation and less regard for the nature of the contrac-tual arrangements. The contract of employment rarely reflects what actually happens and tort always looks more to what the parties do than to what they are entitled to do...

COMMENTARY

In the early stages of the development of vicarious liability 'control' by the employer was the determining test, but as Kahn-Freud pointed out in 1951 ('Servants and Independent-Contractors' (1951) 14 MLR 504):

This distinction was based upon the social conditions of an earlier age: it assumed that the employer of labour was able to direct and instruct the labourer as to the technical methods he should use in performing his work.... The technical and economic developments of all industrial societies have nullified these assumptions.... To say of the captain of a ship, the pilot of an aeroplane, the driver of a railway engine, of a motor vehicle, of a crane, that the employer 'controls' the performance of the work is unrealistic and almost grotesque. If in such a case the employee relied on the employer's instructions 'how to do his work' he would be breaking his contract and possibly be liable to sum-mary dismissal for having misrepresented his skill....

In the case extracted above, Cooke J emphasised that control is now only one of the factors that the courts look to in deciding whether a relationship of employer–employee existed, and considered some of the other factors that might assist in the determination. In *Lee Ting Sang v Chung Chi-Keung* [1990] 2 AC 374, the Privy Council agreed with the Court of Appeal of Hong Kong that these had 'never been better put than by Cooke J'.

Application of Cooke J's Factors in Practice

The modern approach looks to the actual relationship between the parties rather than to form. A good example of the relevant factors being weighed is *Hall (Inspector of Taxes) v*

Lorimer [1994] 1 All ER 250, a case concerned with the appropriate tax schedule for a taxpayer. The taxpayer was trained and employed as a vision mixer, a skilled editing job in the television industry, and went 'freelance' in 1985. During 1985–9 he worked 800 days. He hired no staff but did provide replacements to his employers if he was unavailable. All work was carried out at the studios of the production company who employed him, and the equipment was also provided by those companies. He did not contribute to the cost of production nor was he exposed to profits/loss made by the production company, but he could lose money if a client of that company became insolvent or did not pay. He was assessed for taxation purposes as an employee, but the Court of Appeal affirmed earlier judgments overturning that assessment. Particular attention was paid to the fact that the risk of bad debts and outstanding invoices was not usually associated with a contract of service. It was also significant that the taxpayer had worked for a large number of separate employers for a short period (usually one day).

This case can be constrasted with *Lee Ting Sang v Chung Chi-Keung* [1990] 2 AC 374. The applicant was a stonemason who worked mainly for one subcontractor on short-term contracts. He was paid a piece-work rate (so much for finishing a job) or a daily rate. If he finished early he assisted the subcontractor in sharpening tools. Although he sometimes worked for others, he gave preference to the urgent work of the subcontractor, advising those for whom he was working at that time to replace him. Allowing an appeal from the Court of Appeal of Hong Kong, the Privy Council held him to be an employee. He provided no equipment, did not hire any helpers to assist him, had no responsibility for the management of the job, and did not 'price' the job. He was simply told to turn up for work and was told what to do (although, as a skilled worker, not how to do it). In short (at 384), '[t]he applicant ran no risk whatever save that of being unable to find employment which is, of course, a risk faced by casual employees who move from one job to another...'

The Problem of the Temporary Employee   Dual Vicarious Liability?

What if an employee of one employer is hired to someone else? Which employer is vicariously liable for the torts of the employee? This issue was recently considered by the Court of Appeal.

Viasystems (Tyneside) Ltd v Thermal Transfer (Northern) Ltd
[2006] QB 510

The claimant engaged contractors to install air conditioning on their property. These contractors subcontracted ducting work to A Ltd and labour for this work was supplied to A Ltd by B Ltd. The claimant's property was damaged due to the negligence of one Darren Strang, a fitter's mate supplied by B Ltd to A Ltd. At the time of the accident, Strang was working under the supervision of a Mr Horsley, A Ltd's foreman, and a Mr Megson, a fitter supplied by B Ltd. The trial judge held that only B Ltd was vicariously liable for S's negligence. On appeal, the Court of Appeal asked for submissions as to whether vicarious liability could extend to two employers jointly.

May LJ

18 The relevant negligent act was Darren Strang crawling through the duct. This was a foolish mistake on the spur of the moment. I have said that a central question is: who was entitled, and perhaps in theory obliged, to give orders as to how the work should or should not be

done? Here there is no suggestion, on the facts found by the judge, that either Mr Horsley or Mr Megson had any real opportunity to prevent Darren's momentary foolishness. The judge specifically acquitted Mr Horsley of personal negligence: and we should proceed on the footing that Mr Megson was not personally negligent either. Vicarious liability is liability imposed by a policy of the law upon a party who is not personally at fault. So the core question on the facts of this case is who was entitled, and in theory, if they had had the opportunity, obliged, so to control Darren as to stop him crawling through the duct. In my judgment, the only sensible answer to that question in this case is that both Mr Megson and Mr Horsley were entitled, and in theory obliged, to stop Darren's foolishness. Mr Megson was the fitter in charge of Darren. Mr Horsley was the foreman on the spot. They were both entitled and obliged to control Darren's work, including the act which was his negligence. The second defendants, through Mr Horsley, would, I think, have qualified for vicarious liability, if it had been Mr Megson who foolishly crawled through the duct. It makes no difference to a sensible analysis that it was Darren who was negligent, and that Mr Megson in some respects was interposed. But neither is there any good sense in saying that, because Mr Horsley was relevantly entitled to control Darren, Mr Megson was not: and vice versa...

Rix LJ

76 In my judgment, there is no doubt that there has been a long standing assumption that dual vicarious liability is not possible, and in such a situation it is necessary to pause carefully to consider the weight of that tradition. However, in truth, the issue has never been properly considered. There appears to be a number of possible strands to the assumption...the formal principle that a servant cannot have two masters; and the policy against multiplicity of actions. As for the first, even if it be granted that an employee cannot have contracts of employment with two separate employers at the same time and for the same period and purposes—and yet it seems plain that a person can (a) have two jobs with separate employers at the same time, provided they are compatible with one another; or (b) be employed by a consortium of several employers acting jointly—nevertheless that does not prevent the employee of a general employer being lent to a temporary employer. As was so clearly exposed in *Denham's* case [*Denham v Midland Employers' Mutual Assurance Ltd* [1955] 2 QB 437], it is an inaccurate metaphor to say that the employment or the employee has been transferred: it is rather that the services of the employee have been lent or hired out, or borrowed or bought in, in circumstances where the temporary employer becomes responsible, under the doctrine of vicarious liability (respondeat superior), for the employee's negligence, and does so even though the formal contract or relationship of employment has not been transferred. That demonstrates that the doctrine of vicarious liability may properly be invoked against an employer who is not really, in law, the employee's employer; and that the use of the expression 'transfer' is potentially misleading. As for the policy against multiplicity of actions: no doubt the law does not favour unnecessary complexity which may lead to the suing of unnecessary defendants. But such a policy, while it may inform the formulation of doctrine, cannot determine it; and, in any event, the history of this jurisprudence has demonstrated clearly that it is not safe for a claimant to assume that he can sue one employer only. Whereas the Mersey Docks approach may have discouraged the suing of the temporary employer save in exceptional situations, the problem remains a live one.

77 In my judgment, if consideration is given to the function and purposes of the doctrine of vicarious liability, then the possibility of dual responsibility provides a coherent solution to the problem of the borrowed employee. Both employers are using the employee for the purposes of their business. Both have a general responsibility to select their personnel with care and to encourage and control the careful execution of their employees' duties, and both fall within

the practical policy of the law which looks in general to the employer to organise his affairs in such a way as to make it fair, just and convenient for him to bear the risk of his employees' negligence. I am here using the expression 'employee' in the extended sense used in the authorities relating to the borrowed employee. The functional basis of the doctrine of vicarious liability has become increasingly clear over the years. The Civil Liability (Contribution) Act 1978 now provides a clear and fair statutory basis for the assessment of contribution between the two employers. In my judgment, the existence of the possibility of dual responsibility will be fairer and will also enable cases to be settled more easily.

78 The remaining question is to attempt to define the circumstances in which the liability should be dual. It is possible that where the right to control the method of performance of the employee's duties lies solely on the one side or the other, then the responsibility similarly lies on the same side. That reflects the significance of Lord Esher MR's doctrine of entire and absolute control. If so, then it will only be where the right of control is shared that vicarious liability can be dual. I would agree that the balance of authority is in favour of this solution. On this basis, I agree with May LJ's analysis of the facts in this case as demonstrating a situation of shared control. I would go further and say that it is a situation of shared control where it is just for both employers to share a dual vicarious liability. The relevant employee, Darren, was both part of the temporary employer's team, under the supervision of Mr Horsley, and part of the general employer's small hired squad, under the supervision of its Mr Megson.

79 However, I am a little sceptical that the doctrine of dual vicarious liability is to be wholly equated with the question of control. I can see that, where the assumption is that liability has to fall wholly and solely on the one side or the other, then a test of sole right of control has force to it. Even the *Mersey Docks* case [*Mersey Docks and Harbour Board v Coggins & Griffith (Liverpool) Ltd* [1947] AC 1], however, does not make the control test wholly determinative. Once, however, a doctrine of dual responsibility becomes possible, I am less clear that either the existence of sole right of control or the existence of something less than entire and absolute control necessarily either excludes or respectively invokes the doctrine. Even in the establishment of a formal employer/employee relationship, the right of control has not retained the critical significance it once did. I would prefer to say that I anticipate that subsequent cases may, in various factual circumstances, refine the circumstances in which dual vicarious liability may be imposed. I would hazard, however, the view that what one is looking for is a situation where the employee in question, at any rate for relevant purposes, is so much a part of the work, business or organisation of both employers that it is just to make both employers answer for his negligence. What has to be recalled is that the vicarious liability in question is one which involves no fault on the part of the employer. It is a doctrine designed for the sake of the claimant imposing a liability incurred without fault because the employer is treated by the law as picking up the burden of an organisational or business relationship which he has undertaken for his own benefit.

80 One is looking therefore for practical and structural considerations. Is the employee, in context, still recognisable as the employee of his general employer and, in addition, to be treated as though he was the employee of the temporary employer as well? Thus in the *Mersey Docks* situation, it is tempting to think that liability will not be shared: the employee is used, for a limited time, in his general employer's own sphere of operations, operating his general employer's crane, exercising his own discretion as a crane driver. Even if the right of control were to some extent shared, as in practice it is almost bound to be, one would hesitate to say that it is a case for dual vicarious liability. One could contrast the situation where the employee is contracted-out labour: he is selected and possibly trained by his general employer, hired out by that employer as an integral part of his business, but employed at the temporary employer's site or his customer's site, using the temporary employer's equipment, and subject

to the temporary employer's directions. In such a situation, responsibility is likely to be shared. A third situation, where an employee is seconded for a substantial period of time to the temporary employer, to perform a role embedded in that employer's organisation, is likely to result in the sole responsibility of that employer . . .

COMMENTARY

In reaching its decision that dual vicarious liability is possible the Court of Appeal considered that no previous binding authority prevented such a conclusion. One relevant case was *Mersey Docks and Harbour Board v Coggins & Griffiths (Liverpool) Ltd and McFarlane* [1947] AC 1, where, by and large applying the control test, the House of Lords held that the temporary employer of a lent crane driver (with crane) remained the employee of the permanent (or general) employer and that there was a heavy onus on the latter to prove that the lent employee had become the employee of the hirer. Both May and Rix LJJ thought that in this case—as in the others they considered—it had been assumed rather than decided that dual vicarious liability was not possible. Their Lordships also agreed that, on its facts, *Mersey Docks* was not a case where dual vicarious liability could have been imposed; the control exercised by the permanent employer was not sufficiently altered by the terms on which the employee was lent to change the identity of the employer for the purposes of vicarious liability (cf. *Hawley v Luminar Leisure Ltd* [2006] IRLR 817, a rare case where a temporary employer was held vicariously liable for the actions of a borrowed worker).

How frequently is dual vicarious liability likely to be found? May LJ (at [46]) indicates that in most cases 'a proper application' of the *Mersey Docks* approach would not yield joint control, whilst Rix LJ's approach seems broader, allowing greater scope for dual vicarious liability. Stevens (2006) 122 LQR 201, 204, argues that the level of control necessary to attach liability for the torts or acts of another is low, so that 'the possibility of dual liability for both the regular and temporary employer becomes the logical solution in the majority of cases'. This assertion does not seem to have been borne out in practice. In *Biffa Waste Services Ltd v Maschinenfabrik Ernst Hese GMBH* [2009] QB 725 and *Color Quest Ltd v Total Downstream UK plc* [2009] EWHC 540 (Comm), cases involving vicarious liability for borrowed employees were decided by the application of the *Mersey Docks* test, the permanent employers remaining liable. In neither case was it thought worth arguing dual vicarious liability. If nothing else, these cases demonstrate that the 'heavy onus' on the permanent employer referred to in *Mersey Docks* may also prevent frequent findings of dual vicarious liability as well as findings that the hirer should be vicariously liable for the torts of the borrowed worker.

An alternative ground for determining dual vicarious liability appealed to the Supreme Court of Canada: that the employers were partners (*Blackwater v Plint* [2005] 3 SCR 3). However, as Neyers (2006) 122 LQR 195, 198 points out, there are difficulties in limiting dual vicarious liability to partners: the Supreme Court of Canada clearly saw the partnership relationship as giving rise to joint control but there seems no reason why non-partnership relationships should be excluded from attracting dual vicarious liability if the key question is control.

If dual vicarious liability exists, what should the division of responsibility be between the two employers in contribution proceedings? In *Viasystems*, the Court of Appeal held that, if both employers were not personally at fault, the division could only be 50/50 but the

Supreme Court of Canada in *Plint* thought differently, apportioning responsibility 75/25 between the two employers. Can this be the correct approach? Do you agree with Neyers (2006) 122 LQR 195, 199, that the effect of *Plint* is that 'someone who was held liable without fault, could be more at fault than another person who was held liable without fault'?

Could dual vicarious liability be a satisfactory solution in determining the employer of agency workers? Such workers usually have an express contract only with an employment agency, the agency having a separate contract with the end-user for whom the agency agrees to supply labour. Frequently the contractual arrangements are structured so as to avoid the result that the worker is the employee of either the agency or the end-user, a result the Court of Appeal in *Dacas v Brook Street Bureau (UK) Ltd* [2004] ICR 1347 found difficult to accept. In *Dacas*—a case where there was no contract of service between the agency and the worker—Sedley LJ thought that, for the purposes of a vicarious liability claim, the worker would be regarded as employed by the end-user, especially if the worker had worked for the end-user for some time (see also *Fosse Motor Engineers Ltd v Conde Nast National Magazine Distributors Limited* [2008] EWHC 2037 (TCC)). However, the status of this observation is uncertain as it was linked to his view that, for the purposes of employment law, a contract of employment between the end-user and the worker should be implied in the case of long term placements, a view that was expressly disapproved by the Court of Appeal in *James v London Borough of Greenwich* [2008] EWCA Civ 35; [2008] IRLR 302. If, however, on the facts of the case the worker could be regarded as the employee of the agency (a result thought at least possible by the Court of Appeal in *Cable & Wireless plc v Muscat* [2006[EWCA Civ 220), the degree of control over the worker exercised by the end-user might lead to a finding that, at least for the purposes of vicarious liability, the agency and the end-user are both employers.

Whether or not a hired employee changes employer for the purposes of determining who is vicariously liable does not affect the ability of the temporary and permanent employers, or joint employers, to determine between themselves who shall be liable for any negligence of the hired worker to a third party injured by that negligence (*Arthur White (Contractors) Ltd v Tarmac Civil Engineering* [1967] 1 WLR 1508; *Thompson v T. Lohan (Plant Hire) Ltd* [1987] 1 WLR 649; *Jose v MacSalvors Plant Hire Ltd* [2009] EWCA Civ 1329). However, in *Phillips Products v Hyland* [1987] 1 WLR 659, the plaintiff was the temporary employer whose property had been damaged by the negligence of the employee. When sued the defendant permanent employer attempted to raise as a defence a clause in the contract with the plaintiff providing that the plaintiff would be responsible for any negligence of the hired employee. The Court of Appeal held the clause fell foul of the Unfair Contract Terms Act 1977 as an attempt to restrict liability. This case was distinguished in *Thompson*, above, because in *Thompson* a liability had already been established (to the wife of the person killed by the employee's negligence) so the clause could not be said to restrict or exclude liability, unlike in *Phillips*, where its effect was to deprive the plaintiff of a claim it would otherwise have had against the defendant.

Should the status of the worker be determined by the parties' own description of their relationship? The Court of Appeal in *Dacas*—where the parties stipulated that the worker was not employed under a contract of service—noted the well-established rule that this was only one factor to be considered: it was not determinative. In *Ferguson v John Dawson & Partners (Contractors) Ltd* [1976] 1 WLR 1213, all three members of the Court of Appeal agreed that the intention of the parties was a relevant but not conclusive factor but a majority (Megaw and Browne LJJ) would have gone further, Megaw LJ stating (obiter): 'I find difficulty in accepting that the parties, by a mere expression of intention as to what the legal relationship should be, can in any way influence the conclusion of law as to what the relationship is.' In that case builders who were employed as 'labour only sub-contractors' were held to be employees for the purpose of the Construction (Working Places) Regulations 1966 because the remainder of the terms of employment suggested they were employees. Lawton LJ (dissenting) held that:

I can see no reason why in law a man cannot sell his labour without becoming another man's servant even though he is willing to accept control as to how, when and where he shall work. If he makes his intention not to be a servant sufficiently clear, the implications which would normally arise from implied terms do not override the prime object of the bargain.

Do you agree that the parties' intention should be given more of a role in determining the relationship between the parties?

An Alternative Approach?

It is clear that modern employment practices may make the classification of a worker as an employee or an independent contractor a difficult, and perhaps artificial, task. In *Dacas v Brook Street Bureau (UK) Ltd* [2004] ICR 1347 Mummery LJ noted that as yet 'unclassified' contracts of employment may best describe the relationship between the parties, such as a 'semi-dependent worker's contract' or 'quasi dependent worker's contract' although how these classifications might relate to vicarious liability is unclear. An alternative approach to solving these difficulties was advocated in the Australian case of *Hollis v Vabu Pty Ltd* (2001) 207 CLR 21, where the plaintiff was injured when he was hit by a cycle courier wearing the distinctive apparel of the defendant ('Crisis Couriers'). Although the plaintiff could not identify the individual courier who hit him, he sued the defendant on the basis that it was vicariously liable for the negligence of the courier. The defendant argued that the courier was an independent contractor, a finding which had been made by the New South Wales Court of Appeal in relation to questions of taxation. The majority of the High Court of Australia held that, contrary to the earlier decision, on a true construction of the contract, the couriers were employees of the defendant and hence it was vicariously liable. However, although he agreed with the result, McHugh J adopted a different approach:

It is true that the couriers employed by Vabu are neither employees nor independent contractors in the strict sense. But there is no reason in policy for upholding the strict classification of employees and non-employees in the law of vicarious liability and depriving Mr Hollis of compensation. Rather than expanding the definition of employee or accepting the employee/independent contractor dichotomy, the preferable course is to hold that employers can be vicariously liable for the tortious conduct of agents who are neither employees nor independent contractors ... To hold that an employer is vicariously liable for the conduct of a worker who is not an employee or independent contractor does not affect their relationship in other areas of the law or their freedom to contract between themselves or to arrange their business affairs. And it has the great advantage of ensuring that the doctrine of vicarious liability remains relevant in a world of rapidly changing work practices.

The doctrinal explanation for this new approach to making the employer liable was to be found not in describing the relationship as one of employer/employee but in the concept of agency. Quoting from his earlier judgment in *Scott v Davis* (2000) 204 CLR 333, McHugh J argued that a principal was liable for the wrongful acts of a person who was acting on the principal's behalf as a representative and not as an independent principal. Applying this to the facts, the courier could be described as an agent, thus making the principal liable, because it was fair to hold Vabu liable (the courier was 'on the business' and was wearing a Crisis Couriers uniform, a requirement that, from the terms of its contract with its couriers, it clearly considered important) and because the imposition of liability would deter Vabu from ignoring the safety obligations of its couriers.

Although McHugh J's approach remains a minority view, even in Australia (see *Sweeney v Boylan Nominees Pty Ltd* (2006) 80 ALJR 900), do you think this a better approach to determining when an employer is liable for the acts of one he employs? See further pp. 854, below.

III. The Course of Employment

An employer is not liable for every act of an employee; there must be some connection between the act and the purpose for which the employee is employed. As employees are not employed to perform their duties in an unlawful manner, it could be argued that a tortious act is never in the course of employment. Such an approach would make the doctrine redundant for, as noted below, an employer is liable as a primary tortfeasor if the wrongful act has been expressly authorised. Vicarious liability came to depend on the implied authority of the employee (see below), and the employer's liability on whether the act of the employee was within that authority, or in the modern form, within the course or scope of employment. Thus the key question was thought to be whether the act of the employee was a wrongful or unauthorised mode of doing some act authorised by the master (*Salmond & Heuston*, p. 443). However, the House of Lords in *Lister v Hesley Hall* [2002] 1 AC 215 held that this is the wrong approach. Instead, the question that had to be answered was whether the employee's tort had a close connection with the employment. It has been said that the change will lead to a different result in only a handful of cases (Hopkins [2001] CLJ 458; cf. Glofchevski (2004) 12 Tort L Rev 18), and it is also the case that, at the margins, it will be as difficult to distinguish between whether the tort bore a close connection with the employment as it was to answer the question whether the tort was an unauthorised mode of carrying out an authorised task. Nonetheless, the adoption of the close connection test has been described as a genuine advance, at least in the context of intentional wrongdoing by an employee (Cane (2000) 116 LQR 21, 24). Accordingly, it must be remembered that most of the decisions discussed below were decided by the application of a different test, but it is probably the case that the same results would have been reached if the close connection test had been applied. No matter what the appropriate legal principle may be, it must be recognised that many decisions have been influenced by the practical reality that, if the employer was not found vicariously liable, the victim would be left with a claim against the (probably) worthless employee, although since the introduction of widespread social security benefits in the early part of this century and the National Health Service in 1948 the possibility of a destitute victim without funds to pay either for his medical treatment or day-to-day living expenses has receded. However, awards of tort damages are higher than benefits payable under the social security system, and in areas where the employer will have insurance against tort liabilities there remain practical benefits in seeking to establish vicarious liability.

1. Carelessness and the Motive for the Employee's Act

Century Insurance Company Limited v Northern Ireland Transport Board [1942] AC 509

The case arose out of a fire at a petrol station caused by a petrol delivery driver (Davison) throwing a lighted match onto the floor after using it to light a cigarette. The fire caused damage to property. One issue for the House of Lords was whether, assuming the driver was an employee of the delivery company, the negligent act of throwing the match to the ground was within the course of employment.

Viscount Simon LC

On the second question, every judge who has had to consider the matter in Northern Ireland agrees with the learned arbitrator in holding that Davison's careless act which caused the conflagration and explosion was an act done in the course of his employment. Admittedly, he was serving his master when he put the nozzle into the tank and turned on the tap. Admittedly, he would be serving his master when he turned off the tap and withdrew the nozzle from the tank. In the interval, spirit was flowing from the tanker to the tank, and this was the very delivery which the respondents were required under their contract to effect. Davison's duty was to watch over the delivery of the spirit into the tank, to see that it did not overflow, and to turn off the tap when the proper quantity had passed from the tanker. In circumstances like these, 'they also serve who only stand and wait'. He was presumably close to the apparatus, and his negligence in starting smoking and in throwing away a lighted match at that moment is plainly negligence in the discharge of the duties on which he was employed by the respondents. This conclusion is reached on principle and on the evidence, and does not depend on finding a decided case which closely resembles the present facts, but the decision of the English Court of Appeal twenty years ago in *Jefferson v Derbyshire Farmers Ltd* [1921] 2 KB 281 provides a very close parallel. As for the majority decision, nearly sixty years before that, of the Exchequer Chamber in *Williams v Jones* (1865) 3 H&C 60 it may be possible to draw distinctions, as the court in *Jefferson's case* sought to do, but this House is free to review the earlier decision, and for my part I prefer the view expressed in that case by the minority, which consisted of Blackburn and Mellor JJ. The second question must also be answered adversely to the appellants. I move that the appeal be dismissed with costs.

Lord Wright

On the other question, namely, whether Davison's negligence was in the course of his employment, all the decisions below have been against the appellants. I agree with them and need add little. The act of a workman in lighting his pipe or cigarette is an act done for his own comfort and convenience and, at least generally speaking, not for his employer's benefit, but that last condition is no longer essential to fix liability on the employer: *Lloyd v Grace, Smith & Co* [1912] AC 716. Nor is such an act *prima facie* negligent. It is in itself both innocent and harmless. The negligence is to be found by considering the time when and the circumstances in which the match is struck and thrown down. The duty of the workman to his employer is so to conduct himself in doing his work as not negligently to cause damage either to the employer himself or his property or to third persons or their property, and thus to impose the same liability on the employer as if he had been doing the work himself and committed the negligent act. This may seem too obvious as a matter of common sense to require either argument or authority. I think what plausibility the contrary argument might seem to possess results from treating the act of lighting the cigarette in abstraction from the circumstances as a separate act. This was the line taken by the majority judgment in *Williams v Jones,* but Mellor and Blackburn JJ dissented, rightly as I think. I agree also with the decision of the Court of Appeal in *Jefferson v Derbyshire Farmers Ltd* [1921] 2 KB 281, which is in substance on the facts indistinguishable from the present case. In my judgment the appeal should be dismissed.

Lord Porter agreed with Viscount Simon and Lord Wright.

Appeal dismissed.

COMMENTARY

The importance of this decision lies in its treatment of what can be classed as 'collateral' acts of negligence of an employee; the fact that the employee was doing an act for his own benefit, and not necessarily the employer's, was not fatal to a finding that the act was in the course of employment. Earlier cases had suggested otherwise. In *Williams v Jones* (1865) 3 H & C 602, 159 ER 668, the Court of Exchequer Chamber held, by a majority, that the act of an employee who dropped a lighted wood shaving in a shed (having used it to light a pipe), causing a fire which damaged the shed, was not in the course of employment. This was so even though he was making a signboard in the shed as part of his employment. Even if it was accepted that the act committed in the shed was dangerous, this made it 'more difficult to connect it with the act of making the signboard, and less likely to have been in furtherance of the master's business' (at 612; 672). The minority judgments of Blackburn and Mellor JJ looked to the circumstances that made the act negligent, that is, that the employee was working in a shed which contained inflammable materials in the course of his employment, and it was only in that setting that the act was negligent; hence it was carried out in the course of employment. A similar position had been reached in respect of the liability of principals for acts of their agents: in *Barwick v English Joint Stock Bank* (1867) LR 2 Ex 259, the Court of Exchequer Chamber held that a principal could only be liable for the act of an agent if it was done for the principal's benefit and was within the scope of his authority, but the former requirement was rejected by the House of Lords in *Lloyd v Grace, Smith & Co* [1912] AC 716. When the same question arose in the context of employees in the extracted case, both *Lloyd v Grace, Smith & Co* and the minority judgments in *Williams v Jones* were preferred by the House of Lords.

The issue is now one of the link between the tortious act and the course of employment (or scope of authority) rather than the motive with which the employee/agent committed the act in question. In *Kay v ITW Ltd* [1968] 1 QB 140, the employee was employed to drive trucks and small vans around his employer's worksite. Whilst driving a fork-lift truck he found the only entry to a warehouse where he wanted to go was blocked by a lorry not belonging to his employer. Although he had no right to do so he attempted to move the lorry and as a result of his negligence injured the plaintiff. The Court of Appeal held that the act was within the scope of his employment, because he was attempting to return the fork-lift truck to the defendant's warehouse, which was within the scope of his employment, and his misconduct was not so gross and extreme as to take his act outside the scope of his employment. This can be contrasted with *Mason v Essex County Council,* unreported, CA Civil Division, 29 March 1988. The 16-year-old employee was employed to help lift some mattresses into a van, and in an effort to assist his employer he attempted to drive the van to his employer's house, in doing which he negligently caused injury. This was held to be outside the scope of employment; driving had nothing to do with his employment, even though it was done for his employer's benefit. What is the difference between the two cases?

However, the motive of the employee is not entirely irrelevant. In *General Engineering Services Ltd v Kingston and St Andrew Corporation* [1989] 1 WLR 69, the plaintiff's property was damaged by a fire. Local fire-fighters would normally have arrived at the property in three and a half minutes after an emergency call, but, in furtherance of an industrial dispute with their employer, the fire-fighters were on a 'go-slow' with the result that they arrived seventeen minutes after the call. Concurring with the trial judge and the Court of Appeal of Jamaica, the Privy Council held the fire-fighters' employers were not vicariously liable for the acts of the brigade. The 'go-slow' was in furtherance of an industrial dispute, not related to their employer's business, and this was the very negation of carrying out some act authorised by the employer. Thus, whilst it is not a pre-requisite to vicarious liability that the act be done to further the employer's interest, the motive with which the act is done is relevant in determining whether the act was within the employee's course of employment.

Two apprentices (D and P) were attending a carpentry training course as part of their employment. One part of the course required pairs of apprentices to work together on a project. D and P were one pair and were nearing completion of their project when other apprentices attending the course, who had finished their work earlier, came over to talk to them. One of these, G, started digging a chisel into D and P's project. To stop him P attempted to grab the chisel, but as he was doing so G let go, with the result that P's hand went over his shoulder and the chisel struck D in the eye. Were either P, in attempting to stop G from damaging the project, or G, in engaging in horseplay with other apprentices, acting in the course of their employment? (See *Duffy v Thanet District Council* (1983) 134 NLJ 680.)

2. Employee's Use of Vehicles on Unauthorised Journey

Smith v Stages [1989] AC 928

An employee was employed by the employers, the second defendant, as a peripatetic lagger to install insulation at power stations. In August 1977 he was working on a power station in central England when he was taken off that job and sent with another employee, the first defendant, to carry out an urgent job on a power station in Wales. The two employees were paid eight hours' pay for the travelling time to Wales and eight hours' pay for the journey back, as well as the equivalent of the rail fare for the journey, although no stipulation was made as to the mode of travel. The two employees travelled to Wales in the first defendant's car and stayed a week in Wales while working on the power station there. At the end of the job, after working for twenty-four hours without a break in order to finish the job, they decided to drive straight back to the Midlands. On the way back the car, driven by the first defendant, left the road and crashed through a brick wall. The employee was seriously injured and he brought an action against the first defendant, who was uninsured, and against the employers alleging that they were vicariously liable for the first defendant's negligence since he had been acting in the course of his employment while driving the two employees back to central England. The employee subsequently died from unrelated causes and his widow continued the action on behalf of his estate. The trial judge held that the accident had not occurred in the course of employment, but this was reversed by the Court of Appeal.

Lord Goff

There are, however, circumstances in which, when a man is travelling to (or from) a place where he is doing a job for his employer, he will be held to be acting in the course of his employment....So, if a man is employed to do jobs for his employer at various places during the day, such as a man who goes from door to door canvassing for business, or who distributes goods to customers, or who services equipment like washing machines or dishwashers, he will ordinarily be held to be acting in the course of his employment when travelling from one destination to another, and may also be held to do so when travelling from his home to his first destination and home again after his last. Again, it has been held that, in certain circumstances, a man who is called out from his home at night to deal with an emergency may be acting in the course of his employment when travelling from his home to his place of work to deal with the emergency: see *Blee v London and North Eastern Rly Co* [1938] AC 126. There are many other cases.

But how do we distinguish the cases in this category in which a man is acting in the course of his employment from those in which he is not? The answer is, I fear, that everything depends on the circumstances....

I approach the matter as follows. I do not regard this case as an ordinary case of travelling to work. It would be more accurate to describe it as a case where an employee, who has for a short time to work for his employers at a different place of work some distance away from his usual place of work, has to move from his ordinary base to a temporary base (here lodgings in Pembroke) from which he will travel to work at the temporary place of work each day. For the purpose of moving base, a normal working day was set aside for Mr Stages's journey, for which he was paid as for an eight-hour day. In addition to his day's pay he was given a travel allowance for his journey, and an allowance for his lodgings at his temporary base in Pembroke. In my opinion, in all the circumstances of the case, Mr Stages was required by the employers to make this journey, so as to make himself available to do his work at the Pembroke power station, and it would be proper to describe him as having been employed to do so. The fact that he was not required by his employer to make the journey by any particular means, nor even required to make it on the particular working day made available to him, does not detract from the proposition that he was employed to make the journey. Had Mr Stages wished, he could have driven down on the afternoon of Sunday 21 August, and have devoted the Monday to (for example) visiting friends near Pembroke. In such circumstances it could, I suppose, be said that Stages was not travelling 'in his employers' time'. But this would not matter; for the fact remains that the Monday, a normal working day, was made available for the journey, with full pay for that day to perform a task which he was required by the employers to perform.

I have it very much in mind that Mr Machin and Mr Stages were described by counsel for the employers as peripatetic laggers working at such sites as were available. This may well be an accurate description of their work. If so, their contracts of service may have provided at least an indication as to how far they would be acting in the course of their employment when changing from one power station to another. Indeed, accepting the description as correct, it is difficult to know how much weight to give to it in the absence of their contracts of service. However, the present case can in any event be differentiated on the basis that it was a departure from the norm in that it was concerned with a move to a temporary base to deal with an emergency, on the terms I have described.

I turn to Mr Stages's journey back. Another ordinary working day, Tuesday 30 August, was made available for the journey, with the same pay, to enable him to return to his base in the Midlands to be ready to travel to work on the Wednesday morning. In my opinion, he was employed to make the journey back, just as he was employed to make the journey out to Pembroke. If he had chosen to go to sleep on the Monday morning and afternoon for eight hours or so, and then to drive home on the Monday evening so that he could have Tuesday free . . . that would not have detracted from the proposition that his journey was in the course of his employment. For this purpose, it was irrelevant that Monday was a bank holiday. Of course, it was wrong for him to succumb to the temptation of driving home on the Monday morning, just after he had completed so long a spell of work; but once again that cannot alter the fact that his journey was made in the course of his employment.

For these reasons, I would dismiss the appeal.

Lord Lowry

The paramount rule is that an employee travelling on the highway will be acting in the course of his employment if, and only if, he is at the material time going about his employer's business. One must not confuse the duty to turn up for one's work with the concept of already being 'on duty' while travelling to it.

It is impossible to provide for every eventuality and foolish, without the benefit of argument, to make the attempt, but some *prima facie* propositions may be stated with reasonable confidence.

(1) An employee travelling from his ordinary residence to his regular place of work, whatever the means of transport and even if it is provided by the employer, is not on duty and is not acting in the course of his employment, but, if he is obliged by his contract of service to use the employer's transport, he will normally, in the absence of an express condition to the contrary, be regarded as acting in the course of his employment while doing so.

(2) Travelling in the employer's time between workplaces (one of which may be the regular workplace) or in the course of a peripatetic occupation, whether accompanied by goods or tools or simply in order to reach a succession of workplaces (as an inspector of gas meters might do), will be in the course of the employment.

(3) Receipt of wages (though not receipt of a travelling allowance) will indicate that the employee is travelling in the employer's time and for his benefit and is acting in the course of his employment, and in such a case the fact that the employee may have discretion as to the mode and time of travelling will not take the journey out of the course of his employment.

(4) An employee travelling in the employer's time from his ordinary residence to a workplace other than this regular workplace or in the course of a peripatetic occupation or to the scene of an emergency (such as a fire, an accident or a mechanical breakdown of plant) will be acting in the course of his employment.

(5) A deviation from or interruption of a journey undertaken in the course of employment (unless the deviation or interruption is merely incidental to the journey) will for the time being (which may include an overnight interruption) take the employee out of the course of his employment.

(6) Return journeys are to be treated on the same footing as outward journeys.

All the foregoing propositions are subject to any express arrangements between the employer and the employee or those representing his interests. They are not, I would add, intended to define the position of salaried employees, with regard to whom the touchstone of payment made in the employer's time is not generally significant . . . .

Lord Keith, **Lord Brandon** and **Lord Griffiths** agreed with Lord Goff and Lord Lowry.

Appeal dismissed.

COMMENTARY

Particular problems have arisen in relation to passengers or bystanders injured by an employee driving a form of transport provided by the employer where the accident occurred in the course of an unauthorised detour taken by the employee. Although the cases are difficult to reconcile, whether the employer will be liable depends on the degree of deviance from the authorised journey. As Parke B stated in *Joel v Morison* (1834) 6 C & P 501 at 503: 'If he [the employee] was going out of his way, against his master's implied commands, when driving on his master's business, he will make his master liable; but if he was going on a frolic of his own, without being at all on his master's business, the master will not be liable...'. The difference between departing from the master's implied command so as to make the master liable and a 'frolic of one's own' is hard to tell, to say the least, and the cases only show how difficult such a distinction is in practice (compare *Harvey v R. G. O'Dell* [1958] 2 QB 78—journey by workmen to get a meal during working hours was 'fairly incidental' to their work—with *Hilton v Burton (Rhodes) Ltd* [1961] 1 WLR 705—journey of the employees was seven or eight miles from their work site for tea after they had returned from lunch in a public house and accident occurred on the return trip from the café; held not in the course of employment). See also *Nottingham v Aldridge* [1971] 2 QB 739.

Can the journey be both authorised and unauthorised at the same time? In *A. & W. Hemphill Ltd v Williams* [1966] 2 Lloyd's Rep 101, the pursuer was a member of the Boy's Brigade of Glasgow, which was returning from a summer camp. The boys were being driven to Glasgow by the employee of the defender, who had express instructions as to the route he should take. At the request of some of the boys (not the pursuer) he deviated from this route and took a journey he had expressly been prohibited to take, and in the course of this deviation an accident occurred in which the pursuer was injured. The House of Lords upheld the decision holding the defender vicariously liable. If the lorry had been empty the deviation might have amounted to a 'frolic of his own', but whilst the passengers remained on the lorry transportation of them was the dominant purpose of the driving. Lord Pearce held (at 104):

But when there are passengers whom the servant on his master's behalf has taken on board for transport to Glasgow, their transport and safety does not cease at a certain stage of the journey to be the master's business, or part of his enterprise merely because the servant has for his own purposes chosen some route which is contrary to his instructions.

The reason the responsibility did not cease was presumably that the employer had undertaken to provide a service to the passengers (transport) and unless the acts of the employee were clearly outside the scope of what he was employed to do the employer should remain liable (reasoning analogous to that pertaining to non-delegable duties of care). This was not the case here, because the driver was still doing the job he was paid to do and the accident might just as easily have occurred on an authorised route. Of course, this latter reasoning could apply where pedestrians are injured by employees driving on an unauthorised route, but in that case the employer has not undertaken a responsibility toward the pedestrian in the same way as for a passenger; hence Lord Pearce's distinction between an empty lorry and one carrying passengers. If the driver in *Hemphill* had injured a pedestrian would the deviation have been held to be outside the course of employment? If so, this seems to make the pedestrian's right to recover against the employer dependent on the fortuitous circumstance that the driver was carrying passengers at the time of the accident. Can this be correct? (See *Morris v Martin* (below) per Lord Denning MR, and also the criticism of this part of Lord Pearce's judgment by the Lord Ordinary (Lord Robertson) in *Angus v Glasgow Corporation*

1977 SLT 206, although the First Division of the Inner House made no comment on this aspect of the Lord Ordinary's judgment on appeal. *Hemphill* was applied without comment by the Lord Ordinary (Lord Wylie) in *R. J. McLeod (Contractors) Ltd v South of Scotland Electricity Board* 1982 SLT 274.)

3. Employee Acting Contrary to Express Instructions

Rose v Plenty [1976] 1 WLR 141

The plaintiff was a 13-year-old child who had been employed by a milkman to help deliver milk from a van. This was contrary to a notice that the defendant, the milkman's employer, had exhibited at the depot expressly prohibiting the employment of children to assist the performance of milkmen's duties and from giving lifts on the milk van. As a consequence of assisting the milkman, the plaintiff rode on the milk van and was injured when the milkman drove the float negligently. The plaintiff brought an action for damages for negligence against the milkman and the employers, obtaining judgment against the milkman, but failing against the employers on the ground that the milkman had been acting outside the scope of his employment in employing the plaintiff and carrying him on the float contrary to the employers' instructions. The plaintiff appealed.

Lord Denning MR

In considering whether a prohibited act was within the course of the employment, it depends very much on the purpose for which it is done. If it is done for his employers' business, it is usually done in the course of his employment, even though it is a prohibited act.... But if it is done for some purpose other than his master's business, as, for instance, giving a lift to a hitchhiker, such an act, if prohibited, may not be within the course of his employment.... In the present case it seems to me that the course of Mr Plenty's employment was to distribute the milk, collect the money and to bring back the bottles to the van. He got or allowed this young boy, Leslie Rose, to do part of that business which was the employers' business. It seems to me that although prohibited, it was conduct which was within the course of the employment; and on this ground I think the judge was in error. I agree it is a nice point in these cases on which side of the line the case falls; but, as I understand the authorities, this case falls within those in which the prohibition affects only the conduct within the sphere of the employment and did not take the conduct outside the sphere altogether. I would hold this conduct of Christopher Plenty to be within the course of his employment and the master is liable accordingly, and I would allow the appeal.

Scarman LJ

I think it important to realise that the principle of vicarious liability is one of public policy. It is not a principle which derives from a critical or refined consideration of other concepts in the common law, e.g. the concept of trespass or indeed the concept of agency. No doubt in particular cases it may be relevant to consider whether a particular plaintiff was or was not a trespasser. Similarly, when, as I shall indicate, it is important that one should determine the course of employment of the servant, the law of agency may have some marginal relevance. But basically, as I understand it, the employer is made vicariously liable for the tort of his employee not because the plaintiff is an invitee, nor because of the authority possessed by the servant, but because it is a case in which the employer, having put matters into motion, should be liable if the motion that he has originated leads to damage to another. What is the approach which the cases identify as the correct approach in order to determine this question of public policy? First, as Lord Denning MR has already said, one looks to see whether the servant has committed a tort on the plaintiff. In the present case it is clear that the first defendant, the servant of the dairy company, who are the second defendants, by the negligent driving of the milk float, caused injury to the plaintiff, a boy 13½ years old, who was on the float at his invitation. There was therefore a tort committed by the servant. The next question, as Lord Denning MR has said, is whether the employer should shoulder the liability for compensating the person injured by the tort. With all respect to the points developed by Lawton LJ, it does appear to me to be clear, since the decision of *Limpus v London General Omnibus Co* (1862) 1 H&C 542; 158 ER 993, that that question has to be answered by directing attention to what the first defendant was employed to do when he committed the tort that has caused damage to the plaintiff. The first defendant was, of course, employed at the time of the accident to do a whole number of operations. He was certainly not employed to give the plaintiff a lift, and if one confines one's analysis of the facts to the incident of injury to the plaintiff, then no doubt one would say that carrying the plaintiff on the float—giving him a lift—was not in the course of the first defendant's employment. But in *Ilkiw v Samuels* [1963] 1 WLR at 1004 Diplock LJ indicated that the proper approach to the nature of the servant's employment is a broad one. He said:

> As each of these nouns implies [he is referring to the nouns used to describe course of employment, sphere, scope and so forth] the matter must be looked at broadly, not dissecting the servant's task into its component activities—such as driving, loading, sheeting and the like—by asking: What was the job on which he was engaged for his employer? and answering that question as a jury would.

Applying those words to the employment of the first defendant, I think it is clear from the evidence that he was employed as a roundsman to drive his float round his round and to deliver milk, to collect empties and to obtain payment. That was his job. He was under an express prohibition—a matter to which I shall refer later—not to enlist the help of anyone doing that work. And he was also under an express prohibition not to give lifts on the float to anyone. How did he choose to carry out the task which I have analysed? He chose to disregard the prohibition and to enlist the assistance of the plaintiff. As a matter of common sense, that does seem to me to be a mode, albeit a prohibited mode, of doing the job with which he was entrusted. Why was the plaintiff being carried on the float when the accident occurred? Because it was necessary to take him from point to point so that he could assist in delivering milk, collecting empties and, on occasions, obtaining payment. The plaintiff was there because it was necessary that he should be there in order that he could assist, albeit in a way prohibited by the employers, in the job entrusted to the first defendant by his employers....

It does seem to me that the principle that I have been attempting to describe is to be found in the case law, notably in *Limpus v London General Omnibus Co, Hilton v Thomas Burton (Rhodes) Ltd* [1961] 1 WLR 705 and *Ilkiw v Samuels* [1963] 1 WLR 991. Yet it is said that the flow of this current of authority must be damned and the stream of the law diverted because of the two decisions to which Lawton LJ has referred: *Twine v Bean's Express Ltd* (1946) 175 LT 131 and *Conway v George Wimpey & Co Ltd* [1951] 2 KB 266. Both of those decisions seem to me distinguishable on their facts. In *Twine's case* (at 132), at the very end of the judgment, Lord Greene MR said: 'The other thing that he [ie the servant] was doing simultaneously was something totally outside the scope of his employment, namely, giving a lift to a person who had no right whatsoever to be there.' In that case the conclusion of fact was that the express prohibition on giving lifts was not only a prohibition but was also a limiting factor on the scope of the employment; and, of course, once a prohibition is properly to be treated as a defining or limiting factor on the scope of employment certain results follow. In *Twine's case* the driver was engaged to drive his employers' van, his employers having a contract with the Post Office. When so doing, he gave Mr Twine a lift from A to B. True A and B happened to be, both of them, offices of the Post Office. Yet I can well understand why the court reached the conclusion that in the circumstances of that case it was not possible to say that the driver in giving Mr Twine a lift was acting within the scope of his employment or doing improperly that which he was employed to do. Similarly when one looks at *Conway's case*, one again sees that on the facts of that case the court considered it right so to define the scope of employment that what was done, namely giving somebody a lift, was outside it and was not a mode of doing that which the servant was employed to do. That also was a case of a lift: the person lifted was not in any way engaged, in the course of the lift or indeed otherwise, in doing the master's business or in assisting the servant to do the master's business; and no doubt it was for that reason that Asquith LJ was able to say ([1951] 2 KB at 276) that what was done—that is giving somebody else's employee a lift from the airport home—was not a mode of performing an act which the driver was employed to do, but was the performance of an act which he was not employed to perform. In the present case the first defendant, the servant, was employed to deliver milk, to collect empties, to obtain payment from customers. The plaintiff was there on the float in order to assist the first defendant to do those jobs. I would have thought therefore that whereas *Conway v George Wimpey & Co Ltd* was absolutely correctly decided on its facts, the facts of the present case lead to a very different conclusion. The dividing factor between, for instance, the present case and the decisions in *Twine v Bean's Express Ltd* and *Conway v George Wimpey & Co Ltd* is the category into which the court, on the study of the facts of the case, puts the express prohibition issued by the employers to their servant....

Now there was nothing of that sort [a prohibition on the sphere of employment] in the prohibition in this case. The prohibition is twofold: (1) that the first defendant was not to give lifts on his float; and (2) that he was not to employ others to help him in delivering the milk and so forth. There was nothing in those prohibitions which defined or limited the sphere of his employment. The sphere of his employment remained precisely the same after as before the prohibitions were brought to his notice. The sphere was as a roundsman to go round the rounds delivering milk, collecting empties and obtaining payment. Contrary to instructions, this roundsman chose to do what he was employed to do in an improper way. But the sphere of his employment was in no way affected by his express instructions....

Lawton LJ (dissenting)

If a general principle should be needed to support my opinion in this case, I would adopt the same approach as Lord Greene MR in *Twine's case*. What duty did the second defendants owe to the plaintiff? Counsel for the plaintiff says: 'Oh well, they put the driver with the milk float on the road; they put him into a position to take passengers if he were minded to disobey his instructions and therefore it is socially just that they should be responsible.' I do not agree. When they put the first defendant with his float on the road they put him into a position where he had to take care not to injure those with whom he was reasonably likely to have dealings or to meet, that is all other road users and his customers. They expressly excluded anyone travelling as a passenger on his milk float. He was instructed expressly that he was not to carry passengers. Had he obeyed his instructions, he would not have had a passenger to whom he owed a duty of care. It was his disobedience which brought the injured plaintiff into the class of persons to whom the second defendants vicariously owed a duty of care. He had not been employed to do anything of the kind. In my judgment, the plaintiff has failed to establish that the second defendants owed him any duty of care.

Appeal allowed.

COMMENTARY

Where the employee acts contrary to an express prohibition by the employer, whether by so acting the employee is within or without the course of employment depends upon the construction of the prohibition: 'there are prohibitions which limit the sphere of employment, and prohibitions which only deal with conduct within the sphere of employment' (*Plumb v Cobden Flour Mills Co Ltd* [1914] AC 62 at 67, per Lord Dunedin). The extracted case deals with the latter situation, but two earlier cases, distinguished by the majority, represent the former. In *Twine v Bean's Express Ltd* (1946) 175 LT 131, an employee driver was prohibited from allowing anyone to travel with him in his employer's van, but in breach of this prohibition gave a lift to T, who was killed as result of the driver's negligence. The Court of Appeal held that the employer was not liable for the negligence of its driver. Even though driving the van was clearly within the course of employment, giving a lift to another was equally clearly outside it. This case was applied in *Conway v George Wimpey & Co Ltd* [1951] 2 KB 266. The employee drove his employer's vehicle but with the express provision that it should only be used to provide transport for the employer's employees. However, it was common practice for other workers at the site to be given lifts by the drivers, although the employer did not know of this practice. Applying *Twine*, the Court of Appeal refused to hold the employer vicariously liable. In *Conway* the passenger had not seen the prohibitory notice in the cabin of the lorry (and, as he lost, its effect did not arise for decision) but would it make any difference if a passenger accepted a lift from an employee knowing that this was contrary to an express prohibition of the employer? In *Stone v Taffe* [1974] 1 WLR 1575, Stephenson LJ held (at 1581) that, assuming the prohibition was one that limited the scope of employment, '[A]n employer could escape liability by proving that the prohibition was likely to be known to the injured person.' If, however, the question whether the prohibition limits the scope of employment or not must first be decided, the question of notice of the prohibition appears to add nothing to the question of vicarious liability, although it may operate as some form of *volenti* defence.

Despite the attempt of Scarman LJ to rationalise the cases, the line between some appears fine. In *Iqbal v London Transport Executive, The Times*, 6 June 1973, a conductor attempted to move a bus that was blocking the entry route for his bus contrary to an express prohibition that conductors should not drive buses. This action was held to fall outside his course of employment (see also *Beard v London General Omnibus Company* [1900] 2 QB 530). However, in *Ilkiw v Samuels* [1963] 1 WLR 991 a lorry driver had had strict instructions from his employers not to allow the lorry to be driven by anybody else. After receiving a delivery of sugar the lorry had to be moved to make room for another lorry, and, notwithstanding his instructions, the driver allowed a workman to move the lorry. The worker drove the lorry carelessly and the plaintiff was injured. The Court of Appeal held that the lorry driver had been negligent in allowing the workman to drive, and that this negligence arose in the course of his employment. He was employed to have charge and control of the lorry while engaged on the task, and the prohibition on allowing anyone else to drive was merely a prohibition on the mode of doing his job, disregard of which did not take the negligent act of driving outside the course of his employment. Would it have made any difference in *Iqbal* if, instead of acting of his own volition, the conductor had been asked by the driver to move the bus?

Although it is no longer required that the employee be acting for his employer's benefit to make the employer vicariously liable, the purpose of the employee's act is not irrelevant. As Lord Denning MR suggests in the extracted case, if the act is done for the employer's business it is usually done in the course of employment. But what is the 'master's benefit' in this context? The driver in *Conway v George Wimpey* (above) was driving his lorry from one place to another for the benefit of his employer (he was not doing it for his own gratification) and would undoubtedly have been acting in the course of employment if his negligence had injured a pedestrian; yet he was held not to be acting in the course of employment *vis-à-vis* the unauthorised passenger who was injured. Conversely, in *Limpus v London General Omnibus Co* (1862) 1 H & C 526, 158 ER 993, an omnibus driver who obstructed a rival omnibus in contravention of his employer's stated wishes was none the less held to be acting for his employer's benefit (although the intense rivalry between omnibus companies at the time suggests that there may be more to the decision than meets the eye, especially as the London General Omnibus Company, founded as a French-controlled company, was perceived as being a foreign invader—for a fascinating account, see Barker and Robbins, *History of London Transport*, Vol. 1 (London: Allen & Unwin, 1963), pp. 69–98). More generally, how can an act be for the employer's benefit if it has been expressly prohibited by the employer? If an employer prohibits his employees from acting in an unlawful manner, is an employer none the less vicariously liable, for example, for a battery committed by an employee who shoots another in the course of robbing a bank for the employer's benefit? The simple answer is that it is unlikely that robbing a bank will be in the course of employment, but this is circular, for whether an act is within the course of employment is affected (although not decided) by the motive with which it was done. Perhaps all that can be said is that, at various times and in various circumstances, judicial policy has pulled judges in different directions; hence the divergence in the case law. On one hand it seems unfair to hold an employer to what is effectively absolute liability where the employee acts contrary to instructions. On the other, as Willes J (at 539) noted in *Limpus*:

> It is well known that there is virtually no remedy against the driver of an omnibus, and therefore it is necessary that, for injury resulting from an act done by him in the course of his master's service, the master should be responsible; for there ought to be a remedy against some person capable of paying damages to those injured by improper driving....

Is this reasoning as persuasive as it once was in light of compulsory third party motor vehicle insurance?

Would the application of the 'close connection' test lead to different results in the above cases? In *Fosse Motor Engineers Ltd v Conde Nast National Magazine Distributors Limited* [2008] EWHC 2037 (TCC) it was held (at [115]), obiter, that smoking on the job contrary to an express prohibition was not closely connected with the employment so as to impose vicarious liability on the employer. Do you think this result is consistent with the pre-*Lister* case law? (Consider whether the result in *Century Insurance* would have been different if the employer had expressly prohibited smoking on the job?) Perhaps not too much should be read into this obiter conclusion and it remains unlikely that the close connection test will lead to radically different results in cases of express prohibitions.

4. Criminal Acts of the Employee

Lister v Hesley Hall Ltd [2002] 1 AC 215

Between 1979 and 1982 the claimants were resident in Axeholme House, a boarding house attached to a school owned and managed by the defendants. The warden of the boarding house employed by them, without their knowledge, systematically sexually abused the claimants. The claimants claimed damages against the defendants for the personal injuries involved, contending that the defendants had been negligent in their care, selection and control of the warden, alternatively that they were vicariously liable for the torts committed by him. The judge dismissed the direct claims in negligence. He held that the defendants could not be held vicariously liable for the warden's torts but that they were vicariously liable for the warden's failure to report to them his intentions to commit acts of abuse and the harmful consequences to the claimants of those acts. The Court of Appeal allowed an appeal by the defendants, holding that the warden's acts could not be regarded as an unauthorised mode of carrying out his authorised duties.

Lord Steyn

The central question before the House is whether as a matter of legal principle the employers of the warden of a school boarding house, who sexually abused boys in his care, may depending on the particular circumstances be vicariously liable for the torts of their employee....

Since the decision in the Court of Appeal the law reports of two landmark decisions in the Canadian Supreme Court, which deal with vicarious liability of employers for sexual abuse of children, have become available: *Bazley v Curry* (1999) 174 DLR (4th) 45; *Jacobi v Griffiths* (1999) 174 DLR (4th) 71. Enunciating a principle of 'close connection' the Supreme Court unanimously held liability established in *Bazley's case* and by a four to three majority came to the opposite conclusion in *Jacobi's case*. The Supreme Court judgments examine in detail the circumstances in which, though an employer is not 'at fault', it may still be 'fair' that it should bear responsibility for the tortious conduct of its employees. These decisions have been described as 'a genuine advance on the unauthorised conduct/unauthorised mode distinction': Peter Cane, 'Vicarious Liability for Sexual Abuse' (2000) 116 LQR 21, 24. Counsel for the appellants invited your Lordships to apply the test developed in *Bazley's case* and in *Jacobi's case* and to conclude that the employers are vicariously liable for the sexual torts of their employee....

Vicarious liability is legal responsibility imposed on an employer, although he is himself free from blame, for a tort committed by his employee in the course of his employment. Fleming observed that this formula represented 'a compromise between two conflicting policies: on the one hand, the social interest in furnishing an innocent tort victim with recourse against a financially responsible defendant; on the other, a hesitation to foist any undue burden on business enterprise': *The Law of Torts*, 9th edn (1998), pp 409–410.

For nearly a century English judges have adopted Salmond's statement of the applicable test as correct. Salmond said that a wrongful act is deemed to be done by a 'servant' in the course of his employment if 'it is either (a) a wrongful act authorised by the master, or (b) a wrongful and unauthorised *mode* of doing some act authorised by the master': Salmond, *Law of Torts*, 1st edn (1907), p 83; and *Salmond & Heuston on the Law of Torts*, 21st edn, p 443. Situation (a) causes no problems. The difficulty arises in respect of cases under (b). Salmond did, however, offer an explanation which has sometimes been overlooked. He said (*Salmond on Torts*, 1st edn, pp 83–84) that 'a master ... is liable even for acts which he has not authorised, provided they are *so connected* with acts which he has authorised, that they may rightly *be regarded* as modes—although improper modes—of doing them' (my emphasis) ... *Salmond's* explanation is the germ of the close connection test adumbrated by the Canadian Supreme Court in *Bazley v Curry* and *Jacobi v Griffiths*.

It is not necessary to embark on a detailed examination of the development of the modern principle of vicarious liability. But it is necessary to face up to the way in which the law of vicarious liability sometimes may embrace intentional wrongdoing by an employee. If one mechanically applies *Salmond's* test, the result might at first glance be thought to be that a bank is not liable to a customer where a bank employee defrauds a customer by giving him only half the foreign exchange which he paid for, the employee pocketing the difference. A preoccupation with conceptualistic reasoning may lead to the absurd conclusion that there can only be vicarious liability if the bank carries on business in defrauding its customers. Ideas divorced from reality have never held much attraction for judges steeped in the tradition that their task is to deliver principled but practical justice...

Our law no longer struggles with the concept of vicarious liability for intentional wrongdoing. Thus the decision of the House of Lords in *Racz v Home Office* [1994] 2 AC 45 is authority for the proposition that the Home Office may be vicariously liable for acts of police officers which amounted to misfeasance in public office—and hence for liability in tort involving bad faith. It remains, however, to consider how vicarious liability for intentional wrongdoing fits in with *Salmond*'s formulation. The answer is that it does not cope ideally with such cases. It must, however, be remembered that the great tort writer did not attempt to enunciate precise propositions of law on vicarious liability. At most he propounded a broad test which deems as within the course of employment 'a wrongful and unauthorised mode of doing some *act* authorised by the master'. And he emphasised the connection between the authorised *acts* and the 'improper modes' of doing them. In reality it is simply a practical test serving as a dividing line between cases where it is or is not just to impose vicarious liability. The usefulness of the *Salmond* formulation is, however, crucially dependent on focusing on the right act of the employee...

[After considering *Rose v Plenty*, extracted above, his Lordship continued:]

If this approach to the nature of employment is adopted, it is not necessary to ask the simplistic question whether in the cases under consideration the acts of sexual abuse were modes of doing authorised acts. It becomes possible to consider the question of vicarious liability on the basis that the employer undertook to care for the boys through the services of the warden and that there is a very close connection between the torts of the warden and his employment. After all, they were committed in the time and on the premises of the employers while the warden was also busy caring for the children....

My Lords, I have been greatly assisted by the luminous and illuminating judgments of the Canadian Supreme Court in *Bazley v Curry* and *Jacobi v Griffiths*. Wherever such problems are considered in future in the common law world these judgments will be the starting point. On the other hand, it is unnecessary to express views on the full range of policy considerations examined in those decisions.

Employing the traditional methodology of English law, I am satisfied that in the case of the appeals under consideration the evidence showed that the employers entrusted the care of the children in Axeholme House to the warden. The question is whether the warden's torts were so closely connected with his employment that it would be fair and just to hold the employers vicariously liable. On the facts of the case the answer is yes. After all, the sexual abuse was inextricably interwoven with the carrying out by the warden of his duties in Axeholme House. Matters of degree arise. But the present cases clearly fall on the side of vicarious liability...

Lord Hobhouse of Woodborough

What these cases [*Bazley v Curry*, above, and *Trotman v North Yorkshire County Council* [1999] LGR 584] in truth illustrate is a situation where the employer has assumed a relationship to the plaintiff which imposes specific duties in tort upon the employer and the role of the employee (or servant) is that he is the person to whom the employer has entrusted the performance of those duties. These cases are examples of that class where the employer, by reason of assuming a relationship to the plaintiff, owes to the plaintiff duties which are more extensive than those owed by the public at large and, accordingly, are to be contrasted with the situation where a defendant is simply in proximity to the plaintiff so that it is foreseeable that his acts may injure the plaintiff or his property and a reasonable person would have taken care to avoid causing such injury. The category into which the present cases fall is recognised by the agreed facts and the useful summary of Judge Harry Walker adopted by Swinton Thomas LJ:

> The defendant admits it had a duty of care towards the plaintiffs. That duty of care was to take all reasonable steps to safeguard the plaintiffs (and other pupils) in their physical, moral and educational development whilst at the school. In carrying out that duty of care the defendant, a limited company, necessarily had to appoint a hierarchy of responsible agents . . . each of whom had either general or particular responsibilities which bore upon this duty of care. Mr Grain in particular was responsible for the boys while at Axeholme House . . .

The fact that sexual abuse was involved does not distinguish this case from any other involving the care of the young and vulnerable and the duty to protect them from the risk of harm. The classes of persons or institutions that are in this type of special relationship to another human being include schools, prisons, hospitals and even, in relation to their visitors, occupiers of land. They are liable if they themselves fail to perform the duty which they consequently owe. If they entrust the performance of that duty to an employee and that employee fails to perform the duty, they are still liable. The employee, because he has, through his obligations to his employers, adopted the same relationship towards and come under the same duties to the plaintiff, is also liable to the plaintiff for his own breach of duty. The liability of the employers is a *vicarious* liability because the actual breach of duty is that of the employee. The employee is a tortfeasor. The employers are liable for the employee's tortious act or omission because it is to him that the employers have entrusted the performance of their duty. The employers' liability to the plaintiff is also that of a tortfeasor. I use the word 'entrusted' in preference to the word 'delegated' which is commonly, but perhaps less accurately, used. Vicarious liability is sometimes described as a 'strict' liability. The use of this term is misleading unless it is used just to explain that there has been no *actual* fault on the part of the employers. The liability of the employers derives from their voluntary assumption of the relationship towards the plaintiff and the duties that arise from that relationship and their choosing to entrust the performance of those duties to their servant. Where these conditions are satisfied, the motive of the employee and the fact that he is doing something expressly forbidden and is serving only his own ends does not negative the vicarious liability for his breach of the 'delegated' duty . . . .

My Lords, the correct approach to answering the question whether the tortious act of the servant falls within or without the scope of the servant's employment for the purposes of the principle of vicarious liability is to ask what was the duty of the servant towards the plaintiff which was broken by the servant and what was the contractual duty of the servant towards his employer. The second limb of the classic *Salmond* test is a convenient rule of thumb which provides the answer in very many cases but does not represent the fundamental criterion which is the comparison of the duties respectively owed by the servant to the plaintiff and to his employer. Similarly, I do not believe that it is appropriate to follow the lead given by the Supreme Court of Canada in *Bazley v Curry*. The judgments contain a useful and impressive discussion of the social and economic reasons for having a principle of vicarious liability as part of the law of tort which extends to embrace acts of child abuse. But an exposition of the policy reasons for a rule (or even a description) is not the same as defining the criteria for its application. Legal rules have to have a greater degree of clarity and definition than is provided by simply explaining the reasons for the existence of the rule and the social need for it, instructive though that may be . . .

Lord Millett

Vicarious liability is a species of strict liability. It is not premised on any culpable act or omission on the part of the employer; an employer who is not personally at fault is made legally answerable for the fault of his employee. It is best understood as a loss-distribution device: (see Cane's edition of *Atiyah's Accidents, Compensation and the Law*, 6th ed (1999), p 85 and the articles cited by Atiyah in his monograph on *Vicarious Liability in the Law of Torts*, at p 24.) The theoretical underpinning of the doctrine is unclear. Glanville Williams wrote ('Vicarious Liability and the Master's Indemnity' (1957) 20 MLR 220, 231):

> Vicarious liability is the creation of many judges who have had different ideas of its justification or social policy, or no idea at all. Some judges may have extended the rule more widely, or confined it more narrowly than its true rationale would allow; yet the rationale, if we can discover it, will remain valid so far as it extends.

Fleming observed (*The Law of Torts*, 9th ed, p 410) that the doctrine cannot parade as a deduction from legalistic premises. He indicated that it should be frankly recognised as having its basis in a combination of policy considerations, and continued: 'Most important of these is the belief that a person who employs others to advance his own economic interest should in fairness be placed under a corresponding liability for losses incurred in the course of the enterprise . . .' Atiyah, *Vicarious Liability in the Law of Torts* wrote to the same effect. He suggested, at p 171: 'The master ought to be liable for all those torts which can fairly be regarded as reasonably incidental risks to the type of business he carries on.' These passages are not to be read as confining the doctrine to cases where the employer is carrying on business for profit. They are based on the more general idea that a person who employs another for his own ends inevitably creates a risk that the employee will commit a legal wrong. If the employer's objectives cannot be achieved without a serious risk of the employee committing the kind of wrong which he has in fact committed, the employer ought to be liable. The fact that his employment gave the employee the opportunity to commit the wrong is not enough to make the employer liable. He is liable only if the risk is one which experience shows is inherent in the nature of the business.

While this proposition has never, so far as I am aware, been adopted in so many words as a test of vicarious liability in any of the decided cases, it does I think form the unspoken rationale of the principle that the employer's liability is confined to torts committed by an employee in the course of his employment. The problem is that, as Townshend-Smith has observed (2000) 8 Tort L Rev 108, 111), none of the various tests which have been proposed to determine this essentially factual question is either intellectually satisfying or effective to enable the outcome of a particular case to be predicted. The danger is that in borderline situations, and especially in cases of intentional wrongdoing, recourse to a rigid and possibly inappropriate formula as a test of liability may lead the court to abandon the search for legal principle.

In the very first edition of his book on *Torts* Sir John Salmond wrote, at p 83:

> 1. A master is not responsible for a wrongful act done by his servant unless it is done in the course of his employment. It is deemed to be so done if it is either (a) a wrongful act authorised by the master, or (b) a wrongful and unauthorised *mode* of doing some act authorised by the master.

This passage has stood the test of time. It has survived unchanged for 21 editions, and has probably been cited more often than any other single passage in a legal textbook. Yet it is not without blemish. As has often been observed, the first of the two alternatives is not an example of vicarious liability at all. Its presence (and the word 'deemed') may be an echo of the discredited theory of implied authority. More pertinently, the second is not happily expressed if it is to serve as a test of vicarious liability for intentional wrongdoing.

In the present case the warden was employed to look after the boys in his care and secure their welfare. It is stretching language to breaking-point to describe the series of deliberate sexual assaults on them on which he embarked as merely a wrongful and unauthorised mode of performing that duty . . .

In a passage which is unfortunately less often cited, however, Sir John Salmond (Salmond, *Law of Torts*, 1st ed (1907)) continued his exposition as follows, at pp 83–84:

> But a master, as opposed to the employer of an independent contractor, is liable even for acts which he has not authorised, provided they are so connected with acts which he has authorised, that they may rightly be regarded as modes—although improper modes—of doing them.

One of these steps in this analysis could, I think, usefully be elided to impose vicarious liability where the unauthorised acts of the employee are so connected with acts which the employer has authorised that they may properly be regarded as being within the scope of his employment. Such a formulation would have the advantage of dispensing with the awkward reference to 'improper modes' of carrying out the employee's duties; and by focusing attention on the connection between the employee's duties and his wrongdoing it would accord with the underlying rationale of the doctrine and be applicable without straining the language to accommodate cases of intentional wrongdoing.

But the precise terminology is not critical. The *Salmond* test, in either formulation, is not a statutory definition of the circumstances which give rise to liability, but a guide to the principled application of the law to diverse factual situations. What is critical is that attention should be directed to the closeness of the connection between the employee's duties and his wrongdoing and not to verbal formulae. This is the principle on which the Supreme Court of Canada recently decided the important cases of *Bazley v Curry* 174 DLR (4th) 45 and *Jacobi v Griffiths* 174 DLR (4th) 71 which provide many helpful insights into this branch of the law and from which I have derived much assistance . . .

In the present case the warden's duties provided him with the opportunity to commit indecent assaults on the boys for his own sexual gratification, but that in itself is not enough to make the school liable. The same would be true of the groundsman or the school porter. But there was far more to it than that. The school was responsible for the care and welfare of the boys. It entrusted that responsibility to the warden. He was employed to discharge the school's responsibility to the boys. For this purpose the school entrusted them to his care. He did not merely take advantage of the opportunity which employment at a residential school gave him. He abused the special position in which the school had placed him to enable it to discharge its own responsibilities, with the result that the assaults were committed by the very employee to whom the school had entrusted the care of the boys. It is not necessary to conduct the detailed dissection of the warden's duties of the kind on which the Supreme Court of Canada embarked in *Bazley v Curry* and *Jacobi v Griffiths*. I would hold the school liable.

I would regard this as in accordance not only with ordinary principle deducible from the authorities but with the underlying rationale of vicarious liability. Experience shows that in the case of boarding schools, prisons, nursing homes, old people's homes, geriatric wards, and other residential homes for the young or vulnerable, there is an inherent risk that indecent assaults on the residents will be committed by those placed in authority over them, particularly if they are in close proximity to them and occupying a position of trust . . .

Lord Clyde delivered a separate speech agreeing that the appeal should be allowed. **Lord Hutton** agreed with Lord Steyn.

Appeal allowed.

COMMENTARY

In *Trotman v North Yorkshire County Council* [1999] LGR 584 the Court of Appeal refused to hold a special school vicariously liable for the sexual assaults of one its teachers on a dependant child who was mentally disabled and suffered from epilepsy. Relying on the *Salmond* test as traditionally understood, Butler-Sloss LJ thought the conduct of the teacher was a negation of the task of caring for the plaintiff, not an unauthorised mode of carrying out an authorised task. The House of Lords in *Lister* overruled *Trotman*, holding that the Court of Appeal had asked the wrong question. If it could be said that the act of the carer had a close connection with the employment this would be enough to impose liability. It should be noted, however, that the traditional interpretation—unauthorised mode of performing an authorised task—had been used, at least implicity, to sheet home liability to the employer where an employee stole goods that had been bailed to his employer (*Morris v Martin* [1966] 2 QB 716) or where a solicitor's clerk defrauded his employer's client for his own benefit (*Lloyd v Grace, Smith & Co* [1912] AC 716). In *Morris*, the plaintiff's mink coat was stolen by an employee of the sub-bailee of the coat to whom it had been given to clean. The Court of Appeal held the defendant employer liable for its employee's act, Lord Denning MR for breach of the employer's non-delegable duty as a bailee for reward to take care of the goods and not to do any act inconsistent with the rights of the owner, and Diplock and Salmon LJJ on the basis that the defendant was in breach of its duty to the bailor because of its employee's breach. The latter two judges explicitly (and Lord Denning implicitly) held that the position might have been different if the theft had been carried out by another employee, because the employment would have given that employee only the opportunity of carrying out the theft. Such an employee would not be acting in the course of his employment, unlike the employee to whom the coat was given to clean, even though the latter employee had carried out his employment in an unauthorised way (by stealing it).

After *Lister*, it now seems clear that the basis of this decision is vicarious liability. Whilst the *Salmond* 'unauthorised mode' was the dominant explanatory concept behind course of employment, *Morris v Martin* was hard to justify: in reality, liability was being imposed for giving the employee the opportunity to cause the harm, because only on a perverse view could stealing an object be regarded as a manner of cleaning it. However, the House of Lords in *Lister* stressed that the proper approach was to look at the connection between the employment and the tort. It was for this reason that it was important the employee who was employed to care for the children (or, in *Martin*, to clean the coat) committed the tort. However, it is clear that 'close connection' is a composite concept, involving not just physical proximity but also a consideration of the task the employee was performing, the causal relationship between that task and the tort, and ultimately (as Lord Nicholls pointed out in *Dubai Aluminium Co Ltd v Salaam* [2003] 2 AC 366) a value judgement as to whether vicarious liability should be imposed. Using these guidelines, several of their Lordships in *Lister* thought the result would be different if the assault had been committed by the gardener or school porter as the employment would only have provided such employees with the opportunity to commit the tort.

To a greater or lesser degree all of their Lordship in *Lister* thought the nature of the responsibility assumed by the employer to the claimant was relevant to the question of the former's vicarious liability. If this is correct, however, is it akin to imposing a non-delegable duty of care on the employer to ensure the responsibility is carried out? Giliker, 'Making the right connection: Vicarious liability and institutional philosophy' (2009) 17 TLJ 35 argues that this is not what was intended. Rather, the question is asked to determine the nature of the obligation with which the employee is entrusted as only certain sorts of obligation could give rise to vicarious liability for criminal acts (see also Yap, 'Enlisting close connections: a matter of course for vicarious liability' (2008) 28 LS 197, 200–1). In Giliker's view (pp. 53–4):

Vicarious liability for intentional torts should therefore only arise where the employee is entrusted with a protective or fiduciary discretion, that is, where the employee is entrusted to protect the employer's property, customers, employees, or specific individuals for whom the employer has taken responsibility.

If this was the case (as it was in *Lister*, where the employee had a protective discretion for a specific individual—the child—for whom the employer had taken responsibility), vicarious liability would arise where the act in question was undertaken in the purported exercise of the discretion. A broad notion of a protective or fiduciary discretion vested in the employee has also been used in Australia to determine when vicarious liability for a criminal act should be allowed (see Teague, 'Vicarious liability: A comparative review of the common law after *Ffrench*' (2008) 16 Tort L Rev 39). However, it does not assist the court in answering the second question Giliker poses: whether the act was done in the purported exercise of the discretion. Is it any less a misuse of language to say that abusing a child is an exercise of discretion in caring for the child than to say that it was an unauthorised mode of caring for him? While the extent of any relationship between the employer and the claimant may be relevant in determining whether it is the *type* of case where vicariously liability may be imposed for a criminal act, it does not of itself relieve the court from the task of deciding whether the closeness of connection between the act and the discretion is sufficient.

If the employee is entrusted with a protective or fiduciary duty towards the claimant, should this be sufficient of itself to impose vicarious liability for any acts of the employee which breach that duty? Criticising *Jacobi v Griffiths* (1999) 174 DLR (4th) 71, discussed below, Feldthusen (2001) 9 Tort L Rev 173 argues that in cases where the activity of the employer materially increased the risk of the sexual abuse occurring, the close connection test should be considered satisfied merely by the employee committing sexual abuse against the person to whom the duty was owed because the twin goals of deterrence and loss distribution, set out in *Bazley* would be satisfied. No further enquiry into the connection between the employee's sexual abuse and the employment was necessary. Do you agree with this approach?

The Application of the Close Connection Test outside *Lister*

In *New South Wales v Lepore* (2003) 212 CLR 511 the High Court of Australia divided over the value of the close connection test in determining vicarious liability for criminal conduct, and it must be admitted that *Lister* gives little guidance on how to apply the test outside the facts of the case (see Giliker, *op.cit.*). In *Dubai Aluminium Co Ltd v Salaam* [2003] 2 AC 366 Lord Nicholls noted that the best guide to its application would be previous court decisions (although, as his Lordship thought that the crucial feature or features either producing or negativing vicarious liability varied widely from one case or type of case to the next, the precedential value of previous authority must be limited). In *Bazley v Curry* (1999) 174 DLR (4th) 45, a decision of the Supreme Court of Canada referred to with approval in *Lister*, McLachlin J provided a number of factors to be taken into account: apart from the twin goals of loss-distribution and deterrence, the court should look at the extent to which the tort may have furthered the aims of the employer's enterprise; the extent to which friction, confrontation or intimacy between employees and the potential victims of their torts was inherent in the enterprise; the amount of power which employees had over potential victims by reason of their employment; and the level of vulnerability of potential victims to that power. Even with guidelines, however, it may be doubted whether the outcomes of cases can be predicted with any certainty. For example, in the companion case to *Bazley, Jacobi v Griffiths* (1999) 174 DLR (4th) 71, a majority of the Supreme Court of Canada refused to hold an employer vicariously liable for the acts of its employee. Unlike in *Bazley*, where the sexual abuse had taken place in the home run by the employer, the sexual assaults took place outside work hours and outside work premises. Similar reasoning was employed in *Maga v Roman Catholic Archdiocese of Birmingham* [2009] EWHC 780 (QB), an action against the defendant church for the alleged sexual abuse of a young adult by one of its priests. Although the priest had initially come into contact with the claimant through 'youth work', the association with the claimant arose through his use of the claimant to wash his car, do cleaning for him in the Presbytery and iron his clothes. Jack J held (at [100]) that the association 'was not part of evangelisation' and was not so closely connected with the priest's employment to make it fair and just to hold the church liable. Do you agree? Note that the Court of Appeal reached a different conclusion: [2010] EWCA Civ 256. For an example of these factors being applied outside the sexual abuse context see *Gravil v Carroll* [2008] EWCA Civ 689 where the Court of Appeal held the defendant rugby club liable for its employee player's punch which caused serious injury to an opposing player. Whilst the Court of Appeal stressed that the basis of liability remained the closeness of connection between the employment and the wrong, Sir Anthony Clarke MR (at [28]) noted that imposing vicarious liability would serve the goal of deterrence (the rugby club would be prompted to act to prevent or minimise the risk of foul play) and providing an adequate and just remedy (as clubs would be better placed that individual players to obtain insurance against liability of this kind). Would the same reasoning have justified imposing vicarious liability if a player took offence at the comments of a spectator and hit him on the spur of the moment?

The problem with the broad factors that now determine liability in this area of vicarious liability, however, is that is that their application can easily lead to different conclusions. As Weekes [2004] CLJ 53, 61 argues: 'Where any of the above factors [sc.as set out by McLachlin J] has met divergent judicial opinion and generated conflicting precedent, this is because the courts have disagreed as to its significance in policy terms for determining the imposition of vicarious liability.' A good example is *Jacobi* itself, where, speaking for the majority of the Supreme Court of Canada, Binnie J doubted whether the imposition of liability on the employer, a non-profit organisation, would lead to equitable loss-spreading or that imposing liability would act as a deterrent; it might, in fact, result in over-deterrence by encouraging the closure of this kind of charity. Is this disagreement just an inevitable by-product of the nature of vicarious liability? Commenting on *Bazley* and *Jacobi*, Cane (2000) 116 LQR 21 at 25 writes: 'At the end of the day, the judge must decide, on the facts of the case before the court, whether the connection between the employee's tort and the employer's activity was close enough to justify holding the employer vicariously liable. To this extent, at least, judicial decision-making in such cases is irreducibly "pragmatic".'

Although motive has been disregarded as the sole test for deciding whether an employee's act is in the course of employment, it may still be a relevant factor in deciding if there is a close connection between the tort and the employment. Prior to *Lister*, where employers had been held vicariously liable for prima facie unlawful acts of their employees the acts had normally been done in the employer's interest, a contrast being drawn with cases where the employee's act was one of personal vengeance (*Poland v John Parr* [1927] 1 KB 236; *Vasey v Surrey Free Inns plc*, CA Civil Division, 5 May 1995; cf. *Warren v Henlys Ltd* [1948] 2 All ER 932). In the post-*Lister* case of *Mattis v Pollock* [2003] 1 WLR 2158, the Court of Appeal held that the employer was liable for the act of the employee doorman when returning to the nightclub to assault a patron, having previously gone home to collect a knife. In truth, it is difficult to see the employee's conduct as serving the employer's interests as opposed to being a private act of vengeance, but post-*Lister* there is no reason why private acts of vengeance should necessarily be excluded. The question is simply the closeness of the connection between the act and the employment; in *Mattis* the employee was authorised to use some violence to maintain order, and his conduct was sufficiently connected with the exercise of that authority so as to justify imposing vicarious liability even if, as seems unarguable, the attack was motivated by personal spite. But personal motives retain some relevance; in *N v Chief Constable of Merseyside Police* [2006] EWHC 3041 (QB), the defendant police authority was held not to be vicariously liable for the sexual assaults of a probationary constable even though the constable was wearing full uniform and abused this position to carry out the assaults. Unlike *Mattis*, the constable was off-duty at the time and outside the area where he regularly worked; in these circumstances one reason for holding that the acts did not bear a close connection to the employment was that he was pursuing 'his own misguided personal aims' (cf. *Attorney General v Hartwell* [2004] UKPC 12; *Bernard v Attorney General of Jamaica* [2005] IRLR 398).

It is difficult to resist the conclusion that many of the above decisions are based on the court's perception of the justice or otherwise of allowing the plaintiff to recover—a conclusion that might be equally apt to describe much of the law relating to vicarious liability. For comment on the 'assault' cases, see Rose, 'Liability for an Employee's Assaults' (1977) 40 MLR 420. Do you agree with the author of this article that, although the claimant should not benefit merely because his assailant has an employer, 'there seems to be no reason why he should not benefit in cases where it can be considered justifiable to impose liability on an employer whether for reasons of compensation, deterrence, loss distribution...'? If these are the factors that liability is in fact based on, why should courts continue to go through the charade of determining whether an act was in the course of employment at all? Would explicitly addressing these issues lead to a more principled, better informed debate as to the circumstances in which an employer should bear the costs of an employee's civil liability? (See Stevens (2006) 122 LQR 201.)

It should be noted that whether an employee's act is within the course of employment may vary in statutory contexts. In *Jones v Tower Boot Co* [1997] 2 All ER 395 the complainant sued for racial discrimination under the Race Relations Act 1976, which makes employers liable for racial abuse by their employees carried out in the course of employment. The Court of Appeal held that, as a matter of statutory construction, the term 'the course of employment' was not to be given the same meaning as it bears in the common law of vicarious liability; in this context, looking at the purpose of the 1976 Act, the term bore a wider meaning than at common law.

IV. Primary Liability and Liability for Agents and Non-Employees

1. Primary Liability

Turberville v Stampe (1697) 1 Ld Raym 264, 91 ER 1072

The court was considering the liability arising out of a fire negligently lit by a servant.

> **Holt CJ**
>
> [I]f a stranger set fire to my house, and it burns my neighbour's house, no action will lie against me.... But if my servant throws dirt into the highway, I am indictable. So in this case if the defendant's servant kindled the fire in the way of husbandry and proper for his employment, though he had no express command of his master, yet his master shall be liable to an action for damage done to another by the fire; for it shall be intended, that the servant had authority from his master, it being for the master's benefit.

COMMENTARY

If the master had commanded the servant to perform the act in a negligent way, the master would be liable, not under the principles of vicarious liability, but as a primary tortfeasor, that is, based on the master himself committing a tort. This principle would apply to anyone who commanded another to commit a tort. This case of 'express command' is widened in the extracted case by Holt CJ to 'implied command', that is, the servant had implied authority to carry out acts that were 'proper for his employment'. As *Winfield & Jolowicz* notes (para. 20–2), in time the term 'implied authority' gave way to 'scope of employment' signalling the arrival of the modern doctrine of vicarious liability.

The development of a true 'secondary' vicarious liability, however, has not affected liability as a principal or primary tortfeasor. Thus liability as a principal extends to those who conspire with, procure, authorise or induce another to commit a tort, and also to those who have joined in a common design pursuant to which the tort was committed (*Crédit Lyonnais Bank Nederland NV v Export Credit Guarantee Corporation* [2000] 1 AC 486; Carty (1999) 19 LS 489). What conduct will amount to 'joining in a common design' is less clear. In *Brooke v Bool* [1928] 2 KB 578 the defendant requested M to help him search for a gas leak. M did this by illuminating a gas pipe with a naked flame, causing an explosion. The defendant had previously searched a lower part of the pipe in this way. One ground on which the defendant was held liable was that M's negligence (which constituted a tort) was committed as part of a joint enterprise with the defendant.

2. Liability for Torts of Agents

Although the results produced can be similar, the legal concept of agency is both narrower and wider than that of vicarious liability. It is narrower in the sense that the law of agency is primarily concerned with the circumstances in which one party may enter into a binding contract on behalf of another, whilst vicarious liability is concerned with acts done in the course of employment, a much wider concept. On the other hand, a person who performs a task on behalf of another (which may have nothing to do with binding the principal to any contract made by the agent) can also be described as an 'agent' of that other, irrespective of whether there is an employer–employee relationship.

Whilst vicarious liability restricts the acts for which the employer may be liable to those within the course of employment, the law of agency uses a different limitation—that of authority. A principal will only be liable for torts committed by an agent within the actual or ostensible authority of that agent, but the converse does not necessarily follow; all that can be said with certainty is that torts committed by an agent within authority may make the principal liable. There can, however, be an overlap between vicarious liability and agency. A principal may be liable if an agent commits a tort in the course of entering a contract which he has the principal's authority to enter, but it is equally the case that, assuming an employer–employee relationship exists, the agent's action will be within the course of employment, and hence the principal is also liable under the rules relating to vicarious liability. Whether a principal is generally liable for the torts of a non-employee agent acting within authority is a difficult question beyond the scope of this chapter (see Atiyah, *Vicarious Liability* (London: Butterworths, 1967), ch. 9), but where there is an employer–employee relationship, as a general rule it can be asserted that the liability of the principal by the law of agency is simply a specific application of the more general rules of vicarious liability (see *Armagas Ltd v Mundogas SA* [1986] AC 717; *HSBC v Soh* [2009] EWCA Civ 296). It is for this reason that courts confronted with this issue sometimes use the terms interchangeably. But the difference between the concepts should be kept in mind: an employee who negligently injures another whilst working for his employer is not an agent of the employer in the sense above (although note *Morgans v Launchberry* [1973] AC 127, below) but the employer will none the less be liable if the conditions for the imposition of vicarious liability are established.

There is, however, another situation where an agency relationship may be created at a more general level. The grounds on which a person may be held to be the agent of another for a particular purpose are difficult to state with certainty and have led to some confusion over whether such liability is a primary or secondary liability. In *Scarsbrook v Mason* [1961] 3 All ER 767 the defendant passenger was held liable for the negligent driving of the car's driver even though he had not incited or procured it. The purpose of the journey was a pleasure trip to Southend and to assist this purpose the defendant contributed 4 shillings towards the cost of petrol. Although some have viewed the case as an example of liability for a tort committed as part of a joint enterprise (Atiyah, *Vicarious Liability*, 124), Glyn-Jones J decided that the driver was the agent of the passengers (including the defendant) so it seems the liability was secondary rather than the primary liability which attaches to joint participants. The distinction is important and is recognised by Glanville Williams, *Joint Torts and Contributory Negligence* (London: Stevens, 1951) where, in considering examples of joint liability, agency/vicarious liability is distinguished from joint enterprise liability. In *Scarsbrook*, whilst the liability of the passenger may be described as being joint, this should not be confused with a primary liability: the passenger was jointly (and severally) liable in the sense of being liable as well as the driver, but his liability arose from another's (the driver's) wrong in which he was not a participant; hence the liability is secondary (and different from the primary liability attaching to participants in a joint enterprise).

Whether there were any grounds on which to hold the driver the agent of all the passengers is another matter (see *S v Walsall Metropolitan Borough Council* [1985] 1 WLR 1150), but the idea of the driver of a vehicle being the agent of another for this specific purpose has a respectable lineage (Atiyah, *Vicarious Liability*, ch. 13; *Ormrod v Crosville Motor Services Ltd* [1953] 1 WLR 1120; cf. *Scott v Davis* (2000) 204 CLR 333, where Gummow J of the High Court of Australia thought the doctrine was based on a misunderstanding of nineteenth-century cases). In *Morgans v Launchbury* [1973] AC 127 the defendant's husband died in a car crash in which several other passengers were injured. The car was owned by the defendant but was used by her husband to drive to work, but at the time of the accident it was being driven by a friend of her husband as her husband had consumed too much alcohol to drive safely and so had asked the friend to drive him home. The defendant was at home at the time of the accident and had no knowledge of any of the events leading up to it, but it was held that there was an understanding between the defendant and her husband that he would not drive if he had had too much to drink. A majority of the Court of Appeal ([1971] 2 QB 245) held the wife liable as the driver was her agent for the purpose of driving her husband home. Lord Denning MR held that the owner of a car was responsible at common law for all injury or damage done as a result of negligent driving by a driver whom he had permitted to use it, and could only be excused if the car was being driven by the driver on an occasion on which the owner had no interest and for which no permission had been given. He also held that, in relation to secondary liability, the words 'principal' and 'agent' did not bear the connotation which they have in the law of contract or in the business community but were used as short-hand to denote the circumstances in which secondary liability was imposed. However, the House of Lords held that to establish the existence of an agency relationship it was necessary to show that the driver was using the car at the owner's request, express or implied, or on his instructions, and was doing so in performance of the task or duty thereby delegated to him by the owner. Using the car with the owner's permission for a purpose in which the owner had an interest or concern was not sufficient to establish vicarious liability. Hence neither her husband when driving to work nor his friend when driving at the time of the accident was the agent of the defendant. That this kind of agency is different from the traditional principal–agent relationship is illustrated by the speech of Lord Wilberforce (at 135):

> I accept entirely that agency in contexts such as these is merely a concept, the meaning and purpose of which is to say 'is vicariously liable' and that either expression reflects a judgment of value—*respondeat superior* is the law saying that the owner ought to pay.

The utility of using a concept that has an established meaning in one branch of the law (that of contract) for the purpose of imposing vicarious liability may be doubted (see Reynolds (2001) 117 LQR 180; Handford (2001) 9 Tort L Rev 97; Del Pont, 'Agency: definitional challenges through the law of tort' (2003) 11 TLJ 68). Certainly there is no general rule that someone who performs a task at the request and for the benefit of another is that person's agent so as to impose liability on the requestor. Whilst agreeing that the term 'agency' is inappropriate, Stevens (2006) 122 LQR 201, 205 has argued that the recognition of dual vicarious liability—which may make a person liable as an employer even if there is no formal contract of service with the worker—supports a general principle of attribution where one person carries out a task for the benefit of another, at least where there is an element of control by the beneficiary over the identity and conduct of the person carrying out the task. However, it may be doubted whether the Court of Appeal in *Viasystems* (extracted above, p. 827) would have reached the same conclusion if the worker had not been an employee of *anyone*. The reasoning in that case reflects the pragmatism of vicarious liability: a formal transfer of the worker's contract of employment does not determine of itself whether the original or the new employer is vicariously responsible for the torts of the employee. Accordingly, we remain of the view that the cases involving motor vehicles are best seen as pragmatic attempts to ensure that victims of road accidents receive compensation from an insured party, although in practice the circumstances in which it will be necessary to resort to the owner of the vehicle as opposed to the driver will be rare (Atiyah, *Vicarious Liability*, pp. 134–5, *Winfield & Jolowicz*, para. 20–20). This was the view of the High Court of Australia in *Scott v Davis* (2000) 204 CLR 333, where the majority refused to extend the doctrine to an aeroplane in circumstances where it appeared that the owner of the plane neither had insurance cover for the accident for which the plaintiff claimed nor was required to by law. The absurdity of extending the case law to its logical conclusion is shown by the Irish case of *Moynihan v Moynihan* [1975] IR 192, where the owner of a teapot was held vicariously liable for her daughter's negligence in pouring tea. For comment on *Scott*, see Reynolds (2001) 117 LQR 180, and Handford (2001) 9 Tort L Rev 97.

3. Non-Delegable Duty of Care

Although an employer–employee relationship is required before the employer can be made vicariously liable for the employee's torts, in certain circumstances the employer may also be held liable for the acts of a non-employee. The nature of the employer's liability in these circumstances is far from clear. Sometimes it is based on agency. It may also be based on the imposition of a non-delegable duty of care placed on the employer in respect of the activity that has been or is about to be carried out. In *Alcock v Wraith & Others* (1991) 59 BLR 16 Neill LJ recognised seven situations in which non-delegable duties had been imposed: (1) statutory duties that could not be delegated; (2) withdrawal of support from neighbouring land; (3) escape of fire; (4) liability under the rule in *Rylands v Fletcher*; (5) operations on the highway which may cause danger to persons using the highway; (6) non-delegable duties of an employer for the safety of his employees; and (7) cases involving extra-hazardous acts.

One area omitted from this list is the liability of hospitals to patients for the negligence of non-employees, a liability that found some support from, amongst others, Denning LJ (as he then was) in *Cassidy v Ministry of Health* [1951] 2 KB 342 and *Roe v Minister of Health* [1954] 2 QB 66. This question, and the nature of non-delegable duties, is considered in the following extract.

Farraj v King's Healthcare NHS Trust [2009] EWCA Civ 1203

The claimants were the parents of a child born with a genetic disability. To avoid this possibility, the claimants' doctor in Jordan had sent a sample from the mother for testing to the first defendant, KCH Healthcare NHS Trust ("KCH"), to determine if the foetus carried the offending gene. The first defendant had doubts whether the sample was suitable for testing and sent it to the second defendant ("CSL"), a cytogenics laboratory, for further foetal cells to be cultured from the sample. Although the second defendant's employee had doubts as to whether foetal (as opposed to maternal) cells had been cultured, these doubts were not communicated to KCH, with the result that KCH in fact tested maternal cells and communicated, inaccurately, a test result that the gene was not present in the foetus. The claimants sued both defendants and were successful against both at first instance. The Court of Appeal allowed KCH's appeal against the finding that it was negligent. The extract is concerned with the claimant's alternative argument that KCL was under a non-delegable duty in respect of its testing of the sample.

Dyson LJ

67. It is the claimants' case that KCH owed them a personal non-delegable duty of care and that KCH is liable for the negligence of CSL, despite the fact that KCH is not criticised for having delegated the task of cleaning and culturing the sample or having delegated that task to CSL. Thus, it is said, KCH is liable to the claimants for the shortcomings in CSL's performance even though CSL was reputable and experienced and ran a laboratory which was apparently competent to undertake the task entrusted to it by KCH...

[Dyson LJ considered a number of authorities, including *Cassidy* and *Roe*, mentioned above, and continued:]

88. I am prepared to assume (without deciding) . . . that English law has now reached the stage that the approach advocated by . . . Denning LJ should be adopted. It is true that the extent to which a hospital owes a non-delegable duty to ensure that its patients are treated with due skill and care will depend on the facts of the particular case. But I shall assume that a hospital generally owes a non-delegable duty to its patients to ensure that they are treated with skill and care regardless of the employment status of the person who is treating them . . . [T]he rationale for this is that the hospital undertakes the care, supervision and control of its patients who are in special need of care. Patients are a vulnerable class of persons who place themselves in the care and under the control of a hospital and, as a result, the hospital assumes a particular responsibility for their well-being and safety. To use the language of *Caparo Industries plc v Dickman* [1990] 2 AC 605, 618 it is therefore fair, just and reasonable that a hospital should owe such a duty of care to its patients in these circumstances . . .

92. Even on the assumption that I have made as to the effect of the hospital cases, I do not consider that they justify the conclusion that, on the facts of this case, KCH owed the claimants a non-delegable duty to ensure that CSL carried out the task entrusted to it with due skill and care. I do not accept that it follows from the fact that KCH is a hospital that the jurisprudence to be found in the hospital cases should be applied. The claimants were not admitted to KCH for treatment. KCH has at all material times provided diagnostic and interpretative services for chorionic villus sampling. But there is no reason to suppose that these services could not have been provided by a specialist laboratory or testing house rather than a hospital. In my judgment, there is a significant difference between treating a patient who is admitted to hospital for that purpose and carrying out tests on samples which are provided by a person who is a patient. Such tests are not necessarily carried out in a hospital. The special duty that exists between a patient and a hospital arises because the hospital undertakes the care, supervision and control of persons who, as patients, are in special need of care. I accept that, if a patient who is admitted to hospital for treatment has tests carried out in the hospital, then the non-delegable duty of care, which for present purposes I am assuming to exist, would extend to the carrying out of the tests. But that is because the conducting of the tests is part of the treatment that the patient is receiving in the hospital.

93. The general rule is an important feature of our law of negligence. It recognises that the duty to take reasonable care may be discharged by entrusting the performance of a task to an apparently competent independent contractor . . . In my view, any departure from the general rule must be justified on policy grounds. If the position were to be otherwise, there is a danger that the general rule would become the exception rather than the rule. As I understand it, that is not our law.

94. There is no basis for finding that a special duty was owed by KCH to the claimants in this case. There are no policy reasons for departing from the general rule here. The claimants were not being treated by KCH. Mrs Farraj was receiving treatment from the King Hussein Medical Centre in Amman. There is not even any evidence that the claimants were aware that Dr Batayneh was sending or had sent the sample to KCH. KCH did not undertake any special responsibilities to the claimants (such as those undertaken by employers to their employees, hospitals to the patients whom they treat and schools to the children who are placed in their care) . . .

Sedley LJ delivered a short concurring judgment. **Smith LJ** agreed with both Dyson and Sedley LJJ.

Appeal allowed; cross-appeal dismissed

COMMENTARY

The 'general rule' referred to by the Court of Appeal is that when a duty of care is imposed on a defendant it can ordinarily be discharged by carefully selecting someone to discharge it on the defendants' behalf. That was KCH's argument in *Farraj*: as they did not have the expertise to culture the sample to produce extra cells (and might have been careless if they had tried) they were not in breach of any duty owed to the claimants by sending it out to a reputable specialist laboratory to perform that task. In accepting this argument, the Court of Appeal manifested a reluctance to extend non-delegable duties beyond existing categories and was able to decide the case without affirming that the hospital–patient relationship was one such category. A similar reluctance exists to expand their application beyond negligence. Although there are examples of non-delegable duties being imposed for torts other than negligence (see Witting, 'Breach of the Non-Delegable Duty: Defending Limited Strict Liability in Tort' (2006) 29 UNSWLJ 33), many of the cases involve the imposition of a non-delegable *duty of care* so that liability arises only where the non-employee has been careless. Moreover, there is authority that a non-delegable duty only extends to negligence by the independent contractor in carrying out that duty and does not extend to collateral negligence. *Salmond & Heuston* (p. 466) argue that the rule as to collateral negligence probably

means nothing more than that the negligence required to impose liability upon the employer of an independent contractor must be negligence committed in the doing of the act itself which he is employed to do. . . . If this is all that 'collateral negligence' means, it is only an obscure way of saying that an employer is only liable for acts which are within the scope of the contractor's authority— which is obvious, but unhelpful in any particular case.

If collateral acts of *negligence* can take the contractor outside the scope of a non-delegable duty, it is difficult to see how deliberately wrongful acts by the contractor could be within the scope of such a duty (cf. Section III.4 above). Ceretainly modern attempts to extend the doctrine to other torts have met with little success (see, e.g., the refusal of the majority of the High Court of Australia in *New South Wales v Lepore* (2003) 212 CLR 511 to impose a non-delegable duty in respect of intentional conduct; for criticism see White and Orr (2003) 11 TLJ 101).

Critics of liability for non-delegable duties have referred to it as 'a disguised form of vicarious liability': *Fleming*, p. 433. Others, however, have stressed the differences between conventional vicarious liability and liability for non-delegable duties; amongst other things, vicarious liability does not require the employer to owe an independent duty to the victim, an essential ingredient of liability for many non-delegable duties (see Stevens, 'Non-Delegable Duties and Vicarious Liability' and Murphy, 'Juridical Foundations of Common Law Non-Delegable Duties', both in Neyers, Chamberlain and Pitell (eds), *Emerging Issues in Tort Law* (Oxford: Hart, 2007), chs 13 and 14 respectively). Some of this disagreement stems from the different meanings of 'vicarious liability': undoubtedly breach of a non-delegable duty is—by definition—a different liability from that of an employer for the tort of an employee, but, equally, the primary role of non-delegable duties has been to make one party liable for the wrongdoing of another where the original party has not been at fault, a result which imposes a form of vicarious liability on that party. Whether vicarious liability—in the narrow sense of an employer's liability for the tort of an employee—and liability for breach of non-delegable duties share more than a functional equivalence is a more difficult question but there are at least some other similarities: the exercise of due care in the selection of the employee, or of the person to whom the task is delegated, does not prevent liability, and in both cases the conduct of the employee or delegate must be wrongful to establish liability on the employer. Additionally, as Sedley LJ explicitly pointed out in *Farraj*, at [99]–[103], historically the theory of non-delegable duties developed very substantially as a means of providing for an employer's liability for the negligence of an employee in cases where vicarious liability was precluded by the (now abolished) defence of common employment (see pp. 549, above).

Stevens, above, suggests that breach of a non-delegable duty can be present in two-party cases (involving just the party on whom the duty is imposed and the victim) hence wrongful conduct by a delegate is not an essential part of the claim, but it may be wondered why the non-delegable nature of the duty is of any importance in these cases; the question is not whether the duty can be delegated—it has not been—but whether the duty imposed on the party has been discharged. Thus, if a stranger enters school premises and abuses a child pupil, the liability of the school is not dependent on any question of delegation (unless security has been delegated to an independent contractor) but simply on whether the school has exercised reasonable care to protect the students, which may include the implemention of a system to ensure the security of the school grounds (cf. Stevens, above, p. 364).

Is liability for breach of a non-delegable duty an independent tort? Witting (*op. cit.*) argues that it is, although the duties it protects are derived from negligence and nuisance. Such an approach clearly differentiates the action from vicarious liability but it requires an acceptance that the duties recognised by this new tort are substantively different from the underlying torts which have formed the bases of these actions in the past (such as negligence and nuisance). However, although one function of the action for breach of a non-delegable duty is to 'respond to the inadequacies in the reach of negligence' (Witting, p. 39) it does so by extending the *class* of persons who can be sued for the tort of negligence rather than to protect a new kind of duty, and in this it mirrors closely the aim of vicarious liability. The 'independent tort' approach did not appeal to Kirby J in *Leichhardt Municipal Council v Montgomery* (2007) 81 ALJR 686 at [73].

The significance of finding a non-delegable duty of care is that, as Dyson LJ points out in the extract, any negligence by a person employed to discharge that duty, be it servant or independent contractor, in attempting to discharge the duty amounts to a breach of the duty by the employer. The breach of such a duty is a personal wrong by the employer. Many of the categories of non-delegable duties date from the nineteenth century and apply to narrow categories, established for a specific purpose to overcome a perceived injustice in the law. For example, the non-delegable duty owed by an employer to his employees arose as a way of avoiding the harsh consequences of the 'common employment' rule (see Ch. 11). A similar concern could justify the non-delegable duty imposed on hospitals, for it would seem arbitrary to allow the claimant an action against the hospital when the negligence was that of an employee but not where an independent consultant (for example) was involved, especially where, as Dyson LJ noted, it is the *hospital* that has assumed an obligation to treat the patient. However, it seems the non-delegable duty in relation to testing only applies to patients actually admitted to hospital for treatment and where the tests are carried out in the hospital (see [92]). Even if the non-delegable duty is to be limited to those admitted to hospital, it hard to see why the location of the testing should make a difference. Why is testing not regarded as part of the treatment for which the hospital has assumed an obligation to the patient? (Cf. Sedley LJ at [103] who thought the provision of analytical and diagnostic laboratory services did not fit the paradigm of patient and healthcare provider). Alternatively, do you think that this category of non-delegable duty would impose too great a liability on hospitals unless this kind of arbitrary line is drawn? Do you think this concern influenced the Court of Appeal?

The most open-ended of the cases where non-delegable duties have been imposed relates to the performance of extra-hazardous activities. Exactly what this category embraces is considered below.

Glanville Williams, 'Liability for Independent Contractors'
[1956] CLJ 180

If the doctrine of non-delegable duty is no reason for, or even limitation of, vicarious liability for contractors, the jurist is faced with the task of finding some rule underlying a series of decisions when no such rule was expressed in them. Most of the nineteenth century cases can be restrictively explained as turning on the creation of dangers in the highway.... Yet even this explanation, though perhaps the best that can be done, leaves the law fundamentally incomprehensible. Almost the greatest danger that can be created on the highway is to drive an automobile along it; yet there is no vicarious liability for the negligence of a contractor in his manner of driving. Were it otherwise, a person who posted a letter would be liable for the negligent driving of the Post-Office employee who is carrying the letter; and the passengers on a bus would be vicariously liable for their driver....

[After considering some cases involving statutory functions, he continued:]

Irrespective of statutory power or duty, there is now vicarious liability wherever a contractor is employed to perform what Slesser LJ in *Honeywill & Stein v Larkin Bros* [1934] 1 KB 102 called 'extra-hazardous or dangerous operations'. The liability was held in that case to exist where a photographer was employed to take a flashlight picture in a theatre, the magnesium flash causing a fire in which the theatre suffered damage. It seems rather remarkable to regard the taking of an indoor photograph, even with magnesium powder, as 'extra-hazardous or dangerous'; of course it would be dangerous if performed negligently, but is that fact sufficient to create liability for contractors? The equation of 'extra hazardous' and 'dangerous' is also worthy of remark. One would think that 'hazardous' and 'dangerous' are synonyms; if so, 'extra-hazardous' must mean something specially dangerous. Even if one goes so far as to say that the use of flashlight powder is 'dangerous', it is hyperbolical to describe it as 'extra-hazardous'. If this is extra-hazardous, we are left with no language to describe really dangerous conduct...

Surveying these various instances of liability for contractors, it may be said generally that the law is quite unduly difficult to apply, and divided against itself without any reason. The concept of 'extra-hazardous acts' is not a suitable one for legal rules; the distinction between delegable and nondelegable duties means that the whole law of negligence must be covered by specific judicial decision (often with changes of judicial mind) before the extent of liability can be stated...

COMMENTARY

The unsatisfactory nature of a non-delegable duty for extra-hazardous activities led the Court to Appeal in *Biffa Waste Services Ltd v Maschinenfabrik Ernst Hese GMBH* [2009] QB 725 to hold that its application should be kept as narrow as possible and applied only to activities that are exceptionally dangerous whatever precautions are taken. Commenting on the case, Stanton (2009) 17 Tort L Rev 9, 12 notes:

[H]oneywill is confined to the rare (and probably non-existent) category of cases in relation to which proper precautions fail to reduce the risk below that of being 'exceptionally dangerous'. It thus becomes arguable that, to take an extreme example, conducting maintenance work on a nuclear reactor is not an extra-hazardous activity such as would invoke the Honeywill principle because proper precautions can be taken which eliminate or minimize the risks. In essence, Honeywill has been distinguished out of existence rather than being overruled.

A less controversial application of non-delegable duties relates to fires. As long ago as 1401 it was held that the occupier of land was responsible for a fire lit by himself, his servants, or his guests (*Beaulieu v Finglam*, extracted in Baker and Milsom, *Sources of English Legal History* (London: Butterworths, 1986), p. 557). As *Baker* postulates, 'Perhaps the standard [of care] varied in fact from one type of case to another; fire was particularly feared in a world of timber-framed buildings' (p. 408). Whether the reasons for the rule still apply is arguable, but it has been applied in recent times (*H. & N. Emmanuel Ltd v Greater London Council* [1971] 2 All ER 835). In *Balfour v Barty King* [1957] 1 QB 496 the defendant employed independent contractors to unfreeze some pipes, but they did so negligently with the result that a fire was started which damaged the plaintiff's adjoining premises. Even though the contractors were not employed to light a fire (indeed the negligence consisted in using a blow-torch in close proximity to flammable material), the Court of Appeal held the defendant liable for the contractor's negligence in starting a fire. Would the same result have been reached if, in attempting to unfreeze the pipes, the contractors had negligently caused them to burst, flooding the claimant's property. If so, why?

The most important context in which non-delegable duties operate today lies in the employer's duties to an employee, on which see Chapter 11.

Some attempts have been made to identify a common thread in cases where a non-delegable duty of care has been held to exist. In *Burnie Port Authority v General Jones Pty Ltd* (1994) 179 CLR 520, a majority of the Australian High Court held that in most cases where a non-delegable duty was imposed, '[i]t will be convenient to refer to [the] common element as "the central element of control". Viewed from the perspective of the person to whom the duty is owed, the relationship of proximity giving rise to the non-delegable duty of care in such cases is marked by special dependence or vulnerability on the part of that person' (at 346). In the context of occupiers (the position of the defendants in *Burnie*), this meant that a person who took advantage of the control of premises to introduce a dangerous substance, to carry on a dangerous activity, or to allow another to do one of those things, owed a duty of reasonable care which extended to ensuring that care was taken. However, if this is correct, a non-expert home-owner who employs an electrician to carry out repairs to faulty electrical wiring which, if the repairs are done negligently, might foreseeably cause damage to another, is under a non-delegable duty, yet, if he does nothing, might also be liable for failing to make the repairs. Does this put the homeowner in an impossible position? The result might be avoided by arguing that the electrician's task is not a dangerous activity, but, as critics have noted, most jobs carried out with care are not dangerous *per se*; conversely any task done with negligence poses danger. Perhaps it is not surprising that a later decision of the Australian High Court (*Northern Sandblasting Pty Ltd v Harris* (1997) 188 CLR 313) found, by majority, that a landlord did not owe a non-delegable duty of care to a tenant in respect of electrical repair work to the premises carried out by an electrician.

Do you think dependence or vulnerability are suitable factors on which to establish a non-delegable duty of care? See further Murphy (*op. cit.*), who argues that where the defendant's enterprise creates a substantial risk to the class of which the claimant is a member, and where the defendant has assumed a positive responsibility to protect the claimant from harm, a non-delegable duty of care might be imposed (a view accepted by Kirby J of the High Court of Australia in *Leichhardt Municipal Council v Montgomery* (2007) 230 CLR 22 at [117]–[121]).

16 DAMAGES FOR PERSONAL INJURY

I. Introduction

The tortious infliction of injury to another person is remedied by the award of damages by way of compensation. Damages are not the only weapon to be found in the law's remedial armoury, but in the tort context they are the principal remedy (although in some contexts, e.g. a continuing nuisance or a threatened defamation, the award of an injunction may be of greater significance: see Chs 12.II.5 and 13.V.2 respectively). The normal measure of damages is the compensatory measure, but other types of damages may also be awarded.

II. Different Types of Damages

1. Compensatory Damages

According to Lord Scarman, 'the principle of the law is that compensation should as nearly as possible put the party who has suffered in the same position as he would have been in if he had not sustained the wrong' (*Lim v Camden & Islington Area Health Authority* [1980] AC 174 at 187). The law's object here is sometimes described using the Latin phrase *restitutio in integrum* (indicating an attempt to restore the claimant to a 'whole' state), but this threatens to obscure the important distinction between compensation, which seeks to replace something that the claimant has lost, and restitution, which forces the defendant to give up something gained at the claimant's expense (see further, below). Compensatory damages focus upon the claimant's loss rather than the defendant's gain.

2. Restitutionary Damages

Restitutionary damages, by way of contrast, do focus on the defendant's gain. They oblige the defendant to give up some benefit—an 'unjust enrichment'—which he has derived at the expense of the claimant. The most notable examples of the law of tort awarding damages of a restitutionary nature are the torts of trespass to land and conversion (not covered in this book). Thus if a person steals a car from its owner (an act which would constitute the tort of conversion by the thief) and uses it to conduct a mini-cab business, the owner would be able to claim damages based on the profits made by the thief in using the car rather than having to prove he had suffered any loss from being deprived of it. However, the scope for the award of restitutionary damages in the modern law of tort is a matter of some debate that is beyond the scope of this book (see further Law Commission, *Aggravated, Exemplary and Restitutionary Damages* (Law Com. No. 247, 1997); J. Edelman, *Gain-Based Damages* (Oxford: OUP, 2002); Rotherham, 'The Conceptual Structure of Restitution for Wrongs' [2007] CLJ 172).

3. Exemplary or Punitive Damages

Although the award of damages in the law of tort serves a primarily compensatory purpose, the court may exceptionally seek to punish (or make an example of) the defendant by the award of exemplary or punitive damages. The jurisdiction to award such damages dates back at least to the eighteenth century: two cases arising out of the printing of the radical newspaper, the *North Briton*, provide noteworthy examples (see *Wilkes v Wood* (1763) Lofft 1; *Huckle v Money* (1763) 2 Wils 205). The award of exemplary damages against agents of the State served to reinforce the courts' affirmation of the rule of law in the course of the same saga (*Entick v Carrington* (1765) 19 State Tr 1029). The old authorities were analysed and categorised in the influential speech of Lord Devlin in *Rookes v Barnard*, extracted below. This is the starting point for any discussion of the availability of exemplary damages in the modern law.

(a) The Current Law

Rookes v Barnard [1964] AC 1129

The facts of this case—which arose out of an industrial dispute—are not relevant for present purposes.

Lord Devlin

[T]here are certain categories of cases in which an award of exemplary damages can serve a useful purpose in vindicating the strength of the law and thus affording a practical justification for admitting into the civil law a principle which ought logically to belong to the criminal. I propose to state what these two categories are; and I propose also to state three general considerations which, in my opinion, should always be borne in mind when awards of exemplary damages are being made. I am well aware that what I am about to say will, if accepted, impose limits not hitherto expressed on such awards and that there is powerful, though not compelling, authority for allowing them a wider range...

   The first category is oppressive, arbitrary or unconstitutional action by the servants of the government. I should not extend this category—I say this with particular reference to the facts of this case—to oppressive action by private corporations or individuals. Where one man is more powerful than another, it is inevitable that he will try to use his power to gain his ends; and if his power is much greater than the other's, he might, perhaps, be said to be using it oppressively. If he uses his power illegally, he must of course pay for his illegality in the ordinary way; but he is not to be punished simply because he is the more powerful. In the case of the government it is different, for the servants of the government are also the servants of the people and the use of their power must always be subordinate to their duty of service. It is true that there is something repugnant about a big man bullying a small man and, very likely, the bullying will be a source of humiliation that makes the case one for aggravated damages, but it is not, in my opinion, punishable by damages.

Cases in the second category are those in which the defendant's conduct has been calculated by him to make a profit for himself which may well exceed the compensation payable to the plaintiff. It is a factor that is taken into account in damages for libel; one man should not be allowed to sell another man's reputation for profit. Where a defendant with a cynical disregard for a plaintiff's rights has calculated that the money to be made out of his wrongdoing will probably exceed the damages at risk, it is necessary for the law to show that it cannot be broken with impunity. This category is not confined to moneymaking in the strict sense. It extends to cases in which the defendant is seeking to gain at the expense of the plaintiff some object—perhaps some property which he covets—which either he could not obtain at all or not obtain except at a price greater than he wants to put down. Exemplary damages can properly be awarded whenever it is necessary to teach a wrongdoer that tort does not pay.

To these two categories which are established as part of the common law there must of course be added any category in which exemplary damages are expressly authorised by statute.

I wish now to express three considerations which I think should always be borne in mind when awards of exemplary damages are being considered. First, the plaintiff cannot recover exemplary damages unless he is the victim of the punishable behaviour. The anomaly inherent in exemplary damages would become an absurdity if a plaintiff totally unaffected by some oppressive conduct which the jury wished to punish obtained a windfall in consequence.

Secondly, the power to award exemplary damages constitutes a weapon that, while it can be used in defence of liberty can also be used against liberty. Some of the awards that juries have made in the past seem to me to amount to a greater punishment than would be likely to be incurred if the conduct were criminal; and, moreover, a punishment imposed without the safeguard which the criminal law gives to an offender. I should not allow the respect which is traditionally paid to an assessment of damages by a jury to prevent me from seeing that the weapon is used with restraint. It may even be that the House may find it necessary to place some arbitrary limit on awards of damages that are made by way of punishment. Exhortations to be moderate may not be enough.

Thirdly, the means of the parties, irrelevant in the assessment of compensation, are material in the assessment of exemplary damages. Everything which aggravates or mitigates the defendant's conduct is relevant.

Thus a case for exemplary damages must be presented quite differently from one for compensatory damages; and the judge should not allow it to be left to the jury unless he is satisfied that it can be brought within the categories I have specified. But the fact that the two sorts of damage differ essentially does not necessarily mean that there should be two awards. In a case in which exemplary damages are appropriate, a jury should be directed that if, but only if, the sum which they have in mind to award as compensation (which may, of course, be a sum aggravated by the way in which the defendant has behaved to the plaintiff) is inadequate to punish him for his outrageous conduct, to mark their disapproval of such conduct and to deter him from repeating it, then it can award some larger sum. If a verdict given on such direction has to be reviewed upon appeal, the appellate court will first consider whether the award can be justified as compensation and if it can, there is nothing further to be said. If it cannot, the court must consider whether or not the punishment is, in all the circumstances, excessive. There may be cases in which it is difficult for a judge to say whether or not he ought to leave to the jury a claim for exemplary damages. In such circumstances, and in order to save the possible expense of a new trial, I see no objection to his inviting the jury to say what sum they would fix as compensation and what additional sum, if any, they would award if they were entitled to give exemplary damages.

COMMENTARY

Oppressive, Arbitrary or Unconstitutional Action by the Servants of the Government

A classic example of this would be wrongful arrest by a police officer. According to Lord Reid, 'the category was never intended to be limited to Crown servants. The contrast is between "the government" and private individuals. Local government is as much government as national government, and the police and many other persons are exercising governmental functions' (*Cassell v Broome* [1972] AC 1027 at 1088). It has been held that this category does not extend to the commercial activities of nationalised enterprises (*AB v South West Services Ltd* [1993] QB 507), though some have questioned whether companies—especially large international concerns capable of exercising considerable power—should always be immune from exemplary damages (see, e.g., *Kuddus v Chief Constable of Leicestershire* [2002] 2 AC 122 at [66], per Lord Nicholls).

Conduct Calculated to Make a Profit in Excess of any Compensation Payable

The classic example here is of a newspaper that prints a libellous story in order to boost its circulation. Outside the libel context, the most common exemplary awards under this head are in respect of wrongful harassment or eviction of tenants by landlords (where the latter commit the tort of trespass). Exemplary damages have also been awarded in this category in respect of the unlawful imprisonment and sexual exploitation of foreign women coerced into prostitution in the UK with a view to making profits for the defendants: *AT v Dulghieru* [2009] EWHC 225, noted by Keren-Paz (2010) 18 TLJ 87. Such damages are awarded not merely to reverse the defendant's unjust enrichment (the function of restitutionary damages), but—in Lord Devlin's words—'to teach a wrongdoer that tort does not pay'. If the award were only to reverse the defendant's gain, then the defendant would have 'nothing to lose' by going ahead with the tortious conduct. However, in *Kuddus v Chief Constable of Leicestershire* [2002] 2 AC 122, both Lord Nicholls, at [67], and Lord Scott, at [109], queried whether this category was necessary as the circumstances in which restitutionary damages could be awarded had increased and in most cases the profit of the wrongdoer could be disgorged in this way. Does this meet the criticism that the defendant is insufficiently deterred by an award of restitutionary damages?

Exemplary Damages Limited to Certain Causes of Action

In *AB v South West Water Services Ltd* [1993] QB 507, the Court of Appeal introduced a 'cause of action' test for the award of exemplary damages. It took the view that the development of the law had been frozen into a rigid posture by *Rookes v Barnard* and that exemplary damages could only be awarded in relation to tortious causes of action in which such damages had been awarded prior to that case. Accordingly, inhabitants of Camelford in Cornwall who alleged that they were ill as a result of drinking contaminated water supplied by the defendant failed in their bid for exemplary damages. The causes of action they relied upon (negligence, nuisance, and the rule in *Rylands v Fletcher*) did not allow the award of such damages. The decision was subjected to considerable academic criticism (see, e.g., Pipe (1994) 57 MLR 91) and was subsequently overruled by the House of Lords in *Kuddus v Chief Constable of Leicestershire* [2002] 2 AC 122. It does not follow, however, that a claimant need now prove only that his case falls into one of Lord Devlin's categories to be able to ask for exemplary damages. *Kuddus* does not preclude the courts adopting a revised 'cause of action' test based on a reasoned analysis of which torts should permit exemplary damages and which should not, rather than on the accidents of litigation prior to *Rookes v Barnard*. In *Kuddus*, only Lord Scott adverted to this possibility, at [122], stating that he preferred 'a pragmatic solution' whereby exemplary damages would be allowed in respect of all torts except negligence, nuisance, breach of statutory duty (in the absence of express statutory authorisation), and all torts of strict liability. It is not clear where this would leave defamation, often thought of as a tort of strict liability, but also the tort for which awards of exemplary damages are more common than for any other. It is doubtful that Lord Scott intended to change this well-established position.

Subsequently, in *Mosley v News Group Newspapers Ltd* [2008] EMLR 20 (noted p. 812, above), at [172]–[211], Eady J was obliged to consider whether exemplary damages were available for the unlawful disclosure of private information. He ruled that they were not. His reasoning was partly that there was no authority for such an extension (is this aspect of Eady J's argument consistent with *Kuddus*?), partly because it is undesirable for exemplary damages to be available in an area governed to so large an extent by the Convention rights to privacy and freedom of expressions (Articles 8 and 10, ECHR) when the idea of punitive or exemplary damages is alien to the Strasbourg court. Do you think it is justifiable to retain exemplary damages for defamation but at the same time to exclude their availability for unlawful disclosure of private information?

Limits on Awards of Exemplary Damages against the Police

At common law, a civil claimant has a prima facie right to trial by jury in four causes of action, two of which are false imprisonment and malicious prosecution. As actions against the police can involve such claims, it is not uncommon for them to be heard by a civil jury, together with any associated claims for assault and battery. The traditional approach adopted by the courts prevented counsel or judges referring the jury to awards in similar cases, so it was left to the jury to arrive at an appropriate level of damages, including exemplary damages. The result, unsurprisingly, was a divergence between levels of award.

Until 1990 the only remedy available to the Court of Appeal where it thought the jury's award of damages was irrational was to order a retrial but the Courts and Legal Services Act 1990, s. 8 gave the court the power to substitute its own award in these circumstances. The Court of Appeal has used its powers under this section to provide guidelines to juries in cases of false imprisonment or malicious prosecution against the police. In *Thompson v Commissioner of Police of the Metropolis* [1998] QB 498 the Court of Appeal set out a number of points to be explained to the jury by the judge, including:

(i)   an award of exemplary damages would rarely be less than £5,000, otherwise it was probably not justified;

(ii) conduct had to be particularly deserving of condemnation for an award of £25,000, and £50,000 was to be the absolute maximum, reserved for conduct directly involving officers of at least the rank of superintendent;

(iii) a rough upper-limit guide is three times the total of compensatory and aggravated damages (see Section 4, below) except where basic damages are modest.

Although these guidelines were given in the context of a jury trial they are equally applicable for trial by judge alone.

(b) Analysis

Whether an award of exemplary damages can be justified has been a matter of continued debate, with the House of Lords returning to the matter in *Cassell v Broome*, and more recently in *Kuddus v Chief Constable of Leicestershire* [2002] 2 AC 2002, both extracted below. The Law Commission also issued a report on exemplary damages in 1997.

Cassell v Broome [1972] AC 1027

The facts of this case are not relevant for present purposes.

Lord Reid

That [sc. an award of exemplary damages] meant that the plaintiff, by being given more than on any view could be justified as compensation, was being given a pure and undeserved windfall at the expense of the defendant, and that in so far as the defendant was being required to pay more than could possibly be regarded as compensation he was being subjected to pure punishment.

I thought and still think that that is highly anomalous. It is confusing the function of the civil law which is to compensate with the function of the criminal law which is to inflict deterrent and punitive penalties...

I think that the objections to allowing juries to go beyond compensatory damages are over-whelming. To allow pure punishment in this way contravenes almost every principle which has been evolved for the protection of offenders. There is no definition of the offence except that the conduct punished must be oppressive, high-handed, malicious, wanton or its like—terms far too vague to be admitted to any criminal code worthy of the name. There is no limit to the punishment except that it must not be unreasonable. The punishment is not inflicted by a judge who has experience and at least tries not to be influenced by emotion; it is inflicted by a jury without experience of law or punishment and often swayed by considerations which every judge would put out of his mind. And there is no effective appeal against sentence. All that a reviewing court can do is to quash the jury's decision if it thinks the punishment awarded is more than any 12 reasonable men could award. The court cannot substitute its own award. The punishment must then be decided by another jury and if they too award heavy punishment the court is virtually powerless. It is no excuse to say that we need not waste sympathy on people who behave outrageously. Are we wasting sympathy on vicious criminals when we insist on proper legal safeguards for them? The right to give punitive damages in certain cases is so firmly embedded in our law that only Parliament can remove it. But I must say that I am surprised by the enthusiasm of Lord Devlin's critics in supporting this form of palm tree justice.

Lord Wilberforce

It cannot lightly be taken for granted, even as a matter of theory, that the purpose of the law of tort is compensation, still less that it ought to be, an issue of large social import, or that there is something inappropriate or illogical or anomalous (a question-begging word) in including a punitive element in civil damages, or, conversely that the criminal law, rather than the civil law is in these cases the better instrument for conveying social disapproval, or for redressing a wrong to the social fabric, or that damages in any case can be broken down into the two separate elements. As a matter of practice English law has not committed itself to any of these theories; it may have been wiser than it knew.

Kuddus v Chief Constable of Leicestershire [2002] 2 AC 122

The question for the House of Lords was whether the tort of misfeasance in public office was one in which exemplary damages could be awarded. Both parties argued the case on the basis that *Rookes v Barnard* and *Cassell v Broome* [1972] AC 1027 represented the law, and the specific issue was the correctness of the Court of Appeal decision in *AB v South West Water* (see above). However, several of their Lordships commented more generally on whether there was a role for exemplary damages in the modern law.

Lord Nicholls

The availability of exemplary damages has played a significant role in buttressing civil liberties, in claims for false imprisonment and wrongful arrest. From time to time cases do arise where awards of compensatory damages are perceived as inadequate to achieve a just result between the parties. The nature of the defendant's conduct calls for a further response from the courts. On occasion conscious wrongdoing by the defendant is so outrageous, his disregard of the plaintiff's rights so contumelious, that something more is need to show that the law will not tolerate such behaviour. Without an award of exemplary damages, justice will not have been done. Exemplary damages, as a remedy of last resort, fill what would otherwise be a regrettable lacuna...

In *Rookes v Barnard* Lord Devlin drew a distinction between oppressive acts by government officials and similar acts by companies or individuals. He considered that exemplary damages should not be available in the case of non-governmental oppression or bullying. Whatever may have been the position 40 years ago, I am respectfully inclined to doubt the soundness of this distinction today. National and international companies can exercise enormous power. So do some individuals. I am not sure it would be right to draw a hard and fast line which would always exclude such companies and persons from the reach of exemplary damages. Indeed, the validity of the dividing line drawn by Lord Devlin when formulating his first category is somewhat undermined by his second category, where the defendants are not confined to, and normally would not be, government officials or the like...

Lord Scott

The law regarding exemplary damages did not become fossilised and set in stone when Lord Devlin pronounced in 1964...or when the seven members of the House pronounced in 1972...Since then the common law has flowed on. One of the great developments of the common law since the time of *Rookes v Barnard* has been in the area of public law and judicial review to which Lord Diplock [in *Cassell v Broome*] referred. Oppressive, arbitrary and unconstitutional acts by members of the executive can be remedied through civil proceedings brought in the High Court. The remedies the court can provide include awards of damages, declarations of right and, in most cases, injunctions. The developments since Lord Diplock's remarks in *Broome v Cassell* have transformed the ability of the ordinary citizen to obtain redress. The continuing need in the year 2001 for exemplary damages as a civil remedy in order to control, deter and punish acts falling within Lord Devlin's first category is not in the least obvious.

My noble and learned friend, Lord Hutton, has referred, as examples, to two cases in Northern Ireland where in his view the award of exemplary damages served a valuable purpose in restraining the arbitrary and outrageous use of executive power and in vindicating the strength of the law. In one case (*Lavery v Ministry of Defence* [1984] NI 99) a soldier was the wrongdoer. The Ministry of Defence was the defendant. In the other case (*Pettigrew v Northern Ireland Office* [1990] NI 179) prison officers were the wrongdoers. The Northern Ireland Office was the defendant. In each case the conduct of the wrongdoer, or wrongdoers, was outrageous and fell squarely within Lord Devlin's first category. But I do not follow why an appropriate award of aggravated damages [see Section 4 below] would not have served to vindicate the law just as effectively as the fairly moderate awards of exemplary damages that were made. The condemnation of the trial judge of the conduct in question would have been expressed no differently. As to deterrence, in a case where the defendant is not the wrongdoer, and the damages are in any event going to be met out of public funds, how can it be supposed that the award of exemplary damages adds anything at all to the deterrent effect of the trial judge's finding of fact in favour of the injured person and his condemnation of the conduct in question? The proposition that exemplary damage awards against such defendants as the Ministry of Defence or the Northern Ireland Office, or, for that matter, the Chief Constable of Leicestershire Constabulary, can have a deterrent effect is, in my respectful opinion, fanciful...

My Lords, I view the prospect of any increase in the cases in which exemplary damages can be claimed with regret. I have explained already why I regard the remedy as no longer serving any useful function in our jurisprudence. Victims of tortious conduct should receive due compensation, not windfalls at public expense.

COMMENTARY

As the extracts from the two cases illustrate, judicial opinion on the desirability of awards of exemplary damages remains as polarised today as it did 40 years ago. In *Kuddus* their Lordships clearly felt that the underlying justifications for exemplary damages *should* have been argued before them, but the parties (no doubt for reasons of cost) limited the dispute to a narrow point. Nonetheless, two of the three Lords who proffered (obiter) comments on exemplary damages were broadly in favour, although Lord Nicholls thought Lord Devlin's categories in *Rookes v Barnard* did not represent a satisfactory basis on which to make such awards. Conversely, the speeches of Lord Reid in *Cassell* and Lord Scott in *Kuddus* reflect a reluctance to admit such awards into civil law, albeit for different reasons.

It may be noted that, when the issue of exemplary damages subsequently came before a panel of Law Lords wearing their other hats as members of the Judicial Committee of the Privy Council, a majority of them took an expansive view of the circumstances in which exemplary damages could be awarded under the common law of New Zealand: their award was not to be limited to cases where the defendant intended to cause the harm or was consciously reckless as to the risks involved, but extended to cases of negligence amounting to outrageous conduct (*A v Bottrill* [2002] UKPC 44, [2003] 1 AC 449). Given continued divergences of judicial opinion, it cannot be said that the decision provides any real indication of how the new UK Supreme Court might approach the issue in English law should it be invited to overrule *Rookes v Barnard*.

For an argument that exemplary damages are inconsistent with the nature of private law and should be abolished, see Beever, 'The structure of aggravated and exemplary damages' (2003) 23 OJLS 87.

When the question of exemplary damages was considered by the Law Commission (*Aggravated, Exemplary and Restitutionary Damages* (Law Com. No. 247, 1997)), it recommended that punitive damages should be retained but placed on a clear, principled, but tightly controlled, footing. It concluded that 'civil punishment can be adequately distinguished from criminal punishment, and has an important and distinctive role to play ... The argument of principle for retaining exemplary damages is content ... with a "fuzzy" line [sc. between the civil law and the criminal law], with a range of punishments from civil punishment, through criminal fines, to imprisonment' (para. 5.25).

The Law Commission proposed a statutory scheme, the core elements of which it summarised as follows:

(i) Punitive damages should be available for a legal wrong (other than breach of contract) if the defendant has deliberately and outrageously disregarded the claimant's rights. (The 'cause of action' and 'categories' tests should be abolished.)

(ii) The decision to award punitive damages, and their amount, should be matters for judges to decide; even where a civil trial is otherwise by jury, these matters should never be decided by a jury.

(iii) Punitive damages should be a 'last resort' remedy, which should not be awarded where the defendant has been convicted of a criminal offence for the same conduct, or where another available remedy is adequate punishment.

The government subsequently indicated that, because of the diversity of opinion displayed during the consultation period for the report, it did not intend to introduce legislation to give effect to these recommendations. However, it noted that further judicial development of the law might clarify some of the issues (Hansard, HC vol. 337 col. 502, 9 November 1999 WA). See further DCA, *The Law on Damages* (2007), paras 196–9.

Relevance of Criminal Conviction

If one purpose of exemplary damages is to punish, should such awards be precluded if a criminal sanction has already been imposed? The Law Commission, as noted above, thought they should. The issue seems not to have arisen for decision in English law, but in *Gray v Motor Accident Commission* (1998) 196 CLR 1 a majority of the Australian High Court held, at [40], that '[w]here ... the criminal law has been brought to bear upon the wrongdoer and substantial punishment inflicted, we consider that exemplary damages may not be awarded'. As the defendant had been sentenced to seven years' imprisonment in a prior criminal trial, the plaintiff's claim for exemplary damages was rejected. Although agreeing with the result, Kirby and Callinan JJ adopted a slightly more flexible approach. While both agreed that the imposition of a criminal sanction was an important factor in deciding whether to award exemplary damages, Callinan J noted (at [143]):

A court would also be entitled to take into account that lesser punishments may have been, or might be imposed as a consequence of the acceptance of a lesser plea, the availability (for what might be sound policy reasons in and for the purposes of the criminal law) of a small penalty only, the desirability of the less condemnatory process by way of civil rather than criminal proceedings, the need to encourage compliance with the law, and the fact that the possibility of any criminal sanction is illusory.

Do you think that judges and juries should have some discretion to award exemplary damages even if a criminal sanction has been imposed?

Exemplary Damages and Vicarious Liability

In a passage of his opinion in *Kuddus* not extracted above, Lord Scott stated that an award of exemplary damages against a defendant whose liability is merely vicarious was contrary to principle. Of the remaining members of the House, only Lord Hutton considered this issue. He took the contrary view that exemplary awards made against such a defendant could indeed have a deterrent effect, a position that appealed to the High Court of Australia in *New South Wales v Ibbett* (2006) 229 CLR 638. His Lordship felt that this was particularly so where the individual at fault could not be identified but it was known the wrongdoer was one of a number of people employed by the defendant. The issue came for decision by the Court of Appeal in *Rowlands v Chief Constable of Merseyside Police* [2007] 1 WLR 1065, the Court ruling that exemplary damages should indeed be available even when the defendant's liability was vicarious. On the facts, the question was a chief constable of police's liability for one of his officers. Moore-Bick LJ, with whom Richards and Ward LJJ agreed, stated (at [47]):

[S]ince the power to award exemplary damages rests on policy rather than principle, it seems to me that the question whether awards can be made against persons whose liability is vicarious only must also be answered by resort to considerations of policy rather than strict principle. While the common law continues to recognise a power to award exemplary damages in respect of wrongdoing by servants of the government of a kind that has a direct effect on civil liberties, which for my own part I think it should, I think that it is desirable as a matter of policy that the courts should be able to make punitive awards against those who are vicariously liable for the conduct of their subordinates without being constrained by the financial means of those who committed the wrongful acts in question. Only by this means can awards of an adequate amount be made against those who bear public responsibility for the conduct of the officers concerned.

Do you agree that vicarious liability for exemplary damages, though contrary to principle, can be justified on grounds of public policy?

Punitive Damages in the United States

In the United States, the attachment to punitive damages (as they tend to be known) is very strong in some sectors of society, where they are seen as 'the only practical method of exercising social control over economically formidable offenders... because criminal penalties are no substitute' (Galanter and Luban, 'Poetic Justice: Punitive Damages and Legal Pluralism' (1993) 42 Am U LR 1393 at 1440). Law enforcement agencies, it is argued, cannot be relied upon to identify and prosecute egregious corporate wrongdoing. The punitive damages system is necessary to give injured parties and their lawyers the incentive to carry out necessary investigative work themselves so as to bring the wrongdoer to justice. See also S. Daniels and J. Martin, *Civil Juries and the Politics of Reform* (Evanston: Northwestern University Press, 1995) p. 202ff; Sebok, 'Punitive Damages: From Myth to Theory', (2007) 92 Iowa L Rev 957.

Of course, these arguments are controversial. It has been argued on the other side of the debate that jury awards of punitive damages are errative, arbitrary and unpredictable (Sunstein et al., 'Assessing Punitive Damages', (1998) 107 Yale LJ 2071), that it is unconstitutional to give private actors the power to exercise the power to punish as they are inevitably motivated by their own narrow interests rather than the public interest (Redish and Mathews, 'Why Punitive Damages are Unconstitutional', (2004) 53 Emory LJ 1), and that they cause economic harm because they discourage risk assessment (which inevitably involves a balancing of costs and benefits and so may be thought offensive by jurors), promote counterproductive spending and wasteful precautions that may lead to increased risk, and discourage innovation (Viscusi, 'The Social Costs of Punitive Damages against Corporations in Environmental and Safety Torts', (1998) 87 Georgetown LJ 285).

The arguments against punitive damages have prevailed to some extent in several US states (see Magnus, 'Why is US Tort Law so Different?' (2010) 1 JETL 102, 105). Some have abolished punitive damages, some have introduced caps to limit their amount, and others require the successful claimant to pay a proportion of any punitive award to the state. Additionally, the US Supreme Court has enunciated a constitutional principle that punitive damages must be proportional to the loss for which compensatory damages are available. Punitive awards that exceed compensatory damages by a ratio or more than 10:1 are now regularly found to be excessive and must be reduced on challenge. In the leading case of *BMW of North America Inc v Gore*, 116 S Ct 1589 (1996) BMW had a policy of not advising its dealers, and hence their customers, of pre-delivery damage to new cars when the cost of repair did not exceed 3 per cent of the car's suggested retail price. Gore bought such a car and later discovered it had been damaged. He successfully sued the car manufacturer for fraud. The jury awarded compensatory damages of $4,000, and $4 million in punitive damages, reduced to $2 million on appeal. On further appeal to the US Supreme Court the award of punitive damages was overturned as infringing the rights of due process guaranteed to the defendant by the fourteenth amendment to the US Constitution. One ground for the decision was that the ratio of compensatory damages to punitive damages was excessive (1:500); another was the lack of equivalence between the criminal sanction for the manufacturer's conduct ($2,000) and the punitive award. See also *State Farm v Campbell*, 538 US 408 (2003). Despite the above-mentioned restrictions, however, most US states still allow punitive damages in one form or another.

Punitive Damages in Civilian Legal Systems

Punitive damages are a creature of the common law, and are wholly alien to civilian legal systems. More than one European supreme court has refused to enforce an award of punitive damages made by a US court against a European defendant on the grounds that they offend public policy (see Wurmnest, 'Recognition and Enforcement of US Money Judgments in Germany', (2005) 23 Berkeley J Int'l L 175; Quarta, 'Recognition and Enforcement of US Punitive Damages Awards in Continental Europe: The Italian Supreme Court's Veto', (2008) 31 Hastings Int'l and Comp L Rev 753). For a comparative survey, and further criticism of the use of civil law to effect punishment, see H. Koziol and V. Wilcox (eds), *Punitive Damages: Common Law and Civil Law Perspectives* (Springer, 2009).

4. Aggravated Damages

In some cases, the manner in which the defendant acts may cause additional injury to the claimant. Aggravated damages compensate the claimant for the additional loss he or she has suffered because of the defendant's reprehensible conduct. They are of limited scope: in *Kralj v McGrath* [1986] 1 All ER 54, it was held that aggravated damages are never appropriate in actions in negligence even if the negligence is 'crass'. Aggravated damages occupy a murky middle ground between normal compensatory damages and exemplary damages. They are designed to compensate the claimant for any hurt to his or her feelings and dignity occasioned by the manner in which the defendant committed the tort or by the manner of the defendant's conduct of the litigation. Aggravated damages therefore serve a compensatory function, as was emphasised by Lord Devlin in *Rookes v Barnard* [1964] AC 1129. But they are not normal compensatory damages, for they allow compensation for matters that would not fall under the head of pain and suffering attributable to the tortious injury itself (e.g. the distress suffered as a result of a hostile cross-examination at trial). Furthermore, aggravated damages have a punitive aspect, as it is a traditional requirement that the defendant should be guilty of some exceptional misconduct if aggravated damages are to be awarded. It cannot yet be said that the tension between the compensatory and punitive elements of aggravated damages has been entirely resolved.

A more principled approach is advanced by the Law Commission in its report *Aggravated, Exemplary and Restitutionary Damages* (Law Com No 247, 1997). This recommended that aggravated damages should be viewed as purely compensatory and assessed with reference to what is necessary to compensate the loss suffered by the claimant. They should not be assessed with reference to what is necessary to punish a defendant for his or her conduct. The Commission was not persuaded that legislative abolition of aggravated damages (and, with it, the exceptional conduct requirement) was desirable, because it might tend to limit the availability of damages for mental distress. The Commission argued that it was not the case that losses which would be compensated by an award of aggravated damages could always be compensated under another, already-recognised head of damages for a particular tort. Some losses might only be compensated once it was found that the defendant had acted in a particularly bad manner; abolishing aggravated damages would prevent recovery for such losses. Accordingly, the Commission recommended legislation which clarified the true role of aggravated damages (see paras 2.39–42). However, in 2007, the Government announced that subsequent decisions had introduced sufficient clarity to the law to obviate the need for a statutory definition so as to clarify that the purpose of aggravated damages is compensatory and not punitive (DCA, *The Law of Damages* (CP 9/07, 2007), para. 205).

Limits have been placed on the award of aggravated damages against the police (*Thompson v Commissioner of Police of the Metropolis* [1998] QB 498). The Court of Appeal thought an award of aggravated damages, where appropriate, would rarely be less than £1,000 but would normally not be as much as twice ordinary compensatory damages unless these damages were modest.

It must also be noted that, in any case where distress, humiliation and injury to feelings are treated as part of the basic damages, there should be no further award for the same intangible injuries under the head of aggravated damages as this would give the claimant double recovery (*Rowlands v Chief Constable of Merseyside Police* [2007] 1 WLR 1065 at [26], per Moore-Blick LJ).

5. Nominal Damages

Where a tort is actionable *per se*, the award of nominal damages denotes that the claimant's rights have been infringed by the defendant's tortious conduct even though the claimant has suffered no loss as a result of the tort. The claimant having suffered no loss is entitled to no substantial compensation, and is awarded no more than a few pounds, although the successful claimant will normally obtain a costs order in his favour. The award nevertheless performs the important function of vindicating the claimant's rights. Cf. the possible availability in serious cases of substantial 'vindicatory damages' to signal that the infringement of the claimant's right should not have occurred, as contemplated by Lord Scott in *Ashley v Chief Constable of Sussex Police* [2008] 1 AC 962 at [22]–[23] and [29]. See also *Stevens*, p.59ff.

6. Contemptuous Damages

These are damages of a very small amount—very often the coin of lowest denomination in current circulation—which are designed to express contempt for the claimant's conduct, notwithstanding his (technical) victory on the law. They are very rarely awarded other than in defamation actions. In cases where contemptuous damages are awarded the successful claimant may not obtain a costs order in his favour. A recent example is that of the former Liverpool goalkeeper Bruce Grobbelaar, who sued *The Sun* over allegations that he had accepted bribes to let in goals from the opposition. After protracted legal proceedings the House of Lords in October 2002 reinstated the jury's original verdict in favour of Grobbelaar but reduced the damages from £85,000 to just £1 (*Grobbelaar v News Group Newspapers Ltd* [2002] 1 WLR 3024). Although *The Sun* had technically defamed Grobbelaar, because it had not demonstrated that he had sought to influence the result of any game in which he had played, other evidence showed that he had acted 'in a way in which no decent or honest footballer would act and in a way which could, if not exposed and stamped on, undermine the integrity of a game which earns the loyalty and support of millions': [2002] 1 WLR 3024 at 3036, per Lord Bingham). The following month their Lordships ordered Grobbelaar to pay two-thirds of *The Sun*'s legal costs—about £1m (*Guardian*, 27 November 2002). Although the winner in civil proceedings normally has his costs paid by the loser, an award of this nature justifies a change from the usual rule. As Lord Steyn explained in the October decision [2002] 1 WLR 3024 at 3038: 'By recovering only derisory damages Mr Grobbelaar has (effectively) lost the action to clear his name.' See further p. 734, above.

III. Lump Sums and Periodical Payments

Traditionally damages were recoverable once only and awarded as a lump sum. Where the loss was continuing, the court had to anticipate all that the future held in store for the claimant and adjust the lump sum accordingly. In a personal injury case, the greater the chance of recovery, the smaller the lump sum; the greater the chance of long-term disability, the larger the payment.

Lump sums are still the general rule. The lump sum received by the claimant includes compensation for both losses already suffered and those which are expected in the future. Each requires special adjustment in the light of a number of factors. Compensation for past losses needs adjustment to take account of the lapse of time between the date the losses were sustained and the date at which damages are awarded. The right to damages accrues at the time the loss is sustained, so claimants are deprived of money that is rightfully theirs when they have to wait until trial for their compensation. They thereby lose the opportunity to use the money to their own advantage and will have seen it lose its value because of inflation. To make up for this, the courts require the defendant to pay interest on top of the sum assessed as compensation for the claimant's pre-trial losses.

Where compensation for future losses is included in a lump sum award, it attracts no award of interest but does require adjustment to take into account the fact that the claimant's receipt of money is accelerated (the 'acceleration element'). Additionally, an adjustment must be made in respect of various uncertainties as to the future (the 'vicissitudes of life'). In *Lim Poh Choo v Camden & Islington Area Health Authority* [1980] AC 174 at 182–3, Lord Scarman noted that 'insuperable problems' arose from the operation of the lump-sum rule in the system of compensation for personal injuries:

> The award, which covers past, present and future injury and loss, must, under our law, be of a lump sum assessed at the conclusion of the legal process. The award is final; it is not susceptible to review as the future unfolds, substituting fact for estimate. Knowledge of the future being denied to mankind, so much of the award as is to be attributed to future loss and suffering (in many cases the major part of the award) will almost surely be wrong. There is really only one certainty: the future will prove the award to be either too high or too low.

Lord Scarman emphasises the point that claimants cannot bring a second action on the same facts simply because their injuries turn out to be worse than was originally thought. As damages are, in general, assessed on a once-and-for-all basis, the court must make a guess as to how long the claimant's losses will continue into the future and how serious they will be. If the claimant's condition deteriorates (or improves) unexpectedly, that is of no significance (see *Fetter v Beal* (1701) 1 Ld Raym 339). As Lord Scarman observed, '[t]he award is final'.

The lump-sum, once-and-for-all rule was criticised by the Pearson Commission (1978), which considered that in cases of death or serious and lasting injury a system of periodic payments should be introduced, but this did not attract political support at the time. However, the Administration of Justice Act 1982, s. 6 made a slight inroad on the lump-sum rule by allowing for the award of so-called 'provisional damages'. Section 32A of the Senior Courts Act 1981 (as inserted; see also County Courts Act 1984, s. 51) provides:

(1) This section applies to an action for damages for personal injuries in which there is proved or admitted to be a chance that at some definite or indefinite time in the future the injured person will, as a result of the act or omission which gave rise to the cause of action, develop some serious disease or suffer some serious deterioration in his physical or mental condition.

(2) Subject to [minor exceptions]..., as regards any action for damages to which this section applies in which a judgment is given in the High Court, provision may be made by rules of court for enabling the court, in such circumstances as may be prescribed, to award the injured person

 (a) damages assessed on the assumption that the injured person will not develop the disease or suffer the deterioration in his condition; and

 (b) further damages at a future date if he develops the disease or suffers the deterioration.

The scheme consequently established (see CPR r 41.2, 3 and Practice Direction 41) may be invoked by a person who has already suffered an injury, and fears a further disease or deterioration in future (e.g. epilepsy following a head injury), but not by a person for whom the risk of injury is entirely prospective: see *Rothwell v Chemical & Insulating Co Ltd* [2008] 1 AC 281 (noted p. 222, above). The procedure has the severe limitation that only one application for further damages can be made in respect of the type of injury or disease specified in the original action. Awards of provisional damages are rare and one commentator has described the procedure as 'a backwater of personal injury litigation' (Lewis (1997) 60 MLR 230 at 237).

Another attempt to get around the problems created by the lump-sum, once-and-for-all rule was the 'structured settlement' in which the parties agree that a portion of the damages is used to buy the claimant a life-assurance policy assuring a regular flow of income until the claimant's death or some other suitable date (see Law Commission, *Structured Settlements and Interim and Provisional Damages,* Law Com. No. 224, Cm. 2646, 1994, and R. Lewis, *Structured Settlements: The Law and Practice* (1993)). The big limitation of structured settlements, however, was that they depended on the voluntary agreement of the parties: there was no judicial power to compel the parties to accept a 'structure'. The Law Commission tentatively suggested in its consultation paper preceding the just-mentioned report (CP No. 125, 1992) that courts should have the power to impose a structure on the parties whether they wanted it or not, but the Commission's final report retreated from the idea, observing that the existing law gave rise to no significant injustices that called out urgently to be addressed (para. 3.48). However, continuing concerns over lump sum awards led to fresh calls for the greater use of periodical payments, and the question of allowing the courts to order compulsory periodical payments was considered in a Lord Chancellor's Department (LCD) Consultation Paper published in March 2002, which paved the way to the legislative introduction of 'periodical payment orders' (PPOs) by the Courts Act 2003, amending s. 2 of the Damages Act 1996. (In 2003, the LCD became part of the Department for Constitutional Affairs (DCA), which in turn was incorporated in the new Ministry of Justice in 2007.)

Lord Chancellor's Department, *Damages for Future Loss: Giving the Courts the Power to Order Periodical Payments for Future Loss and Care Costs in Personal Injury Cases,* Consultation Paper (March 2002)

Lump Sums or Periodical Payments?

14. When successful claimants are awarded a lump sum they are paid for all past and future losses at once. However carefully the claimant's likely future losses and needs are estimated, they can never be known with certainty in advance. An underestimate will cause the claimant to suffer; an overestimate will unfairly penalise the defendant. We consider that greater use of periodical payments offers scope to reflect claimants' actual needs and losses more closely than is possible with lump sums.

15. The most significant area of uncertainty is the future life expectancy of the claimant. Unless claimants live for exactly the number of years expected, they will invariably be either over- or under-compensated by a lump sum. Periodical payments, on the other hand, continue for the actual lifetime of a permanently injured claimant, and cease on the claimant's death (unless the terms of a particular order or annuity provide otherwise).

16. The issue of life expectancy, and whether a lump sum will run out because they might live longer than expected, can be of concern to claimants. In particular, this concern can result in an overly cautious approach being adopted to spending money, leading to seriously injured or disabled claimants not receiving the required level of care or full benefits intended by the award. If the money runs out, either because they live for longer than expected, or they dissipate their award, claimants may need to fall back upon the State, causing an additional burden to the Government purse and the taxpayer.

17. If a claimant dies much earlier than expected, a lump sum award will provide a windfall for the heirs of that claimant, and it will be they who benefit most from the award. It is sometimes argued that this does not matter because the lump sum payment still serves to penalise the defendant. But the purpose of tort law in these cases is to compensate claimants for loss, in particular by restoring them, so far as possible, to the financial position they enjoyed before the accident: it is not to punish defendants or provide heirs of the deceased with a financial

gain beyond any compensation that was awarded to them by the court. And the cost of any 'windfall' or 'profit' is ultimately borne, for example, by other insurance premium payers or by users of the NHS.

18. Lump sum compensation for future financial losses is a crude mechanism for restoring the claimant's position. Care costs are incurred over time, not all at once. Similarly, damages for lost earnings are intended to compensate for a stream of income that would have been earned in the future, not for the loss of an existing fortune. For these reasons, lump sums can place inappropriate pressures on claimants. There is a risk that claimants will be overawed by the amount awarded or that receipt of a very large sum may encourage a false sense of security. Claimants may also come under pressure from family or friends to spend the award inappropriately, for example by using money intended for their future care to help out someone in financial difficulties or to invest in a risky business venture. Although most adult claimants are free to spend their money as they choose, the system should not rely on a form of payment that enables, and arguably encourages, claimants to use their awards inappropriately.

19. Lump sums also impose on claimants the burden of investing the award (assuming they choose to do so) in a way that will enable them to purchase the care they require and to restore the income they have foregone because of the accident. It would be difficult for anyone to manage an entire lifetime's income so that it lasted until the day they died. That is why large awards often include provision for financial advice. But claimants may not seek or receive sound financial advice—lump sums can be difficult to manage, but easy to spend. This difficulty is magnified when accident victims have to cope with the stress of ongoing disabilities and usually the knowledge that they have no alternative source of income.

20. Periodical payments, on the other hand, provide a guaranteed income and claimants will know exactly how much they are going to receive and when, without the need for expensive investment advice. They will know that they can spend the money on immediate needs, without the risk of depletion or worries about investment. Instead, periodical payments require the defendant or the defendant insurer to provide funds or invest in a manner that ensures successful claimants receive certain and ongoing streams of payments for the remainder of their lives. This places the risk associated with investment where it belongs, namely on the negligent party. And, in most cases, where that risk can be more effectively managed, namely on an insurance company or other large organisation. For example, insurance companies should be able to invest to meet their liabilities across a large portfolio of annuities or claims, with much lower overall expenditure on financial advice and other administrative costs compared to individuals each investing a single lump sum. Public sector defendants, in particular the NHS, will be better placed to manage their budgets effectively, because the total amounts paid out in damages in any given year will be more predictable. So periodical payments could offer advantages over lump sums for defendants, defendant insurers, and the NHS and its users, as well as for claimants.

21. It is sometimes argued that an advantage of lump sums is that they provide a clean break between the claimant and the defendant, putting an end to adversarial contact. The desire for a clean break is understandable. But where the defendant is insured, or is uninsured but has purchased an annuity, it will be a general insurer or life office making the stream of payments to the claimant, not the defendant. Similarly, with most clinical negligence cases, it is not the doctor or medical team that pay the compensation, but rather the NHS Litigation Authority. There is rarely an ongoing relationship with the negligent party in person. Moreover, facilities for electronic transfer of money can remove any personal element to the transaction. A more pertinent point concerning the clean break issue is considered in paragraph 58 below in the context of the question of whether it should be possible to review awards of periodical payments.

22. To sum up, we consider that in most circumstances periodical payments are, in principle, the more appropriate means for paying compensation for significant future financial losses. They better reflect the purpose of compensation which is to restore the claimant's prior position. They place the risks associated with life expectancy and investment on defendants rather than claimants. This ensures that claimants who live longer than expected enjoy the quality of life they are entitled to, and do not have fall back on social security when the money runs out. It should also benefit defendants by allowing awards to be managed more cost-effectively. Lump sums invariably penalise one of the parties whereas periodical payments can provide better justice for both.

Damages Act 1996 (as amended by Courts Act 2003, s. 100)

Section 2: periodical payments

(1) A court awarding damages for future pecuniary loss in respect of personal injury—
   (a) may order that the damages are wholly or partly to take the form of periodical payments, and
   (b) shall consider whether to make that order.

(2) A court awarding other damages in respect of personal injury may, if the parties consent, order that the damages are wholly or partly to take the form of periodical payments.

(3) A court may not make an order for periodical payments unless satisfied that the continuity of payment under the order is reasonably secure.

(4) For the purpose of subsection (3) the continuity of payment under an order is reasonably secure if—
   (a) it is protected by a guarantee given under section 6 of or the Schedule to this Act,
   (b) it is protected by a scheme under section 213 of the Financial Services and Markets Act 2000 (compensation) . . . or
   (c) the source of payment is a government or health service body.

(5) An order for periodical payments may include provision—
   (a) requiring the party responsible for the payments to use a method (selected or to be selected by him) under which the continuity of payment is reasonably secure by virtue of subsection (4);
   (b) about how the payments are to be made, if not by a method under which the continuity of payment is reasonably secure by virtue of subsection (4);
   (c) requiring the party responsible for the payments to take specified action to secure continuity of payment, where continuity is not reasonably secure by virtue of subsection (4);
   (d) enabling a party to apply for a variation of provision included under paragraph (a), (b) or (c).
   . . .

(8) An order for periodical payments shall be treated as providing for the amount of payments to vary by reference to the retail prices index . . . at such times, and in such a manner, as may be determined by or in accordance with Civil Procedure Rules.

(9) But an order for periodical payments may include provision—
   (a) disapplying subsection (8), or
   (b) modifying the effect of subsection (8).

Damages (Variation of Periodical Payments) Order 2005, SI 2005/841

Article 1: Citation, commencement, interpretation and extent

...(2) In this Order—

- (a) "the Act" means the Damages Act 1996;
- (b) "agreement" means an agreement by parties to a claim or action for damages which settles the claim or action and which provides for periodical payments;
- (c) "damages" means damages for future pecuniary loss in respect of personal injury...
- (f) "variable order" means an order for periodical payments which contains a provision referred to in Article 2...

Article 2: Power to make variable orders

If there is proved or admitted to be a chance that at some definite or indefinite time in the future the claimant will—

- (a) as a result of the act or omission which gave rise to the cause of action, develop some serious disease or suffer some serious deterioration, or
- (b) enjoy some significant improvement, in his physical or mental condition, where that condition had been adversely affected as a result of that act or omission,

the court may, on the application of a party, with the agreement of all the parties, or of its own initiative, provide in an order for periodical payments that it may be varied...

Article 5: Contents of variable order

Where the court makes a variable order—

- (a) the damages must be assessed or agreed on the assumption that the disease, deterioration or improvement will not occur;
- (b) the order must specify the disease or type of deterioration or improvement;
- (c) the order may specify a period within which an application for it to be varied may be made;
- (d) the order may specify more than one disease or type of deterioration or improvement and may, in respect of each, specify a different period within which an application for it to be varied may be made;
- (e) the order must provide that a party must obtain the court's permission to apply for it to be varied, unless the court otherwise orders...

Article 7: Limit on number of applications to vary

A party may make only one application to vary a variable order in respect of each specified disease or type of deterioration or improvement.

COMMENTARY

The Courts Act 2003, amending s. 2 of the Damages Act 1996, introduced a new judicial power to make a periodical payment order (PPO) with or without the consent of the parties. The court's coercive power is limited to damages for future pecuniary loss (s. 2(1)), although it may make an order for periodical payments in respect of other heads of damage with the consent of the parties (s. 2(2)). As was the case with structured settlements, the court must be convinced that the continuity of the payments is reasonably secure (s. 2(3)), e.g. because it is protected by a ministerial guarantee (s. 2(4)(a)), covered by the statutory scheme providing an indemnity in the event of an insurer's insolvency (s. 2(4)(b)), or to be paid by a government or health service body (s. 2(4)(c)). From the claimant's perspective, PPOs may be attractive not just because they protect against the risk that the compensation monies will run out, but also because (like structured settlements before them) they are accorded tax-free status by HM Revenue and Customs.

The criteria to be used, and the procedure to be adopted, in determining whether to make a PPO are set out in Part 41 of the Civil Procedure Rules (as amended). Rule 41.7 states that the court must have regard to the form of award that best meets the claimant's needs. Further elaboration is to be found in a Practice Direction (PD41B), which states that the court must have regard to (amongst other things) the reasons for both the claimant's and defendant's preferences as to the form of award. Of course, it is not necessarily the case that the claimant will prefer a PPO (see Lush, 'Damages for Personal Injury: Why some claimants prefer a conventional lump sum to periodical payments' (2005) 1 London L Rev 187), and there has been judicial recognition that a PPO may not be appropriate where there is contributory negligence and the annual sum, reduced accordingly, would not fully cover the claimant's continuing care and other needs (*Rowe v Dolman* [2008] EWCA Civ 1040). For most claimants, a further key concern will be to ensure a sufficient contingency fund—whether instead of or in addition to periodical payments—to meet unexpected needs.

According to the official guidance (DCA, *Guidance on Periodical Payments*, 2005, para. 8) the calculation of the periodical sum is to be effected by a new 'bottom-up' approach:

> An important principle underlying the introduction of the power to order periodical payments was that it should lead to a fundamental change in the way in which these payments are calculated. Instead of the traditional 'top-down' approach used for structured settlements, requiring uncertain assumptions about life expectancy and investment, it is intended that where a periodical payments order is made or agreed, a 'bottom-up' approach will be adopted, which focuses instead on calculating the annual future needs of the claimant... Moving from a 'top-down' to a 'bottom-up' approach means that the claimant should no longer need financial advice on how to 'structure' the payments or on the best priced annuity available to meet his or her needs. The 'bottom-up' approach places the onus on the defendant to decide how to meet the terms of the court order or settlement.

The Guidance states that a top-down approach would preserve many of the disadvantages associated with lump sums, and—after the application of multipliers to allow for inflation, life expectancy and a discount rate—would produce payments which were unlikely to match the original assessment of the claimant's annual needs (paras 24–5).

By the Damages (Variation of Periodical Payments) Order 2005, a court may make a 'variable order' where there is a chance that the claimant will in future develop some serious disease or suffer some serious deterioration in his condition as a result of the tortious conduct, or that he will enjoy some significant improvement in his condition (Article 2). There is also provision for parties to a structured settlement to make it a 'variable agreement' in like circumstances (Article 9). But there can be no variation of a PPO or structured settlement except where the initial order or agreement was specified to be variable. The scope of the current provisions is thus the same as that governing the award of provisional lump sum damages (see p. 877, above), except that they allow for the significant improvement of the claimant's condition, not just its deterioration. The Order follows the LCD's earlier recommendation that the power of variation should be limited to cases where the change in condition was foreseen and specified. In its Consultation Paper of 2002, the LCD stated that allowing variation in respect of unforeseen medical changes would introduce unacceptably high levels of uncertainty and potential cost for both parties (see especially para. 58). But the Order does not adopt the LCD's associated recommendation (paras 67–71) that variation should be allowed in other cases of significant unforeseen change (e.g. the death of a carer).

Independently of the 'variable order' procedure, the court may provide that the PPO may take the form of a 'stepped' order by stipulating in advance that the annual payment should increase or decrease in anticipation of changes in the claimant's condition or other significant changes of circumstances (e.g. when the claimant reaches the age of 18). (See CPR, r. 41.8(3).)

Under the new provisions, the claimant is not allowed to assign or charge the right to receive periodical payments without the approval of the court and any attempt to do so is void (s. 2(6)). Thus the claimant may not foil the order of the court by selling his right to periodical payments in return for a lump sum. However, this presupposes that there has in fact been a judicial order for periodical payments. An important limitation on the court's power to override the wishes of the parties is that the vast majority of damages claims—even for very serious personal injuries—never reach the court at all but are the subject of out-of-court settlement. (See Ch. 18.I.2, below.) Except in cases involving children or 'patients' unable to manage their own affairs, there is no judicial control over the form of the settlement agreed by the parties. One commentator (Lewis (2006) 69 MLR 418 at 425) has accordingly concluded that lump sums will likely be used even in the majority of serious injury cases, but he notes that the reform will still affect *all* serious injury cases because 'the possibility of imposing a PPO substantially influences the bargaining position of the parties' (e.g. because one side may be able to exploit the other's preference for a lump sum).

The new PPO regime was strongly supported by claimants' organisations, but received a more guarded response from the liability insurance sector which fears that it will cost substantially more to fund a PPO than a traditional lump sum. One burning issue between claimants and insurers is the court's power (s. 2(9)) to disapply the presumptive linking of PPOs with the RPI (s. 2(8)). In *Flora v Wakom (Heathrow) Ltd* [2007] 1 WLR 482, the claimant sought a PPO under which the sums payable would vary by reference to average earnings, not prices, as the main heads of his claim were future loss of earnings (necessarily wage-related) and the cost of future care (largely, if not entirely, wage-related). The Court of Appeal rejected the defendant's application to strike out this part of the claim, noting that there was nothing to limit s. 2(9) to exceptional cases. In *Thompstone v Tameside and Glossop Acute Services NHS Trust* [2008] 1 WLR 2207, the Court of Appeal rejected a challenge to its *Flora* decision and for the first time exercised the s. 2(9) power, accepting after an exhaustive review the appropriateness of indexation of future care costs on the basis of the Annual Survey of Hours and Earnings (ASHE), which tracks pay-rates by occupational category (here, care assistants and home carers).

It is too simplistic, however, to describe the reform as a victory for claimants over liability insurers. As Lewis suggests, in the extract below, the short-term interests of the government in its management of public finances arguably provided the crucial impetus.

R. Lewis, 'The Politics and Economics of Tort Law: Judicially Imposed Periodical Payments of Damages' (2006) 69 MLR 418

[T]he catalysts for reform lay within Government itself...Claimants' interests were very much secondary to those involving public finance and the demands of the NHS. Far from being what they appear on the surface, the reforms in fact were politically driven.

The political and economic advantages to Government of periodical payments are as follows. In contrast to the problems faced by liability insurers, Government bodies such as the Ministry of Defence and especially the NHS will make immediate gains. This is because their budgets will no longer be denuded by the loss of large capital sums paid as damages. Their cash-flow will be improved because they can self-fund the periodical payments and they are not required to enter the expensive annuity market. It was forecast that in the first year of the new regime the NHS could save as much as £245 million out of the £330 million they would otherwise have to pay for the larger claims. This cash-flow saving will continue at a diminishing rate for 24 years until the accumulated liabilities reach, and thereafter outgrow, what would have been the capital sums needed to dispose of the claims entirely...

No matter what the short-term gains for the Treasury and the NHS, ultimately the taxpayer will have to pick up the total damages bill. There are at least two reasons to be concerned about this. First, the payments eventually are likely to be higher than they would have been if the traditional lump sums had continued to be used. This is because the move towards bottom-up assessments irrespective of the capital cost of providing the index-linked periodical payments drives up the ultimate cost of an award, and this will have an effect even upon those able to self-fund. Moreover, the tax and benefits savings made by the claimant in receiving payments in this way also occurs at a cost to the Exchequer. Secondly, the deferring of payments accumulates a debt which eventually will have to be met. The projection is that after 24 years the impact upon the cash-flow will be negative. That is, at that time not only will the good times come to an end and have to be paid for, but also there will be a real and increasing additional cost to the public purse. This cost may be relatively small in relation to the entire NHS budget, but Government finances should beware of these contingent liabilities, especially in the light of current concern about whether we should be paying more to fund future pensions in general. In effect, it will be our children who will have to find the money to pay for the full cost of today's medical negligence...

COMMENTARY

In Lewis's view, the reform can be considered amongst others of recent years that effect a transfer of the rising cost of tort damages from the public to the private sphere (e.g. to liability insurers). Other reforms that may be mentioned here include the costs recoverability of the claimant's 'success fee' under a conditional fee agreement, plus the insurance premium paid against the possibility of losing (see Ch. 18.I.3(c), below), and the state's recoupment of social security benefits paid to successful claimants (see Section IV.4(b), below), and more recently the costs of their NHS treatment (see Section IV.3(b), below). Of course, these costs are further dispersed throughout the private sphere. As Lewis observes (p. 441), 'the transfer results in a "stealth tax" which all premium payers and, ultimately, society at large must pay'. This brings us back—yet again—to one of the fundamental questions for all students of tort law: who is it that *really* pays the costs of the tort system?

IV. Damages for Personal Injury

A successful claimant is entitled to recover all losses—pecuniary or non-pecuniary (i.e. financial or non-financial)—that flow from the defendant's tort. Financial losses (e.g. loss of earnings or medical expenses) incurred up to the date of trial can be added up accurately and are termed 'special damages'. This means that the sums claimed must be specified in the claimant's initial schedule of damages. Damages for financial losses that the claimant expects to incur in the future cannot be specified accurately and together with damages for non-pecuniary loss are termed 'general damages'.

For each head of loss the claimant is also entitled to the payment of interest as compensation for the diminution of the real value of money in the pre-trial period. Interest is normally awarded on special damages at half the special investment rate for money paid into court, from the date of the accident to the date of the trial (*Cookson v Knowles* [1979] AC 556; Law Commission, *Damages for Personal Injury: Medical, Nursing and Other Expenses; Collateral Benefits*, Law Com. No. 262 (1999), paras 7.1–7.16) and on non-pecuniary loss at a rate of 2 per cent, from date of service of the writ to the date of the trial (*Wright v British Railways Board* [1983] 2 AC 773; see also the Law Commission report on *Damages for Personal Injury: Non-Pecuniary Loss* (Law Com. No. 257 (1999)), paras 2.29–2.58).

1. Non-Pecuniary Losses

(a) General

No amount of money can fully compensate for the loss of a limb or for extreme pain. Indeed, the assessment of damages for non-pecuniary losses has been described as an 'intrinsically impossible task' (*Cassell v Broome* [1972] AC 1027 at 1070, per Lord Hailsham LC). Nevertheless, 'slowly and painfully English law has evolved ways of assessing the incalculable' (*West v Shephard* [1964] AC 326 at 359, per Lord Devlin).

Royal Commission on Civil Liability and Compensation for Personal Injury, Chairman: Lord Pearson, *Report* Cm. 7054 (1978)

The function of damages for non-pecuniary loss

359 By definition, money cannot make good a non-pecuniary loss. Yet damages for non-pecuniary loss are recoverable in both English law and, as *solatium*, in Scots law. Indeed they are recoverable in some form in almost all tort systems.

360 What, then, is the purpose of an award for non-pecuniary loss? Clearly it cannot provide full compensation—no amount of money can drive away pain and suffering, or restore a lost limb. But at least three functions may be suggested. First, a conventional award may serve as a palliative. Pain and suffering and loss of amenity are real enough, at least for the seriously injured plaintiff; and he may well feel entitled to some reparation where these misfortunes

befall him because of an injury for which someone else is liable. Secondly, an award for non-pecuniary loss may enable the plaintiff to purchase alternative sources of satisfaction to replace those he has lost. Thirdly, it may help to meet hidden expenses caused by his injury. Although in theory all expenses resulting from injury are recoverable as pecuniary loss, in practice some of them may well be unquantifiable or unforeseen.

Heil v Rankin [2001] QB 272

The facts are not relevant to the extract.

Lord Woolf MR

In the case of pecuniary loss, the courts have progressively been prepared to adopt ever more sophisticated calculations in order to establish the extent of a claimant's loss. The House of Lords' decision in *Wells v Wells* [see p. 895, below] is a recent example of the analytical approach the courts will now adopt. In the case of non-pecuniary damages, the scale of damages has remained a 'jury question'. This is the position notwithstanding section 6 of the Administration of Justice (Miscellaneous Provisions) Act 1933, as a result of which the use of a jury to try personal injury cases became discretionary. In practice, since the 1960's, the assessment of damages has been carried out primarily by the judiciary. The assessment requires the judge to make a value judgment. That value judgment has been increasingly constrained by the desire to achieve consistency between the decisions of different judges. Consistency is important, because it assists in achieving justice by facilitating settlements. The courts have become increasingly aware that this is in the interests of the litigants and society as a whole, particularly in the personal injury field. Delay in resolving claims can be a source of great injustice as well as the cause for expense to the parties and the justice system. It is for this reason that the introduction by the Judicial Studies Board ('J.S.B.') in 1992 of its *Guidelines for the Assessment of General Damages in Personal Injury Cases* was such a welcome development . . .

Excessive importance must not, however, be attached to consistency. Care must be exercised not to freeze the compensation for non-pecuniary loss at a level which the passage of time and changes in circumstances make inadequate. The compensation must remain fair, reasonable and just. Fair compensation for the injured person. The level also must not result in injustice to the defendant, and it must not be out of accord with what society as a whole would perceive as being reasonable.

Whilst recognising the dangers which can arise from too rigid an application of tariffs, it has been the continuous responsibility of the courts not only to set tariffs for damages for non-pecuniary loss in the case of personal injuries, but also, having done so, to keep the tariffs up to date. The courts sought to achieve this by deciding guideline cases and subsequently making allowance for inflation, that is, the depreciation in the value of money, since the guideline was laid down. This usually involved doing no more than applying the guideline decision the appropriate difference between the R.P.I. [Retail Price Index] at the date on which the guideline case was decided and the R.P.I. at the date on which the guideline was applied.

However, the changes which take place in society are not confined to changes in the R.P.I. Other changes in society can result in a level of damages which was previously acceptable no longer providing fair, reasonable and just compensation, taking into account the interests of the claimants, the defendants and society as a whole. For this reason, it is clearly desirable for the courts at appropriate intervals to review the level of damages so as to consider whether what was previously acceptable remains appropriate.

COMMENTARY

It is now generally accepted that the most the law can do is provide for an award that is 'fair'. As is indicated in the extract, fairness is achieved in part through consistency in the level of awards, and this is ensured by awarding 'conventional' sums for non-financial losses, assessed after comparison with awards made in like cases in the past. Details of current awards appear in the practitioners' work *Kemp & Kemp on Damages*, and, as noted in the extract, the Judicial Studies Board has produced a set of guidelines for awards (*Guidelines for the Assessment of General Damages in Personal Injury Cases*, 9th edn. (2008)). Some illustrative figures may be cited from the *Guidelines*: quadriplegia—£206,750–257,750; loss of both arms—£154,000–191,500; total blindness—in the region of £172,500; total deafness and loss of speech—£70,000–90,000; loss of smell—£16,000–21,000; total impotence and loss of sexual function in the case of a young man—in the region of £95,000; a woman's infertility with severe depression and anxiety, pain and scarring—£73,500–108,000 (the awards are much smaller for men and women who have already had children); severe post-traumatic stress disorder—£40,000–64,250; loss of or serious damage to several front teeth—£5,600–7,250. What criteria do you think are employed in assessing the guideline figures? Do you think that the law attaches *the right* value to these very different injuries? (For an attempt to value non-pecuniary losses objectively—with concepts borrowed from the field of health economics—see Karapanou and Visscher, 'Towards a Better Assessment of Pain and Suffering Damages' (2010) 1 JETL 48.)

Whilst endorsing the current general approach to the assessment of awards for non-pecuniary loss, the Court of Appeal in *Heil v Rankin* agreed with a then-recent Law Commission Report (*Damages for Personal Injury: Non-Pecuniary Loss* (Law Com. No. 257 (1999)) that there should be an increase in the general levels of awards, though it stopped short of the Commission's recommendation of a tapered increase of up to 100 per cent (for the most serious injuries), adopting instead a tapered increase of up to 30 per cent. Awards under £10,000 were not affected (cf. the Law Commission's £2,000 threshold). Lewis ('Increasing the Cost of Pain' (2001) 64 MLR 100), observing that a large majority of damages awards for personal injury are for sums under £10,000, and the proportion of damages awarded for non-pecuniary loss is highest in small-value claims, criticises both the Law Commission and the Court of Appeal for failing to engage with fundamental questions as to the priority, in terms of general social policy, that should be given to the compensation of non-pecuniary losses. As *Atiyah* (p. 414) has pointed out, few compensation systems other than tort provide compensation as a palliative or to pay for alternative sources of satisfaction, and the reality is that the tort system is largely financed by insurance premiums paid by a substantial section of the public: 'one is forced to ask whether there are not other claims on society's resources which deserve priority…It is hard to justify compensation for mental distress and deprivation of pleasure when many disabled people receive little or no compensation even for income losses.' The Pearson Commission reached a similar conclusion:

382 We were struck by the high cost of compensation for non-pecuniary loss. It accounts for more than half of all tort compensation for personal injury, and for a particularly high proportion of small payments.

383 We think it likely that payments for minor non-pecuniary loss represent, in part, the price of a settlement. It may well be in the interests of the defendant's insurance company to offer more than a court would award as compensation for the plaintiff's pain and suffering and loss of amenity, in order to avoid the expense of continuing argument and possible litigation. We think this is wasteful.

> 384 Most of us find it hard to justify payments for minor or transient non-pecuniary losses, such as may equally be incurred through sickness or some everyday mishap. We find it impossible to justify their use as bargaining counters. The emphasis in compensation for non-pecuniary loss should in our view be on serious and continuing losses, especially loss of faculty.

The Commission recommended, by a majority, that no damages should be recoverable for non-pecuniary loss suffered during the first three months after the date of injury (para. 388). It estimated that this would produce a saving in the cost of tort compensation of about one-fifth of all awards for personal injury. The proposal was specifically rejected by the Law Commission, which took the view that it lacked any principled basis (*Damages for Personal Injury: Non-Pecuniary Loss*, Law Com. No. 257, 1999, paras 2.25–2.28), and has not been implemented (cf. the position in Australia, where most jurisdictions have eliminated claims for non-pecuniary loss for minor injury; see, e.g., Civil Liability Act 2002 (NSW), s. 16).

(b) Two forms of Non-Financial Loss

Two categories of non-financial loss must be distinguished: pain and suffering, on the one hand, and loss of amenities, on the other. As Lord Scarman observed in *Lim Poh Choo v Camden & Islington AHA* [1980] AC 174 at 188:

> [The authorities] draw a clear distinction between damages for pain and suffering and damages for loss of amenities. The former depend on the plaintiff's personal awareness of pain, her capacity for suffering. But the latter are awarded for the fact of deprivation, a substantial loss, whether the plaintiff is aware of it or not.

Pain and suffering, then, is assessed subjectively: the damages measure the degree of pain actually felt by the claimant (and reflect therefore his or her capacity for suffering). Under this head, the claimant may recover damages to represent the trauma of knowing that his or her life expectancy has been shortened by the accident (Administration of Justice Act 1982, s. 1(1)(b)). Note that the previous, objectively assessed and conventional figure awarded for loss of expectation of life (see *Benham v Gambling* [1941] AC 157) was abolished in Administration of Justice Act 1982, s. 1(1)(a).

Loss of amenities by contrast is assessed objectively. The sum awarded depends on the degree of deprivation—that is, the extent to which the victim is unable to do those things which but for the injury he or she would have been able to do (note the definition of loss of amenities given by the Law Commission Consultation Paper No. 140, *Damages for Personal Injury: Non-Pecuniary Loss*, 1995, para. 2.10). The claimant's lifestyle will be crucial here. As Lord Pearce has remarked, '[i]f there is loss of amenity apart from the obvious and normal loss inherent in the deprivation of the limb—for instance, the claimant's main interest in life was some sport or hobby from which he will in future be debarred, that…increases the assessment' (*West v Shephard*, extracted below, at 365).

The English approach to damages for non-pecuniary loss represents, then, a compromise between subjective and objective approaches, with the former applying to the calculation of damages for pain and suffering, and the latter to the award for loss of amenities. The competing merits of the two approaches were debated in a succession of cases dealing with claimants who were left with impaired consciousness as a result of the tortious conduct in question: *Wise v Kay* [1962] 1 QB 638; *H. West & Son Ltd v Shephard* [1964] AC 326 and *Lim Poh Choo v Camden and Islington Area Health Authority* [1980] AC 174. The present approach was decisively adopted by the House of Lords in *West v Shephard* (confirmed by the subsequent decision of the House of Lords in *Lim*).

H West & Son Ltd v Shephard [1964] AC 326

The plaintiff, a 41-year-old woman, sustained very severe injuries in a motor vehicle accident caused by the negligence of the defendant driver. She was left with cerebral atrophy on her right side and paralysis of all four limbs. As a result, she was no longer able to speak, and such communications as she was able to make were limited to movements of the eyes, face, and right hand. She showed a very limited ability to understand what was said to her and might, to some extent, have been able to appreciate the condition she was in, but she suffered from a severe degree of dementia and there was no prospect of further improvement. She was unable to feed herself and required full time hospital nursing care. At the date of the trial, some two years after the accident, her life expectancy was assessed at five years.

The House of Lords was obliged to rule on the correctness of the decision of the Court of Appeal in *Wise v Kay* [1962] 1 QB 638 to the effect that substantial damages may be awarded for loss of amenity even to a plaintiff who is unconscious.

Lord Morris

My Lords, the damages which are to be awarded for a tort are those which 'so far as money can compensate, will give the injured party reparation for the wrongful act and for all the natural and direct consequences of the wrongful act' (*Admiralty Comrs v Susquehanna (Owners), The Susquehanna* [1926] AC 655 at 661 per Viscount Dunedin). The words 'so far as money can compensate' point to the impossibility of equating money with human suffering or personal deprivations. A money award can be calculated so as to make good a financial loss. Money may be awarded so that something tangible may be procured to replace something else of like nature which has been destroyed or lost. But money cannot renew a physical frame that has been battered and shattered. All that judges and courts can do is to award sums which must be regarded as giving reasonable compensation. In the process there must be the endeavour to secure some uniformity in the general method of approach. By common assent awards must be reasonable and must be assessed with moderation. Furthermore, it is eminently desirable that so far as possible comparable injuries should be compensated by comparable awards. When all this is said it still must be that amounts which are awarded are to a considerable extent conventional.

In the process of assessing damages judges endeavour to take into account all the relevant changes in a claimant's circumstances which have been caused by the tortfeasor. These are often conveniently described as 'heads of damage' ... If there has been some serious physical injury which, as the result of skilled medical attention, has happily not necessitated the enduring of pain, then it will follow that there will be no question of including in an award any sum as compensation for the enduring of pain. If someone has been made unconscious so that pain is not felt the like result will follow. Damages are awarded as a fair compensation for that which has in fact happened and will not arise in respect of anything that has not happened ...

Certain particular questions have been raised. How are general damages affected, if at all, by the fact that the sufferer is unconscious? How are they affected, if at all, if it be the fact that the sufferer will not be able to make use of any money which is awarded?

The first of these questions may be largely answered if it is remembered that damages are designed to compensate for such results as have actually been caused. If someone has been caused pain then damages to compensate for the enduring of it may be awarded. If, however, by reason of an injury someone is made unconscious either for a short or for a prolonged period with the result that he does not feel pain then he needs no monetary compensation in respect of pain because he will not have suffered it. Apart from actual physical pain it may often be that some physical injury causes distress or fear or anxiety. If, for example, personal injuries include the loss of a leg, there may be much physical suffering, there will be the actual loss of the leg (a loss the gravity of which will depend on the particular circumstances of the particular case) and there may be (depending on particular circumstances) elements of consequential worry and anxiety. One part of the affliction (again depending on particular circumstances) may be an inevitable and constant awareness of the deprivations which the loss of the leg entails. These are all matters which judges take into account. In this connexion also the length of the period of life during which the deprivations will continue will be a relevant factor (see *Rose v Ford* [1937] AC 826). To the extent to which any of these last-mentioned matters depend for their existence on an awareness in the victim it must follow that they will not exist and will not call for compensation if the victim is unconscious. An unconscious person will be spared pain and suffering and will not experience the mental anguish which may result from knowledge of what has in life been lost or from knowledge that life has been shortened. The fact of unconsciousness is therefore relevant in respect of, and will eliminate, those heads or elements of damage which can only exist by being felt or thought or experienced. The fact of unconsciousness does not, however, eliminate the actuality of the deprivations of the ordinary experiences and amenities of life which may be the inevitable result of some physical injury.

If damages are awarded to a plaintiff on a correct basis, it seems to me that it can be of no concern to the court to consider any question as to the use that will thereafter be made of the money awarded. If follows that if damages are assessed on a correct basis, there should not then be a paring down of the award because of some thought that a particular plaintiff will not be able to use the money. In assessing damages there may be items which will only be awarded if certain needs of a claimant are established. A particular plaintiff may have provision made for some future form of transport: a particular plaintiff may have to have provision made for some special future attention or some special treatment or medication. If, however, some reasonable sum is awarded to a plaintiff as compensation for pain endured or for the loss of past or future earnings or for ruined years of life or lost years of life, the use to which a plaintiff puts such sum is a matter for the plaintiff alone. A rich man, merely because he is rich and is not in need, is not to be denied proper compensation: nor is a thrifty man merely because he may keep and not spend...

Lord Pearce

The loss of happiness of the individual plaintiff is not, in my opinion, a practicable or correct guide to reasonable compensation in cases of personal injury to a living plaintiff. A man of fortitude is not made less happy because he loses a limb. It may alter the scope of his activities and force him to seek his happiness in other directions. The cripple by the fireside reading or talking with friends may achieve happiness as great as that which, but for the accident, he would have achieved playing golf in the fresh air of the links. To some ancient philosophers the former kind of happiness might even have seemed of a higher nature than the latter, provided that the book or the talk were such as they would approve. Some less robust persons on the other hand are prepared to attribute a great loss of happiness to a quite trivial event. It would be lamentable if the trial of a personal injury claim put a premium on protestations of misery and if a long face was the only safe passport to a large award. Under the present practice there is no call for a parade of personal unhappiness. A plaintiff who cheerfully admits that he is as happy as he was, may yet receive a large award as reasonable compensation for the grave injury and loss of amenity over which he has managed to triumph.

Lord Reid (dissenting)

What is the basis on which damages for serious injuries are awarded? The determination of that question in the ordinary case where the injured person is fully conscious of his disability will go far to decide how to deal with a case like *Wise v Kaye* where the injured person was wholly unconscious with no prospect of ever regaining consciousness or like the present case where the respondent is only conscious to a slight extent.

In the ordinary case of a man losing a leg or sustaining a permanent internal injury, he is entitled to recover in respect of his pain and suffering: if he is fortunate in suffering little pain, he must get a smaller award. So it is not disputed that where an injured person does not suffer at all because of unconsciousness he gets no award under this head. Nothing was awarded in *Wise*'s case and nothing has been awarded in this case. On the other hand no one doubts that damages must be awarded irrespective of the man's mental condition or the extent of his suffering where there is financial loss. That will cover the cost of treatment or alleviation of his condition just as much as it covers the cost of repairing or renewing his property. And it will cover loss of earning power: there may be a question whether some deduction should be made where his outgoings will be less than they would have been if there had been no accident, so as to reach his net financial loss, but that does not arise in the present case. The difficulty is in connexion with what is often called loss of amenity and with curtailment of his expectation of life. If there had been no curtailment of his expectation of life, the man whose injuries are permanent has to look forward to a life of frustration and handicap and he must be compensated, so far as money can do it, for that and for the mental strain and anxiety which results. But I would agree with Sellers LJ in *Wise*'s case that a brave man who makes light of his disabilities and finds other outlets to replace activities no longer open to him must not receive less compensation on that account.

There are two views about the true basis for this kind of compensation. One is that the man is simply being compensated for the loss of his leg or the impairment of his digestion. The other is that his real loss is not so much his physical injury as the loss of those opportunities to lead a full and normal life which are now denied to him by his physical condition—for the multitude of deprivations and even petty annoyances which he must tolerate. Unless I am prevented by authority I would think that the ordinary man is, at least after the first few months, far less concerned about his physical injury than about the dislocation of his normal life. So I would think that compensation should be based much less on the nature of the injuries than on the extent of the injured man's consequential difficulties in his daily life. It is true that in practice one tends to look at the matter objectively and to regard the physical loss of an eye or a limb as the subject for compensation. But I think that is because the consequences of such a loss are very much the same for all normal people. If one takes the case of injury to an internal organ, I think that the true view becomes apparent. It is more difficult to say there that the plaintiff is being paid for the physical damage done to his liver or stomach or even his brain, and much more reasonable to say that he is being paid for the extent to which that injury will prevent him from living a full and normal life and for what he will suffer from being unable to do so.

If that is so, then I think it must follow that if a man's injuries make him wholly unconscious so that he suffers none of these daily frustrations or inconveniences, he ought to get less than the man who is every day acutely conscious of what he suffers and what he has lost. I do not say that he should get nothing. This is not a question that can be decided logically. I think that there are two elements, what he has lost and what he must feel about it, and of the two I think the latter is generally the more important to the injured man. To my mind there is something unreal in saying that a man who knows and feels nothing should get the same as a man who has to live with and put up with his disabilities, merely because they have sustained comparable physical injuries. It is no more possible to compensate an unconscious man than it is to compensate a dead man. The fact that the damages can give no benefit or satisfaction to the injured man and can only go to those who inherit the dead man's estate would not be a good reason for with-holding damages which are legally due. But it is, in my view, a powerful argument against the view that there is no analogy between a dead man and a man who is unconscious and that a man who is unconscious ought to be treated as if he were fully conscious . . .

Lord Tucker concurred with Lord Morris. **Lord Devlin** delivered a separate dissenting opinion.

Appeal dismissed.

COMMENTARY

In *Lim Poh Choo v Camden and Islington Area Health Authority* [1980] AC 174, the House of Lords rejected a challenge to the authority of *West*. The plaintiff, a 36-year-old senior psychiatric registrar employed by the NHS, suffered serious injuries when she had a minor operation at the defendant's hospital. Following the operation her breathing stopped and she suffered a cardiac arrest, leaving her 'the wreck of a human being . . . only intermittently, and then barely, sentient and totally dependent on others' (at 182, per Lord Scarman). Although she was a helpless invalid needing total care, her life expectancy remained substantially as it had been before the accident. At trial, she was awarded £20,000 plus interest in respect of pain, suffering, and loss of amenities (in addition to various sums awarded in respect of pecuniary losses). This award was upheld by the House of Lords. Lord Scarman, who deliv-ered the leading speech, stated (at 188):

[I]t would be wrong now to reverse by judicial decision the two rules which were laid down by the majority of the House in *H West & Son Ltd v Shephard*, namely (1) that the fact of unconsciousness does not eliminate the actuality of the deprivation of the ordinary experiences and amenities . . . and (2) that, if damages are awarded on a correct basis, it is of no concern to the court to consider any question as to the use that will thereafter be made of the money awarded.

A Functional Approach to the Assessment of Damages for Non-Pecuniary Loss?

English law, as the above extract demonstrates, ignores the use to which an injured claimant may be expected to put any damages recovered (but cf. Lord Reid's dissent). By contrast, a dif-ferent approach prevails in Canada where what is known as a 'functional' approach has been adopted (see *Andrews v Grand & Toy Alberta Ltd* (1978) 83 DLR (3d) 452, *Thornton v Board of School Trustees of School District No 57* (1978) 83 DLR (3d) 480, and *Arnold v Teno* (1978) 83 DLR (3d) 609). It was described in the following terms by Dickson J in *Andrews* (at 476–7):

The . . . 'functional' approach . . . attempts to assess the compensation required to provide the injured person 'with reasonable solace for his misfortune'. 'Solace' in this sense is taken to mean physical arrangements which can make his life more endurable rather than 'solace' in the sense of sympathy. To my mind, this . . . approach has much to commend it, as it provides a rationale as to why money is considered compensation for non-pecuniary losses such as loss of amenities, pain and suffering, and loss of expectation of life. Money is awarded because it will serve a useful func-tion in making up for what has been lost in the only way possible, accepting that what has been lost is incapable of being replaced in any direct way . . . If damages for non-pecuniary loss are viewed from a functional perspective, it is reasonable that large amounts should not be awarded once a person is properly provided for in terms of future care for his injuries and disabilities. The money for future care is to provide physical arrangements for assistance, equipment and facilities directly related to the injuries. Additional money to make life more endurable should then be seen as providing more general physical arrangements above and beyond those relating directly to the injuries. The result is a co-ordinated and interlocking basis for compensation, and a more rational justification for non-pecuniary loss compensation.

The functional approach has twice been rejected by the Law Commission (*Personal Injuries Litigation: Assessment of* Damages (Law Com. No. 56, 1973), para. 31; *Damages for Personal Injury: Non-Pecuniary Loss* (Law Com. No. 257, 1999), para. 2.7). One of the Commission's particular concerns (expressed in Consultation Paper No. 149, *Damages for Personal Injury: Non-Pecuniary Loss* (1995), para. 4.09) is that 'it is unrealistic to assume that substitute pleasures can provide full solace to a plaintiff... Even if one thinks in terms of some of the damages being used to provide substitute pleasures, a sum would still seem to be required to make up for the loss of capacity to enjoy life that inevitably remains after "substitutes" have been bought.' Additionally, the Commission feared that awarding damages according to the uses to which a particular claimant could be expected to put the money would leave too much to the circumstances of the individual case, entail the abandonment of the tariff system, and result in inconsistency in awards (*ibid.*).

Effect of Unconsciousness on Award of Damages for Non-Pecuniary Loss

Although the Law Commission rejected the functional approach of the Canadian courts, it did not regard the English 'diminution in value' approach as entirely satisfactory either. Considering the situation of the unconscious claimant, it stated (*ibid.*, para. 4.14):

[W]e are attracted by the view that non-pecuniary loss should be rationalised in terms of the mental suffering and loss of happiness caused to the plaintiff. If the plaintiff is so badly injured that he or she is incapable of suffering, then we consider it strongly arguable that, just as if the plaintiff had been instantly killed, the plaintiff should be regarded as incurring no non-pecuniary loss at all; that, in other words, all non-pecuniary loss should be assessed subjectively (through the plaintiff's awareness of it) and not objectively (irrespective of the plaintiff's awareness of it).

The Commission indicated that this approach—which it termed 'the personal approach'—did not entail that claimants who made light of their injury would receive lower damages than others who failed to come to terms with their condition (para. 4.15). Why should this not follow?

The Commission rejected three possible objections to its approach:

(i) to the objection that the award of substantial damages to an unconscious claimant is necessary because it can never be certain that the plaintiff is not suffering, the Commission replied that medical science is indeed capable of determining whether an individual patient is sentient of his or her condition (para. 4.16);

(ii) against the argument that the Commission's approach would produce the perverse result that it is cheaper to injure someone more seriously than less seriously, the Commission responded that 'this begs the question as to what are the relevant criteria for determining the seriousness of an injury: the basis of the "personal" approach is that the plaintiff who cannot feel anything is in a better position than someone who experiences pain and suffering' (para. 4.17);

(iii) to the objection that the introduction of a nil award for loss of amenity in such cases would produce a lacuna in the rights of a claimant's dependants, the Commission maintained that the rights of dependants should be addressed directly, and that an award in respect of their distress should not be disguised through an award to the injured claimant (para. 4.18).

After receiving responses from consultees, however, the final recommendation of the Commission was that no change in the law was required (*Damages for Personal Injury: Non-Pecuniary Loss* (Law Com. No. 257 (1999), para. 2.19). Arguments in favour of the present position included the concern that a subjective approach would lead to a lower award for non-pecuniary loss in respect of catastrophic injuries than for less serious ones. Further, consultees were not convinced by the Commission's arguments summarised above: many expressed the concern that an allegedly unconscious claimant may have some level of awareness (para. 2.14), and some feared that the failure to award damages for loss of amenity to an unconscious claimant would in fact result in the dependants being deprived of compensation (para. 2.15). Which arguments do you find convincing?

See further Ogus, 'Damages for Lost Amenities: for a Foot, a Feeling or a Function?' (1972) 35 MLR 1, and cf. *Skelton v Collins* (1966) 115 CLR 94.

2. Loss of Earnings

In cases of serious and lasting injury, the sum awarded for loss of earnings may be the most significant element of the damages. In the case of a young employed adult claiming in respect of practically the whole of his or her working life, the damages for loss of earnings can easily run to hundreds of thousands of pounds, and awards of over a million pounds are increasingly common. As we have seen, damages for loss of earnings up to the date of trial fall under the head of 'special damages' as they can be assessed accurately and without undue difficulty; to the extent that the claimant has been 'kept out of his or her money' by being made to wait for receipt of this sum, the courts take account of this by the award of interest. It is in respect of future losses (i.e. those after the date of trial) that real difficulties arise.

(a) Future Losses

Only in a very small minority of claims (5.5 per cent, according to *Pearson*, vol. 2, para. 44) does a tort damages payment include compensation for future loss of earnings. But the injuries in such cases are likely to be among the most serious, and it is therefore necessary to take particular care to ensure the award is adequate. Where the loss is expected to continue for a period of years, there are two ways of calculating the appropriate award, depending on whether the claimant is to receive a lump sum or a periodical payment. Both methods may also be applied to other financial losses, for example, medical costs, that are expected to continue into the future.

The traditional approach is the 'multiplier method' used for lump-sum compensation. The sum awarded is the product of two figures. The multiplicand is the annual loss (net of deductions) that the court expects the claimant to suffer. The multiplier reflects the number of years that the court estimates the loss will continue, discounted to take account of the 'vicissitudes of life' and the fact of accelerated payment (the claimant receives a lump sum immediately and is therefore given investment opportunities that would not otherwise have presented themselves). Because of the claimant's ability to invest the money received, staving off the depreciatory effects of inflation, no special allowance should be made to compensate for the depreciation over time of the value of money. In practice, the maximum multiplier—applied if the claimant is aged around 20—is 26 or 27. This decreases to around 16.5 for those aged 40 and to around 11 for those aged 50.

The alternative approach is for the court to make a periodical payment order. A PPO is 'a wholly different creature... [T]here is neither a multiplicand nor a multiplier' (*Thompstone v Tameside and Glossop Acute Services NHS Trust* [2008] 1 WLR 2207 at [61], per Waller LJ). The court simply prescribes an annual amount that is to be paid at specified intervals for a stated period of time (e.g. until the claimant reaches a particular age or the claimant's death). A crucial advantage of the PPO is that it takes away the risk that the claimant's investment strategy might not provide sufficient protection against the effects of inflation (*Flora v Wakom*, at [27]–[28] per Brooke LJ).

As can be seen from the following extract, the determination of the correct 'discount rate' to be used in assessing a lump sum by the multiplier method is of crucial importance. The case considers the discount rate of 4.5 per cent conventionally employed at the time.

Wells v Wells; Thomas v Brighton Health Authority; Page v Sheerness Steel Co plc [1999] 1 AC 345

The facts of the case are not relevant for present purposes.

Lord Lloyd

The approach to the basic calculation of the lump sum has been explained in many cases... The starting point is the multiplicand, that is to say the annual loss of earnings or the annual cost of care, as the case may be... The medical evidence may be that the need for care will increase or decrease as the years go by, in which case it may be necessary to take different multiplicands for different periods covered by the award. But to simplify the illustration, one can take an average annual cost of care of £10,000 on a life expectancy of 20 years. If one assumes a constant value for money, then if the court were to award 20 times £10,000 it is obvious that the plaintiff would be overcompensated. For the £10,000 needed to purchase care in the 20th year should have been earning interest for 19 years. The purpose of the discount is to eliminate this element of overcompensation. The objective is to arrive at a lump sum which by drawing down both interest and capital will provide exactly £10,000 a year for 20 years, and no more. This is known as the annuity approach. It is a simple enough matter to find the answer by reference to standard tables. The higher the assumed return on capital, net of tax, the lower the lump sum. If one assumes a net return of 5 per cent the discounted figure would be £124,600 instead of £200,000. If one assumes a net return of 3 per cent the figure would be £148,800.

The same point can be put the other way round. £200,000 invested at 5 per cent will produce £10,000 a year for 20 years. But there would still be £200,000 left at the end.

So far there is no problem. The difficulty arises because, contrary to the assumption made above, money does not retain its value. How is the court to ensure that the plaintiff receives the money he will need to purchase the care he needs as the years go by despite the impact of inflation? In the past the courts have solved this problem by assuming that the plaintiff can take care of future inflation in a rough and ready way by investing the lump sum sensibly in a mixed 'basket' of equities and gilts. But the advent of the index-linked government stock (they were first issued in 1981) has provided an alternative. The return of income and capital on index-linked government stock (ILGS) is fully protected against inflation. Thus the purchaser of £100 of ILGS with a maturity date of 2020 knows that his investment will then be worth £100 plus x per cent of £100, where x represents the percentage increase in the retail price index between the date of issue and the date of maturity (or, more accurately, eight months before the two dates). Of course if the plaintiff were to invest his £100 in equities it might then be worth much more. But it might also be worth less. The virtue of ILGS is that it provides a risk-free investment.

The first instance judges in these appeals have broken with the past. They have each assumed for the purpose of the calculation that the plaintiffs will go into the market, and purchase the required amount of ILGS so as to provide for his or her future needs with the minimum risk of their damages being eroded by inflation. How the plaintiffs will in fact invest their damages is, of course, irrelevant. That is a question for them. It cannot affect the calculation. The question for decision therefore is whether the judges were right to assume that the plaintiffs would invest in ILGS with a low average net return of 2.5 per cent, instead of a mixed portfolio of equities and gilts. The Court of Appeal has held not. They have reverted to the traditional 4 to 5 per cent with the consequential reduction in the sums awarded...

[His Lordship proceeded to consider the defendants' argument that the ordinary prudent investor would invest substantially in equities, which could be assumed to produce a higher rate of return than ILGS.]

Granted that a substantial proportion of equities is the best long term investment for the ordinary prudent investor, the question is whether the same is true for these plaintiffs. The ordinary investor may be presumed to have enough to live on. He can meet his day-to-day requirements. If the equity market suffers a catastrophic fall, as it did in 1972, he has no immediate need to sell. He can abide his time, and wait until the equity market eventually recovers.

The plaintiffs are not in the same happy position. They are not 'ordinary investors' in the sense that they can wait for long-term recovery, remembering that it was not until 1989 that equity prices regained their old pre-1972 level in real terms. For they need the income, and a portion of their capital, every year to meet their current cost of care. A plaintiff who invested the whole of his award in equities in 1972 would have found that their real value had fallen by 41 per cent in 1973 and by a further 62 per cent in 1974. The real value of the income on his equities had also fallen.

So it does not follow that a prudent investment for the ordinary investor is a prudent investment for the plaintiffs. Equities may well prove the best long-term investment. But their volatility over the short term creates a serious risk... [E]very long period starts with a short period. If there is a substantial fall in equities in the first five or 10 years, during which the plaintiff will have had to call on part of his capital to meet his needs, and will have had to realise that part of his capital in a depressed market, the depleted fund may never recover.

While therefore I agree with the Court of Appeal that, in calculating the lump sum, courts are entitled to assume that the plaintiff will behave prudently, I do not agree that what is prudent for the ordinary investor is necessarily prudent for the plaintiff. Indeed the opposite may be the case. What the prudent plaintiff needs is an investment which will bring him the income he requires without the risks inherent in the equity market; which brings us back to ILGS...

In the end it comes back to the question of risk. Ex hypothesi equities are riskier than gilts. That is the very reason why the return on equities is likely to be greater. The plaintiffs say that they are not obliged to bear that extra risk for the benefit of the defendants...

[G]uidelines as to the rate of interest for economic and non-economic loss should be simple to apply, and broad enough to allow for the special features of individual cases. Such guidelines are not to be regarded as rules of law or even rules of practice. They set no binding precedent, and can be altered as circumstances alter...

Conclusion

My conclusion is that the judges in these three cases were right to assume for the purpose of their calculations that the plaintiffs would invest their damages in ILGS for the following reasons.

(1) Investment in ILGS is the most accurate way of calculating the present value of the loss which the plaintiffs will actually suffer in real terms.

(2) Although this will result in a heavier burden on these defendants, and, if the principle is applied across the board, on the insurance industry in general, I can see nothing unjust. It is true that insurance premiums may have been fixed on the basis of the 4 to 5 per cent discount rate indicated in *Cookson v Knowles* [1979] AC 556 and the earlier authorities. But this was only because there was then no better way of allowing for future inflation. The objective was always the same. No doubt insurance premiums will have to increase in order to take account of the new lower rate of discount. Whether this is something which the country can afford is not a subject on which your Lordships were addressed. So we are not in a position to form any view as to the wider consequences.

(3) The search for a prudent investment will always depend on the circumstances of the particular investor. Some are able to take a measure of risk, others are not. For a plaintiff who is not in a position to take risks, and who wishes to protect himself against inflation in the short term of up to ten years, it is clearly prudent to invest in ILGS It cannot therefore be assumed that he will invest in equities and gilts. Still less is it his duty to invest in equities and gilts in order to mitigate his loss.

(4) Logically the same applies to a plaintiff investing for the long term. In any event it is desirable to have a single rate applying across the board, in order to facilitate settlements and to save the expense of expert evidence at the trial. I take this view even though it is open to the Lord Chancellor under s 1(3) of the 1996 Act to prescribe different rates of return for different classes of case . . .

(5) How the plaintiff, or the majority of plaintiffs, in fact invest their money is irrelevant. The research carried out by the Law Commission [*Personal Injury Compensation: How Much is Enough?* (Law Com No 225, 1994)] does not suggest that the majority of plaintiffs in fact invest in equities and gilts, but rather in a building society or a bank deposit.

(6) There was no agreement between the parties as to how much greater, if at all, the return on equities is likely to be in the short or long term. But it is at least clear that an investment in ILGS will save up to 1 per cent per annum by obviating the need for continuing investment advice . . .

Consequences

Once it is accepted that the lump sum should be calculated on the basis of the rate of return available on ILGS, then an assessment of the average rate of return at the relevant date presents no problem. The rates are published daily in the *Financial Times*.

[His Lordship adopted a net discount rate of 3 per cent, accepting that this figure was to some extent an approximation, but he felt that it 'sounded right' and was an appropriate guideline figure to apply in subsequent cases. It was, however, necessary to retain flexibility to depart from this figure if, for example, the average rate of return on ILGS should rise or fall significantly.]

Lord Steyn, **Lord Hope**, **Lord Clyde** and **Lord Hutton** delivered speeches in favour of allowing the appeals.

Appeals allowed.

COMMENTARY

Section 1 of the Damages Act 1996 provides:

In determining the return to be expected from the investment of a sum awarded as damages for future pecuniary loss in an action for personal injury the court shall, subject to and in accordance with rules of court made for the purposes of this section, take into account such rate of return (if any) as may from time to time be prescribed by an order made by the Lord Chancellor . . .

The Lord Chancellor exercised his power to make such an order in June 2001 (Damages (Personal Injury) Order 2000, SI 2001/2301), adopting a discount rate of 2.5 per cent. Economic circumstances had changed since the time of the House of Lords' decision, and ILGS could no longer be expected to achieve a net yield of 3 per cent. In a statement setting out his reasons (*Setting the Discount Rate: Lord Chancellor's Reasons*, July 2001), he indicated that he considered the *Wells v Wells* approach to be broadly correct, as tort claimants who had suffered severe injuries could not be expected to take even moderate risks when they invested their damages. However, he said he could not ignore the likelihood that those receiving large awards would invest in a mixed portfolio of equities and gilts (including ILGS), albeit one involving very low risks, and not in risk-free ILGS alone. For this reason, he set the discount rate at the top end of the range of estimates of what ILGS could be expected to yield. He indicated that it was desirable to set a single rate to cover all cases, even though this meant ignoring the widely differing personal and financial circumstance of individual claimants, as this would promote certainty and facilitate the negotiation of settlements.

Although s. 1 allows the parties in an individual case to argue that a different discount rate is appropriate, the Court of Appeal in *Warriner v Warriner* [2002] 1 WLR 1703 made it clear that such circumstances would be rare; the claimant would need to show that there were special features of the case which had not been considered by the Lord Chancellor in making his order. This is consistent with the approach previously adopted by the Court of Appeal to attempts by claimants to argue that the 3 per cent discount rate set out in *Wells v Wells* should be varied (*Warren v Northern General Hospital NHS Trust* [2000] 1 WLR 1404).

The insurance industry estimated that the change in discount rate from 4.5 per cent to 3 per cent after *Wells v Wells* increased the cost of motor insurance by about 1 per cent, employers' liability insurance by 2 per cent, and public liability insurance by 7 per cent (Lord Chancellor's Department, *Damages: The Discount Rate and Alternatives to Lump Sum Payments (a consultation paper)*, 2000, para. 14). It appears that the further reduction in the discount rate to 2.5 per cent will entail additional rises of 0.5 per cent in motor insurance premiums, 1.1 per cent in employers' liability premiums, and 0.4 per cent in public liability premiums (Lord Chancellor's Department, *Regulatory Impact Assessment (Damages Act 1996: Analysis of the Impact of the Prescribed Discount Rate of 2.5%)*, March 2002). Taken in isolation, these rises may not appear that significant, but they in fact form part of a wider pattern of reforms that have increased the average size of damages payments in recent years. (See also *Heil v Rankin*, p. 886, above, and Lewis, Morris and Oliphant, 'Tort personal injury claims statistics: Is there a compensation culture in the United Kingdom' (2006) 14 TLJ 158 at pp. 172–4.) Ultimately, of course, these costs are borne not just by defendants and their liability insurers but by the community at large.

The Ogden Tables

In assessing the appropriate multiplier to use, the courts have in recent years made use of actuarial calculations (which are used in the insurance industry to work out the cost of annuities for persons of different ages in the light of an assessment of average life expectancies). There was some initial scepticism on the part of the courts as to the value of such calculations, as expressed memorably in Oliver LJ's view that 'as a method of providing a reliable guide to individual behaviour patterns, or to future economic and political events, the predictions of an actuary can be only a little more likely to be accurate (and will almost certainly be less entertaining) than those of an astrologer' (*Auty v National Coal Board* [1985] 1 WLR 784 at 800–1; see also *Taylor v O'Connor* [1971] AC 115, *Hunt v Severs* [1994] 2 AC 350). However, it is now commonplace to refer to tables of actuarial calculations specially adapted for use in the assessment of damages by an official working party chaired by Sir Michael Ogden, and in *Wells* Lord Lloyd commented: 'the tables should now be regarded as the starting-point, rather than as a check'. The tables indicate the appropriate multiplier to use for the average person across the whole range of ages in assessing damages both for lost earnings and for the cost of life-long medical care. Different tables are provided for various assumed rates of return on investment, so the tables are just as compatible with the approach of the House of Lords in *Wells v Wells* as they were with the previous approach stemming from *Cookson v Knowles*. Note that Civil Evidence Act 1995, s. 10(1) specifically provides that the Ogden tables are to be admissible in evidence for the purpose of assessing, in an action for personal injury, the sum to be awarded as general damages for future pecuniary loss, but at the date of writing this section has not been brought into force, presumably because use of the tables has become commonplace in practice. This may be seen as another factor which has served to increase the amount of damages payments in recent years.

Child Claimants

The position of child claimants warrants special attention.

(i) *Annual amount* Where a child suffers injuries that will impair his or her earning capacity in later life, the court may take average national earnings as the starting-point in assessing the multiplicand (*Croke v Wiseman* [1982] 1 WLR 71) or, presumably, the annual amount to be awarded under a PPO. Deviation from average earnings might however be appropriate if the child were nearing the end of a job training scheme or embarking on a university law degree or if he or she enjoyed a career as a child TV star. Where there is simply too much uncertainty as to what the claimant would have earned in the absence of the tortious act, the court should simply calculate the damages as a global sum (*Clarke v Devon County Council* [2005] 2 FLR 747, a case of failure to diagnose and treat dyslexia: it was uncertain what the claimant would have earned if he had received special education). Conversely, in one—surely a very exceptional—case, the Court of Appeal approved a multiplicand of almost 2.5 times national average earnings even though the claimant was injured at birth and was only eight at the time of the trial (*Cassel v Riverside Health Authority* [1992] PIQR Q168). The court took account of the claimant's favourable family circumstances (caring, close-knit, happy and well-to-do) and heredity—several of his forbears had achieved success in commerce, the arts and the professions, including an uncle, grandfather and great grandfather who all became Queen's Counsel, his parents both achieved several 'O' and 'A' Levels at school, and his father had increased his assets by prudent investment in property, as others in the family had done in the past. The claimant therefore likely possessed 'legal, … artistic and entrepreneurial genes': [1992] PIQR Q1 at Q15 per Rose J. He would also have had as good an education as money could buy, having been put down for Eton (the famous private school) at or before birth. All things considered, it was reasonable to assume that he would have enjoyed earnings equivalent to the salary of a partner in a medium-sized City law firm. Do you think it is justified to compensate for loss of a career that the claimant could not even have embarked on for another dozen years or more?

(ii) *The multiplier* Where the court wishes to award a lump sum calculated by the multiplier method, an additional reduction will be made in the multiplier, over and above those made in the case of an adult claimant, to reflect the passage of time before the child reaches working age. There are two reasons for this:

(i) the uncertainties in a child's case are greater than in that of an adult, as many things might happen to the child before he or she reaches working age;

(ii) the receipt of the money is even more 'accelerated' than is the case with an adult, giving the child an even greater opportunity to invest the money profitably.

These problems were faced in *Croke v Wiseman* [1982] 1 WLR 71 in which the plaintiff, aged 21 months at the time of his accident and seven years at the time of his trial, had suffered severe brain damage, rendering him incapable of working and reducing his life expectation so that he was expected to live only until 40. The court based the multiplicand on average national earnings but used a multiplier of only five (far lower than it would in the case of an adult expected to survive for another 20 years or more of working life).

(b) The Lost Years

Where a person's life expectancy is reduced by an accident, do damages for loss of future earnings reflect the pre- or post-accident life expectancy? If the former, they may be styled 'wages in heaven', that is, they will compensate for a period in which the claimant is now expected to be dead. Lord Denning has described the problem as follows (*What Next in the Law* (London: Butterworths, 1982), p. 146):

> Take a man of thirty. If he had not been injured, he would have expected to live, say, till seventy-five. But owing to his injury, he will probably die at fifty. No doubt he should get damages for his loss of earnings from age thirty to age fifty. But is he to get damages for loss of earnings from age fifty to age sixty-five when he would have retired? Those fifteen years from fifty to sixty-five are 'lost years'—lost to him by reason of the accident. Ought damages be awarded for the 'lost years'?

The conclusion reached by the House of Lords in *Pickett v British Rail Engineering* [1980] AC 136 was that damages should indeed be awarded for the lost years. These would be calculated by taking the annual amount appropriate for the time during which, but for the accident, the claimant would have been alive and deducting from it the money the claimant would save by being dead, that is his or her living expenses. Alternatively, the court may now make a PPO, providing for the payment of the full annual loss until the claimant dies, and then a reduced amount to the claimant's dependants until a specified date (e.g. when the claimant would have reached retirement age).

Pickett v British Rail Engineering Ltd [1980] AC 136

The deceased contracted the asbestos-related cancer, mesothelioma, while working for the defendant and as a result of the defendant's admitted negligence. Before his death, he issued a writ against the defendant claiming damages for personal injuries. The defendant contested the quantum of liability. The judge awarded the deceased damages under various heads, including a sum in respect of loss of earnings which covered only the one year from the date of trial for which the deceased was expected to survive (here the trial judge was bound by the previous Court of Appeal decision in *Oliver v Ashman* [1962] 2 QB 210). The deceased's estate appealed, arguing that damages for loss of future earnings should cover the whole period of the deceased's pre-tort working life expectancy.

Lord Wilberforce

In 1974, when his symptoms became acute, the deceased was a man of 51 with an excellent physical record. He was a champion cyclist of Olympic standard, he kept himself very fit and was a non-smoker. He was leading an active life and cycled to work every day. He had a wife and two children. There was medical evidence at the trial as to his condition and prospects, which put his then expectation of life at one year: this the judge accepted. There can be no doubt that but for his exposure to asbestos dust in his employment he could have looked forward to a normal period of continued employment up to retiring age. That exposure, for which the defendant accepts liability, has resulted in this period being shortened to one year. It seems, therefore, strange and unjust that his claim for loss of earnings should be limited to that one year (the survival period) and that he should recover nothing in respect of the years of which he has been deprived (the lost years). But this is the result of authority binding on the judge and the Court of Appeal, *Oliver v Ashman*. The present is, in effect, an appeal against that decision.

Oliver v Ashman is part of a complex of law which has developed piecemeal and which is neither logical nor consistent. Judges do their best to make do with it but from time to time cases appear, like the present, which do not appeal to a sense of justice. I shall not review in any detail the state of the authorities for this was admirably done by Holroyd Pearce LJ in *Oliver v Ashman*. The main strands in the law as it then stood were: (1) the Law Reform (Miscellaneous Provisions) Act 1934 abolished the old rule *actio personalis moritur cum persona* and provided for the survival of causes of action in tort for the benefit of the victim's estate; (2) the decision of this House in *Rose v Ford* [1937] AC 826 that a claim for loss of expectation of life survived under the 1934 Act, and was not a claim for damages based on the death of a person and so barred at common law (cf. *Admiralty Comrs v Owners of Steamship Amerika* [1917] AC 38); (3) the decision of this House in *Benham v Gambling* [1941] AC 157 that damages for loss of expectation of life could only be given up to a conventional figure, then fixed at £200; (4) the Fatal Accidents Acts under which proceedings may be brought for the benefit of dependants to recover the loss caused to those dependants by the death of the breadwinner; the amount of this loss is related to the probable future earnings which would have been made by the deceased during 'lost years'.

This creates a difficulty. It is assumed in the present case, and the assumption is supported by authority, that if an action for damages is brought by the victim during his lifetime, and either proceeds to judgment or is settled, further proceedings cannot be brought after his death under the Fatal Accidents Acts. If this assumption is correct, it provides a basis, in logic and justice, for allowing the victim to recover for earnings lost during his lost years.

This assumption is based on the wording of s. 1 of the 1846 Act (now s. 1 of the Fatal Accidents Act 1976) and is not supported by any decision of this House. It cannot however be challenged in this appeal, since there is before us no claim under the Fatal Accident Acts. I think therefore, that we must for present purposes act on the basis that it is well founded, and that if the present claim, in respect of earnings during the lost years, fails it will not be possible for a fresh action to be brought by the deceased's dependants in relation to them.

With this background, *Oliver v Ashman* may now be considered. I shall deal with it on authority and on principle...

[Having considered whether the decision in *Oliver v Ashman* was justified by the authorities, and found that it was not, his Lordship proceeded:] As to principle, the passage which best summarises the underlying reasons for the decision in *Oliver v Ashman* is the following (at 240, per Willmer LJ):

> ... what has been lost by the person assumed to be dead is the opportunity to enjoy what he would have earned, whether by spending it or saving it. Earnings themselves strike me

as being of no significance without reference to the way in which they are used. To inquire what would have been the value to a person in the position of this plaintiff of any earnings which he might have made after the date when ex hypothesi he will be dead strikes me as a hopeless task.

Or as Holroyd Pearce LJ put it ([1962] 2 QB 210 at 230): 'What is lost is an expectation, not the thing itself.'

My Lords, I think that these are instinctual sentences, not logical propositions or syllogisms, none the worse for that because we are not in the field of pure logic. It may not be unfair to paraphrase them as saying: 'Nothing is of value except to a man who is there to spend or save it. The plaintiff will not be there when these earnings hypothetically accrue: so they have no value to him.' Perhaps there are additional strands, one which indeed Willmer LJ had earlier made explicit, that the whole process of assessment is too speculative for the courts to undertake; another that the only loss is a subjective one, an emotion of distress. But if so I would disagree with them. Assumptions, chances, hypotheses enter into most assessments, and juries had, we must suppose, no difficulties with them; the judicial approach, however less robust, can manage too. And to say that what calls for compensation is injured feelings does not provide an answer to the vital question which is whether, in addition to this subjective element, there is something objective which has been lost.

But is the main line of reasoning acceptable? Does it not ignore the fact that a particular man, in good health, and sound earning, has in these two things an asset of present value quite separate and distinct from the expectation of life which every man possesses? Compare him with a man in poor health and out of a job. Is he not, and not only in the immediate present, a richer man? Is he not entitled to say, at one moment I am a man with existing capability to earn well for 14 years, the next moment I can only earn less well for one year? And why should he be compensated only for the immediate reduction in his earnings and not for the loss of the whole period for which he has been deprived of his ability to earn them? To the argument that 'they are of no value because you will not be there to enjoy them' can he not reply, 'Yes they are; what is of value to me is not only my opportunity to spend them enjoyably, but to use such part of them as I do not need for my dependants, or for other persons or causes which I wish to support. If I cannot do this, I have been deprived of something on which a value, a present value, can be placed'?

I do not think that the problem can be solved by describing what has been lost as an 'opportunity' or a 'prospect' or an 'expectation'. Indeed these words are invoked both ways, by the Lords Justices as denying a right to recover (on grounds of remoteness, intangibility or speculation), by those supporting the appellant's argument as demonstrating the loss of some real asset of true value. The fact is that the law sometimes allows damages to be given for the loss of things so described (e.g. *Chaplin v Hicks* [1911] 2 KB 786), sometimes it does not. It always has to answer a question which in the end can hardly be more accurately framed than as: 'Is the loss of this something for which the claimant should and reasonably can be compensated?'

The defendant, in an impressive argument, urged on us that the real loss in such cases as the present was to the victim's dependants and that the right way in which to compensate them was to change the law (by statute; judicially it would be impossible) so as to enable the dependants to recover their loss independently of any action by the victim. There is much force in this, and no doubt the law could be changed in this way. But I think that the argument fails because it does not take account, as in an action for damages account must be taken, of the interest of the victim. Future earnings are of value to him in order that he may satisfy legitimate desires, but these may not correspond with the allocation which the law makes of money recovered by dependants on account of his loss. He may wish to benefit some dependants more than, or to the exclusion of, others; this (subject to family inheritance legislation) he is entitled to do. He may not have dependants, but he may have others, or causes, whom he would wish to benefit, for whom he might even regard himself as working. One cannot make a distinction, for the purposes of assessing damages, between men in different family situations.

There is another argument, in the opposite sense; that which appealed to Streatfeild J in *Pope v D Murphy & Son Ltd* [1960] 2 All ER 873. Why, he asked, should the tortfeasor benefit from the fact that as well as reducing his victim's earning capacity he has shortened his victim's life? Good advocacy but unsound principle, for damages are to compensate the victim not to reflect what the wrongdoer ought to pay.

My Lords, in the case of the adult wage earner with or without dependants who sues for damages during his lifetime, I am convinced that a rule which enables the 'lost years' to be taken into account comes closer to the ordinary man's expectations than one which limits his interest to his shortened span of life. The interest which such a man has in the earnings he might hope to make over a normal life, if not saleable in a market, has a value which can be assessed. A man who receives that assessed value would surely consider himself and be considered compensated; a man denied it would not. And I do not think that to act in this way creates insoluble problems of assessment in other cases. In that of a young child (cf. *Benham v Gambling*) neither present nor future earnings could enter into the matter; in the more difficult case of adolescents just embarking on the process of earning (cf. *Skelton v Collins* (1966) 115 CLR 94) the value of 'lost' earnings might be real but would probably be assessable as small.

There will remain some difficulties. In cases, probably the normal, where a man's actual dependants coincide with those for whom he provides out of the damages he receives, whatever they obtain by inheritance will simply be set off against their own claim. If on the other hand this coincidence is lacking, there might be duplication of recovery. To that extent injustice may be caused to the wrongdoer. But if there is a choice between taking a view of the law which mitigates a clear and recognised injustice in cases of normal occurrence, at the cost of the possibility in fewer cases of excess payments being made, or leaving the law as it is, I think that our duty is clear. We should carry the judicial process of seeking a just principle as far as we can, confident that a wise legislator will correct resultant anomalies.

Lord Salmon, **Lord Edmund-Davies** and **Lord Scarman** delivered separate concurring speeches. **Lord Russell of Killowen** dissented on the question of the 'lost years'.

Appeal allowed.

COMMENTARY

The question of the appropriate deduction in respect of living expenses under the rule in *Pickett* was considered by the Court of Appeal in *Harris v Empress Motors* [1984] 1 WLR 212. It held that the court should only deduct those sums spent by the plaintiff exclusively on himself; money that was spent on dependants should not be deducted even if it could be regarded as benefiting the plaintiff too (e.g. paying the bills for a common residence). Compare the position with regard to such sums under the Fatal Accidents Act 1976 (see Ch. 17).

As Lord Wilberforce intimated, child claimants again raise special problems. The general position of the courts here—exemplified by the decision of the Court of Appeal in *Croke v Wiseman* (above)—has been to regard earnings in the lost years as too speculative to make any award under this heading, although in the case of a child claimant with an established earning capacity an award might be justified (see Lord Scarman's example of a five-year-old child TV star in *Gammell v Wilson* [1982] AC 27). It would also be unfair to ignore the lost years where their number is very large—as in the case of a child claimant whose post-accident life expectancy only just reaches adulthood—and in such a case they may be compensated through a small adjustment in the multiplier applied to the basic multiplicand, rather than by a separate calculation (*Neale v Queen Mary's Sidcup NHS Trust* [2003] EWHC 1471; see further *Housecroft v Burnett* [1986] 1 All ER 332 at 345, per O'Connor LJ).

In *Pickett* Lord Wilberforce expressed the generally-held view that, once a claimant had successfully brought an action for his injuries while he was alive, this prevented his dependants from suing for loss of dependency under the fatal accidents legislation, even if the death was the result of the original tort. The solution reached in *Pickett* was to allow the living claimant a claim for 'lost years' but in *Gregg v Scott* [2005] 2 AC 176 at [182], Lord Phillips stated that a better solution would be to allow the dependants a claim even if the deceased had already successfully brought an action during his lifetime. From the dependants' point of view, using the lost years claim as a means of providing for them after the claimant's premature death carries two risks—at least where the claimant's damages are awarded in a lump sum. First, the claimant may spend the lost years component of the award before he dies, with the result that there is nothing left for the dependants on his death. Secondly, even if the claimant has not dissipated this portion of his award by his death, whatever is left over will fall to be distributed under his will. Whilst the dependants may well be beneficiaries under the will, they do not have to be—and if they are not none of the lost years award will filter down to them. Given that one reason given in *Pickett* for allowing the lost years award was to provide for the dependants, do you agree with Lord Phillips' assessment that the protection of their interests by an award for the lost years is 'a poor substitute' for a direct claim for loss of dependency under the Fatal Accidents Act 1976? Note, however, that the court now has power to make a periodic payment order in cases where damages for lost years are awarded (see CPR, r 41.8(2)). The order may provide, for example, for the payment of the full annual loss to the claimant until he dies, and then a reduced amount to his dependants until a specified date (e.g. for the period during which the claimant would have been alive and providing financial support). Such an order would provide far greater protection for the dependants' interests than a lump sum awarded to the claimant, but not as much as an independent claim under the Fatal Accidents Act (where the amount of the award is calculated more generously than in a lost years claim: see Ch. 17.III, below).

3. Medical Care

(a) General

The cost of medical care is recovered in the same way as any other form of financial loss. In the case of future medical care, the courts again have a choice between the traditional multiplier method and a PPO. In both cases, the period of loss may be longer than that for the loss of earnings, because the victim's care needs may continue past retirement age.

One issue that arises here, and has been touched on before, is that 'inflation-proofing' the award by reference to movements in the retail price index may be inadequate, because care costs have historically risen faster than the RPI (see *Wells v Wells* [1999] 1 AC 345 at 369,

Lord Lloyd). The courts have already addressed this concern in respect of PPOs by opting to link the annual amount awarded for future medical care to average earnings, rather than prices (see p. 883, above). This contrasts with the approach taken to the award of lump sum damages, where no adjustment to either multiplier or multiplicand has yet been permitted. In *Cooke v United Bristol Healthcare NHS Trust* [2004] 1 WLR 251 the Court of Appeal ruled that the Lord Chancellor in setting the standard discount rate of 2.5 per cent under the Damages Act 1996, s. 1 had plainly intended it to apply to care costs, not just lost earnings. His aim was to prescribe a single discount rate even at the expense of a somewhat 'rough and ready' approach to future pecuniary losses. There was no warrant for treating claims where future care costs were likely to be very high as 'exceptional' under s. 1(2) and applying a different discount rate to them (see further p. 898, above). Nor was it permissible to allow for future rises in care costs by stepped increases in the multiplicand, as this would be an illicit attempt to subvert the Lord Chancellor's order indirectly. Do you think it is justifiable to take a different approach to the inflation-proofing of future care costs depending on whether the award is made by PPO or lump sum?

A particular problem arises where the claimant is spared certain expenses as an incidental by-product of medical care. Where the claimant is in hospital, many of his or her day-to-day needs may be satisfied by the hospital. Thus, for example, there may be no need to spend money on meals as food is provided. If the claimant is being treated on the NHS, the position is governed by s. 5 of the Administration of Justice Act 1982. This section seeks to avoid double recovery by providing that maintenance at the public expense is to be taken into account by way of a set-off to damages awarded for lost earnings. If the claimant elects for private treatment, then the courts will deduct a 'domestic element' from the cost of the treatment so as to avoid overlap with that proportion of the claimant's lost earnings that would have gone on living expenses (per Lord Scarman in *Lim* at 191). In *Lim*, Lord Scarman concluded that the plaintiff was entitled to recover a sum representing her loss of earnings and her cost of care, but an amount reflecting the domestic element was deducted from the latter head of damages.

(b) Mitigation of Loss and the State Provision of Care

There is no duty to mitigate by seeking treatment on the NHS rather than privately. Law Reform (Personal Injuries) Act 1948, s. 2(4) provides:

> In an action for damages for personal injuries (including any such action arising out of a contract), there shall be disregarded, in determining the reasonableness of any expenses, the possibility of avoiding those expenses or part of them by taking advantage of facilities available under [the National Health Service Act 2006] . . .

A claimant is therefore quite free to opt for private medical care instead of that which is offered free by the state, and cannot be accused of failing to mitigate in exercising that option. The subsection does not apply to the provision of care and assistance by local authorities, but a claimant who wishes to 'go private' in preference to reliance on statutory care or assistance provided by a local authority is also entitled to damages for the cost as of right: *Peters v East Midlands Strategic Health Authority* [2010] QB 48. Of course, if the claimant has in fact received state care he cannot claim for private treatment. As regards future medical treatment, if the claimant's needs cannot fully be met in the private sector, so that at some stage he will have to rely on the state, then a claim for the cost of private medical care will be reduced, and if the only way that treatment can be provided is through the NHS no claim for private treatment will be allowed (see *Housecroft v Burnett* [1986] 1 All ER 332; *Woodrup v Nicol* [1993] PIQR Q104). The prospect of the claimant claiming for the cost of future private medical care but in fact using the NHS prompted the Pearson Commission to recommend the repeal of s. 2(4) (para. 342) but the Law Commission recommended the section be retained, considering it unlikely that problems would arise in practice (*Damages for Personal Injury: Medical, Nursing, and Other Expenses* (CP No. 144, 1996) paras 3.10–3.13, 3.18; *Damages for Personal Injury: Medical, Nursing and Other Expenses: Collateral Benefits* (Law Com. No. 262 (1999), para 3.18; see also DCA, *The Law on Damages* (CP 9/07, 2007), paras 146–63).

In a related development the government in 2001 requested that the Chief Medical Officer (CMO)—in a review of clinical negligence law and practice—consider whether the care costs element of NHS compensation payments should continue to be based on the costs of private rather than NHS care. In his subsequent report (*Making Amends*, 2003), the CMO noted concern expressed by claimant and patient groups at the NHS's capacity to provide care in accident cases currently handled in the private sector, and at the range of treatments and services the NHS was able to provide (para. 4.32). He also accepted that empirical investigation of how claimants used their damages did not support the contention that claimants who received damages reflecting the cost of private treatment in fact made frequent use of NHS services to provide their care (para. 4.30). Nevertheless, he submitted that the NHS was in a different position from other defendants, and recommended that clinical negligence claims arising from NHS treatment should be exempted from s. 2(4) (recommendation 17). In response to obvious concerns about the equity of exempting a state defendant from a responsibility imposed on defendants generally, the proposal was substantially watered down. The NHS Redress Act 2006 now provides for the creation of a scheme enabling redress to be provided to the victims of NHS negligence without recourse to civil proceedings, with 'redress' expressly extended beyond financial compensation to cover contracts to provide care or treatment (s. 3(3)(a)). In other words, the redress scheme may offer the aggrieved party a special NHS care package—perhaps equivalent to private health care—in addition to financial compensation, making it less likely that the latter will opt for private care and seek to recover the costs in ordinary civil proceedings. What the impact will be on ordinary NHS care, and whether it is desirable to have a two-tier NHS, are large questions which we cannot address here. At time of writing, the Act was not yet in effect.

If the claimant does opt for state care, can the NHS (or whatever public body provides the care) pursue the tortfeasor for its own consequential costs? Such claims are for purely economic loss, and at common law are caught by the general exclusion of such claims from the tort of negligence (*Islington LBC v University College London Hospital NHS Trust* [2006] PIQR P3). But the position is of course different where there is express statutory provision, such as has applied for some considerable time in cases of hospital treatment following a road traffic accident. Successive Road Traffic Acts have accorded the provider of hospital treatment the right to recover expenses from the vehicle owner or the insurer where compensation has been paid in respect of death or injury arising out of a road accident, though the amount recoverable is capped at a relatively low level—£2,949 for each person treated as an in-patient (see Road Traffic Act 1988, s. 157). (Further small sums may be recovered by a practitioner giving emergency treatment to a traffic accident victim: ss. 158 and 159.) For many years, responsibility for seeking recovery was left with the individual hospital, but the Road Traffic (NHS Charges) Act 1999 shifted responsibility for collecting these sums, in respect of NHS hospitals, to the same central department (the Compensation Recovery

Unit) that is responsible for recouping social security benefits using a similar procedure (see below). The Act also increased the charges recoverable to reflect more closely actual costs. (See further Lewis, 'Recovery of NHS Accident Costs' (1999) 62 MLR 903.) Subsequently, the scheme was extended beyond road traffic cases to all personal injury (but not disease) claims by the Health and Social Care (Community Health and Standards) Act 2003, which repeals the relevant provisions of the 1999 Act.

Health and Social Care (Community Health and Standards) Act 2003

Section 150: Liability to pay NHS charges

(1) This section applies if—
  (a) a person makes a compensation payment to or in respect of any other person (the 'injured person') in consequence of any injury, whether physical or psychological, suffered by the injured person, and
  (b) the injured person has—
    (i) received NHS treatment at a health service hospital as a result of the injury.
    (ii) been provided with NHS ambulance services as a result of the injury for the purpose of taking him to a health service hospital for NHS treatment (unless he was dead on arrival at that hospital), or
    (iii) received treatment as mentioned in sub-paragraph (i) and been provided with ambulance services as mentioned in sub-paragraph (ii).

(2) The person making the compensation payment is liable to pay the relevant NHS charges—
  (a) in respect of—
    (i) the treatment, in so far as received at a hospital in England or Wales,
    (ii) the ambulance services, in so far as provided to take the injured person to such a hospital,
  to the Secretary of State...

(3) 'Compensation payment' means a payment, including a payment in money's worth, made—
  (a) by or on behalf of a person who is, or is alleged to be, liable to any extent in respect of the injury, or
  (b) in pursuance of a compensation scheme for motor accidents,
  but does not include a payment mentioned in Schedule 10.

(4) Subsection (1)(a) applies—
  (a) to a payment made—
    (i) voluntarily, or in pursuance of a court order or an agreement, or otherwise, and
    (ii) in the United Kingdom or elsewhere, and
  (b) if more than one payment is made, to each payment.

(5) 'Injury' does not include any disease.

(6) Nothing in subsection (5) prevents this Part from applying to—
  (a) treatment received as a result of any disease suffered by the injured person, or
  (b) ambulance services provided as a result of any disease suffered by him, if the disease in question is attributable to the injury suffered by the injured person (and accordingly that treatment is received or those services are provided as a result of the injury)...

COMMENTARY

The scheme came into force on 29 January 2007. The across-the-board recovery of NHS hospital charges accords with the recommendation of the Law Commission in its report on *Damages for Personal Injury: Medical, Nursing and Other Expenses; Collateral Benefits* (Law Com. No. 262 (1999), para. 3.43) and with subsequent Department of Health consultations. The government's Regulatory Impact Assessment (RIA) estimated that the scheme could allow the NHS to augment the sums recovered under the previous road traffic accident (RTA) scheme by up to 165 per cent per year (the additional sums being the cost of treating non-RTA personal injury cases), causing a 1.5 per cent increase in insurance premiums for businesses (RIA, para. 5.36). The 'fundamental principle' underlying the scheme is that 'the NHS, and therefore the taxpayer, should not have to subsidise those responsible for causing injury to others' (para. 11.2). The reform can be seen as an aspect of a broader transfer of the costs of accidental injury from the public to the private sector (see p. 884, above). It is also expected that the scheme will contribute to better accident prevention (para. 2.3). The costs of primary NHS care (e.g. GPs' services), however, do not fall within the scheme and the NHS's 'subsidy' of tort defendants will therefore remain to that extent, with a consequent distortion of the incentives for accident prevention.

Schedule 10, mentioned in s. 150(3) above, provides for certain 'exempted payments' including payments under compensation orders made against convicted persons by the criminal courts, payments by the claimant's own (first-party) insurer, and payments under the Fatal Accidents Act 1976 (i.e. damages for loss of dependency and bereavement), so there is no recovery of NHS costs where the primary victim's family brings a claim consequent on his or her death. As the dependants' claim under the 1976 Act does not extend to any medical expenses incurred by the deceased prior to his or her death, the tortfeasor's payment *to them* cannot reflect any benefit the tortfeasor may have gained by the deceased using NHS services before death; hence the exclusion of such payments.

The reference in s. 150(3)(b) to 'a compensation scheme for motor accidents' makes it clear that the recovery scheme extends to payments by the Motor Insurers Bureau in respect of road traffic accidents caused by uninsured or untraceable drivers (see further p. 979, below).

Compensation payments in respect of disease are excluded by s. 150(5), though sub-s. (6) qualifies this to a limited extent. If the claimant is injured and the injury itself triggers a disease (e.g. by infection), the costs of treating the disease are recoverable under the scheme. But if the claimant suffers a free-standing disease for which he or she receives compensation (e.g. employment-related asbestosis), all consequent NHS treatment falls outside the scheme. One concern was that the difficulties inherent in calculating treatments costs in disease cases might result in a burden on NHS information systems outweighing the benefits of the scheme, especially where the patient is suffering from other illnesses too (see Department of Health, *The recovery of National Health Service costs in cases involving personal injury compensation: a consultation* (2002), paras 5.2 and 5.3, also noting that many of the costs are likely to occur within the primary care sector and so be unrecoverable). Insurers and business also objected to the inclusion of disease claims because many cases would have retrospective costs (Department of Health, *The Recovery of National Health Service Costs in Cases Involving Personal Injury Compensation: Consultation Summary of Outcome*, September 2003, para. 5.16).

The recoverable charges are specified in the Personal Injuries (NHS Charges) (Amounts) Regulations 2007, reg. 2 (as amended): £177 for each ambulance journey, £585 for treatment as an outpatient and £719 per day where the claimant is admitted to hospital, subject to a maximum of £42,999. The amounts are reduced to the extent of any contributory negligence by the injured person (s. 153(3)). Payment of the charge may be sought from individual tort-feasors, not just liability insurers, but may be waived on grounds of excessive hardship (s. 157(5)).

(c) Gratuitous Provision of Care

A problem which all legal systems have to consider concerns care given gratuitously (e.g. by a relative) to the claimant because of injuries attributable to the defendant's negligence.

Hunt v Severs [1994] 2 AC 350

The plaintiff was seriously injured in a road accident whilst riding on the pillion of a motorcycle driven by the defendant, who admitted negligence. The plaintiff, aged 22 at the time of the accident, suffered paraplegia as a result and subsequently spent long periods in various hospitals. Whenever she was not in hospital, she and the defendant lived together and five years after the accident they were married. At trial, the plaintiff was awarded damages under various heads. Included in the award of special damages was a sum of £17,000 representing the value of the past services rendered by the defendant in caring for the plaintiff when she was at home. Included in the award for future loss was a sum of £60,000 representing the estimated value of the services which would be rendered by the defendant in caring for the plaintiff in future. The defendant appealed against a number of heads of damages awarded to the plaintiff, including the award of the two sums specified above.

Lord Bridge

My Lords, a plaintiff who establishes a claim for damages for personal injury is entitled in English law to recover as part of those damages the reasonable value of services rendered to him gratuitously by a relative or friend in the provision of nursing care or domestic assistance of the kind rendered necessary by the injuries the plaintiff has suffered. The major issue which arises for determination in this appeal is whether the law will sustain such a claim in respect of gratuitous services in the case where the voluntary carer is the tortfeasor himself . . .

The law with respect to the services of a third party who provides voluntary care for a tortiously injured plaintiff has developed somewhat erratically in England. The voluntary carer has no cause of action of his own against the tortfeasor. The justice of allowing the injured plaintiff to recover the value of the services so that he may recompense the voluntary carer has been generally recognised, but there has been difficulty in articulating a consistent juridical principle to justify this result . . .

In *Cunningham v Harrison* [1973] QB 942 and *Donnelly v Joyce* [1974] QB 454 judgments were delivered by different divisions of the Court of Appeal on successive days. In *Cunningham* the wife of a severely disabled plaintiff, who had initially looked after him, had died before the trial. Lord Denning MR said, at pp 951–952:

> Before dealing with [the claim for future nursing expenses] I would like to consider what the position would have been if the wife had not died and had continued to look after her husband, as she had been doing. The plaintiff's advisers seem to have thought that a husband could not claim for the nursing services rendered by a wife unless the husband was legally bound to pay her for them. So, on their advice on 11 July 1972, an agreement was signed

whereby the husband agreed to pay his wife £2,000 per annum in respect of her nursing services. We were told that such advice is often given by counsel in such cases as these when advising on evidence. I know the reason why such advice is given. It is because it has been said in some cases that a plaintiff can only recover for services rendered to him when he was legally liable to pay for them … But, I think that view is much too narrow. It seems to me that when a husband is grievously injured—and is entitled to damages—then it is only right and just that, if his wife renders services to him, instead of a nurse, he should recover compensation for the value of the services that his wife has rendered. It should not be necessary to draw up a legal agreement for them. On recovering such an amount, the husband should hold it on trust for her and pay it over to her. She cannot herself sue the wrongdoer … but she has rendered services necessitated by the wrongdoing, and should be compensated for it. If she had given up paid work to look after him, he would clearly have been entitled to recover on her behalf; because the family income would have dropped by so much: see *Wattson v Port of London Authority* [1969] 1 Lloyd's Rep 95, 102, per Megaw J. Even though she had not been doing paid work but only domestic duties in the house, nevertheless all extra attendance on him certainly calls for compensation.

In *Donnelly v Joyce* [1974] QB 454, the injured plaintiff was a boy of six. His mother gave up her work for a period to provide necessary care for him and the disputed item in his claim related to the mother's loss of wages. The judgment of the court delivered by Megaw LJ contains a lengthy review of the authorities, but the key passage relied on by the trial judge and the Court of Appeal in the instant case is at pp 461–462, and reads:

> We do not agree with the proposition, inherent in Mr. Hamilton's submission, that the plaintiff's claim, in circumstances such as the present, is properly to be regarded as being, to use his phrase, 'in relation to someone else's loss,' merely because someone else has provided to, or for the benefit of, the plaintiff—the injured person—the money, or the services to be valued as money, to provide for needs of the plaintiff directly caused by the defendant's wrongdoing. The loss is the plaintiff's loss. The question from what source the plaintiff's needs have been met, the question who has paid the money or given the services, the question whether or not the plaintiff is or is not under a legal or moral liability to repay, are, so far as the defendant and his liability are concerned, all irrelevant. The plaintiff's loss, to take this present case, is not the expenditure of money to buy the special boots or to pay for the nursing attention. His loss is the existence of the need for those special boots or for those nursing services, the value of which for purposes of damages—for the purpose of the ascertainment of the amount of his loss—is the proper and reasonable cost of supplying those needs. That, in our judgment, is the key to the problem. So far as the defendant is concerned, the loss is not someone else's loss. It is the plaintiff's loss.

Hence it does not matter, so far as the defendant's liability to the plaintiff is concerned, whether the needs have been supplied by the plaintiff out of his own pocket or by a charitable contribution to him from some other person whom we shall call the 'provider'; it does not matter, for that purpose, whether the plaintiff has a legal liability, absolute or conditional, to repay to the provider what he has received, because of the general law or because of some private agreement between himself and the provider; it does not matter whether he has a moral obligation, however ascertained or defined, so to do. The question of legal liability to reimburse the provider may be very relevant to the question of the legal right of the provider to recover from the plaintiff. That may depend on the nature of the liability imposed by the general law or the particular agreement. But it is not a matter which affects the right of the plaintiff against the wrongdoer.

With respect, I do not find this reasoning convincing. I accept that the basis of a plaintiff's claim for damages may consist in his need for services but I cannot accept that the question from what source that need has been met is irrelevant. If an injured plaintiff is treated in hospital as a private patient he is entitled to recover the cost of that treatment. But if he receives free treatment under the National Health Service, his need has been met without cost to him and he cannot claim the cost of the treatment from the tortfeasor. So it cannot, I think, be right to say that in all cases the plaintiff's loss is 'for the purpose of damages . . . the proper and reasonable cost of supplying [his] needs' . . .

[I]t is . . . important to recognise that the underlying rationale of the English law, as all the cases before *Donnelly v Joyce* [1974] QB 454 demonstrate, is to enable the voluntary carer to receive proper recompense for his or her services and I would think it appropriate for the House to take the opportunity [to adopt] the view of Lord Denning MR in *Cunningham v Harrison* [1973] QB 942 that . . . the injured plaintiff who recovers damages under this head should hold them on trust for the voluntary carer.

By concentrating on the plaintiff's need and the plaintiff's loss as the basis of an award in respect of voluntary care received by the plaintiff, the reasoning in *Donnelly v Joyce* diverts attention from the award's central objective of compensating the voluntary carer. Once this is recognised it becomes evident that there can be no ground in public policy or otherwise for requiring the tortfeasor to pay to the plaintiff, in respect of the services which he himself has rendered, a sum of money which the plaintiff must then repay to him . . .

[B]efore your Lordships Mr McGregor [for the plaintiff], recognising the difficulty of formulating any principle of public policy which could justify recovery against the tortfeasor who has to pay out of his own pocket, advanced the bold proposition that such a policy could be founded on the liability of insurers to meet the claim. Exploration of the implications of this proposition in argument revealed the many difficulties which it encounters. But I do not think it necessary to examine these in detail. The short answer, in my judgment, to Mr McGregor's contention is that its acceptance would represent a novel and radical departure in the law of a kind which only the legislature may properly effect. At common law the circumstance that a defendant is contractually indemnified by a third party against a particular legal liability can have no relevance whatever to the measure of that liability . . .

Lord Keith, **Lord Jauncey**, **Lord Browne-Wilkinson** and **Lord Nolan** agreed with Lord Bridge.

Appeal allowed.

COMMENTARY

This decision met with a chorus of disapproval. For analysis, see Kemp (1994) 110 LQR 524, and Matthews and Lunney, 'A Tortfeasor's Lot is Not a Happy One' (1995) 58 MLR 395, and note the Australian High Court's preference for the former 'claimant need' approach in *Kars v Kars* (1996) 187 CLR 354 (noted by Lunney (1997–8) 8 KCLJ 115). One problem highlighted by Matthews and Lunney is the failure of the House of Lords to distinguish between pre-trial and post-trial caring services. Whilst it might have been justifiable to make no award in respect of pre-trial services—although the authors argue otherwise—different considerations apply to post-trial services because the defendant tortfeasor may become incapable of providing the same services in future; in such a case, the *Hunt v Severs* approach provides the claimant with no financial means to purchase alternative care. There are also several problems with the Law Lords' view that, in the normal case of gratuitous care rendered by a third party, the notional care costs should be held on trust for the carer, for example, because the latter will receive an undeserved windfall if the victim dies unexpectedly.

For these and other reasons, the Law Commission (*Damages for Personal Injury: Medical, Nursing and Other Expenses; Collateral Benefits* (Law Com. No. 262, 1999), paras 3.62, 3.76) subsequently recommended legislation to reverse the result in *Hunt v Severs* in so far as it concerned gratuitous care rendered by the defendant. In all cases, the claimant would have a personal obligation to account to the carer (whether the tortfeasor or not) for pre-trial care, rather than an obligation under a trust. There would be no obligation to account to the carer for post-trial gratuitous care. The government accepted that reform was necessary (see DCA, *The Law on Damages* (2007), paras 114–20) and included the following clause in its draft Civil Law Reform Bill presented in December 2009:

7 Damages for gratuitous services

(1) Subsection (2) applies if, on a claim for damages for personal injury, a court awards damages to the injured person in respect of a gratuitous provision of services to that person.

(2) The injured person must account to—

   (a) such persons as provided the services before the date of the award, and

   (b) such persons as provided the services on or after that date.

(3) A court must not refuse to award damages in respect of a gratuitous provision of services merely because the person providing the services is the defendant.

(4) But a court may not award damages in respect of a gratuitous provision of services by the defendant to the injured person for any period before the date of the award (and accordingly subsection (2)(a) does not apply) . . .

Does this provision implement the Law Commission's proposals? How would it be applied on the facts of *Hunt v Severs* itself?

For an argument that the basis of the carer's entitlement to compensation lies in the law of unjust enrichment rather than tort, see S. Degeling, *Restitutionary Rights to Share in Damages: Carers' Claims* (Cambridge: CUP, 2003). Degeling submits that the law should afford the carer, like an insurer exercising a right of subrogation, the power to compel the victim to sue. Do you think it is desirable that the law should intrude on private relations in such a way?

What if the defendant's tort, rather than necessitating the provision of gratuitous services *to the claimant*, prevents the claimant from providing gratuitous services *for others*? Can the claimant claim for the value of these services he or she can no longer provide? In *Daly v General Steam Navigation Ltd* [1981] 1 WLR 120 it was held that the plaintiff could recover the substitute value of unpaid household services which she could no longer perform as a result of the tort. As a dependant can recover for the value of the household services gratuitously provided before his or her death by the deceased under the Fatal Accidents Act 1976 (see Ch. 17.III), the decision in *Daly* ensures that damages are also recovered where the services cannot be provided as a result of the tortfeasor injuring rather than killing the gratuitous provider of the services (although they are recovered by the claimant rather than by the claimant's dependants). The limits of these claims, however, are more difficult to determine: they extend to gratuitous household services that the claimant provided for him- or herself (e.g. mowing the lawn) but would the cost of hiring a substitute dog walker be included? These and other difficulties lead the High Court of Australia in *CSR v Eddy* (2005) 226 CLR 1 to reject any such awards, even in respect of household services: the failure to provide services to another simply reflected a change in the ability of the plaintiff to live her life in the way that she had previously lived, and there was no justification for taking this one aspect of loss of amenity—loss of the ability to provide caring services to others—and to compensate that aspect by reference to the pecuniary value of the services to the recipient. Such a loss was compensated as part of an award of general damages for loss of amenity. Do you agree? (Note that some jurisdictions in Australia have now introduced legislation allowing the value of gratuitous domestic services provided to dependants to be recovered, e.g. Civil Liability Act 2002 (NSW), s. 15B.)

4. Deductions

The aim of compensation is to replace what the claimant has lost. Hence lost income is assessed net of tax (*BTC v Gourley* [1956] AC 185). Furthermore, the court must inquire whether the claimant has taken up alternative, perhaps less demanding, employment after the accident and will award only the difference between the level of earnings if the accident had not occurred and that which the claimant will now earn.

In addition, various saved expenses must be taken into account, for example where the claimant is saved substantial costs incurred in going to work (see *Dews v National Coal Board* [1988] AC 1 at 12–13, per Lord Griffiths). We have already noted that a similar problem arises where the claimant is spared certain expenses as a result of her medical treatment.

In order to avoid double compensation, it may be necessary to deduct from the damages the amount of benefits received as a result of the accident from other sources ('collateral benefits'). Hence, where an employee receives sick pay after an accident has rendered her unfit for work, this is generally deducted from the amount of damages received. But the law here is not straightforward, as the following section reveals.

(a) Collateral Benefits: General Principles

In *Hussain v New Taplow Paper Mills Ltd* [1988] AC 514 at 527, the House of Lords recognised two exceptions to the rule requiring full deduction of collateral benefits (per Lord Bridge):

> [T]o the prima facie rule there are two well-established exceptions. First, where a plaintiff recovers under an insurance policy for which he has paid the premiums, the insurance moneys are not deductible from damages payable by the tortfeasor...Second, when the plaintiff receives money from the benevolence of third parties prompted by sympathy for his misfortune, as in the case of a beneficiary from a disaster fund, the amount received is again to be disregarded...

Tricky questions arise as to whether certain benefits received by the claimant from her employer as a result of her injury are appropriately regarded as 'insurance' payments which are non-deductible. Disability pensions and employers' sickness benefit schemes, for example, might be regarded as insurance schemes taken out by the employer on the employee's behalf and paid for by the employee whose wages are reduced as a consequence. In *Hussain*, Lord Bridge drew a distinction between:

(i) benefits which represent a partial substitute for earnings, such as sick pay, and

(ii) benefits ('pensions') which are only payable after employment ceases.

In his view, only the latter could be regarded as the fruits of insurance.

On the facts of the case before him, Lord Bridge held that an occupational long-term sickness benefit scheme was a substitute for earnings rather than the fruits of insurance. Under the scheme benefits were paid to employees incapacitated from work for the duration of the incapacity (until death or retirement age) so long as the employee remained in employment with the employer. This can be contrasted with the decision in *Parry v Cleaver* [1970] AC 1, where the House of Lords held that an occupational disability pension, whether contributory or non-contributory, was not deductible, because a pension is analogous to private insurance. Whether there should be a difference between occupational sick pay and occupational disability pensions is another matter; as Lord Morris pointed out, in his dissenting opinion in *Parry* (at 32):

> If under the terms of a contract of employment the time comes when instead of having full pay or half pay or sick pay a person retires with a pension, the loss which he suffers is the difference between the amount of his pay and the amount of his pension. If it is said that a pension is neither pay nor insurance benefit then I would say that where there is no discretionary element and where the arrangements leading to a pension are an essential part of the contract of employment then the pension payments are very much more akin to pay than to anything else.

Note that *Parry* was upheld in *Smoker v London Fire & Civil Defence Authority* [1991] 2 AC 502 on the basis that pension benefits were the fruits of money set aside in respect of past work and the defendant was not entitled to reduce his liability by appropriating these amounts. See also *Longden v British Coal Corporation* [1998] AC 653.

The reason for the exception of insurance payments from the normal rule of deductibility of collateral benefits was classically stated by Pigott B in *Bradburn v Great Western Railway Co* (1874) LR 10 Exch 1 at 3:

> [T]here is no reason or justice in setting off what the plaintiff has entitled himself to under a contract with third persons, by which he has bargained for the payment of a sum of money in the event of an accident happening to him. He does not receive that sum of money because of the accident, but because he has made a contract providing for the contingency; an accident must occur to entitle him to it, but it is not the accident, but his contract, which is the cause of his receiving it.

The reason charitable payments are not deducted was clearly stated by Lord Reid in *Parry v Cleaver* [1970] AC 1 at 14:

> It would be revolting to the ordinary man's sense of justice, and therefore contrary to public policy, that the sufferer should have his damages reduced so that he would gain nothing from the benevolence of his friends or relatives or of the public at large, and that the only gainer would be the wrongdoer.

The Law Commission found in 1999 that there was no need for statutory reform of the common law approach (*Damages for Personal Injury: Medical, Nursing and Other Expenses; Collateral Benefits* (Law Com. No. 262, 1999), para. 11.53.) Subsequently, the government endorsed the principal exceptions to the general rule of deductibility but proposed that the claimant should, wherever practicable, be compensated at the expense of the tortfeasor rather than the collateral benefit payer (DCA, *The Law on Damages*, CP 9/07 (2007), paras 103 and 107). Collateral benefits should be disregarded in the assessment of damages—bringing the law into line with the treatment of Fatal Accidents Act claims (see Ch. 17.III.3, below)—with benefits already paid being refunded by the claimant from the damages, while the obligation to provide further benefits would be extinguished (para. 108). This proposal was not, however, included in the government's draft Civil Law Reform Bill of 2009.

For general discussion of these issues, see Lewis, 'Deducting collateral benefits from damages: principle and policy' (1998) 18 LS 15.

(b) Social Security Benefits

Special statutory rules apply to the deduction of social security benefits. The basic provisions are now set out in the Social Security (Recovery of Benefits) Act 1997. A particular area of controversy has been the introduction in 1989 of a 'recoupment' regime, whereby the state is able to 'claw back' from the defendant certain benefits paid to the claimant under the social security system. Concern that this regime was unduly diminishing the compensation monies paid to tortiously injured persons led to reform of the rules in 1997.

Social Security (Recovery of Benefits) Act 1997

Section 1: Cases in which this Act applies

(1) This Act applies in cases where—
    (a) a person makes a payment (whether on his own behalf or not) to or in respect of any other person in consequence of any accident, injury or disease suffered by the other, and
    (b) any listed benefits have been, or are likely to be, paid to or for the other during the relevant period in respect of the accident, injury or disease.

(2) The reference above to a payment in consequence of any accident, injury or disease is to a payment made—
    (a) by or on behalf of a person who is, or is alleged to be, liable to any extent in respect of the accident, injury or disease, or—
    (b) in pursuance of a compensation scheme for motor accidents; but does not include a payment mentioned in Part I of Schedule 1.

(3) Subsection (1)(a) applies to a payment made—
    (a) voluntarily, or in pursuance of a court order or an agreement, or otherwise, and
    (b) in the United Kingdom or elsewhere.

(4) In a case where this Act applies—
    (a) the 'injured person' is the person who suffered the accident, injury or disease,
    (b) the 'compensation payment' is the payment within subsection (1)(a), and
    (c) 'recoverable benefit' is any listed benefit which has been or is likely to be paid as mentioned in subsection (1)(b) ...

Section 3: 'The relevant period'

(1) In relation to a person ('the claimant') who has suffered any accident, injury or disease, 'the relevant period' has the meaning given by the following subsections.

(2) Subject to subsection (4), if it is a case of accident or injury, the relevant period is the period of five years immediately following the day on which the accident or injury in question occurred.

(3) Subject to subsection (4), if it is a case of disease, the relevant period is the period of five years beginning with the date on which the claimant first claims a listed benefit in consequence of the disease.

(4) If at any time before the end of the period referred to in subsection (2) or (3)—
    (a) a person makes a compensation payment in final discharge of any claim made by or in respect of the claimant and arising out of the accident, injury or disease, or
    (b) an agreement is made under which an earlier compensation payment is treated as having been made in final discharge of any such claim,
    the relevant period ends at that time.

(5) The reference above to a payment in consequence of any accident, injury or disease is to a payment made—

Section 4: Applications for certificates of recoverable benefits

(1) Before a person ('the compensator') makes a compensation payment he must apply to the Secretary of State for a certificate of recoverable benefits . . .

Section 6: Liability to pay Secretary of State amount of benefits

(1) A person who makes a compensation payment in any case is liable to pay to the Secretary of State an amount equal to the total amount of the recoverable benefits . . .

Section 8: Reduction of compensation payment

(1) This section applies in a case where, in relation to any head of compensation listed in column 1 of Schedule 2—
    (a) any of the compensation payment is attributable to that head, and
    (b) any recoverable benefit is shown against that head in column 2 of the Schedule.

(2) In such a case, any claim of a person to receive the compensation payment is to be treated for all purposes as discharged if—
    (a) he is paid the amount (if any) of the compensation payment calculated in accordance with this section, and
    (b) if the amount of the compensation payment so calculated is nil, he is given a statement saying so by the person who (apart from this section) would have paid the gross amount of the compensation payment.

(3) For each head of compensation listed in column 1 of the Schedule for which paragraphs (a) and (b) of subsection (1) are met, so much of the gross amount of the compensation payment as is attributable to that head is to be reduced (to nil, if necessary) by deducting the amount of the recoverable benefit or, as the case may be, the aggregate amount of the recoverable benefits shown against it.

(4) Subsection (3) is to have effect as if a requirement to reduce a payment by deducting an amount which exceeds that payment were a requirement to reduce that payment to nil.

(5) The amount of the compensation payment calculated in accordance with this section is—
    (a) the gross amount of the compensation payment, less
    (b) the sum of the reductions made under subsection (3), (and, accordingly, the amount may be nil).

Schedule 2:Calculation of compensation payment

(1) Head of compensation	(2) Benefit
1. Compensation for earnings lost during the relevant period.	Disablement pension...; Incapacity benefit; Income support; Invalidity pension and allowance; Jobseeker's allowance; Reduced earnings allowance; Severe disablement allowance; Sickness benefit; Statutory sick pay; Unemployability supplement; Unemployment benefit.
2. Compensation for cost of care incurred during the relevant period.	Attendance allowance; Care component of disability living allowance; Disablement pension increase...
3. Compensation for loss of mobility during the relevant period.	Mobility allowance, Mobility component of disability living allowance.

COMMENTARY

This statutory scheme, created in largely its present form in 1989, replaces the previous scheme implemented by s. 2(1) of the Law Reform (Personal Injuries) Act 1948. The essence of the earlier scheme was a 50 per cent rule, whereby the defendant was entitled to offset half of any specified benefits received or to be received, for five years from the date the cause of action accrued. After this period, the question of deduction was left to the common law, which adopted a principle of no deduction in many cases (e g. in relation to the state retirement pension: *Hewson v Downs* [1970] 1 QB 73). There was no provision for the state to 'claw back' any of the benefits paid to the claimant.

The current law regarding the deduction of social security benefits can be summarised in the following (somewhat simplified) propositions:

(i) The compensation received by the victim is reduced by the full value of specified benefits (defined in Sch. 2, col. 2) received during the relevant period (s. 8). The deduction only applies to heads of compensation with which the particular benefit is matched (explained further below).

(ii) The relevant period (defined in s. 3) is five years from the injury, or, in the case of a disease, five years from the date of the first claim for benefit as a result of the disease. However, a payment in final discharge of the claim brings the relevant period to an end.

(iii) No deduction at all is made in respect of benefits falling outside the relevant period, i.e. after the lapse of five years or the date of settlement, whichever is earlier (because s. 8 allows reduction of the compensation payment only in respect of 'recoverable benefits', which are defined in terms of 'the relevant period': s. 1(1)(b) and (4)(c)).

(iv) The 'compensator' (normally the tortfeasor or his insurer) is liable to pay the amount deducted from the compensation to the Secretary of State for Work and Pensions (s. 6). The compensator must apply for a 'certificate of recoverable benefit' before making any compensation payment (s. 4(1)). This should normally be granted within 28 days, after which the compensator has 14 days in which to pay (ss. 5–6, not extracted).

The original scheme of 1989 allowed for the deduction of recoverable benefits from the total amount of compensation payable, rather than from particular heads of claim. This was perceived to be unfair, especially because it could result in a nil award even though there was substantial pain and suffering, which social security benefits are not designed to compensate. The 1997 Act aimed to address this concern by dividing the award of damages into the components listed in column 1 of Sch. 2, extracted above, for the purpose of deduction. No deduction may be made against awards for pain and suffering, whilst only specified benefits may be deducted against awards for loss of earnings, cost of care and loss of mobility. One important change made by the 1997 Act relates to where the amount of recoverable benefit is greater than the amount that can be deducted from the damages award. The compensator must, in every case, pay the Secretary of State the full amount of recoverable benefit (s. 6(1)), even if this results in a total payment in excess of the original damages award. For example, if the claimant receives an award of £10,000 (£5,000 for pain and suffering, £5,000 for loss of earnings) and the relevant benefit payable is £8,000, the result will be as follows. Assuming the relevant benefit is one that can be deducted against loss of earnings, the claimant's compensation for loss of earnings will be reduced to zero. This still leaves £3,000 of relevant benefit which cannot be deducted (because no deductions can be made against damages for pain and suffering). The result will be that the compensator will pay £5,000 to the claimant and £8,000 to the Secretary of State (a total of £13,000), even though the original damages award was only £10,000.

Another change from before 1997 was the abolition of an exemption in respect of small payments, being payments of less than £2,500, though the Act provides for regulations to restore the exemption if this is deemed necessary (see s. 1(2) and Sch. 1).

The Scheme is operated by a government agency, the Compensation Recovery Unit, whose website provides additional information: www.dwp.gov.uk/cru/. (The same agency now works with NHS bodies to recover treatment costs arising from accidental personal injury: see above.) See further R. Lewis, *Deducting Benefits from Damages for Personal Injury* (Oxford: OUP, 1999), chs 12–17.

17 DEATH AND DAMAGES

The death of a person raises two questions in respect of liability in the law of tort. First, does the death of one of the parties to a tort action extinguish that action? At common law the general rule for a tort claim was that it did, but this has now been changed by statute (Law Reform (Miscellaneous Provisions) Act 1934, below). Death here does not create the cause of action; the question is what effect it has on an existing cause of action, and the person who brings any action under this Act does so as representative of the deceased. The second question is whether the death of another as a result of a tort gives rise to a new cause of action in those who have suffered damage as a result of the death. In this situation death is the factor that creates the cause of action, and the claimant in such an action sues for a loss suffered by him personally. Again the common law frowned on such actions (*Baker v Bolton* (1808) 1 Camp 493), but a statutory cause of action was created in 1846, although both the plaintiffs and the damage for which they could sue were limited, and remain so in the modern version of the 1846 legislation (Fatal Accidents Act 1976).

I. The Effect of Death on Existing Causes of Action

Law Reform (Miscellaneous Provisions) Act 1934

1. EFFECT OF DEATH ON CERTAIN CAUSES OF ACTION

(1) Subject to the provisions of this section, on the death of any person after the commencement of this Act all causes of action subsisting against or vested in him shall survive against, or, as the case may be, for the benefit of, his estate. Provided that this subsection shall not apply to causes of action for defamation...

(1A) The right of a person to claim under section 1A of the Fatal Accidents Act 1976 (bereavement) shall not survive for the benefit of his estate on his death.

(2) Where a cause of action survives as aforesaid for the benefit of the estate of a deceased person, the damages recoverable for the benefit of the estate of that person—
    (a) shall not include—
        (i) any exemplary damages;
        (ii) any damages for loss of income in respect of any period after that person's death;...
    (b) ...
    (c) where the death of that person has been caused by the act or omission which gives rise to the cause of action, shall be calculated without reference to any loss or gain to

his estate consequent on his death, except that a sum in respect of funeral expenses may be included...

(4) Where damage has been suffered by reason of any act or omission in respect of which a cause of action would have subsisted against any person if that person had not died before or at the same time as the damage was suffered, there shall be deemed, for the purposes of this Act, to have been subsisting against him before his death such cause of action in respect of that act or omission as would have subsisted if he had died after the damage was suffered.

(5) The rights conferred by this Act for the benefit of the estates of deceased persons shall be in addition to and not in derogation of any rights conferred on the dependants of deceased persons by the Fatal Accidents Acts 1846 to 1976...and so much of this Act as relates to causes of action against the estates of deceased persons shall apply in relation to causes of action under the said Acts as it applies in relation to other causes of action not expressly excepted from the operation of subsection (1) of this section.

Hicks v Chief Constable of the South Yorkshire Police
[1992] 2 All ER 65

The two deceased, spectators at the Hillsborough football stadium at the time of the tragic events there of April 1989, were killed when they and many others were crushed to death by the press of people in the pens at one end of the ground as a result of the defendant's negligence. Each suffered traumatic asphyxia which deprived them of their ability to breathe, and the medical evidence was that once the asphyxia had set in, unconsciousness would have followed within seconds and death would have occurred within five minutes. There was no indication in the post mortem reports on either of the deceased of physical injuries attributable to anything other than the fatal crushing which caused the asphyxia, save for some superficial bruising in respect of one of the deceased which could have occurred either before or after loss of consciousness. The plaintiffs, administrators of the deceased's estates, brought actions for the benefit of the estates under s. 1(1) of the Law Reform (Miscellaneous Provisions) Act 1934, claiming damages from the defendant for the deceased's pre-death pain and suffering caused by the injury, including suffering from the awareness of impending death, that being a recoverable head of damage by virtue of s. 1(1)(b) of the Administration of Justice Act 1982. The trial judge and Court of Appeal dismissed the claim.

Lord Bridge of Harwich

My Lords, the appellants are the parents of two girls, Sarah and Victoria Hicks, who died in the disaster at Hillsborough Football Stadium on 15 April 1989 when they were respectively 19 and 15 years of age. In this action they claim damages under the Law Reform (Miscellaneous Provisions) Act 1934 for the benefit of the estate of each daughter of which they are in each case the administrators. The respondent is the Chief Constable of the South Yorkshire Police who does not contest his liability to persons who suffered damage in the disaster. The basis of the claim advanced here is that at the moment of death Sarah and Victoria each had an accrued cause of action for injuries suffered prior to death which survived for the benefit of their respective estates....

The evidence here showed that both girls died from traumatic asphyxia. They were in the pens at one end of the Hillsborough Stadium to which access was through a tunnel some 23 metres in length. When the pens were already seriously overcrowded a great number of additional spectators, anxious to see the football match which was about to start, were admitted through the turnstiles and surged through the tunnel causing the dreadful crush in the pens in which 95 people died. Medical evidence which the judge accepted was to the effect that in cases of death from traumatic asphyxia caused by crushing the victim would lose consciousness within a matter of seconds from the crushing of the chest which cut off the ability to breathe and would die within five minutes. There was no indication in the post-mortem reports on either girl of physical injuries attributable to anything other than the fatal crushing which caused the asphyxia, save, in the case of Sarah, some superficial bruising which, on the evidence, could have occurred either before or after loss of consciousness. Hidden J was not satisfied that any physical injury had been sustained before what he described as the 'swift and sudden [death] as shown by the medical evidence'. Unless the law were to distinguish between death within seconds of injury and unconsciousness within seconds of injury followed by death within minutes, which I do not understand to be suggested, these findings, as Hidden J himself said 'with regret', made it impossible for him to award any damages.

Mr Hytner sought to persuade your Lordships, as he sought to persuade the Court of Appeal, that on the whole of the evidence the judge ought to have found on a balance of probabilities that there was a gradual build-up of pressure on the bodies of the two girls causing increasing breathlessness, discomfort and pain from which they suffered for some 20 minutes before the final crushing injury which produced unconsciousness. This should have led, he submitted, to the conclusion that they sustained injuries which caused considerable pain and suffering while they were still conscious and which should attract a substantial award of damages. The Court of Appeal, in a judgment delivered by Parker LJ with which both Stocker and Nolan LJJ agreed, carefully reviewed the evidence and concluded, in agreement with Hidden J, that it did not establish that any physical injury was caused before the fatal crushing injury. I do not intend myself to embark on a detailed review of the evidence. In the circumstances I think it sufficient to say that, in my opinion, the conclusion of fact reached by Hidden J and the Court of Appeal was fairly open to them and it is impossible to say that they were wrong.

A good deal of argument in the courts below and before your Lordships was addressed to the question whether damages for physical injuries should be increased on account of the terrifying circumstances in which they were inflicted. This may depend on difficult questions of causation. But on the facts found in this case the question does not arise for decision. It is perfectly clear law that fear by itself, of whatever degree, is a normal human emotion for which no damages can be awarded. Those trapped in the crush at Hillsborough who were fortunate enough to escape without injury have no claim in respect of the distress they suffered in what must have been a truly terrifying experience. It follows that fear of impending death felt by the victim of a fatal injury before that injury is inflicted cannot by itself give rise to a cause of action which survives for the benefit of the victim's estate.

Lords Goff, **Browne-Wilkinson**, **Griffiths** and **Templeman** agreed with Lord Bridge.

Appeal dismissed.

COMMENTARY

The practical outcome of the case was that the estates of the deceased, sisters aged 15 and 19, recovered nothing in respect of their fear of impending death and nothing for their pain, suffering and loss of amenity in the time between injury and death. Neither could the estates recover for the sisters' loss of expectation of life, as this is not a recoverable head of damages under English law (Administration of Justice Act 1982, s. 1(1)(a)). The parents could recover funeral expenses and they had a statutory claim for bereavement damages, then worth £3,500, under s. 1A of the Fatal Accident Act 1976 (see further below), but this arose only in respect of their younger daughter as the death of an adult child is not covered. Add to this the rejection in separate proceedings of the Hillsborough relatives' personal claims for post-traumatic stress (see p. 342, above). Do you think that the law's response to the sisters' tragic loss of life and their parents' consequent grief was really adequate? (Cf. *Keenan v United Kingdom,* discussed p. 934, below.) Note, however, the House of Lords has recently affirmed the gist of *Hicks*, holding that a living claimant has no claim for anxiety at the prospect of future injury (*Rothwell v Chemical & Insulating Co Ltd* [2007] UKHL 39; [2008] AC 281).

The case illustrates the anomaly that, in English law, it may be cheaper to kill than to maim. An old legal joke poses the question: what's the best advice you can give to a driver who's just knocked down and injured a pedestrian? Answer: back up and make sure you finish off the job properly.

What damages are recoverable by the estate under the 1934 Act? The simple answer is all damages that the deceased could have claimed up to and including the date of his death (with the addition of funeral expenses—s. 1(2)(c)). This will include any expenses incurred by the deceased from the date of the tort until the date of the death as well as loss of earnings during that time. In *Pickett v British Engineering Ltd* [1980] AC 136 the House of Lords held that a living plaintiff could recover damages for the loss of earnings during the period which, as a result of the tort, he would now be dead, and this claim was held to survive for the benefit of the deceased's estate under the 1934 Act in *Gammell v Wilson* [1982] AC 27. One reason for their Lordships' decision in *Pickett* was to provide benefits for the dependants of the plaintiff, for once the living plaintiff had been awarded damages the dependants could not bring a later claim against the defendant in respect of the same tort (see p. 930, below). Thus if the (living) plaintiff did not receive any damages for the loss of earnings during the lost years the dependants would be uncompensated for the loss of dependency during those years. However, this policy ground did not apply where the victim of the tort died before bringing a claim, because in this case the dependants had an independent right to sue under the fatal accidents legislation (see below). There was concern that if the lost years claim continued to survive for the benefit of the estate, the tortfeasor might in certain circumstances have to pay out twice to compensate for the same loss (the lost years claim to the estate and loss of dependency to the dependants). The 1934 Act was accordingly amended by the Administration of Justice Act 1982, s. 4. However, in *Gregg v Scott* [2005] 2 AC 176 at [182], Lord Phillips opined that the preferable solution would be to disallow the claim of the living claimant for loss of earnings during the lost years but to allow an action under the Fatal Accidents Act to the dependants if the claimant later died even though the claimant had brought a successful action during his lifetime. If the reason for allowing the claim for lost years was to benefit the dependants of the claimant, his Lordship argued that the *Pickett* claim was a 'poor substitute' for allowing the dependants their own action under the Fatal Accidents Act. His Lordship thought that this result could be achieved by a 'purposive interpretation' of s. 1(1) of the Fatal Accidents Act. (Cf. *Thompson v Arnold* [2008] PIQR P1.) Note, however, that one concern with using the lost years claim as a means of providing for dependants after the claimant's death—that the claimant might spend the lost years award during his own shortened life so that there is nothing left for dependants at his death—can be avoided by use of a periodical payment order (see p. 932, below).

The 1982 Act in s. 1(1)(a) abolished the claim for 'loss of expectation of life', available to a living plaintiff where life expectancy had been reduced as a result of the tort but limited to the notional amount of £200 since *Benham v Gambling* [1941] AC 157. However, s. 1(1)(b) allows for an award of pain and suffering damages to be increased to reflect the fact that a victim may suffer increased distress from the knowledge that his life-span is now reduced. But when can damages for pain and suffering be awarded in the first place? It is trite law that a claimant who has suffered physical injury can recover damages for the pain and suffering associated with that injury, but a physical injury there must be. In *Hicks* (above) the House of Lords affirmed that the short period of pain between the commencement of the crushing and unconsciousness or death did not amount to a physical injury for the purposes of awarding damages for the associated pain and suffering of that injury. This seems to apply a *de minimis* requirement: the gap between the commencement of the injury and death must be sufficiently long so that the court can find that the claimant suffered, as a matter of law, a 'physical' injury for which pain and suffering damages can be awarded. Do you agree with Handford, *Mullany and Handford's Tort Liability for Psychiatric Damage*, 2nd edn. (Sydney: Law Book Co, 2006), para. 4.140, that the duration of the discomfort 'has been afforded an undeserved prominence'? For example, would it be fair to deny pre-death pain and suffering damages to the estate of an air crash victim depending on the length of time it takes the plane to crash? For a discussion of US cases where recovery of these damages by the estate has been allowed, see Handford, above, para. 4.140.

Defamation

Section 1 of the 1934 Act provides generally for the survival of actions in tort, with the exception of defamation. Given that the exception applies to both claimants and defendants it might seem curious that a defendant should be excused from liability by the fortuitous death of the claimant. The Faulks Committee (1975), Cmnd 5909 explained the exception of the cause of action in defamation on the basis of a wish to avoid controversial areas and a desire to expedite the introduction of legislation to deal with the problem of deaths in road accidents. The Committee recommended survival of claims against the estate of a deceased defamer as well as a right of action in the personal representatives of a person defamed to seek an injunction and damages for pecuniary loss. A further right in relatives to seek a declaration, an injunction against publication, and costs in respect of defamation of a deceased person within five years of the death was also proposed, but none of these proposals found favour with the Committee on Supreme Court Practice and Procedure (1991, the 'Neill Report').

II. Death as a Cause of Action

1. Common Law

Clark v London General Omnibus Company Limited [1906] 2 KB 648

The plaintiff's daughter was killed as a result of an accident with one of the defendant's omnibuses. At trial the plaintiff recovered for, amongst other things, the cost of burying his unmarried daughter. The Court of Appeal allowed an appeal against this head of damage both under

Lord Campbell's Act (the predecessor of the current Fatal Accidents Act) and at common law. The extract is concerned with the common law position.

Lord Alvertsone CJ

But on the main question, if it was intended in *Baker v Bolton* (1808) 1 Camp 493 to enunciate the proposition that no action lies in respect of death apart from statutory enactment, it would, of course, be an authority in favour of the present defendants. What right can be said to be infringed? What is the *injuria* which has caused the *damnum*? The father has no right of property in the child in the sense that he can recover if his property is injured. In this case it seems to me that there is no duty towards the father which has been broken. There is no property of the father which has been injured, and no contract with the father which has been broken. Some breach of duty must be made out, and I can see no ground for any suggestion that there is any duty to the father that has been infringed, or any property of the father which has been injured. It seems to me that this case falls within that class to which reference is made in the notes to *Ashby v White* (1703) 2 Ld Raym 938, where there are certain wrongful acts which may place persons in the position of spending money and yet will not involve a legal liability to make that expenditure good. I am therefore of opinion that the plaintiff's action fails at common law. . . .

W. S. Holdsworth, 'The Origin of the Rule in *Baker v Bolton*'
(1916) 32 LQR 431

In 1808 Lord Ellenborough decided [in *Baker v Bolton*] that 'in a civil court the death of a human being could not be complained of as an injury'. . . . The principle as laid down by Lord Ellenborough is very wide and admits of two perfectly distinct applications. Firstly, it covers part of the ground covered by the maxim *actio personalis moritur cum persona*—the representative of a deceased victim of a tort, which has caused his (the victim's) death cannot sue in his representative capacity. Secondly, it makes it impossible for a plaintiff to sue a defendant for a wrong committed by the defendant to the plaintiff, when that wrong consists in damage causing the death of a person in the continuance of whose life the plaintiff had an interest. It is clear that the second application of the principle has nothing to do with the maxim *actio personalis, &c.*, as both plaintiff and defendant are still alive. The death is simply an element of the cause of action. . . .

It is probable that the origin of the second application of this principle is to be found in the rule that, if a cause of action in tort disclosed a felony, the right of action in tort was affected [either by being suspended or lost]. . . .

[After considering the cases on this rule, Holdsworth continued:]

It would seem to follow; therefore, that the mere fact that a felonious tort to the person results in death should not debar a person, who has suffered loss by the death, from suing in tort for such damages as he can prove that he has sustained, provided that the felony has been prosecuted. *A fortiori* he ought to be able to sue if the tortious act causing death does not amount to a felony. . . . But logic has been disregarded; and in cases where the tort results in death a right of action is denied. What, then, is the reason for a rule which, even on technical grounds, seems to be illogical. . . .

In the great majority of cases in which death ensues as a result of a tort felony has been committed. In a large number of cases also the persons damaged by the tort are the deceased's near relatives. I would like to suggest, therefore, that the rule based upon the maxim *actio personalis, &c.*, became confused with the rule based upon the fact that the tortious act was a felony....I should like to suggest, therefore, that when Lord Ellenborough gave his ruling in *Baker v Bolton* he was the victim of the same confusion of ideas.

COMMENTARY

The reason the felony might affect the tort claim was that the lesser wrong 'drowned' in the more serious felony: *Higgins v Butcher* (1607) Yelv 89, 80 ER 61.

Although it was common for felony to be prosecuted on indictment, there also existed a process known as an *'appeal of felony'* which was 'essentially an oral accusation of crime made by someone closely affected' (*Baker*, p. 503). As felonies were particularly serious crimes a successful prosecution resulted in the death of the accused and forfeiture of his property. Although this did not provide compensation for the relatives, Holdsworth argues that the threat of an appeal of felony by the relatives against the tortfeasor might in practice have encouraged the tortfeasor to provide them with some compensation for the death. This possibility was eliminated when appeals of felony were abolished in 1819.

Whatever the historical explanation, a more modern rationale of the rule that death gives rise to no cause of action can be provided. The common law has never been keen to allow claims for 'relational' loss, that is, a loss caused as a consequence of an injury to someone else. Generally such claims are for pure economic loss and are subject to the restrictive rules applicable for that type of loss (*Cattle v Stockton Waterworks* (1875) LR 10 QB 453). So where the defendant's tort results in another's death the claim of those financially dependent upon him is relational (related to the death) and is for pure economic loss, hence the usual reluctance of the common law to allow a claim. The reasoning behind this restrictive approach is a concern as to the appropriate level of liability of the defendant: it may be fair to compensate a person who has suffered physical injury or property damage but if the defendant must also pay for all consequential economic losses which resulted from the original injury this would be imposing too great a burden, notwithstanding the defendant's admitted negligence. The problem with this approach, as applied to torts causing death, was twofold. First, the defendant was better off if the tort killed the victim rather than merely injuring him. Secondly, the death of a husband often resulted in the immediate family being deprived of their 'breadwinner' and hence their means of support. These two factors were influential in convincing Parliament that statutory change was necessary.

2. Statutory Change to the Common Law Rule

R. Kostal, *English Law and Railway Capitalism* (Oxford: OUP, 1994), pp. 289-90

At the same time [by 1845], however, some prominent politicians and law reformers led by Lord John Campbell recognised that the revival of deodands [see commentary, below] by coroner's juries had not been sheer whimsy; it was a symptom of growing public anxiety about railway safety. Jurors had deliberately conscripted the deodand to the cause of punishing and deterring railway company negligence. They had done so because statutory and common law were seen as ineffective sources of safety regulation and financial compensation. Mindful of the need to maintain a legal deterrent to negligence, Lord Campbell introduced a bill to Parliament in 1845 designed to modify the common law principles concerning the right to sue in the case of a fatal accident. The bill enabled the immediate relatives of the deceased to bring an action for 'such damages . . . proportioned to the injury resulting from such death'. If enacted, the legislation instantly stood to give many accidental deaths monetary values. Although the railway industry appears to have offered some resistance to Lord Campbell's bill, its attention was greatly distracted by the railway promotional mania and subsequent stock market crash. The fact that the fate of the Deodands Abolition Bill was linked to Lord Campbell's bill appears also to have diminished opposition to the measure. Both bills were passed into law in August 1846. This was a major turning-point in the history of English personal injury litigation.

W. Cornish and G. Clarke, *Law and Society in England 1750–1950* (London: Sweet & Maxwell, 1989), pp. 503–4

One complaint which the Select Committee on Railway Labourers [1846] endorsed was the lack of protection or assistance offered to dependants of those who were killed. Even before that Committee's Report, Lord Campbell had taken up the cause, but could not be persuaded to do more than seek a remedy for this small part of the whole injustice. Accordingly two bills became law. One abolished deodands, the other gave dependants certain opportunities to claim compensation by civil action. This Fatal Accidents Act, although in many respects obscure, was nonetheless drawn with a degree of cunning. For it did not give dependants of the deceased their own right of action, as would have followed from the Scots example of the solatium [see below under bereavement]. Instead, the personal representatives of the deceased person were permitted to maintain an action in any case where, if he had not died, he himself might have sued. Nevertheless the damages were to compensate those dependants who fell within a limited range—wife, husband, parent or child of the deceased. . . .

Any defence that would have been open to the defendant against the deceased ran equally against a claim by his estate on his dependant's behalf; not only contributory negligence, but also common employment, were to prevent claims from succeeding under the Act. In 1846 *Priestley v Fowler* [the case which introduced the defence of common employment] was still a unique precedent standing against a wholly unfamiliar type of action and it was certainly assumed by some employers that they were being made vicariously liable to dead employees' relatives under the new Act. Yet the first case to reiterate the *Priestley v Fowler* rule refused relief under the Fatal Accidents Act to the widow of a deceased railwayman who, as administratrix, sought to make her husband's employers vicariously liable for the negligence of a fellow worker. In the mines, where colliers died in their hundreds each year, the position was the same. . . .

The families of deceased passengers did gain some benefit from the Act—indeed verdicts of £13,000 in 1871 and £16,000 in 1880 are recorded. But even they found that the courts interpreted the Act cautiously. Thus the judges refused to allow that the 'injury' suffered by the dependants could include their distress as well as their financial loss. The Scots precedent of the solatium was rejected, Coleridge J pointing out [in *Blake v Midland Railway Company* (1852) 18 QB 93 at 111] that the Act applied 'not only to great railway companies but to little tradesmen who sent out a horse and cart in the care of an apprentice'.

COMMENTARY

'The basic idea of the deodand was that if an animal or inanimate object caused or occasioned the accidental death of a human being, often by moving to the death, it would be confiscated' (Sutton, 'The Deodand and Responsibility for Death' (1997) 18 J Leg His 44). A reason why railway companies may have been prepared to accept Lord Campbell's bill in return for abolishing deodands is suggested by Sutton:

This revival [in the use of deodands] consisted of a series of high-profile nineteenth century cases often involving steam engines and other new forms of transport. In these cases deodands, which were often for extremely large sums of money, were imposed on the vehicle or engine causing death.... These types of cases represent the final adaptation of the deodand concept. They also point to the two key reasons why the deodand was abolished in 1846—that it was an expensive inconvenience for some transport enterprises and that a more appropriate means of dealing with fatal accidents was now required.

The new way of dealing with fatal accidents was provided by Lord Campbell's Act, and the basic principle of giving the dependants a derivative, as opposed to an independent, action has been retained in all subsequent legislation dealing with tort liability for fatal accidents.

III. Current Legislation

Fatal Accidents Act 1976

1. RIGHT OF ACTION FOR WRONGFUL ACT CAUSING DEATH

(1) If death is caused by any wrongful act, neglect or default which is such as would (if death had not ensued) have entitled the person injured to maintain an action and recover damages in respect thereof, the person who would have been liable if death had not ensued shall be liable to an action for damages, notwithstanding the death of the person injured.

(2) Subject to section 1A(2) below, every such action shall be for the benefit of the dependants of the person ('the deceased') whose death has been so caused.

(3) In this Act 'dependant' means—
    (a) the wife or husband or former wife or husband of the deceased;
    (aa)the civil partner or former civil partner of the deceased;
    (b) any person who—
        (i) was living with the deceased in the same household immediately before the date of the death; and
        (ii) had been living with the deceased in the same household for at least two years before that date; and
        (iii) was living during the whole of that period as the husband or wife or civil partner of the deceased;
    (c) any parent or other ascendant of the deceased;
    (d) any person who was treated by the deceased as his parent;
    (e) any child or other descendant of the deceased;

(f) any person (not being a child of the deceased) who, in the case of any marriage to which the deceased was at any time a party, was treated by the deceased as a child of the family in relation to that marriage;

(fa) any person (not being a child of the deceased) who, in the case of any civil partnership in which the deceased was at any time a civil partner, was treated by the deceased as a child of the family in relation to that civil partnership;

(g) any person who is, or is the issue of, a brother, sister, uncle or aunt of the deceased.

(4) The reference to the former wife or husband of the deceased in subsection (3)(a) above includes a reference to a person whose marriage to the deceased has been annulled or declared void as well as a person whose marriage to the deceased has been dissolved.

(4A) The reference to the former civil partner of the deceased in subsection (3)(aa) above includes a reference to a person whose civil partnership with the deceased has been annulled as well as a person whose civil partnership with the deceased has been dissolved.

(5) In deducing any relationship for the purposes of subsection (3) above—

(a) any relationship by marriage or civil partnership shall be treated as a relationship by consanguinity, any relationship of the half blood as a relationship of the whole blood, and the stepchild of any person as his child; and

(b) an illegitimate person shall be treated as the legitimate child of his mother and reputed father.

(6) Any reference in this Act to injury includes any disease and any impairment of a person's physical or mental condition.

1A. BEREAVEMENT

(1) An action under this Act may consist of or include a claim for damages for bereavement.

(2) A claim for damages for bereavement shall only be for the benefit—

(a) of the wife or husband or civil partner of the deceased; and

(b) where the deceased was a minor who was never married or a civil partner—

(i) of his parents, if he was legitimate; and

(ii) of his mother, if he was illegitimate.

(3) Subject to subsection (5) below, the sum to be awarded as damages under this section shall be £10,000.

(4) Where there is a claim for damages under this section for the benefit of both the parents of the deceased, the sum awarded shall be divided equally between them (subject to any deduction falling to be made in respect of costs not recovered from the defendant).

(5) The Lord Chancellor may by order made by statutory instrument, subject to annulment in pursuance of a resolution of either House of Parliament, amend this section by varying the sum for the time being specified in subsection (3) above.

2. PERSONS ENTITLED TO BRING THE ACTION

(1) The action shall be brought by and in the name of the executor or administrator of the deceased.

(2) If—

(a) there is no executor or administrator of the deceased, or

(b) no action is brought within six months after the death by and in the name of an executor or administrator of the deceased the action may be brought by and in the name of all or any of the persons for whose benefit an executor or administrator could have brought it.

(3) Not more than one action shall lie for and in respect of the same subject matter of complaint.

(4) The plaintiff in the action shall be required to deliver to the defendant or his solicitor full particulars of the persons for whom and on whose behalf the action is brought and of the nature of the claim in respect of which damages are sought to be recovered.

3. ASSESSMENT OF DAMAGES

(1) In the action such damages, other than damages for bereavement, may be awarded as are proportioned to the injury resulting from the death to the dependants respectively.

(2) After deducting the costs not recovered from the defendant any amount recovered otherwise than as damages for bereavement shall be divided among the dependants in such shares as may be directed.

(3) In an action under this Act where there fall to be assessed damages payable to a widow in respect of the death of her husband there shall not be taken account the re-marriage of the widow or her prospects of re-marriage.

(4) In an action under this Act where there fall to be assessed damages payable to a person who is a dependant by virtue of section 1(3)(b) above in respect of the death of the person with whom the dependant was living as husband or wife or civil partner there shall be taken into account (together with any other matter that appears to the court to be relevant to the action) the fact that the dependant had no enforceable right to financial support by the deceased as a result of their living together.

(5) If the dependants have incurred funeral expenses in respect of the deceased, damages may be awarded in respect of those expenses

(6) Money paid into court in satisfaction of a cause of action under this Act may be in one sum without specifying any person's share.

4. ASSESSMENT OF DAMAGES: DISREGARD OF BENEFITS

In assessing damages in respect of a person's death in an action under this Act, benefits which have accrued or will or may accrue to any person from his estate or otherwise as a result of his death shall be disregarded.

5. CONTRIBUTORY NEGLIGENCE

Where any person dies as the result partly of his own fault and partly of the fault of any other person or persons, and accordingly if an action were brought for the benefit of the estate under the Law Reform (Miscellaneous Provisions) Act 1934 the damages recoverable would be reduced under section 1(1) of the Law Reform (Contributory Negligence) Act 1945, any damages recoverable in an action . . . under this Act shall be reduced to a proportionate extent.

COMMENTARY

Under s. 1(1) if the deceased, had he not died, would have had an action against the defendant for damages, then the dependants (as defined) have a right of action under the Act. As noted above, the claim of the dependants is derivative, not independent, with the result that any defence available against the deceased would also be available under the Fatal

Accidents Act. As Cornish and Clarke point out, this was problematic where the defence was common employment (see Ch. 11) or contributory negligence, the former involving no fault by the deceased and the latter only some small degree of fault. The result was that one arbitrary restriction replaced another: the fate of the dependants rested on whether the tort was caused by a fellow employee or the presence of some carelessness of the deceased, rather than on whether the tort killed the victim or not. However, with apportionment of damages for contributory negligence introduced in 1945 and of the defence of common employment abolished in 1948 the lot of the dependants became more secure.

Nonetheless, contributory negligence of the deceased will still reduce the award to the dependants (s. 5). Also any contributory negligence of a dependant will reduce that dependant's award and may even eliminate it if the dependant was wholly responsible for the death, although the contributory negligence of one dependant has no effect on the claims of the others (see *Mulholland v McCrea* [1961] NI 135; *Dodds v Dodds* [1978] QB 543). The deceased may have no action other than by reason of a defence; he may have settled the case or obtained judgment before death. As noted above (p. 922), this interpretation was questioned by Lord Phillips in *Gregg v Scott* [2005] 2 AC 176. However, in *Thompson v Arnold* [2008] PIQR P1 Langstaff J held (at [86]) that the right given to the dependants to sue under s1(1) 'deals with the case in which a victim has not had the opportunity of obtaining funds which, indirectly, might benefit those for whom the victim cares, and those who depend upon his income'. Under the current law, this prevents the defendant from being liable twice over. This is because some of the settlement or judgment damages awarded to a living claimant (for example loss of future earnings during the lost years) would go towards maintaining dependants, and it would be anomalous if, once the claimant died, the dependants could have a second bite by claiming damages for a loss for which the defendant had already paid compensation. Of course, it would not be anomalous if, as Lord Phillips suggested, a living claimant could not claim damages for loss of earnings during the lost years. No doubt his Lordship's suggestion for reform was based on the fact that damages for loss of dependency under the Fatal Accidents Act are calculated more generously than the claim for loss of earnings in the lost years (see *Thompson v Arnold* [2008] PIQR P1 at [22]–[25]). As the primary rationale for allowing the lost years claim to a living claimant is to provide for dependants after the claimant's death, this difference is difficult to justify, although it may require an amendment to Fatal Accidents Act for Lord Phillips's suggestions to be implemented.

Although the dependant's claim is derivative, it is not the same as the deceased's would have been if he had lived. In *Gray v Barr* [1971] 2 QB 554 Lord Denning explained:

> If [the deceased] had lived, i.e., only been injured and not died, and living would have been entitled to maintain an action and recover damages—then his widow and children can do so. They stand in his shoes in regard to liability, but not as to damages.

1. Who May Claim and for What?

Who is entitled to the benefit of an action under the Act? Section 1(2) provides that the action is for the benefit of 'dependants' but then provides an exhaustive list of persons who qualify as such. The current list now includes (after amendments introduced by the Civil Partnership Act 2004) cohabitees in both heterosexual and same-sex relationships. However, the current legislation retains the strictures on claims by cohabitees that were imposed when such claims were first recognised by amending legislation in 1982: the person must have been living with the deceased in the same household as husband or wife or as a civil partner at the time of the death and for two years previously. But should the list be extended to include those who cohabit without being in any kind of relationship (e.g. house-sharers)? After considering the recommendations of a Law Commission Report (*Claims for Wrongful Death* (Law Com. No. 263, 1999) and a Department for Constitutional Affairs (DCA) Consultation Paper (*The Law of Damages* (CP 9/07, 2007)), the government has indicated that it will add to the list of dependants a residual category of people being wholly or partly maintained by the deceased immediately before the death (Ministry of Justice, Civil Law Reform Bill Consultation Paper (CP53/09, 2009), Draft Bill cl. 1(2)).

If this change is implemented, would it mean that a person who received lifts to work or birthday presents from the deceased was 'partly dependent' and hence entitled to claim? See Law Commission Consultation Paper No. 148 (*Claims for Wrongful Death*), para. 3.31.

How much is each qualifying dependant able to claim? The case extracted below deals with this issue.

Franklin v South Eastern Railway (1858) 3 H & N 211, 157 ER 448

The issue for the court was the assessment of damages under Lord Campbell's Act.

Pollock CB

The statute does not in terms say on what principle the action it gives is to be maintainable, nor on what principle the damages are to be assessed....

It has been held that these damages are not to be given as a solatium; but are to be given in reference to a pecuniary loss. That was so decided for the first time *in banc*, in *Blake v The Midland Railway Co* (1852) 18 QB 93. That case was tried before Parke B, who told the jury that the Lord Chief Baron had frequently ruled...without objection, that the claim for damage must be founded on pecuniary loss, actual or expected, and that mere injury to feelings could not be considered. It is also clear that damages are not to be given merely in reference to the loss of a legal right, for they are to be distributed among relations only, and not to all individuals sustaining a loss....If then the damages are not to be calculated on either of these principles, nothing remains except that they should be calculated in reference to a reasonable expectation of pecuniary benefit, as of right or otherwise, from the continuance of the life.

COMMENTARY

Although this case represents the general principle, 'pecuniary benefit' should not be read too strictly: it is well established that a dependant may claim for loss of services provided by the deceased (e.g. the caring services provided by a parent to a child—see below). There are limits, however, on what can be claimed. In *Burns v Edman* [1970] QB 541 Crichton J disallowed the claim by a widow and her children in respect of her husband's death: although it had been caused by the defendant's negligence the support the husband provided was from the proceeds of his criminal activity and hence the *ex turpi causa* maxim prevented the widow's claim.

Although the dependency will normally result from a dependence upon the deceased's own income, this is not a necessary condition for a claim under the Act. In *Cox v Hockenhull* [2000] 1 WLR 750 it was held that a dependency could be founded on the state benefits payable to the deceased, although it was accepted that in the majority of such cases the dependant would suffer no loss as the level of support would be the same even if the amount was reduced to reflect the fact that one less adult was being supported. See also *Hunter v Butler, The Times*, 28 December 1995.

What amounts to a reasonable expectation of pecuniary benefit is a question of fact but not of past fact. The court is asking what would have happened if the deceased had lived. In *Davies v Taylor* [1974] AC 207 the widow, who had been having an adulterous affair for the previous two years, had left her spouse five weeks before his death and, as Lord Reid put it, 'there was no immediate prospect of her returning to him'. Following his death she had an *ex post mortem* burst of affection for him and attempted to convince the courts that she might have returned to him (despite telling the deceased shortly before his death that she would not do so). The House of Lords rejected the proposition that she had to show, on the balance of probability, that she would have returned to her husband. As long as there was a not insubstantial chance that she might return, the court could evaluate that chance, although on the facts the widow did not satisfy this requirement.

Even where no such complicating factors arise, the court is still faced with the task of valuing the dependency. As in the case of personal injury actions, there are now two methods of calculation: the multiplier approach and periodical payments. When the multiplier approach is used, the annual value of the dependency is calculated and is multiplied by the multiplier. The multiplier is calculated from the date of death, not the date of trial (but see *Corbett v Barking et al. Health Authority* [1991] 2 QB 408). Whilst based on the length of time the dependency will last, the multiplier is discounted to reflect the fact that the dependant is getting a lump sum and the possibility that the dependency would have ended for other reasons. The uncertainty is even greater here than in the assessment of a claimant's loss of future earnings; not only is there the possibility that the deceased may have died anyway but also that the dependant may die before the normal period of dependency has expired. The normal practice is to calculate a single multiplicand (representing the value of the dependency for all dependants) and to then apply a single multiplier, apportioning the total arrived at between the dependants (see CPR Part 41.3A), although separate multiplicands and multipliers can be calculated for each dependant (*Creswell v Eaton* [1991] 1 WLR 1113). Where the issue is the value of the services provided by the deceased, the Court of Appeal in *Spittle v Bunney* [1988] 1 WLR 847 stressed that a court must consider the decreasing need for those services in the case of a child dependant; as the child grows older the need for the services decreases and the ultimate award to the dependant should reflect this.

One problem with the multiplier method in this context is that, as the multiplier (which is calculated allowing for a discount for early receipt of the money) is applied from the date of death, there is a discount for the accelerated receipt of payments from the date of death. However, in respect of the value of the dependency attributable to the period between the date of death and the date of trial, there is in reality no early payment; in fact, the dependant is getting the money later than he would have done if the deceased had lived. The Law Commission recommended reform, but it has been held that such reform may only be carried out by the House of Lords (now the Supreme Court), this being the only court able to review the decisions requiring the multiplier to be calculated as at the date of death (see *White v ESAB Group (UK) Ltd* [2002] PIQR Q76; *H v S* [2003] QB 965; *Fletcher v A Train & Sons Ltd* [2008] EWCA Civ 413).

Periodical payments may also be ordered in actions under the Fatal Accidents Act (Damages Act 1996, ss. 2, 7). The method of calculating the value of the periodical payment is the same as in personal injury actions by a living claimant (see p. 881, above) with the exception that the annual loss on which the periodical payment is based will be the value of the dependency to each dependant.

Section 3(5) allows for the dependants to recover funeral expenses, although the estate of the deceased can also recover such expenses. It will be preferable for the estate to claim these expenses where the dependant's award will be reduced because of the dependant's contribu tory negligence, because such negligence will not affect the estate's claim (Law Commission Consultation Paper, para. 2.61). Where the dependant's award will be reduced because of the deceased's contributory negligence it does not matter who brings the claim as both are affected by the contributory negligence.

Bereavement

Under the civil law of Scotland a pursuer is allowed to claim a moderate sum in acknowl- edgement of the grief felt at a relative's death (known as solatium; see now Damages (Scotland) Act 1976 s. 1(4)). No such claim was known to the common law, and, while courts may have extended pecuniary benefit to include the loss of services by the deceased, no amount of verbal manipulation could extend a pecuniary benefit to include grief so that an award could be made under this head in a Fatal Accidents Act claim. This rigid position was changed by the Administration of Justice Act 1982, s. 3, which created a statutory right for a limited class of dependants to claim a fixed sum for bereavement, originally £3,500, and most recently increased to £11,800 for causes of action accruing after 1 January 2008 (SI 2007/3489).

The class who may claim for bereavement is currently much more limited than the general class of dependants in s. 1(2) and is somewhat anomalous: allowing the claim of the mother but not the father of an illegitimate child seems difficult to defend (Law Commission Consultation Paper, para. 3.144). The only change to the original class of claimants has been the addition of the civil partner upon the introduction of the Civil Partnership Act 2004 but the government has now indicated its intention to widen the class to allow the father of the illegitimate child to claim in most circumstances. It is also proposed to extend the class to (1) children of the deceased under the age of 18 years (who would receive half the amount specified in s. 1(3)); and (2) a person who had been living with the deceased as the deceased's husband or wife or civil partner for a period of at least two years ending with the date of the death (Ministry of Justice, Civil Law Reform Bill Consultation Paper (CP53/09), Draft Bill cl. 5(2)). The Law Commission had earlier rec- ommended that bereavement damages should be recoverable by a spouse, parent, child, brother, or sister of the deceased, and perhaps also a cohabitee, and that it should continue to be unnecessary (as under the present law) to 'prove' grief as a requirement of receiving these damages (*Claims for Wrongful Death* (Law Com. No. 263, 1999), paras 6.31, 6.34 and 6.41). The latter was accepted by the government but not the former, with the result that adult children and siblings will remain excluded from claiming for bereavement. This was justified on the basis that the bereavement award needed to be kept within finite limits and any extension of the class of eligible claimants would dilute the value of the award to be paid to those closest to the deceased (DCA CP 9/07, paras 59–65). Do you think that this concern justifies excluding adult children and siblings? (Note that the total cost of widening the class of claimants as proposed is estimated at just over £5 million (Ministry of Justice, CP53/09, p. 71).

Although the class of claimants who can claim for bereavement under the Fatal Accidents Act is limited, a wider class may be eligible to claim a similar remedy if the death arises from a breach of Article 2 of the ECHR. In two cases, *Keenan v United Kingdom* (2001) 33 EHRR 38 and *Bubbins v United Kingdom* (2005) 41 EHRR 458, the ECtHR suggested that an effective remedy for breach of Article 2 would require the victim to have a claim in damages that should in principle extend to non-pecuniary loss, including anxiety and distress caused by the death. With the implementation of the HRA, such claims may now be brought in domestic legal proceedings (ss. 7–8), assuming that the bereaved relative is a 'victim' of the unlawful act, as the statute requires (s. 7(1), (7)). It remains to be seen what sort of ties with the deceased will enable such a claim to be brought, and what levels of compensation will be regarded as appropriate. Note that in actions under the HRA, damages are calculated taking into account the principles applied by the ECtHR in relation to the award of compensation under Article 41 of the Convention. These principles do not provide for a fixed sum to be awarded for non-pecuniary loss so it is possible (but perhaps not likely) that an award for non-pecuniary loss under the HRA may exceed the £11,800 that is payable for bereavement under the Fatal Accidents Act.

Given the statutory remedy for breach of Article 2 under the HRA and the reluctance of the courts to adapt the common law of negligence to provide a remedy for breach of the ECHR (see pp. 150–1, above), it is unlikely that the availability of this remedy will force the courts (in accordance with s. 3 HRA) to interpret the class of claimants in s. 1A more widely in order to comply with the ECHR. The result is that there are different classes of claimants, and potentially different amounts of damages, for bereavement depending on whether the death results from a tort or from breach of Article 2. Is this a defensible distinction?

Benefits Arising from the Death

Although the death of the deceased may cause loss to the dependants, it may also cause benefits to accrue to them that they would not otherwise have received. For example, a dependant may be a beneficiary under the deceased's will or under a life insurance policy. Are these benefits to be taken into account? One benefit is dealt with specifically in s. 3(3)— the remarriage of a widow or prospects of remarriage are not to be taken into account in assessing the widow's claim. The *Pearson Commission* described the failure to take into account the actual remarriage of a widow as a 'manifest absurdity' (para. 411). Conversely, a majority of the High Court of Australia has held that no separate discount for the prospects of remarriage should be made to an award to the surviving spouse; the general discount for vicissitudes would cover the possibility of re-partnering and there was no reason for selecting one contingency—re-partnering—and treating it differently from the myriad of other contingencies that might possibly affect the award (*De Sales v Ingrilli* (2002) 212 CLR 338). The Law Commission Consultation Paper noted that the rationale behind the section was that 'taking into account widows' prospects of remarriage exposed the widows to distressing cross-examination and consideration by the judiciary of their appearance' (para. 3.57). However, as the Commission noted, the section does not prevent this kind of questioning in relation to a child dependant's claim (the possible remarriage of the widow being relevant to her ability to provide for the child), nor does it prevent a court considering benefits received by the widow from her partner in a de facto relationship. A number of alternative reforms were suggested, the most radical being to take into account the fact of the widow's remarriage and to apply a rebuttable presumption as to the prospects of remarriage based on objective statistical probability (so that a widow engaged to be married at the date of the trial would have a greater likelihood of remarriage than one who was unattached at the trial). The difficulty with such an approach is that it may encourage delay and subterfuge (because a widow with no immediate prospect of remarriage will get a higher award than one who is married or about to be married) but in practice such concerns may be overstated. In its final report the Commission recommended the abolition of s. 3(3) in favour of taking into account future marriage where the claimant had in fact remarried or was engaged to be married (*Claims for Wrongful Death* (Law Com. No. 263, 1999), para. 4.53). After considering the responses to the DCA consultation paper (see p. 931, above) the government has indicated (Ministry of Justice, Civil Law Reform Bill Consultation Paper (CP53/09, 2009), Draft Bill cl. 2) that it will amend s. 3(3) to provide that the fact (but not the prospect) of a person's remarriage, entry into a civil partnership and financially supportive cohabitation of at least two years' duration following the death must be taken into account in assessing the value of the dependency of that person (cf. the position for children of the deceased, where it is a factor that may be considered where the judge considers it appropriate to do so).

If prospects of remarriage are not taken into account it might be thought that neither should the prospects of divorce. However, the Court of Appeal in *Owen v Martin* [1992] PIQR Q151 took the view that such prospects had to be taken into account (recognising as well that divorce might not have ended the other party's entitlement to financial support). However, both the Law Commission and the DCA Consultation Paper took the view that it was as distasteful to assess prospects of divorce as prospects of remarriage. The draft Civil Law Reform Bill provides that these prospects may be taken into account only if either party at the time of the death had petitioned for divorce, judicial separation or nullity of the marriage, had applied for a dissolution or annulment of a civil partnership, or were not living together immediately before the death (cl. 3).

A different approach is taken to a wife's prospects of earning remuneration after the death of a spouse, where it has recently been held that these prospects (or, if actually working, the remuneration) should be taken into account when valuing the dependency, at least where the wife intended to work in the future irrespective of the death (*Wolfe v De Innocenti* [2006] EWHC 2694 (QB)). Is it more or less objectionable to question the prospects of future employment or the prospects of remarriage or divorce? Perhaps the different treatment can be defended because the prospects of future earnings can usually be assessed with more certainty than prospects of remarriage although considerable uncertainty may attach to both issues.

More generally, benefits arising from the deceased's death are dealt with in s. 4—any benefits which have accrued or may accrue to the dependant as a result of the death must be disregarded. This 1982 amendment to the Act changed the way in which benefits were dealt with, as previously the relevant section had listed a number of defined benefits which were not to be taken into account. Difficulties have arisen in relation to the gratuitous provision of services to a dependant after the deceased's death. If those services are equal to or an improvement on what the dependant was in fact receiving from the deceased, must the court nonetheless disregard the replacement services and award the dependant damages for the value of the deceased's services? In *Stanley v Saddique* [1992] QB 1 a child's parents were estranged at the time when he was born, and he lived with his mother. When his mother died in a road traffic accident the child was taken in by his father, who shortly afterwards met and married a young woman who accepted the boy as a member of their new family and provided services to the child that were at least as good as those provided by the deceased. The Court of Appeal held that on its proper construction the word 'benefit' in s. 4 of the 1976 Act was not restricted to direct pecuniary benefit but included the benefit accruing to the plaintiff as a result of his absorption into a new family unit consisting of his father, step-mother and siblings, and was thus to be disregarded. However, in *Hayden v Hayden* [1992] 1 WLR 986 a differently constituted Court of Appeal (although Sir David Croom-Johnson sat on both panels) decided that the replacement services provided to the deceased's children by her partner, the children's father, who was also the tortfeasor, could be taken into account in assessing the award that should be made to the child dependant. These two cases are considered in the case extracted below.

R v Criminal Injuries Compensation Board, ex p. K [1999] QB 1131

The issue for the Divisional Court was how substituted caring services provided by the aunt and uncle of the deceased to the deceased's children should be taken into account in assessing the children's claim under the Criminal Injuries Compensation Scheme (which for this purpose required the court to consider the position under the Fatal Accidents Act 1976).

Brooke LJ

In September 1989 a mother was murdered by her husband. Her three young children, then aged 3, 2 and 1 years old, were taken into the family of her husband's brother and his wife, and have lived there ever since. They have been very well looked after. In July 1993 a single member of the Criminal Injuries Compensation Board, Mr Conrad Seagroatt QC, awarded them £35,000 in respect of the loss of their mother's services, based on a multiplier of seven and an annual loss of £5,000. The Official Solicitor, who represented them, sought an oral hearing because he considered that the multiplier was too low. On 3 February 1997 a panel of the Board (Sir Jonathan Clarke and Mr Roderick Macdonald QC) reduced the award to £9,000. They did so because they considered themselves bound by the majority decision of the Court of Appeal in *Hayden v Hayden* [1992] 1 WLR 986 to hold that the general parental services provided by their uncle and aunt were at least as good as those provided by their mother before her death, so that the children had suffered no loss, and that those substituted services should not be disregarded by reason of the operation of section 4 of the Fatal Accidents Act 1976 (as substituted by section 3(1) of the Administration of Justice Act 1982) . . .

[S]ection 4 of the Fatal Accidents Act 1976, as substituted by section 3(1) of the Administration of Justice Act 1982, now reads:

> In assessing damages in respect of a person's death in an action under this Act, benefits which have accrued or will or may accrue to any person from his estate or otherwise as a result of his death shall be disregarded.

In *Stanley v Saddique (Mohammed)* [1992] QB 1 the Court of Appeal unanimously held that this wide wording was not to be cut down by reason of its juxtaposition to section 3 of the Act of 1976, as amended. In that case a child's parents were estranged at the time when he was born, and he lived with his mother, but when his mother died in a road traffic accident the boy, then three months old, was taken in by his father, who shortly afterwards met and then married a young woman who accepted the boy as a member of their new family. The Court of Appeal held that on its proper construction the word 'benefit' in section 4 of the Act of 1976, as amended, was not restricted to direct pecuniary benefit but included the benefit accruing to the plaintiff as a result of his absorption into a new family unit consisting of his father, stepmother and siblings. In those circumstances, by virtue of section 4, that benefit was to be wholly disregarded for the purposes of assessing damages for loss of dependency. . . .

If that decision had stood alone, there would not have been the slightest difficulty about the present case. The benefit conferred on the applicants by their uncle and aunt taking them into their own home would fall to be disregarded, and the applicants would be entitled to recover for the loss of their mother's services, however those might be valued. The difficulty arises from the decision of the Court of Appeal in *Hayden v Hayden* [1992] 1 WLR 986, and it is important, in my judgment, to see what that case was all about, and what it appears to have decided....

It is necessary to avoid thinking that *Hayden v Hayden* sets out any principles of law of general application to the valuation of children's claims for three reasons. The first is that the assessment of damages is a jury question and the Court of Appeal had no power to interfere with the judge's award of £20,000 unless it was plainly too high or too low. The second is that in that case the father was the tortfeasor who was liable to pay the damages for the benefit of his child. The third was that there was no third party who stepped in to look after the orphaned child, like the grandmother in *Hay v Hughes* [1975] QB 790, the estranged father's new wife in *Stanley v Saddique* [1992] QB 1, or the uncle and aunt in the present case: it was the father himself who expanded the scope of his parental duties towards his daughter in the home they shared.

Both McCowan LJ (who dissented) and Sir David Croom-Johnson said that the court was bound by the earlier decision in *Stanley v Saddique*....

What divided Sir David Croom-Johnson from McCowan LJ was their application of the law, as explained in *Stanley v Saddique*, to the particular facts of the case before them. Sir David Croom-Johnson considered that the court should first ask itself: 'Has the plaintiff suffered any loss at all?' and then: 'Are there any benefits which accrued to the child as a result of the death which are to be disregarded?'

The judge did not reveal the process by which he arrived at his figure of £20,000. Sir David Croom-Johnson said that he had plainly included in his award an element of financial benefit from the mother's earnings, but he was not persuaded that the judge distinguished the element in respect of the loss of services provided by the mother which were replaced by the defendant from the element in respect of the loss of those which were not. He rejected the proposition that a jury would have valued the lost services by reference to the cost of a 'notional nanny'. It would simply have gone on the established facts of what had happened in the past and was likely to happen in the future. He said [1992] 1 WLR 986, 998:

> If the result of making an allowance for the fact that the defendant has himself continued to act as a loving father means that his ultimate financial liability to the plaintiff is smaller, there is nothing wrong or objectionable in that. Emotive phrases like allowing the defendant 'to profit from his wrongdoing' are beside the point. It is preferable to say that what he had done has had, as one result, the reduction of his liability. Mr Crowther has submitted that to award any damages under his heading (i) [for the loss of services provided by the deceased which were replaced by the defendant] was wrong in law, but I do not think it was. There must be a claim for loss of the mother's services, in the special circumstances of this case, over and above what the defendant has been able to replace. The judge has included it, and rightly so, although he has not particularised the amount.

This, then, was what Sir David Croom-Johnson held the child had lost in the particular context of a case in which she had remained at home and her father had replaced the mother's services to a certain extent. He then went on to consider whether at the second stage of the exercise there were any benefits which had to be disregarded under section 4 of the Act of 1976. He said, at pp. 999–1000:

> The facts in the instant case, however, are wholly different from those in *Stanley v Saddique* [1992] QB 1. The plaintiff remained in the family home with her father and, for a time, with

her older brothers and sisters until they left home. She continued to be looked after by him. No reasonable judge or jury would regard the defendant, in doing what he did, as doing other than discharge his parental duties, many of which he had been carrying out in any event, and would be expected to continue to do. The reasoning of the trial judge in the instant case seems to be that he was making the first of Diplock LJ's two estimates, that is, of the initial loss to the plaintiff caused by the death of the mother. Whether that is so or not, the continuing services of the father are not a benefit which has accrued as a result of the death. In the end, what is a 'benefit' must be a question of fact.

It follows that both Sir David Croom-Johnson and McCowan LJ agreed that they were bound by *Stanley v Saddique* [1992] QB 1 but were unable to agree on the way in which the principles established in that case were to be applied to the facts in *Hayden v Hayden* [1992] 1 WLR 986; for McCowan LJ's dissenting view, see p. 993.

Parker LJ, for his part, adopted a rather different approach. He started his judgment, at p. 1000, by saying that when faced with claims by dependent children under the Fatal Accidents Act 1976 the court was faced with the task of quantifying in money that which in reality could not be so quantified, even in cases without complications. The facts of the case in *Hayden v Hayden* were such that the difficulties of reaching a just solution were greatly increased. After summarising the rival contentions he added:

> For the defendant it is pointed out that if his services are to be disregarded he will in effect be paying damages three times over. First he will be providing replacement services free of charge, secondly, he will be paying for the services which he has so provided, and thirdly he will have lost his employment in order to provide such services. This is true and on the face of it appears not to be in accordance with justice. Furthermore in cases in which it is shown that the services of the father are in every respect as good as, or even better than the services previously provided by the mother it is, again on the face of it, difficult to see that the child has suffered a recoverable loss. He will or she will of course have been deprived of the mother's love and affection but it is not and could not be suggested that this loss sounds in damages.

This passage shows that Parker LJ was concentrating his mind on the way to find a just solution in an unusual case where the father in a united family was not only providing the replacement services given by the mother, but was also the defendant tortfeasor from whom compensation was being sought.

Parker LJ, at pp. 1001–1003, reviewed the authorities and concluded that the court was entitled to prefer *Hay v Hughes* [1975] QB 790 to *Stanley v Saddique* [1992] QB 1, and to hold that the gratuitous services of a relative do not constitute a benefit resulting from the death of the deceased. I have already explained why, in my judgment, this court is bound to follow the decision in *Stanley v Saddique*, buttressed as it is by the opinion of two members of the Court of Appeal in *Hayden v Hayden* [1992] 1 WLR 986....

[W]e are bound by *Stanley v Saddique* [1992] QB 1 to hold that in so far as the value of the replacement services formed a benefit resulting from the death (like the stepmother's services in that case) we must disregard them when assessing damages. In other words at the first stage of the inquiry we cannot say that the children have suffered no loss because the only way in which we could do so would be to take into account something which we are not allowed to take into account. The factual position is quite different from the factual position in *Hayden v Hayden* [1992] 1 WLR 986, in which the majority of the Court of Appeal held that the value of the tortfeasor father's replacement services was not to be disregarded under section 4(1), whether because section 4(1) did not apply at all (Parker LJ) or because this situation was totally different from a case in which the replacement services are voluntarily provided by a third party (Sir David Croom-Johnson)....

The effect of this judgment will enable the Board to revert to compensating child claimants for the most part as they used to do before this panel of the Board thought that the decision of the Court of Appeal in *Hayden v Hayden* [1992] 1 WLR 986 had made a much more radical change in the law. The correct way to resolve a claim by a child whose needs are met after its mother's death by someone who already owed parental duties to it before the death will have to be resolved by the courts on another occasion....

Rougier J

The affidavit of Mr. Macdonald QC does not suggest that the Board progressed beyond the first question—namely whether or not the children had suffered any loss. But if and in so far as they had considered section 4, it seems to me that they could only have reached a conclusion adverse to the applicants in reliance on a further obiter remark by Parker LJ in *Hayden v Hayden* [1992] 1 WLR 986, where, having quoted the judgment of Purchas LJ in *Stanley v Saddique*, Parker LJ said, at p. 1003:

> It is thus clear that he regarded the services of the stepmother as being a benefit resulting from the death of the deceased which is directly contrary to the decision in *Hay v Hughes* [1975] QB 790. On the point of construction Ralph Gibson LJ with hesitation agreed with Purchas LJ and Croom-Johnson LJ agreed with both judgments. With conflicting decisions on the point whether the gratuitous services of a relative do or do not result from the death of a mother I for my part have no hesitation in following *Hay v Hughes* [1975] QB 790 rather than *Stanley v Saddique* [1992] QB 1 and if this is right section 4 does not apply.

It seems to me that if and in so far as the Board may have been relying on this observation in support of a decision that section 4 does not apply, they were overlooking two factors. First, the majority of the court in *Hayden v Hayden* [1992] 1 WLR 986 declared that *Stanley v Saddique* [1992] QB 1 was binding upon them. Secondly, they were able to distinguish *Hayden v Hayden* on two specific differences of fact: (1) that the defendant himself was the tortfeasor who was continuing to provide the services, so that to make him pay for them would effectively be awarding triple damages, and (2) that the defendant, as the father of the children, had been providing services before the death by reason of no more than parental duty, so that the services he provided after death could not be said to arise as a result of the death.

To my mind the facts of the present case, in so far as they deal with the quality of substituted care, are far more akin to those of *Stanley v Saddique* [1992] QB 1 and there is no effective comparison to be drawn with the facts of *Hayden v Hayden* [1992] 1 WLR 986. For those reasons I think this application succeeds and the matter should be remitted to the Board for the purposes suggested by Brooke LJ.

Application granted.

COMMENTARY

Can the services provided by a parent to a child ever be replaced? Commenting on Parker LJ's reasoning in *Hayden* that the provision of the replacement services meant it was at least arguable that the child had suffered no loss, Kemp (1993) 109 LQR 173 notes (at p. 175): 'The child undoubtedly lost her mother's services. That is a loss.' Do you agree? Compare Parker LJ's reasoning in *Hayden* with that of Sir David Croom-Johnson, who rejected an argument that it was wrong to award *any* damages for the loss of the services of a parent which were replaced by the surviving parent, holding that '[t]here must be a claim for loss of the mother's services, in the special circumstances of the case, over and above what the defendant has been able to replace'. This assumes that some services can never be replaced, in which case no substituted services could eliminate a claim under this head (in fact conventional awards can be made to reflect the value of services only a mother can provide).

The Divisional Court preferred *Stanley v Saddique* on the facts of the case before them, distinguishing *Hayden* on the grounds that: (1) the duties that the father took on after the mother's death were simply an extension of the existing parental duties of the father and hence did not arise as a result of the death; and (2) the provider of the substituted services was the tortfeasor. The result of these three decisions appears to be that, where the substituted caring services provided to the dependant are provided by a third party and are equivalent to or better than those provided by the deceased, such a benefit results from the death and, as a result of s. 4, is disregarded when calculating the value of the dependency.

The position is more complicated where a surviving parent provides the substituted services. In *H v S* [2003] QB 965 it was held by the Court of Appeal that if, at the time of death, the surviving parent was providing no support or caring services and there was no prospect of such services being provided in the future, any support or services provided by the surviving parent after the death fell within s. 4 and were to be disregarded. Although the Court did not explicitly say so, this seems to be the ground for distinguishing *Hayden*, where the surviving parent had been providing services prior to the death. This suggests that, if the parents of the child had been living together at the time of the death, or one parent had a legal obligation to support the child financially, substituted services provided by the surviving parent may be taken into account, as such services are the result of ordinary parental duties and do not result from the death. Thus the dependant child's award is reduced, either because the dependant suffers no loss or because the substituted services do not fall within s. 4. This result appears odd, because a father who provides support for his children that was, before her death, provided by the mother is clearly doing substantially more than simply performing his ordinary parental duties. The current situation also results in the paradox that, in terms of a dependency award under the Fatal Accidents Act 1976, it may be better to be a child of single parent rather than of stable parents who both care for the child. In the former case, if the surviving parent does provide substitute services after the death they will be disregarded, but in the latter the services will be considered as an extension of parental duties and taken into account, with the result that (1) the surviving parent and child have lost a partner and parent; and (2) the family income is doubly reduced because no damages are awarded for the substituted services and because the surviving parent may have given up remunerative work to perform the services. Can this be justified?

However, it should be noted that *Hayden* can also be distinguished even where the surviving parent takes on additional parental duties after the death. The Court of Appeal in *Hayden* was clearly influenced by the fact that the *tortfeasor* was the provider of the substituted services, although the tortfeasor was also the surviving spouse in that case (although see now Ministry of Justice, Civil Law Reform Bill Consultation Paper (CP53/09, 2009), Draft Bill cl. 8). In light of the above criticism, if the tortfeasor was not the surviving spouse, it may be wondered whether the award to the dependant would be reduced if the surviving spouse provided substituted services; that is, would the court hold that the spouse was only acting out of an existing parental duty and hence the benefit was not caught by s. 4 and could be taken into account?

It will be remembered that the House of Lords in *Hunt v Severs* [1994] 2 AC 350 held that damages paid to a living claimant in respect of gratuitously-provided caring services were held on trust for the carer (except where, as in that case, the carer was the tortfeasor). Despite criticism of that decision by academics and the recommendation of an alternative approach to compensating the carer by the Law Commission (see Law Commission, *Claims for Wrongful Death* (Law Com. No. 263, 1999), paras 7.22–7.2.3), the Court of Appeal has held that the same rule applies to the provision of gratuitous substitute caring services in claims under the Fatal Accidents Act. In *H v S* [2003] QB 965 it was held that the only basis on which such damages could be awarded was that they were used to reimburse the voluntary carer for services already rendered and were available to pay for such services in the future. Such amounts were to be held on trust, such trust being legally enforceable by the carer beneficiaries (cf. *Bordin v St Mary's NHS Trust* [2000] Lloyd's Rep 287, where the judge thought that the trust was not enforceable in the courts). Apart from the inappropriateness of the trust in this setting (demonstrated in this case by making an uncle and two of the elder children of the child claimants trustees), the consequences of giving the carer a proprietary right to the fund may be seen as undesirable. Should those who take on the responsibility for caring for another's children as part of the relationship with one of the parents expect financial remuneration for it? What if the services provided are poorer than those provided by the deceased, but better than nothing? Should the temporary partner of the surviving parent have a claim for substitute services actually provided, even if such services have ceased to be provided by the time of the trial because he/she had run off with someone else, leaving the surviving parent destitute? For comment on *H v S* see Lunney (2002) 13 KCLJ 219.

After considering responses to its consultation paper (see p. 931, above), the government indicated (Ministry of Justice, *The Law of Damages* (CP(R) 9/07, 2009, p. 53) that its view was that damages should be able to awarded in respect of gratuitous services provided to a dependant that replace the deceased's services, but that the dependant should be under a personal obligation to account to the gratuitous service provider (noting that this would bring the position under the Fatal Accidents Act in line with personal injury cases where it was recommending similar reform). This has been incorporated in the draft Civil Law Reform Bill, which also provides that the fact that the provider of the replacement services is the tortfeasor does not prevent the dependant from claiming for the value of those services but that the claim is limited to services to be provided post-trial (cl. 8). A similar amendment is proposed for damages awarded for gratuitous services to a claimant in a personal injury action (cl. 7: see further Ch. 16.IV.3(c)), the effect of which is that (if the bill in its current form is enacted), awards in respect of gratuitously provided services will be made on the same basis in both personal injury actions and in claims by dependants under the Fatal Accidents Act. Do you think these changes are preferable to the 'trust' solution?

18 HOW TORT WORKS

This chapter focuses on the role played by the law of tort in the compensation and prevention of personal injuries. The question addressed is how tort works, both at a descriptive and an evaluative level (i.e. both how does it in fact work and also how well does it work). We begin in Section I by examining the way that tort operates in practice: when are claims for compensation actually made; how are these claims settled or otherwise disposed of; how much does it cost and how long does it take; is the compensation adequate; and who pays for it? A question of recurring importance here is whether the statistical evidence supports the contention that there has been an explosion in the numbers and costs of tort personal injury claims, feeding a 'compensation culture'. We conclude Section I by looking at tort law in context, considering in particular its role in the 'mixed system' of accident compensation that operates in this country. In Section II, we turn to evaluation, and focus upon the so-called fault principle that is enshrined in the law of tort, that is the principle that compensation should only be paid to a person injured by another's fault. In this section, we shall consider how the law might depart from the fault principle by the development of strict liability or no-fault compensation, concluding with an examination of radical reform options involving the abolition of tort as a means of compensating for personal injuries.

I. Tort Law in Operation

1. When are Claims for Compensation Made?

D. Harris et al., *Compensation and Support for Illness and Injury* (Oxford: OUP, 1984)

[The extract summarises some of the findings of an empirical study conducted by the Oxford Centre for Socio-Legal Studies in 1976–7 ('the Oxford survey'). The researchers obtained general information about the incidence of illness, injury, and handicap from a large-scale household survey and follow-up interviews with individuals incapacitated by illness or accident. The extract focuses upon the research team's analysis of the factors associated with claiming and obtaining damages (written up by Hazel Genn) and of accident victims' perspectives on fault and liability (written up by Sally Lloyd-Bostock).]

The survey showed that only a small minority of all accident victims initiate legal claims and obtain damages for the losses they have suffered....For all types of accident taken together, the figure is 12 per cent of cases, but there are important differences in the success rates between different categories of accident. While fewer than one in three of road accident victims, and one in five of work accident victims obtained damages, fewer than one in fifty of all other types of accident victims obtained damages, despite the fact that this represented the largest category of accidents suffered by victims in the sample. Although the chances of obtaining damages were very high once there had been contact with a solicitor about the possibility of making a claim, the vast majority of victims either never considered the question of claiming compensation, or if they did so, failed to take any positive steps to make a definite claim.

Elderly victims and young victims appeared on the whole to be reluctant to claim damages, irrespective of the type of accident suffered, and, for elderly victims at least, irrespective of the degree of residual disability suffered as a result of the accident. Women suffering work accidents claimed less often than men suffering work accidents, although for road and other accidents the proportions were similar. In general, accident victims in full- or part-time employment were considerably more likely to claim damages than those not in employment. Contrary to our expectations, accident victims in lower status socio-economic groups were proportionately more likely to obtain damages than victims in professional or managerial groups. The seriousness of injury in both physical terms and the amount of time taken off work was not consistently associated with the likelihood that damages would be obtained, underlining the fact that the tort system is based on the cause of accidents rather than on the consequences.

Detailed analysis of what steps were involved in actually perceiving an accident as a problem for which legal advice should be sought indicated that women and the elderly were both less likely to consider the question of compensation, and having done so, were less likely than other groups actually to seek legal advice. For those accident victims who did succeed in obtaining damages it was clear that advice obtained before getting in touch with a solicitor was very important in providing or reinforcing the incentive to claim damages. More than two-thirds of those people in contact with a solicitor claimed that the idea of obtaining legal advice first came from another person. For victims who have accidents on the road or at work there are normally certain procedures for reporting the accident which have to be followed and during which advice about claiming may spontaneously be offered. For victims who have accidents elsewhere there are no such procedures and the people who disproportionately suffer these types of accidents—women, the elderly, children—are more isolated than those at work from networks of information and advice. Trade union activity in pressing claims for damages provides an important example of both the value of immediate advice and easy access to the legal system.

The reasons given for not proceeding with a claim by those people who had at some time considered the possibility indicate that lack of claims-consciousness, problems about providing evidence, and fear of the legal costs involved in making a claim represent important constraints....

Our data showed that it was not victims' attributions of fault which motivated them to make a damages claim.... Fault was not always seen as appropriate grounds for compensation, nor was it necessarily seen as a precondition if a claim was to be made. In only half those cases where the victim took steps to initiate a claim for damages had he also attributed fault to the person against whom the claim would be made. Only about half of those who said their accident was someone else's fault said they had at any time thought that that person should compensate them. Moreover, the pattern of responses for different types of accidents suggested that even in those cases where attributions of fault did coincide with the initiation of a claim, the attribution of fault was a justification rather than a reason for the claim, and that, without the prospect of a possible damages award, fault might have been attributed differently, if at all. The question of fault was certainly not unimportant to the victims. In particular, holding someone to blame was clearly seen as threatening to a relationship. However, the factors determining whether or not fault was attributed to someone else, and if so how, were extremely complex, and included many factors besides the causes and circumstances of the accident. Rather than the law reflecting the ordinary man's view of fault and liability, the victims' attributions of fault and liability reflected legal norms and the likelihood of a successful damages claim. The findings also confirmed that the attribution of fault in the context of a particular damages claim is very much a function of that context. It cannot be assumed that the type of attribution of fault generated by the tort system will be appropriate also for purposes of deterrence or accident prevention, where it may be far more effective to focus on quite different causal factors.

COMMENTARY

The survey is now rather out of date, but no more recent survey has collected data on the same range of issues, and it remains the best evidence we have of the reasons why some people claim for their injuries while others do not. The findings are broadly consistent with those of other empirical studies of the tort system in operation. Another valuable—though also dated—source of information about the workings of the system is the Pearson Report (Royal Commission on Civil Liability and Compensation for Personal Injury, Chairman: Lord Pearson, *Report*, Cm. 7054, 1978). Combining data from interviews with victims of accidental injury or work-related illness in the years up to 1973 with figures derived from analyses of court records, a survey carried out by the insurance industry, and other publicly available information, the Pearson Commission found that, of some three million people injured in the United Kingdom every year, only about 250,000 brought an action for damages, of whom only about 215,000 obtained tort compensation (*Pearson,* vol. 2, paras 50 and 59). This figure, which corresponds to a finding that tort damages are recovered by only about 6.5 per cent of those suffering personal injury, is even more striking than that obtained by the Oxford Survey, in whose study 12 per cent recovered damages, the difference being explicable on the basis that the latter considered only those injuries which prevented the victims from carrying out their normal activities for a period of two weeks or more.

   More recent studies indicate that the number of claims has risen substantially since the Pearson survey. In 1998, the annual number of claims was estimated by the Civil Justice Review to be 340,000 (*Report of the Review Body on Civil Justice*, Cm. 394, London: HMSO, 1988, para. 391). Only since 2000, however, has there been an accurate annual count of the number of tort personal injury claims. The relevant data is collected by the Compensation Recovery Unit (CRU), established in 1990 to administer the 'claw back' of social security benefits paid to those subsequently receiving tort compensation for the same injury. Initially small compensation claims (under £2,500) were excluded, but the claw back regime now applies to personal injury claims of all sizes. Anyone receiving a claim—whether they accept liability or not—must report it to CRU, and in the overwhelming majority of cases this is done through the automated systems of liability insurers. We can therefore have a high degree of confidence in the reliability of the figures reported below.

Compensation Recovery Unit: Tort Personal Injury Claims Statistics

Number of personal injury claims for damages

Year	Accident claims	Disease claims	Total
2000/01	612,120	123,811	735,931
2001/02	614,126	74,189	688,315
2002/03	615,546	91,151	706,697
2003/04	557,186	213,057	770,243
2004/05	579,282	176,593	755,875
2005/06	629,981	44,441	674,422
2006/07	682,498	28,286	710,784
2007/08	713,440	19,310	732,750
2008/09	797,007	15,341	812,348
2009/10	846,946	14,379	861,325

Type of personal injury claims for damages, 2008/09

	Number of claims	Percentage of claims
Motor liability	625,072	76.9
Clinical negligence	9,880	1.2
Employer's liability	86,957	10.7
Public liability	86,164	10.6
Other	3,415	0.4
Unknown	860	0.1
TOTAL	812,348	100.0

R. Lewis, A. Morris and K. Oliphant, 'Tort Personal Injury Claims Statistics: Is There a Compensation Culture in the United Kingdom?' (2006) 14 TLJ 158

The increased frequency of claims since Pearson and prior to the current period of relative stability is likely to be attributable to a wide variety of factors. At one end of the spectrum, increased social understanding of injuries and their causes has meant that we are more likely to characterise symptoms as injuries and to attribute responsibility for that injury to another individual or entity. For example, it is now common knowledge that whiplash can result from a road traffic accident and indeed insurers have suggested that as many as 80 per cent of all road accident claims involve a claim for whiplash injury. At the other end of the spectrum, there has been an extension in the number of people who can qualify for compensation through the tort system. This is in part a consequence of legal developments. For example, liability for psychiatric harm, consequent upon involvement in or witnessing an accident has been widened in crucial respects, and the Motor Insurers' Bureau uninsured drivers' agreement has extended the categories of claims for which it (and indirectly the insurance industry) is responsible. In addition, the Crown Proceedings (Armed Forces) Act 1987 allowed service personnel to claim for the first time against the Ministry of Defence...

It is not only, however, that the law has expanded but also that the increased specialisation of lawyers in personal injury claims has enabled them to become increasingly adept at identifying and developing grounds for pursuing claims within the current legal framework...

The reasons underlying our increased propensity to respond to injury by seeking legal redress are likely to be numerous, complex and inter-related. Perhaps the most important factor is the increased social awareness of the possibility of claiming compensation following an accident... Our increased assertiveness is unlikely, however, just to stem from increased social awareness and is probably also due to changes in our relationships with, and in our expectations of, each other, our employers and the state. Another possible factor, for which we have not been able to test, is changes over time in the value of and entitlement to social security benefits...

The conclusions we draw from the evidence we have presented can be summarised as follows. First, there is no evidence that the tort system has been flooded with an increasing number of personal injury claims in recent years. In fact the number of claims has been relatively stable since at least 1997–1998, the first year for which reliable CRU statistics are available. The swelling of the headline total claims figure from 2003 to 2005 is entirely due to a surge in disease claims prior to the closure of the Coal Health compensation schemes. In the same years, the number of accident claims actually fell. Nor can it be said that the introduction of CFAs and advertising for legal services has led to any measurable increase in claims during this period.

Secondly, and by way of contrast, consideration of a longer timeframe reveals that there has undoubtedly been a very substantial increase in the number of personal injury claims. Comparison of the CRU figures with the Pearson Commission's estimates from the 1970s shows an approximately three-fold rise in total claims numbers over 30 years, though not all categories of claim follow this pattern. Unfortunately there is no reliable data source which tracks the increase from year to year and therefore no means of determining whether it proceeded by steady increments or in fits and starts as a result of particular causative factors. It must be emphasised, however, that a mere rise in claims numbers is insufficient to establish the existence of a damaging compensation culture, as this insinuates that a significant proportion of claims are fraudulent, exaggerated or otherwise lacking in merit. We are not aware of any data that would support such a contention. The rise in claims numbers from the 1970s is equally consistent with there having been significant *under*-claiming at that time, with a subsequent increase in the proportion of those with genuine claims who chose to initiate legal action.

COMMENTARY

The above article presents statistical evidence drawn from a number of sources, of which CRU is the most important. Since it was written, there has been a significant surge in the number of motor liability claims and hence the overall total (see figures above), but a very pronounced fall in the number of claims for work-related disease. As the extract notes, the number in this category was artificially inflated for a number of years by the Coal Health Compensation schemes, established following successful High Court test cases by former miners in the late 1990s. The schemes processed a very large backlog of claims relating to work-related respiratory disease and 'vibration white finger', potentially dating back as far as 1954. In total, some 750,000 coal health claims were registered from 1999 to 2004 (the cut-off date for registration). See further Committee of Public Accounts, 'Coal Health Compensation Schemes', HC (2007–08) 350.

Road accident claims are now by far the biggest single category of personal injury claiming, and their number continues to rise. Conversely, the number of work accident claims has reduced very considerably since the time of the Pearson Commission's survey, when they were the most numerous of all. This probably reflects changes in the nature of the UK economy and workforce, and improvements in workplace health and safety. As work claims have fallen, public liability claims have increased. This category covers, amongst other things, occupiers' liability and product liability: the word 'public' reflects insurance industry terminology, and does not indicate that the defendant is a public body, though 'tripping and slipping' and many other claims against local authorities do fall in this category. The number of clinical negligence claims is still relatively low compared with other categories, though it is very much higher than the Pearson Commission's estimate of 500 claims per year in the early 1970s, and these claims undoubtedly have an importance in public debates that outstrips their numerical representation.

Propensity to sue

Why some injured people sue, and others do not, may be explained by a number of factors. The Pearson Commission found that the most common reasons given by injured persons for not bringing a claim were that they did not consider the injury serious enough, that they did not know that they could claim or how to do so, that they considered it 'just an accident', and that they thought suing would be too much trouble or too upsetting, or 'did not want to make a fuss' (*Pearson*, vol. 2, table 84).

The process by which an injury is 'transformed' into an action for damages is described in a famous sociological analysis by Felstiner, Abel and Sarat, 'The Emergence and Transformation of Disputes. Naming, Blaming and Claiming' (1981) 15 L & Soc Rev 631. They identify the following three stages in the emergence of legal disputes (pp. 635–6):

[The] first transformation—saying to oneself that a particular experience has been injurious—we call *naming*...For instance, asbestosis only became an acknowledged 'disease' and the basis of a claim for compensation when shipyard workers stopped taking for granted that they would have trouble breathing after ten years of installing insulation and came to view their condition as a problem. The next step is the transformation of a perceived injurious experience into a grievance. This occurs when a person attributes an injury to the fault of another individual or social entity...We call the transformation from perceived injurious experience to grievance *blaming*: our diseased shipyard worker makes this transformation when he holds his employer or the manufacturer of asbestos insulation responsible for his asbestosis. The third transformation occurs when someone with a grievance voices it to the person or entity believed to be responsible and asks for some remedy. We call this communication *claiming*. A claim is transformed into a dispute when it is rejected in whole or in part.

In an important recent contribution to the debate about compensation culture Annette Morris has applied this transformational account to an analysis of the factors that are alleged to have increased the general propensity to sue for personal injury ('Spiralling or Stabilising? The "Compensation Culture" and our Propensity to Claim Damages for Personal Injury' (2007) 70 MLR 349). 'Levels of claiming depend,' she says (p. 373), 'on the prevalence of external factors and conditions which affect our ability and willingness to transform injuries into claims. It also depends on legal consciousness shaping perceptions of the ability and informing the willingness to claim.' Her particular focus is the influence of 'no win no fee' advertising by solicitors and claims management companies, which may be said to have increased our *ability* to name, blame and claim, because previously many injured people did not know they had a potential claim or how to pursue it, and our *willingness* to do so, especially by raising our awareness of the availability of compensation. Advertising also 'seeks to legitimise and normalise claiming by portraying the claims process as routine and administrative' (p. 374), and to suppress concerns about claiming by portraying the process as consumer-friendly, stress-free and costless.

In the extract above, Lewis et al. observed that there was no evidence of an explosion in the number of claims in recent years—contrary to popular belief—though it will have to be seen whether the surge in claims from 2008 on is merely a 'blip' or part of a longer term trend. It seems in any case that the proliferation of 'no win no fee' advertising has had little discernible impact on propensity to sue. Although people may now be more aware of their rights than in the past, the influence of the adverts may actually have been offset by the 'dampening' effect of the compensation culture debate itself (see Morris, *op. cit.*, p. 376). Negative publicity about tort claims may have had the paradoxical outcome of dissuading the genuinely injured from bringing well-founded actions at the same time as encouraging a small 'have a go' minority to exaggerate or fabricate claims.

This analysis may usefully be compared with the final paragraph of the extract from the Oxford survey, above, reporting empirical evidence that it was rarely the defendant's fault, rather than the likelihood of winning damages, that motivated victims to make a claim.

2. How are Compensation Claims Dealt With?

Most claims brought to solicitors are settled without proceedings ever being started. Where proceedings are started, most are settled: only in a very small minority of cases is judgment handed down. The Oxford survey found that in only 2.7 per cent of accident claims in which compensation was paid was there a court hearing. Far from being regarded as unsatisfactory, this situation may actually be beneficial to the proper resolution of claims, and the promotion of out-of-court settlements has in fact been a major theme of recent reforms of the civil justice system (see below). In 1996, the Woolf Report on the civil justice system stated that it was part of its purpose 'to develop measures which will encourage reasonable and early settlement of proceedings'. Lord Woolf noted the paradox that, although most claims end in settlement, the existing rules of the court were mainly directed towards preparation for trial: 'My aim', he responded, 'is to increase the emphasis on resolution otherwise than by trial' (*Access to Justice*, p. 194).

D. Harris, D. Campbell and R. Halson, *Remedies in Contract and Tort*, 2nd edn. (London: Butterworths, 2000)

[Drawing upon earlier empirical studies (see esp. the Oxford survey cited above, and H. Genn, *Hard Bargaining: Out of Court Settlement in Personal Injury Actions* (Oxford: OUP, 1987)) Harris et al. explain how the damages system works in practice. They examine, in particular, the out-of-court settlement process by which the vast majority of claims are resolved.]

The Damages System in Practice...

Nearly all claims are settled out of court as the result of negotiations between the parties' representatives (usually between C's solicitor and a claims inspector from D's insurance company). In these negotiations there are many pressures on claimants to accept sums which heavily discount the amount which a judge would award if he found D 'fully' liable, viz. if he decided every disputed question in C's favour. There will be a discount for every risk or uncertainty facing C: the risk that he does not have adequate evidence to prove C's fault (C can only guess the strength of the evidence available to D); that he might be found to have been partly at fault himself; that the medical reports on his side about his prognosis may not be accepted by the judge; that his evidence about his future employment prospects may not be accepted. Added to these are the uncertainties about how much further delay there would be in waiting for a court hearing; about how much the legal costs might amount to and whether part or all of them might fall on P himself; and about how much the judge might award for intangible losses, such as pain and suffering and loss of amenity. Every one of these risks or uncertainties is a negotiating weapon in the hands of D's insurance representative....

The impact of these risks and uncertainties on the parties differs greatly, because there is a structural imbalance between them which puts C into an unequal bargaining position. First, insurance companies have the resources to collect all the available evidence as soon as possible, and to arrange for experts to report on the accident. Even while P is on his way to hospital, D will often be reporting the accident to his insurance company, which can then immediately arrange for assessors to take photographs of the scene and to seek out witnesses.... Secondly, insurance companies are...'repeat players' to whom any particular case is merely one of many. They can afford to take a detached, neutral view of C's individual case, because they are concerned with the overall results of all the cases they handle. They can 'average' or spread their risks over them all and so can be risk-neutral in their attitude to the individual case. But what is routine to the insurance man is unique to C. He is...a 'one-shotter' who is almost invariably risk-averse: if he is seriously injured the case is of crucial importance to him and the risk of losing it is a powerful incentive on him to compromise for a smaller sum than he could hope to win in court on the basis of 'full' liability. He cannot spread his risk and is also likely to be under financial and psychological pressure. If he is not back at work he may be in urgent need of money....

Insurance companies obviously try to settle claims as cheaply as possible; they operate within the existing fault-based system, and their principal responsibility is to their premium payers (and shareholders), not to protect the interests of accident victims....They consider it legitimate to take advantage of any rule, whether of substance or procedure, which will assist them in minimising their expenditure. They search for and then expose any weakness in C's case; and they take advantage of the inexperience of solicitors who handle claims only infrequently....

[I]n a personal injury claim C is almost completely dependent on his solicitor's advice at all stages of the claim and particularly in regard to the amount he could expect to recover. The process of bringing a claim is so complicated, and the formal rules create such uncertainty, that C has no option except to give his solicitor effective control over all the crucial decisions— whether to go to court, to settle (and if to settle, for which amount), or to abandon the claim. The large number of uncertainties surrounding the claim has the effect of nearly always protecting the solicitor from criticism, no matter what advice he gives. Almost no case is so certain in regard to the amount of damages to be expected that his advice can be shown to be negligent: in practice, he can be held negligent only if he flagrantly fails to take a necessary step in the litigation procedure or fails to meet a specified time limit....

COMMENTARY

As Harris et al. note, even experienced solicitors will advise their clients to settle out of court, if there is a reasonable offer on the table. A number of reasons can be advanced why claims are settled out of court (see further Harris et al., *Compensation and Support*, pp. 12–14):

(1) *Cost.* It is cheaper to settle than to fight it out in court. Out-of-court settlements save the parties the expenditure of legal fees, time and inconvenience. These savings represent a 'bonus' that can be split between the parties if they can agree a settlement. And there is also a saving of societal resources (to the extent that court fees do not cover the full cost of court proceedings).

(2) *Flexibility.* Outcomes are more varied than the all-or-nothing solution imposed by the court; the parties can agree a compromise. Furthermore, an out-of-court settlement allows the parties to impose conditions on each other that could not be ordered in court, e.g. as to publicity. For instance, in the Opren multiparty litigation (about the alleged side-effects of the anti-arthritis drug, Opren), it was a term of the settlement that the plaintiffs' solicitors should not act in any subsequent cases arising out of the use of the drug (see *Davies v Eli Lilly & Co* (1987) 137 NLJ 1181).

(3) *Harmful effects of litigation on continuing relationships.* Litigation can be damaging to the health of a continuing relationship, and tends to be viewed as a parting shot (e.g. where an employee is injured at work, the working relationship is more likely to be preserved if there is a negotiated agreement).

(4) *Harmful effects of litigation on individuals.* Litigation may result in psychological pressure on individuals involved in it, perhaps leading to what is known as 'compensation neurosis'.

(5) *Uncertainty of litigation.* Settlement ends the inevitable uncertainty as to the outcome of litigation and enables parties to organise their affairs without having to bear in mind the risk of winning or losing in subsequent court proceedings.

The Mechanics of the Settlement Process

The process by which out-of-court settlements are reached may be summarised as follows. First, the parties start with the figure the claimant would get if successful. Then they make a discount for settlement, that is a reduction to reflect the possibility of failure in the action and the fact of immediate payment. In the Opren litigation referred to above, for example, one-third was subtracted from the sums that the plaintiffs would have got if successful. The amount of the discount will of course vary according to the extent of the uncertainties surrounding the claimant's case, and in particular whether the defendant is contesting liability or only the quantum of damages. Although the emphasis in most tort books is on the elements of liability, liability issues are comparatively rare in practice. One recent survey found, for example, that there was no or no significant dispute over liability in 78 per cent of personal injury claims, other than for clinical negligence, conducted under a conditional fee agreement (P. Fenn et al., *The funding of personal injury litigation: comparisons over time and across jurisdictions* (DCA, 2006), para. 5.1.2).

Inequality of Bargaining Power and the Role of the Solicitor

It has been said that 'tort law in action is differentiated from the formal law by its greater simplicity, liberality and inequity' (H. L. Ross, *Settled Out of Court: The Social Process of*

Insurance Claims Adjustment, 2nd edn. (New York: Aldine, 1980), p. 237). Tort law in action is simpler that the law in the books because it involves the routine processing of claims on the basis of rules of thumb, more liberal because claims may be paid out even when it is doubtful that the claimant can prove fault (e.g. because of their nuisance value), and liable to cause inequity because it rewards those who get effective legal representation, while those who do not lose out. Further possible inequity results from the 'structural imbalance', or inequality of bargaining power, that Harris, Campbell and Halson explain in the above extract. Insurance claims adjusters can—entirely within the law—exploit the relative weakness of the other side, for whom the difference between winning and losing may be overwhelming.

Claimants must rely upon the legal expertise of their solicitors to redress this imbalance, but they may be let down for a number of reasons. First, there is inexperience. Some generalist high-street practices lack experience in personal injury work (see Genn, *op. cit.*, pp. 40–50). They tend to take a conciliatory approach and assume the insurer is acting reasonably; specialists, by contrast, take a more adversarial approach and assume that the insurer will offer negligible sums unless it sees that the claimant is serious about going to court. Secondly, there may be a conflict of interest between solicitor and client. Solicitors might want to settle quickly in order to increase their turnover, recognising that further expense or effort might be disproportionate to the benefit gained. They may also want to settle to ensure that their costs are met, as insurers generally pay costs in addition to compensation. Furthermore, they might decline to use legal aid even where the claimant is entitled to it as they may wish to avoid the extra administrative work and reduction in fees that such work entails. By doing so they lose the chance of insulating their client from the financial risks of pursuing a claim. However, this latter point should not be overstated: a solicitor who prefers his own interests to those of his client is in breach of his fiduciary duty to the client and may also be disciplined by the Law Society, and in any event, after the reforms of the Access to Justice Act 1999, the availability of legal aid for personal injury claims has been greatly reduced. But the fact remains that there are a number of factors that may limit the effectiveness of the solicitor's representation, and these are aggravated by the lack of any practical way for clients to monitor their solicitor's performance.

It has become commonplace to view defendants and their insurers as the somewhat ruthless 'bad guys' in the settlement process. Genn, for example, states: 'Defendants adopt a theoretically uncompromising approach which includes taking advantage of whatever opportunities may be presented for avoiding or minimizing expenditure on claims' (p. 53). But a more recent study by Dingwall et al. ('Firm handling: the litigation strategies of defence lawyers in personal injury cases' (2000) 20 LS 1) draws a rather different picture, on the basis of data derived from (*inter alia*) interviews with various parties involved in the asbestos disease litigation of the late 1980s. The authors conclude (p. 17):

Where Genn sees homogeneity among defendants, we have shown that they are also a diverse group with diverse interests. In the asbestos study, large general insurers, small regional insurers, self-insured companies, government agencies, and Lloyds brokers were all reported as behaving in rather different ways. Even within these categories, different enterprises had different traditions and cultures.... Their responses [to claims] were mediated in different ways through their legal representatives, from enthusiastic hired guns dedicated to winning to cooler professionals who saw their job as properly testing the victims' claims and requiring justification for spending their client's money rather than minimising pay-outs by every available means. A category like 'repeat players' occludes these differences. In PI work, defendants are indeed almost all repeat players but this structural location does not indicate a uniform strategy....

The authors also criticise the tendency to regard 'hard bargaining' (aggressive and unco-operative negotiating) as invariably the best strategy for claimant solicitors to adopt. In fact, it is their view that '[h]ard bargaining…is not particularly effective *as a universal strategy* because of the amount of variation among both plaintiffs and defendants…The real skill for lawyers *on either side* is to produce a correct analysis of the other's position and to develop a litigation strategy appropriate to it. Sometimes this may be adversarial, sometimes it may be co-operative, often it may be some combination' (p. 16). The empirical work on which Dingwall et al. base their conclusions predates the Woolf reforms of the civil justice system (see below) and it may be, given the emphasis placed in those reforms on co-operation between the parties, that stereotypical hard bargaining will fare even worse in the new litigation environment.

Legal Costs

Another area in which it has been argued that a structural imbalance exists in favour of defendants and their insurers is the law regarding legal costs. The traditional rule that costs follow the event (i.e. are borne by the losing side) serves to increase the stakes for the claimant: 'It makes winning more victorious and losing more disastrous' (Jacob, *The Fabric of English Civil Justice* (London: Stevens, 1987), p. 46). As risk-averse claimants are more concerned with the 'downside' risk (i.e. the risk of financial catastrophe), it has generally been thought that the rule tends to promote earlier and lower settlements. Say the claimant's claim is for £10,000; the defendant alleges he is not liable at all but offers £5,000. Should the claimant accept the offer? If she carries on she may win an extra £5,000. But she may alternatively lose the £5,000 that has been offered to her and have to pay the defendant's costs, which may run to thousands of pounds. Fear of financial ruin may induce her to accept an offer that does not reflect her true prospects of success.

Changes in the civil justice system in the late 1990s, however, created a rather different environment. The Access to Justice Act 1999 heralded an enormous increase in the number of cases that may be taken on a conditional fee (or 'no win no fee') basis (see below). Under such arrangements, claimants typically take out an insurance policy that will cover their liability in costs to the other side in the event that their claim is unsuccessful ('after-the-event insurance'). To that extent, their 'downside risk' is reduced. At the same time, the defendant is exposed to potentially higher costs than before. If unsuccessful, he will be liable for his own legal costs, the claimant's legal costs (including the 'success fee' that the claimant's solicitor may charge for taking the case on a 'no win no fee' basis: Courts and Legal Services Act 1990, s. 58A(6)), and the cost of the after-the-event (ATE) insurance (Access to Justice Act 1999, s. 29).

In December 2009, Jackson LJ reported the results of an official review into the costs of civil litigation, which had been set up by the Master of the Rolls, Sir Anthony Clarke, in response to concern at rising civil justice costs. A key finding of the *Jackson Report* was that the current 'costs shifting' rule has a tendency to increase overall costs (para. 4.3.23):

The costs shifting rule creates perverse incentives in two situations.

   (i) Sometimes the consequence of the costs shifting rule is that while each party is running up costs, it does not know who will be paying the bill. In some instances a litigant may believe that the more he or she spends in costs, the less likely he or she is to foot the ultimate bill because the costs liability will be shifted. If both parties take this view, then costs escalate upwards without any proper control and ultimately result in one or other party picking up an enormous and disproportionate bill…

(ii) Sometimes both parties know that the defendant will be paying costs, for example where there is no defence on liability (or liability has been admitted) and no Part 36 offer [see below] has been made. In such a situation the claimant has no incentive to control costs. The only restraint upon the claimant's lawyers will be their perception of what may be disallowed on assessment.

In Jackson's view, while the basic rule was justified in principle and should be retained, modifications were necessary to prevent parties recovering disproportionate costs, especially in cases where there was a conditional fee arrangement (CFA). The specific recommendations on CFAs are considered in Section I.3(c) below. Here it is enough to note that the Report recommends the abolition of the successful claimant's current right under a CFA to recover both the success fee and the ATE premium from the losing defendant (paras 9.4.1ff and 10.4.1ff). The Report considered that ATE insurance was not the best way as a matter of social policy to protect claimants against the risk of adverse costs; its preferred option was 'one way costs shifting', i.e. the defendant pays the claimant's costs if the claim succeeds, but the claimant pays the defendant nothing if the claim fails. Though this approach would not be appropriate in all areas—the Report specifically excludes commercial and construction litigation (para. 9.5.5)—it was justified in personal injury cases as injured persons might otherwise be deterred from bringing claims for compensation. The Report explains:

19.1.2 *Important features of personal injuries litigation.* There are two important features of personal injuries litigation. First and self-evidently, the claimant is an individual. For the vast majority of individuals it would be prohibitively expensive to meet an adverse costs order in fully-contested litigation. The most recent *Social Trends* report shows that 73% of all households have savings (made up of securities, shares, currency and deposits) of less than £10,000. Defence costs can easily be many times higher than £10,000 in fully-contested litigation. This would mean that for three quarters of households their other financial assets (their own home in most cases) would be at risk from an adverse costs order. Secondly, the defendant is almost invariably either insured or self insured. By 'self insured', I mean that the defendant is a large organisation which has adopted the policy of paying out on personal injury claims as and when they arise, rather than paying substantial liability insurance premiums every year.

19.1.3 *Factors pointing towards one way costs shifting.* The factors which make one way costs shifting a serious candidate for consideration in relation to personal injuries litigation are the following:

(i) Claimants are successful in the majority of personal injury claims. Defendants seldom recover costs, so they derive little benefit from two way costs shifting.
(ii) Personal injuries litigation is the paradigm instance of litigation in which the parties are in an asymmetric relationship . . . [This is a reference to the inequality of bargaining power between claimant and the defendant's insurer.]
(iii) The principal objective of recoverable ATE insurance premiums is to protect claimants against adverse costs orders. One way costs shifting would be a less expensive method of achieving the same objective.
(iv) One way costs shifting is not a novel concept in personal injuries litigation. Between 1949 and 2000, the vast majority of personal injury claims proceeded under a one way costs shifting regime, namely the legal aid shield.

This 'shield' (see now Access to Justice Act 1999, s. 11) provides that costs ordered against a legally-aided individual 'shall not exceed the amount (if any) which is a reasonable one to pay having regard to all the circumstances including: (a) the financial resources of all the parties to the proceedings, and (b) their conduct in connection with the dispute…' The *Jackson Report* notes that the protection is therefore not absolute, though it is rare indeed for a successful opponent even to attempt recovery against a legally aided party. Bearing in mind the need to deter frivolous claims and to encourage claimants to accept reasonable offers, the Report recommends that one-way costs shifting should be qualified by a provision modeled on s. 11 (para. 19.4.1ff).

Offers to Settle

The course of out-of-court negotiations may also be influenced by the making of a formal 'offer to settle' under provisions contained in CPR Part 36. The procedure is open to both parties to a dispute. If the claimant makes an offer to settle at a particular figure, and this is rejected by the defendant, then the defendant bears the risk of being held responsible for unnecessarily prolonging the litigation. If the judge ultimately awards the claimant a sum that is more than the claimant had offered to accept (say, the judge awards £10,000 but the claimant had offered to settle at £5,000) then the defendant can be penalised in the assessment of costs. As the defendant, having lost on the question of liability, would ordinarily be expected to bear the costs of the action anyway, the sanction is an increase in the costs he has to bear over their normal amount: the judge has the discretion to award costs on an indemnity basis rather than on the (less generous) standard basis, or to award interest on the sum recovered at an enhanced rate substantially above that which would normally be payable. The *Jackson Report* thought this did not go far enough in terms of incentivising defendants to accept offers made by claimants and, to provide greater incentives for defendants to accept settlement offers, recommended that where a defendant fails to beat a claimant's offer, the claimant's damages should be increased by 10 per cent.

Where it is the claimant who fails to do better than the defendant's offer, he may (at the court's discretion) be held liable as before for the defendant's costs incurred after the last date the offer could have been accepted without judicial approval. The introduction of offers to settle has been well received: in research carried out for the Law Society and Civil Justice Council (Goriely, Moorhead and Abrams, *More Civil Justice? The impact of the Woolf reforms on pre-action behaviour* (London: Law Society, 2002)) the reform was praised by both claimants, who saw them as a useful way of obtaining a response from the defendant, and defendants, who appreciated them for setting an upper limit to the bargaining range.

Prior to 1999, it was only the defendant who could make a formal offer of settlement, which had to be backed by payment of the amount of the offer into a court-administered account, but this was felt to offend against the principle of equality (see Woolf, *Access to Justice: Interim Report*, 1995, ch. 24). Under the new procedure, it is not necessary for a defendant who offers to settle to make a payment into court.

Pre-Action Protocols

Another of the Woolf reforms designed to promote informal negotiation and settlement between the parties was the introduction of pre-action protocols. These set out, as a matter of best practice, the steps that a solicitor should take for the benefit of his client before any claim is issued. The aim was to increase the degree of contact between the two sides to a dispute and to encourage the exchange of information in the hope that the matter can be resolved without the initiation of legal proceedings. A party failing to follow the steps prescribed in the relevant protocol may be penalised in an order for costs (at the judge's discretion). Pre-action protocols have been published in respect of personal injury and clinical negligence cases, and they have generally been positively received by practitioners in the personal injury field (see Goriely, Moorhead and Abrams, *op. cit.*, p. v; see also *Jackson Report*, para. 35.5.8).

3. Cost and Delay

(a) The Problem

Royal Commission on Civil Liability and Compensation for Personal Injury Chairman: Lord Pearson, *Report*, Cmnd. **7054** (1978)

We estimate that the operating costs of the tort system amount to about 85 per cent of the value of tort compensation payments, or about 45 per cent of the combined total of compensation and operating costs. Of these operating costs, about 40 per cent is accounted for by the costs of insurers in handling claims and on general administration. The remaining elements are the commissions paid by insurers to brokers and agents, claimants' legal fees, and profit. Each represents about a fifth. On small claims, the expenses can be greater than the damages paid. . . .

Nearly half of all claims on insurers are dealt with within twelve months of the injury. Some payment is made in respect of 97 per cent of these claims. Generally the sums of money involved are small, accounting in all for less than a quarter of the total amount paid. As the length of time from injury to settlement increases, so the proportion of claims in which payment is made decreases, falling to about two thirds for claims not disposed of within two years of the injury. At the same time the average size of payment increases, reflecting the fact that it is the more serious cases which take the longest time.

Eighty six per cent of claims were settled without the issue of a writ. Only three per cent were set down for trial, and only 1 per cent reached the courts. . . . The average time interval between the injury and the disposal of the claim for cases set down for trial was three years. About 10 per cent of claims were disposed of in less than a year; nearly a quarter took more than four years. Cases in the county courts were disposed of more quickly than those in the High Court. On average, claims involving medical negligence took longer than others. . . .

COMMENTARY

The excessive costs of litigation have been a regular target of critics of the legal system. The Pearson Commission's findings that for every £1 that was paid out in compensation for personal injury some 85p was eaten up in operating costs (legal costs and insurers' administration costs) are matched by more recent evidence. The sources considered by Lewis, Morris and Oliphant (*op. cit.*, p. 174) suggest that legal costs alone (excluding insurers' costs) amount to approximately 30 per cent of the total costs of a tort claim, a significant proportion even if it is not perhaps sufficient to warrant Lord Woolf's conclusion, in his landmark report on *Access to Justice*, that 'the present system provides higher benefits to lawyers than to their clients' (*Final Report*, s. II, ch. 1, para. 11). Still, costs of this magnitude suggest that litigants get poor value for money from the legal system and risk putting the courts beyond the reach of ordinary individuals. (See also *Jackson Report*, ch. 2.) As the *Civil Justice Review* noted, 'fear of costs is one of the greatest deterrents to using the courts' (para. 70).

One of the main factors contributing to costs is the duration of litigation. The Pearson Commission's personal injury survey found that only a minority of claims (48.9 per cent), generally involving only small sums of money, were settled within a year, and that 7.3 per cent of claims took more than three years to conclude (*Pearson*, vol. 2, table 17). The claims lasting the longest were for the largest amounts, and had lower prospects of success. The 7.3 per cent of claims lasting more than three years had less than a two-thirds prospect of success (cf. the 97 per cent of claims settled within a year in which some payment was made) but resulted in the payment of 19.1 per cent of the total amount of compensation.

The typical case that goes to trial suffers from even longer delays. According to evidence presented to the *Civil Justice Review*, half of all personal injury cases in the High Court took at least four years to complete from the commencement of proceedings to final disposal. The average time taken from the date of the accident (or other incident giving rise to the action) to trial was over five years in the High Court and almost three years in the county court.

A protracted litigation process is not necessarily undesirable. The Pearson Commission thought it a popular misconception that delay was never justified (vol. 1, para. 181): 'It may be in the plaintiff's own interests that the case should not be settled before his medical condition has sufficiently stabilised to allow of a proper prognosis; and a quick settlement may well result in less compensation being paid. Delay does not always indicate a fault in the system.' Delay may also be justified in order to give the parties due opportunity to discover the gist of the other side's case and to prepare their own case accordingly, and to allow time for negotiations out of court (see above). However, there is a general consensus that the extent of the delays encountered in the civil justice system go beyond what is justified. Evidence before the *Civil Justice Review* led it to the conclusion that '[d]elay...undermines justice' (paras 67–8). In particular, it considered that delay reduces the availability of evidence and erodes the reliability of that which is available; denies compensation to those who are entitled to it until long after it is most needed; causes stress, anxiety and financial hardship to ordinary people and their families; and induces economically weaker parties to accept unfair settlements. At the same time delay legitimises inefficiency on the part of courts and lawyers and saps public confidence in the courts' ability to do justice.

Delay is particularly undesirable in the context of personal injury litigation because of the inequality of bargaining power as between defendants and their insurers and claimants. The view is often expressed that insurance claims adjusters unnecessarily draw out litigation in order to increase the pressure on claimants, although this is vigorously disputed by claims adjusters themselves (see Genn, *op. cit.*, pp. 100–8; cf. Goriely, Moorhead and Abrams, *op. cit.*, p. viii and p. 951ff above). Whatever the truth of this view, it is apparent that delay does exacerbate the psychological and financial strain that claimants find themselves under (though it should be noted that the award of interest on damages serves to protect the real value of compensation from being eroded by inflation). A claimant who is in immediate need of cash to pay expenses arising out of an accident, and to cover any income lost as a result of inability to work, will be particularly vulnerable in the face of any delays in the conduct of the litigation. This plight is aggravated by a number of legal rules. On the one hand, it is the claimant who has responsibility for the expeditious conduct of litigation and who may therefore be penalised for unnecessary delay (e.g. by a reduction in the award of interest on any damages recovered); there is no equivalent sanction for an insurer who delays. On the other hand, the law in fact encourages insurers to delay because the interest they have to pay on the damages is generally less than the rate of return on money invested as working capital. Accordingly, it in one sense pays insurers to prolong proceedings as long as possible, although there may be countervailing pressures, for example the desire of the insurance claims adjuster to be seen to be 'getting the job done' by resolving claims swiftly (see Ross, *op. cit.*).

(b) The Solution—Civil Justice Reform?

In recent years, a number of official reports have made criticisms of the way in which civil matters are dealt with by the courts, and their recommendations have led to several important reforms. Of greatest significance are the reforms implemented as a result of Lord Woolf's report on *Access to Justice*. Lord Woolf summarised the defects he identified in the civil justice system as follows (*Access to Justice (Final Report)*, 1996, section I, para. 2):

> [O]ur present system . . . is too expensive in that the costs often exceed the value of the claim; too slow in bringing cases to a conclusion and too unequal: there is a lack of equality between the powerful, wealthy litigant and the under-resourced litigant. It is too uncertain: the difficulty of forecasting what litigation will cost and how long it will last induces the fear of the unknown; and it is incomprehensible to many litigants. Above all it is too fragmented in the way it is organised since there is no one with clear overall responsibility for the administration of civil justice; and too adversarial as cases are run by the parties, not by the courts and the rules of court, all too often, are ignored by the parties and not enforced by the court.

Lord Woolf's response was to urge a move away from the traditional approach to civil litigation, which applied the policy that 'time and money are no object'. In his view, it was important to balance the achievement of the right result against the expenditure of time and money needed to achieve that result, and the means of the parties. In some cases, a 'no-frills' approach would be more appropriate.

The central reform was the allocation of civil claims into one of three 'tracks' (CPR, r. 26.6). Small claims up to £5,000 (subject to a maximum of £1,000 in respect of any claim for personal injury damages) are dealt with informally, with very limited costs recovery, building upon the previous county court arbitration scheme introduced in 1973. Claims of moderate value (up to £25,000) are put on a 'fast-track', with scaled-down procedures to cut down the length and cost of litigation. Complex or high-value claims are reserved for the 'multi-track', with full procedures but hands-on judicial control ('case management'). The proposal for a fast track was perhaps the most revolutionary—and controversial—aspect of Lord Woolf's reforms. It is here that his ambition to move away from the 'time and money are no object' approach of the past is most obvious. The key features of the fast-track (CPR, r. 28) are:

(i) *Limited procedures*, e.g. in relation to disclosure and inspection of documents.

(ii) *Fixed timetables*. A period of no more than 30 weeks will usually be stipulated between allocation of the claim to the fast track and trial.

(iii) *Limited trials*. The trial should normally be concluded on one day, and the judge will specify the time allowed for cross-examination of witnesses (on the basis of written witness statements) and legal submissions by each side.

(iv) *Fixed costs*. The initial proposal was for costs to be fixed in advance as a percentage of the claim, subject to a basic fixed minimum. The aim was to enable parties to anticipate their potential liabilities in advance, to remove the need for taxation of costs, and to allow solicitors to work to a known budget (*Access to Justice*, p. 45). But the issue proved to be very controversial, and the proposal has yet to be fully implemented, though a tariff of fixed recoverable costs now applies to fast-track trial costs (CPR, r. 46) and to solicitors' charges in respect of road traffic accident claims concluded by a default or summary judgment where the damages do not exceed £10,000 (CPR, r. 45). In 2009, the *Jackson Report* recommended that a fixed costs system should be introduced in all fast-track cases, fixing all the costs of personal injuries litigation, and stipulating an overall limit on recoverable costs in all non-personal injury cases (ch. 15).

Lord Woolf, *Access to Justice (Final Report)* (1996)

[In the following extract, Lord Woolf summarises and responds to criticisms made by the Association of Personal Injury Lawyers (APIL) of the proposed use of fast track procedures in personal injury claims.]

First . . . [APIL] argues that it is impossible to investigate and to prove personal injury claims in a way that is proportionate to the compensation eventually awarded because insurers are prepared to throw unlimited sums of money into the defence of quite small claims. Secondly, it argues that disproportionate cost is immaterial since the majority of personal injury claims succeed and the costs of litigating the action are in any event reimbursed to the claimant by the defendant. I accept that the first argument will have weight in a minority of cases; an example is where there are pioneering types of action such as vibration white finger. Actions involving new areas of industrial disease or other cases which are effectively test cases should not come within the fast track. However, in the majority of cases, the insurers will have little scope to deploy excessive resources even if they want to do so, which I doubt will happen, because of the limited procedure. In those cases where a defendant unexpectedly pursues a small action at great expense to the claimant, the judge will provide the protection needed by exercising his discretion to disapply the limit on recoverable costs.

The second point goes to the root of the Inquiry and is not to be accepted. A system which usually pays those who litigate cases as much as, and sometimes more than, the victims receive in compensation simply fails to command public confidence. One of the objectives of the Inquiry is to restructure the work that solicitors have to do so that there will be a greater degree of proportionality between the amount of a claim and the cost of pursuing it . . . [T]he only way to limit the costs of a case is to limit the amount of work that the solicitor has to do on the case. That is what the fast track will achieve.

Even where individual litigants receive back the full cost of achieving their compensation, that cost must be borne in the first place by the insurers, in the second place by the insured and in the third place by society generally. I accept that the cost of litigating and awarding compensation has a regulatory role in influencing awards of compensation and the costs associated with them may well play a part in deterring employers from perpetuating unsafe practices. But that is also likely to be achieved by proportionate costs, and in any event is more a matter for the insurance industry to achieve through appropriate loading of premiums than through accepting excessive litigation costs. In addition, when insurers consider settling cases they tend to look at the total cost of the claim (the damages payable plus costs). Excessive cost tends to reduce the sum available for damages. Finally, the pattern of high spending on personal injury contaminates other areas of litigation where the costs are less likely to be borne by insurers.

COMMENTARY

The Woolf reforms were substantially implemented when a new set of Civil Procedure Rules came into effect in 1999. Even after more than 10 years, it is difficult to assess how effective the reforms have been in their aim of reducing cost and delay. What research there has been on the operation of the reforms in practice has been equivocal (see J. Peysner and M. Seneviratne, *The management of civil cases: the courts and the post-Woolf landscape* (DCA, 2005); Strategic Research Unit, *Civil Litigation Survey* (Spring 2002), p. 12; Goriely, Moorhead and Abrams, *op. cit.*). The latter study found that some practitioners felt that courts were still inefficient and responsible for delays, but that 'case management' procedures were more positively received in London than elsewhere, perhaps because of the numbers and experience of the judiciary in the capital. The study also found that defendant liability insurers complained that the Woolf reforms had failed to reduce the cost of litigation. In both pre- and post-Woolf cases in the survey, the costs of small cases amounted to 68 per cent of damages. The reforms have also led to increased time arguing over costs, which have been exacerbated by the greatly increased role played by conditional fee agreements (CFAs) since 2000.

(c) Legal Aid and Conditional Fees

The above sections make clear the great importance of securing adequate legal representation; even in the out-of-court settlement process, good legal representation is vital to ensuring that defendants or, more likely, insurers take the claimant's case seriously. However, the cost of legal representation threatens to obstruct private individuals in their search for justice through the tort system. Even if procedural reforms designed to reduce the cost of civil litigation are effective, it seems inevitable that the cost of even the simplified Woolf procedures will be beyond the means of most private litigants. Therefore it is necessary to look at ways in which private litigation can be funded, be it by the taxpayer or otherwise. Traditionally, the public purse has played a very significant role in this area through its funding of the legal aid system. However, over several years a very large number of people fell out of the legal aid 'safety net' as successive governments limited the class of those benefiting from the scheme in an effort to control public expenditure. At the same time, government attempted to shift the burden of providing the necessary finance from the public to the private sector, especially by the introduction and promotion of conditional fee agreements ('CFAs'). Under these arrangements, it is solicitors who provide the necessary up-front funding for litigation and who bear the risk of loss, as they take on cases on the basis that their client pays no fee if the litigation is unsuccessful. 'No win no fee' agreements of this nature were first introduced by statutory instrument in 1995. In 1998, the Labour government announced that it planned to abolish legal aid for personal injury litigation almost altogether and to place near exclusive reliance on conditional fee arrangements as the means of ensuring access to justice. It claimed that conditional fees would enable those on middle incomes, who over the previous 15 or 20 years had had their entitlement to legal aid withdrawn, to pursue actions for damages that would otherwise be beyond their financial means.

Lord Chancellor's Department, *Consultation Paper on Access to Justice with Conditional Fees* (4 March 1998)

What are Conditional Fees?

Conditional fee agreements, also known as no-win-no-fee agreements, allow a lawyer to agree to take a case on the understanding that if the case is lost, he will not charge his client for the work he has done. If, however, the case is won, the lawyer is entitled to charge a success fee calculated as a percentage of his normal costs, to recompense him for the risk he has run of not being paid. Clients sometimes have to pay for the expenses, known as disbursements (medical or other expert reports, court fees or enquiry agent's fees) that the lawyer has had to pay, although in some cases the lawyer may agree to fund these costs as well as part of the agreement. Conditional fees allow lawyers and clients to share the risk of litigation. The success fee is set according to the risk the lawyer is taking. The higher the chance of winning, the lower the success fee should be set, and vice versa. This helps to ensure that the risks are managed by those who are in the best position to know what the risks are—the lawyers.

Lawyers working under a conditional fee agreement are likely to be more concerned to ensure that they do not take on cases where the chances of success are not sufficiently good. Conversely, in the cases that are taken on, the lawyer is encouraged to achieve a favourable outcome for his client to earn his success fee. The introduction of conditional fees is a significant step towards removing the barrier of high costs that deters so many people from starting legal proceedings however good their claims might be. To provide peace of mind against the possibility of having to pay his opponent's costs, a client can take out insurance to pay the opponent's costs, and the disbursements the client has paid his lawyer....

The reforms we plan will begin to redress the unfairness of the present legal aid system...Lawyers who are sharing risks with clients will assess more carefully the merits of cases. Some weak cases presently brought under legal aid will not find lawyers who are willing to act. This is to be welcomed: the Government does not believe that weak cases should be brought using legal aid which would not be brought privately. Removing these cases will reduce the costs not only to the legal aid fund but to all defendants who presently face these speculative claims.

COMMENTARY

The ending of legal aid for most cases of personal injury (other than clinical negligence) was effected from 1 April 2000 by the Access to Justice Act 1999, which at the same time increased very considerably the number of cases in which CFAs are permitted (s. 27). An explicit aim was to limit the call on legal aid funds by providing an alternative means of access to justice for which the state did not have pay. The solicitor is given the incentive to accept a case on a 'no win no fee' basis by the prospect of receiving a success fee, and the claimant can eliminate the risk of being ordered to pay the defendant's costs if he loses the case by taking out insurance against that risk (known as 'after-the-event' or 'ATE' insurance). If the claim is successful, the success fee and the ATE premium can be recovered from the defendant by way of costs (see p. 952, above). CFAs are now employed in the overwhelming majority of personal injury claims other than for clinical negligence, including 93 per cent of claims referred to solicitors by claims management companies ('claims farmers'), 99 per cent of trade union cases, 91 per cent of claims covered by before-the-event legal expenses insurance, and 86 per cent of the 'other' caseload (P. Fenn et al., *The funding of personal injury litigation: comparisons over time and across jurisdictions*, DCA Research Series 2/06 (2006), para. 5.1). Funding of clinical negligence claims is split in roughly equal shares between CFAs, legal aid and private hourly fee (*ibid.*, para. 5.2).

Despite this apparent measure of success, CFAs have proved very controversial. Shortly after their introduction, liability insurers began a series of legal challenges to costs orders against them, alleging that the success fee agreed by the claimant and his or her solicitors was unreasonable (see, e.g., *Callery v Gray* [2002] 1 WLR 2000, where a majority of the House of Lords affirmed the Court of Appeal's reduction of the success fee from 60 per cent to 20 per cent). This 'costs war', as it was styled, was temporarily brought to an end by the Civil Justice Council's negotiation of agreements between the representatives of the main insurance and solicitors' organisations and the Bar. The agreements cover the success fees to be charged in employers' liability and road traffic accident claims by both solicitors and barristers (e.g. a standard 25 per cent of solicitors' costs for employers' liability accident claims settled without trial (12.5 per cent in road traffic accident claims) rising to 100 per cent if there is a trial). See further CPR Part 45.

Hostilities have been re-opened with the publication of the *Jackson Report* in December 2009. The Report states that 'the CFA regime has emerged as one of the major drivers of excessive costs' in the civil justice system (para. 4.3.26), and highlights its major flaws:

10.4.12 The first flaw in the recoverability regime is that it is unfocused. There is no eligibility test for entering into a CFA, provided that a willing solicitor can be found.

10.4.13 The second flaw is that the party with a CFA generally has no interest in the level of costs being incurred in his or her name. Whether the case is won or lost, the client will usually pay nothing. If the case is lost, the solicitors waive their costs and pay the disbursements, in so far as not covered by ATE insurance. If the case is won, the lawyers will recover whatever they can from the other side either (a) by detailed or summary assessment or (b) by negotiation based upon the likely outcome of such an assessment.

10.4.14 This circumstance means that the client exerts no control … over costs when they are being incurred. The entire burden falls upon the judge who assesses costs retrospectively at the end of the case, when it is too late to 'control' what is spent.

10.4.15 The third flaw in the recoverability regime is that the costs burden placed upon opposing parties is excessive and sometimes amounts to a denial of justice …

10.4.16 If the opposing party contests a case to trial (possibly quite reasonably) and then loses, its costs liability becomes grossly disproportionate. Indeed the costs consequences of the recoverability rules can be so extreme as to drive opposing parties to settle at an early stage, despite having good prospects of a successful defence. This effect is sometimes described as 'blackmail', even though the claimant is using the recoverability rules in a perfectly lawful way …

10.4.19 … [I]t is a [fourth] flaw of the recoverability regime that it presents an opportunity to lawyers substantially to increase their earnings by cherry picking [i.e. taking on only the most potentially lucrative cases and rejecting others]. This is a feature which tends to demean the profession in the eyes of the public

Jackson consequently recommends abolition of recoverability as regards success fees and ATE premiums (para. 10.4.20). In return, so as to prevent personal injury claimants being left worse off, Jackson makes two countervailing proposals. First, a 'qualified one way costs shifting rule' should apply, meaning that losing claimants will normally have no liability to pay the successful defendant's costs, and hence there will be no need for ATE insurance (see p. 953, above). Secondly, because successful claimants will—if the proposal is implemented—end up paying their lawyers' success fee out of the damages they recover, there should be a one-off and across-the-board increase in the level of general damages for pain, suffering and loss of amenity of 10 per cent, and a cap on the amount of success fee that lawyers may deduct at 25 per cent of damages, excluding damages for future economic losses (para. 10.5.3ff). The same increase would apply to general damages for nuisance, defamation and any other tort which causes suffering to individuals (para. 10.5.6).

The proposals are sure to provoke fierce debate in the coming months and years. Who do you think stands to gain the most from the proposals? Who will lose the most? Consider in particular who will end up having to subsidise the cost of *unsuccessful* claims.

4. The Cost and Adequacy of Tort Damages

Law Commission, *Personal Injury Compensation: How Much is Enough? (A study of the compensation experiences of victims of personal injury)* Law Com. No. 225 (1994)

[As part of its review of the law of damages, the Law Commission commissioned a survey of the adequacy of tort compensation in the light of the subsequent experiences of recipients. The survey, which was conducted by Professor Hazel Genn, considered claims at every level from the small to the very large, dividing them into a number of 'settlement ranges', but it focused upon cases involving the payment of more than £50,000 by way of compensation, typically involving serious and long-lasting injury, and sampled disproportionately fewer awards under this figure. The evidence suggested that even large awards of damages often proved inadequate, especially in view of the unexpectedly large proportion of accident victims who did not return permanently to work after their accident.]

The Failure to Return to Work and Adequacy of Damages

A particular concern is the high proportion of accident victims in all settlement ranges who did not return to work at all after their accident, or who returned for a period and were then forced to leave work as a result of the continuing effects of their injuries. For many of these victims, the amount of damages received did not cover their past losses and will not cover their future loss of earnings and the extra expenses resulting from their injury. It is notable that many accident victims fail to realise, in the period after settlement, just how little they have received, relative to their potential losses, and for how long they are likely to be affected by their injuries. Accident victims are often not aware of the extent to which they will be dependent on their damages in the future. In this respect, victims of catastrophic injury may be in a more favourable position because their permanent inability to carry out normal work is evident at the time of settlement. For many others, however, it appears that at the time of settlement their own expectations of their ability to return to work in the future are unrealistic. It is not entirely clear whether this is because experts fail to anticipate the extent of future incapacity, or whether the effect of a prolonged recovery period reduces the chances of finding work, or whether appropriate work is unavailable. What is clear, however, is that many respondents are unprepared for the impact of their injuries on their long-term capacity for work.

This problem is reflected most clearly in respondents' changing perceptions of the value of damages. Although most respondents are satisfied at settlement when presented with what appears to be a very substantial sum of money, this sense of satisfaction alters dramatically over time as accident victims are faced with the reality of long-term ill-effects of their injuries and a reduced capacity for work.

COMMENTARY

The Law Commission's finding that, in high value claims involving serious and long-lasting injury, the amount of damages awarded is prone to fall short of what is necessary to compensate fully for the claimant's losses is corroborated by empirical evidence about the operation of the labour market collated by Lewis et al., 'Court Awards of Damages for Loss of Future Earnings' (2002) 29 J Law Soc 406. This article submits that the courts currently make insufficient allowance for two factors in particular: first, the extent to which the claimant's earnings might have increased as he grew older, perhaps partly because of economy-wide earnings growth; secondly, the extent of the disadvantage the claimant will now suffer in the market for jobs as a result of his disability.

In the above study, the Law Commission noted that the difficulties of calculating the lump sum were particularly significant in so far as compensation for future needs was concerned, for example because there was virtually no possibility of the award being modified at a later stage because of deterioration or improvement in the claimant's condition or circumstances (para. 1.2). Do you think that the replacement of lump sum awards with periodic payment will improve the chances of achieving full compensation for the victims of serious long-term injuries? (See further Ch. 16.III)

In the recent debate about compensation culture, there has been a change of emphasis in discussion of levels of compensation. A dominant concern today is that damages may be too high, rather than too low.

R. Lewis, A. Morris and K. Oliphant, 'Tort Personal Injury Claims Statistics: Is There a Compensation Culture in the United Kingdom?' (2006) 14 TLJ 158

The cost of individual claims has risen sharply in recent years and appears to be due to increases in both damages paid and legal costs incurred. Damages are likely to have increased for a number of reasons.

Firstly, the decision in *Heil v Rankin* [2001] QB 272 increased damages for non-pecuniary loss in order to bring such awards in line with inflation. The effect of this judgment was to increase the highest levels of award for pain and suffering by one third from £150,000 to £200,000. Awards below £10,000 were not increased but tapered increases were applied for injuries falling between £10,000 and the highest awards. The Department of Health estimated that, because of the disproportionate number of high value claims brought against the NHS, this judgment would cost it £74 million in future liabilities. Given that the vast majority of general claims in tort are below £10,000, however, the impact of *Heil v Rankin* should not be exaggerated.

Of much more importance is the second reason. This is that damages have increased as a result of the reduction in the discount rate applied to future pecuniary losses. The rate makes allowance for the investment return upon lump sum damages. For 30 years prior to 1998 the rate was 4.5% but this was then reduced by the House of Lords in *Wells v Wells* [1999] 1 AC 345 to 3%. In 2001 the Lord Chancellor used his power to reduce the rate still further to 2.5%. As a result of the last change alone, the NHS predicted an increase in their liabilities of £100 million a year, being about a quarter of its total expenditure on damages for clinical negligence at that time. Apart from a £4 million increase in the value of MoD claims, other Government departments and local authorities predicted that the effect would be negligible as they mainly dealt with relatively minor slips and trips. Although the effect upon the insurance industry was substantial, the Association of British Insurers was much more conservative in its estimates than the NHS. It predicted an increase of only £57 million in the annual bill, even though it pays out six times as much in claims for damages over £100,000 compared to the NHS.

Thirdly, the use of the Ogden tables, which was approved by the House of Lords in *Wells v Wells*, has increased the multipliers applied in claims and, therefore, the level of damages paid. The multipliers in the Ogden tables provide an aid for those assessing the current capital value of future pecuniary losses or expenses on the basis of various assumptions, including rates of mortality. Whilst they used to be based on historical mortality rates, they are now based on reasonable estimates of future mortality. In effect, the forecast that those living today will survive longer than their forebears increases the cost of compensating them for life.

Fourthly, damages have also increased due to the introduction of legislation which has considerably increased compensators' liability to pay for the claimant's social security benefits and NHS hospital charges. Since 1990 the state has been able to recover benefits paid to the claimant as a result of an accident in which damages for personal injury are paid. The scheme, administered by CRU, was extended in 1997 so as to apply to all cases no matter what the level of damages involved. Two years later another Act introduced a similarly centralised and efficient system for the recovery of NHS charges in road traffic accident claims. Prior to this, NHS costs were recovered by individual hospitals many of which did not use their powers and recovered very little. This scheme has also since been extended. Fixed sums have been set for the recovery of ambulance and care costs, and these will soon apply to all types of accident.

Finally, a large part of the damages award reflects income. Not only lost wages themselves but also those costs of care which reflect income levels have increased at rates well above inflation in prices. On average, real earnings growth has exceeded price inflation by almost two per cent a year for almost the last 60 years. As a result, it is to be expected that damages in serious injury cases will rise in real terms.

COMMENTARY

Evidence that compensation costs per claim have increased in recent years may be derived from a number of different sources (analysed elsewhere in the above article). The *UK Bodily Injury Awards Studies* (1997, 1999, 2003 and 2007) provide insurance industry figures in respect of personal injury claims arising from motor accidents between 1991 and 2006. The most recent study shows an increase in the total costs of bodily injury claims paid out by UK motor insurers of 9.5 per cent per annum between 1996 and 2006, compared with an increase in national average earnings of 4.3 per cent per annum. The average value of claims increased at an annual rate of 6.5% in the period, with higher claims inflation in larger value claims. Annual increases of on average nearly 3 per cent in the number of claims also contributed to the rise in the overall costs. Another useful source of statistic information here is the National Health Service Litigation Authority (NHSLA), which now has responsibility for the defence of all compensation claims against the NHS. The earliest year for which reliable information about NHS clinical negligence compensation costs is available is 1990–91, in which they were put at £53.2 million. By 1996–97 this had risen to £235 million. In 2008–09, the figure was £807 million. (See www.nhsla.com.) It will be apparent that these rises are massively higher than both price and earnings inflation in the periods in question.

In large part, the increase in average compensation costs has stemmed from English law's commitment to the principle of full compensation, whereby every effort is made to put the claimant into the position he would have been in had he not suffered the tort, in so far as this can be achieved in money terms. Even in the quite recent past, as demonstrated by the extracted Law Commission study, *How Much is Enough?*, it appears that seriously-injured claimants were being significantly under-compensated. But, as noted in the second extract, a number of subsequent changes have greatly increased the costs of compensation, and required liability insurers to raise premiums as a consequence (though it is also alleged that insurers have used this as an excuse for premium rises motivated by quite distinct concerns: see p. 39, above). The impact on public funds has also been considerable, though this has been mitigated by a number of reforms—e.g. the claw back of benefits and treatment costs—that have transferred costs from the public to private-sector insurers (see p. 884, above).

No-one has yet succeeded in making a reliable estimate of the total annual costs of the tort system in the United Kingdom or its constituent nations. The figure of £10 billion, or just over 1 per cent of GDP, advanced by an Institute of Actuaries working party in 2002 ('The Cost of Compensation Culture', /www.actuaries.org.uk/__data/assets/pdf_file/0007/18736/Lowe.pdf) relies to a very large extent on guesswork. The American insurance consultants, Tillinghast Towers Perrin, estimated that total tort costs in the United Kingdom, covering compensation payments, legal costs and administrative expenses, were 0.69 per cent of GDP in 2003, having risen from 0.53 per cent in 2000 (*US Tort Costs and Cross-Border Perspectives: 2005 Update* (2005), 13). Compared with the other countries surveyed, the costs for 2003 were lower than in Belgium, France, Germany, Italy, Japan, Spain and Switzerland (and, of course, the United States), and higher only than Denmark and Poland. The report notes, however, that the data available outside the United States was limited and that the figures 'should not be overanalysed'. Tillinghast has greater confidence in the reliability of its figures for the United States, and its most recent study (*2009 Update on US Tort Cost Trends*) estimates that US tort costs totalled $254.7 billion in 2008, representing about 1.79 per cent of GDP, or $838 per person. The cost as a percentage of GDP may be compared with the respective percentages for 2000 (1.82), 1990 (2.24), 1980 (1.53), 1970 (1.34), 1960 (1.03) and 1950 (0.62). The current trend—after a long period of rising costs as a proportion of GDP—is thus in a downwards direction, though costs today are significantly higher than even 30 years ago. For criticism of the Tillinghast analyses, see L. Chimerine and R. Eisenbrey, 'The Frivolous Case for Tort Law Change', Economic Policy Institute Briefing Paper, 2005 (www.epinet.org/briefingpapers/157/bp157.pdf). Tillinghast's response may be found at www.towersperrin.com/tillinghast/pdf/response_0517.pdf.

5. Who Pays Damages?

P. S. Atiyah, *The Damages Lottery* (Oxford: Hart, 1997) pp. 108–13

The Guilty Parties Do Not Pay . . .

[I]n serious cases the wrongdoers never pay. In fact the only kind of case where the wrongdoers—the negligent parties—commonly pay are in very minor road accidents where a car is slightly damaged but no injuries are caused. In these cases, reasonable motorists will often admit their fault and pay out of their own pockets to save claiming against their insurance, with consequent loss of no-claims bonus. But in more serious cases, and in virtually all injury claims, the parties guilty of negligence will not pay. In fact solicitors acting for a plaintiff will not usually bother to claim against them. They will simply extract the name of the defendant's insurance company and address their claim straight to the insurers. From then on, the whole procedure will be dealt with by the insurers on the defendant's side, and the plaintiff's solicitor on his side. The insurers will decide whether to admit blame, whether to settle, how much to offer, how to fight the case if it goes to trial, what barrister to brief, whether to appeal if they lose, and so on, all without troubling to consult the nominal defendant. . . . Insurers may even chose to settle a case against the wishes of the insured who might prefer to defend it. . . .

Some might think that, at least where damages are awarded against companies, the companies themselves are often seriously to blame and it is fair therefore that they should pay for their own faults. This is a very popular viewpoint. . . . But this is one of those areas where the popular viewpoint and the legal viewpoint both seem founded on misconceptions. A company or a government department or other public body is an abstraction. It is real people not abstractions who commit acts of negligence. Generally speaking, the liability of a company involves no imputation at all against the company itself—it is just legally liable for the negligence of its employees. . . .

Paradoxically, there is actually one group of negligent people who do, in a peculiar sense, pay for their own negligence, and these are accident victims themselves. Whenever an accident victim who makes a claim has his damages scaled down because of his own contributory negligence he is paying, in a rather special sense, for his own negligence. People do not insure against the effects of their own contributory negligence so they 'pay' for it themselves. . . .

The Public Pays

If the actual wrongdoers don't pay for the damages, who does? The answer . . . is that, in a broad sense, the whole public pays. . . . It is actually very much like taxation. . . . First, it is clear that businesses have to pay a large part of the cost of damages in the first instance. All large businesses insure against this sort of liability, and indeed, it is legally compulsory for them to insure against their liability to pay damages to their own employees. So in a sense, the damages will actually be paid by insurance companies rather than the businesses themselves. But of course insurance companies have to collect premiums, and the business concerns who insure against this kind of risk have to provide these premiums. Where do they get the money from to pay the premiums? The answer is that finding the money is just an overhead cost of the business, like the rent paid for the premises, or the cost of heating the premises.

The business has to charge—its customers—enough money to cover its overheads, so some small part of what we pay for all the goods and services we buy in the market is actually going to fund this kind of insurance, and ultimately to pay the damages which the insurance companies have to pay out. If the business is unable to pass on the whole cost to its customers for competitive reasons then the shareholders (rather than, or as well as, the customers) will pay. So damages premiums are just like a bit more VAT levied on businesses, and passed onto the public.

There is a simpler, more direct payment route, with regard to private motorists. As everybody knows, an ordinary motorist is legally obliged to insure against third party risks—he has to buy insurance to cover the risk of being held liable to pay damages through use of his car on the road. So here again, the money is paid through insurance companies, but is levied in effect as a charge on the motorist. Since it is compulsory the resemblance to a tax is stronger still. . . . In other cases the route through which the money moves is even simpler, but the ultimate result is much the same. For instance, whenever the government (or a government department) is held liable to pay damages, there is no insurance because the central government never insures, but the money is just paid out of taxes. So here, it is even more clear that damages are just like any other government expenditure which has to be paid from taxes. If the government wants to pay social security benefits, it has to raise taxes to pay for the benefits, and if it is willing to pay damages, it has to do the same.

The Consequence of Recognising that the Public Pays

The fact that damages are ultimately paid for like this, by members of the public, is critically important . . . [I]t means that sympathy for accident victims comes with a price label attached if we want to do anything about it. Sympathy itself is cheap; but if we want to translate that sympathy into more compensation or higher damages, then we, the public, will have to pay more. Some people may be willing to do this; others, looking at the huge damages awarded sometimes awarded for relatively minor injuries, or in dubious circumstances, may feel less sure. . . . The public perception of these matters appears still to be that damages are somehow paid by wrongdoers, negligent and blameworthy parties, and this perception fuels demand for more and higher damages. It is time that the public understood that they themselves are paying for these damages awards.

COMMENTARY

Atiyah proceeds to argue that the fact that tort damages are really, albeit indirectly, paid by the public at large 'makes nonsense of the whole fault principle' (p. 115). This matter is considered further below.

We have already noted the very extensive influence that insurers have over the day-to-day operation of the tort system, and their increasing input into matters of policy (see Ch. 1.III.1). One point raised in the earlier discussion was that an action ostensibly between private individuals may be, in reality, between their insurance companies. In cases of property damage, in particular, the action is often brought by the claimant's (first-party) insurer who, having paid out under the policy of insurance, may exercise a right of subrogation and bring an action—in the claimant's name but for the insurer's sole benefit—against the liability insurer lying behind the nominal defendant. The result is that tort law becomes nothing more than a mechanism for shifting risks between different classes of insurers. The financial burden on members of the public—many of whom are comprehensively insured, i.e. pay both first-party and liability insurance premiums—remains substantially the same. It was an acceptance that there was nothing to be gained from expensive litigation as to which of two insurance companies should bear the costs of compensation that led to the development of so-called 'knock-for-knock' agreements between insurers in respect of collisions between comprehensively insured motorists. Insurers offering comprehensive policies calculated that it would be cheaper for them in the long run if they entered into bilateral agreements whereby, after a collision between vehicles insured by the contracting parties, each would pay compensation to its own insured irrespective of which of the two motorists was actually at fault (i.e. they agreed not to exercise their rights of subrogation). Over time, the number of occasions on which they paid up 'unnecessarily' would balance against the number of occasions on which they were saved having to discharge the liabilities incurred by their insureds (see further *Atiyah*, p. 238). In recent years, however, knock-for-knock agreements have fallen into disuse, partly as a result of a growth in the number of insurers targeting groups of motorists perceived to be safe drivers. Such insurers could only lose out if required to pay the costs of accidents caused by 'dangerous' drivers insured elsewhere.

The 'Tort Tax'

Atiyah's view that tort liability operates as a form of taxation on the general public is shared by a number of other writers. The American commentator, Peter Huber, coined the phrase 'the tort tax' to describe the phenomenon (*Liability: The Legal Revolution and its Consequences* (New York: Basic Books, 1988), p. 4). But the tax is not like other forms of taxation, such as income tax (at least in the United Kingdom), because it is regressive in effect. It produces a system in which the rich get larger awards than the poor—because their income losses are greater, or their damaged property more valuable, or because they are more likely to opt for expensive (and non-deductible) private medical treatment for their injuries—without this being necessarily or adequately reflected in the amounts of money they pay into the tort system by way of liability insurance premiums. As Abel writes ('Tort', in D. Kairys (ed.), *The Politics of Law*, 3rd edn. (New York: Basic Books, 1998), p. 454):

Damages deliberately reproduce the existing distribution of wealth and income . . . [T]he cost of preserving privilege is borne by everyone buying liability insurance, purchasing products and services, and paying taxes. Thus, all insured car owners pay the cost of compensating the privileged few who drive Rolls-Royces or earn a million dollars a year. They also pay for the superior medical care consumed by victims from higher socioeconomic strata.

In effect, then, 'a regressive subsidy . . . is hidden in the operation of the damages system' as average and low earners subsidise the rich (Harris, Campbell and Halson, *op. cit.*, p. 425).

6. The Tort System in Context

Royal Commission on Civil Liability and Compensation for Personal Injury, Chairman: Lord Pearson, *Report*, vol. 1, Cmnd. 7054–1 (1978), paras 28–33

We define compensation for personal injury as the provision of something to the injured person (or to his dependants if he has been killed) in consequence of the injury and for the purpose of removing or alleviating its ill effects. What is provided may be money, services, goods or real property....

Services include the medical and other services provided free of charge or at low cost by the National Health Service and by local authority social service departments. Services may also include help towards rehabilitation, domestic help and travel facilities. Goods may include such things as wheel-chairs, walking aids, special clothing or special equipment. Real property may include a suitable dwelling or adaptation of an existing dwelling. All these diminish the need for cash compensation. If they had to be paid for, more money would be required....

Cash compensation involves a payment to the injured or bereaved person from a source other than his own resources. Within our definition there are several important, and quite different sources of compensation.

To take first the source most obviously covered by our terms of reference, compensation may be paid by the person who has caused or is responsible for the injury, whether directly or indirectly. Payment may be made from that person's own resources or, more usually, by his insurer. This is the province of civil liability in tort or (in Scotland) delict. Usually, but not invariably, the law of tort requires payment only where the person who caused the injury was at 'fault'....

The biggest single source of compensation, however, is the social security system. Social security payments are normally made irrespective of the cause of the injury or death. Even where the cause is relevant, as in the industrial injuries scheme, payments do not depend on whether the injury was due to someone else's fault. Payment is made instead to meet a particular need or other circumstances, which for the injured is most commonly that of incapacity for work....

In addition to the tort system and the state, there are two other important sources of compensation. First, there is the employer, who may compensate an employee through sick pay, through some form of private insurance policy taken out for the employee or through an occupational disability pension. Again, compensation of these kinds is normally paid irrespective of the cause of the injury and irrespective of fault. Secondly, there is private insurance, whereby the injured person has taken out and paid for his own policy, and payment is in effect made from a fund into which others running a risk of injury have also contributed. The terms of the policy will have determined whether or not compensation is payable in the circumstances concerned....

COMMENTARY

What the Pearson Commission described was a 'mixed system' of accident compensation. The Commission affirmed that 'social security should be regarded as the primary method of providing compensation—it is quick, certain and inexpensive to administer, and it already covers a majority of the injured' (vol. 1, para. 275)—and saw the role of tort as limited to 'supplementing the no-fault compensation provided by the state' (para. 311). Certainly, in terms of the numbers benefiting from tort compensation, tort seems a very junior partner of social security indeed: the Pearson Commission found that tort damages were paid to only about 215,000 accident victims each year, as compared with approximately 1,550,000 newly benefiting from social security payments, and 1,000,000 newly benefiting from occupational sick pay (vol. 2, table 10).

We have already noted (Section 1, above) that the number of tort personal injury claims has risen considerably since the time of the Pearson Report, but, unfortunately, there are no reliable statistics about the number of those claims that are successful. Information about the current operation of the social security system, by contrast, is easily accessible via the series, *Social Trends*, published by National Statistics. The most recent edition (*Social Trends*, No. 39, 2009) reports that, in 2007–8, incapacity benefit and severe disablement allowance (SDA) was paid to 2.7 million people of working age who are unable to work because of illness or disability. (SDA is paid only to applicants whose entitlement was recognised prior to April 2001; no new claims are allowed.) In March 2010, the basic weekly rate of incapacity benefit started at £67.75 and rose to £89.80 after 12 months.

It is commonly assumed that the average compensation payments received by successful tort claimants are very much greater than the value of benefits paid through the social security system. Multi-million pound awards of damages are regularly highlighted by the media (see, e.g., the record £20 million damages reported as having been awarded to a 34-year-old dancer, ranked at one stage in the top ten Latin American dancers in the world, who was left profoundly brain-damaged as a result of clinical negligence during the birth of her first child, and in need of 24-hour-a-day care for the rest of her life (*Daily Telegraph*, 15 October 2002)). Such awards, however, are the exception rather than the rule, and the vast majority of personal injury compensation payments are for less than £10,000 (Lewis, Morris and Oliphant, *op. cit.*, p. 172). It must also be remembered that social security benefits are paid by weekly instalments, which can add up to substantial amounts over time, whereas nearly all tort damages awards are paid in a single lump sum (even after the introduction of periodical payment orders). Nevertheless, some disparity in the amounts of compensation offered by tort as compared with social security is to be expected, especially in cases of very serious injury, reflecting a difference in the compensation aims of the two systems. Whereas tort damages are designed to provide full compensation for all the claimant's losses, including non-pecuniary losses, social security benefits are intended only to satisfy basic needs in order to ward off poverty or other hardship, and do not compensate for pain and suffering at all. Whether full compensation of the few, for pecuniary and non-pecuniary losses, leaving the majority to make do with limited compensation for needs, is a goal worth striving for is a question considered in Section II, below.

The Regulatory Context

Although tort law is normally seen in the context of other mechanisms for accident compensation, we should not ignore one other context in which it plays an important role, namely in the field of regulation, especially relating to health and safety. (For a critical evaluation, see Cane, 'Tort Law as Regulation' (2002) 31 Comm L World Rev 305.) Growing scepticism about the value of tort law as a means of compensating the victims of accidents has led proponents of the tort system to highlight its role in the prevention of accidents and the deterrence of wrongful conduct (see p. 20, above). The theory is that even accidental injuries can be avoided if tort law, by threatening potential injurers with the spectre of liability in damages, provides them with the appropriate incentives to invest in safety precautions.

Whether tort law can usefully perform this function again depends upon the existence and effectiveness of other mechanisms operating in the same field. In English law, health and safety regulation is traditionally pursued by the statutory prescription of precautions to be taken by those engaging in various activities, reinforced with criminal sanctions. The task of ensuring that these prescriptions are enforced is divided between various official agencies, of which the inspectorates whose work is co-ordinated by the Health and Safety Executive (the factory inspectorate, railway inspectorate, etc.) are the most important, at least in the accidents context. (Note also the responsibilities of the Environment Agency and local authorities in respect of environmental pollution.) Although they have the power to initiate prosecutions, factory inspectors and others may choose to proceed by various less formal processes, for example by the issue of improvement notices requiring certain action within a specified period (Health and Safety at Work etc. Act 1974, s. 21) or by ordering a person to desist from activities that involve a risk of 'serious personal injury' (s. 22). This reflects a general trend away from traditional regulation by way of highly detailed statutory prescriptions—which is now viewed as likely to impede development and innovation through its reliance upon fixed, excessively specific, and inflexible rules—and towards self-regulation of health and safety by employers, with the advice and assistance of the enforcement agencies. Particularly notable in this respect is the obligation on employers to ensure workplace safety by carrying out 'risk assessments', which identify the hazards arising from work activities or the state of the premises and evaluates the extent of the risks involved in the light of precautions taken to reduce the risks (Management of Health and Safety at Work Regulations 1999, SI 1999/3242, reg. 3). The theoretical foundations of this modern approach were set down by the Committee on Safety and Health at Work chaired by Lord Robens in its report of 1972 (*Report of the Committee on Safety and Health at Work*, London: HMSO, 1972, Cmnd 5034).

Notwithstanding these developments, there remains a measure of scepticism as to the effectiveness of regulatory approaches to accident prevention, for example because of concerns about the under-funding of enforcement agencies. To advocates of the economic analysis of law, in particular, tort law remains the primary means of safeguarding health and safety. Yet empirical evidence of the comparative effectiveness of tort law and regulation is difficult to assess, and seems to support the view that the success of each in providing appropriate incentives to guard against accidents varies from sector to sector. In a major survey of the existing literature, Dewees and Trebilcock, 'The Efficiency of the Tort System and its Alternatives: A Review of the Empirical Evidence' (1992) 30 Osgoode Hall LJ 57, study the deterrent effects of tort law relative to regulation in the context of five different categories of accidents: automobile accidents, medical malpractice, product-related accidents, environmental injuries and workplace injuries. The authors conclude that the deterrent effects of tort law are hard to gauge but appear strongest in relation to automobile accidents and weakest in relation to environmental injuries; in other contexts, the deterrent effects of tort law are variable. Although they also find that the evidence about the effectiveness of regulation is 'decidedly mixed', the authors nevertheless conclude (p. 137):

In the final analysis, our review of the empirical evidence leads us to a relatively bleak judgment about the properties of the tort system as a deterrent mechanism. . . . In most of the accident contexts that we have reviewed, regulatory alternatives seem to hold out more promise than the tort system from the deterrence perspective.

See also the fuller account provided in D. Dewees, D. Duff and M. Trebilcock, *Exploring the Domain of Accident Law: Taking the Facts Seriously* (New York: OUP, 1996).

II. Tort and the Fault Principle Evaluated

In the modern law of tort, liability is premised upon fault, which usually takes the form of the intention to injure another or negligence. The so-called 'fault principle' appears to have taken a hold in the law of tort in the late eighteenth or early nineteenth century, though how this evolution is accounted for is a matter of dispute: some view it as a response to pressure from newly-formed industrial concerns who were anxious to stave off the threat of strict liability (i.e. liability without fault) in respect of statistically inevitable accidents; some as an intellectual attempt to group together a number of disparate liabilities of more limited scope as part of a process of rationalising and developing the law (see Ch. 1.I.6, above). It may be doubted whether a principle of strict liability was ever widely espoused in the pre-industrial law, but it did have a few proponents in the nineteenth century, as the famous decision of *Rylands v Fletcher* demonstrates (see Ch. 12.III). Nevertheless, strict liability is somewhat exceptional in the modern law in which tort liability is predominantly fault-based.

1. The Moral Basis of the Fault Principle

The fault principle has intuitive appeal: to many modern minds, fault is the natural standard of liability. It seems to be morally right that a person who injures another through fault should have to pay compensation. Nevertheless, the moral basis of the fault principle may be disputed.

P. Cane, *Atiyah's Accidents, Compensation and the Law*
7th edn. (Cambridge: CUP, 2006)

[Patrick Atiyah's path-finding work on accidents, compensation, and the law was first published in 1970. Inaugurating the well-known *Law in Context* series, Atiyah took the rules of the law of tort and considered them in the light of the accident compensation system as a whole, dealing not only with tort but also with social security, insurance, and other sources of compensation. Atiyah's criticisms of the tort system were encapsulated in the book in his celebrated 'indictment' of the fault principle (headed more neutrally an 'appraisal' of the fault principle in the most recent editions, prepared by Peter Cane). The following are the most important counts on Atiyah's indictment.]

The compensation payable bears no relation to the degree of fault....

Fault is like a magic talisman; once it is established, all shall be given to the injured party. It is generally immaterial whether the fault was gross or trivial or whether the consequences of the fault were catastrophic or minor. A degree of fault on the part of someone justifies compensating the injured person for all the losses suffered, provided the claimant was in no way personally at fault. Yet the seriousness of the consequences of a negligent action often bear no proportion to the degree of fault which gave rise to it. A piece of momentary thoughtlessness on the road may cost someone their life and cause great loss to their family; but similar acts of thoughtlessness may be committed by scores of others every day with only minor or even no adverse consequences....

[I]t may seem inequitable that the few whose negligence results in injury or loss to others should be required to bear this burden while the majority of negligent people go free.

The compensation payable bears no relation to the means of the tortfeasor

In tort law, the tortfeasor's wealth or financial means are usually irrelevant to liability. The fact that a tortfeasor is rich is no ground for imposing liability, and the fact that they are poor is no ground for not imposing liability. Most people would probably accept as morally right this principle of equality before the law regardless of wealth, which is implicit in the fault principle. But when we take into account the fact that once liability is imposed, the compensation payable will bear no relationship to the means of the tortfeasor, we may begin to doubt whether it really is fair to ignore their financial position.... No criminal court would think of imposing a fine for culpable conduct of the amounts that civil courts award as damages every day, without serious inquiry into the ability of the defendant to pay....

A harm-doer may be held legally liable without being morally culpable and vice versa....

The traditional justification [of the fault principle] is that the legal concept of liability for fault embodies a moral principle to the effect that if a person, by blameworthy conduct, causes damage or loss to an innocent person, the former should compensate the latter for that damage or loss. But there are at least two grounds on which people have questioned whether tort law actually does embody such a moral principle. In the first place, it is said, if tort law was based on fault would it not prohibit liability insurance, vicarious liability and other loss distribution devices by which the burden of paying compensation can be shifted from a party at fault to another party not at fault?...

A second ground on which tort law's adherence to a moral principle of responsibility for fault has been questioned is this: if the law really reflected morality, it would not adopt an objective definition of fault which, on the whole, ignores the personal qualities of the persons involved and which does not require that the harm-doer should have had any consciousness of moral wrongdoing, or even of the risk they were creating or of the dangerousness of their conduct....

But even if the law is out of step with morality, it does not follow that this is a bad thing... [I]f we think that the main purpose of the law is to compensate injured persons, there is no reason why moral fault should be the criterion of liability to pay compensation. Indeed, if this is our aim, the criterion of whether a person is entitled to compensation ought to be whether they have been injured, regardless of how they were injured. From this point of view, the chief shortcoming of the tort system is not that it sometimes compensates people whose injuries were not the result of moral fault, but that it fails to compensate very many other people who have suffered injuries in circumstances which do not fall within the tort system at all....

COMMENTARY

The above extract covers the principal counts on Atiyah's indictment of the fault principle; additional counts not set out in the extract are: the fault principle pays little attention to the conduct or needs of the victim; justice may require the payment of compensation without fault; it is often difficult to adjudicate allegations of fault; and the fault principle contributes to a culture of blaming and discourages people from taking responsibility for their own lives (this last count on the indictment added by Cane in the most recent editions).

Fault and the Objective Standard of Care

In the above extract, Atiyah distinguished moral fault from the objective notion of fault adopted by the law of tort. This is perhaps most evident in the rule that lack of skill or experience is no defence to a claim of tortious liability (see *Nettleship v Weston*, p. 187, above). But it is perhaps necessary to separate out the question whether the defendant has been guilty of moral wrongdoing from the question whether it is morally right to make the defendant pay compensation to the claimant. A line of argument dating from the last century suggests that the imposition of liability on one who is in breach of the law's objective standard of care, but not morally at fault, can be justified on the basis that it serves to maintain general standards of safety and personal security across society as a whole (see, e.g., Oliver Wendell Holmes, *The Common Law* (1881)). Some may object that the individual defendant ought not to be sacrificed to this utilitarian concern when he is not morally culpable. In an attempt to answer this objection, Tony Honoré has developed a theory of 'outcome responsibility' in which he maintains that the imposition of liability without moral fault may be justifiable as a means of reinforcing the moral responsibility of the individual for his or her actions and their outcomes; to accept a plea of 'lack of skill' or 'lack of experience' would undermine the legal subject's status as a morally responsible agent, as it would mean that the ability to take reasonable care of the interests of others could no longer be regarded as an essential aspect of legal personality (see 'Responsibility and Luck' (1988) 104 LQR 530).

Strict Liability

Under a regime of strict liability, it is not necessary for the claimant to prove that his or her injury was attributable to the defendant's fault; it is enough that the defendant has caused the claimant's injury. The modern law has adopted strict liability only in exceptional circumstances. The recognition of a new rule of strict liability in the classic case of *Rylands v Fletcher* was followed shortly afterwards by an effort to restrict greatly its scope (see Ch. 12.III, above). But, although the common law has not developed any practically significant example of strict liability—at least in so far as personal injury is concerned—a number of statutes do impose liabilities of this nature. Under the Nuclear Installations Act 1965 there is strict liability for death, personal injury, or damage to property arising from (*inter alia*) emissions of radiation from nuclear installations (subject to certain statutory maxima). The Civil Aviation Act 1982, s. 76(2) imposes strict liability in respect of loss or damage to persons or property on land or water caused by a civil aircraft while in flight. By virtue of the Gas Act 1965, s. 14 strict liability applies to the underground storage of gas. And the Animals Act 1971, s. 2 subjects the keeper of a dangerous animal to strict liability as well. It should also be noted that in the area of industrial safety a number of duties laid down by statute are strict (see Ch. 11.IV, above).

Proposals for Further Strict Liability Regimes

The Pearson Commission in its report of 1978 recommended the introduction of new strict liability regimes in a number of areas: rail transport, defective products and vaccine damage. It also recommended that strict liability in respect of personal injury caused by dangerous things and activities should be put on a statutory footing (vol. 1, para. 1643). In recommending strict liability in these areas, the Commission's guiding concerns were the insurability of the risk in question ('Can those who may cause an injury take out insurance more conveniently and cheaply than those who may be injured?') and 'whether the victim is likely to experience particular difficulty in proving fault', as in the case of defective products (para. 316).

Although the Pearson Commission proposals were not directly implemented—a special scheme was, however, set up to provide fixed lump-sum payments to the victims of vaccine damage—a statutory regime of strict products liability was ultimately introduced as a result of European Community Directive 85/374 (see further Ch. 11.III).

Generally speaking, other European legal systems are much more willing to countenance tortious liability for damage without proof of fault—or, more accurately, a range of liabilities that are progressively stricter than the ordinary liability for fault. See B.A. Koch and H. Koziol (eds), *Unification of Tort Law: Strict Liability* (Kluwer, 2002).

Arguments For and Against Strict Liability

What are the arguments in favour of strict liability? A classic American exposition of the case for strict liability, in the context of products liability, was given in the California Supreme Court by Justice Traynor in *Escola v Coca Cola Bottling Co of Fresno*, 150 P 2d 436 (1944) (later approved by the entire court in *Greenman v Yuba Power Products, Inc*, 377 P 2d 897 (1963)):

I believe the manufacturer's negligence should no longer be singled out as the basis of a plaintiff's right to recover in cases like the present one.... Even if there is no negligence...public policy demands that responsibility be fixed wherever it will most effectively reduce the hazards to life and health inherent in defective products that reach the market.... The cost of an injury and the loss of time or health may be an overwhelming misfortune to the person injured, and a needless one, for the risk of injury can be insured by the manufacturer and distributed among the public as a cost of doing business.

Traynor J's suggestion that strict liability is simply 'a cost of doing business' suggests a 'licence fee' rationale for strict liability (or 'enterprise liability' as it is often called in this context): the cost of compensating the victims of defective products can be regarded as a licence fee exacted from manufacturers who, after all, are in business in the pursuit of profit. The question for the manufacturer will be whether the profits to be derived from a particular product outweigh the cost of paying compensation claims (see further V. Nolan and E. Ursin, *Understanding Enterprise Liability: Rethinking Tort Reform for the Twenty-first Century* (Philadelphia: Temple University Press, 1995)).

Strict liability has attracted a number of significant opponents. For Oliver Wendell Holmes, '[a]s action cannot be avoided, and tends to the public good, there is obviously no policy in throwing the hazard of what is at once desirable and inevitable upon the actor...[The state's] cumbrous and expensive machinery ought not to be set in motion unless some clear benefit is to be derived from disturbing the *status quo*. State interference is an evil, where it cannot be shown to be a good...' (*The Common Law*, p. 77). Holmes also seems to have viewed it as simply 'unfair' that liability should be imposed in the absence of fault, and many people intuitively sympathise with this point of view. For further criticisms, see Priest, 'The Invention of Enterprise Liability: A Critical History of the Intellectual Foundations of Modern Tort Law', (1985) 14 J Leg Stud 461.

Given the criticisms of the fault principle listed above, do you think that strict liability is any more unfair than liability based on *legal* fault?

2. Alternatives to Tort Law

We have considered above some options for minor reform of the tort system. But if the criticisms made of the tort system by Atiyah and others are taken seriously, more radical reform—perhaps even the replacement of the law of tort—is needed. Reform proposals of this nature are not currently on the table in the United Kingdom, but Lord Woolf warned not long ago that, if his attempts to reduce the cost of personal injury litigation prove unsuccessful, '[m]ore fundamental measures, possibly involving the removal of at least moderate-sized injury claims from the litigation system, would have to be envisaged' (*Access to Justice (Interim Report)*, ch. 7, paras 24–5). This final section considers two radical reform options: the introduction of 'no-fault' compensation alongside or in place of the law of tort; and the abolition of tortious liability for personal injuries in order to encourage an increase in self-reliance through the acquisition of insurance.

(a) No-Fault Compensation: General

Royal Commission on Civil Liability and Compensation for Personal Injury, Chairman: Lord Pearson, *Report*, Cmnd. 7054 (1978)

[T]he term 'no-fault'...refer[s] to compensation which is obtainable without proving fault and is provided outside the tort system. No-fault compensation is a system of obtaining payment from a fund instead of proceeding against the person responsible for the injury.... The relationship between tort compensation and no-fault compensation is a central theme of our report....

[W]e have found a widespread ignorance of the fact that in this country we already have a considerable element of no-fault provisions...[W]e have had no-fault provision on quite a considerable scale since the 1897 Workmen's Compensation Act. Now, as well as the contributory benefits of the social security scheme, we have non-contributory no-fault benefits available to disabled people, the medical benefits of the National Health Service, and local authority social services provision of various kinds.

In some respects, this no-fault provision for the whole population already exceeds that provided by the no-fault schemes of limited scope which have been introduced in other countries. For example, medical and hospital cover under the National Health Service is open ended, whereas most United States no-fault schemes for road accidents provide only limited medical and hospital cover. Additional no-fault schemes for those injured in accidents in the United Kingdom would for most of them be a matter of building on to the no-fault provision which already exists....

A Look Overseas...

For centuries, tort was the only means of obtaining compensation for personal injury. In most countries, compensation is now provided from a variety of no-fault sources, in addition to tort or in partial or total replacement of it....

The break away from tort started in Germany in the nineteenth century with Bismarck's scheme of industrial accident insurance. No-fault provision has since spread all over the world. In many countries, including Canada, Australia and the USA, workmen's compensation has virtually replaced tort as a source of compensation for work injuries.

The twentieth century has seen the introduction of no-fault provision for road injuries. By the middle of the century, as motor cars multiplied and became more powerful and to some extent more lethal, thoughts turned to special provision for victims of road accidents. This time the movement started in North America... Sweden is the only European country operating a no-fault scheme of road accident injuries....

Our Strategy...

The fundamental problem with which we were faced was the balance between no-fault and tort. The extreme options might be thought of as exclusive reliance on one or the other. A total dependence on the tort system, however, would be unrealistic—there could be no question of sweeping away the growing structure of social security provision. On the other hand, the possibility of relying exclusively on no-fault required more careful consideration... asking two main questions—how far no-fault should be extended; and whether tort should be abolished....

[L]eaving aside the merits of the issue and the matter of cost, our terms of reference precluded us from considering whether to recommend a no-fault scheme covering all injuries.... We therefore came of necessity to ask ourselves whether there were persuasive reasons for extending no-fault compensation for particular categories of injury, and whether any new no-fault schemes could be satisfactorily financed.

Our decision to approach the extension of no-fault in this manner had an obvious bearing on the question whether tort should be abolished. It was clear to us that social security should be regarded as the primary method of providing compensation—it is quick, certain and inexpensive to administer, and it already covers a majority of the injured. But, in the absence of a no-fault scheme covering all injuries, the abolition of tort for personal injury would deprive many injured people of a potential source of compensation, without putting anything in its place. We concluded that tort must be retained; and most of us saw good reason for keeping tort even where all injuries in a given category are covered by a no-fault scheme....

We reached three main conclusions on the extension and improvement of no-fault provision. These were that the structure of the industrial injuries scheme should remain basically unchanged, albeit with some improvements; that a new scheme should be introduced for road injuries; and that a new social security benefit should be introduced for severely handicapped children.

We considered the introduction of new no-fault schemes for other categories covered by our terms of reference, but, in broad terms, we thought that the case for such schemes was less compelling; that our proposals as they stood would be enough, for the present at any rate, for the administrative system to absorb; and that the miscellaneous circumstances of accidents would make it difficult, and sometimes impracticable, to construct and finance schemes other than those covered by our main conclusions.

COMMENTARY

Under a no-fault system, compensation is paid out of a centrally-controlled fund to victims of accidents (and perhaps illness) regardless of whether their injuries were the result of anyone else's fault. Although the social security system provides benefits on a no-fault basis, the value of these benefits is limited and they cannot be regarded as full compensation for losses sustained by the claimant (see Section I.6, above). Accordingly, no-fault compensation is normally understood to refer to particular schemes falling outside both the tort and social security systems that aim at compensation at more than bare subsistence levels. Workers' compensation, which could formerly be regarded as a no-fault scheme in this sense, is now more appropriately regarded as part of the social security system as it no longer offers benefits on an earnings-related basis, while the task of dealing with short-term injuries now falls to statutory sick pay (which is not limited to those injured in the course of their employment and pays only flat-rate benefits). Where incapacity lasts more than 15 weeks, industrial injuries disablement benefit can still be claimed, but this reflects only the claimant's degree of disablement, not his or her pre-accident earnings. At the time of writing, the maximum level of benefit was £143.60 per week (cf. £79.15 for statutory sick pay).

Severely Handicapped Children

One of the principal impetuses for the setting up of the Pearson Commission was the public outcry at the Thalidomide tragedy of the 1960s (see *The Thalidomide Children and the Law: A Report by the Sunday Times* (London: André Deutsch, 1973), p. 8; H. Teff and C. Munro, *Thalidomide: The Legal Aftermath* (Farnborough: Saxon House, 1976), p. 18). Thalidomide, a pharmaceutical drug given to pregnant women suffering from morning sickness, was withdrawn from the British market in 1961 having been found to have been the cause of very serious congenital injuries suffered by some 10,000 children across the world (many of them born without arms or without legs, some with no limbs at all). Some 400 claims for damages were made against Distillers Co (Biochemicals) Ltd which made and sold the drug in Britain. In view of legal advice warning that such claims were very speculative—given especially the likely difficulty of proving negligence on the part of Distillers and the legal uncertainty as to whether an unborn child could be owed a duty of care—in 1968, an initial group of plaintiffs settled out-of-court at 40 per cent of the total to which they would have been entitled if the company had been found liable; the average award was £16,129 and the total payment was about £1 million. Subsequently, in 1974 (12 years after the issue of the first writ) another settlement was reached with the remaining plaintiffs by which Distillers paid a total of £20 million, from which immediate cash payments averaging £54,000 were made to each of the children, with the balance of some £14 million going into a charitable trust fund (see Teff and Munro, *op. cit.*, pp. 12, 20). According to Teff and Munro, the litigation 'highlighted some fundamental shortcomings of the tort system', in particular 'the fact that the consumer has to prove negligence to succeed against the manufacturer, and the defects of the procedural framework within which the parties operate' (p. 129).

The litigation stimulated legal change, notably the statutory recognition of the right to sue in respect of congenital disabilities (see p. 132, above). But the Pearson Commission's recommendation of a new (no-fault) social security benefit for severely handicapped children has not been acted upon. However, children are eligible for Disability Living Allowance, paid to their parents to provide help with personal care and/or mobility (up to a maximum £119.45 per week at present rates), while a parent caring for a disabled child may be entitled to a carer's allowance (currently £53.10 per week).

No-Fault Compensation for Road Accidents

A Pearson Commission proposal that wholly awaits implementation is its recommendation of a no-fault compensation scheme for the victims of road accidents. The Commission found that the fault principle operated with 'particular capriciousness' in that area, and was impressed also with the fact that '[r]oad accidents are numerous, particularly likely to be the cause of serious injury, and an unavoidable hazard for most of the population' (vol. 1, paras 286–7). No action was taken to implement the proposal at the time, but a consultation paper, *Compensation for Road Accidents*, published by the Lord Chancellor's Department in

1991 proposed that a person suffering personal injuries as a result of a road accident should be able to recover compensation up to a maximum of £2,500 without having to prove that another person was at fault. Compensation was to be assessed according to normal principles of the law of damages, as any reduction in the level of damages (justified, for example, by the speedier disposal of claims and the more certain entitlement to compensation) might encourage victims to abandon the scheme in favour of ordinary tort litigation. The LCD believed that the range of road accident victims eligible for compensation would be wider than under the tort system, and that disputes over liability for minor injuries would be greatly reduced. The scheme was to be funded and operated by the insurance industry, which would have to increase the level of premiums accordingly, and would not therefore impose any additional costs on public funds.

The LCD proposal appears to have died a quiet death, and may in any case be criticised for preferring those suffering minor injuries, who do not have to prove fault, over the seriously injured, who must do so. It is also unclear whether it would in fact result in any savings in resources, as the scheme would only cover personal injury, leaving accident victims to pursue separate proceedings through the courts in respect of any damage sustained to their property. Overall, the proposals seems to have been designed to reduce the burden on the courts of dealing with road accident claims of small value and to transfer the costs of administering such claims onto road users.

A more general question is whether it is justifiable to give preferential treatment to the victims of road accidents as compared with the victims of accidents in general, on which see Lewis, 'No-Fault Compensation for Victims of Road Accidents: Can it be Justified?' (1981) 10 J Soc Pol 161.

The Motor Insurers' Bureau

In this context, a brief mention is warranted of the Motor Insurers' Bureau (MIB), which was set up by the insurance industry in 1946 in response to pressure from the then Minister of Transport. The idea was that insurers should contribute, *pro rata* to the amount of their motor business, to a fund from which compensation would be paid to victims of uninsured drivers. Uninsured Drivers Agreements between successive Ministers of Transport and the MIB have provided a legal basis for the compensation payments (the most recent being dated 13 August 1999). Since 1968, a separate set of agreements has safeguarded the victims of hit-and-run or otherwise untraceable drivers (the Untraced Drivers Agreements, the most recent being 14 February 2003). The purpose of the agreements is to provide compensation where none would be recovered by means of ordinary tort litigation, but the scheme does not provide for no-fault compensation in the strict sense, as the claimant must still show that the injuries were suffered as a result of the tort of an uninsured or untraced driver. In 2008, the MIB handled some 57,000 new claims and paid compensation totalling £352.7 million, both figures being lower than in the previous year (source: *MIB Annual Report and Accounts 2008*). For further details, see *Atiyah*, pp. 256–9.

Criminal Injuries Compensation

Outside the social security system, the Criminal Injuries Compensation Scheme (introduced in 1964) is perhaps the best example in English law of state-provided compensation in respect of personal injury. It may perhaps be regarded as problematic to regard this as an example of 'no fault', because by definition the compensation is only paid in respect of criminally-inflicted injuries. Nevertheless, the state assumes the obligation to pay compensation in respect of such injuries as a matter of social responsibility, and not as a matter of fault on its part.

The current scheme, operated under the terms of the Criminal Injuries Compensation Act 1995, has been effective since 2008 and is administered by the Criminal Injuries Compensation Authority (CICA). It provides compensation to defined classes of claimants who have been the victim of a 'crime of violence' or other specified criminal injury (CICA, *The Criminal Injuries Compensation Scheme 2008* (2008), paras 8–12). There are eligibility conditions that must be satisfied before an award can be made, and awards can be reduced or withheld on grounds of the applicant's unreasonable conduct (*ibid.*, paras 13–16). Until 2001, awards were assessed in accordance with the rules of assessment for common law damages, but since then there has been a statutory 'tariff' of 25 different levels of compensation, the maximum tariff payable being £250,000. Loss of earnings (beyond the first 28 weeks) and 'special expenses' may also be compensated under the scheme; the rules for calculating these awards are similar to but less generous than those at common law (*ibid.*, paras 23–36). The maximum total amount payable in respect of a single injury is £500,000 (*ibid.*, para. 24). In 2008–09, the scheme decided some 79,000 applications (28,800 were disallowed) and paid out tariff compensation totaling £234.6 million to victims of crime (CICA, *Annual report and accounts 2008–09* (2009)).

For a discussion of the background to the 1995 Act, and the controversy caused by its adoption, see Ganz, 'Criminal Injuries Compensation: The Constitutional Issue' (1996) 59 MLR 95.

After the 7/7 terrorist attacks on London in 2005, there were calls to treat the victims of terrorist violence as a special case, and to restore to them the full compensation entitlements enjoyed by ordinary tort claimants. The government was strongly opposed, reiterating the longstanding policy of treating payments under the scheme as akin to charity rather than the discharge of a liability. See further Miers, 'Rebuilding Lives: operation and policy issues in the compensation of victims of violent and terrorist crimes' [2006] Crim LR 695.

Is it fair that victims of criminal injuries should receive less compensation than the victims of tortious injuries? Is it fair that they should receive more than accident victims who have to rely upon social security?

A No-Fault Scheme for Victims of Medical Misadventure?

The idea of a no-fault scheme for the victims of medical misadventure (including, but going beyond, medical negligence) has been on and off the political agenda for the last couple of decades. No-fault schemes were twice proposed in Private Members' Bills put before Parliament in the early 1990s, though nothing came of either initiative through lack of government support. Notwithstanding this lack of success, the British Medical Association campaigned for many years for the introduction of 'no fault', and remains a vociferous critic of the current clinical negligence regime. The matter returned to the political agenda, largely as a result of recommendations in the report of Sir Ian Kennedy's inquiry into infant deaths in the cardiac unit at the Bristol Royal Infirmary (Bristol Royal Infirmary Inquiry, *Final Report*, 2001: www.bristol-inquiry.org.uk/final_report/index.htm). The report recommended the abolition of the clinical negligence system, which acts as a disincentive to open reporting and the discussion of adverse events and near misses, and its replacement with 'an alternative system for compensating those patients who suffer harm arising out of treatment from the NHS' (para. 119). However, a subsequent report by the Chief Medical Officer (*Making Amends: A consultation paper setting out proposals for reforming the approach to clinical negligence in the NHS* (Department of Health, 2003)) rejected the Kennedy recommendation because it believed that a true no-fault scheme could potentially lead to huge increases in claims numbers and costs, might alternatively offer only limited compensation not meeting the needs of the victim, and might reduce incentives on health professionals to take reasonable care. Curiously, the report thought that there was a case for no-fault compensation to be paid in respect of birth injuries resulting in severe neurological impairment, but this was not taken up in the subsequent Act, whose main purpose was to establish a scheme for the resolution of low-value clinical negligence claims against the NHS without recourse to civil proceedings (NHS Redress Act 2006). One of the aims of the reform was to safeguard public funds by persuading victims of clinical negligence to accept (at their discretion) special care packages offered by the NHS rather than seeking private care, the costs of which would in principle be recoverable from the NHS in an action in tort (see p. 906, above). Implementation of the scheme will require the issue of regulations by the Secretary of State for Health.

(b) Universal No-Fault Compensation

Compared with the piecemeal and secondary approach to no-fault compensation that has so far prevailed in the United Kingdom, a more radical approach would be to introduce 'no-fault' compensation *in place of* liability for personal injuries in the law of tort. The Pearson Commission declined to take such a radical step—construing its terms of reference narrowly so as to preclude a comprehensive reform of this nature—and indicated that the fault principle was still of intuitive appeal to some of its members. In New Zealand, by contrast, this bold reform had already been implemented. In 1974, following a path-finding report by a Royal Commission of Inquiry, the right to recover compensatory damages for personal injury was abolished, and its place taken by a claim under a state-organised, 'no-fault' compensation scheme.

Royal Commission of Inquiry (Chairman: The Honourable Mr Justice Woodhouse), *Compensation for Personal Injury in New Zealand* (Wellington, NZ: Government Printer, 1967)

The toll of personal injury is one of the disastrous incidents of social progress, and the statistically inevitable victims are entitled to receive a co-ordinated response from the nation as a whole. They receive this only from the health service. For financial relief they must turn to three entirely different remedies, and frequently they are aided by none.

The negligence action is a form of lottery. In the case of industrial accidents it provides inconsistent solutions for less than one victim in every hundred. The Workers' Compensation Act provides meagre compensation for workers, but only if their injury occurred at their work. The Social Security Act will assist with the pressing needs of those who remain, provided they can meet the means test. All others are left to fend for themselves.

Such a fragmented and capricious response to a social problem which cries out for co-ordinated and comprehensive treatment cannot be good enough. No economic reason justifies it. It is a situation which needs to be changed. . . .

We have made recommendations which recognise the inevitability of two fundamental principles.

First, no satisfactory system of injury insurance can be organised except on a basis of community responsibility;

Second, wisdom, logic, and justice all require that every citizen who is injured must be included, and equal losses must be given equal treatment. There must be comprehensive entitlement. Moreover, always accepting the obvious need to produce something which the country can afford, it seemed necessary to lay down three further rules which, taken together with the two fundamental matters, would provide the framework for the new system. There must be complete rehabilitation. There must be real compensation—income-related benefits for income losses, payment throughout the whole period of incapacity, recognition of permanent bodily impairment as a loss in itself. And there must be administrative efficiency. . . .

Community Responsibility—If the well-being of the work force is neglected, the economy must suffer injury. For this reason the nation has not merely a clear duty but also a vested interest in urging forward the physical and economic rehabilitation of every adult citizen whose activities bear upon the general welfare. This is the plain answer to any who might query the responsibility of the community in the matter. Of course, the injured worker himself has a moral claim, and further a more material claim based upon his earlier contribution, or his readiness to contribute to the national product. But the whole community has a very real stake in the matter. . . .

Injury, not Cause, is the Issue—Once the principle of community responsibility is recognised the principle of comprehensive entitlement follows automatically. Few would attempt to argue that injured workers should be treated by society in different ways depending upon the cause of injury. Unless economic reasons demanded it the protection and remedy society might have to offer could not in justice be concentrated upon a single type of accident to the exclusion of others. With the admirable exception of the health services this has occurred in the past. There has been such concentration upon the risks faced by men during the working day that the considerable hazards they must face during the rest of each 24 hours (particularly on every road in the country) have been virtually disregarded. But workers do not change their status at 5 p.m., and if injured on the highway or at home they are the same men, and their needs and their country's needs of them are unchanged.

COMMENTARY

The Woodhouse Commission envisaged that the scheme it proposed would be financed by the abolition of tort liability for personal injuries and the application of the funds thereby saved to the new system. The institution of the new no-fault system would make tort law simply 'irrelevant' (para. 280).

New Zealand's Accident Compensation Scheme came into operation on 1 April 1974, enacting—with a few notable exceptions—the proposals of the Woodhouse Committee. In what was viewed as a 'social contract' between the state and the people of New Zealand, the right to sue for compensation for personal injury was abolished in return for the introduction of a system of 'no-fault' compensation. The essential elements of the scheme can be summarised as follows:

(i) Coverage was dependent upon the suffering of a 'personal injury by accident'. It was not necessary to prove that this was occasioned by another's breach of duty: effectively, the requirement of 'fault' was replaced by that of 'accident'.

(ii) Compensation was offered for loss of earnings ('earnings-related compensation', paid on a periodic basis at 80 per cent of pre-accident earnings, at least in so far as these did not exceed a fixed 'cap'); non-pecuniary loss (originally paid in the form of lump sums); medical costs and adjustment expenses; and loss of dependency.

(iii) Levies on employers, motor vehicle licence holders and others provided the principal source of finance for the scheme, with the balance being met out of general taxation.

Reform of the Scheme

The scheme has been subjected to significant reforms on several occasions. In 1992, a number of changes were made to it in an effort to reverse the steady 'cost creep' and resultant financial problems which had afflicted the scheme in the 1980s (see Accident Rehabilitation and Compensation Insurance Act 1992). First, a new and more rigid definition of compensatable personal injury was introduced in order to prevent incremental expansions in the scope of coverage that were thought to have resulted from reliance upon the largely undefined notion of 'personal injury by accident'. Secondly, the benefits payable under the scheme were limited in a number of respects, notably by replacing the right to lump-sum compensation for non-pecuniary loss with an entitlement, in cases of residual disability only, to an independence allowance. Lastly, the funding basis of the scheme was altered in an attempt to impose a greater degree of individual responsibility upon those actually responsible for accidents (especially by providing for experience-rating in the setting of individual levies).

Then, in 1998, new legislation provided for the opening up of workplace injury insurance to a competitive market (Accident Insurance Act 1998). The legislation imposed a requirement on all employers to purchase private accident insurance for work-related personal injuries suffered by their employees, although the state was to continue to provide personal injury insurance cover for injuries not occurring in the workplace. In addition, self-employed persons could opt to continue within the state-run scheme.

A change of government in 2000 heralded another round of changes. Undoing many of the previous reforms, the partial privatisation of the scheme set out above was ended and the state again became responsible for its running (Injury Prevention, Rehabilitation and Compensation Act 2001). Another reversion to the past was the re-introduction of lump sum compensation for permanent impairment in place of the independence allowance introduced in 1992. These changes returned the scheme to something close to its form at the time of its establishment in 1974, and it broadly retains this form notwithstanding further legislative intervention since.

Views of the Scheme

According to Sir Geoffrey Palmer, one of the architects of the scheme and subsequently New Zealand's Prime Minister, the no-fault regime 'signal[led] the achievement of real security upon which a better society can be built' (*Compensation for Incapacity* (Wellington, New Zealand: OUP, 1979), p. 407). The secret of the new scheme's success lay in its very moderate administrative costs—approximately 15 cents per New Zealand dollar of compensation (cf. the administrative costs of tort compensation, above, Section I.(3)(a))—which enabled it to spread its net of compensation far wider than tort for the same total expenditure. Yet, although the scheme has been held up as a model of enlightened reform by critics of the tort system in other jurisdictions, no other jurisdiction in the Anglo-American legal world has followed its lead (arguably, however, the 'social insurance' systems of some civilian jurisdictions, e.g. Sweden, achieve much the same results). The following extract summarises some common criticisms of the New Zealand scheme.

J. Henderson, 'The New Zealand Accident Compensation Reform' (1981) 48 U Chi L Rev 781

[In a review of G. Palmer, *Compensation for Incapacity*, Henderson sets out a series of arguments in an effort to undermine the claims made for the New Zealand scheme by Palmer and other supporters.]

A. The Failure to Compensate Some Accident Victims Was Not a Significant Social Problem

One who believes that accident victims who recover little or nothing through the tort system present a significant social problem probably is thinking of the relatively few instances in which serious and permanent injuries cause great financial hardship for the victims and their families. Such cases do occur, and some are tragic. But there was no strong correlation between suffering accidental injury and experiencing financial hardship. Only a small percentage of accident victims encountered significant financial hardship, because of the availability of free medical care and, for many accident victims, of other benefits, including public welfare and personal savings. (Studies of automobile accident cases in the United States, for example, indicate that a small percentage (no more than five percent) of accident victims suffer significant dislocation costs. . . . It seems reasonable to assume that in New Zealand, with its greater public welfare programs, the percentage was no higher, and probably lower.) To the unfortunate few who fell into the hardship category, of course, the problems were significant. But it would seem more realistic to view this minority as part of the problem of poverty than as part of the problem of uncompensated accident victims. . . . Thus, the New Zealand compensation system can be justified on the basis of social welfare principles only if those principles are expanded to include welfare for those not in particular financial need. . . . [T]his is, in essence, a social welfare system for the middle and upper-classes. . . .

B. The Common Law Tort System Never Purported to Address All Unexpected Financial Hardships of Individuals . . .

The reformers [in New Zealand] understood that the expanded no-fault compensation system could become a reality only if it replaced the tort system, because otherwise the need for new funding would be so great as to render unattractive any expanded commitment to compensation. Thus, there had to be an 'utterly devastating' attack on the common law. If the reformers had focused on the true objectives of tort law—the enhancement of social utility and the promotion of shared notions of fairness—the attack would have fallen short. The reformers possessed no empirical data to support conclusions that the tort system had failed to achieve either of these objectives, so the focus of attention had to be shifted to the compensation objective for the attack to succeed. Indeed, once the compensation objective is considered paramount, it is self-evident that a system promising 'integrated and comprehensive . . . compensation that is usually swift and sure' is preferable to one that offers only '[u]ncertain, uncoordinated, and capricious remedies.'

Thus, the strategy of reform that led to the Act was to attack the tort system for failing to achieve an objective that it never purported to recognize and then to belittle as tangential and ineffective its efforts to enhance utility and fairness. . . .

C. The New Zealand System is an Inadequate Solution to the Problem of Financial Disruptions . . .

[T]here is no reason why victims of misfortunes other than accidents should not have equally valid claims to compensation as accident victims. Why, for example, should the working person whose leg must be amputated because of cancer be denied benefits because he lost his leg through disease rather than by accident? Diseases such as cancer may often cause more significant disruptions in people's lives than accidents....If the New Zealand system is not expanded, what will have emerged from the reforms is a system that violates the principle of compensating victims of unexpected misfortune even as it purports to embody that principle. One may wonder whether the critics who spoke of the 'false morality' of tort law will be able to appreciate the hypocrisy reflected in the system they helped create....

D. The New Zealand System is Likely to have Negative Effects on Allocative Efficiency and Fairness

The tort system's objectives include the enhancement of allocative efficiency and the promotion of shared notions of fairness. The former objective is accomplished by deterring unacceptably risky conduct, the latter by providing private remedies against those who commit wrongs. The tort system does fail to compensate some accident victims who have suffered loss, but it must neglect the compensation objective if it is accomplish the others. Replacing the tort system with a compensation system may well generate benefits only at the cost of detracting from efficiency and fairness....

Generally, if actors are not required to pay a fair share of the costs of their activities, including the accident costs, they will tend to overengage in those activities whose costs they can most successfully escape from paying. Thus, if everyone were required to pay into a universal accident compensation fund on a flat-rate, *per capita* basis, those who engaged in comparatively safe activities would pay more than their share of the total accident costs generated by all activities, and those who engaged in relatively risky activities would pay less. The resulting wealth transfers would encourage actors at the margin (those indifferent to which sort of activities to engage in) to switch from safe to risky activities. Not everyone would switch, but enough would to cause the overall accident costs in the society to increase over what they would have been if those engaging in relatively safe activities had not been required to subsidize their risk-preferring fellow citizens. Resources would be misallocated to relatively risky activities; the increase in accident costs would constitute social waste.

The solution to this problem of waste, one that to a limited extent was incorporated in the New Zealand scheme, is to require contribution to the compensation fund in proportion to the risk of accidents created by the actor. If the amount contributed is appropriate, the proper balance between safe and risky activities will be achieved. The tort system consciously aims at attaching the appropriate price tags to risky conduct, but there is no reason in theory why a system providing universal compensation could not do the same thing....

[Henderson finds, however, that in practice there is 'little likelihood of achieving adequate safety incentives under the New Zealand scheme', mainly because of the very high administrative costs involved in ascertaining the riskiness of different activities and in imposing differential levies on the basis of that information.]

In addition to considering the potentially negative effects on allocative efficiency of moving to a compensation system such as the one adopted in New Zealand, such a move must be assessed from the standpoint of shared notions of fairness. A New Zealand-type system can be criticized on several fairness grounds. First, citizens would no longer have some of the traditional methods of vindicating individual rights in our legal system. A person intentionally struck by another, for example, would no longer be entitled to a legal judgment that his right to personal integrity had been violated. Second, the anomalies created by the Act are open to attack. For example, distinctions drawn between illness and accidental injury under the system cause persons similarly disadvantaged to be treated differently. Third, the measures of recovery include a number of arbitrary limits that cause persons dissimilarly disadvantaged to receive essentially the same benefits. Finally, the procedures under the compensation system reflect a willingness to sacrifice the interests of the individual to the greater good.

COMMENTARY

The New Zealand experience is relied upon by both proponents and opponents of 'no-fault' compensation. It remains an open question whether no-fault is desirable in principle and feasible in practice. It is, however, notable that New Zealand's accident compensation scheme has maintained very broad cross-party political support, as well as the support of the unions, (some) employers' organisations and legal and medical professional bodies in that country.

For further comment, see Miller, 'The Future of New Zealand's Accident Compensation Scheme' (1989) 11 Hawaii L Rev 1; Palmer, 'New Zealand's Accident Compensation Scheme: Twenty Years On' (1994) U of Toronto LJ 223; I. Campbell, *Compensation for Personal Injury in New Zealand: Its Rise and Fall* (Auckland: Auckland University Press, 1996); Gaskins, 'Regulating private law: Socio-legal perspectives on the New Zealand Accident Compensation Scheme' (2009) 17 TLJ 12 For a proposal to introduce comprehensive no-fault compensation in the United States, see S. Sugarman, *Doing Away with Personal Injury Law* (New York: Quorum, 1989).

(c) Compensation for Incapacity to be Exclusively a Matter of Private Insurance

In his classic work, *The Common Law*, Oliver Wendell Holmes rejected the idea of a state-run mutual insurance scheme of the type subsequently introduced in New Zealand on the basis that '[s]tate interference is an evil'. In his view, '[u]niversal insurance, if desired, can be better and more cheaply accomplished by private enterprise' (p. 77). Holmes did not consider the possibility that tort compensation for personal injury might be abolished with a view to letting private insurance provision take its place, but this option has recently been advocated by Patrick Atiyah in his book, *The Damages Lottery (1997)*. Some 30–40 years ago, Atiyah was a well-known proponent of the type of reform adopted in New Zealand in the 1970s, namely, the introduction of a 'no-fault' compensation scheme in place of tort compensation. Indeed, Atiyah actually sat on the Australian Woodhouse Commission that recommended a similar (in fact, more extensive) reform for that country a few years later. (A change of government meant that the reform never took place.) The 'early Atiyah' made his name with his book *Accidents, Compensation and the Law*, which survives in something like its original state in the most recent edition by Peter Cane. Atiyah meanwhile has moved on: from 'woolly liberal', with a belief in the capacity of the state to protect individual welfare, to supporter of the free market, with a deep antipathy to state interference and a preference for individual responsibility. The 'new Atiyah' is to be found in his recent book, *The Damages Lottery*, which decries the extent to which both tort law and no-fault compensation schemes encourage a so-called 'blame culture'. In the following extract, Atiyah presents his new vision for reform.

P. S. Atiyah, *The Damages Lottery* (Oxford: Hart, 1997), pp. 189–93

The action for damages for personal injuries should simply be abolished, and first-party insurance should be left to the free market. This proposal might seem at first little short of revolutionary, but closer examination shows that it is a perfectly natural development of current trends.

For a start, it should not be assumed that the action for damages for personal injuries is in any sense a real cornerstone of our legal system. This type of legal liability is of quite recent origin in the history of modern legal systems. In fact it is little more than a century old, and its rise closely parallels the rise of third-party liability insurance.... Unfortunately, the law got onto the wrong track from the very outset, developing and encouraging third-party insurance instead of first-party insurance. So to abolish the action for damages for personal injuries today would only be to put the law back onto the right lines from which it diverged a hundred years ago. Many countries have already abolished the action for damages for special kinds of injuries, such as road accidents and workers' compensation injuries. There is no evidence that this causes any sense of grievance or public outrage, provided that some kind of alternative insurance system is put in its place... [I]f the case for abolition of the present system is once agreed to be made out [sic], the only really practical alternative today... seems to be to leave the matter largely to the free market. If we don't do this, we shall probably end up with a whole collection of special compensation schemes, one for road accidents, one for workers' compensation, one perhaps for medical injuries, one for sporting injuries and so on. The compensation payable for all these kinds of injuries will doubtless differ from case to case, with just as many anomalies and absurdities as we have today. Only if we allow people the free choice to make their own decisions as to what kind of insurance they want, will these variations become acceptable.

Of course, a transitional period of several years would be needed before such a change could be implemented, and in the interim it would be necessary for the insurance industry, with pressure from the government, to come up with some sensible proposals for first-party insurance schemes to be established which would cover the most ordinary forms of accident. People would in this way be encouraged to insure themselves and their families against these risks. No doubt this would not be done on an individual policy basis—groups of people would be encouraged to take out policies together. For example, schools should take out policies to cover their children against sporting injuries on a no-fault basis (actually this is already beginning). Employers and trade unions should be encouraged to co-operate in taking out policies to cover the workers against industrial accidents. Homeowners' insurance policies should cover people against accidents in the home on a no-fault basis. Pregnant women should be encouraged to insure against the risk of having a disabled baby. And so on....

[T]he basic point must be the gradual encouragement of first-party insurance by more and more people, with the state simply acting as a fall-back protection for those who have no insurance of their own. There would be enormous advantages in this course. First, we should get rid of all the wasteful legal and administrative costs associated with claims for damages and third-party insurance.... Secondly, it will vastly improve the coverage which most people have against a large variety of risks. Instead of being offered a small, often a minuscule chance of recovering enormous damages for some injuries, people will have a much better chance of obtaining reasonable compensation for all, or anyhow, most injuries. What is more, the compensation will be obtainable on a much fairer basis than the present lottery—broadly, you will get what you choose to pay for. Third, this reform would begin the job of getting rid of the artificial distinctions embodied in the present law and practice between accidental injuries and disabilities from other causes....

Fourth, the shift to a free market in insurance would introduce a great deal of consumer choice in an area where it is significantly absent today... [I]t could enable people to decide what level of income they want to insure, whether they want life insurance and so on. For this reason, also, it will distribute more equitably the burden of many accidents, where at present the third-party system favours the more highly-paid and discriminates against the low-paid, the unemployed and the retired. It means that the right people would be paying for the insurance cover for their own possible income losses. . . .

Some may object that this idea is all very well for those who can afford to insure themselves, but what about those who can't? But the answer to this is that almost everybody will actually save more money by abolishing the present system than they will need to pay for their new first-party insurance. The poorest people, especially, will actually save on their motor insurance policies, which should become substantially cheaper for those on low incomes, or for the pensioners who don't need income-loss protection or life insurance cover. And even those who don't have cars will save on the price of goods and services, as businesses will no longer have to pay huge premiums to cover the risk of damages claims. Of course some state social security safety net will still be needed for those who are not otherwise covered at all.

This would indeed be a reform worth striving for.

COMMENTARY

Do you agree with Atiyah that the time has now come to abolish the tort system for compensating personal injuries? Is it satisfactory to leave compensation to the free market, via first-party insurance policies, especially for those on low incomes? (Consider Kalven's comment: 'If the poor were not quite so poor, we could decently ask them to provide their own accident insurance' ((1955) 33 Texas L Rev 778 at 782.)

In fact, Atiyah does suggest one very significant qualification to his proposed turn to the free market: there should be compulsory first-party insurance in respect of road accidents. He seems to view the abolition of tort liability on the roads, and its replacement with such a scheme, as a first step towards the complete abolition of tort. For 'purely pragmatic reasons', namely, 'too many people would probably end up without any cover' if this new kind of insurance were entirely voluntary (p. 187), Atiyah proposes that there should be a compulsory element to it. He suggests, however, that the compulsory element could be limited (e.g. allowing for only modest levels of income replacement) and that it should be possible to acquire 'top up' policies on a voluntary basis.

Why should compulsory first party insurance be limited to the road traffic context? Does the risk that 'too many people would probably end up without any cover' arise in other contexts too? Do you think that there should be a compulsory basic level of insurance protection for everyone, albeit of course with the ability to purchase 'top up' protection as well? Should this reform be pursued wholly outside the social security system, or is there a case for integrating at least the compulsory elements of any reformed system of accident or disability compensation within the social security system?

Following Atiyah, Smillie, 'The Future of Negligence' (2007) 15 TLJ 300 also advocates the abolition of tort of negligence and its replacement with 'nothing', though he would favour higher levels of state income protection than envisaged by Atiyah. For criticism of Atiyah's approach, see Ripstein, 'Some Recent Obituaries of Tort Law' (1998) 48 UTLJ 561; Conaghan and Mansell, 'From the Permissive to the Dismissive Society: Patrick Atiyah's Accidents, Compensation and the Market' (1998) 25 JLS 284.

INDEX